The Oxford English Minidictionary

The Oxford English Minidictionary

FIFTH EDITION, REVISED

Edited by
Lucinda Coventry

with
Martin Nixon

OXFORD
UNIVERSITY PRESS

Great Clarendon Street, Oxford OX2 6DP

Oxford University Press is a department of the University of Oxford. It furthers the University's objective of excellence in research, scholarship, and education by publishing worldwide in

Oxford New York

Auckland Bangkok Buenos Aires Chennai Dar es Salaam Delhi Hong Kong Istanbul Karachi Kolkata Kuala Lumpur Madrid Melbourne Mexico City Mumbai Nairobi São Paulo Shanghai Taipei Tokyo Toronto

Published in the United States by Oxford University Press Inc., New York

First edition 1981
Second edition 1988
Third edition 1991
Revised third edition 1994
Fourth edition 1995
Fifth edition 1999
Revised fifth edition 2003

British Library Cataloguing in Publication Data

Data available

Library of Congress Cataloging in Publication Data

Data available

ISBN 0-19-860712-1

10 9 8 7 6 5 4 3 2 1

Typeset in Nimrod and Arial
by Alliance Phototypesetters
Printed in Great Britain
Charles Letts & Co. Ltd.

Contents

Preface vi
Pronunciation vii
Abbreviations viii

The Oxford English Minidictionary 1

Language tips 606

Preface

The aim of the *Oxford English Minidictionary* is to provide a compact guide to spelling and usage in current everyday English.

Use has been made of extensive research into current English usage carried out by the Oxford Dictionaries Department. In the light of this research, important new words, senses, and phrases have been selected for inclusion. The most common meaning of each word has also been identified and placed first.

The dictionary gives many alternative spellings, including American English variants, which are presented as separate headwords; cases where different British and American uses of the same word might cause confusion are also noted. Guidance on pronunciation has been given for a greater number of words than in previous editions. More help has been given on the spelling of inflected forms: irregular plurals of nouns and comparatives and superlatives of adjectives are shown, and irregular or difficult inflections of verbs are spelt out in full.

The dictionary includes over a hundred notes on the spelling and correct use of individual words and on pairs of words that are easily confused. A new appendix offers useful tips on spelling and punctuation.

L.J.C.

Pronunciation

A guide to pronunciation is given for any word that is difficult to pronounce, or difficult to recognize when read, or spelt the same as another word but pronounced differently. The pronunciation given represents the standard speech of southern England. It is shown in brackets, usually just after the word itself.

Words are broken up into small units, usually of one syllable. The syllable that is spoken with most stress in a word of two or more syllables is shown in heavy letters, like **this**.

The sounds represented are as follows:

a *as in* cat
ă *as in* ago
ah *as in* calm
air *as in* hair
ar *as in* bar
aw *as in* law
ay *as in* say
b *as in* bat
ch *as in* chin
d *as in* day
e *as in* bed
ĕ *as in* taken
ee *as in* meet
eer *as in* beer
er *as in* her
ew *as in* few
ewr *as in* pure
f *as in* fat
g *as in* get
h *as in* hat
i *as in* pin
i *as in* pencil
I *as in* eye
j *as in* jam
k *as in* king
l *as in* leg
m *as in* man
n *as in* not
ng *as in* sing, finger
nk *as in* thank
o *as in* top
ŏ *as in* lemon
oh *as in* most
oi *as in* join
oo *as in* soon
oor *as in* poor
or *as in* corn
ow *as in* cow
p *as in* pen
r *as in* red
s *as in* sit
sh *as in* shop
t *as in* top
th *as in* thin
th as in this
u *as in* cup
ŭ *as in* circus
uu *as in* book
v *as in* van
w *as in* will
y *as in* yes or when preceded by a consonant = I *as in* cry
yoo *as in* unit
yoor *as in* Europe
yr *as in* fire
z *as in* zebra
zh as in vision

A consonant is sometimes doubled to show that the vowel just before it is short (like the vowels in *cat*, *bed*, *pin*, *top*, *cup*). The pronunciation of a word is sometimes indicated by giving a well known word that rhymes with it.

Abbreviations

adj. adjective
abbr. abbreviation
adv. adverb
Amer. American
Austral. Australian
Brit. British
comb. form combining form
conj. conjunction
derog. derogatory
esp. especially
hist. historical
int. interjection
n. noun
N. Engl. northern England
n. pl. noun plural
pl. plural
poss. pron. possesive pronoun
p.p. past participle
pref. prefix
prep. preposition
pron. pronoun
rel. pron. relative pronoun
S. Afr. South African
Scot. Scottish
sing. singular
sp. spelling
symb. symbol
usu. usually
v. verb
var. variant
vars. variants
v.aux auxillary verb

Abbreviations that are in general use (such as cm, RC, and USA) appear in the dictionary itself.

Proprietary terms

This book includes some words which are or are asserted to be proprietary names or trade marks. Their inclusion does not imply that they have acquired for legal purposes a non-proprietary or general significance, nor is any other judgement implied concerning their legal status. In cases where the editor has some evidence that a word is used as a proprietary name or trade mark this is indicated by the label (*trade mark*), but no judgement concerning the legal status of such words is made or implied thereby.

Aa

A *abbr.* **1** ampere(s). **2** answer. ▫ **A1** *informal* excellent, first rate. **A1, A2, A3**, etc. standard sizes for paper, each half as large as the previous one.

a *adj.* (called the *indefinite article*) **1** used in mentioning someone or something not previously referred to; one, any. **2** in, to, or for each; per: *60 words a minute.*

Å *abbr.* angstrom(s).

AA *abbr.* **1** Automobile Association. **2** Alcoholics Anonymous.

aardvark *n.* an African animal with a long snout

aback *adv.* ▫ **taken aback** surprised and disturbed.

abacus (a-bă-kŭs) *n.* an instrument for counting, consisting of a frame with beads sliding on wires or rods.

abandon *v.* leave without intending to return; give up. ● *n.* lack of inhibition. ▫ **abandonment** *n.*

abandoned *adj.* careless, wild, or undisciplined; depraved.

abase *v.* humiliate, degrade. ▫ **abasement** *n.*

abashed *adj.* embarrassed, ashamed.

abate *v.* make or become less intense. ▫ **abatement** *n.*

abattoir (ab-ă-twar) *n.* a slaughterhouse.

abbey *n.* a building occupied by a community of monks or nuns; a church belonging to this.

abbot *n.* a man who is the head of a community of monks.

abbreviate *v.* shorten.

abbreviation *n.* a shortened form of a word or phrase.

ABC *n.* **1** the alphabet; an alphabetical guide. **2** the basic facts of a subject.

abdicate *v.* **1** renounce the throne. **2** fail to fulfil (a duty or responsibility). ▫ **abdication** *n.*

abdomen *n.* the part of the body containing the digestive organs. ▫ **abdominal** *adj.*

abduct *v.* kidnap. ▫ **abduction** *n.*, **abductor** *n.*

aberrant *adj.* deviating from a standard. ▫ **aberrance** *n.*

aberration *n.* a deviation from what is normal.

abet *v.* (**abetted, abetting**) encourage or assist in wrongdoing. ▫ **abettor** *n.*

abeyance *n.* ▫ **in abeyance** in temporary disuse.

abhor *v.* (**abhorred, abhorring**) detest. ▫ **abhorrence** *n.*

abhorrent *adj.* detestable.

abide *v.* **1** endure, tolerate. **2** *archaic* live, dwell. ▫ **abide by** keep (a promise); accept (consequences etc.).

abiding *adj.* lasting, permanent.

ability *n.* (*pl.* **-ies**) **1** the power to do something. **2** cleverness.

ab initio (ab in-ish-i-oh) *adv.* from the beginning.

abject *adj.* wretched; lacking all pride. ▫ **abjectly** *adv.*

abjure *v.* renounce; repudiate.

ablaze *adj.* blazing.

able *adj.* **1** capable of doing something. **2** clever. ▫ **ably** *adv.*

ablutions *n.pl. formal* the action of washing oneself.

abnegate *v.* renounce.

abnormal *adj.* not normal. ▫ **abnormality** *n.*, **abnormally** *adv.*

aboard *adv.* & *prep.* on board.

abode *n. literary* or *humorous* a home, a dwelling place.

abolish *v.* put an end to formally. ▫ **abolition** *n.*

abominable *adj.* causing revulsion. □ **abominably** *adv.*

abominate *v. literary* detest. □ **abomination** *n.*

aboriginal *adj.* existing in a country from its earliest times. ● *n.* an aboriginal inhabitant, esp. (**Aboriginal**) of Australia.

aborigine (ab-er-**ij**-in-ee) *n.* an aboriginal inhabitant, esp. (**Aborigine**) of Australia.

abort *v.* (cause to) expel (a foetus) prematurely; (cause to) end prematurely and unsuccessfully.

abortion *n.* the premature expulsion of a foetus from the womb; an operation to cause this.

abortionist *n.* a person who performs abortions.

abortive *adj.* unsuccessful. □ **abortively** *adv.*

abound *v.* be plentiful.

about *prep.* **1** concerning, in connection with. **2** approximately. **3** surrounding. ● *adv.* **1** so as to face in the opposite direction. **2** in existence; in circulation; in the vicinity. □ **be about to** be on the point of (doing).

about-face *n.* (also **about-turn**) a reversal of direction or policy.

above *adv.* & *prep.* at or to a higher point or level (than); superior to; greater (than). □ **above board** legitimate, honest. **not be above** be capable of (something dishonourable).

abracadabra *n.* a magic formula.

abrasion *n.* rubbing or scraping away; an injury caused by this.

abrasive *adj.* tending to rub or scrape; harsh. ● *n.* a substance used for grinding or polishing.

abreast *adv.* side by side. □ **keep abreast of** keep up to date with.

abridge *v.* shorten by using fewer words. □ **abridgement** *n.*

abroad *adv.* away from one's home country.

abrogate *v.* repeal, abolish. □ **abrogation** *n.*

abrupt *adj.* **1** sudden. **2** curt. **3** steep. □ **abruptly** *adv.*, **abruptness** *n.*

abscess *n.* a swollen, pus- filled area formed in the body.

abscond *v.* leave secretly or illegally.

abseil (ab-sayl) *v.* descend using a rope fixed at a higher point.

absence *n.* **1** the state of being absent. **2** lack.

absent (ab-sĕnt) *adj.* not present; lacking, non- existent. □ **absent oneself** (ab-**sent**) stay away.

absentee *n.* a person who is absent from work etc. □ **absenteeism** *n.*

absent-minded *adj.* forgetful; easily distracted, inattentive.

absinthe (ab-sinth) *n.* a green liqueur.

absolute *adj.* complete; unrestricted.

absolutely *adv.* with no qualification or restriction. ● *int.* yes; definitely.

absolution *n.* a priest's formal declaration of forgiveness of sins.

absolutism *n.* a principle of government with unrestricted powers. □ **absolutist** *n.*

absolve *v.* clear of blame or guilt.

absorb *v.* take in, soak up; assimilate; occupy the attention or interest of. □ **absorption** *n.*

absorbent *adj.* able to absorb moisture.

abstain *v.* **1** refrain, esp. from drinking alcohol. **2** decide not to use one's vote. □ **abstainer** *n.*, **abstention** *n.*

abstemious (ab-stee-mi-ŏs) *adj.* not self-indulgent, esp. in eating and drinking. □ **abstemiously** *adv.*, **abstemiousness** *n.*

abstinence *n.* abstaining, esp. from food or alcohol.

abstract *adj.* (**ab**-strakt) **1** having no material existence; theoretical. **2** (of art) not representing things pictorially. ● *v.* (ăb-**strakt**) **1** remove; extract; separate. **2** make a summary of. ● *n.* (**ab**-strakt) **1** a summary. **2** a piece of abstract art.

□ **in the abstract** with no specific examples or context. □ **abstraction** *n.*

abstruse *adj.* hard to understand, obscure.

absurd *adj.* ridiculous, illogical, nonsensical. □ **absurdity** *n.*, **absurdly** *adv.*

abundant *adj.* plentiful; having plenty of something. □ **abundance** *n.*, **abundantly** *adv.*

abuse *v.* (ă-**bewz**) **1** ill-treat; insult. **2** misuse. ● *n.* (ă-**bewss**) **1** ill-treatment; insults. **2** wrongful use.

abusive *adj.* **1** insulting, offensive. **2** cruel, violent. □ **abusively** *adv.*

abut *v.* **abutted, abutting** border (upon), end or lean (against); have a common boundary.

abysmal (ă-**biz**-măl) *adj.* very bad.

abyss (ăb-**is**) *n.* a bottomless chasm.

AC *abbr.* (also **ac**) alternating current.

Ac *symb.* actinium.

a/c *abbr.* account.

academic *adj.* **1** of a college or university; scholarly. **2** of theoretical interest only. ● *n.* a person engaged in study and teaching. □ **academically** *adv.*

academician *n.* a member of an Academy.

Academy *n.* (*pl.* **-ies**) **1** a society of scholars or artists. **2** (**academy**) a school.

ACAS *abbr.* Advisory, Conciliation, and Arbitration Service.

accede (ak-**seed**) *v. formal* agree (to).

accelerate *v.* increase the speed (of). □ **acceleration** *n.*

accelerator *n.* a pedal on a vehicle for increasing speed.

accent *n.* (**ak**-sĕnt) **1** a style of pronunciation typical of a particular region or country. **2** emphasis. **3** a written mark guiding pronunciation. ● *v.* (ak-**sent**) pronounce with an accent; emphasize.

accentuate *v.* emphasize; make prominent. □ **accentuation** *n.*

accept *v.* say yes (to); take as true; resign oneself to. □ **acceptance** *n.*

acceptable *adj.* tolerable; satisfactory; welcome. □ **acceptability** *n.*, **acceptably** *adv.*

access *n.* a way in; the opportunity to use something; the right to see or enter. ● *v.* retrieve or examine (computerized data or files).

accessible *adj.* able to be reached or obtained. □ **accessibility** *n.*, **accessibly** *adv.*

accession *n.* **1** reaching a rank or position. **2** an addition.

accessory *n.* (*pl.* **-ies**) **1** something added as a supplement or decoration. **2** someone who helps in or knows about a crime.

accident *n.* **1** an unplanned event causing damage or injury. **2** chance, absence of intention.

accidental *adj.* happening by accident. □ **accidentally** *adv.*

acclaim *v.* welcome or applaud enthusiastically. ● *n.* enthusiastic approval or applause. □ **acclamation** *n.*

acclimatize *v.* (also **-ise**) make or become used to new conditions. □ **acclimatization** *n.*

accolade *n.* bestowal of a knighthood; praise, tribute.

accommodate *v.* **1** provide lodging or room for. **2** adapt to.

■ **Usage** *Accommodate, accommodation*, etc. are spelt with two m's not one.

accommodating *adj.* willing to do as asked.

accommodation *n.* a place to live.

accompany *v.* (**accompanied, accompanying**) **1** go with. **2** play an instrumental part supporting (a singer or instrument). □ **accompaniment** *n.*, **accompanist** *n.*

accomplice *n.* a partner in crime.

accomplish *v.* succeed in doing or achieving. □ **accomplishment** *n.*

accomplished *adj.* highly skilled.

accord *v.* be consistent with something. ● *n.* agreement, harmony.

□ **of one's own accord** without being asked.

accordance *n.* conformity.

according *adv.* □ **according to 1** as stated by. **2** in proportion to. □ **accordingly** *adv.*

accordion *n.* a portable musical instrument with bellows and keys or buttons.

accost *v.* approach and speak to.

account *n.* **1** a statement of money paid or owed; a credit arrangement with a bank or firm. **2** a narrative or description. □ **account for 1** explain. **2** form, make up. **on account of** because of.

accountable *adj.* obliged to account for one's actions. □ **accountability** *n.*

accountant *n.* a person who keeps or inspects business accounts. □ **accountancy** *n.*

accoutrements (ă-**koo**-t(r)ĕ-mĕnts) *n.pl.* (*Amer.* also **accouterments**) equipment, trappings.

accredited *adj.* officially recognized or authorized.

accretion *n.* growth by addition of matter; an addition.

accrue *v.* (**accrued, accruing**) accumulate. □ **accrual** *n.*

accumulate *v.* acquire more and more of; increase in amount. □ **accumulation** *n.*

accumulator *n.* **1** a rechargeable electric battery. **2** a series of bets with winnings restaked.

accurate *adj.* free from error. □ **accuracy** *n.*, **accurately** *adv.*

accusative *n.* the grammatical case expressing the direct object.

accuse *v.* represent as responsible for a crime or fault. □ **accusation** *n.*, **accuser** *n.*

accustom *v.* make used (to).

ace *n.* **1** a playing card with a single spot. **2** *informal* an expert. **3** an unreturnable serve in tennis.

acerbic (ă-**ser**-bik) *adj.* harsh and sharp. □ **acerbity** *n.*

acetate (a-si-tayt) *n.* a synthetic textile fibre.

acetic acid (ă-**see**-tik, ă-**set**-ik) *n.* a colourless liquid (also called *ethanoic acid*), an essential ingredient of vinegar.

acetone (a-si-tohn) *n.* a colourless liquid used as a solvent.

acetylene (ă-**set**-i-leen) *n.* a colourless gas burning with a bright flame.

ache *n.* a dull continuous pain. ● *v.* suffer such a pain.

achieve *v.* succeed by effort in doing, reaching, or gaining. □ **achievable** *adj.*, **achievement** *n.*, **achiever** *n.*

Achilles heel *n.* a person's vulnerable point.

Achilles tendon *n.* the tendon attaching the calf muscles to the heel.

acid *adj.* sour. ● *n.* any of a class of substances that contain hydrogen and neutralize alkalis. ● *adj.* containing acid; (of manner) sharp, unkind. □ **acidic** *adj.*, **acidity** *n.*, **acidly** *adv.*

acid rain *n.* rain made acid by pollution.

acknowledge *v.* **1** admit the truth of. **2** confirm receipt of, express thanks for. □ **acknowledgement** *n.*

acme (**ak**-mi) *n.* the height of perfection.

acne (**ak**-ni) *n.* an eruption of pimples.

acolyte (a-kŏ-lIt) *n.* a person assisting a priest in a service; a devoted follower.

acorn *n.* the oval nut of the oak tree.

acoustic (ă-**koo**-stik) *adj.* relating to sound. ● *n.pl.* **(acoustics)** the qualities of a room that affect the way sound carries.

acquaint *v.* make aware of. □ **be acquainted with** know slightly.

acquaintance *n.* a slight knowledge; a person one knows slightly.

acquiesce *v.* agree. □ **acquiescence** *n.*, **acquiescent** *adj.*

acquire *v.* gain possession of.

acquired immune deficiency syndrome *see* **Aids**.

acquisition *n.* something acquired; acquiring.

acquisitive *adj.* eager to acquire things. □ **acquisitiveness** *n.*

acquit *v.* (**acquitted, acquitting**) declare to be not guilty. □ **acquit oneself** fulfil a function, perform. □ **acquittal** *n.*

acre (ay-ker) *n.* a measure of land, 4,840 sq. yds (0.405 hectares). □ **acreage** *n.*

acrid *adj.* bitter.

acrimonious *adj.* angry and bitter. □ **acrimony** *n.*

acrobat *n.* a performer of acrobatics.

acrobatic *adj.* involving spectacular gymnastic feats. ● *n.pl.* **(acrobatics)** acrobatic feats.

acronym (ak-rŏ-nim) *n.* a word formed from the initial letters of others.

acrophobia *n.* an abnormal fear of heights.

acropolis *n.* the fortified upper part of an ancient Greek city.

across *prep.* & *adv.* **1** from side to side (of). **2** on the other side (of).

acrostic *n.* a poem in which the first and/or last letters of lines form a word or words.

acrylic (ă-kri-lik) *n.* a synthetic fibre made from an organic substance.

act *v.* **1** do something; behave; perform actions. **2** play (a part); be an actor. ● *n.* **1** something done. **2** a law made by parliament. **3** a section of a play. **4** an item in a variety show.

acting *adj.* serving temporarily.

actinium *n.* a radioactive element (symbol Ac).

action *n.* **1** the process of doing or functioning; something done. **2** a lawsuit. **3** a battle.

actionable *adj.* giving cause for a lawsuit.

activate *v.* cause to act or work. □ **activation** *n.*, **activator** *n.*

active *adj.* **1** functioning. **2** energetic. □ **actively** *adv.*

activist *n.* a person adopting a policy of vigorous action in politics etc. □ **activism** *n.*

activity *n.* (*pl.* **-ies**) **1** a particular pursuit. **2** lively action.

actor *n.* a performer in a play or film.

actress *n.* a female actor.

actual *adj.* **1** existing in fact. **2** current.

actuality *n.* reality.

actually *adv.* in fact, really.

actuary *n.* (*pl.* **-ies**) an insurance expert who calculates risks and premiums. □ **actuarial** *adj.*

actuate *v.* activate; motivate. □ **actuation** *n.*

acumen *n.* shrewdness.

acupressure *n.* medical treatment involving pressing the body at specific points. □ **acupressurist** *n.*

acupuncture *n.* medical treatment involving pricking the skin at specific points with needles. □ **acupuncturist** *n.*

acute *adj.* **1** intense; (of an illness) short but severe. **2** quick to understand. **3** sharp; (of an angle) less than 90°. □ **acutely** *adv.*, **acuteness** *n.*

AD *abbr.* (in dates) after the supposed date of Christ's birth (from Latin *Anno Domini* = in the year of the Lord).

adage (**ad**-ĭj) *n.* a proverb.

adagio (ă-**dah**-jee-oh) *adv. Music* in slow time.

adamant *adj.* not yielding to requests or arguments.

Adam's apple *n.* the lump of cartilage at the front of the neck.

adapt *v.* make or become suitable for new use or conditions. □ **adaptation** *n.*

adaptable *adj.* able to be adapted or to adapt oneself. □ **adaptability** *n.*

adaptor *n.* a device for connecting several electric plugs to one socket.

ADD *abbr.* attention deficit disorder; a condition characterized by hyperactivity and poor concentration.

add *v.* **1** join to an existing item to increase or enlarge it. **2** say as a further remark. **3** put (numbers) together to calculate a total.

addendum *n.* (*pl.* **addenda**) a section added to a book.

adder *n.* a poisonous snake.

addict *n.* a person addicted to something, esp. a drug.

addicted *adj.* doing or using something as a compulsive habit. □ **addiction** *n.*, **addictive** *adj.*

addition *n.* adding; something added.

additional *adj.* added, extra. □ **additionally** *adv.*

additive *n.* a substance added.

addle *v.* muddle, confuse.

addled *adj.* **1** (of an egg) rotten. **2** muddled.

address *n.* **1** particulars of where a person lives or where mail should be delivered. **2** a speech. ● *v.* **1** write the address on (mail) **2** speak to. **3** apply (oneself) to a task.

addressee *n.* a person to whom a letter etc. is addressed.

adduce *v.* cite as evidence.

adenoids *n.pl.* the enlarged tissue between the back of the nose and the throat. □ **adenoidal** *adj.*

adept *adj.* very skilful.

adequate *adj.* satisfactory in quantity or quality. □ **adequacy** *n.*, **adequately** *adv.*

adhere *v.* **1** stick. **2** support a cause or belief. □ **adherence** *n.*, **adherent** *adj.* & *n.*

adhesion *n.* the process or fact of sticking to something.

adhesive *adj.* sticking, sticky. ● *n.* an adhesive substance.

ad hoc *adv.* & *adj.* for a particular occasion or purpose, not repeated regularly.

adieu (ă-dew) *int.* & *n.* (*pl.* **adieus** or **adieux**) (a) goodbye.

ad infinitum *adv.* for ever.

adipose *adj.* fatty.

adjacent *adj.* adjoining.

adjective *n.* a word ascribing characteristics to a noun. □ **adjectival** *adj.*

adjoin *v.* be next to.

adjourn *v.* move (a meeting etc.) to another place or time. □ **adjournment** *n.*

adjudge *v.* decide judicially.

adjudicate *v.* act as judge (of); adjudge. □ **adjudication** *n.*, **adjudicator** *n.*

adjunct *n.* a non-essential supplement to something.

adjure *v.* command; urge.

adjust *v.* alter slightly; adapt to new conditions. □ **adjustable** *adj.*, **adjustment** *n.*

adjutant *n.* an army officer assisting in administrative work.

ad lib *adv.* & *adj.* **1** without preparation. **2** as much as desired. ● *v.* (**ad-libbed, ad-libbing**) improvise.

administer *v.* **1** manage (business affairs). **2** give or hand out.

administrate *v.* act as manager (of). □ **administrator** *n.*

administration *n.* management of public or business affairs. □ **administrative** *adj.*

admirable *adj.* worthy of admiration. □ **admirably** *adv.*

admiral *n.* a naval officer of the highest rank.

admire *v.* **1** respect highly. **2** look at with pleasure. □ **admiration** *n.*

admissible *adj.* able to be admitted or allowed. □ **admissibility** *n.*

admission *n.* **1** a statement admitting something **2** entering or being allowed to enter.

admit *v.* (**admitted, admitting**) **1** reluctantly state as true. **2** allow to enter. **3** accept as valid.

admittance *n.* admission, esp. to a private place.

admittedly *adv.* as must be admitted.

admixture *n.* something added as an ingredient.

admonish *v.* reprove; warn; exhort. □ **admonition** *n.*

ad nauseam *adv.* to a sickening extent.

ado (ă-doo) *n.* commotion, fuss.

adobe (ă-**doh**-bi) *n.* a sun-dried brick.

adolescent *adj.* & *n.* (a person) between childhood and adulthood. □ **adolescence** *n.*

adopt *v.* **1** bring up (another's child) as one's own. **2** choose to follow (a course of action). **3** accept (a report). □ **adoption** *n.*

adoptive *adj.* related by adoption.

adorable *adj.* delightful; enchanting.

adore *v.* **1** love deeply. **2** worship. □ **adoration** *n.*

adorn *v.* decorate; be an ornament to. □ **adornment** *n.*

adrenal (ă-**dree**-năl) *adj.* close to the kidneys.

adrenalin (ă-**dren**-ă-lin) *n.* (also **adrenaline**) a stimulant hormone produced by the adrenal glands.

adrift *adj.* & *adv.* drifting; without guidance or purpose.

adroit *adj.* skilful, ingenious.

adsorb *v.* attract and hold (a gas or liquid) to a surface.

adulation *n.* excessive flattery. □ **adulatory** *adj.*

adult *adj.* fully grown. ● *n.* an adult person or animal. □ **adulthood** *n.*

adulterate *v.* make impure by adding a substance. □ **adulteration** *n.*

adulterer *n.* a person who commits adultery.

adultery *n.* sexual infidelity to one's wife or husband. □ **adulterous** *adj.*

advance *v.* **1** move forward; (cause to) make progress. **2** lend (money). ● *n.* **1** a forward movement; an improvement. **2** a loan. **3** (**advances**) romantic or sexual approaches to someone. □ **advancement** *n.*

advanced *adj.* **1** far on in development or time. **2** not elementary.

advantage *n.* **1** something putting one in a favourable position. **2** a benefit. □ **take advantage of 1** exploit. **2** use.

advantageous *adj.* beneficial.

Advent *n.* **1** the season before Christmas. **2** (**advent**) an arrival.

adventure *n.* an exciting experience or undertaking. □ **adventurer** *n.*, **adventurous** *adj.*

adverb *n.* a word qualifying a verb, adjective, or other adverb. □ **adverbial** *adj.*, **adverbially** *adv.*

adversary *n.* (*pl.* **-ies**) an opponent. □ **adversarial** *adj.*

adverse *adj.* unfavourable; bringing harm. □ **adversely** *adv.*

■ **Usage** *Adverse* is sometimes confused with **averse**, meaning 'disliking, unwilling'.

adversity *n.* (*pl.* **-ies**) hardship.

advertise *v.* publicize (goods, to promote sales, or a vacancy, to encourage applications).

advertisement *n.* a public notice promoting a product or publicizing a job vacancy.

advice *n.* a suggestion to someone about their best course of action.

advisable *adj.* (of a course of action) prudent, sensible. □ **advisability** *n.*

advise *v.* **1** give advice to; recommend. **2** inform. □ **adviser** *n.*

advisory *adj.* giving advice.

advocate *n.* (**ad**-vŏ-kăt) **1** a person who recommends a policy. **2** a person who speaks in court on behalf of another. ● *v.* (**ad**-vŏ-kayt) recommend. □ **advocacy** *n.*

adze *n.* (*Amer.* also **adz**) an axe with a blade at right angles to the handle.

aegis (ee-jiss) *n.* protection, sponsorship.

aeolian (ee-**oh**-li-ăn) *adj.* relating to wind.

aeon (ee-ŏn) *n.* (also **eon**) an immense time.

aerate *v.* **1** expose to the action of air. **2** add carbon dioxide to.

aerial *adj.* **1** of or like air. **2** existing or moving in the air. **3** by or from aircraft. ● *n.* a wire for transmitting or receiving radio waves. □ **aerially** *adv.*

aero- *comb. form* air; aircraft.

aerobatics *n.pl.* spectacular feats by aircraft in flight. □ **aerobatic** *adj.*

aerobics *n.pl.* vigorous exercises designed to increase oxygen intake. □ **aerobic** *adj.*

aerodynamic *adj.* relating to aerodynamics. □ **aerodynamically** *adv.*

aerodynamics *n.* the study of moving air and its interaction with objects moving through it.

aerofoil *n.* an aircraft wing, fin, or tailplane giving lift in flight.

aeronautics *n.* the study of the flight of aircraft. □ **aeronautical** *adj.*

aeroplane *n.* a power-driven aircraft with fixed wings.

aerosol *n.* a pressurized container holding a substance for release as a fine spray.

aerospace *n.* the branch of technology concerned with aviation and space flight.

aesthete (ees-theet) *n.* (*Amer.* also **esthete**) a person claiming special appreciation of beauty.

aesthetic (ess-the-tik) *adj.* (*Amer.* also **esthetic**) relating to beauty or its appreciation. □ **aesthetically** *adv.*

aesthetics *n.* the study of beauty and its appreciation.

aetiology (ee-ti-ol-ŏji) *n.* (*Amer.* **etiology**) **1** a set of causes. **2** the study of causation.

affable *adj.* polite and friendly. □ **affability** *n.*, **affably** *adv.*

afar *adv.* far away.

affair *n.* **1** an event or series of events. **2** a person's rightful concerns. **3** a temporary sexual relationship.

affect *v.* **1** have an effect on. **2** pretend to feel, have, etc.

■ **Usage** Do not confuse *affect* with *effect*, 'bring about'.

affectation *n.* an artificial and pretentious manner.

affected *adj.* full of affectation.

affection *n.* love, liking.

affectionate *adj.* loving. □ **affectionately** *adv.*

affidavit *n.* a written statement sworn on oath to be true.

affiliate *v.* connect as a subordinate member or branch. □ **affiliation** *n.*

affinity *n.* (*pl.* **-ies**) a close resemblance or attraction.

affirm *v.* **1** state as a fact. **2** declare one's support for. □ **affirmation** *n.*

affirmative *adj.* saying that something is the case; saying 'yes'. ● *n.* an affirmative statement. ● *int.* yes.

affirmative action *n.* a policy of favouring groups often discriminated against.

affix *v.* (ă-**fiks**) attach; add (a signature etc.). ● *n.* (**a**-fiks) a thing affixed; a prefix or suffix.

afflict *v.* cause suffering to.

affliction *n.* a painful condition.

affluent *adj.* wealthy. □ **affluence** *n.*, **affluently** *adv.*

afford *v.* **1** have enough money for. **2** be able to spare. **3** give, provide.

affray *n.* a public fight or riot.

affront *n.* an open insult. ● *v.* insult, offend.

afforest *v.* convert (land) into forest. □ **afforestation** *n.*

afloat *adv.* & *adj.* floating; on a boat.

afoot *adv.* & *adj.* going on.

aforementioned, aforesaid *adj.* mentioned previously.

afraid *adj.* **1** frightened. **2** an expression of apology: *I'm afraid I can't.*

afresh *adv.* making a fresh start.

African *adj.* of Africa or its people. ● *n.* an African person.

Afrikaans *n.* a language of South Africa, developed from Dutch.

Afrikaner *n.* an Afrikaans-speaking white person in South Africa.

aft *adv.* at or towards the rear of a ship or aircraft.

after *prep.* **1** later than. **2** behind; pursuing; following. **3** in imitation of or allusion to. ● *conj.* & *adv.* at a time later (than): ● *n.pl.* (**afters**) *informal* dessert.

afterbirth *n.* the placenta discharged from the womb after childbirth.

after-effect *n.* an effect persisting after its cause has gone.

aftermath *n.* the after-effects.

afternoon *n.* the time between noon and evening.

aftershave *n.* an astringent lotion used after shaving.

afterthought *n.* something thought of or added later.

afterwards *adv.* at a later time.

Ag *symb.* silver.

Aga *n. trademark* a large cooking stove.

again *adv.* **1** once more. **2** besides, too. **3** returning to a previous position: *came back again.*

against *prep.* **1** in opposition or contrast to. **2** in preparation for. **3** colliding with; touching; supported by.

agar (ay-gar) *n.* (also **agar-agar**) a substance obtained from seaweed, used to make jellies etc. set.

agate *n.* a stone with bands of colour.

age *n.* **1** the length of life or existence. **2** a historical period. **3** (usu. **ages**) a very long time. ● *v.* (**aged, ageing**) grow old, show signs of age; cause to do this.

aged *adj.* **1** (ayjd) of a specified age. **2** (ay-jid) old.

ageism *n.* prejudice on grounds of age. □ **ageist** *n.* & *adj.*

ageless *adj.* not growing or seeming to grow old.

agency *n.* (*pl.* **-ies**) **1** an organization providing a particular service. **2** action producing an effect.

agenda *n.* a list of things to be dealt with, esp. at a meeting.

agent *n.* **1** a person who acts on behalf of another. **2** a person or thing producing an effect.

agent provocateur (*azh*-ahn prŏ-vok-ă-ter) *n.* a person who tempts others to do something illegal.

agglomerate *v.* collect into a mass. □ **agglomeration** *n.*

aggrandize *v.* (also **-ise**) increase the power or reputation of. □ **aggrandizement** *n.*

aggravate *v.* **1** make worse. **2** *informal* annoy. □ **aggravation** *n.*

aggregate *n.* (ag-ri-găt) **1** a whole combining several elements. **2** crushed stone used in making concrete. ● *adj.* (ag-ri-găt) formed by combination or addition. ● *v.* (ag-ri-gayt) combine, unite. □ **aggregation** *n.*

aggression *n.* hostile acts or behaviour.

aggressive *adj.* showing aggression. □ **aggressively** *adv.*

aggressor *n.* a person who begins hostilities.

aggrieved *adj.* having a grievance.

aghast *adj.* filled with horror.

agile *adj.* nimble, quick-moving. □ **agility** *n.*

agitate *v.* **1** worry, disturb; campaign to raise concern. **2** shake briskly. □ **agitation** *n.*, **agitator** *n.*

AGM *abbr.* annual general meeting.

agnostic *adj.* & *n.* (a person) believing that nothing can be known about the existence of God. □ **agnosticism** *n.*

ago *adv.* in the past.

agog *adj.* eager, expectant.

agonize *v.* (also **-ise**) worry intensely.

agonizing *adj.* (also **-ising**) causing extreme suffering.

agony *n.* (*pl.* **-ies**) extreme suffering.

agoraphobia *n.* an irrational fear of open spaces. □ **agoraphobic** *n.* & *adj.*

AGR *abbr.* advanced gas-cooled (nuclear) reactor.

agrarian *adj.* of land or agriculture.

agree *v.* (**agreed, agreeing**) **1** hold or express the same opinion. **2** consent. ◻ **agree with 1** suit the health or digestion of. **2** approve of.

agreeable *adj.* **1** pleasant. **2** willing to agree. ◻ **agreeably** *adv.*

agreement *n.* agreeing; consistency; an arrangement agreed between people.

agriculture *n.* the science or practice of farming. ◻ **agricultural** *adj.*

agronomy *n.* soil management and crop production.

aground *adv.* & *adj.* (of a ship) on the bottom in shallow water.

ague (ay-gew) *n. archaic* an illness involving fever and shivering.

ahead *adv.* further forward in position or time.

ahoy *int.* a seaman's shout for attention.

AI *abbr.* **1** artificial intelligence. **2** artificial insemination.

aid *v.* & *n.* help.

aide *n.* an aide-de-camp; an assistant.

aide-de-camp (ayd-dĕ-korm) *n.* (*pl.* **aides-de-camp**) an officer assisting a senior officer.

Aids *abbr.* (also **AIDS**) acquired immune deficiency syndrome, a condition developing after infection with the HIV virus, breaking down a person's natural defences against illness.

aikido (I-kee-doh) *n.* a Japanese form of self-defence.

ail *v.* make or become ill.

aileron *n.* a hinged flap on an aircraft wing.

ailment *n.* a slight illness.

aim *v.* point, send, or direct towards a target; intend, try. ● *n.* aiming; intention.

aimless *adj.* without a purpose. ◻ **aimlessly** *adv.*, **aimlessness** *n.*

ain't *contr. informal* am not, is not, are not; has not, have not.

■ **Usage** The use of *ain't* is incorrect in standard English.

air *n.* **1** a mixture of oxygen, nitrogen, etc., surrounding the earth. **2** a manner; an impression given; (**airs**) an affectation of superiority. **3** a melody. ● *v.* **1** express (an opinion) publicly. **2** expose to air to dry or ventilate. ◻ **airless** *adj.*

air bag *n.* a car safety device that fills with air in a collision to protect the driver.

air bed *n.* an inflatable mattress.

airborne *adj.* carried by air or aircraft; (of aircraft) in flight.

airbrick *n.* a brick perforated to allow ventilation.

air conditioning *n.* a system controlling the humidity and temperature of air in a building or vehicle. ◻ **air-conditioned** *adj.*, **air-conditioner** *n.*

aircraft *n.* (*pl.* **aircraft**) a machine capable of flight in air.

aircraft carrier *n.* a ship acting as a base for aircraft.

aircrew *n.* the crew of an aircraft.

airfield *n.* an area for the take-off and landing of aircraft.

air force *n.* a branch of the armed forces using aircraft.

airframe *n.* the body of an aircraft as distinct from the engine.

airgun *n.* a gun with a missile propelled by compressed air.

airlift *n.* the large-scale transport of supplies by aircraft. ● *v.* transport in this way.

airline *n.* a company providing an air transport service.

airliner *n.* a passenger aircraft.

airlock *n.* **1** a stoppage of the flow in a pipe, caused by an air bubble. **2** an airtight compartment giving access to a pressurized chamber.

airmail *n.* mail carried by aircraft.

airman *n.* (*pl.* **-men**) a member of an air force, esp. one below the rank of officer.

airplane *n. Amer.* = **aeroplane**.

airplay *n.* the playing of a recording on radio.

airport *n.* an airfield with facilities for passengers and goods.

air raid *n.* an attack by aircraft.

airship *n.* a power-driven aircraft that is lighter than air.

airspace *n.* the air and skies above a country.

airstrip *n.* a strip of ground for take-off and landing of aircraft.

airtight *adj.* not allowing air to enter or escape.

airwaves *n.pl.* the radio frequencies used for broadcasting.

airway *n.* **1** a regular route of aircraft. **2** a ventilating passage; a passage for air into the lungs.

airworthy *adj.* (**-worthier, -worthiest**) (of aircraft) fit to fly. □ **airworthiness** *n.*

airy *adj.* (**airier, airiest**) **1** well ventilated. **2** delicate, light. **3** carefree and casual. □ **airily** *adv.*, **airiness** *n.*

aisle (Il) *n.* **1** a passage between rows of seats. **2** a side part of a church.

ajar *adv.* & *adj.* (of a door) slightly open.

aka *abbr.* also known as.

akimbo *adv.* with hands on hips and elbows pointed outwards.

akin *adj.* related; similar.

Al *symb.* aluminium.

à la *prep. informal* in the style of.

alabaster *n.* a soft translucent mineral.

à la carte *adj.* & *adv.* ordered as separate items from a menu.

alacrity *n.* eager readiness.

à la mode *adj.* & *adv.* in fashion.

alarm *n.* **1** fear and anxiety. **2** a warning sound or signal; a device to wake someone at a set time. ● *v.* cause alarm to.

alarmist *n.* a person who raises unnecessary or excessive alarm.

alas *int.* an exclamation of sorrow.

albatross *n.* a large seabird.

albino *n.* (*pl.* **albinos**) a person or animal with no natural colouring in the hair, skin, or eyes.

album *n.* **1** a blank book for holding photographs, stamps, etc. **2** a collection of recordings issued as a single item.

albumen *n.* egg white.

albumin *n.* a protein found in egg white, milk, blood, etc. □ **albuminous** *adj.*

alchemy *n.* a medieval form of chemistry, seeking to turn other metals into gold. □ **alchemist** *n.*

alcohol *n.* a colourless inflammable liquid, the intoxicant in wine, beer, etc.; drink containing this.

alcoholic *adj.* containing or relating to alcohol. ● *n.* a person addicted to drinking alcohol. □ **alcoholism** *n.*

alcopop *n.* a ready-mixed soft drink with alcohol added.

alcove *n.* a recess in a wall.

al dente (al **den**-tay) *adj.* (of pasta) cooked so as to be still firm.

alderman *n.* (*pl.* **-men**) **1** (*hist.*) a co-opted senior member of an English council. **2** an elected member of the municipal governing body in Australian and some American cities.

ale *n.* beer.

alert *adj.* watchful, observant. ● *v.* warn, make aware.

A level *n.* Advanced level, an examination of a higher level than ordinary level or GCSE.

alfalfa *n.* lucerne.

alfresco *adv.* & *adj.* in the open air.

algae *n.pl.* simple water plants with no true stems or leaves.

algebra *n.* a branch of mathematics using letters etc. to represent quantities. □ **algebraic** *adj.*, **algebraically** *adv.*

algorithm *n.* a step by step procedure for calculation.

alias *n.* a false name. ● *adv.* also called.

alibi *n.* evidence that an accused person was elsewhere when a crime was committed.

■ **Usage** *Alibi* is often misused to mean 'an excuse'.

alien *n.* **1** a person who is not a citizen of the country where he or she lives. **2** a being from another world. ● *adj.* **1** foreign; unfamiliar. **2** extraterrestrial.

alienate *v.* cause to become unfriendly or unsympathetic.

alienation *n.* a state of isolation or estrangement.

alight[1] *v.* get down from a vehicle; land, settle.

alight[2] *adj.* & *adv.* on fire.

align *v.* **1** bring into the correct position. **2** ally (oneself). □ **alignment** *n.*

alike *adj.* like one another. ● *adv.* in the same way.

alimentary *adj.* of nourishment.

alimony (a-li-mŏ-ni) *n.* money paid by a divorced person to their former spouse.

alive *adj.* living; lively. □ **alive to** aware of.

alkali *n.* any of a class of substances that neutralize acids. □ **alkaline** *adj.*

alkaloid *n.* an organic compound containing nitrogen.

all *adj.* the whole number, amount, or extent of. ● *pron.* **1** everyone, everything. **2** the only thing: *all I want.* ● *adv.* completely: *all alone.* □ **all along** all the time. **all but** almost. **all in 1** including everything. **2** *informal* exhausted. **all out** using all one's strength. **all right 1** unhurt. **2** satisfactory.

allay *v.* lessen (fears).

all-clear *n.* a signal that danger is over.

allegation *n.* something alleged.

allege *v.* declare without proof.

allegedly *adv.* according to allegation.

allegiance *n.* loyal support.

allegory *n.* (*pl.* **-ies**) a story symbolizing an underlying meaning. □ **allegorical** *adj.*, **allegorically** *adv.*, **allegorize** (**-ise**) *v.*

allegro *adv. Music* briskly.

alleluia *int.* & *n.* (also **hallelujah**) praise to God.

allergen *n.* a substance causing an allergic reaction.

allergic *adj.* having or caused by an allergy.

allergy *n.* (*pl.* **-ies**) a condition causing an unfavourable reaction to certain foods, pollens, etc.

alleviate *v.* ease (pain or distress). □ **alleviation** *n.*

alley *n.* (*pl.* **alleys**) a narrow street; a long enclosure for tenpin bowling.

alliance *n.* an association formed for mutual benefit.

allied *adj.* **1** joined in alliance; working together. **2** related.

alligator *n.* a reptile of the crocodile family.

alliteration *n.* the occurrence of the same sound at the start of adjacent words. □ **alliterative** *adj.*

allocate *v.* allot, assign. □ **allocation** *n.*

allot *v.* (**allotted, allotting**) distribute; give as a share.

allotment *n.* **1** a small piece of land rented for cultivation. **2** an allotted share.

allotrope *n.* one of the forms of an element that exists in different physical forms.

allow *v.* **1** permit; enable, make possible. **2** set aside for a purpose. **3** admit. □ **allow for** take into account.

allowance *n.* **1** a permitted amount. **2** a sum of money paid regularly. □ **make allowances** be tolerant or lenient.

alloy *n.* a mixture of chemical elements at least one of which is a metal. ● *v.* **1** mix with another metal. **2** spoil (pleasure etc.)

allude *v.* refer briefly or indirectly. □ **allusion** *n.*, **allusive** *adj.*

allure *v.* entice, attract. ● *n.* attractiveness.

alluvium *n.* a deposit left by a flood. ◻ **alluvial** *adj.*

ally *n.* (al-I) (*pl.* **allies**) a country or person in alliance with another. ● *v.* (ăl-I) make (oneself) an ally; join, combine.

almanac *n.* (also **almanack**) **1** an annually published calendar containing information on important dates, astronomical data, etc. **2** a yearbook of a particular activity.

almighty *adj.* **1** all-powerful. **2** *informal* enormous.

almond *n.* an edible oval-shaped nut.

almost *adv.* very nearly.

alms (ahmz) *n.pl. formal* money given to the poor.

almshouse *n. hist.* a house built by charity for poor people.

aloe *n.* a plant with bitter juice.

aloft *adv.* high up; upwards.

alone *adj.* not with others; without company or help. ● *adv.* only, uniquely.

along *prep.* moving over the length of; extending beside all or most of. ● *adv.* **1** onward: *moving along.* **2** accompanying someone: *bring him along.*

alongside *adv. prep.* close to the side of (a ship or wharf etc.)

aloof *adj.* unfriendly, distant. ◻ **aloofly** *adv.*, **aloofness** *n.*

alopecia (a-lŏ-pee-shă) *n.* loss of hair; baldness.

aloud *adv.* in a voice that can be heard, not in a whisper.

alpaca *n.* a llama with long wool; its wool.

alpha *n.* the first letter of the Greek alphabet (Α, α).

alphabet *n.* a set of letters in a fixed order representing the sounds of a language. ◻ **alphabetical** *adj.*, **alphabetically** *adv.*

alphabetize *v.* (also **-ise**) put into alphabetical order. ◻ **alphabetization** *n.*

alpine *adj.* of high mountains. ● *n.* a plant growing on mountains or in rock gardens.

already *adv.* before this time; as early as this.

Alsatian *n.* a large dog of a breed often used for police work.

also *adv.* in addition, besides.

altar *n.* a table used in religious service.

altarpiece *n.* a painting behind an altar.

alter *v.* make or become different. ◻ **alteration** *n.*

altercation *n.* a noisy dispute.

alternate *v.* (**awl**-ter-nayt) (cause to) occur in turn repeatedly. ● *adj.* (awl-**ter**-năt) **1** every other, every second. **2** (of two things) repeatedly following and replacing each other. ◻ **alternately** *adv.*, **alternation** *n.*

alternative *adj.* **1** available as another choice. **2** unconventional. ● *n.* a choice, another option. ◻ **alternatively** *adv.*

■ **Usage** Do not confuse *alternative* with *alternate.*

---

alternator *n.* a dynamo producing an alternating current.

although *conj.* despite the fact that.

altimeter *n.* an instrument in an aircraft showing altitude.

altitude *n.* height above sea or ground level.

alto *n.* (*pl.* **altos**) the highest adult male or lowest female voice; a musical instrument with the second or third highest pitch in its group.

altogether *adv.* **1** completely. **2** taking everything into consideration. ◻ **in the altogether** *informal* naked.

altruism *n.* unselfishness. ◻ **altruist** *n.*, **altruistic** *adj.*, **altruistically** *adv.*

alum *n.* a colourless compound used in medicine and dyeing.

aluminium *n.* a metallic element (symbol Al), a lightweight silvery metal.

always *adv.* at all times; whatever the circumstances.

Alzheimer's disease (alts-hy-merz) *n.* a brain disorder causing senility.

AM *abbr.* amplitude modulation.

Am *symb.* americium.

a.m. *abbr.* (Latin *ante meridiem*) before noon.

amalgam *n.* **1** a blend. **2** an alloy of mercury used in dentistry.

amalgamate *v.* unite, combine. □ **amalgamation** *n.*

amass *v.* heap up, collect.

amateur *n.* a person who does something as a pastime rather than as a profession.

amateurish *adj.* unskilful.

amatory *adj.* relating to love.

amaze *v.* overwhelm with wonder. □ **amazement** *n.*

amazon *n.* a strong and aggressive woman.

ambassador *n.* a senior diplomat representing his or her country abroad.

amber *n.* yellowish fossilized resin; its colour.

ambidextrous *adj.* able to use either hand equally well.

ambience *n.* atmosphere, feeling.

ambient *adj.* **1** surrounding. **2** (of music) used to create atmosphere.

ambiguous *adj.* having two or more possible meanings. □ **ambiguity** *n.*, **ambiguously** *adv.*

ambit *n.* scope, bounds.

ambition *n.* a strong desire to achieve something. □ **ambitious** *adj.*, **ambitiously** *adv.*

ambivalent *adj.* with mixed feelings. □ **ambivalence** *n.*, **ambivalently** *adv.*

amble *v.* & *n.* (walk at) a leisurely pace.

ambrosia *n.* something delicious. □ **ambrosial** *adj.*

ambulance *n.* a vehicle equipped to carry sick or injured people.

ambuscade *n. dated* an ambush.

ambush *n.* a surprise attack by people lying in wait. ● *v.* attack in this way.

ameba Amer. sp. of **amoeba**.

ameliorate (ă-mee-lĭŏ-rayt) *v.* make or become better. □ **amelioration** *n.*

amen *int.* (in prayers) so be it.

amenable *adj.* cooperative. □ **amenable to** admitting of. □ **amenability** *n.*, **amenably** *adv.*

amend *v.* make minor alterations in (a text etc.). □ **make amends** compensate for something. □ **amendment** *n.*

■ **Usage** *Amend* is sometimes confused with *emend*, meaning 're-move errors from'.

amenity *n.* (*pl.* **-ies**) a pleasant or useful feature of a place.

American *adj.* of America; of the USA. ● *n.* an American person.

American football *n.* a form of football played with an oval ball and an H-shaped goal on a field marked as a gridiron.

Americanism *n.* an American word or phrase.

americium *n.* an artificially made radioactive metallic element (symbol Am).

amethyst (amĕ-thist) *n.* a precious stone, a purple or violet quartz.

amiable *adj.* likeable; friendly. □ **amiability** *n.*, **amiably** *adv.*

amicable *adj.* friendly. □ **amicably** *adv.*

amid, amidst *prep.* in the middle of; during.

amino acid *n.* an organic acid found in proteins.

amiss *adv.* wrongly, badly. ● *adj.* wrong, faulty.

amity *n.* friendly feeling.

ammeter *n.* an instrument that measures electric current.

ammonia *n.* a strong-smelling gas; a solution of this in water.

ammonite *n.* a fossil of a spiral shell.

ammunition *n.* a supply of bullets, shells, etc.

amnesia *n.* loss of memory. □ **amnesiac** *adj.* & *n.*

amnesty *n.* (*pl.* **-ies**) a general pardon.

amniocentesis (amni-oh-sen-**tee**-sis) *n.* (*pl.* **amniocenteses**) a prenatal test for foetal abnormality involving the withdrawal of a sample of amniotic fluid.

amniotic fluid *n.* the fluid surrounding the foetus in the womb.

amoeba (ă-**mee**-bă) *n.* (*Amer.* also **ameba**) (*pl.* **amoebae** or **amoebas**) a single-celled organism capable of changing shape.

amok *adv.* (also **amuck**) ◻ **run amok** be out of control.

among, amongst *prep.* **1** surrounded by. **2** being one of (a larger group). **3** between (different options, several recipients): *share it amongst you.*

amoral (ay-**mo**-răl) *adj.* not based on moral standards.

amorous *adj.* showing sexual desire.

amorphous *adj.* shapeless.

amortize *v.* (also **-ise**) pay off (a debt) gradually.

amount *n.* a total of anything; a quantity. ◻ **amount to** add up to; be equivalent to.

amour propre (a-moor **prop**-rĕ) *n.* self-respect.

amp *n. informal* **1** an ampere. **2** an amplifier.

ampere (**am**-pair) *n.* a unit of electric current (symbol A).

ampersand *n.* the sign & (= and).

amphetamine *n.* a stimulant drug.

amphibian *n.* an amphibious animal; an amphibious vehicle.

amphibious *adj.* able to live or operate both on land and in water.

amphitheatre *n.* (*Amer.* **amphitheater**) a semicircular unroofed building with tiers of seats round a central arena.

ample *adj.* plentiful, quite enough; large. ◻ **amply** *adv.*

amplify *v.* (**amplified, amplifying**), **1** make louder; intensify. **2** add details to (a statement). ◻ **amplification** *n.*, **amplifier** *n.*

amplitude *n.* breadth; abundance.

ampoule (**am**-pool) *n.* a small sealed container.

amuck var. of **amok**.

amputate *v.* cut off by surgical operation. ◻ **amputation** *n.*

amulet *n.* something worn as a charm against evil.

amuse *v.* cause to laugh or smile; make time pass pleasantly for. ◻ **amusement** *n.*, **amusing** *adj.*

an *adj.* the form of *a* used before vowel sounds.

anabolic steroid *n.* a synthetic steroid hormone used to build up bone and muscle.

anachronism (ă-**na**-krŏ-nizĕm) *n.* something that does not belong in the period in which it is placed. ◻ **anachronistic** *adj.*

anaconda *n.* a large snake of South America.

anaemia (ă-**nee**-miă) *n.* (*Amer.* **anemia**) lack of haemoglobin in the blood.

anaemic (ă-**nee**-mik) (*Amer.* **anemic**) *adj.* suffering from anaemia; pale and lacking in vitality.

anaerobic *adj.* not requiring air or oxygen.

anaesthesia (an-is-**thee**-ziă) *n.* (*Amer.* **anesthesia**) loss of sensation, esp. induced by anaesthetics.

anaesthetic (an-is-**the**-tik) *adj.* & *n.* (*Amer.* **anesthetic**) (a substance) causing loss of sensation.

anaesthetist (ă-**nees**-thĕ-tist) *n.* (*Amer.* **anesthetist**) a medical specialist who administers anaesthetics. ◻ **anaesthetize** *v.*

anagram *n.* a word or phrase formed by rearranging the letters of another word or phrase.

anal (**ay**-năl) *adj.* of the anus.

analgesic *adj.* & *n.* (a drug) relieving pain. ◻ **analgesia** *n.*

analog Amer. sp. of **analogue**.

analogous *adj.* comparable.

analogue *n.* (*Amer.* also **analog**) an analogous thing.

analogy (*pl.* **-ies**) *n.* a comparison; a partial likeness.

analyse *v.* (*Amer.* **analyze**) examine in detail; psychoanalyse. ▫ **analyst** *n.*

analysis *n.* (*pl.* **analyses**) a detailed examination or study.

analytical *adj.* (also **analytic**) of or using analysis. ▫ **analytically** *adv.*

analyze Amer. sp. of **analyse**.

anarchist *n.* a person who believes that government should be abolished. ▫ **anarchism** *n.*

anarchy *n.* total lack of organized control; lawlessness. ▫ **anarchic** *adj.*, **anarchical** *adj.*, **anarchically** *adv.*

anathema (ă-nath-ĕmă) *n.* **1** a detested thing. **2** a formal curse.

anathematize *v.* (also **-ise**) curse.

anatomist *n.* an expert in anatomy.

anatomize *v.* (also **-ise**) examine the anatomy or structure of.

anatomy *n.* (*pl.* **-ies**) bodily structure; a study of structure and functioning. ▫ **anatomical** *adj.*, **anatomically** *adv.*

ANC *abbr.* African National Congress.

ancestor *n.* a person from whom one is descended. ▫ **ancestral** *adj.*

ancestry *n.* (*pl.* **-ies**) one's ancestors collectively.

anchor *n.* a heavy metal structure for mooring a ship to the sea bottom. ● *v.* moor with an anchor; fix firmly.

anchorage *n.* a place where ships may anchor.

anchorman *n.* (*pl.* **-men**) **1** the compère of a radio or TV programme. **2** someone who reliably plays a vital part.

anchovy *n.* (*pl.* **-ies**) a small strong-tasting fish.

ancient *adj.* very old.

ancillary (an-sil-ă-ri) *adj.* helping in a subsidiary way.

and *conj.* **1** together with, added to. **2** next, then.

andante (an-dan-tai) *adv. Music* in moderately slow time.

andiron *n.* a metal stand for supporting wood in a fireplace.

androgynous *adj.* partly male and partly female in appearance.

anecdote *n.* a short amusing or interesting true story.

anemia etc. Amer. sp. of **anaemia** etc.

anemone (ă-ne-mŏ-nee) *n.* a plant with white, red, or purple flowers.

aneroid barometer *n.* a barometer measuring air pressure by the action of air on a box containing a vacuum.

anesthesia etc. Amer. sp. of **anaesthesia** etc.

aneurysm (a-newr-iz-ĕm) *n.* excessive swelling of an artery.

anew *adv.* **1** making a new start. **2** again.

angel *n.* **1** a supernatural being, messenger of God. **2** a kind person; *informal* a benefactor.

angelica *n.* candied stalks of a fragrant plant.

angelus *n.* a Roman Catholic prayer to the Virgin Mary said at morning, noon, and sunset; the bell announcing this.

anger *n.* a strong feeling of displeasure. ● *v.* make angry.

angina (an-JI-nă) *n.* (in full **angina pectoris**) pain in the chest caused by overexertion when the heart is diseased.

angle[1] *n.* **1** the space between two lines or surfaces at the point where they meet; a corner; a slant. **2** a point of view. ● *v.* present from a particular viewpoint; place obliquely.

angle[2] *v.* fish with line and bait as a sport; try to obtain something by hinting. ▫ **angler** *n.*, **angling** *n.*

Anglican *adj.* & *n.* (a member) of the Church of England. ▫ **Anglicanism** *n.*

Anglicism *n.* a uniquely British word or custom.

Anglicize *v.* (also **-ise**) make English in character.

Anglo- *comb. form* English, British.

Anglo-Saxon *n.* & *adj.* (of) an English person or language before the Norman Conquest; (of) a person of English descent.

angora *n.* yarn from the hair of a long-haired goat.

angry *adj.* (**angrier, angriest**) feeling or showing anger. □ **angrily** *adv.*

angst *n.* severe anxiety.

angstrom *n.* a unit of measurement for wavelengths.

anguish *n.* severe physical or mental pain. □ **anguished** *adj.*

angular *adj.* having angles or sharp corners; forming an angle.

anhydrous (an-**hI**-drŭs) *adj.* without water.

aniline (a-ni-leen) *n.* a colourless oily liquid used in making dyes and plastics.

animal *n.* & *adj.* (of) a living being with sense organs, able to move voluntarily; any such being other than a human.

animate *adj.* (an-i-măt) living. ● *v.* (an-i-mayt) bring to life; make vivacious. □ **animated** *adj.*, **animation** *n.*, **animator** *n.*

animism *n.* the belief that all natural things have a living soul.

animosity *n.* hostility.

animus *n.* animosity.

anion *n.* an ion with a negative charge.

aniseed *n.* a fragrant flavouring.

ankle *n.* the joint connecting the foot with the leg.

anklet *n.* a chain or band worn round the ankle.

annals *n.pl.* a narrative of events year by year.

anneal *v.* toughen (metal or glass) by heat and slow cooling.

annex (ă-neks) *v.* **1** take possession of. **2** add as a subordinate part. □ **annexation** *n.*

annexe (a-neks) *n.* an extension to a building.

annihilate *v.* destroy completely. □ **annihilation** *n.*

anniversary *n.* (*pl.* **-ies**) the date on which an event took place in a previous year.

annotate *v.* add explanatory notes to. □ **annotation** *n.*

announce *v.* make known publicly. □ **announcement** *n.*

announcer *n.* a person who announces items in a broadcast.

annoy *v.* cause slight anger to. □ **annoyance** *n.*, **annoyed** *adj.*

annual *adj.* yearly. ● *n.* **1** a plant that lives for one year or one season. **2** a book published in yearly issues. □ **annually** *adv.*

annuity *n.* (*pl.* **-ies**) a yearly allowance.

annul *v.* (**annulled, annulling**) declare invalid, cancel. □ **annulment** *n.*

annular *adj.* ring-shaped.

Annunciation *n.* the announcement by the angel Gabriel to the Virgin Mary that she was to be the mother of Christ.

anode *n.* a positively charged electrode.

anodize *v.* (also **-ise**) coat (metal) with a protective layer by electrolysis.

anodyne (an-o-dIn) *adj.* inoffensive but dull. ● *n.* a painkilling medicine.

anoint *v.* apply ointment or oil etc. to, esp. in religious consecration.

anomaly *n.* (*pl.* **-ies**) something irregular or inconsistent. □ **anomalous** *adj.*

anon *adv.* *archaic* soon.

anon. *abbr.* anonymous.

anonymous *adj.* of unknown or undisclosed name or authorship. □ **anonymity** *n.*, **anonymously** *adv.*

anorak *n.* a waterproof jacket with a hood.

anorexia *n.* reluctance to eat; (in full **anorexia nervosa**) a condition characterized by an obsessive desire to lose weight. □ **anorexic** *adj.* & *n.*

another *adj.* **1** an additional. **2** a different. ● *pron.* another one.

answer *n.* **1** something said or written in response to a previous statement. **2** the solution to a problem; a way of dealing with a difficulty. ● *v.* **1** speak or act in response (to); be or provide a solution to. **2** correspond to (a description); satisfy (a need). □ **answer for** be responsible for.

answerable *adj.* having to account for something.

answering machine *n.* a machine that answers telephone calls and records messages.

ant *n.* a small insect that lives in highly organized groups.

antacid *n.* & *adj.* (a substance) preventing or correcting acidity, esp. in the stomach.

antagonism *n.* hostility. □ **antagonistic** *adj.*

antagonist *n.* an opponent.

antagonize *v.* (also **-ise**) rouse antagonism in.

Antarctic *adj.* & *n.* (of) regions round the South Pole.

■ **Usage** *Antarctic* is spelt and pronounced with a *c* before *-tic*

---

ante *n.* a stake put up by a poker-player at the beginning of a hand.

ante- *pref.* before.

anteater *n.* a mammal that eats ants.

antecedent *n.* something that predates or precedes something else; (**antecedents**) a person's background. ● *adj.* previous.

antechamber *n.* an ante-room.

antedate *v.* **1** precede in time. **2** give an earlier date to.

antediluvian *adj.* of the time before Noah's Flood; *informal* antiquated.

antelope *n.* a deer-like wild animal.

antenatal *adj.* before birth; of or during pregnancy.

antenna *n.* **1** (*pl.* **antennae**) an insect's feeler. **2** (*pl.* **antennas**) a radio or TV aerial.

anterior *adj.* further forward in position or time.

ante-room *n.* a small room leading to a main one.

anthem *n.* **1** a piece of music to be sung in a religious service. **2** a song adopted by a country or by a group as an expression of identity.

anther *n.* a part of a flower's stamen containing pollen.

anthology *n.* (*pl.* **-ies**) a collection of passages from literature, esp. poems.

anthracite *n.* a form of coal burning with little flame or smoke.

anthrax *n.* a serious disease of sheep and cattle, transmissible to humans.

anthropoid *adj.* resembling a human in form. ● *n.* an anthropoid ape.

anthropology *n.* the study of the origin and customs of mankind. □ **anthropological** *adj.*, **anthropologist** *n.*

anthropomorphic *adj.* attributing human form or character to a god or animal. □ **anthropomorphism** *n.*

anti- *pref.* opposed to; counter-acting.

antibiotic *n.* & *adj.* (of) a substance that destroys bacteria.

antibody *n.* (*pl.* **-ies**) a protein formed in the blood in reaction to a substance which it then destroys.

anticipate *v.* expect, look forward to; deal with or respond to in advance. □ **anticipation** *n.*, **anticipatory** *adj.*

anticlimax *n.* a dull ending where a climax was expected.

anticlockwise *adj.* & *adv.* in the direction opposite to clockwise.

antics *n.pl.* ridiculous behaviour.

anticyclone *n.* an outward flow of air from an area of high pressure, producing fine weather.

antidepressant *n.* a drug counteracting mental depression.

antidote *n.* a substance that counteracts the effects of poison.

antifreeze *n.* a substance added to water to prevent freezing.

antigen (an-ti-jĕn) *n.* a foreign substance stimulating the production of antibodies.

anti-hero *n.* (*pl.* **anti-heroes**) a central character in a story, lacking conventional heroic qualities.

antihistamine *n.* a drug counteracting the effect of histamine, used to treat allergies.

anti-lock *adj.* (of brakes) designed to prevent locking of the wheels and skidding.

antimacassar *n.* a protective covering for a chair-back.

antimony *n.* a metallic element (symbol Sb).

antipasto *n.* (*pl.* **antipasti**) an Italian starter or appetizer.

antipathy *n.* (*pl.* **-ies**) strong dislike. ◻ **antipathetic** *adj.*

antiperspirant *n.* a substance that prevents or reduces sweating.

antipodes (an-**tip**-ŏdeez) *n.pl.* places on opposite sides of the earth, esp. Australia and New Zealand. ◻ **antipodean** *adj.*

antiquarian *adj.* relating to antiques and their study. ● *n.* a person who studies antiques.

antiquated *adj.* very old-fashioned.

antique *adj.* belonging to the distant past. ● *n.* an old and usu. valuable object.

antiquity *n.* (*pl.* **-ies**) **1** ancient times. **2** an object dating from ancient times.

anti-Semitic *adj.* hostile to Jews. ◻ **anti-Semitism** *n.*

antiseptic *adj.* & *n.* (a substance) preventing things from becoming septic.

antisocial *adj.* destructive or hostile to other members of society.

antistatic *adj.* counteracting the effects of static electricity.

antithesis *n.* (*pl.* **antitheses**) an opposite; a contrast. ◻ **antithetical** *adj.*

antitoxin *n.* a substance that neutralizes a toxin. ◻ **antitoxic** *adj.*

antler *n.* a branched horn of a deer.

antonym (**an**-tŏ-nim) *n.* a word opposite to another in meaning.

anus (ay-nŭs) *n.* the excretory opening at the end of the alimentary canal.

anvil *n.* an iron block on which a smith hammers metal into shape.

anxiety *n.* (*pl.* **-ies**) the state of being troubled and uneasy.

anxious *adj.* troubled and uneasy. ◻ **anxious to** eager to. ◻ **anxiously** *adv.*

any *adj.* **1** one or some of a quantity or amount: *have you any bread?* **2** an unspecified; expressing indifference as to identity: *any one will do.*

anybody *pron.* any person.

anyhow *adv.* **1** anyway. **2** in a disorganized or untidy way.

anyone *pron.* anybody.

anything *pron.* any item.

anyway *adv.* **1** used to add a further point: *it's too late, anyway.* **2** used to dismiss objections or difficulties: *I did it anyway.* **3** used in introducing a new topic.

anywhere *adv.* & *pron.* (in or to) any place.

AOB *abbr.* any other business.

aorta (ay-or-tă) *n.* the main artery carrying blood from the heart.

apace *adv.* swiftly.

apart *adv.* separately, so as to become separated; to or at a distance; into pieces.

apartheid (ă-par-tayt) *n.* a former policy of racial segregation (esp. in South Africa).

apartment *n.* a set of rooms; *Amer.* a flat.

apathy *n.* lack of interest or concern. ◻ **apathetic** *adj.*

ape *n.* a tailless primate, eg. a gorilla. ● *v.* imitate, mimic.

aperitif *n.* an alcoholic drink taken as an appetizer.

aperture *n.* an opening, esp. one that admits light.

Apex *n.* (also **APEX**) a system of reduced fares for scheduled flights paid for in advance.

apex *n.* the highest point or level.

aphasia *n.* loss of the ability to use language, resulting from brain damage.

aphid (ay-fid) *n.* a small insect destructive to plants.

aphorism (a-fŏr-iz-ĕm) *n.* a short saying expressing a general truth. □ **aphoristic** *adj.*

aphrodisiac *adj.* & *n.* (a substance) arousing sexual desire.

apiary *n.* (*pl.* **-ies**) a place where bees are kept. □ **apiarist** *n.*

apiece *adv.* to, for, or by each.

aplomb (ă-plom) *n.* self-possession, confidence.

apocalypse (ă-po-kă-lips) *n.* the destruction of the world, esp. as described in **the Apocalypse** (the last book of the New Testament); a catastrophic event. □ **apocalyptic** *adj.*

Apocrypha *n.pl.* the books of the Old Testament not accepted as part of the Hebrew scriptures.

apocryphal (ă-po-krŭ-făl) *adj.* of doubtful authenticity.

apogee (a-pŏ-jee) *n.* **1** the point in the moon's orbit furthest from the earth. **2** the climax of something.

apologetic *adj.* expressing regret for having done wrong. □ **apologetically** *adv.*

apologize *v.* (also **-ise**) make an apology.

apology *n.* (*pl.* **-ies**) **1** a statement of regret for having done wrong or hurt someone. □ **an apology for** a poor example of.

apoplectic *adj.* **1** *informal* furious. **2** *dated* relating to apoplexy.

apoplexy *n.* **1** *dated* a stroke. **2** *informal* extreme anger.

apostasy (ă-pos-tă-si) *n.* abandonment of one's former religious belief.

apostate (a-pos-tayt) *n.* a person who renounces a former belief.

a posteriori *adj.* (of reasoning) proceeding from effect to cause.

Apostle *n.* each of the twelve men sent by Christ to preach the gospel; (**apostle**) someone who supports and spreads an idea. □ **apostolic** *adj.*

apostrophe (ă-pos-trŏ-fi) *n.* the sign ' used to show the possessive case or omission of a letter.

apothecary *n.* (*pl.* **-ies**) *archaic* a pharmaceutical chemist.

apotheosis *n.* (*pl.* **apotheoses**) **1** elevation to divine status. **2** a supremely good example.

appal *v.* (*Amer.* **appall**) (**appalled, appalling**) horrify. □ **appalling** *adj.*

apparatus *n.* equipment for scientific or other work.

apparel *n. formal* clothing.

apparent *adj.* **1** clearly seen or understood. **2** seeming but not real. □ **apparently** *adv.*

apparition *n.* a ghost.

appeal *v.* **1** make an earnest or formal request. **2** refer a decision to a higher court. **3** seem attractive. ● *n.* **1** an act of appealing. **2** attractiveness.

appear *v.* **1** become visible. **2** seem, give an impression. □ **appearance** *n.*

appease *v.* pacify (someone) by giving what they ask for. □ **appeasement** *n.*

appellant *n.* a person who appeals to a higher court.

append *v.* add at the end.

appendage *n.* a thing appended.

appendectomy *n.* (*pl.* **-ies**) the surgical removal of the appendix.

appendicitis *n.* inflammation of the intestinal appendix.

appendix *n.* (*pl.* **appendices** or **appendixes**) **1** a section at the end of a book, giving extra information. **2** the small closed tube of tissue attached to the large intestine.

appertain *v.* be relevant.

appetite *n.* desire, esp. for food.

appetizer *n.* (also **-iser**) something eaten or drunk to stimulate the appetite.

appetizing *adj.* (also **-ising**) stimulating the appetite.

applaud *v.* express approval, esp. by clapping. □ **applause** *n.*

apple *n.* a round fruit with firm juicy flesh.

appliance *n.* a piece of equipment for a specific task.

applicable *adj.* appropriate; relevant. □ **applicability** *n.*

applicant *n.* a person who applies for a job.

application *n.* **1** a formal request. **2** sustained hard work. **3** the action of applying something. **4** a computer program designed for a particular purpose.

applicator *n.* a device for inserting or spreading something.

applied *adj.* put to practical use.

appliqué (ap-lee-kay) *n.* needle work in which pieces of fabric are attached to a background to make a design.

apply *v.* (**applied, applying**) **1** make a formal request. **2** be relevant. **3** spread over a surface. **4** bring into operation. □ **apply oneself** devote one's energy and attention.

appoint *v.* choose (a person) for a job. □ **appointee** *n.*

appointment *n.* **1** an arrangement to meet or visit at a specified time. **2** a job.

apportion *v.* share out.

apposite (a-pŏ-zIt) *adj.* appropriate, relevant.

apposition *n.* a grammatical relationship in which a word or phrase is placed immediately after another referring to the same thing and identifying it differently, e.g. *Elizabeth, our Queen.*

appraise *v.* estimate the value or quality of. □ **appraisal** *n.*

■ **Usage** Do not confuse *appraise* with *apprise*, 'inform'.

---

appreciable *adj.* considerable. □ **appreciably** *adv.*

appreciate *v.* **1** recognize the good qualities of; understand; be grateful for. **2** increase in value. □ **appreciation** *n.*, **appreciative** *adj.*

apprehend *v.* **1** seize, arrest. **2** perceive, understand.

apprehension *n.* **1** anxiety. **2** understanding. **3** arrest.

apprehensive *adj.* anxious, nervous. □ **apprehensively** *adv.*

apprentice *n.* a person learning a craft. □ **apprenticeship** *n.*

apprise *v.* inform.

■ **Usage** Do not confuse *apprise* with *appraise*

---

approach *v.* **1** come nearer to. **2** make a request or suggestion to. **3** start to deal with (a task). ● *n.* an act or manner of approaching; a path leading to a place.

approachable *adj.* easy to talk to.

approbation *n.* approval.

appropriate *adj.* (ă-**proh**-pri-ăt) suitable, proper. ● *v.* (ă-**proh**-pri-ayt) take and use; set aside for a special purpose. □ **appropriately** *adv.*, **appropriation** *n.*

approval *n.* approving.

approve *v.* **1** regard something as good or acceptable. **2** formally authorize or accept.

approx. *abbr.* approximate(ly).

approximate *adj.* (ă-**prok**-sim-ăt) almost but not quite exact. ● *v.* (ă-**prok**-sim-ayt) be very similar. □ **approximately** *adv.*, **approximation** *n.*

APR *abbr.* annual percentage rate (of interest).

Apr. *abbr.* April.

après-ski (ap-ray-**skee**) *n.* social activities following a day's skiing.

apricot *n.* a soft stone fruit related to the peach; its orange-yellow colour.

April *n.* the fourth month.

a priori *adj.* involving theoretical deduction from cause to effect. ● *adv.* without observation, using only theory.

apron *n.* **1** a garment worn over the front of the body to protect clothes. **2** part of a theatre stage in front of the curtain. **3** an area on an airfield for manoeuvring and loading aircraft.

apropos (aprŏ-**poh**) *adv.* concerning.

apse *n.* a recess with an arched or domed roof in a church.

apt *adj.* appropriate. □ **apt to** having, a tendency to. □ **aptly** *adv.*, **aptness** *n.*

aptitude *n.* natural ability.

aqualung *n.* a portable underwater breathing apparatus.

aquamarine *n.* a bluish-green gemstone.

aquaplane *n.* a board on which a person can be towed by a speedboat. ● *v.* (of a vehicle) glide uncontrollably on a wet road surface.

aquarium *n.* (*pl.* **aquariums** or **aquaria**) a tank for keeping living fish etc.; a building containing such tanks.

aquarobics *n.pl.* aerobic exercises performed in water.

aquatic *adj.* living or taking place in or on water.

aqua vitae *n.* alcoholic spirit, esp. brandy.

aqueduct *n.* a structure carrying a waterway over a valley.

aqueous (**ay**-kwi-ŭs) *adj.* of or like water.

aquifer *n.* a layer of water-bearing rock or soil.

aquiline *adj.* like an eagle; curved like an eagle's beak.

Ar *symb.* Argon.

Arab *n.* & *adj.* (a member) of a Semitic people of the Middle East.

arabesque *n.* **1** a ballet position in which one leg is lifted and extended backwards. **2** an ornamental design of intertwined lines.

Arabian *adj.* of Arabia.

Arabic *adj.* & *n.* (of) the language of the Arabs.

Arabic numerals *n.pl.* the symbols 1, 2, 3, etc.

arable *adj.* & *n.* (land) suitable for growing crops.

arachnid *n.* a spider or other member of the same class, e.g. a scorpion.

arbiter *n.* a person with power to judge in a dispute.

arbitrary *adj.* based on random choice. □ **arbitrarily** *adv.*

arbitrate *v.* act as arbitrator. □ **arbitration** *n.*

arbitrator *n.* an impartial person chosen to settle a dispute.

arbor Amer. sp. of **arbour**.

arboreal (ah-**bor**-ree-ăl) *adj.* of or living in trees.

arboretum *n.* (*pl.* **arboretums** or **arboreta**) a place where trees are grown for study and display.

arbour *n.* (*Amer.* **arbor**) a shady shelter under trees or a framework with climbing plants.

arc *n.* **1** part of a curve, esp. of the circumference of a circle. **2** a luminous electric current crossing a gap between terminals.

arcade *n.* a covered walk between shops; an enclosed place containing games machines etc.

arcane *adj.* mysterious.

arch[1] *n.* a curved structure, esp. as a support; a curved shape. ● *v.* make or become arch-shaped.

arch[2] *adj.* affectedly playful. □ **archly** *adv.*, **archness** *n.*

arch- *pref.* chief, principal, main.

archaeology *n.* (*Amer.* **archeology**) the study of earlier civilizations through their material remains. □ **archaeological** *adj.*, **archaeologist** *n.*

archaic *adj.* belonging to former or ancient times.

archaism *n.* an archaic word or phrase.

archangel *n.* an angel of the highest rank.

archbishop *n.* a chief bishop.

archdeacon *n.* a priest ranking next below bishop.

archduke *n. hist.* the son of an Austrian Emperor.

archeology Amer. sp. of **archaeology**.

archer *n.* a person who shoots with bow and arrows. □ **archery** *n.*

archetype (ar-ki-typ) *n.* a typical example; an original model. ▫ **archetypal** *adj.*

archipelago (ah-ki-pe-lă-goh) *n.* (*pl.* **archipelagos** or **archipelagoes**) a group of islands; the sea round this.

architect *n.* a designer of buildings.

architecture *n.* the designing of buildings; the style of a building. ▫ **architectural** *adj.*

architrave (ah-ki-tragv) *n.* a moulded frame round a doorway or window.

archive (ar-kyv) *n.* (usu. **archives**) a collection of historical documents.

archivist (ar-kiv-ist) *n.* a person trained to deal with archives.

archway *n.* an arched entrance or passage.

Arctic *adj.* **1** of regions round the North Pole. **2** (**arctic**) *informal* very cold.

▪ **Usage** *Arctic* is spelt and pronounced with a *c* before *-tic*.

ardent *adj.* passionate, enthusiastic. ▫ **ardently** *adv.*

ardour *n.* (*Amer.* **ardor**) passion; enthusiasm.

arduous *adj.* needing much effort.

area *n.* **1** a region; a space for a specific use. **2** the extent of a surface or piece of land.

arena *n.* a level area in the centre of an amphitheatre or sports stadium; the scene of a conflict.

arête *n.* a sharp mountain ridge.

argon *n.* a chemical element (symbol Ar), an inert gas.

argot (ar-goh) *n.* jargon, slang.

arguable *adj.* **1** able to be asserted or maintained. **2** open to question. ▫ **arguably** *adv.*

argue *v.* **1** express disagreement; exchange angry words. **2** give reasons for an opinion.

argument *n.* **1** a discussion involving disagreement; a quarrel. **2** a reason put forward; a chain of reasoning.

argumentative *adj.* given to arguing.

aria *n.* a solo in an opera.

arid *adj.* dry, parched. ▫ **aridity** *n.*, **aridly** *adv.*

arise *v.* (**arose, arisen, arising**) **1** come into existence or to people's notice. **2** *literary* rise.

aristocracy *n.* (*pl.* **-ies**) the hereditary upper classes. ▫ **aristocrat** *n.* **aristocratic** *adj.*

arithmetic *n.* calculating by means of numbers.

ark *n.* **1** (in the Bible) the ship built by Noah to escape the Flood. **2** (in full **Ark of the Covenant**) a wooden chest in which the writings of Jewish Law were kept.

arm *n.* **1** an upper limb of the body. **2** a raised side part of a chair. **3** a division of a company or organization. **4** (**arms**) weapons. ● *v.* equip with weapons; make (a bomb) ready to explode.

armada *n.* a fleet of warships.

armadillo *n.* (*pl.* **armadillos**) a mammal of South America with a body encased in bony plates.

Armageddon *n.* a final disastrous conflict; in the Bible, the last battle between good and evil before the Day of Judgement.

armament *n.* military weapons.

armature *n.* the wire-wound core of a dynamo or electric motor.

armchair *n.* an upholstered chair with supports for the arms at the sides.

armistice *n.* an agreement to stop fighting temporarily.

armlet *n.* a band worn round a person's arm.

armor etc. Amer. sp. of **armour** etc.

armorial *adj.* of heraldry.

armour *n.* (*Amer.* **armor**) a protective metal covering, esp. that formerly worn in battle.

armoured *adj.* (*Amer.* **armored**) protected by armour.

armoury *n.* (*pl.* **-ies**) (*Amer.* **armory**) a place where weapons are kept.

armpit *n.* the hollow under the arm at the shoulder.

army *n.* (*pl.* **-ies**) **1** an organized force for fighting on land. **2** a vast group.

arnica *n.* a plant substance used to treat bruises.

aroma *n.* a smell, esp. a pleasant one. □ **aromatic** *adj.*

aromatherapy *n.* the use of essential plant oils for healing.

arose past of **arise**.

around *adv.* & *prep.* **1** on every side (of). **2** in the vicinity (of). **3** approximately. **4** to many places throughout (an area); so as to encircle. **5** so as to face in the opposite direction

arouse *v.* waken; stir; stimulate.

arpeggio *n.* (ah-pe-jee-oh) (*pl.* **arpeggios**) the notes of a musical chord played in succession.

arraign (ă-rayn) *v.* accuse; find fault with. □ **arraignment** *n.*

arrange *v.* **1** put into order. **2** organize; settle; prepare. **3** adapt (a piece of music). □ **arrangement** *n.*

arrant *adj.* utter: *arrant nonsense.* □ **arrantly** *adv.*

array *n.* **1** a display or wide range. **2** an arrangement. **3** *literary* fine clothing. ● *v.* **1** arrange. **2** dress finely.

arrears *n.pl.* money owed and overdue for repayment; work overdue for being finished.

arrest *v.* **1** seize (someone) by legal authority. **2** stop, delay. ● *n.* the legal seizure of an offender.

arrival *n.* arriving; a person or thing that has arrived.

arrive *v.* reach the end of a journey; (of time) come; be recognized as having achieved success.

arrogant *adj.* exaggerating one's importance or abilities; proud. □ **arrogance** *n.*, **arrogantly** *adv.*

arrogate *n.* take or claim for oneself without justification.

arrow *n.* a straight shaft with a sharp point, shot from a bow; a sign shaped like this.

arrowroot *n.* a form of edible starch.

arse *n.* (*Amer.* **ass**) *vulgar slang* the buttocks or anus.

arsenal *n.* a place where weapons are stored or made.

arsenic *n.* a semi-metallic element (symbol As); a strongly poisonous compound of this. □ **arsenical** *adj.*

arson *n.* the intentional and unlawful setting on fire of a building. □ **arsonist** *n.*

art *n.* **1** the creation of something beautiful and expressive; paintings and sculptures. **2** (**arts**) subjects other than sciences; creative activities (e.g. painting, music, writing). **3** a skill.

artefact *n.* (*Amer.* **artifact**) a man-made object.

arterial *adj.* of an artery.

arterial road *n.* a major road.

arteriosclerosis (ah-teer-ioh-skleer-**oh**-sis) *n.* a thickening of the artery walls, hindering blood circulation.

artery *n.* (*pl.* **-ies**) a large blood vessel carrying blood away from the heart.

artesian well *n.* a well that is bored vertically into oblique strata so that water rises naturally with little or no pumping.

artful *adj.* crafty. □ **artfully** *adv.*

arthritis *n.* a condition in which there is pain and stiffness in the joints. □ **arthritic** *adj.*

arthropod *n.* an animal with a segmented body and jointed limbs (e.g. a crustacean).

artichoke *n.* **1** (also **globe artichoke**) a plant with a flower of leaflike scales used as a vegetable. **2** (**Jerusalem artichoke**) a type of sunflower with a root eaten as a vegetable.

article *n.* **1** an individual object. **2** a piece of writing in a newspaper or journal. **3** a clause in an agreement. □ **definite article** the word 'the'. **indefinite article** the word 'a' or 'an'.

articled clerk *n. dated* a trainee solicitor.

articulate *adj.* (ar-**tik**-yoo-lăt) able to express oneself coherently; (of speech) clear and coherent. ● *v.* (ar-**tik**-yoo-layt) **1** speak or express clearly. **2** form a joint, connect by joints. ◻ **articulately** *adv.*, **articulation** *n.*

articulated lorry *n.* a lorry with sections connected by a flexible joint.

artifact Amer. sp. of **artefact**.

artifice *n.* a clever deception; skill.

artificial *adj.* not originating naturally; man-made. ◻ **artificiality** *n.*, **artificially** *adv.*

artificial intelligence *n.* the development of computers to do things normally requiring human intelligence.

artillery *n.* (*pl.* **-ies**) large guns used in fighting on land; a branch of an army using these.

artisan *n.* a skilled manual worker, a craftsperson.

artist *n.* **1** a person who creates works of art, esp. paintings. **2** a person skilled at a particular task. **3** a professional entertainer. ◻ **artistry** *n.*

artiste (ar-**teest**) *n.* a professional entertainer.

artistic *adj.* **1** of art or artists. **2** skilled in art. **3** aesthetically pleasing. ◻ **artistically** *adv.*

artless *adj.* simple and natural. ◻ **artlessly** *adv.*, **artlessness** *n.*

artwork *n.* pictures and diagrams in published material.

arty *adj.* (**artier artiest**) *informal* pretentiously displaying one's interest in the arts.

As *symb.* arsenic.

as *adv.* & *conj.* **1** used in comparisons to indicate extent or degree: *as old as you*; used to indicate manner: *do as you like*. **2** while. **3** because. **4** although: *much as I'd like to, I can't*. ● *prep.* in the role or form of: *speaking as a friend*. ◻ **as for, as to** with regard to. **as well** in addition.

asafoetida *n.* (also **asafetida**) a strong-smelling spice.

a.s.a.p. *abbr.* as soon as possible.

asbestos *n.* a soft fibrous mineral substance used to make fireproof material.

asbestosis *n.* a lung disease caused by inhaling asbestos particles.

ascend *v.* rise; climb.

ascendant *adj.* rising.

ascension *n.* an ascent, esp. (**Ascension**) that of Christ to heaven.

ascent *n.* going up; away up.

ascertain (as-ser-**tayn**) *v.* find out. ◻ **ascertainable** *adj.*

ascetic *adj.* & *n.* (a person) abstaining from pleasures and luxuries. ◻ **asceticism** *n.*

ASCII *abbr. Computing* American Standard Code for Information Interchange; a code assigning a different number to each letter and character.

ascorbic acid *n.* vitamin C.

ascribe *v.* attribute. ◻ **ascription** *n.*

asepsis *n.* an aseptic condition.

aseptic *adj.* free from harmful bacteria. ◻ **aseptically** *adv.*

asexual *adj.* without sex. ◻ **asexually** *adv.*

ash *n.* **1** a tree with silver-grey bark. **2** powder that remains after something has burnt.

ashamed *adj.* feeling shame.

ashcan *n. Amer.* a dustbin.

ashen *adj.* pale as ashes; grey.

ashlar *n.* masonry made of large square-cut stones.

ashore *adv.* to or on the shore.

ashram *n.* (originally in India) a place of religious retreat.

Asian *adj.* of Asia or its people. ● *n.* an Asian person.

Asiatic *adj.* of Asia.

aside *adv.* to or on one side. ● *n.* a remark made so that only certain people will hear.

asinine (a-si-nIn) *adj.* silly.

ask *v.* **1** try to obtain an answer (to) or information (from). **2** make a request. **3** invite (someone).

askance *adv.* ◻ **look askance at** regard with disapproval.

askew *adv.* & *adj.* crooked(ly).

asleep *adv.* & *adj.* in or into a state of sleep.

asp *n.* a small poisonous snake.

asparagus *n.* a plant whose shoots are used as a vegetable.

aspect *n.* **1** a feature or part of something. **2** the appearance of something. **3** the direction in which a building faces.

aspen *n.* a poplar tree.

asperity *n.* harshness.

aspersion *n.* a derogatory remark.

asphalt *n.* a black tar-like substance mixed with gravel for surfacing roads.

asphyxia (ăs-fix-i-ă) *n.* suffocation.

asphyxiate *v.* suffocate. ◻ **asphyxiation** *n.*

aspic *n.* a savoury jelly for coating cooked meat, eggs, etc.

aspidistra *n.* an ornamental plant.

aspirant *n.* a person aiming to achieve something.

aspirate *n.* (ass-pi-răt) the sound of *h.* ● *v.* (ass-pi-rayt) pronounce with an *h.*

aspiration *n.* **1** an earnest desire or ambition. **2** aspirating.

aspire *v.* have a hope or ambition.

aspirin *n.* a drug that relieves pain and reduces fever.

ass *n.* **1** a donkey. **2** *informal* a stupid person. **3** *Amer.* = **arse**.

assail *v.* attack violently.

assailant *n.* an attacker.

assassin *n.* a killer of an important person.

assassinate *v.* kill (an important person) by violent means. ◻ **assassination** *n.*

assault *n.* & *v.* attack.

assay *n.* a test of metal for quality. ● *v.* make an assay of.

assemble *v.* bring or come together; put together the parts of.

assembly *n.* an assembled group; assembling.

assent *n.* agreement. ● *v.* express agreement.

assert *v.* **1** state, declare to be true. **2** exercise (rights or authority). ◻ **assert oneself** behave forcefully. ◻ **assertion** *n.*, **assertive** *adj.*, **assertiveness** *n.*

assess *v.* decide the amount or value of; estimate the worth or likelihood of. ◻ **assessment** *n.*, **assessor** *n.*

asset *n.* **1** a property with money value. **2** a useful or valuable thing, person, or quality.

assiduous *adj.* diligent and persevering. ◻ **assiduity** *n.*, **assiduously** *adv.*, **assiduousness** *n.*

assign *v.* allot to a person or purpose; designate to perform a task.

assignation *n.* an arrangement to meet.

assignment *n.* a task assigned.

assimilate *v.* absorb or be absorbed into the body, into a larger group, or into the mind as knowledge. ◻ **assimilation** *n.*

assist *v.* help. ◻ **assistance** *n.*

assistant *n.* a helper; a person who serves customers in a shop. ● *adj.* assisting, esp. as a subordinate.

assizes *n.pl.* formerly, a county court.

associate *v.* (ă-soh-si-ayt) **1** connect in one's mind; (**be associated**) occur together, be linked. **2** mix socially; (**associate oneself**) be involved with something. ● *n.* (ă-soh-si-ăt) **1** a business companion, a partner. **2** a subordinate member.

association *n.* **1** a group organized for a shared purpose; a link, a connection. **2** feelings or ideas commonly connected with another idea.

assonance *n.* the rhyming of vowels but not consonants in neighbouring syllables. ◻ **assonant** *adj.*

assorted *adj.* of several sorts.

assortment *n.* a collection composed of several sorts.

assuage (ă-swayj) *v.* soothe; satisfy (a desire).

assume *v.* **1** accept as true without proof. **2** take on (a responsibility, quality, etc.).

assumption *n.* something assumed to be true.

assurance *n.* **1** an assertion, a promise. **2** self-confidence. **3** life insurance.

assure *v.* tell confidently, promise.

assured *adj.* **1** sure, confident. **2** insured.

assuredly *adv.* certainly.

astatine (ass-tă-teen) *n.* a radioactive element (symbol At).

asterisk *n.* a star-shaped symbol (*).

astern *adv.* at or towards the stern; backwards.

asteroid *n.* one of many small rocky bodies orbiting the sun between Mars and Jupiter.

asthma *n.* a chronic condition causing difficulty in breathing. □ **asthmatic** *adj.* & *n.*

astigmatism *n.* a defect in an eye, preventing proper focusing. □ **astigmatic** *adj.*

astonish *v.* surprise very greatly. □ **astonishment** *n.*

astound *v.* amaze, stun.

astral *adj.* of or from the stars.

astray *adv.* & *adj.* away from the proper path.

astride *adv.* & *prep.* with one leg on each side (of).

astringent *adj.* **1** causing tissue to contract. **2** harsh, severe. ● *n.* an astringent substance or drug. □ **astringency** *n.*

astro- *comb. form* of the stars.

astrology *n.* the study of the supposed influence of stars on human affairs. □ **astrologer** *n.*, **astrological** *adj.*

astronaut *n.* a person trained to travel in a spacecraft.

astronautics *n.* the study of space travel and its technology.

astronomical *adj.* **1** of astronomy. **2** *informal* enormous in amount. □ **astronomically** *adv.*

astronomy *n.* the study of stars and planets and their movements. □ **astronomer** *n.*

astrophysics *n.* the study of the physics and chemistry of heavenly bodies. □ **astrophysicist** *n.*

astute *adj.* shrewd. □ **astutely** *adv.*, **astuteness** *n.*

asunder *adv. literary* apart.

asylum *n.* **1** refuge, protection. **2** *dated* a mental institution.

asymmetrical *adj.* lacking symmetry. □ **asymmetrically** *adv.*, **asymmetry** *n.*

At *symb.* astatine.

at *prep.* **1** expressing position in space or time. **2** denoting the object of a movement; engaged in: *at work*. **3** denoting a state: *at an advantage*. **4** having as a price.

atavistic *adj.* reverting to ancient ancestral characteristics. □ **atavism** *n.*

ataxia *n.* difficulty in controlling body movements.

ate past of **eat**.

atheist *n.* a person who does not believe in God. □ **atheism** *n.*

atherosclerosis (a-thĕ-roh-skleer-oh-sis) *n.* damage to the arteries caused by a build-up of fatty deposits.

athlete *n.* a person who is good at athletics.

athlete's foot *n.* an infectious fungal condition of the foot.

athletic *adj.* **1** strong, fit, and active. **2** of athletics. ● *n.* (**athletics**) track and field sports. □ **athletically** *adv.*, **athleticism** *n.*

atlas *n.* a book of maps.

atmosphere *n.* **1** the mixture of gases surrounding a planet; air. **2** a unit of pressure. **3** the feeling given by a place, situation, etc. □ **atmospheric** *adj.*

atoll *n.* a ring-shaped coral reef enclosing a lagoon.

atom *n.* the smallest particle of a chemical element; a very small quantity. ◻ **atomic** *adj.*

atomic bomb *n.* a bomb deriving its power from atomic energy.

atomic energy *n.* energy obtained from nuclear fission.

atomize *v.* (also **-ise**) reduce to atoms or fine particles. ◻ **atomization** *n.*, **atomizer** *n.*

atonal (ay-**toh**-năl) *adj.* (of music) not written in any key. ◻ **atonality** *n.*

atone *v.* make amends for a fault. ◻ **atonement** *n.*

atrium *n.* (*pl.* **atria** or **atriums**) **1** either of the two upper heart cavities. **2** the central court of an ancient Roman house.

atrocious *adj.* very bad. ◻ **atrociously** *adv.*

atrocity *n.* (*pl.* **-ies**) wickedness; a cruel act.

atrophy *v.* (**atrophied, atrophying**) (cause to) waste away from lack of use or nourishment. ● *n.* wasting away.

attach *v.* fix to something else; join; ascribe; be ascribed. ◻ **attachment** *n.*

attaché (ă-**tash**-ay) *n.* a person attached to an ambassador's staff.

attaché case *n.* a small case for carrying documents.

attached *adj.* fastened on. ◻ **attached to** fond of

attack *n.* a violent attempt to hurt or defeat a person; strong criticism; a sudden onset of illness. ● *v.* make an attack (on). ◻ **attacker** *n.*

attain *v.* achieve. ◻ **attainable** *adj.*, **attainment** *n.*

attar *n.* a fragrant oil from rose-petals.

attempt *v.* try. ● *n.* an effort.

attend *v.* **1** be present at; accompany. **2** take notice; (**attend to**) deal with, look after. ◻ **attendance** *n.*

attendant *n.* an assistant; a person providing service in a particular place. ● *adj.* occurring with something; accompanying.

attention *n.* **1** concentrating one's mind on something; notice; care. **2** an erect attitude in military drill.

attentive *adj.* paying attention; considerate, helpful. ◻ **attentively** *adv.*, **attentiveness** *n.*

attenuate *v.* make thin or weaker. ◻ **attenuation** *n.*

attest *v.* provide proof of; declare true or genuine. ◻ **attestation** *n.*

attic *n.* a room in the top storey of a house.

attire *n. literary* clothes. ● *v.* clothe.

attitude *n.* **1** a fixed way of thinking. **2** a position of the body. **3** *informal* uncooperative behaviour. **4** *informal* individuality, self-confidence.

attorney *n.* (*pl.* **attorneys**) *Amer.* a lawyer.

Attorney-General *n.* the chief legal officer in England and some other countries.

attract *v.* cause to come somewhere or do something by offering advantage; arouse interest or liking in. ◻ **attraction** *n.*

attractive *adj.* pleasing in appearance. ◻ **attractively** *adv.*, **attractiveness** *n.*

attribute *n.* (**at**-ri-bewt) a characteristic quality. ◻ **attribute to** (ă-**tri**-bewt) regard as belonging to or caused by. ◻ **attributable** *adj.*, **attribution** *n.*

attributive *adj. Grammar* (of a word) placed before the word it describes.

attrition *n.* wearing away.

attune *v.* make or become sensitive.

atypical *adj.* not typical. ◻ **atypically** *adv.*

Au *symb.* gold.

aubergine (**oh**-ber-*zheen*) *n.* (also **eggplant**) a dark purple tropical vegetable.

auburn *adj.* (of hair) reddish brown.

auction *n.* a public sale where articles are sold to the highest bidder. ● *v.* sell by auction.

auctioneer *n.* a person who conducts an auction.

audacious *adj.* daring. □ **audaciously** *adv.*, **audacity** *n.*

audible *adj.* loud enough to be heard. □ **audibly** *adv.*

audience *n.* **1** a group of listeners or spectators. **2** a formal interview.

audio *n.* sound or the reproduction of sound.

audiotape *n.* (also **audio tape**) a magnetic tape for recording sound; a recording on this.

audio-visual *adj.* using both sight and sound.

audit *n.* an official examination of accounts. ● *v.* make an audit of. □ **auditor** *n.*

audition *n.* a test of a performer's ability for a particular part. ● *v.* test or be tested in an audition.

auditorium *n.* (**auditoriums** or **auditoria**) the part of a theatre or concert hall where the audience sits.

auditory *adj.* of hearing.

au fait (oh fay) *adj.* □ **au fait with** having good knowledge of (a subject).

Aug. *abbr.* August.

auger (or-gĕ) *n.* a boring tool with a spiral point.

augment *v.* add to, increase. □ **augmentation** *n.*, **augmentative** *adj.*

au gratin (oh gra-tan) *adj.* cooked with a topping of breadcrumbs or grated cheese.

augur *v.* be an omen.

augury *n.* (*pl.* **-ies**) an omen; interpretation of omens.

August *n.* the eighth month.

august (aw-**gust**) *adj.* majestic.

auk (ork) *n.* a northern seabird.

aunt *n.* the sister or sister-in-law of one's father or mother.

au pair *n.* a young person from overseas helping with housework in return for board and lodging.

aura *n.* the atmosphere surrounding a person or thing.

aural (or-ăl, ow-răl) *adj.* of the ear. □ **aurally** *adv.*

■ **Usage** *Aural* is sometimes confused with *oral*, 'spoken'.

aureole *n.* (also **aureola**) a halo.

au revoir (oh rĕ-vwah) *int.* goodbye (until we meet again).

auscultation (or-skŭl-tay-shŏn) *n.* listening to the sound of the heart or other organs for medical diagnosis.

auspices *n.pl.* □ **under the auspices of** with the support of.

auspicious *adj.* conducive to success; being an omen of success. □ **auspiciously** *adv.*, **auspiciousness** *n.*

austere *adj.* severely simple and plain. □ **austerity** *n.*

Australasian *adj.* & *n.* (a native or inhabitant) of Australia, New Zealand, and neighbouring islands.

Australian *adj.* & *n.* (a native or inhabitant) of Australia.

authentic *adj.* genuine, known to be true. □ **authentically** *adv.*, **authenticity** *n.*

authenticate *v.* prove the authenticity of. □ **authentication** *n.*

author *n.* the writer of a book etc.; an originator of something. □ **authorship** *n.*

authoritarian *adj.* favouring complete obedience to authority. □ **authoritarianism** *n.*

authoritative *adj.* **1** reliably accurate or true. **2** commanding obedience and respect. □ **authoritatively** *adv.*

authority *n.* (*pl.* **-ies**) **1** power to enforce obedience; a person with this. **2** a person with specialized knowledge.

authorize *v.* (also **-ise**) give official permission for. □ **authorization** *n.*

autistic (or-tis-tik) *adj.* suffering from a mental disorder that prevents normal communication and relationships. □ **autism** *n.*

auto- *comb. form* self; own.

autobiography *n.* (*pl.* **-ies**) the story of a person's life written by that person. □ **autobiographical** *adj.*

autocracy *n.* (*pl.* **-ies**) rule by an autocrat.

autocrat *n.* a ruler with unrestricted power. □ **autocratic** *adj.*, **autocratically** *adv.*

autocross *n.* motor racing across country or on dirt tracks.

autocue *n. trademark* a device showing a speaker's script on a television screen unseen by the audience.

autograph *n.* a person's signature. ● *v.* write one's name in or on.

autoimmune *adj.* (of diseases) caused by antibodies produced against substances naturally present in the body.

automat *n. Amer. historical* a cafeteria in which food was obtained from slot machines.

automate *v.* introduce automation to (a process).

automatic *adj.* functioning without human intervention; done without thinking. ● *n.* an automatic machine or firearm. □ **automatically** *adv.*

automation *n.* the use of automatic equipment in industry.

automaton *n.* (*pl.* **automatons** or **automata**) a robot.

automobile *n. Amer.* a car.

automotive *adj.* concerned with motor vehicles.

autonomous *adj.* self-governing. □ **autonomy** *n.*

autopilot *n.* a device for keeping an aircraft or ship on a set course automatically.

autopsy *n.* (*pl.* **-ies**) a post-mortem.

autumn *n.* the season between summer and winter. □ **autumnal** *adj.*

auxiliary *adj.* giving help or support. ● *n.* (*pl.* **-ies**) a helper.

auxiliary verb *n. Grammar* a verb used in forming the tenses of other verbs.

avail *v.* be of use or help. □ **avail oneself of** make use of. **to no avail** without success.

available *adj.* ready to be used; obtainable. □ **availability** *n.*

avalanche *n.* a mass of snow pouring down a mountain.

avant-garde (av-ahn-**gard**) *adj.* new, experimental, progressive. ● *n.* a group of innovators, esp. in the arts.

avarice *n.* greed for gain. □ **avaricious** *adj.*, **avariciously** *adv.*

Ave. *abbr.* avenue.

avenge *v.* take vengeance for. □ **avenger** *n.*

avenue *n.* a wide road, usu. tree-lined; a method of approach.

aver *v.* (**averred, averring**) state as true.

average *n.* a value arrived at by adding several quantities together and dividing by the number of these; a standard regarded as usual. ● *adj.* found by making an average; ordinary, usual.

averse *adj.* having a strong dislike.

aversion *n.* a strong dislike.

avert *v.* **1** turn away. **2** ward off.

aviary *n.* (*pl.* **-ies**) a large cage or building for keeping birds.

aviation *n.* the practice or science of flying an aircraft.

avid *adj.* having a strong desire. □ **avidity** *n.*, **avidly** *adv.*

avionics *n.* electronics in aviation.

avocado *n.* (*pl.* **avocados**) a pear-shaped tropical fruit.

avocet *n.* a wading bird with a long upturned bill.

avoid *v.* keep oneself away from; refrain from. □ **avoidable** *adj.*, **avoidance** *n.*

avoirdupois (av-wah-dyou-**pwah**) *n.* a system of weights based on a pound of 16 ounces.

avow *v.* declare. □ **avowal** *n.*

avuncular *adj.* of or like a kindly uncle.

AWACS *abbr.* airborne warning and control system.

await *v.* wait for; be in store for.

awake *v.* (**awoke, awoken, awaking**) wake. ● *adj.* not asleep; alert.

awaken *v.* awake.

award *v.* give by official decision as a prize or penalty. ● *n.* something awarded; awarding.

aware *adj.* having knowledge or realization. □ **awareness** *n.*

awash *adj.* covered or flooded with water.

away *adv.* **1** to or at a distance; into non-existence. **2** constantly: *toiling away.* ● *adj.* (of a match) played on an opponent's ground.

awe *n.* respect combined with fear or wonder. ● *v.* fill with awe.

aweigh *adj.* (of an anchor) raised clear of the sea bottom.

awesome *adj.* causing awe.

awful *adj.* **1** extremely bad or unpleasant. **2** *informal* very great; utter.

awfully *adv.* **1** very much; extremely. **2** very badly.

awhile *adv.* for a short time.

awkward *adj.* **1** difficult to use, do, or handle; inconvenient; clumsy. **2** uncooperative. **3** embarrassed; embarrassing. □ **awkwardly** *adv.*, **awkwardness** *n.*

awl *n.* a tool for making holes in leather or wood.

awning *n.* a canvas shelter.

awoke, awoken past. & p.p. of **awake**.

AWOL *abbr.* absent without leave.

awry (ă-ry) *adv.* & *adj.* **1** twisted to one side. **2** wrong, amiss.

axe (*Amer.* usu. **ax**) *n.* a chopping tool with a sharp blade. ● *v.* (**axed, axing**) remove by abolishing or dismissing.

axiom *n.* an accepted general principle. □ **axiomatic** *adj.*

axis *n.* (*pl.* **axes**) a line through the centre of an object, round which it rotates if spinning. □ **axial** *adj.*

axle *n.* a rod on which wheels turn.

ayatollah *n.* a Muslim religious leader in Iran.

aye (also **ay**) *adv. archaic* or *dialect* yes. ● *n.* a vote in favour.

Aztec *n.* a member of a former Indian people ruling Mexico before the Spanish conquest in the 16th century.

azure *adj.* & *n.* (of) a deep sky-blue colour.

Bb

B *abbr.* (B, 2B, 3B, etc.) black (denoting a pencil lead softer than H and HB). ● *symb.* boron.

b. *abbr.* born.

BA *abbr.* Bachelor of Arts.

ba *symb.* barium.

baa *n.* & *v.* (**baaed, baaing**) (utter) a bleat.

babble *v.* chatter indistinctly or foolishly; (of a stream) murmur. ● *n.* babbling talk or sound.

babe *n.* a baby; *informal* an attractive young woman.

babel *n.* a confused noise.

baboon *n.* a large monkey.

baby *n.* (*pl.* **-ies**) a very young child or animal; *informal* an affectionate address to a girl friend. ● *adj.* small of its kind, miniature. □ **babyish** *adj.*

babysit *v.* (**babysat, babysitting**) look after a child while its parents are out. □ **babysitter** *n.*

baccalaureate (bak-ă-*lor*-iăt) *n.* the final school examination in France.

baccarat (*bak*-er-ah) *n.* a gambling card game.

bachelor *n.* **1** an unmarried man. **2** used in names of university degrees.

bacillus (ba-si-lŭs) *n.* (*pl.* **bacilli**) a rod-shaped bacterium.

back *n.* the surface or part furthest from the front; the rear part of the human body from shoulders to hips; the corresponding part of an animal's body; a defensive player positioned near the goal in football etc. ● *adv.* **1** at or towards the rear; in or into a previous time, position, or state. **2** in return: *ring me back.* ● *v.* **1** support, help. **2** move backwards. **3** lay a bet on. ● *adj.* **1** situated at the back. **2** of or relating to the past: *back numbers.* □ **back down** withdraw a claim or argument. **back out** withdraw from a commitment. **back up 1** support. **2** make a copy of (a computer disc). □ **backer** *n.*

backache *n.* a pain in one's back.

backbencher *n.* an ordinary MP not holding a senior office.

backbiting *n.* spiteful talk.

backbone *n.* the column of small bones down the centre of the back.

backchat *n. informal* answering back rudely.

backcloth *n.* a painted cloth at the back of a stage or scene.

backdate *v.* declare to be valid from a previous date.

backdrop *n.* a backcloth; a background.

backfire *v.* **1** make an explosion in an exhaust pipe. **2** produce an undesired effect.

backgammon *n.* a boardgame played with draughts and dice.

background *n.* the back part of a scene or picture; the circumstances surrounding something.

backhand *n.* a backhanded stroke.

backhanded *adj.* **1** performed with the back of the hand turned forwards. **2** said with underlying sarcasm.

backhander *n.* **1** a backhanded stroke. **2** *informal* a bribe.

backlash *n.* a hostile reaction.

backlist *n.* a publisher's list of books available.

backlog *n.* arrears of work.

backpack *n.* a rucksack.

back-pedal *v.* (**back-pedalled, pedalling**; *Amer.* **back-pedaled**) reverse one's previous action or opinion.

back seat *n.* an inferior position or status. □ **back-seat driver** someone who gives unwanted advice on someone else's actions.

backside *n. informal* the buttocks.

backslide *v.* slip back from good behaviour into bad.

backspace *v.* move a computer cursor or typewriter carriage one space back.

backspin *n.* a backward spinning movement of a ball.

backstage *adj.* & *adv.* behind a theatre stage.

backstreet *n.* a side street. ● *adj.* secret and illegal.

backstroke *n.* a swimming stroke performed on the back.

backtrack *v.* retrace one's route; reverse one's opinion.

backup *n.* a support, a reserve; *Computing* a copy of data made in case of loss or damage.

backward *adj.* **1** directed to the rear. **2** having made less than normal progress. **3** diffident. ● *adv.* backwards. □ **backwardness** *n.*

backwards *adv.* towards the back; with the back foremost; in reverse.

backwash *n.* **1** receding waves created by a ship etc. **2** a reaction.

backwater *n.* **1** a part of a river that is stagnant because not reached by the current. **2** a place unaffected by progress.

backwoods *n.pl.* a remote or backward region.

backyard *n.* a yard behind a house; *informal* the area near where one lives.

bacon *n.* salted or smoked meat from a pig.

bacterium *n.* (*pl.* **bacteria**) a microscopic organism. □ **bacterial** *adj.*, **bacteriological** *adj.*, **bacteriologist** *n.*, **bacteriology** *n.*

bad *adj.* (**worse, worst**) **1** of poor quality; having undesirable characteristics. **2** wicked; naughty. **3** harmful; serious. **4** decayed. □ **badness** *n.*

bade past of **bid**[2].

badge *n.* something worn to show membership, rank, etc.

badger *n.* a large burrowing animal with a black and white striped head. ● *v.* pester.

badly *adv.* **1** in an unsatisfactory, undesirable, or evil way. **2** very intensely □ **badly off** in a difficult situation, esp. financially.

badminton *n.* a game played with rackets and a shuttlecock over a high net.

baffle *v.* be too difficult for; frustrate. □ **bafflement** *n.*

bag *n.* **1** a flexible container; a hand bag. **2** (**bags**) *informal* a large amount. **3** *offensive* an unpleasant or annoying woman. **4** the amount of game shot by a hunter. ● *v.* (**bagged, bagging**) *informal* take or reserve for oneself.

bagatelle *n.* **1** a board game in which balls are struck into holes. **2** something trivial. **3** a short piece of music.

baggage *n.* luggage.

baggy *adj.* (**baggier, baggiest**) hanging in loose folds.

bagpipes *n.pl.* a wind instrument with air stored in a bag and pressed out through pipes.

baguette (ba-get) *n.* a long thin French loaf.

bail (*see also* **bale**) *n.* **1** money pledged as security that an accused person will return for trial. **2** each of two crosspieces resting on the stumps in cricket. ● *v.* (also **bale**) scoop water out of. □ **bail out** obtain or allow the release of (a person) on bail; relieve by financial help.

bailey *n.* the outer wall of a castle.

bailiff *n.* a law officer empowered to seize goods for non-payment of fines or debts.

bailiwick *n.* an area of authority or interest.

bain-marie (ban mă-ree) *n.* (*pl.* **bains-marie**) a pan of hot water in which a dish of food is placed for slow cooking.

bairn *n. Scot. & N. Engl.* a child.

bait *n.* food etc. placed to attract prey; an attraction, an inducement. ● *v.* **1** place bait on or in. **2** torment; taunt.

baize *n.* thick woollen green cloth.

bake *v.* cook or harden by dry heat.

baker *n.* a person who bakes or sells bread. □ **bakery** *n.*

baker's dozen *n.* thirteen.

baking powder *n.* a mixture used to make cakes rise.

baksheesh *n.* a tip; a bribe.

balaclava (helmet) *n.* a woollen cap covering the head and neck.

balalaika (bal-ă-lI-kă) *n.* a Russian guitar-like instrument.

balance *n.* **1** an even distribution of weight; stability; proportion. **2** the difference between credits and debits; a remainder. **3** a weighing apparatus. **4** the regulating apparatus of a clock. ● *v.* **1** make or stay stable, without falling. **2** compare.

balcony *n.* (*pl.* **-ies**) a projecting platform with a rail or parapet; the upper floor of seats in a theatre etc.

bald *adj.* **1** with the scalp wholly or partly hairless; (of tyres) with the tread worn away. **2** without details. □ **baldly** *adv.*, **baldness** *n.*

balderdash *n.* nonsense.

balding *adj.* becoming bald.

bale (*see also* **bail**) *n.* a large bound bundle of straw etc. ● *v.* make into bales. □ **bale out** (or **bail out**) make an emergency parachute jump from an aircraft.

baleful *adj.* menacing, destructive. □ **balefully** *adv.*

balk var. of **baulk**.

ball *n.* **1** a spherical object used in games; a rounded part or mass; a single delivery of a ball by a bowler; (**balls**) *vulgar slang* testicles. **2** a formal social gathering for dancing. □ **on the ball** alert, aware.

ballad *n.* a song telling a story.

ballast *n.* heavy material placed in a ship's hold to steady it; coarse stones as the base of a railway or road.

ball-bearing *n.* a ring of small steel balls reducing friction between moving parts of a machine; one of these balls.

ballcock *n.* a valve attached to a floating ball, controlling the water level in a cistern.

ballerina *n.* a female ballet dancer.

ballet *n.* an artistic dance form performed to music. □ **balletic** *adj.*

ballistic missile *n.* a powered missile, directed at its launch, then falling by gravity to its target.

ballistics *n.pl.* the study of projectiles and firearms. □ **ballistic** *adj.*

balloon *n.* a rubber bag inflated with air or lighter gas. ● *v.* swell like such a bag.

ballot *n.* a vote recorded on a slip of paper; voting by this. ● *v.* (**balloted, balloting**) (cause to) vote by ballot.

ballpark *n.* **1** a baseball ground. **2** *informal* an area or range. ● *adj. informal* approximate.

ballpoint *n.* a pen with a tiny ball as its writing point.

ballroom *n.* a large room where dances are held.

ballyhoo *n. informal* a fuss.

balm *n.* **1** a soothing influence; a fragrant ointment. **2** a fragrant herb.

balmy *adj.* (**balmier, balmiest**) **1** (of air or weather) pleasantly warm. **2** var. of **barmy**.

baloney *n.* (also **boloney**) *informal* nonsense.

balsa *n.* lightweight wood from a tropical American tree.

balsam *n.* **1** a soothing oil. **2** a kind of flowering plant.

baluster *n.* a short pillar in a balustrade.

balustrade *n.* a row of short pillars supporting a rail or coping.

bamboo *n.* a giant tropical grass with hollow stems.

bamboo shoot *n.* the young shoot of a bamboo, eaten as a vegetable.

bamboozle *v. informal* mystify, trick.

ban *v.* (**banned, banning**) forbid officially. ● *n.* an order banning something.

banal (bă-**nahl**) *adj.* commonplace, uninteresting. □ **banality** *n.*

banana *n.* a curved yellow fruit.

band[1] *n.* **1** a strip, a hoop, a loop. **2** a range of values or wavelengths. □ **banded** *adj.*

band[2] *n.* an organized group of people; a set of musicians. ● *v.* form a band. □ **bandleader** *n.*, **bandmaster** *n.*, **bandsman** *n.*

bandage *n.* a strip of material for binding a wound. ● *v.* bind with this.

bandanna *n.* a large coloured neckerchief.

b. & b. *abbr.* bed and breakfast.

bandit *n.* a member of a band of robbers.

bandstand *n.* a covered outdoor platform for a band playing music.

bandwagon *n.* □ **climb on the bandwagon** join a fashionable or successful movement.

bandy[1] *v.* (**bandied, bandying**) spread (gossip); exchange (words).

bandy[2] *adj.* (**bandier, bandiest**) (of legs) curving apart at the knees.

bane *n.* a cause of annoyance or misfortune.

bang *n.* a sudden loud sharp noise; a sharp blow. ● *v.* strike, esp. noisily; close or put down noisily; make a banging noise. ● *adv.* with a bang.

banger *n.* **1** a firework that explodes noisily; *informal* a noisy old car. **2** *informal* a sausage.

bangle *n.* a bracelet of rigid material.

banish *v.* condemn to exile; dismiss from one's presence or thoughts. □ **banishment** *n.*

banisters *n.pl.* (also **bannisters**) the uprights and handrail of a staircase.

banjo *n.* (*pl.* **banjos**) a guitar-like musical instrument with a circular body.

bank *n.* **1** a slope, esp. at the side of a river; a raised mass of earth etc. **2** a row of lights, switches, etc. **3** an establishment for safe keeping of money; a stock or store. ● *v.* **1** build up into a mound or bank. **2** tilt sideways. **3** place (money) in a bank. ▫ **bank on** rely on.

banker's card = **cheque card**.

banker's order *n.* an instruction to a bank to pay money or deliver property.

banknote *n.* a printed strip of paper issued as currency.

bankrupt *adj.* & *n.* (a person) unable to pay their debts. ● *v.* make bankrupt. ▫ **bankruptcy** *n.*

banner *n.* a flag; a piece of cloth bearing a slogan.

bannisters var. of **banisters**.

banns *n.pl.* an announcement of a forthcoming marriage.

banquet (bang-kwit) *n.* an elaborate ceremonial meal.

banquette (bang-**ket**) *n.* a long upholstered seat attached to a wall.

banshee *n.* a spirit whose wail is said to foretell a death.

bantam *n.* a small chicken.

bantamweight *n.* a weight between featherweight and flyweight (esp. in boxing).

banter *n.* good-humoured joking. ● *v.* joke in this way.

Bantu *adj.* & *n.* (*pl.* **Bantu** or **Bantus**) (a member) of a group of indigenous African peoples.

bap *n.* a large soft bread roll.

baptism *n.* a religious rite of sprinkling with water as a sign of purification, usu. with name-giving. ▫ **baptismal** *adj.*

Baptist *n.* a member of a Protestant sect believing in adult baptism by total immersion in water.

baptize *v.* (also **-ise**) perform baptism on; name, nickname.

bar *n.* **1** a length of solid rigid material. **2** a stripe. **3** a counter or room where alcohol is served. **4** a barrier. **5** one of the short units into which a piece of music is divided. **6** (**the Bar**) barristers or their profession. **7** a unit of atmospheric pressure. ● *v.* (**barred, barring**) **1** fasten with bars. **2** forbid, exclude; obstruct. ● *prep.* apart from.

barb *n.* **1** a backward-pointing part of an arrow, fish-hook, etc. **2** a wounding remark.

barbarian *n.* an uncivilized person.

barbaric *adj.* **1** primitive. **2** savagely cruel.

barbarity *n.* savage cruelty.

barbarous *adj.* **1** uncivilized. **2** cruel. ▫ **barbarism** *n.*, **barbarously** *adv.*

barbecue *n.* an open-air party where food is cooked on a frame above an open fire; this frame. ● *v.* cook on a barbecue.

barbed *adj.* having barbs; (of a remark) hurtful.

barbed wire *n.* wire with sharp points at intervals along it.

barber *n.* a men's hairdresser.

barber-shop *n.* close harmony singing for four male voices.

barbican *n.* an outer defence to a city or castle; a double tower over a gate or bridge.

barbiturate *n.* a sedative drug.

bar code *n.* a pattern of printed stripes used as a machine-readable code.

bard *n.* *literary* a poet. ▫ **bardic** *adj.*

bare *adj.* **1** not clothed or covered; not adorned. **2** scanty, just sufficient. ● *v.* reveal.

bareback *adv.* & *adj.* on horseback without a saddle.

barefaced *adj.* shameless, undisguised.

barely *adv.* only just, hardly.

bargain *n.* **1** an agreement where each side does something for the other. **2** something obtained cheaply. ● *v.* discuss the terms of an agreement. □ **bargain on** (or **for**) rely on, expect.

barge *n.* a large flat-bottomed boat used on rivers and canals. □ **barge in** intrude.

baritone *n.* a male voice between tenor and bass.

barium *n.* a white metallic element (symbol Ba).

bark *n.* **1** a sharp harsh sound made by a dog. **2** the outer layer of a tree. ● *v.* **1** make the sharp harsh sound of a dog; utter in a sharp commanding voice. **2** scrape skin off (a limb) accidentally.

barley *n.* a cereal plant; its grain.

barley sugar *n.* a sweet made of boiled sugar.

barmaid *n.* a woman serving in a pub etc.

barman *n.* (*pl.* **-men**) a man serving in a pub etc.

bar mitzvah *n.* a Jewish ceremony in which a boy of 13 takes on the responsibilities of an adult.

barmy *adj.* (**barmier, barmiest**) *informal* crazy.

barn *n.* a simple roofed farm building for storing grain etc.

barnacle *n.* a shellfish that attaches itself to objects under water.

barney *n.* (*pl.* **barneys**) *informal* a noisy argument.

barometer *n.* an instrument measuring atmospheric pressure, used in forecasting weather. □ **barometric** *adj.*

baron *n.* **1** a member of the lowest rank of nobility. **2** an influential businessman. □ **baronial** *adj.*

baroness *n.* a woman of the rank of baron; a baron's wife or widow.

baronet *n.* the holder of a hereditary title below a baron but above a knight. □ **baronetcy** *n.*

baroque (bă-**rok**) *adj.* of the ornate architectural or musical style of the 17th-18th centuries; complicated, elaborate. ● *n.* this style.

barque (bahk) *n.* a sailing ship.

barrack *v.* shout protests; jeer at.

barracks *n.pl.* buildings for soldiers to live in.

barracuda *n.* a large voracious tropical sea fish.

barrage *n.* **1** a heavy bombardment. **2** an artificial barrier across a river.

barre *n.* a horizontal bar used for support in ballet exercises.

barrel *n.* **1** a cylindrical container with flat ends. **2** a tube-like part esp. of a gun.

barrel organ *n.* a mechanical instrument producing music by a pin-studded cylinder acting on pipes or keys.

barren *adj.* **1** not fertile or fruitful. **2** bleak; pointless; worthless. □ **barrenness** *n.*

barricade *n.* a barrier. ● *v.* block or defend with a barricade.

barrier *n.* something that prevents advance or access.

barring *prep.* except for, apart from.

barrister *n.* a lawyer representing clients in court.

barrow *n.* **1** a wheelbarrow; a cart pushed or pulled by hand. **2** a prehistoric burial mound.

barter *n.* & *v.* (engage in) trade by exchange of goods.

basal (**bay**-săl) *adj.* of or at the base of something.

basalt (**ba**-sawlt) *n.* a dark rock of volcanic origin.

base *n.* **1** the lowest part; a part on which a thing rests or is supported; a starting point. **2** headquarters; a centre of organization. **3** a substance capable of combining with an acid to form a salt. **4** each of four stations to be reached by a batter in baseball. **5** the number on which a system of counting is based. ● *v.* make something the foundation or supporting evidence for. ● *adj.* dishonourable; of inferior value.

baseball *n.* a team game in which the batter has to hit the ball and run round a circuit.

baseless *adj.* without foundation. □ **baselessly** *adv.*

basement *n.* a storey below ground level.

bash *informal v.* strike violently; attack. ● *n.* a violent blow.

bashful *adj.* shy. □ **bashfully** *adv.*, **bashfulness** *n.*

BASIC *n.* a computer programming language using familiar English words.

basic *adj.* **1** forming an essential foundation. **2** without elaboration or luxury. □ **basically** *adv.*

basil *n.* a sweet-smelling herb.

basilica *n.* an oblong hall or church with an apse at one end.

basilisk *n.* a mythical reptile said to cause death by its glance or breath.

basin *n.* **1** a washbasin. **2** a round open container for food or liquid; a sunken place where water collects; an area drained by a river. □ **basinful** *n.*

basis *n.* (*pl.* **bases**) **1** a foundation or support. **2** a system of proceeding: *on a regular basis.*

bask *v.* sit or lie comfortably exposed to pleasant warmth.

basket *n.* a container for holding or carrying things, made of interwoven cane or wire.

basketball *n.* a team game in which the aim is to throw the ball through a high hooped net.

basketwork *n.* material woven in the style of a basket.

Basque (bahsk) *n.* & *adj.* (a member, the language) of a people living in the western Pyrenees.

bas-relief *n.* a carving with figures standing out slightly from the background.

bass[1] (bayss) *adj.* deep-sounding; of the lowest pitch in music. ● *n.* the lowest male voice.

bass[2] (bass) *n.* (*pl.* **bass**) an edible fish.

bassoon *n.* a woodwind instrument with a deep tone.

bast *n.* the inner bark of the lime tree used as fibre for matting.

bastard *n.* **1** *offensive* an illegitimate child. **2** *vulgar slang* an unpleasant or difficult person or thing. □ **bastardy** *n.*

baste *v.* **1** moisten with fat during cooking. **2** sew together temporarily with loose stitches.

bastion *n.* a projecting part of a fortified place; a stronghold.

bat *n.* **1** a wooden implement for hitting a ball in games; a batsman. **2** a flying animal with a mouselike body. **3** *informal* a women regarded as unpleasant or unattractive. ● *v.* (**batted, batting**) perform or strike with the bat in cricket etc.

batch *n.* a set of people or things dealt with as a group.

bated *adj.* □ **with bated breath** very anxiously.

bath *n.* a container used for washing the body; a wash in this. ● *v.* wash in a bath.

bathe *v.* **1** immerse in or clean with liquid. **2** swim for pleasure. ● *n.* a swim. □ **bather** *n.*

bathos (bay-thos) *n.* an anticlimax, a descent from an important thing to a trivial one. □ **bathetic** *adj.*

bathroom *n.* a room containing a bath, shower, washbasin, etc.

batik *n.* a method of printing textiles by waxing parts not to be dyed; fabric printed in this way.

batman *n.* (*pl.* **-men**) a soldier acting as an officer's personal servant.

baton *n.* a short stick, esp. one used by a conductor.

batrachian (bă-tray-kiăn) *n.* a frog or toad.

batsman *n.* (*pl.* **-men**) a player batting in cricket etc.

battalion *n.* an army unit of several companies.

batten *n.* a bar of wood or metal, esp. holding something in place. ● *v.* fasten with battens. □ **batten on** thrive at the expense of.

batter *v.* hit hard and often. ● *n.* **1** a beaten mixture of flour, eggs, and milk, used in cooking. **2** a player batting in baseball.

battering ram *n.* an iron-headed beam formerly used for breaking through walls or gates.

battery *n.* (*pl.* **-ies**) **1** a device containing and supplying electric power. **2** a group of big guns; an artillery unit. **3** a set of similar or connected units of equipment; a series of small cages for intensive rearing of livestock. **4** an unlawful blow or touch.

battle *n.* a fight between large organized forces; a contest. ● *v.* engage in a battle, struggle.

battleaxe *n.* a heavy axe used as a weapon in ancient times; *informal* an aggressive woman.

battlefield *n.* the scene of a battle.

battlements *n.pl.* a parapet with openings for firing from.

battleship *n.* a warship of the most heavily armed kind.

batty *adj.* (**battier, battiest**) *informal* crazy.

bauble *n.* a small coloured sphere used for decoration; a valueless ornament.

baulk (also **balk**) *v.* be reluctant; hinder. ● *n.* the starting area on a billiard table.

bauxite (**bork**-sIt) *n.* a mineral from which aluminium is obtained.

bawdy *adj.* (**bawdier, bawdiest**) humorously indecent. ◻ **bawdiness** *n.*

bawl *v.* shout; weep noisily. ◻ **bawl out** *informal* reprimand.

bay *n.* **1** part of the sea within a wide curve of the shore. **2** a recess. **3** a laurel, esp. a type used as a herb. **4** the deep cry of a large dog or of hounds in pursuit. ● *v.* (of a dog) give a deep howling cry. ● *adj.* (of a horse) reddish brown. ◻ **at bay** forced to face attackers.

bayonet *n.* a stabbing blade fixed to a rifle.

bay window *n.* a window projecting from an outside wall.

bazaar *n.* **1** a market in an eastern country. **2** a sale of goods to raise funds.

bazooka *n.* a portable weapon firing anti-tank rockets.

BBC *abbr.* British Broadcasting Corporation.

BC *abbr.* (of a date) before Christ.

Be *symb.* beryllium.

be *v.* **1** exist; occur; be present. **2** have a specified quality, position, or condition. ● *v.aux.* used to form tenses of other verbs.

beach *n.* the shore. ● *v.* bring on shore from water.

beachcomber *n.* a person who salvages things on a beach.

beachhead *n.* a fortified position set up on a beach by an invading army.

beacon *n.* a signal fire on a hill.

bead *n.* a small shaped piece of hard material pierced for threading with others on a string; a rounded drop of liquid.

beading *n.* a decorative strip of wood etc. for the edges of furniture etc.

beadle *n.* (formerly) a minor parish official.

beady *adj.* (**beadier, beadiest**) (of eyes) small and bright.

beagle *n.* a small hound.

beak *n.* **1** a bird's horny projecting jaws; any similar projection. **2** *informal* a magistrate.

beaker *n.* a tall cup; a tumbler.

beam *n.* **1** a long piece of timber or metal carrying the weight of part of a building. **2** a ray of light or other radiation. **3** a bright smile. **4** a ship's breadth. ● *v.* **1** send out (radio signals). **2** shine brightly; smile radiantly.

bean *n.* a plant with kidney-shaped seeds in long pods; a seed of this or of coffee. ◻ **full of beans** *informal* very cheerful.

beanfeast *n.* *informal* a celebratory party.

bear[1] *n.* a large heavy animal with thick fur; a child's toy resembling this.

bear[2] *v.* (**bore, borne**) **1** carry; support; shoulder (responsibilities etc.). **2** endure, tolerate. **3** be fit for (specified treatment): *does not bear repeating*. **4** produce (children, young, or fruit). **5** take a specified direction. ▫ **bear down** exert pressure; approach someone purposefully. **bear in mind** remember. **bear up** remain cheerful in adversity. **bring to bear** exert; make use of.

bearable *adj.* endurable.

beard *n.* the hair around a man's chin. ● *v.* confront boldly.

bearing *n.* **1** a way of standing, moving, or behaving. **2** relevance. **3** a compass direction. **4** a device in a machine reducing friction where a part turns.

bearskin *n.* a tall furry cap worn by some troops.

beast *n.* **1** a large animal. **2** *informal* an unpleasant person or thing.

beastly *adj.* (**beastlier, beastliest**) *informal* very unpleasant. ▫ **beastliness** *n.*

beat *v.* (**beat, beaten, beating**) **1** hit repeatedly; move or pulsate rhythmically. **2** defeat; out do. **3** mix (cooking ingredients) vigorously. ● *n.* **1** an accent in music; strong rhythm; throbbing, pulsating. **2** the sound of a drum being struck. **3** an area regularly patrolled by a policeman. ▫ **beat it** *informal* go away. **beat up** assault violently.

beatific (bee-ă-ti-fik) *adj.* showing great happiness. ▫ **beatifically** *adv.*

beatify (bee-a-ti-fI) *v.* (**beatified, beatifying**) (in the RC Church) declare (a dead person) blessed, as the first step in canonization. ▫ **beatification** *n.*

beatitude (bee-a-ti-tyood) *n.* blessedness.

beauteous *adj. poetic* beautiful.

beautician *n.* a person who gives beauty treatment.

beautiful *adj.* **1** having beauty. **2** excellent. ▫ **beautifully** *adv.*

beautify *v.* (**beautified, beautifying**) make beautiful. ▫ **beautification** *n.*

beauty *n.* (*pl.* **-ies**) a combination of qualities giving pleasure to the sight, mind, etc.; a beautiful person; an excellent specimen of something.

beaver *n.* an amphibious rodent that builds dams. ▫ **beaver away** work hard.

becalmed *adj.* unable to move because there is no wind.

because *conj.* for the reason that. ▫ **because of** by reason of.

beck[1] *n. N. Engl.* a stream.

beck[2] *n.* ▫ **at someone's beck and call** doing whatever someone asks.

beckon *v.* make a summoning gesture.

become *v.* (**became, become, becoming**) **1** turn into; begin to be. **2** suit; befit. ▫ **becoming** *adj.*

becquerel (bek-er-el) *n.* a unit of radioactivity.

bed *n.* **1** a thing to sleep or rest on; a framework with a mattress and coverings. **2** a flat base, a foundation; the bottom of a sea or river etc. **3** a garden plot.

B.Ed. *abbr.* Bachelor of Education.

bedclothes *n.pl.* sheets, blankets, etc.

bedding *n.* beds and bedclothes.

bedding plant *n.* a plant grown to be planted when in flower and discarded at the end of the season.

bedevil *v.* (**bedevilled, bedevilling**; *Amer.* **bedeviled**) afflict with difficulties.

bedfellow *n.* **1** a person sharing one's bed. **2** an associate.

bedlam *n.* a scene of uproar.

Bedouin (bed-oo-in) (also **Beduin**) *n.* (*pl.* **Bedouin**) a member of a nomadic Arab people of the desert.

bedpan *n.* a pan for use as a lavatory by a person confined to bed.

bedraggled *adj.* limp and untidy.

bedridden *adj.* permanently confined to bed through illness.

bedrock *n.* **1** solid rock beneath loose soil. **2** basic facts or principles.

bedroom *n.* a room for sleeping in.

bedsitter *n.* (also **bedsit**, **bedsitting room**) a room used for both living and sleeping in.

bedsore *n.* a sore developed by lying in bed in one position for a long time.

bedspread *n.* a covering for a bed.

bedstead *n.* the framework of a bed.

Beduin var. of **Bedouin**.

bee *n.* an insect that produces honey.

beech *n.* a tree with smooth bark and glossy leaves.

beef *n.* **1** meat from an ox, bull, or cow. **2** muscular strength. **3** *informal* a complaint. ● *v. informal* complain.

beefburger *n.* a fried cake of minced beef.

beefeater *n.* a warder in the Tower of London, wearing Tudor dress.

beefy *adj.* (**beefier, beefiest**) *informal* having a solid muscular body.

beehive *n.* a structure in which bees live.

beeline *n.* □ **make a beeline for** go straight or rapidly towards.

beep *n.* a high-pitched sound like that of a car horn. ● *v.* make a beep. □ **beeper** *n.*

beer *n.* an alcoholic drink made from malt and hops. □ **beery** *adj.*

beeswax *n.* a yellow substance secreted by bees, used as polish.

beet *n.* a plant with a fleshy root used as a vegetable (**beetroot**) or for making sugar (**sugar beet**).

beetle *n.* **1** an insect with hard wing-covers. **2** a tool for ramming or crushing. ● *v. informal* move hurriedly.

beetling *adj.* overhanging; projecting.

beetroot *n.* the dark red root of a beet as a vegetable.

befall *v.* (**befell, befallen, befalling**) *poetic* happen; happen to.

befit *v.* (**befitted, befitting**) be proper for.

before *adv., prep., & conj.* at an earlier time (than); ahead, in front of; in preference to, with a higher priority than.

beforehand *adv.* in advance.

befriend *v.* be supportive and friendly towards.

befuddle *v.* confuse.

beg *v.* (**begged, begging**) **1** ask earnestly or humbly (for); ask for food or money as charity. **2** (of a dog) sit up expectantly with forepaws off the ground. □ **beg the question** assume the truth of a thing to be proved.

■ **Usage** The correct use of *beg the question* is illustrated in *The proposed changes beg the question of whether change is needed.* The expression is often wrongly used to mean 'raise or invite a question', as in *The changes beg the question of why nothing was done earlier.*

beget *v.* (**begot, begotten, begetting**) *literary* be the father of; give rise to.

beggar *n.* a person who lives by asking for charity. ● *v.* reduce to poverty. □ **beggary** *n.*

beggarly *adj.* mean and insufficient.

begin *v.* (**began, begun, beginning**) **1** perform the first or earliest part of (an activity); be the first to do a thing. **2** come into existence.

beginner *n.* a person beginning to learn a skill.

beginning *n.* a first part; a source or origin.

begrudge *v.* be unwilling to give or allow.

beguile *v.* **1** charm, esp. deceptively. **2** pass (time) pleasantly.

begum (bay-gum) *n.* the title of a married Muslim woman.

behalf *n.* □ **on behalf of** as the representative of; in the interests of.

behave *v.* act or react in a specified way; (also **behave oneself**) show good manners.

behaviour *n.* (*Amer.* **behavior**) a way of behaving.

behead *v.* cut the head off.

beheld past & p.p. of **behold**.

behind *adv.* & *prep.* **1** in or to the rear (of); following; less advanced (than). **2** remaining (after). **3** supporting. **4** late; in arrears. ● *n. informal* the buttocks.

behold *v.* (**beheld, beholding**) *archaic & literary* see, observe. □ **beholder** *n.*

beholden *adj.* indebted.

behove *v. formal* be a duty of; befit.

beige *n.* a light fawn colour.

being *n.* existence; a thing that exists and has life, a person.

belabour *v.* (*Amer.* **belabor**) **1** attack. **2** argue (a point) at excessive length.

belated *adj.* coming very late or too late. □ **belatedly** *adv.*

belay *v.* secure (a rope) by winding it round something.

belch *v.* send out wind noisily from the stomach through the mouth. ● *n.* an act or sound of belching.

beleaguer *v.* besiege; harass.

belfry *n.* (*pl.* **-ies**) a space for bells in a tower.

belie *v.* (**belied, belying**) contradict, fail to confirm.

belief *n.* believing; something believed.

believe *v.* accept as true or as speaking truth; think, suppose. □ **believe in 1** have faith in the truth or existence of. **2** regard as right or desirable. □ **believer** *n.*

Belisha beacon *n.* a flashing amber globe marking a pedestrian crossing.

belittle *v.* disparage.

bell *n.* **1** a cup-shaped metal instrument that makes a ringing sound when struck. **2** a device making a ringing or buzzing sound as a signal.

belladonna *n.* deadly night-shade; a medicinal drug made from this.

belle *n.* a beautiful woman.

belles-lettres (bel-letr) *n.pl.* literary writings or studies.

bellicose *adj.* eager to fight.

belligerent *adj.* **1** aggressive. **2** engaged in a war. □ **belligerence** *n.*, **belligerently** *adv.*

bellow *n.* a loud deep sound made by a bull; a deep shout. ● *v.* make this sound.

bellows *n.pl.* an apparatus for pumping air into something.

belly *n.* (*pl.* **-ies**) the abdomen; the stomach. ● *v.* (**bellied, bellying**) (cause to) swell

bellyful *n.* □ **have a bellyful of** *informal* have more than enough of.

belong *v.* be rightly placed or assigned; fit in a particular environment. □ **belong to 1** be owned by. **2** be a member of.

belongings *n.pl.* personal possessions.

beloved *adj.* dearly loved.

below *adv.* & *prep.* extending underneath; at or to a lower position or level (than).

belt *n.* a strip of cloth or leather etc. worn round the waist; a long narrow strip or region. ● *v.* **1** put a belt round. **2** *informal* hit. **3** *informal* rush. □ **below the belt** unfair.

bemoan *v.* complain about.

bemused *adj.* bewildered. □ **bemusement** *n.*

bench *n.* **1** a long seat of wood or stone; a long working-table. **2** the office of judge or magistrate.

benchmark *n.* a surveyor's mark; a standard, a criterion.

bend *v.* (**bent, bending**) make or become curved; stoop; turn in a new direction; distort (rules). ● *n.* a curve, a turn. □ **bendy** *adj.*

bender *n. informal* a wild drinking spree.

beneath *adv.* & *prep.* below, underneath; not worthy of.

benediction *n.* a spoken blessing.

benefactor *n.* a person who gives financial or other help. □ **benefaction** *n.*, **benefactress** *n.*

beneficent *adj.* doing good; actively kind. □ **beneficence** *n.*

beneficial *adj.* resulting in good; advantageous. □ **beneficially** *adv.*

beneficiary *n.* (*pl.* **-ies**) one who receives a benefit or legacy.

benefit *n.* **1** an advantage or profit. **2** a state payment to the poor, ill, or unemployed. ● *v.* (**benefited, benefiting**; *Amer.* **benefitted**) profit from something; give an advantage to.

benevolent *adj.* kindly, helpful. □ **benevolence** *n.*, **benevolently** *adv.*

benighted *adj.* in darkness; ignorant.

benign (bi-nIn) *adj.* kindly, mild; (of a tumour) not malignant. □ **benignity** *n.*, **benignly** *adv.*

bent past & p.p. of **bend** ● *n.* a natural skill or liking. □ **bent on** determined to do or attain.

benzene *n.* a liquid obtained from petroleum and coal tar, used as a solvent, fuel, etc.

benzine *n.* a liquid mixture of hydrocarbons used in dry-cleaning.

benzol *n.* unrefined benzene.

bequeath *v.* leave in one's will.

bequest *n.* a legacy.

berate *v.* scold.

bereave *v.* deprive, esp. of a relative, by death. □ **bereavement** *n.*

bereft *adj.* deprived; deserted and lonely.

beret (be-ray) *n.* a round flat cap with no peak.

beriberi *n.* a disease caused by lack of vitamin B.

berk *n. informal* a stupid person.

berkelium *n.* a man-made radioactive metallic element (symbol Bk).

berry *n.* (*pl.* **-ies**) a small round juicy fruit with no stone.

berserk (bĕ-zerk) *adj.* □ **go berserk** go into an uncontrollable destructive rage.

berth *n.* **1** a bunk or sleeping place in a ship or train. **2** a place for a ship to tie up at a wharf. ● *v.* moor at a berth. □ **give a wide berth to** keep a safe distance from.

beryl *n.* a transparent green gem.

beryllium *n.* a light metallic element (symbol Be).

beseech *v.* (**besought, beseeching**) beg earnestly.

beset *v.* (**beset, besetting**) trouble persistently; surround, hem in.

beside *prep.* **1** at the side of. **2** compared with. □ **beside oneself** distraught. **beside the point** irrelevant.

besides *prep.* **1** in addition to. **2** apart from. ● *adv.* also.

besiege *v.* lay siege to.

besmirch *v.* dirty; dishonour.

besom (bee-zŏm) *n.* a broom made from a bundle of twigs tied to a handle.

besotted *adj.* infatuated.

besought past & p.p. of **beseech**.

bespeak *v.* (**bespoke, bespoken, bespeaking**) **1** be evidence of. **2** reserve in advance.

bespoke *adj.* made to order.

best *adj.* most excellent or desirable; most beneficial. ● *adv.* **1** better than any others. **2** to the highest degree. ● *v.* get the better of. ● *n.* the highest standard that one can reach: *do one's best*. □ **best part of** most of.

bestial *adj.* of or like a beast, savage. □ **bestiality** *n.*

bestir *v.* (**bestirred, bestirring**) □ **bestir oneself** exert oneself.

best man *n.* a bridegroom's chief attendant.

bestow *v.* present as a gift. □ **bestowal** *n.*

bestride *v.* (**bestrode, bestridden, bestriding**) stand astride over.

bet *v.* (**bet** or **betted, betting**) **1** stake money on the outcome of a future event. **2** *informal* feel certain. ● *n.* an act of betting; the amount staked.

beta *n.* the second letter of the Greek alphabet (Β, β).

beta blocker *n.* a drug used to control heartbeat rhythms and treat high blood pressure.

betake *v.* (**betook, betaken, betaking**) □ **betake oneself** *formal* go.

bête noire (bet nwar) *n.* (*pl.* **bêtes noires**) something greatly disliked.

betide *v. literary* happen (to).

betimes *adv. literary* early.

betoken *v.* be a sign of.

betray *v.* hand over to an enemy; be disloyal to; reveal (a secret). □ **betrayal** *n.*, **betrayer** *n.*

betroth *v.* cause to be engaged to marry. □ **betrothal** *n.*

better[1] *adj.* **1** more excellent. **2** recovered from illness. ● *adv.* more excellently or effectively. ● *n.* (**betters**) one's superiors. ● *v.* outdo, surpass. □ **better half** *informal* a spouse. **better oneself** reach a higher position in society. **better part of** more than half. **get the better of** overcome; outwit.

better[2] *n.* a person who bets.

between *prep.* **1** in the space or time bounded by (two limits); separating; to and from. **2** indicating division or difference. **3** indicating connection or collision; indicating a shared action or outcome. ● *adv.* between points or limits.

bevel *n.* a sloping edge. ● *v.* (**bevelled, bevelling;** *Amer.* **beveled**) give a sloping edge to.

beverage *n.* a drink.

bevvy *n.* (*pl.* **-ies**) *informal* an alcoholic drink.

bevy *n.* (*pl.* **-ies**) a large group.

bewail *v.* lament (a misfortune).

beware *v.* be on one's guard.

bewilder *v.* puzzle, confuse. □ **bewilderment** *n.*

bewitch *v.* put under a magic spell; delight greatly.

beyond *prep.* at or to the far side of (a point in space or time); more advanced than; greater than; too hard for. ● *adv.* at or to the far side.

bezel *n.* a ring holding a watch cover in place.

bhaji (bah-jee) *n.* an Indian dish of vegetables fried in batter.

b.h.p. *abbr.* brake horsepower.

Bi *symb.* bismuth.

bi- *comb. form* two; twice.

biannual *adj.* happening twice a year. □ **biannually** *adv.*

bias *n.* **1** a prejudice unfairly influencing treatment. **2** (in bowls) a tendency to swerve caused by a bowl's irregular shape. **3** a cut across the weave of a fabric. ● *v.* (**biased, biasing** or **biassed, biassing**) give a bias to, influence.

bib *n.* a covering put under a young child's chin to protect its clothes while feeding.

Bible *n.* the Christian or Jewish scriptures; *informal* a book regarded as authoritative.

biblical *adj.* of or in the Bible.

bibliography *n.* (*pl.* **-ies**) a list of books about a subject or by a specified author. □ **bibliographer** *n.*, **bibliographical** *adj.*

bibliophile *n.* a book-lover.

bicarbonate *n.* a salt containing a double proportion of carbon dioxide.

bicentenary *n.* (*pl.* **-ies**) a 200th anniversary.

bicentennial *adj.* happening every 200 years. ● *n.* a bicentenary.

biceps (bI-seps) *n.* the large muscle at the front of the upper arm.

bicker *v.* quarrel about unimportant things.

bicycle *n.* a two-wheeled vehicle driven by pedals. ● *v.* ride a bicycle.

bid[1] *n.* **1** an offer of a price, esp. at an auction. **2** a statement of the number of tricks a player proposes to win in a card game. **3** an attempt. ● *v.* (**bid, bidding**) **1** offer (a price). **2** try to achieve something. □ **bidder** *n.*

bid[2] *v.* (**bid** or **bade, bidden, bidding**) **1** utter (a greeting or farewell. **2** *archaic* command.

biddable *adj.* meekly obedient.

bide *v.* □ **bide one's time** wait patiently for an opportunity.

bidet (bee-day) *n.* a low basin used for washing the genital and anal regions.

biennial *adj.* happening every two years. ● *n.* a plant that flowers and dies in its second year. □ **biennially** *adv.*

bier (beer) *n.* a movable stand for a coffin.

biff *n. informal* a sharp blow. ● *v.* hit (a person).

bifocals *n.pl.* spectacles with lenses that have two segments, assisting both distant and close focusing.

bifurcate *v.* split into two branches. □ **bifurcation** *n.*

big *adj.* (**bigger, biggest**) of great size, amount, or intensity; important; serious; grown up.

bigamy *n.* the crime of going through a form of marriage while a previous marriage is still valid. □ **bigamist** *adj.*, **bigamous** *adj.*

bigot *n.* a person who is prejudiced and intolerant of differing views. □ **bigoted** *adj.*, **bigotry** *n.*

bijou (bee-*zhoo*) *adj.* small and elegant.

bike *n. informal* a bicycle or motorcycle. □ **biker** *n.*

bikini *n.* a woman's two-piece swimming costume.

bilateral *adj.* **1** involving two parties. **2** of two sides. □ **bilaterally** *adv.*

bile *n.* **1** a bitter yellowish liquid produced by the liver. **2** bad temper.

bilge *n.* **1** a ship's bottom; water collecting there. **2** *informal* nonsense.

bilharzia (bil-**hahts**-i-ă) *n.* a disease caused by a tropical parasitic flatworm.

bilingual *adj.* written in or able to speak two languages.

bilious *adj.* **1** sick, esp. from trouble with the bile or liver. **2** spiteful, bad-tempered. □ **biliousness** *n.*

bill *n.* **1** a written statement of charges to be paid. **2** a draft of a proposed law. **3** a programme of entertainment. **4** *Amer.* a banknote. **5** a poster. **6** a bird's beak. □ **bill and coo** exchange caresses. **fill the bill** meet requirements.

billabong *n. Austral.* a backwater.

billboard *n.* a hoarding for advertisements.

billet *n.* a lodging for troops. ● *v.* (**billeted, billeting**) place in a billet.

billhook *n.* a tool with a broad curved blade for lopping trees.

billiards *n.* a game played on a table, with three balls which are struck with cues into pockets at the edge of the table.

billion *n.* a thousand million or (less commonly) a million million.

billow *n.* a great wave. ● *v.* rise or move like waves; swell out.

bimbo *n.* (*pl.* **bimbos**) *informal* an attractive but unintelligent young woman.

bi-media *adj.* involving or working in two media of mass communication.

bimetallic *adj.* made of two metals.

bin *n.* a large rigid container or receptacle. ● *v.* (**binned, binning**) discard.

binary *adj.* of two.

binary digit *n.* either of the two digits (0 and 1) of the **binary system**, a number system used in computing.

bind *v.* (**bound, binding**) **1** tie together; unite (a group); secure a cover round (a book); cover the edge of (cloth). **2** tie up. **3** place under an obligation. ● *n. informal* something irritating or tedious.

binding *n.* **1** a book cover. **2** braid etc. used to bind an edge.

binge *n. informal* a bout of excessive eating and drinking.

bingo *n.* a gambling game using cards marked with numbered squares.

binocular *adj.* using two eyes. ● *n.pl.* (**binoculars**) an instrument with lenses for both eyes, for viewing distant objects.

binomial *adj.* & *n.* (an expression or name) consisting of two terms.

bio- *comb. form* of living things.

biochemistry *n.* the chemistry of living organisms. □ **biochemical** *adj.*, **biochemist** *n.*

biodegradable *adj.* able to be decomposed by bacteria.

biodiversity *n.* the variety of living things in an environment.

bioengineering *n.* **1** genetic engineering. **2** the use of artificial body parts to replace damaged ones.

bioethics *n.* the ethics of medical and biological research.

biography *n.* (*pl.* **-ies**) the story of a person's life. □ **biographer** *n.*, **biographical** *adj.*

biology *n.* the study of the life and structure of living things. □ **biological** *adj.*, **biologist** *n.*

biomass *n.* the total quantity or weight of organisms in a given area.

bionic *adj.* having electronically operated artificial body parts.

biopic *n. informal* a biographical film.

biopsy *n.* (*pl.* **-ies**) an examination of tissue cut from a living body.

biorhythm *n.* a recurring cycle of physical, intellectual, or emotional activity thought to affect human behaviour.

biotechnology *n.* the use of micro-organisms and biological processes in industrial production.

bipartisan *adj.* involving two parties.

bipartite *adj.* consisting of two parts; involving two groups.

biped *n.* a two-footed animal such as man.

biplane *n.* an aeroplane with two pairs of wings.

birch *n.* a tree with thin peeling bark.

bird *n.* **1** a feathered egg-laying animal, usu. able to fly. **2** *informal* a young woman.

birdie *n. Golf* a score of one stroke under par for a hole.

biro *n.* (*pl.* **biros**) *trademark* a ball-point pen.

birth *n.* the emergence of young from its mother's body; origin, ancestry.

birth control *n.* contraception.

birthday *n.* the anniversary of the day of one's birth.

birthmark *n.* an unusual coloured mark on the skin at birth.

birthright *n.* a right or privilege possessed from birth.

biscuit *n.* a small, flat, crisp unleavened cake.

bisect *v.* divide into two equal parts. □ **bisection** *n.*, **bisector** *n.*

bisexual *adj.* & *n.* (a person) sexually attracted to members of both sexes. □ **bisexuality** *n.*

bishop *n.* **1** a senior clergyman **2** a mitre-shaped chess piece.

bishopric *n.* the district under a bishop's control.

bismuth *n.* a metallic element (symbol Bi); a compound of this used in medicines.

bison *n.* (*pl.* **bison**) a wild ox; a buffalo.

bistro *n.* (*pl.* **bistros**) a small informal restaurant.

bit[1] *n.* **1** a small piece or quantity; a short time or distance. **2** the mouthpiece of a bridle. **3** a tool for drilling or boring. **4** *Computing* a binary digit. □ **a bit** rather, to some extent.

bit[2] past of *bite*.

bitch *n.* **1** a female dog. **2** *informal* a spiteful woman; something difficult or unpleasant. ● *v. informal* make spiteful comments. □ **bitchiness** *n.*, **bitchy** *adj.*

bite *v.* (**bit, bitten, biting**) **1** cut with the teeth to eat or injure. **2** take hold on a surface. **3** cause pain or distress. ● *n.* **1** an act of biting; a wound made by this. **2** a small meal.

biting *adj.* causing a smarting pain; sharply critical.

bitter *adj.* **1** tasting sharp, not sweet or mild. **2** resentful; very distressing. **3** piercingly cold. ● *n.* beer flavoured with hops and slightly bitter. □ **bitterly** *adv.*, **bitterness** *n.*

bittern *n.* a marsh bird.

bitty *adj.* (**bittier, bittiest**) lacking unity, disconnected. □ **bittiness** *n.*

bitumen *n.* a black substance made from petroleum. □ **bituminous** *adj.*

bivalve *n.* a shellfish with a hinged double shell.

bivouac (**bi**-voo-ak) *n.* a temporary camp without tents or other cover. ● *v.* (**bivouacked, bivouacking**) camp in a bivouac.

bizarre *adj.* strikingly odd in appearance or effect.

Bk *symb.* berkelium.

blab *v.* (**blabbed, blabbing**) talk indiscreetly.

black *adj.* **1** of the very darkest colour, like coal; having a dark skin; (of tea or coffee) without milk. **2** gloomy; hostile; evil; (of humour) macabre. ● *n.* a black colour or thing; a member of a dark-skinned race. □ **in the black** with a credit balance, not in debt. **black out 1** lose consciousness. **2** cover windows so that no light can penetrate.

blackberry *n.* (*pl.* **-ies**) an edible dark berry growing on a prickly bush.

blackbird *n.* a European songbird, the male of which is black.

blackboard *n.* a dark board for writing on with chalk, used esp. in schools.

black economy *n.* (*pl.* **-ies**) unofficial and untaxed business activity.

blacken *v.* **1** make or become black. **2** say evil things about.

black eye *n.* a bruised eye.

blackguard (**blag**-ard) *n.* a dishonourable man.

blackhead *n.* a small dark lump blocking a pore in the skin.

black hole *n.* a region in outer space from which matter and radiation cannot escape.

blackleg *n.* a person who works while fellow workers are on strike.

blacklist *n.* a list of people considered untrustworthy or unacceptable.

blackmail *v.* extort money from (someone) by threatening to reveal compromising information. ● *n.* the offence of doing this. □ **blackmailer** *n.*

black market *n.* illegal trading in officially controlled goods.

blackout *n.* a temporary loss of consciousness or memory.

black pudding *n.* a sausage of blood and suet.

black sheep *n.* a member of a family regarded as a disgrace.

blacksmith *n.* a person who makes and repairs things in iron.

bladder *n.* **1** the sac in which urine collects in the body. **2** an inflatable bag.

blade *n.* the flattened cutting part of a knife or sword; the flat part of an oar or propeller; a long narrow leaf of grass.

blame *v.* hold responsible for a fault. ● *n.* responsibility for a fault. □ **blameless** *adj.*, **blameworthy** *adj.*

blanch *v.* **1** make or become white or pale. **2** immerse (vegetables) briefly in boiling water; peel (almonds) by scalding.

blancmange (blă-**monj**) *n.* a flavoured jelly-like dessert.

bland *adj.* **1** dull, uninteresting; not strongly flavoured. **2** gentle; not showing strong emotion. □ **blandly** *adv.*

blandishments *n.pl.* flattering or coaxing words.

blank *adj.* **1** not marked or decorated. **2** showing no interest, understanding, or reaction. ● *n.* a blank space; a cartridge containing no bullet. □ **draw a blank** be unsuccessful.

blank cheque *n.* a cheque with the amount left for the payee to fill in.

blanket *n.* a warm covering made of woollen or similar material; a thick covering mass. ● *adj.* total and inclusive.

blank verse *n.* verse without rhyme.

blare *v.* & *n.* (make) a loud harsh sound.

blarney *n.* charming and persuasive talk.

blasé (blah-zay) *adj.* unimpressed through familiarity with something.

blaspheme *v.* talk blasphemously. □ **blasphemer** *n.*

blasphemy *n.* (*pl.* **-ies**) irreverent talk about sacred things. □ **blasphemous** *adj.*, **blasphemously** *adv.*

blast *n.* **1** a wave of air from an explosion; a strong gust. **2** a loud note on a whistle or horn. **3** *informal* a reprimand. ● *v.* **1** blow up with explosives. **2** produce a loud sound. **3** *informal* reprimand severely. **4** blight, shrivel. □ **blast off** (of a rocket etc.) take off from a launching site.

blatant (blay-tănt) *adj.* very obvious; shameless. □ **blatantly** *adv.*

blather *v.* (also **blether**) chatter foolishly.

blaze *n.* **1** a bright flame or fire; a bright light; an outburst or display. **2** a white mark on an animal's face; a mark chipped in the bark of a tree to mark a route. ● *v.* burn or shine brightly. □ **blaze a trail** mark out a route; pioneer.

blazer *n.* a loose-fitting jacket, esp. in the colours or bearing the badge of a school, team, etc.

blazon *v.* display or proclaim publicly. ● *n.* a description of a coat of arms.

bleach *v.* whiten by sunlight or chemicals. ● *n.* a bleaching substance or process.

bleak *adj.* cold and cheerless; not hopeful or encouraging. □ **bleakly** *adv.*, **bleakness** *n.*

bleary *adj.* (**blearier, bleariest**) (of eyes) dull and unfocused. □ **blearily** *adv.*, **bleariness** *n.*

bleat *n.* the cry of a sheep or goat. ● *v.* utter this cry; speak or complain feebly.

bleed *v.* (**bled, bleeding**) leak blood or other fluid; draw blood or fluid from; extort money from.

bleep *n.* a short high-pitched sound. ● *v.* make this sound, esp. as a signal. □ **bleeper** *n.*

blemish *n.* a flaw or defect. ● *v.* spoil the appearance of.

blench *v.* flinch.

blend *v.* mix smoothly; mingle. ● *n.* a mixture.

blender *n.* an appliance for purée-ing food.

bless *v.* call God's favour upon; consecrate; praise (God); feel deep gratitude to. □ **be blessed with** be fortunate in having.

blessed (bles-id) *adj.* **1** holy. **2** very welcome, much desired. **3** *informal* euphemism for **damned**. □ **blessedly** *adv.*

blessing *n.* **1** God's favour; a prayer for this. **2** approval, support. **3** something one is glad of.

blether var. of **blather**.

blew past of **blow**.

blight *n.* a disease or fungus that withers plants; a malignant influence. ● *v.* affect with blight; spoil.

blimey *int. informal* an exclamation of surprise.

blimp *n.* a small airship.

blind *adj.* **1** unable to see; lacking discernment; unreasoning, not guided by reason. **2** (of a road etc.) hidden. ● *v.* make blind; rob of judgement. ● *n.* **1** a screen, esp. on a roller, for a window. **2** a pretext. □ **bake blind** bake a pastry case with no filling. **not a blind (or the blindest)** *informal* not the slightest. □ **blindly** *adv.*, **blindness** *n.*

blindfold *n.* a cloth used to cover the eyes and block the sight. ● *v.* cover the eyes of (a person) with this.

blink *v.* open and shut one's eyes rapidly; shine unsteadily. ● *n.* an act of blinking; a quick gleam.

blinker *n.* a leather piece fixed to a bridle to prevent a horse from seeing sideways. ● *v.* obstruct the sight or understanding of.

blip *n.* **1** a slight error or deviation. **2** a short high-pitched sound; a small image on a radar screen.

bliss *n.* perfect happiness. ◻ **blissful** *adj.*, **blissfully** *adv.*

blister *n.* a bubble-like swelling on the skin; a raised swelling on a surface. ● *v.* raise a blister on; be affected with blister(s).

blithe *adj.* casual and carefree. ◻ **blithely** *adv.*

blitz *n.* a sudden intensive attack; an energetic and concerted effort. ● *v.* attack in a blitz.

blitzkrieg *n.* an intense military campaign aimed at a swift victory.

blizzard *n.* a severe snowstorm.

bloat *v.* swell with fat, gas, or liquid.

bloater *n.* a salted smoked herring.

blob *n.* a drop of liquid; a round mass.

bloc *n.* a group of parties or countries who combine for a purpose.

block *n.* **1** a solid piece of a hard substance, usu. with flat sides. **2** a large building divided into flats or offices; a group of buildings enclosed by roads. **3** a large quantity of related items treated as a unit. **4** an obstruction. **5** a pad of writing paper. **6** *informal* a person's head. **7** a pulley mounted in a case. ● *v.* obstruct, prevent the movement or use of.

blockade *n.* the blocking of access to a place, to prevent entry of goods. ● *v.* set up a blockade of.

blockage *n.* an obstruction.

blockbuster *n.* *informal* a very successful book or film.

blockhead *n.* a stupid person.

block letters *n.pl.* plain capital letters.

bloke *n.* *informal* a man.

blonde *adj.* (also **blond**) fair-haired; (of hair) fair. ● *n.* a fair-haired woman (**blonde**) or man (**blond**).

blood *n.* **1** the red liquid circulating in the bodies of animals. **2** family, descent. **3** spirit, temper. ● *v.* give a first taste of blood to (a hound); initiate (a person). ◻ **in cold blood** deliberately and ruthlessly.

blood count *n.* the number of corpuscles in a sample of blood.

blood-curdling *adj.* horrifying.

bloodhound *n.* a large keen-scented dog, formerly used in tracking.

bloodless *adj.* without bloodshed. ◻ **bloodlessly** *adv.*

bloodshed *n.* killing or wounding.

bloodshot *adj.* (of eyes) red from dilated veins.

blood sports *n.pl.* sports involving killing.

bloodstock *n.* thoroughbred horses.

bloodstream *n.* blood circulating in the body.

bloodsucker *n.* a creature that sucks blood; *informal* a person who extorts money.

bloodthirsty *adj.* eager for bloodshed.

blood vessel *n.* a tubular structure conveying blood within the body.

bloody *adj.* (**bloodier, bloodiest**) **1** covered in blood. **2** involving much bloodshed. **3** *vulgar slang* cursed. ● *adv.* *vulgar slang* extremely. ● *v.* stain with blood.

bloody-minded *adj.* *informal* deliberately uncooperative.

bloom **1** a flower. **2** youthful beauty; perfection. ● *v.* **1** bear flowers. **2** be healthy and attractive.

bloomer *n.* **1** *informal* a blunder. **2** a long loaf with diagonal marks. **3** (**bloomers**) loose knee-length knickers.

blossom *n.* flowers, esp. of a fruit tree. ● *v.* open into flowers; develop and flourish.

blot *n.* a stain of ink etc.; an eyesore; a disgrace. ● *v.* (**blotted, blotting**) **1** make a blot on. **2** soak up with absorbent material. □ **blot out** erase, destroy; obscure.

blotch *n.* a large irregular mark. □ **blotchy** *adj.*

blotto *adj. informal* very drunk.

blouse *n.* a shirt-like garment worn by women.

blouson *n.* a short full jacket gathered at the waist.

blow *v.* (**blew, blown, blowing**) **1** send out a current of air or breath; move as a current of air; carry on air or breath. **2** break or displace with explosives. **3** play (a wind instrument). **4** use air to shape (glass). **5** (of a fuse) burn out. **6** *informal* spend, squander. **7** *informal* bungle; waste (an opportunity). ● *n.* **1** a wind; an act of blowing. **2** a stroke with the hand or a weapon; a shock, disappointment, or setback. □ **blow up 1** explode; shatter. **2** inflate; enlarge; exaggerate. **3** *informal* lose one's temper.

blowfly *n.* (*pl.* **-ies**) a fly that lays its eggs on meat.

blow lamp *n.* (also **blowtorch**) a portable burner with a very hot flame for removing old paint.

blowout *n.* **1** a burst tyre. **2** a melted fuse. **3** an uprush of oil from a well. **4** *informal* a huge meal. **5** *Amer.* an easy victory.

blowpipe *n.* a tube through which air etc. is blown, e.g. to heat a flame or send out a missile.

blowy *adj.* (**blowier, blowiest**) windy.

blowzy (blow-zi) *adj.* (**blowzier, blowziest**) red-faced and coarse-looking.

blub *v.* (**blubbed, blubbing**) *informal* sob.

blubber *n.* whale fat. ● *v. informal* sob noisily.

bludgeon *n.* a heavy stick used as a weapon. ● *v.* strike with a bludgeon; compel forcefully.

blue *adj.* **1** of a colour like the cloudless sky. **2** *informal* unhappy. **3** *informal* indecent. ● *n.* **1** a blue colour or thing. **2** (**blues**) melancholy jazz melodies; a state of depression. ● *v. informal* spend (money) recklessly. □ **out of the blue** unexpectedly. □ **bluish** *adj.*

bluebell *n.* a plant with blue bell-shaped flowers.

blue-blooded *adj.* of aristocratic descent.

bluebottle *n.* a large bluish fly.

blueprint *n.* a design plan; a model.

bluestocking *n.* a learned woman.

bluff *v.* pretend; deceive. ● *n.* **1** bluffing. **2** a broad steep cliff or headland. ● *adj.* **1** with a broad steep front. **2** abrupt, frank, and hearty.

blunder *v.* move clumsily and uncertainly; make a mistake. ● *n.* a stupid mistake.

blunderbuss *n.* an old type of gun firing many balls at one shot.

blunt *adj.* **1** without a sharp edge or point. **2** speaking or expressed plainly. ● *v.* make or become blunt. □ **bluntly** *adv.*, **bluntness** *n.*

blur *n.* something perceived indistinctly. ● *v.* (**blurred, blurring**) make or become indistinct.

blurb *n.* a written description and advertisement of something.

blurt *v.* utter abruptly or tactlessly.

blush *v.* become red-faced from shame or embarrassment. ● *n.* blushing; a pink tinge.

blusher *n.* a cosmetic giving a rosy colour to cheeks.

bluster *v.* **1** blow in gusts. **2** make aggressive but empty threats. ● *n.* blustering talk. □ **blustery** *adj.*

BMA *abbr.* British Medical Association.

BMX *n.* cross-country bicycle racing; a bicycle for this.

BO *abbr.* body odour.

boa (boh-ă) *n.* a large South American snake that crushes its prey.

boar *n.* a wild pig; a male pig.

board *n.* **1** a long piece of sawn wood; a flat piece of wood or stiff material. **2** daily meals supplied in return for payment or services. **3** a committee. ● *v.* **1** get on (a ship, aircraft, train, etc.). **2** receive or provide accommodation and meals for payment. **3** cover or block with boards. □ **go by the board** be lost or abandoned. **on board** on or in a ship, aircraft, or vehicle.

boarder *n.* a person who boards with someone; a resident pupil.

boarding house *n.* a house at which board and lodging can be obtained for payment.

boarding school *n.* a school where pupils live during term time.

boardroom *n.* a room where a board of directors meets.

boast *v.* **1** talk with pride about one's achievements or possessions. **2** possess (a desirable feature). ● *n.* a boastful statement; a thing one is proud of. □ **boastful** *adj.*, **boastfully** *adv.*, **boastfulness** *n.*

boat *n.* a vessel for travelling on water. □ **burn one's boats** do something irreversible. **push the boat out** be extravagant.

boater *n.* a flat-topped straw hat.

boathouse *n.* a shed at the water's edge for boats.

boating *n.* rowing or sailing for pleasure.

boatman *n.* (*pl.* **-men**) a man who hires out boats or provides transport by boat.

boat people *n.pl.* refugees who have fled their own country by boat.

boatswain (boh-sŭn) (also **bosun, bo'sun**) *n.* a ship's officer in charge of rigging, boats, etc.

bob *v.* (**bobbed, bobbing**) **1** move quickly up and down. **2** cut (hair) in a bob. ● *n.* **1** a bobbing movement. **2** a hairstyle with the hair at the same length just above the shoulders.

bobbin *n.* a small spool holding thread or wire in a machine.

bobble *n.* a small woolly ball as an ornament.

bobsleigh *n.* a mechanically steered sledge with two sets of runners.

bode *v.* be a portent of, foreshadow.

bodice *n.* part of a dress from shoulder to waist; an undergarment for this part of the body.

bodily *adj.* of the body; physical, material. ● *adv.* **1** by taking hold of the body. **2** in one mass or whole.

body *n.* (*pl.* **-ies**) **1** the physical form of a person or animal. **2** a corpse. **3** the main part of something. **4** a collection; a group. **5** a distinct object. **6** fullness; strong flavour or texture.

body blow *n.* a severe setback.

bodyguard *n.* a personal guard for an important person.

bodysuit *n.* a close-fitting one-piece stretch garment for women.

bodywork *n.* the outer shell of a motor vehicle.

Boer *n.* a South African of Dutch descent.

boffin *n. informal* a person engaged in scientific research.

bog *n.* **1** permanently wet spongy ground. **2** *informal* a lavatory. □ **bog down** (**bogged**) make or become stuck and unable to progress. □ **bogginess** *n.*, **boggy** *adj.*

bogey *n.* (*pl.* **-bogeys**) **1** *Golf* a score of one stroke over par at a hole. **2** (also **bogy**) something causing fear.

boggle *v.* be amazed or alarmed.

bogus *adj.* false.

bohemian *adj.* socially unconventional.

boil *v.* bubble up with heat; heat (liquid) until it does this; cook in boiling water. ● *n.* an inflamed swelling producing pus.

boiler *n.* **1** a container in which water is heated. **2** a fowl too tough to roast.

boiler suit *n.* a one-piece garment for rough work.

boisterous *adj.* cheerfully noisy or rough. □ **boisterously** *adv.*

bold *adj.* **1** confident and courageous. **2** (of a colour or design) strong and vivid. □ **boldly** *adv.*, **boldness** *n.*

bole *n.* the trunk of a tree.

bolero (bo-**lair**-oh) *n.* (*pl.* **boleros**) **1** a Spanish dance. **2** a woman's short jacket with no fastening.

boll *n.* a round seed vessel of cotton, flax, etc.

bollard *n.* a short thick post.

bollocks *vulgar slang n.pl.* testicles. ● *int.* rubbish, nonsense.

boloney var. of **baloney**.

bolshie *adj.* (also **bolshy**) *informal* deliberately uncooperative.

bolster *n.* a long pad placed under a pillow. ● *v.* support, prop.

bolt *n.* **1** a sliding bar for fastening a door; a strong metal pin used with a nut to hold things together. **2** a shaft of lightning. **3** a roll of cloth. **4** an arrow from a crossbow. ● *v.* **1** fasten with a bolt. **2** run away. **3** gulp (food) hastily.

bolt-hole *n.* a place into which one can escape.

bomb *n.* a case of explosive or incendiary material to be set off by impact or a timing device. ● *v.* **1** attack with bombs. **2** *informal* move quickly. **3** *informal* be a failure. □ **cost a bomb** *informal* be very expensive.

bombard *v.* attack with artillery; attack with questions etc. □ **bombardment** *n.*

bombardier *n.* an artillery noncommissioned officer.

bombastic *adj.* using pompous words. □ **bombast** *n.*

bomber *n.* an aircraft that carries and drops bombs; a person who places bombs.

bombshell *n.* a great shock.

bona fide (boh-nă **fy**-di) *adj.* genuine.

bonanza *n.* a sudden increase in wealth or luck.

bond *n.* **1** something that unites or restrains; a binding agreement; an emotional link. **2** a document issued by a government or public company acknowledging that money has been lent to it and will be repaid with interest. ● *v.* join or be joined with a bond. □ **in bond** stored in a customs warehouse until duties are paid.

bondage *n.* slavery, captivity.

bone *n.* each of the hard parts making up the vertebrate skeleton. ● *v.* remove bones from. □ **bone up on** *informal* study intensively.

bonfire *n.* a fire built in the open air.

bongo *n.* (*pl.* **bongos**) or **bongoes**) each of a pair of small drums played with the fingers.

bonhomie (**bon**-ŏmi) *n.* cheerful friendliness.

bonk *v.* **1** make an abrupt thudding sound; bump. **2** *informal* have sexual intercourse (with). ● *n.* **1** a thudding sound. **2** *informal* an act of sexual intercourse.

bonnet *n.* **1** a hat with strings that tie under the chin. **2** a hinged cover over the engine of a motor vehicle.

bonny *adj.* (**bonnier, bonniest**) healthy-looking; *Scot. & N. Engl.* good-looking.

bonsai *n.* (*pl.* **bonsai**) an ornamental miniature tree or shrub; the art of growing these.

bonus *n.* an extra payment or benefit.

bon voyage (bon vwa-**yah***zh*) *int.* an expression of good wishes to a person starting a journey.

bony *adj.* (**bonier, boniest**) like bones; having many bones; so thin that the bones show.

boo *int.* an exclamation of disapproval; an exclamation to startle someone. ● *v.* shout 'boo' (at).

boob *n. informal* **1** a blunder. **2** a breast.

booby *n.* (*pl.* **-ies**) a foolish person.

booby prize *n.* a prize given to the competitor with the lowest score.

booby trap *n.* a disguised bomb; a trap set as a practical joke.

boogie *v.* (**boogied, boogieing**) dance to fast rock or pop music.

book *n.* **1** a set of sheets of paper bound in a cover; a literary work filling this; a main division of a literary work. **2** a record of bets made. ● *v.* **1** reserve, buy, or engage in advance. **2** record details of (an offender).

bookcase *n.* a piece of furniture with shelves for books.

bookie *n. informal* a bookmaker.

bookkeeping *n.* the systematic recording of business transactions.

booklet *n.* a small thin book.

bookmaker *n.* a person whose business is the taking of bets.

bookmark *n.* a strip of paper etc. to mark a place in a book.

bookworm *n.* **1** *informal* a person fond of reading. **2** a grub that eats holes in books.

boom *v.* **1** make a deep resonant sound. **2** have a period of prosperity. ● *n.* **1** a booming sound. **2** a period of prosperity. **3** a long pole; a floating barrier.

boomerang *n.* an Australian missile of curved wood that can be thrown so as to return to the thrower.

boon *n.* a benefit.

boor *n.* an ill-mannered person. ◻ **boorish** *adj.*, **boorishness** *n.*

boost *v.* improve or increase; support, encourage. ● *n.* encouragement, help; an increase.

booster *n.* **1** a small supplementary dose of a vaccine. **2** a rocket giving extra speed to a spacecraft as it takes off.

boot *n.* **1** a shoe covering both foot and ankle. **2** the luggage compartment at the back of a car. **3** (**the boot**) *informal* dismissal. ● *v.* **1** kick. **2** start up (a computer).

bootee *n.* a baby's woollen boot.

booth *n.* a small enclosed compartment; a stall or stand.

bootleg *adj.* smuggled, illicit. ◻ **bootlegger** *n.*, **bootlegging** *n.*

booty *n.* loot.

booze *informal v.* drink alcohol. ● *n.* alcoholic drink ◻ **boozer** *n.*, **boozy** *adj.*

borax *n.* a compound of boron used in detergents.

border *n.* a boundary, an edge; a flower bed round part of a garden. ● *v.* put or be a border to. ◻ **border on** come close to being.

borderline *n.* a line marking a boundary.

bore[1] past of bear.

bore[2] *v.* **1** tire by dullness. **2** make (a hole) with a revolving tool. ● *n.* **1** a tedious person or thing. **2** the hollow inside of a gun barrel; its diameter. **3** a hole bored. **4** a tidal wave in an estuary. ◻ **boredom** *n.*

boric *adj.* of boron.

born *adj.* **1** existing as a result of birth. **2** naturally having a specified ability.

born-again *adj.* converted to a religion (esp. Christianity).

borne p.p. of **bear**.

boron *n.* a chemical element (symbol B).

borough (**bu**-rĕ) *n.* a town or district with rights of local government.

borrow *v.* take (something needed) from someone, with the intention of returning it. ◻ **borrower** *n.*

Borstal *n.* the former name of an institution for young offenders.

bortsch *n.* (also **borsch**) beetroot soup.

bosom *n.* the breast.

boss *n.* **1** *informal* an employer; a person in charge. **2** a projecting knob. ● *v. informal* give orders to in a domineering way.

boss-eyed *adj.* blind in one eye; cross-eyed.

bosun, bo'sun vars. of **boatswain**.

bossy *adj.* (**bossier, bossiest**) domineering. ◻ **bossily** *adv.*, **bossiness** *n.*

botany *n.* the study of plants. □ **botanical** *adj.*, **botanist** *n.*

botch *v.* do (a task) badly.

both *adj.*, *pron.*, & *adv.* the two.

bother *v.* **1** cause trouble, worry, or annoyance to; pester. **2** take trouble. ● *n.* **1** effort; (a cause of) inconvenience. **2** trouble; violence. □ **bothersome** *adj.*

bottle *n.* a narrow-necked container for liquid. ● *v.* store in bottles; preserve in jars.

bottleneck *n.* a narrow point in a road where congestion occurs.

bottom *n.* **1** the lowest part or point; the ground under a stretch of water. **2** the buttocks. ● *adj.* lowest in position, rank, or degree. □ **bottomless** *adj.*

botulism *n.* poisoning caused by bacteria in food.

bougainvillea (*boo*-gĕn-*vi*-lee-ă) *n.* a tropical shrub with large red or purple bracts.

bough *n.* a main branch of a tree.

bought past & p.p. of **buy**.

bouillon (boo-yawn) *n.* thin clear soup.

boulder *n.* a large rounded stone.

boulevard *n.* a wide street.

bounce *v.* **1** rebound; move up and down; move in a light, lively manner. **2** *informal* (of a cheque) be sent back by a bank as worthless. ● *n.* a rebound; a bouncing movement; resilience, liveliness.

bouncer *n.* a person employed to eject troublemakers from a club etc.

bound[1] past & p.p. of **bind**.

bound[2] *v.* **1** run with a leaping movement. **2** form the boundary of. ● *n.* **1** a leap. **2** a boundary; a limitation. ● *adj.* heading in a specified direction. □ **bound to** certain to. **out of bounds** outside where one is permitted to be.

boundary *n.* (*pl.* **-ies**) the limit of an area or the line marking it; a hit to the boundary in cricket.

boundless *adj.* unlimited.

bountiful *adj.* giving generously; abundant. □ **bountifully** *adv.*

bounty *n.* (*pl.* **-ies**) generosity; a generous gift. □ **bounteous** *adj.*

bouquet (boo-kay) *n.* **1** a bunch of flowers. **2** the perfume of wine.

bouquet garni (boo-kay gar-ni) *n.* (*pl.* **bouquets garnis**) a bunch of herbs for flavouring stews etc.

bourbon (ber-bŏn) *n.* an American whisky made from maize.

bourgeois (boor-*zh*wah) *adj.* conventionally middle-class.

bourgeoisie (boor-*zh*wah-zi) *n.* the bourgeois class.

bout *n.* **1** a period of exercise, work, or illness. **2** a boxing contest.

boutique *n.* a small shop selling fashionable clothes etc.

bovine *adj.* **1** of oxen or cattle. **2** dull and stupid.

bow[1] (boh) *n.* **1** a weapon for shooting arrows. **2** a rod with horsehair stretched between its ends, for playing a violin etc. **3** a knot with two loops, for fastening or decoration.

bow[2] (bow) *n.* an inclination of the head or body in greeting, respect, etc. ● *v.* bend in this way; cause to bend downwards under weight; submit.

bow[3] (bow) *n.* the front end of a boat or ship.

bowdlerize *v.* (also **-ise**) remove sections considered improper from (a book etc.). □ **bowdlerization** *n.*

bowel *n.* the intestine; (**bowels**) the innermost parts.

bower *n.* a leafy shelter.

bowl *n.* **1** a round, deep dish for food or liquid; the hollow rounded part of a spoon etc. **2** a heavy ball weighted to roll in a curve; (**bowls**) a game played with such balls; a ball used in skittles. ● *v.* **1** send rolling along the ground; go fast and smoothly. **2** send a ball to a batsman; dismiss (a batsman) by knocking bails off with the ball. □ **bowl over** knock down; overwhelm with surprise or emotion.

bowler *n.* **1** a person who bowls in cricket; one who plays at bowls.

2 (in full **bowler hat**) a hard felt hat with a rounded top.

bowling *n.* playing bowls, skittles, or a similar game.

box *n.* **1** a container with a flat base and sides, usu. square and with a lid; a space enclosed by straight lines on a page or screen; a compartment at a theatre; *informal* television. **2** a facility at a newspaper office or post office for receiving replies to an advertisement or letters. **3** a small evergreen shrub; its wood. ● *v.* **1** put into a box. **2** fight with the fists as a sport. □ **boxing** *n.*

boxer *n.* **1** a person who engages in the sport of boxing. **2** a dog of a breed resembling a bulldog.

boxer shorts *n.pl.* men's loose underpants like shorts.

box office *n.* an office for booking seats at a theatre etc.

boxroom *n.* a small spare room.

boy *n.* a male child. ● *int.* an exclamation of surprise or pleasure. □ **boyhood** *n.*, **boyish** *adj.*

boycott *v.* refuse to deal with or trade with. ● *n.* boycotting.

boyfriend *n.* a person's regular male companion or lover.

Bq *abbr.* becquerel.

Br *symb.* bromine.

bra *n.* a woman's undergarment worn to support the breasts.

brace *n.* **1** a device that holds things together or in position; (**braces**) straps to keep trousers up, passing over the shoulders; a wire device worn in the mouth to straighten the teeth. **2** a pair. ● *v.* give support or firmness to.

bracelet *n.* an ornamental band worn on the arm.

bracing *adj.* invigorating.

bracken *n.* a large fern.

bracket *n.* **1** any of the marks used in pairs to enclose and separate off words or figures, ( ), [ ], { }; a group or category falling within certain limits. **2** a support for a shelf or lamp, projecting from a wall. ● *v.* enclose in brackets; group together.

brackish *adj.* slightly salty.

bract *n.* a brightly coloured leaflike part of a plant.

brag *v.* (**bragged, bragging**) boast.

braggart *n.* a person who brags.

Brahman *n.* (also **Brahmin**) a member of the highest Hindu caste, the priestly caste.

braid *n.* **1** a woven ornamental trimming. **2** a plait of hair. ● *v.* **1** trim with braid. **2** plait.

Braille *n.* a system of representing letters etc. by raised dots which blind people read by touch.

brain *n.* the mass of soft grey matter in the skull, the centre of the nervous system in animals; (also **brains**) the mind, intelligence.

brainchild *n.* a person's invention or plan.

brainstorm *n.* **1** a violent mental disturbance; a sudden mental lapse. **2** a spontaneous discussion in search of new ideas; *Amer.* a clever idea.

brainwash *v.* pressurize (someone) into changing their beliefs by means other than rational argument.

brainwave *n.* a bright idea.

brainy *adj.* (**brainier, brainiest**) clever.

braise *v.* cook slowly with little liquid in a closed container.

brake *n.* a device for reducing speed or stopping motion. ● *v.* stop or slow by the use of this.

bramble *n.* a prickly shrub on which blackberries grow.

bran *n.* the ground inner husks of grain, sifted from flour.

branch *n.* **1** a part of a tree growing out from the trunk; a division of a road, river, etc. **2** a subdivision of a subject. **3** a local shop or office belonging to a large organization. ● *v.* send out or divide into branches.

brand *n.* goods of a particular make; an identifying mark made on skin with hot metal. ● *v.* mark with a brand.

brandish *v.* wave, flourish.

brand new *adj.* completely new.

brandy *n.* (*pl.* **-ies**) a strong alcoholic spirit distilled from wine or fermented fruit juice.

brash *adj.* aggressively self-assertive. □ **brashly** *adv.*, **brashness** *n.*

brass *n.* a yellow alloy of copper and zinc; musical instruments made of this; a memorial tablet made of this; *informal* money. ● *adj.* made of brass.

brasserie (bra-sĕ-ree) *n.* an informal licensed restaurant.

brassica *n.* a plant of the cabbage family.

brassière (bras-i-air) *n.* a bra.

brassy *adj.* (**brassier, brassiest**) **1** like brass. **2** bold and vulgar. □ **brassiness** *n.*

brat *n. derog.* a child.

bravado *n.* a show of boldness.

brave *adj.* able to face and endure danger or pain. ● *v.* face and endure bravely. ● *n. dated* an American Indian warrior. □ **bravely** *adv.*, **bravery** *n.*

bravo *int.* well done!

bravura *n.* brilliant style and technique in performing.

brawl *n.* a noisy quarrel or fight. ● *v.* take part in a brawl.

brawn *n.* **1** muscular strength. **2** pressed meat from a pig's or calf's head.

brawny *adj.* (**brawnier, brawniest**) muscular.

bray *n.* a donkey's cry; a harsh, loud sound. ● *v.* make this cry or sound.

braze *v.* solder with an alloy of brass.

brazen *adj.* **1** shameless, impudent. **2** *literary* made of brass. □ **brazen it out** behave (after doing wrong) as if one has no need to be ashamed. □ **brazenly** *adv.*

brazier *n.* a basket-like stand for holding burning coals.

breach *n.* **1** failure to observe a rule or contract. **2** separation, estrangement. **3** a gap in a defence. ● *v.* break through, make a breach in.

bread *n.* food made of baked dough of flour and liquid, usu. leavened by yeast.

breadline *n.* □ **on the breadline** living in extreme poverty.

breadth *n.* width, broadness.

breadwinner *n.* the member of a family who earns money to support the others.

break *v.* (**broke, broken, breaking**) **1** separate or cause to separate as a result of a blow or strain; suffer a fracture in (a limb); interrupt (a sequence or habit). **2** fail to keep (a promise or law). **3** crush, defeat. **4** reveal (bad news). **5** surpass (a record). **6** (of a wave) fall on the shore. **7** (of a boy's voice) deepen at puberty. **8** (of a ball) change direction after touching the ground. ● *n.* **1** a gap; an interruption of continuity; a rest, a holiday. **2** a fracture. **3** a sudden dash. **4** *informal* an opportunity. **5** points scored consecutively in snooker. □ **break down 1** cease to function; collapse; give way to emotion. **2** analyse, separate. **break even** have equal profits and costs. **break in 1** force entry. **2** familiarize.

breakable *adj.* able to be broken.

breakage *n.* breaking; something broken.

breakdown *n.* **1** a mechanical failure; a collapse of health or mental stability. **2** an analysis.

breaker *n.* a heavy ocean wave that breaks on the coast.

breakfast *n.* the first meal of the day.

breakneck *adj.* dangerously fast.

breakthrough *n.* a sudden major advance in an undertaking.

breakwater *n.* a wall built out into the sea to break the force of waves.

breast *n.* the upper front part of the body; either of the two milk-producing organs on a woman's chest;

a joint of meat from the upper front part of the body.

breastbone *n.* the bone down the upper front of the body.

breaststroke *n.* a swimming stroke performed on one's front with circular arm and leg movements.

breath *n.* air drawn into and sent out of the lungs in breathing; a slight movement of wind. □ **hold one's breath** temporarily cease breathing; be in suspense. **out of breath** panting after exercise. **under one's breath** in a whisper. □ **breathy** *adj.*

breathalyser *n.* (*Amer.* **breathalyzer**) *trademark* a device measuring the alcohol in a person's breath. □ **breathalyse** *v.* (*Amer.* **-yze**).

breathe *v.* **1** draw (air) into the lungs and send it out again. **2** whisper.

breather *n.* a pause for rest; a short period in fresh air.

breathless *adj.* out of breath.

breathtaking *adj.* amazing.

bred past & p.p. of **breed**.

breech *n.* the back part of a gun barrel, where it opens.

breeches *n.pl.* trousers reaching to just below the knees.

breed *v.* (**bred, breeding**) produce offspring; control the mating of (animals), esp. to produce young with particular qualities; train, rear; give rise to. ● *n.* a variety of animals within a species; a sort. □ **breeder** *n.*

breeding *n.* good manners resulting from training or background.

breeze *n.* a light wind. □ **breezy** *adj.*

breeze-block *n.* a lightweight building block.

brethren *n.pl. archaic* brothers.

Breton *adj.* & *n.* (a native) of Brittany.

breve *n.* **1** a mark (˘) over a short vowel. **2** (in music) a long note.

breviary *n.* (*pl.* **-ies**) a book of prayers to be said by Roman Catholic priests.

brevity *n.* briefness; conciseness.

brew *v.* **1** make (beer) by boiling and fermentation; make (tea) by infusion. **2** (of an unpleasant situation) begin to develop. ● *n.* a liquid or amount brewed.

brewer *n.* a person whose trade is brewing beer.

brewery *n.* (*pl.* **-ies**) a place where beer is made commercially.

briar var. of **brier**.

bribe *n.* a gift offered to influence a person to act in favour of the giver. ● *v.* persuade by this. □ **bribery** *n.*

bric-a-brac *n.* odd items of ornaments, furniture, etc.

brick *n.* **1** a block of baked or dried clay used to build walls; a rectangular block. **2** *informal, dated* a kind and helpful person. ● *v.* block with a brick structure.

brickbat *n.* a missile hurled at someone; a criticism.

bricklayer *n.* a workman who builds with bricks.

bridal *adj.* of a bride or wedding.

bride *n.* a woman on her wedding day or when newly married.

bridegroom *n.* a man on his wedding day or when newly married.

bridesmaid *n.* a girl or unmarried woman attending a bride.

bridge *n.* **1** a structure providing a way over a gap or other obstacle; a connection between two points or groups. **2** the captain's platform on a ship. **3** the bony upper part of the nose. **4** a card game developed from whist. ● *v.* make or be a bridge over.

bridgehead *n.* a fortified area established in enemy territory, esp. on the far side of a river.

bridgework *n.* a dental structure covering a gap.

bridle *n.* a harness on a horse's head. ● *v.* **1** put a bridle on; restrain. **2** draw up one's head in pride or scorn.

bridle path *n.* (also **bridleway**) a path for riders or walkers.

brief *adj.* lasting only for a short time; concise; short. ● *n.* a set of instructions and information, esp. to a barrister about a case. ● *v.* inform or instruct in advance. □ **briefly** *adv.*, **briefness** *n.*

briefcase *n.* a case for carrying documents.

briefs *n.pl.* short pants or knickers.

brier *n.* (also **briar**) a thorny bush, a wild rose.

brig *n.* a square-rigged sailing vessel with two masts.

brigade *n.* an army unit forming part of a division; *informal* a group with a shared purpose or interest.

brigadier *n.* an officer commanding a brigade or of similar status.

brigand *n.* a member of a band of robbers.

bright *adj.* **1** giving out or reflecting much light, shining. **2** clever. **3** cheerful; encouraging. □ **brightly** *adv.*, **brightness** *n.*

brighten *v.* make or become brighter.

brilliant *adj.* **1** very bright, sparkling. **2** very clever. ● *n.* a cut diamond with many facets. □ **brilliance** *n.*, **brilliantly** *adv.*

brim *n.* the edge of a cup or hollow; the projecting edge of a hat. ● *v.* (**brimmed, brimming**) be full to the brim.

brimstone *n. archaic* sulphur.

brindled *adj.* brown with streaks of another colour.

brine *n.* salt water; sea water.

bring *v.* (**brought, bringing**) cause to come or move in a particular direction; accompany; cause to be in a particular state. □ **bring about** cause to happen. **bring off** achieve. **bring on** cause. **bring oneself** force oneself to do something. **bring out 1** produce, publish. **2** make more obvious. **bring up** look after and educate.

brink *n.* the edge of a steep place or of a stretch of water; the point just before an event or state.

brinkmanship *n.* a policy of pursuing a dangerous course to the brink of catastrophe.

briny *adj.* of brine or sea water; salty.

briquette (bri-**ket**) *n.* a block of compressed coal dust.

brisk *adj.* **1** energetic, moving quickly. **2** curt. □ **briskly** *adv.*

brisket *n.* a joint of beef from the breast.

bristle *n.* a short stiff hair; one of the stiff pieces of hair or wire in a brush. ● *v.* (of hair) stand upright as a result of anger or fear; show indignation; be thickly set with something.

Britannic *adj.* of Britain.

British *adj.* of Britain or its people.

Briton *n.* a British person.

brittle *adj.* hard but easily broken. □ **brittleness** *n.*

broach *v.* open and start using; begin discussion of.

broad *adj.* **1** wide, large from side to side; extensive, inclusive. **2** in general terms; not precise or detailed. **3** (of humour) rather coarse. **4** (of an accent) strong.

broad-minded *adj.* not easily shocked.

broadcast *v.* (**broadcast, broadcasting**) **1** send out by radio or television; make generally known. **2** sow (seed) by scattering. ● *n.* a broadcast programme. □ **broadcaster** *n.*

broaden *v.* make or become broader.

broadly *adv.* in general; with few exceptions.

broadsheet *n.* a large-sized newspaper.

broadside *n.* the firing of all guns on one side of a ship; a strongly worded criticism.

brocade *n.* a fabric woven with raised patterns.

broccoli *n.* a vegetable with tightly-packed green or purple flower heads.

brochure (**broh**-shewr) *n.* a booklet or leaflet giving information.

broderie anglaise (*broh*-dě-ri *ong*-layz) *n.* open embroidery on white cotton or linen.

brogue *n.* **1** a strong shoe with ornamental perforated bands. **2** a strong regional accent, esp. Irish.

broil *v.* grill.

broiler *n.* a chicken suitable for broiling.

broke past of **break**. ● *adj. informal* having spent all one's money; bankrupt.

broken p.p. of **break**. ● *adj.* (of a language) badly spoken by a foreigner.

broken-hearted *adj.* overwhelmed with grief.

broker *n.* an agent who buys and sells on behalf of others. ● *v.* arrange, negotiate (a deal).

brokerage *n.* a broker's fee.

brolly *n.* (*pl.* **-ies**) *informal* an umbrella.

bromide *n.* a compound used to calm nerves.

bromine *n.* a dark red poisonous liquid element (symbol Br).

bronchial *adj.* of the branched tubes into which the windpipe divides.

bronchitis *n.* inflammation of the bronchial tubes.

bronco *n.* (*pl.* **broncos**) a wild or half-tamed horse of western North America.

brontosaurus *n.* a large plant-eating dinosaur.

bronze *n.* a brown alloy of copper and tin; something made of this; its colour. ● *v.* make suntanned.

brooch (brohch) *n.* an ornamental hinged pin fastened with a clasp.

brood *n.* young produced at one hatching or birth; a family. ● *v.* **1** sit on (eggs) and hatch them. **2** think long, deeply, and sadly.

broody *adj.* (**broodier, broodiest**) **1** (of a hen) wanting to brood; *informal* (of a woman) wanting children. **2** thoughtful and unhappy.

brook *n.* a small stream. ● *v.* tolerate, allow.

broom *n.* **1** a long-handled brush. **2** a shrub with yellow flowers.

broomstick *n.* a broom-handle.

Bros. *abbr.* Brothers.

broth *n.* a thin meat or fish soup.

brothel *n.* a house where people pay to have sex with prostitutes.

brother *n.* **1** the son of the same parents as another person. **2** a man who is a fellow member of a group, trade union, or Church. **3** a monk who is not a priest. □ **brotherly** *adj.*

brotherhood *n.* the relationship of brothers; comradeship; an association with a common interest.

brother-in-law *n.* (*pl.* **brothers-in-law**) the brother of one's husband or wife; the husband of one's sister.

brought past & p.p. of **bring**.

brow *n.* an eyebrow; a forehead; the summit of a hill.

browbeat *v.* (**browbeat, browbeaten, browbeating**) intimidate.

brown *adj.* of a colour between orange and black, like earth or wood. ● *v.* make or become brown.

browned off *adj. informal* bored or annoyed.

brownfield *adj.* (of a site) having had previous development on it.

browse *v.* **1** look around casually; read or scan superficially. **2** feed on leaves or grass.

bruise *n.* an injury that discolours skin without breaking it. ● *v.* cause a bruise on.

bruiser *n.* a tough brutal person.

brunch *n.* a meal combining breakfast and lunch.

brunette *n.* a woman with brown hair.

brunt *n.* the worst stress or chief impact.

brush *n.* **1** an implement for cleaning, arranging hair, etc., consisting of bristles set into a block; an act of using this; a light touch. **2** a fox's tail. **3** a dangerous or unpleasant encounter. **4** undergrowth. ● *v.* clean, arrange, etc., with a brush; touch lightly in passing. □ **brush aside** dismiss. **brush off** reject, snub. **brush up** improve; improve one's knowledge.

brushwood *n.* undergrowth; cut or broken twigs.

brusque (broosk) *adj.* curt and off-hand. □ **brusquely** *adv.*

Brussels sprout *n.* the edible bud of a kind of cabbage.

brutal *adj.* cruel, without mercy. □ **brutality** *n.*, **brutally** *adv.*

brutalize *v.* (also **-ise**) make brutal; treat brutally. □ **brutalization** *n.*

brute *n.* **1** an animal other than man. **2** a brutal person; *informal* an unpleasant person or thing. ● *adj.* without reason; merely physical. □ **brutish** *adj.*

BS *abbr.* British Standard(s).

BSE *abbr.* bovine spongiform encephalopathy, a fatal brain disease of cattle.

BST *abbr.* British Summer Time.

Bt. *abbr.* Baronet.

bubble *n.* a thin sphere of liquid enclosing air or gas; an air-filled cavity. ● *v.* **1** rise in bubbles; contain bubbles. **2** show great liveliness. □ **bubbly** *adj.*

bubonic plague *n.* a plague characterized by swellings.

buccaneer *n.* a pirate; an adventurer.

buck *n.* **1** the male of a deer, hare, or rabbit. **2** an article placed before the dealer in a game of poker. **3** *Amer. & Austral.* a dollar. ● *v.* **1** (of a horse) jump with the back arched. **2** *informal* resist, oppose, or reverse. □ **buck up 1** cheer up. **2** hurry. **pass the buck** shift the responsibility (and possible blame).

bucket *n.* a cylindrical open container with a handle, for carrying liquid; (**buckets**) *informal* a large amount of liquid. ● *v. informal* rain heavily.

buckle *n.* a device through which a belt or strap is threaded to secure it. ● *v.* **1** fasten with a buckle. **2** crumple under pressure. □ **buckle down to** set about doing.

buckram *n.* stiffened cloth for binding books.

bucolic *adj.* rustic.

bud *n.* a leaf or flower not fully open. ● *v.* (**budded, budding**) put forth buds; begin to develop.

Buddhism *n.* an Asian religion based on the teachings of Buddha. □ **Buddhist** *adj & n.*

budding *adj.* beginning to develop or be successful.

buddleia *n.* a tree or shrub with purple or yellow flowers.

buddy *n.* (*pl.* **-ies**) *Amer. informal* a friend.

budge *v.* move slightly.

budgerigar *n.* an Australian parakeet often kept as a pet.

budget *n.* a plan of income and expenditure; the amount of money someone has available. ● *v.* allow or provide for in a budget.

budgie *n. informal* a budgerigar.

buff *n.* **1** a fawn colour. **2** *informal* an expert and enthusiast. ● *v.* polish with soft material. □ **in the buff** *informal* naked.

buffalo *n.* (*pl.* **buffaloes** or **buffalo**) a wild ox; a North American bison.

buffer *n.* **1** something that lessens the effect of impact. **2** *informal* an elderly and foolish man. ● *v.* act as a buffer to.

buffet[1] (buuf-ay) *n.* a meal where guests serve themselves; a counter where food and drink are served.

buffet[2] (buff-it) *v.* strike repeatedly. ● *n. dated* a blow.

buffoon *n.* a person who plays the fool. □ **buffoonery** *n.*

bug *n.* **1** a small insect; *informal* a micro-organism causing illness; *informal* an infection; *informal* a fault in a computer system. **2** *informal* a hidden microphone. ● *v.* (**bugged, bugging**) *informal* **1** install a hidden microphone in. **2** annoy.

bugbear *n.* something feared or disliked.

bugger *vulgar slang int.* damn. ● *n.* **1** an unpleasant person or thing; a person of a specified type. **2** a person who commits buggery.

buggery *n.* anal intercourse.

buggy *n.* (*pl.* **-ies**) a small light vehicle; a lightweight folding pushchair.

bugle *n.* a brass instrument like a small trumpet. □ **bugler** *n.*

build *v.* (**built, building**) construct by putting parts or material together. ● *n.* bodily shape. □ **build up** establish gradually; increase. □ **builder** *n.*

building *n.* a house or similar structure.

building society *n.* an organization that accepts deposits and lends money, esp. to people buying houses.

built-in *adj.* forming part of a structure.

built-up *adj.* covered with buildings.

bulb *n.* the rounded base of the stem of certain plants; something shaped like this; the glass part giving light in an electric lamp. □ **bulbous** *adj.*

bulge *n.* a rounded swelling. ● *v.* form a bulge, swell.

bulimia *n.* (in full **bulimia nervosa**) an eating disorder in which overeating alternates with self-induced vomiting, dieting, or purging. □ **bulimic** *adj.*

bulk *n.* mass; something large and heavy; the majority. ● *v.* be or seem large or important; increase the size of.

bulkhead *n.* a partition in a ship etc.

bulky *adj.* (**bulkier, bulkiest**) taking up much space.

bull *n.* **1** the male of the ox, whale, elephant, etc. **2** the bullseye of a target. **3** a pope's official edict. **4** *informal* nonsense.

bulldog *n.* a powerful dog with a short thick neck.

bulldozer *n.* a powerful tractor with a device for clearing ground.

bullet *n.* **1** a small missile fired from a rifle or revolver. **2** a small solid circle printed before each item in a list.

bulletin *n.* a short official statement of news.

bullfight *n.* the baiting and killing of bulls as an entertainment.

bullion *n.* gold or silver in bulk or bars.

bullock *n.* a castrated bull.

bullseye *n.* the centre of a target.

bullshit *n. vulgar slang* nonsense.

bully *n.* (*pl.* **-ies**) a person who hurts or intimidates others who are weaker. ● *v.* (**bullied, bullying**) behave as a bully towards. □ **bully off** put the ball into play in hockey by two opponents striking sticks together.

bulrush *n.* a rush with a velvety head.

bulwark *n.* **1** a defensive wall; a defence. **2** a ship's side above the deck.

bum *n. informal* **1** the buttocks. **2** a tramp; an idler.

bumble *v.* move or act clumsily or incompetently.

bumblebee *n.* a large bee.

bumf *n.* (also **bumph**) *informal* documents, papers.

bump *v.* **1** knock or collide with. **2** travel with a jolting movement. ● *n.* **1** a knock or collision; the dull sound of this. **2** a swelling, a raised area on a surface. **3** a jolt. □ **bumpy** *adj.*

bumper *n.* a horizontal bar at the front or back of a motor vehicle to lessen the damage in collision. ● *adj.* unusually large or successful.

bumpkin *n.* a country person with awkward manners.

bumptious *adj.* conceited.

bun *n.* **1** a small sweet cake. **2** hair twisted into a coil at the back of the head.

bunch *n.* a number of things growing or fastened together; a group.

● *v.* form or be formed into a bunch.

bundle *n.* **1** a collection of things loosely fastened or wrapped together. **2** *informal* a large amount of money. ● *v.* **1** make into a bundle. **2** move or push hurriedly.

bung *n.* a stopper for a jar or barrel. ● *v.* **1** block, close. **2** *informal* throw, put.

bungalow *n.* a one-storeyed house.

bungee jumping *n.* the sport of jumping from a height attached to an elasticated rope (a **bungee**).

bungle *v.* spoil by lack of skill, mismanage. ● *n.* a bungled attempt. □ **bungler** *n.*

bunion *n.* a painful swelling at the base of the big toe.

bunk *n.* a shelflike bed. □ **do a bunk** *informal* run away.

bunker *n.* **1** a container for fuel. **2** a sandy hollow forming an obstacle on a golf course. **3** a reinforced underground shelter.

bunkum *n. informal, dated* nonsense.

Bunsen burner *n.* a small adjustable gas burner used in laboratories.

bunting *n.* **1** a bird related to the finches. **2** decorative flags.

buoy (boy) *n.* an anchored floating object serving as a navigation mark. □ **buoy up** keep afloat; make cheerful.

buoyant (boy-ănt) *adj.* **1** able to float. **2** cheerful. □ **buoyancy** *n.*

bur *n.* (also **burr**) a prickly seed case that clings to clothing etc.

burble *v.* make a gentle murmuring sound; speak lengthily and foolishly.

burden *n.* something carried; an obligation causing hardship. ● *v.* load; oppress.

bureau (bew-roh) *n.* (*pl.* **bureaux** or **bureaus**) **1** a writing desk with drawers. **2** an office, a department.

bureaucracy (bew-rok-ră-si) *n.* (*pl.* **-ies**) government by unelected officials; excessive administration. □ **bureaucratic** *adj.*

bureaucrat *n.* a government official.

burgeon (ber-jĕn) *v.* begin to grow rapidly.

burger *n. informal* a hamburger.

burglar *n.* a person who breaks into a building in order to steal. □ **burglary** *n.*, **burgle** *v.*

burgundy *n.* (*pl.* **-ies**) a red wine; a purplish red colour.

burial *n.* the burying of a corpse.

burlesque *n.* a mocking imitation. ● *v.* parody.

burly *adj.* (**burlier, burliest**) with a strong heavy body. □ **burliness** *n.*

burn[1] *v.* (**burned** or **burnt, burning**) be on fire, produce heat or light; damage or destroy by fire, heat, or acid; use (fuel); feel hot and painful; feel passionate emotion. ● *n.* a mark or injury made by burning.

burn[2] *n. Scot.* a stream.

burner *n.* a part that shapes the flame in a lamp, cooker, etc.

burning *adj.* **1** intense. **2** (of an issue) keenly discussed.

burnish *v.* polish by rubbing.

burnt past & p.p. of **burn**.

burp *n.* & *v. informal* (make) a belch.

burr *n.* **1** a whirring sound; the strong pronunciation of 'r'; a country accent using this. **2** var. of **bur**. ● *v.* make a whirring sound.

burrow *n.* a hole dug by an animal as a dwelling. ● *v.* dig a burrow; advance by tunnelling; inquire or search thoroughly.

bursar *n.* a person who manages the finances and other business of a college or school.

bursary *n.* (*pl.* **-ies**) **1** a scholarship or grant given to a student. **2** a bursar's office.

burst *v.* (**burst, bursting**) break suddenly and violently apart; force or be forced open; be very full; appear or come suddenly and forcefully; suddenly begin to do something. ● *n.* an instance of breaking; a brief violent or energetic outbreak; a spurt.

bury *v.* (**buried, burying**) put underground; place (a dead body) in the earth or a tomb; cover, conceal; involve (oneself) deeply, be absorbed.

bus *n.* (*pl.* **buses**; *Amer.* **busses**) a large motor vehicle for public transport by road. ● *v.* (**buses** or **busses, bussed, bussing**) travel by bus; transport by bus.

busby *n.* (*pl.* **-ies**) a tall fur hat.

bush *n.* **1** a shrub; uncultivated land or the vegetation on it; an untidy clump of hair. **2** a metal lining for a hole in a machine; an insulating sleeve. □ **beat about the bush** talk without coming to the point.

bushy *adj.* (**bushier, bushiest**) covered with bushes; growing thickly.

business *n.* **1** an occupation, profession, or trade; something that is someone's duty or concern. **2** trade, commerce; a commercial establishment. **3** *informal* a set of events, an affair.

businesslike *adj.* practical, systematic, efficient.

businessman *n.* (*pl.* **-men**) a man engaged in trade or commerce.

businesswoman *n.* (*pl.* **-women**) a woman engaged in trade or commerce.

busker *n.* a street entertainer performing for donations. □ **busk** *v.*

busman's holiday *n.* leisure time spent doing something similar to one's work.

bust *n.* a woman's chest measured around the breasts; a sculptured head, shoulders, and chest. ● *v. informal* burst, break. □ **go bust** *informal* become bankrupt.

bustle *v.* make a show of activity or hurry. ● *n.* **1** excited activity. **2** *hist.* padding to puff out the top of a skirt at the back.

bust-up *n. informal* a quarrel.

busy *adj.* (**busier, busiest**) having much to do; occupied; full of activity. □ **busily** *adv.*

busybody *n.* (*pl.* **-ies**) a meddlesome person.

but *conj.* introducing contrast; however; except. ● *prep.* apart from. ● *adv.* merely, only.

butane *n.* an inflammable gas used in liquid form as fuel.

butch *adj. informal* ostentatiously and aggressively masculine.

butcher *n.* a person who cuts up and sells animal flesh for food; a savage killer. ● *v.* kill needlessly or brutally. □ **butchery** *n.*

butler *n.* a chief manservant.

butt *n.* **1** a cask. **2** the thick end of a tool or weapon; a cigarette stub. **3** *informal* the buttocks. **4** a target for ridicule or teasing. **5** (**butts**) a shooting range. ● *v.* **1** push with the head. **2** meet or place end to end. □ **butt in** interrupt.

butter *n.* a fatty food substance made from milk and used as a spread. ● *v.* spread with butter. □ **butter up** *informal* flatter.

buttercup *n.* a wild plant with yellow cup-shaped flowers.

butterfly *n.* (*pl.* **-ies**) **1** an insect with four large often brightly coloured wings; a frivolous person. **2** a swimming stroke with both arms lifted at the same time.

buttermilk *n.* liquid left after butter is churned from milk.

butterscotch *n.* a hard toffee-like sweet.

buttock *n.* either of the two fleshy rounded parts at the lower end of the back of the body.

button *n.* a disc or knob sewn to a garment as a fastener or ornament; a small rounded object; a knob pressed to operate a device. ● *v.* fasten with button(s).

buttonhole *n.* a slit through which a button is passed to fasten clothing; a flower worn in the buttonhole of a lapel. ● *v.* accost and talk to.

buttress *n.* a support built against a wall; something that supports. ● *v.* reinforce, prop up.

butty *n.* (*pl.* **-ies**) *informal* a sandwich.

buxom *adj.* (of a woman) plump, large-breasted.

buy *v.* (**bought, buying**) **1** obtain in exchange for money. **2** *informal* accept as true. ● *n.* a purchase. □ **buyer** *n.*

buyout *n.* the purchase of a controlling share in a company; the buying of a company by people who work for it.

buzz *n.* **1** a vibrating humming sound; *informal* a telephone call. **2** *informal* a rumour. **3** *informal* a thrill; an exciting atmosphere. ● *v.* **1** make a buzzing sound. **2** be full of activity; move quickly. **3** fly close to at high speed.

buzzard *n.* a large hawk.

buzzer *n.* a device that produces a buzzing sound as a signal.

buzzword *n. informal* a fashionable technical word.

by *prep.* **1** beside; near. **2** through the agency or means of. **3** not later than. **4** during: *by night*. **5** indicating extent or margin: *by far the best*. **6** past; via. ● *adv.* going past. □ **by and by** before long. **by and large** on the whole. **by oneself** alone. **put by** keep in reserve.

bye *n.* **1** a run scored from a ball not hit by the batsman. **2** the transfer of a competitor to a higher round in the absence of an opponent.

by-election *n.* an election of an MP to replace one who has died or resigned.

bygone *adj.* belonging to the past. □ **let bygones be bygones** forgive past offences.

by-law *n.* a regulation made by a local authority or corporation.

byline *n.* a line naming the writer of a newspaper article.

bypass *n.* a road taking traffic round a town; (an operation providing) an alternative passage for blood. ● *v.* provide with a bypass; go round, avoid.

by-product *n.* something produced incidentally while making something else.

byre *n.* a cowshed.

byroad *n.* a minor road.

bystander *n.* a person standing near when something happens.

byte *n. Computing* a fixed number of bits (usually eight).

byway *n.* a minor road.

byword *n.* a famous or typical example; a familiar saying.

Cc

C *abbr.* **1** Celsius; centigrade. **2** coulomb(s). ● *symb.* carbon. ● *n.* (as a Roman numeral) 100.

c. *abbr.* **1** century. **2** cent(s). **3** circa. **4** copyright.

Ca *symb.* calcium.

cab *n.* **1** a taxi. **2** a compartment for the driver of a train, lorry, etc.

cabal (kă-**bahl**) *n.* (a group involved in) a plot; a small, exclusive, influential group.

cabaret (**kab**-ăray) *n.* entertainment provided in a nightclub etc.

cabbage *n.* a vegetable with a round head of green or purple leaves.

cabby *n.* (*pl.* **-ies**) *informal* a taxi driver.

caber *n.* a roughly trimmed tree trunk thrown as a trial of strength.

cabin *n.* a compartment in a ship or aircraft; a small hut.

cabinet *n.* **1** a cupboard with drawers or shelves. **2** (**the Cabinet**) the group of ministers chosen to be responsible for government policy.

cabinetmaker *n.* a maker of high-quality furniture.

cable *n.* **1** a thick rope of fibre or wire; a set of insulated wires for carrying electricity or signals. **2** a telegram.

cable car *n.* a vehicle pulled by a moving cable for carrying passengers up and down mountains.

cable television *n.* television transmission by cable to subscribers.

cabriolet (**kab**-ree-oh-lay) *n.* a car with a folding top; a light two-wheeled carriage with a hood.

cacao *n.* the bean from which cocoa and chocolate are made

cache (kash) *n.* a hidden store; a hiding place. ● *v.* store secretly.

cachet (**kash**-ay) *n.* **1** prestige. **2** a distinguishing mark.

cackle *n.* the clucking of hens; chattering talk; a loud silly laugh. ● *v.* utter a cackle.

cacophony (ka-**ko**-fŏ-nee) *n.* (*pl.* **-ies**) a discordant mixture of sounds. ◻ **cacophonous** *adj.*

cactus *n.* (*pl.* **cacti** or **cactuses**) a fleshy plant, often with prickles, from a hot dry climate.

cad *n. dated* a dishonourable man.

cadaver *n.* a corpse.

cadaverous *adj.* gaunt and pale.

caddie *n.* (also **caddy**) a golfer's attendant carrying clubs. ● *v.* act as caddie.

caddy *n.* (*pl.* **-ies**) **1** a small box for tea. **2** var. of **caddie**.

cadence *n.* **1** the rise and fall of the voice in speech. **2** a sequence of notes ending a musical phrase.

cadenza *n.* an elaborate passage for a solo instrument or singer.

cadet *n.* **1** a young trainee in the armed forces or police. **2** a junior branch of a family.

cadge *v.* ask for as a gift, beg.

cadmium *n.* a metallic element (symbol Cd).

cadre (**kah**-drĕ) *n.* a small group of specially trained people; an activist in a revolutionary organization.

caecum (see-kŭm) *n.* (*Amer.* **cecum**) (*pl.* **caeca**) a small pouch at the first part of the large intestine.

Caesarean section *n.* (*Amer.* **Cesarean, Cesarian**) an operation to deliver a child by an incision through the walls of the mother's abdomen and womb.

caesium (see-zi-ŭm) *n.* (*Amer.* **cesium**) a soft metallic element (symbol Cs).

café *n.* a small informal tea shop or restaurant.

cafeteria *n.* a self-service restaurant.

cafetière (ka-fĕ-**tyair**) *n.* a coffee pot with a plunger to keep the ground coffee separate from the liquid.

caffeine *n.* a stimulant found in tea and coffee.

caftan var. of **kaftan**.

cage *n.* an enclosure of wire or with bars, esp. for birds or animals. ● *v.* confine in a cage.

cagey *adj.* (**cagier, cagiest**) *informal* secretive, reticent. ◻ **cagily** *adv.*, **caginess** *n.*

cagoule (kă-**gool**) *n.* a light hooded water-proof jacket.

cahoots *n. informal* ◻ **in cahoots with** in league with.

caiman var. of **cayman**.

cairn *n.* a mound of stones as a memorial or landmark.

caisson (*kay*-sĕn) *n.* a watertight chamber used in underwater construction work.

cajole *v.* coax. ◻ **cajolery** *n.*

Cajun (*kay*-jĕn) *adj.* in the style of French Louisiana.

cake *n.* **1** a sweet food made from a baked mixture of flour, eggs, sugar, and fat. **2** a flat compact mass. ● *v.* form a crust (on).

calamine *n.* a soothing skin lotion containing zinc carbonate.

calamity *n.* (*pl.* **-ies**) a disaster. ◻ **calamitous** *adj.*, **calamitously** *adv.*

calcify *v.* (**calcified, calcifying**) harden by a deposit of calcium salts. ◻ **calcification** *n.*

calcium *n.* a whitish metallic element (symbol Ca).

calculate *v.* **1** reckon mathematically; estimate. **2** intend, plan. ◻ **calculation** *n.*

calculating *adj.* ruthlessly scheming.

calculator *n.* an electronic device for mathematical calculations.

calculus *n.* **1** (*pl.* **calculuses**) a branch of mathematics dealing with rates of variation. **2** (*pl.* **calculi**) a stone formed in the body.

caldron var. of **cauldron**.

Caledonian *adj.* of Scotland.

calendar *n.* a chart showing dates of days of the year.

calendar year *n.* 1 January to 31 December inclusive.

calf *n.* (*pl.* **calves**) **1** the young of cattle, elephants, whales, etc. **2** the fleshy back of the human leg below the knee.

calibrate *v.* mark the units of measurement on or check the accuracy of (a gauge). □ **calibration** *n.*

calibre *n.* (*Amer.* **caliber**) **1** degree of quality or ability. **2** the diameter of a gun, tube, or bullet.

calico *n.* a cotton cloth.

californium *n.* a radioactive metallic element (symbol Cf).

caliper var. of **calliper**.

caliph (kay-lif) *n.* (formerly) a Muslim ruler.

calisthenics var. of **callisthenics**.

calk var. of **caulk**.

call *v.* **1** shout to attract the attention (of); summon; waken. **2** (of a bird) utter a characteristic cry. **3** telephone. **4** pay a visit. **5** name; describe or address in a specified way. ● *n.* **1** a brief visit. **2** a shout; a bird's cry; a summons. **3** a telephone communication. **4** a vocation. **5** a need. □ **call off** cancel. **call on 1** visit. **2** necessitate. **call the shots (or tune)** control the action. □ **caller** *n.*

call box *n.* a telephone kiosk.

calligraphy *n.* (beautiful) handwriting. □ **calligrapher** *n.*

calliper *n.* (also **caliper**) **1** a metal support for a weak leg. **2** (**callipers**) an instrument for measuring diameters.

callisthenics *n.pl.* (also **calisthenics**) exercises to develop strength and grace.

callous *adj.* feeling no pity or sympathy. □ **callously** *adv.*, **callousness** *n.*

callow *adj.* immature and inexperienced.

callus *n.* a patch of hardened skin.

calm *adj.* **1** not excited or agitated. **2** not windy or disturbed by wind. ● *n.* a calm condition. ● *v.* make calm. □ **calmly** *adv.*, **calmness** *n.*

Calor gas *n. trademark* liquefied butane stored under pressure in containers.

calorie *n.* a unit of heat; a unit of the energy-producing value of food.

calorific *adj.* of heat or calories.

calumniate *v.* slander.

calumny *n.* (*pl.* **-ies**) slander.

calve *v.* give birth to a calf.

Calvinism *n.* a branch of Protestantism following the teachings of John Calvin. □ **Calvinist** *n.*

calypso *n.* (*pl.* **calypsos**) West Indian song with syncopated music and topical words.

calyx *n.* (*pl.* **calyxes** or **calyces**) a ring of leaves (sepals) covering a flower bud.

cam *n.* a projecting part on a wheel or shaft changing rotary to to-and-fro motion.

camaraderie *n.* comradeship.

camber *n.* a slight convex curve given to a surface, esp. of a road.

cambric *n.* thin linen or cotton cloth.

camcorder *n.* a combined video and sound recorder.

came past of **come**.

camel *n.* a large animal with one hump or two; its fawn colour.

camellia *n.* an evergreen flowering shrub.

cameo *n.* (*pl.* **cameos**) **1** a piece of jewellery with a portrait carved in relief on a background of a different colour. **2** a small part in a play or film taken by a famous actor or actress.

camera *n.* an apparatus for taking photographs or film pictures. □ **in camera** with the public excluded. □ **cameraman** *n.*

camiknickers *n.pl.* a woman's one-piece undergarment combining camisole and knickers.

camisole *n.* a woman's bodice-like undergarment with shoulder straps.

camomile *n.* (also **chamomile**) an aromatic herb.

camouflage (ka-mĕ-flahzh) *n.* disguise or concealment by colouring or covering. ● *v.* disguise or conceal in this way.

camp *n.* **1** a place with temporary accommodation in tents; a place where troops are lodged or trained. **2** a group of people with the same ideals. **3** affected or histrionic behaviour. ● *v.* sleep in a tent; lodge temporarily. ● *adj.* affected, histrionic; ostentatiously effeminate.

campaign *n.* a connected series of military operations; an organized course of action to achieve a goal. ● *v.* conduct or take part in a campaign. □ **campaigner** *n.*

campanology *n.* the study of bells; bell-ringing. □ **campanologist** *n.*

camp bed *n.* a portable folding bed.

camper *n.* a person who is camping; a large vehicle with beds, cooking facilities, etc.

camphor *n.* a strong-smelling white substance used in medicine and mothballs.

campsite *n.* a place for camping.

campus *n.* the grounds of a university or college.

camshaft *n.* a shaft carrying cams.

can[1] *n.* a cylindrical metal container for holding liquid or preserving food. ● *v.* (**canned, canning**) preserve in a can.

can[2] *v.aux.* (**can, could**) be able or allowed to.

Canadian *adj.* & *n.* (a native or inhabitant) of Canada.

canal *n.* an artificial watercourse; a duct in the body.

canalize *v.* (also **-ise**) convert into a canal; direct through a channel. □ **canalization** *n.*

canapé (kan-ăpay) *n.* a small piece of bread or pastry with savoury topping.

canard *n.* a false rumour.

canary *n.* (*pl.* **-ies**) a small yellow songbird, often kept as a pet.

cancan *n.* a lively high-kicking dance performed by women.

cancel *v.* (**cancelled, cancelling**; *Amer.* **canceled**) **1** declare that (something arranged) will not take place; put an end to. **2** mark (a ticket or stamp) to prevent re-use. □ **cancel out** offset, neutralize. □ **cancellation** *n.*

cancer *n.* a malignant tumour; a disease in which these form. □ **cancerous** *adj.*

candela *n.* a unit measuring the brightness of light.

candelabrum *n.* (also **candelabra**) (*pl.* **candelabra**; *Amer.* **candelabras** or **candelabrums**) a large branched candlestick or stand for lights.

candid *adj.* frank. □ **candidly** *adv.*, **candidness** *n.*

candidate *n.* a person applying for a job, standing for election, or taking an examination. □ **candidacy** *n.*, **candidature** *n.*

candied *adj.* encrusted or preserved in sugar.

candle *n.* a stick of wax enclosing a wick which is burnt to give light. □ **hold a candle to** compare or compete with.

candlestick *n.* a holder for a candle.

candour *n.* (*Amer.* **candor**) frankness.

candy *n.* (*pl.* **-ies**) *Amer.* sweets, a sweet.

candyfloss *n.* a fluffy mass of spun sugar.

candy stripe *n.* alternate stripes of white and colour. □ **candy-striped** *adj.*

cane *n.* a stem of a tall reed or grass; a light walking stick; a stick used for corporal punishment. ● *v.* beat with a cane.

canine (kay-nyn) *adj.* of dogs. ● *n.* (in full **canine tooth**) a pointed tooth between the incisors and molars.

canister *n.* a small metal container.

canker *n.* a disease of animals or plants; a persistent corrupting influence.

cannabis *n.* the hemp plant; a drug made from this.

canned past & p.p. of **can**[1].

cannelloni *n.pl.* rolls of pasta with a savoury filling.

cannibal *n.* a person who eats human flesh. □ **cannibalism** *n.*

cannibalize *v.* (also **-ise**) use parts from (a machine) to repair another.

cannon *n.* **1** (*pl.* usu. **cannon**) a large gun. **2** the hitting of two balls in one shot in billiards. ● *v.* bump heavily (into).

■ **Usage** Do not confuse *cannon* with *canon*.

cannonade *n.* continuous gunfire. ● *v.* bombard with this.

cannot *v. aux* the negative form of **can**[2].

canny *adj.* (**cannier, canniest**) **1** shrewd. **2** *Scot. & N. Engl.* pleasant, attractive. □ **cannily** *adv.*

canoe *n.* a light boat propelled by paddling. ● *v.* (**canoed, canoeing**) go in a canoe. □ **canoeist** *n.*

canon *n.* **1** a member of cathedral clergy. **2** a general rule or principle. **3** a set of writings accepted as genuine. □ **canonical** *adj.*

■ **Usage** Do not confuse *canon* with *cannon*.

canonize *v.* (also **-ise**) declare officially to be a saint. □ **canonization** *n.*

canoodle *v. informal* kiss and cuddle.

canopy *n.* (*pl.* **-ies**) an ornamental cloth held up as a covering.

cant *n.* insincere talk; jargon.

cantabile (kan-**tah**-bi-lay) *adv.* *Music* smooth and flowing.

cantankerous *adj.* bad-tempered, perverse. □ **cantankerously** *adv.*

cantata *n.* a choral composition.

canteen *n.* **1** a restaurant for employees. **2** a case of cutlery.

canter *n.* a gentle gallop. ● *v.* go at a canter.

cantilever *n.* a projecting beam or girder supporting a structure.

canto *n.* (*pl.* **cantos**) a division of a long poem.

canton *n.* a political division of a country, esp. Switzerland.

canvas *n.* a strong coarse cloth; a painting on this.

canvass *v.* **1** ask for votes. **2** propose (a plan) for discussion.

canyon *n.* a deep gorge.

CAP *abbr.* Common Agricultural Policy.

cap *n.* **1** a soft brimless hat, often with a peak; a headdress worn as part of a uniform; a cover or top; an upper limit. **2** an explosive device for a toy pistol. ● *v.* (**capped, capping**) put a lid on; cover; set an upper limit to; surpass.

capable *adj.* **1** able or fit to do something. **2** competent, efficient. □ **capability** *n.*, **capably** *adv.*

capacious *adj.* roomy.

capacitance *n.* the ability to store an electric charge.

capacitor *n.* a device storing a charge of electricity.

capacity *n.* (*pl.* **-ies**) **1** the amount that something can contain. **2** ability to do something. **3** a role or function.

caparison (kă-pa-ri-sŏn) *v.* deck out. ● *n.* finery.

cape *n.* **1** a sleeveless cloak; this as part of a coat. **2** a coastal promontory.

caper *v.* jump about friskily. ● *n.* **1** a frisky movement; *informal* a foolish or illicit activity. **2** (**capers**) the pickled buds of a bramble-like shrub.

capillarity *n.* (also **capillary action**) the rise or fall of a liquid in a narrow tube.

capillary *n.* (*pl.* **-ies**) a very fine hairlike tube or blood vessel.

capital *adj.* **1** chief, very important. **2** (of a letter of the alphabet) of the kind used to begin a name or sentence. **3** involving the death penalty. **4** *dated, informal* excellent. ● *n.* **1** the chief town of a country etc. **2** a capital letter. **3** money with which a business is started. **4** the top part of a pillar.

capitalism *n.* a system in which trade and industry are controlled by private owners.

capitalist *n.* a person who invests in trade and industry; a supporter of capitalism.

capitalize *v.* (also **-ise**) **1** convert into or provide with capital. **2** write as or with a capital letter. □ **capitalize on** make advantageous use of. □ **capitalization** *n.*

capitation *n.* a fee paid per person.

capitulate *v.* surrender, yield. □ **capitulation** *n.*

capo *n.* (*pl.* **capos**) a device fitted across the strings of an instrument to raise their pitch.

capon (**kay**-pŏn) *n.* a domestic cock castrated and fattened.

cappuccino (ka-poo-**chee**-noh) *n.* (*pl.* **cappuccinos**) coffee made with frothy steamed milk.

caprice (kă-**prees**) *n.* a whim; a short lively piece of music.

capricious *adj.* acting on whims; unpredictable. □ **capriciously** *adv.*, **capriciousness** *n.*

capsicum *n.* a sweet pepper.

capsize *v.* (of a boat) overturn.

capstan *n.* a revolving post or spindle on which a cable etc. winds.

capsule *n.* **1** a small soluble gelatin case enclosing medicine for swallowing. **2** a detachable compartment of a spacecraft. **3** a plant's seed case.

captain *n.* a person commanding a ship or aircraft; the leader of a group or team; a naval officer next below rear admiral; an army officer next below major. ● *v.* be captain of. □ **captaincy** *n.*

caption *n.* a short title or heading; an explanation on an illustration.

captious *adj.* fond of finding fault, esp. about trivial matters.

captivate *v.* capture the fancy of, charm. □ **captivation** *n.*

captive *adj.* taken prisoner, unable to escape. ● *n.* a captive person or animal. □ **captivity** *n.*

captor *n.* one who takes a captive.

capture *v.* **1** gain control of by force; take prisoner. **2** record accurately in words or pictures. **3** cause (data) to be stored in a computer. ● *n.* capturing.

car *n.* a motor vehicle for a small number of passengers; a compartment in a cable railway, lift, etc.

carafe (kă-**raf**) *n.* a glass bottle for serving wine or water.

caramel *n.* brown syrup made from heated sugar; toffee tasting like this. □ **caramelization** *n.*, **caramelize** (also **-ise**) *v.*

carapace *n.* the upper shell of a tortoise.

carat *n.* a unit of purity of gold; a unit of weight for precious stones.

caravan *n.* **1** a vehicle equipped for living in, able to be towed by a horse or car. **2** a company travelling together across desert. □ **caravanning** *n.*

caraway *n.* a plant with spicy seeds used as flavouring.

carbine *n.* an automatic rifle.

carbohydrate *n.* an energy-producing compound (e.g. starch) in food.

carbolic *n.* a disinfectant.

carbon *n.* a chemical element (symbol C) occurring as diamond, graphite, and charcoal, and in all living matter.

carbonate *n.* a compound releasing carbon dioxide when mixed with acid. ● *v.* dissolve carbon dioxide in (a liquid).

carbon copy *n.* a copy made with carbon paper; an exact copy.

carbon dating *n.* a method of deciding the age of something by measuring the decay of radiocarbon in it.

carboniferous *adj.* producing coal.

carbon paper *n.* paper coated with carbon, used to make copies of typed or written matter.

carborundum *n.* a compound of carbon and silicon used for grinding and polishing things.

carboy *n.* a large round bottle surrounded by a protective framework.

carbuncle *n.* **1** a severe abscess. **2** a garnet cut in a round knob shape.

carburettor *n.* (*Amer.* **carburetor**) a device mixing air and petrol in a motor engine.

carcass *n.* (also **carcase**) the dead body of an animal; the framework or basic structure of something.

carcinogen (kah-**sin**-ŏ-jin) *n.* a cancer-producing substance. ▫ **carcinogenic** *adj.*

carcinoma (kah-si-**noh**-mă) *n.* (*pl.* **carcinomata** or **carcinomas**) a cancerous tumour.

card *n.* a piece of cardboard or thick paper; this used to send a message or greeting; this printed with someone's identifying details; a playing card; a credit card; (**cards**) any card game. ● *v.* clean or comb (wool) with a wire brush or toothed instrument. ▫ **on the cards** *informal* probable.

cardamom *n.* a cooking spice.

cardboard *n.* pasteboard or stiff paper. ● *adj.* (of a fictional character) unconvincing, lacking depth.

cardboard city *n.* (*pl.* **-ies**) an urban area where homeless people congregate under shelters made from cardboard boxes.

cardiac *adj.* of the heart.

cardigan *n.* a knitted jacket.

cardinal *adj.* chief, most important. ● *n.* a member of the Sacred College of the RC Church which elects the Pope.

cardinal number *n.* a number denoting quantity rather than order (1, 2, 3, etc.); contrast **ordinal**.

cardiogram *n.* a record of heart movements.

cardiograph *n.* an instrument recording heart movements.

cardiology *n.* the study of diseases of the heart. ▫ **cardiological** *adj.*, **cardiologist** *n.*

cardphone *n.* a public telephone operated by a plastic machine-readable card.

card sharp *n.* (also **card-sharper**) a swindler at card games.

care *n.* **1** protection and provision of necessities; supervision. **2** serious attention and thought; caution to avoid damage or loss. ● *v.* feel concern or interest. ▫ **care for 1** look after. **2** feel affection for; like, enjoy.

careen *v.* tilt or keel over.

career *n.* the way someone makes their living over a significant period of their life; the progress and development of a person or thing. ● *v.* move swiftly or wildly.

careerist *n.* a person intent on advancement in a career.

carefree *adj.* light-hearted and free from worry.

careful *adj.* showing attention or caution. ▫ **carefully** *adv.*

careless *adj.* showing insufficient attention or concern. ▫ **carelessly** *adv.*, **carelessness** *n.*

carer *n.* a person who looks after a sick or disabled person at home.

caress *n.* a gentle loving touch. ● *v.* give a caress to.

caret (**kar**-rĕt) *n.* a mark (γ) indicating an insertion in text.

caretaker *n.* a person employed to look after a building.

careworn *adj.* showing signs of prolonged worry.

cargo *n.* (*pl.* **cargoes** or **cargos**) goods carried by ship, aircraft, or motor vehicle.

Caribbean *adj.* of the West Indies or their inhabitants.

caribou *n.* (*pl.* **caribou**) a North American reindeer.

caricature *n.* a portrayal exaggerating someone's characteristics for comic effect. ● *v.* portray in this way. □ **caricaturist** *n.*

caries (kair-eez) *n.* decay of a tooth or bone.

carillon (kă-ril-yŏn) *n.* a set of bells sounded mechanically; a tune played on these.

carjacking *n.* violently taking over an occupied car. □ **carjack** *v.*, **carjacker** *n.*

carmine *adj.* & *n.* vivid crimson.

carnage *n.* great slaughter.

carnal *adj.* of the body or flesh, not spiritual. □ **carnally** *adv.*

carnation *n.* a cultivated fragrant pink.

carnelian var. of **cornelian**.

carnet (kar-nay) *n.* a permit.

carnival *n.* a public festival, usu. with a procession.

carnivore *n.* an animal feeding on flesh. □ **carnivorous** *adj.*

carob *n.* a chocolate substitute made from the pods of a Mediterranean evergreen tree.

carol *n.* a Christmas hymn. ● *v.* (**carolled, carolling**; *Amer.* **caroled**) sing carols; sing joyfully.

carotene *n.* an orange-coloured pigment found in carrots, tomatoes, etc.

carotid (kă-rot-id) *n.* an artery carrying blood to the head.

carouse (kă-rowz) *v.* drink and be merry. □ **carousal** *n.*, **carouser** *n.*

carousel (ka-roo-sel) *n.* **1** *Amer.* a merry-go-round. **2** a rotating conveyor, esp. for luggage at an airport.

carp *n.* a freshwater fish. ● *v.* keep finding fault.

carpel *n.* the part of a flower in which the seeds develop.

carpenter *n.* a person who makes or repairs wooden objects and structures. □ **carpentry** *n.*

carpet *n.* a textile fabric for covering a floor; a covering. ● *v.* (**carpeted, carpeting**) **1** cover with a carpet. **2** *informal* reprimand. □ **on the carpet** *informal* being reprimanded.

carport *n.* a roofed open-sided shelter for a car.

carpus *n.* (*pl.* **carpi**) the set of small bones forming the wrist.

carriage *n.* **1** a section of a train; a horse-drawn vehicle. **2** transport of goods. **3** a person's way of standing and moving. **4** a part of a machine that carries other parts into position.

carriage clock *n.* a small portable clock with a handle on top.

carriageway *n.* the part of the road on which vehicles travel.

carrier *n.* a person or thing carrying something; a company transporting goods; a bag with handles for shopping.

carrion *n.* dead decaying flesh.

carrot *n.* **1** a tapering orange root vegetable. **2** *informal* an incentive.

carry *v.* (**carried, carrying**) **1** transport, support and move; have on one's person; transmit (a disease). **2** support; assume (responsibility). **3** entail (a consequence). **4** take (a process) to a particular point. **5** approve (a measure); gain the support of. **6** stock (goods). **7** be audible at a distance. □ **carry on 1** continue. **2** *informal* behave excitedly. **3** *informal* have a love affair. **carry out** put into practice. **get carried away** lose self-control.

cart *n.* a wheeled vehicle for carrying loads. ● *v.* carry, transport.

carte blanche (kart **blahnsh**) *n.* full power to do as one thinks best.

cartel *n.* a manufacturers' or producers' union to control prices.

carthorse *n.* a horse of heavy build.

cartilage *n.* the firm elastic tissue in skeletons of vertebrates, gristle.

cartography *n.* map-drawing. □ **cartographer** *n.*, **cartographic** *adj.*

carton *n.* a cardboard or plastic container.

cartoon *n.* **1** a humorous drawing. **2** a film consisting of an animated sequence of drawings. **3** a sketch for a painting. □ **cartoonist** *n.*

cartridge *n.* **1** a case containing explosive for firearms. **2** a sealed cassette.

cartridge paper *n.* thick strong paper.

cartwheel *n.* a handspring with limbs spread like the spokes of a wheel.

carve *v.* cut (hard material) to make (an object or pattern); cut (meat) into slices for eating.

carvery *n.* (*pl.* **-ies**) a restaurant where meat is served from a joint as required.

Casanova *n.* a man noted for his love affairs.

cascade *n.* a waterfall; something falling like this; a large quantity of related things. ● *v.* fall like a waterfall.

case *n.* **1** an instance of something's occurring; an instance of a disease. **2** a lawsuit; a set of arguments supporting a position. **3** a container or protective covering; a suitcase. **4** the form of a noun, adjective, or pronoun indicating its grammatical role in a sentence; this role. ● *v.* **1** enclose in a case. **2** *informal* examine (a building etc.) in preparation for a crime. □ **in case** lest.

casement *n.* a window opening on vertical hinges.

case-sensitive *adj.* (of a computer operation) differentiating between capital and lower-case letters.

cash *n.* money in the form of coins or banknotes. ● *v.* give or obtain cash for (a cheque etc.). □ **cash in (on)** get profit or advantage (from).

cashback *n.* a facility offered by retailers allowing customers to withdraw cash when paying by credit card.

cash card *n.* a plastic card with magnetic code for drawing money from a machine.

cashew *n.* an edible nut.

cashier *n.* a person employed to handle money. ● *v.* dismiss from military service in disgrace.

cashmere *n.* very fine soft wool; fabric made from this.

cashpoint *n.* (also **cash machine, cash dispenser**) a machine dispensing cash.

casino *n.* (*pl.* **casinos**) a public building or room for gambling.

cask *n.* a barrel for liquids.

casket *n.* a small usu. ornamental box for valuables; *Amer.* a coffin.

cassava *n.* (flour made from) the starchy root of a tropical tree.

casserole *n.* a covered dish in which meat etc. is cooked and served; food cooked in this. ● *v.* cook in a casserole.

cassette *n.* a small case containing a reel of magnetic tape or film.

cassis *n.* a blackcurrant-flavoured usu. alcoholic syrup.

cassock *n.* a long robe worn by clergy and choristers.

cassowary *n.* (*pl.* **-ies**) a large flightless bird.

cast *v.* (**cast, casting**) **1** throw; discard; direct, cause to appear on or affect something. **2** register (a vote). **3** shape (molten metal) in a mould. **4** select actors for (a play or film); assign a role to. **5** phrase (statements); calculate (a horoscope). ● *n.* **1** a throw of dice, a fishing line, etc. **2** an object made by casting molten metal. **3** a set of actors in a play etc. **4** a type, a quality: *an inquiring cast of mind.* **5** a slight squint.

castanets *n.pl.* a pair of shell-shaped pieces of wood clicked in the hand to accompany Spanish dancing.

castaway *n.* a shipwrecked person.

caste *n.* a social class, esp. in the Hindu system.

castellated *adj.* having turrets or battlements.

caster var. of **castor**.

castigate *v.* reprimand severely. ◻ **castigation** *n.*

casting vote *n.* a deciding vote when those on each side are equal.

cast iron *n.* a hard alloy of iron cast in a mould. ● *adj.* (**cast-iron**) made of cast iron; unbreakable, unchangeable.

castle *n.* a large fortified residence.

cast-off *n.* a discarded thing.

castor *n.* (also **caster**) **1** a small swivelling wheel on a leg of furniture. **2** a small container with a perforated top for sprinkling sugar etc.

castor oil *n.* a purgative and lubricant oil from the seeds of a tropical plant.

castor sugar *n.* finely granulated white sugar.

castrate *v.* remove the testicles of. ◻ **castration** *n.*

castrato *n.* (*pl.* **castrati**) *hist.* a male singer castrated to retain a soprano or alto voice.

casual *adj.* **1** relaxed, not worried. **2** happening by chance. **3** not regular or permanent; not serious or formal. ◻ **casually** *adv.*, **casualness** *n.*

casualty *n.* (*pl.* **-ies**) **1** a person killed or injured; something lost or destroyed. **2** (in full **casualty department**) part of a hospital treating accident victims.

casuistry *n.* **1** clever but unsound argument. **2** the application of moral rules to particular instances. ◻ **casuist** *n.*

cat *n.* a small furry domesticated animal; a wild animal related to this.

cataclysm *n.* a violent upheaval or disaster. ◻ **cataclysmic** *adj.*

catacomb (**kat**-ăkoom) *n.* an underground gallery with recesses for tombs.

catafalque (**kat**-ă-falk) *n.* a platform for the coffin of a distinguished person before or during a funeral.

catalepsy *n.* (*pl.* **-ies**) a seizure or trance in which the body goes rigid. ◻ **cataleptic** *adj.*

catalogue *n.* (*Amer.* also **catalog**) a systematic list of items. ● *v.* (**catalogued, cataloguing**) list in a catalogue.

catalyse *v.* (*Amer.* **catalyze**) subject to the action of a catalyst. ◻ **catalysis** *n.*

catalyst *n.* a substance that aids a chemical reaction while remaining unchanged.

catalytic converter *n.* part of an exhaust system that reduces the harmful effects of pollutant gases.

catamaran *n.* a boat with parallel twin hulls.

catapult *n.* a device with elastic fitted to a forked stick for shooting small stones. ● *v.* hurl from or as if from a catapult.

cataract *n.* **1** a large waterfall. **2** an opaque area clouding the lens of the eye.

catarrh (kă-**tah**) *n.* inflammation of a mucous membrane, esp. of the nose, with a watery discharge.

catastrophe (kă-tas-trŏ-fi) *n.* a sudden great disaster. ◻ **catastrophic** *adj.*, **catastrophically** *adv.*

catcall *n.* a whistle of disapproval.

catch *v.* **1** grasp and hold (a moving object). **2** capture; detect. **3** be in time for (a train etc.). **4** become infected with. **5** hear; understand. **6** succeed in expressing. **7** hit. ● *n.* **1** an act of catching; something caught or worth catching. **2** a fastener for a door or window. **3** *in-*

formal a hidden drawback. □ **catch on** *informal* **1** become popular. **2** understand. **catch out** detect in a mistake. **catch up** reach those ahead of one; complete arrears of work.

catching *adj.* infectious.

catchment area *n.* an area from which rainfall drains into a river; an area from which a hospital draws patients or a school draws pupils.

catchphrase *n.* a phrase in frequent current use, a slogan.

catch-22 *n.* a dilemma in which either choice will cause suffering.

catchword *n.* a catchphrase.

catchy *adj.* (**catchier, catchiest**) (of a tune) pleasant and easy to remember.

catechism *n.* a series of questions and answers, esp. on the principles of a religion.

catechize *v.* (also **-ise**) put a series of questions to.

categorical *adj.* unconditional, absolute. □ **categorically** *adv.*

categorize *v.* (also **-ise**) place in a category. □ **categorization** *n.*

category *n.* (*pl.* **-ies**) a class of things.

cater *v.* supply food; provide what is needed or wanted. □ **caterer** *n.*

caterpillar *n.* **1** the larva of a butterfly or moth. **2** (in full **caterpillar track** or **tread**) *trademark* a steel band passing round the wheels of a tractor etc. for travel on rough ground.

caterwaul (ka-tě-worl) *v.* make a cat's howling cry.

catgut *n.* material used for instrument strings etc., made from horse or sheep gut.

catharsis *n.* (*pl.* **catharses**) a release of strong feeling or tension. □ **cathartic** *adj.*

cathedral *n.* the principal church of a diocese.

Catherine wheel *n.* a rotating firework.

catheter *n.* a tube inserted into the bladder to extract urine.

cathode *n.* an electrode by which current leaves a device.

cathode ray tube *n.* a vacuum tube in which beams of electrons produce a luminous image on a fluorescent screen.

catholic *adj.* **1** all-embracing, universal. **2** (**Catholic**) Roman Catholic; of all Churches or Christians. □ **Catholicism** *n.*

cation (kat-I-ŏn) *n.* a positively charged ion.

catkin *n.* a hanging flower of willow, hazel, etc.

catnap *n.* a short nap.

cat's cradle *n.* a child's game in which string is wound round the fingers; a complex intertwining of threads.

Catseye *n.* *trademark* a reflector stud on a road.

cat's-paw *n.* a person used as a tool by another.

catsup *Amer.* = **ketchup**.

cattery *n.* (*pl.* **-ies**) a place where cats are boarded.

cattle *n.pl.* cows, bulls, and oxen.

catty *adj.* (**cattier, cattiest**) slightly spiteful. □ **cattily** *adv.*, **cattiness** *n.*

catwalk *n.* a narrow platform extending into an auditorium, used in fashion shows.

caucus (kor-kŭs) *n.* a group with shared interests within a political party; *Amer.* a meeting of party leaders.

caught past & p.p. of **catch**.

caul *n.* a membrane enclosing a foetus in the womb.

cauldron *n.* (also **caldron**) a large deep cooking pot.

cauliflower *n.* a cabbage with a large white flower head.

caulk *v.* (also **calk**) stop up (a ship's seams) with waterproof material.

causal *adj.* relating to or acting as a cause.

causality *n.* the relation between cause and effect.

cause *n.* **1** something that brings about something else; a reason, a motive. **2** a principle or movement supported. ● *v.* bring about, give rise to. □ **causation** *n.*

cause célèbre (kohz se-lebr) *n.* (*pl.* **causes célèbres**) an issue arousing great interest.

causeway *n.* a raised road across low or wet ground.

caustic *adj.* **1** burning by chemical action. **2** sarcastic. ● *n.* a caustic substance. □ **caustically** *adv.*

caustic soda *n.* sodium hydroxide.

cauterize *v.* (also **-ise**) burn (tissue) to destroy infection or stop bleeding. □ **cauterization** *n.*

caution *n.* **1** care to avoid danger or error. **2** a warning. ● *v.* warn; reprimand.

cautionary *adj.* conveying a warning.

cautious *adj.* having or showing caution. □ **cautiously** *adv.*

cavalcade *n.* a procession.

cavalier *adj.* arrogant, offhand. ● *n.* (**Cavalier**) *hist.* a supporter of Charles I in the English Civil War.

cavalry *n.* (*pl.* **-ies**) mounted troops; troops in armoured vehicles.

cave *n.* a hollow in a cliff or hillside. □ **cave in** collapse; yield.

caveat (kav-iat) *n.* a warning.

caveat emptor *n.* the principle that the buyer alone is responsible for checking the quality of goods.

caveman *n.* (*pl.* **-men**) a person of prehistoric times living in a cave.

cavern *n.* a large cave.

cavernous *adj.* like a cavern, large and hollow.

caviar *n.* the pickled roe of sturgeon or other large fish.

cavil *v.* (**cavilled, cavilling**; *Amer.* **caviled**) raise petty objections. ● *n.* a petty objection.

caving *n.* the sport of exploring caves.

cavity *n.* (*pl.* **-ies**) a hollow within a solid object.

cavort *v.* leap about excitedly.

caw *n.* the harsh cry of a rook or crow. ● *v.* utter this cry.

cayenne *n.* a hot red pepper.

cayman *n.* (*pl.* **caymans**) (also **caiman**) a South American alligator.

CB *abbr.* citizens' band (radio frequencies).

CBE *abbr.* Commander of the Order of the British Empire.

CBI *abbr.* Confederation of British Industry.

cc *abbr.* (also **c.c.**) **1** carbon copy or copies. **2** cubic centimetre(s).

CD *abbr.* compact disc.

Cd *symb.* cadmium.

CD-ROM *n.* a compact disc holding data for display on a computer screen.

Ce *symb.* cerium.

cease *v.* come to an end; stop doing something; discontinue.

ceasefire *n.* a truce; a signal to stop shooting.

ceaseless *adj.* not ceasing.

cecum Amer. sp. of **caecum**.

cedar *n.* an evergreen tree.

cede *v.* surrender (territory etc.).

cedilla *n.* a mark written under c (ç) to show that it is pronounced as s.

ceilidh (**kay**-li) *n. Scot. & Irish* an informal gathering for traditional music and dancing.

ceiling *n.* the upper interior surface of a room; an upper limit.

celandine *n.* a small wild plant with yellow flowers.

celebrant *n.* an officiating priest.

celebrate *v.* mark or honour with festivities. □ **celebration** *n.*

celebrated *adj.* famous.

celebrity *n.* (*pl.* **-ies**) a famous person; fame.

celerity *n. literary* swiftness.

celery *n.* a plant with edible crisp stems.

celestial *adj.* of the sky; of heaven.

celiac Amer. sp. of **coeliac**.

celibate *adj.* abstaining from sexual intercourse. □ **celibacy** *n.*

cell *n.* **1** a small room for a prisoner or monk; a compartment in a honeycomb. **2** a microscopic unit of living matter; a small group as a nucleus of political activity. **3** a device for producing electric current chemically.

cellar *n.* an underground room; a stock of wine.

cello (che-loh) *n.* (*pl.* **cellos**) a bass instrument of the violin family. □ **cellist** *n.*

cellophane *n. trademark* a thin transparent wrapping material.

cellphone *n.* a small portable radio-telephone.

cellular *adj.* **1** of living cells. **2** woven with an open mesh.

cellular phone (or **radio**) *n.* a system of mobile communication over an area served by several short-range radio stations.

cellulite *n.* a lumpy form of fat producing puckering of the skin.

celluloid *n.* transparent plastic formerly used for cinematographic film; the world of cinema, films.

cellulose *n.* a substance in plant tissues, used in making plastics.

Celsius *adj.* of a centigrade scale with 0° as the freezing point and 100° as the boiling point of water.

Celt *n.* a member of an ancient European people or their descendants. □ **Celtic** *adj.*

cement *n.* a substance of lime and clay used to make mortar or concrete; an adhesive; a substance for filling cavities in teeth. ● *v.* join with cement; unite firmly.

cemetery *n.* (*pl.* **-ies**) a burial ground other than a churchyard.

cenotaph *n.* a monument to people buried elsewhere.

censer *n.* a container for burning incense.

censor *n.* a person authorized to examine letters, books, films, etc., and suppress any parts regarded as socially or politically unacceptable. ● *v.* examine and alter in this way. □ **censorial** *adj.*, **censorship** *n.*

■ **Usage** Do not confuse the verbs *censor* and *censure*.

censorious *adj.* severely critical.

censure *n.* hostile criticism and rebuke. ● *v.* criticize harshly.

census *n.* an official count of the population.

cent *n.* a 100th part of a dollar or other currency; a coin worth this.

centaur *n.* a mythical creature, half man, half horse.

centenarian *n.* a person 100 years old or more.

centenary *n.* (*pl.* **-ies**) a 100th anniversary.

centennial *adj.* of a centenary. ● *n.* a centenary.

center etc. Amer. sp. of **centre** etc.

centigrade *adj.* using a temperature scale of 100°; = Celsius.

centigram *n.* (also **centigramme**) a 100th of a gram.

centilitre *n.* (*Amer.* **centiliter**) a 100th of a litre.

centime *n.* a 100th of a franc.

centimetre *n.* (*Amer.* **centimeter**) a 100th of a metre, about 0.4 inch.

centipede *n.* a small crawling creature with many legs.

central *adj.* of, at, or forming a centre; most important. □ **centrality** *n.*, **centrally** *adv.*

central heating *n.* heating of a building from one source.

centralism *n.* a system that centralizes an administration.

centralize *v.* (also **-ise**) bring under the control of a central authority. □ **centralization** *n.*

central nervous system *n.* the brain and the spinal cord.

centre (*Amer.* **center**) *n.* **1** a point or part in the middle of something; a position avoiding extremes. **2** a place where a specified activity takes place; a point where something begins or is most intense. ● *v.* (**centred, centring**) **1** have or cause to have something as a major concern or theme. **2** place in the middle; base at a particular place.

centrefold *n.* (*Amer.* **centerfold**) the two middle pages of a magazine, newspaper, etc.

centrifugal *adj.* moving away from the centre.

centrifuge *n.* a machine using centrifugal force for separating substances.

centripetal *adj.* moving towards the centre.

centurion *n.* a commander in the ancient Roman army.

century *n.* (*pl.* **-ies**) **1** a period of 100 years; this reckoned from the traditional date of the birth of Christ. **2** 100 runs at cricket.

cephalic *adj.* of the head.

cephalopod *n.* a mollusc with tentacles (e.g. an octopus).

ceramic *adj.* of pottery or a similar substance. ● *n.* (**ceramics**) pottery; pottery-making.

cereal *n.* a grass plant with edible grain; this grain; breakfast food made from it.

cerebellum *n.* (*pl.* **cerebellums** or **cerebella**) a small part of the brain at the back of the skull.

cerebral *adj.* of the brain; intellectual. ▫ **cerebrally** *adv.*

cerebral palsy *n.* paralysis resulting from brain damage before or at birth.

cerebrum *n.* (*pl.* **cerebra**) the main part of the brain.

ceremonial *adj.* of or used in ceremonies, formal. ● *n.* rules to be observed at a formal occasion. ▫ **ceremonially** *adv.*

ceremonious *adj.* of or appropriate to ceremonies. ▫ **ceremoniously** *adv.*

ceremony *n.* (*pl.* **-ies**) a grand occasion on which special acts are performed; such ritual acts; formal politeness.

cerise (se-reez) *adj.* & *n.* light clear red.

cerium *n.* a metallic element (symbol Ce).

certain *adj.* **1** definite, reliable. **2** feeling sure. **3** specific but not named: *certain people disagreed.*

certainly *adv.* of course; yes.

certainty *n.* (*pl.* **-ies**) conviction; definite truth or reliability; something that is certain.

certifiable *adj.* **1** able or needing to be certified. **2** *informal* mad.

certificate *n.* an official document attesting certain facts.

certify *v.* (**certified, certifying**) declare formally; recognize as meeting certain standards; declare insane.

certitude *n.* a feeling of certainty.

cerulean (se-roo-lee-ăn) *adj. literary* deep blue like a clear sky.

cervix *n.* (*pl.* **cervices**) the neck; a necklike structure, esp. of the womb. ▫ **cervical** *adj.*

Cesarean, Cesarian Amer. sp. of **Caesarean**.

cesium Amer. sp. of **caesium**.

cessation *n.* ceasing.

cession *n.* ceding, giving up.

cesspit *n.* (also **cesspool**) a covered pit designed to receive liquid waste or sewage.

cetacean (si-tay-shăn) *adj.* & *n.* (a member) of the whale family.

Cf. *symb.* californium.

cf. *abbr.* compare.

CFC *abbr.* chlorofluorocarbon, a gaseous compound thought to harm the ozone layer.

chador (chah-dor) *n.* a piece of cloth worn by Muslim women around the head and upper body.

chafe *v.* **1** warm by rubbing; make or become sore by rubbing. **2** make or become irritated or impatient.

chafer *n.* a large beetle.

chaff *n.* **1** corn husks separated from seed. **2** banter. ● *v.* banter, tease.

chaffinch *n.* a pink-breasted finch.

chafing dish *n.* a heated pan for keeping food warm at the table.

chagrin *n.* annoyance and embarrassment.

chain *n.* **1** a series of connected metal links; a connected series or sequence; a group of hotels or shops owned by the same company. **2** a unit of measurement (66 feet). ● *v.* fasten with chain(s).

chain reaction *n.* a series of events in which each causes the next.

chainsaw *n.* a saw with teeth set on a circular chain.

chair *n.* **1** a movable seat for one person, usu. with a back and four legs. **2** (the position of) a chairperson; the position of a professor. ● *v.* act as chairman of.

chairlift *n.* a series of chairs on a cable for carrying people up a mountain.

chairman *n.* (*pl.* **-men**) a person who presides over a meeting or board of directors.

chairperson *n.* a chairman or chairwoman.

chairwoman *n.* (*pl.* **-women**) a woman who presides over a meeting or board of directors.

chaise longue (shayz **lawng**) *n.* (*pl.* **chaises longues** or **chaise longues**) a sofa with a backrest at only one end.

chalcedony (kal-**sed**-ŏ-nee) *n.* a type of quartz.

chalet (**sha**-lay) *n.* a Swiss hut or cottage; a small cabin in a holiday camp.

chalice *n.* a large goblet.

chalk *n.* white soft limestone; a piece of this or similar coloured substance used for drawing. □ **by a long chalk** by far. □ **chalky** *adj.*

challenge *n.* **1** a call to try one's skill or strength, esp. in a competition; a demanding task. **2** an objection or query. **3** an order to identify oneself or give a password. ● *v.* **1** invite to a contest; test the ability of. **2** dispute, query. □ **challenger** *n.*

challenged *adj.* impaired or deficient in a specified respect (used euphemistically or humorously).

chamber *n.* a hall used for meetings of a council, parliament, etc.; *archaic* a room, a bedroom; (**chambers**) rooms used by a barrister; an enclosed space, a cavity.

chamberlain *n.* an official managing a sovereign's or noble's household.

chambermaid *n.* a woman employed to clean hotel bedrooms.

chamber music *n.* music written for a small group of players.

chamber pot *n.* a bedroom receptacle for urine.

chameleon (kă-**mee**-li-ŏn) *n.* a small lizard that changes colour according to its surroundings.

chamfer (**cham**-fĕ) *v.* bevel the edge of.

chamois *n.* **1** (**sham**-wah) a small mountain antelope. **2** (**sha**-mi) a piece of soft leather used for cleaning windows, cars, etc.

chamomile var. of **camomile**.

champ *v.* munch noisily, make a chewing action. □ **champ at the bit** show impatience.

champagne *n.* a sparkling white French wine.

champion *n.* **1** a person or thing that defeats all others in a competition. **2** a person who fights or speaks in support of another or of a cause. ● *v.* support. ● *adj. dialect* excellent. □ **championship** *n.*

chance *n.* **1** a possibility, an opportunity; a degree of likelihood. **2** development of events without planning or obvious reason. ● *v.* **1** try (something uncertain or dangerous). **2** happen; happen to do something. ● *adj.* unplanned, happening by chance.

chancel *n.* the part of a church near the altar.

chancellor *n.* the government minister in charge of the nation's budget; a state or law official of various other kinds; the non-resident head of a university. □ **chancellorship** *n.*

Chancery *n.* a division of the British High Court of Justice.

chancy *adj.* (**chancier, chanciest**) *informal* risky, uncertain.

chandelier *n.* a hanging light with branches for several bulbs or candles.

chandler *n.* a dealer in ropes, canvas, etc. for ships.

change *v.* make or become different; exchange, substitute, replace; go from one of two (trains, sides, etc.) to the other; put a clean nappy on (a baby); get or give small money or different currency for. ● *n.* changing; money in small units or returned as balance. □ **change one's mind** adopt a new opinion or plan. □ **changeable** *adj.*

changeling *n.* a child or thing believed to have been substituted secretly for another.

channel *n.* **1** a stretch of water connecting two seas; a passage for water. **2** a medium of communication. **3** a band of broadcasting frequencies. ● *v.* (**channelled, channelling**; *Amer.* **channeled**) direct to a particular end or by a particular route.

chant *n.* a monotonous song; a rhythmic shout of a repeated phrase; a melody for psalms. ● *v.* sing, intone; shout rhythmically and repeatedly.

chanter *n.* the melody-pipe of bagpipes.

chanterelle *n.* a yellow edible funnel-shaped fungus.

chantry *n.* (*pl.* **-ies**) a chapel founded for priests to sing Masses for the founder's soul.

chaos *n.* great disorder. □ **chaotic** *adj.*, **chaotically** *adv.*

chap *n. informal* a man. ● *v.* (**chapped, chapping**) (of the skin) split or crack.

chapatti *n.* (also **chapati**) a thin flat circle of unleavened bread, used in Indian cookery.

chapel *n.* **1** a place used for Christian worship, other than a cathedral or parish church; a place with a separate altar within a church. **2** a branch of a printers' trade union.

chaperone *n.* (also **chaperon**) an older woman looking after a young unmarried woman on social occasions. ● *v.* act as chaperone to.

chaplain *n.* a clergyman of an institution, private chapel, ship, regiment, etc. □ **chaplaincy** *n.*

chapter *n.* **1** a division of a book. **2** the canons of a cathedral.

char *n.* **1** *informal* a charwoman. **2** *Brit. informal* tea. ● *v.* (**charred, charring**) make or become black by burning.

charabanc (sha-ră-bang) *n.* an early form of bus with bench seats.

character *n.* **1** the distinctive qualities of someone or something; moral strength. **2** a person in a novel, play, or film; an individual and original person. **3** a physical characteristic. **4** a printed or written letter or sign. **5** *dated* a testimonial.

characteristic *n.* a feature typical of and helping to identify a person or thing. ● *adj.* typical of or distinguishing a person or thing. □ **characteristically** *adv.*

characterize *v.* (also **-ise**) **1** describe the character of. **2** be a characteristic of. □ **characterization** *n.*

charade (shă-**rahd**) *n.* **1** an absurd pretence. **2** (**charades**) a game involving guessing words from acted clues.

charcoal *n.* a black substance made by burning wood slowly.

charge *n.* **1** the price asked for goods or services. **2** an accusation. **3** responsibility and care; someone or something for which one is responsible. **4** a rushing attack. **5** the electricity contained in a substance. **6** a quantity of explosive. ● *v.* **1** ask for (a specified price) from (someone). **2** accuse formally. **3** entrust with a task or responsibility. **4** rush forward in attack. **5** give an electric charge to. **6** load with explosive. □ **in charge**

in command. **take charge** take control.

charge card *n.* a credit card.

chargé d'affaires *n.* (*pl.* **chargés d'affaires**) an ambassador's deputy.

charger *n.* **1** a cavalry horse. **2** a device for charging a battery.

chariot *n.* a two-wheeled horse-drawn vehicle used in ancient times in battle and in racing.

charioteer *n.* a driver of a chariot.

charisma (kă-riz-mă) *n.* the power to inspire devotion and enthusiasm; great charm.

charismatic *adj.* having charisma; (of worship) emphasizing spontaneity and divine inspiration. ◻ **charismatically** *adv.*

charitable *adj.* **1** relating to charities. **2** lenient, kindly. ◻ **charitably** *adv.*

charity *n.* (*pl.* **-ies**) **1** an organization helping the needy; gifts or voluntary work for the needy. **2** kindness and tolerance in judging others.

charlady *n.* (*pl.* **-ies**) a charwoman.

charlatan *n.* a person falsely claiming to be an expert.

charm *n.* **1** the power to attract, delight, or fascinate. **2** an act, object, or words believed to have magic power; a small ornament worn on a bracelet etc. ● *v.* **1** delight; influence by personal charm. **2** control by magic. ◻ **charmer** *n.*

charming *adj.* delightful.

charnel house *n.* a place containing corpses or bones.

chart *n.* **1** a table, graph, or diagram; a map for navigators. **2** (**the charts**) a weekly list of the current best-selling pop records. ● *v.* record or show on a chart.

charter *n.* **1** an official document granting rights. **2** hiring an aircraft etc. for a special purpose. ● *v.* **1** grant a charter to. **2** let or hire (an aircraft, ship, or vehicle).

chartered *adj.* (of an accountant, engineer, etc.) qualified according to the rules of an association holding a royal charter.

charter flight *n.* a flight by a chartered aircraft as opposed to a scheduled flight.

chartreuse (shah-trerz) *n.* a green or yellow liqueur.

charwoman *n.* (*pl.* **-women**) a woman employed to clean a house etc.

chary *adj.* (**charier, chariest**) cautious. ◻ **charily** *adv.*, **chariness** *n.*

chase *v.* go quickly after in order to capture, overtake, or drive away. ● *n.* **1** a pursuit; hunting. **2** a steeplechase.

chaser *n.* a drink taken after a drink of another kind.

chasm (kaz-ŭm) *n.* a deep cleft.

chassis (sha-see) *n.* (*pl.* **chassis**) the base frame of a vehicle.

chaste *adj.* **1** virgin, celibate; sexually pure. **2** simple in style, not ornate. ◻ **chastely** *adv.*, **chastity** *n.*

chasten *v.* subdue, restrain; punish, discipline.

chastise *v.* punish, esp. by beating; reprimand severely. ◻ **chastisement** *n.*

chat *n.* an informal conversation. ● *v.* (**chatted, chatting**) have a chat.

chateau (sha-toh) *n.* (*pl.* **chateaux**) a French castle or large country house.

chatelaine (sha-tĕ-layn) *n.* the mistress of a large house.

chattel *n.* a movable possession.

chatter *v.* **1** talk quickly and continuously about unimportant matters. **2** (of teeth) rattle together. ● *n.* chattering talk; a series of short high-pitched sounds. ◻ **chatterer** *n.*

chatterbox *n.* a talkative person.

chatty *adj.* (**chattier, chattiest**) fond of chatting; (of a letter etc.) informal and lively. ◻ **chattily** *adv.*, **chattiness** *n.*

chauffeur (shoh-fer) *n.* a person employed to drive a car. ● *v.* drive as a chauffeur.

chauvinism (shoh-vin-izm) *n.* prejudiced belief in the superiority of one's own race, sex, etc. □ **chauvinist** *n.*, **chauvinistic** *adj.*

cheap *adj.* low in cost or value; poor in quality; contemptible; worthless. □ **cheaply** *adv.*, **cheapness** *n.*

cheapen *v.* make or become cheap; degrade.

cheapskate *n. informal* a stingy person.

cheat *v.* act dishonestly or unfairly to win profit or advantage; trick, deprive by deceit. ● *n.* a person who cheats; a deception.

check *v.* **1** examine, test, verify. **2** stop, slow the motion of. **3** *Amer.* correspond when compared. ● *n.* **1** an inspection. **2** a hindrance; a control or restraint. **3** the exposure of a chess king to capture. **4** *Amer.* a bill in a restaurant; a cheque. **5** a pattern of squares or crossing lines. □ **check in** register on arrival. **check out** register on departure or dispatch. □ **checked** *adj.*

checker *n.* **1** var. of **chequer**. **2** (**checkers**) *Amer.* the game of draughts. **3** a person who or thing that checks things.

checkmate *n.* the situation in chess where capture of a king is inevitable; complete defeat, deadlock. ● *v.* put into checkmate; defeat, foil.

checkout *n.* a desk where goods are paid for in a supermarket.

checkpoint *n.* a place where security checks are made on travellers, esp. at a border.

cheek *n.* **1** the side of the face below the eye. **2** bold or impudent speech. ● *v.* speak cheekily to. □ **cheek by jowl** close together.

cheeky *adj.* (**cheekier, cheekiest**) mischievously impudent. □ **cheekily** *adv.*

cheep *n.* a weak shrill cry like that of a young bird. ● *v.* make this cry.

cheer *n.* **1** a shout of applause. **2** cheerfulness. ● *v.* **1** applaud with a cheer, utter a cheer. **2** make happier. □ **cheer up** make or become more cheerful.

cheerful *adj.* **1** happy, optimistic. **2** expressing or inspiring cheerfulness. □ **cheerfully** *adv.*, **cheerfulness** *n.*

cheerio *int. informal* goodbye.

cheerless *adj.* gloomy, dreary.

cheery *adj.* (**cheerier, cheeriest**) cheerful. □ **cheerily** *adv.*, **cheeriness** *n.*

cheese *n.* **1** food made from pressed milk curds. **2** a thick, smooth, sweet spread. □ **hard cheese** *informal* an expression of sympathy. □ **cheesy** *adj.*

cheeseburger *n.* a hamburger with cheese on it.

cheesecake *n.* **1** an open tart filled with flavoured cream cheese or curd cheese. **2** *informal* the portrayal of women in a sexually attractive manner.

cheesecloth *n.* a thin loosely-woven cotton fabric.

cheesed off *adj. informal* bored, exasperated.

cheese-paring *adj.* stingy. ● *n.* stinginess.

cheetah *n.* a swift large animal of the cat family.

chef *n.* a professional cook.

chef-d'oeuvre (shay-**dervr**) *n.* (*pl.* **chefs-d'oeuvre**) a masterpiece.

chemical *adj.* of or made by chemistry. ● *n.* a substance obtained by or used in a chemical process. □ **chemically** *adv.*

chemise (shĕ-**meez**) *n.* a woman's loose-fitting undergarment or dress.

chemist *n.* **1** a person authorized to sell medicinal drugs; a shop where such drugs and items such as toiletries are sold. **2** an expert in chemistry.

chemistry *n.* (*pl.* **-ies**) **1** the study of substances and their reactions; its application in forming new substances; the structure and properties of a substance. **2** complex emotional interaction between people.

chemotherapy (kee-moh-**the**-ră-pi) *n.* treatment of disease, esp. cancer, by drugs etc.

chenille (shĕ-**neel**) *n.* a fabric with a velvety pile.

cheque *n.* (*Amer.* **check**) a written order to a bank to pay out money from an account; a printed form for this.

cheque card *n.* (also **banker's card**) a card guaranteeing payment of cheques.

chequer *n.* (also **checker**) a pattern of squares, esp. of alternating colours.

chequered *adj.* **1** marked with a chequer pattern. **2** having frequent changes of fortune.

cherish *v.* **1** take loving care of. **2** cling to (hopes etc.)

cheroot (shĕ-**root**) *n.* a cigar with both ends open.

cherry *n.* (*pl.* **-ies**) a small soft round fruit with a stone; a tree bearing this or grown for its ornamental flowers; bright red.

cherub *n.* **1** (*pl.* **cherubim**) an angelic being. **2** (in art) a chubby infant with wings; an angelic child. □ **cherubic** *adj.*

chess *n.* a game of skill for two players using 32 pieces on a chequered board.

chest *n.* **1** a large strong box. **2** the upper front surface of the body.

chestnut *n.* **1** a nut which can be roasted and eaten; the tree on which it grows. **2** reddish brown; a horse of this colour. **3** an old joke or anecdote.

chest of drawers *n.* a piece of furniture with drawers for clothes etc.

cheval glass (shĕ-**val**) *n.* a tall mirror mounted on a frame so that it can be tilted.

chevron *n.* a V-shaped symbol.

chew *v.* work or grind between the teeth

chewing gum *n.* flavoured gum used for prolonged chewing.

chewy *adj.* (**chewier, chewiest**) tough; needing or suitable for chewing. □ **chewiness** *n.*

chez (shay) *prep.* at the home of.

chiaroscuro (ki-arŏ-**skoor**-oh) *n.* the use of contrasting light and shade in painting etc.

chic (sheek) *adj.* stylish and elegant. ● *n.* stylishness, elegance.

chicane (shi-**kayn**) *n.* a sharp double bend on a motor-racing track.

chicanery *n.* trickery.

chick *n.* a newly hatched young bird.

chicken *n.* **1** a young domestic fowl; its flesh as food. **2** *informal* a coward. ● *adj. informal* cowardly. ● *v.* **chicken out** *informal* withdraw through cowardice.

chicken feed *n. informal* a trifling amount of money.

chickenpox *n.* an infectious illness with a rash of small red blisters.

chickpea *n.* a pea with yellow seeds used as a vegetable.

chicory *n.* a blue-flowered plant grown for its salad leaves and its root which is used as a flavouring with coffee.

chide *v.* (**chided** or **chid, chidden, chiding**) *archaic* rebuke.

chief *n.* a leader, a ruler; the person with the highest rank. ● *adj.* most important; highest in rank.

chiefly *adv.* mainly.

chieftain *n.* the chief of a clan or tribe.

chiffon (**shif**-on) *n.* a thin almost transparent fabric.

chignon (**sheen**-yon) *n.* a coil of hair worn at the back of the head.

chihuahua (chi-**wah**-wă) *n.* a very small smooth-haired dog.

chilblain *n.* a painful swelling caused by exposure to cold.

child *n.* (*pl.* **children**) a young human being; a son or daughter. □ **childhood** *n.*, **childless** *adj.*

childbirth *n.* the process of giving birth to a child.

childish *adj.* appropriate to a child; silly and immature.

childlike *adj.* simple and innocent.

chili Amer. sp. of **chilli**.

chill *n.* **1** an unpleasant coldness. **2** a feverish cold. **3** unfriendliness. ● *adj.* chilly. ● *v.* **1** make cold; cool in a refrigerator. **2** *informal* relax.

chiller *n.* a cold cabinet, a refrigerator.

chilli *n.* (*Amer.* **chili**) (*pl.* **chillies**) a hot-tasting dried pod of red or green pepper.

chilly *adj.* (**chillier, chilliest**) rather cold; unfriendly in manner.

chime *n.* the sound of a tuned set of bells; such a set. ● *v.* ring as a chime. □ **chime in** put in a remark.

chimera (ky-**meer**-ă) *n.* a legendary monster with a lion's head, goat's body, and serpent's tail; a fantastic product of the imagination.

chimney *n.* (*pl.* **chimneys**) a structure for carrying off smoke or gases from a fire or furnace.

chimney breast *n.* a projecting wall surrounding a chimney.

chimney pot *n.* a short pipe on top of a chimney.

chimp *n. informal* a chimpanzee.

chimpanzee *n.* an African ape.

chin *n.* the protruding part of the face below the mouth.

china *n.* fine earthenware, porcelain; things made of this.

chinchilla *n.* a small squirrel-like South American animal; its grey fur.

chine *n.* **1** an animal's backbone. **2** (in southern England) a ravine.

Chinese *adj.* & *n.* (*pl.* **Chinese**) (a native, the language) of China.

chink *n.* **1** a narrow opening, a slit. **2** the sound of glasses or coins striking together. ● *v.* make this sound.

chinless *adj. informal* weak or feeble in character.

chinoiserie (shin-**wah**-zĕ-ree) *n.* imitation Chinese motifs as decoration.

chintz *n.* glazed cotton cloth used for furnishings.

chip *n.* **1** a small piece cut or broken off something hard; a small hole left by breaking off such a piece. **2** a fried oblong strip of potato. **3** a counter used in gambling. ● *v.* (**chipped, chipping**) cut (small pieces) off (hard material); break, flake. □ **chip in** *informal* **1** interrupt. **2** make a contribution. **chip on one's shoulder** a long-held grievance.

chipboard *n.* board made of compressed wood chips.

chipmunk *n.* a striped squirrel-like animal of North America.

chipolata *n.* a small sausage.

chippings *n.pl.* chips of stone etc. for surfacing a path or road.

chiropody (ki-**rop**-ŏdi) *n.* treatment of minor ailments of the feet. □ **chiropodist** *n.*

chiropractic (ky-rŏ-**prak**-tik) *n.* treatment of certain physical disorders by manipulation of the joints. □ **chiropractor** *n.*

chirp *n.* a short sharp sound made by a small bird or grasshopper. ● *v.* make this sound.

chirpy *adj.* (**chirpier, chirpiest**) *informal* lively and cheerful.

chisel *n.* a tool with a sharp bevelled end for shaping wood or stone etc. ● *v.* (**chiselled, chiselling**; *Amer.* **chiseled**) cut with this.

chit *n.* **1** a young and impudent girl. **2** a short written note.

chitterlings *n.pl.* the small intestines of a pig, cooked as food.

chivalry *n.* courtesy and considerate behaviour, esp. towards weaker people. □ **chivalrous** *adj.*

chive *n.* a herb with onion-flavoured leaves.

chivvy *v.* (**chivvied, chivvying**) urge, nag, pester.

chloride *n.* a compound of chlorine and another element.

chlorinate *v.* treat or sterilize with chlorine. □ **chlorination** *n.*

chlorine *n.* a chemical element (symbol Cl), a poisonous gas.

chlorofluorocarbon *see* **CFC**.

chloroform *n.* a liquid giving off vapour that causes unconsciousness when inhaled.

chlorophyll (klor-ŏ-fil) *n.* green colouring matter in plants.

choc ice *n.* a bar of ice cream coated with chocolate.

chock *n.* a block or wedge for preventing a wheel from moving. ● *v.* wedge with chocks.

chock-a-block *adj.* & *adv. informal* crammed, crowded together.

chocolate *n.* an edible substance made from cacao seeds; a sweet made or coated with this, a drink made with this; a dark brown colour.

choice *n.* choosing; the right or opportunity to choose; a variety from which to choose; a person or thing chosen. ● *adj.* of especially good quality.

choir *n.* an organized band of singers, esp. in church; part of a church where these sit, the chancel.

choirboy *n.* a boy singer in a church choir.

choke *v.* stop (a person) breathing by squeezing or blocking the windpipe; have difficulty breathing; clog, smother. ● *n.* a valve controlling the flow of air into a petrol engine.

choker *n.* a close-fitting necklace.

cholera *n.* a serious often fatal disease caused by bacteria.

choleric *adj.* easily angered.

cholesterol *n.* a fatty animal substance thought to cause hardening of arteries.

chomp *v.* munch noisily.

choose *v.* (**chose, chosen, choosing**) select out of a number of things; decide (on), prefer.

choosy *adj.* (**choosier, choosiest**) *informal* excessively fastidious. □ **choosiness** *n.*

chop *v.* (**chopped, chopping**) cut by a blow with an axe or knife; cut into small pieces; hit with a short downward movement. ● *n.* **1** a downward cutting blow. **2** a thick slice of meat, usu. including a rib.

chopper *n.* **1** a chopping tool. **2** *informal* a helicopter.

choppy *adj.* (**choppier, choppiest**) full of short broken waves.

chopstick *n.* each of a pair of sticks used as eating utensils in China, Japan, etc.

chop suey *n.* a Chinese dish of meat fried with vegetables.

choral *adj.* for or sung by a choir.

chorale *n.* **1** a choral composition using the words of a hymn. **2** a choir.

chord *n.* **1** a combination of notes sounded together. **2** a straight line joining two points on a curve. □ **strike (or touch) a chord with** appeal to the emotions of.

chore *n.* a routine or irksome task.

choreography (ko-ri-og-răfi) *n.* the composition of stage dances. □ **choreographer** *n.*, **choreographic** *adj.*

chorister *n.* a member of a choir.

chortle *n.* a loud chuckle. ● *v.* utter a chortle.

chorus *n.* **1** a group of singers; a group of singing dancers in a musical etc.; an utterance by many people simultaneously. **2** the refrain of a song. ● *v.* say (the same thing) as a group.

chose, chosen past & p.p. of **choose**.

choux pastry (shoo) *n.* very light pastry enriched with eggs.

chow *n.* **1** a long-haired dog of a Chinese breed. **2** *informal* food.

chowder *n.* a thick soup usu. containing clams or fish.

chow mein (mayn) *n.* a Chinese-style dish of fried noodles and shredded meat etc.

christen *v.* admit to the Christian Church by baptism; name.

Christendom *n.* all Christians or Christian countries.

Christian *adj.* of or believing in Christianity; *informal* kindly, humane. ● *n.* a believer in Christianity.

Christianity *n.* a religion based on the teachings of Christ.

Christian name *n.* an individual's distinguishing name, a first name.

Christian Science *n.* a religious system by which health and healing are sought by Christian faith, without medical treatment.

Christmas *n.* a festival (25 Dec.) commemorating Christ's birth.

Christmas tree *n.* an evergreen or artificial tree decorated at Christmas.

chromatic *adj.* of colour, in colours. □ **chromatically** *adv.*

chromatic scale *n.* a music scale proceeding by semitones.

chromatography *n.* separation of substances by slow passage through material that absorbs them at different rates.

chrome *n.* **1** chromium plating. **2** a yellow pigment made from a compound of chromium.

chromium *n.* a metallic element (symbol Cr) that does not rust.

chromosome *n.* a threadlike structure carrying genes in animal and plant cells.

chronic *adj.* **1** constantly present or recurring; having a chronic disease or habit. **2** *informal* very bad. □ **chronically** *adv.*

chronicle *n.* a record of events. ● *v.* record in a chronicle. □ **chronicler** *n.*

chronological *adj.* following the order in which things happened. □ **chronologically** *adv.*

chronology *n.* arrangement of events in order of occurrence.

chronometer *n.* a time-measuring instrument.

chrysalis *n.* (*pl.* **chrysalises** or **chrysalides**) a form of an insect in the stage between larva and adult insect; the case enclosing it.

chrysanthemum *n.* a garden plant flowering in autumn.

chubby *adj.* (**chubbier, chubbiest**) round and plump. □ **chubbiness** *n.*

chuck *v.* **1** *informal* throw carelessly; discard. **2** touch gently under the chin. ● *n.* **1** part of a lathe holding the drill; part of a drill holding the bit. **2** a cut of beef from neck to ribs.

chuckle *v.* & *n.* (utter) a quiet laugh.

chuff *v.* (of an engine) work with a regular puffing noise.

chuffed *adj. informal* pleased.

chug *v.* (**chugged, chugging**) (of a boat etc.) make repeated dull short sounds while moving.

chum *n. informal* a close friend. □ **chummy** *adj.*

chump *n. informal* a stupid person.

chunk *n.* a thick piece; *informal* a substantial amount.

chunky *adj.* (**chunkier, chunkiest**) **1** containing chunks in liquid. **2** short and thick or sturdy. □ **chunkiness** *n.*

chunter *v. informal* **1** grumble monotonously. **2** move slowly.

church *n.* a building for public Christian worship; a religious service in this; (**the Church**) Christians collectively; a particular group of these.

churchwarden *n.* a parish representative, assisting with church business.

churchyard *n.* enclosed land round a church, used for burials.

churlish *adj.* ill-mannered, surly. □ **churlishly** *adv.*, **churlishness** *n.*

churn *n.* a machine in which milk is beaten to make butter; a very large milk can. ● *v.* beat (milk) or make (butter) in a churn; move and turn violently. □ **churn out** produce large quantities of (something) without thought or care.

chute *n.* a sloping channel down which things can be slid or dropped.

chutney *n.* (*pl.* **chutneys**) a seasoned mixture of fruit, vinegar, spices, etc.

Ci *abbr.* curie.

CIA *abbr.* (in the USA) Central Intelligence Agency.

ciabatta (chĭă-**bah**-tă) *n.* an Italian bread made with olive oil.

ciao (chow) *int. informal* a greeting on meeting or parting.

cicada (si-**kah**-dă) *n.* a chirping insect resembling a grasshopper.

cicatrice (**si**-kă-tris) *n.* a scar.

CID *abbr.* Criminal Investigation Department.

cider *n.* a fermented drink made from apples.

cigar *n.* a cylinder of tobacco in tobacco leaves for smoking.

cigarette *n.* a roll of shredded tobacco in thin paper for smoking.

cinch *n. informal* a very easy task; a certainty.

cinder *n.* a piece of partly burnt coal or wood.

cine- *comb. form* cinematographic.

cinema *n.* a theatre where films are shown; films as an art form or industry.

cinematography *n.* the process of making and projecting moving pictures. ▫ **cinematographic** *adj.*

cinnamon *n.* a spice.

cipher *n.* (also **cypher**) **1** a symbol (0) representing nought or zero; a numeral; a person of no importance. **2** a system of letters or numbers used to represent others for secrecy.

circa *prep.* about, approximately.

circle *n.* **1** a perfectly round plane figure. **2** a curved tier of seats at a theatre etc. **3** a group with similar interests or shared acquaintances ● *v.* move in a circle (round); form a circle round.

circlet *n.* a circular band worn on the head as an ornament.

circuit *n.* **1** a roughly circular route returning to its starting point. **2** an itinerary regularly followed. **3** the path of an electric current.

circuitous (sir-**kew**-itŭs) *adj.* roundabout, indirect. ▫ **circuitously** *adv.*

circuitry *n.* electric circuits.

circular *adj.* **1** shaped like or moving round a circle. **2** (of an argument) assuming what is to be proved. ● *n.* a letter or leaflet sent to a large number of people. ▫ **circularity** *n.*

circulate *v.* (cause to) move around an area; (cause to) pass from one place or person to another.

circulation *n.* **1** circulating; the movement of blood round the body. **2** the extent to which something is known about or available; the number of copies sold of a newspaper. ▫ **circulatory** *adj.*

circumcise *v.* cut off the foreskin of. ▫ **circumcision** *n.*

circumference *n.* the boundary of a circle, the distance round this.

circumflex accent *n.* the accent ˆ.

circumlocution *n.* an evasively or pointlessly verbose expression. ▫ **circumlocutory** *adj.*

circumnavigate *v.* sail completely round. ▫ **circumnavigation** *n.*, **circumnavigator** *n.*

circumscribe *v.* restrict; draw a line round.

circumspect *adj.* cautious and watchful, wary. ▫ **circumspection** *n.*, **circumspectly** *adv.*

circumstance *n.* an occurrence or fact relevant to an event or situation.

circumstantial *adj.* **1** (of evidence) suggesting but not proving something. **2** detailed.

circumvent *v.* evade (a difficulty etc.). ▫ **circumvention** *n.*

circus *n.* a travelling show with performing animals, acrobats, etc.

cirque (serk) *n.* a bowl-shaped hollow on a mountain.

cirrhosis (si-**roh**-sis) *n.* a disease of the liver.

cirrus (**sir**-rŭs) *n.* (*pl.* **cirri**) a high wispy white cloud.

cistern *n.* a tank for storing water.

citadel *n.* a fortress overlooking a city.

cite *v.* quote; mention as an example. □ **citation** *n.*

citizen *n.* **1** a person with full rights in a country. **2** an inhabitant of a city. □ **citizenship** *n.*

citrus *n.* a tree or fruit of a group including lemon, orange, etc. □ **citric** *adj.*

city *n.* (*pl.* **-ies**) **1** an important town; a town with special rights given by charter and containing a cathedral. **2** (**the City**) the financial and commercial institutions of the City of London.

civet *n.* (in full **civet cat**) a catlike animal of central Africa; a musky substance obtained from its glands.

civic *adj.* of a city or citizenship.

civil *adj.* **1** of citizens; not of the armed forces or the Church. **2** polite and obliging. □ **civilly** *adv.*

civil engineering *n.* the design and construction of roads, bridges, etc.

civilian *n.* & *adj.* (a person) not in the armed forces.

civility *n.* (*pl.* **-ies**) politeness; a polite remark.

civilization *n.* (also **-isation**) **1** an advanced stage of social development; progress towards this; comfort and convenience. **2** the culture and way of life of a particular area or period.

civilize *v.* (also **-ise**) **1** cause to improve to a developed stage of society. **2** improve the behaviour of.

Civil List *n.* an annual allowance for the royal family's household expenses.

civil servant *n.* an employee of the **civil service**, government departments other than the armed forces.

civil war *n.* war between citizens of the same country.

civvies *n.pl. informal* ordinary clothes, not uniform.

CJD *abbr.* Creutzfeldt-Jakob Disease, a fatal degenerative brain disease.

Cl *symb.* chlorine.

cl *abbr.* centilitre(s).

clack *n.* a short sharp sound of two objects hitting each other. ● *v.* make this sound.

clad *adj.* clothed.

cladding *n.* boards or metal plates as a protective covering.

claim *v.* **1** demand as one's right. **2** assert. ● *n.* **1** a demand; a right to something. **2** an assertion.

claimant *n.* a person making a claim.

clairvoyance *n.* the power of seeing the future. □ **clairvoyant** *n.* & *adj.*

clam *n.* a shellfish with a hinged shell. □ **clam up** (**clammed, clamming**) *informal* refuse to talk.

clamber *v.* climb with difficulty.

clammy *adj.* (**clammier, clammiest**) unpleasantly moist and sticky.

clamour *n.* (*Amer.* **clamor**) a loud confused noise; a loud protest etc. ● *v.* shout loudly; demand or protest vehemently. □ **clamorous** *adj.*

clamp *n.* a device for holding things tightly; a device for immobilizing an illegally parked car. ● *v.* grip with a clamp, fix firmly; immobilize (an illegally parked car) with a clamp. □ **clamp down on** become firmer about, put a stop to.

clan *n.* a group of families with a common ancestor. □ **clannish** *adj.*

clandestine *adj.* kept secret, done secretly.

clang *n.* & *v.* (make) a loud ringing sound.

clanger *n. informal* a blunder.

clangour *n.* (*Amer.* **clangor**) a clanging noise.

clank *n.* a sound like metal striking metal. ● *v.* make or cause to make this sound.

clap *v.* (**clapped, clapping**) **1** strike the palms of the hands loudly together, esp. in applause. **2** place (a hand etc.) quickly; slap on the back. ● *n.* **1** an act of clapping. **2** a sharp noise of thunder. ▫ **clapped out** *informal* worn out.

clapper *n.* the tongue or striker of a bell.

clapperboard *n.* a device of hinged boards struck together at the start of filming to synchronize the starting of picture and sound machinery.

claptrap *n.* pretentious talk; nonsense.

claret *n.* a dry red wine.

clarify *v.* (**clarified, clarifying**) **1** make more intelligible. **2** remove impurities from (fats) by heating. ▫ **clarification** *n.*

clarinet *n.* a woodwind instrument. ▫ **clarinettist** *n.*

clarion *adj.* loud, rousing.

clarity *n.* clearness.

clash *n.* a violent confrontation, a conflict; discordant sounds or colours. ● *v.* come into conflict; be incompatible; be discordant.

clasp *n.* a device for fastening things, with interlocking parts; a grasp, a handshake. ● *v.* grasp tightly; embrace closely; fasten with a clasp.

class *n.* **1** a set of people or things with shared characteristics; a standard of quality; a social rank; a set of students taught together. **2** *informal* excellence; style. ● *v.* assign to a particular category.

classic *adj.* **1** of recognized high quality. **2** typical. **3** simple in style. ● *n.* **1** a classic author or work etc. **2** (**classics**) the study of ancient Greek and Roman literature, history, etc. ▫ **classicism** *n.*, **classicist** *n.*

classical *adj.* **1** of ancient Greek and Roman civilization. **2** traditional in form and style. ▫ **classically** *adv.*

classify *v.* (**classified, classifying**) **1** arrange systematically, class. **2** designate as officially secret. ▫ **classifiable** *adj.*, **classification** *n.*, **classified** *adj.*

classless *adj.* without distinctions of social class.

classroom *n.* a room where a class of students is taught.

classy *adj.* (**classier, classiest**) *informal* of high quality, stylish.

clatter *n.* & *v.* (make) a rattling sound.

clause *n.* **1** a single part in a treaty, law, or contract. **2** a distinct part of a sentence, with its own verb.

claustrophobia *n.* abnormal fear of being in an enclosed space. ▫ **claustrophobic** *adj.*

clavichord *n.* an early keyboard instrument.

clavicle *n.* the collarbone.

claw *n.* a pointed nail on an animal's or bird's foot; a clawlike device for grappling or holding things. ● *v.* scratch or clutch with a claw or hand.

clay *n.* stiff sticky earth, used for making bricks and pottery. ▫ **clayey** *adj.*

clay pigeon *n.* a breakable disc thrown up as a target for shooting.

clean *adj.* free from dirt or impurities; not soiled or used; not indecent or obscene. ● *v.* make clean. ▫ **cleaner** *n.*, **cleanly** *adv.*

cleanly (klen-li) *adj.* (**cleanlier, cleanliest**) attentive to cleanness, with clean habits. ▫ **cleanliness** *n.*

cleanse (klenz) *v.* make clean; rid of undesirable elements. ▫ **cleanser** *n.*

clear *adj.* **1** easily perceived or understood. **2** transparent. **3** free of obstructions. **4** free from blemishes, doubts, or anything undesirable. ● *v.* **1** free or become free from obstacles etc. **2** prove innocent. **3** get past or over. **4** give official approval for. **5** make as net profit. ▫ **clear off** *informal* go away. **clear out 1** empty, tidy. **2** *informal* go away. ▫ **clearly** *adv.*

clearance *n.* **1** clearing. **2** official permission. **3** space allowed for one object to pass another.

clearing *n.* a space cleared of trees in a forest.

clearing house *n.* an office at which banks exchange cheques; an agency collecting and distributing information.

clearway *n.* a road where vehicles must not stop.

cleat *n.* a projecting piece for fastening ropes to.

cleavage *n.* a split, a separation; the hollow between full breasts.

cleave[1] *v.* (**cleaved** or **cleft** or **clove, cleft** or **cloven, cleaving**) *literary* split, divide.

cleave[2] *v. literary* stick, cling.

cleaver *n.* a chopping tool.

clef *n.* a symbol on a stave in music, showing the pitch of notes.

cleft *adj.* split. ● *n.* a split, a cleavage.

cleft palate *n.* a defect in the roof of the mouth where two sides of the palate failed to join.

clematis *n.* a climbing plant with showy flowers.

clemency *n.* mercy. □ **clement** *adj.*

clementine *n.* a small variety of orange.

clench *v.* close (the teeth or fingers) tightly.

clerestory *n.* (*pl.* **-ies**) an upper row of windows in a large church.

clergy *n.* people ordained for religious duties. □ **clergyman** *n.*

cleric *n.* a member of the clergy.

clerical *adj.* **1** of routine office work. **2** of clergy.

clerk *n.* a person employed to do written work in an office.

clever *adj.* quick at learning and understanding things; showing skill. □ **cleverly** *adv.*, **cleverness** *n.*

cliché (klee-shay) *n.* an overused phrase or idea. □ **clichéd** *adj.*

click *n.* a short sharp sound. ● *v.* **1** make or cause to make such a sound; press (a button on a computer mouse). **2** *informal* quickly become friendly. **3** *informal* become intelligible.

client *n.* **1** a person using the services of a professional person. **2** a desktop computer capable of obtaining information from a server.

clientele (klee-ahn-**tel**) *n.* clients.

cliff *n.* a steep rock face, esp. on a coast.

cliffhanger *n.* an ending to an episode of a serial that leaves the audience in suspense.

climate *n.* the regular weather conditions of an area. □ **climatic** *adj.*

climax *n.* the most intense or exciting point; the culmination. □ **climactic** *adj.*

climb *v.* go up; rise. ● *n.* an ascent; a route for ascent; an increase. □ **climber** *n.*

clime *n. literary* a climate; a region.

clinch *v.* settle conclusively; fasten; grapple. ● *n.* a close hold or embrace. □ **clincher** *n.*

cling *v.* (**clung, clinging**) hold on tightly; stick.

cling film *n.* thin polythene wrapping that adheres to surfaces.

clinic *n.* a place or session at which medical treatment is given; a private or specialized hospital.

clinical *adj.* **1** of or used in treatment of patients. **2** unemotional and efficient. □ **clinically** *adv.*

clink *n.* **1** a sharp ringing sound. **2** *informal* prison. ● *v.* make this sound.

clinker *n.* fused coal ash.

clip *n.* **1** a device for holding things together or in place. **2** an act of cutting; an excerpt. **3** *informal* a sharp blow. ● *v.* (**clipped, clipping**) **1** fasten with a clip. **2** cut with shears or scissors. **3** *informal* hit sharply.

clipper *n.* **1** a fast sailing ship. **2** (**clippers**) an instrument for clipping things.

clipping *n.* a piece clipped off; a newspaper cutting.

clique (kleek) *n.* a small exclusive group. □ **cliquey** *adj.*, **cliquish** *adj.*

clitoris *n.* the small erectile part of the female genitals.

Cllr. *abbr.* Councillor.

cloak *n.* a loose sleeveless outer garment. ● *v.* cover, conceal.

cloakroom *n.* **1** a room where outer garments can be left. **2** a lavatory.

clobber *informal n.* equipment; belongings. ● *v.* hit hard; defeat heavily.

cloche (klosh) *n.* a translucent cover for protecting plants.

clock *n.* an instrument indicating time. □ **clock in** or **on, out** or **off** register one's time of arrival or departure. **clock up** *informal* reach, register (a speed or total).

clockwise *adv.* & *adj.* moving in the direction of the hands of a clock.

clockwork *n.* a mechanism with wheels and springs. □ **like clockwork** smoothly and easily; predictably.

clod *n.* a lump of earth.

clog *n.* a wooden-soled shoe. ● *v.* (**clogged, clogging**) cause an obstruction in; become blocked.

cloister *n.* a covered walk in a monastery etc.; life in a monastery or convent.

cloistered *adj.* shut away, sheltered, secluded.

clone *n.* a group of organisms or cells produced asexually from one ancestor; an identical copy. ● *v.* produce (a clone) (of); make an identical copy of.

close (klohss) *adj.* **1** near in space or time. **2** very affectionate or intimate. **3** airless, humid. **4** detailed, careful. **5** secretive; stingy. ● *adv.* in or into a near position; leaving little space. ● *v.* (klohz). **1** shut; cover (an opening), cause to cover an opening. **2** bring or come to an end. **3** come nearer together. ● *n.* **1** (klohz) an ending. **2** (klohss) a street closed at one end; the precinct surrounding a cathedral. □ **closely** *adv.*, **closeness** *n.*

closet *n.* a cupboard; a storeroom. ● *v.* (**closeted, closeting**) shut away in private conference or study. ● *adj.* secret, unacknowledged.

close-up *n.* a photograph etc. showing a subject at close range.

closure *n.* closing or being closed; conclusion.

clot *n.* **1** a thickened mass of liquid. **2** *informal* a stupid person. ● *v.* (**clotted, clotting**) form clots.

cloth *n.* **1** woven or felted material; a piece of this for cleaning etc. **2** the clergy; the clerical profession.

clothe *v.* put clothes on, provide with clothes.

clothes *n.pl.* things worn to cover the body.

clothier *n.* a maker or seller of clothes or cloth.

clothing *n.* clothes for the body.

clotted cream *n.* very thick cream, thickened by scalding.

cloud *n.* **1** a visible mass of watery vapour floating in the sky; a mass of smoke or dust. **2** something spoiling happiness or peace. ● *v.* become covered with clouds or gloom.

cloudburst *n.* a sudden violent rain storm.

cloudy *adj.* (**cloudier, cloudiest**) covered with clouds; (of liquid) not transparent. □ **cloudiness** *n.*

clout *informal n.* **1** a blow. **2** influence. ● *v.* hit.

clove[1] past of **cleave**[1]

clove[2] *n.* **1** a dried bud of a tropical tree, used as a spice. **2** one division of a compound bulb such as garlic.

clove hitch *n.* a knot used to fasten a rope round a pole etc.

cloven hoof *n.* a divided hoof like that of sheep, cows, etc.

clover *n.* a flowering plant with three-lobed leaves. □ **in clover** in luxury.

clown *n.* a person who does comical tricks. ● *v.* perform or behave as a clown.

cloy *v.* sicken by glutting with sweetness or pleasure.

club *n.* **1** a group who meet for social or sporting purposes; their premises; an organization offering benefits to subscribers. **2** a heavy stick used as a weapon; a stick with a wooden or metal head, used in golf. **3** (**clubs**) a suit of playing cards marked with black clover leaves. ● *v.* (**clubbed, clubbing**) **1** strike with a club. **2** go to nightclubs. □ **club together** join together to collect a sum of money.

club class *n.* a class of air travel designed for business travellers.

cluck *n.* the throaty cry of a hen. ● *v.* utter a cluck.

clue *n.* something that helps solve a puzzle or problem.

clump *n.* a cluster, a mass. ● *v.* **1** tread heavily. **2** form into a clump.

clumsy *adj.* (**clumsier, clumsiest**) moving or done without grace or skill; awkward to handle. □ **clumsily** *adv.*, **clumsiness** *n.*

clung past & p.p. of **cling**.

cluster *n.* a small close group. ● *v.* form a cluster.

clutch *v.* grasp tightly. ● *n.* **1** a tight grasp. **2** a device for connecting and disconnecting moving parts. **3** a set of eggs laid at one time; chickens hatched from these.

clutter *n.* things lying about untidily. ● *v.* crowd untidily.

Cm *symb.* curium.

cm *abbr.* centimetre.

CND *abbr.* Campaign for Nuclear Disarmament.

Co *symb.* cobalt.

Co. *abbr.* **1** Company. **2** County.

c/o *abbr.* care of.

co- *comb. form* joint, jointly.

coach *n.* **1** a long-distance bus; a horse-drawn carriage; a railway carriage. **2** a private tutor; an instructor in sports. ● *v.* train, teach.

coagulate (koh-ag-yoo-layt) *v.* change from liquid to semi-solid, clot. □ **coagulant** *n.*, **coagulation** *n.*

coal *n.* a hard black mineral burnt as fuel.

coalesce *v.* form a single mass; combine. □ **coalescence** *n.*

coalfield *n.* an area where coal is mined.

coalition *n.* a union, esp. a temporary union of political parties.

coal tar *n.* tar produced when gas is made from coal.

coarse *adj.* **1** composed of large particles; rough in texture. **2** crude, vulgar. □ **coarsely** *adv.*, **coarseness** *n.*

coarse fish *n.* any freshwater fish other than salmon and trout.

coarsen *v.* make or become coarse.

coast *n.* the seashore and land near it. ● *v.* **1** move easily without using power. **2** sail along a coast. □ **coastal** *adj.*

coaster *n.* **1** a ship trading along a coast. **2** a mat for a glass.

coastguard *n.* an officer of an organization that keeps watch on the coast.

coat *n.* a long outer garment with sleeves; the fur or hair covering an animal's body; a covering layer. ● *v.* cover with a layer.

coating *n.* a covering layer.

coat of arms *n.* a design on a shield as the emblem of a family or institution.

coax *v.* persuade gently; manipulate carefully or slowly.

coaxial (koh-aks-iăl) *adj.* (of cable) containing two conductors, one surrounding but insulated from the other.

cob *n.* **1** a sturdy short-legged horse. **2** a hazelnut. **3** the central part of an ear of maize. **4** a small round loaf. **5** a male swan.

cobalt *n.* a metallic element (symbol Co); a deep blue pigment made from it.

cobber *n.* *Austral. informal* a friend, a mate.

cobble *n.* a rounded stone formerly used for paving roads. ● *v.* mend or assemble roughly.

cobbler *n.* a shoe-mender.

cobra *n.* a poisonous snake of India and Africa.

cobweb *n.* a spider's web.

cocaine *n.* a drug used illegally as a stimulant.

coccyx (**kok**-siks) *n.* the bone at the base of the spinal column.

cochineal (ko-chi-**neel**) *n.* red food colouring made from dried insects.

cock *n.* **1** a male bird. **2** a stopcock. **3** a firing lever in a gun. **4** *vulgar slang* a penis. ● *v.* **1** tilt (the head etc.); bend. **2** set (a gun) for firing.

cockade *n.* a rosette worn on a hat as a badge.

cock-a-hoop *adj.* very pleased, triumphant.

cockatoo *n.* (*pl.* **cockatoos**) a crested parrot.

cockatrice *n.* a basilisk; a dragon with a cock's head.

cockerel *n.* a young male fowl.

cock-eyed *adj. informal* **1** crooked. **2** absurd, crazy.

cockle *n.* an edible shellfish.

cockney *n.* (*pl.* **cockneys**) a native of the East End of London; their accent or dialect.

cockpit *n.* **1** the compartment for the pilot in a plane, or for the driver in a racing car. **2** a pit for cockfighting.

cockroach *n.* a beetle-like insect.

cockscomb *n.* the crest of of a male fowl.

cocksure *adj.* over-confident.

cocktail *n.* a mixed alcoholic drink; a dish of mixed small pieces of food; a mixture.

cocky *adj.* (**cockier, cockiest**) conceited and arrogant. □ **cockily** *adv.*

cocoa *n.* powder of crushed cacao seeds; a drink made from this.

coconut *n.* a nut of a tropical palm.

cocoon *n.* a silky sheath round a chrysalis; a protective wrapping. ● *v.* wrap in something soft and warm; protect, cherish.

COD *abbr.* cash (or *Amer.* collect) on delivery.

cod *n.* a large edible sea fish.

coda *n.* the final part of a musical composition.

coddle *v.* **1** cherish and protect. **2** cook (eggs) in water just below boiling point.

code *n.* **1** a system of words or symbols used to represent others for secrecy; a sequence of numbers or letters for identification. **2** a set of laws, standards, etc.

codeine (**koh**-deen) *n.* a pain-killing drug.

codex *n.* (*pl.* **codices** or **codexes**) **1** an ancient manuscript text in book form. **2** a pharmaceutical description of drugs.

codicil *n.* an appendix to a will.

codify *v.* (**codified, codifying**) arrange (laws etc.) into a code. □ **codification** *n.*

co-education *n.* education of boys and girls in the same classes. □ **co-educational** *adj.*

coefficient *n.* a multiplier; the constant multiplying the variable in an algebraic expression.

coelacanth (**seel**-ă-kanth) *n.* a large sea fish formerly thought to be extinct.

coeliac disease (**seel**-iak) *n.* (*Amer.* **celiac**) a disease causing inability to digest gluten.

coerce *v.* compel by threats or force. □ **coercion** *n.*, **coercive** *adj.*

coeval (koh-**eev**-ăl) *adj.* of the same age or epoch.

coexist *v.* exist together, esp. harmoniously. □ **coexistence** *n.*, **coexistent** *adj.*

coffee *n.* the beanlike seeds of a tropical shrub, roasted and ground for making a drink; this drink; a pale brown colour.

coffee table *n.* a small low table.

coffer *n.* a large strong box for holding money and valuables; (**coffers**) financial resources.

cofferdam *n.* an enclosure pumped dry to enable construction work to be done within it.

coffin *n.* a box in which a corpse is placed for burial or cremation.

cog *n.* one of a series of projections on the edge of a wheel, engaging with those of another.

cogent *adj.* logical and convincing. ◻ **cogency** *n.*, **cogently** *adv.*

cogitate *v.* think deeply. ◻ **cogitation** *n.*

cognac (**kon**-yak) *n.* French brandy.

cognate *adj.* akin, related.

cognition *n.* gaining knowledge by thought or perception. ◻ **cognitive** *adj.*

cognizant *adj.* aware, having knowledge. ◻ **cognizance** *n.*

cognoscente (kon-yŏ-**shen**-ti) *n.* (*pl.* **cognoscenti**) a connoisseur.

cohabit *v.* live together as man and wife. ◻ **cohabitation** *n.*

cohere *v.* stick together.

coherent *adj.* connected logically; articulate; forming a consistent whole. ◻ **coherence** *n.* **coherently** *adv.*

cohesion *n.* being coherent. ◻ **cohesive** *adj.*, **cohesively** *adv.*

cohort *n.* a tenth part of a Roman legion; a group or set of people.

coiffure (kwa-**fyoor**) *n.* a hairstyle.

coil *v.* wind into rings or a spiral. ● *n.* **1** something wound in a spiral; one ring or turn in this. **2** a contraceptive device inserted into the womb.

coin *n.* a piece of metal money. ● *v.* **1** make (coins) by stamping metal; *informal* get (money) in large quantities as profit. **2** invent (a word or phrase). ◻ **coiner** *n.*

coinage *n.* **1** coins, a system of coins; making coins. **2** a coined word or phrase.

coincide *v.* occupy the same portion of time or space; be in agreement or identical.

coincidence *n.* **1** the chance occurrence of events which are similar or interrelate to affect developments. **2** coinciding. ◻ **coincidental** *adj.* **coincidentally** *adv.*

coir (**koi**-ĕ) *n.* coconut fibre.

coitus *n.* (also **coition**) sexual intercourse.

coke *n.* **1** a solid substance left after gas and tar have been extracted from coal, used as fuel. **2** *informal* cocaine.

col *n.* the lowest point in a ridge between two mountain peaks.

cola *n.* (also **kola**) a West African tree with seeds containing caffeine; a drink flavoured with these.

colander *n.* a bowl-shaped perforated container for draining food.

cold *adj.* **1** at or having a low temperature. **2** not affectionate; not enthusiastic. **3** not prepared or rehearsed. ● *n.* **1** low temperature; a cold condition. **2** an illness causing catarrh and sneezing. ◻ **coldly** *adv.*, **coldness** *n.*

cold-blooded *adj.* **1** having a blood temperature varying with that of the surroundings. **2** unfeeling, ruthless.

cold calling *n.* a sales technique involving contacting people who have not previously shown interest.

cold feet *n.pl. informal* loss of confidence.

cold-shoulder *v.* treat with deliberate unfriendliness.

cold turkey *n. informal* sudden withdrawal of drugs from an addict.

cold war *n.* hostility between nations without fighting.

coleslaw *n.* a salad of shredded raw cabbage in dressing.

coley *n.* an edible fish.

colic *n.* severe abdominal pain.

colitis *n.* inflammation of the colon.

collaborate *v.* work in partnership. ◻ **collaboration** *n.*, **collaborator** *n.*, **collaborative** *adj.*

collage (kol-**ahzh**) *n.* a picture formed by fixing various items to a backing; this art form.

collagen *n.* a protein substance found in bone and tissue.

collapse *v.* fall down suddenly; lose strength suddenly; fold. ● *n.* collapsing; breakdown.

collapsible *adj.* made so as to fold up.

collar *n.* **1** a band round the neck of a garment. **2** a band holding part of a machine. **3** a cut of bacon from near the head. ● *v. informal* seize; take illicitly.

collate *v.* **1** collect and combine. **2** compare in detail. ◻ **collator** *n.*

collateral *adj.* **1** additional but subordinate. **2** descended from the same ancestor by a different line. ● *n.* security for repayment of a loan. ◻ **collaterally** *adv.*

collation *n.* **1** collating. **2** a light meal.

colleague *n.* a fellow worker in a business or profession.

collect *v.* bring or come together; obtain specimens of, esp. as a hobby; fetch. ● *adv.* & *adj. Amer.* (of a telephone call) paid for by the person receiving it. ● *n.* a short prayer. ◻ **collectable** or **collectible** *adj.* & *n.*, **collector** *n.*

collected *adj.* calm and controlled.

collection *n.* collecting; a set of objects or money collected.

collective *adj.* of or denoting a group taken or working as a unit. ◻ **collectively** *adv.*

collective noun *n. Grammar* a noun (singular in form) denoting a group (e.g. *army, herd*).

colleen *n. Irish* a girl.

college *n.* an educational establishment for higher or professional education; an organized body of professional people. ◻ **collegiate** *adj.*

collide *v.* hit when moving.

collie *n.* a breed of dog often used as a sheepdog.

colliery *n.* (*pl.* **-ies**) a coal mine.

collision *n.* **1** the striking of one thing against another when at least one is moving. **2** conflict.

collocate *v.* place (words) together. ◻ **collocation** *n.*

colloquial *adj.* suitable for informal speech or writing. ◻ **colloquialism** *n.*, **colloquially** *adv.*

collusion *n.* an agreement made for a deceitful or fraudulent purpose.

cologne (kŏ-**lohn**) *n.* a light perfume.

colon *n.* **1** a punctuation mark (:). **2** the lower part of the large intestine. ◻ **colonic** *adj.*

colonel (ker-nĕl) *n.* an army officer next below brigadier.

colonial *adj.* of a colony or colonies. ● *n.* an inhabitant of a colony.

colonialism *n.* a policy of acquiring or maintaining colonies.

colonize *v.* (also **-ise**) acquire as a colony; establish a colony in. ◻ **colonist** *n.*, **colonization** *n.*

colonnade *n.* a row of columns.

colony *n.* (*pl.* **-ies**) a country under the control of another and occupied by settlers from there; a group of settlers; people of shared nationality or occupation living as a community; a community of animals or plants of one kind.

color, colorful etc. Amer. sp. of **colour, colourful** etc.

coloration *n.* (also **colouration**) colouring.

coloratura *n.* elaborate ornamentation of a vocal melody; a singer (esp. a soprano) skilled in such singing.

colossal *adj.* immense. ◻ **colossally** *adv.*

colossus *n.* (*pl.* **colossi** or **colossuses**) an immense statue.

colostomy *n.* (*pl.* **-ies**) an operation to form an opening from the colon onto the surface of the abdomen, through which the bowel can empty.

colour (*Amer.* **color**) *n.* the effect on something's appearance of the way it reflects light; pigment, paint; (usu. **colours**) the flag of a ship or regiment. ● *v.* put colour on; paint, stain, dye; blush; give a special character or bias to (an outlook, account, etc.)

colourant *n.* (also **colorant**) a dye etc.

colour-blind *adj.* unable to distinguish between certain colours.

coloured *adj.* (*Amer.* **colored**) **1** having a colour. **2** wholly or partly of non-white descent.

colourful *adj.* (*Amer.* **colorful**) **1** full of colour. **2** vivid, lively; (of language) rude. ▫ **colourfully** *adv.*

colourless *adj.* (*Amer.* **colorless**) without colour; lacking vividness.

colt *n.* a young male horse.

column *n.* **1** a round pillar; something resembling this. **2** a vertical division of a page; material printed in this. **3** a long narrow formation of troops, vehicles, etc.

columnist *n.* a journalist who regularly writes a column of comments.

coma *n.* deep unconsciousness.

comatose *adj.* in a coma; *informal* very lethargic.

comb *n.* **1** a toothed strip of stiff material for tidying hair. **2** a fowl's fleshy crest. ● *v.* tidy with a comb; search thoroughly.

combat *n.* a battle, a contest. ● *v.* (**combated, combating**) oppose, try to stop or destroy. ▫ **combative** *adj.*

combatant *adj.* & *n.* (a person or nation) engaged in fighting.

combe var. of **coomb**.

combination *n.* **1** combining or being combined; a set of united but distinct elements. **2** (**combinations**) *dated* an undergarment covering the body and legs.

combination lock *n.* a lock controlled by a series of positions of dials.

combine *v.* (kŏm-**byn**) put together, join, unite. ● *n.* (**kom**-byn). **1** a combination of people or firms acting together. **2** (in full **combine harvester**) a combined reaping and threshing machine.

combining form *n.* a word or partial word used in combination with another to form a different word, e.g. *Anglo-*.

combustible *adj.* capable of catching fire.

combustion *n.* burning; the process in which substances combine with oxygen and produce heat.

come *v.* (**came, come, coming**) move towards the speaker or a place or point; arrive; occur; pass into a specified state; originate from a specified place; have a specified place in an ordering. ▫ **come about** happen. **come across 1** find by chance. **2** make a particular impression. **come by** obtain. **come into** inherit. **come off** be successful. **come out** become known; cease to be secretive. **come round. 1** recover consciousness. **2** be persuaded. **come to** regain consciousness. **come up** occur; arise for discussion. ▫ **coming** *adj.*

comeback *n.* **1** a return to a former successful position. **2** a retort.

comedian *n.* a humorous entertainer or actor.

comedienne *n.* a female comedian.

comedown *n.* a fall in status.

comedy *n.* (*pl.* **-ies**) an amusing book, film, or play; the amusing aspect of a series of events etc.

comely *adj.* (**comelier, comeliest**) *archaic* attractive. ▫ **comeliness** *n.*

comestibles *n.pl. formal* food.

comet *n.* a heavenly body with a luminous tail of gas and dust.

come-uppance *n. informal* deserved punishment.

comfort *n.* a state of ease and contentment; relief of suffering or grief; a person or thing giving this. ● *v.* relieve the grief of. ▫ **comforter** *n.*

comfortable *adj.* **1** providing or enjoying physical or mental ease. **2** adequate; easy. ▫ **comfortably** *adv.*

comfy *adj.* (**comfier, comfiest**) *informal* comfortable.

comic *adj.* causing amusement; of comedy. ● *n.* **1** a comedian. **2** a children's paper with a series of strip cartoons. □ **comical** *adj.*, **comically** *adv.*

comic strip *n.* a sequence of drawings telling a story.

comma *n.* a punctuation mark (,).

command *n.* **1** an order, an instruction; authority; forces or a district under a commander. **2** skill in using something. ● *v.* **1** give an order to; have authority over. **2** be reliably able to get or control.

commandant *n.* an officer in command of a military establishment.

commandeer *v.* seize for use.

commander *n.* a person in command; a naval officer next below captain; a police officer next below commissioner.

commandment *n.* a rule to be strictly observed.

commando *n.* (*pl.* **commandos**) a member of a military unit specially trained for making raids and assaults.

commemorate *v.* keep in the memory by a celebration or memorial. □ **commemoration** *n.*, **commemorative** *adj.*

commence *v.* begin. □ **commencement** *n.*

commend *v.* **1** praise. **2** entrust. □ **commendation** *n.*

commendable *adj.* worthy of praise. □ **commendably** *adv.*

commensurable *adj.* measurable by the same standard. □ **commensurability** *n.*, **commensurably** *adv.*

commensurate *adj.* proportionate, corresponding.

comment *n.* an expression of opinion; an explanatory note. ● *v.* make a comment.

commentary *n.* (*pl.* **-ies**) **1** the making of comments; a set of notes on a text. **2** an account of an event, given as it occurs.

commentator *n.* a person who gives a commentary on an event. □ **commentate** *v.*

commerce *n.* all forms of trade and business.

commercial *adj.* of or engaged in commerce; intended to make a profit. □ **commercially** *adv.*

commercialize *v.* (also **-ise**) operate (a business etc.) so as to make a profit. □ **commercialization** *n.*

commiserate *v.* sympathize, express pity. □ **commiseration** *n.*

commissariat *n.* a military department supplying food.

commission *n.* **1** a task, an instruction; an order for a piece of work; a group of people given official authority to do something. **2** a sum paid to an agent selling goods or services. **3** a warrant conferring the rank of officer in the armed forces. **4** committing an offence. ● *v.* **1** give an instruction to; authorize; create an officer. **2** place an order for. □ **in commission** ready for service. **out of commission** not in working order.

commissionaire *n.* a uniformed attendant at the door of a theatre, business premises, etc.

commissioner *n.* a member of, or a person appointed by, a commission; a government official in charge of a district abroad.

commit *v.* (**committed, committing**) **1** do, carry out (a crime etc.). **2** bind to a course of action. **3** entrust, consign.

commitment *n.* dedication; an obligation; a binding pledge.

committal *n.* committing to prison etc.

committee *n.* a group of people appointed to attend to special business or manage the affairs of a club etc.

■ **Usage Committee** is spelt with two *m*'s and two *t*'s

commode *n.* **1** a seat containing a chamber pot. **2** a chest of drawers.

commodious *adj.* roomy.

commodity *n.* (*pl.* **-ies**) an article to be bought and sold; something valuable.

commodore *n.* a naval officer next below rear admiral; a president of a yacht club.

common *adj.* **1** found or done often; not rare. **2** generally or widely shared. **3** ordinary, undistinguished. **4** vulgar. ● *n.* an area of unfenced grassland for public use.

commoner *n.* one of the common people, not a noble.

common law *n.* an unwritten law based on custom and former court decisions.

commonly *adv.* usually, frequently.

Common Market *n.* the European Community.

commonplace *adj.* ordinary; lacking originality. ● *n.* something widely recognized; a trite remark.

common room *n.* a room shared by students or workers for social purposes.

common sense *n.* normal good sense in practical matters.

commonwealth *n.* an independent state; a federation of states; (**the Commonwealth**) an association of Britain and independent states formerly under British rule.

commotion *n.* uproar, confusion, disturbance.

communal *adj.* shared among a group. □ **communally** *adv.*

commune *v.* (kŏ-**mewn**) communicate mentally or spiritually. ● *n.* (**kom**-yoon) **1** a group (not all of one family) sharing accommodation and goods. **2** a district of local government in France etc.

communicable *adj.* able to be made known or transmitted to others.

communicant *n.* a person who receives Holy Communion.

communicate *v.* **1** exchange news and information; pass on (information); transmit, convey. **2** (of two rooms) have a common connecting door. **3** receive Holy Communion. □ **communicator** *n.*

communication *n.* sharing or imparting information; a letter or message; (**communications**) means of communicating or of travelling.

communicative *adj.* talkative, willing to give information.

communion *n.* **1** sharing thoughts and feelings, communing. **2** a branch of the Christian Church; (**(Holy) Communion**) a sacrament in which bread and wine are shared.

communiqué (kŏ-**mew**-ni-kay) *n.* an official announcement or statement.

communism *n.* a social system based on common ownership of property, means of production, etc.; a political doctrine or movement seeking a form of this. □ **communist** *n.* & *adj.*

community *n.* (*pl.* **-ies**) **1** a body of people living in one place or united by origin, interests, etc.; the public, society. **2** similarity or identity.

commutable *adj.* **1** enabling one to commute between home and work. **2** exchangeable.

commute *v.* **1** travel regularly between one's home and workplace. **2** exchange, replace; make (a sentence) less severe. □ **commuter** *n.*

compact *adj.* (kŏm-**pakt**) closely or neatly packed together; concise. ● *v.* (kŏm-**pakt**) compress. ● *n.* (**kom**-pakt) **1** a small flat case for face powder. **2** a pact, a contract.

compact disc *n.* a small disc from which sound etc. is reproduced by laser action.

companion *n.* a person living or travelling with another; a thing designed to complement another. □ **companionship** *n.*

companionable *adj.* sociable.

companionway *n.* a staircase from a ship's deck to cabins etc.

company *n.* (*pl.* **-ies**) **1** being with other people; companionship; a group of people. **2** a commercial business. **3** a subdivision of an infantry battalion.

comparable *adj.* suitable to be compared, similar. ▫ **comparability** *n.*, **comparably** *adv.*

comparative *adj.* involving comparison; based on or judged by comparing; of the grammatical form expressing 'more'. ● *n.* a comparative form of a word. ▫ **comparatively** *adv.*

compare *v.* **1** assess the similarity of. **2** declare to be similar. **3** be of equal quality with something. ▫ **beyond compare** outstanding, unparalleled.

comparison *n.* comparing.

compartment *n.* a partitioned space. ▫ **compartmental** *adj.*

compass *n.* **1** a device showing the direction of the magnetic or true north. **2** range, scope. **3** (**compasses**) a hinged instrument for drawing circles. ● *v.* **1** surround; include. **2** achieve.

compassion *n.* a feeling of pity. ▫ **compassionate** *adj.*, **compassionately** *adv.*

compatible *adj.* able to exist or be used together; consistent. ▫ **compatibility** *n.*, **compatibly** *adv.*

compatriot *n.* a fellow countryman.

compel *v.* (**compelled, compelling**) force.

compelling *adj.* very interesting, fascinating; irresistible; very convincing.

compendious *adj.* giving much information concisely.

compendium *n.* (*pl.* **compendia** or **compendiums**) a summary; a collection of information etc.

compensate *v.* make payment to (a person) in return for loss or damage; counterbalance, offset something. ▫ **compensation** *n.*, **compensatory** *adj.*

compère (**kom**-pair) *n.* a person who introduces performers in a variety show. ● *v.* act as compère to.

compete *v.* try to win something by defeating others; take part in a competition.

competence *n.* **1** ability, efficiency. **2** authority.

competent *adj.* **1** skilled and efficient. **2** authorized to do something. ▫ **competently** *adv.*

competition *n.* an event in which people try to outdo others; competing; one's rivals in a competition.

competitive *adj.* involving competition; enjoying competition, anxious to win. ▫ **competitively** *adv.*, **competitiveness** *n.*

competitor *n.* one who competes.

compile *v.* collect and arrange into a list or book; make (a book) in this way. ▫ **compilation** *n.*, **compiler** *n.*

complacent *adj.* not worrying about one's abilities, a situation, etc.; self-satisfied. ▫ **complacency** *n.*, **complacently** *adv.*

▪ **Usage** Do not confuse *complacent* with *complaisant.*

complain *v.* express dissatisfaction or pain. ▫ **complainant** *n.*

complaint *n.* **1** a declaration of dissatisfaction or annoyance. **2** an illness.

complaisant *adj.* willing to please others. ▫ **complaisance** *n.*

▪ **Usage** Do not confuse *complaisant* with *complacent.*

complement *n.* a thing that completes or balances something else; the full number required. ● *v.* form a complement to. ▫ **complementary** *adj.*

▪ **Usage** See note at *compliment.*

complete *adj.* having all its parts, entire; finished; total, absolute. ● *v.* make complete; fill in (a form). ▫ **completely** *adv.*, **completeness** *n.*, **completion** *n.*

complex *adj.* made up of many parts; complicated, hard to understand. ● *n.* **1** a complex whole; a group of buildings. **2** a set of unconscious feelings affecting behaviour. □ **complexity** *n.*

complexion *n.* the colour and texture of the skin of the face; the general character of things.

compliant *adj.* complying, obedient. □ **compliance** *n.*

complicate *v.* make complicated.

complicated *adj.* difficult because complex and confused.

complication *n.* being complicated; a factor causing this; a secondary disease aggravating an existing one.

complicity *n.* involvement in wrongdoing.

compliment *n.* a polite expression of praise. ● *v.* pay a compliment to.

■ **Usage** *Compliment* and *complimentary* are often confused with *complement* and *complementary*. The correct usage is shown in *He complimented her on the way her coat complemented her suit*; one can have *complimentary tickets* but not *complimentary medicine*.

---

complimentary *adj.* **1** expressing a compliment. **2** free of charge.

compline *n.* (esp. in the RC Church) the last service of the day.

comply *v.* (**complied, complying**) act in accordance with a request.

component *n.* one of the parts of which a thing is composed.

comport *v.* □ **comport oneself** conduct oneself, behave.

compose *v.* **1** create (a work of music or literature). **2** (of parts) make up (a whole). **3** calm; cause to appear calm. **4** prepare (a text) for printing. □ **composer** *n.*

composite *adj.* made up of parts.

composition *n.* **1** something's elements and the way it is made up; composing. **2** a musical or literary work. **3** a compound artificial substance.

compositor *n.* a typesetter.

compos mentis *adj.* sane.

compost *n.* decayed organic matter used as fertilizer.

composure *n.* calmness.

compote *n.* fruit in syrup.

compound *adj.* (**kom**-pownd) made up of two or more elements. ● *n.* (**kom**-pownd) **1** a compound substance. **2** a fenced-in enclosure. ● *v.* (kŏm-**pownd**) **1** combine; make by combining. **2** make worse. **3** settle by agreement.

comprehend *v.* **1** understand. **2** include.

comprehensible *adj.* intelligible. □ **comprehensibility** *n.*, **comprehensibly** *adv.*

comprehension *n.* understanding.

comprehensive *adj.* including much or all. ● *n.* (in full **comprehensive school**) a school providing secondary education for children of all abilities. □ **comprehensively** *adv.*, **comprehensiveness** *n.*

compress *v.* (kŏm-**press**) squeeze, force into less space. ● *n.* (**kom**-press) a pad to stop bleeding or to reduce inflammation. □ **compression** *n.*, **compressor** *n.*

comprise *v.* consist of.

■ **Usage** It is a mistake to use *comprise* to mean 'to compose or make up'.

---

compromise *n.* a settlement reached by concessions on each side. ● *v.* **1** make a settlement in this way. **2** expose to suspicion, scandal, or danger.

comptroller (kŏn-**troh**-ler) *n.* (in titles) a financial controller.

compulsion *n.* forcing or being forced; an irresistible urge.

compulsive *adj.* **1** resulting from or driven by an irresistible urge. **2** fascinating, gripping. □ **compulsively** *adv.*

compulsory *adj.* required by a law or rule. □ **compulsorily** *adv.*

compunction *n.* regret, scruple.

compute *v.* calculate; use a computer. □ **computation** *n.*

computer *n.* an electronic device for analysing or storing data, making calculations, etc.

computerize *v.* (also **-ise**) equip with, perform, or operate by computer. ◻ **computerization** *n.*

comrade *n.* a companion, an associate. **comradeship** ● *n.*

con *v.* (**conned, conning**) **1** *informal* trick, cheat. **2** (*Amer.* **conn**) direct the steering of (a ship). ● *n. informal* a confidence trick. ◻ **pros and cons** *see* **pro.**

concatenation *n.* a connected series.

concave *adj.* curving inwards like the inner surface of a ball.

conceal *v.* hide, keep secret. ◻ **concealment** *n.*

concede *v.* admit to be true; grant (a privilege etc.); admit defeat in (a contest); yield.

conceit *n.* **1** excessive pride in oneself. **2** a fanciful idea or figure of speech.

conceited *adj.* vain, arrogant.

conceivable *adj.* able to be imagined or grasped. ◻ **conceivably** *adv.*

conceive *v.* **1** become pregnant (with). **2** form (an idea etc.) in the mind.

concentrate *v.* **1** focus all one's attention. **2** gather together in a small area; make less dilute. ● *n.* a concentrated substance. ◻ **concentrated** *adj.*, **concentration** *n.*

concentration camp *n.* a prison camp for political prisoners etc., esp. associated with Nazi Germany.

concentric *adj.* having the same centre. ◻ **concentrically** *adv.*

concept *n.* an idea, a general notion. ◻ **conceptual** *adj.*

conception *n.* **1** conceiving. **2** an idea.

conceptualize *v.* (also **-ise**) form a concept of. ◻ **conceptualization** *n.*

concern *v.* **1** be about. **2** be relevant to; involve. **3** make anxious. ● *n.* **1** anxiety. **2** something in which one is interested or involved. **3** a business, a firm.

concerned *adj.* anxious.

concerning *prep.* on the subject of.

concert *n.* a musical entertainment.

concerted *adj.* done in combination.

concertina *n.* a portable musical instrument with bellows and buttons. ● *v.* (**concertinaed, concertinaing**) fold or collapse like concertina bellows.

concerto (kŏn-**chair**-toh) *n.* (*pl.* **concertos** or **concerti**) a musical composition for solo instrument and orchestra.

concession *n.* something granted; granting, yielding; an allowance or reduced price.

conch *n.* a spiral shell.

conciliate *v.* make less hostile or angry. ◻ **conciliation** *n.*, **conciliatory** *adj.*

concise *adj.* saying briefly all that is needed. ◻ **concisely** *adv.*, **conciseness** *n.*

conclave *n.* a private meeting.

conclude *v.* **1** end; settle finally. **2** reach an opinion by reasoning.

conclusion *n.* **1** an ending. **2** an opinion reached.

conclusive *adj.* decisive; settling an issue. ◻ **conclusively** *adv.*

concoct *v.* prepare from ingredients; invent. ◻ **concoction** *n.*

concomitant *adj.* accompanying, associated.

concord *n.* agreement, harmony.

concordance *n.* **1** an index of the words in a text. **2** *formal* agreement.

concordant *adj.* in agreement.

concourse *n.* **1** a large open area at a railway station etc. **2** *formal* a crowd.

concrete *n.* a mixture of gravel and cement etc., used for building. ● *adj.* material, physical, not abstract; definite. ● *v.* cover or fix with concrete.

concubine *n.* a secondary wife (in polygamous societies); a woman who lives with a man as his wife but is not married to him.

concur *v.* (**concurred, concurring**) **1** agree in opinion. **2** happen together, coincide. □ **concurrence** *n.*, **concurrent** *adj.*, **concurrently** *adv.*

concuss *v.* affect with concussion.

concussion *n.* temporary unconsciousness caused by a blow on the head.

condemn *v.* **1** express strong disapproval of; declare unfit for use. **2** sentence; doom; prove guilty. □ **condemnation** *n.*

condensation *n.* **1** droplets of water formed on a cold surface in contact with humid air. **2** condensing.

condense *v.* **1** make denser or briefer. **2** change from gas or vapour to liquid.

condenser *n.* **1** an apparatus for condensing vapour. **2** *Electricity* = **capacitor**.

condescend *v.* behave patronizingly; do something one believes to be beneath one. □ **condescending** *adj.*, **condescension** *n.*

condiment *n.* a seasoning for food.

condition *n.* **1** the state something is in; (**conditions**) circumstances. **2** something that is necessary if something else is to exist or occur. ● *v.* **1** influence, determine; train, accustom. **2** bring into the desired condition.

conditional *adj.* subject to specified conditions. □ **conditionally** *adv.*

conditioner *n.* a substance that improves the condition of hair, fabric, etc.

condole *v.* express sympathy. □ **condolence** *n.*

condom *n.* a contraceptive sheath.

condominium *n.* **1** the joint control of a state's affairs by other states. **2** *Amer.* a building containing flats which are individually owned.

condone *v.* forgive or overlook (a fault etc.).

condor *n.* a large vulture.

conduce *v.* help to cause or produce something. □ **conducive** *adj.*

conduct *v.* (kŏn-**dukt**) **1** lead, guide; be the conductor of. **2** manage; carry out. **3** transmit (heat or electricity). ● *n.* (**kon**-dukt) behaviour; a way of conducting business etc.

conduction *n.* the conducting of heat or electricity. □ **conductive** *adj.*, **conductivity** *n.*

conductor *n.* **1** a person who directs an orchestra's or choir's performance. **2** a substance that conducts heat or electricity. **3** a person collecting fares on a bus.

conduit *n.* **1** a channel for liquid. **2** a tube protecting electric wires.

cone *n.* **1** an object with a circular base, tapering to a point. **2** a dry scaly fruit of a pine or fir.

coney (also **cony**) *n.* a rabbit; its fur.

confection *n.* an elaborate sweet dish; an elaborately constructed thing.

confectioner *n.* a maker or seller of confectionery.

confectionery *n.* sweets, cakes, and pastries.

confederacy *n.* (*pl.* **-ies**) a league of states.

confederate *adj.* joined by treaty or agreement. ● *n.* a member of a confederacy; an accomplice.

confederation *n.* a union of states, people, or organizations.

confer *v.* (**conferred, conferring**) **1** grant (a title etc.). **2** hold a discussion. □ **conferment** *n.*

conference *n.* a meeting for discussion.

confess *v.* acknowledge, admit; declare one's sins to a priest.

confession *n.* an acknowledgement of a fact, sin, guilt, etc.; a statement of beliefs.

confessional *n.* an enclosed stall in a church for hearing confessions.

confessor *n.* a priest who hears confessions and gives counsel.

confetti *n.* bits of coloured paper thrown at a bride and bridegroom.

confidant *n.* a person in whom one confides.

■ **Usage** The nouns *confidant*, *confidante* are spelt with an *a*; the adjective *confident* is spelt with an *e*.

---

confidante *n.* a woman in whom one confides.

confide *v.* tell someone about a secret; entrust to someone.

confidence *n.* trust; certainty; boldness; something told in secret.

confidence trick *n.* a swindle worked by gaining a person's trust.

confident *adj.* feeling confidence. □ **confidently** *adv.*

confidential *adj.* to be kept secret; entrusted with secrets. □ **confidentiality** *n.*, **confidentially** *adv.*

configuration *n.* an arrangement, a form, an outline.

confine *v.* keep within limits; keep shut up.

confinement *n.* **1** confining, being confined. **2** the time of childbirth.

confines *n.pl.* boundaries.

confirm *v.* **1** establish the truth of; make definite. **2** administer the rite of confirmation to. □ **confirmatory** *adj.*

confirmation *n.* **1** confirming, being confirmed. **2** a Christian rite admitting a baptized person to full church membership.

confiscate *v.* take or seize by authority. □ **confiscation** *n.*

conflagration *n.* a great fire.

conflate *v.* combine into one. □ **conflation** *n.*

conflict *n.* (**kon**-flikt) a fight, a struggle; disagreement. ● *v.* (kŏn-**flikt**) clash, be incompatible.

confluence *n.* a place where two rivers unite.

confluent *adj.* merging.

conform *v.* comply with rules, standards, or conventions. □ **conformity** *n.*

conformable *adj.* **1** ready to conform. **2** consistent with something. □ **conformably** *adv.*

conformist *n.* a person who conforms to rules or custom. □ **conformism** *n.*

confound *v.* surprise and confuse; prove wrong; defeat.

confront *v.* be or come or bring face to face with; face boldly. □ **confrontation** *n.*

confuse *v.* **1** bewilder. **2** mix up, identify wrongly. **3** make muddled or unclear. □ **confusion** *n.*

confute *v.* prove wrong. □ **confutation** *n.*

conga *n.* a dance in which people form a long winding line.

congeal *v.* coagulate, solidify.

congenial *adj.* pleasant, agreeable to oneself. □ **congenially** *adv.*

congenital *adj.* being so from birth. □ **congenitally** *adv.*

conger *n.* a large sea eel.

congested *adj.* over full; blocked up; (of the nose) blocked with mucus. □ **congestion** *n.*

conglomerate *n.* (kŏn-**glom**-er-ăt) a number of things grouped together; a corporation formed from a merger of firms. ● *adj.* (kŏn-**glom**-ĕr-ăt) massed together. ● *v.* (kŏn-**glom**-er-ayt) gather into a mass; form a conglomerate. □ **conglomeration** *n.*

congratulate *v.* express pleasure at the good fortune of; praise the achievements of. □ **congratulation** *n.*, **congratulatory** *adj.*

congregate *v.* flock together.

congregation *n.* people assembled at a church service.

congress *n.* a formal meeting of delegates for discussion; (**Congress**) a law-making assembly, esp. of the USA. □ **congressional** *adj.*

congruent *adj.* **1** consistent. **2** *Geometry* of identical shape and size. □ **congruence** *n.*

conic *adj.* of a cone.

conical *adj.* cone-shaped.

conifer *n.* a tree bearing cones. ▫ **coniferous** *adj.*

conjecture *n.* & *v.* (a) guess.

conjugal *adj.* of marriage.

conjugate *v. Grammar* give the different forms of (a verb). ▫ **conjugation** *n.*

conjunction *n.* **1** a word such as 'and' or 'or' that connects others. **2** a combination; simultaneous occurrence.

conjunctivitis *n.* inflammation of the membrane connecting the eyeball and eyelid.

conjure *v.* produce as though by magic; summon, evoke.

conjuror (also **conjurer**) *n.* a person who performs sleight-of-hand tricks for entertainment.

conk *informal n.* the nose; the head. ● *v.* hit. ▫ **conk out** break down.

conn *v.* Amer. sp. of **con** (*sense 2*).

connect *v.* join, be joined; associate mentally; put into contact by telephone; (of a train, coach, or flight) arrive so that passengers are in time to catch another. ▫ **connective** *adj.*, **connector** *n.*

connection *n.* **1** a link, linking; a place where things connect; connecting trains etc. **2** (**connections**) influential friends or relatives.

connive *v.* ▫ **connive at** secretly allow. ▫ **connivance** *n.*

connoisseur (kon-ŏ-**ser**) *n.* an expert, esp. in artistic subjects.

connote *v.* (of a word) imply in addition to its literal meaning. ▫ **connotation** *n.*

conquer *v.* overcome in war or by effort. ▫ **conqueror** *n.*

conquest *n.* conquering; something won by conquering.

conscience *n.* a sense of right and wrong guiding a person's actions.

conscientious *adj.* **1** diligent in one's duty. **2** relating to conscience. ▫ **conscientiously** *adv.*, **conscientiousness** *n.*

conscientious objector *n.* a person who refuses to serve in the armed forces for moral reasons.

conscious *adj.* **1** awake and alert; aware. **2** intentional. ▫ **consciously** *adv.*, **consciousness** *n.*

conscript *v.* (kŏn-**skript**) summon for compulsory military service. ● *n.* (**kon**-skript) a conscripted person. ▫ **conscription** *n.*

consecrate *v.* make sacred; *informal* devote to a particular purpose. ▫ **consecration** *n.*

consecutive *adj.* following in unbroken sequence. ▫ **consecutively** *adv.*

consensus *n.* general agreement.

consent *v.* agree; give permission. ● *n.* permission; agreement.

consequence *n.* **1** a result. **2** importance.

consequent *adj.* resulting.

consequential *adj.* **1** resulting. **2** important. ▫ **consequentially** *adv.*

consequently *adv.* as a result.

conservancy *n.* (*pl.* **-ies**) **1** an authority controlling a river etc. **2** official conservation.

conservation *n.* conserving; preservation of the natural environment.

conservationist *n.* a person who seeks to preserve the natural environment.

conservative *adj.* **1** opposed to change; (**Conservative**) of the Conservative Party. **2** (of an estimate) purposely low. ● *n.* a conservative person; (**Conservative**) a member of the Conservative Party. ▫ **conservatively** *adv.*, **conservatism** *n.*

Conservative party *n.* a British political party promoting free enterprise and private ownership.

conservatoire *n.* a school of music or other arts.

conservatory *n.* (*pl.* **-ies**) a greenhouse built on to a house.

conserve *v.* (kŏn-**serv**) keep from harm, decay, or loss. ● *n.* (**kon**-serv) jam. ▫ **conservator** *n.*

consider *v.* **1** think about, esp. in order to decide. **2** believe; think. **3** take into account.

considerable *adj.* great in amount or importance. ▫ **considerably** *adv.*

considerate *adj.* careful not to hurt or inconvenience others. ▫ **considerately** *adv.*

consideration *n.* **1** careful thought; a factor taken into account in making a decision; being considerate. **2** a payment or reward.

considering *prep.* taking into account.

consign *v.* deliver, send; put for disposal.

consignee *n.* a person to whom goods are sent.

consignment *n.* **1** a batch of goods sent to someone. **2** consigning.

consist *v.* ▫ **consist of** be composed of.

consistency *n.* (*pl.* **-ies**) **1** being consistent. **2** the degree of thickness or solidity of semi-liquid matter.

consistent *adj.* **1** unchanging. **2** not conflicting; free from contradictions. ▫ **consistently** *adv.*

console[1] (kŏn-**sohl**) *v.* comfort in time of sorrow. ▫ **consolable** *adj.*, **consolation** *n.*

console[2] (**kon**-sohl) *n.* **1** a panel holding controls for electronic equipment. **2** a bracket supporting a shelf.

consolidate *v.* **1** make stronger or more secure. **2** combine. ▫ **consolidation** *n.*

consommé (kŏn-**som**-ay) *n.* clear soup.

consonant *n.* a sound made by obstructing the breath, a sound other than a vowel; a letter representing this. ● *adj.* in agreement. ▫ **consonance** *n.*, **consonantal** *adj.*

consort *n.* (**kon**-sort) a husband or wife, esp. of a monarch. ● *v.* (kŏn-**sort**) associate with someone.

consortium *n.* (*pl.* **consortia** or **consortiums**) a combination of firms acting together.

conspicuous *adj.* easily seen, attracting attention. ▫ **conspicuously** *adv.*

conspiracy *n.* (*pl.* **-ies**) a secret plan made by a group; conspiring.

conspire *v.* **1** plot secretly in a group to do something wrong. **2** (of events) combine to produce an effect as though deliberately. ▫ **conspirator** *n.*, **conspiratorial** *adj.*, **conspiratorially** *adv.*

constable *n.* a police officer of the lowest rank.

constabulary *n.* (*pl.* **-ies**) a police force.

constancy *n.* **1** faithfulness. **2** the quality of being unchanging.

constant *adj.* occurring continuously or repeatedly; unchanging; faithful. ● *n.* an unvarying quantity. ▫ **constantly** *adv.*

constellation *n.* a group of stars.

consternation *n.* great surprise and anxiety or dismay.

constipation *n.* difficulty in emptying the bowels. ▫ **constipated** *adj.*

constituency *n.* (*pl.* **-ies**) a body of voters who elect a representative; an area represented in this way.

constituent *adj.* forming part of a whole. ● *n.* **1** a constituent part. **2** a member of a constituency.

constitute *v.* be the parts of.

constitution *n.* **1** the principles by which a state is organized. **2** the general condition of the body. **3** the composition of something.

constitutional *adj.* of or in accordance with a constitution. ● *n.* *dated* a walk taken for exercise.

constrain *v.* compel, oblige.

constraint *n.* a restriction; stiffness and embarrassment.

constrict *v.* make or become narrower; squeeze; restrict. ▫ **constriction** *n.*, **constrictor** *n.*

construct *v.* (kŏn-**strukt**) make by placing parts together. ● *n.* (**kon**-strukt) something constructed, esp. in the mind. ▫ **constructor** *n.*

construction *n.* **1** constructing; a thing constructed. **2** an interpretation. **3** the arrangement of words in a sentence etc.

constructive *adj.* (of criticism etc.) helpful, giving advice. □ **constructively** *adv.*

construe *v.* interpret; analyse word for word.

consul *n.* an official representative of a state in a foreign city. □ **consular** *adj.*

consulate *n.* a consul's position or premises.

consult *v.* seek information or advice from. □ **consultation** *n.*

consultant *n.* a specialist consulted for professional advice. □ **consultancy** *n.*

consultative *adj.* of or for consultation; advisory.

consume *v.* eat or drink; use up; (of fire) destroy; absorb, obsess.

consumer *n.* a person who buys or uses goods or services.

consummate *v.* (**kon**-sŭ-mayt) accomplish; complete (esp. marriage by sexual intercourse). ● *adj.* (kon-**sum**-măt) highly skilled, perfect. □ **consummation** *n.*

consumption *n.* **1** consuming. **2** *dated* tuberculosis.

consumptive *adj.* & *n.* *dated* (a person) suffering from tuberculosis.

cont. *abbr.* continued.

contact *n.* touching; communication; an electrical connection; a person who may be contacted for information or help. ● *v.* get in touch with.

contact lens *n.* a small lens worn directly on the eyeball to correct the vision.

contagion *n.* spreading of disease by contact. □ **contagious** *adj.*

contain *v.* **1** have within itself; include. **2** control, restrain.

container *n.* a receptacle; a metal box of standard design for transporting goods.

containment *n.* restricting the growth of something dangerous or hostile.

contaminate *v.* pollute. □ **contaminant** *n.*, **contamination** *n.*

contemplate *v.* **1** gaze at. **2** consider as a possibility, intend; meditate. □ **contemplation** *n.*

contemplative *adj.* meditative; of religious meditation.

contemporaneous *adj.* existing or occurring at the same time.

contemporary *adj.* **1** living or occurring at the same time. **2** modern. ● *n.* (*pl.* **-ies**) a person of the same age or living at the same time.

contempt *n.* despising or being despised; disrespectful disregard or disobedience.

contemptible *adj.* deserving contempt.

contemptuous *adj.* showing contempt. □ **contemptuously** *adv.*

contend *v.* **1** struggle; compete. **2** assert, argue. □ **contender** *n.*

content[1] (kŏn-**tent**) *adj.* satisfied with what one has. ● *n.* satisfaction. ● *v.* satisfy. □ **contented** *adj.*, **contentment** *n.*

content[2] (**kon**-tent) *n.* (also **contents**) what is contained in something; the subject matter of a book etc.

contention *n.* **1** disagreement, conflict. **2** an assertion.

contentious *adj.* quarrelsome; disputed heatedly.

contest *v.* (kŏn-**test**) compete for or in; oppose; argue about. ● *n.* (**kon**-test) a struggle for victory; a competition. □ **contestant** *n.*

context *n.* what precedes or follows a word or statement and fixes its meaning; circumstances. □ **contextual** *adj.*

contiguous *adj.* adjacent, touching. □ **contiguity** *n.*

continent[1] *n.* one of the earth's main land masses. □ **continental** *adj.*

continent[2] *adj.* able to control the excretion of one's urine and faeces; self-restrained. □ **continence** *n.*

contingency *n.* (*pl.* **-ies**) a possible but unpredictable occurrence.

contingent *adj.* **1** subject to chance. **2** depending on other circumstances. **3** not logically necessary. ● *n.* a body of troops contributed to a larger group.

continual *adj.* constantly or frequently recurring. □ **continually** *adv.*

continue *v.* **1** not cease; remain in existence, in a place or condition. **2** resume; extend. □ **continuance** *n.*, **continuation** *n.*

continuo *n.* (*pl.* **continuos**) *Music* a (keyboard) accompaniment providing a bass line.

continuous *adj.* without interval, uninterrupted. □ **continuity** *n.*, **continuously** *adv.*

continuum *n.* (*pl.* **continua**) a sequence with gradual development from one extreme to another.

contort *v.* force or twist out of normal shape. □ **contortion** *n.*

contortionist *n.* a performer who can twist his or her body dramatically.

contour *n.* an outline; a line on a map showing height above sea level.

contra- *pref.* against.

contraband *adj.* & *n.* smuggled (goods).

contraception *n.* the prevention of pregnancy, birth control.

contraceptive *adj.* & *n.* (a drug or device) preventing conception.

contract *n.* (**kon**-trakt) a formal agreement. ● *v.* (kŏn-**trakt**) **1** make or become smaller or shorter. **2** make a contract; arrange by contract for (work) to be done. **3** catch (an illness). □ **contractor** *n.*, **contractual** *adj.*

contractable *adj.* (of a disease) able to be contracted.

contractible *adj.* able to be shrunk or drawn together.

contractile *adj.* able to contract or to produce contraction.

contraction *n.* making or becoming smaller; a shortened form of a word or words; a shortening of the uterine muscles during childbirth.

contradict *v.* say that (a statement) is untrue or (a person) is wrong; conflict with. □ **contradiction** *n.*

contradictory *adj.* inconsistent; containing inconsistencies.

contraflow *n.* a flow (esp. of traffic) in a direction opposite to and alongside the usual flow.

contralto *n.* (*pl.* **contraltos**) the lowest female voice.

contraption *n.* a strange device or machine.

contrapuntal *adj.* of or in counterpoint.

contrariwise *adv.* on the other hand; in the opposite way.

contrary (**kon**-tră-ri) *adj.* **1** opposite in nature, tendency, or direction. **2** (kŏn-**trair**-i) *informal* perverse, doing the opposite of what is desired. ● *n.* the opposite. □ **contrary to** conflicting with. **on the contrary** as the opposite of what was just stated. □ **contrarily** *adv.*, **contrariness** *n.*

contrast *n.* (**kon**-trahst) a striking difference; a comparison drawing attention to this. ● *v.* (kŏn-**trahst**) be strikingly different; point out the difference between (two things).

contravene *v.* break (a rule etc.). □ **contravention** *n.*

contretemps (**kon**-trĕ-tahn) *n.* (*pl.* **contretemps**) a minor disagreement.

contribute *v.* give to a common fund or effort; help to cause something. □ **contribution** *n.*, **contributor** *n.*, **contributory** *adj.*

contrite *adj.* remorseful. □ **contritely** *adv.*, **contrition** *n.*

contrivance *n.* contriving; something skilfully made to serve a purpose; artificiality.

contrive *v.* skilfully make or bring about; manage to do.

contrived *adj.* artificial; feeling false.

control *n.* the power to direct, influence, or restrain something; a means of restraining or regulating; a standard for checking the results of an experiment. ● *v.* (**controlled, controlling**) influence; regulate; restrain.

controversial *adj.* causing controversy. □ **controversially** *adv.*

controversy *n.* (*pl.* **-ies**) a prolonged and heated disagreement.

controvert *v.* deny the truth of. □ **controvertible** *adj.*

contumacy (kon-tyoo-mă-see) *n.* stubborn refusal to obey. □ **contumacious** *adj.*

contusion *n.* a bruise.

conundrum *n.* a riddle, a puzzle.

conurbation *n.* a large urban area formed where towns have spread and merged.

convalesce *v.* regain health after illness. □ **convalescence** *n.*, **convalescent** *adj.* & *n.*

convection *n.* the transmission of heat within a liquid or gas by movement of heated particles.

convene *v.* call together; assemble. □ **convener** or **convenor** *n.*

convenience *n.* **1** ease, lack of effort; something contributing to this. **2** a lavatory.

convenient *adj.* involving little trouble or effort; easily accessible. □ **conveniently** *adv.*

convent *n.* a community of nuns; their residence.

convention *n.* **1** an accepted custom; behaviour generally considered correct. **2** an assembly. **3** a formal agreement. □ **conventional** *adj.*, **conventionally** *adv.*

converge *v.* come to or towards the same point. □ **convergence** *n.*, **convergent** *adj.*

conversant *adj.* □ **conversant with** having knowledge of.

conversation *n.* informal talk between people. □ **conversational** *adj.*, **conversationally** *adv.*

converse[1] *v.* (kŏn-vers) hold a conversation.

converse[2] (kon-verss) *adj.* opposite, contrary. ● *n.* the opposite, the reverse. □ **conversely** *adv.*

convert *v.* (kŏn-vert) (cause to) change from one form or use to another; cause to change an attitude or belief. ● *n.* (kon-vert) a person persuaded to adopt a new faith or other belief. □ **conversion** *n.*, **converter** or **convertor** *n.*

convertible *adj.* able to be converted. ● *n.* a car with a folding or detachable roof.

convex *adj.* curved like the outer surface of a ball. □ **convexity** *n.*

convey *v.* transport, carry; communicate; express.

conveyance *n.* **1** transport; a means of transport. **2** the transfer of ownership of property.

conveyancing *n.* the branch of law concerned with transferring ownership of property.

conveyor *n.* a person or thing that conveys; (in full **conveyor belt**) a continuous moving belt conveying objects.

convict *v.* (kŏn-vikt) prove or declare guilty. ● *n.* (kon-vikt) a convicted person in prison.

conviction *n.* **1** a firm belief; confidence. **2** convicting or being convicted.

convince *v.* make (a person) feel certain that something is true.

■ **Usage** *Convince* is often misused to mean 'persuade to do something'.

convivial *adj.* sociable and lively.

convocation *n.* an assembly; summoning an assembly.

convoke *v.* summon to assemble.

convoluted *adj.* complicated; intricately coiled. □ **convolution** *n.*

convolvulus *n.* a twining plant with trumpet-shaped flowers.

convoy *n.* ships or vehicles travelling under escort or together. ● *v.* escort (ships etc.) for protection.

convulse *v.* suffer violent muscle spasms; cause violent movement in; throw into upheaval.

convulsion *n.* a violent involuntary movement of the body; (**convulsions**) uncontrollable laughter. □ **convulsive** *adj.*

cony var. of **coney**.

coo *v.* make a soft murmuring sound like a dove. ● *n.* this sound. ● *int.* an expression of surprise.

cooee *int.* a cry to attract attention.

cook *v.* **1** prepare (food) by heating; undergo this process. **2** *informal* falsify (accounts etc.). ● *n.* a person who cooks, esp. as a job. □ **cook up** *informal* invent (a story etc.).

cooker *n.* a stove for cooking food.

cookery *n.* the art and practice of cooking.

cookie *n. Amer.* a sweet biscuit.

cool *adj.* **1** fairly cold. **2** calm; not enthusiastic or friendly. **3** *informal* sophisticated; excellent. **4** *informal* emphasizing an amount: *a cool five thousand.* ● *n.* **1** low temperature. **2** *informal* calmness; sophistication. ● *v.* make or become cool. □ **coolly** *adv.*, **coolness** *n.*

coolant *n.* fluid for cooling machinery.

cool bag *n.* (also **cool box**) an insulated container for keeping food cool.

coolie *n. dated* a native labourer in Eastern countries.

coomb (koom) *n.* (also **combe**) a valley in a hillside.

coop *n.* a cage for poultry. ● *v.* confine, shut in.

co-op *n. informal* a cooperative society; a shop run by this.

cooper *n.* a person who makes or repairs casks and barrels.

cooperate *v.* work together for a common end. □ **cooperation** *n.*

cooperative *adj.* helpful; involving mutual help; (of a firm etc.) run collectively, based on economic cooperation. ● *n.* a farm or firm etc. run on this basis.

co-opt *v.* appoint to a committee by invitation of existing members, not election.

coordinate *v.* (koh-**ord**-i-nayt) arrange the elements of (a complex whole) to achieve efficiency; negotiate and work with others. ● *adj.* (koh-**ord**-i-năt) equal in importance. ● *n.* (koh-**ord**-i-năt) **1** any of the numbers used to indicate the position of a point. **2** (**coordinates**) matching items of clothing. □ **coordination** *n.*, **coordinator** *n.*

coot *n.* a waterbird.

cop *informal n.* a police officer. ● *v.* (**copped, copping**) catch or arrest. □ **cop it** get into trouble. **cop out** avoid doing something that one ought to.

cope *v.* □ **cope with** deal successfully with; manage successfully.

copeck *n.* var. of **kopeck**.

copier *n.* a copying machine.

coping *n.* the sloping top row of masonry of a wall.

copious *adj.* plentiful. □ **copiously** *adv.*

copper *n.* **1** a reddish-brown metallic element (symbol Cu); a coin containing this; its colour. **2** *informal* a police officer. ● *adj.* made of or coloured like copper.

copper-bottomed *adj.* reliable, esp. financially; genuine.

copperplate *n.* neat round handwriting.

coppice *n.* (also **copse**) a group of small trees and undergrowth.

Coptic *adj.* of the Egyptian branch of the Christian Church.

copula *n. Grammar* the verb *be*.

copulate *v.* have sexual intercourse. □ **copulation** *n.*

copy *n.* (*pl.* **-ies**) a thing made to look like another; a specimen of a book etc.; matter to be printed in a newspaper etc. ● *v.* (**copied, copying**) make a copy of; imitate.

copyright *n.* the sole right to publish a work. ● *v.* secure copyright for.

copywriter *n.* a person who writes advertising copy.

coquette *n.* a woman who flirts. □ **coquetry** *n.*, **coquettish** *adj.*

coracle *n.* a small wicker boat.

coral *n.* a hard red, pink, or white substance built by tiny sea creatures; a reddish-pink colour.

cor anglais (kor **ahng**-lay) *n.* (*pl.* **cors anglais**) a woodwind instrument

corbel *n.* a stone or wooden support projecting from a wall.

cord *n.* **1** long thin flexible material made from twisted strands; a piece of this; an anatomical structure like this. **2** corduroy.

cordial *adj.* warm and friendly. ● *n.* a fruit-flavoured drink. □ **cordially** *adv.*

cordite *n.* a smokeless explosive.

cordless *adj.* (of an electrical appliance or telephone) working without connection to a mains supply.

cordon *n.* **1** a line of police, soldiers, etc., enclosing something. **2** a fruit tree pruned to grow as a single stem. □ **cordon off** enclose with a cordon; isolate.

cordon bleu (kor-don **bler**) *adj.* of the highest class in cookery.

corduroy *n.* cloth with velvety ridges.

core *n.* the central or most important part; the tough central part of an apple etc., containing seeds. ● *v.* remove the core from.

co-respondent *n.* the person with whom the respondent in a divorce suit is said to have committed adultery.

corgi *n.* a dog of a small breed with short legs.

coriander *n.* a fragrant herb.

cork *n.* the light tough bark of a Mediterranean oak; a piece of this used as a float; a bottle stopper. ● *v.* stop up with a cork.

corkage *n.* a restaurant's charge for serving wine brought from elsewhere.

corked *adj.* (of wine) contaminated by a decayed cork.

corkscrew *n.* a device with a spiral rod for extracting corks from bottles; a spiral thing.

corm *n.* a bulb-like underground stem from which buds grow.

cormorant *n.* a large black seabird.

corn *n.* **1** wheat, oats, or maize; grain. **2** *informal* sentimentality; triteness. **3** a small painful area of hardened skin, esp. on the foot.

cornea *n.* the transparent outer covering of the eyeball. □ **corneal** *adj.*

cornelian *n.* (also **carnelian**) a reddish or white semi-precious stone.

corner *n.* an angle where two lines or sides meet; the area around this; a part or aspect; a free kick or hit from the corner of the field in football or hockey. ● *v.* **1** force into a position from which there is no escape. **2** drive round a corner. **3** obtain a monopoly of (a commodity).

cornerstone *n.* a basis; a vital foundation.

cornet *n.* **1** a brass instrument like a small trumpet. **2** a cone-shaped wafer holding ice cream.

cornflour *n.* fine flour made from maize.

cornflower *n.* a blue-flowered plant.

cornice *n.* an ornamental moulding round the top of an indoor wall.

Cornish *adj.* & *n.* (the ancient language) of Cornwall.

cornucopia *n.* a horn-shaped container overflowing with fruit and flowers, symbolizing abundance; a plentiful supply.

corny *adj.* (**cornier, corniest**) *informal* sentimental; hackneyed.

corolla *n.* the petals of a flower.

corollary *n.* (*pl.* **-ies**) a proposition that follows logically from another.

corona *n.* (*pl.* **coronae**) a ring of light round the sun or moon.

coronary *adj.* of the arteries supplying blood to the heart. ● *n.* (*pl.* **-ies**) a blockage in one of these arteries, caused by a blood clot.

coronation *n.* the ceremony of crowning a monarch or consort.

coroner *n.* an officer holding inquests.

coronet *n.* a small crown.

corpora *pl.* of **corpus**.

corporal *n.* a non-commissioned officer next below sergeant. ● *adj.* of the body.

corporal punishment *n.* punishment by whipping or beating.

corporate *adj.* shared by members of a group; united in a group.

corporation *n.* a group in business or elected to govern a town.

corporeal (kor-**por**-ee-ăl) *adj.* having a body, tangible. □ **corporeally** *adv.*

corps (kor) *n.* (*pl.* **corps**) a military unit; an organized body of people.

corpse *n.* a dead body.

corpulent *adj.* fat. □ **corpulence** *n.*

corpus *n.* (*pl.* **corpora**) a collection of writings.

corpuscle *n.* a blood cell.

corral *n. Amer.* an enclosure for cattle. ● *v.* (**corralled, corralling**) put or keep in a corral.

correct *adj.* **1** true; free from errors. **2** conforming to an accepted standard of behaviour. ● *v.* mark or rectify errors in; put right; reprove. □ **correctly** *adv.*, **correctness** *n.*

correction *n.* correcting; an alteration correcting something; *dated* punishment.

corrective *adj.* & *n.* (something) correcting what is bad or harmful.

correlate *v.* be systematically related; analyse such a relation between (two things). □ **correlation** *n.*

correspond *v.* **1** be similar, equivalent, or in harmony. **2** write letters to each other.

correspondence *n.* **1** similarity. **2** writing letters; letters written.

correspondent *n.* **1** a person who writes letters. **2** a person employed by a newspaper or TV news station to gather news and send reports.

corridor *n.* a passage in a building or train giving access to rooms or compartments; a strip of territory giving access to somewhere.

corrie *n.* a round hollow on a mountainside.

corroborate *v.* support, confirm. □ **corroboration** *n.*, **corroborative** *adj.*

corrode *v.* destroy (a metal etc.) gradually by chemical action. □ **corrosion** *n.*, **corrosive** *adj.*

corrugated *adj.* shaped into alternate ridges and grooves. □ **corrugation** *n.*

corrupt *adj.* **1** accepting bribes, dishonest; immoral. **2** (of a text) full of errors. ● *v.* **1** bribe; influence into bad habits.

corruption *n.* **1** decay. **2** bribery; dishonesty. **3** error.

corsair *n.* a pirate ship; a pirate.

corset *n.* a close-fitting undergarment worn to shape or support the body.

cortège (kor-**tayzh**) *n.* a funeral procession.

cortex *n.* (*pl.* **cortices**) the outer part of the brain; an outer layer of tissue. □ **cortical** *adj.*

cortisone *n.* a hormone used in treating allergies.

corvette *n.* a small fast gunboat.

cos *abbr.* cosine.

cosh *n.* a weighted weapon for hitting people. ● *v.* hit with a cosh.

cosine (**koh**-sIn) *n. Maths* the ratio of the side adjacent to an acute angle (in a right-angled triangle) to the hypotenuse.

cosmetic *n.* a substance for beautifying the complexion etc. ● *adj.* improving the appearance; superficial.

cosmic *adj.* of the universe.

cosmic rays *n.pl.* (also **cosmic radiation**) radiation from outer space.

cosmogony *n.* (*pl.* **-ies**) (a theory of) the origin of the universe.

cosmology *n.* the science or theory of the universe. □ **cosmological** *adj.*

cosmonaut *n.* a Russian astronaut.

cosmopolitan *adj.* free from national prejudices; including people from all parts of the world. ● *n.* a cosmopolitan person.

cosmos *n.* the universe.

Cossack *n.* & *adj.* (a member) of a people of southern Russia, famous as horsemen.

cosset *v.* (**cosseted, cosseting**) pamper.

cost *v.* **1** (**cost, costing**) have as its price; involve the sacrifice or loss of; require (someone) to do or give something. **2** (**costed, costing**) estimate the cost of. ● *n.* what a thing costs.

costal *adj.* of the ribs.

co-star *n.* a celebrity performing with another of equal status.

costermonger *n.* a person selling fruit etc. from a barrow in the street.

costly *adj.* (**costlier, costliest**) expensive.

costume *n.* a style of clothes, esp. that of a historical period; garments for a special activity.

cosy *adj.* (*Amer.* **cozy**) (**cosier, cosiest**) **1** warm and comfortable. **2** mutually advantageous. ● *n.* (*pl.* **-ies**) a cover to keep a teapot etc. hot. □ **cosy up to 1** snuggle up to. **2** *informal* ingratiate oneself with. □ **cosily** *adv.*, **cosiness** *n.*

cot *n.* a child's bed with high sides.

cot death *n.* (also **SIDS**) the unexplained death of a sleeping baby.

coterie (koh-ter-ee) *n.* a select group.

cottage *n.* a small simple house, esp. in the country.

cottage cheese *n.* soft white lumpy cheese made from curds.

cottage pie *n.* a dish of minced meat topped with mashed potato.

cotton *n.* a soft white substance round the seeds of a tropical plant; this plant; thread or fabric made from cotton. □ **cotton on** *informal* understand.

cotton wool *n.* fluffy wadding, originally made from raw cotton, used to clean wounds etc.

cotyledon (koti-**lee**-dŏn) *n.* the first leaf growing from a seed.

couch *n.* a sofa. ● *v.* express in a specified way.

couchette (koo-**shet**) *n.* a railway carriage with seats convertible into sleeping berths.

couch potato *n. informal* a person who takes very little exercise and watches a lot of television.

cougar (**koo**-ger) *n. Amer.* a puma.

cough *v.* expel air etc. from the lungs with a sudden sharp sound. ● *n.* the act or sound of coughing; an illness causing coughing. □ **cough up** *informal* say or give something reluctantly.

could past of **can**[2].

coulomb (**koo**-lom) *n.* a unit of electric charge.

council *n.* a formal group meeting regularly for debate and administration; the body governing a town.

■ **Usage** Do not confuse *council*, a formal group which may give advice, with *counsel*, advice given.

councillor *n.* (*Amer.* **councilor**) a member of a council.

council tax *n.* a UK local tax based on property value.

counsel *n.* **1** advice. **2** (*pl.* **counsel**) a barrister. ● *v.* (**counselled, counselling**; *Amer.* **counseled**) advise; give professional psychological help to. □ **counsellor** *n.*

count *v.* **1** find the total of; say numbers in order. **2** include. **3** be important. **4** regard in a specified way. ● *n.* **1** counting; a total reached by counting. **2** a point to consider; a charge. **3** a foreign nobleman. □ **count on** rely on.

countdown *n.* counting seconds backwards to zero; the final period before an important event.

countenance *n.* **1** the face; an expression. **2** approval. ● *v.* give approval to.

counter *n.* **1** a flat-topped fitment over which goods are sold or business transacted with customers. **2** a small disc used in board games. ● *adv.* in the opposite direction; in conflict. ● *adj.* responding; opposed. ● *v.* speak or act against. □ **under the counter** (of trade) secret and illegal.

counter- *pref.* retaliatory; rival; opposite; corresponding.

counteract *v.* reduce or prevent the effects of. □ **counteraction** *n.*

counter-attack *n.* & *v.* (make) an attack in reply to an opponent's attack.

counterbalance *n.* a weight or influence balancing or neutralizing another. ● *v.* act as a counterbalance to.

counterblast *n.* a powerful retort.

counterfeit *adj.* forged, not genuine. ● *n.* a forgery. ● *v.* forge.

counterfoil *n.* a section of a cheque or receipt kept as a record by the person issuing it.

countermand *v.* cancel.

counterpane *n.* a bedspread.

counterpart *n.* a person or thing corresponding to another.

counterpoint *n. Music* a technique of combining melodies; a contrasting theme or element.

counter-productive *adj.* having the opposite of the desired effect.

countersign *v.* add a second signature to (a document already signed by one person).

countersink *v.* (**countersunk, countersinking**) sink (a screw-head) into a shaped cavity so that the surface is level.

counter-tenor *n.* a male alto.

countess *n.* a count's or earl's wife or widow; a woman with the rank of count or earl.

countless *adj.* too many to be counted.

countrified *adj.* (also **countryfied**) rustic in appearance etc.; unsophisticated.

country *n.* (*pl.* **-ies**) **1** a nation with its own government and territory; its people; the state of which one is a member; a region. **2** land outside large towns. □ **go to the country** call a general election.

countryman *n.* (*pl.* **-men**) **1** a person living in the country. **2** a person of one's own country.

countryside *n.* a rural district.

countrywoman *n.* (*pl.* **-women**) **1** a woman living in the country. **2** a woman of one's own country.

county *n.* (*pl.* **-ies**) **1** a major administrative division of some countries. **2** families of high social class long established in a county.

coup (koo) *n.* a very successful action; a coup d'état.

coup de grâce (koo dĕ **grahs**) *n.* a finishing stroke.

coup d'état (koo day-**tah**) *n.* (*pl.* **coups d'état**) the sudden, violent, and illegal overthrow of a government.

coupé *n.* (*Amer.* **coupe**) a closed two-door car with a sloping back.

couple *n.* two people or things; a married or romantically involved pair. ● *v.* fasten or link together; copulate.

couplet *n.* two successive rhyming lines of verse.

coupling *n.* a connecting device.

coupon *n.* a form or ticket entitling the holder to something; an entry form for a football pool.

courage *n.* the ability to control fear when facing danger or pain. □ **courageous** *adj.*, **courageously** *adv.*

courgette (kor-**zhet**) *n.* a small vegetable marrow.

courier (**ku**-ree-ĕ) *n.* **1** a messenger carrying documents **2** a person employed to guide and assist tourists.

course *n.* **1** onward progress; a direction taken or intended. **2** a series of lessons or treatments. **3** an area on which golf is played or a race takes place. **4** a layer of stone etc. in a building. **5** one part of a meal. ● *v.* **1** move or flow freely. **2** pursue (hares etc.) with hounds. □ **a matter of course** a regular and unremarkable procedure. **in course of** undergoing; during. **of course** certainly; naturally; without doubt. **on course for** heading for; likely to achieve.

court *n.* **1** a body of people hearing legal cases; the place where they meet. **2** a courtyard; an area for playing squash, tennis, etc. **3** a sovereign's establishment with attendants. ● *v.* try to win the love or support of; risk (danger etc.).

courteous (ker-tee-ŭs) *adj.* polite. □ **courteously** *adv.*, **courteousness** *n.*

courtesan (kor-ti-zan) *n. literary* a prostitute with high-class clients.

courtesy (ker-tĕ-see) *n.* politeness.

courtier *n.* a sovereign's companion or attendant at court.

courtly *adj.* dignified and polite.

court martial *n.* (*pl.* **courts martial**) a court trying offences against military law; a trial by this. ● *v.* (**court-martial**) (**-martialled, -martialling**; *Amer.* **martialed**) try by such a court.

courtship *n.* courting, wooing.

courtyard *n.* a space enclosed by walls or buildings.

couscous (koos-koos) *n.* a North African dish of crushed wheat.

cousin *n.* (also **first cousin**) a child of one's uncle or aunt. □ **second cousin** a child of one's parent's cousin.

couture (koo-tyewr) *n.* the design and making of fashionable clothes.

couturier (koo-tyewr-ee-ay) *n.* a designer of fashionable clothes.

cove *n.* a small bay.

coven (kuv-ĕn) *n.* an assembly of witches.

covenant (kuv-ĕ-nănt) *n.* a formal agreement, a contract. ● *v.* make a covenant.

cover *v.* **1** be or place something over; conceal or protect in this way; disguise. **2** deal with (a subject); report on for a newspaper etc. **3** be enough to pay for; protect by insurance. **4** travel over (a distance). **5** keep a gun aimed at. **6** take over someone's job temporarily. ● *n.* **1** a thing that covers; a wrapper, envelope, or binding of a book; a shelter or protection; a disguise. **2** protection by insurance. **3** a place laid at a meal. □ **cover up** conceal (a thing or fact). □ **cover-up** *n.*

coverage *n.* **1** dealing with or protecting something. **2** an area covered.

covering letter *n.* an explanatory letter enclosed with goods.

coverlet *n.* a cover lying over other bedclothes.

covert *n.* thick undergrowth where animals hide. ● *adj.* concealed, done secretly. □ **covertly** *adv.*

covet *v.* (**coveted, coveting**) desire (a thing belonging to another person). □ **covetous** *adj.*

covey (ku-vee) *n.* (*pl.* **coveys**) a group of game birds.

cow *n.* **1** a fully grown female of cattle or certain other large animals (e.g. the elephant or whale). **2** *informal* an unpleasant woman. ● *v.* intimidate.

coward *n.* a person who lacks courage. □ **cowardly** *adj.*

cowardice *n.* lack of courage.

cowboy *n.* **1** a man in charge of cattle on a ranch. **2** *informal* a person with careless or dishonest methods in business.

cower *v.* crouch or shrink in fear.

cowl *n.* a monk's hood or hooded robe; a hood-shaped covering on a chimney.

cowling *n.* a removable metal cover on an engine.

cowrie *n.* a type of seashell.

cowslip *n.* a wild plant with small yellow flowers.

cox *n.* a coxswain. ● *v.* act as cox of (a racing boat).

coxcomb *n. dated* a conceited person.

coxswain (**kok**-sŭn) *n.* **1** a person who steers a boat. **2** a senior petty officer in the Royal Navy.

coy *adj.* pretending to be shy or embarrassed. ◻ **coyly** *adv.*

coyote (koy-**oh**-ti) *n.* a North American wolflike wild dog.

coypu *n.* a beaver-like aquatic rodent.

cozy Amer. sp. of **cosy**.

CPU *abbr. Computing* central processing unit.

Cr *symb.* chromium.

crab *n.* a ten-legged shellfish.

crab apple *n.* a small sour apple.

crabbed *adj.* (also **crabby**) **1** bad-tempered. **2** (of handwriting) hard to read.

crack *n.* **1** a line where a thing is broken but not separated; a narrow opening; a sharp blow. **2** a sudden sharp noise. **3** *informal* a joke. **4** a strong form of cocaine. ● *v.* **1** break without separating; knock sharply; give way under strain; (of a voice) become harsh. **2** make or cause to make the sound of a crack. **3** solve (a problem). **4** tell (a joke). ● *adj.* excellent. ◻ **crack down on** *informal* take severe measures against. **crack up** *informal* **1** have an emotional breakdown. **2** praise. **have a crack at** *informal* attempt.

crack-brained *adj. informal* crazy.

crackdown *n. informal* severe measures against something.

cracker *n.* **1** a small explosive firework; a paper tube giving an explosive crack when pulled apart, containing a small gift. **2** a thin dry biscuit.

crackers *adj. informal* crazy.

crackle *v.* make or cause to make a series of light cracking sounds. ● *n.* these sounds.

crackling *n.* crisp skin on roast pork.

crackpot *informal n.* an eccentric person. ● *adj.* mad.

cradle *n.* **1** a baby's bed usu. with rockers; a place where something originates. **2** a supporting structure. ● *v.* hold or support gently.

craft *n.* **1** a skill; an occupation requiring this. **2** cunning, deceit. **3** (*pl.* **craft**) a ship or boat.

craftsman *n.* (*pl.* **-men**) a worker skilled in a craft. ◻ **craftsmanship** *n.*

crafty *adj.* (**craftier, craftiest**) cunning, using underhand methods. ◻ **craftily** *adv.*, **craftiness** *n.*

crag *n.* a steep or rugged rock.

craggy *adj.* (**craggier, craggiest**) rugged.

cram *v.* (**crammed, cramming**) **1** force into too small a space; overfill. **2** study intensively for an examination.

cramp *n.* **1** a painful involuntary tightening of a muscle. **2** a metal bar with bent ends for holding things together. ● *v.* keep within too narrow limits.

crampon *n.* a spiked plate worn on boots for climbing on ice.

crane *n.* **1** a large wading bird. **2** a machine for lifting and moving heavy objects. ● *v.* stretch (one's neck) to see something.

cranium *n.* (**craniums** or **crania**) the skull.

crank *n.* **1** an L-shaped part for converting to-and-fro into circular motion. **2** an eccentric person. ● *v.* turn (a crank) to start (an engine). ◻ **cranky** *adj.*

crankshaft *n.* a shaft driven by a crank.

cranny *n.* (*pl.* **-ies**) a crevice.

crap *vulgar slang n.* faeces; nonsense, rubbish. ● *v.* (**crapped, crapping**) defecate.

craps *n.pl. Amer.* a gambling game played with a pair of dice.

crash *n.* a loud noise of collision or breakage; a violent collision; a financial collapse. ● *v.* **1** make a crash; be or cause to be involved in a crash; move noisily. **2** *informal* gatecrash. ● *adj.* involving intense effort to achieve something rapidly: *a crash course.*

crash helmet *n.* a padded helmet worn esp. by a motorcyclist to protect the head in a crash.

crashing *adj. informal* great, absolute: *a crashing bore.*

crash-land *v.* (of an aircraft) land in an emergency, causing damage.

crass *adj.* gross; very stupid; insensitive.

crate *n.* a packing case made of wooden slats; a container divided into individual units for bottles. ● *v.* pack in crate(s).

crater *n.* a bowl-shaped cavity; the mouth of a volcano.

cravat *n.* a short scarf; a necktie.

crave *v.* feel an intense longing (for); ask earnestly for.

craven *adj.* cowardly.

craving *n.* an intense longing.

craw *n.* a bird's crop.

crawfish *n.* = **crayfish**.

crawl *v.* **1** move on hands and knees or with the body on the ground; move very slowly. **2** *informal* seek favour by servile behaviour. ● *n.* a crawling movement or pace; an overarm swimming stroke. □ **crawling with** very crowded with. □ **crawler** *n.*

crayfish *n.* (*pl.* **crayfish**) a freshwater shellfish like a small lobster.

crayon *n.* a stick of coloured wax etc. for drawing. ● *v.* draw or colour with crayons.

craze *n.* a temporary enthusiasm.

crazy *adj.* (**crazier, craziest**) insane; very foolish; *informal* madly eager. □ **crazily** *adv.*, **craziness** *n.*

crazy paving *n.* paving made of irregular pieces.

creak *n.* a harsh squeak. ● *v.* make this sound. □ **creaky** *adj.*

cream *n.* the fatty part of milk; its colour, yellowish white; a cream-like ointment etc.; the best part. ● *adj.* yellowish white. ● *v.* beat to a creamy consistency. □ **cream off** take (the best part of something). □ **creamy** *adj.*

cream cheese *n.* a soft rich cheese.

cream cracker *n.* a crisp unsweetened biscuit.

creamery *n.* (*pl.* **-ies**) a factory producing butter and cheese.

cream of tartar *n.* a compound of potassium used in baking powder.

crease *n.* **1** a line made in cloth or paper by crushing or pressing. **2** a line marking the limit of the bowler's or batsman's position in cricket. ● *v.* make a crease in; develop creases.

create *v.* **1** bring into existence; produce by what one does; give a specified title to. **2** *informal* make a fuss. □ **creation** *n.*, **creator** *n.*

creative *adj.* involving creation or invention; showing imagination and originality. □ **creatively** *adv.*, **creativity** *n.*

creature *n.* an animal; a person.

crèche (kresh) *n.* a day nursery.

credence *n.* belief.

credentials *n.pl.* qualifications, qualities, etc.; documents attesting to these.

credible *adj.* believable. □ **credibly** *adv.*, **credibility** *n.*

■ **Usage** Do not confuse *credible* with *credulous*, 'gullible'.

credit *n.* **1** a system of deferring payment for purchases. **2** a record in an account of a sum received; having money in one's bank account. **3** acknowledgement or honour for an achievement; a source of honour or pride; (**credits**) acknowledgements of contributors to a film; good reputation, esp. for trustworthiness. ● *v.* (**credited, crediting**) **1** attribute. **2** enter in an account. **3** believe.

creditable *adj.* deserving praise. □ **creditably** *adv.*

■ **Usage** Do not confuse *creditable* with *credible.*

credit card *n.* a plastic card containing machine-readable magnetic code, allowing the holder to make purchases on credit.

creditor *n.* a person to whom money is owed.

credulous *adj.* too ready to believe things; gullible. □ **credulity** *n.*

creed *n.* a set of beliefs or principles.

creek *n.* a narrow inlet of water, esp. on a coast; *Amer.* a tributary.

creep *v.* (**crept, creeping**) **1** move slowly, quietly, and stealthily; develop or increase gradually; (of a plant) grow along the ground or a wall etc. **2** (of skin) have an unpleasant sensation through fear or disgust. ● *n.* **1** *informal* an unpleasant person. **2** slow and stealthy or imperceptible movement. **3** (**the creeps**) *informal* a nervous sensation.

creepy *adj.* (**creepier, creepiest**) *informal* frightening; disturbing.

cremate *v.* burn (a corpse) to ashes. □ **cremation** *n.*

crematorium *n.* (*pl.* **crematoria** or **crematoriums**) a place where corpses are cremated.

crème de la crème (krem dĕ la krem) *n.* the very best.

crème de menthe (krem dĕ month) *n.* a peppermint-flavoured liqueur.

crenellated *adj.* having battlements. □ **crenellation** *n.*

Creole (kree-ohl) *n.* a descendant of European settlers in the West Indies or South America; their dialect; a hybrid language.

creosote *n.* a brown oily liquid distilled from coal tar, used as a preservative for wood.

crêpe *n.* **1** (krayp) a fabric with a wrinkled surface. **2** (krep) a pancake.

crept past & p.p. of **creep**.

crepuscular *adj.* of or like twilight; active at twilight.

Cres. *abbr.* Crescent.

crescendo (kri-shen-doh) *adv.* gradually becoming louder. ● *n.* (*pl.* **crescendos** or **crescendi**) a gradual increase in loudness.

crescent *n.* a narrow curved shape tapering to a point at each end; a curved street of houses.

cress *n.* a plant with small leaves used in salads.

crest *n.* **1** a tuft or outgrowth on a bird's or animal's head; a plume on a helmet. **2** the top of a slope or hill; a white top of a large wave. **3** a design above a shield on a coat of arms.

crestfallen *adj.* disappointed at failure.

cretaceous (kri-taysh-ŭs) *adj.* chalky.

cretin *n. dated* a person who is deformed and mentally handicapped; *informal* a stupid person. □ **cretinous** *adj.*

crevasse *n.* a deep open crack esp. in a glacier.

crevice *n.* a narrow gap in a surface.

crew[1] *n.* the people working a ship or aircraft; a group working together; a gang. ● *v.* act as a crew member (of).

crew[2] past of **crow**.

crew cut *n.* a very short haircut.

crib *n.* **1** a rack for fodder; a model of the manger scene at Bethlehem; a cot. **2** *informal* a translation of a text for students' use. ● *v.* (**cribbed, cribbing**) *informal* copy unfairly; plagiarize.

cribbage *n.* a card game.

crick *n.* a sudden painful stiffness in the neck or back.

cricket *n.* **1** an outdoor game for two teams of 11 players with ball, bats, and wickets. **2** a brown insect resembling a grasshopper. □ **cricketer** *n.*

crier *n.* (also **cryer**) an official making public announcements.

crikey *int. informal* an exclamation of astonishment.

crime *n.* a serious offence, an act that breaks a law; illegal acts.

criminal *n.* a person guilty of a crime. ● *adj.* of or involving crime. □ **criminality** *n.*, **criminally** *adv.*

criminology *n.* the study of crime. □ **criminologist** *n.*

crimp *v.* press into ridges.

crimson *adj.* & *n.* deep red.

cringe *v.* cower; behave obsequiously.

crinkle *n.* & *v.* (a) wrinkle.

crinoline *n.* a light framework formerly worn to make a long skirt stand out.

cripple *n.* a disabled or lame person. ● *v.* make lame; weaken seriously.

crisis *n.* (*pl.* **crises**) a time of intense danger or difficulty; the decisive moment in an illness.

crisp *adj.* **1** firm, dry, and brittle. **2** cold and bracing. **3** brisk and decisive. ● *n.* a thin slice of potato fried crisp. □ **crisply** *adv.*, **crispness** *n.*, **crispy** *adj.*

crispbread *n.* a thin crisp unsweetened biscuit.

criss-cross *n.* a pattern of intersecting lines. ● *adj.* & *adv.* in this pattern. ● *v.* form a criss-cross pattern (on).

criterion *n.* (*pl.* **criteria**) a standard of judgement.

critic *n.* **1** a person who points out faults. **2** a person who appraises artistic works and performances.

critical *adj.* **1** looking for faults. **2** of literary or artistic criticism. **3** of or at a crisis. □ **critically** *adv.*

criticism *n.* **1** the pointing out of faults. **2** an evaluation of literary or artistic work.

criticize *v.* (also **-ise**) **1** find fault with. **2** analyse and evaluate.

critique *n.* an analysis and assessment.

croak *n.* a deep hoarse cry or sound like that of a frog. ● *v.* **1** utter or speak with a croak. **2** *informal* die.

crochet (**kroh**-shay) *n.* lacy fabric produced from thread worked with a hooked needle. ● *v.* (**crocheted, crocheting**) make by or do such work.

crock *n.* **1** an earthenware pot; a broken piece of this. **2** *informal* a weak or disabled person; a worn-out vehicle etc.

crockery *n.* household china.

crocodile *n.* **1** a large predatory amphibious tropical reptile. **2** *Brit.* a line of people walking in pairs.

crocodile tears *n.pl.* insincere sorrow.

crocus *n.* a small spring-flowering plant.

croft *n.* a small rented farm in Scotland.

crofter *n.* the tenant of a croft.

croissant (**krwa**-son) *n.* a rich crescent-shaped roll.

crone *n.* an old and ugly woman.

crony *n.* (*pl.* **-ies**) a close friend or companion.

crook *n.* **1** a hooked stick; an angle. **2** *informal* a criminal. ● *v.* bend (a finger).

crooked *adj.* **1** not straight. **2** *informal* dishonest. □ **crookedly** *adv.*

croon *v.* sing softly or sentimentally. □ **crooner** *n.*

crop *n.* **1** a plant cultivated on a large scale for its produce; a harvest from this; a group or amount produced at one time. **2** a pouch in a bird's gullet where food is broken up for digestion. **3** the handle of a whip. **4** a very short haircut. ● *v.* (**cropped, cropping**) **1** cut or bite off. **2** produce or gather as harvest. □ **crop up** occur unexpectedly.

cropper *n.* □ **come a cropper** *informal* fall heavily; fail badly.

croquet (**kroh**-kay) *n.* a game played on a lawn with balls driven through hoops with mallets.

croquette (kroh-**ket**) *n.* a small ball of potato etc. fried in bread crumbs.

crosier *n.* (also **crozier**) a bishop's hooked staff.

cross *n.* **1** a mark or shape formed by two intersecting lines or pieces; an upright post with a transverse bar, formerly used in crucifixion. **2** an unavoidable affliction. **3** a hybrid; a mixture of two things. **4** a transverse blow or pass of a ball. ● *v.* **1** go or extend across; draw a line across; mark (a cheque) so that it must be paid into a named account. **2** (cause to) intersect; mark with a cross. **3** (of a letter) be dispatched while a letter from the addressee is already in the post. **4** cause to interbreed. **5** oppose the wishes of. ● *adj.* annoyed. □ **at cross purposes** misunderstanding or with different aims. □ **crossly** *adv.*, **crossness** *n.*

crossbar *n.* a horizontal bar between uprights.

cross-bench *n.* a seat in the House of Lords for members independent of any political party.

crossbow *n.* a mechanical bow fixed across a wooden support.

cross-breed *n.* an animal produced by interbreeding. □ **cross-bred** *adj.*

cross-check *v.* verify (figures etc.) by an alternative method.

cross-dressing *n.* wearing the clothes of the opposite sex.

cross-examine *v.* question (a witness in court) to check a testimony already given. □ **cross-examination** *n.*

cross-eyed *adj.* squinting.

crossfire *n.* gunfire crossing another line of fire.

crossing *n.* a place where things cross; a journey across water; moving across something; a place to cross a road, border, etc.

crosspatch *n. informal* a bad-tempered person.

cross-ply *adj.* (of a tyre) having fabric layers with cords lying crosswise.

cross-reference *n.* a reference to another place in the same book.

crossroads *n.* a place where roads intersect.

cross-section *n.* a surface or shape revealed by cutting across something; a representative sample.

crosswise *adv.* (also **crossways**) in the form of a cross; intersecting; diagonally.

crossword *n.* a puzzle in which intersecting words have to be inserted into a grid of squares.

crotch *n.* the fork between the legs where they join the trunk; a fork in a tree etc.

crotchet *n.* a note in music, half a minim.

crotchety *adj.* peevish, irritable. □ **crotchetiness** *n.*

crouch *v.* stoop low with the legs tightly bent. ● *n.* this position.

croup (kroop) *n.* **1** an inflammation of the windpipe in children, causing coughing and breathing difficulty. **2** the rump of a horse etc.

croupier (**kroop**-i-ay, **kroop**-i-ĕ) *n.* a person who rakes in stakes and pays out winnings at a gaming table.

crouton *n.* a small piece of fried or toasted bread as a garnish.

crow *n.* **1** a large black bird. **2** a cock's call; a triumphant cry. ● *v.* (**crowed** or **crew, crowing**) utter a cock's cry; express triumph and glee.

crowbar *n.* an iron bar with a bent end, used as a lever.

crowd *n.* a large group. ● *v.* fill completely or excessively; move or gather in a crowd.

crown *n.* **1** a monarch's ceremonial headdress; (**the Crown**) the supreme governing power in a monarchy. **2** the top of a head, hill, etc. ● *v.* **1** place a crown on (a new monarch). **2** form the top of; be the climax of. **3** *informal* hit on the head.

Crown prince, Crown princess *n.* the heir to a throne.

crozier var. of **crosier**.

cruces pl. of **crux**.

crucial *adj.* very important, decisive. □ **crucially** *adv.*

crucible *n.* a container in which metals are melted.

crucifix *n.* a model of a cross with a figure of Christ on it.

crucifixion *n.* crucifying; (**the Crucifixion**) that of Christ.

cruciform *adj.* cross-shaped.

crucify *v.* (**crucified, crucifying**) put to death by nailing or binding to a cross; cause anguish to.

crude *adj.* in a natural or raw state; roughly made; offensively coarse or rude. □ **crudely** *adv.*, **crudity** *n.*

crudités *n.pl.* sliced mixed raw vegetables to dip into a sauce.

cruel *adj.* (**crueller** or **crueler, cruellest** or **cruelest**) deliberately causing suffering; hard-hearted; harsh. □ **cruelly** *adv.*, **cruelty** *n.*

cruet *n.* a set of containers for salt, pepper, etc. at the table.

cruise *v.* **1** sail for pleasure or on patrol. **2** travel at a moderate economical speed. **3** *informal* search for casual sexual partners. ● *n.* a cruising voyage.

cruiser *n.* a fast warship; a motor boat with a cabin.

crumb *n.* a small fragment of bread etc.; a tiny piece.

crumble *v.* (cause to) break into small fragments. ● *n.* a pudding of stewed fruit topped with a crumbly mixture of flour, fat, and sugar.

crumbly *adj.* (**crumblier, crumbliest**) easily crumbled.

crummy *adj.* (**crummier, crummiest**) *informal* of poor quality.

crumpet *n.* **1** a flat soft yeast cake eaten toasted. **2** *informal* a sexually attractive person.

crumple *v.* crush or become crushed into creases; collapse.

crunch *v.* crush noisily with the teeth; make a muffled grinding sound. ● *n.* **1** the sound of crunching. **2** *informal* a crucial point or situation.

crunchy *adj.* (**crunchier, crunchiest**) crisp; making a crunching sound when crushed.

crupper *n.* a strap looped under a horse's tail from the saddle.

crusade *n.* a medieval Christian military expedition to recover the Holy Land from Muslims; a campaign for a cause. ● *v.* take part in a crusade. □ **crusader** *n.*

crush *v.* press so as to break, injure, or wrinkle; pound into fragments; defeat or subdue completely. ● *n.* **1** a crowded mass of people. **2** *informal* an infatuation.

crust *n.* a hard outer layer, esp. of bread.

crustacean (krust-**aysh**-ŭn) *n.* a creature with a hard shell (e.g. a lobster).

crusty *adj.* (**crustier, crustiest**) **1** with a crisp crust. **2** irritable.

crutch *n.* **1** a support for a lame person. **2** the crotch.

crux *n.* (*pl.* **cruces** or **cruxes**) a vital part of a problem; a difficult point.

cry *n.* (*pl.* **cries**) **1** a loud inarticulate shout expressing emotion; a call; an appeal. **2** a spell of weeping. ● *v.* (**cries, cried, crying**) **1** shed tears. **2** call loudly; scream; appeal. □ **cry off** *informal* fail to do what one has arranged to.

cryer var. of **crier**.

cryogenics (krI-oh-jen-iks) *n.* a branch of physics dealing with very low temperatures. □ **cryogenic** *adj.*

crypt (kript) *n.* a room below the floor of a church.

cryptic *adj.* hard to interpret; puzzling.

cryptogram *n.* something written in cipher.

cryptography *n.* the study of ciphers. □ **cryptographer** *n.*

crystal *adj.* a glasslike mineral; high-quality glass; a symmetrical piece of a solidified substance.

crystalline *adj.* **1** like or made of crystal. **2** *literary* clear.

crystallize *v.* (also **-ise**) form into crystals; make or become definite in form; preserve (fruit) in sugar. □ **crystallization** *n.*

Cs *symb.* caesium.

CSE *abbr.* Certificate of Secondary Education.

CS gas *n.* a gas causing tears and choking, used to control riots etc.

Cu *symb.* copper.

cu. *abbr.* cubic.

cub *n.* **1** the young of foxes, lions, etc. **2** (**Cub**, in full **Cub Scout**) a member of the junior branch of the Scout Association.

cubby hole *n.* a very small room or space.

cube *n.* **1** a solid object with six equal square sides. **2** the product of a number multiplied by itself twice. ● *v.* **1** find the cube of (a number). **2** cut into cubes.

cube root *n.* a number which produces a given number when cubed.

cubic *adj.* cube-shaped; (of measurements) of three dimensions.

cubicle *n.* a small area partitioned off in a large room.

cubism *n.* a style of painting in which objects are shown as geometrical shapes. □ **cubist** *n.*

cuckold *n.* a man whose wife commits adultery. ● *v.* make a cuckold of.

cuckoo *n.* a bird that lays its eggs in other birds' nests.

cucumber *n.* a long green-skinned fruit eaten as salad.

cud *n.* food that cattle bring back from the stomach into the mouth and chew again.

cuddle *v.* hug lovingly; nestle together. ● *n.* a gentle hug. □ **cuddly** *adj.*

cudgel *n.* a short thick stick used as a weapon. ● *v.* (**cudgelled, cudgelling**; *Amer.* **cudgeled**) beat with a cudgel.

cue *n.* **1** a signal to do something, esp. for an actor to begin a speech. **2** a long rod for striking balls in billiards etc. ● *v.* (**cued, cueing**) **1** give a signal to (someone). **2** use a billiards cue.

cuff *n.* **1** a band of cloth round the edge of a sleeve. **2** a blow with the open hand. ● *v.* strike with the open hand. □ **off the cuff** *informal* without preparation.

cuff link *n.* a device of two linked discs etc. to hold cuff edges together.

cuisine (kwi-zeen) *n.* a style of cooking.

cul-de-sac *n.* a street closed at one end.

culinary *adj.* of or for cooking.

cull *v.* gather, select; select and kill (animals) to reduce numbers.

culminate *v.* reach a climax. □ **culmination** *n.*

culottes (kyuu-lots) *n.pl.* women's trousers styled to resemble a skirt.

culpable *adj.* deserving blame. □ **culpability** *n.*, **culpably** *adv.*

culprit *n.* a person who has committed an offence.

cult *n.* a system of religious worship; excessive admiration of a person or thing.

cultivate *v.* **1** prepare and use (land) for crops; produce (crops) by tending them. **2** develop (a skill etc.) by practice. **3** try to win the friendship or support of. □ **cultivation** *n.*, **cultivator** *n.*

culture *n.* **1** a developed understanding of literature, art, music, etc.; the art, customs, etc. of a particular country or society. **2** artificial rearing of bacteria; bacteria grown for study. ● *v.* grow in artificial conditions. □ **cultural** *adj.*, **culturally** *adv.*

culvert *n.* a drain under a road.

cum *prep.* as well as; also used as; *a bedroom-cum-study*.

cumbersome *adj.* heavy and awkward to carry or use.

cumin *n.* (also **cummin**) a spice.

cummerbund *n.* a sash for the waist.

cumquat var. of **kumquat**.

cumulative *adj.* increasing by additions. □ **cumulatively** *adv.*

cumulus (kyoo-myuu-lŭs) *n.* (*pl.* **cumuli**) clouds formed in heaped-up rounded masses.

cuneiform (kyoo-ni-form) *n.* ancient writing done in wedge-shaped strokes cut into stone etc.

cunning *adj.* skilled at deception, crafty; ingenious. ● *n.* craftiness, ingenuity. □ **cunningly** *adv.*

cup *n.* **1** a drinking vessel usu. with a handle at the side; a trophy shaped like this. **2** wine or fruit juice with added flavourings. ● *v.* (**cupped, cupping**) form (one's hands) into a cuplike shape. □ **cupful** *n.*

cupboard *n.* a recess or piece of furniture with a door, in which things may be stored.

cupidity *n.* greed for gain.

cupola *n.* a small dome.

cupreous (kyoo-pree-ŭs) *adj.* of or like copper.

cur *n.* a mongrel dog; a contemptible person.

curaçao (kewr-ăsoh) *n.* an orange-flavoured liqueur.

curacy *n.* (*pl.* **-ies**) the position of curate.

curare (kyoo-**rah**-ri) *n.* a vegetable poison that induces paralysis.

curate *n.* a member of the clergy who assists a parish priest.

curate's egg *n. informal* something that is good only in parts.

curator *n.* a person in charge of a museum or other collection.

curb *n.* a means of restraint. ● *v.* restrain.

curds *n.pl.* the thick soft substance formed when milk turns sour.

curdle *v.* form or cause to form curds.

cure *v.* **1** restore to health; get rid of (a disease or trouble etc.). **2** preserve by salting, drying, etc. ● *n.* a substance or treatment curing disease; restoration to health.

curette (kyou-**ret**) *n.* a surgical scraping instrument. □ **curettage** *n.*

curfew *n.* a law requiring people to stay indoors after a stated time; this time.

curie *n.* a unit of radioactivity.

curio *n.* (*pl.* **curios**) an unusual and interesting object.

curiosity *n.* (*pl.* **-ies**) **1** desire to find something out. **2** a curio.

curious *adj.* **1** eager to learn or know something. **2** strange, unusual. □ **curiously** *adv.*, **curiousness** *n.*

curium *n.* a radioactive metallic element (symbol Cm).

curl *v.* (cause to) take a curved or spiral shape. ● *n.* a curled thing or shape; a coiled lock of hair. □ **curly** *adj.*

curler *n.* a small tube round which hair is wound to make it curl.

curlew *n.* a wading bird with a long curved bill.

curlicue *n.* a curly ornamental line.

curling *n.* a game like bowls played on ice.

curmudgeon *n.* a bad-tempered person.

currant *n.* **1** a dried grape used in cookery. **2** a small round edible berry; a shrub producing this.

currency *n.* (*pl.* **-ies**) **1** money in use in a particular area. **2** being widely used or known.

current *adj.* **1** belonging to the present time. **2** in general use. ● *n.* a body of water or air moving in one direction; a flow of electricity. □ **currently** *adv.*

curriculum *n.* (*pl.* **curricula**) a course of study.

curriculum vitae *n.* a brief account of one's career.

curry *n.* (*pl.* **-ies**) a savoury dish cooked with hot spices. ● *v.* (**curried, currying**) **1** make into such a dish. **2** groom (a horse) with a curry-comb. □ **curry favour** win favour by flattery.

curry-comb *n.* a rubber comb, for grooming horses.

curse *n.* a call for evil to come on a person or thing; something causing suffering or annoyance; an offensive word expressing anger. ● *v.* utter a curse (against); afflict. □ **cursed** *adj.*

cursive *adj.* & *n.* (writing) done with joined letters.

cursor *n.* a movable indicator on a VDU screen.

cursory *adj.* hasty and not thorough. □ **cursorily** *adv.*

curt *adj.* noticeably or rudely brief. □ **curtly** *adv.*, **curtness** *n.*

curtail *v.* cut short, reduce. □ **curtailment** *n.*

curtain *n.* a piece of cloth hung as a screen, esp. at a window.

curtsy *n.* (*pl.* **-ies**) (also **curtsey**) a woman's movement of respect made by bending the knees. ● *v.* (**curtsied, curtsying**) make a curtsy.

curvaceous *adj.* (of a woman) having a shapely curved figure.

curvature *n.* curving; a curved form.

curve *n.* a line or surface with no part straight or flat. ● *v.* form (into) a curve. □ **curvy** *adj.*

curvilinear *adj.* contained by or consisting of curved lines.

cushion *n.* a stuffed bag used for sitting or leaning on; a support or protection; a body of air supporting a hovercraft. ● *v.* protect with a pad; lessen the impact of.

cushy *adj.* (**cushier, cushiest**) *informal* pleasant and easy.

cusp *n.* **1** a pointed part where curves meet. **2** a point of transition, esp. between astrological signs.

cuss *informal n.* a curse; a difficult person. ● *v.* curse.

cussed (cuss-id) *adj. informal* stubborn.

custard *n.* a sweet sauce made with milk and eggs or flavoured cornflour.

custodian *n.* a guardian, a keeper.

custody *n.* **1** protective care. **2** imprisonment.

custom *n.* **1** the usual way of behaving or acting. **2** regular dealing by customers. **3** (**customs**) duty on imported goods.

customary *adj.* usual. □ **customarily** *adv.*

customer *n.* a person buying goods or services from a shop etc.

cut *v.* (**cut, cutting**) **1** open, wound, divide, or shape by pressure of a sharp edge; remove or reduce in this way. **2** intersect. **3** divide (a pack of cards). **4** avoid or ignore. **5** have (a tooth) coming through the gum. ● *n.* **1** cutting; an incision or wound. **2** a piece cut off; *informal* a share. **3** a reduction. **4** a style of cutting. □ **a cut above** superior to. **cut off** isolated. **cut out for** suited to.

cute *adj. informal* **1** attractive, endearing. **2** clever □ **cutely** *adv.*, **cuteness** *n.*

cuticle *n.* the skin at the base of a nail.

cutlass *n.* a short curved sword.

cutler *n.* a maker of cutlery.

cutlery *n.* table knives, forks, and spoons.

cutlet *n.* a lamb or veal chop from behind the neck; a flat cake of minced meat or nuts and breadcrumbs etc.

cut-throat *adj.* ruthless, unscrupulous. ● *n.* a murderer.

cutting *adj.* (of remarks) hurtful. ● *n.* **1** a passage cut through high ground for a railway etc. **2** a piece of a plant for replanting. **3** a piece cut out of a newspaper etc.

cuttlefish *n.* a sea creature that ejects black fluid when attacked.

CV *abbr.* curriculum vitae.

cwt *abbr.* hundredweight.

cyan (sI-ăn) *n.* a greenish-blue colour.

cyanide *n.* a strong poison.

cyber- *comb. form* relating to electronic communication and virtual reality.

cybernetics *n.* the science of systems of control and communication in animals and machines.

cycle *n.* **1** a recurring series of events. **2** a bicycle or motorcycle. ● *v.* ride a bicycle. □ **cyclist** *n.*

cyclic *adj.* (also **cyclical**) recurring regularly. □ **cyclically** *adv.*

cyclone *n.* a violent wind rotating round a central area. □ **cyclonic** *adj.*

cyclotron (sIk-lŏ-tron) *n.* an apparatus for accelerating charged particles in a spiral path.

cygnet (sig-nĕt) *n.* a young swan.

cylinder *n.* an object with straight sides and circular ends. □ **cylindrical** *adj.*, **cylindrically** *adv.*

cymbal *n.* a brass plate struck against another or with a stick as a percussion instrument.

cynic *n.* a person who believes people's motives are usually bad or selfish. □ **cynical** *adj.*, **cynically** *adv.*, **cynicism** *n.*

cynosure (sin-o-syewr, sIn-o-syewr) *n.* a centre of attention.

cypher var. of **cipher**.

cypress *n.* an evergreen tree.

cyst (sist) *n.* a growth on the body containing fluid or soft matter.

cystic *adj.* of the bladder or gall bladder.

cystic fibrosis *n.* a hereditary disease usu. resulting in respiratory infections.

cystitis *n.* inflammation of the bladder.

cytology (sI-to-lŏ-ji) *n.* the study of biological cells. □ **cytological** *adj.*

czar var. of **tsar**.

Dd

D *n.* (as a Roman numeral) 500. ● *symb.* deuterium.

d. *abbr.* (until 1971) penny, pence.

dab *v.* (**dabbed, dabbing**) wipe with quick strokes using something absorbent; apply with quick strokes. ● *n.* a quick stroke; a small amount applied.

dabble *v.* **1** splash about gently or playfully. **2** work at something in a casual or superficial way.

dab hand *n. informal* an expert.

da capo *adv. Music* repeat from the beginning.

dacha *n.* a Russian country cottage.

dachshund *n.* a small dog with a long body and short legs.

dad *n. informal* father.

daddy *n.* (*pl.* **-ies**) *informal* father.

daddy-long-legs *n. informal* a long-legged flying insect.

dado (day-doh) *n.* (*pl.* **dados**) the lower part of a wall decorated differently from the upper part.

daffodil *n.* a yellow flower with a trumpet-shaped central part.

daft *adj. informal* silly, crazy.

dagger *n.* a short pointed two-edged weapon used for stabbing.

dago (day-goh) *n.* (*pl.* **dagos** or **dagoes**) *informal, offensive* a person from southern Europe (esp. Spain or Italy).

daguerrotype (dă-ger-rŏ-tIp) *n.* an early kind of photograph.

Dáil (doil) *n.* (in full **Dáil Éireann**) the lower House of Parliament in the Republic of Ireland.

daily *adj.* happening or appearing on every day or every weekday. ● *adv.* once a day. ● *n.* (*pl.* **-ies**) **1** a daily newspaper. **2** *informal* a domestic cleaner.

dainty *adj.* (**daintier, daintiest**) **1** delicate, small, and pretty. **2** fastidious. □ **daintily** *adv.*, **daintiness** *n.*

dairy *n.* (*pl.* **-ies**) a place where milk and its products are processed or sold.

dais (day-iss) *n.* a low platform, esp. at the end of a hall.

daisy *n.* (*pl.* **-ies**) a flower with many ray-like petals.

daisy wheel *n.* a device with radiating spokes ending in letters, used in printers.

dal var. of **dhal**.

dale *n.* a valley.

dally *v.* (**dallied, dallying**) idle, dawdle; flirt. □ **dalliance** *n.*

Dalmatian *n.* a dog of a large white breed with dark spots.

dam *n.* **1** a barrier built across a river to hold back water. **2** the mother of an animal, esp. a mammal. ● *v.* (**dammed, damming**) build a dam across; obstruct, hold back.

damage *n.* **1** harm, injury, esp. reducing something's value, usefulness, or attractiveness. **2** (**damages**) money as compensation for injury. ● *v.* cause damage to.

damask *n.* a fabric woven with a pattern visible on either side.

dame *n.* **1** (**Dame**) the title of a woman with an order of knighthood. **2** *Amer. informal* a woman.

damn *v.* condemn to hell; condemn, criticize; swear at. ● *int. informal* an exclamation of annoyance. ● *adj.* & *adv.* (also **damned**) *informal* **1** annoying(ly) **2** extreme(ly).

damnable *adj.* hateful, annoying. □ **damnably** *adv.*

damnation *n.* eternal punishment in hell. ● *int. informal* an exclamation of annoyance.

damp *adj.* slightly wet. ● *n.* moistness. ● *v.* **1** dampen. **2** restrain, discourage. **3** reduce the vibration and volume of (a piano string etc.). □ **dampness** *n.*

dampen *v.* make or become damp. □ **dampener** *n.*

damper *n.* **1** something that depresses or subdues. **2** a pad silencing a piano string. **3** a metal plate controlling the draught in a flue.

damsel *n. archaic* a young woman.

damson *n.* a small purple plum.

dance *v.* move with rhythmical steps and gestures, usu. to music; move in a quick or lively way. ● *n.* a piece of dancing; music for this; a social gathering for dancing. □ **dance attendance on** follow about and help dutifully. □ **dancer** *n.*

D and C *abbr.* dilatation and curettage, a minor operation to clean the womb.

dandelion *n.* a wild plant with bright yellow flowers.

dandified *adj.* like a dandy.

dandle *v.* dance or nurse (a child) in one's arms.

dandruff *n.* flakes of dead skin from the scalp.

dandy *n.* (*pl.* **-ies**) a man who pays excessive attention to his appearance. ● *adj. informal* excellent. □ **dandyism** *n.*

Dane *n.* a native or inhabitant of Denmark.

danger *n.* likelihood of harm or death; something causing this.

dangerous *adj.* causing or involving danger. □ **dangerously** *adv.*

dangle *v.* hang or swing loosely; hold out temptingly. □ **dangler** *n.*, **dangly** *adj.*

Danish *adj.* & *n.* (the language) of Denmark.

dank *adj.* damp and cold. □ **dankly** *adv.*, **dankness** *n.*

dapper *adj.* neat and precise in dress or movement.

dapple *v.* mark with patches of colour or shade.

dapple grey *adj.* (of a horse etc.) grey or white with darker spots.

dare *v.* be bold enough (to do something); challenge to do something risky. ● *n.* this challenge. □ **I dare say** I think it likely.

daredevil *n.* a recklessly daring person. ● *adj.* recklessly daring.

daring *adj.* bold. ● *n.* boldness. □ **daringly** *adv.*

dark *adj.* **1** with little or no light; closer to black than to white; having dark hair or skin. **2** gloomy, tragic; evil. **3** hidden, mysterious. ● *n.* absence of light; night. □ **darkly** *adv.*, **darkness** *n.*

darken *v.* make or become dark.

dark horse *n.* a successful competitor of whom little is known.

darkroom *n.* a darkened room for processing photographs.

darling *n.* a loved or lovable person or thing; a favourite. ● *adj.* beloved, lovable; favourite.

darn *v.* mend (a hole in fabric) by weaving thread across it. ● *n.* a darned area in material. ● *adj.* (also **darned**) *informal* damn.

dart *n.* **1** a small pointed missile; (**darts**) a game in which such missiles are thrown at a target. **2** a sudden run. **3** a tuck shaping a garment. ● *v.* run suddenly; send out (a glance etc.) rapidly.

dartboard *n.* a target in the game of darts.

dash *v.* **1** run rapidly. **2** strike or throw violently against something; destroy (hopes etc.). ● *n.* **1** a rapid run, a rush. **2** a small amount of liquid etc. added to something. **3** a punctuation mark (-) marking a pause or break in the sense or representing omitted letters. **4** flamboyance and liveliness. **5** a dashboard.

dashboard *n.* the instrument panel of a motor vehicle.

dashing *adj.* stylish; spirited, gallant.

dastardly *adj.* wicked, vile.

DAT *abbr.* digital audio tape.

data *n.* facts collected for reference or analysis; facts to be processed by computer.

data bank *n.* a large store of computerized data.

database *n.* an organized store of computerized data.

date[1] *n.* **1** a specified day of a month or year; the day or year of something's occurrence; the period to which something belongs. **2** *informal* an appointment to meet someone socially or romantically; (esp. *Amer.*) the person to be met. ● *v.* **1** establish the date of; originate from a specified date; mark with a date; become or show to be old-fashioned. **2** *informal* go out with (a romantic partner). □ **to date** until now.

date[2] *n.* a small brown edible fruit.

dated *adj.* old-fashioned.

date rape *n.* the rape of a woman by a person with whom she is on a date.

dative *n.* the grammatical case expressing the indirect object.

datum *n.* (*pl.* **data**) an item of data.

daub (dorb) *v.* smear roughly. ● *n.* a crudely painted picture; a smear.

daughter *n.* a female in relation to her parents.

daughter-in-law *n.* (*pl.* **daughters-in-law**) a son's wife.

daunt *v.* intimidate, discourage.

dauntless *adj.* fearless and determined.

dauphin (**doh**-fah, **dor**-fin) *n.* the title of the eldest son of former kings of France.

davit *n.* a small crane on a ship.

dawdle *v.* walk slowly; idle. □ **dawdler** *n.*

dawn *n.* the first light of day; a beginning. ● *v.* begin; grow light; be realised or understood. □ **dawning** *n.*

day *n.* **1** a period of 24 hours; the part of this when the sun is above the horizon; the part of this spent working. **2** a time, a period. □ **in one's day** at an earlier and better point in one's life.

daybreak *n.* the first light of day.

daydream *n.* pleasant idle thoughts. ● *v.* have daydreams.

daze *v.* cause to feel stunned or bewildered. ● *n.* a dazed state.

dazzle *v.* blind temporarily with bright light; impress with splendour. □ **dazzlement** *n.*

dB *abbr.* decibel(s).

DC *abbr.* direct current.

DD *abbr.* Doctor of Divinity.

DDT *abbr.* a chlorinated hydrocarbon used as an insecticide.

de- *pref.* implying removal or reversal.

deacon *n.* a member of the clergy ranking below priest; a lay person attending to church business in Nonconformist churches.

dead *adj.* **1** no longer alive. **2** lacking sensation or emotion; lacking excitement; lacking resonance. **3** no longer functioning; no longer relevant. **4** total, absolute. ● *adv.* absolutely; exactly.

dead beat *adj. informal* tired out.

deaden *v.* make less intense; deprive of sensation or sensitivity; deprive of vitality.

dead end *n.* a cul-de-sac; an occupation with no prospect of development or progress.

dead heat *n.* a race in which two or more competitors finish exactly even.

dead letter *n.* a law or rule no longer observed.

deadline *n.* a time limit.

deadlock *n.* a state when no progress can be made. ● *v.* bring to such a state.

deadly *adj.* (**deadlier, deadliest**) **1** causing death. **2** absolute: *in deadly earnest.* **3** *informal* very boring. ● *adv.* **1** so as to appear dead. **2** extremely. □ **deadliness** *n.*

deadpan *adj.* expressionless.

deaf *adj.* wholly or partly unable to hear; refusing to listen. □ **deafen** *v.*, **deafness** *n.*

deal *v.* (**dealt, dealing**) **1** distribute (playing cards) to players; hand out; inflict (a blow, a misfortune, etc.). **2** engage in trade. ● *n.* **1** a bargain, a transaction. **2** dealing cards. **3** fir or pine timber. □ **a great deal** a large amount. **a raw deal** *informal* unfair or harsh treatment. **big deal** *informal* an ironic expression of contempt. **deal with 1** take action about. **2** have as a topic.

dealer *n.* a person who deals; a trader.

dean *n.* **1** a clergyman who is head of a cathedral chapter. **2** a university official.

deanery *n.* (*pl.* **-ies**) a dean's residence.

dear *adj.* **1** much loved, cherished. **2** expensive. ● *n.* a dear person. ● *int.* an exclamation of surprise or distress. □ **dearly** *adv.*, **dearness** *n.*

dearth (derth) *n.* a scarcity, a lack.

death *n.* the process of dying; the state of being dead; an end; ruin.

death duty (*pl.* **-ies**) *n.* a tax levied on property after the owner's death.

deathly *adj.* (**deathlier, deathliest**) as of death: *a deathly hush.*

death trap *n.* a very dangerous place.

death-watch beetle *n.* a beetle whose larvae bore into wood and make a ticking sound.

deb *n. informal* a debutante.

debacle (day-**bah**-kl) *n.* an utter and ignominious failure.

debar *v.* (**debarred, debarring**) exclude.

debase *v.* lower in quality or value. □ **debasement** *n.*

debatable *adj.* questionable.

debate *n.* a formal discussion. ● *v.* discuss formally; consider.

debauchery *n.* over-indulgence in harmful or immoral pleasures. □ **debauched** *adj.*

debenture (di-**bent**-chĕ) *n.* a long-term security bearing a fixed rate of interest.

debilitate *v.* weaken. □ **debilitation** *n.*

debility *n.* physical weakness.

debit *n.* an entry in an account for a sum owing. ● *v.* (**debited, debiting**) enter as a debit, charge.

debonair *adj.* having a carefree self-confident manner.

debouch (di-**bowsh**, di-**boosh**) *v.* come out from a narrow into an open area.

debrief *v.* question to obtain facts about a completed mission.

debris (**deb**-ree) *n.* scattered broken pieces or rubbish.

debt (det) *n.* something owed. □ **in debt** owing something.

debtor *n.* a person who owes money.

debunk *v. informal* show up as exaggerated or false.

debut (**day**-bew) *n.* a first public appearance.

debutante *n.* a young upper-class woman making her first formal appearance in society.

Dec. *abbr.* December.

deca- *comb. form* ten.

decade *n.* a ten-year period.

decadent *adj.* in a state of moral deterioration. □ **decadence** *n.*

decaffeinated *adj.* with caffeine removed or reduced.

decagon *n.* a geometric figure with ten sides.

Decalogue *n.* the Ten Commandments.

decamp *v.* go away suddenly or secretly.

decant *v.* pour (liquid) into another container, leaving sediment behind.

decanter *n.* a bottle into which wine may be decanted before serving.

decapitate *v.* behead. □ **decapitation** *n.*

decarbonize *v.* (also **-ise**) remove carbon deposit from (an engine). □ **decarbonization** *n.*

decathlon *n.* an athletic contest involving ten events.

decay *v.* rot; decline, deteriorate. ● *n.* rot; deterioration.

decease *n.* death.

deceased *adj.* dead.

deceit *n.* deception. □ **deceitful** *adj.*, **deceitfully** *adv.*

deceive *v.* **1** cause to believe something that is not true. **2** be sexually unfaithful to. □ **deceiver** *n.*

decelerate *v.* reduce the speed (of). □ **deceleration** *n.*

December *n.* the twelfth month.

decennial (di-sen-iăl) *adj.* happening every tenth year; lasting ten years. □ **decennially** *adv.*

decent *adj.* **1** conforming to accepted standards of propriety; respectable, fitting. **2** of an acceptable standard. **3** *informal* kind, generous. □ **decency** *n.*, **decently** *adv.*

decentralize *v.* (also **-ise**) transfer from central to local control. □ **decentralization** *n.*

deception *n.* deceiving; a trick.

deceptive *adj.* misleading. □ **deceptively** *adv.*

deci- *comb. form* one-tenth.

decibel *n.* a unit for measuring the intensity of sound.

decide *v.* make up one's mind; settle (a contest or argument).

decided *adj.* having firm opinions; clear, definite. □ **decidedly** *adv.*

deciduous *adj.* (of a tree) shedding its leaves annually.

decimal *adj.* reckoned in tens or tenths. ● *n.* a decimal fraction.

decimal currency *n.* currency with each unit 10 or 100 times the value of the one next below it.

decimal fraction *n.* a fraction based on powers of ten, shown as figures after a dot.

decimalize *v.* (also **-ise**) convert into a decimal. □ **decimalization** *n.*

decimal point *n.* the dot used in a decimal fraction.

decimate *v.* destroy one-tenth of; *informal* destroy a large proportion of. □ **decimation** *n.*

decipher *v.* make out the meaning of (code, bad handwriting).

decision *n.* a conclusion, reached after consideration; reaching this; the ability to decide quickly and confidently.

decisive *adj.* **1** settling an issue definitively. **2** able to decide quickly and confidently. □ **decisively** *adv.*, **decisiveness** *n.*

deck *n.* **1** a floor or storey of a ship or bus. **2** the part of a cassette- or record-player that holds and plays the cassettes or records. ● *v.* decorate, dress up.

deckchair *n.* a folding canvas chair.

declaim *v.* speak or say impressively. □ **declamation** *n.*, **declamatory** *adj.*

declare *v.* announce openly or formally; state firmly. □ **declaration** *n.*, **declaratory** *adj.*

declassify *v.* (**declassified, declassifying**) cease to classify as officially secret. ▫ **declassification** *n.*

declension *n. Grammar* a class of nouns and adjectives having the same inflectional forms.

decline *v.* **1** decrease in size or number; lose strength or quality. **2** refuse politely. **3** slope downwards. ● *n.* a gradual decrease or loss of strength.

declivity *n.* (*pl.* **-ies**) a downward slope.

declutch *v.* disengage the clutch of a motor.

decoction *n.* an essence extracted by boiling; extracting this. ▫ **decoct** *v.*

decode *v.* put (a coded message) into plain language; make (an electronic signal) intelligible. ▫ **decoder** *n.*

décolleté *adj.* having a low neckline.

decompose *v.* (cause to) rot or decay. ▫ **decomposition** *n.*

decompress *v.* **1** reduce air pressure in or on. **2** expand (computer data) so it can be processed. ▫ **decompression** *n.*

decongestant *n.* a medicinal substance that relieves congestion.

decontaminate *v.* free from radioactivity, germs, etc. ▫ **decontamination** *n.*

decor (**day**-kor, **de**-kor) *n.* the style of decoration used in a room.

decorate *v.* **1** make attractive by adding ornaments; paint or paper the walls of. **2** confer a medal or award on. ▫ **decoration** *n.*

decorative *adj.* ornamental. ▫ **decoratively** *adv.*

decorator *n.* a person who paints and papers rooms etc. professionally.

decorous *adj.* decent; restrained. ▫ **decorously** *adv.*

decorum (di-**kor**-ŭm) *n.* correctness and dignity of behaviour.

decoy *n.* a person or animal used to lure others into a trap. ● *v.* lure by a decoy.

decrease *v.* make or become smaller or fewer. ● *n.* decreasing; the extent of this.

decree *n.* an order given by a government or other authority. ● *v.* order by decree.

decrepit *adj.* made weak by age or use; dilapidated. ▫ **decrepitude** *n.*

decriminalize *v.* (also **-ise**) cease to treat (an action) as criminal.

decry *v.* (**decried, decrying**) denounce publicly.

dedicate *v.* devote to a cause or task; address (a book etc.) to a person as a tribute. ▫ **dedication** *n.*

dedicated *adj.* serious in one's commitment to a task; exclusively set aside for a particular purpose.

deduce *v.* arrive at (a conclusion) by reasoning; infer. ▫ **deducible** *adj.*

deduct *v.* subtract.

deduction *n.* **1** deducting; something deducted. **2** deducing; a conclusion deduced.

deductive *adj.* based on reasoning.

deed *n.* **1** something done, an act. **2** a legal document.

deem *v.* consider to be of a specified character.

deep *adj.* **1** extending or situated far down or in from the top or surface. **2** intense, extreme. **3** profound. **4** low-pitched. ▫ **deep in** fully absorbed in. ▫ **deepen** *v.*, **deeply** *adv.*, **deepness** *n.*

deer *n.* (*pl.* **deer**) a hoofed animal, the male of which usu. has antlers.

deerstalker *n.* a cloth cap with a peak in front and at the back.

deface *v.* spoil or damage the surface of. ▫ **defacement** *n.*

de facto *adj.* & *adv.* (existing) in fact, whether by right or not.

defame *v.* attack the good reputation of. ▫ **defamation** *n.*, **defamatory** *adj.*

default *v.* fail to fulfil an obligation, esp. to pay debts or appear in court. ● *n.* **1** failure to fulfil an obligation. **2** a pre-selected option adopted by a computer program unless otherwise instructed. □ **by default** in the absence of competition or other options. **in default of** in the absence of. □ **defaulter** *n.*

defeat *v.* win victory over; cause to fail. ● *n.* defeating; being defeated.

defeatist *n.* a person who pessimistically expects or accepts failure. □ **defeatism** *n.*

defecate *v.* discharge faeces from the body. □ **defecation** *n.*

defect *n.* (dee-fekt) an imperfection. ● *v.* (di-**fekt**) desert one's country or cause. □ **defection** *n.*, **defector** *n.*

defective *adj.* imperfect, faulty; incomplete. □ **defectively** *adv.*, **defectiveness** *n.*

defence *n.* (*Amer.* **defense**) protecting; equipment or resources for protection; arguments against an accusation. □ **defenceless** *adj.*, **defencelessness** *n.*

defend *v.* protect from attack; uphold by argument; represent (the defendant). □ **defender** *n.*

defendant *n.* a person accused or sued in a lawsuit.

defensible *adj.* able to be defended. □ **defensibility** *n.*, **defensibly** *adv.*

defensive *adj.* **1** intended for defence. **2** sensitive to criticism. □ **defensively** *adv.*, **defensiveness** *n.*

defer *v.* (**deferred, deferring**) **1** postpone. **2** yield to a person's wishes or authority. □ **deferment** *n.*, **deferral** *n.*

deference *n.* polite respect. □ **deferential** *adj.*, **deferentially** *adv.*

defiance *n.* resistance, disobedience. □ **defiant** *adj.*, **defiantly** *adv.*

deficiency *n.* (*pl.* **-ies**) a lack, a shortage; an imperfection.

deficient *adj.* not having enough; insufficient, inadequate.

deficit *n.* an amount by which a total falls short of what is required.

defile *v.* make dirty or impure, pollute. ● *n.* a narrow pass or gorge.

define *v.* state precisely; give the meaning of; mark the boundary of.

definite *adj.* clearly and firmly decided or stated; certain, unambiguous; with a clear shape or outline. □ **definitely** *adv.*

definite article *see* **article**.

definition *n.* a statement of precise meaning; distinctness, clearness of outline.

definitive *adj.* settling something finally and authoritatively; most authoritative. □ **definitively** *adv.*

deflate *v.* (cause to) collapse through release of air; make less confident; reduce the price levels in (an economy). □ **deflation** *n.*

deflect *v.* turn aside. □ **deflection** or **deflexion** *n.*, **deflector** *n.*

deflower *v.* *literary* deprive of virginity.

defoliate *v.* remove the leaves of. □ **defoliant** *n.*, **defoliation** *n.*

deforest *v.* clear of trees. □ **deforestation** *n.*

deform *v.* spoil the shape of. □ **deformation** *n.*

deformity *n.* (*pl.* **-ies**) abnormality of shape, esp. of a part of the body.

defraud *v.* deprive by fraud.

defray *v.* provide money to pay (costs). □ **defrayal** *n.*

defrost *v.* remove ice from (a refrigerator); thaw.

deft *adj.* skilful and quick. □ **deftly** *adv.*

defunct *adj.* no longer existing or functioning.

defuse *v.* remove the fuse from (an explosive); reduce the dangerous tension in (a situation).

■ **Usage** Do not confuse *defuse* with *diffuse*.

defy *v.* (**defied, defying**) resist, disobey; challenge; make difficult or impossible: *defies belief*.

degenerate *v.* (di-jen-er-ayt) become worse physically, mentally, or morally. ● *adj.* (di-**jen**-er-ăt) having degenerated. ● *n.* a degenerate person. □ **degeneracy** *n.*, **degeneration** *n.*

degrade *v.* **1** treat disrespectfully, humiliate; *archaic* reduce to a lower rank. **2** decompose. □ **degradation** *n.*

degree *n.* **1** the extent to which something is true or present; a stage in a series. **2** a unit of measurement for angles or temperature. **3** an award given by a university or college.

dehumanize *v.* (also **-ise**) remove human qualities from; make impersonal. □ **dehumanization** *n.*

dehydrate *v.* (cause to) lose a large amount of moisture; preserve (food) by doing this. □ **dehydration** *n.*, **dehydrator** *n.*

deify *v.* (**deified, deifying**) treat as a god. □ **deification** *n.*

deign (dayn) *v.* condescend.

deity *n.* (*pl.* **-ies**) a divine being.

déjà vu (day-*zhah* **voo**) *n.* a feeling of having experienced a present situation before.

dejected *adj.* in low spirits.

dejection *n.* lowness of spirits.

de jure (dee **joo**-ri) *adj.* & *adv.* rightful, by right.

delay *v.* make late; be slow; postpone. ● *n.* delaying; time lost by delaying.

delayering *n.* the reduction of the number of levels in the hierarchy of an organization.

delectable *adj.* delicious, delightful. □ **delectably** *adv.*

delectation *n.* enjoyment.

delegate *n.* (**del**-i-găt) a representative. ● *v.* (**del**-i-gayt) entrust (a task or power) to an agent.

delegation *n.* a group of representatives; delegating.

delete *v.* strike out (a word etc.); remove. □ **deletion** *n.*

deleterious *adj.* harmful.

delft *n.* glazed earthenware.

deliberate *adj.* (di-**lib**-er-ăt) **1** intentional. **2** slow and careful. ● *v.* (di-**lib**-er-ayt) engage in careful discussion or consideration (of). □ **deliberately** *adv.*, **deliberation** *n.*

delicacy *n.* (*pl.* **-ies**) **1** being delicate. **2** a choice food.

delicate *adj.* **1** fine, intricate. **2** fragile; prone to illness or injury. **3** requiring or showing tact. □ **delicately** *adv.*

delicatessen *n.* a shop selling speciality groceries, cheeses, cooked meats, etc.

delicious *adj.* delightful, esp. to taste or smell. □ **deliciously** *adv.*

delight *n.* great pleasure; a source of this. ● *v.* please greatly; feel delight. □ **delightful** *adj.*, **delightfully** *adv.*

delimit *v.* determine the limits or boundaries of. □ **delimitation** *n.*

delineate *v.* outline. □ **delineation** *n.*, **delineator** *n.*

delinquent *adj.* & *n.* (a person) guilty of persistent law-breaking. □ **delinquency** *n.*

deliquesce (de-li-**kwes**) *v.* become liquid, melt.

delirium *n.* a disordered state of mind, esp. during fever; wild excitement. □ **delirious** *adj.*, **deliriously** *adv.*

deliver *v.* **1** take to an addressee or purchaser; hand over; utter (a speech etc.); aim (a blow or attack). **2** rescue, set free. **3** assist in the birth of. □ **deliverer** *n.*, **delivery** *n.*

deliverance *n.* rescue, freeing.

dell *n.* a small wooded hollow.

delta *n.* **1** the fourth letter of the Greek alphabet (Δ, δ). **2** a triangular patch of deposited earth at the mouth of a river, formed by its diverging outlets.

delude *v.* deceive, mislead.

deluge *n.* a flood; a heavy fall of rain; a large quantity of something coming at the same time. ● *v.* flood; overwhelm.

delusion *n.* a false belief or impression. □ **delusory** *adj.*

delusive *adj.* giving a false impression.

de luxe *adj.* of superior quality; luxurious.

delve *v.* search deeply.

demagogue *n.* a political leader who wins support by appealing to popular feelings and prejudices. □ **demagogic** *adj.*, **demagogy** *n.*

demand *n.* a firm or official request; customers' desire for goods or services; a claim. ● *v.* make a demand for; need.

demanding *adj.* **1** difficult, requiring great skill or effort. **2** expecting a lot from other people.

demarcation *n.* the marking of a boundary or limits, esp. of work for different trades.

demean *v.* lower the dignity of.

demeanour *n.* (*Amer.* **demeanor**) the way a person behaves.

demented *adj.* driven mad, crazy.

dementia *n.* a mental disorder.

demerara *n.* brown raw cane sugar.

demesne (dĕ-**mayn**) *n.* a landed estate.

demi- *pref.* half.

demilitarize *v.* (also **-ise**) remove military forces from. □ **demilitarization** *n.*

demise *n.* death; failure.

demisemiquaver *n.* a note equal to half a semiquaver.

demo *n.* (*pl.* **demos**) *informal* a demonstration.

demob *informal v.* (**demobbed, demobbing**) demobilize. ● *n.* demobilization.

demobilize *v.* (also **-ise**) release from military service. □ **demobilization** *n.*

democracy *n.* (*pl.* **-ies**) government by all the people, usu. through elected representatives; a country governed in this way. □ **democratic** *adj.*, **democratically** *adv.*

democrat *n.* a person favouring democracy.

demography *n.* the statistical study of human populations. □ **demographic** *adj.*

demolish *v.* pull or knock down; destroy. □ **demolition** *n.*

demon *n.* a devil, an evil spirit; a cruel person; an energetic and forceful person. □ **demoniac** *adj.*, **demoniacal** *adj.*, **demonic** *adj.*

demonstrable *adj.* able to be proved or shown. □ **demonstrability** *n.*, **demonstrably** *adv.*

demonstrate *v.* **1** prove, show clearly; give an exhibition of. **2** take part in a public protest. □ **demonstrator** *n.*

demonstration *n.* **1** proving; exhibiting. **2** a public protest.

demonstrative *adj.* **1** showing feelings openly. **2** giving proof, conclusive. □ **demonstratively** *adv.*

demoralize *v.* (also **-ise**) dishearten. □ **demoralization** *n.*

demote *v.* reduce to a lower rank or category. □ **demotion** *n.*

demur *v.* (**demurred, demurring**) raise objections. ● *n.* objecting.

demure *adj.* quiet and modest or pretending to be so. □ **demurely** *adv.*, **demureness** *n.*

den *n.* a wild animal's lair; a person's small private room.

denary *adj.* of ten; decimal.

denationalize *v.* (also **-ise**) privatize. □ **denationalization** *n.*

denature *v.* **1** change the properties of. **2** make (alcohol) unfit for drinking.

dendrochronology *n.* the dating of timber by study of the annual growth rings.

deniable *adj.* able to be denied.

denial *n.* denying; a statement that a thing is not true.

denier (**den**-yer) *n.* a unit of weight for measuring the fineness of yarn.

denigrate *v.* disparage; criticize unfairly. □ **denigration** *n.*

denim *n.* a strong twilled fabric; (**denims**) trousers made of this.

denizen *n. formal* an inhabitant.

denominate *v. formal* name.

denomination *n.* **1** a branch of the Christian Church or another religion. **2** the face value of a coin or bank note. **3** *formal* a name. □ **denominational** *adj.*

denominator *n.* a number below the line in a vulgar fraction.

denote *v.* be a sign or symbol of; indicate. □ **denotation** *n.*

denouement (day-**noo**-mahn) *n.* the final outcome of a play or story.

denounce *v.* condemn, criticize; inform against.

dense *adj.* **1** thick, closely massed. **2** compressed and hard to understand. **3** stupid. □ **densely** *adv.*, **denseness** *n.*

density *n.* the degree to which something is full or closely packed; the relation of weight to volume.

dent *n.* a hollow left by a blow or pressure. ● *v.* mark with a dent; diminish, discourage.

dental *adj.* of or for teeth; of dentistry.

dental floss *n.* thread for cleaning between the teeth.

dentate *adj.* toothed, notched.

dentifrice *n.* a paste or powder for cleaning teeth.

dentine *n.* the hard tissue forming the teeth.

dentist *n.* a person qualified to treat decay and malformations of teeth.

dentistry *n.* a dentist's work.

dentition *n.* the arrangement of the teeth.

denture *n.* a plate holding an artificial tooth or teeth.

denude *v.* strip of covering or property. □ **denudation** *n.*

denunciation *n.* a public condemnation; informing against someone.

deny *v.* (**denied, denying**) **1** say that (something) is not true; refuse to admit as belonging or attaching to one. **2** refuse; prevent from having. □ **deny oneself** practise abstinence.

deodorant *n.* a substance that removes or conceals unwanted odours. ● *adj.* deodorizing.

deodorize *v.* (also **-ise**) remove unpleasant smells from. □ **deodorization** *n.*

deoxyribonucleic acid *see* **DNA**.

depart *v.* go away, leave.

departed *adj.* dead.

department *n.* a section of an organization with a special function or concern. □ **departmental** *adj.*

department store *n.* a large shop selling many kinds of goods.

departure *n.* departing; setting out on a new course of action.

depend *v.* □ **depend on 1** be determined by. **2** trust confidently. **3** be unable to do without.

■ **Usage** Do not use *depend* without *on*: *It depends on what you want*, not *It depends what you want*.

---

dependable *adj.* reliable.

dependant *n.* one who depends on another for support.

■ **Usage** *Dependant* with an *a* is a noun; *dependent* with an *e* is an adjective.

---

dependency *n.* (*pl.* **-ies**) being dependent; a country controlled by another.

dependent *adj.* depending; controlled by another. □ **dependence** *n.*

depict *v.* represent in a picture or in words. □ **depiction** *n.*

depilatory *adj.* & *n.* (*pl.* **-ies**) (a substance) removing hair.

deplete *v.* reduce the number of by overuse. □ **depletion** *n.*

deplorable *adj.* shockingly bad. □ **deplorably** *adv.*

deplore *v.* feel or express strong disapproval of.

deploy *v.* move into position for action; utilize. □ **deployment** *n.*

depopulate *v.* reduce the population of. □ **depopulation** *n.*

deport *v.* remove (a person) from a country. □ **deportation** *n.*

deportment *n.* behaviour; bearing.

depose *v.* remove from power.

deposit *v.* (**deposited, depositing**) **1** put down; leave (a layer of earth etc.). **2** entrust for safe keeping; pay into a bank or as a guarantee. ● *n.* **1** a sum paid into a bank; a first instalment of payment. **2** a layer of sediment etc. ▫ **depositor** *n.*

depositary *n.* (*pl.* **-ies**) a person to whom something is entrusted.

deposition *n.* **1** deposing. **2** depositing. **3** a sworn statement.

depository *n.* (*pl.* **-ies**) **1** a storehouse. **2** a depositary.

depot (de-poh) *n.* a storage area, esp. for vehicles; *Amer.* a bus or railway station.

depraved *adj.* morally corrupt. ▫ **deprave** *v.*

depravity *n.* moral corruption, wickedness.

deprecate *v.* **1** express disapproval of. **2** disclaim politely. ▫ **deprecation** *n.*, **deprecatory** *adj.*

■ **Usage** Do not confuse *deprecate* and *depreciate*.

---

depreciate *v.* diminish in value; belittle. ▫ **depreciation** *n.*, **depreciatory** *adj.*

depredation *n.* plundering, destruction.

depress *v.* **1** cause to feel dispirited. **2** press down. **3** reduce the strength or activity of. ▫ **depressant** *adj.* & *n.*

depression *n.* **1** sadness, gloominess. **2** a long period of inactivity in trading. **3** pressing down; lowering, reduction; a hollow on a surface; an area of low atmospheric pressure. ▫ **depressive** *adj.*

deprive *v.* prevent from using or enjoying something. ▫ **deprivation** *n.*

depth *n.* **1** distance downwards or inwards from a surface. **2** profundity; detailed treatment; intensity. **3** the deepest or most central part. ▫ **in depth** thoroughly, in detail. **out of one's depth** in water too deep for one to stand; unable to understand or cope.

depth charge *n.* a bomb that will explode under water.

deputation *n.* a body of people sent to represent others.

depute *v.* appoint to act as one's representative.

deputize *v.* (also **-ise**) act as deputy.

deputy *n.* (*pl.* **-ies**) a person appointed to act as a substitute or representative.

derail *v.* cause (a train) to leave the rails. ▫ **derailment** *n.*

derange *v.* **1** make insane. **2** throw into confusion. ▫ **derangement** *n.*

derelict *adj.* left to fall into ruin.

dereliction *n.* **1** being derelict. **2** failure to do one's duty.

derestrict *v.* remove restrictions from.

deride *v.* mock, scorn.

de rigueur (dĕ rig-er) *adj.* required by custom or etiquette.

derision *n.* scorn, ridicule. ▫ **derisive** *adj.*, **derisively** *adv.*

derisory *adj.* **1** ridiculously or insultingly small. **2** derisive.

derivative *adj.* derived from another source; lacking originality. ● *n.* something derived from another source; a financial contract whose value is dependent on a variable asset.

derive *v.* obtain from a source; originate. ▫ **derivation** *n.*

dermatitis *n.* inflammation of the skin.

dermatology *n.* the study of the skin and its diseases. ▫ **dermatologist** *n.*

derogatory *adj.* disparaging.

derrick *n.* a crane with a pivoted arm; a framework over an oil well etc.

derris *n.* an insecticide made from the root of a tropical plant.

derv *n.* fuel for diesel engines.

dervish *n.* a member of a Muslim religious order known for their whirling dance.

DES *abbr.* Department of Education and Science.

desalinate *v.* remove salt from (esp. sea water). □ **desalination** *n.*

descant *n.* a treble accompaniment to a main melody.

descend *v.* go or come down; stoop to unworthy behaviour; make an attack or a sudden visit. □ **be descended from** have as one's ancestor(s).

descendant *n.* a person descended from another.

descent *n.* descending; a downward route or slope; ancestry.

describe *v.* **1** give a description of. **2** mark the outline of (a geometrical figure).

description *n.* **1** a statement of what a person or thing is like. **2** a kind, a sort: *cars of all descriptions*

descriptive *adj.* describing.

descry *v.* (**descried, descrying**) *literary* catch sight of.

desecrate *v.* defile (a sacred place or object) by irreverent treatment. □ **desecration** *n.*, **desecrator** *n.*

desegregate *v.* abolish segregation in or of. □ **desegregation** *n.*

deselect *v.* **1** reject (an MP) as a candidate for re-election. **2** turn off (a selected feature) on a list of options on a computer menu. □ **deselection** *n.*

desert[1] (dez-ert) *n.* a barren uninhabited often sandy area.

desert[2] (di-zert) *v.* abandon; leave one's service in the armed forces without permission. □ **deserter** *n.*, **desertion** *n.*

deserts (di-zerts) *n.pl.* what one deserves.

deserve *v.* be worthy of through one's actions or qualities. □ **deservedly** *adv.*

deserving *adj.* worthy of good treatment or fortune.

déshabillé (day-za-bee-ay) *n.* (also **dishabille**) the state of being only partly dressed.

desiccate *v.* dry out moisture from. □ **desiccation** *n.*

desideratum *n.* (*pl.* **desiderata**) something required.

design *n.* **1** a drawing that shows how a thing is to be made; a general form or arrangement; a decorative pattern. **2** an intention; planning. ● *v.* prepare a design for; plan, intend. □ **have designs on** aim to acquire, esp. illicitly. □ **designedly** *adv.*, **designer** *n.*

designate *v.* (dez-ig-nayt) appoint to a position; officially assign a status to. ● *adj.* (dez-ig-năt) appointed but not get installed. □ **designation** *n.*

designing *adj.* scheming, crafty.

desirable *adj.* **1** arousing desire, attractive. **2** advisable, beneficial. □ **desirability** *n.*

desire *n.* a feeling of wanting something strongly; sexual appetite; a thing desired. ● *v.* feel a desire for.

desirous *adj.* desiring.

desist *v.* cease, stop.

desk *n.* a piece of furniture for reading or writing at; a counter; a section of a newspaper office etc.

desktop *n.* **1** the working surface of a desk. **2** (in full **desktop computer**) a computer small enough for use on a desk.

desktop publishing *n.* producing documents, booklets, etc. with a desktop computer and high-quality printer.

desolate *adj.* deserted, lonely; very unhappy. □ **desolation** *n.*

desolated *adj.* feeling very distressed.

despair *n.* complete lack of hope. ● *v.* feel despair.

despatch var. of **dispatch**.

desperado *n.* (*pl.* **desperadoes**; *Amer.* **desperados**) a reckless criminal.

desperate *adj.* **1** hopeless; very bad or serious; made reckless by despair. **2** feeling an intense desire or need. □ **desperately** *adv.*, **desperation** *n.*

■ **Usage** *Desperate* is spelt with *-per*, not *-par*.

despicable *adj.* contemptible. ▫ **despicably** *adv.*

despise *v.* regard as worthless.

despite *prep.* in spite of.

despoil *v. literary* plunder. ▫ **despoilment** *n.*, **despoliation** *n.*

despondent *adj.* dejected and discouraged. ▫ **despondency** *n.*, **despondently** *adv.*

despot *n.* a dictator. ▫ **despotic** *adj.*, **despotically** *adv.*, **despotism** *n.*

dessert (di-zert) *n.* the sweet course of a meal.

dessertspoon *n.* a medium-sized spoon for eating puddings etc. ▫ **dessertspoonful** *n.*

destabilize *v.* (also **-ise**) make unstable or insecure.

destination *n.* the place to which a person or thing is going.

destine *v.* set apart for a purpose; doom to a particular fate.

destiny *n.* (*pl.* **-ies**) fate; one's future destined by fate.

destitute *adj.* extremely poor; without means to live. ▫ **destitution** *n.*

destroy *v.* pull or break down; ruin; kill (an animal). ▫ **destruction** *n.*, **destructive** *adj.*

destroyer *n.* **1** a fast warship. **2** a person or thing that destroys.

destruct *v.* destroy (esp. a rocket) deliberately.

destructible *adj.* able to be destroyed.

desuetude *n. formal* disuse.

desultory (dez-ŭl-tĕ-ree) *adj.* without purpose or enthusiasm; moving at random between subjects. ▫ **desultorily** *adv.*

detach *v.* **1** separate, unfasten. **2** send (a group of soldiers) on a separate mission. ▫ **detachable** *adj.*

detached *adj.* **1** separate; not connected. **2** free from bias or emotion.

detachment *n.* **1** objectivity. **2** detaching. **3** a group sent on a military mission.

detail *n.* **1** a small individual fact or item; such items collectively. **2** a small military detachment. ● *v.* **1** describe in detail. **2** assign to a special duty.

detain *v.* keep in official custody; delay. ▫ **detainment** *n.*

detainee *n.* a person detained in custody.

detect *v.* discover the presence of. ▫ **detection** *n.*, **detector** *n.*

detective *n.* a person whose job is to investigate crimes.

détente (day-**tahnt**) *n.* an easing of tension between nations.

detention *n.* detaining; imprisonment.

deter *v.* (**deterred, deterring**) discourage from action. ▫ **determent** *n.*

detergent *n.* a cleansing substance, esp. other than soap.

deteriorate *v.* become worse. ▫ **deterioration** *n.*

determinant *n.* a decisive factor.

determination *n.* **1** resolution, firmness of purpose. **2** discovering, establishing. **3** controlling, deciding.

determine *v.* **1** control. **2** resolve firmly. **3** establish precisely.

determined *adj.* full of determination.

determinism *n.* a theory that actions are determined by external forces.

deterrent *n.* & *adj.* (something) deterring or intended to deter. ▫ **deterrence** *n.*

detest *v.* dislike intensely. ▫ **detestable** *adj.*, **detestation** *n.*

dethrone *v.* remove from power. ▫ **dethronement** *n.*

detonate *v.* (cause to) explode. ▫ **detonation** *n.*, **detonator** *n.*

detour *n.* a deviation from a direct or intended course.

detoxify *v.* (**detoxified, detoxifying**) remove harmful substances from.

detract *v.* □ **detract from** reduce the credit that is due to; lessen. □ **detraction** *n.*

detractor *n.* a person who criticizes something.

detriment *n.* harm. □ **detrimental** *adj.*, **detrimentally** *adv.*

detritus (di-trI-tŭs) *n.* debris; loose stones.

de trop (dĕ troh) *adj.* not wanted.

deuce (dyoos) *n.* **1** a score of 40 all in tennis. **2** *informal* (in exclamations) the Devil.

deuterium *n.* a heavy form of hydrogen.

Deutschmark (doich-mark) *n.* the former unit of money in Germany.

devalue *v.* reduce the value of; disparage. □ **devaluation** *n.*

devastate *v.* cause great destruction to. □ **devastation** *n.*

devastating *adj.* very destructive; shocking and distressing; very impressive or effective.

develop *v.* (**developed, developing**) **1** make or become larger, more mature, or more advanced; begin to exist or have. **2** make (land etc.) usable or profitable. **3** treat (a film) so as to make a picture visible. □ **developer** *n.*, **development** *n.*

deviant *adj.* & *n.* (a person or thing) deviating from accepted standards.

deviate *v.* diverge from a route, course of action, etc. □ **deviation** *n.*

device *n.* a thing made or used for a purpose; a scheme.

devil *n.* an evil spirit; (**the Devil**) the supreme spirit of evil; a cruel person; a person of mischievous energy or cleverness; *informal* a difficult person or problem. □ **devilish** *adj.*

devilled *adj.* (*Amer.* **deviled**) cooked with hot spices.

devilment *n.* mischief.

devilry *n.* wickedness; mischief.

devil's advocate *n.* a person who tests a proposition by arguing against it.

devious *adj.* underhand; (of a route) indirect. □ **deviously** *adv.*, **deviousness** *n.*

devise *v.* plan; invent. □ **devisor** *n.*

devoid *adj.* □ **devoid of** lacking, free from.

devolution *n.* delegation of power esp. from central to local administration.

devolve *v.* transfer (power) to a lower level; (of duties etc.) pass to a deputy.

devote *v.* give or use exclusively for a particular purpose.

devoted *adj.* showing devotion.

devotee *n.* an enthusiast; a worshipper.

devotion *n.* great love, loyalty, or commitment; religious worship; (**devotions**) prayers.

devotional *adj.* used in worship.

devour *v.* eat hungrily or greedily; consume, destroy; take in avidly. □ **devourer** *n.*

devout *adj.* earnestly religious; earnest, sincere. □ **devoutly** *adv.*

dew *n.* drops of condensed moisture forming on cool surfaces at night. □ **dewy** *adj.*

dewclaw *n.* a small claw on the inner side of a dog's leg.

dewlap *n.* a fold of loose skin on the throat of cattle etc.

dexterity *n.* skill. □ **dexterous** *adj.* (also **dextrous**), **dexterously** *adv.*

dextrose *n.* a form of glucose.

dhal *n.* (also **dal**) an Indian dish of split pulses.

di- *pref.* two; double.

diabetes *n.* a disease in which sugar and starch are not properly absorbed by the body. □ **diabetic** *adj.* & *n.*

diabolic *adj.* of the Devil.

diabolical *adj.* very wicked; *informal* extremely bad. □ **diabolically** *adv.*

diabolism *n.* worship of the Devil.

diachronic *adj.* concerned with the historical development of a subject.

diaconate *n.* the office of deacon; a body of deacons. □ **diaconal** *adj.*

diacritic *n.* a sign on a letter indicating a difference in pronunciation, e.g. an accent.

diadem *n.* a crown.

diaeresis *n.* (*Amer.* **dieresis**) a mark over a vowel sounded separately.

diagnose *v.* make a diagnosis of.

diagnosis *n.* (*pl.* **diagnoses**) the identification of a disease or condition after observing its symptoms. □ **diagnostic** *adj.*, **diagnostician** *n.*

diagonal *adj.* & *n.* (a line) joining opposite corners of a square or rectangle. □ **diagonally** *adv.*

diagram *n.* a schematic drawing that shows the parts or operation of something. □ **diagrammatic** *adj.*, **diagrammatically** *adv.*

dial *n.* the face of a clock or watch; a similar plate or disc with a movable pointer; a movable disc manipulated to connect one telephone with another. ● *v.* (**dialled, dialling**; *Amer.* **dialed**) select or operate by using a dial or numbered buttons.

dialect *n.* a local form of a language. □ **dialectal** *adj.*

dialectic *n.* investigation of truths esp. by examining contradictions. □ **dialectical** *adj.*

dialogue *n.* (*Amer.* **dialog**) a conversation or discussion.

dialysis *n.* purification of blood by filtering it through a membrane.

diamanté (dee-ă-**mon**-tay) *adj.* decorated with artificial jewels.

diameter *n.* a straight line from side to side through the centre of a circle or sphere; its length.

diametrical *adj.* **1** (of opposites) total, absolute. **2** of or along a diameter. □ **diametrically** *adv.*

diamond *n.* **1** a very hard brilliant precious stone. **2** a four-sided figure with equal sides and with angles that are not right angles; a playing card marked with such shapes.

diamond wedding *n.* a 60th anniversary.

diaper *n. Amer.* a baby's nappy.

diaphanous (dI-**af**-ă-nŭs) *adj.* almost transparent. □ **diaphanously** *adv.*

diaphragm (**dy**-ă-fram) *n.* **1** the muscular partition between the chest and abdomen. **2** a contraceptive cap fitting over the cervix.

diarrhoea (dyă-**ree**-ă) (*Amer.* **diarrhea**) *n.* a condition with frequent fluid faeces.

diary *n.* (*pl.* **-ies**) a daily record of events; a book for this or for noting appointments. □ **diarist** *n.*

diatribe *n.* a violent verbal attack.

dibber *n.* (also **dibble**) a tool to make holes in the ground for young plants.

dice *n.* (*pl.* **dice**) a small cube marked on each side with 1–6 spots, used in games of chance. ● *v.* cut into small cubes. □ **dice with death** take great risks.

dicey *adj.* (**dicier, diciest**) *informal* risky, unpredictable.

dichotomy (dy-**kot**-ŏ-mi) *n.* (*pl.* **-ies**) a division into two absolutely opposed parts. □ **dichotomous** *adj.*

dicky *informal adj.* (**dickier, dickiest**) weak, unhealthy. ● *n.* (*pl.* **-ies**) a false shirt-front.

dicta pl. of **dictum**.

dictate *v.* **1** say (words) aloud to be written or recorded. **2** give orders officiously; control, prescribe. ● *n. pl.* (**dictates**) commands. □ **dictation** *n.*

dictator *n.* a ruler with unrestricted authority; a domineering person. □ **dictatorship** *n.*

dictatorial *adj.* of or like a dictator. □ **dictatorially** *adv.*

diction *n.* a manner of uttering or pronouncing words.

dictionary *n.* (*pl.* **-ies**) a book that lists and gives the meaning of the words of a language; an alphabetically arranged reference book.

dictum *n.* (*pl.* **dicta**) a formal statement; a saying.

did past of **do**.

didactic *adj.* meant or meaning to instruct. ◻ **didactically** *adv.*

diddle *v. informal* cheat.

die[1] *v.* (**died, dying**) cease to be alive; cease to exist; *informal* stop functioning; fade away. ◻ **be dying for** or **to** *informal* long for or to.

die[2] *n.* a device for cutting or moulding metal or for stamping a design on coins etc.

diehard *n.* a stubbornly conservative person.

dieresis Amer. sp. of **diaeresis**.

diesel *n.* (also **diesel engine**) an oil-burning engine in which ignition is produced by the heat of compressed air; fuel used in this.

diet *n.* **1** a person's usual food; a special restricted course of food adopted to lose weight or for medical reasons. **2** a congress, a parliamentary assembly in certain countries. ● *v.* (**dieted, dieting**) restrict what one eats. ● *adj.* designed for a weight-reducing diet; low in sugar and fat. ◻ **dietary** *adj.*, **dieter** *n.*

dietetic *adj.* of diet and nutrition. ● *n.* (**dietetics**) the study of diet and nutrition.

dietitian *n.* (also **dietician**) an expert in dietetics.

differ *v.* be unlike; disagree.

difference *n.* **1** a way in which things are not the same; being different; the extent of a difference, the remainder when one sum is subtracted from another. **2** a disagreement.

different *adj.* not the same; distinct; novel. ◻ **differently** *adv.*

differential *adj.* of, showing, or depending on a difference; distinctive. ● *n.* **1** an agreed difference in wage-rates. **2** an arrangement of gears allowing a vehicle's wheels to revolve at different speeds when cornering.

differentiate *v.* distinguish between; be a difference between; make or become different. ◻ **differentiation** *n.*

difficult *adj.* needing much effort or skill to do, deal with, or understand; hard to please, uncooperative. ◻ **difficulty** *n.*

diffident *adj.* lacking self-confidence. ◻ **diffidence** *n.*, **diffidently** *adv.*

diffract *v.* break up (a beam of light) into a series of coloured or dark-and-light bands. ◻ **diffraction** *n.*, **diffractive** *adj.*

diffuse *adj.* (di-**fewss**) spread widely, not concentrated. ● *v.* (di-**fewz**) spread widely or thinly. ◻ **diffusely** *adv.*, **diffuser** *n.*, **diffusion** *n.*, **diffusive** *adj.* **diffusible** *adj.*

■ **Usage** Do not confuse the verbs *diffuse* and *defuse*.

dig *v.* (**dug, digging**) **1** break up and move soil; make (a hole etc.) in this way; extract from the ground in this way. **2** push, poke. **3** search for; find. **4** *informal* like. ● *n.* **1** digging; an excavation. **2** a poke with the finger etc. **3** a cutting remark. **4** (**digs**) *informal* lodgings.

digest *v.* (dy-**jest**) break down (food) in the body; absorb into the mind. ● *n.* (**dy**-jest) a methodical summary. ◻ **digester** *n.*, **digestible** *adj.*, **digestibility** *n.*

digestion *n.* the process or power of digesting food.

digestive *adj.* of or aiding digestion.

digger *n.* a person who digs; a mechanical excavator.

digit *n.* **1** any numeral from 0 to 9. **2** a finger or toe.

digital *adj.* of or using digits; (of a clock) showing the time by a row of figures; (of a recording) converting sound into electrical pulses. ◻ **digitally** *adv.*

digitalis *n.* a heart stimulant prepared from foxglove leaves.

dignified *adj.* showing dignity.

dignify *v.* (**dignified, dignifying**) treat as important or deserving respect.

dignitary *n.* (*pl.* **-ies**) a person holding high rank or position.

dignity *n.* (*pl.* **-ies**) being worthy of respect; a calm and serious manner; a high rank or position.

digress *v.* depart from the main subject temporarily. ▫ **digression** *n.*, **digressive** *adj.*

dike var. of **dyke**.

diktat *n.* a firm statement or order.

dilapidated *adj.* in disrepair.

dilapidation *n.* disrepair due to neglect.

dilate *v.* make or become wider. ▫ **dilation, dilatation** *n.*, **dilator** *n.*

dilatory (dil-ă-ter-i) *adj.* slow to act; causing delay.

dilemma *n.* a situation in which a difficult choice has to be made.

dilettante (dili-tan-ti) *n.* (*pl.* **dilettanti** or **dilettantes**) a person who dabbles in a subject for pleasure.

diligent *adj.* working or done with care and effort. ▫ **diligence** *n.*, **diligently** *adv.*

dill *n.* a herb.

dilly-dally *v.* (**dilly-dallied, -dallying**) *informal* waste time by dawdling or being indecisive.

dilute *v.* reduce the strength of (fluid) by adding water etc.; reduce the forcefulness of. ● *adj.* diluted. ▫ **dilution** *n.*

dim *adj.* (**dimmer, dimmest**) **1** not bright, indistinct. **2** *informal* stupid. ● *v.* (**dimmed, dimming**) make or become less bright or distinct. ▫ **dimly** *adv.*, **dimness** *n.*

dime *n.* a 10-cent coin of the USA.

dimension *n.* **1** an aspect or feature. **2** a measurement such as length or breadth; (**dimensions**) size, extent. ▫ **dimensional** *adj.*

diminish *v.* make or become less.

diminuendo *n.* (*pl.* **diminuendos** or **diminuendi**) *Music* a gradual decrease in loudness.

diminution *n.* a decrease.

diminutive *adj.* tiny. ● *n.* a form of a word suggesting smallness.

dimple *n.* a small dent, esp. in the skin. ● *v.* (cause to) show dimples.

din *n.* a loud annoying noise. ● *v.* (**dinned, dinning**) impress (information) on someone by constant repetition.

dinar (dee-nar) *n.* a unit of money in some Balkan and Middle Eastern countries.

dine *v.* eat dinner. ▫ **dine out on** frequently relate (an experience) at social occasions. ▫ **diner** *n.*

ding-dong *n.* **1** the sound of bells. **2** *informal* an argument. ● *adj.* & *adv.* **1** with a chiming sound. **2** *informal* with intense competition between well-matched opponents.

dinghy *n.* (*pl.* **-ies**) a small open boat or inflatable rubber boat.

dingle *n. literary* a deep dell.

dingo *n.* (*pl.* **dingoes**) an Australian wild dog.

dingy *adj.* (**dingier, dingiest**) dull, drab. ▫ **dingily** *adv.*, **dinginess** *n.*

dining room *n.* a room in which meals are eaten.

dinky *adj.* (**dinkier, dinkiest**) *informal* attractively small and neat.

dinner *n.* the chief meal of the day; a formal evening meal.

dinner jacket *n.* a man's jacket for formal evening wear.

dinosaur *n.* an extinct prehistoric reptile, often of enormous size.

dint *n.* a dent. ▫ **by dint of** by means of.

diocese *n.* a district under the care of a bishop. ▫ **diocesan** *adj.*

diode *n.* a semiconductor allowing the flow of current in one direction only and having two terminals.

dioptre (dy-op-ter) *n.* (*Amer.* **diopter**) a unit of refractive power of a lens.

dioxide *n.* an oxide with two atoms of oxygen to one of a metal or other element.

dip *v.* (**dipped, dipping**) **1** plunge briefly into liquid; put (a hand etc.) briefly into something. **2** move or slope downwards; lower; lower the beam of (headlights). ● *n.* **1** a short swim; a brief immersion; a liquid in which sheep are dipped to guard against infection; a creamy sauce in which crudités etc. are dipped. **2** hollow. □ **dip into** casually read parts of (a book).

diphtheria *n.* an infectious disease with inflammation of the throat.

diphthong *n.* a compound vowel sound (as *ou* in *loud*).

diploma *n.* a certificate awarded on completion of a course of study.

diplomacy *n.* handling of international relations; tact.

diplomat *n.* **1** an official representing a country abroad. **2** a tactful person. □ **diplomatic** *adj.*, **diplomatically** *adv.*

dipper *n.* **1** a diving bird. **2** a ladle.

dipsomania *n.* an uncontrollable craving for alcohol. □ **dipsomaniac** *n.*

diptych (dip-tik) *n.* a pair of pictures on two panels hinged together.

dire *adj.* extreme, serious; *informal* very bad.

direct *adj.* **1** straight, without interruptions or diversions; with nothing intervening or mediating; frank. **2** absolute: *the direct opposite.* ● *adv.* with no interruption, intermediary, etc. ● *v.* **1** control, manage; order. **2** aim in a particular direction; address (a letter etc.); tell (someone) how to reach a place; instruct. □ **directness** *n.*

direct action *n.* the use of strikes, public protests, etc. rather than negotiation to achieve one's demands.

direct debit *n.* an instruction to one's bank to make regular payments to a third party.

direction *n.* **1** a course along which someone or something moves; the way something faces. **2** control; (**directions**) instructions. □ **directional** *adj.*

directive *n.* an official instruction.

directly *adv.* **1** in a direct line or manner. **2** immediately. ● *conj.* as soon as.

direct object *n.* *Grammar* the primary object of a transitive verb, the person or thing directly affected.

director *n.* a person in charge of an activity or organization; a member of a board directing a business; one who supervises acting and filming. □ **directorship** *n.*

directorate *n.* a board of directors; a section of a government department dealing with a particular area.

directory *n.* (*pl.* **-ies**) a book listing telephone subscribers etc.; a computer file listing other files.

direct speech *n.* speech reported by quoting the exact words spoken.

dirge *n.* a mournful song.

dirham (deer-ĕm) *n.* the unit of money in Morocco and the United Arab Emirates.

dirigible *n.* an airship. ● *adj.* able to be steered or guided.

dirndl *n.* a full gathered skirt.

dirt *n.* unclean matter; loose soil; excrement; *informal* scandalous information; obscene material.

dirty *adj.* (**dirtier, dirtiest**) marked or covered with dirt; producing dirt or pollution; obscene; dishonourable, unfair. ● *v.* (**dirtied, dirtying**) make dirty. ● *adv.* *informal* emphasizing size: *a dirty great rock.* □ **dirtily** *adv.*, **dirtiness** *n.*

disability *n.* (*pl.* **-ies**) a physical or mental incapacity; a legal disadvantage.

disable *v.* impair the capacities or activity of; keep from functioning or from doing something.

disabled *adj.* having a physical disability. □ **disablement** *n.*

disabuse *v.* disillusion.

disadvantage *n.* an unfavourable condition or position in relation to others; something diminishing one's chances of success or effectiveness. □ **disadvantaged** *adj.*, **disadvantageous** *adj.*

disaffected *adj.* discontented and no longer loyal. □ **disaffection** *n.*

disagree *v.* have a different opinion; argue; be inconsistent. □ **disagree with** (of food etc.) make ill. □ **disagreement** *n.*

disagreeable *adj.* unpleasant; bad-tempered. □ **disagreeably** *adv.*

disallow *v.* refuse to sanction.

disappear *v.* pass from sight or existence. □ **disappearance** *n.*

disappoint *v.* fail to fulfil the hopes or expectations of. □ **disappointment** *n.*

disapprobation *n.* disapproval.

disapprove *v.* consider something bad or immoral. □ **disapproval** *n.*

disarm *v.* **1** deprive of weapons; reduce armed forces. **2** make less hostile; win over.

disarmament *n.* a reduction of a country's forces or weapons.

disarrange *v.* make untidy. □ **disarrangement** *n.*

disarray *n.* disorder, confusion.

disassociate *v.* = **dissociate**.

disaster *n.* a sudden great misfortune or failure. □ **disastrous** *adj.*, **disastrously** *adv.*

disavow *v.* deny any connection with. □ **disavowal** *n.*

disband *v.* (cause to) separate.

disbar *v.* (**disbarred, disbarring**) deprive (a barrister) of the right to practise law.

disbelieve *v.* refuse or be unable to believe. □ **disbelief** *n.*

disburse *v.* pay out (money). □ **disbursement** *n.*

■ **Usage** Do not confuse *disburse* with *disperse*.

disc *n.* a thin, flat round object; a record bearing recorded sound; a layer of cartilage between the vertebrae; *Computing* = **disk**.

discard *v.* (dis-**kard**) reject as useless or unwanted. ● *n.* (**dis**-kard) something rejected.

discern *v.* perceive with the mind or senses. □ **discernible** *adj.*, **discernibly** *adv.*, **discernment** *n.*

discerning *adj.* with good judgement or understanding.

discharge *v.* **1** dismiss; release; free from obligation. **2** allow (liquid etc.) to flow out; unload. **3** pay (a debt); fulfil (an obligation). ● *n.* discharging; material flowing from something.

disciple *n.* a pupil or follower; one of the original followers of Christ.

disciplinarian *n.* a person who enforces strict discipline.

disciplinary *adj.* of or for discipline.

discipline *n.* **1** controlled and obedient behaviour; training and punishment producing this. **2** a branch of learning. ● *v.* train to be orderly; punish.

disc jockey *n.* a person who introduces and plays pop records on the radio or at a disco.

disclaim *v.* refuse to acknowledge.

disclaimer *n.* a denial of responsibility.

disclose *v.* reveal. □ **disclosure** *n.*

disco *n.* (*pl.* **discos**) a place where recorded pop music is played for dancing; equipment for playing this.

discolour *v.* (*Amer.* **discolor**) become a less attractive colour; stain. □ **discoloration** *n.*

discomfit *v.* (**discomfited, discomfiting**) make uneasy; embarrass. □ **discomfiture** *n.*

discomfort *n.* lack of physical or mental ease; slight pain.

discommode *v.* inconvenience.

disconcert *v.* upset the self-confidence of, unsettle.

disconnect *v.* break the connection of; cut off the power supply of. □ **disconnection** *n.*

disconsolate *adj.* very unhappy. □ **disconsolately** *adv.*

discontent *n.* dissatisfaction. □ **discontented** *adj.*

discontinue *v.* put an end to; cease. □ **discontinuance** *n.*

discontinuous *adj.* having gaps or breaks. ◻ **discontinuity** *n.*

discord *n.* **1** disagreement, quarrelling. **2** inharmonious noise. ◻ **discordance** *n.*, **discordant** *adj.*

discotheque *n.* a disco.

discount *n.* (dis-kownt) an amount of money taken off something's full price. ● *v.* (dis-**kownt**) **1** reduce the price of. **2** disregard as unreliable.

discourage *v.* dishearten; deter, dissuade. ◻ **discouragement** *n.*

discourse *n.* (dis-korss) communication, debate; a treatise or lecture. ● *v.* (dis-**korss**) speak or write authoritatively.

discourteous *adj.* impolite. ◻ **discourteously** *adv.*, **discourtesy** *n.*

discover *v.* find; learn; be the first to find. ◻ **discovery** *n.*

discredit *v.* (**discredited, discrediting**) damage the reputation of; cause to be disbelieved. ● *n.* (something causing) damage to a reputation.

discreditable *adj.* bringing discredit.

discreet *adj.* unobtrusive; cautious; not giving away secrets. ◻ **discreetly** *adv.*

discrepancy *n.* (*pl.* **-ies**) a difference, a failure to match.

discrete *adj.* separate, distinct. ◻ **discretely** *adv.*

■ *Usage* Do not confuse *discrete* with *discreet.*

discretion *n.* **1** being discreet. **2** freedom to decide something.

discretionary *adj.* done or used at a person's discretion.

discriminate *v.* distinguish; make an unfair difference in one's treatment of people. ◻ **discrimination** *n.*, **discriminatory** *adj.*

discriminating *adj.* having good judgement.

discursive *adj.* rambling, not keeping to the main subject.

discus *n.* a heavy disc thrown in an athletic contest.

discuss *v.* examine by argument, talk or write about. ◻ **discussion** *n.*

disdain *v.* & *n.* scorn. ◻ **disdainful** *adj.*, **disdainfully** *adv.*

disease *n.* an illness, an unhealthy condition. ◻ **diseased** *adj.*

disembark *v.* (cause to) leave a ship, train, etc. ◻ **disembarkation** *n.*

disembodied *adj.* (of a voice) with no obvious physical source.

disembowel *v.* (**disembowelled, disembowelling**; *Amer.* **disemboweled**) take out the entrails of. ◻ **disembowelment** *n.*

disenchant *v.* disappoint, disillusion. ◻ **disenchantment** *n.*

disenfranchise *v.* (also **disfranchise**) deprive of the right to vote. ◻ **disenfranchisement** *n.*

disengage *v.* detach; release. ◻ **disengagement** *n.*

disentangle *v.* free from tangles or confusion; separate. ◻ **disentanglement** *n.*

disestablish *v.* deprive (an organization, esp. a Church) of an official connection with the state.

disfavour *n.* (*Amer.* **disfavor**) dislike, disapproval.

disfigure *v.* spoil the appearance of. ◻ **disfigurement** *n.*

disfranchise var. of **disenfranchise**.

disgorge *v.* eject, pour forth. ◻ **disgorgement** *n.*

disgrace *n.* (something causing) loss of respect. ● *v.* bring disgrace upon. ◻ **disgraceful** *adj.*, **disgracefully** *adv.*

disgruntled *adj.* annoyed, resentful. ◻ **disgruntlement** *n.*

disguise *v.* conceal the identity of. ● *n.* a means of concealing one's identity; being disguised.

disgust *n.* a feeling that something is offensive or unpleasant; loathing. ● *v.* cause disgust in. ◻ **disgusting** *adj.*

dish *n.* **1** a shallow bowl, esp. for food; food prepared according to a recipe. **2** *informal* an attractive person. ▫ **dish out** serve (food); *informal* distribute casually. **dish up** serve (food).

dishabille var. of **déshabillé**.

disharmony *n.* lack of harmony.

dishearten *v.* cause to lose hope or confidence.

dished *adj.* concave.

dishevelled *adj.* (*Amer.* **disheveled**) ruffled and untidy. ▫ **dishevelment** *n.*

dishonest *adj.* not honest. ▫ **dishonestly** *adv.*, **dishonesty** *n.*

dishonour *v.* & *n.* (*Amer.* **dishonor**) disgrace.

dishonourable *adj.* (*Amer.* **dishonorable**) shameful, deserving disgrace. ▫ **dishonourably** *adv.*

dishwasher *n.* a machine for washing dishes.

dishy *adj.* (**dishier, dishiest**) *informal* attractive.

disillusion *v.* rid of pleasant but mistaken beliefs. ▫ **disillusionment** *n.*

disincentive *n.* something that discourages an action or effort.

disinclination *n.* unwillingness.

disinclined *adj.* reluctant.

disinfect *v.* cleanse by destroying harmful bacteria. ▫ **disinfection** *n.*

disinfectant *n.* a substance used for disinfecting things.

disinformation *n.* deliberately misleading information.

disingenuous *adj.* insincere.

disinherit *v.* cancel a bequest to. ▫ **disinheritance** *n.*

disintegrate *v.* break into small pieces. ▫ **disintegration** *n.*

disinter *v.* (**disinterred, disinterring**) dig up; discover. ▫ **disinterment** *n.*

disinterested *adj.* **1** unbiased, impartial. **2** uninterested. ▫ **disinterest** *n.*

▪ **Usage** The use of *disinterested* to mean 'uninterested' is common in informal use but is widely considered incorrect.

---

disjointed *adj.* lacking coherent connection.

disjunctive *adj.* **1** lacking connection. **2** involving mutually exclusive possibilities.

disk *n.* a flat circular device on which computer data can be stored.

diskette *n.* *Computing* a small floppy disk.

dislike *n.* distaste, hostility. ● *v.* feel dislike for.

dislocate *v.* disturb the arrangement or position of; disrupt. ▫ **dislocation** *n.*

dislodge *v.* remove from an established position.

disloyal *adj.* not loyal. ▫ **disloyally** *adv.*, **disloyalty** *n.*

dismal *adj.* gloomy; *informal* very bad. ▫ **dismally** *adv.*

dismantle *v.* take to pieces.

dismay *n.* a feeling of shock and distress. ● *v.* cause to feel this.

dismember *v.* remove the limbs of; split into pieces. ▫ **dismemberment** *n.*

dismiss *v.* send away from one's presence or employment; disregard. ▫ **dismissal** *n.*

dismissive *adj.* treating something as unworthy of consideration. ▫ **dismissively** *adv.*

dismount *v.* get off a thing on which one is riding.

disobedient *adj.* not obedient. ▫ **disobediently** *adv.*, **disobedience** *n.*

disobey *v.* disregard orders.

disobliging *adj.* uncooperative, unhelpful. ▫ **disoblige** *v.*

disorder *n.* **1** untidiness. **2** a breakdown of discipline. **3** an ailment. ● *v.* disarrange, disrupt. ▫ **disorderly** *adj.*, **disorderliness** *n.*

disorganized *adj.* (also **-ized**) not properly planned or arranged; muddled. ▫ **disorganization** *n.*, **disorganize** *v.*

disorientate *v.* (also **disorient**) cause (a person) to lose his or her sense of direction. □ **disorientation** *n.*

disown *v.* refuse to acknowledge; reject all connection with.

disparage *v.* belittle; criticize. □ **disparagement** *n.*

disparate *adj.* different in kind. □ **disparately** *adv.*

■ **Usage** Do not confuse *disparate* with *desperate*.

disparity *n.* (*pl.* **-ies**) a great difference.

dispassionate *adj.* unemotional and objective. □ **dispassionately** *adv.*

dispatch (also **despatch**) *v.* **1** send off to a destination or for a purpose. **2** complete (a task) quickly. **3** kill. ● *n.* **1** sending off. **2** promptness. **3** an official report; a news report.

dispatch box *n.* a container for carrying official documents.

dispatch rider *n.* a messenger who travels by motorcycle.

dispel *v.* (**dispelled, dispelling**) drive or clear away.

dispensable *adj.* not essential.

dispensary *n.* (*pl.* **-ies**) a place where medicines are dispensed.

dispensation *n.* **1** exemption. **2** a system of government, organization, etc. **3** distribution.

dispense *v.* deal out; prepare and give out (medicine). □ **dispense with** do without; abandon. □ **dispenser** *n.*

disperse *v.* go or send in different directions, scatter. □ **dispersal** *n.*, **dispersion** *n.*

dispirited *adj.* dejected. □ **dispiriting** *adj.*

displace *v.* take the place of; move from its place or home. □ **displacement** *n.*

display *v.* show, make conspicuous. ● *n.* displaying; thing(s) displayed.

displease *v.* irritate; annoy.

displeasure *n.* annoyance.

disport *v.* (also **disport oneself**) frolic; enjoy oneself.

disposable *adj.* **1** designed to be thrown away after use. **2** available for use. □ **disposability** *n.*

disposal *n.* **1** getting rid of something. **2** arrangement. □ **at one's disposal** available for one's use.

dispose *v.* **1** place, arrange. **2** make willing or ready to do something. □ **dispose of** get rid of. **be well disposed** be friendly or favourable.

disposition *n.* **1** a person's character; a tendency. **2** arrangement; control.

dispossess *v.* deprive (someone) of something they own. □ **dispossession** *n.*

disproportionate *adj.* relatively too large or too small. □ **disproportionately** *adv.*

disprove *v.* show to be false.

disputable *adj.* questionable. □ **disputably** *adv.*

disputant *n.* a person engaged in a dispute.

disputation *n.* an argument, a debate.

disputatious *adj.* fond of arguing.

dispute *v.* argue, debate; question the truth of; compete for. ● *n.* a debate; a disagreement.

disqualify *v.* (**disqualified, disqualifying**) cause or judge to be ineligible or unsuitable. □ **disqualification** *n.*

disquiet *n.* uneasiness, anxiety. ● *v.* make uneasy.

disquisition *n.* a long elaborate discussion or explanation.

disregard *v.* pay no attention to. ● *n.* lack of attention.

disrepair *n.* bad condition caused by lack of repair.

disreputable *adj.* not respectable. □ **disreputably** *adv.*

disrepute *n.* a bad reputation.

disrespect *n.* lack of respect. □ **disrespectful** *adj.*, **disrespectfully** *adv.*

disrobe *v.* get undressed.

disrupt *v.* interrupt the flow, continuity, or organization of. □ **disruption** *n.*, **disruptive** *adj.*

dissatisfaction *n.* lack of satisfaction or of contentment.

dissatisfied *adj.* not pleased or contented.

dissect *v.* cut apart so as to examine the internal structure. □ **dissection** *n.*, **dissector** *n.*

dissemble *v.* conceal one's feelings etc. □ **dissemblance** *n.*

disseminate *v.* spread widely. □ **dissemination** *n.*

dissension *n.* disagreement that gives rise to strife.

dissent *v.* disagree, esp. with a widely or officially held view. ● *n.* disagreement. □ **dissenter** *n.*

dissertation *n.* a lengthy essay.

disservice *n.* an unhelpful or harmful action.

dissident *adj.* & *n.* (a person) disagreeing, esp. with an established government. □ **dissidence** *n.*

dissimilar *adj.* unlike. □ **dissimilarity** *n.*, **dissimilitude** *n.*

dissimulate *v.* conceal, disguise. □ **dissimulation** *n.*

dissipate *v.* dispel; fritter away.

dissipated *adj.* living a dissolute life.

dissipation *n.* **1** a dissipated lifestyle. **2** dispersal, squandering.

dissociate *v.* regard as separate; declare to be unconnected. □ **dissociation** *n.*

dissolute *adj.* lacking moral restraint or self-discipline.

dissolution *n.* the dissolving of an assembly or partnership.

dissolve *v.* make or become liquid or dispersed in liquid, disappear gradually; disperse (an assembly); end (a partnership, esp. marriage).

dissonant *adj.* lacking harmony. □ **dissonance** *n.*, **dissonantly** *adv.*

dissuade *v.* deter by argument. □ **dissuasion** *n.*

distaff *n.* a cleft stick holding wool etc. in spinning. □ **the distaff side** the mother's side of the family.

distance *n.* the length of space or time between two points; being far away; a far point or part; the full length (of a race etc.). ● *v.* separate, make remote.

distant *adj.* far away; at a specified distance; cool, aloof. □ **distantly** *adv.*

distaste *n.* dislike, disapproval.

distasteful *adj.* arousing distaste. □ **distastefully** *adv.*

distemper *n.* **1** a disease of dogs. **2** a kind of paint for use on walls. ● *v.* paint with distemper.

distend *v.* (cause to) swell from internal pressure. □ **distension** *n.*

distil *v.* (*Amer.* **distill**) (**distilled, distilling**) treat or make by distillation; undergo distillation; capture the essence of.

distillation *n.* the process of vaporizing and condensing a liquid so as to purify it or to extract elements; something distilled.

distiller *n.* one who makes alcoholic liquor by distillation.

distillery *n.* (*pl.* **-ies**) a place where alcohol is distilled.

distinct *adj.* **1** different in kind. **2** clearly perceptible; definite. □ **distinctly** *adv.*

distinction *n.* **1** a contrast or difference; difference in treatment or attitude. **2** excellence; an honour; a high grade in an examination.

distinctive *adj.* distinguishing, characteristic. □ **distinctively** *adv.*

distinguish *v.* **1** perceive a difference; be a characteristic of, differentiate. **2** discern. □ **distinguish oneself** behave in a notable and admirable way. □ **distinguishable** *adj.*

distinguished *adj.* commanding respect; famous for great achievements.

distort *v.* pull out of shape; misrepresent. □ **distortion** *n.*

distract *v.* draw away the attention of.

distracted *adj.* preoccupied, unable to concentrate.

distraction *n.* **1** something that distracts; an entertainment. **2** extreme distress and agitation.

distraint *n.* seizure of a debtor's possessions as payment for the debt. □ **distrain** *v.*

distraught *adj.* nearly crazy with grief or worry.

distress *n.* **1** unhappiness; pain; hardship. **2** = **distraint**. ● *v.* **1** make unhappy. **2** make (wood or furniture) look old and worn. □ **in distress** in danger and needing help.

distribute *v.* divide and share out; spread over an area. □ **distribution** *n.*, **distributive** *adj.*

distributor *n.* a person or thing that distributes; a device in an engine for passing electric current to the spark plugs.

district *n.* an area (of a country, county, or city) with a particular feature or regarded as an administrative unit.

distrust *n.* lack of trust; suspicion. ● *v.* feel distrust in. □ **distrustful** *adj.*, **distrustfully** *adv.*

disturb *v.* interfere with the arrangement of; break the rest or privacy of; make anxious. □ **disturbance** *n.*

disturbed *adj.* mentally or emotionally unstable or abnormal.

disuse *n.* a state of not being used.

disused *adj.* no longer used.

ditch *n.* a long narrow trench for drainage. ● *v.* **1** make or repair ditches. **2** *informal* abandon.

dither *v.* hesitate indecisively.

ditto *n.* (in lists) the same again.

ditty *n.* (*pl.* **-ies**) a short simple song.

diuretic *n.* a drug that causes more urine to be excreted.

diurnal *adj.* of or in the day.

diva *n.* a famous female singer.

divan *n.* a couch without a back or arms; a bed resembling this.

dive *v.* plunge head first into water; swim under water using breathing apparatus; move quickly downwards or in a specified direction. ● *n.* **1** an act of diving. **2** *informal* a disreputable nightclub etc.

diver *n.* a person who dives or swims under water; a diving bird.

diverge *v.* separate and go in different directions; depart from a path etc. □ **divergence** *n.*, **divergent** *adj.*

diverse *adj.* of differing kinds.

diversify *v.* (**diversified, diversifying**) make or become more varied; (of a company) enlarge its range of products. □ **diversification** *n.*

diversion *n.* **1** diverting; an alternative route avoiding a closed road. **2** a recreation or entertainment.

diversity *n.* (*pl.* **-ies**) being varied; a wide range.

divert *v.* **1** turn from a course or route. **2** entertain; distract.

divest *v.* □ **divest of** strip of.

divide *v.* **1** separate into parts or from something else. **2** cause to disagree. **3** find how many times one number contains another; be divisible by a number without remainder. ● *n.* a divergence; a boundary.

dividend *n.* a sum paid to a company's shareholders out of its profits; a benefit from an action.

divider *n.* **1** a thing that divides. **2** (**dividers**) measuring compasses.

divine *adj.* **1** of, from, or like God or a god. **2** *informal* wonderful. ● *v.* discover by intuition or magic. □ **divination** *n.*, **divinely** *adv.*, **diviner** *n.*

divining rod *n.* a dowser's stick.

divinity *n.* (*pl.* **-ies**) being divine; a god.

divisible *adj.* able to be divided. □ **divisibility** *n.*

division *n.* dividing, being divided; a dividing line, a partition; one of the parts into which something is divided. □ **divisional** *adj.*

divisive *adj.* tending to cause disagreement.

divisor *n.* a number by which another is to be divided.

divorce *n.* the legal termination of a marriage; separation. ● *v.* end the marriage of (a person) by divorce; separate.

divorcee *n.* a divorced person.

divulge *v.* reveal (information).

Diwali *n.* a Hindu festival at which lamps are lit, held between September and November.

DIY *abbr.* do-it-yourself.

dizzy *adj.* (**dizzier, dizziest**) giddy, feeling confused; causing giddiness. □ **dizzily** *adv.*, **dizziness** *n.*

DJ *abbr.* **1** disc jockey. **2** dinner jacket.

djellaba (jel-ăbă) *n.* an Arab cloak.

D.Litt. *abbr.* Doctor of Letters.

DM *abbr.* Deutschmark.

D.Mus. *abbr.* Doctor of Music.

DNA *abbr.* deoxyribonucleic acid, a substance storing genetic information.

D notice *n.* an official order not to publish specific items for security reasons.

do *v.* (**does, did, done, doing**) **1** perform, complete; work at, deal with; provide, make. **2** act, proceed; fare. **3** be suitable or acceptable. ● *v.aux.* used to form the present or past tense, in questions, for emphasis, or to avoid repeating a verb just used. ● *n.* (*pl.* **dos** or **do's**) *informal* a party. □ **do away with** abolish. **do for** *informal* destroy, ruin. **do in** *informal* kill; injure; tire out. **do out** *informal* redecorate. **do out of** *informal* deprive of unfairly. **do up 1** fasten; wrap. **2** *informal* redecorate. **do without** manage without. **to do with** concerning; connected with.

docile *adj.* submissive, easily managed. □ **docilely** *adv.*, **docility** *n.*

dock *n.* **1** an enclosed body of water where ships are loaded, unloaded, or repaired. **2** an enclosure for the prisoner in a criminal court. **3** a weed with broad leaves. ● *v.* **1** (of a ship) come into dock; bring into dock. **2** (of a space craft) join with another craft in space. **3** deduct, take away; cut short.

docker *n.* a labourer who loads and unloads ships in a dockyard.

docket *n.* a document listing goods delivered; a voucher. ● *v.* (**docketed, docketing**) label with a docket.

dockyard *n.* the area and buildings round a shipping dock.

doctor *n.* **1** a person qualified to give medical treatment. **2** a person holding a doctorate. ● *v.* **1** tamper with, falsify; adulterate. **2** *informal* treat medically; castrate or spay (an animal); repair.

doctorate *n.* the highest degree at a university. □ **doctoral** *adj.*

doctrinaire *adj.* applying theories or principles rigidly.

doctrine *n.* a principle or the beliefs of a religious, political, or other group. □ **doctrinal** *adj.*

docudrama *n.* a television drama based on real events.

document *n.* a piece of written, printed, or electronic material giving information or evidence. ● *v.* **1** record. **2** provide written evidence for. □ **documentation** *n.*

documentary *adj.* **1** consisting of documents. **2** giving a factual report. ● *n.* (*pl.* **-ies**) a documentary film.

dodder *v.* totter because of age or frailty. □ **dodderer** *n.*, **doddery** *adj.*

dodecagon *n.* a geometric figure with twelve sides.

dodge *v.* avoid by a quick sideways movement; move in this way; evade. ● *n.* a dodging movement; *informal* a cunning trick. □ **dodger** *n.*

dodgem *n.* a small electric car driven in an enclosure with the aim of bumping into others as a funfair amusement.

dodo *n.* (*pl.* **dodos**) a large extinct bird.

DoE *abbr.* Department of the Environment.

doe *n.* the female of the deer, hare, or rabbit.

does *see* **do**.

doff *v. dated* take off (one's hat).

dog *n.* **1** a four-legged carnivorous wild or domesticated animal; the male of this or of the fox or wolf. **2** (**the dogs**) *informal* greyhound racing. ● *v.* (**dogged, dogging**) follow persistently. ◻ **go to the dogs** *informal* deteriorate shockingly.

dog cart *n.* a two-wheeled cart with back-to-back seats.

dog collar *n. informal* a clerical collar fastening at the back of the neck.

dog-eared *adj.* with page-corners crumpled through use.

dogfish *n.* a small shark.

dogged (dog-id) *adj.* persistent, undeterred. ◻ **doggedly** *adv.*

doggerel *n.* bad verse.

doggo *adv.* ◻ **lie doggo** *informal* remain motionless to escape detection.

doggy *adj.* of or like a dog. ● *n.* (*pl.* **-ies**) (also **doggie**) a child's word for a dog.

doggy bag *n. informal* a bag for taking home leftovers from a restaurant etc.

doghouse *n. Amer.* a dog's kennel. ◻ **in the doghouse** *informal* in disgrace or disfavour.

dogma *n.* doctrines put forward by authority to be accepted without question.

dogmatic *adj.* not admitting doubt or questions. ◻ **dogmatically** *adv.*

do-gooder *n. informal* a well-meaning but unrealistic promoter of social work or reform.

dog rose *n.* a wild hedge-rose.

dogsbody *n.* (*pl.* **-ies**) *informal* a drudge.

doh *n. Music* the first note of a major scale, or the note C.

doily *n.* (*pl.* **-ies**) (also **doyley**) a small ornamental lace or paper mat.

Dolby *n. trademark* a system for reducing unwanted sounds in a tape-recording.

doldrums *n.pl.* inactivity; depression; an equatorial region of the Atlantic with little or no wind.

dole *n. informal* unemployment benefit. ◻ **dole out** distribute.

doleful *adj.* mournful. ◻ **dolefully** *adv.*, **dolefulness** *n.*

doll *n.* a small model of a human figure, esp. as a child's toy. ◻ **dolled up** *informal* finely dressed.

dollar *n.* the unit of money in the USA and various other countries.

dollop *n. informal* a mass of a soft substance.

dolly *n.* (*pl.* **-ies**) **1** a child's name for a doll. **2** a movable platform for a cine-camera.

dolmen *n.* a megalithic structure of a large flat stone laid on two upright ones.

dolomite *n.* a type of limestone rock. ◻ **dolomitic** *adj.*

dolour *n.* (*Amer.* **dolor**) *literary* sorrow. ◻ **dolorous** *adj.*

dolphin *n.* a sea animal like a large porpoise, with a beaklike snout.

dolt *n. dated* a stupid person. ◻ **doltish** *adj.*

domain *n.* an area under a person's control; a field of activity.

dome *n.* a rounded roof with a circular base; something shaped like this. ◻ **domed** *adj.*

domestic *adj.* of home or household; of one's own country; domesticated. ● *n.* a servant in a household. ◻ **domestically** *adv.*

domesticate *v.* train (an animal) to live with humans; accustom to household work and home life. ◻ **domestication** *n.*

domesticity *n.* family life.

domicile *n.* a place of residence. ◻ **domiciliary** *adj.*

dominant *adj.* dominating. ◻ **dominance** *n.*

dominate *v.* have a commanding influence over; be most influential or conspicuous in; tower over. □ **domination** *n.*

domineer *v.* control people arrogantly.

dominion *n.* authority to rule, control; a ruler's territory.

domino *n.* (*pl.* **dominoes**) a small oblong piece marked with 0-6 pips, used in the game of **dominoes**, where the aim is to match pieces with the same value.

don *v.* (**donned, donning**) put on. ● *n.* **1** a head, fellow, or tutor of a college. **2** (**Don**) a Spanish title put before a man's Christian name. □ **donnish** *adj.*

donate *v.* give as a donation.

donation *n.* a gift (esp. of money) to a fund or institution.

done p.p. of **do**. ● *adj. informal* socially acceptable.

donkey *n.* (*pl.* **donkeys**) a long-eared animal of the horse family.

donkey jacket *n.* a thick weatherproof jacket.

donkey's years *n.pl. informal* a very long time.

donkey work *n. informal* drudgery.

Donna *n.* the title of an Italian, Spanish, or Portuguese lady.

donor *n.* one who gives or donates something.

donut Amer. sp. of **doughnut**.

doodle *v.* & *n.* (make) an idle drawing.

doom *n.* a grim fate; death or ruin. ● *v.* destine to a grim fate.

doomsday *n.* the day of the Last Judgement.

door *n.* a hinged, sliding, or revolving barrier at the entrance to a room, building, etc.; a doorway.

doorway *n.* an entrance to a room, building, etc.

dope *informal n.* **1** a drug; a narcotic. **2** information. **3** a stupid person. ● *v.* drug.

dopey *adj.* (also **dopy**) (**dopier, dopiest**) *informal* half asleep; stupid.

dormant *adj.* temporarily inactive; with physical functions slowed down. □ **dormancy** *n.*

dormer *n.* an upright window under a small gable on a sloping roof.

dormitory *n.* (*pl.* **-ies**) a room with several beds in a school, hostel, etc.

dormitory town *n.* a town from which most residents travel to work elsewhere.

Dormobile *n. trademark* a motor caravan.

dormouse *n.* (*pl.* **dormice**) a mouselike animal that hibernates.

dorsal *adj.* of or on the back.

DOS *abbr.* a computer operating system.

dosage *n.* the size of a dose.

dose *n.* an amount of medicine to be taken at one time; an amount of radiation received. ● *v.* give a dose of medicine to.

doss *v. informal* **1** sleep in rough accommodation. **2** idle. □ **dosser** *n.*

dosshouse *n. informal* a cheap hostel.

dossier *n.* a set of documents about a person or event.

DoT *abbr.* Department of Transport.

dot *n.* a small round mark. ● *v.* (**dotted, dotting**) mark with dots; scatter here and there. □ **dot the is and cross the t's** *informal* make sure that all details are correct. **on the dot** *informal* exactly on time.

dotage *n.* senility.

dote *v.* □ **dote on** be extremely and uncritically fond of. □ **doting** *adj.*

dot matrix printer *n.* a computer printer that forms letters etc. from a number of tiny dots.

dotty *adj.* (**dottier, dottiest**) *informal* slightly mad; infatuated. □ **dottily** *adv.*, **dottiness** *n.*

double *adj.* consisting of two equal parts; twice the usual size; occurring twice; for two people. ● *adv.* twice as much. ● *n.* **1** a double quantity or thing. **2** a person very like another. **3** (**doubles**) a game with two players on each side. ● *v.* **1** make or become twice as much or as many; fold in two; act two parts; have two uses. **2** go back in the direction one came from. ▫ **at the double** very fast. **see double** see two images of something when there is only one of it. ▫ **doubly** *adv.*

double bass *n.* the largest and lowest-pitched instrument of the violin family.

double-breasted *adj.* (of a coat) with fronts overlapping.

double chin *n.* a chin with a roll of fat below.

double cream *n.* thick cream with a high fat content.

double-cross *v.* cheat, deceive.

double-dealing *n.* deceit, esp. in business.

double-decker *n.* a bus with two decks.

double Dutch *n. informal* incomprehensible talk.

double entendre (doobl ahntahndr) *n.* a phrase with two meanings, one of which is usu. indecent.

double figures *n.pl.* numbers from 10 to 99.

double glazing *n.* two sheets of glass in a window, designed to reduce heat loss.

double negative *n. Grammar* a statement containing two negative expressions which neutralize each other to give a positive meaning, eg. *I didn't do nothing*, logically meaning *I did something*.

doublet *n.* **1** each of a pair of similar things. **2** *hist.* a man's short close-fitting jacket.

double take *n.* a delayed reaction just after one's first reaction.

doubletalk *n.* talk with deliberately ambiguous meaning.

double time *n.* a rate of pay equal to double the standard rate, paid e.g. for working on holidays.

double whammy *n. informal* a twofold blow or setback.

doubloon *n.* a former Spanish gold coin.

doubt *n.* a feeling of uncertainty or disbelief. ● *v.* feel uncertain of the truth or existence of; disbelieve. ▫ **doubter** *n.*

doubtful *adj.* feeling doubt; not known for certain; unlikely. ▫ **doubtfully** *adv.*

doubtless *adj.* certainly.

douche (doosh) *n.* a jet of water applied to the body for cleansing or medical purposes; a device for applying this. ● *v.* use a douche (on).

dough (doh) *n.* **1** a thick mixture of flour etc. and liquid, for baking. **2** *informal* money. ▫ **doughy** *adj.*

doughnut (doh-nut) *n.* (*Amer.* **donut**) a small cake of fried sweetened dough.

doughty (dow-ti) *adj.* (**doughtier, doughtiest**) brave and determined.

dour (door) *adj.* stern, gloomy-looking. ▫ **dourly** *adv.*, **dourness** *n.*

douse (dowss) *v.* **1** drench with a liquid. **2** extinguish (a light).

dove *n.* **1** a bird with a thick body and short legs. **2** a person favouring negotiation rather than violence.

dovecote *n.* (also **dovecot**) a shelter for domesticated pigeons.

dovetail *n.* a wedge-shaped joint interlocking two pieces of wood. ● *v.* combine easily and conveniently.

dowager (dow-ij-ĕ) *n.* a woman holding a title or property from her dead husband.

dowdy *adj.* (**dowdier, dowdiest**) not smart or fashionable. ▫ **dowdily** *adv.*, **dowdiness** *n.*

dowel *n.* a headless wooden or metal pin holding pieces of wood or stone together.

dowelling *n.* (*Amer.* **doweling**) rods for cutting into dowels.

down[1] *adv.* **1** to, in, or at a lower place or position. **2** to or at a lower level of intensity; to a smaller size.

3 from an earlier to a later point in time or order. **4** in or into a worse or weaker position. **5** in writing. **6** as (partial) payment at the time of purchase. ● *prep.* from a higher to a lower point of; at a point further along; along, throughout. ● *adj.* **1** directed downwards; travelling away from a central place. **2** depressed. **3** (of a computer system) not functioning. ● *v. informal* **1** knock down. **2** swallow. ● *n.* a period of misfortune or depression. □ **down to** attributable to; the responsibility of. **down under** in the Antipodes, esp. Australia. **have a down on** *informal* be hostile to.

down² *n.* **1** very fine soft furry feathers or short hairs. **2** an area of open undulating land; (**downs**) chalk uplands.

down-and-out *adj.* destitute. ● *n.* a destitute person.

down beat *adj.* **1** gloomy. **2** relaxed, understated. ● *n. Music* an accented beat.

downcast *adj.* dejected; (of eyes) looking downwards.

downfall *n.* a loss of prosperity or power; something causing this.

downgrade *v.* reduce to a lower grade.

downhearted *adj.* discouraged and depressed.

downhill *adj.* & *adv.* going downwards; becoming worse.

download *v.* transfer (data) from one computer to another using a direct link.

downmarket *adj.* & *adv.* of or towards lower prices and quality.

downpour *n.* a heavy fall of rain.

downright *adj.* & *adv.* completely as described, utter.

downshift *v.* change to a less profitable but more relaxed way of life.

downside *n.* a negative aspect.

downsize *v.* reduce the number of staff employed by a company.

Down's syndrome *n.* a congenital disorder characterized by a broad face, sloping eyes, and learning difficulties.

downstairs *adv.* & *adj.* to or on a lower floor.

downstream *adj.* & *adv.* in the direction in which a stream or river flows.

down-to-earth *adj.* sensible and practical.

downtown *adj.* & *n. Amer.* (of) the lower or more central part of a city.

downtrodden *adj.* oppressed.

downward *adj.* moving or leading down. ● *adv.* (also **downwards**) towards what is lower, less important, or later.

downy *adj.* (**downier, downiest**) covered with or resembling soft down.

dowry *n.* (*pl.* **-ies**) property or money brought by a bride to her husband on marriage.

dowse (dowz) *v.* search for underground water or minerals by using a stick which dips when these are present. □ **dowser** *n.*

doxology *n.* (*pl.* **-ies**) a formula of praise to God.

doyen (doi-ĕn) *n.* the most important or highly regarded men in a particular field.

doyenne (doi-enn) *n.* the most important or highly regarded woman in a particular field.

doyley var. of **doily**.

doze *v.* sleep lightly. ● *n.* a short light sleep.

dozen *n.* a set of twelve; (**dozens**) very many.

dozy *adj.* (**dozier, doziest**) not fully awake or alert.

D.Phil *abbr.* Doctor of Philosophy.

DPP *abbr.* Director of Public Prosecutions.

Dr *abbr.* Doctor.

drab *adj.* (**drabber, drabbest**) dull and unexciting; not brightly coloured.

drachma *n.* (*pl.* **drachmas** or **drachmae**) the former unit of money in Greece.

draconian *adj.* harsh, strict.

draft *n.* **1** a preliminary written version. **2** a written order to a bank to pay money. **3** *Amer.* military conscription. **4** Amer. sp. of **draught**. ● *v.* **1** prepare a draft of. **2** *Amer.* conscript for military service.

draftsman Amer. sp. of **draughtsman**.

drafty Amer. sp. of **draughty**.

drag *v.* (**dragged, dragging**) **1** pull or bring with effort; (of time) pass slowly. **2** trail on the ground. **3** search (water) with nets or hooks. ● *n.* **1** something that impedes progress; *informal* something irritating or tedious. **2** *informal* women's clothes worn by men. **3** *informal* an act of inhaling on a cigarette.

dragnet *n.* a net for dragging water.

dragon *n.* **1** a mythical reptile able to breathe out fire. **2** a bad-tempered and intimidating person.

dragonfly *n.* (*pl.* **-ies**) a long-bodied insect with gauzy wings.

dragoon *n.* a cavalryman or (formerly) mounted infantryman. ● *v.* force into action.

drag race *n.* an acceleration race between cars over a short distance.

drain *v.* **1** draw liquid out of; become dry; draw off (liquid) by channels or pipes; flow away. **2** gradually deprive of strength or resources. **3** drink all the contents of. ● *n.* **1** a channel or pipe carrying off water or liquid waste. **2** something that deprives one of energy or resources.

drainage *n.* draining; a system of drains; what is drained off.

drake *n.* a male duck.

dram *n.* a small drink of spirits.

drama *n.* a play; plays and acting; an exciting series of events; a striking and exciting quality.

dramatic *adj.* **1** of plays and acting. **2** exciting, striking, impressive. ◻ **dramatically** *adv.*

dramatist *n.* a writer of plays.

dramatize *v.* (also **-ise**) present in dramatic form. ◻ **dramatization** *n.*

drank past of **drink**.

drape *v.* spread (covers) loosely over something. ● *n.pl.* (**drapes**) *Amer.* curtains.

drastic *adj.* having an extreme or violent effect. ◻ **drastically** *adv.*

drat *int. informal* an expression of annoyance.

dratted *adj. informal* cursed; wretched; damn.

draught *n.* (*Amer.* **draft**) **1** a current of air in a confined space. **2** an amount of liquid swallowed at one time; *archaic* a medicinal drink. **3** (**draughts**) a game played with 24 round pieces on a chessboard. **4** the depth of water needed to float a ship. ● *adj.* used for pulling loads.

draught beer *n.* beer drawn from a cask.

draughtsman *n.* (*pl.* **-men**) (*Amer.* **draftsman**) **1** a person who draws plans or diagrams. **2** *Brit.* a piece used in draughts.

draughty *adj.* (*Amer.* **drafty**) (**draughtier, draughtiest**) letting in cold currents of air. ◻ **draughtily** *adv.*, **draughtiness** *n.*

draw *v.* (**drew, drawn, drawing**) **1** create a picture or diagram by marking a surface. **2** pull; take out or from a store; take in (breath). **3** attract. **4** finish a contest with scores equal. **5** pick lots to decide an outcome. **6** make one's way, come: *draw near*. **7** write out (a cheque). **8** require (a specified depth) in which to float. **9** infuse. **10** (of a chimney) allow an upward current of air, enabling a fire to burn. ● *n.* **1** a lottery; an act of drawing lots. **2** a contest with equal closing scores. **3** something that attracts. **4** an act of inhaling. ◻ **draw in** (of days) become shorter. **draw on** use as a resource. **draw out 1** prolong; (of days) become longer. **2** encourage to talk. **draw up 1** come to a halt. **2** compose (a contract etc.)

drawback *n.* a disadvantage.

drawbridge *n.* a bridge over a moat, hinged for raising.

drawer *n.* **1** a lidless compartment sliding horizontally into and out of a piece of furniture. **2** a person who draws. **3** a person who writes a cheque. **4** (**drawers**) knickers, underpants.

drawing *n.* a picture made with a pencil or pen.

drawing pin *n.* a pin for fastening paper to a surface.

drawing room *n.* a formal sitting room.

drawl *v.* speak slowly with drawn-out vowel sounds. ● *n.* a drawling manner of speaking.

drawn p.p. of **draw**. ● *adj.* looking strained from tiredness or worry.

drawstring *n.* a string that can be pulled to close an opening.

dray *n.* a low cart for heavy loads.

dread *n.* great fear. ● *v.* fear greatly. ● *adj.* greatly feared.

dreadful *adj.* very bad or unpleasant. ◻ **dreadfully** *adv.*

dream *n.* a series of pictures or events in a sleeping person's mind; something greatly desired; something unreal or impossible. ● *v.* (**dreamed** or **dreamt, dreaming**) have a dream while asleep; have an ambition or desire; think of or contemplate something as possible. ◻ **dream up** invent or imagine (something foolish or improbable). ◻ **dreamer** *n.*, **dreamless** *adj.*

dreamy *adj.* (**dreamier, dreamiest**) **1** absorbed in a day dream; distracted, vague. **2** *informal* very attractive or pleasant. ◻ **dreamily** *adv.*, **dreaminess** *n.*

dreary *adj.* (**drearier, dreariest**) depressingly dull; gloomy. ◻ **drearily** *adv.*, **dreariness** *n.*

dredge *v.* **1** clear (an area of water) of (mud or silt). **2** sprinkle (food) with flour or sugar.

dredger *n.* **1** a machine or boat for dredging. **2** a container with a perforated lid for sprinkling flour or sugar.

dregs *n.pl.* sediment at the bottom of a drink; a last small remnant; the least useful, attractive, or valuable part.

drench *v.* wet all through.

dress *n.* **1** a woman's or girl's garment with a bodice and skirt. **2** clothing. ● *v.* **1** clothe oneself; clothe. **2** put a dressing on. **3** decorate; arrange. ◻ **dress up 1** put on fancy dress. **2** put on smart or formal clothes.

dressage (**dress**-ah*zh*) *n.* exercises to show off a horse's obedience and deportment.

dress circle *n.* the first gallery in a theatre.

dresser *n.* **1** a person who helps actors with their costumes. **2** a person who dresses in a particular style: *a smart dresser*. **3** a sideboard with shelves above for dishes etc.

dressing *n.* **1** a sauce for salad. **2** a protective covering for a wound. **3** fertilizer etc. spread over land.

dressing down *n. informal* a scolding.

dressing gown *n.* a loose robe worn when one is not fully dressed.

dressing table *n.* a table topped by a mirror, used while dressing or applying make-up.

dressmaker *n.* a person whose job is making women's clothes. ◻ **dressmaking** *n.*

dress rehearsal *n.* a final rehearsal, in full costume, of a dramatic production.

dress shirt *n.* a man's shirt for formal wear.

dressy *adj.* (**dressier, dressiest**) stylish, smart; wearing stylish clothes.

drew past of **draw**.

drey *n.* (*pl.* **dreys**) a squirrel's nest.

dribble *v.* **1** (cause to) flow in drops; have saliva flowing from the mouth. **2** (in football etc.) move the ball forward with slight touches. ● *n.* a thin stream of liquid; saliva running from the mouth.

dried *adj.* (of food) preserved by removal of moisture.

drier *n.* (also **dryer**) a device for drying things.

drift *v.* be carried by a current of water or air; go casually or aimlessly; pass gradually into a particular state. ● *n.* **1** a drifting movement. **2** a mass of snow piled up by the wind. **3** the general meaning of a speech etc.

drifter *n.* an aimless person.

driftwood *n.* wood floating on the sea or washed ashore.

drill *n.* **1** a tool or machine for boring holes or sinking wells. **2** training; repeated exercises; routine. **3** a strong twilled cotton fabric. ● *v.* **1** use a drill, make (a hole) with a drill. **2** train, be trained.

drily *adv.* (also **dryly**) **1** with irony. **2** without moisture.

drink *v.* (**drank, drunk, drinking**) swallow (liquid); consume alcoholic drink, esp. in excess; express good wishes in a toast. ● *n.* a liquid for drinking; alcoholic liquor. ◻ **drink in** watch or listen to eagerly. ◻ **drinker** *n.*

drink-driver *n.* a person who drives having drunk more than the legal limit of alcohol.

drip *v.* (**dripped, dripping**) **1** fall or let fall in drops. **2** be conspicuously full of or covered in. ● *n.* **1** a regular fall of drops of liquid; the sound of this; (also **drip-feed**) an apparatus for administering a liquid at a very slow rate into the body, esp. intravenously. **2** *informal* an ineffectual person.

drip-dry *adj.* (of clothes) capable of drying without creasing if hung up wet after washing. ● *v.* (**-dried, -drying**) dry (clothes) in this way.

dripping *n.* fat melted from roast meat.

drive *v.* (**drove, driven, driving**) **1** operate (a vehicle), controlling its direction and speed; travel or convey in a private vehicle. **2** propel or carry forcefully; provide the energy to work (a machine); urge onwards; compel; cause to work too hard. **3** make (a bargain). ● *n.* **1** a journey in a private vehicle. **2** an innate urge or motive; determination; an organized effort to achieve something; the transmission of power to machinery. **3** a short road leading to a house etc. ◻ **drive at** try to convey as a meaning.

drive-in *adj.* (of a cinema etc.) able to be used without getting out of one's car.

drivel *n.* silly talk, nonsense.

driver *n.* **1** a person who drives. **2** a golf club for striking the ball from a tee.

drizzle *n.* very fine drops of rain. ● *v.* rain very lightly.

droll *adj.* strange and amusing. ◻ **drollery** *n.*, **drolly** (*pl.* **-ies**) *adv.*

dromedary *n.* a camel with one hump, bred for riding.

drone *n.* **1** a deep humming sound. **2** a male bee. **3** an idle person living off others. ● *v.* make a humming sound; speak monotonously.

drool *v.* **1** slaver, dribble. **2** show gushing appreciation.

droop *v.* bend or hang down limply. ● *n.* a drooping attitude. ◻ **droopy** *adj.*

drop *n.* **1** a small rounded mass of liquid; a very small amount of liquid; (**drops**) liquid medicine measured in drops. **2** a fall; letting something fall; an abrupt slope. **3** something that drops, eg. a stage curtain. ● *v.* (**dropped, dropping**) **1** let (something) fall; fall vertically; *informal* collapse from weariness; make or become lower, weaker, or smaller. **2** give up (a habit); discard, reject; *informal* stop associating with. **3** utter casually. **4** set down (a passenger or load). ◻ **drop in** pay a casual visit. **drop off** fall asleep. **drop out** cease to participate.

droplet *n.* small drop of liquid.

drop-out *n.* a person who abandons a course of study or rejects conventional society.

dropper *n.* a device for measuring out drops of medicine etc.

droppings *n.pl.* animal dung.

dropsy *n. dated* oedema. □ **dropsical** *adj.*

dross *n.* rubbish, worthless matter; scum on molten metal.

drought (drowt) *n.* a long spell of dry weather; a shortage of water.

drove[1] past of **drive**.

drove[2] a flock or herd; a crowd.

drover *n.* a person who drives cattle.

drown *v.* kill or be killed by suffocating in water or other liquid; submerge; deaden (grief etc.) with drink; (of a sound) be louder than (another sound) and make it inaudible.

drowse *v.* be lightly asleep.

drowsy *adj.* (**drowsier, drowsiest**) sleepy, lethargic. □ **drowsily** *adv.*, **drowsiness** *n.*

drub *v.* (**drubbed, drubbing**) thrash; defeat thoroughly.

drudge *n.* a person who does laborious or menial work. □ **drudgery** *n.*

drug *n.* a substance used in medicine or as a stimulant or narcotic. ● *v.* (**drugged, drubbing**) treat with drugs; add a drug to.

drugstore *n. Amer.* a chemist's shop also selling toiletries etc.

Druid *n.* an ancient Celtic priest. □ **Druidic, Druidical** *adj.*

drum *n.* a round frame with a membrane stretched across, used as a percussion instrument; a sound of or as of this; a cylindrical object. ● *v.* (**drummed, drumming**) play a drum; make a continuous rhythmic noise; tap (one's fingers etc.) repeatedly on a surface. □ **drum up** obtain by canvassing or requesting.

drum majorette *n.* a female member of a parading group.

drummer *n.* a person who plays drums.

drumstick *n.* **1** a stick for beating a drum. **2** the lower part of a cooked fowl's leg.

drunk p.p. of **drink**. ● *adj.* deprived of the control of one's faculties by alcohol. ● *n.* a drunken person.

drunkard *n.* a person who is often drunk.

drunken *adj.* intoxicated; often in this condition. □ **drunkenly** *adv.*, **drunkenness** *n.*

dry *adj.* (**drier, driest**) **1** without moisture or liquid; thirsty. **2** uninteresting. **3** (of humour) subtle, understated. **4** not allowing the sale of alcohol. **5** (of wine etc.) not sweet. **6** (of bread) without butter etc. ● *v.* (**dries, dried, drying**) make or become dry; preserve (food) by removing its moisture; wipe tears from (the eyes). □ **dry up 1** dry washed dishes etc. **2** *informal* stop talking; decrease and stop. □ **dryness** *n.*

dryad *n.* a wood nymph.

dry-clean *v.* clean with solvents without using water.

dryer var. of **drier**.

dryly var. of **drily**.

dry rot *n.* decay of wood that is not ventilated.

dry run *n. informal* a rehearsal.

drystone wall *n.* a wall built without mortar.

DSS *abbr.* Department of Social Security.

DTI *abbr.* Department of Trade and Industry.

DTP *abbr.* desktop publishing.

dual *adj.* composed of two parts; double. □ **duality** *n.*

dual carriageway *n.* a road with a central strip separating traffic travelling in opposite directions.

dub *v.* (**dubbed, dubbing**) **1** give (a film) a soundtrack in a language other than the original. **2** give a nickname to. **3** confer a knighthood on.

dubbin *n.* (also **dubbing**) a thick grease for softening and waterproofing leather.

dubiety *n. literary* being doubtful or unknown.

dubious *adj.* **1** hesitant; uncertain. **2** suspect, questionable. □ **dubiously** *adv.*

ducal *adj.* of a duke.

ducat *n.* a former gold coin of various European countries.

duchess *n.* a woman with the rank of duke; a duke's wife or widow.

duchy *n.* (*pl.* **-ies**) the territory of a duke.

duck *n.* **1** a water bird with a broad blunt bill and webbed feet; the female of this. **2** a batsman's score of 0. **3** a quick dip or lowering of the head. ● *v.* **1** push (a person) or dip one's head under water. **2** lower one's head or body to avoid a blow or so as not to be seen; avoid (a blow); *informal* evade (a duty).

duckboards *n.pl.* boards forming a narrow path over mud etc.

duckling *n.* a young duck.

duct *n.* a channel or tube conveying liquid or air; a vessel in the body carrying secreted or excreted matter. □ **ductless** *adj.*

ductile *adj.* (of metal) able to be drawn into fine strands; easily moulded. □ **ductility** *n.*

dud *informal n.* something that fails to work; an ineffectual person. ● *adj.* useless; counterfeit.

dude *n. informal*, esp. *Amer.* a fellow; a dandy.

dudgeon *n.* a feeling of offence: *a high dudgeon.*

due *adj.* **1** expected or scheduled at a particular time. **2** owed, to be paid; deserved. **3** deserving; entitled to expect. ● *n.* **1** what is owed to or deserved by someone. **2** (**dues**) fees. ● *adv.* directly, exactly: *due north.* □ **due to** because of, caused by.

duel *n.* a fight or contest between two persons or sides. ● *v.* (**duelled, duelling**; *Amer.* **dueled**) fight a duel. □ **duellist** *n.*

duenna *n.* an older women chaperoning a younger one.

duet *n.* a musical composition for two performers.

duff *adj. informal* worthless; incorrect.

duffel coat *n.* a heavy woollen coat with a hood.

duffer *n. informal* an inefficient or stupid person.

dug[1] past & p.p. of **dig**

dug[2] *n.* an udder, a teat.

dugong (**dew**-gong) *n.* an Asian sea mammal.

dugout *n.* **1** an underground shelter. **2** a canoe made from a hollowed tree trunk.

duke *n.* a nobleman of the highest hereditary rank; a ruler of certain small states. □ **dukedom** *n.*

dulcet *adj.* sounding sweet.

dulcimer *n.* a musical instrument with strings struck with hand-held hammers.

dull *adj.* **1** not interesting or exciting. **2** not bright or resonant; not sharp. **3** stupid. ● *v.* make or become less intense, sharp, or bright. □ **dully** *adv.*, **dullness** *n.*

dullard *n.* a stupid person.

duly *adv.* as is required or appropriate; as might be expected.

dumb *adj.* **1** unable to speak; silent. **2** *informal* stupid. □ **dumb down** *informal* make or become less intellectually challenging. □ **dumbly** *adv.*, **dumbness** *n.*

■ **Usage** The use of *dumb* to mean 'unable to speak' is found offensive by many people.

dumb-bell *n.* a short bar with weighted ends, lifted to exercise muscles.

dumbfound *v.* astonish.

dumdum bullet *n.* a soft-nosed bullet that expands on impact.

dummy *n.* (*pl.* **-ies**). **1** a model of the human figure used to display clothes or in an exhibition; a model of something used as a substitute. **2** a rubber teat for a baby to suck. **3** *informal* a stupid person.

dummy run *n.* a trial or rehearsal.

dump *v.* **1** deposit as rubbish; put down carelessly; *informal* end a relationship with; sell (unsaleable goods) abroad at a lower price. **2** *Computing* copy (data) to a different location; print out the contents of (a store). ● *n.* **1** a site for depositing rubbish or waste; a temporary store; *informal* a dull or unpleasant place. **2** *Computing* an act of dumping data; a print-out.

dumpling *n.* a ball of dough cooked in stew or with fruit inside.

dun *adj.* & *n.* greyish brown. ● *v.* (**dunned, dunning**) *informal* demand payment from.

dunce *n.* a person slow at learning.

dune *n.* a mound of drifted sand.

dung *n.* animal excrement.

dungarees *n.pl.* overalls of coarse cotton cloth.

dungeon *n.* a strong underground cell for prisoners.

dunk *v.* dip (bread etc.) into soup or a drink before eating it.

duo *n.* (*pl.* **duos**) a pair of performers; a duet.

duodecimal *adj.* reckoned in twelves or twelfths.

duodenum (dyoo-ŏ-**dee**-nŭm) *n.* the part of the intestine next to the stomach. □ **duodenal** *adj.*

dupe *v.* deceive, trick. ● *n.* a duped person.

duple *adj.* (in music) having two beats to the bar.

duplex *adj.* having two elements.

duplicate *n.* (**dew**-pli-kăt) an exact copy. ● *adj.* (**dew**-pli-kăt) exactly like something specified; having two identical parts; doubled. ● *v.* (**dew**-pli-kayt) make or be an exact copy of; do (work already done) again unnecessarily. □ **duplication** *n.*, **duplicator** *n.*

duplicity *n.* deceitfulness.

durable *adj.* lasting; withstanding damage. ● *n.pl.* (**durables**) goods that can be kept without immediate consumption or replacement. □ **durably** *adv.*, **durability** *n.*

duration *n.* the time during which a thing continues.

duress *n.* the use of force or threats.

during *prep.* throughout; at a point in the duration of.

dusk *n.* a darker stage of twilight.

dusky *adj.* (**duskier, duskiest**) darkish in colour. □ **duskiness** *n.*

dust *n.* fine particles of earth or other matter. ● *v.* **1** wipe dust from the surface of. **2** cover lightly with a powdered substance.

dustbin *n.* a bin for household rubbish.

dust bowl *n.* an area denuded of vegetation and reduced to desert.

dust jacket *n.* (also **dust cover**) a paper cover used to protect a book.

duster *n.* a cloth for wiping dust from things.

dustman *n.* (*pl.* **-men**) a person employed to empty dustbins.

dustpan *n.* a container into which dust is brushed from a floor.

dusty *adj.* (**dustier, dustiest**) **1** covered with dust. **2** like dust; (of colours) dull. □ **dustiness** *n.*

Dutch *adj.* & *n.* (the language) of the Netherlands. □ **go Dutch** share expenses on an outing. □ **Dutchman** *n.*, **Dutchwoman** *n.*

Dutch courage *n.* false courage obtained by drinking alcohol.

dutiable *adj.* on which customs or other duties must be paid.

dutiful *adj.* obedient and conscientious. □ **dutifully** *adv.*

duty *n.* (*pl.* **-ies**) **1** a moral or legal obligation; a task that one is required to perform. **2** a tax on imports etc. □ **on duty** at work.

duvet (doo-vay) *n.* a thick soft bed quilt.

dwarf *n.* (*pl.* **dwarfs** or **dwarves**) a mythical human-like being of small size and with magic powers; a person or thing much below the usual size. ● *v.* **1** cause to seem small by comparison. **2** stunt.

dwell *v.* (**dwelt, dwelling**) live as an inhabitant. ▫ **dwell on** write, speak, or think lengthily about. ▫ **dweller** *n.*

dwelling *n.* a house etc. to live in.

dwindle *v.* gradually become less or smaller.

Dy *symb.* dysprosium.

dye *v.* (**dyed, dyeing**) colour, esp. by dipping in liquid. • *n.* a substance used for dyeing things; a colour given by dyeing. ▫ **dyer** *n.*

dying present participle of **die**.

dyke *n.* (also **dike**) a wall or embankment to prevent flooding; a drainage ditch.

dynamic *adj.* characterized by constant change or activity; energetic, forceful; *Physics* of force producing motion. ▫ **dynamically** *adv.*

dynamics *n.* **1** the branch of mechanics dealing with the motion of bodies under the action of forces; forces stimulating growth and change. **2** the variations in volume in a musical work.

dynamism *n.* energizing power.

dynamite *n.* a powerful explosive made of nitroglycerine. • *v.* blow up with dynamite.

dynamo *n.* (*pl.* **dynamos**) a small generator producing electric current.

dynasty *n.* (*pl.* **-ies**) a line of hereditary rulers. ▫ **dynastic** *adj.*

dysentery *n.* a disease causing severe diarrhoea.

dysfunction *n.* abnormal functioning; deviation from accepted behaviour. ▫ **dysfunctional** *adj.*

dyslexia *n.* a condition causing difficulty in reading and spelling. ▫ **dyslexic** *adj.* & *n.*

dyspepsia *n.* indigestion. ▫ **dyspeptic** *adj.* & *n.*

dysprosium *n.* a metallic element (symbol Dy).

dystrophy *n.* wasting of a part of the body. *See also* **muscular dystrophy**.

Ee

E *abbr.* **1** east, eastern. **2** *informal* the drug Ecstasy.

e- *comb. form* involving electronic communication.

each *adj.* & *pron.* every one of two or more, taken separately. • *adv.* to or for each one individually. ▫ **each way** (of a bet) backing a horse to win or be placed.

eager *adj.* full of desire, interest, or enthusiasm. ▫ **eagerly** *adv.*, **eagerness** *n.*

eagle *n.* a large, keen-sighted bird of prey.

ear *n.* **1** the organ of hearing; the external part of this; the ability to distinguish sounds accurately. **2** the seed-bearing part of corn.

eardrum *n.* a membrane inside the ear, vibrating when sound waves strike it.

earl *n.* a British nobleman ranking between marquess and viscount. ▫ **earldom** *n.*

early • *adj.* (**earlier, earliest**) & *adv.* before the usual or expected time; near the beginning of a series, period, etc.

earmark *n.* a distinguishing mark. • *v.* designate for a particular purpose.

earn *v.* get or deserve for work or merit; (of invested money) gain as interest. ▫ **earner** *n.*

earnest *adj.* showing serious feeling or intention. • *n.* a sign or guarantee of future actions etc. ▫ **in earnest** seriously. ▫ **earnestly** *adv.*, **earnestness** *n.*

earphone *n.* a device worn on the ear to receive radio or telephone communications or to listen privately to a radio etc.

earring *n.* a piece of jewellery worn on the ear.

earshot *n.* the distance over which something can be heard.

earth *n.* **1** (also **Earth**) the planet we live on; its surface; soil. **2** a connection of an electrical circuit to ground. **3** a fox's den. ● *v.* connect (an electrical circuit) to ground. □ **cost the earth** *informal* be very expensive. **run to earth** find after a long search.

earthen *adj.* made of earth or of baked clay.

earthenware *n.* pottery made of coarse baked clay.

earthly *adj.* **1** of this earth, of man's life on it. **2** used to emphasize a negative: *no earthly reason.*

earthquake *n.* a violent movement of part of the earth's crust.

earthwork *n.* a large defensive bank built of earth.

earthworm *n.* a worm living in the soil.

earthy *adj.* (**earthier, earthiest**) **1** (of humour etc.) unrefined, uninhibited. **2** like soil.

earwig *n.* a small insect with pincers at the end of its body.

ease *n.* lack of difficulty; freedom from anxiety or pain. ● *v.* **1** make or become less severe or intense. **2** move gradually and carefully; make (something) happen easily.

easel *n.* a frame to support a painting, blackboard, etc.

easement *n.* a right of way over another's property.

east *n.* the point on the horizon where the sun rises; the direction in which this lies; an eastern part. ● *adj.* at the eastern end or side; (of wind) from the east. ● *adv.* towards the east.

Easter *n.* a spring festival commemorating Christ's resurrection.

easterly *adj.* towards the east; blowing from the east.

eastern *adj.* of or in the east.

easternmost *adj.* furthest east.

eastward *adj.* towards the east. □ **eastwards** *adv.*

easy *adj.* (**easier, easiest**) achieved without great effort; free from worries or problems; relaxed, not awkward. ● *adv. informal* in an easy way. □ **take it easy** go slowly; relax. □ **easily** *adv.*, **easiness** *n.*

easy chair *n.* a large comfortable chair.

easy-going *adj.* relaxed in manner, not strict.

eat *v.* (**ate, eaten, eating**) chew and swallow (food); have a meal; use up, consume; erode, destroy. ● *n.* (**eats**) *informal* light food. □ **eater** *n.*

eatable *adj.* fit to be eaten. ● *n.pl.* (**eatables**) food.

eating disorder *n.* any of a range of psychological disorders characterized by abnormal eating habits.

eau de Cologne (oh-dĕ-kŏ-**lohn**) *n.* a delicate perfume.

eaves *n.pl.* the overhanging edge of a roof.

eavesdrop *v.* (**eavesdropped, eavesdropping**) listen secretly to a private conversation. □ **eavesdropper** *n.*

ebb *n.* **1** the movement of the tide out to sea. **2** a decline. ● *v.* **1** flow away. **2** decline. □ **at a low ebb** in a poor or weak state.

ebonite *n.* vulcanite.

ebony *n.* the hard black wood of a tropical tree. ● *adj.* black as ebony.

ebullient *adj.* full of high spirits. □ **ebullience** *n.*, **ebulliently** *adv.*

EC *abbr.* European Community; European Commission.

eccentric *adj.* **1** unconventional and strange. **2** not concentric; (of an orbit or wheel) not circular. ● *n.* an eccentric person. □ **eccentrically** *adv.*, **eccentricity** *n.*

ecclesiastical *adj.* of the Church or clergy.

ECG *abbr.* electrocardiogram.

echelon (esh-ĕlon) *n.* **1** a level in a hierarchy. **2** a wedge-shaped formation of troops etc.

echo *n.* (*pl.* **echoes**) a repetition of sound caused by reflection of sound waves; a close imitation. ● *v.* (**echoed, echoing**) resound, be repeated by echo; repeat (someone's words); be very like.

éclair *n.* a finger-shaped pastry cake with cream filling.

eclampsia *n.* a condition involving convulsions, affecting women in pregnancy.

eclectic *adj.* choosing or accepting from various sources.

eclipse *n.* the blocking of light from one heavenly body by another; a loss of influence or prominence. ● *v.* cause an eclipse of; outshine.

ecliptic *n.* the sun's apparent path.

eclogue *n.* a short pastoral poem.

eco- *comb. form* relating to ecology.

eco-friendly *adj.* not harmful to the environment.

ecology *n.* (the study of) relationships of living things to each other and to their environment. □ **ecological** *adj.*, **ecologically** *adv.*, **ecologist** *n.*

economic *adj.* **1** of economics or the economy. **2** profitable, not wasteful.

economical *adj.* thrifty, avoiding waste. □ **economically** *adv.*

economics *n.* the science of the production and use of goods or services; (as *pl.*) the financial aspects of a region or group. □ **economist** *n.*

economize *v.* (also **-ise**) reduce one's expenses.

economy *n.* (*pl.* **-ies**) **1** a country's system of using its resources to produce wealth. **2** being economical. ● *adj.* (of a product) giving the best value for money; economical to use.

ecosystem *n.* a system of interacting organisms and their environment.

ecru *n.* a light fawn colour.

ecstasy *n.* (*pl.* **-ies**) **1** intense delight. **2** (**Ecstasy**) a hallucinogenic drug. □ **ecstatic** *adj.*, **ecstatically** *adv.*

ECT *abbr.* electroconvulsive therapy.

ectopic pregnancy *n.* an unsuccessful pregnancy in which the egg develops outside the womb.

ecu *n.* (also **Ecu**) former term for **euro**.

ecumenical *adj.* of the whole Christian Church; seeking worldwide Christian unity.

eczema *n.* a skin disease causing scaly itching patches.

eddy *n.* (*pl.* **-ies**) a circular movement in water or air etc. ● *v.* swirl in eddies.

edelweiss (ay-dĕl-vys) *n.* an alpine plant.

edema Amer. sp. of **oedema**.

edge *n.* **1** the outer limit of an area or object; a rim; the area next to a steep drop. **2** the sharpened side of a blade; the narrow side of a thin, flat object. **3** a position of advantage: *I had the edge over him.* **4** a sharp or anxious note; an exciting quality. ● *v.* **1** provide with a border. **2** move slowly and carefully. □ **on edge** tense, nervous.

edgeways *adv.* (also **edgewise**) with the edge forwards or outwards. □ **get a word in edgeways** say something with difficulty because someone else hardly stops talking.

edging *n.* a decorative border.

edgy *adj.* (**edgier, edgiest**) tense and irritable. □ **edgily** *adv.*, **edginess** *n.*

edible *adj.* suitable for eating. □ **edibility** *n.*

edict (ee-dikt) *n.* an order issued by someone in authority.

edifice *n.* a large building.

edify *v.* (**edified, edifying**) improve morally or intellectually. □ **edification** *n.*

edit *v.* (**edited, editing**) prepare (written material) for publication; choose and arrange material for (a film etc.).

edition *n.* a version of a published text; all the copies of a text etc. issued at one time; one instance of a regular broadcast programme; a version or copy.

editor *n.* a person responsible for the contents of a newspaper etc. or a section of this; a person who edits.

editorial *adj.* of an editor. ● *n.* a newspaper article giving the editor's comments.

educate *v.* train the mind, character, and abilities of; teach. ▫ **education** *n.*, **educational** *adj.*

edutainment *n.* material or an activity intended both to entertain and to inform.

Edwardian *adj.* & *n.* (a person) of the reign of Edward VII (1901–10).

EEC *abbr.* European Economic Community.

EEG *abbr.* electroencephalogram.

eel *n.* a snakelike fish.

eerie *adj.* (**eerier, eeriest**) mysterious and frightening. ▫ **eerily** *adv.*, **eeriness** *n.*

efface *v.* rub out, obliterate; make inconspicuous. ▫ **effacement** *n.*

effect *n.* **1** a change produced by an action or cause; an impression; (**effects**) lighting, sound, etc. in a film, broadcast, etc. **2** a state of being operative. **3** (**effects**) property. ● *v.* bring about, cause.

▪ **Usage** Do not confuse the verbs *effect* and *affect*. *He effected an entrance* means 'He got in (somehow)', but *This won't affect me* means 'My life won't be changed by this'.

effective *adj.* **1** achieving the intended result; operative. **2** fulfilling a function in fact though not officially. ▫ **effectively** *adv.*, **effectiveness** *n.*

effectual *adj.* effective. ▫ **effectually** *adv.*

effeminate *adj.* (of a man) feminine in appearance or manner. ▫ **effeminacy** *n.*, **effeminately** *adv.*

effervescent *adj.* fizzy, bubbling; vivacious, high-spirited. ▫ **effervesce** *v.*, **effervescence** *n.*

effete *adj.* having lost vitality; feeble. ▫ **effeteness** *n.*

efficacious *adj.* producing the desired result. ▫ **efficaciously** *adv.*, **efficacy** *n.*

efficient *adj.* producing results with little waste of effort; competent, organized. ▫ **efficiency** *n.*, **efficiently** *adv.*

effigy *n.* (*pl.* **-ies**) a model of a person.

effloresce *v.* **1** (of a substance) lose moisture and turn to powder. **2** reach a peak of development. ▫ **efflorescence** *n.*

effluent *n.* outflow, sewage.

effluvium *n.* (*pl.* **effluvia**) an unpleasant or harmful smell or outflow.

effort *n.* a vigorous attempt; use of energy, hard work. ▫ **effortless** *adj.*

effrontery *n.* bold insolence.

effusion *n.* an outpouring.

effusive *adj.* expressing emotion in an unrestrained way. ▫ **effusively** *adv.*, **effusiveness** *n.*

EFL *abbr.* English as a foreign language.

EFTA *abbr.* European Free Trade Association.

e.g. *abbr.* (Latin *exempli gratia*) for example.

egalitarian *adj.* & *n.* (a person) holding the principle of equal rights for all. ▫ **egalitarianism** *n.*

egg *n.* an oval or round object laid by a female bird, reptile, etc., containing an embryo; an ovum; a hen's egg as food. ▫ **egg on** urge, encourage.

egghead *n. informal* an intellectual person.

eggshell *n.* the shell of an egg. ● *adj.* **1** (of china) fragile. **2** (of paint) with a slightly glossy finish.

eggplant *n.* (esp. *Amer.*) an aubergine.

ego *n.* self; self-esteem.

egocentric *adj.* self-centred.

egoism *n.* self-centredness. ▫ **egoist** *n.*, **egoistic** *adj.*

egotism *n.* the practice of talking too much about oneself, conceit.

□ **egotist** *n.*, **egotistic** *adj.*, **egotistical** *adj.*

egregious (i-gree-jŭs) *adj.* outstandingly bad, shocking.

egress (ee-gress) *n.* departure; a way out.

Egyptian *adj.* & *n.* (a native) of Egypt.

Egyptology *n.* the study of Egyptian antiquities. □ **Egyptologist** *n.*

eider *n.* a large northern duck.

eiderdown *n.* a quilt stuffed with soft material.

eight *adj.* & *n.* one more than seven (8, VIII). □ **eighth** *adj.* & *n.*

eighteen *adj.* & *n.* one more than seventeen (18, XVIII). □ **eighteenth** *adj.* & *n.*

eighty *adj.* & *n.* ten times eight (80, LXXX). □ **eightieth** *adj.* & *n.*

einsteinium *n.* a radioactive metallic element (symbol Es).

eisteddfod (I-sted-vĕd, I-steth-vĕd) *n.* a Welsh festival of music, poetry, and dance.

either *adj.* & *pron.* one or other of two; each of two. ● *adv.* & *conj.* **1** as the first alternative. **2** likewise (used with negatives): *I don't like him and she doesn't either.*

ejaculate *v.* **1** utter suddenly. **2** eject (semen). □ **ejaculation** *n.*

eject *v.* throw or force out. □ **ejection** *n.*, **ejector** *n.*

eke *v.* □ **eke out** make (a supply etc.) last longer by careful use; make (a living) laboriously.

elaborate *adj.* (i-lab-ĕr-ăt) complicated, with many parts or details; exaggerated, emphasized. ● *v.* (i-lab-ĕr-ayt) develop in detail; add detail to. □ **elaborately** *adv.*, **elaboration** *n.*

élan (ay-lan) *n.* vivacity, vigour.

elapse *v.* (of time) pass, go by.

elastic *adj.* going back to its original length or shape after being stretched or squeezed; adaptable. ● *n.* cord or material made elastic by interweaving strands of rubber etc. □ **elasticity** *n.*

elated *adj.* very happy and excited. □ **elate** *v.*, **elation** *n.*

elbow *n.* the joint between the forearm and upper arm; the part of a sleeve covering this; a sharp bend. ● *v.* thrust with one's elbow; clear one's way by pushing with one's elbows.

elbow grease *n.* vigorous polishing, hard work.

elbow room *n.* enough space to move or work in.

elder *adj.* older. ● *n.* **1** an older person; an official in certain Churches. **2** a tree with small dark berries.

elderly *adj.* old.

eldest *adj.* first-born, oldest.

eldorado *n.* (*pl.* **eldorados**) a place of prosperity and abundance.

elect *v.* choose by vote; decide on a course of action. ● *adj.* chosen; elected but not yet in office.

election *n.* an occasion when representatives, office-holders, etc. are chosen by vote; electing, being elected.

electioneer *v.* take part in an election campaign.

elective *adj.* **1** working by elections; chosen by election. **2** optional.

elector *n.* a person entitled to vote in an election. □ **electoral** *adj.*

electorate *n.* a body of electors.

electric *adj.* of, producing, or worked by electricity.

electrical *adj.* of electricity. □ **electrically** *adv.*

electrician *n.* a person whose job is to deal with electrical equipment.

electricity *n.* a form of energy occurring in certain particles; a supply of electric current.

electrics *n.pl.* electrical fittings.

electrify *v.* (**electrified, electrifying**) charge with electricity; convert to the use of electric power; cause a sudden thrill to. □ **electrification** *n.*

electrocardiogram *n.* a record of the electric current generated by heartbeats.

electroconvulsive therapy *n.* treatment of mental illness by electric shocks producing convulsions.

electrocute *v.* kill by electric shock. □ **electrocution** *n.*

electrode *n.* a solid conductor through which electricity enters or leaves a vacuum tube etc.

electroencephalogram *n.* a record of the electrical activity of the brain.

electrolysis *n.* the decomposition of a substance by the application of an electric current; the destruction of hair-roots etc. by this process.

electrolyte *n.* a solution that conducts an electric current.

electromagnet *n.* a magnet consisting of a metal core magnetized by a current-carrying coil round it.

electromagnetic *adj.* of the interrelation of electric and magnetic fields. □ **electromagnetically** *adv.*, **electromagnetism** *n.*

electromotive *adj.* producing an electric current.

electron *n.* a particle with a negative electric charge.

electronic *adj.* **1** having many small components, e.g. microchips, that control an electric current; concerned with electronic equipment; carried out using a computer or other electronic device. **2** of electrons. □ **electronically** *adv.*

electronics *n.* the branch of physics and technology concerned with the behaviour of electric currents in electronic equipment; (as *pl.*) electronic circuits or devices.

electronic tagging *n.* the attaching of electronic markers to people or goods enabling them to be traced.

electron microscope *n.* a very powerful microscope using a focused beam of electrons instead of light.

electroplate *v.* coat (metal) with a thin layer of silver etc. by electrolysis.

elegant *adj.* graceful and stylish, tasteful. □ **elegantly** *adv.*, **elegance** *n.*

elegy *n.* (*pl.* **-ies**) a sorrowful poem. □ **elegiac** *adj.*

element *n.* **1** a part or aspect, esp. an essential one; a small amount; (**elements**) basic principles of a subject. **2** a substance that cannot be broken down into other substances; earth, air, fire, and water, regarded as basic. **3** (**the elements**) weather, esp. when bad. **4** a wire that gives out heat in an electrical appliance. □ **in one's element** in a situation or activity that suits one perfectly. □ **elemental** *adj.*

elementary *adj.* dealing with the simplest facts of a subject.

elephant *n.* a very large animal with a trunk and ivory tusks.

elephantine *adj.* huge.

elevate *v.* raise to a higher position or level.

elevation *n.* **1** raising, being raised; altitude; a hill. **2** one side of a building etc.; a drawing of this.

elevator *n. Amer.* a lift.

eleven *adj.* & *n.* one more than ten (11, XI). □ **eleventh** *adj.* & *n.*

elevenses *n. informal* a midmorning snack.

elf *n.* (*pl.* **elves**) an imaginary small being with magic powers.

elfin *adj.* (of a face etc.) small and delicate.

elicit *v.* draw out (a response).

eligible *adj.* **1** qualified or having the right to something. **2** desirable as a marriage partner. □ **eligibility** *n.*

eliminate *v.* get rid of; exclude. □ **elimination** *n.*, **eliminator** *n.*

elision *n.* omission of part of a word in pronunciation.

elite (ay-leet) *n.* a group regarded as superior and favoured.

elitism (ay-leet-izm) *n.* favouring of or dominance by a selected group. □ **elitist** *n.* & *adj.*

elixir *n.* a liquid used for medicinal or magical purposes.

Elizabethan *adj.* & *n.* (a person) of Elizabeth I's reign (1558–1603).

elk *n.* a large deer.

ellipse *n.* a regular oval.

ellipsis *n.* (*pl.* **ellipses**) omission of words; dots indicating this.

elliptical *adj.* **1** shaped like an ellipse. **2** with a word or words omitted. □ **elliptically** *adv.*

elm *n.* a tree with rough serrated leaves; its wood.

elocution *n.* the art of clear and expressive speech; a style of speaking. □ **elocutionary** *adj.*

elongate *v.* lengthen.

elope *v.* run away secretly with a lover. □ **elopement** *n.*

eloquence *n.* fluent and persuasive use of language. □ **eloquent** *adj.*, **eloquently** *adv.*

else *adv.* **1** in addition. **2** instead, other. □ **or else** otherwise, if not.

elsewhere *adv.* in another place.

elucidate *v.* throw light on, explain. □ **elucidation** *n.*

elude *v.* escape skilfully from; escape the memory or understanding of; be unattainable by. □ **elusion** *n.*, **elusive** *adj.*

elver *n.* a young eel.

emaciated *adj.* thin from illness or starvation. □ **emaciation** *n.*

e-mail *n.* (also **email**) electronic mail, messages sent from one computer user to another and displayed on-screen. ● *v.* send (a message) to (someone).

emanate *v.* issue, originate from a source. □ **emanation** *n.*

emancipate *v.* liberate, free from restraint. □ **emancipation** *n.*

emasculate *v.* deprive of force, weaken. □ **emasculation** *n.*

embalm *v.* preserve (a corpse) by using spices or chemicals. □ **embalmment** *n.*

embankment *n.* a bank or stone structure to keep a river from spreading or to carry a railway.

embargo *n.* (*pl.* **embargoes**) an official ban on trade or another activity. ● *v.* (**embargoed, embargoing**) impose an official ban on.

embark *v.* board a ship. □ **embark on** begin (an undertaking). □ **embarkation** *n.*

embarrass *v.* cause to feel awkward or ashamed; cause financial difficulties to. □ **embarrassment** *n.*

embassy *n.* (*pl.* **-ies**) the official residence or offices of an ambassador.

embattled *adj.* prepared for war; beset by conflicts or problems.

embed *v.* (also **imbed**) (**embedded**, **embedding**) fix firmly in a surrounding mass.

embellish *v.* ornament; invent exciting details for (a story). □ **embellishment** *n.*

embers *n.pl.* small pieces of live coal or wood in a dying fire.

embezzle *v.* take (company funds etc.) fraudulently for one's own use. □ **embezzlement** *n.*, **embezzler** *n.*

embittered *adj.* resentful, bitter. □ **embitterment** *n.*

emblem *n.* a symbol, a design used as a badge etc.

emblematic *adj.* serving as an emblem. □ **emblematically** *adv.*

embody *v.* (**embodied**, **embodying**) **1** give a tangible or visible form to. **2** include. □ **embodiment** *n.*

embolden *v.* make bold

embolism *n.* obstruction of a blood vessel by a clot or air bubble.

emboss *v.* decorate by a raised design; mould in relief.

embrace *v.* **1** hold closely in one's arms as a sign of affection; hold each other in this way. **2** accept, adopt; include. ● *n.* an act of embracing, a hug.

embrocation *n.* liquid for rubbing on the body to relieve aches.

embroider *v.* ornament with needlework; embellish (a story). □ **embroidery** *n.*

embroil *v.* involve in an argument or quarrel etc.

embryo *n.* (*pl.* **embryos**) an animal developing in a womb or egg; something in an early stage of development. ▫ **embryology** *n.*, **embryonic** *adj.*

emend *v.* alter to remove errors. ▫ **emendation** *n.*, **emendatory** *adj.*

■ **Usage** Do not confuse *emend* with *amend*, meaning 'make slight alterations to'.

emerald *n.* a bright green precious stone; its colour.

emerge *v.* come up or out into view; become known; recover from a difficult situation. ▫ **emergence** *n.*, **emergent** *adj.*

emergency *n.* (*pl.* **-ies**) a serious situation needing prompt attention.

emeritus *adj.* retired and retaining a title as an honour.

emery *n.* a coarse abrasive.

emery board *n.* a strip of cardboard coated with emery, used for filing the nails.

emetic *n.* & *adj.* (a medicine) causing vomiting.

emf *abbr.* electromotive force.

emigrate *v.* leave one country and go to settle in another. ▫ **emigrant** *n.*, **emigration** *n.*

émigré (em-i-gray) *n.* an emigrant, esp. a political exile.

eminence *n.* **1** fame, superiority; an important person; (**Eminence**) a title of a cardinal. **2** *formal* a hill.

eminent *adj.* famous, distinguished. ▫ **eminently** *adv.*

emir (em-eer) *n.* a Muslim ruler.

emirate *n.* the territory of an emir.

emissary *n.* (*pl.* **-ies**) a person sent to conduct negotiations.

emit *v.* (**emitted**, **emitting**) send out (light, heat, fumes, etc.); utter. ▫ **emission** *n.*, **emitter** *n.*

emollient *adj.* softening; soothing. ● *n.* a cream to soften the skin.

emolument *n.* a fee; a salary.

emotion *n.* an intense feeling; feeling contrasted with reason.

emotional *adj.* of emotions; readily feeling or showing emotion; expressing strong feelings. ▫ **emotionally** *adv.*

emotive *adj.* rousing emotion.

■ **Usage** Do not confuse *emotive* with *emotional*, 'feeling or showing emotion'.

empathize *v.* (also **-ise**) share and understand another's feelings.

empathy *n.* the ability to share and understand another's feelings.

emperor *n.* a male ruler of an empire.

emphasis *n.* (*pl.* **emphases**) special importance or prominence; stress on a sound or word; intensity of expression.

emphasize *v.* (also **-ise**) stress; treat as important; make more noticeable.

emphatic *adj.* using or showing emphasis. ▫ **emphatically** *adv.*

emphysema (em-fi-see-mă) *n.* enlargement of the air sacs in the lungs, causing breathlessness.

empire *n.* a group of countries ruled by a supreme authority; a large organization controlled by one person or group.

empirical *adj.* based on observation or experiment, not on theory. ▫ **empirically** *adv.*, **empiricism** *n.*, **empiricist** *n.*

emplacement *n.* a platform for a gun or battery of guns.

employ *v.* give work to; make use of. ▫ **employer** *n.*, **employment** *n.*

employee *n.* a person employed by another in return for wages.

emporium *n.* (*pl.* **emporia** or **emporiums**) a large shop selling a variety of goods.

empower *v.* authorize, enable.

empress *n.* a female ruler of an empire; the wife of an emperor.

empty *adj.* (**emptier**, **emptiest**) **1** containing nothing; without occupants. **2** having no meaning or value. ● *v.* make or become empty.

● *n. informal* an empty glass or bottle. ▫ **emptiness** *n.*

EMU *abbr.* European Monetary Union.

emu *n.* a large flightless Australian bird resembling an ostrich.

emulate *v.* match or surpass; imitate. ▫ **emulation** *n.*, **emulator** *n.*

emulsify *v.* (**emulsified, emulsifying**) convert or be converted into emulsion. ▫ **emulsification** *n.*, **emulsifier** *n.*

emulsion *n.* **1** finely dispersed droplets of one liquid in another. **2** a light-sensitive coating on photographic film.

enable *v.* give the means or authority to do something.

enact *v.* **1** make into a law. **2** play (a part or scene). ▫ **enactment** *n.*

enamel *n.* **1** a glasslike coating for metal or pottery. **2** glossy paint. **3** the hard outer covering of teeth. ● *v.* (**enamelled, enamelling**; *Amer.* **enameled**) coat with enamel.

enamoured *adj.* (*Amer.* **enamored**) fond.

en bloc (ahn **blok**) *adv.* as a whole, all at the same time.

encamp *v.* settle in a camp.

encampment *n.* a camp.

encapsulate *v.* **1** enclose (as) in a capsule. **2** summarize. ▫ **encapsulation** *n.*

encase *v.* enclose in a case.

encephalitis *n.* inflammation of the brain.

enchant *v.* delight; bewitch. ▫ **enchanter** *n.*, **enchantment** *n.*, **enchantress** *n.*

encircle *v.* surround. ▫ **encirclement** *n.*

enclave *n.* a small territory wholly within the boundaries of another.

enclose *v.* **1** shut in on all sides. **2** include with other contents.

enclosure *n.* **1** an enclosed area; enclosing; fencing off land. **2** something placed in an envelope together with a letter.

encode *v.* put into code; put (data) into computerized form. ▫ **encoder** *n.*

encomium *n.* (*pl.* **encomiums** or **encomia**) a formal expression of praise.

encompass *v.* **1** encircle. **2** include.

encore (ong-kor) *n.* a repeated or additional performance. ● *int.* a call for this. ● *v.* call for (a performance) to be repeated.

encounter *v.* meet by chance; be faced with. ● *n.* a chance meeting; a battle.

encourage *v.* give hope, confidence, or stimulus to; urge. ▫ **encouragement** *n.*

encroach *v.* intrude on someone's territory or rights. ▫ **encroachment** *n.*

encrust *v.* cover with a crust of hard material. ▫ **encrustation** *n.*

encumber *v.* be a burden to, hamper. ▫ **encumbrance** *n.*

encyclical *n.* a pope's letter for circulation to churches.

encyclopedia *n.* (also **encyclopaedia**) a book containing information on many subjects. ▫ **encyclopedic** *adj.*

end *n.* **1** the point after which something no longer exists or happens; a furthest or final part or point; a remnant. **2** death. **3** a goal. ● *v.* bring or come to an end. ▫ **end up** eventually reach a particular place or state. **make ends meet** earn enough money to support oneself. **on end** continuing for a long time: *it rained for days on end.*

endanger *v.* cause danger to.

endear *v.* cause to be loved.

■ **Usage** *Endear* is sometimes wrongly used to mean 'make fond of'. It is correctly used in *Her charm endeared her to me* (not *endeared me to her*).

endearment *n.* words expressing love.

endeavour *v.* & *n.* (*Amer.* **endeavor**) (make) an earnest attempt.

endemic *adj.* commonly found in a specified area or people.

ending *n.* the final part.

endive *n.* a curly-leaved plant used in salads; *Amer.* chicory.

endless *adj.* without end; continual; *informal* countless. □ **endlessly** *adv.*

endocrine gland *n.* a gland secreting hormones into the blood.

endorse *v.* **1** declare approval of. **2** sign (a cheque) on the back. **3** record an offence on (a driving licence). □ **endorsement** *n.*

endow *v.* provide with a permanent income or property. □ **endowed with** possessing (a desirable quality). □ **endowment** *n.*

endurance *n.* the power of enduring.

endure *v.* experience and survive (pain or hardship); tolerate; last. □ **endurable** *adj.*

enema *n.* liquid injected into the rectum, esp. to empty the bowels.

enemy *n.* (*pl.* **-ies**) one who is hostile to and seeks to harm another.

energetic *adj.* possessing, showing, or requiring a great deal of energy. □ **energetically** *adv.*

energize *v.* (also **-ise**) give energy to; supply electricity to.

energy *n.* the strength and vitality needed for vigorous activity; the ability of matter or radiation to do work; power derived from physical resources to provide light, heat, etc.

enervate *v.* cause to lose vitality. □ **enervation** *n.*

enfant terrible (ahn-fahn tereebl) *n.* (*pl.* **enfants terribles**) a person who embarrasses others by unconventional behaviour.

enfeeble *v.* make weak. □ **enfeeblement** *n.*

enfold *v.* surround; embrace.

enforce *v.* compel obedience to (a law etc.); force to happen or be done. □ **enforceable** *adj.*, **enforcement** *n.*

enfranchise *v.* give the right to vote. □ **enfranchisement** *n.*

engage *v.* **1** occupy, involve; employ. **2** promise. **3** establish contact; move (part of a machine) into working position; begin a battle with. □ **engage in** occupy oneself with.

engaged *adj.* **1** having promised to marry a specified person. **2** occupied; in use.

engagement *n.* **1** a promise to marry a specified person. **2** an appointment. **3** engaging, being engaged. **4** a battle.

engaging *adj.* charming.

engender *v.* give rise to.

engine *n.* a machine with moving parts that converts energy into motion; a railway locomotive.

engineer *n.* a person skilled in engineering; one in charge of machines and engines. ● *v.* design and build (a machine); contrive to bring about (an event).

engineering *n.* the application of science for the design and building of machines and structures.

English *n.* the language of Britain, the USA, and several other countries; (**the English**) the people of England. ● *adj.* of England or its language. □ **Englishman** *n.*, **Englishwoman** *n.*

engrave *v.* cut (a design) into a hard surface; ornament in this way. □ **engraver** *n.*

engraving *n.* a print made from an engraved metal plate.

engross *v.* absorb the attention of. □ **engrossment** *n.*

engulf *v.* swamp.

enhance *v.* increase the quality, value, or extent of. □ **enhancement** *n.*

enigma *n.* a mysterious person or thing. □ **enigmatic** *adj.*, **enigmatically** *adv.*

enjoy *v.* **1** take pleasure in. **2** possess and benefit from. □ **enjoy**

oneself have a pleasant time. □ **enjoyable** *adj.*, **enjoyment** *n.*

enlarge *v.* make or become larger. □ **enlarge upon** say more about. □ **enlargement** *n.*, **enlarger** *n.*

enlighten *v.* make more knowledgeable or comprehending. □ **enlightenment** *n.*

enlist *v.* enrol for military service; secure (support, service). □ **enlistment** *n.*

enliven *v.* make more interesting or interested. □ **enlivenment** *n.*

en masse (ahn **mass**) *adv.* all together; in a group.

enmesh *v.* entangle.

enmity *n.* hostility; hatred.

ennoble *v.* give a noble rank to. □ **ennoblement** *n.*

ennui (ahn-wee) *n.* boredom.

enormity *n.* (*pl.* **-ies**) **1** great wickedness. **2** great size.

enormous *adj.* very large.

enough *adj., adv.,* & *n.* as much or as many as necessary.

enquire *v.* ask. □ **enquiry** *n.*

enrage *v.* make furious.

enrapture *v.* delight intensely.

enrich *v.* **1** enhance; make more rewarding, nourishing, etc. **2** make wealthier. □ **enrichment** *n.*

enrol *v.* (*Amer.* **enroll**) (**enrolled, enrolling**) admit as or become a member. □ **enrolment** *n.*

en route (ahn **root**) *adv.* on the way.

ensconce *v.* establish securely or comfortably.

ensemble (ahn-**sahmbl**) *n.* a thing viewed as a whole; a group of performers; an outfit.

enshrine *v.* preserve and respect. □ **enshrinement** *n.*

ensign *n.* a military or naval flag.

enslave *v.* take away the freedom of. □ **enslavement** *n.*

ensnare *v.* snare; trap.

ensue *v.* happen afterwards or as a result.

en suite (ahn **sweet**) *adv.* & *adj.* (of a bedroom and bathroom) adjoining and forming a single unit.

ensure *v.* make certain (that); secure.

entail *v.* involve as a necessary part or consequence.

entangle *v.* tangle; entwine and trap. □ **entanglement** *n.*

entente (on-tont) *n.* (also **entente cordiale**) friendly understanding between countries.

enter *v.* **1** go or come in or into; become involved in; register as a competitor (in). **2** record (information) in a book, computer, etc.

enteritis *n.* inflammation of the intestines.

enterprise *n.* a bold undertaking; boldness; a business activity.

enterprising *adj.* full of initiative.

entertain *v.* **1** amuse. **2** offer hospitality to. **3** consider (an idea etc.). □ **entertainer** *n.*, **entertainment** *n.*

enthral *v.* (*Amer.* **enthrall**) (**enthralled, enthralling**) hold spellbound. □ **enthralment** *n.*

enthrone *v.* place on a throne; install in a position of power. □ **enthronement** *n.*

enthuse *v.* fill with or show enthusiasm.

enthusiasm *n.* eager liking or interest.

enthusiast *n.* a person who is full of enthusiasm for something. □ **enthusiastic** *adj.*, **enthusiastically** *adv.*

entice *v.* attract by offering something pleasant; tempt. □ **enticement** *n.*

entire *adj.* complete. □ **entirely** *adv.*

entirety *n.* □ **in its entirety** as a whole.

entitle *v.* **1** give (a person) a right or claim. **2** give (a book etc.) a particular title. □ **entitlement** *n.*

entity *n.* (*pl.* **-ies**) a distinct and individual thing.

entomology *n.* the study of insects. □ **entomological** *adj.*, **entomologist** *n.*

entourage (on-toor-ah*zh*) *n.* people accompanying an important person.

entr'acte (on-trakt) *n.* an interval between acts of a play.

entrails *n.pl.* intestines.

entrance[1] (en-trăns) *n.* a door, passage, etc., through which one enters; coming in; a right of admission, the fee for this.

entrance[2] (en-trahns) *v.* fill with intense delight.

entreat *v.* request earnestly or emotionally. ◻ **entreaty** *n.*

entrée (on-tray) *n.* **1** a dish served between the fish and meat courses of a meal. **2** the right of admission.

entrench *v.* establish firmly. ◻ **entrenchment** *n.*

entrepreneur (on-trĕ-prĕ-ner) *n.* a person who sets up a business at considerable risk. ◻ **entrepreneurial** *adj.*

entropy *n.* a measure of the amount of a system's thermal energy not available for conversion into mechanical work.

entrust *v.* give as a responsibility, place in a person's care.

entry *n.* (*pl.* **-ies**) **1** entering; an entrance. **2** an item entered in a record. **3** an item entered in a competition.

entwine *v.* twist together.

E-number *n.* E followed by a number, the EC designation for permitted food additives.

enumerate *v.* mention (items) one by one. ◻ **enumeration** *n.*

enunciate *v.* pronounce; state clearly. ◻ **enunciation** *n.*

envelop *v.* (**enveloped, enveloping**) wrap up; surround. ◻ **envelopment** *n.*

envelope *n.* a paper holder for a letter, with a sealable flap.

enviable *adj.* desirable enough to arouse envy. ◻ **enviably** *adv.*

envious *adj.* full of envy. ◻ **enviously** *adv.*

environment *n.* **1** surroundings, setting. **2** the natural world. ◻ **environmental** *adj.*, **environmentally** *adv.*

environmentalist *n.* a person seeking to protect the natural environment.

environs *n.pl.* the surrounding districts, esp. of a town.

envisage *v.* imagine; foresee.

envoy *n.* a messenger, esp. to a foreign government.

envy *n.* discontent aroused by another's possessions or success; the object of this: *he is the envy of us all.* ● *v.* (**envied, envying**) feel envy of.

enzyme *n.* a protein formed in living cells and assisting chemical processes.

eon var. of **aeon**.

epaulette *n.* an ornamental shoulder-piece on a uniform.

ephemera (e-fem-ĕ-ră) *n.pl.* things of only short-lived usefulness.

ephemeral *adj.* lasting only a short time. ◻ **ephemerally** *adv.*

epic *n.* a long poem, story, or film about heroic deeds or history. ● *adj.* of or like an epic; on a grand or heroic scale.

epicene (e-pi-seen) *adj.* appropriate to either sex.

epicentre *n.* (*Amer.* **epicenter**) the point on the earth's surface above the focus of an earthquake.

epicure *n.* a person who enjoys fine food and drink. ◻ **epicurean** *adj.* & *n.*, **epicureanism** *n.*

epidemic *n.* an outbreak of a disease etc. spreading through a community. ◻ **epidemiology** *n.*

epidermis *n.* the outer layer of the skin.

epidural *n.* a spinal anaesthetic affecting the lower part of the body, esp. used in child birth.

epiglottis *n.* a cartilage that covers the larynx in swallowing.

epigram *n.* a short witty saying. ◻ **epigrammatic** *adj.*

epilepsy *n.* a disorder of the nervous system, causing fits. ◻ **epileptic** *adj.* & *n.*

epilogue *n.* a short concluding section of a book etc.

episcopal *adj.* of or governed by bishops.

episcopalian *adj.* & *n.* (a member) of an episcopal church.

episiotomy (e-pi-si-o-tŏ-mi) *n.* (*pl.* **-ies**) a cut made at the opening of the vagina during childbirth.

episode *n.* an event forming one part of a sequence; one part of a serial. □ **episodic** *adj.*, **episodically** *adv.*

epistle *n.* a letter. □ **epistolary** *adj.*

epitaph *n.* words in memory of a dead person, esp. inscribed on a tomb.

epithet *n.* a descriptive word.

epitome (i-pit-ŏmi) *n.* **1** a perfect example. **2** a summary.

epitomize *v.* (also **-ise**) be a perfect example of. □ **epitomization** *n.*

epoch (ee-pok) *n.* a period marked by particular characteristics.

eponymous (e-pon-i-mŭs) *adj.* after whom something is named.

equable *adj.* **1** calm, not easily angered. **2** free from extremes. □ **equably** *adv.*

■ **Usage** not confuse *equable* with *equitable*, 'fair'.

---

equal *adj.* the same in size, amount, value, etc.; having the same rights or status; free from discrimination or disadvantage. ● *n.* a person or thing of the same status or quality as another. ● *v.* (**equalled, equalling**; *Amer.* **equaled**) be the same as in number or amount; match, rival. □ **equal to** able to deal with. □ **equality** *n.*, **equally** *adv.*

equalize *v.* (also **-ise**) make or become equal; match an opponent's score. □ **equalization** *n.*

equalizer *n.* (also **-iser**) something that equalizes; a goal making scores even.

equal opportunity *n.* absence of discrimination in the competition for jobs etc.

equanimity *n.* calmness of mind or temper.

equate *v.* consider to be equal or equivalent.

equation *n.* a mathematical statement that two expressions are equal.

equator *n.* an imaginary line round the earth at an equal distance from the North and South Poles. □ **equatorial** *adj.*

equerry *n.* (*pl.* **-ies**) an officer attending the British royal family.

equestrian *adj.* of horse-riding; on horseback.

equidistant *adj.* at an equal distance.

equilateral *adj.* having all sides equal.

equilibrium *n.* (*pl.* **equilibria**) a balanced state.

equine (ek-wyn) *adj.* of or like a horse.

equinox *n.* the time of year when night and day are of equal length. □ **equinoctial** *adj.*

equip *v.* (**equipped, equipping**) supply with what is needed.

equipage *n. hist.* a carriage, horses, and attendants.

equipment *n.* the tools etc. needed for a purpose; supplying these.

equipoise *n.* equilibrium.

equitable *adj.* fair and just. □ **equitably** *adv.*

■ **Usage** Do not confuse *equitable* with *equable*

---

equitation *n. formal* horse-riding.

equity *n.* **1** fairness, impartiality. **2** (**equities**) stocks and shares not bearing fixed interest.

equivalent *adj.* equal in amount, value, meaning, etc. ● *n.* an equivalent thing. □ **equivalence** *n.*

equivocal *adj.* ambiguous. □ **equivocally** *adv.*

equivocate *v.* use words ambiguously. □ **equivocation** *n.*

ER *abbr.* Elizabeth Regina.

Er *symb.* erbium.

era *n.* a period of history.

eradicate *v.* wipe out. ▫ **eradicable** *adj.*, **eradication** *n.*

erase *v.* rub out. ▫ **eraser** *n.*, **erasure** *n.*

erbium *n.* a soft metallic element (symbol Er).

ere (air) *prep.* & *conj. poetic* before.

erect *adj.* upright; (of the penis or nipples) rigid from sexual excitement. ● *v.* set upright; construct. ▫ **erection** *n.*

erectile *adj.* capable of becoming erect.

erg *n.* a unit of work or energy.

ergo *adv.* therefore.

ergonomics *n.* the study of people's efficiency in their working environment. ▫ **ergonomic** *adj.*, **ergonomically** *adv.*

ERM *abbr.* Exchange Rate Mechanism.

ermine *n.* a stoat; its white winter fur.

erode *v.* wear away gradually. ▫ **erosion** *n.*, **erosive** *adj.*

erogenous *adj.* arousing sexual excitement.

erotic *adj.* of or arousing sexual desire. ▫ **erotically** *adv.*

eroticism *n.* being erotic.

err *v.* (**erred, erring**) make a mistake; do wrong.

errand *n.* a short journey to do a job for someone.

errant *adj. formal* misbehaving.

erratic *adj.* irregular, uneven. ▫ **erratically** *adv.*

erratum *n.* (*pl.* **errata**) an error in printing or writing.

erroneous *adj.* incorrect. ▫ **erroneously** *adv.*

error *n.* a mistake; being wrong.

ersatz *adj.* used as a substitute.

erstwhile *adj.* former.

eructation *n. formal* belching.

erudite *adj.* learned. ▫ **erudition** *n.*

erupt *v.* (of a volcano) eject lava; burst out; express an emotion violently. ▫ **eruption** *n.*

erythrocyte (e-rith-ro-sIt) *n.* a red blood cell.

Es *symb.* einsteinium.

escalate *v.* increase in intensity or extent. ▫ **escalation** *n.*

escalator *n.* a moving staircase.

escalope *n.* a thin slice of boneless meat, esp. veal.

escapade *n.* a piece of reckless or mischievous conduct.

escape *v.* get free (from); avoid (danger); leak from a container; fail to be remembered by. ● *n.* an act or means of escaping.

escapee *n.* one who escapes.

escapement *n.* a mechanism regulating a clock movement.

escapism *n.* a tendency to ignore the realities of life. ▫ **escapist** *n.* & *adj.*

escapologist *n.* an entertainer whose act involves escaping from bonds etc. ▫ **escapology** *n.*

escarpment *n.* a steep slope at the edge of a plateau etc.

eschew *v. literary* abstain from, avoid.

escort *n.* (ess-kort) a group of people or vehicles accompanying another as a protection or honour; a person accompanying a person of the opposite sex to a social event. ● *v.* (i-**skort**) act as escort to.

escritoire (es-kri-**twah**) *n.* a writing desk with drawers.

escudo *n.* (*pl.* **escudos**) a former unit of money in Portugal.

escutcheon *n.* **1** a shield bearing a coat of arms. **2** the protective plate around a keyhole or door handle.

Eskimo *n.* (*pl.* **Eskimos** or **Eskimo**) a member of a people living near the Arctic coast of America and eastern Siberia; their language.

■ **Usage** The Eskimos of North America prefer the term *Inuit*.

---

esophagus Amer. sp. of **oesophagus**.

esoteric *adj.* intended only for a few people with special knowledge or interest.

ESP *abbr.* extrasensory perception.

espadrille *n.* a canvas shoe with a sole of plaited fibre.

espalier *n.* a tree trained on a trellis against a wall.

esparto *n.* a coarse grass used in making paper.

especial *adj.* special; particular.

especially *adv.* **1** more than any other; particularly, individually. **2** to a great extent.

Esperanto *n.* an artificial international language.

espionage *n.* spying.

esplanade *n.* a promenade.

espouse *v.* **1** support (a cause). **2** *archaic* marry. □ **espousal** *n.*

espresso *n.* (also **expresso**) (*pl.* **espressos**) strong coffee made by forcing steam through powdered coffee beans.

esprit de corps (es-pree dĕ **kor**) *n.* loyalty uniting a group.

espy *v.* (**espied, espying**) catch sight of.

Esq. *abbr.* Esquire, a courtesy title placed after a man's surname.

essay *n.* (ess-ay) a short literary composition in prose. ● *v.* (e-**say**) attempt.

essence *n.* the qualities or elements making something what it is; a concentrated extract. □ **of the essence** critically important.

essential *adj.* **1** absolutely necessary. **2** central to something's nature. ● *n.* something absolutely necessary; (**the essentials**) the basic facts. ● *n.* an essential thing. □ **essentially** *adv.*

establish *v.* set up; make permanent or secure; prove.

established *adj.* officially recognized as the national Church.

establishment *n.* **1** establishing, being established. **2** an organization; its staff; (**the Establishment**) influential people in a social system.

estate *n.* landed property; a residential or industrial district planned as a unit; property left at someone's death.

estate car *n.* a car with a door at the back and extended luggage space.

esteem *v.* think highly of. ● *n.* a favourable opinion, respect.

esthete, esthetic Amer. sp. of **aesthete, aesthetic**.

estimable *adj.* worthy of esteem.

estimate *v.* (ess-ti-mayt) make an approximate judgement of (something's quantity, value, etc.). ● *n.* (ess-ti-măt) such a judgement. □ **estimation** *n.*

estrange *v.* cause to be no longer friendly or loving. □ **estrangement** *n.*

estrogen Amer. sp. of **oestrogen**.

estuary *n.* (*pl.* **-ies**) the mouth of a large river, affected by tides. □ **estuarine** *adj.*

et al. *abbr.* and others.

etc. *abbr.* et cetera, and other similar things.

etch *v.* **1** produce (a picture) by engraving (a metal plate) with acid. **2** impress deeply on the mind. □ **etcher** *n.*, **etching** *n.*

eternal *adj.* existing always; unchanging. □ **eternally** *adv.*

eternity *n.* (*pl.* **-ies**) infinite time; the endless period of life after death; *informal* a long time.

ethanol *n.* alcohol.

ether *n.* **1** the upper air. **2** a liquid used as an anaesthetic and solvent.

ethereal *adj.* light, delicate, and other worldly. □ **ethereally** *adv.*

ethic *n.* a moral principle or framework; (**ethics**) moral principles; the discussion of these.

ethical *adj.* of ethics; morally correct. □ **ethically** *adv.*

ethnic *adj.* of a group sharing a common origin, culture, or language. □ **ethnically** *adv.*, **ethnicity** *n.*

ethnic cleansing *n.* the mass expulsion or killing of members of one ethnic group in an area by those of another.

ethnology *n.* the study of human races and their characteristics.

□ **ethnological** *adj.*, **ethnologist** *n.*

ethos (ee-thoss) *n.* the characteristic spirit and beliefs of a community.

ethylene *n.* a hydrocarbon occurring in natural gas, used in manufacturing polythene.

etiolated (ee-ti-ŏ-lay-tĕd) *adj.* pale through being deprived of light. □ **etiolation** *n.*

etiology Amer. sp. of **aetiology**.

etiquette *n.* conventions of behaviour accepted as polite.

étude *n.* a short musical composition.

etymology *n.* (*pl.* **-ies**) an account of a word's origin and development. □ **etymological** *adj.*, **etymologically** *adv.*, **etymologist** *n.*

EU *abbr.* European Union.

Eu *symb.* europium.

eucalyptus *n.* (also **eucalypt**) a tree, native to Australia, with leaves that yield a strong-smelling oil.

Eucharist *n.* the Christian sacrament commemorating the Last Supper, in which bread and wine are consumed; this bread and wine. □ **Eucharistic** *adj.*

eugenics *n.* the science of controlling breeding to produce a healthier, more intelligent, etc. race.

eulogy *n.* (*pl.* **-ies**) a speech or work praising someone. □ **eulogistic** *adj.*, **eulogize** *v.*

eunuch *n.* a castrated man.

euphemism *n.* a mild expression substituted for an improper or blunt one. □ **euphemistic** *adj.*, **euphemistically** *adv.*

euphony *n.* pleasantness of sounds, esp. in words.

euphoria *n.* excited happiness. □ **euphoric** *adj.*, **euphorically** *adv.*

Eurasian *adj.* of Europe and Asia; of mixed European and Asian parentage. ● *n.* a Eurasian person.

eureka (yoor-eek-ă) *int.* I have found it! (announcing a discovery etc.).

eurhythmics *n.* (*Amer.* **eurythmics**) physical exercises to music.

Euro- *comb. form* European.

euro *n.* the single European currency, which replaced some national currencies in 2002.

European *adj.* of Europe or its people. ● *n.* a European person.

europium *n.* a soft metallic element (symbol Eu).

eurythmics Amer. sp. of **eurhythmics**.

Eustachian tube (yoo-stay-shăn) *n.* the passage between the ear and the throat.

euthanasia *n.* painless killing, esp. of someone with a terminal illness.

evacuate *v.* **1** send from a dangerous to a safer place. **2** empty. □ **evacuation** *n.*

evacuee *n.* an evacuated person.

evade *v.* avoid by cleverness or trickery.

evaluate *v.* find out or state the value of; assess. □ **evaluation** *n.*

evanescent *adj.* quickly fading. □ **evanesce** *v.*, **evanescence** *n.*

evangelical *adj.* **1** of the gospel. **2** of a branch of Protestantism emphasizing biblical authority. **3** zealously advocating something. □ **evangelicalism** *n.*

evangelist *n.* any of the authors of the four Gospels; a person who tries to convert others. □ **evangelism** *n.*, **evangelistic** *adj.*

evaporate *v.* turn (liquid) into vapour; (of something abstract) disappear. □ **evaporation** *n.*

evasion *n.* evading; an evasive answer or excuse.

evasive *adj.* evading; not frank. □ **evasively** *adv.*, **evasiveness** *n.*

eve *n.* an evening, day, or time just before a special event.

even *adj.* **1** level; regular; equally balanced. **2** exactly divisible by two. **3** not easily upset or annoyed. ● *v.* make or become even. ● *adv.* used for emphasis or in comparisons: *even faster*. □ **evenly** *adv.*, **evenness** *n.*

evening *n.* the latter part of the day, before nightfall.

evensong *n.* an evening service in the Church of England.

event *n.* something that happens; an organized social occasion; an item in a sports programme.

eventful *adj.* full of exciting events.

eventual *adj.* ultimate, final.

eventually *adv.* in the end, at last.

eventuality *n.* (*pl.* **-ies**) a possible event.

ever *adv.* **1** at any time: *have you ever been there?* **2** always.

evergreen *adj.* & *n.* (a plant) having green leaves throughout the year.

everlasting *adj.* lasting for ever or for a very long time.

evermore *adv.* for all the future.

every *adj.* each without exception; all possible; indicating an interval at which something regularly occurs: *every three months.* □ **every other** each alternate.

everybody *pron.* every person.

everyday *adj.* used or occurring on ordinary days; ordinary.

everyone *pron.* everybody.

everything *pron.* all things; all that is important.

everywhere *adv.* in every place.

evict *v.* expel (a tenant) by legal process. □ **eviction** *n.*, **evictor** *n.*

evidence *n.* signs of something's truth or existence; statements made in a law court to support a case. ● *v.* be evidence of. □ **be in evidence** be conspicuous. □ **evidential** *adj.*

evident *adj.* obvious to the eye or mind. □ **evidently** *adv.*

evil *adj.* morally bad; harmful; very unpleasant. ● *n.* wickedness; something wicked. □ **evilly** *adv.*

evince *v.* show, indicate.

eviscerate (i-vis-ĕ-rayt) *v.* disembowel. □ **evisceration** *n.*

evoke *v.* **1** cause someone to think of. **2** elicit (a response). □ **evocation** *n.*, **evocative** *adj.*

evolution *n.* the process of developing into a different form; the origination of living things by such development. □ **evolutionary** *adj.*

evolve *v.* develop or work out gradually. □ **evolvement** *n.*

ewe *n.* a female sheep.

ewer *n.* a water jug.

ex *prep.* **1** (of goods) as sold from (a factory etc.). **2** without, excluding. ● *n. informal* a former husband, wife, or partner.

ex- *pref.* **1** out, away. **2** thoroughly. **3** former.

exacerbate (ig-zass-er-bayt) *v.* make worse □ **exacerbation** *n.*

■ **Usage** *Exacerbate* is sometimes confused with *exasperate.*

exact *adj.* completely accurate; giving all details. ● *v.* insist on and obtain. □ **exactness** *n.*

exacting *adj.* making great demands, requiring great effort.

exactitude *n.* exactness.

exactly *adv.* **1** without vagueness or discrepancy. **2** expressing total agreement.

exaggerate *v.* represent as greater than is the case. □ **exaggeration** *n.*, **exaggerator** *n.*

exalt *v.* regard or praise highly; raise in rank.

■ **Usage** Do not confuse *exalt* and *exult.*

exaltation *n.* **1** extreme happiness. **2** praising; raising in rank.

exam *n. informal* an examination.

examination *n.* an inspection or investigation; a formal test of knowledge or ability.

examine *v.* look at closely; question as a formal test of knowledge. □ **examiner** *n.*

examinee *n.* a person being tested in an examination.

example *n.* something seen as typical of its kind or of a general rule; a person or thing worthy of imitation. □ **make an example of** punish as a warning to others.

exasperate *v.* annoy greatly. □ **exasperation** *n.*

excavate *v.* make (a hole) by digging, dig out; reveal (buried remains) by digging (a site). □ **excavation** *n.*, **excavator** *n.*

exceed *v.* be greater than; go beyond the limit of.

exceedingly *adv.* very.

excel *v.* (**excelled, excelling**) be very good at something. □ **excel oneself** do better than one ever has.

Excellency *n.* the title of an ambassador, governor, etc.

excellent *adj.* extremely good. □ **excellence** *n.*, **excellently** *adv.*

except *prep.* not including. ● *v.* exclude.

excepting *prep.* except.

exception *n.* something that does not follow a general rule. □ **take exception to** object to.

exceptionable *adj. formal* open to objection.

exceptional *adj.* very unusual; outstandingly good. □ **exceptionally** *adv.*

excerpt *n.* (ek-serpt) an extract from a book, film, etc. ● *v.* (ek-**serpt**) make (a short extract).

excess *n.* too large an amount of something; the amount by which one quantity exceeds another; lack of moderation. ● *adj.* exceeding a limit.

excessive *adj.* too much. □ **excessively** *adv.*

exchange *v.* give or receive in place of another thing. ● *n.* **1** exchanging; giving money for its equivalent in another currency; a brief conversation. **2** a place for trading a particular commodity. **3** a centre where telephone lines are connected. □ **exchangeable** *adj.*

exchequer (eks-**chek**-ĕ) *n.* a national treasury.

excise *n.* (**ek**-syz) duty or tax on certain goods and licences. ● *v.* (ek-syz) cut out or away. □ **excision** *n.*

excitable *adj.* easily excited. □ **excitability** *n.*, **excitably** *adv.*

excitation *n.* arousing, being aroused.

excite *v.* cause to feel eager and pleasantly agitated; arouse sexually; cause (a feeling or reaction). □ **excitement** *n.*

exclaim *v.* cry out suddenly.

exclamation *n.* a sudden utterance, esp. expressing an emotion. □ **exclamatory** *adj.*

exclamation mark *n.* a punctuation mark (!) placed after an exclamation.

exclude *v.* keep out from a place, group, privilege, etc.; omit, ignore as irrelevant; make impossible. □ **exclusion** *n.*

exclusive *adj.* **1** excluding something. **2** limited to one or a few people; catering only for the wealthy. ● *n.* a story published in only one newspaper. □ **exclusive of** not including. **exclusive to** found only in. □ **exclusively** *adv.*, **exclusiveness** *n.*

excommunicate *v.* officially exclude from a Church or its sacraments. □ **excommunication** *n.*

excoriate *v.* **1** strip skin from. **2** criticize severely. □ **excoriation** *n.*

excrement *n.* faeces.

excrescence *n.* an outgrowth on an animal or plant; an unnecessary or unattractive addition.

excreta *n.pl.* matter (esp. faeces) excreted from the body.

excrete *v.* expel (waste matter) from the body or tissues. □ **excretion** *n.*, **excretory** *adj.*

excruciating *adj.* intensely painful or unpleasant.

excursion *n.* a short journey, esp. for pleasure.

excuse *v.* (ek-**skewz**) **1** justify, defend (an action etc.); forgive. **2** exempt. ● *n.* (ek-**skewss**) a reason put forward to justify a fault; a pretext. □ **excusable** *adj.*, **excusably** *adv.*

ex-directory *adj.* deliberately not listed in a telephone directory.

execrable *adj.* very bad or unpleasant. □ **execrably** *adv.*

execrate *v.* express loathing for. □ **execration** *n.*

execute *v.* **1** carry out (an order); produce or perform (a work of art). **2** put (a condemned person) to death. □ **execution** *n.*

executioner *n.* an official who executes condemned people.

executive *n.* a person or group with managerial powers, or with authority to put government decisions into effect. ● *adj.* having such power or authority.

executor *n.* a person appointed to carry out the terms of a will.

exemplar *n.* a typical example, a model.

exemplary *adj.* **1** serving as a desirable model. **2** serving as a warning to others.

exemplify *v.* (**exemplified, exemplifying**) serve as an example of. □ **exemplification** *n.*

exempt *adj.* free from an obligation etc. imposed on others. ● *v.* make exempt. □ **exemption** *n.*

exercise *n.* **1** physical activity. **2** a task designed to practise a skill. **3** use of one's powers or rights. ● *v.* **1** use (a right etc.). **2** (cause to) take physical exercise. **3** occupy the thoughts of.

exercise book *n.* a book for writing in.

exert *v.* apply (a force, influence, etc.). □ **exert oneself** make an effort.

exertion *n.* **1** an effort. **2** applying a force etc.

exeunt (eks-iunt) *v.* (as a stage direction) they (actors) leave the stage.

exfoliate *v.* come off in scales or layers; remove dead layers of skin from. □ **exfoliation** *n.*

ex gratia (eks gray-shă) *adj.* & *adv.* done or given as a favour, without legal obligation.

exhale *v.* breathe out; give off in vapour. □ **exhalation** *n.*

exhaust *v.* **1** tire out. **2** use up completely. ● *n.* waste gases from an engine etc; a device through which they are expelled. □ **exhaustible** *adj.*

exhaustion *n.* **1** extreme tiredness. **2** using, being used up.

exhaustive *adj.* attending to every detail. □ **exhaustively** *adv.*

exhibit *v.* put on show publicly; display (a quality etc.). ● *n.* a thing on public show. □ **exhibitor** *n.*

exhibition *n.* **1** a public show; a display of a quality etc. **2** *Brit.* a scholarship at a college.

exhibitionism *n.* a tendency to behave in a way designed to attract attention. □ **exhibitionist** *n.*

exhilarate *v.* make joyful or lively. □ **exhilaration** *n.*

exhort *v.* urge or advise earnestly. □ **exhortation** *n.*, **exhortative** *adj.*

exhume *v.* dig up (a buried corpse). □ **exhumation** *n.*

exigency *n.* (*pl.* **-ies**) (also **exigence**) an urgent need.

exigent *adj. formal* demanding, taxing.

exiguous *adj.* very small, scanty.

exile *n.* banishment or long absence from one's country or home, esp. as a punishment; an exiled person. ● *v.* send into exile.

exist *v.* have being; occur; live, survive. □ **existence** *n.*, **existent** *adj.*

existentialism *n.* a philosophical theory emphasizing individuals' freedom to choose their actions. □ **existentialist** *n.* & *adj.*

exit *n.* a way out; a departure; an actor's going off stage. ● *v.* go away; (as a stage direction) he or she leaves the stage.

exodus *n.* a departure of many people.

ex officio (eks ŏ-**fish**-ioh) *adv.* & *adj.* because of one's official position.

exonerate *v.* show to be blameless. □ **exoneration** *n.*

exorbitant *adj.* (of a price) unreasonably high. □ **exorbitantly** *adv.*, **exorbitance** *n.*

exorcize *v.* (also **-ise**) drive out (an evil spirit) by prayer; free (a person or place) of an evil spirit. □ **exorcism** *n.*, **exorcist** *n.*

exotic *adj.* belonging to a foreign country; attractively unusual, striking. □ **exotically** *adv.*

exotica *n.* strange or rare objects.

expand *v.* **1** make or become larger; give a more detailed account. **2** become less reserved. □ **expandable** *adj.*, **expander** *n.*, **expansion** *n.*

expanse *n.* a wide area or extent.

expansive *adj.* **1** covering a wide area. **2** genial and communicative. □ **expansiveness** *n.*

expatiate (eks-**pay**-shi-ayt) *v.* speak or write at length about a subject. □ **expatiation** *n.*

expatriate *adj.* & *n.* (a person) living abroad.

expect *v.* believe that (a person or thing) will come or (a thing) will happen; require, see as due; suppose, believe.

expectant *adj.* **1** filled with anticipation. **2** pregnant. □ **expectancy** *n.*, **expectantly** *adv.*

expectation *n.* a belief that something will happen; a hope.

expectorant *n.* a medicine for causing a person to expectorate.

expectorate *v.* cough and spit phlegm; spit. □ **expectoration** *n.*

expedient *adj.* advantageous rather than right or just. ● *n.* a means of achieving something. □ **expediency** *n.*

expedite *v.* help or hurry the progress of.

expedition *n.* a journey for a purpose; people and equipment for this. □ **expeditionary** *adj.*

expeditious *adj.* speedy and efficient. □ **expeditiously** *adv.*

expel *v.* (**expelled, expelling**) **1** deprive of membership; force to leave. **2** force out (breath etc.).

expend *v.* spend; use up.

expendable *adj.* not causing serious loss if abandoned.

expenditure *n.* the expending of money etc.; an amount expended.

expense *n.* money spent on something; something on which one spends money; (**expenses**) the amount spent doing a job; reimbursement of this.

expensive *adj.* involving great expenditure; costing or charging more than average. □ **expensively** *adv.*, **expensiveness** *n.*

experience *n.* practical involvement in an activity, event, etc.; knowledge or skill gained through this; an event or action from which one learns. ● *v.* undergo, be involved in.

experienced *adj.* having had much experience.

experiment *n.* a scientific test to find out or prove something; a trial of something new. ● *v.* conduct an experiment. □ **experimentation** *n.*

experimental *adj.* of or used in experiments; still being tested. □ **experimentally** *adv.*

expert *n.* & *adj.* (a person) with great knowledge or skill in a particular area. □ **expertly** *adv.*

expertise *n.* expert knowledge or skill.

expiate *v.* make amends for. □ **expiation** *n.*, **expiatory** *adj.*

expire *v.* **1** die; cease to be valid. **2** breathe out (air). □ **expiration** *n.*

expiry *n.* termination of validity.

explain *v.* make clear, show the meaning of; account for. □ **explanation** *n.*, **explanatory** *adj.*

expletive *n.* a violent exclamation, an oath.

explicable *adj.* able to be explained. □ **explicability** *n.*

explicit *adj.* speaking or stated plainly. ◻ **explicitly** *adv.*, **explicitness** *n.*

explode *v.* **1** (cause to) expand and break with a loud noise; show sudden violent emotion; increase suddenly. **2** destroy the credibility of (a theory etc.). ◻ **explosion** *n.*

exploit *n.* (**eks**-ployt) a notable deed. ● *v.* (eks-**ployt**) make full use of; use selfishly and unfairly. ◻ **exploitable** *adj.*, **exploitation** *n.*, **exploiter** *n.*

explore *v.* travel into (a country etc.) in order to learn about it; examine. ◻ **exploration** *n.*, **exploratory** *adj.*, **explorer** *n.*

explosive *adj.* & *n.* (a substance) able or liable to explode.

exponent *n.* **1** a person who holds and argues for a theory etc. **2** a raised figure beside a number indicating how many times the number is to be multiplied by itself.

exponential *adj.* **1** of a mathematical exponent. **2** (of an increase) more and more rapid.

export *v.* (eks-**port**) send (goods etc.) to another country for sale; transfer (data) from one computer system to another. ● *n.* (**eks**-port) exporting; a thing exported. ◻ **exportation** *n.*, **exporter** *n.*

expose *v.* leave uncovered or unprotected; subject to a risk etc.; allow light to reach (film etc.); reveal. ◻ **exposure** *n.*

exposé (eks-**poh**-zay) *n.* a statement of facts; a disclosure.

exposition *n.* **1** an account and explanation. **2** a large exhibition.

expostulate *v.* protest, argue. ◻ **expostulation** *n.*, **expostulatory** *adj.*

expound *v.* explain in detail.

express *v.* **1** convey (feelings etc.) by words or gestures; represent by symbols. **2** squeeze out (liquid or air). ● *adj.* **1** definitely stated; precisely identified. **2** travelling or operating at high speed. ● *n.* a fast train or bus making few stops. ● *adv.* by express train or special delivery service. ◻ **expressible** *adj.*

expression *n.* **1** expressing. **2** a look on someone's face conveying feeling. **3** a word or phrase.

expressionism *n.* a style of art seeking to express feelings rather than represent objects realistically. ◻ **expressionist** *n.*

expressive *adj.* conveying feelings etc. clearly; expressing something. ◻ **expressively** *adv.*

expressly *adv.* precisely, definitely.

expresso var. of **espresso**.

expressway *n. Amer.* an urban motorway.

expropriate *v.* (esp. of the state) deprive (an owner) of (property). ◻ **expropriation** *n.*

expulsion *n.* expelling; being expelled. ◻ **expulsive** *adj.*

expunge *v.* wipe out.

expurgate *v.* remove (objectionable matter) from (a book etc.). ◻ **expurgation** *n.*, **expurgator** *n.*, **expurgatory** *adj.*

exquisite *adj.* **1** extremely beautiful and delicate. **2** acute; keenly felt. ◻ **exquisitely** *adv.*

extant *adj.* still existing.

extemporize *v.* (also **-ise**) speak, perform, or produce without preparation. ◻ **extemporization** *n.*

extend *v.* **1** make longer or larger; stretch and straighten (part of the body); reach over an area. **2** offer. ◻ **extendable** *adj.* (also **extendible, extensible**).

extension *n.* **1** a part added to and enlarging something. **2** extending. **3** a subsidiary telephone; its number. **4** the items to which a concept applies.

extensive *adj.* large in area or scope. ◻ **extensively** *adv.*

extensor *n.* a muscle that extends a part of the body.

extent *n.* the area covered by something; scope, scale; the degree to which something is true.

extenuate *v.* make (an offence) seem less serious or more forgivable. □ **extenuation** *n.*

exterior *adj.* on or coming from the outside. ● *n.* an outer surface or appearance.

exterminate *v.* destroy completely; kill. □ **extermination** *n.*, **exterminator** *n.*

external *adj.* of or on the outside. ● *n.* an outward or superficial feature. □ **externally** *adv.*

externalize *v.* (also **-ise**) express, see, or present as existing outside oneself.

extinct *adj.* with no living members; no longer active or alight.

extinction *n.* being, becoming, or making extinct.

extinguish *v.* put out (a light or flame); put an end to.

extinguisher *n.* a device for discharging liquid chemicals or foam to extinguish a fire.

extirpate *v.* root out, destroy. □ **extirpation** *n.*

extol *v.* (**extolled, extolling**) praise enthusiastically.

extort *v.* obtain by force or threats. □ **extortion** *n.*, **extortioner** *n.*

extortionate *adj.* excessively high in price, exorbitant. □ **extortionately** *adv.*

extra *adj.* additional, more than is usual or expected. ● *adv.* more than usually; in addition. ● *n.* an additional item; a person employed as one of a crowd in a film.

extra- *pref.* outside, beyond.

extract *v.* (eks-**trakt**) take out or obtain by force or effort; obtain by chemical treatment etc.; select (a passage from a book etc.). ● *n.* (**eks**-trakt) a passage quoted from a book, film, etc.; the concentrated essence of a substance. □ **extractor** *n.*

extraction *n.* **1** extracting. **2** ancestry, origin.

extra-curricular *adj.* not part of the normal curriculum.

extradite *v.* hand over (an accused person) for trial in the country where a crime was committed. □ **extraditable** *adj.*, **extradition** *n.*

extramarital *adj.* occurring outside marriage.

extramural *adj.* for students who are not members of a university.

extraneous *adj.* **1** irrelevant. **2** of external origin. □ **extraneously** *adv.*

extraordinary *adj.* very unusual or surprising; special, extra. □ **extraordinarily** *adv.*

extrapolate *v.* extend (a conclusion etc.) beyond what is known, on the basis of available data. □ **extrapolation** *n.*

extrasensory *adj.* achieved by some means other than the known senses.

extraterrestrial *adj.* of or from outside the earth or its atmosphere.

extravagant *adj.* spending or using excessively; very expensive; going beyond what is reasonable. □ **extravagance** *n.*, **extravagantly** *adv.*

extravaganza *n.* a lavish spectacular display.

extreme *adj.* **1** very great or intense; reaching a very high degree; very severe; drastic or immoderate; (of a sport) involving great physical danger. **2** furthest, outermost. ● *n.* an extreme point; one end of a scale; a very high degree. □ **extremely** *adv.*

extremist *n.* a person holding extreme views. □ **extremism** *n.*

extremity *n.* (*pl.* **-ies**) **1** an extreme degree; extreme hardship or danger. **2** an outermost point; (**the extremities**) the hands and feet.

extricate *v.* free from an entanglement or difficulty. □ **extricable** *adj.*, **extrication** *n.*

extrinsic *adj.* not intrinsic; extraneous. □ **extrinsically** *adv.*

extrovert *n.* a lively sociable person. □ **extroversion** *n.*

extrude *v.* thrust or squeeze out. □ **extrusion** *n.*, **extrusive** *adj.*

exuberant *adj.* **1** full of high spirits. **2** growing profusely. □ **exuberance** *n.*, **exuberantly** *adv.*

exude *v.* ooze; give off like sweat or a smell. □ **exudation** *n.*

exult *v.* feel or show delight. □ **exultant** *adj.*, **exultation** *n.*

▪ **Usage** Do not confuse *exult* and *exalt.*

eye *n.* **1** the organ of sight; the iris of this; the region round it; the power of seeing. **2** something compared to an eye in shape, centrality, etc. ● *v.* (**eyed, eyeing**) look at, watch.

eyeball *n.* the whole of the eye within the eyelids.

eyebrow *n.* the fringe of hair on the ridge above the eye socket.

eyelash *n.* one of the hairs fringing the eyelids.

eyelet *n.* a small hole through which a lace can be threaded.

eyelid *n.* either of the two folds of skin that can be moved together to cover the eye.

eyeliner *n.* a cosmetic applied in a line around the eye.

eye-opener *n. informal* something that brings enlightenment or great surprise.

eyepiece *n.* the lens to which the eye is applied in a telescope or microscope etc.

eyeshadow *n.* a cosmetic applied to the skin round the eyes.

eyesight *n.* the ability to see; the range of vision.

eyesore *n.* an ugly thing.

eye-tooth *n.* a canine tooth in the upper jaw, below the eye.

eyewash *n. informal* insincere talk; nonsense.

eyewitness *n.* a person who saw something happen.

eyrie (eer-i) *n.* an eagle's nest; a high and inaccessible place.

Ff

F *abbr.* Fahrenheit. ● *symb.* fluorine.

f *abbr.* **1** female; feminine. **2** *Music* forte.

FA *abbr.* Football Association.

fable *n.* a story not based on fact, often with a moral.

fabled *adj.* famous; legendary.

fabric *n.* **1** woven or knitted cloth. **2** the essential structure of a building etc.

fabricate *v.* **1** invent (a story etc.). **2** construct. □ **fabrication** *n.*, **fabricator** *n.*

fabulous *adj.* **1** extraordinarily great. **2** mythical. **3** *informal* very good. □ **fabulously** *adv.*

façade (fŭ-sahd) *n.* the front of a building; an outward appearance, esp. a misleading one.

face *n.* **1** the front of the head; an expression on its features; a grimace: *make a face.* **2** an aspect. **3** a surface; a side of a mountain; the surface of a coal-seam. **4** the dial of a clock. ● *v.* **1** have one's face or front towards; confront boldly. **2** put a facing on. □ **lose face** become less respected.

facecloth *n.* a small towelling cloth for washing the face and body.

faceless *adj.* **1** impersonal, not identifiable. **2** without character.

facelift *n.* an operation tightening the skin of the face to remove wrinkles; an alteration that improves the appearance.

facet *n.* one of many sides of a cut stone or jewel; one aspect.

facetious *adj.* inappropriately humorous about serious subjects. □ **facetiously** *adv.*, **facetiousness** *n.*

facia (fay-shŭ) *n.* (also **fascia**) **1** the instrument panel of a vehicle. **2** a nameplate over a shop front.

facial *adj.* of the face. ● *n.* a beauty treatment for the face.

facile (fa-syl) *adj.* misleadingly simple; superficial, glib.

facilitate *v.* make easy or easier. ▫ **facilitation** *n.*

facility *n.* (*pl.* **-ies**) **1** space etc. for doing something; an amenity or resource. **2** absence of difficulty.

facing *n.* an outer covering; a layer of material at the edge of a garment for strengthening, contrast, neatening, etc.

facsimile (fak-**sim**-ili) *n.* an exact copy of a document etc.

fact *n.* something known to be true. ▫ **facts of life** information about sex and reproduction. **in fact** actually.

faction *n.* **1** an organized group within a larger one; dissension between such groups. **2** a blend of fact and fiction in a book etc. ▫ **factious** *adj.*

factitious *adj.* (of a quality, emotion, etc.) artificial.

factor *n.* **1** a circumstance that contributes towards a result. **2** a number by which a given number can be divided exactly.

factory *n.* (*pl.* **-ies**) a building in which goods are manufactured.

factotum *n.* a general servant or assistant.

factual *adj.* based on or containing facts. ▫ **factually** *adv.*

faculty *n.* (*pl.* **-ies**) **1** a mental or physical power. **2** a department teaching a specified subject in a university or college.

fad *n.* a craze, a whim.

faddy *adj.* (**faddier, faddiest**) *Brit.* having petty likes and dislikes, esp. about food.

fade *v.* (cause to) lose colour, freshness, or vigour; disappear gradually.

faeces (fee-seez) *n.pl.* (*Amer.* **feces**) waste matter discharged from the bowels. ▫ **faecal** *adj.*

faff *n. informal* fuss; pointless activity. ▫ **faff about** fuss; dither.

fag *informal v.* (**fagged, fagging**) toil; make tired. ● *n.* **1** a tiring or tedious task. **2** a cigarette.

faggot *n.* (*Amer.* **fagot**) **1** a tied bundle of sticks or twigs. **2** a ball of chopped seasoned liver etc., baked or fried.

fah *n. Music* the fourth note of a major scale, or the note F.

Fahrenheit *adj.* of a temperature scale with the freezing point of water at 32° and boiling point at 212°.

faience (fy-ahns) *n.* painted glazed earthenware.

fail *v.* **1** be unsuccessful; declare to be unsuccessful. **2** neglect one's duty; disappoint (someone relying on one). **3** become weak; cease functioning; become bankrupt. ● *n.* a mark too low to pass an examination.

failing *n.* a weakness or fault. ● *prep.* if (a thing) does not happen.

failure *n.* failing, lack of success; a deficiency; a person or thing that fails.

fain *adv. archaic* willingly.

faint *adj.* **1** indistinct, not clear or intense. **2** weak; about to faint. ● *v.* collapse unconscious. ● *n.* the act or state of fainting. ▫ **faintly** *adv.*, **faintness** *n.*

faint-hearted *adj.* timid.

fair *n.* **1** a funfair. **2** a gathering for a sale of goods, often with entertainments; an exhibition of commercial goods. ● *adj.* **1** light in colour, having light-coloured hair. **2** (of weather) fine; (of wind) favourable. **3** just, unbiased. **4** of moderate quality or amount. ● *adv.* without cheating.

fairground *n.* an open space where a fair is held.

fairing *n.* a streamlining structure added to a ship, vehicle, etc.

fairly *adv.* **1** justly. **2** to some extent; quite.

fairway *n.* **1** a navigable channel. **2** part of a golf course between tee and green.

fairy *n.* (*pl.* **-ies**) an imaginary small being with magical powers.

fairy godmother *n.* a benefactress providing help in times of difficulty.

fairyland *n.* an ideally beautiful place.

fairy lights *n.pl.* strings of small coloured lights used as decorations.

fait accompli (fayt ŭ-kom-**plee**) *n.* something already done and not reversible.

faith *n.* reliance, trust; belief in religious doctrine. □ **break (or keep) faith** be disloyal (or loyal).

faithful *adj.* **1** loyal. **2** true, accurate. □ **faithfully** *adv.*, **faithfulness** *n.*

faith healing *n.* healing achieved through religious belief rather than medicine. □ **faith healer** *n.*

faithless *adj.* disloyal.

fake *n.* a person or thing that is not genuine. ● *adj.* counterfeit. ● *v.* make an imitation of; pretend. □ **faker** *n.*

fakir (fay-keer) *n.* a Muslim or Hindu religious ascetic living on alms.

falcon *n.* a small long-winged hawk.

falconry *n.* the breeding and training of hawks. □ **falconer** *n.*

fall *v.* (**fell, fallen, falling**) **1** move downwards without control; lose one's balance; (of land) slope downwards. **2** decrease. **3** pass into a specified state. **4** lose power; be captured or conquered; die in battle. **5** (of the face) show distress. **6** occur. ● *n.* **1** falling; the distance or amount of this; something fallen; (**falls**) a waterfall **2** *Amer.* autumn. □ **fall back on** have recourse to. **fall for** *informal* **1** fall in love with. **2** be deceived by. **fall out 1** quarrel. **2** happen. **fall short** be inadequate. **fall through** (of a plan) fail.

fallacy *n.* (*pl.* **-ies**) unsound reasoning; a false belief. □ **fallacious** *adj.*

fallible *adj.* liable to make mistakes. □ **fallibility** *n.*

Fallopian tube *n.* either of the two tubes from the ovary to the womb.

fallout *n.* airborne radioactive debris.

fallow *adj.* & *n.* (land) left unplanted to restore its fertility.

false *adj.* **1** not true; incorrect; not genuine, sham. **2** unfaithful. □ **play false** cheat, deceive. □ **falsely** *adv.*, **falseness** *n.*

falsehood *n.* a lie; being untrue.

falsetto *n.* (*pl.* **falsettos**) a voice above one's natural range.

falsify *v.* (**falsified, falsifying**) **1** alter fraudulently. **2** prove to be false. □ **falsification** *n.*

falsity *n.* falseness; falsehood.

falter *v.* become weaker; move or function unsteadily; speak hesitantly.

fame *n.* being widely known about; good reputation. □ **famed** *adj.*

familial *adj.* of a family.

familiar *adj.* **1** well known. **2** having knowledge or experience. **3** friendly, intimate; too informal. □ **familiarity** *n.*, **familiarly** *adv.*

familiarize *v.* (also **-ise**) make familiar. □ **familiarization** *n.*

family *n.* (*pl.* **-ies**) parents and their children; a person's children; a set of relatives; a group of related plants, animals, or things.

famine *n.* extreme scarcity of food.

famished *adj.* extremely hungry.

famous *adj.* **1** known to very many people. **2** *informal* excellent. □ **famously** *adv.*

fan *n.* **1** a hand-held or mechanical device to create a current of air. **2** an enthusiastic admirer or supporter. ● *v.* (**fanned, fanning**) **1** cool with a fan; make (a fire etc.) stronger by fanning. **2** spread from a central point.

fanatic *n.* a person with excessive enthusiasm for something. □ **fan-**

atical *adj.*, **fanatically** *adv.*, **fanaticism** *n.*

fan belt *n.* a belt driving a fan that cools a car engine.

fancier *n.* a person with special knowledge and love of something specified.

fanciful *adj.* imaginative; imaginary. ◻ **fancifully** *adv.*

fancy *n.* (*pl.* **-ies**) **1** imagination; something imagined, an unfounded idea. **2** a desire, a whim. ● *adj.* (**fancier, fanciest**) ornamental, elaborate. ● *v.* (**fancied, fancying**) **1** imagine; suppose. **2** *informal* feel a desire for (something); be attracted to (someone).

fancy dress *n.* a costume representing an animal, historical character, etc., worn for a party.

fanfare *n.* a short ceremonious sounding of trumpets.

fang *n.* a long sharp tooth; a snake's tooth that injects venom.

fanlight *n.* a small window above a door or larger window.

fantasia *n.* an improvisatory musical composition.

fantasize *v.* (also **-ise**) day-dream.

fantastic *adj.* **1** imaginative; bizarre, exotic. **2** *informal* excellent. ◻ **fantastically** *adv.*

fantasy *n.* (*pl.* **-ies**) **1** imagination; a day-dream; fiction involving magic and adventure. **2** a fantasia.

far *adv.* at, to, or by a great distance; for a long way; by a great deal. ● *adj.* distant, remote.

farad *n.* a unit of electrical capacitance.

farce *n.* a light comedy; an absurd situation. ◻ **farcical** *adj.*, **farcically** *adv.*

fare *n.* **1** the price charged for a passenger to travel; a passenger paying this. **2** food provided. ● *v.* get on or be treated in a specified way.

Far East *n.* China, Japan, and other countries of east Asia.

farewell *int.* goodbye. ● *n.* a parting; parting good wishes.

far-fetched *adj.* unconvincing, very unlikely.

farinaceous (fa-ri-nay-shŭs) *adj.* starchy.

farm *n.* a unit of land used for raising crops or livestock. ● *v.* grow crops, raise livestock; use (land) for this. ◻ **farm out** subcontract (work) to others. ◻ **farmer** *n.*

farmhouse *n.* a farmer's house.

farmstead *n.* a farm and its buildings.

farmyard *n.* an enclosed area round farm buildings.

farrago (fŭ-rah-goh) *n.* (*pl.* **farragos** or **farragoes**) a confused mixture.

farrier *n.* a smith who shoes horses.

farrow *v.* give birth to (piglets). ● *n.* a litter of pigs; farrowing.

fart *v.* *informal* send out wind from the anus.

farther, farthest vars. of **further, furthest**.

farthingale *n.* *hist.* a hooped petticoat.

fascia var. of **facia**.

fascinate *v.* **1** irresistibly interest and attract. **2** make motionless with fear. ◻ **fascination** *n.*

Fascism (fash-izm) *n.* (also **fascism**) a system of extreme right-wing dictatorship. ◻ **Fascist** *n.* & *adj.*, **Fascistic** *adj.*

fashion *n.* **1** a manner of doing something. **2** a popular trend; producing and marketing styles of clothing etc. ● *v.* make into a particular shape.

fashionable *adj.* currently popular; following popular trends. ◻ **fashionably** *adv.*

fast[1] *adj.* **1** moving or able to move quickly; working or done quickly; allowing quick movement. **2** (of a clock etc.) showing a time ahead of the correct one. **3** firmly fixed. ● *adv.* **1** quickly. **2** securely, tightly; soundly.

fast[2] *v.* go without food. ● *n.* a period without eating.

fastback *n.* a car with a long sloping back.

fasten *v.* fix firmly, tie or join together; be closed or done up.

fastener *n.* (also **fastening**) a device to close or secure something.

fast food *n.* food that is sold pre-prepared for a quick meal.

fastidious *adj.* attentive to details; hard to please; easily disgusted. □ **fastidiously** *adv.*, **fastidiousness** *n.*

fastness *n.* a stronghold, a secure refuge.

fat *n.* a greasy substance occurring in animal bodies and certain seeds; this as used in cooking or an element in diet; excess of this in the body, corpolence. ● *adj.* (**fatter, fattest**) excessively plump; containing much fat; thick; substantial. □ **fat chance** *informal* no chance. □ **fatness** *n.*, **fatty** *adj.*

fatal *adj.* causing death or disaster □ **fatally** *adv.*

fatalist *n.* a person believing that whatever happens is predestined and inescapable. □ **fatalism** *n.*, **fatalistic** *adj.*

fatality *n.* (*pl.* **-ies**) a death caused by accident or in war etc.

fate *n.* a power thought to control all events; a person's destiny.

fated *adj.* destined by fate.

fateful *adj.* leading to great usu. unpleasant events. □ **fatefully** *adv.*

father *n.* a male parent or ancestor; a founder, an originator; a title of certain priests. ● *v.* beget; originate. □ **fatherhood** *n.*, **fatherless** *adj.*, **fatherly** *adj.*

father-in-law *n.* (*pl.* **fathers-in-law**) the father of one's wife or husband.

fatherland *n.* one's native country.

fathom *n.* a measure (1.82 m) of the depth of water. ● *v.* understand. □ **fathomable** *adj.*

fathomless *adj.* **1** too deep to measure. **2** incomprehensible.

fatigue *n.* **1** tiredness. **2** weakness in metal etc., caused by stress. **3** a soldier's non-military task; (**fatigues**) soldiers' clothes for specific tasks. ● *v.* tire or weaken.

fatstock *n.* livestock fattened for slaughter as food.

fatten *v.* make or become fat.

fatuous *adj.* foolish, silly. □ **fatuously** *adv.*, **fatuousness** *n.*

fatwa *n.* a ruling made by an Islamic leader.

faucet (for-sit) *n.* esp. *Amer.* a tap.

fault *n.* **1** a defect, an imperfection. **2** responsibility for something wrong; a weakness or offence. **3** a break in layers of rock. ● *v.* criticize, find defects in. □ **at fault** responsible for a mistake etc. □ **faultless** *adj.*, **faulty** *adj.*

faun *n.* a Roman god of the countryside with a goat's legs and horns.

fauna *n.* (*pl.* **faunas** or **faunae**) the animals of an area or period.

faux pas (foh **pah**) *n.* (*pl.* **faux pas**) an embarrassing social blunder or breach of etiquette.

favour (*Amer.* **favor**) *n.* **1** liking, approval. **2** a kindly or helpful act beyond what is due. **3** favouritism. ● *v.* **1** like, approve of, support. **2** gratify. **3** *informal* resemble (a parent etc.).

favourable *adj.* (*Amer.* **favorable**) **1** showing approval; giving consent. **2** advantageous. **3** (of weather) fine; (of a wind) in the right direction. □ **favourably** *adv.*

favourite *adj.* (*Amer.* **favorite**) liked above others. ● *n.* a favoured person or thing; a competitor expected to win.

favouritism *n.* (*Amer.* **favoritism**) unfairly generous treatment of one at the expense of others.

fawn *n.* **1** a deer in its first year. **2** light yellowish brown. ● *adj.* fawn-coloured. ● *v.* try to win favour by obsequiousness; (of a dog) show extreme affection.

fax *n.* transmission of exact copies of documents by electronic scanning; a copy produced in this way; a machine for sending and receiving faxes. ● *v.* transmit (a document) by this process.

fay *n.* *literary* a fairy.

faze *v.* *informal* disconcert; daunt.

FBI *abbr.* (in the USA) Federal Bureau of Investigation.

FC *abbr.* Football Club.

Fe *symb.* iron.

fealty *n.* loyalty, allegiance.

fear *n.* an unpleasant sensation caused by nearness of danger or pain. ● *v.* be afraid (of); be deterred.

fearful *adj.* **1** terrible. **2** feeling fear. **3** *informal* very great or bad. □ **fearfully** *adv.*

fearless *adj.* feeling no fear. □ **fearlessly** *adv.*, **fearlessness** *n.*

fearsome *adj.* frightening.

feasible *adj.* able to be done, possible. □ **feasibility** *n.*, **feasibly** *adv.*

■ **Usage** *Feasible* should not be used to mean 'likely'. *Possible* or *probable* should be used instead.

---

feast *n.* a large elaborate meal; an annual religious celebration. ● *v.* eat heartily; give a feast to.

feat *n.* a remarkable achievement.

feather *n.* each of the structures with a central shaft and fringe of fine strands, growing from a bird's skin. ● *v.* turn (an oar) to pass through the air edgeways. □ **a feather in one's cap** an achievement to be proud of. **feather one's nest** enrich oneself illicitly. □ **feathery** *adj.*

feather-bed *v.* (**-bedded, -bedding**) make things financially easy for.

feathered *adj.* covered or decorated with feathers.

featherweight *n.* a very lightweight thing or person; a boxing weight between bantamweight and lightweight.

feature *n.* **1** a distinctive part of the face. **2** a noticeable attribute or aspect. **3** a newspaper article on a particular topic. **4** a full-length cinema film. ● *v.* have as a feature; be a feature of or in.

Feb. *abbr.* February.

febrile (fee-bryl) *adj.* feverish; tense and excited.

February *n.* the second month.

feces Amer. sp. of **faeces**.

feckless *adj.* incompetent and irresponsible. □ **fecklessness** *n.*

fecund *adj.* fertile. □ **fecundity** *n.*

fed past & p.p. of **feed**.

federal *adj.* of a system in which states unite under a central authority but are independent in internal affairs. □ **federalism** *n.*, **federalist** *n.*, **federally** *adv.*

federate *v.* (fed-er-ayt) unite on a federal basis or for a common purpose. ● *adj.* (fed-er-ŭt) united in this way. □ **federative** *adj.*

federation *n.* federating; a federated society or group of states.

fed up *adj. informal* annoyed and resentful.

fee *n.* a sum payable for professional services, or for a privilege.

feeble *adj.* weak; ineffective. □ **feebly** *adv.*, **feebleness** *n.*

feed *v.* (**fed, feeding**) give (food) to (a person or animal); eat; supply (a necessary resource) to (someone or something). ● *n.* food for animals; an act of feeding.

feedback *n.* return of part of a system's output to its source; return of information about a product, a piece of work, etc. to the producer.

feeder *n.* **1** a person or thing that feeds; a baby's feeding bottle; a feeding apparatus in a machine. **2** a road, railway line, etc. linking outlying areas to a central system.

feel *v.* (**felt, feeling**) **1** perceive or examine by touch; give a specified sensation when touched. **2** experience an emotion or sensation. **3** have an opinion or belief. ● *n.* the sense of touch; an act of touching; a sensation given by something touched. □ **feel like** be inclined to have or do.

feeler *n.* **1** a long slender organ of touch in certain animals. **2** a tentative suggestion.

feeling *n.* **1** an emotion; (**feelings**) emotional susceptibilities; sympathy, sensitivity. **2** a belief not based on reason. **3** the power of sensation.

feet pl. of **foot**.

feign (fayn) *v.* pretend.

feint (faynt) *n.* a sham attack made to divert attention. ● *v.* make a feint. ● *adj.* (of paper) printed with faint ruled lines.

feisty (fī-sti) *adj.* (**feistier, feistiest**) *informal* boldly determined and energetic.

feldspar *n.* (also **felspar**) a white or red mineral.

felicitate *v.* congratulate. □ **felicitation** *n.*

felicitous *adj.* well-chosen, apt. □ **felicitously** *adv.*, **felicitousness** *n.*

felicity *n.* (*pl.* **-ies**) happiness; an apt or pleasing feature.

feline *adj.* of cats; catlike. ● *n.* an animal of the cat family.

fell[1] past of **fall**.

fell[2] *n.* a stretch of moor or hilly land, esp. in northern England. ● *v.* cut or knock down.

fellow *n.* **1** *informal* a man or boy. **2** an associate or equal; a thing like another. **3** a member of a learned society or governing body of a college.

fellowship *n.* **1** friendly association with others. **2** a society. **3** the position of a college fellow.

felon *n.* a person who has committed a serious violent crime. □ **felony** *n.*

felspar var. of **feldspar**.

felt[1] past & p.p. of **feel**.

felt[2] *n.* cloth made by matting and pressing fibres. ● *v.* make into felt; cover with felt.

felt-tip pen *n.* (also **felt-tipped pen**) a pen with a writing point made of fibre.

female *adj.* **1** of the sex that can bear offspring or produce eggs; (of plants) fruit-bearing. **2** (of a machine part etc.) hollow. ● *n.* a female animal or plant.

feminine *adj.* **1** of, like, or traditionally considered suitable for women. **2** having the grammatical form of the female gender. □ **femininity** *n.*

feminist *n.* a supporter of women's claims to be given rights equal to those of men. □ **feminism** *n.*

femme fatale (fam fŭ-tahl) *n.* (*pl.* **femmes fatales**) a dangerously seductive woman.

femur *n.* (*pl.* **femurs** or **femora**) the thigh bone. □ **femoral** *adj.*

fen *n.* a low-lying marshy or flooded tract of land.

fence *n.* **1** a barrier round the boundary of a field or garden etc. **2** *informal* a person who deals in stolen goods. ● *v.* **1** surround with a fence. **2** engage in the sport of fencing. □ **fencer** *n.*

fencing *n.* **1** the sport of fighting with swords, esp. foils. **2** fences; their material.

fend *v.* □ **fend for oneself** support oneself. **fend off** ward off.

fender *n.* **1** a low frame bordering a fireplace. **2** a pad hung over a moored vessel's side to protect against bumping. **3** *Amer.* the mudguard or bumper of a motor vehicle.

fennel *n.* an aniseed-flavoured plant.

fenugreek *n.* a plant with fragrant seeds used for flavouring.

feral *adj.* wild.

ferment *v.* (fer-**ment**) undergo fermentation; cause fermentation in; stir up (unrest or excitement). ● *n.* (fer-mĕnt) excitement, agitation.

fermentation *n.* a chemical change caused by an organic substance, producing effervescence and heat.

fermium *n.* a radioactive metallic element (symbol Fm).

fern *n.* a flowerless plant with feathery green leaves. □ **ferny** *adj.*

ferocious *adj.* fierce, savage. □ **ferociously** *adv.*, **ferocity** *n.*

ferrel var. of **ferrule**.

ferret *n.* a small animal of the weasel family. ● *v.* (**ferreted, fer-**

reting) search tenaciously, rummage. □ **ferrety** *adj.*

ferric *adj.* (also **ferrous**) of or containing iron.

Ferris wheel *n.* a giant revolving vertical wheel with passenger cars for funfair rides.

ferroconcrete *n.* concrete reinforced with steel.

ferrule *n.* (also **ferrel**) a metal cap strengthening the end of a stick or tube.

ferry *n.* (*pl.* **-ies**) a boat for transporting passengers and goods; the service it provides; the place where it operates. ● *v.* (**ferried, ferrying**) convey in a ferry; transport.

fertile *adj.* able to produce vegetation, fruit, or young; capable of developing into a new plant or animal; productive, inventive. □ **fertility** *n.*

fertilize *v.* (also **-ise**) **1** introduce pollen or sperm into. **2** add fertilizer to. □ **fertilization** *n.*

fertilizer *n.* (also **fertiliser**) material added to soil to make it more fertile.

fervent *adj.* showing intense feeling. □ **fervency** *n.*, **fervently** *adv.*

fervid *adj.* fervent. □ **fervidly** *adv.*

fervour *n.* (*Amer.* **fervor**) intensity of feeling.

fester *v.* **1** make or become septic. **2** (of ill-feeling) continue and grow worse.

festival *n.* **1** a day or period of celebration. **2** a series of concerts, plays, etc.

festive *adj.* of or suitable for a festival; cheerful. □ **festively** *adv.*, **festiveness** *n.*

festivity *n.* (*pl.* **-ies**) a festive occasion; celebration.

festoon *n.* a hanging chain of flowers or ribbons etc. ● *v.* decorate with hanging ornaments.

feta *n.* a white salty Greek cheese.

fetch *v.* **1** go for and bring back; cause to come. **2** be sold for (a specified price).

fetching *adj.* attractive.

fête (fayt) *n. Brit.* an outdoor entertainment or sale, esp. in aid of charity; *Amer.* a festival. ● *v.* honour and entertain lavishly.

fetid *adj.* (also **foetid**) stinking.

fetish *n.* an object worshipped as having magical powers; something given excessive respect.

fetlock *n.* a horse's leg above and behind the hoof.

fetter *n.* a shackle for the ankles; a restraint. ● *v.* put into fetters; restrict, hinder.

fettle *n.* condition: *in fine fettle.*

fetus Amer. sp. of **foetus**.

feud *n.* a state of lasting hostility. ● *v.* be involved in a feud.

feudalism *n.* a medieval social system involving a strict hierarchy in which lower orders gave services to higher in return for land or protection. □ **feudal** *adj.*, **feudalistic** *adj.*

fever *n.* an abnormally high body temperature; a disease causing it; nervous excitement. □ **fevered** *adj.*, **feverish** *adj.*, **feverishly** *adv.*

few *adj.* & *n.* not many. □ **a few** some. **a good few** a fairly large number.

fey *adj.* uncanny; clairvoyant. □ **feyness** *n.*

fez *n.* (*pl.* **fezzes**) a high flattopped red cap worn by some Muslim men.

ff *abbr. Music* fortissimo.

ff. *abbr.* the following pages.

fiancé, fiancée *n.* a man (*fiancé*) or woman (*fiancée*) one is engaged to marry.

fiasco *n.* (*pl.* **fiascos**) a total and ludicrous failure.

fiat (fy-at) *n.* an order; an authorization.

fib *n.* a trivial lie. ● *v.* (**fibbed, fibbing**) tell a fib. □ **fibber** *n.*

fibre *n.* (*Amer.* **fiber**) **1** a threadlike strand; a substance formed of fibres; fibrous material in food, roughage. **2** strength of character. □ **fibrous** *adj.*

fibreglass *n.* (*Amer.* **fiberglass**) material made of or containing glass fibres.

fibre optics *n.* transmission of information by light along thin flexible glass fibres.

fibril *n.* a small fibre.

fibroid *adj.* consisting of fibrous tissue. ● *n.* a benign fibroid tumour.

fibrositis *n.* rheumatic pain in tissue other than bones and joints.

fibula *n.* (*pl.* **fibulae** or **fibulas**) the bone on the outer side of the shin.

fiche (feesh) *n.* (*pl.* **fiche** or **fiches**) a microfiche.

fickle *adj.* inconstant, not loyal. □ **fickleness** *n.*

fiction *n.* literature describing imaginary events and people; an invented story. □ **fictional** *adj.*

fictitious *adj.* imaginary, not true or real.

fiddle *informal n.* **1** a violin. **2** a swindle. ● *v.* **1** fidget with something. **2** falsify (figures etc.). □ **fiddler** *n.*

fiddlesticks *int.* nonsense.

fiddly *adj.* (**fiddlier**, **fiddliest**) *informal* awkward or complicated.

fidelity *n.* **1** faithfulness, loyalty. **2** accuracy in a copy etc.

fidget *v.* (**fidgeted**, **fidgeting**) make small restless movements; be or make uneasy. ● *n.* a person who fidgets. □ **fidgety** *adj.*

fiduciary *adj.* held or given in trust. ● *n.* (*pl.* **-ies**) a trustee.

fief (feef) *n. hist.* an estate held by a noble under feudalism.

field *n.* **1** an enclosed area of open ground, esp. for pasture or cultivation; a sports ground. **2** an area rich in a natural product. **3** a sphere of action or interest. **4** all the competitors in a race or contest. ● *v.* **1** (in cricket etc.) stop and return the ball to prevent scoring. **2** put (a team) into a contest.

field day *n.* an opportunity for successful unrestrained action.

fielder *n.* (in cricket etc.) a member of the side not batting.

field events *n.* athletic contests other than races.

field glasses *n.pl.* binoculars.

field marshal *n.* an army officer of the highest rank.

fieldwork *n.* practical research done outside libraries and laboratories. □ **fieldworker** *n.*

fiend (feend) *n.* **1** an evil spirit; a cruel or mischievous person. **2** *informal* a devotee or addict: *a fitness fiend.*

fiendish *adj.* cruel; extremely difficult. □ **fiendishly** *adv.*

fierce *adj.* violent, aggressive; intense; powerful and destructive. □ **fiercely** *adv.*, **fierceness** *n.*

fiery *adj.* (**fierier**, **fieriest**) **1** consisting of or like fire. **2** passionate, intense. □ **fierily** *adv.*, **fieriness** *n.*

fiesta *n.* a festival in Spanish-speaking countries.

fife *n.* a small shrill flute.

fifteen *adj.* & *n.* one more than fourteen (15, XV). □ **fifteenth** *adj.* & *n.*

fifth *adj.* & *n.* the next after fourth. □ **fifthly** *adv.*

fifty *adj.* & *n.* five times ten (50, L). □ **fiftieth** *adj.* & *n.*

fifty-fifty *adj.* & *adv.* half-and-half, equally.

fig *n.* a soft, sweet pear-shaped fruit.

fig. *abbr.* figure.

fight *v.* (**fought**, **fighting**) struggle (against), esp. in physical combat or war; strive to obtain or accomplish something; argue. ● *n.* fighting; a battle, a contest, a struggle; a boxing match.

fighter *n.* one who fights; an aircraft designed for attacking others.

figment *n.* something that exists only in the imagination.

figurative *adj.* metaphorical. □ **figuratively** *adv.*

figure *n.* **1** a number; an amount of money; a numerical symbol; (**figures**) arithmetic. **2** bodily shape; a representation of a person or animal. **3** a well-known person. **4** a geometric shape; a diagram or illustration; a pattern. ● *v.* **1** appear; play a part. **2** calculate; *Amer. informal* suppose, think.

figured *adj.* with a woven pattern.

figurehead *n.* a carved image at the prow of a ship; a leader with only nominal power.

figure of speech *n.* an expression used for effect rather than literally.

figurine *n.* a statuette.

filament *n.* a slender thread; a fine wire giving off light in an electric lamp.

filbert *n.* a hazelnut.

filch *v. informal* steal (something small).

file *n.* **1** a folder or box for keeping documents; its contents. **2** a set of data in a computer. **3** a line of people or things one behind another. **4** a tool with a rough surface for smoothing things. ● *v.* **1** place (a document) in a file; place on record. **2** march in a long line. **3** shape or smooth (a surface) with a file.

filial *adj.* of or due from a son or daughter. □ **filially** *adv.*

filibuster *v.* delay the passage of a bill by making long speeches. ● *n.* delaying progress in this way.

filigree *n.* ornamental work of fine gold or silver wire.

filings *n.pl.* thin chips removed with a file.

Filipino *n.* & *adj.* (*pl.* **Filipinos**) (a native) of the Philippine Islands.

fill *v.* **1** make or become full; stop up (a cavity). **2** occupy; appoint someone to (a vacant post). ● *n.* enough of a substance to fill a container. □ **fill in 1** complete (a form etc.). **2** act as someone's substitute. **3** tell (someone) more details. **fill out 1** put on weight. **2** *Amer.* complete (a form etc.). **fill up** fill completely. **one's fill** as much as one wants or can bear.

filler *n.* a thing or material used to fill a gap or increase bulk.

fillet *n.* a piece of boneless meat or fish. ● *v.* (**filleted, filleting**) remove bones from.

filling *n.* a substance used to fill a cavity etc. ● *adj.* (of food) satisfying hunger.

filling station *n.* a place selling petrol to motorists.

fillip *n.* a stimulus or incentive.

filly *n.* (*pl.* **-ies**) a young female horse.

film *n.* **1** a thin flexible strip of light-sensitive material for taking photographs. **2** a story told through a sequence of images projected on a screen. **3** a thin layer. ● *v.* photograph with a cine-camera or video camera; make a film of. □ **film over** become covered with a thin layer of something.

filmstrip *n.* a series of transparencies in a strip for projection.

filmy *adj.* (**filmier, filmiest**) thin and almost transparent.

filo (fee-loh) *n.* pastry in very thin sheets.

Filofax *n. trademark* a loose-leaf note book for recording appointments, addresses, etc.

filter *n.* a device or substance for holding back impurities in liquid or gas passing through it; a screen for absorbing or modifying light or electrical or sound waves; an arrangement allowing traffic to filter. ● *v.* pass through a filter; remove (impurities) in this way; pass gradually in or out; (of traffic) be allowed to turn left while traffic going straight on is held up.

filth *n.* disgusting dirt; obscenity. □ **filthily** *adv.*, **filthiness** *n.*, **filthy** *adj.*

filtrate *n.* a filtered liquid. □ **filtration** *n.*

fin *n.* a thin projection from a fish's body, used for propelling and steering itself; a similar projection to improve the stability of aircraft etc.

final *adj.* coming at the end of a series or process; allowing no dispute. ● *n.* the last contest in a series; the last edition of a day's newspaper; (**finals**) examinations at the end of a degree course. □ **finally** *adv.*

finale (fi-nah-li) *n.* the closing section of a performance or musical composition.

finalist *n.* a competitor in a final.

finality *n.* the quality or fact of being final.

finalize *v.* (also **-ise**) complete, put in definitive form. □ **finalization** *n.*

finance *n.* management of money; (**finances**) money resources. ● *v.* fund. □ **financial** *adj.*, **financially** *adv.*

financier *n.* a person engaged in financing businesses.

finch *n.* a small bird.

find *v.* (**found, finding**) **1** discover; learn. **2** reach; obtain: *find time to write.* **3** judge (something) to have a particular quality; declare a verdict. ● *n.* something found, esp. something valuable. □ **find out** detect; learn, discover. □ **finder** *n.*

fine[1] *adj.* **1** of very high quality; satisfactory; acceptable; in good health. **2** bright, free from rain etc. **3** thin; in small particles; subtle. **4** (of feelings) noble, refined. ● *adv.* very well. □ **finely** *adv.*, **fineness** *n.*

fine[2] *n.* a sum of money to be paid as a penalty. ● *v.* punish with a fine.

finery *n.* showy clothes etc.

finesse *n.* delicate manipulation; tact.

finger *n.* each of the five parts extending from each hand; any of these other than the thumb; an object compared to a finger; a measure (about 20 mm) of alcohol in a glass. ● *v.* touch or feel with the fingers.

fingerboard *n.* a flat strip on a stringed instrument against which the strings are pressed with the fingers to produce different notes.

fingerprint *n.* an impression of the ridges on the pad of a finger, used for identification.

finger-stall *n.* a sheath to cover an injured finger.

finial *n.* an ornament at the apex of a gable, pinnacle, etc.

finicky *adj.* (also **finicking**) fussy; detailed and fiddly.

finish *v.* **1** bring or come to an end; consume the whole or the remains of; reach the end of a race etc. **2** complete; put final touches to. ● *n.* **1** the final part or stage; the end of a race. **2** the way in which something is made; a surface appearance. □ **finish off 1** complete. **2** consume; kill. □ **finisher** *n.*

finite (fI-nIt) *adj.* limited.

Finn *n.* a native of Finland.

Finnish *n.* & *adj.* (the language) of Finland.

fiord var. of **fjord**.

fir *n.* an evergreen cone-bearing tree.

fire *n.* **1** combustion; destructive burning; fuel burned to provide heat; a gas or electrical heater. **2** the firing of guns. **3** passionate feeling. ● *v.* **1** send a bullet or shell from (a gun); launch (a missile). **2** *informal* dismiss from a job. **3** excite. **4** supply fuel to. **5** bake (pottery) in a kiln.

firearm *n.* a gun, pistol, etc.

firebrand *n.* a person who causes trouble and unrest.

firebreak *n.* an obstacle to the spread of fire.

fire brigade *n.* an organized body of people employed to extinguish fires.

firecracker *n. Amer.* an explosive firework.

firedamp *n.* an explosive mixture of methane and air in mines.

firedog *n.* an iron support for logs in a fireplace.

fire engine *n.* a vehicle with equipment for putting out fires.

fire escape *n.* a special staircase or apparatus for escape from a burning building.

firefly *n.* (*pl.* **-ies**) a phosphorescent beetle.

fireman *n.* (*pl.* **-men**) (also **firefighter**) a member of a fire brigade.

fireplace *n.* a recess with a chimney for a domestic fire.

fireside *n.* the area round a fireplace.

firework *n.* a device containing chemicals that explode producing spectacular colours etc.

firing squad *n.* a group ordered to shoot a condemned person.

firkin *n.* a small barrel.

firm *adj.* not yielding when pressed or pushed; securely in place; (of a hold etc.) steady and strong; not giving way to argument, intimidation, etc. ● *adv.* firmly. ● *v.* make or become firm. ● *n.* a business company.

firmament *n.* the sky with the stars etc.

first *adj.* coming before all others in time, order, or importance. ● *n.* **1** the first thing or occurrence; the first day of a month. **2** a top grade in an examination. ● *adv.* before all others or another; before doing something else; for the first time. ▫ **at first** at the beginning.

first aid *n.* basic treatment given for an injury etc. before a doctor arrives.

first-class *adj.* & *adv.* of the best quality; in the best category of accommodation; (of mail) delivered most quickly.

first cousin *see* **cousin**.

first-hand *adv.* & *adj.* directly from the original source.

firstly *adv.* as the first point or consideration.

first name *n.* a personal name.

first-rate *adj.* excellent.

firth *n.* (also **frith**) an estuary or narrow inlet of the sea in Scotland.

fiscal *adj.* of public revenue.

fish *n.* (*pl.* **fish** or **fishes**) a cold-blooded vertebrate living wholly in water; its flesh as food. ● *v.* try to catch fish; do this in (an area of water); reach into a receptacle to find something; say something to elicit a compliment etc.

fishery *n.* (*pl.* **-ies**) a place where fish are reared commercially; an area of sea where fishing is done; fishing as an industry.

fishmeal *n.* ground dried fish used as a fertilizer or animal feed.

fishmonger *n.* a shopkeeper who sells fish.

fishnet *adj.* (of fabric) of a coarse open mesh.

fishy *adj.* (**fishier, fishiest**) **1** like fish. **2** *informal* arousing suspicion.

fissile *adj.* tending to split; capable of undergoing nuclear fission.

fission *n.* splitting (esp. of an atomic nucleus, with release of energy).

fissure *n.* a cleft.

fist *n.* a tightly closed hand.

fisticuffs *n.pl.* fighting with fists.

fistula *n.* (*pl.* **fistulae** or **fistulas**) a pipe-like ulcer; a pipe-like passage in the body.

fit *adj.* (**fitter, fittest**) **1** suitable; right and proper; competent or qualified. **2** in good health. ● *v.* (**fitted, fitting**) **1** be the right size and shape for; try on and adjust; be small or few enough to get into a space. **2** fix in place; join or be joined. **3** make or be appropriate; make competent. ● *n.* **1** the way a garment etc. fits. **2** a sudden outburst of emotion, activity, etc.; a sudden attack of convulsions or loss of consciousness. ▫ **fitness** *n.*

fitful *adj.* irregular; occurring in short periods. ▫ **fitfully** *adv.*

fitment *n.* a piece of fixed furniture.

fitter *n.* **1** a person who supervises the fitting of clothes. **2** a mechanic.

fitting *adj.* right and proper. ● *n.* **1** the process of having a garment fitted. **2** (**fittings**) items of furniture fixed in a house but removable when the owner moves.

five *adj.* & *n.* one more than four (5, V).

fiver *n.* *informal* a five-pound note.

fix *v.* **1** fasten securely in position; direct (the eyes or attention) steadily. **2** repair. **3** agree on, settle. **4** *informal* arrange, deal with; influence (a result etc.) dishonestly. ● *n.* **1** an awkward situation. **2** *informal* a dose of something to which one is addicted. **3** *informal* a solution to a problem, esp. a makeshift one. **4** a position determined by taking bearings. □ **fix up** organize; provide for.

fixated *adj.* having an obsession.

fixation *n.* **1** an obsession. **2** fixing.

fixative *n.* a substance for keeping things in position, or preventing fading or evaporation.

fixedly *adv.* without changing or wavering.

fixity *n.* being unchanging or permanent.

fixture *n.* a thing fixed in position; a firmly established person or thing.

fizz *v.* **1** (of liquid) produce bubbles of gas with a hissing sound. **2** be exciting and lively. ● *n.* bubbliness; the sound of this; an effervescent drink. □ **fizziness** *n.*, **fizzy** *adj.*

fizzle *v.* hiss or splutter feebly. □ **fizzle out** end feebly.

fjord (fi-ord) *n.* (also **fiord**) a narrow inlet of sea between cliffs, esp. in Norway.

fl. *abbr.* **1** floruit. **2** fluid.

flab *n. informal* flabbiness, fat.

flabbergast *v. informal* astound.

flabby *adj.* (**flabbier**, **flabbiest**) fat and limp, not firm. □ **flabbiness** *n.*

flaccid (flas-sid) *adj.* soft, loose, and limp. □ **flaccidity** *n.*, **flaccidly** *adv.*

flag *n.* a piece of cloth attached by one edge to a staff or rope as a signal or symbol; a device used as a marker. ● *v.* (**flagged, flagging**) **1** mark or signal (as) with a flag. **2** become tired or weak.

flag day *n.* a day on which small emblems are sold for a charity.

flagellate (fla-jĕ-layt) *v.* whip, flog. □ **flagellant** *n.*, **flagellation** *n.*

flageolet (fla-jĕ-**let**) *n.* a small wind instrument.

flagged *adj.* paved with flagstones.

flagon *n.* a large bottle for wine or cider; a container with a handle, lip, and lid for serving wine.

flagrant (**flay**-grŭnt) *adj.* (of an offence or offender) very bad and obvious. □ **flagrantly** *adv.*

flagship *n.* an admiral's ship; the most important product of an organization etc.

flagstone *n.* a large paving stone.

flail *n.* an implement formerly used for threshing grain. ● *v.* thrash or swing about wildly.

flair *n.* natural ability.

flak *n.* **1** anti-aircraft shells. **2** harsh criticism.

flake *n.* a thin, flat piece of something. ● *v.* come off in flakes; break (food) into flakes. □ **flake out** *informal* faint; fall asleep from exhaustion. □ **flakiness** *n.*, **flaky** *adj.*

flambé (**flom**-bay) *adj.* (of food) served covered in flaming alcohol.

flamboyant *adj.* showy in appearance or manner. □ **flamboyance** *n.*, **flamboyantly** *adv.*

flame *n.* a hot, glowing quantity of burning gas coming from something on fire; an orange-red colour. ● *v.* burn with flames; be bright, become bright red. □ **fan the flames** make a feeling more intense. **old flame** *informal* a former sweetheart.

flamenco *n.* (*pl.* **flamencos**) a Spanish style of singing and dancing.

flamingo *n.* (*pl.* **flamingos** or **flamingoes**) a wading bird with long legs and pink feathers.

flammable *adj.* able to be set on fire. □ **flammability** *n.*

■ **Usage** *Flammable* is often used because *inflammable* could be taken mistakenly to mean 'not flammable'. The negative of *flammable* is *non-flammable*.

---

flan *n.* an open pastry or sponge case with filling.

flange (flanj) *n.* a projecting rim. ◻ **flanged** *adj.*

flank *n.* a side, esp. of the body between ribs and hip; a side of an army etc. ● *v.* be on either side of.

flannel *n.* **1** soft, slightly raised fabric. **2** a facecloth. **3** (**flannels**) trousers of flannel. **4** *informal* evasive and meaningless talk. ● *v.* (**flannelled**, **flannelling**; *Amer.* **flanneled**) *informal* talk meaninglessly to avoid an issue.

flannelette *n.* a heavy brushed cotton fabric.

flap *v.* (**flapped, flapping**) **1** move (wings, arms, etc.) up and down; flutter or sway. **2** *informal* be anxious, panic. ● *n.* **1** a piece of cloth, metal, etc., covering an opening and moving (as) on a hinge. **2** a flapping movement. **3** *informal* a panic.

flapjack *n.* a biscuit made with oats.

flare *v.* **1** blaze suddenly; burst into activity or anger. **2** grow wider towards one end; dilate. ● *n.* **1** a sudden blaze; a device producing flame as a signal or illumination. **2** a flared shape. **3** (**flares**) trousers with legs widening from the knee down.

flash *v.* give out a sudden bright light; cause to shine briefly; show suddenly, briefly, or ostentatiously; move or send rapidly. ● *n.* a sudden burst of flame or light; a bright patch; a sudden, brief show of wit, feeling, etc.; a brief news item; a very short time; a device producing a brief bright light in photography. ● *adj. informal* ostentatiously expensive, smart, etc. ◻ **a flash in the pan** a success that is not repeated or continued.

flashback *n.* a scene in a story, film, etc., set at a time earlier than the main narrative.

flasher *n. informal* a man who indecently exposes himself.

flash flood *n.* a sudden destructive flood.

flashing *n.* a strip of metal covering a joint in a roof etc.

flashlight *n.* an electric torch.

flashpoint *n.* **1** a point at which violence often flares up. **2** the temperature at which a vapour ignites.

flashy *adj.* (**flashier, flashiest**) ostentatiously smart, expensive, etc. ◻ **flashily** *adv.*, **flashiness** *n.*

flask *n.* a narrow-necked bottle; a vacuum flask.

flat *adj.* (**flatter, flattest**) **1** level, even, without irregularities; broad and shallow; horizontal. **2** lacking enthusiasm or energy; monotonous; having lost effervescence; having lost power to generate electric current. **3** absolute: *a flat refusal*; (of a price) unvarying. **4** *Music* below the correct pitch; (of a note) a semitone lower than a specified note. ● *adv.* **1** so as to be flat. **2** *informal* absolutely, definitely. ● *n.* **1** a flat surface or object; level ground. **2** a set of rooms on one floor, used as a residence. **3** *Music* (a sign indicating) a note lowered by a semitone. ◻ **flat out** at top speed; with maximum effort.

flatfish *n.* a sea fish with a flattened body and both eyes on one side.

flatmate *n.* a person with whom one shares a flat.

flatten *v.* make or become flat.

flatter *v.* compliment insincerely; represent as or cause to appear more attractive than is the case. ◻ **flatterer** *n.*, **flattery** *n.*

flatulent *adj.* causing or suffering from formation of gas in the digestive tract. ◻ **flatulence** *n.*

flaunt (flórnt) *v.* display ostentatiously; show off.

■ **Usage** Do not confuse *flaunt* with *flout*, which means 'to disobey contemptuously'.

---

flautist (**flor**-tist) *n.* a flute-player.

flavour (*Amer.* **flavor**) *n.* a distinctive taste; a special characteristic. ● *v.* give flavour to. ◻ **flavourless** *adj.*

flavouring *n.* (*Amer.* **flavoring**) a substance used to give flavour to food.

flaw *n.* an imperfection. ● *v.* spoil, weaken. ▫ **flawed** *adj.*, **flawless** *adj.*

flax *n.* a blue-flowered plant; a textile fibre from its stem.

flaxen *adj.* made of flax; *literary* pale yellow like dressed flax.

flay *v.* **1** strip off the skin or hide of. **2** criticize severely.

flea *n.* a small jumping blood-sucking insect.

flea market *n.* a market for second-hand goods.

fleck *n.* a very small mark; a speck. ● *v.* mark with flecks.

fled past & p.p. of **flee**.

fledged *adj.* (of a young bird) with fully grown wing-feathers, able to fly. ▫ **fully (or newly) fledged** completely (or recently) trained, appointed, etc. in a particular capacity.

fledgeling *n.* (also **fledgling**) a bird just fledged.

flee *v.* (**fled, fleeing**) run or hurry away (from).

fleece *n.* a sheep's woolly hair. ● *v.* *informal* rob by trickery. ▫ **fleecy** *adj.*

fleet *n.* a navy; ships sailing together; vehicles or aircraft under one command or ownership. ● *adj.* *poetic* swift and nimble. ▫ **fleetly** *adv.*, **fleetness** *n.*

fleeting *adj.* passing quickly, brief.

flesh *n.* **1** the soft substance of animal bodies; meat; the body as opposed to the mind or soul. **2** the pulpy part of fruits and vegetables. ▫ **flesh and blood** human nature; a real person. **flesh out** add details to. **one's own flesh and blood** a relative.

fleshy *adj.* (**fleshier, fleshiest**) **1** plump. **2** thick, pulpy. **3** like flesh.

fleur-de-lis (fler dĕ lee) *n.* (also **fleur-de-lys**) (*pl.* **fleurs-de-lis**) a heraldic design of a lily with three petals.

flew past of **fly**.

flex *n.* a flexible insulated wire for carrying electric current. ● *v.* bend; move (a muscle) so that it bends a joint. ▫ **flexion** *n.*

flexible *adj.* able to bend easily; adaptable, changing readily. ▫ **flexibility** *n.*, **flexibly** *adv.*

flexitime *n.* a system of working a set number of hours but with variable starting and finishing times.

flibbertigibbet *n.* a gossiping or frivolous person.

flick *n.* **1** a quick, sharp, small movement; a light blow. **2** *informal* a cinema film. ● *v.* move, strike, or remove with a flick.

flicker *v.* burn or shine unsteadily; make small rapid movements; occur or appear briefly. ● *n.* an unsteady light; a tiny movement; a brief or slight occurrence.

flier var. of **flyer**.

flight *n.* **1** flying; a journey through air or space; the path of an object moving through the air; a group of birds or aircraft. **2** a series of stairs. **3** feathers etc. on a dart or arrow. **4** running away, escape.

flight deck *n.* **1** the cockpit of a large aircraft. **2** the deck of an aircraft carrier.

flightless *adj.* unable to fly.

flight recorder *n.* an electronic device in an aircraft recording details of its flight.

flighty *adj.* (**flightier, flightiest**) unreliable, irresponsible. ▫ **flightily** *adv.*, **flightiness** *n.*

flimsy *adj.* (**flimsier, flimsiest**) light and thin; fragile; unconvincing. ▫ **flimsily** *adv.*, **flimsiness** *n.*

flinch *v.* make a nervous movement in pain or fear; shrink from something.

fling *v.* (**flung, flinging**) throw violently; say forcefully. ● *n.* a spell of indulgence in pleasure; a brief sexual relationship.

flint *n.* very hard stone; a piece of a hard alloy producing sparks when struck.

flintlock *n.* an old type of gun.

flip *v.* (**flipped, flipping**) **1** (cause to) turn over suddenly and swiftly. **2** *informal* lose one's self-control. ● *n.* **1** a sudden sharp movement. **2** *informal* a quick tour. ● *adj. informal* glib, flippant.

flippant *adj.* not showing proper seriousness. ◻ **flippancy** *n.*, **flippantly** *adv.*

flipper *n.* a sea animal's limb used in swimming; a large flat rubber attachment to the foot for underwater swimming.

flirt *v.* behave in a frivolously amorous way; consider an idea etc. without committing oneself to it. ● *n.* a person who flirts. ◻ **flirtation** *n.*, **flirtatious** *adj.*, **flirtatiously** *adv.*

flit *v.* (**flitted, flitting**) **1** move swiftly and lightly. **2** leave one's home, esp. secretly. ● *n. informal* an act of leaving one's home.

flitch *n.* a side of bacon.

flitter *v.* flit about.

float *v.* **1** rest or drift on the surface of liquid; be supported in air; move aimlessly. **2** make (a suggestion) to test reactions. **3** offer the shares of (a company) for sale. **4** (of currency) have a variable rate of exchange. ● *n.* **1** a thing designed to float on liquid. **2** money for minor expenditure or giving change. **3** *Brit.* a small vehicle.

floatation var. of **flotation**.

flocculent *adj.* like tufts of wool.

flock *n.* **1** a number of animals or birds together; a large number of people; a congregation. **2** a tuft of wool or cotton; wool or cotton waste as stuffing. ● *v.* gather or go in a group.

floe *n.* a sheet of floating ice.

flog *v.* (**flogged, flogging**) **1** beat severely. **2** *informal* sell. ◻ **flogging** *n.*

flood *n.* an overflow of water on a place usually dry; a great outpouring; a large quantity; the inflow of the tide. ● *v.* cover with flood water; overflow; arrive in great quantities; overwhelm.

floodlight *n.* a lamp producing a broad bright beam. ● *v.* (**floodlit, floodlighting**) illuminate with this.

floor *n.* **1** the lower surface of a room. **2** a storey. **3** the right to speak in a debate: *have the floor.* ● *v.* **1** provide with a floor. **2** *informal* knock down; baffle.

flooring *n.* material for a floor.

floor show *n.* a cabaret.

floozie *n.* (also **floozy**) *informal* a woman regarded as promiscuous.

flop *v.* (**flopped, flopping**) **1** hang or fall heavily and loosely. **2** *informal* be a failure. ● *n.* **1** a flopping movement or sound. **2** *informal* a failure.

floppy *adj.* (**floppier, floppiest**) not firm or stiff.

floppy disk *n.* a magnetic disk for storing machine-readable data.

flora *n.* (*pl.* **florae** or **floras**) the plants of an area or period.

floral *adj.* of flowers.

floret *n.* each of the small flowers of a composite flower.

florid *adj.* **1** red, flushed. **2** over-elaborate. ◻ **floridity** *n.*

florin *n.* a former British coin worth two shillings; a Dutch guilder.

florist *n.* a person who sells flowers.

floruit *n.* & *v.* (the period at which a person) was alive and working.

floss *n.* **1** a mass of silky fibres. **2** dental floss. ◻ **flossy** *adj.*

flotation *n.* (also **floatation**) floating; the sale of new shares in a company to the public.

flotilla *n.* a small fleet.

flotsam *n.* floating wreckage. ◻ **flotsam and jetsam** odds and ends.

flounce *v.* go in an impatient annoyed manner. ● *n.* **1** a flouncing movement. **2** a deep frill. ◻ **flounced** *adj.*

flounder *v.* move clumsily, as in mud; become confused; be in difficulty. ● *n.* a small flatfish.

flour *n.* fine powder made from grain, used in cooking. ● *v.* sprinkle with flour. □ **floury** *adj.*

flourish *v.* **1** grow vigorously; prosper, be successful. **2** wave dramatically. ● *n.* a dramatic gesture; an ornamental curve; a fanfare.

flout *v.* disobey (a law etc.) contemptuously.

■ **Usage** Do not confuse *flout* with *flaunt*, which means 'to display proudly or show off'.

---

flow *v.* glide along as a stream; move steadily; (of hair etc.) hang loosely; be supplied and drunk in large quantities: *wine flowed at the party.* ● *n.* a flowing movement; a continuous stream; its speed. □ **go with the flow** follow a general tendency.

flow chart *n.* a diagram showing the sequence of events in a process.

flower *n.* **1** the part of a plant where fruit or seed develops, usu. brightly coloured and decorative; a plant grown for this. **2** the best among a group of people. ● *v.* produce flowers.

flowered *adj.* ornamented with a design of flowers.

flowerpot *n.* a pot in which plants are grown.

flowery *adj.* **1** full of flowers. **2** full of ornamental phrases.

flown p.p. of **fly**.

flu *n.* influenza.

fluctuate *v.* vary irregularly. □ **fluctuation** *n.*

flue *n.* a smoke-duct in a chimney; a channel for conveying heat.

fluent *adj.* speaking or spoken smoothly and readily. □ **fluency** *n.*, **fluently** *adv.*

fluff *n.* a soft mass of fibres or down. ● *v.* **1** make (something) appear fuller and softer. **2** *informal* bungle, do unsuccessfully. □ **fluffiness** *n.*, **fluffy** *adj.*

fluid *adj.* flowing easily; not fixed or settled. ● *n.* a liquid. □ **fluidity** *n.*, **fluidly** *adv.*

fluid ounce *n.* one-twentieth (in the USA, one-sixteenth) of a pint (about 28 ml, in the USA 35 ml).

fluke *n.* **1** a lucky accident. **2** the barbed arm of an anchor etc.; a lobe of a whale's tail. **3** a flat parasitic worm. **4** a flatfish.

flummery *n.* **1** nonsense, empty compliments. **2** a type of pudding.

flummox *v. informal* baffle.

flung past & p.p. of **fling**.

flunk *v. Amer. informal* fail.

flunkey *n.* (also **flunky**) (*pl.* **flunkeys** or **flunkies**) a liveried servant; a person who does menial work.

fluorescent *adj.* taking in radiations and sending them out as light. □ **fluoresce** *v.*, **fluorescence** *n.*

fluoridate *v.* add fluoride to (a water supply) to combat tooth decay. □ **fluoridation** *n.*

fluoride *n.* a compound of fluorine with metal.

fluorine *n.* a chemical element (symbol F), a pungent corrosive gas.

fluorspar *n.* a colourless mineral.

flurry *n.* (*pl.* **-ies**) a short rush of wind, rain, or snow; a commotion.

flush *v.* **1** make or become red; blush. **2** cleanse or dispose of with a flow of water. **3** drive out from cover. ● *n.* **1** a blush. **2** a rush of emotion. **3** an act of cleansing something with a rush of water. ● *adj.* **1** level, even with another surface. **2** *informal* wealthy.

fluster *v.* make agitated and confused. ● *n.* a flustered state.

flute *n.* **1** a wind instrument consisting of a pipe with holes along it and a mouth-hole at the side. **2** an ornamental groove. **3** a tall narrow wine glass.

flutter *v.* move wings hurriedly; wave or flap quickly; (of the heart) beat irregularly. ● *n.* **1** a fluttering movement; a state of nervous excitement. **2** *informal* a small bet.

fluvial *adj.* of or found in rivers.

flux *n.* **1** flowing; a discharge; continuous change. **2** a substance mixed with a solid to lower its melting point.

fly *v.* (**flew, flown, flying**) **1** move through the air on wings or in an aircraft; be thrown through the air; control the flight of. **2** display (a flag); flutter, be blown about. **3** (of time) pass rapidly; *archaic* run away. ● *n.* (*pl.* **flies**) **1** a two-winged insect. **2** (also **flies**) a fastening down the front of trousers. □ **a fly in the ointment** something that spoils a situation or thing. **no flies on someone** *informal* used of an alert and astute person. **with flying colours** with great credit or success.

flyblown *adj.* tainted by flies' eggs.

flyer *n.* (also **flier**) **1** a thing that flies; an airman or airwoman; something that moves fast. **2** a small hand bill advertising something.

flying *adj.* able to fly.

flying buttress *n.* a buttress based on a structure separate from the wall it supports.

flying fish *n.* a tropical fish with winglike fins for gliding through the air.

flying fox *n.* a large fruit-eating bat.

flying saucer *n.* an unidentified flying object, supposedly a craft from outer space.

flying squad *n.* a group of police etc. organized to reach an incident quickly.

flyleaf *n.* (*pl.* **flyleaves**) a blank leaf at the beginning or end of a book.

flyover *n.* a bridge carrying one road or railway over another.

fly-post *v.* display (posters etc.) in unauthorized places.

flysheet *n.* an outer cover for a tent.

fly-tip *v.* (**-tipped, -tipping**) *Brit.* dump waste illegally.

flyweight *n.* a weight below bantamweight, in amateur boxing between 48 and 51 kg.

flywheel *n.* a heavy wheel revolving on a shaft to regulate machinery.

FM *abbr.* frequency modulation.

Fm *symb.* fermium.

foal *n.* the young of a horse or related animal. ● *v.* give birth to a foal.

foam *n.* **1** a mass of small bubbles; a bubbly substance prepared for shaving etc.; saliva. **2** spongy rubber or plastic. ● *v.* form or produce foam. □ **foamy** *adj.*

fob *n.* a chain for a watch; an ornament hanging from it; a tab on a key ring. □ **fob off** (**fobbed, fobbing**) give (something inferior) to (someone); deceitfully pacify.

focal *adj.* of or at a focus.

fo'c's'le var. of **forecastle**.

focus *n.* (*pl.* **focuses** or **foci**) **1** the centre of interest or activity; concentration of attention. **2** clear visual definition; the distance at which an object is most clearly seen; an adjustment on a lens to produce a clear image. **3** a point where rays meet. ● *v.* (**focused, focusing** or **focussed, focussing**) **1** adjust the focus of; bring into focus. **2** concentrate.

fodder *n.* food for animals.

foe *n.* an enemy.

foetid var. of **fetid**.

foetus (fee-tŭs) *n.* (*Amer.* **fetus**) (*pl.* **foetuses**) a developed embryo in a womb or egg. □ **foetal** *adj.*

fog *n.* thick mist. ● *v.* (**fogged, fogging**) cover or become covered with fog or condensed vapour; make obscure. □ **fogginess** *n.*, **foggy** *adj.*

fogey *n.* (also **fogy**) (*pl.* **fogeys** or **fogies**) an old-fashioned person.

foghorn *n.* a device making a deep sound to warn ships of hidden rocks etc. in fog.

foible *n.* a harmless peculiarity in a person's character.

foil *n.* **1** a very thin flexible sheet of metal. **2** a person or thing emphasizing another's qualities by contrast. **3** a long thin sword with a button on the point. ● *v.* thwart, frustrate.

foist *v.* cause a person to accept (an inferior or unwelcome thing).

fold *v.* **1** bend (something thin and flat) so that one part of it lies over another. **2** wrap; clasp. **3** mix (an ingredient) gently into a mixture. **4** *informal* (of a business etc.) fail, cease operating. **5** enclose (sheep) in a fold. ● *n.* **1** a shape or line made by folding. **2** a pen for sheep; a close and protected community.

folder *n.* **1** a folding cover for loose papers. **2** *Amer.* a leaflet.

foliage *n.* leaves.

foliate *adj.* decorated with leaves.

folio *n.* (*pl.* **folios**) a folded sheet of paper making two leaves of a book; a book of such pages; the page number of a book.

folk *n.* (*pl.* **folk** or **folks**) **1** *informal* people; relatives. **2** folk music. ● *adj.* (of music, song, etc.) in the traditional style of a country or region.

folklore *n.* the traditional beliefs and tales of a community.

folksy *adj.* (**folksier, folksiest**) **1** in the style of traditional culture, esp. artificially. **2** informal and friendly.

follicle *n.* a very small cavity containing a hair-root. □ **follicular** *adj.*

follow *v.* **1** go or come after; go along (a route); happen after. **2** act according to (instructions etc.); accept the ideas of. **3** pay close attention to, take an interest in. **4** be a consequence or conclusion. □ **follow suit** follow someone's example. **follow up** investigate further. □ **follower** *n.*

following *n.* a body of believers or supporters. ● *adj.* **1** about to be mentioned. **2** next in time. ● *prep.* as a sequel to.

folly *n.* (*pl.* **-ies**) **1** foolishness, a foolish act. **2** an impractical ornamental building.

foment *v.* stir up (trouble). □ **fomentation** *n.*

fond *adj.* **1** liking someone or something; doting. **2** (of hope) unlikely to be fulfilled. □ **fondly** *adv.*, **fondness** *n.*

fondant *n.* a soft sugary sweet.

fondle *v.* stroke lovingly.

fondue *n.* a dish of flavoured melted cheese.

font *n.* **1** a basin in a church, holding water for baptism. **2** (also **fount**) a size and style of printing type.

fontanelle *n.* (*Amer.* **fontanel**) a soft spot where the bones of an infant's skull have not yet grown together.

food *n.* a substance (esp. solid) that can be taken into the body of an animal or plant to maintain its life.

foodie *n. informal* a gourmet.

food processor *n.* a machine for chopping and mixing food.

foodstuff *n.* a substance used as food.

fool *n.* **1** a foolish person. **2** a creamy fruit-flavoured pudding. ● *v.* trick, deceive; behave frivolously, joke.

foolery *n.* foolish behaviour.

foolhardy *adj.* recklessly bold.

foolish *adj.* lacking good sense or judgement; ridiculous. □ **foolishly** *adv.*, **foolishness** *n.*

foolproof *adj.* unable to go wrong or be misused.

foolscap *n.* a large size of paper.

foot *n.* (*pl.* **feet**) **1** the part of the leg below the ankle; a lower end; a base. **2** a measure of length = 12 inches (30.48 cm). **3** a unit of rhythm in verse. ● *v. informal* pay (a bill). □ **foot it** travel on foot. **put one's foot down** be firm in dealing with bad behaviour.

footage *n.* **1** a length of film. **2** length measured in feet.

foot-and-mouth disease *n.* a contagious viral disease of cattle.

football *n.* a large round or elliptical inflated ball; a game played with this. □ **footballer** *n.*

football pools *n.pl.* a form of gambling on the results of football matches.

footfall *n.* the sound of footsteps.

foothills *n.pl.* low hills near the bottom of a mountain or range.

foothold *n.* a place just wide enough for one's foot; a secure position as a basis for progress.

footing *n.* **1** a secure grip with one's feet: *I lost my footing*. **2** a way of operating; a position: *put us on an equal footing*.

footlights *n.pl.* a row of lights along the front of a stage floor.

footling (foot-ling) *adj. informal* trivial.

footloose *adj.* independent, without responsibilities.

footman *n.* (*pl.* **-men**) a manservant, usu. in livery.

footnote *n.* a note printed at the bottom of a page.

footpath *n.* a path for pedestrians; a pavement.

footplate *n.* the platform for the crew of a locomotive.

footprint *n.* an impression left by a foot or shoe.

footsie *n. informal* flirtatious touching of another's feet with one's own.

footsore *adj.* with feet sore from walking.

footstep *n.* a step; the sound of this.

footstool *n.* a stool for resting the feet on while sitting.

footwear *n.* shoes, socks, etc.

footwork *n.* a manner of moving or using the feet in sports etc.

fop *n.* an affectedly fashionable man. □ **foppery** *n.*, **foppish** *adj.*

for *prep.* **1** in support of; on behalf of. **2** to be received or used by. **3** relating to, in respect of. **4** having as a purpose, goal, or destination; on account of. **5** in place of; as a price or penalty of; representing. **6** over (a period or distance). ● *conj. poetic* because.

forage (fo-rij) *v.* search for food. ● *n.* **1** fodder. **2** a search.

foray *n.* a sudden attack, a raid. ● *v.* make a foray.

forbade past of **forbid**.

forbear *v.* (**forbore, forborne, forbearing**) refrain (from).

forbearing *adj.* patient, tolerant. □ **forbearance** *n.*

forbid *v.* (**forbade, forbidden, forbidding**) order not to do something; refuse to allow.

forbidding *adj.* daunting, uninviting.

force *n.* **1** strength, power; someone or something exerting an influence; *Physics* an influence tending to cause movement. **2** violent compulsion. **3** validity. **4** a body of troops or police; an organized group. ● *v.* **1** make one's way by effort or violence. **2** compel. **3** strain; produce with an effort.

forceful *adj.* powerful; assertive, strong-willed. □ **forcefully** *adv.*, **forcefulness** *n.*

forcemeat *n.* finely chopped seasoned meat used as stuffing.

forceps *n.pl.* pincers used in surgery etc.

forcible *adj.* **1** done by force. **2** powerful. □ **forcibly** *adv.*

ford *n.* a shallow place where a stream may be crossed by wading or driving through. ● *v.* cross (a stream etc.) in this way.

fore *adj.* & *adv.* in, at, or towards the front. ● *n.* the front part. □ **to the fore** in front; conspicuous.

forearm *n.* (for-arm) the arm from the elbow downwards. ● *v.* (for-**arm**) arm or prepare in advance against possible danger.

forebears *n.pl.* ancestors.

foreboding *n.* a feeling that trouble is coming.

forecast *v.* (**forecast, forecasting**) predict (future weather, events, etc.). ● *n.* a statement that does this. □ **forecaster** *n.*

forecastle (fohk-sŭl) *n.* (also **fo'c's'le**) the forward part of certain ships.

foreclose *v.* take possession of property when a loan secured on it is not repaid. □ **foreclosure** *n.*

forecourt *n.* an open area in front of a building.

forefathers *n.pl.* ancestors.

forefinger *n.* the finger next to the thumb.

forefoot *n.* (*pl.* **forefeet**) an animal's front foot.

forefront *n.* the very front.

foregather *v.* (also **forgather**) assemble.

forego var. of **forgo**.

foregoing *adj.* preceding.

foregone conclusion *n.* a predictable result.

■ **Usage** *Foregone* is spelt with an *e*. *Forgone* is the past participle of *forgo*.

---

foreground *n.* the part of a scene etc. that is nearest to the observer. ● *v.* give prominence to.

forehand *n.* (in tennis etc.) a stroke played with the palm of the hand turned forwards. ● *adj.* played in this way.

forehead *n.* the part of the face above the eyes.

foreign *adj.* of, from, or in a country that is not one's own; relating to other countries; strange, out of place.

foreigner *n.* a person born in or coming from another country.

foreknowledge *n.* knowledge of a thing before it occurs.

foreleg *n.* an animal's front leg.

forelock *n.* a lock of hair just above the forehead.

foreman *n.* (*pl.* **-men**) a worker supervising others; the president and spokesman of a jury.

foremost *adj.* most advanced in position or rank; most important. ● *adv.* first; in the most important position.

forename *n.* a first name.

forenoon *n. literary* the morning.

forensic (fŏ-ren-sik) *adj.* of or used in law courts.

forensic medicine *n.* medical knowledge used in police investigations etc.

foreplay *n.* stimulation preceding sexual intercourse.

forerunner *n.* a person or thing coming before and foreshadowing another.

foresee *v.* (**foresaw, foreseen, foreseeing**) be aware of or realize beforehand. □ **foreseeable** *adj.*

foreshadow *v.* be an advance sign of (a future event etc.).

foreshore *n.* the part of the shore between high and low water marks.

foreshorten *v.* show or portray (an object) as shorter than it is, as an effect of perspective.

foresight *n.* the ability to foresee and prepare for future needs.

foreskin *n.* the fold of skin covering the end of the penis.

forest *n.* a large area covered with trees and undergrowth.

forestall *v.* prevent or foil by taking action first.

forester *n.* a person in charge of a forest or of growing timber.

forestry *n.* the science of planting and caring for forests.

foretaste *n.* a sample or indication of what is to come.

foretell *v.* (**foretold, foretelling**) forecast.

forethought *n.* careful planning for the future.

forever *adv.* **1** for all time. **2** continually.

forewarn *v.* warn beforehand.

foreword *n.* an introduction to a book.

forfeit *n.* something that has to be paid or given up as a penalty. ● *v.* give or lose as a forfeit. ● *adj.* forfeited. □ **forfeiture** *n.*

forgather var. of **foregather**.

forgave past of **forgive**.

forge *n.* a blacksmith's workshop; a furnace where metal is heated. ● *v.* **1** shape (metal) by heating and hammering. **2** make a fraudulent copy of. **3** force one's way. □ **forger** *n.*

forgery *n.* (*pl.* **-ies**) forging; something forged.

forget *v.* (**forgot, forgotten, forgetting**) cease to remember or think about. □ **forget oneself** behave improperly or uncontrolledly.

forgetful *adj.* tending to forget. □ **forgetfully** *adv.*, **forgetfulness** *n.*

forget-me-not *n.* a plant with small blue flowers.

forgive *v.* (**forgave, forgiven, forgiving**) cease to feel angry or bitter towards or about. □ **forgivable** *adj.*, **forgiveness** *n.*

forgo *v.* (also **forego**) (**forwent, forgone, forgoing**) give up; go without.

fork *n.* a pronged implement for holding food or tool for digging; a point where a road, river, etc., divides; one of its branches. ● *v.* **1** (of a road etc.) divide into two branches; follow one branch. **2** lift or dig with a fork. □ **fork out** *informal* give money. □ **forked** *adj.*

forklift truck *n.* a truck with a forked device for lifting and carrying loads.

forlorn *adj.* left alone and unhappy. □ **forlornly** *adv.*

forlorn hope *n.* a desperate enterprise.

form *n.* **1** shape, appearance; structure. **2** a type or variety; the way in which something exists: *what form did it take?* **3** correct behaviour. **4** a document with blank spaces for information. **5** a school class or year. **6** a bench. ● *v.* create; shape; develop; be the parts of, constitute.

formal *adj.* **1** in accordance with rules or conventions; of or for official occasions; stiff, prim. **2** of structure or appearance as opposed to content. □ **formally** *adv.*

formaldehyde (for-mal-di-hId) *n.* a colourless gas used in solution as a preservative and disinfectant.

formalin *n.* a solution of formaldehyde in water, used as a preservative for biological specimens.

formalism *n.* excessive attention to prescribed form or outward appearance.

formality *n.* (*pl.* **-ies**) being formal; something done only because required by a rule.

formalize *v.* (also **-ise**) make official. □ **formalization** *n.*

format *n.* the way something is arranged; the shape and size of a book; *Computing* a structure for the processing etc. of data. ● *v.* (**formatted, formatting**) arrange in a format; prepare (a disk) to receive data.

formation *n.* forming, being formed; a structure or pattern.

formative *adj.* influencing development; relating to development.

former *adj.* of an earlier period; mentioned first of two.

formerly *adv.* in former times.

formic acid *n.* a colourless acid in fluid emitted by ants.

formidable *adj.* inspiring fear or awe; difficult to achieve. □ **formidably** *adv.*

formula *n.* (*pl.* **formulae** or **formulas**) **1** symbols showing chemical constituents or a mathematical statement. **2** a fixed series of words for use on social or ceremonial occasions. **3** a list of ingredients. **4** a classification of a racing car. □ **formulaic** *adj.*

formulate *v.* **1** create, devise. **2** express precisely. □ **formulation** *n.*

fornicate *v. formal* have sexual intercourse outside marriage. □ **fornication** *n.*, **fornicator** *n.*

forsake *v.* (**forsook, forsaken, forsaking**) withdraw one's help or companionship from; give up, abandon.

forsooth *adv. archaic* indeed.

forswear *v.* (**forswore, forsworn, forswearing**) renounce.

forsworn *adj.* having sworn falsely.

fort *n.* a fortified building.

forte (for-tay) *n.* something at which a person excels. ● *adv. Music* loudly.

forth *adv.* **1** outwards and forwards. **2** onwards from a point in time. ▫ **back and forth** to and fro.

forthcoming *adj.* **1** about to occur or appear. **2** communicative.

forthright *adj.* frank, outspoken.

forthwith *adv.* immediately.

fortification *n.* a defensive wall or building; fortifying.

fortify *v.* (**fortified, fortifying**) **1** strengthen against attack. **2** strengthen, invigorate. **3** increase the alcohol content or nutritive value of.

fortissimo *adv. Music* very loudly.

fortitude *n.* courage in bearing pain or trouble.

fortnight *n.* a period of two weeks.

fortnightly *adj.* & *adv.* (happening or appearing) once a fortnight.

Fortran *n.* a computer programming language used esp. for scientific work.

fortress *n.* a fortified building or town.

fortuitous *adj.* happening by chance. ▫ **fortuitously** *adv.*

▪ **Usage** *Fortuitous* should not be used to mean *fortunate.*

fortunate *adj.* lucky. ▫ **fortunately** *adv.*

fortune *n.* **1** chance seen as affecting people's lives; luck; (**fortunes**) what happens to someone. **2** a large amount of money.

fortune-teller *n.* a person who claims to foretell future events in people's lives.

forty *adj.* & *n.* four times ten (40, XL). ▫ **fortieth** *adj.* & *n.*

forty winks *n.pl. informal* a short sleep.

forum *n.* a place or meeting where a public discussion is held.

forward *adv.* towards the front; in the direction one is facing or moving; onward, making progress; towards the future; so as to happen sooner. ● *adj.* **1** facing the front or the line of motion. **2** bold, presumptuous. **3** having made faster than usual progress; advanced. **4** concerning the future. ● *n.* an attacking player in football, hockey, etc. ● *v.* **1** send on (a letter etc.) to another destination. **2** help, advance (interests). ▫ **forwardness** *n.*

forwards *adv.* forward.

fosse *n.* a long fortification ditch.

fossil *n.* the petrified remains or traces of a prehistoric animal or plant. ▫ **fossilization** *n.* (also **-isation**), **fossilize** *v.* (also **-ise**).

fossil fuel *n.* fuel such as coal or gas, formed from the remains of living organisms.

foster *v.* **1** encourage or help the development of. **2** bring up (a child that is not one's own).

foster child *n.* a child brought up by parents other than its own.

foster parent *n.* a person who fosters a child.

fought past & p.p. of **fight**.

foul *adj.* **1** causing disgust; very bad; dirty. **2** wicked; against the rules of a game. ● *adv.* unfairly. ● *n.* an action that breaks the rules of a game. ● *v.* **1** make dirty. **2** commit a foul against (a sporting opponent). **3** (of a ship) collide with (another); obstruct, entangle. ▫ **foully** *adv.*, **foulness** *n.*

found[1] past & p.p. of **find**.

found[2] *v.* **1** establish (an institution etc.); set on a base or basis. **2** melt and mould (metal or glass); make (an object) in this way.

foundation *n.* **1** a base, a lowest layer; an underlying principle. **2** founding; an institution etc. that is founded.

founder *v.* stumble or fall; (of a ship) sink; fail completely. ● *n.* a person who has founded an institution etc.

foundling *n.* a deserted child of unknown parents.

foundry *n.* (*pl.* **-ies**) a workshop where metal or glass founding is done.

fount *n.* **1** *literary* a fountain; a source. **2** var. of **font** (*sense* 2).

fountain *n.* **1** an ornamental structure pumping out a jet of water. **2** a source.

fountainhead *n.* a source.

fountain pen *n.* a pen with a container supplying ink to the nib.

four *adj.* & *n.* one more than three (4, IV).

fourfold *adj.* & *adv.* four times as great or as many; having four parts.

four-poster *n.* a bed with four posts that support a canopy.

foursome *n.* a party of four people.

fourteen *adj.* & *n.* one more than thirteen (14, XIV). ▫ **fourteenth** *adj.* & *n.*

fourth *adj.* next after the third. ● *n.* **1** a fourth thing, class, etc. **2** a quarter. ▫ **fourthly** *adv.*

four-wheel drive *n.* motive power acting on all four wheels of a vehicle.

fowl *n.* a bird kept to supply eggs and flesh for food.

fox *n.* **1** a wild animal of the dog family with a bushy tail; its fur. **2** a cunning person. ● *v.* *informal* baffle, deceive.

foxglove *n.* a tall plant with flowers like glove-fingers.

foxhole *n.* a small trench as a military shelter.

foxhound *n.* a hound bred to hunt foxes.

foxtrot *n.* a dance with slow and quick steps; music for this.

foyer (foi-yay) *n.* an entrance hall of a theatre, cinema, or hotel.

Fr *symb.* francium.

fracas (fra-kah) *n.* (*pl.* **fracas**) a noisy quarrel or disturbance.

fraction *n.* a number that is not a whole number; a small part or amount. ▫ **fractional** *adj.*, **fractionally** *adv.*

fractious *adj.* irritable; hard to control. ▫ **fractiously** *adv.*, **fractiousness** *n.*

fracture *n.* a break, esp. in a bone; breaking. ● *v.* break.

fragile *adj.* easily broken or damaged; delicate. ▫ **fragility** *n.*

fragment *n.* (**frag**-měnt) a piece broken off something; an isolated part. ● *v.* (frag-**ment**) (cause to) break into fragments. ▫ **fragmentation** *n.*

fragmentary *adj.* consisting of fragments.

fragrance *n.* a pleasant smell. ▫ **fragrant** *adj.*

frail *adj.* weak; fragile. ▫ **frailty** *n.*

frame *n.* **1** a rigid structure supporting other parts; a basis for a system, theory, etc.; a person's body. **2** a rigid structure surrounding a picture, window, etc. **3** a single exposure on a cinema film. **4** a single game of snooker. ● *v.* **1** put or form a frame round. **2** construct. **3** *informal* arrange false evidence against. ▫ **frame of mind** a temporary state of mind.

framework *n.* a supporting frame.

franc *n.* a unit of money in Switzerland (formerly in France, Belgium, etc.).

franchise *n.* **1** the right to vote in public elections. **2** authorization to sell a company's goods or services in a certain area. ● *v.* grant a franchise to.

francium *n.* a radioactive metallic element (symbol Fr).

Franco- *comb. form* French.

frank *adj.* honest in expressing one's thoughts and feelings. ● *v.* mark (a letter etc.) to show that postage has been paid. ▫ **frankly** *adv.*, **frankness** *n.*

frankfurter *n.* a smoked sausage.

frankincense *n.* a sweet-smelling gum burnt as incense.

frantic *adj.* wildly agitated or excited. ▫ **frantically** *adv.*

fraternal *adj.* of a brother or brothers. ▫ **fraternally** *adv.*

fraternity *n.* (*pl.* **-ies**) **1** a group of people with a common interest. **2** brotherhood.

fraternize *v.* (also **-ise**) associate with others in a friendly way. □ **fraternization** *n.*

fratricide *n.* the killing of one's own brother or sister; a person who does this. □ **fratricidal** *adj.*

Frau (frow) *n.* the title of a German married woman.

fraud (frord) *n.* criminal deception; a dishonest trick; a person carrying this out. □ **fraudulence** *n.*, **fraudulent** *adj.*, **fraudulently** *adv.*

fraught (frort) *adj.* causing or suffering anxiety. □ **fraught with** filled with, involving.

Fräulein (**froi**-lyn) *n.* the title of a German unmarried woman.

fray *v.* (of fabric, rope, etc.) unravel, become worn; (of nerves) be strained. ● *n.* a fight, a conflict.

frazzle *n. informal* an exhausted state: *worn to a frazzle.* □ **frazzled** *adj.*

freak *n.* **1** an abnormal person, thing, or event. **2** *informal* an enthusiast for something specified. □ **freak out** *informal* (cause to) behave wildly and irrationally. □ **freakish** *adj.*, **freaky** *adj.*

freckle *n.* a light brown spot on the skin. ● *v.* spot or become spotted with freckles. □ **freckled** *adj.*

free *adj.* (**freer, freest**) **1** not captive, confined, or restricted; not in another's power. **2** not busy or taken up; not in use; not prevented from doing something. **3** not subject to something; without. **4** costing nothing. **5** giving or spending without restraint. ● *adv.* at no cost. ● *v.* **1** set free. **2** rid of something undesirable. □ **a free hand** authority to do what one thinks fit. **make free with** use or handle carelessly and without restraint. □ **freely** *adv.*

freebie *n. informal* something provided free.

freebooter *n.* a pirate.

freedom *n.* **1** being free; independence. **2** unrestricted use. **3** honorary citizenship. **4** frankness, familiarity.

free fall *n.* unrestricted falling under the force of gravity, esp. the part of a parachute descent before the parachute opens.

Freefone *n. trademark* (also **Freephone**) a system whereby an organization pays for incoming calls made by customers.

freehand *adj.* (of drawing) done by hand without ruler or compasses etc.

freehold *n.* the holding of land or a house etc. in absolute ownership. ● *adj.* owned in this way. □ **freeholder** *n.*

free house *n.* a public house not controlled by one brewery.

freelance *adj.* & *n.* (a person) working for various employers rather than permanently employed by one.

freeloader *n. informal* a person who lives off others' generosity.

Freemason *n.* a member of a fraternity for mutual help, with elaborate secret rituals. □ **Freemasonry** *n.*

Freephone var. of **Freefone**.

Freepost *n.* a system in which postage is paid by the addressee.

free-range *adj.* (of hens) allowed to range freely in search of food; (of eggs) from such hens.

freestyle *n.* a swimming race allowing any stroke.

freeway *n. Amer.* a motorway.

freewheel *v.* ride a bicycle without pedalling.

freeze *v.* (**froze, frozen, freezing**) **1** change or be changed from liquid to solid by extreme cold; (of weather etc.) be so cold that water turns to ice; (cause to) feel very cold or die of cold. **2** preserve (food etc.) at a very low temperature. **3** become motionless; stop (a moving image); hold (prices or wages) at a fixed level; prevent (assets) from being used; anaesthetize. ● *n.*

1 the freezing of prices etc. **2** *informal* a very cold spell. □ **freezing** *adj.*

freeze-dry *v.* (**-dried, -drying**) preserve by freezing and evaporating ice in a vacuum.

freezer *n.* a refrigerated container for preserving and storing food.

freight (frayt) *n.* goods transported in bulk; a charge for transport. ● *v.* transport (goods).

freighter (fray-tĕ) *n.* a ship or aircraft carrying mainly freight.

freightliner *n. Brit. trademark* a train carrying goods in containers.

French *adj.* & *n.* (the language) of France. □ **Frenchman** *n.*, **Frenchwoman** *n.*

French bread *n.* white bread in a long crisp loaf.

French dressing *n.* a salad dressing of oil and vinegar.

French fries *n.pl.* potato chips.

French horn *n.* a brass wind instrument with a coiled tube.

French leave *n. informal* absence without permission.

French polish *n.* polish producing a high gloss on wood.

French window *n.* a window reaching to the ground, used also as a door.

frenetic *adj.* wild, agitated, uncontrolled. □ **frenetically** *adv.*

frenzy *n.* (*pl.* **-ies**) a state of wild excitement or agitation. □ **frenzied** *adj.*

frequency *n.* (*pl.* **-ies**) the rate at which something occurs or is repeated; frequent occurrence; *Physics* the number of cycles of a carrier wave per second; a band or group of these.

frequent *adj.* (free-kwĕnt) happening or appearing often. ● *v.* (fri-**kwent**) go frequently to, be often in (a place). □ **frequently** *adv.*

fresco *n.* (*pl.* **frescos** or **frescoes**) a picture painted on a wall or ceiling before the plaster is dry.

fresh *adj.* **1** new; not faded or stale; not tired. **2** (of food) not tinned, frozen, etc. **3** (of water) not salty. **4** refreshing; vigorous. **5** *informal* impudent. □ **freshen** *v.*, **freshener** *n.*, **freshly** *adv.*, **freshness** *n.*

fresher *n. informal* (also **freshman**) a first-year university student.

freshwater *adj.* of fresh water, not of the sea.

fret *v.* (**fretted, fretting**) **1** (cause to) feel anxious. **2** erode, wear away. ● *n.* each of the ridges on the fingerboard of a guitar etc.

fretful *adj.* distressed or irritable. □ **fretfully** *adv.*

fretsaw *n.* a narrow saw used for fretwork.

fretwork *n.* woodwork cut in decorative patterns.

Fri. *abbr.* Friday.

friable (frI-ă-bĕl) *adj.* easily crumbled. □ **friability** *n.*

friar *n.* a member of certain religious orders of men.

friary *n.* (*pl.* **-ies**) a building occupied by friars.

fricassee *n.* a dish of pieces of meat served in a thick sauce. ● *v.* (**fricasseed, fricasseeing**) make a fricassee of.

friction *n.* **1** rubbing; resistance of one surface to another that moves over it. **2** conflict of people who disagree. □ **frictional** *adj.*

Friday *n.* the day following Thursday.

fridge *n. informal* a refrigerator.

fried past & p.p. of **fry**.

friend *n.* a person (other than a relative or lover) with whom one is on terms of mutual affection; a supporter of a cause; a person on the same side in a conflict. □ **friendship** *n.*

friendly *adj.* (**friendlier, friendliest**) kindly, encouraging; (of people or their relationship) affectionate; *Brit.* (of a game) not part of a serious competition; favourable, not harmful. □ **friendliness** *n.*

frieze (freez) *n.* a band of decoration round a wall.

frigate *n.* a small fast naval ship.

fright *n.* sudden great fear; an experience of this. □ **look a fright** *informal* be very untidy or grotesque.

frighten *v.* make afraid; deter through fear.

frightened *adj.* afraid.

frightful *adj.* very bad or unpleasant; *informal* extreme (esp. of something bad). □ **frightfully** *adv.*, **frightfulness** *n.*

frigid *adj.* intensely cold; very cold in manner; unresponsive sexually. □ **frigidity** *n.*, **frigidly** *adv.*

frill *n.* a gathered or pleated strip of material attached at one edge to a garment etc. for decoration; *informal* an unnecessary extra feature or luxury. □ **frilled** *adj.*, **frilly** *adj.*

fringe *n.* **1** an ornamental edging of hanging threads; front hair cut short to hang over the forehead. **2** the outer part of an area, group, etc. ● *adj.* (of theatre etc.) unconventional. ● *v.* give or form a fringe to.

fringe benefit *n.* a benefit provided in addition to wages.

frippery *n.* showy unnecessary finery or ornament.

frisbee *n. trademark* a plastic disc for skimming through the air as an outdoor game.

frisk *v.* **1** leap or skip playfully. **2** feel over or search (a person) for concealed weapons etc. ● *n.* a playful leap or skip.

frisky *adj.* (**friskier, friskiest**) lively, playful. □ **friskily** *adv.*, **friskiness** *n.*

frisson (free-son) *n.* a thrill.

frith var. of **firth**.

fritter *v.* waste (money or time) on trivial things. ● *n.* a fried batter-coated slice of fruit or meat etc.

frivolous *adj.* not serious; purely for or interested in pleasure. □ **frivolity** *n.*, **frivolously** *adv.*

frizz *v.* form (hair) into a mass of small curls; curl in this way. ● *n.* such curls. □ **frizziness** *n.*, **frizzy** *adj.*

frizzle *v.* sizzle while frying; fry (food) until crisp.

frock *n.* a woman's or girl's dress.

frock coat *n.* a man's long-skirted coat not cut away in front.

frog *n.* a small amphibian with long web-footed hind legs. □ **frog in one's throat** *informal* hoarseness.

frogman *n.* (*pl.* **-men**) a swimmer with a rubber suit and oxygen supply for working under water.

frogmarch *v.* hustle (a person) forcibly, holding the arms.

frogspawn *n.* the eggs of a frog, surrounded by transparent jelly.

frolic *v.* (**frolicked, frolicking**) play about in a lively way. ● *n.* such play.

from *prep.* **1** having as the starting point, source, material, or cause. **2** as separated, distinguished, or unlike.

fromage frais (from-a*zh* **fray**) *n.* a smooth low-fat soft cheese.

frond *n.* a long leaf or leaflike part of a fern, palm tree, etc.

front *n.* **1** the side or part normally nearer or towards the spectator or line of motion; any side of a building. **2** a battle line. **3** an outward appearance; a cover for secret activities. **4** a boundary between warm and cold air-masses. **5** a promenade at a seaside resort. ● *adj.* of or at the front. ● *v.* **1** face, have the front towards; give (an object) a front of a specified type. **2** lead (a group etc.). **3** act as a cover for secret activities. □ **in front** at the front.

frontage *n.* the front of a building; land bordering this.

frontal *adj.* of or on the front.

frontbencher *n.* an MP entitled to sit on the front benches in Parliament, reserved for ministers and the Shadow Cabinet.

frontier *n.* a boundary between countries.

frontispiece *n.* an illustration opposite the title-page of a book.

front runner *n.* the contestant most likely to win.

frost *n.* small white ice crystals on grass etc.; a period cold enough for these to form. ● *v.* cover or be covered with frost.

frostbite *n.* injury to body tissues due to freezing. □ **frostbitten** *adj.*

frosted *adj.* (of glass) having its surface roughened to make it opaque.

frosting *n. Amer.* sugar icing.

frosty *adj.* (**frostier, frostiest**) **1** cold with frost; covered with frost. **2** unfriendly. □ **frostily** *adv.*, **frostiness** *n.*

froth *n.* & *v.* foam. □ **frothy** *adj.*

frown *v.* wrinkle one's brow in thought or disapproval. ● *n.* a frowning movement or look. □ **frown on** disapprove of.

frowsty (frow-sti) *adj.* (**frowstier, frowstiest**) stuffy, oppressive.

frowzy (frow-zi) *adj.* (also **frowsy**) (**frowzier, frowziest**) scruffy, dingy.

froze, frozen past & p.p. of **freeze**.

fructose *n.* a sugar found in honey and fruit.

frugal *adj.* economical; simple and costing little. □ **frugality** *n.*, **frugally** *adv.*

fruit *n.* **1** the seed-containing part of a plant; this used as food. **2** (**fruits**) the product of labour. ● *v.* produce fruit. □ **bear fruit** have good results.

fruiterer *n.* a shopkeeper selling fruit.

fruitful *adj.* producing much fruit or good results. □ **fruitfully** *adv.*, **fruitfulness** *n.*

fruition (froo-ish-ŏn) *n.* the fulfilment of a hope, plan, or project.

fruitless *adj.* producing little or no result. □ **fruitlessly** *adv.*, **fruitlessness** *n.*

fruit machine *n.* a coin-operated gambling machine.

fruity *adj.* (**fruitier, fruitiest**) **1** like or containing fruit; (of a voice) deep and rich. **2** *Brit. informal* sexually suggestive. □ **fruitiness** *n.*

frump *n.* a dowdy woman. □ **frumpish** *adj.*, **frumpy** *adj.*

frustrate *v.* prevent from achieving something or from being achieved. □ **frustration** *n.*

fry[1] *v.* (**fries, fried, frying**) cook or be cooked in very hot fat; be very hot. ● *n.* a fried meal. □ **fryer** *n.*

fry[2] *n.* (*pl.* **fry**) young fish. □ **small fry** unimportant or powerless people.

ft *abbr.* foot or feet (as a measure).

FT-SE *abbr.* Financial Times-Stock Exchange 100 share index.

fuchsia (few-shŭ) *n.* a plant with drooping flowers.

fuck *v. vulgar slang* have sexual intercourse (with). □ **fuck off** go away.

fucking *adj.* & *adv. vulgar slang* damned.

fuddle *v.* confuse or stupefy, esp. with alcoholic drink.

fuddy-duddy *adj.* & *n.* (*pl.* **fuddy-duddies**) *informal* (a person who is) old-fashioned.

fudge *n.* **1** a soft sweet made of milk, sugar, and butter. **2** a makeshift way of dealing with a problem. ● *v.* present or deal with in an inadequate and evasive way.

fuel *n.* material burnt as a source of energy; something that increases anger etc. ● *v.* (**fuelled, fuelling**; *Amer.* **fueled**) supply with fuel.

fug *n.* a stuffy atmosphere in a room etc. □ **fugginess** *n.*, **fuggy** *adj.*

fugitive *n.* a person who is fleeing or escaping. ● *adj.* passing or vanishing quickly.

fugue (fewg) *n.* a musical composition using repeated themes in increasingly complex patterns.

fulcrum (fuul-krŭm) *n.* (*pl.* **fulcra** or **fulcrums**) the point of support on which a lever pivots.

fulfil *v.* (*Amer.* **fulfill**) (**fulfilled, fulfilling**) accomplish, carry out (a task); satisfy, do what is required by (a contract etc.). □ **fulfil one-**

self develop and use one's abilities fully. ▫ **fulfilment** *n.*

full *adj.* **1** holding or containing as much as is possible; having a lot of something; obsessed with something. **2** complete. **3** plump; (of a garment) using much material in folds or gathers; (of a tone) deep and mellow. ● *adv.* directly; very. ▫ **fully** *adv.*, **fullness** *n.*

full-back *n.* (in football etc.) a defensive player positioned near the goal.

full-blooded *adj.* vigorous, hearty.

full-blown *adj.* fully developed.

full moon *n.* the moon with the whole disc illuminated.

full-scale *adj.* (of a model etc.) the same size as what it represents.

full stop *n.* a dot used as a punctuation mark at the end of a sentence or abbreviation; a complete stop.

fulminate *v.* protest loudly and bitterly. ▫ **fulmination** *n.*

fulsome *adj.* excessively flattering.

▪ **Usage** *Fulsome* is sometimes wrongly used to mean 'generous', as in *fulsome praise*, or 'generous with praise', as in *a fulsome tribute*.

fumble *v.* use one's hands clumsily; grope about.

fume *n.* pungent smoke or vapour. ● *v.* **1** emit fumes; subject to fumes. **2** be very angry.

fumigate *v.* disinfect with chemical fumes. ▫ **fumigation** *n.*, **fumigator** *n.*

fun *n.* light-hearted amusement. ▫ **make fun of** cause people to laugh at.

function *n.* **1** the special activity or purpose of a person or thing. **2** an important ceremony. **3** (in mathematics) a relation involving variables; a quantity whose value depends on varying values of others. ● *v.* perform a function; work, operate.

functional *adj.* of uses or purposes; practical, not decorative; working, operating. ▫ **functionally** *adv.*

functionary *n.* (*pl.* **-ies**) an official.

fund *n.* a sum of money for a special purpose; (**funds**) financial resources; a stock, a supply. ● *v.* provide with money.

fundamental *adj.* basic; essential. ● *n.* a fundamental fact or principle. ▫ **fundamentally** *adv.*

fundamentalist *n.* a person who upholds a strict or literal interpretation of traditional religious beliefs. ▫ **fundamentalism** *n.*

fundholder *n.* a medical practice controlling its own budget.

funeral *n.* a ceremony of burial or cremation.

funerary *adj.* of or used for a burial or funeral.

funereal *adj.* mournful, dismal.

funfair *n.* a fair consisting of amusements and sideshows.

fungicide *n.* a substance that kills fungus. ▫ **fungicidal** *adj.*

fungus *n.* (*pl.* **fungi**) a plant without green colouring matter (e.g. a mushroom or mould). ▫ **fungal** *adj.*, **fungous** *adj.*

funicular (fyoo-**nik**-guu-lŭ) *adj.* (of a railway) operating by cable up and down a mountainside.

funk *n. informal* dance music with a heavy rhythmical beat. ▫ **funky** *adj.*

funnel *n.* **1** a tube with a wide top for pouring liquid into small openings. **2** a chimney on a steam engine or ship. ● *v.* (**funnelled, funnelling**; *Amer.* **funneled**) guide (as) through a funnel.

funny *adj.* (**funnier, funniest**) **1** causing amusement. **2** puzzling, odd. ▫ **funnily** *adv.*

funny bone *n. informal* the part of the elbow where a very sensitive nerve passes.

fur *n.* **1** the short fine hair of certain animals; a skin with this used for clothing. **2** a coating on the inside of a kettle etc. ● *v.* (**furred, furring**) cover or become covered with fur.

furbish *v.* clean up; renovate.

furious *adj.* very angry; intense, violent. □ **furiously** *adv.*

furl *v.* roll up and fasten (a piece of fabric).

furlong *n.* an eighth of a mile.

furlough (fer-loh) *n.* leave of absence.

furnace *n.* an enclosed fireplace for intense heating or smelting.

furnish *v.* **1** equip with furniture. **2** supply (someone) with (something).

furnishings *n.pl.* furniture and fitments etc.

furniture *n.* movable articles (e.g. chairs, beds) for use in a room.

furore (few-ror-i) *n.* (*Amer.* **furor**) an outbreak of public anger or excitement.

furrier (fu-ri-ĕ) *n.* a person who deals in furs.

furrow *n.* a long cut in the ground; a groove. ● *v.* make furrows in.

furry *adj.* (**furrier, furriest**) like fur; covered with fur. □ **furriness** *n.*

further *adv.* & *adj.* (also **farther**) **1** at, to, or over a greater distance; more distant. **2** to a greater extent. **3** additional(ly). ● *v.* help the progress of.

furtherance *n.* assistance, advancement.

further education *n.* education provided for persons above school age but usu. below degree level.

furthermore *adv.* moreover.

furthest (also **farthest**) *adj.* most distant. ● *adv.* at, to, or by the greatest distance.

furtive *adj.* stealthy, secretive. □ **furtively** *adv.*, **furtiveness** *n.*

fury *n.* (*pl.* **-ies**) wild anger, rage; violence.

furze *n.* gorse.

fuse *v.* **1** blend (metals etc.); become blended; unite. **2** *Brit.* (of an electrical appliance) stop working when a fuse melts. **3** fit (an appliance) with a fuse. ● *n.* **1** a strip of wire placed in an electric circuit to melt and interrupt the current when the circuit is overloaded. **2** (also **fuze**) a length of easily burnt material for igniting a bomb or explosive. □ **fusibility** *n.*, **fusible** *adj.*

fuselage *n.* the body of an aeroplane.

fusilier (fyoo-zi-leer) *n.* a soldier of certain regiments.

fusillade *n.* a continuous discharge of firearms; an outburst of criticism etc.

fusion *n.* fusing; the union of atomic nuclei, with release of energy.

fuss *n.* unnecessary excitement or activity; a vigorous protest. ● *v.* show excessive concern; move about restlessly; disturb.

fussy *adj.* (**fussier, fussiest**) **1** hard to please. **2** with much unnecessary detail or decoration. □ **fussily** *adv.*, **fussiness** *n.*

fustian *n.* **1** thick twilled cotton cloth. **2** pompous language.

fusty *adj.* (**fustier, fustiest**) **1** smelling stale and stuffy. **2** old-fashioned. □ **fustiness** *n.*

futile *adj.* pointless, useless. □ **futilely** *adv.*, **futility** *n.*

futon (foo-ton) *n.* a Japanese quilted mattress laid on the floor for use as a bed; this with a wooden frame convertible into a sofa.

future *n.* **1** time still to come; what may happen then. **2** a prospect of success. **3** (**futures**) goods or shares bought at an agreed price but paid for later. ● *adj.* of time to come. □ **in future** from now on.

futuristic *adj.* with very modern technology or design. □ **futuristically** *adv.*

fuze var. of **fuse** *n.* (*sense* 2).

fuzz *n.* **1** a fluffy or frizzy mass; a blur. **2** *informal* the police.

fuzzy *adj.* (**fuzzier, fuzziest**) **1** fluffy or frizzy. **2** indistinct. □ **fuzzily** *adv.*, **fuzziness** *n.*

G *abbr.* giga-; gauss.

g *abbr.* gram(s); gravity.

Ga *symb.* gallium.

gabble *v.* talk quickly and indistinctly.

gable *n.* a triangular upper part of a wall, between sloping roofs. □ **gabled** *adj.*

gad *v.* (**gadded, gadding**) □ **gad about** go about idly in search of pleasure.

gadabout *n.* an idle pleasure-seeker.

gadfly *n.* (*pl.* **-flies**) a fly that bites cattle.

gadget *n.* a small mechanical device or tool. □ **gadgetry** *n.*

gadolinium *n.* a metallic element (symbol Gd).

Gaelic (gay-lik, ga-lik) *n.* the Celtic language of the Scots or Irish.

gaff *n.* a hooked stick for landing large fish.

gaffe *n.* an embarrassing blunder.

gaffer *n. informal* **1** a person in charge of others. **2** an old man.

gag *n.* **1** something put over a person's mouth to silence them; a surgical device to hold the mouth open. **2** a joke. ● *v.* (**gagged, gagging**) **1** put a gag on; deprive of freedom of speech. **2** retch.

gaga (gah-gah) *adj. informal* slightly mad; senile.

gage Amer. sp. of **gauge**.

gaggle *n.* a flock of geese; a disorderly group.

gaiety *n.* (*pl.* **-ies**) cheerfulness, bright appearance; merrymaking.

gaily *adv.* **1** cheerfully. **2** thoughtlessly.

gain *v.* **1** obtain, secure; acquire gradually; profit. **2** reach (a place). **3** increase in value. **4** (of a clock) become fast. ● *n.* an increase in wealth or value; something gained. □ **gain on** get nearer to (someone or something pursued).

gainful *adj.* profitable. □ **gainfully** *adv.*

gainsay *v.* (**gainsaid, gainsaying**) deny, contradict.

gait *n.* a manner of walking or running.

gaiter *n.* a covering for the lower leg.

gala (gah-lă) *n.* an occasion with special entertainments; a sports gathering.

galaxy *n.* (*pl.* **-ies**) a system of stars, esp. (**the Galaxy**) the one containing the sun and the earth. □ **galactic** *adj.*

gale *n.* a very strong wind; a noisy outburst.

gall (gawl) *n.* **1** boldness, impudence. **2** bile. **3** something very hurtful. **4** a sore made by rubbing; an abnormal growth on a plant. ● *v.* make sore by rubbing; annoy.

gallant *adj.* brave; chivalrous. □ **gallantly** *adv.*, **gallantry** *n.*

gall bladder *n.* an organ attached to the liver, storing bile.

galleon *n.* a large Spanish sailing ship of the 15th-17th centuries.

galleria (ga-lĕ-ree-ă) *n.* a group of small shops under one roof.

gallery *n.* (*pl.* **-ies**) **1** a building for displaying works of art. **2** a balcony in a theatre or hall. **3** a long room or passage.

galley *n.* (*pl.* **galleys**) **1** an ancient ship, usu. rowed by slaves. **2** a kitchen on a boat or aircraft. **3** (also **galley proof**) a printer's proof before division into pages.

Gallic *adj.* **1** French. **2** of ancient Gaul.

galling (gawl-ing) *adj.* annoying.

gallium *n.* a metallic element (symbol Ga).

gallivant *v. informal* go about looking for fun.

gallon *n.* a measure for liquids = 8 pints (4.546 litres, or 3.785 litres in the USA).

gallop *n.* a horse's fastest pace; a ride at this pace. ● *v.* (**galloped, galloping**) go at a gallop; go fast.

gallows *n.* a framework with a noose for hanging criminals.

gallstone *n.* a small hard mass forming in the gall bladder.

Gallup poll *n. trademark* an assessment of public opinion by questioning a sample group.

galore *adv.* in plenty.

galosh *n.* a rubber overshoe.

galvanize *v.* (also **-ise**) **1** stimulate into activity. **2** coat (iron or steel) with zinc.

galvanometer *n.* an instrument measuring electric current.

gambit *n.* an opening move; *Chess* an opening involving the sacrifice of a pawn.

gamble *v.* play games of chance for money; risk (money etc.) in hope of gain. ● *n.* an act of gambling; a risky undertaking. □ **gambler** *n.*

gambol *v.* (**gambolled, gambolling**; *Amer.* **gamboled**) jump about playfully.

game *n.* **1** a form of play or sport; a period of play with a closing score. **2** *informal* a secret plan: *what's your game?* **3** wild animals hunted for sport or food; their flesh as food. ● *adj.* **1** willing, eager. **2** *dated* lame. □ **gamely** *adv.*

gamekeeper *n.* a person employed to protect and breed game.

gamelan (gam-ĕ-lan) *n.* a SE Asian percussion orchestra.

gamesmanship *n.* the art of winning games by upsetting an opponent's confidence.

gamete *n.* a reproductive cell.

gamine (ga-**meen**) *n.* a girl with mischievous or boyish charm.

gamma *n.* the third letter of the Greek alphabet (Γ, γ); a thirdclass mark.

gammon *n.* cured or smoked ham.

gammy *adj. informal* lame, injured.

gamut (gam-ŭt) *n.* the whole range or scope: *the whole gamut of emotions.*

gamy *adj.* (**gamier, gamiest**) smelling or tasting of game kept till it is high.

gander *n.* **1** a male goose. **2** *informal* a look, a glance.

gang *n.* an organized group, esp. of criminals or workers. □ **gang up (on)** form a group (to intimidate someone).

gangling *adj.* tall and awkward.

ganglion *n.* (*pl.* **ganglia** or **ganglions**) **1** a group of nerve cells. **2** a cyst on a tendon.

gangplank *n.* a plank for walking to or from a boat.

gang rape *n.* the rape of one person by several men.

gangrene *n.* decay of body tissue. □ **gangrenous** *adj.*

gangster *n.* a member of a gang of violent criminals.

gangway *n.* a passage, esp. between rows of seats; a movable bridge from a ship to land.

gannet *n.* a large seabird; *informal* a greedy person.

gantry *n.* (*pl.* **-ies**) an overhead framework supporting railway signals, road signs, a crane etc.

gaol etc. var. of **jail** etc.

gap *n.* **1** a space, an opening; an interval. **2** a deficiency; a wide difference. □ **gappy** *adj.*

gape *v.* open one's mouth wide; be wide open.

garage *n.* a building for storing a vehicle; an establishment selling petrol or repairing and selling vehicles.

garb *n.* clothing. ● *v.* clothe.

garbage *n.* rubbish.

garbled *adj.* (of a message or story) distorted or confused.

garden *n.* a piece of cultivated ground by a house; (**gardens**) ornamental public grounds. ● *v.* tend a garden. □ **gardener** *n.*

gargantuan *adj.* gigantic.

gargle *v.* wash the throat with liquid held there by breathing out through it. ● *n.* an act of gargling; a liquid for this.

gargoyle *n.* a waterspout in the form of a grotesque carved face on a building.

garish (gair-ish) *adj.* too bright and harsh. □ **garishly** *adv.*

garland *n.* a wreath of flowers as a decoration. ● *v.* decorate with garlands.

garlic *n.* an onion-like plant. □ **garlicky** *adj.*

garment *n.* a piece of clothing.

garner *v.* gather, collect.

garnet *n.* a red semi-precious stone.

garnish *v.* decorate (food). ● *n.* something used for garnishing.

garotte var. of garrotte.

garret *n.* an attic.

garrison *n.* troops stationed in a town or fort; the building they occupy. ● *v.* guard (a town etc) with a garrison.

garrotte *n.* (also **garotte**; *Amer.* **garrote**) a wire or a metal collar used to strangle a victim. ● *v.* strangle with this.

garrulous *adj.* talkative. □ **garrulously** *adv.*, **garrulousness** *n.*

garter *n.* a band worn round the leg to keep up a stocking; (**the Garter**) the highest order of English knighthood.

gas *n.* (*pl.* **gases**) **1** an airlike substance (not a solid or liquid); such a substance used as fuel. **2** *Amer.* petrol. ● *v.* (**gassed, gassing**) **1** attack or kill with poisonous gas. **2** *informal* talk at length.

gas chamber *n.* a room filled with poisonous gas to kill people.

gas mask *n.* a device worn over the face as protection against poisonous gas.

gaseous (gay-see-ŭs, ga-see-ŭs) *adj.* of or like a gas.

gash *n.* a long deep cut. ● *v.* make a gash in.

gasify *v.* (**gasified, gasifying**) change into gas.

gasket *n.* a piece of rubber etc. sealing a joint between metal surfaces. □ **blow a gasket** *informal* lose one's temper.

gasoline *n. Amer.* petrol.

gasp *v.* draw in breath sharply; speak breathlessly. ● *n.* a sharp intake of breath.

gastric *adj.* of the stomach.

gastroenteritis *n.* inflammation of the stomach and intestines.

gastropod *n.* a mollusc, such as a snail, that moves by means of a single muscular foot.

gate *n.* **1** a movable barrier in a wall or fence; an entrance. **2** the number of spectators paying to attend a sporting event; the amount of money taken.

-gate *comb. form* denoting a scandal involving deception and concealment.

gateau (gat-oh) *n.* (*pl.* **gateaux** or **gateaus**) a large rich cream cake.

gatecrash *v.* go to (a private party) uninvited. □ **gatecrasher** *n.*

gateway *n.* an opening closed by a gate; a means of entry or access.

gather *v.* **1** come or bring together; collect; pick up; summon up: *gather strength.* **2** conclude, infer. **3** draw (fabric) together in folds by running a thread through it. ● *n.* a small fold in a garment.

gathering *n.* people assembled.

GATT *abbr.* General Agreement on Tariffs and Trade, an international trade treaty.

gauche (gohsh) *adj.* socially awkward. □ **gaucherie** *n.*

gaucho (gow-choh) *n.* (*pl.* **gauchos**) a South American cowboy.

gaudy (gaw-di) *adj.* (**gaudier, gaudiest**) showy or bright, but tasteless. □ **gaudily** *adv.*, **gaudiness** *n.*

gauge (gayj) *n.* (*Amer.* **gage**) **1** a measuring device; a standard measure of thickness etc. **2** the distance between the rails of a railway track. ● *v.* estimate; measure.

gaunt (gawnt) *adj.* lean and haggard; grim, desolate.

gauntlet *n.* a glove with a long wide cuff. □ **run the gauntlet** be exposed to something dangerous or unpleasant.

gauss (gowss) *n.* (*pl.* **gauss**) a unit of magnetic flux density.

gauze (gawz) *n.* thin transparent fabric; fine wire mesh. □ **gauzy** *adj.*

gave past of **give**.

gavel *n.* a mallet used by an auctioneer or chairman to call for attention.

gawky *adj.* (**gawkier, gawkiest**) awkward and ungainly.

gay *adj.* **1** homosexual. **2** merry, light-hearted; brightly coloured. ● *n.* a homosexual person. □ **gayness** *n.*

gaze *v.* look long and steadily. ● *n.* a long steady look.

gazebo (gă-zee-boh) *n.* (*pl.* **gazebos**) a summer house with a wide view.

gazelle *n.* a small antelope.

gazette *n.* an official journal of an institution; the title of some newspapers.

gazetteer *n.* an index of places, rivers, mountains, etc.

gazump *v.* make a higher offer for a property than (someone whose offer had been accepted).

GB *abbr.* Great Britain.

Gb *abbr.* gigabyte.

GBH *abbr.* grievous bodily harm.

GCE *abbr.* General Certificate of Education.

GCSE *abbr.* General Certificate of Secondary Education.

Gd *abbr.* gadolinium.

GDP *abbr.* gross domestic product.

Ge *symb.* germanium.

gear *n.* **1** a set of toothed wheels working together to change the speed of machinery; a particular adjustment of these: *top gear*. **2** *informal* equipment; belongings, clothes. ● *v.* **1** design or adjust the gears in (a machine). **2** intend or direct to a particular purpose. □ **in gear** with the gear mechanism engaged.

gearbox *n.* a case enclosing a gear mechanism.

gecko *n.* (*pl.* **geckos**) a tropical lizard.

geese pl. of **goose**.

Geiger counter (gy-ger) *n.* a device for measuring radioactivity.

geisha (gay-shă) *n.* a Japanese hostess trained to entertain men.

gel (jel) *n.* a jelly-like substance. ● *v.* set, become firm.

gelatin *n.* (also **gelatine**) a clear substance made by boiling bones and used in making jelly etc. □ **gelatinous** *adj.*

geld *v.* castrate.

gelding *n.* a castrated horse.

gelignite *n.* an explosive containing nitroglycerine.

gem *n.* a precious stone; something of great beauty or excellence.

gender *n.* **1** being male or female. **2** the classification of nouns as masculine, feminine, or neuter.

gene *n.* each of the factors controlling heredity, carried by a chromosome.

genealogy *n.* (*pl.* **-ies**) a line of descent; the study of family pedigrees. □ **genealogical** *adj.*, **genealogist** *n.*

genera pl. of **genus**.

general *adj.* **1** of or involving all or most parts, things, or people; not detailed or specific. **2** (in titles) chief. ● *n.* an army officer next below field marshal. □ **in general** **1** mostly, with few exceptions. **2** as a whole, all together: *things in general*. □ **generally** *adv.*

general election *n.* an election of parliamentary representatives from the whole country.

generality *n.* (*pl.* **-ies**) **1** a general statement; being general. **2** the majority.

generalize *v.* (also **-ise**) **1** speak in general terms. **2** make generally available. □ **generalization** *n.*

general practitioner *n.* a community doctor treating cases of all kinds.

generate *v.* bring into existence, produce.

generation *n.* **1** all the people born at roughly the same time; one stage in the descent of a family; a period of about 30 years. **2** generating. □ **generational** *adj.*

generator *n.* a machine converting mechanical energy into electricity.

generic (jĕn-e-rik) *adj.* of a whole genus or group. □ **generically** *adv.*

generous *adj.* giving freely; large, plentiful. □ **generosity** *n.*, **generously** *adv.*

genesis *n.* a beginning or origin.

genetic *adj.* of genes or genetics; of origin. ● *n.* (**genetics**) the science of heredity. □ **genetically** *adv.*, **geneticist** *n.*

genetic engineering *n.* manipulation of DNA to change hereditary features.

genetic fingerprinting *n.* identifying individuals by their DNA patterns.

genial (jee-ni-ăl) *adj.* kindly and cheerful; (of climate etc.) pleasantly mild. □ **geniality** *n.*, **genially** *adv.*

genie *n.* (*pl.* **genii**) a spirit in Arabian folk lore.

genital *adj.* of animal reproduction or sex organs. ● *n.pl.* (**genitals**) (also **genitalia**) the external sex organs.

genitive *n.* the grammatical case expressing possession or source.

genius *n.* (*pl.* **geniuses**) exceptionally great intellectual or creative power; a person with this.

genocide *n.* deliberate extermination of a race of people.

genre (*zh*ahnr) *n.* a style of art or literature.

genteel *adj.* polite and refined, often affectedly so. □ **genteelly** *adv.*, **gentility** *n.*

gentian (jen-shăn) *n.* an alpine plant with deep blue flowers.

Gentile *n.* a non-Jewish person.

gentle *adj.* kind and mild. (of climate etc.) moderate, not harsh. □ **gentleness** *n.*, **gently** *adv.*

gentleman *n.* (*pl.* **-men**) a well-mannered man; a man of good social position. □ **gentlemanly** *adj.*

gentrify *v.* (**gentrified, gentrifying**) alter (an area) to conform to middle-class tastes.

gentry *n.* people next below nobility.

genuflect *v.* bend the knee and lower the body, esp. in worship.

genuine *adj.* really what it is said to be. □ **genuinely** *adv.*, **genuineness** *n.*

genus *n.* (*pl.* **genera**) a group of similar animals or plants, usu. containing several species; a kind.

geocentric *adj.* having the earth as a centre; as viewed from the earth's centre.

geode (jee-ohd) *n.* a cavity lined with crystals; a rock containing this.

geodesy (jee-o-de-si) *n.* the study of the earth's shape and size.

geography *n.* the study of the earth's physical features, climate, etc.; the features and arrangement of a place. □ **geographer** *n.*, **geographical** *adj.*, **geographically** *adv.*

geology *n.* the study of the earth's structure; the rocks etc. of a district. □ **geological** *adj.*, **geologically** *adv.*, **geologist** *n.*

geometry *n.* the branch of mathematics dealing with lines, angles, surfaces, and solids. □ **geometric** *adj.*, **geometrical** *adj.*, **geometrically** *adv.*

Georgian *adj.* of the time of the Georges, kings of England, esp. 1714–1830.

geranium *n.* a cultivated flowering plant.

gerbil *n.* (also **jerbil**) a rodent with long hind legs, often kept as a pet.

geriatric *adj.* of old people. ● *n.* an old person; (**geriatrics**) the branch of medicine dealing with the diseases and care of old people.

germ *n.* **1** a micro-organism causing disease. **2** a portion of an organism capable of developing into a new organism; a basis from which a thing may develop.

German *adj.* & *n.* (a native, the language) of Germany.

germane *adj.* relevant.

Germanic *adj.* **1** of the Scandinavians, Anglo-Saxons, or Germans. **2** having characteristics commonly associated with Germans.

germanium *n.* a semi-metallic element (symbol Ge).

German measles *n.* (also **rubella**) a disease like mild measles.

germinate *v.* begin or cause to grow. □ **germination** *n.*

gerontology *n.* the study of ageing.

gerrymander *v.* arrange boundaries of (a constituency) to gain unfair electoral advantage.

gerund *n. Grammar* a verbal noun (ending in *-ing* in English).

Gestapo *n.* the German secret police of the Nazi regime.

gestation *n.* the period when a foetus is developing in the womb.

gesticulate *v.* make expressive movements with the hands and arms. □ **gesticulation** *n.*

gesture *n.* **1** a movement designed to convey a meaning. **2** something done to display good intentions etc., with no practical value. ● *v.* make a gesture.

get *v.* (**got, getting**) **1** come to possess; receive; succeed in attaining. **2** fetch. **3** experience (pain etc.); catch (a disease). **4** bring or come into a specified state; arrive or bring somewhere. **5** persuade, induce, or order: *get him to come.* **6** capture. **7** *informal* understand. **8** *informal* annoy. □ **get by** manage to survive. **get off** be acquitted. **get on 1** make progress. **2** be friendly. **3** *informal* grow old. **get over** recover from. **get round 1** overcome (a difficulty). **2** persuade. **get up 1** get out of bed; stand up. **2** organize, arrange. **get up to** *Brit. informal* be involved in (something secret or disreputable).

getaway *n.* an escape after a crime.

get-together *n.* a social gathering.

get-up *n. informal* an outfit.

geyser (gee-zer) *n.* **1** a spring spouting hot water or steam. **2** a water heater.

ghastly *adj.* (**ghastlier, ghastliest**) **1** causing horror; *informal* very unpleasant. **2** very pale. □ **ghastliness** *n.*

ghee (gee) *n.* clarified butter used in Indian cooking.

gherkin *n.* a small pickled cucumber.

ghetto *n.* (*pl.* **ghettos**) an area in which members of a minority racial etc. group are segregated.

ghetto blaster *n.* a large portable stereo radio etc.

ghost *n.* an apparition of a dead person; a faint trace. ● *v.* write as a ghost writer.

ghostly *adj.* like a ghost; eerie. □ **ghostliness** *n.*

ghost writer *n.* a person who writes a book etc. for another to pass off as his or her own.

ghoul (gool) *n.* an evil spirit said to rob graves and eat corpses; a person morbidly interested in death and injury. □ **ghoulish** *adj.*

giant *n.* (in fairy tales) a being of superhuman size; an abnormally large person, animal, or thing; a person of outstanding ability. ● *adj.* very large.

gibber *v.* make meaningless sounds in shock or terror.

gibberish *n.* unintelligible talk; nonsense.

gibbet *n.* a gallows.

gibbon *n.* a long-armed ape.

gibe *v.* (also **jibe**) jeer. ● *n.* a jeering remark.

giblets (**jib**-lits) *n.pl.* the liver, heart, etc., of a fowl.

giddy *adj.* (**giddier, giddiest**) having or causing the feeling that everything is spinning; excitable, flighty. ▫ **giddily** *adv.*, **giddiness** *n.*

gift *n.* **1** something given or received without payment; a very easy task. **2** a natural talent.

gifted *adj.* having great natural ability.

gig (gig) *n.* **1** a light two-wheeled horse-drawn carriage. **2** *informal* a live performance by popular or jazz musicians.

giga- *comb. form* one thousand million, 10^9.

gigantic *adj.* very large.

giggle *v.* laugh quietly. ● *n.* such a laugh. ▫ **giggly** *adj.*

gigolo (jig-ŏ-loh) *n.* (*pl.* **gigolos**) a man paid by a woman to be her escort or lover.

gild *v.* cover with a thin layer of gold or gold paint. ● *n.* var. of **guild**.

gill (jil) *n.* one-quarter of a pint.

gills (gilz) *n.* **1** the organ with which a fish breathes. **2** the vertical plates on the underside of a mushroom.

gilt *adj.* gilded. ● *n.* **1** gold leaf or paint used in gilding. **2** a gilt-edged investment.

gilt-edged *adj.* (of an investment etc.) very safe.

gimbals (jim-bălz) *n.pl.* a contrivance of rings to keep instruments horizontal on a ship.

gimcrack (jim-krak) *adj.* cheap and poorly made.

gimlet (gim-lit) *n.* a small tool with a screw-like tip for boring holes.

gimmick *n.* a trick or device to attract attention. ▫ **gimmicky** *adj.*

gin *n.* an alcoholic spirit flavoured with juniper berries.

ginger *n.* **1** a hot-tasting root used as a spice. **2** spirit; excitement. ● *adj.* reddish yellow in colour.

gingerbread *n.* ginger-flavoured cake.

ginger group *n.* a group urging a more active policy.

gingerly *adj.* & *adv.* cautious(ly).

gingham (ging-ăm) *n.* cotton fabric with a checked or striped pattern.

gingivitis (jin-ji-vy-tiss) *n.* inflammation of the gums.

ginseng (jin-seng) *n.* a medicinal plant with a fragrant root.

gipsy var. of **gypsy**.

giraffe *n.* a long-necked African animal.

gird *v. literary* encircle with a belt or band.

girder *n.* a metal beam supporting a structure.

girdle *n.* a belt; an elastic corset; something surrounding something else; *Anatomy* a ring of bones. ● *v.* surround.

girl *n.* a female child; a young woman. ▫ **girlhood** *n.*

girlfriend *n.* a female friend; a woman with whom someone has a romantic relationship.

giro (jy-roh) *n.* (*pl.* **giros**) a banking system in which payment can be made by transferring credit from one account to another; a cheque or payment made by this.

girth *n.* the measurement round something, esp. someone's stomach; a band under a horse's belly holding a saddle in place.

gist (jist) *n.* the essential points or general sense of a speech etc.

gîte (*zh*eet) *n.* (in France) a holiday cottage.

give *v.* (**gave, given, giving**) **1** hand over; cause (someone) to receive (something); devote to a cause; cause (someone) to experience (something); make available. **2** do; utter. **3** yield under pressure, be flexible. ● *n.* elasticity. ▫ **give and take** mutual compromise. **give away** reveal unintentionally. **give in** acknowledge defeat. **give out 1** announce; distribute. **2** be used up or exhausted. **give over** *informal* cease. **give up** hand over; sacrifice; abandon hope or an effort. **give way** yield; allow other traffic to go first. ▫ **giver** *n.*

giveaway *n.* **1** a free gift. **2** *informal* an unintentional disclosure.

given p.p. of **give**. ● *adj.* **1** specified. **2** having a tendency: *given to swearing.* ● *prep.* considering, taking into account: *given the circumstances.* ● *n.* something already existing, known, or assumed.

given name *n.* a first name.

gizmo *n.* (*pl.* **gizmos**) *informal* a gadget.

gizzard *n.* a bird's second stomach, in which food is ground.

glacé (gla-say) *adj.* preserved in sugar.

glacial (glay-see-ăl) *adj.* of or from glaciers; icy, very cold. ◻ **glacially** *adv.*

glaciated *adj.* covered with or affected by a glacier. ◻ **glaciation** *n.*

glacier (gla-see-ĕ, glay-see-ĕ) *n.* a mass or river of ice moving very slowly.

glad *adj.* pleased, joyful. ◻ **gladly** *adv.*, **gladness** *n.*

gladden *v.* make glad.

glade *n.* an open space in a forest.

gladiator *n.* a man trained to fight at public shows in ancient Rome. ◻ **gladiatorial** *adj.*

glamour *n.* (*Amer.* **glamor**) alluring beauty; attractive exciting qualities. ◻ **glamorize** *v.*, **glamorous** *adj.*, **glamorously** *adv.*

glance *v.* **1** look briefly. **2** strike something and bounce off at an angle; (of light) reflect off a surface. ● *n.* a brief look.

gland *n.* an organ that secretes substances to be used or expelled by the body. ◻ **glandular** *adj.*

glare *v.* stare angrily or fiercely; shine with a harsh dazzling light. ● *n.* a fierce stare; a harsh light.

glaring *adj.* conspicuous.

glasnost (glaz-nost) *n.* a policy of more openness in news reporting etc.

glass *n.* **1** a hard brittle transparent substance; a drinking container made of this; such containers collectively; a mirror; a barometer. **2** (**glasses**) spectacles; binoculars. ◻ **glassful** *n.* **glassy** *adj.*

glass ceiling *n.* an unacknowledged barrier to advancement in a profession.

glasshouse *n.* **1** a greenhouse. **2** *informal* a military prison.

glaucoma (glow-**koh**-mă) *n.* a condition causing gradual loss of sight.

glaze *v.* **1** fit or cover with glass. **2** coat with a glossy surface. **3** (of eyes etc.) lose brightness and animation. ● *n.* a shiny surface or coating. ◻ **glazed** *adj.*

glazier *n.* a person whose job is to fit glass in windows.

gleam *n.* a briefly shining light; a brief or faint show of a quality. ● *v.* shine brightly; reflect light.

glean *v.* pick up (grain left by harvesters); collect, gather. ◻ **gleaner** *n.*, **gleanings** *n.pl.*

glebe *n. hist.* a portion of land allocated to, and providing revenue for, a clergyman.

glee *n.* lively or triumphant joy. ◻ **gleeful** *adj.*, **gleefully** *adv.*

glen *n.* a narrow valley.

glib *adj.* (**glibber, glibbest**) articulate but insincere or superficial.

glide *v.* move smoothly; fly in a glider or aircraft without engine power. ● *n.* a gliding movement.

glider *n.* an aeroplane with no engine.

glimmer *n.* a faint gleam. ● *v.* gleam faintly.

glimpse *n.* a brief view. ● *v.* catch a glimpse of.

glint *n.* a brief flash of light. ● *v.* send out a glint.

glisten *v.* shine like something wet.

glitch *n. informal* a malfunction; a setback.

glitter *v.* & *n.* sparkle.

glitterati (glit-tĕ-**rah**-tee) *n.pl. informal* rich famous people.

glitz *n. informal* superficial glamour and ostentation. ◻ **glitzy** *adj.*

gloaming *n. poetic* twilight.

gloat *v.* exult in one's own success or another's misfortune.

global *adj.* worldwide; of or affecting an entire group. □ **globally** *adv.*

global warming *n.* an increase in the temperature of the earth's atmosphere.

globe *n.* a ball-shaped object, esp. one with a map of the earth on it; the world.

globetrotter *n.* *informal* a person who travels widely. □ **globetrotting** *n.* & *adj.*

globular *adj.* globe-shaped.

globule *n.* a small round drop.

globulin *n.* a protein found in animal and plant tissue.

glockenspiel (glok-ĕn-shpeel) *n.* a musical instrument of metal bars or tubes struck by hammers.

gloom *n.* **1** semi-darkness. **2** depression, sadness. □ **gloomily** *adv.*, **gloomy** *adj.*

glorify *v.* (**glorified, glorifying**) **1** praise highly; worship. **2** make (something) seem grander than it is. □ **glorification** *n.*

glorious *adj.* having or bringing glory; beautiful, splendid. □ **gloriously** *adv.*

glory *n.* (*pl.* **-ies**) fame, honour, and praise; beauty, splendour; a source of fame and pride. ● *v.* take pride or pleasure in something.

gloss *n.* **1** a shine on a smooth surface. **2** a translation or explanation. □ **gloss over** try to conceal (a fault etc.). □ **glossily** *adv.*, **glossiness** *n.*, **glossy** *adj.*

glossary *n.* (*pl.* **-ies**) a list of technical or special words with definitions.

glottis *n.* the opening at the upper end of the windpipe between the vocal cords. □ **glottal** *adj.*

glove *n.* a covering for the hand with separate divisions for fingers and thumb.

glow *v.* send out light and heat without flame; have a warm or flushed look or colour; feel deep pleasure. ● *n.* a glowing state.

glower (glow-ĕ) *v.* scowl.

glow-worm *n.* a beetle that can give out a greenish light.

glucose *n.* a form of sugar found in fruit juice.

glue *n.* a sticky substance used for joining things. ● *v.* (**glued, gluing**) fasten with glue; attach closely. □ **gluey** *adj.*

glue-sniffing *n.* inhaling glue fumes for their narcotic effects.

glum *adj.* (**glummer, glummest**) sad and gloomy. □ **glumly** *adv.*, **glumness** *n.*

glut *v.* (**glutted, glutting**) supply or fill to excess. ● *n.* an excessive supply.

gluten *n.* a protein found in cereals.

glutinous *adj.* glue-like, sticky. □ **glutinously** *adv.*

glutton *n.* a greedy person; one who is eager for something. □ **gluttonous** *adj.* **gluttony** *n.*

glycerine (gli-sĕ-reen) *n.* (*Amer.* **glycerin**) a thick sweet liquid used in medicines etc.

glycerol *n.* = **glycerine**.

gm *abbr.* gram(s).

GMT *abbr.* Greenwich Mean Time.

gnarled *adj.* knobbly; twisted and misshapen.

gnash *v.* (of teeth) strike together; grind (one's teeth).

gnat (nat) *n.* a small biting fly.

gnaw *v.* bite persistently at something hard.

gnome *n.* a dwarf in fairy tales.

gnomic (**noh**-mik) *adj.* expressed in or using brief maxims.

gnomon (**noh**-mon) *n.* the rod of a sundial.

gnostic (**noss**-tik) *adj.* of or having mystical knowledge.

GNP *abbr.* gross national product.

gnu (noo) *n.* a large heavy antelope.

GNVQ *abbr.* General National Vocational Qualification.

go *v.* (**goes, went, gone, going**) **1** move, travel. **2** depart; (of time) pass. **3** pass into a specified state; proceed in a specified way: *the party went well.* **4** be regularly kept in a particular place; fit into a space. **5** (of a machine etc.) function; (of a bell etc.) sound. **6** cease functioning; die. **7** (of a story etc.) have a particular content. ● *n.* (*pl.* **goes**) **1** an attempt; a turn to do something. **2** energy. □ **go back on** fail to keep (a promise). **go for 1** like, be attracted by; choose. **2** *informal* attack. **go into** study, investigate. **go off 1** explode. **2** (of food etc.) become stale or bad. **3** *informal* begin to dislike. **go on 1** continue. **2** happen. **go out** be extinguished. **go round** be enough for everyone. **go under** collapse, fail. **go with** harmonize with. **make a go of** *informal* be successful in. **on the go** *informal* active. **to go** *Amer.* (of food) to be taken away for eating.

goad *n.* a pointed stick for driving cattle; a stimulus to activity. ● *v.* provoke to action.

go-ahead *informal n.* permission to proceed. ● *adj.* enterprising.

goal *n.* **1** a structure or area into which players send the ball to score a point in certain games; a point scored. **2** something aimed at; an ambition.

goalie *n. informal* a goalkeeper.

goalkeeper *n.* a player whose job is to keep the ball out of the goal.

goalpost *n.* either of the posts marking the limit of a goal. □ **move the goalposts** unfairly alter conditions or rules of a procedure once it has started.

goat *n.* a horned animal, sometimes domesticated for milk etc. □ **get someone's goat** *informal* irritate someone.

go-between *n.* a messenger or negotiator.

gobble *v.* **1** eat quickly and greedily. **2** make a throaty sound like a turkeycock.

gobbledegook *n. informal* unintelligible language.

goblet *n.* a drinking glass with a stem and a foot.

goblin *n.* a mischievous ugly elf.

go-cart var. of **go-kart**.

god *n.* a superhuman being worshipped as having power over nature and human affairs; a person or thing greatly admired or adored; (**God**) the creator and ruler of the universe in Christian, Jewish, and Muslim teaching.

godchild *n.* (*pl.* **-children**) a child in relation to its godparent(s).

god-daughter *n.* a female godchild.

goddess *n.* a female deity.

godfather *n.* **1** a male godparent. **2** a head of an illegal organization, esp. the Máfia.

God-fearing *adj.* sincerely religious.

godforsaken *adj.* with no merit or attractiveness.

godhead *n.* divine nature; a deity.

godmother *n.* a female godparent.

godparent *n.* a person who represents a child at baptism and takes responsibility for its religious education.

godsend *n.* a very helpful thing, person, or event.

godson *n.* a male godchild.

go-getter *n. informal* an aggressively enterprising person.

goggle *v.* stare with wide-open eyes.

goggles *n.pl.* spectacles for protecting the eyes.

goitre (goy·ter) *n.* (*Amer.* **goiter**) an enlarged thyroid gland causing a swelling on the neck.

go-kart *n.* (also **go-cart**) a miniature racing car.

gold *n.* a chemical element (symbol Au); a yellow metal of high value; coins or articles made of this; its colour; a gold medal (awarded as first prize); something very valuable. ● *adj.* made of or coloured like gold.

golden *adj.* **1** gold. **2** precious, excellent; very happy: *golden days.* □ **golden boy** (or **girl**) a very popular or successful man (or woman).

golden handshake *n.* a generous cash payment given on redundancy or early retirement.

golden jubilee *n.* the 50th anniversary of a sovereign's reign.

golden wedding *n.* the 50th anniversary of a wedding.

goldfield *n.* an area where gold is mined.

goldfish *n.* (*pl.* **goldfish** or **goldfishes**) a small reddish carp kept in a bowl or pond.

gold leaf *n.* gold beaten into a very thin sheet.

gold rush *n.* a rush to a newly discovered goldfield.

goldsmith *n.* a person who makes gold articles.

gold standard *n.* something setting the standard of excellence for things of its type.

golf *n.* a game in which a ball is struck with clubs into a series of holes. □ **golfer** *n.*

golf course *n.* (also **golf links**) an area of land on which golf is played.

golliwog *n.* a black-faced soft doll with fuzzy hair.

gonad (**goh**-nad) *n.* an animal organ producing gametes.

gondola *n.* a boat with high pointed ends, used on canals in Venice.

gondolier *n.* a man who propels a gondola with a pole.

gone p.p. of **go**.

gong *n.* a metal plate that resounds when struck; *informal* a medal.

gonorrhoea (gon-ŏ-**ree**-ă) *n.* (*Amer.* **gonorrhea**) a venereal disease with a discharge from the genitals.

goo *n. informal* a sticky wet substance.

good *adj.* (**better**, **best**) **1** to be desired or approved of; pleasing, welcome. **2** having the right or necessary qualities; performing a particular function well; beneficial. **3** morally correct; kind; well-behaved. **4** (of food etc.) enjoyable. **5** valid. **6** complete, thorough: *a good wash.* **7** *informal* at least as many as: *a good twenty minutes.* ● *n.* **1** that which is morally right. **2** benefit, advantage. **3** (**goods**) movable property; articles for trade; items to be transported. □ **as good as** almost. **good at** talented at.

goodbye *int.* & *n.* an expression used when parting.

good-for-nothing *adj.* worthless. ● *n.* a worthless person.

Good Friday *n.* the Friday before Easter, commemorating the Crucifixion.

goodie var. of **goody.**

goodness *n.* the quality of being good; the wholesome or beneficial part of food.

goodwill *n.* friendly feeling; the established popularity of a business, treated as a saleable asset.

goody *n.* (also **goodie**) (*pl.* **-ies**) *informal* **1** a good person in a story etc. **2** something pleasant, esp. to eat.

goody-goody *n.* (*pl.* **goody-goodies**) *informal* a smugly virtuous person.

gooey *adj.* (**gooier, gooiest**) *informal* wet and sticky.

goose *n.* (*pl.* **geese**) a web-footed bird larger than a duck; the female of this.

gooseberry *n.* (*pl.* **-ies**) **1** an edible berry growing on a thorny bush. **2** *informal* an unwelcome third person in the company of two lovers.

goose-flesh *n.* (also **goose pimples**) bristling bumpy skin caused by cold or fright.

goose-step *v.* march without bending the knees. ● *n.* this style of marching.

gopher *n.* **1** an American burrowing rodent. **2** *Computing* a system for searching for information on the Internet.

gore *n.* **1** blood from a wound. **2** a triangular or tapering section of a skirt or sail. ● *v.* pierce with a horn or tusk.

gorge *n.* a narrow steep-sided valley. ● *v.* eat greedily.

gorgeous *adj.* beautiful; richly coloured or decorated; *informal* very pleasant or attractive. ▫ **gorgeously** *adv.*

gorgon *n.* a mythical monster able to turn people into stone; an intimidating woman.

gorilla *n.* a large powerful ape.

gorse *n.* a wild evergreen thorny shrub with yellow flowers.

gory *adj.* (**gorier, goriest**) covered with blood; involving bloodshed.

gosling *n.* a young goose.

go-slow *n.* working slowly as a protest.

gospel *n.* **1** the teachings of Christ; (**Gospel**) any of the first four books of the New Testament. **2** something regarded as definitely true.

gossamer *n.* a fine piece of cobweb.

gossip *n.* casual talk about other people's affairs; a person fond of such talk. ● *v.* (**gossiped, gossiping**) engage in gossip.

got past & p.p. of **get**.

Gothic *adj.* **1** of an architectural style of the 12th-16th centuries, with pointed arches. **2** (of a novel etc.) in a horrific style popular in the 18th-19th centuries.

gotten *Amer.* = **got**.

gouache (goo-**ash**, gwash) *n.* painting with opaque pigments in water thickened with a gluey substance.

gouge (gowj, gooj) *n.* a chisel with a concave blade. ● *v.* cut out with a gouge; scoop or force out.

goulash *n.* a stew of meat and vegetables, seasoned with paprika.

gourd *n.* a fleshy fruit of a climbing plant; a container made from its dried rind.

gourmand (**goor**-mond) *n.* a food lover; a glutton.

gourmet (**goor**-may) *n.* a connoisseur of good food and drink.

gout *n.* a disease causing inflammation of the joints.

govern *v.* conduct the policy etc. of (a country, its people), rule; control, influence, direct. ▫ **governable** *adj.*, **governor** *n.*

governance *n.* governing, control.

governess *n.* a woman employed to teach children in a private household.

government *n.* the governing body of a state; the system by which a state is governed. ▫ **governmental** *adj.*

gown *n.* a long dress; a loose overgarment; an official robe.

GP *abbr.* general practitioner.

grab *v.* (**grabbed, grabbing**) grasp suddenly; take greedily. ● *n.* a sudden clutch or attempt to seize something; a mechanical device for gripping things.

grace *n.* **1** elegance of movement. **2** courtesy; an attractive manner. **3** mercy; undeserved favour, esp. from God. **4** a short prayer of thanks for a meal. ● *v.* honour (a place etc.) with one's presence; be an ornament to.

graceful *adj.* **1** moving elegantly. **2** polite, charming. ▫ **gracefully** *adv.*

graceless *adj.* inelegant.

gracious *adj.* kind and pleasant, esp. towards inferiors. ▫ **graciously** *adv.*, **graciousness** *n.*

gradation *n.* a series of changes; a stage in such a series.

grade *n.* **1** a level of rank or quality; a mark indicating standard of work. **2** *Amer.* a class in school. ● *v.* arrange in grades; assign a grade to. ▫ **make the grade** *informal* be successful.

gradient *n.* a slope; the angle of a slope.

gradual *adj.* taking place by degrees, not sudden. ▫ **gradually** *adv.*

graduate *n.* (**grad**-yoo-ăt) a person who has a university degree. ● *v.* (**grad**-yoo-ayt) **1** obtain a university degree. **2** arrange in a series or according to a scale; change (colour etc.) by small stages. □ **graduation** *n.*

graffiti *n.pl.* words or drawings scribbled or sprayed on a wall.

graft *n.* **1** a plant shoot fixed into a cut in another plant to form a new growth; living tissue transplanted surgically. **2** *informal* hard work. **3** *informal* bribery, corrupt practice. ● *v.* **1** insert (a graft) in a plant; transplant (tissue); join, add. **2** *informal* work hard.

grain *n.* **1** small seed(s) of a food plant such as wheat or rice; these plants; a small hard particle; a very small amount. **2** a unit of weight (about 65 mg). **3** the pattern of fibres in wood etc. □ **against the grain** contrary to one's natural inclination. □ **grainy** *adj.*

gram *n.* (also **gramme**) one-thousandth of a kilogram.

grammar *n.* (the rules governing) the use of words in their correct forms and relationships; a book analysing this; the basic elements of an area of knowledge.

■ **Usage** *Grammar* is not spelt with an *e*.

grammatical *adj.* conforming to the rules of grammar. □ **grammatically** *adv.*

grampus *n.* a dolphin-like sea animal.

gran *n. informal* grandmother.

granary *n.* (*pl.* **-ies**) a storehouse for grain.

grand *adj.* large and imposing; ambitious; chief of its kind; *informal* excellent. ● *n.* **1** a grand piano. **2** *informal* a thousand dollars or pounds. □ **grandly** *adv.*, **grandness** *n.*

grandchild *n.* (*pl.* **-children**) a child of one's son or daughter.

granddad *n. informal* grandfather.

granddaughter *n.* a female grandchild.

grandeur (gran-dewr) *n.* splendour, grandness.

grandfather *n.* a male grandparent.

grandfather clock *n.* a clock in a tall wooden case.

grandiloquent *adj.* using pompous language. □ **grandiloquence** *n.*

grandiose *adj.* imposing; planned on a large scale.

grandma *n. informal* grandmother.

grandmother *n.* a female grandparent.

grandpa *n. informal* grandfather.

grandparent *n.* a parent of one's father or mother.

grand piano *n.* a large piano with horizontal strings.

grand slam *n.* the winning of all the major championships in a sport in one season.

grandson *n.* a male grandchild.

grandstand *n.* the principal stand for spectators at a sports ground.

grange *n.* a country house with farm buildings.

granite *n.* a hard grey stone.

granny *n.* (also **grannie**) (*pl.* **-ies**) *informal* grandmother.

granny flat *n. informal* part of a house made into self-contained accommodation for a relative.

grant *v.* **1** give or allow as a privilege. **2** admit to be true. ● *n.* a sum of money given from public funds for a particular purpose. □ **take for granted 1** fail to appreciate or be grateful for. **2** assume to be true.

granular *adj.* like or consisting of grains.

granulated *adj.* formed into grains.

granule *n.* a small grain.

grape *n.* a green or purple berry growing in clusters, used for making wine.

grapefruit *n.* a large round yellow citrus fruit.

grapevine *n.* a vine bearing grapes. □ **on the grapevine** *informal* by a rumour spread unofficially.

graph *n.* a diagram showing the relationship between quantities.

graphic *adj.* **1** of drawing, painting, or engraving. **2** giving a vivid description. ● *n.* (**graphics**) diagrams used in calculation and design; drawings; computer images.

graphical *adj.* **1** in the form of a graph. **2** of visual art or computer graphics. ◻ **graphically** *adv.*

graphic equalizer *n.* a device controlling individual frequency bands of a stereo system.

graphite *n.* a form of carbon.

graphology *n.* the study of handwriting. ◻ **graphologist** *n.*

grapnel *n.* a small anchor with several hooks; a hooked device for dragging a river bed.

grapple *v.* wrestle; seize; struggle.

grappling iron *n.* a grapnel.

grasp *v.* **1** seize and hold. **2** understand. ● *n.* **1** a firm hold or grip. **2** an understanding.

grasping *adj.* greedy, avaricious.

grass *n.* **1** a plant with green blades; a species of this (e.g. a cereal plant); ground covered with grass. **2** *informal* marijuana. **3** *informal* an informer. ● *v.* **1** cover with grass. **2** *informal* act as an informer. ◻ **grassy** *adj.*

grasshopper *n.* a jumping insect that makes a chirping noise.

grassland *n.* a wide grasscovered area with few trees.

grass roots *n.pl.* the fundamental level or source; ordinary people, rank-and-file members.

grass widow *n.* a wife whose husband is absent for some time.

grate *n.* a metal framework keeping fuel in a fireplace. ● *v.* **1** shred finely by rubbing against a jagged surface. **2** make a harsh noise; have an irritating effect.

grateful *adj.* valuing a kindness or benefit received; thankful. ◻ **gratefully** *adv.*

grater *n.* a device for grating food.

gratify *v.* (**gratified, gratifying**) give pleasure to; satisfy (wishes). ◻ **gratification** *n.*

grating *n.* a screen of spaced bars placed across an opening.

gratis *adj.* & *adv.* free of charge.

gratitude *n.* being grateful.

gratuitous *adj.* **1** without reason, uncalled for. **2** free of charge. ◻ **gratuitously** *adv.*

gratuity *n.* (*pl.* **-ies**) money given for services rendered, a tip.

grave[1] *n.* a hole dug to bury a corpse.

grave[2] *adj.* **1** causing anxiety, serious. **2** solemn. ◻ **gravely** *adv.*

grave accent (grahv) *n.* the accent (`).

gravel *n.* small stones, used for paths etc.

gravelly *adj.* **1** like or consisting of gravel. **2** rough-sounding.

graven *adj.* **1** carved. **2** firmly fixed (in the memory).

gravestone *n.* a stone placed over a grave.

graveyard *n.* a burial ground.

gravitate *v.* move or be attracted towards a person, place, or thing.

gravitation *n.* gravitating; *Physics* attraction between particles. ◻ **gravitational** *adj.*

gravity *n.* **1** the force that attracts bodies towards the centre of the earth. **2** seriousness; solemnity.

gravy *n.* (*pl.* **-ies**) juice from cooked meat; a sauce made from this.

gravy train *n.* *informal* an easy way of making money.

gray Amer. sp. of **grey**.

graze *v.* **1** feed on growing grass; pasture animals in (a field); *informal* frequently eat snacks. **2** injure by scraping the skin; touch or scrape lightly in passing. ● *n.* a grazed place on the skin.

grease *n.* a fatty or oily substance, a lubricant. ● *v.* put grease on. ◻ **greasy** *adj.*

greasepaint *n.* make-up used by actors.

great *adj.* much above average in size, amount, or intensity; of outstanding ability or character, important; *informal* very good. ◻ **greatness** *n.*

great- *comb. form* (of a family relationship) one generation removed in ancestry or descent.

greatly *adv.* very much.

grebe *n.* a diving bird.

Grecian *adj.* Greek.

Grecian nose *n.* a straight nose.

greed *n.* excessive desire for food, wealth, power, etc. □ **greedily** *adv.*, **greedy** *adj.*

Greek *adj.* & *n.* (an inhabitant, the language) of Greece.

green *adj.* **1** of the colour of growing grass; covered with growing grass; consisting of fresh green vegetables. **2** concerned with protecting the environment. **3** unripe; inexperienced, naïve. ● *n.* a green colour; a piece of grassy public land; (**greens**) green vegetables. □ **greenish** *adj.*, **greenness** *n.*

green belt *n.* an area of open land round a town.

green card *n.* **1** (in the UK) an international insurance document for motorists. **2** (in the US) a work and residence permit.

greenery *n.* green foliage or plants.

green fingers *n.pl. informal* skill in growing plants.

greenfly *n.* (*pl.* **greenfly**) a small green insect that sucks juices from plants.

greengage *n.* a round plum with a greenish skin.

greengrocer *n.* a shopkeeper selling vegetables and fruit.

greenhorn *n. informal* an inexperienced person.

greenhouse *n.* a glass building for rearing plants.

greenhouse effect *n.* the trapping of the sun's radiation by pollution in the atmosphere, causing a rise in temperature.

greenhouse gas *n.* a gas contributing to the greenhouse effect.

green light *n. informal* a signal or permission to proceed.

Green Paper *n.* a preliminary report of government proposals.

green room *n.* a room in a theatre used by actors when off stage.

greenstick fracture *n.* a bent and partially broken bone.

greet *v.* address politely on meeting; welcome; react to; become apparent to (sight or hearing). □ **greeting** *n.*

gregarious *adj.* fond of company; living in flocks. □ **gregariousness** *n.*

gremlin *n.* an imaginary mischievous spirit blamed for mechanical faults; *informal* a fault or problem.

grenade *n.* a small bomb thrown by hand or fired from a rifle.

grenadine *n.* a sweet syrup.

grew past of **grow**.

grey *adj.* (*Amer.* **gray**) of the colour between black and white; dull, depressing. ● *n.* a grey colour; a grey or white horse. □ **grey area** a problem or situation that has no clear rules or definition. □ **greyish** *adj.*, **greyness** *n.*

greyhound *n.* a slender smooth-haired dog noted for its swiftness.

grey matter *n. informal* intelligence.

grid *n.* a grating; a system of numbered squares for map references; a network of lines, power cables, etc.; a gridiron.

gridiron *n.* a framework of metal bars for cooking on; a field for American football, marked with parallel lines.

gridlock *n.* a traffic jam affecting intersecting streets; a situation in which no progress can be made.

grief *n.* deep sorrow. □ **come to grief** meet with disaster; fail.

grievance *n.* a cause for complaint.

grieve *v.* cause grief to; feel grief.

grievous *adj.* very serious or distressing. □ **grievous bodily harm** the offence of inflicting serious injury. □ **grievously** *adv.*

griffin *n.* (also **griffon, gryphon**) a mythological creature with an eagle's head and wings and a lion's body.

griffon *n.* **1** a small terrier-like dog. **2** a vulture. **3** a griffin.

grill *n.* **1** a device on a cooker for radiating heat downwards; food cooked on this. **2** a grille. ● *v.* **1** cook under a grill or on a gridiron. **2** *informal* question closely and severely.

grille *n.* (also **grill**) a grating; a grid protecting a vehicle's radiator.

grim *adj.* (**grimmer, grimmest**) stern, severe; forbidding; disagreeable. □ **grimly** *adv.*, **grimness** *n.*

grimace *n.* a contortion of the face in pain or amusement. ● *v.* make a grimace.

grime *n.* ingrained dirt. ● *v.* blacken with grime. □ **grimily** *adv.*, **griminess** *n.*, **grimy** *adj.*

grin *v.* (**grinned, grinning**) smile broadly. ● *n.* a broad smile.

grind *v.* (**ground, grinding**) **1** crush into grains or powder. **2** sharpen or smooth by friction; rub together gratingly. **3** oppress cruelly. ● *n. informal* hard or tedious work.

grindstone *n.* a revolving disc for sharpening or grinding things.

grip *v.* (**gripped, gripping**) hold firmly; hold the attention of; affect deeply. ● *n.* **1** a firm grasp; a method of holding; a part that is held. **2** understanding of or skill in something. **3** a travelling bag.

gripe *v. informal* grumble. ● *n.* **1** *informal* a complaint. **2** colic pain.

gripping *adj.* very interesting or exciting; enthralling.

grisly *adj.* (**grislier, grisliest**) causing fear, horror, or disgust.

grist *n.* grain to be ground. □ **grist to the mill** something that one can exploit.

gristle *n.* tough inedible tissue in meat. □ **gristly** *adj.*

grit *n.* **1** particles of stone or sand. **2** *informal* courage and endurance. ● *v.* (**gritted, gritting**) **1** clench (the teeth) to aid endurance or restraint. **2** spread grit on (a road etc.) **3** make a grating sound. □ **grittiness** *n.*, **gritty** *adj.*

grizzle *v. informal* whimper, whine; complain.

grizzled *adj.* grey-haired.

groan *v.* make a long deep sound in pain or disapproval; make a deep creaking sound. ● *n.* such a sound. □ **groan under** be oppressed by.

grocer *n.* a shopkeeper selling food and household goods.

grocery *n.* (*pl.* **-ies**) a grocer's shop; (**groceries**) a grocer's goods.

grog *n.* a drink of spirits mixed with water.

groggy *adj.* (**groggier, groggiest**) *informal* weak and unsteady, esp. after illness. □ **groggily** *adv.*

groin *n.* **1** the place where the thighs join the abdomen. **2** a curved edge where two vaults meet. **3** Amer. sp. of **groyne**.

grommet *n.* **1** a ring to protect a rope etc. passing through a hole in a panel. **2** a tube placed through the eardrum to drain the ear.

groom *n.* **1** a person employed to look after horses. **2** a bridegroom. ● *v.* **1** clean and brush (an animal); make neat and tidy. **2** prepare (a person) for a career or position.

groove *n.* a long narrow channel; the track for a stylus on a gramophone record; a fixed routine. ● *v.* cut grooves in.

grope *v.* feel about as one does in the dark.

gross *adj.* **1** unattractively large or fat. **2** vulgar; *informal* repulsive. **3** (of income etc.) total, without deductions. ● *n.* (*pl.* **gross**) twelve dozen. ● *v.* produce or earn as total profit. □ **grossly** *adv.*, **grossness** *n.*

grotesque (groh-tesk) *adj.* very odd or ugly. ● *n.* a comically distorted figure; a design using fantastic forms. □ **grotesquely** *adv.*, **grotesqueness** *n.*

grotto *n.* (*pl.* **grottoes** or **grottos**) a picturesque cave.

grouch *informal v.* grumble. ● *n.* a grumbler; a complaint. □ **grouchy** *adj.*

ground[1] past & p.p. of **grind**.

ground[2] *n.* **1** the solid surface of the earth; an area of this; land of a specified type or used for a specified purpose; (**grounds**) land belonging to a large house. **2** (**grounds**) the reason or justification for a belief or action. **3** (**grounds**) coffee dregs. ● *v.* **1** prevent (an aircraft or a pilot) from flying. **2** give a basis to. **3** instruct thoroughly in a subject.

ground glass *n.* glass made opaque by grinding.

grounding *n.* basic training.

groundless *adj.* without basis or good reason.

groundnut *n.* a peanut.

ground rent *n.* rent paid by the owner of a building to the owner of the land on which it is built.

groundsheet *n.* a waterproof sheet for spreading on the ground.

groundsman *n.* (*pl.* **-men**) a person employed to look after a sports ground.

groundswell *n.* **1** slow heavy waves. **2** an increasingly forceful public opinion.

groundwork *n.* preliminary or basic work.

group *n.* a number of people or things near, categorized, or working together. ● *v.* form or gather into group(s); classify.

grouse *n.* **1** a game bird. **2** *informal* a complaint. ● *v. informal* grumble.

grout (growt) *n.* thin fluid mortar. ● *v.* fill with grout.

grove *n.* a group of trees.

grovel *v.* (**grovelled, grovelling**; *Amer.* **groveled**) crawl face downwards; behave humbly; apologize profusely.

grow *v.* (**grew, grown, growing**) **1** increase in size or amount; allow (hair etc.) to grow. **2** exist as a living plant; cultivate (crops etc.). **3** develop a specified characteristic, become: *grow fat.* ▫ **grow on** gradually start to appeal to. **grow up** become adult; start to behave maturely. ▫ **grower** *n.*

growl *v.* make a low threatening sound as a dog does. ● *n.* this sound.

grown p.p. of **grow**. ● *adj.* adult, fully developed.

grown-up *adj.* adult. ● *n.* an adult.

growth *n.* the process of growing; something that grows or has grown; a tumour.

groyne *n.* (*Amer.* **groin**) a solid structure built out into the sea to prevent erosion.

grub *n.* **1** the worm-like larva of certain insects. **2** *informal* food. ● *v.* (**grubbed, grubbing**) **1** dig the surface of soil; dig up by the roots. **2** rummage.

grubby *adj.* (**grubbier, grubbiest**) dirty. ▫ **grubbiness** *n.*

grudge *n.* a feeling of resentment or ill will. ● *v.* begrudge, resent.

gruel *n.* thin oatmeal porridge.

gruelling *adj.* (*Amer.* **grueling**) very tiring.

gruesome *adj.* horrifying, disgusting.

gruff *adj.* (of the voice) low and hoarse; (of a person) appearing bad-tempered. ▫ **gruffly** *adv.*, **gruffness** *n.*

grumble *v.* **1** complain in a bad-tempered way. **2** rumble. ● *n.* **1** a complaint. **2** a rumbling sound. ▫ **grumbler** *n.*

grumpy *adj.* (**grumpier, grumpiest**) bad-tempered. ▫ **grumpily** *adv.*, **grumpiness** *n.*

grunge *n.* a style of rock music with a raucous guitar sound; torn and untidy clothing as a fashion associated with this.

grunt *n.* a gruff snorting sound made or like that made by a pig. ● *v.* make this sound.

gryphon *n.* var. of **griffin**.

GSOH *abbr.* good sense of humour (used in advertisements).

G-string *n.* a narrow strip of cloth covering the genitals, attached to a string round the waist.

G-suit *n.* a pressurized suit worn by astronauts and some pilots.

guano (gwah-noh) *n.* the dung of seabirds, used as manure.

guarantee *n.* a formal promise to do something or that a thing is of a specified quality; something offered as security; a guarantor. ● *v.* give or be a guarantee (of).

guarantor *n.* the giver of a guarantee.

guard *v.* watch over to protect, prevent escape, etc.; take precautions. ● *n.* **1** a person guarding someone or something; *Brit.* a railway official in charge of a train; a protective part or device. **2** a state of watchfulness; a defensive posture in boxing, cricket, etc.

guarded *adj.* cautious, discreet.

guardian *n.* one who guards or protects; a person undertaking legal responsibility for an orphan. □ **guardianship** *n.*

guardsman *n.* (*pl.* **-men**) a soldier of a Guards regiment.

guava (gwah-vă) *n.* a tropical fruit.

gudgeon *n.* **1** a small freshwater fish. **2** a pivot; a socket for a rudder; a metal pin.

guerrilla (gĕ-ril-lă) *n.* (also **guerilla**) a member of a small fighting force, taking independent irregular action.

guess *v.* form an opinion without definite knowledge; think likely. ● *n.* an opinion formed by guessing.

guesstimate *n.* (also **guestimate**) *informal* an estimate based on guesswork and reasoning.

guesswork *n.* guessing.

guest *n.* a person entertained at another's house, or staying at a hotel; a visiting performer.

guest house *n.* a private house offering accommodation to paying guests.

guestimate var. of **guesstimate**.

guffaw *n.* a coarse noisy laugh. ● *v.* laugh in this way.

guidance *n.* guiding; advice.

guide *n.* **1** a person who shows others the way; one employed to point out sights to travellers. **2** a thing helping one to make a decision; a book of information, maps, etc.; a structure marking the correct position or direction of something. ● *v.* act as a guide to.

guidebook *n.* a book of information about a place.

guild *n.* (also **gild**) a society for mutual aid or with a common purpose; *hist.* an association of craftsmen or merchants.

guilder *n.* a former unit of money of the Netherlands.

guile *n.* treacherous cunning, craftiness. □ **guileless** *adj.*

guillotine *n.* **1** a machine for beheading criminals; a machine for cutting paper or metal. **2** the fixing of times for voting in Parliament, to prevent a lengthy debate. ● *v.* behead, cut, or limit with a guillotine.

guilt *n.* the fact of having committed an offence; a feeling that one is to blame. □ **guiltless** *adj.*

guilty *adj.* (**guiltier, guiltiest**) having done wrong; having committed a particular offence; feeling or showing guilt. □ **guiltily** *adv.*

guinea *n.* a former British coin worth 21 shillings (£1.05).

guinea pig *n.* **1** a small domesticated rodent. **2** *informal* a person or thing used as a subject for an experiment.

guise (gIz) *n.* a false outward appearance; a pretence.

guitar *n.* a stringed musical instrument. □ **guitarist** *n.*

gulf *n.* **1** a large area of sea partly surrounded by land. **2** a deep ravine; a wide difference in opinion.

gull *n.* a seabird with long wings. ● *v.* fool, deceive.

gullet *n.* the passage by which food goes from mouth to stomach.

gullible *adj.* easily deceived. □ **gullibility** *n.*, **gullibly** *adv.*

gully *n.* (*pl.* **-ies**) a narrow channel cut by water or carrying rainwater from a building.

gulp *v.* swallow (food etc.) hastily or greedily; make a gulping movement. ● *n.* the act of gulping; a large mouthful of liquid gulped.

gum *n.* **1** the firm flesh in which teeth are rooted. **2** a sticky substance exuded by certain trees; adhesive; chewing gum. ● *v.* (**gummed, gumming**) smear or stick together with gum. □ **gummy** *adj.*

gum tree *n.* a tree that exudes gum, esp. a eucalyptus.

gumboots *n.pl. informal* rubber boots, wellingtons.

gumdrop *n.* a hard gelatin sweet.

gumption *n. informal* resourcefulness, spirit.

gun *n.* a weapon that fires shells or bullets from a metal tube; a device forcing out a substance through a tube. ● *v.* (**gunned, gunning**) **1** shoot (someone) with a gun. **2** *informal* accelerate. □ **gun for 1** pursue with hostility. **2** try determinedly to achieve. **jump the gun** *informal* act prematurely. **stick to one's guns** *informal* refuse to give way to criticism.

gunboat diplomacy *n.* foreign policy combining diplomacy with the threat of force.

gunfire *n.* the firing of guns.

gunge *informal n.* an unpleasantly sticky and messy substance. ● *v.* cloy or coat with this.

gunman *n.* (*pl.* **-men**) a person armed with a gun.

gunnel var. of **gunwale**.

gunner *n.* an artillery soldier; a member of an aircraft crew operating a gun.

gunnery *n.* the construction and operating of large guns.

gunny *n.* coarse material for making sacks.

gunpowder *n.* an explosive of saltpetre, sulphur, and charcoal.

gunrunning *n.* the smuggling of firearms. □ **gunrunner** *n.*

gunshot *n.* a shot fired from a gun; the range of a gun.

gunsmith *n.* a maker and repairer of small firearms.

gunwale (gun-ăl) *n.* (also **gunnel**) the upper edge of a boat's side.

gurdwara (gerd-**wah**-ră) *n.* a Sikh temple.

gurgle *n.* & *v.* (make) a low bubbling sound.

Gurkha *n.* a Hindu of Nepal; a Nepalese soldier serving in the British army.

guru *n.* (*pl.* **gurus**) a Hindu spiritual teacher; a revered teacher.

gush *v.* **1** (of liquid) flow out suddenly and in large quantities. **2** express excessive or insincere enthusiasm. ● *v.* **1** a gushing stream. **2** effusiveness.

gusset *n.* a piece of cloth inserted to strengthen or enlarge a garment. □ **gusseted** *adj.*

gust *n.* a sudden rush of wind, rain, or smoke. ● *v.* blow in gusts. □ **gusty** *adj.*

gusto *n.* zest, enthusiasm.

gut *n.* **1** the belly; the intestine; thread made from animal intestines; (**guts**) the internal parts or essence of something. **2** (**guts**) *informal* courage, determination. ● *v.* (**gutted, gutting**) remove the guts from (fish); remove or destroy the internal parts of (a building etc.). □ **gut reaction** an emotional rather than reasoned response.

gutsy *adj.* (**gutsier, gutsiest**) *informal* **1** brave, spirited. **2** greedy.

gutta-percha *n.* a rubbery substance made from the juice of various Malaysian trees.

gutter *n.* a trough round a roof, or a channel beside a road, for carrying away rainwater. ● *v.* (of a candle) burn unsteadily. □ **the gutter** a life of poverty.

guttersnipe *n.* a street urchin.

guttural *adj.* throaty, harshsounding. □ **gutturally** *adv.*

guv *n.* an informal address to a man.

guy *n.* **1** *informal* a man. **2** *Brit.* an effigy of Guy Fawkes burnt on 5 Nov. **3** a rope or chain to keep a thing steady or secured. ● *v.* imitate mockingly.

guzzle *v.* eat or drink greedily.

gybe *v.* (*Amer.* **jibe**) (of a sail or boom) swing across the wind; (of a boat) change course in this way. ● *n.* this movement.

gym *n.* a gymnasium; gymnastics.

gymkhana *n.* a horse-riding competition.

gymnasium *n.* (*pl.* **gymnasia** or **gymnasiums**) a room equipped for physical training and gymnastics.

gymnast *n.* an expert in gymnastics.

gymnastics *n.* & *n.pl.* exercises to develop the muscles or demonstrate agility. □ **gymnastic** *adj.*

gynaecology (gy-ni-**kol**-ŏji) *n.* (*Amer.* **gynecology**) the study of the physiological functions and diseases of women. □ **gynaecological** *adj.*, **gynaecologist** *n.*

gypsum *n.* a chalk-like mineral used in building etc.

gypsy *n.* (*pl.* **-ies**) (also **gipsy**) a member of a travelling people.

gyrate *v.* move in circles or spirals, revolve. □ **gyration** *n.*

gyratory *adj.* gyrating, following a circular or spiral path.

gyrocompass *n.* a navigation compass using a gyroscope.

gyroscope *n.* a device used to keep navigation instruments steady, consisting of a disc rotating on an axis. □ **gyroscopic** *adj.*

Hh

H *abbr.* (of pencil lead) hard. ● *symb.* hydrogen.

ha *int.* an exclamation of triumph. ● *abbr.* hectare(s).

habeas corpus (hay-bee-ăs) *n.* an order requiring a person to be brought to court after arrest.

haberdasher *n.* a seller of sewing materials etc. □ **haberdashery** *n.*

habit *n.* **1** a regular way of behaving; *informal* an addiction. **2** a monk's or nun's long dress; a woman's riding-dress.

habitable *adj.* suitable for living in.

habitat *n.* an animal's or plant's natural environment.

habitation *n.* a place to live in.

habitual *adj.* done regularly or constantly; usual. □ **habitually** *adv.*

habituate *v.* accustom.

hacienda *n.* a ranch or large estate in South America.

hack *n.* **1** a writer producing dull and unoriginal work. **2** a horse for ordinary riding. ● *v.* **1** cut, chop, or hit roughly. **2** gain unauthorized access to computer files. **3** ride on horseback for pleasure and exercise.

hacker *n.* *informal* a computer enthusiast, esp. one gaining unauthorized access to files.

hacking *adj.* (of a cough) dry and frequent.

hackles *n.pl.* the hairs on the back of an animal's neck, raised in anger.

hackneyed *adj.* (of a phrase etc.) over-used and lacking impact.

hacksaw *n.* a saw for metal.

had past & p.p. of **have**.

haddock *n.* (*pl.* **haddock**) an edible sea fish.

hadji var. of **hajji**.

haem- *pref.* (*Amer.* **hem-**) of the blood.

haematology (heemă-) *n.* the study of blood. □ **haematologist** *n.*

haemoglobin (heem-ŏ-gloh-bin) *n.* the red oxygen-carrying substance in blood.

haemophilia (heemŏ-) *n.* failure of the blood to clot causing excessive bleeding. □ **haemophiliac** *n.*

haemorrhage (hem-ŏ-rij) *n.* heavy bleeding. ● *v.* bleed heavily.

haemorrhoids (hem-ŏ-roidz) *n.pl.* varicose veins at or near the anus.

hafnium *n.* a metallic element (symbol Hf).

haft *n.* the handle of a knife or dagger.

hag *n.* an ugly old woman.

haggard *adj.* looking pale and exhausted.

haggis *n.* a Scottish dish made from offal boiled in a sheep's stomach.

haggle *v.* argue about the price or terms of a deal.

ha-ha *n.* a boundary to an estate, consisting of a ditch with a sunken wall in it.

haiku (**hy**-koo) *n.* a Japanese three-line poem of 17 syllables.

hail *n.* a shower of frozen rain; a shower of blows, questions, etc. ● *v.* **1** pour down as or like hail. **2** call out to; welcome or acclaim. ● *int. archaic* an expression of greeting or acclamation.

hailstone *n.* a pellet of frozen rain.

hair *n.* one of the fine thread-like strands growing from the skin; these strands on a person's head. □ **let one's hair down** *informal* behave uninhibitedly. **not turn a hair** not be at all worried or surprised.

haircut *n.* shortening of hair by cutting it; an act of cutting a person's hair; a style of this.

hairdo *n.* (*pl.* **hairdos**) *informal* an arrangement of the hair.

hairdresser *n.* a person who cuts and arranges hair. □ **hairdressing** *n.*

hairgrip *n.* a springy hairpin.

hairline *n.* **1** the edge of the hair on the forehead etc. **2** a very narrow crack or line.

hairpin *n.* a U-shaped pin for keeping hair in place.

hairpin bend *n.* a sharp U-shaped bend.

hair-raising *adj.* terrifying.

hair-trigger *n.* a trigger operated by the slightest pressure.

hairy *adj.* (**hairier, hairiest**) **1** covered with hair. **2** *informal* frightening and difficult. □ **hairiness** *n.*

Haitian (**hay**-shăn) *adj.* & *n.* (a native) of Haiti.

hajji *n.* (also **hadji**) a Muslim who has been to Mecca on pilgrimage.

haka (**ha**-kă) *n.* a Maori war dance with chanting.

hake *n.* (*pl.* **hake**) an edible sea fish.

halal (hă-**lahl**) *n.* (also **hallal**) meat from an animal killed according to Muslim law.

halcyon (**hal**-si-ŏn) *adj.* (of a period) happy and peaceful.

hale *adj.* strong and healthy.

half *n.* (*pl.* **halves**) **1** each of two equal parts into which something is divided. **2** half a pint, half a pound, etc. **3** *informal* a child's fare on a bus etc. ● *adj.* & *pron.* amounting to half of something. ● *adv.* to the extent of a half; partly. □ **half a dozen** six. **half and half** half one thing and half another.

half-back *n.* a player between forwards and full-back(s).

half board *n.* bed, breakfast, and evening meal at a hotel etc.

half-brother *n.* a brother with whom one has only one parent in common.

half-caste *n. offensive* a person of mixed race.

half-hearted *adj.* not very enthusiastic.

half-life *n.* the time taken for radioactivity to reach half its original level.

half mast *n.* the position of a flag lowered in mourning.

half nelson *n.* a wrestling hold.

halfpenny (**hayp**-ni) *n.* (*pl.* **halfpennies** for single coins, **halfpence** for a sum of money) *hist.* a coin worth half a penny.

half-sister *n.* a sister with whom one has only one parent in common.

half-term *n.* a short holiday halfway through a school term.

half-timbered *adj.* (of a house etc.) built with a timber frame and brick or plaster filling.

half-time *n.* the interval between two halves of a game.

half-tone *n.* a black and white illustration with grey shades shown by dots.

half-volley *n.* (in tennis etc.) the return of the ball as soon as it bounces.

halfway *adj.* & *adv.* at a point equidistant between two others.

halfwit *n.* a stupid person. ▫ **half-witted** *adj.*

halibut *n.* (*pl.* **halibut**) a large edible flatfish.

halitosis (hal-i-**toh**-sis) *n.* breath that smells unpleasant.

hall *n.* **1** the room or space inside the front entrance of a house. **2** a large room or building for meetings, concerts, etc. **3** *Brit.* a large country house.

hallal var. of **halal**.

hallelujah var. of **alleluia**.

halliard var. of **halyard**.

hallmark *n.* an official mark on precious metals to indicate their standard; a distinguishing characteristic. ▫ **hallmarked** *adj.*

hallo *int.* & *n.* var. of **hello**.

Hallowe'en *n.* 31 Oct., eve of All Saints' Day.

hallucinate *v.* experience hallucinations.

hallucination *n.* an illusion of seeing or hearing something. ▫ **hallucinatory** *adj.*

hallucinogenic *adj.* causing hallucinations.

halm var. of **haulm**.

halo *n.* (*pl.* **haloes**) a circle of light, esp. one round the head of a sacred figure.

halogen *n.* any of a group of various non-metallic elements including chlorine and iodine.

halon (hay-lon) *n.* a gaseous compound of halogens used to extinguish fires.

halt *v.* come or bring to a stop. ● *n.* a temporary stop; *Brit.* a minor stopping place on a railway.

halter *n.* a strap round the head of a horse for leading or holding it.

halting *adj.* slow and hesitant.

halve *v.* divide equally between two; reduce by half.

halyard (hal-yăd) *n.* (also **halliard**) a rope for raising or lowering a sail or flag.

ham *n.* **1** smoked or salted meat from a pig's thigh. **2** (**hams**) the thighs and buttocks. **3** a bad actor. **4** *informal* an amateur radio operator. ● *v.* (**hammed, hamming**) *informal* overact.

hamburger *n.* a flat round cake of minced beef.

ham-fisted *adj.* clumsy.

hamlet *n.* a small village.

hammer *n.* **1** a tool with a head for hitting nails etc. **2** a metal ball attached to a wire, thrown in an athletic contest. ● *v.* hit or beat with a hammer; hit something forcefully; impress (an idea etc.) on people.

hammock *n.* a hanging bed of canvas or netting.

hamper *n.* a large lidded basket for carrying food etc. on a picnic; a selection of food packed as a gift. ● *v.* keep from moving or acting freely.

hamster *n.* a small domesticated rodent.

hamstring *n.* a tendon at the back of a knee or hock. ● *v.* (**hamstrung, hamstringing**) cripple by cutting the hamstring(s); cripple the activity of.

hand *n.* **1** the part of the arm below the wrist. **2** a pointer on a clock, dial, etc. **3** control, influence; (**a hand**) help. **4** a manual worker. **5** the cards dealt to a player in a card game; a round of a game. **6** a round of applause. **7** a person's handwriting. **8** a unit of measurement of a horse's height. ● *v.* give, pass. ▫ **at hand** close by. **hand out** distribute. **hands down** easily; decisively. **on hand** available. **out of hand** out of control. **to hand** within reach.

handbag *n.* a small bag to hold a purse and personal articles.

handball *n.* **1** a game with a ball with the hand or arms thrown by hand. **2** the intentional touching of the ball with the hand or arm in football (a foul).

handbill *n.* a printed notice circulated by hand.

handbook *n.* a small book giving useful facts.

handcuff *n.* a metal ring linked to another, for securing a prisoner's wrists. ● *v.* put handcuffs on.

handful *n.* **1** a quantity that fills the hand; a few. **2** *informal* a person hard to deal with or control.

handicap *n.* a physical or mental disability; something that makes progress difficult; a disadvantage imposed on a superior competitor to equalize chances; a race etc. in which handicaps are imposed. ● *v.* (**handicapped, handicapping**) be a handicap to; place at a disadvantage.

handkerchief *n.* (*pl.* **-chiefs** or **-chieves**) a small square of cloth for wiping the nose etc.

handle *n.* a part by which a thing is held, carried, or controlled. ● *v.* touch or move with the hands; deal with; manage.

handlebar *n.* a steering bar of a bicycle etc.

handler *n.* a person in charge of a trained dog etc.

handout *n.* a quantity of financial aid; information etc. given free of charge.

handrail *n.* a rail beside stairs etc. for people to hold for support.

handshake *n.* the act of shaking hands as a greeting etc.

handsome *adj.* (**handsomer, handsomest**) **1** good-looking; striking, imposing. **2** (of a sum etc.) ample, substantial; generous. □ **handsomely** *adv.*

handstand *n.* balancing on one's hands with feet in the air.

handwriting *n.* writing by hand with pen or pencil; a style of this.

handy *adj.* (**handier, handiest**) **1** ready to hand; convenient; easy to use. **2** skilled with one's hands. □ **come in handy** prove to be useful. □ **handily** *adv.*, **handiness** *n.*

handyman *n.* (*pl.* **-men**) a person who does minor repairs etc.

hang *v.* (**hung, hanging**; in sense 2 **hanged, hanging**) **1** support or be supported from above; fasten to a wall; remain static in the air. **2** kill or be killed by suspension on a rope tied round the neck. ● *n.* the way something hangs. □ **get the hang of** *informal* learn how to do. **hang about** loiter. **hang back** hesitate; remain behind. **hang on 1** hold tightly. **2** *informal* wait. **3** depend on. **hang out** *informal* spend time relaxing.

hangar *n.* a building for aircraft.

hangdog *adj.* shamefaced.

hanger *n.* a shaped piece of wood, metal, etc. to hang a garment on.

hang-glider *n.* an unpowered flying device for one person, consisting of a frame with a fabric aerofoil above it.

hang-gliding *n.* the sport of flying in a hang-glider.

hangings *n.pl.* draperies hung on walls.

hangman *n.* (*pl.* **-men**) a person whose job is to hang people condemned to death.

hangnail *n.* torn skin at the base of a fingernail.

hangover *n.* unpleasant after-effects from drinking too much alcohol.

hank *n.* a coil or length of thread.

hanker *v.* crave, feel a longing.

hanky *n.* (*pl.* **-ies**) *informal* a handkerchief.

Hanukkah (han-oo-kă) *n.* a Jewish festival of lights, beginning in December.

haphazard *adj.* done or chosen at random. □ **haphazardly** *adv.*

hapless *adj.* unlucky.

happen *v.* take place; occur by chance. □ **happen on** find by chance. **happen to** be the fate or experience of.

happy *adj.* (**happier, happiest**) **1** pleased, contented. **2** fortunate. □ **happy medium** a satisfactory compromise. □ **happily** *adv.*, **happiness** *n.*

happy-go-lucky *adj.* cheerfully casual.

harangue *v.* lecture earnestly and at length.

harass *v.* worry or annoy continually; make repeated attacks on. □ **harassment** *n.*

harbour (*Amer.* **harbor**) *n.* a place for ships to moor; a refuge. ● *v.* **1** keep (a thought etc.) in one's mind. **2** shelter.

hard *adj.* **1** firm to the touch; rigid, not easily cut or dented; (of a person) strong-minded; severe; (of information) reliable. **2** difficult; requiring effort; harsh; causing suffering. **3** powerful; (of drinks) strongly alcoholic; (of drugs) strong and addictive; (of currency) not likely to drop suddenly in value; (of water) containing minerals that prevent soap from lathering freely. ● *adv.* **1** with effort, diligently; with force. **2** so as to be firm: *the cement set hard.* □ **hard of hearing** slightly deaf. **hard up** *informal* short of money. **the hard sell** aggressive salesmanship. □ **hardness** *n.*

hardbitten *adj.* tough and cynical.

hardboard *n.* stiff board made of compressed wood pulp.

hard-boiled *adj.* **1** (of eggs) boiled until the yolk and white are set. **2** (of people) callous.

hard copy *n.* material produced in printed form from a computer.

harden *v.* make or become hard or hardy.

hard-headed *adj.* practical, not sentimental.

hard-hearted *adj.* unfeeling.

hardly *adv.* only with difficulty; scarcely.

hardship *n.* suffering, poverty.

hard shoulder *n.* an extra strip of road beside a motorway, for use in an emergency.

hardware *n.* **1** tools and household implements sold by a shop. **2** machinery used in a computer system.

hardwood *n.* the hard heavy wood of deciduous trees.

hardy *adj.* (**hardier, hardiest**) capable of enduring cold or harsh conditions. □ **hardiness** *n.*

hare *n.* a field animal like a large rabbit. ● *v.* run rapidly.

hare-brained *adj.* wild and foolish, rash.

harelip *n.* a deformed lip with a vertical slit.

■ **Usage** *Cleft lip* is less likely to be offensive than *harelip*.

---

harem (har-eem) *n.* the women's quarters in a Muslim household; the wives of a polygamous man.

hark *v. poetic* listen. □ **hark back** recall something from the past.

harlequin *n.* a character in traditional pantomime. ● *adj.* variegated like this character's costume.

harm *n.* damage, injury. ● *v.* cause harm to. □ **harmful** *adj.*, **harmless** *adj.*

harmonica *n.* a mouth organ.

harmonium *n.* a musical instrument like a small organ.

harmonize *v.* (also **-ise**) **1** add notes to (a melody) to form chords. **2** make consistent: go well together. □ **harmonization** *n.*

harmony *n.* (*pl.* **-ies**) the combination of musical notes to form chords; pleasing tuneful sound; agreement, peace; consistency. □ **harmonic** *adj.*, **harmonious** *adj.*, **harmoniously** *adv.*

harness *n.* straps and fittings by which a horse is controlled; fastenings for a parachute etc. ● *v.* put (a horse) in harness, attach to a cart etc.; control and use (resources).

harp *n.* a musical instrument with strings in a triangular frame.

□ **harp on** *informal* talk repeatedly about. □ **harpist** *n.*

harpoon *n.* a spear-like missile with a rope attached. ● *v.* spear with a harpoon.

harpsichord *n.* a piano-like instrument.

harpy *n.* (*pl.* **-ies**) a grasping unscrupulous woman.

harridan *n.* a bad-tempered old woman.

harrier *n.* **1** a hound used for hunting hares. **2** a falcon. **3** a cross-country runner.

harrow *n.* a heavy frame with metal spikes or discs for breaking up soil. ● *v.* **1** draw a harrow over (soil). **2** distress greatly. □ **harrowing** *adj.*

harry *v.* (**harried, harrying**) harass.

harsh *adj.* disagreeably rough to touch, hear, etc.; severe, cruel; grim. □ **harshly** *adv.*, **harshness** *n.*

hart *n.* an adult male deer.

harvest *n.* the gathering of crop(s); the season for this; a season's yield of a natural product. ● *v.* gather (a crop). □ **harvester** *n.*

has 3rd sing. of **have**.

has-been *n. informal* a person or thing that has lost a former importance or popularity.

hash *n.* **1** a dish of chopped recooked meat. **2** *informal* hashish. □ **make a hash of** *informal* do or make badly, make a mess of.

hashish *n.* cannabis.

hasp (hahsp) *n.* a metal plate fitting over a U-shaped staple as part of a door fastening.

hassle *informal n.* inconvenience, annoyance; harassment. ● *v.* harass; bother.

hassock *n.* a thick firm cushion for kneeling on.

haste *n.* hurry.

hasten *v.* hurry; cause to go faster.

hasty *adj.* (**hastier, hastiest**) hurried; acting or done too quickly. □ **hastily** *adv.*, **hastiness** *n.*

hat *n.* a covering for the head.

hatch[1] *n.* an opening in a deck, ceiling, etc., to allow passage.

hatch[2] *v.* emerge from an egg; cause to do this; devise (a plot).

hatch[3] *v.* shade (an area) with close parallel lines. □ **hatching** *n.*

hatchback *n.* a car with a back door that opens upwards.

hatchery *n.* (*pl.* **-ies**) a place for hatching eggs, especially for fish.

hatchet *n.* a small axe. □ **bury the hatchet** stop quarrelling.

hatchway *n.* an opening in a ship's deck for loading cargo.

hate *n.* hatred. ● *v.* feel hatred towards; dislike greatly.

hateful *adj.* arousing hatred.

hatred *n.* intense dislike.

hat-trick *n.* three successes in a row, esp. in sports.

haughty (hor-ti) *adj.* (**haughtier, haughtiest**) proud and looking down on others. □ **haughtily** *adv.*, **haughtiness** *n.*

haul *v.* **1** pull or drag forcibly. **2** transport by truck etc. ● *n.* a quantity of goods stolen. □ **a long haul** a long way to travel.

haulage *n.* transport of goods.

haulier *n.* a person or firm transporting goods by road.

haulm (horm) *n.* (also **halm**) a stalk or stem.

haunch *n.* the fleshy part of the buttock and thigh; a leg and loin of meat.

haunt *v.* (of a ghost) appear regularly at or to; frequent (a place); linger in the mind of. ● *n.* a place often visited by a particular person.

haute couture (oht koo-**tewr**) *n.* high fashion.

haute cuisine (oht kwi-**zeen**) *n.* high-class cookery.

have *v.* (**has, had, having**) **1** possess; hold; contain. **2** experience; suffer from (an illness etc.). **3** cause to be or be done: *have the house painted.* **4** be obliged or compelled: *I have to go.* **5** give birth to. **6** allow, tolerate. **7** *informal* cheat. ● *v.aux.* used with the past participle to form past tenses: *he has gone*. ▫ **have had it** *informal* be past recovery or survival. **have it out** discuss a problem frankly. **have on 1** be wearing. **2** have as an engagement. **3** *informal* tease, try to fool. **haves and have-nots** people with and without wealth or privilege. **have up** *informal* bring (someone) to trial.

haven *n.* a refuge.

haversack *n.* a strong bag carried on the back or shoulder.

havoc *n.* great destruction or disorder.

haw *n.* a hawthorn berry.

hawk *n.* **1** a bird of prey. **2** a person who favours an aggressive policy.

hawk-eyed *adj.* having very keen sight.

hawser *n.* a heavy rope or cable for mooring or towing a ship.

hawthorn *n.* a thorny tree with small red berries.

hay *n.* grass cut and dried for fodder.

hay fever *n.* an allergy caused by pollen and dust.

haystack *n.* a pile of hay stacked in a large block shape for storing.

haywire *adj.* ▫ **go haywire** *informal* become erratic; cease functioning.

hazard *n.* a risk, a danger; an obstacle. ● *v.* risk; venture. ▫ **hazardous** *adj.*

haze *n.* thin mist.

hazel *n.* **1** a tree with small edible nuts. **2** light brown. ▫ **hazelnut** *n.*

hazy *adj.* (**hazier, haziest**) misty; indistinct; vague. ▫ **hazily** *adv.*, **haziness** *n.*

HB *abbr.* (of a pencil lead) hard black.

H-bomb *n.* a hydrogen bomb.

He *symb.* helium.

he *pron.* the male previously mentioned. ● *n.* a male.

head *n.* **1** the part of the body containing the eyes, nose, mouth, and brain. **2** the intellect. **3** the front or top end of something. **4** something shaped like a head. **5** a leader, a chief; a head teacher. **6** a person considered as a unit: *six pounds a head*. **7** (**heads**) the side of a coin showing a head, turned upwards after being tossed. **8** a body of water or steam confined for exerting pressure. **9** the foam on top of beer. ● *v.* **1** lead, control, be at the head of; give a heading to. **2** move in a specified direction. **3** (in football) strike (the ball) with one's head. ▫ **come to a head** reach a crisis. **head off** go in front of (someone), forcing them to turn.

headache *n.* a continuous pain in the head; *informal* a worrying problem.

headdress *n.* an ornamental covering worn on the head.

header *n.* **1** a heading of the ball in football. **2** *informal* a headlong fall or dive.

headgear *n.* a hat or headdress.

headhunt *v.* seek to recruit (senior staff) from another firm.

heading *n.* **1** word(s) at the top of written matter as a title; a division of a subject. **2** a direction, a bearing.

headlamp *n.* a headlight.

headland *n.* a promontory.

headlight *n.* a powerful light on the front of a vehicle etc.

headline *n.* a heading in a newspaper; (**headlines**) a summary of broadcast news.

headlong *adj.* & *adv.* falling or plunging with the head first; in a hasty and rash way.

headmaster *n.* a man who is a head teacher.

headmistress *n.* a woman who is a head teacher.

head-on *adj.* & *adv.* involving the front of a vehicle; involving direct confrontation.

headphones *n.pl.* a set of earphones for listening to audio equipment.

headquarters *n.pl.* a place from which an organization is controlled.

headstone *n.* a memorial stone set up at the head of a grave.

headstrong *adj.* self-willed and obstinate.

head teacher *n.* the principal teacher in a school, responsible for organizing it.

headway *n.* progress.

headwind *n.* a wind blowing from directly in front.

heady *adj.* (**headier, headiest**) intoxicating; exciting.

heal *v.* make or become healthy after injury; cure. □ **healer** *n.*

health *n.* the state of being well and free from illness; mental or physical condition: *poor health.*

health centre *n.* a doctors' surgery with several doctors, a nurse, a pharmacy, etc.

health farm *n.* an establishment offering controlled regimes of diet, exercise, massage, etc. to improve health.

health visitor *n.* a trained nurse who visits invalids at home.

healthy *adj.* (**healthier, healthiest**) having or showing good health; producing good health; functioning well. □ **healthily** *adv.*, **healthiness** *n.*

heap *n.* **1** a number of things or articles lying one on top of another. **2** (**heaps**) *informal* plenty. ● *v.* pile or become piled in a heap; load with large quantities.

hear *v.* (**heard, hearing**) perceive (sounds) with the ear; be informed of; pay attention to; judge (a legal case). □ **hear from** be contacted by. **hear! hear!** I agree. □ **hearer** *n.*

hearing *n.* **1** ability to hear. **2** an opportunity to state one's case; a trial in court.

hearing aid *n.* a small sound-amplifier worn by a partially deaf person to improve the hearing.

hearsay *n.* rumour or gossip.

hearse (hers) *n.* a vehicle carrying the coffin at a funeral.

heart *n.* **1** the muscular organ that keeps blood circulating. **2** the centre of a person's emotions or inner thoughts; courage; enthusiasm. **3** a central or essential part. **4** a figure representing a heart; a playing card of the suit marked with these. □ **at heart** really, fundamentally. **break a person's heart** cause someone overwhelming grief. **by heart** memorized thoroughly.

heartache *n.* deep sorrow.

heart attack *n.* (also **heart failure**) sudden failure of the heart to function normally.

heartbeat *n.* the pulsation of the heart.

heartbreak *n.* overwhelming grief.

heartbroken *adj.* very sad.

heartburn *n.* a burning sensation in the lower part of the chest from indigestion.

hearten *v.* encourage.

heartfelt *adj.* felt deeply, sincere.

hearth *n.* the floor of a fireplace; the fireside.

heartless *adj.* not feeling pity or sympathy. □ **heartlessly** *adv.*

heart-rending *adj.* very distressing.

heart-searching *n.* examination of one's own feelings and motives.

heart-throb *n.* *informal* an attractive person inspiring romantic feelings.

heart-to-heart *adj.* frank and personal. ● *n.* a conversation of this nature.

heart-warming *adj.* emotionally moving and encouraging.

heartwood *n.* the dense, hardest, inner part of a tree trunk.

hearty *adj.* (**heartier, heartiest**) **1** vigorous; enthusiastic; heartfelt. **2** (of a meal or an appetite) large. □ **heartily** *adv.*, **heartiness** *n.*

heat *n.* **1** being hot; high temperature; a source of this; *Physics* energy produced by movement of molecules. **2** intense feeling. **3** a preliminary contest in a sporting competition. ● *v.* make or become hot. □ **on heat** (of female mammals) ready to mate.

heated *adj.* (of a person or discussion) angry. □ **heatedly** *adv.*

heater *n.* a device supplying heat.

heath *n.* flat uncultivated land with low shrubs; a shrub typically growing on this.

heathen *n.* a person who does not believe in an established religion. ● *adj.* believed in by such people.

heather *n.* an evergreen shrub with purple, pink, or white flowers.

heatstroke *n.* an illness caused by overexposure to sun.

heatwave *n.* a long period of hot weather.

heave *v.* **1** lift or haul with great effort; *informal* throw. **2** utter (a sigh). **3** rise and fall like waves. **4** retch. ● *n.* an act of heaving. □ **heave in sight** (**hove, heaving**) come into view. **heave to** (**hove, heaving**) bring a ship to a standstill with its head to the wind.

heaven *n.* **1** the abode of God; a place or state of bliss. **2** (**the heavens**) *poetic* the sky.

heavenly *adj.* **1** of heaven; divine; *informal* very pleasing. **2** of the sky. □ **heavenly bodies** the sun, stars, planets, etc.

heavy *adj.* (**heavier, heaviest**) **1** having great weight; requiring physical effort. **2** unusually great, forceful, or intense. **3** dense, thick; (of food) hard to digest. **4** serious; oppressive; sad. □ **heavy going** a situation in which it is hard to make headway. □ **heavily** *adv.*, **heaviness** *n.*

heavy-hearted *adj.* sad.

heavy industry *n.* industry producing metal or heavy machines etc.

heavy metal *n.* a type of loud rock music.

heavyweight *adj.* having great weight; very serious or important. ● *n.* a heavyweight person; a boxer etc. of the highest weight.

Hebrew *n.* & *adj.* (a member) of a Semitic people in ancient Palestine; (of) their language or a modern form of this. □ **Hebraic** *adj.*

heckle *v.* interrupt (a public speaker) with aggressive questions or abuse. □ **heckler** *n.*

hectare *n.* a unit of area, 10,000 sq. metres (2.471 acres).

hectic *adj.* full of frantic activity. □ **hectically** *adv.*

hectogram *n.* 100 grams.

hector *v.* intimidate by bullying.

hedge *n.* a barrier or boundary of bushes or shrubs. ● *v.* **1** surround with a hedge; make or trim hedges. **2** avoid giving a direct answer or commitment.

hedgehog *n.* a small animal covered in stiff spines.

hedgerow *n.* bushes etc. forming a hedge.

hedonism *n.* the pursuit of pleasure as the chief good. □ **hedonist** *n.*, **hedonistic** *adj.*

heed *v.* pay attention to. ● *n.* careful attention. □ **heedful** *adj.*, **heedless** *adj.*, **heedlessly** *adv.*

heel *n.* **1** the back part of the human foot; part of a shoe supporting this; (**heels**) high-heeled shoes. **2** *informal, dated* a scoundrel. ● *v.* **1** make or repair the heel(s) of. **2** (of a boat) tilt to one side. □ **down at heel** shabby. **take to one's heels** run away.

hefty *adj.* (**heftier, heftiest**) large, heavy, and powerful. □ **heftily** *adv.*, **heftiness** *n.*

hegemony (hi-jem-ŏni) *n.* dominance, esp. of one country over others.

Hegira (hej-iră) (also **Hejira**) *n.* Muhammad's flight from Mecca (AD 622), from which the Muslim era is reckoned.

heifer (hef-er) *n.* a young cow.

height *n.* **1** measurement from base to top or foot to head; distance above ground or sea level. **2** being tall; a high place; the highest degree of something.

heighten *v.* make or become higher or more intense.

heinous (hay-nŭss, hee-nŭs) *adj.* very wicked.

heir (air) *n.* a person entitled to inherit property or a rank etc.

heiress (air-ess) *n.* a female heir.

heirloom (air-loom) *n.* a possession handed down in a family for several generations.

Hejira var of **Hegira**.

held past & p.p. of **hold**.

helical *adj.* like a helix.

helicopter *n.* an aircraft with horizontally rotating overhead rotors.

heliport *n.* a helicopter station.

helium *n.* a light colourless gas (symbol He) that does not burn.

helix (hee-liks) *n.* (*pl.* **helices**) a spiral.

hell *n.* a place of punishment for the wicked after death; a place or state of misery. ● *int.* an exclamation of anger. □ **hell for leather** very fast. □ **hellish** *adj.*

hell-bent *adj.* recklessly determined.

hello *int.* & *n.* (also **hallo, hullo**) (*pl.* **hellos**) an exclamation used in greeting or to call attention.

helm *n.* the tiller or wheel by which a ship's rudder is controlled.

helmet *n.* a protective head-covering.

helmsman *n.* (*pl.* **-men**) a person controlling a ship's helm.

help *v.* **1** make a task etc. easier for (someone); improve or ease; benefit. **2** serve with food. **3** avoid; stop oneself: *I can't help laughing.* ● *n.* helping; someone or something that helps. □ **help oneself** take what one wants. □ **helper** *n.*

helpful *adj.* giving help, useful. □ **helpfully** *adv.*, **helpfulness** *n.*

helping *n.* a portion of food served.

helpless *adj.* unable to manage without help; powerless. □ **helplessly** *adv.*, **helplessness** *n.*

helpline *n.* a telephone service providing help with problems.

helter-skelter *adv.* in disorderly haste. ● *n.* a spiral slide at a funfair.

hem *n.* an edge (of cloth) turned under and sewn down. ● *v.* (**hemmed, hemming**) sew a hem on. □ **hem in** surround and restrict.

hem-, hematology, etc. Amer. sp. of **haem-, haematology,** etc.

hemisphere *n.* half a sphere; half of the earth. □ **hemispherical** *adj.*

hemlock *n.* a poisonous plant.

hemp *n.* a plant with coarse fibres used in making rope and cloth; a narcotic drug made from this.

hen *n.* a female bird, esp. of the domestic fowl.

hence *adv.* **1** for this reason. **2** from this time. **3** *archaic* from here.

henceforth *adv.* (also **henceforward**) from this time on, in future.

henchman *n.* (*pl.* **-men**) a supporter, a follower.

henna *n.* a reddish dye used esp. on the hair. □ **hennaed** *adj.*

hen party *n.* (*pl.* **-ies**) *informal* a party for women only.

henpecked *adj. informal* (of a man) nagged by his wife.

henry *n.* (*pl.* **henries** or **henrys**) *Physics* a unit of electric inductance.

hepatic *adj.* of the liver.

hepatitis *n.* inflammation of the liver.

heptagon *n.* a geometric figure with seven sides. □ **heptagonal** *adj.*

heptathlon *n.* an athletic contest involving seven events.

her *pron.* the objective case of **she**. ● *adj.* belonging to a female already mentioned.

herald *v.* be a sign of; proclaim the approach of. ● *n.* a person or thing heralding something.

heraldry *n.* the study of coats of arms. □ **heraldic** *adj.*

herb *n.* a plant used as a flavouring or in medicine.

herbaceous (her-**bay**-shŭs) *adj.* soft-stemmed.

herbaceous border *n.* a border containing esp. perennial plants.

herbal *adj.* of herbs. ● *n.* a book about herbs.

herbalist *n.* a dealer in medicinal herbs.

herbicide *n.* a substance used to destroy plants.

herbivorous *adj.* feeding on plants. ▫ **herbivore** *n.*

herculean (her-kyoo-**lee**-ăn) *adj.* needing or showing great strength or effort.

herd *n.* a group of animals feeding or staying together; a mob. ● *v.* (cause to) move in a group; look after (livestock).

herdsman *n.* (*pl.* **-men**) a man who looks after livestock.

here *adv.* in, at, or to this place; at this point.

hereabouts *adv.* near here.

hereafter *adv.* from now on. ▫ **the hereafter** life after death.

hereby *adv.* by this means; as a result of this.

hereditary *adj.* inherited; holding a position by inheritance.

heredity *n.* inheritance of characteristics from parents.

herein *adv.* in this document etc.; in a feature just mentioned.

heresy *n.* (*pl.* **-ies**) a belief, esp. a religious one, contrary to orthodox doctrine.

heretic *n.* a person who believes in a heresy. ▫ **heretical** *adj.*, **heretically** *adv.*

hereto *adv. formal* to this.

herewith *adv. formal* with this.

heritage *n.* inherited property; a nation's historic buildings etc.

hermaphrodite *n.* a creature with male and female sexual organs.

hermetic *adj.* airtight, sealed. ▫ **hermetically** *adv.*

hermit *n.* a person living in solitude.

hermitage *n.* a hermit's dwelling.

hernia *n.* a protrusion of part of an organ through the wall of the cavity (esp. the abdomen) containing it.

hero *n.* (*pl.* **heroes**) a man admired for his brave deeds; the chief male character in a story.

heroic *adj.* very brave. ● *n.pl.* (**heroics**) over-dramatic behaviour. ▫ **heroically** *adv.*

heroin *n.* a powerful addictive drug derived from morphine.

heroine *n.* a woman admired for her brave deeds; the chief female character in a story.

heroism *n.* heroic conduct.

heron *n.* a long-legged wading bird.

herpes (**her**-peez) *n.* a viral disease causing blisters.

Herr *n.* (*pl.* **Herren**) the title of a German man, corresponding to Mr.

herring *n.* an edible North Atlantic fish.

herringbone *n.* a zigzag pattern or arrangement.

hers *poss. pron.* belonging to her.

herself *pron.* the emphatic and reflexive form of **she** and **her**.

hertz *n.* (*pl.* **hertz**) *Physics* a unit of frequency of electromagnetic waves.

hesitant *adj.* uncertain, reluctant. ▫ **hesitancy** *n.*, **hesitantly** *adv.*

hesitate *v.* pause doubtfully; be reluctant, scruple. ▫ **hesitation** *n.*

hessian *n.* a strong coarse cloth of hemp or jute.

heterodox *adj.* not in accordance with what is generally accepted.

heterogeneous (het-ĕ-ro-**jee**-nee-ŭs) *adj.* made up of people or things of various sorts. ▫ **heterogeneity** *n.*

■ Usage *Heterogeneous* is spelt with an *e* before *-ous*.

---

heterosexual *adj.* & *n.* (a person) sexually attracted to people of the opposite sex. ▫ **heterosexuality** *n.*

hew *v.* (**hewed, hewn** or **hewed, hewing**) chop or cut with an axe etc.; cut into shape.

hex *n.* a magic spell; a curse.

hexadecimal *adj. Computing* of a number system using 16 rather than 10 as a base.

hexagon *n.* a geometric figure with six sides. ▫ **hexagonal** *adj.*

hexagram *n.* a six-pointed star formed of two intersecting triangles.

hey *int.* an exclamation of surprise or inquiry, or calling attention.

heyday *n.* the time of someone's or something's greatest success.

Hf *symb.* hafnium.

Hg *symb.* mercury.

hg *abbr.* hectogram.

HGV *abbr.* heavy goods vehicle.

HH *abbr.* (of pencil lead) extra hard.

hi *int.* an informal greeting or call to attract attention.

hiatus (hy-**ay**-tus) *n.* (*pl.* **hiatuses**) a break or gap in a sequence.

hibernate *v.* spend the winter in a sleep-like state. ▫ **hibernation** *n.*

Hibernian *adj.* & *n.* (a native) of Ireland.

hiccup *n.* (also **hiccough**) a sudden stopping of breath with a 'hic' sound; *informal* a temporary setback. • *v.* (**hiccuped, hiccuping**) suffer from a hiccup.

hide *v.* (**hid, hidden, hiding**) put or keep out of sight; keep secret; conceal oneself. • *n.* **1** a hiding place used when birdwatching etc. **2** an animal's skin.

hidebound *adj.* rigidly conventional.

hideous *adj.* very ugly. ▫ **hideously** *adv.*, **hideousness** *n.*

hideout *n.* a hiding place.

hiding *n. informal* a severe beating.

hierarchy (**hI**-ĕ-rah-ki) *n.* a system with grades ranking one above another. ▫ **hierarchical** *adj.*

hieroglyphics (hI-ĕ-rŏ-**glif**-iks) *n.pl.* writing consisting of pictorial symbols. ▫ **hieroglyph** *n.*, **hieroglyphic** *adj.*

hi-fi *adj.* high-fidelity, reproducing sound accurately. • *n.* a set of hi-fi equipment.

higgledy-piggledy *adj.* & *adv.* in complete confusion.

high *adj.* **1** extending far upwards or a specified distance upwards; far above ground or sea level. **2** greater or more intense than normal. **3** great in status. **4** (of a sound) not deep or low. **5** (of an opinion) favourable. **6** (of meat) slightly decomposed. **7** *informal* excited; under the influence of drugs. • *n.* **1** a high level; an area of high pressure. **2** *informal* a euphoric state. • *adv.* in, at, or to a high level. ▫ **high time** at or past the time when something should happen.

highbrow *adj.* intellectual, cultured. • *n.* a highbrow person.

higher education *n.* education at university etc.

highfalutin *adj.* (also **highfaluting**) *informal* pompous, pretentious.

high-handed *adj.* using authority arrogantly.

highlands *n.pl.* a mountainous region. ▫ **highland** *adj.*, **highlander** *n.*

highlight *n.* **1** an outstandingly good part of something. **2** a bright area in a picture; a light streak in the hair. • *v.* emphasize.

highlighter *n.* a coloured marker pen.

highly *adv.* **1** to a high degree. **2** favourably: *highly regarded.*

highly-strung *adj.* nervous, easily upset.

high-rise *adj.* (of a building) with many storeys.

high road *n.* a main road; the best or most direct way to achieve something.

high school *n.* a secondary school.

high seas *n. pl.* the sea outside a country's territorial waters.

high season *n.* the busiest season at a hotel etc.

high-spirited *adj.* lively.

high street *n.* the principal shopping street of a town.

high tea *n.* an early evening meal with tea and cooked food.

high-tech *adj.* (also **hi-tech**) involving advanced technology and electronics.

high tide *n.* the tide at its highest level.

high water *n.* = **high tide**.

highway *n.* a public road; a main route.

highwayman *n.* (*pl.* **-men**) a person who robbed travellers in former times.

hijack *v.* illegally seize control of (a vehicle or aircraft in transit). ● *n.* hijacking. □ **hijacker** *n.*

hike *n.* **1** a long walk. **2** a sharp increase in price etc. ● *v.* **1** go for a hike. **2** raise. □ **hiker** *n.*

hilarious *adj.* very funny; boisterous and merry. □ **hilariously** *adv.*, **hilarity** *n.*

hill *n.* a raised part of the earth's surface, lower than a mountain; a slope in a road etc.

hillock *n.* a small hill.

hilt *n.* the handle of a sword or dagger. □ **to the hilt** completely.

him *pron.* the objective case of **he**.

himself *pron.* the emphatic and reflexive form of **he** and **him**.

hind[1] *adj.* situated at the back.

hind[2] *n.* a female deer.

hinder *v.* obstruct, make difficulties for.

Hindi *n.* the most widely spoken language of northern India.

hindmost *adj.* furthest behind.

hindrance *n.* something that hinders; difficulty, obstruction.

hindsight *n.* wisdom about an event after it has occurred.

Hinduism *n.* the principal religion and philosophy of India. □ **Hindu** *adj.* & *n.*

Hindustani *n.* a group of languages of NW India.

hinge *n.* a movable joint such as that on a door or lid. ● *v.* attach or be attached by hinge(s). □ **hinge on** depend on.

hint *n.* a slight or indirect suggestion; a piece of practical information; a slight trace. ● *v.* suggest, indicate.

hinterland *n.* the district behind a coast or served by a port or other centre.

hip *n.* **1** the projection of the pelvis on each side of the body. **2** the fruit of the rose.

hip hop *n.* a style of popular music featuring rap with electronic backing; culture associated with this.

hippie var. of **hippy**.

hippopotamus *n.* (*pl.* **hippopotamuses** or **hippopotami**) a large African river animal with a thick skin.

hippy *n.* (*pl.* **-ies**) (also **hippie**) a young person rejecting convention and supporting peace and free love.

hire *v.* purchase the temporary use of. ● *n.* hiring. □ **hire out** grant temporary use of for payment.

hireling *n.* a hired helper.

hire purchase *n. Brit.* a system of purchase by payment in instalments.

hirsute (**herss**-yoot) *adj.* hairy.

his *adj.* & *poss.pron.* belonging to a male already mentioned.

Hispanic *adj.* & *n.* (a native) of Spain or a Spanish-speaking country.

hiss *n.* a sound like 's'. ● *v.* make this sound; utter with a hiss; express disapproval in this way.

histamine *n.* a substance in the body, associated with allergic reactions.

histology *n.* the study of organic tissues.

historian *n.* an expert on history.

historic *adj.* **1** important in the development of events. **2** relating to history.

■ **Usage** Both *historic* and *historical* can mean 'relating to history'. Only *historic* can mean 'significant, important'.

---

historical *adj.* of or concerned with history; belonging to the past. □ **historically** *adv.*

history *n.* (*pl.* **-ies**) the study of past events; the past, someone's or something's past; a narrative. □ **make history** do something important and memorable.

histrionic *adj.* excessively theatrical in manner; *formal* of acting. ● *n.pl.* (**histrionics**) theatrical behaviour.

hit *v.* (**hit, hitting**) **1** strike with a blow or missile; strike forcefully against. **2** affect badly. **3** reach (a target etc.). ● *n.* **1** a blow, a stroke; a shot that hits its target. **2** *informal* a success. □ **hit it off** *informal* like one another. □ **hitter** *n.*

hitch *v.* **1** move (something) with a jerk. **2** hitch-hike; obtain (a lift). **3** tether, fasten. ● *n.* **1** a temporary problem or setback. **2** a kind of knot. □ **get hitched** *informal* marry.

hitch-hike *v.* travel by seeking free lifts in passing vehicles. □ **hitch-hiker** *n.*

hi-tech *adj.* var. of **high-tech**.

hither *adv.* to or towards this place.

hitherto *adv.* until this time.

hit list *n. informal* a list of prospective victims.

HIV *abbr.* human immuno-deficiency virus (causing Aids).

hive *n.* **1** a structure in which bees live. **2** (**hives**) a skin eruption, esp. nettle-rash. □ **hive off** separate from a larger group.

HMG *abbr.* Her (or His) Majesty's Government.

HMS *abbr.* Her (or His) Majesty's Ship.

HNC *abbr.* Higher National Certificate.

HND *abbr.* Higher National Diploma.

Ho *symb.* holmium.

hoard *v.* save and store away. ● *n.* a store, esp. of valuable things.

hoarding *n.* a large board for displaying advertisements.

hoar frost *n.* white frost.

hoarse *adj.* (of a voice) rough and dry-sounding. □ **hoarsely** *adv.*, **hoarseness** *n.*

hoary *adj.* (**hoarier, hoariest**) grey with age; (of a joke etc.) old.

hoax *v.* deceive jokingly. ● *n.* a joking deception. □ **hoaxer** *n.*

hob *n.* a cooking surface with hotplates.

hobble *v.* **1** walk lamely. **2** fasten the legs of (a horse) to limit its movement. ● *n.* **1** a hobbling walk. **2** a rope etc. used to hobble a horse.

hobby *n.* (*pl.* **-ies**) something done for pleasure in one's spare time.

hobby horse *n.* **1** a stick with a horse's head, as a toy. **2** *informal* a favourite topic.

hobgoblin *n.* a mischievous imp.

hobnail *n.* a heavy-headed nail for boot-soles.

hobnob *v.* (**hobnobbed, hobnobbing**) *informal* mix socially with people of a different class etc.

Hobson's choice *n.* no alternative to the thing offered.

hock *n.* **1** the middle joint of an animal's hind leg. **2** German white wine. ● *v. informal* pawn.

hockey *n.* a field game played with curved sticks and a small hard ball.

hocus-pocus *n.* mystifying and often deceptive talk or behaviour.

hod *n.* **1** a trough on a pole for carrying mortar or bricks. **2** a tall container for coal.

hodgepodge var. of **hotchpotch**.

hoe *n.* a tool for loosening soil or scraping up weeds. ● *v.* (**hoed, hoeing**) dig or scrape with a hoe.

hog *n.* **1** a castrated male pig reared for meat. **2** a greedy person. ● *v.* (**hogged, hogging**) take greedily. □ **go the whole hog** *informal* do something thoroughly.

Hogmanay *n. Scot.* New Year's Eve.

hoick *v. informal* lift or bring out with a jerk.

hoi polloi *n.* ordinary people.

hoist *v.* raise or haul up. ● *n.* an apparatus for hoisting things.

hoity-toity *adj.* haughty.

hokum *n. informal* sentimental or unreal material in a story; nonsense.

hold *v.* (**held, holding**) **1** keep or support in one's hands or arms; contain; support in position; bear the weight of. **2** keep in one's possession; detain, keep captive. **3** remain unmoved or unbroken under pressure; remain true or valid. **4** consider to be of a particular nature. **5** arrange and take part in: *hold a meeting.* ● *n.* **1** an act, manner, or means of holding; a means of exerting influence. **2** a storage cavity below a ship's deck. ◻ **hold on** wait; endure. **hold out 1** resist, survive, last; persist in making a demand. **2** offer. **hold up 1** delay. **2** rob with violence. **hold with** *informal* approve of. ◻ **holder** *n.*

holdall *n.* a large soft travel bag.

holding *n.* **1** land held by lease. **2** (**holdings**) stocks, property, etc. owned by someone.

hold-up *n.* **1** a delay. **2** a robbery.

hole *n.* **1** a hollow in a surface; a burrow; an opening; a tear in cloth etc. **2** *informal* an unpleasant place; an awkward situation. ● *v.* make a hole in. ◻ **holey** *adj.*

holiday *n.* a period of recreation. ● *v.* spend a holiday.

holism *n.* (also **wholism**) treating the whole person rather than just particular isolated symptoms. ◻ **holistic** *adj.*

hollow *adj.* **1** empty within, not solid; sunken; echoing as if in something hollow. **2** worthless. ● *n.* a cavity; a sunken place; a valley. ● *v.* make hollow. ◻ **hollowly** *adv.*, **hollowness** *n.*

holly *n.* an evergreen shrub with prickly leaves and red berries.

holmium *n.* a metallic element (symbol Ho).

holocaust *n.* destruction or slaughter on a mass scale.

hologram *n.* a three-dimensional photographic image.

holograph *adj.* & *n.* (a document) written wholly in the handwriting of the author.

holography *n.* the study of holograms.

holster *n.* a leather case holding a pistol or revolver.

holy *adj.* (**holier, holiest**) dedicated to God; pious, virtuous. ◻ **holiness** *n.*

homage *n.* things said or done as a mark of respect or loyalty.

home *n.* **1** the place where one lives. **2** an institution where people needing care may live. **3** the finishing point in a race. ● *adj.* of one's home or country; (of a match) played on a team's own ground. ● *adv.* at or to one's home; to the point aimed at. ● *v.* make its way home or to a target. ◻ **homeless** *adj.*, **homelessness** *n.*

homeland *n.* one's native land.

homely *adj.* (**homelier, homeliest**) **1** *Brit.* simple but comfortable. **2** *Amer.* plain, not beautiful. ◻ **homeliness** *n.*

homeopathy Amer. sp. of **homoeopathy**.

home page *n. Computing* an individual's or organization's introductory document on the World Wide Web.

homesick *adj.* longing for home.

home truth *n.* an unpleasant truth about oneself.

homeward *adj.* & *adv.* going towards home. ◻ **homewards** *adv.*

homework *n.* work set for a pupil to do away from school.

homicide *n.* killing of one person by another. ◻ **homicidal** *adj.*

homily *n.* (*pl.* **-ies**) a moralizing lecture.

hominid *adj.* & *n.* (a member) of the family of existing and fossil man.

homoeopathy (hohm-i-**op**-ăthi) *n.* (*Amer.* **homeopathy**) treatment of a disease by very small doses of a substance that would produce the same symptoms in a healthy person. ◻ **homoeopath** *n.*, **homoeopathic** *adj.*

homogeneous (hom-ŏ-**jeen**-ee-ŭs) *adj.* of the same kind, uniform. □ **homogeneity** *n.*, **homogeneously** *adv.*

■ **Usage** *Homogeneous* is often confused with *homogenous*, but that is a term in biology meaning 'similar owing to common descent'.

homogenize *v.* (also **-ise**) treat (milk) so that cream does not separate and rise to the top.

homograph *n.* (also **homonym**) a word spelt the same way as another.

homophobia *n.* hatred or fear of homosexuals. □ **homophobe** *n.*, **homophobic** *adj.*

homophone *n.* a word with the same sound as another.

Homo sapiens (hoh-moh **sap**-i-enz) *n.* modern humans.

homosexual *adj.* & *n.* (a person) sexually attracted to people of the same sex. □ **homosexuality** *n.*

hone *v.* sharpen on a whetstone.

honest *adj.* truthful, trustworthy; fairly earned. □ **honesty** *n.*

honestly *adv.* **1** in an honest way. **2** really (emphasizing an opinion).

honey *n.* (*pl.* **honeys**) **1** a sweet substance made by bees from nectar. **2** *informal* darling.

honey bee *n.* the common hivebee.

honeycomb *n.* a bees' wax structure holding their honey and eggs; a pattern of six-sided sections.

honeydew *n.* **1** a sticky substance on plants, secreted by aphids. **2** a variety of melon.

honeyed *adj.* flattering, pleasant.

honeymoon *n.* a holiday for a newly married couple; an initial period of goodwill. ● *v.* spend a honeymoon.

honeysuckle *n.* a climbing shrub with fragrant pink and yellow flowers.

honk *n.* the cry of a wild goose; the harsh sound of a car horn. ● *v.* make this noise.

honor Amer. sp. of **honour**.

honorarium (*n. pl.* **honorariums** or **honoraria**) a voluntary payment made where no fee is legally required.

honorary *adj.* **1** given as an honour, without the usual requirements. **2** (of an office-holder) unpaid.

honour *n.* (*Amer.* **honor**) great respect or public regard; a mark of this, a privilege; honesty, integrity. ● *v.* **1** respect; confer a mark of honour on. **2** keep (an agreement); pay (a cheque).

honourable *adj.* (*Amer.* **honorable**) honest; deserving honour. □ **honourably** *adv.*

honours degree *n.* a degree of a higher standard than a pass.

hood *n.* **1** a covering for the head and neck. **2** a hood-like thing or cover; a folding roof over a car; *Amer.* a car bonnet. **3** *Amer. informal* a gangster or gunman.

hoodlum *n.* a hooligan or gangster.

hoodoo *n.* bad luck; something causing this.

hoodwink *v.* deceive.

hoof *n.* (*pl.* **hoofs** or **hooves**) the horny part of a horse's foot.

hook *n.* **1** a curved device for catching hold of or hanging things on; a bent piece of metal for catching fish; a curved implement for reaping etc. **2** a short blow made with the elbow bent. ● *v.* **1** attach with a hook. **2** catch with a hook. **3** bend or be bent into a hooked shape. □ **off the hook 1** (of a telephone) off its rest. **2** *informal* no longer in difficulty.

hookah *n.* an oriental tobacco pipe with a long tube passing through water.

hooked *adj.* **1** hook-shaped. **2** *informal* addicted.

hook-up *n.* an interconnection of broadcasting equipment.

hookworm *n.* a parasitic worm with hooklike mouthparts.

hooligan *n.* a young ruffian. □ **hooliganism** *n.*

hoop *n.* a circular band of metal or wood; a metal croquet arch.

hoopla *n.* a game in which rings are thrown to encircle a prize.

hoopoe *n.* a crested bird.

hooray *int.* & *n.* var. of **hurrah**.

hoot *n.* **1** an owl's cry; the sound of a hooter; a cry of laughter or disapproval. **2** *informal* an amusing person or thing. ● *v.* utter or make a hoot.

hooter *n.* a siren or steam whistle; a car horn.

Hoover *n. trademark* a vacuum cleaner. ● *v.* (**hoover**) clean with a vacuum cleaner.

hop[1] *v.* (**hopped, hopping**) **1** jump on one foot; (of an animal) jump with all feet together. **2** *informal* make a short journey; move quickly to a new position. ● *n.* a hopping movement; a short journey. □ **on the hop** *informal* unprepared.

hop[2] *n.* a plant used to flavour beer.

hope *n.* expectation of something desired; something giving grounds for this; something hoped for. ● *v.* feel hope. □ **hopeful** *adj.*

hopefully *adv.* **1** in a hopeful way. **2** it is to be hoped.

■ **Usage** The use of *hopefully* to mean 'it is to be hoped' is widely considered incorrect.

hopeless *adj.* **1** without hope. **2** inadequate, incompetent. □ **hopelessly** *adv.*, **hopelessness** *n.*

hopper *n.* **1** a container with an opening at the base for discharging its contents. **2** one who hops.

hopscotch *n.* a game involving hopping over marked squares.

horde *n.* a large group or crowd.

horizon *n.* **1** the line at which earth and sky appear to meet. **2** the limit of someone's knowledge or interests.

horizontal *adj.* parallel to the horizon, going across rather than up and down. □ **horizontally** *adv.*

hormone *n.* a substance produced by the body or a plant to stimulate growth or an organ's functions. □ **hormonal** *adj.*

horn *n.* **1** a hard pointed growth on the heads of certain animals; the substance of this; something resembling these growths. **2** a wind instrument with a trumpet-shaped end; a device for sounding a warning signal. □ **horned** *adj.*

hornblende *n.* a dark mineral constituent of granite etc.

hornet *n.* a large wasp.

hornpipe *n.* a lively solo dance traditionally performed by sailors.

horn-rimmed *adj.* with frames of horn or similar material.

horny *adj.* (**hornier, horniest**) **1** of or like horn; hardened and calloused. **2** *informal* sexually excited.

horology *n.* the measurement of time; the making of clocks. □ **horologist** *n.*

horoscope *n.* a forecast of events based on the positions of stars.

horrendous *adj.* horrifying. □ **horrendously** *adv.*

horrible *adj.* causing horror; very unpleasant. □ **horribly** *adv.*

horrid *adj.* horrible.

horrific *adj.* horrifying. □ **horrifically** *adv.*

horrify *v.* (**horrified, horrifying**) arouse horror in.

horror *n.* intense shock and fear or disgust; a terrible event or situation; *informal* a naughty child.

hors d'oeuvre (or **dervr**) *n.* food served as an appetizer.

horse *n.* **1** a four-legged animal with a mane and tail. **2** a padded structure for vaulting over in a gym. □ **horse around** *informal* fool about.

horseback *n.* □ **on horseback** riding on a horse.

horsebox *n.* a vehicle for transporting horses.

horse chestnut *n.* a brown shiny nut; the tree bearing this.

horsefly *n.* (*pl.* **-flies**) a large biting fly.

horseman *n.* (*pl.* **-men**) a male rider on horseback. □ **horsemanship** *n.*

horseplay *n.* boisterous play.

horsepower *n.* (*pl.* **horsepower**) a unit for measuring the power of an engine.

horseradish *n.* a plant with a hot-tasting root used to make sauce.

horse sense *n. informal* common sense.

horseshoe *n.* a U-shaped strip of metal nailed to a horse's hoof; something shaped like this.

horsewoman *n.* (*pl.* **-women**) a woman rider on horseback.

horsy *adj.* (**horsier, horsiest**) (also **horsey**) **1** of or like a horse. **2** interested in horses.

horticulture *n.* the art of garden cultivation. □ **horticultural** *adj.*, **horticulturist** *n.*

hose *n.* **1** (also **hosepipe**) a flexible tube for conveying water. **2** stockings and socks. ● *v.* water or spray with a hosepipe.

hosiery *n.* stockings, socks, etc.

hospice *n.* a hospital or home for the terminally ill.

hospitable *adj.* friendly and welcoming. □ **hospitably** *adv.*

hospital *n.* an institution for treatment of sick or injured people.

hospitality *n.* friendly and generous entertainment of guests.

hospitalize *v.* (also **-ise**) send or admit to a hospital. □ **hospitalization** *n.*

host *n.* **1** a person entertaining guests; a place or person providing facilities for visitors. **2** an organism on which another lives as a parasite. **3** a large number of people or things. ● *v.* act as host at (an event).

hostage *n.* a person held as security that the holder's demands will be satisfied.

hostel *n.* a lodging house for students, nurses, homeless people, etc.

hostess *n.* a woman entertaining guests.

hostile *adj.* unfriendly; of an enemy; opposed to something.

hostility *n.* (*pl.* **-ies**) enmity, unfriendliness; (**hostilities**) acts of warfare.

hot *adj.* **1** at or having a high temperature. **2** producing a burning sensation when tasted. **3** passionate; eager, excited; angry; arousing strong feelings. **4** (of news) fresh; *informal* popular. □ **hot air** *informal* empty talk designed to impress. **hot button** *Amer.* an issue arousing strong feelings. **hot up** (**hotted, hotting**) *informal*) make or become hotter or more intense. **in hot water** in trouble.

hotbed *n.* a place encouraging vice, intrigue, etc.

hotchpotch *n.* (also **hodgepodge**) a confused mixture.

hot-desking *n.* the sharing of office desks by workers on a rota.

hot dog *n.* a hot sausage in a bread roll.

hotel *n.* an establishment providing rooms and meals for tourists and travellers.

hotelier *n.* a hotel-keeper.

hotfoot *adv.* in eager haste.

hothead *n.* an impetuous person. □ **hot-headed** *adj.*

hothouse *n.* a heated green-house; an environment encouraging rapid development.

hotline *n.* a direct telephone line for speedy communication.

hotly *adv.* **1** angrily; passionately. **2** closely and quickly: *hotly pursued.*

hotplate *n.* a heated surface on a cooker or hob.

hotting *n. informal* joyriding in stolen cars.

hoummos var. of **hummus**.

hound *n.* a dog used in hunting. ● *v.* pursue, harass.

hour *n.* **1** one twenty-fourth part of a day and night. **2** a point in time. **3** (**hours**) time fixed or set aside for work or an activity.

hour glass *n.* two connected glass globes containing sand that takes an hour to pass from the upper to the lower.

houri (hoor-i) *n.* a beautiful young woman of the Muslim paradise.

hourly *adj.* done or occurring once an hour; reckoned by the hour. ● *adv.* **1** once an hour. **2** very frequently.

house *n.* (howss) **1** a building for people to live in, or for a specific purpose; a household; a family or dynasty. **2** a legislative assembly; a business firm; a theatre audience or performance. **3** a style of popular dance music using drum machines. ● *v.* (howz) provide accommodation or storage space for; encase. ◻ **on the house** (of drinks in a bar etc.) provided free of charge.

house arrest *n.* detention in one's own home.

houseboat *n.* a boat fitted up as a dwelling.

housebound *adj.* unable to leave one's house, esp. through illness.

housebreaker *n.* a burglar. ◻ **housebreaking** *n.*

housecoat *n.* a woman's dressing gown.

household *n.* the occupants of a house regarded as a unit.

householder *n.* a person owning or renting a house or flat.

household word *n.* (also **household name**) a widely known saying or name.

housekeeper *n.* a person employed to look after a household.

housekeeping *n.* management of household affairs; money to be used for this.

housemaster *n.* a male teacher in charge of a school boarding house.

housemistress *n.* a female teacher in charge of a school boarding house.

house-proud *adj.* giving great attention to the appearance of one's home.

house-trained *adj.* (of a pet) trained to be clean in the house.

house-warming *n.* a party to celebrate moving into a new home.

housewife *n.* (*pl.* **-wives**) a woman managing a household.

housework *n.* cleaning and cooking etc. in a house.

housing *n.* **1** accommodation. **2** a rigid case enclosing machinery.

hove *see* **heave**.

hovel *n.* a small miserable dwelling.

hover *v.* (of a bird, aircraft, etc.) remain in one place in the air; wait close by, linger.

hovercraft *n.* a vehicle supported by air thrust downwards from its engines.

how *adv.* **1** by what means, in what way. **2** to what extent or degree. **3** of what kind, in what condition: *how was the holiday?*

howdah (how-dă) *n.* a seat with a canopy on an elephant's back.

however *adv.* **1** nevertheless, despite this. **2** in whatever way, to whatever extent.

howitzer *n.* a short gun firing shells at high elevation.

howl *n.* a long loud wailing cry or sound. ● *v.* make or utter with a howl; weep loudly.

howler *n. informal* a stupid mistake.

hoyden *n. dated* a boisterous girl.

h.p. *abbr.* **1** hire purchase. **2** horse power.

HQ *abbr.* headquarters.

HRH *abbr.* His or Her Royal Highness.

HRT *abbr.* hormone replacement therapy.

hub *n.* the central part of a wheel; the centre of activity.

hubbub *n.* a confused noise of voices.

hubcap *n.* the cover for the hub of a car wheel.

hubris (hew-bris) *n.* arrogant pride.

huddle *v.* crowd into a small place. ● *n.* a close group or mass.

hue *n.* a colour, a tint. ▫ **hue and cry** public outcry or outrage.

huff *n.* a fit of annoyance. ● *v.* blow, breathe heavily. ▫ **huffily** *adv.*, **huffy** *adj.*

hug *v.* (**hugged, hugging**) squeeze in one's arms; hold closely; keep close to: *hug the shore.* ● *n.* an embrace.

huge *adj.* extremely large. ▫ **hugely** *adv.*

hula hoop (*trademark*) *n.* a large hoop for spinning round the body.

hulk *n.* the body of an old ship; a large clumsy-looking person or thing.

hulking *adj. informal* large and clumsy.

hull *n.* **1** the framework of a ship. **2** the pod of a pea or bean; the cluster of leaves on a strawberry. ● *v.* remove the hulls of (beans, strawberries, etc.).

hullabaloo *n. informal* an uproar.

hullo var. of **hello**.

hum *v.* (**hummed, humming**) **1** make a low continuous sound; sing with closed lips. **2** be in a state of activity. ● *n.* a humming sound.

human *adj.* of mankind; of people; not impersonal or insensitive. ● *n.* a human being. ▫ **humanly** *adv.*

humane *adj.* kind-hearted, merciful. ▫ **humanely** *adv.*

humanism *n.* a system of thought emphasizing human rather than divine matters and seeking rational solutions to human problems. ▫ **humanist** *n.*, **humanistic** *adj.*

humanitarian *adj.* promoting human welfare and reduction of suffering. ▫ **humanitarianism** *n.*

humanity *n.* **1** human nature; the human race. **2** kindness. **3** (**humanities**) arts subjects.

humanize *v.* (also **-ise**) make human; make humane.

human resources *n.pl.* the department of an organization dealing with the management and training of employees.

humble *adj.* **1** having a low opinion of one's importance or deserts. **2** of low rank; not large or expensive. ● *v.* lower the rank of; make less proud. ▫ **humbly** *adv.*

humbug *n.* **1** hypocritical talk or behaviour. **2** a hard usu. peppermint-flavoured sweet.

humdrum *adj.* dull, commonplace.

humerus *n.* (*pl.* **humeri**) the bone in the upper arm. ▫ **humeral** *adj.*

humid *adj.* (of air) damp. ▫ **humidity** *n.*

humidify *v.* (**humidified, humidifying**) increase the moisture in (air). ▫ **humidifier** *n.*

humiliate *v.* cause to feel ashamed and foolish. ▫ **humiliation** *n.*

humility *n.* a humble attitude of mind.

hummock *n.* a hump in the ground.

hummus *n.* (also **hoummos**) a paste of ground chickpeas, sesame oil, lemon juice, and garlic.

humour *n.* (*Amer.* **humor**) **1** the quality of being amusing; the ability to perceive and enjoy this. **2** a state of mind. ● *v.* keep (a person) contented by doing as he or she wishes. ▫ **humorous** *adj.*, **humorously** *adv.*

hump *n.* a rounded projecting part; a curved deformity of the spine. ● *v.* **1** form into a hump. **2** *informal* hoist and carry.

humpback *n.* a hunchback; a whale with a hump on its back.

humpback bridge *n.* a small steeply arched bridge.

humus (hyoo-mŭs) *n.* rich dark organic material in soil, formed by decay of dead leaves and plants.

hunch *v.* draw (one's shoulders) up; bend one's body forward. ● *n.* **1** an intuitive feeling. **2** a hunched position.

hunchback *n.* a person with a humped back.

▪ **Usage** The term *hunchback* is often found offensive.

hundred *n.* ten times ten (100, C). ▫ **hundredth** *adj.* & *n.*

hundredfold *adj.* & *adv.* 100 times as much or as many.

hundredweight *n.* a measure of weight, 112 lb (50.802 kg), or in America 100 lb (45.359 kg); a metric unit of weight equal to 50 kg.

hung past & p.p. of **hang**. ● *adj.* (of a council, parliament, etc.) with no party having a clear majority.

Hungarian *adj.* & *n.* (a native, the language) of Hungary.

hunger *n.* **1** discomfort and weakness felt when one has not eaten for some time; lack of food. **2** a strong desire. ● *v.* feel hunger.

hunger strike *n.* refusal of food as a form of protest.

hung-over *adj. informal* suffering from a hangover.

hungry *adj.* (**hungrier, hungriest**) feeling hunger; causing hunger. ▫ **hungrily** *adv.*

hunk *n.* **1** a large piece broken off. **2** *informal* an attractive man.

hunt *v.* **1** pursue (wild animals) for food or sport; pursue with hostility; seek; search. **2** (of an engine) run unevenly. ● *n.* an act of hunting; a hunting group.

hunter *n.* one who hunts; a horse used for hunting.

hurdle *n.* a portable fencing panel; a frame to be jumped over in a race; an obstacle, a difficulty. ▫ **hurdler** *n.*

hurl *v.* throw violently.

hurly-burly *n.* bustling activity.

hurrah *int.* & *n.* (also **hurray, hooray**) an exclamation of joy or approval.

hurricane *n.* a violent storm-wind.

hurricane lamp *n.* a lamp with the flame protected from the wind.

hurried *adj.* done with great haste. ▫ **hurriedly** *adv.*

hurry *v.* (**hurried, hurrying**) move or act with great or excessive haste; cause to do this. ● *n.* hurrying.

hurt *v.* (**hurt, hurt, hurting**) cause pain, injury, or grief to; feel pain; offend. ● *n.* injury, harm, or distress.

hurtful *adj.* causing distress.

hurtle *v.* move or hurl rapidly.

husband *n.* a married man in relation to his wife. ● *v.* use economically, try to save.

husbandry *n.* **1** farming. **2** economical management of resources.

hush *v.* make or become silent. ● *n.* silence. ▫ **hush up** suppress discussion of or information about.

husk *n.* the dry outer covering of certain seeds and fruits. ● *v.* remove the husk from.

husky *adj.* (**huskier, huskiest**) **1** (of a voice) low and hoarse. **2** strong, burly. ● *n.* (*pl.* **-ies**) an Arctic sledge-dog. ▫ **huskily** *adv.*, **huskiness** *n.*

hustle *v.* push roughly; force to move hurriedly. ● *n.* hustling.

hustings *n.* a meeting for political candidates to address voters.

hut *n.* a small simple or roughly made house or shelter.

hutch *n.* a box-like cage for rabbits.

hyacinth *n.* a plant with fragrant bell-shaped flowers.

hyaena var. of **hyena**.

hybrid *n.* the offspring of two different species or varieties; something made by combining different elements. ● *adj.* composed of different elements.

hybridize *v.* (also **-ise**) cross-breed; produce hybrids. ▫ **hybridism** *n.*, **hybridization** *n.*

hydrant *n.* a pipe from a water main in a street to which a hose can be attached.

hydrate *n.* a chemical compound of water with another substance.

hydraulic (hI-dror-lik) *adj.* **1** operated by pressure of fluid conveyed in pipes. **2** hardening under water. ● *n.* (**hydraulics**) the science of hydraulic operations. ▫ **hydraulically** *adv.*

hydrocarbon *n.* a compound of hydrogen and carbon.

hydrochloric acid *n.* a corrosive acid containing hydrogen and chlorine.

hydrodynamic *adj.* of the forces exerted by liquids in motion.

hydroelectric *adj.* using water-power to produce electricity.

hydrofoil *n.* a boat with a structure that raises its hull out of the water when in motion.

hydrogen *n.* an odourless gas, the lightest element (symbol H).

hydrogen bomb *n.* a powerful bomb releasing energy by fusion of hydrogen nuclei.

hydrolysis *n.* decomposition by chemical reaction with water. □ **hydrolytic** *adj.*

hydrometer *n.* a device measuring the density of liquids.

hydrophobia *n.* abnormal fear of water; rabies.

hydroponics *n.* growing plants in water impregnated with chemicals rather than in soil.

hydrostatic *adj.* of the pressure and other characteristics of liquid at rest.

hydrotherapy *n.* therapeutic exercise in water.

hydrous *adj.* containing water.

hyena *n.* (also **hyaena**) a wolf-like animal with a howl that sounds like laughter.

hygiene (**hI**-jeen) *n.* cleanliness as a means of preventing disease. □ **hygienic** *adj.*, **hygienically** *adv.*, **hygienist** *n.*

hymen *n.* the membrane partly closing the opening of the vagina of a virgin girl or woman.

hymn *n.* a song used in worship.

hype *n. informal* intensive promotion of a product.

hyper- *pref.* **1** excessively. **2** *Computing* relating to hypertext.

■ **Usage** The pronunciations of *hyper-* and *hypo-* are similar, but confusing them can reverse the meaning of a word, for example if *hypertension* is confused with *hypotension*.

hyperactive *adj.* abnormally active. □ **hyperactivity** *n.*

hyperbola (hI-per-bŏ-lă) *n.* (*pl.* **hyperbolas** or **hyperbolae**) the curve produced by a cut made through a cone at an angle with the base greater than that of the side of the cone.

hyperbole *n.* (hy-**per**-bŏli) an exaggerated statement.

hyperglycaemia (hy-per-gly-**see**-miă) *n.* (*Amer.* **hyperglycemia**) excess glucose in the blood.

hyperlink *n. Computing* a link from a hypertext document to another location.

hypermarket *n.* a very large supermarket.

hypersonic *adj.* of speeds more than five times that of sound.

hypertension *n.* **1** abnormally high blood pressure. **2** extreme tension.

hypertext *n. Computing* a system allowing simultaneous use of, and cross-reference between, several texts.

hyperventilation *n.* abnormally rapid breathing.

hyphen *n.* a sign (-) used to join words together or mark the division of a word at the end of a line.

hyphenate *v.* join or divide with a hyphen. □ **hyphenation** *n.*

hypnosis *n.* the production of a sleep-like condition in a person who then obeys suggestions. □ **hypnotic** *adj.*, **hypnotically** *adv.*

hypnotism *n.* hypnosis. □ **hypnotist** *n.*

hypnotize *v.* (also **-ise**) control by or as though by hypnosis.

hypo- *pref.* under; below normal.

hypo-allergenic *adj.* unlikely to cause an allergic reaction.

hypochondria *n.* the state of constantly imagining that one is ill. □ **hypochondriac** *n.*

hypocrisy *n.* (*pl.* **-ies**) falsely pretending to be virtuous; insincerity.

hypocrite *n.* a person guilty of hypocrisy. □ **hypocritical** *adj.*, **hypocritically** *adv.*

hypodermic *adj.* injected beneath the skin; used for such injections. ● *n.* a hypodermic syringe.

hypotension *n.* abnormally low blood pressure.

hypotenuse (hI-pot-ĕ-nyooz) *n.* the longest side of a right-angled triangle.

hypothermia *n.* the condition of having an abnormally low body temperature.

hypothesis *n.* (*pl.* **hypotheses**) a supposition put forward as a basis for reasoning or investigation.

hypothetical *adj.* supposed but not necessarily true. □ **hypothetically** *adv.*

hysterectomy (his-tĕr-**ek**-tŏm-i) *n.* (*pl.* **-ies**) the surgical removal of the womb.

hysteria *n.* wild uncontrollable emotion. □ **hysterical** *adj.*, **hysterically** *adv.*

hysterics *n.pl.* an outburst of hysteria; *informal* uncontrollable laughter.

Hz *abbr.* hertz.

Ii

I *pron.* the person speaking or writing and referring to himself or herself. ● *symb.* iodine.

iambic (I-**am**-bik) *adj.* & *n.* (verse) using iambuses, metrical feet of one short and one long syllable.

Iberian (I-**beer**-i-ăn) *adj.* of the peninsula comprising Spain and Portugal.

ibex *n.* (*pl.* **ibex** or **ibexes**) a mountain goat.

ibid. *abbr.* in a source just referred to.

ice *n.* **1** frozen water; an ice cream. **2** *informal* diamonds. ● *v.* cover with icing. □ **break the ice** start a conversation, relieve shyness. **ice over** become covered with ice. **ice up** become blocked with ice.

iceberg *n.* a mass of ice floating in the sea.

icebox *n.* the freezing compartment in a fridge; *Amer.* a fridge.

ice cream *n.* a sweet creamy frozen food.

Icelandic *adj.* & *n.* (the language) of Iceland. □ **Icelander** *n.*

ichthyology (ik-thi-**ol**-ŏji) *n.* the study of fishes. □ **ichthyologist** *n.*

icicle *n.* a piece of ice hanging downwards.

icing *n.* a mixture of powdered sugar and liquid or fat used to decorate cakes.

icon *n.* (also **ikon**) a sacred painting or mosaic; a greatly admired person; *Computing* a graphic symbol on a computer screen.

iconoclast *n.* a person who attacks established traditions. □ **iconoclasm** *n.*, **iconoclastic** *adj.*

icy *adj.* (**icier, iciest**) covered with ice; very cold; very unfriendly. □ **icily** *adv.*, **iciness** *n.*

ID *abbr.* identification.

idea *n.* a plan etc. formed in the mind; an opinion; a mental impression; a vague belief.

ideal *adj.* satisfying one's idea of what is perfect. ● *n.* a person or thing regarded as perfect; an aim, principle, or standard. □ **ideally** *adv.*

idealist *n.* a person with high ideals. □ **idealism** *n.*, **idealistic** *adj.*

idealize *v.* (also **-ise**) regard or represent as perfect.

identical *adj.* the same; exactly alike. □ **identically** *adv.*

identification *n.* identifying; something used as a proof of identity.

identify *v.* (**identified**, **identifying**) recognize as being a specified person or thing; reveal the identity of; associate (someone) closely with someone or something else; feel sympathy for someone. □ **identifiable** *adj.*, **identifiably** *adv.*

identikit *n.* a set of pictures of features that can be put together to form a likeness of a person.

identity *n.* (*pl.* **-ies**) **1** who or what someone or something is. **2** being the same.

ideogram *n.* a symbol or picture representing an idea, e.g. Chinese characters or road signs.

ideology *n.* (*pl.* **-ies**) ideas that form the basis of a political or economic theory. □ **ideological** *adj.*

idiocy *n.* (*pl.* **-ies**) extreme stupidity.

idiom *n.* a phrase whose meaning cannot be deduced from the words in it; an expression natural to a language.

idiomatic *adj.* using idioms; sounding natural. □ **idiomatically** *adv.*

idiosyncrasy *n.* (*pl.* **-ies**) a way of behaving distinctive of a particular person. □ **idiosyncratic** *adj.*

idiot *n.* a very stupid person. □ **idiotic** *adj.*, **idiotically** *adv.*

idle *adj.* not employed or in use; lazy; aimless. ● *v.* be idle; move slowly and aimlessly; (of an engine) run slowly in neutral gear. □ **idleness** *n.*, **idler** *n.*, **idly** *adv.*

idol *n.* an image worshipped as a god; an idolized person or thing.

idolatry *n.* worship of idols. □ **idolater** *n.*, **idolatrous** *adj.*

idolize *v.* (also **-ise**) love or admire excessively.

idyll (id-il) *n.* a peaceful or romantic scene; a description of this, usu. in verse. □ **idyllic** *adj.*, **idyllically** *adv.*

i.e. *abbr.* that is.

if *conj.* **1** on condition that; supposing that. **2** whether: *ask if they can come.* ● *n.* a condition or supposition.

iffy *adj.* (**iffier, iffiest**) *informal* uncertain; of doubtful quality.

igloo *n.* a dome-shaped Eskimo snow house.

igneous *adj.* (of rock) formed by volcanic action.

ignite *v.* set fire to; catch fire.

ignition *n.* igniting; a mechanism producing a spark to ignite the fuel in an engine.

ignoble *adj.* **1** not honourable. **2** of low status. □ **ignobly** *adv.*

ignominy (ig-nŏ-mi-ni) *n.* disgrace, humiliation. □ **ignominious** *adj.*, **ignominiously** *adv.*

ignoramus *n.* (*pl.* **ignoramuses**) an ignorant person.

ignorant *adj.* lacking knowledge; behaving rudely through not knowing good manners. □ **ignorance** *n.*, **ignorantly** *adv.*

ignore *v.* take no notice of.

iguana *n.* a large tropical lizard.

ikon var. of **icon**.

ileum *n.* a part of the small intestine.

ilk *n.* □ **of that ilk** of that kind.

ill *adj.* **1** in poor health, sick. **2** of poor quality. **3** harmful; unfavourable. ● *adv.* badly, wrongly. ● *n.* harm; a misfortune or problem. □ **ill at ease** uncomfortable, embarrassed.

ill-advised *adj.* unwise.

illegal *adj.* against the law. □ **illegality** *n.*, **illegally** *adv.*

illegible *adj.* not readable. □ **illegibility** *n.*, **illegibly** *adv.*

illegitimate *adj.* **1** born of parents not married to each other. **2** contrary to a law or rule. □ **illegitimacy** *n.*, **illegitimately** *adv.*

ill-gotten *adj.* gained by evil or unlawful means.

illicit *adj.* unlawful, not allowed. □ **illicitly** *adv.*

illiterate *adj.* unable to read and write; uneducated. □ **illiteracy** *n.*

ill-mannered *adj.* having bad manners.

illness *n.* the state of being ill; a particular form of ill health.

illogical *adj.* not logical. □ **illogicality** *n.*, **illogically** *adv.*

ill-treat *v.* treat badly or cruelly. □ **ill-treatment** *n.*

illuminate *v.* light up; decorate with lights; explain, clarify (a subject). □ **illumination** *n.*

illumine *v. literary* light up; enlighten.

illusion *n.* a false belief; a deceptive appearance; an error of perception.

illusionist *n.* a conjuror.

illusory *adj.* (also **illusive**) based on illusion; not real.

illustrate *v.* supply (a book etc.) with drawings or pictures; make clear by example(s) or picture(s); serve as an example of. □ **illustration** *n.*, **illustrative** *adj.*, **illustrator** *n.*

illustrious (il-lus-tri-ŭs) *adj.* well known and respected.

ill will *n.* hostility, unkind feeling.

image *n.* a picture or other representation; an optical appearance produced in a mirror or through a lens; a mental picture; a reputation; a simile or metaphor.

imaginary *adj.* existing only in the imagination, not real.

imagination *n.* imagining; the ability to imagine or to plan creatively. □ **imaginative** *adj.*, **imaginatively** *adv.*

imagine *v.* form a mental image of; think, suppose; guess. □ **imaginable** *adj.*

imago (i-may-goh) *n.* (*pl.* **imagines** or **imagos**) an insect in its fully developed adult stage.

imam (i-mahm) *n.* a leader of prayers in a mosque.

imbalance *n.* lack of balance.

imbecile *n.* a stupid person.

imbed var. of **embed**.

imbibe *v.* drink; absorb (ideas).

imbroglio (im-broh-lyoh) *n.* (*pl.* **imbroglios**) a confused or embarrassing situation.

■ **Usage** *Imbroglio* is spelt with a *g*.

imbue *v.* fill with feelings, qualities, or emotions.

IMF *abbr.* International Monetary Fund.

imitable *adj.* able to be imitated.

imitate *v.* try to act or be like; copy. □ **imitation** *n.*, **imitator** *n.*

imitative *adj.* imitating; not original.

immaculate *adj.* spotlessly clean and tidy; free from blemish or fault. □ **immaculately** *adv.*

immanent *adj.* inherent; present in everything. □ **immanence** *n.*

immaterial *adj.* **1** having no physical substance. **2** of no importance.

immature *adj.* **1** not fully grown. **2** childish, irresponsible. □ **immaturity** *n.*

immeasurable *adj.* too large or extreme to measure. □ **immeasurably** *adv.*

immediate *adj.* **1** done or occurring without delay. **2** nearest, with nothing between. □ **immediacy** *n.*

immediately *adv.* **1** without delay. **2** directly, with nothing in between. ● *conj.* as soon as.

immemorial *adj.* extremely old.

immense *adj.* extremely great. □ **immensely** *adv.*, **immensity** *n.*

immerse *v.* put completely into liquid; involve deeply in an activity etc.

immersion *n.* immersing.

immersion heater *n.* an electric heater placed in the liquid to be heated.

immigrate *v.* come to live permanently in a foreign country. □ **immigrant** *adj.* & *n.*, **immigration** *n.*

imminent *adj.* about to occur. □ **imminence** *n.*, **imminently** *adv.*

immiscible (im-miss-i-bĕl) *adj.* not able to be mixed (with another substance).

immobile *adj.* not moving; unable to be moved. □ **immobility** *n.*, **im-**

mobilize *v.* (also **-ise**), **immobilization** *n.*

immoderate *adj.* excessive. □ **immoderately** *adv.*

immolate *v.* kill as a sacrifice.

immoral *adj.* morally wrong. □ **immorality** *n.*, **immorally** *adv.*

immortal *adj.* living for ever, not mortal; famous for all time. □ **immortality** *n.*, **immortalize** *v.* (also **-ise**)

immovable *adj.* unable to be moved; unyielding. □ **immovably** *adv.*

immune *adj.* resistant to infection; exempt from an obligation etc.; not affected. □ **immunity** *n.*, **immunize** *v.* (also **-ise**), **immunization** *n.*

immunodeficiency *n.* (also **immune deficiency**) a reduction in normal resistance to infection.

immunology *n.* the study of resistance to infection. □ **immunological** *adj.*, **immunologist** *n.*

immure *v.* imprison, shut in.

immutable *adj.* unchangeable. □ **immutability** *n.*, **immutably** *adv.*

imp *n.* a small devil; a mischievous child.

impact *n.* (im-pakt) a collision, the force of this; a strong effect. ● *v.* (im-**pakt**) **1** collide forcefully with something. **2** press firmly.

impair *v.* damage, weaken. □ **impairment** *n.*

impale *v.* fix or pierce with a pointed object. □ **impalement** *n.*

impalpable *adj.* not easily grasped by the mind; unable to be felt by touch. □ **impalpably** *adv.*

impart *v.* make (information) known; give (a quality).

impartial *adj.* not favouring one side more than another. □ **impartiality** *n.*, **impartially** *adv.*

impassable *adj.* impossible to travel on or over.

impasse (am-pahss) *n.* a deadlock.

impassioned *adj.* passionate.

impassive *adj.* not feeling or showing emotion. □ **impassively** *adv.*, **impassivity** *n.*

impatient *adj.* **1** intolerant, easily irritated. **2** not ready to wait; eager. □ **impatience** *n.*, **impatiently** *adv.*

impeach *v.* **1** accuse of a serious crime against the state and bring for trial. **2** question, challenge (a privilege etc.). □ **impeachment** *n.*

impeccable *adj.* faultless. □ **impeccability** *n.*, **impeccably** *adv.*

impecunious *adj.* having little or no money.

impedance (im-**peed**-ăns) *n.* resistance of an electric circuit to the flow of current.

impede *v.* hinder.

impediment *n.* a hindrance or obstruction; a defect in speech, e.g. a lisp or stammer.

impel *v.* (**impelled, impelling**) urge or force to do something; drive forward.

impending *adj.* imminent.

impenetrable *adj.* **1** impossible to enter or pass through. **2** incomprehensible. □ **impenetrability** *n.*, **impenetrably** *adv.*

imperative *adj.* **1** essential, vital. **2** giving a command. ● *n.* **1** an essential thing. **2** a command; the grammatical case used for commands.

imperceptible *adj.* too slight to be noticed. □ **imperceptibly** *adv.*

imperfect *adj.* **1** flawed, faulty; not complete. **2** *Grammar* (of a tense) implying action going on and not completed. □ **imperfection** *n.*, **imperfectly** *adv.*

imperial *adj.* **1** of an empire or emperor; majestic. **2** (of measures) belonging to the British official non-metric system. □ **imperially** *adv.*

imperialism *n.* the policy of having or extending an empire. □ **imperialist** *n.*, **imperialistic** *adj.*

imperil *v.* (**imperilled, imperilling**; *Amer.* **imperiled**) endanger.

imperious *adj.* arrogantly giving orders. □ **imperiously** *adv.*, **imperiousness** *n.*

impermeable *adj.* not able to be penetrated by liquid.

impersonal *adj.* **1** not showing or influenced by personal feeling. **2** not existing as a person. □ **impersonality** *n.*, **impersonally** *adv.*

impersonate *v.* pretend to be (another person). □ **impersonation** *n.*, **impersonator** *n.*

impertinent *adj.* **1** disrespectful, rude. **2** *formal* irrelevant. □ **impertinence** *n.*, **impertinently** *adv.*

imperturbable *adj.* not excitable, calm.

impervious *adj.* impermeable. □ **impervious to** not able to be penetrated or influenced by. □ **imperviousness** *n.*

impetigo (im-pi-**ty**-goh) *n.* a contagious skin disease.

impetuous *adj.* acting or done quickly and recklessly. □ **impetuosity** *n.*, **impetuously** *adv.*

impetus *n.* a moving or driving force.

impiety *n.* (*pl.* **-ies**) lack of reverence.

impinge *v.* make an impact; encroach.

impious *adj.* not reverent, esp. towards a god; wicked. □ **impiously** *adv.*

implacable *adj.* unable to be placated; relentless. □ **implacability** *n.*, **implacably** *adv.*

implant *v.* (im-**plahnt**) insert (tissue or a device) into a living thing; fix (an idea) in the mind. ● *n.* (**im**-plahnt) something implanted. □ **implantation** *n.*

implausible *adj.* not persuasive, improbable. □ **implausibly** *adv.*

implement *n.* a tool. ● *v.* put (a decision etc.) into effect. □ **implementation** *n.*

implicate *v.* show or cause to be involved in a crime etc.

implication *n.* **1** something implied. **2** being implicated.

implicit *adj.* **1** implied but not stated. **2** absolute; total and unquestioning. □ **implicitly** *adv.*

implode *v.* (cause to) burst inwards. □ **implosion** *n.*

implore *v.* beg, ask earnestly.

imply *v.* (**implied, implying**) convey without stating directly.

impolite *adj.* bad-mannered, rude.

impolitic *adj.* unwise; risky.

imponderable *adj.* & *n.* (a thing) not able to be estimated or assessed.

import *v.* (im-**port**) bring from abroad or from an outside source. ● *n.* (**im**-port) **1** something imported; importing. **2** meaning; importance. □ **importation** *n.*, **importer** *n.*

important *adj.* having great significance or value; having a high and influential position. □ **importance** *n.*

importunate *adj.* making annoyingly persistent requests. □ **importunity** *n.*

importune *v.* make insistent requests to; (of a prostitute) solicit.

impose *v.* force (something unwelcome) on someone; put (a restriction, tax, etc.) into effect. □ **impose on** take unfair advantage of.

imposing *adj.* impressive.

imposition *n.* imposing something; being imposed; a burden imposed unfairly.

impossible *adj.* not able to exist, occur, or be done; very hard to deal with. □ **impossibility** *n.*, **impossibly** *adv.*

impostor *n.* a person who fraudulently pretends to be someone else.

imposture *n.* fraudulently pretending to be someone else.

impotent *adj.* powerless; (of a male) unable to copulate successfully. □ **impotence** *n.*

impound *v.* **1** take (property) into legal custody. **2** shut up, imprison.

impoverish *v.* cause to become poor; exhaust the strength or fertility of. ▫ **impoverishment** *n.*

impracticable *adj.* not able to be put into practice.

■ **Usage** *Impracticable* is sometimes confused with *impractical*.

impractical *adj.* not showing realism or common sense; not sensible or useful.

imprecation *n.* a spoken curse.

imprecise *adj.* not precise.

impregnable *adj.* safe against attack. ▫ **impregnability** *n.*

impregnate *v.* **1** introduce sperm or pollen into and fertilize. **2** saturate with a substance. ▫ **impregnation** *n.*

impresario (im-pri-**sah**-ri-oh) *n.* (*pl.* **impresarios**) an organizer of public entertainment.

impress *v.* **1** cause or feel admiration. **2** make a mark on (something) with a seal etc.; fix (an idea) in the mind.

impression *n.* **1** an idea or opinion about someone or something; an effect produced on the mind. **2** an imitation done for entertainment. **3** a mark impressed on a surface. ▫ **under the impression** believing (something).

impressionable *adj.* easily influenced.

impressionism *n.* a style of art giving a general impression without detail. ▫ **impressionist** *n.*, **impressionistic** *adj.*

impressive *adj.* inspiring admiration; grand or awesome. ▫ **impressively** *adv.*, **impressiveness** *n.*

imprint *n.* (im-print) **1** a mark made by pressing on a surface. **2** a publisher's name etc. on a title-page. ● *v.* (im-**print**) impress or stamp (a mark) on a surface.

imprison *v.* put into prison; keep in confinement. ▫ **imprisonment** *n.*

improbable *adj.* not likely to be true or to happen. ▫ **improbability** *n.*, **improbably** *adv.*

improbity (im-**proh**-bi-ti) *n.* dishonesty.

impromptu *adj.* & *adv.* without preparation or rehearsal.

improper *adj.* not conforming to accepted rules or standards; not decent or modest. ▫ **improperly** *adv.*, **impropriety** *n.*

improve *v.* make or become better. ▫ **improvement** *n.*

improvident *adj.* not providing for future needs. ▫ **improvidence** *n.*, **improvidently** *adv.*

improvise *v.* perform (drama, music etc.) without preparation or a script; make from whatever materials are at hand. ▫ **improvisation** *n.*

imprudent *adj.* unwise, rash. ▫ **imprudence** *n.*, **imprudently** *adv.*

impudent *adj.* disrespectful. ▫ **impudence** *n.*, **impudently** *adv.*

impugn (im-**pewn**) *v.* express doubts about the truth or honesty of.

impulse *n.* **1** a sudden urge to do something. **2** a driving force. **3** a pulse of electrical energy.

impulsion *n.* a strong urge; a driving force.

impulsive *adj.* acting or done on impulse, without prior thought. ▫ **impulsively** *adv.*, **impulsiveness** *n.*

impunity *n.* freedom from punishment or injury.

impure *adj.* **1** mixed with another substance. **2** dirty; morally wrong.

impurity *n.* (*pl.* **-ies**) being impure; a substance that makes another impure.

impute *v.* attribute (a fault) to someone. ▫ **imputation** *n.*

In *symb.* indium.

in *prep.* **1** enclosed or surrounded by; within (limits of space or time); contained by. **2** having as a condition etc.: *in love.* **3** having as a language or medium: *in English, in writing.* **4** into. ● *adv.* so as to be enclosed or surrounded; reaching a destination; entering a position etc. ● *adj.* **1** at home. **2** *informal* fashionable. □ **in for** about to experience **in on** sharing (a secret). **ins and outs** *informal* details. **in so far as** to the extent that. **in with** *informal* friendly with.

in. *abbr.* inch(es).

inability *n.* being unable.

in absentia *adv.* in his, her, or their absence.

inaccessible *adj.* hard or impossible to reach; unfriendly.

inaccurate *adj.* not accurate. □ **inaccuracy** *n.*, **inaccurately** *adv.*

inaction *n.* lack of action.

inactive *adj.* not active; not working or taking effect. □ **inactivity** *n.*

inadequate *adj.* not of sufficient quantity or quality; weak and incompetent. □ **inadequacy** *n.*, **inadequately** *adv.*

inadmissible *adj.* not allowable.

inadvertent *adj.* unintentional. □ **inadvertency** *n.*, **inadvertently** *adv.*

inalienable *adj.* not able to be given or taken away.

inane *adj.* silly, lacking sense. □ **inanely** *adv.*, **inanity** *n.*

inanimate *adj.* lacking animal life; showing no sign of being alive.

inappropriate *adj.* unsuitable. □ **inappropriately** *adv.*, **inappropriateness** *n.*

inarticulate *adj.* not expressed in words; unable to speak distinctly; unable to express ideas clearly. □ **inarticulacy** *n.*, **inarticulately** *adv.*

inasmuch *adv.* □ **inasmuch as** seeing that, because.

inattentive *adj.* not paying attention. □ **inattentively** *adv.*

inaudible *adj.* unable to be heard. □ **inaudibly** *adv.*

inaugurate (in-org-ewr-ayt) *v.* begin, introduce (a policy etc.); admit formally to office; open (a building etc.) formally. □ **inaugural** *adj.*, **inauguration** *n.*, **inaugurator** *n.*

inboard *adj.* & *adv.* (of an engine) inside a boat.

inborn *adj.* existing in a person or animal from birth, natural.

inbred *adj.* **1** produced by inbreeding. **2** inborn.

inbreeding *n.* breeding from closely related individuals.

inbuilt *adj.* essentially and naturally part of something.

Inc. *abbr.* incorporated.

incalculable *adj.* unable to be calculated; unpredictable. □ **incalculably** *adv.*

incandescent *adj.* glowing with heat. □ **incandescence** *n.*

incantation *n.* words or sounds uttered as a magic spell.

incapable *adj.* unable to do something; helpless. □ **incapability** *n.*

incapacitate *v.* prevent from functioning, disable.

incapacity *n.* mental or physical inability to do something; legal disqualification.

incarcerate (in-**kahs**-ĕr-ayt) *v.* imprison. □ **incarceration** *n.*

incarnate (in-**kah**-năt) *adj.* embodied, esp. in human form.

incarnation *n.* embodiment, esp. in human form; (**the Incarnation**) that of God as Christ.

incautious *adj.* rash.

incendiary *adj.* designed to cause fire; tending to provoke conflict. ● *n.* an incendiary bomb; an arsonist.

incense[1] (**in**-sens) *n.* a substance burnt to produce fragrant smoke, esp. in religious ceremonies.

incense[2] (in-**sens**) *v.* make angry.

incentive *n.* something that encourages action or effort.

inception *n.* the beginning of something.

incessant *adj.* not ceasing. □ **incessantly** *adv.*

incest *n.* sexual intercourse between very closely related people. □ **incestuous** *adj.*

inch *n.* a measure of length (= 2.54 cm). ● *v.* move gradually.

inchoate (in-koh-ăt, in-**koh**-ayt) *adj.* **1** not fully developed. **2** confused, incoherent.

incidence *n.* **1** the rate at which a thing occurs. **2** *Physics* the falling of a ray, line, etc. on a surface.

incident *n.* an event, esp. one causing trouble.

incidental *adj.* **1** minor, not essential. **2** occurring as a consequence of something else.

incidentally *adv.* **1** used to introduce a further or unconnected remark. **2** as a chance occurrence.

incidental music *n.* background music composed for a film.

incinerate *v.* burn to ashes. □ **incineration** *n.*, **incinerator** *n.*

incipient (in-**sip**-i-ĕnt) *adj.* in its early stages; beginning.

incise *v.* make a cut in; engrave. □ **incision** *n.*

incisive *adj.* clear and decisive. □ **incisively** *adv.*, **incisiveness** *n.*

incisor *n.* a sharp-edged front tooth.

incite *v.* urge on to action; stir up. □ **incitement** *n.*

incivility *n.* (*pl.* **-ies**) rudeness.

inclement *adj.* (of weather) unpleasant.

inclination *n.* **1** a tendency; a liking or preference. **2** a slope; bending.

incline *v.* (in-**klIn**) lean; bend. ● *n.* (**in**-klIn) a slope. □ **inclined to** **1** having a tendency to. **2** wanting to, preferring to.

include *v.* **1** contain as part of a whole; regard as part of something. **2** put in as part of a group or set. □ **inclusion** *n.*

inclusive *adj.* including all charges, services, etc.; (of language) designed to be non-sexist. □ **inclusive of** including. □ **inclusively** *adv.*, **inclusiveness** *n.*

incognito (in-kog-**nee**-toh) *adj.* & *adv.* with one's identity kept secret.

incoherent *adj.* disconnected; shapeless; unclear, confused. □ **incoherence** *n.*, **incoherently** *adv.*

incombustible *adj.* not able to be burnt.

income *n.* money received as wages, interest, etc.

incoming *adj.* coming in.

incommunicado (in-kom-yoo-ni-**kah**-doh) *adj.* not allowed or not wishing to communicate with others.

incomparable *adj.* beyond comparison, without an equal. □ **incomparably** *adv.*

incompatible *adj.* conflicting, inconsistent, unable to exist together. □ **incompatibility** *n.*

incompetent *adj.* lacking skill; not legally qualified to do something. □ **incompetence** *n.*

incomplete *adj.* not complete.

incomprehensible *adj.* not able to be understood. □ **incomprehensibly** *adv.*, **incomprehension** *n.*

inconceivable *adj.* unable to be imagined; most unlikely.

inconclusive *adj.* not fully convincing; not decisive. □ **inconclusively** *adv.*

incongruous *adj.* out of keeping, inappropriate. □ **incongruity** *n.*, **incongruously** *adv.*

inconsequential *adj.* unimportant. □ **inconsequentially** *adv.*

inconsiderable *adj.* of small size or value.

inconsiderate *adj.* not thinking of others' feelings or convenience. □ **inconsiderately** *adv.*

inconsistent *adj.* not consistent. □ **inconsistency** *n.*

inconsolable *adj.* not able to be comforted. □ **inconsolably** *adv.*

inconstant *adj.* frequently changing; irregular; disloyal. □ **inconstancy** *n.*

incontestable *adj.* indisputable.

incontinent *adj.* unable to control one's excretion of urine and/or faeces. □ **incontinence** *n.*

incontrovertible *adj.* indisputable, undeniable. □ **incontrovertibly** *adv.*

inconvenience *n.* difficulty and discomfort; a cause of this. ● *v.* cause inconvenience to.

inconvenient *adj.* difficult or troublesome. □ **inconveniently** *adv.*

incorporate *v.* **1** include as a part. **2** form (a company etc.) into a corporation. □ **incorporation** *n.*

incorrect *adj.* **1** not right or true. **2** not in accordance with standards. □ **incorrectly** *adv.*

incorrigible *adj.* not able to be reformed or improved. □ **incorrigibly** *adv.*

incorruptible *adj.* **1** not susceptible to bribery. **2** not subject to decay.

increase *v.* (in-**kreess**) make or become greater. ● *n.* (**in**-kreess) increasing; the amount by which a thing increases.

increasingly *adv.* more and more.

incredible *adj.* unbelievable; very surprising. □ **incredibly** *adv.*

incredulous *adj.* unbelieving, showing disbelief. □ **incredulity** *n.*, **incredulously** *adv.*

increment *n.* an increase, an added amount. □ **incremental** *adj.*

incriminate *v.* cause to appear guilty, imply the guilt of. □ **incrimination** *n.*, **incriminatory** *adj.*

incrustation *n.* a crust or deposit formed on a surface.

incubate *v.* hatch (eggs) by warmth; cause (bacteria etc.) to develop. □ **incubation** *n.*

incubator *n.* an apparatus for incubating eggs or bacteria; an enclosed heated compartment in which a premature baby can be kept.

inculcate (**in**-kul-kayt) *v.* implant (ideas or habits) by constant urging.

incumbent *adj.* forming an obligation or duty. ● *n.* the holder of an office, esp. a rector or a vicar.

incur *v.* (**incurred, incurring**) bring (something unpleasant) on oneself.

incurable *adj.* unable to be cured.

incursion *n.* a brief invasion, a raid.

indebted *adj.* owing money or gratitude.

indecent *adj.* offending against standards of decency; improper, inappropriate. □ **indecency** *n.*, **indecently** *adv.*

indecent assault *n.* sexual assault not involving rape.

indecent exposure *n.* exposing one's genitals in public.

indecipherable *adj.* unable to be read or interpreted.

indecision *n.* inability to decide, hesitation.

indecorous *adj.* improper; not in good taste.

indeed *adv.* in truth, really.

indefatigable (in-di-**fat**-ig-ă-bĕl) *adj.* untiring.

indefensible *adj.* **1** not justifiable. **2** not able to be defended.

indefinable *adj.* unable to be defined or described clearly.

indefinite *adj.* not clearly stated or fixed; vague; (of time) not limited.

indefinite article *see* **article**.

indefinitely *adv.* for an unlimited period; to an unlimited extent.

indelible *adj.* (of a mark) unable to be removed or washed away; (of ink) making such a mark. □ **indelibly** *adv.*

indelicate *adj.* slightly indecent; tactless. □ **indelicacy** *n.*, **indelicately** *adv.*

indemnify *v.* (**indemnified, indemnifying**) protect or insure (a person) against penalties that he or she might incur; compensate. □ **indemnification** *n.*

indemnity *n.* (*pl.* **-ies**) protection against penalties incurred by one's actions; money paid as compensation.

indent *v.* **1** start (a line of text) inwards from a margin; form recesses in (a surface). **2** place an official order for goods etc. □ **indentation** *n.*

indenture *n.* a written contract, esp. of apprenticeship. ● *v.* bind by this.

independent *adj.* **1** not ruled or controlled by another. **2** not relying on another; not connected, separate. □ **independence** *n.*, **independently** *adv.*

indescribable *adj.* too extreme, unusual, etc., to be described. □ **indescribably** *adv.*

indestructible *adj.* unable to be destroyed.

indeterminable *adj.* impossible to discover or decide.

indeterminate *adj.* not known; vague, not fixed or definite. □ **indeterminacy** *n.*

index *n.* (*pl.* **indexes** or **indices**) **1** a list (usu. alphabetical) of names, subjects, etc., with references. **2** an indicator of something; a figure indicating the current level of prices etc. compared with a previous level. **3** *Maths* the exponent of a number. ● *v.* **1** record in an index. **2** adjust (wages etc.) according to a price index.

indexation *n.* the practice of making wages and benefits index-linked.

index finger *n.* the finger next to the thumb.

index-linked *adj.* (of wages and benefits) increased in line with the cost-of-living index.

Indian *adj.* of India or Indians. ● *n.* **1** a native of India. **2** any of the original inhabitants of the American continent or their descendants.

Indian ink *n.* deep black ink.

Indian summer *n.* dry sunny weather in autumn.

India rubber *n.* natural rubber.

indicate *v.* point out; be a sign of; state briefly. □ **indication** *n.*, **indicative** *adj.*

indicator *n.* a thing that indicates; a pointer; a flashing light on a vehicle showing when it is going to turn.

indices pl. of **index**.

indict (in-**dyt**) *v.* make a formal accusation against. □ **indictable** *adj.*, **indictment** *n.*

indifferent *adj.* **1** showing no interest or sympathy. **2** neither good nor bad; not very good. □ **indifference** *n.*, **indifferently** *adv.*

indigenous (in-**dij**-i-nŭs) *adj.* native.

indigent (in-dij-ĕnt) *adj.* poor. □ **indigence** *n.*

indigestible *adj.* difficult or impossible to digest.

indigestion *n.* discomfort caused by difficulty in digesting food.

indignant *adj.* feeling or showing indignation. □ **indignantly** *adv.*

indignation *n.* anger aroused by something unjust or wicked.

indignity (*pl.* **-ies**) humiliating treatment or circumstances.

indigo (in-di-goh) *n.* a deep blue dye or colour.

indirect *adj.* not direct. □ **indirectly** *n.*

indirect object *n.* *Grammar* a word or phrase referring to someone or something indirectly affected by an action, e.g. *him* in *give it to him.*

indirect speech *n.* = **reported speech**.

indirect taxes *n.pl.* taxes paid on goods and services, not on income or capital.

indiscernible *adj.* unable to be perceived.

indiscreet *adj.* incautious; revealing secrets. □ **indiscreetly** *adv.*, **indiscretion** *n.*

indiscriminate *adj.* done or acting at random; not making a careful choice. □ **indiscriminately** *adv.*

indispensable *adj.* essential.

indisposed *adj.* **1** slightly ill. **2** unwilling. □ **indisposition** *n.*

indisputable *adj.* undeniable. □ **indisputably** *adv.*

indissoluble *adj.* firm and lasting, not able to be destroyed.

indistinct *adj.* unclear; obscure. □ **indistinctly** *adv.*

indistinguishable *adj.* unable to be told apart.

indium *n.* a metallic element (symbol In).

individual *adj.* single, separate; of or for one person or thing; original, not influenced by others. ● *n.* one person, animal, or plant considered separately; a person. □ **individuality** *n.*, **individually** *adv.*

individualist *n.* a person who is very independent in thought or action. □ **individualism** *n.*

indivisible *adj.* not able to be divided.

Indo- *comb. form* Indian (and).

indoctrinate *v.* teach (someone) to accept a set of beliefs uncritically. □ **indoctrination** *n.*

indolent *adj.* lazy. □ **indolence** *n.*, **indolently** *adv.*

indomitable *adj.* impossible to subdue or defeat. □ **indomitably** *adv.*

indoor *adj.* situated, used, or done inside a building. ● *adv.* (**indoors**) inside a building.

indubitable *adj.* that cannot reasonably be doubted. □ **indubitably** *adv.*

induce *v.* **1** persuade. **2** give rise to; bring on (child birth) artificially.

inducement *n.* an incentive; a bribe.

induct *v.* install (a clergyman) ceremonially into a benefice.

inductance *n.* the property of producing an electric current by induction.

induction *n.* **1** inducting. **2** causing; inducing childbirth. **3** reasoning to a general law from individual cases. **4** the production of an electric or magnetic state by proximity of an electrified or magnetic object. **5** drawing of a fuel mixture into the cylinder(s) of an engine.

inductive *adj.* **1** (of reasoning) proceeding from the individual to the general. **2** of electric or magnetic induction.

indulge *v.* satisfy (a desire); allow (someone) to have what they want. □ **indulge in** allow oneself (something pleasant). □ **indulgence** *n.*

indulgent *adj.* indulging a person's wishes too freely; kind, lenient. □ **indulgently** *adv.*

industrial *adj.* of, for, or full of industries. □ **industrially** *adv.*

industrial action *n.* a strike or similar protest.

industrial estate *n.* an area of land developed for business and industry.

industrialism *n.* an economic system in which manufacturing industries are predominant.

industrialist *n.* an owner or manager of an industrial business.

industrialized *adj.* (also **-ised**) full of industries.

industrial relations *n.pl.* relations between management and workers.

industrious *adj.* hard-working. □ **industriously** *adv.*

industry *n.* (*pl.* **-ies**) **1** manufacture or production of goods; business activity. **2** being industrious.

inebriated *adj.* drunk.

inedible *adj.* not edible, not suitable for eating.

ineducable *adj.* incapable of being educated.

ineffable *adj.* too great or extreme to be described.

ineffective *adj.* not producing the desired effect. □ **ineffectively** *adv.*

ineffectual *adj.* ineffective; unable to deal with a role or situation. □ **ineffectually** *adv.*

inefficient *adj.* not efficient; wasteful. □ **inefficiency** *n.*, **inefficiently** *adv.*

inelegant *adj.* not elegant; unrefined. □ **inelegantly** *adv.*

ineligible *adj.* not eligible or qualified.

ineluctable *adj.* inescapable, unavoidable.

inept *adj.* clumsy, unskilful. □ **ineptitude** *n.*, **ineptly** *adv.*, **ineptness** *n.*

inequality *n.* (*pl.* **-ies**) lack of equality.

inequitable *adj.* unfair, unjust. □ **inequitably** *adv.*

inert *adj.* without power to move; without active properties; not moving or taking action. □ **inertly** *adv.*, **inertness** *n.*

inertia (in-er-shă) *n.* **1** being inert; slowness to act. **2** the property by which matter continues in its existing state of rest or line of motion unless acted upon by a force.

inertia reel *n.* a reel allowing a seat belt to unwind freely unless pulled suddenly.

inescapable *adj.* unavoidable. □ **inescapably** *adv.*

inessential *adj.* not essential. ● *n.* an inessential thing.

inestimable *adj.* too great to be estimated. □ **inestimably** *adv.*

inevitable *adj.* unavoidable, sure to happen or appear. □ **inevitability** *n.*, **inevitably** *adv.*

inexact *adj.* not exact. □ **inexactitude** *n.*, **inexactly** *adv.*

inexcusable *adj.* unable to be excused or justified.

inexhaustible *adj.* available in unlimited quantity.

inexorable *adj.* impossible to prevent; impossible to persuade. □ **inexorably** *adv.*

inexpensive *adj.* not expensive.

inexperienced *adj.* lacking experience. □ **inexperience** *n.*

inexpert *adj.* not expert, unskilful. □ **inexpertly** *adv.*

inexplicable *adj.* impossible to explain. □ **inexplicability** *n.*, **inexplicably** *adv.*

inexpressible *adj.* unable to be expressed in words. □ **inexpressibly** *adv.*

in extremis *adj.* at the point of death; in an emergency.

inextricable *adj.* impossible to disentangle; impossible to escape from. □ **inextricably** *adv.*

infallible *adj.* incapable of being wrong; never failing. □ **infallibility** *n.*, **infallibly** *adv.*

infamous (in-fă-mŭs) *adj.* having a bad reputation. □ **infamously** *adv.*, **infamy** *n.*

infancy *n.* early childhood, babyhood; an early stage of development.

infant *n.* a child during the earliest stage of its life.

infanticide *n.* the killing or killer of an infant soon after its birth.

infantile *adj.* of infants or infancy; very childish.

infantry *n.* troops who fight on foot.

infatuated *adj.* filled with intense unreasoning love. □ **infatuation** *n.*

infect *v.* affect or contaminate with a disease or its germs; affect with one's feeling.

infection *n.* infecting; being infected; a disease spread in this way.

infectious *adj.* (of disease) able to spread by air or water; infecting others. □ **infectiously** *adv.*, **infectiousness** *n.*

infer *v.* (**inferred, inferring**) work out from evidence; conclude. □ **inference** *n.*

■ **Usage** It is a mistake to use *infer* to mean 'imply', as in *Are you inferring that I'm a liar?*

inferior *adj.* of lower rank, status, or quality; of low standard. ● *n.* a person inferior to another. □ **inferiority** *n.*

infernal *adj.* **1** of hell. **2** *informal* detestable, tiresome. □ **infernally** *adv.*

inferno *n.* (*pl.* **infernos**) a raging fire; an intensely hot place; hell.

infertile *adj.* unable to have offspring; (of soil) not producing vegetation. □ **infertility** *n.*

infest *v.* be present in (a place) in large numbers, esp. harmfully. ▫ **infestation** *n.*

infidel *n.* a person who does not believe in a religion.

infidelity *n.* (*pl.* **-ies**) unfaithfulness, esp. adultery.

infighting *n.* conflict within an organization.

infill *n.* (also **infilling**) material used to fill a hole; buildings constructed to fill a gap.

infiltrate *v.* make one's way into (a group etc.) secretly and gradually. ▫ **infiltration** *n.*, **infiltrator** *n.*

infinite *adj.* having no end or limit; very great, very many. ▫ **infinitely** *adv.*

infinitesimal *adj.* very small. ▫ **infinitesimally** *adv.*

infinitive *n.* the form of a verb not indicating tense, number, or person (e.g. *to go*).

infinity *n.* (*pl.* **-ies**) being infinite; an infinite number, space, or time.

infirm *adj.* weak from age or illness. ▫ **infirmity** *n.*

infirmary *n.* (*pl.* **-ies**) a hospital.

inflame *v.* **1** provoke or intensify (feelings). **2** cause inflammation in.

inflammable *adj.* easily set on fire. ▫ **inflammability** *n.*

▪ **Usage** Because *inflammable* could be taken to mean 'not easily set on fire', *flammable* is often used instead. The negative of *inflammable* is *non-inflammable*.

inflammation *n.* redness, heat, and pain in a part of the body.

inflammatory *adj.* arousing strong feeling or anger.

inflatable *adj.* able to be inflated. ● *n.* an object needing to be inflated before use.

inflate *v.* **1** (cause to) swell by filling with air or gas. **2** increase excessively and artificially; exaggerate.

inflation *n.* **1** inflating; being inflated. **2** a general increase in prices and fall in the purchasing power of money. ▫ **inflationary** *adj.*

inflect *v.* **1** change the pitch of (a voice) in speaking. **2** *Grammar* change the ending or form of (a word). ▫ **inflection** *n.*

inflexible *adj.* impossible to bend; unwilling to yield or compromise; unable to be changed. ▫ **inflexibility** *n.*, **inflexibly** *adv.*

inflict *v.* cause (something painful or unpleasant) to be suffered. ▫ **infliction** *n.*

inflorescence *n.* flowering; the complete flower head of a plant.

influence *n.* power to produce an effect, esp. on character, beliefs, or actions; a person or thing with this power. ● *v.* exert influence on.

influential *adj.* having great influence. ▫ **influentially** *adv.*

influenza *n.* a viral disease causing fever, muscular pain, and catarrh.

influx *n.* an arrival of large numbers of people or things.

inform *v.* **1** give information to; reveal criminal activities to the authorities. **2** be an essential principle or quality of.

informal *adj.* relaxed; unofficial; casual; without ceremony. ▫ **informality** *n.*, **informally** *adv.*

informant *n.* a giver of information.

information *n.* facts told or discovered.

information technology *n.* (also **information science**) the study and use of computers, microelectronics, etc. for storing and transferring information.

informative *adj.* giving information. ▫ **informatively** *adv.*

informed *adj.* having a good knowledge of something.

informer *n.* a person who reveals criminal activity to the authorities.

infra dig *adj.* *informal* beneath one's dignity.

infrared *adj.* of or using radiation with a wavelength longer than that of visible light rays.

infrastructure *n.* the basic structural parts of something; roads, sewers, etc. regarded as a country's basic facilities.

infrequent *adj.* not frequent. ▫ **infrequently** *adv.*

infringe *v.* break (a rule or agreement); encroach. ▫ **infringement** *n.*

infuriate *v.* make very angry.

infuse *v.* **1** fill (with a quality). **2** soak (tea or herbs) to bring out flavour.

infusion *n.* **1** a drink etc. made by infusing leaves. **2** introducing a new element into something.

ingenious *adj.* clever at inventing things; cleverly contrived. ▫ **ingeniously** *adv.*, **ingenuity** *n.*

▪ **Usage** *Ingenious* is sometimes confused with *ingenuous*.

ingenuous (in-jen-you-ŭs) *adj.* innocent, guileless; naive. ▫ **ingenuously** *adv.*, **ingenuousness** *n.*

ingest *v.* take in as food.

inglenook *n.* a space for sitting within a very large fireplace.

inglorious *adj.* **1** shameful. **2** not famous.

ingot *n.* a brick-shaped lump of cast metal.

ingrained *adj.* deeply embedded in a surface or in a person's character.

ingratiate *v.* bring (oneself) into a person's favour, esp. to gain advantage.

ingratitude *n.* lack of gratitude.

ingredient *n.* any of the parts in a mixture.

ingress *n.* going in; the right of entry; an entrance.

ingrowing *adj.* (of a toenail) growing abnormally into the flesh.

inhabit *v.* live in as one's home. ▫ **inhabitable** *adj.*, **inhabitant** *n.*

inhalant *n.* a medicinal substance to be inhaled.

inhale *v.* breathe in (air, smoke, gas, etc.). ▫ **inhalation** *n.*

inhaler *n.* a device for administering a vapour to be inhaled to relieve asthma etc.

inherent *adj.* existing in a thing as a natural or permanent quality. ▫ **inherently** *adv.*

inherit *v.* receive from a predecessor, esp. from someone who has died; receive (a characteristic) from one's parents. ▫ **inheritance** *n.*, **inheritor** *n.*

inhibit *v.* restrain, prevent; cause inhibitions in. ▫ **inhibited** *adj.*, **inhibitor** *n.*

inhibition *n.* a sense of embarrassment and self-consciousness keeping one from behaving naturally.

inhospitable *adj.* not hospitable; (of a place) with a harsh climate or landscape.

in-house *adj.* & *adv.* within an organization.

inhuman *adj.* (also **inhumane**) brutal, extremely cruel. ▫ **inhumanity** *n.*, **inhumanly** *adv.*

inimical *adj.* hostile; harmful. ▫ **inimically** *adv.*

inimitable *adj.* impossible to imitate. ▫ **inimitably** *adv.*

iniquity *n.* (*pl.* **-ies**) great injustice; wickedness. ▫ **iniquitous** *adj.*

initial *n.* the first letter of a word or name. ● *v.* (**initialled, initialling**; *Amer.* **initialed**) mark or sign with initials. ● *adj.* first, existing at the beginning. ▫ **initially** *adv.*

initiate *v.* (in-**ish**-i-ayt) **1** cause (a process etc.) to begin. **2** admit to membership of a secret group; introduce to a skill or activity. ● *n.* (in-**ish**-i-ăt) someone who has been admitted to a secret society etc. ▫ **initiation** *n.*, **initiator** *n.*, **initiatory** *adj.*

initiative *n.* **1** the capacity to invent and initiate ideas. **2** a position from which one can act to forestall others. **3** a fresh approach to a problem.

inject *v.* **1** force (liquid) into the body with a syringe. **2** introduce (a new element) into a situation etc. ▫ **injection** *n.*

injudicious *adj.* unwise. ◻ **injudiciously** *adv.*

injunction *n.* an authoritative order, esp. one made by a judge.

injure *v.* cause injury to.

injurious *adj.* harmful.

injury *n.* (*pl.* **-ies**) harm, damage; a wound, broken bone, etc.; unjust treatment.

injustice *n.* lack of justice; an unjust action.

ink *n.* coloured liquid used in writing, printing, etc. ● *v.* apply ink to. ◻ **inky** *adj.*

inkling *n.* a slight suspicion.

inlaid past of **inlay**.

inland *adj.* & *adv.* in or towards the interior of a country.

in-laws *n.pl. informal* one's relatives by marriage.

inlay *v.* (in-**lay**) (**inlaid, inlaying**) decorate (a surface) by setting pieces of another material in it so that the surfaces are flush. ● *n.* (**in**-lay) inlaid material or design.

inlet *n.* **1** an arm of the sea etc. extending inland. **2** a way in (e.g. for water into a tank).

in loco parentis *adv.* acting in the place of a parent.

inmate *n.* a person living in a prison or other institution.

in memoriam *prep.* in memory of (a dead person).

inmost *adj.* furthest inward.

inn *n.* a public house esp. one in the country offering accommodation.

innards *n.pl. informal* the stomach and bowels; the inner parts.

innate *adj.* inborn; natural. ◻ **innately** *adv.*

inner *adj.* nearer to the centre or inside; interior, internal.

inner city *n.* the central area of a city.

innermost *adj.* furthest inward.

innings *n.* (in cricket) a batsman's or side's turn at batting.

innocent *adj.* **1** not guilty; not intended to cause harm; morally pure. **2** without experience or knowledge, esp. of something bad. ◻ **innocence** *n.*, **innocently** *adv.*

innocuous *adj.* harmless. ◻ **innocuously** *adv.*

innovate *v.* introduce something new. ◻ **innovation** *n.*, **innovative** *adj.*, **innovator** *n.*

innuendo (in-yoo-**end**-oh) *n.* (*pl.* **innuendoes** or **innuendos**) a remark indirectly suggesting something discreditable or indecent.

innumerable *adj.* too many to be counted.

innumerate *adj.* without knowledge of basic arithmetic. ◻ **innumeracy** *n.*

inoculate *v.* protect against disease with vaccines or serums. ◻ **inoculation** *n.*

inoperable *adj.* unable to be cured by surgical operation.

inoperative *adj.* not functioning.

inopportune *adj.* happening at an unsuitable time.

inordinate *adj.* excessive; disproportionate. ◻ **inordinately** *adv.*

inorganic *adj.* of mineral origin, not organic. ◻ **inorganically** *adv.*

in-patient *n.* a patient staying in a hospital during treatment.

input *n.* something put in or contributed for use or processing; supplying, putting in. ● *v.* (**input** or **inputted, inputting**) supply (data etc.) to a computer.

inquest *n.* a judicial investigation, esp. of a sudden death.

inquire *v.* make an inquiry.

inquiry *n.* (*pl.* **-ies**) an investigation.

inquisition *n.* an act of detailed or relentless questioning. ◻ **inquisitor** *n.*, **inquisitorial** *adj.*

inquisitive *adj.* curious; prying. ◻ **inquisitively** *adv.*, **inquisitiveness** *n.*

inroad *n.* a hostile attack. ◻ **make inroads on** or **into** encroach on; use up, destroy.

insalubrious (in-să-**loob**-ri-ŭs) *adj.* unhealthy, unwholesome.

insane *adj.* mad; extremely foolish. ◻ **insanely** *adv.*, **insanity** *n.*

insanitary *adj.* dirty and unhygienic.

insatiable *adj.* impossible to satisfy. ▫ **insatiability** *n.*, **insatiably** *adv.*

inscribe *v.* write or carve (words) on a surface; write a dedication on or in; *Geometry* draw (a figure) inside another.

inscription *n.* words inscribed.

inscrutable *adj.* baffling, impossible to interpret. ▫ **inscrutability** *n.*, **inscrutably** *adv.*

insect *n.* a small creature with six legs, no backbone, and a segmented body.

insecticide *n.* a substance for killing insects.

insectivorous *adj.* insect-eating.

insecure *adj.* **1** not firmly fixed or attached. **2** lacking confidence.

inseminate *v.* insert semen into. ▫ **insemination** *n.*

insensible *adj.* **1** unconscious; unaware. **2** imperceptible. ▫ **insensibility** *n.*, **insensibly** *adv.*

insensitive *adj.* not sensitive. ▫ **insensitively** *adv.*, **insensitivity** *n.*

inseparable *adj.* impossible to separate or treat separately; (of friends) reluctant to part. ▫ **inseparability** *n.*, **inseparably** *adv.*

insert *v.* (in-**sert**) put into something else; include or enclose. ● *n.* (**in**-sert) something inserted, esp. pages inserted in a magazine etc. ▫ **insertion** *n.*

in-service *adj.* (of training) for people working in the profession concerned.

inset *n.* (**in**-set) a small picture included in a larger one; an insert in a magazine; a thing fitted in something else. ● *v.* (in-**set**) (**inset, insetting**) put in as an inset; decorate with an inset.

inshore *adj.* & *adv.* at sea but near or towards the shore.

inside *n.* the inner part of something; the inner side or surface; *informal* a position giving access to confidential information; (**insides**) the stomach and bowels. ● *adj.* on or from the inside. ● *adv.* on, in, or to the inside; *informal* in prison. ● *prep.* within, contained by; into; in less than (a specified time). ▫ **inside out 1** with the inner side turned outwards; confused; utterly changed. **2** thoroughly: *know the subject inside out.*

insider dealing *n.* the illegal practice of using confidential information to gain advantage in buying stocks and shares.

insidious *adj.* imperceptibly spreading or developing with harmful effect. ▫ **insidiously** *adv.*, **insidiousness** *n.*

insight *n.* intuitive perception and understanding.

insignia *n.pl.* symbols of authority or office; an identifying badge.

insignificant *adj.* trivial, not worth considering. ▫ **insignificance** *n.*, **insignificantly** *adv.*

insinuate *v.* **1** indirectly suggest something discreditable. **2** gradually and artfully manoevre (something, esp. oneself) into position. ▫ **insinuation** *n.*, **insinuator** *n.*

insipid *adj.* lacking flavour, interest, or liveliness. **insipidity** *n.*

insist *v.* demand or state emphatically.

insistent *adj.* insisting; forcing itself on one's attention. ▫ **insistence** *n.*, **insistently** *adv.*

in situ (in sit-yoo) *adv.* in its original place.

insolent *adj.* disrespectful, arrogant. ▫ **insolence** *n.*, **insolently** *adv.*

insoluble *adj.* **1** impossible to solve. **2** unable to be dissolved.

insolvent *adj.* unable to pay one's debts. ▫ **insolvency** *n.*

insomnia *n.* inability to sleep. ▫ **insomniac** *n.*

insouciant (in-soo-si-ĕnt) *adj.* carefree, unconcerned. ▫ **insouciance** *n.*

inspect *v.* examine critically or officially. ▫ **inspection** *n.*

inspector *n.* **1** a person who inspects. **2** a police officer above sergeant.

inspiration *n.* **1** being inspired; a sudden brilliant idea; someone or something inspiring. **2** breathing in. □ **inspirational** *adj.*

inspire *v.* **1** stimulate to activity; encourage (a feeling); cause to feel uplifted. **2** inhale.

inst. *abbr.* instant, of the current month.

instability *n.* lack of stability.

install *v.* place (a person) into office ceremonially; set in position and ready for use; establish.

installation *n.* the process of installing; an apparatus etc. installed.

instalment *n.* (*Amer.* **installment**) one of the regular payments made to clear a debt paid over a period of time; one part of a serial.

instance *n.* an example; a particular case. ● *v.* mention as an example.

instant *adj.* happening or done immediately; (of food) quickly and easily prepared. ● *n.* an exact moment; a very short time. □ **instantly** *adv.*

instantaneous (in-stăn-**tay**-ni-ŭs) *adj.* occurring or done instantly. □ **instantaneously** *adv.*

instead *adv.* as an alternative.

instep *n.* the middle part of the foot.

instigate *v.* bring about (an action); urge to act. □ **instigation** *n.*, **instigator** *n.*

instil *v.* (*Amer.* **instill**) (**instilled, instilling**) introduce (ideas etc.) into a person's mind gradually. □ **instillation** *n.*

instinct *n.* an inborn impulse; a natural tendency or ability. □ **instinctive** *adj.*, **instinctively** *adv.*

institute *n.* an organization for promotion of a specified activity; its premises. ● *v.* set up; establish.

institution *n.* **1** an institute. **2** a home in which people with special needs are cared for. **3** an established rule or custom. **4** instituting; being instituted. □ **institutional** *adj.*

institutionalize *v.* (also **-ise**) **1** establish as a custom etc. **2** place in a residential institution. □ **institutionalized** *adj.*

instruct *v.* **1** teach a subject or skill to. **2** give instructions to. □ **instructor** *n.*

instruction *n.* **1** the process of teaching. **2** an order; (**instructions**) an explanation of how to do or use something. □ **instructional** *adj.*

instructive *adj.* informative, enlightening. □ **instructively** *adv.*

instrument *n.* **1** a tool for delicate work. **2** a measuring device of an engine or vehicle. **3** a device for producing musical sounds.

instrumental *adj.* **1** serving as a means. **2** performed on musical instruments.

instrumentalist *n.* a player of a musical instrument.

insubordinate *adj.* disobedient, rebellious. □ **insubordination** *n.*

insubstantial *adj.* lacking reality or solidity.

insufferable *adj.* intolerable. □ **insufferably** *adv.*

insufficient *adj.* not enough; inadequate. □ **insufficiency** *n.*, **insufficiently** *adv.*

insular *adj.* **1** of an island. **2** narrow-minded. □ **insularity** *n.*

insulate *v.* **1** cover with a substance that prevents the passage of electricity, sound, or heat. **2** protect from outside influences, pressures, etc. □ **insulation** *n.*, **insulator** *n.*

insulin *n.* a hormone controlling the body's absorption of sugar.

insult *v.* (in-**sult**) speak or act so as to offend (a person). ● *n.* (**in**-sult) an insulting remark or action. □ **insulting** *adj.*

insuperable *adj.* impossible to overcome. □ **insuperably** *adv.*

insupportable *adj.* unbearable.

insurance *n.* a contract to provide compensation for loss, damage, or death; a sum payable as a premium or in compensation; a safeguard against loss or failure.

insure *v.* **1** protect by insurance. **2** *Amer.* ensure. □ **insurer** *n.*

insurgent *adj.* rebellious, rising in revolt. ● *n.* a rebel. □ **insurgency** *n.*

insurmountable *adj.* too great to be overcome.

insurrection *n.* a rebellion. □ **insurrectionist** *n.*

intact *adj.* undamaged, complete.

intake *n.* an amount of a substance taken into the body; people entering an establishment at a particular time; taking in.

intangible *adj.* unable to be touched or grasped; vague, indefinable.

integer *n.* a whole number, not a fraction.

integral *adj.* necessary to make a whole complete.

integrate *v.* combine (parts) into a whole; bring or come into full membership of a community. □ **integration** *n.*

integrity *n.* **1** honesty. **2** being complete and unified.

intellect *n.* the mind's power of reasoning and acquiring knowledge.

intellectual *adj.* of the intellect; appealing to the intellect; having a strong intellect. ● *n.* an intellectual person. □ **intellectually** *adv.*

intelligence *n.* **1** mental ability to learn and understand things. **2** information, esp. that of military value; people collecting this.

intelligent *adj.* having great mental ability. □ **intelligently** *adv.*

intelligentsia *n.* educated and cultured people.

intelligible *adj.* able to be understood. □ **intelligibility** *n.*, **intelligibly** *adv.*

intend *v.* have in mind as what one wishes to achieve; plan a particular use or destiny for (someone or something).

intense *adj.* **1** extreme; in a high degree. **2** having strong feelings. □ **intensely** *adv.*, **intensity** *n.*

■ **Usage** *Intense* is sometimes confused with *intensive*, and wrongly used to describe a course of study etc.

intensifier *n. Grammar* a word used to give emphasis, e.g. *really* in *I'm really hot.*

intensify *v.* (**intensified, intensifying**) make or become more intense. □ **intensification** *n.*

intensive *adj.* **1** achieving a great deal in a short time; concentrated. **2** intended to achieve the highest level of production possible in an area. **3** making much use of something specified: *labour-intensive.* □ **intensively** *adv.*, **intensiveness** *n.*

intensive care *n.* medical treatment with constant attention for a seriously ill patient.

intent *n.* intention. ● *adj.* with concentrated attention. □ **intent on** determined to. □ **intently** *adv.*, **intentness** *n.*

intention *n.* what one intends to do.

intentional *adj.* done on purpose. □ **intentionally** *adv.*

inter *v.* (**interred, interring**) bury (a dead body).

inter- *pref.* between, among.

interact *v.* have an effect upon each other. □ **interaction** *n.*, **interactive** *adj.*

inter alia *adv.* among other things.

interbreed *v.* (**interbred, interbreeding**) breed with each other, cross-breed.

intercede (in-tĕ-**seed**) *v.* intervene on someone's behalf.

intercept *v.* stop or catch between a starting point and destination. □ **interception** *n.*, **interceptor** *n.*

intercession *n.* interceding.

interchange *v.* (inter-**chaynj**) **1** (of two people) exchange (things).

2 cause to change places. ● *n.* (**inter**-chaynj) **1** a process of interchanging. **2** a road junction designed so that streams of traffic do not cross on the same level. ▫ **interchangeable** *adj.*

intercom *n.* an electrical device allowing one-way or two-way communication.

interconnect *v.* connect with each other. ▫ **interconnection** *n.*

intercontinental *adj.* between continents.

intercourse *n.* **1** dealings between people or countries. **2** sexual intercourse, copulation.

interdenominational *adj.* involving more than one religious denomination.

interdependent *adj.* dependent on each other.

interdict (in-tĕ-dikt) *n.* a formal prohibition.

interdisciplinary *adj.* involving different branches of knowledge.

interest *n.* **1** wanting to learn about or do something; something about which one feels this; being interesting. **2** money paid for use of money borrowed. **3** advantage: *in my own interest.* **4** a share in an undertaking. ● *v.* arouse the curiosity of, be interesting to.

interested *adj.* **1** feeling interest. **2** not impartial.

interesting *adj.* arousing interest.

interface *n.* **1** a place where interaction occurs. **2** *Computing* a program or apparatus connecting two machines or enabling a user to use a program.

interfere *v.* **1** prevent something's progress or proper functioning. **2** become involved in others' affairs without invitation. ▫ **interfere with** molest sexually.

interference *n.* interfering; disturbance of radio signals.

interferon *n.* a protein preventing the development of a virus.

intergalactic *adj.* between galaxies.

interim *n.* an intervening period. ● *adj.* of or in such a period, temporary.

interior *adj.* inner. ● *n.* the inner part; the inside.

interject *v.* put in (a remark) when someone is speaking.

interjection *n.* a remark interjected; an exclamation.

interlace *v.* weave or lace together.

interlink *v.* link together.

interlock *v.* (of two things) fit into each other. ● *n.* a fine machine-knitted fabric.

interloper *n.* an intruder.

interlude *n.* **1** an interval. **2** music or other entertainment provided during an interval.

intermarry *v.* (**intermarried, intermarrying**) (of members of different groups) marry one another; (of close relations) marry. ▫ **intermarriage** *n.*

intermediary *n.* (*pl.* **-ies**) a mediator, a messenger. ● *adj.* intermediate.

intermediate *adj.* coming between two things in time, place, or order; having achieved a basic level in a subject or skill.

interment *n.* burial.

intermezzo (inter-**mets**-oh) *n.* (*pl.* **intermezzos** or **intermezzi**) a short piece of music.

interminable *adj.* endless; very long. ▫ **interminably** *adv.*

intermission *n.* an interval; a pause.

intermittent *adj.* occurring at irregular intervals. ▫ **intermittently** *adv.*

intern *v.* confine (esp. an enemy alien). ● *n.* (also **interne**) *Amer.* a resident junior doctor at a hospital.

internal *adj.* of or in the inside; inside the body; of a country's domestic affairs; applying within an organization. ▫ **internally** *adv.*

internal-combustion engine *n.* an engine producing power from fuel exploded within a cylinder.

internalize *v.* (also **-ise**) learn, absorb into the mind.

international *adj.* between countries; involving several countries. ● *n. Brit.* a sports contest between players of different countries; one of these players. □ **internationally** *adv.*

interne var. of **intern** *n.*

internecine (inter-nee-syn) *adj.* destructive to both sides in a conflict; of conflict within a group.

internee *n.* an interned person.

Internet *n.* an international computer network with information accessible to the public via modem links.

internment *n.* interning; being interned.

interplay *n.* interaction.

interpolate (in-ter-pŏ-layt) *v.* insert; add to a text; interject. □ **interpolation** *n.*

interpose *v.* **1** place between one thing and another. **2** intervene between opponents.

interpret *v.* explain the meaning of; understand in a particular way; act as interpreter. □ **interpretation** *n.*, **interpretative** *adj.*, **interpretive** *adj.*

interpreter *n.* a person who orally translates speech between people speaking different languages.

interracial *adj.* involving different races.

interregnum *n.* a period between the rule of two successive rulers.

interrelated *adj.* related to each other.

interrogate *v.* question closely. □ **interrogation** *n.*, **interrogator** *n.*

interrogative *adj.* forming a question; used in questions. □ **interrogatively** *adv.*

interrupt *v.* break the continuity of; break the flow of (speech etc.) by a remark. □ **interruption** *n.*

intersect *v.* divide or cross by passing or lying across. □ **intersection** *n.*

intersperse *v.* insert here and there; vary by adding something different at intervals.

interstate *adj.* between states, esp. of the USA.

interval *n.* a time between events, a break in activity; the time between acts of a play etc.; a space between two things; a difference in musical pitch. □ **at intervals** with spaces or time in between.

intervene *v.* **1** become involved in a situation to change its course; form an obstacle or delay. **2** occur between events. □ **intervention** *n.*

interview *n.* a formal conversation with someone, designed to extract information or assess their suitability for a position. ● *v.* hold an interview with. □ **interviewee** *n.*, **interviewer** *n.*

interweave *v.* (**interwove, interwoven, interweaving**) weave together; blend.

intestate (in-tes-tayt) *adj.* not having made a valid will. □ **intestacy** *n.*

intestine *n.* a long tubular section of the alimentary canal between the stomach and anus. □ **intestinal** *adj.*

intimate[1] (in-ti-măt) *adj.* **1** closely acquainted or familiar; having a sexual relationship (esp. outside marriage); private and personal. **2** (of knowledge) thorough, detailed. ● *n.* an intimate friend. □ **intimacy** *n.*, **intimately** *adv.*

intimate[2] (in-ti-mayt) *v.* make known, esp. by hinting. □ **intimation** *n.*

intimidate *v.* influence by frightening. □ **intimidation** *n.*

into *prep.* **1** to the inside of, to a point within. **2** so as to touch: *he bumped into me.* **3** becoming, developing into; resulting in: *changed into a frog.* **4** concerned with, focussing on: *an inquiry into the incident.* **5** dividing (a number) mathematically. **6** *informal* interested in, enthusiastic about.

intolerable *adj.* unbearable. □ **intolerably** *adv.*

intonation *n.* the rise and fall of the voice in speaking.

intone *v.* chant, esp. on one note.

intoxicant *adj.* & *n.* (a substance) causing intoxication.

intoxicate *v.* make drunk; make greatly excited. □ **intoxication** *n.*

intra- *pref.* within.

intractable *adj.* hard to deal with or control. □ **intractability** *n.*

intramural *adj.* **1** within the walls of an institution etc. **2** part of ordinary university work.

intransigent *adj.* stubborn. □ **intransigence** *n.*, **intransigently** *adv.*

intransitive *adj. Grammar* (of a verb) not followed by a direct object.

intrauterine *adj.* within the uterus.

intravenous *adj.* in or administered into a vein. □ **intravenously** *adv.*

in-tray *n.* a tray holding documents that need attention.

intrepid *adj.* fearless, brave. □ **intrepidly** *adv.*

intricate *adj.* very complicated. □ **intricacy** *n.*, **intricately** *adv.*

intrigue *v.* (in-treeg) **1** arouse the curiosity of. **2** plot secretly. ● *n.* (in-treeg) a plot; a secret love affair. □ **intriguing** *adj.*

intrinsic *adj.* existing in a thing as a natural or permanent quality; essential. □ **intrinsically** *adv.*

introduce *v.* **1** make (a person) known to another; present to an audience. **2** bring into use. **3** insert. **4** occur at the start of.

introduction *n.* introducing; an introductory part.

introductory *adj.* introducing a person or thing; preliminary.

introspection *n.* examination of one's own thoughts and feelings. □ **introspective** *adj.*

introvert *n.* an introspective and shy person. □ **introverted** *adj.*

intrude *v.* come or join in without being invited or wanted; thrust in. □ **intrusion** *n.*, **intrusive** *adj.*

intruder *n.* a person who intrudes; a burglar.

intuition *n.* the power of knowing without learning or reasoning; a belief based on instinct or emotion. □ **intuitive** *adj.*, **intuitively** *adv.*

Inuit (in-yoo-it) *n.* (*pl.* **Inuit** or **Inuits**) a North American Eskimo.

inundate *v.* flood; overwhelm.

inure *v.* **1** accustom, esp. to something unpleasant. **2** (in law) take effect.

invade *v.* enter (territory) with hostile intent; crowd into, encroach on; penetrate harmfully. □ **invader** *n.*

invalid[1] (in-vă-lid) *n.* a person suffering from ill health.

invalid[2] (in-val-id) *adj.* not valid.

invalidate *v.* make no longer valid.

invaluable *adj.* having a value too great to be measured.

invariable *adj.* not variable, always the same. □ **invariably** *adv.*

invasion *n.* a hostile or harmful intrusion. □ **invasive** *adj.*

invective *n.* abusive language.

invent *v.* make or design (something new); make up (a lie, a story). □ **inventor** *n.*

invention *n.* something invented; inventing.

inventive *adj.* able to invent things. □ **inventiveness** *n.*

inventory *n.* (*pl.* **-ies**) a detailed list of goods or furniture.

inverse *adj.* opposite, contrary. □ **inverse proportion** a relation such that one item decreases to the extent that the other increases. □ **inversely** *adv.*

invert *v.* turn upside down; reverse the position, order, or relationship of. □ **inversion** *n.*

invertebrate *adj.* & *n.* (an animal) having no backbone.

inverted commas *n.pl.* quotation marks.

invest *v.* **1** use (money, time, etc.) to earn interest or bring profit. **2** confer rank or office upon.

3 endow with a quality. □ **investment** *n.*, **investor** *n.*

investigate *v.* study carefully; inquire into. □ **investigation** *n.*, **investigative** *adj.*, **investigator** *n.*

investiture *n.* investing a person with honours or rank.

inveterate *adj.* habitual; firmly established.

invidious *adj.* liable to cause resentment. □ **invidiously** *adv.*

invigilate *v.* supervise examination candidates. □ **invigilator** *n.*

invigorate *v.* fill with vigour, give strength or courage to.

invincible *adj.* unconquerable.

inviolable *adj.* never to be broken or dishonoured.

inviolate *adj.* not violated; safe.

invisible *adj.* not able to be seen. □ **invisibility** *n.*, **invisibly** *adv.*

invite *v.* ask (a person) politely to come or to do something; ask for; risk provoking: *his behaviour invited criticism.* □ **invitation** *n.*

inviting *adj.* pleasant and tempting. □ **invitingly** *adv.*

in vitro *adj.* & *adv.* in a test tube or other laboratory environment: *in vitro fertilization.*

invocation *n.* invoking; an incantation used to summon supernatural forces.

invoice *n.* a bill for goods or services. ● *v.* send an invoice to.

invoke *v.* call for the help or protection of; summon (a spirit).

involuntary *adj.* done without intention. □ **involuntarily** *adv.*

involve *v.* have as a part or consequence; cause to participate; require. □ **involvement** *adj.*

involved *adj.* **1** concerned in something; in a relationship with someone. **2** complicated.

invulnerable *adj.* not vulnerable.

inward *adj.* situated on or going towards the inside; in the mind or spirit. ● *adv.* towards the inside. □ **inwardly** *adv.*, **inwards** *adv.*

iodine *n.* a chemical (symbol I) used in solution as an antiseptic.

iodize *v.* (also **-ise**) treat or impregnate with iodine.

ion *n.* an electrically charged atom that has lost or gained an electron. □ **ionic** *adj.*

ionize *v.* (also **-ise**) convert or be converted into ions.

ionosphere *n.* the ionized region of the atmosphere. □ **ionospheric** *adj.*

iota *n.* **1** a Greek letter (Ι, ι). **2** a very small amount: *not an iota of difference.*

IOU *n.* a signed paper given as a receipt for money borrowed.

ipso facto *adv.* by that very fact.

IQ *abbr.* intelligence quotient, a number showing how a person's intelligence compares with the average.

Ir *symb.* iridium.

irascible (irr-ass-i-bĕl) *adj.* hot-tempered. □ **irascibly** *adv.*

irate *adj.* angry. □ **irately** *adv.*

ire *n.* anger.

iridescent (irr-id-ess-ĕnt) *adj.* shimmering with many colours. □ **iridescence** *n.*

iridium *n.* a metallic element (symbol Ir).

iris *n.* **1** the coloured part of the eyeball, round the pupil. **2** a plant with showy flowers.

Irish *adj.* & *n.* (the language) of Ireland. □ **Irishman** *n.*, **Irishwoman** *n.*

irk *v.* annoy, be tiresome to.

irksome *adj.* irritating.

iron *n.* **1** an element (symbol Fe), a strong hard metal; a tool made of this. **2** an implement with a flat base heated for smoothing cloth. **3** (**irons**) fetters. ● *adj.* made of iron; as strong as iron. ● *v.* smooth (clothes etc.) with an iron. □ **iron out** remove (creases) by ironing; solve (problems).

ironmonger *n.* a shopkeeper selling tools and household implements.

iron rations *n.pl.* a small emergency food supply.

irony *n.* (*pl.* **-ies**) the expression of a meaning through words whose literal sense is the opposite; the development of events in the opposite way to that intended or expected. □ **ironic** *adj.*, **ironical** *adj.*, **ironically** *adv.*

irradiate *v.* **1** expose to radiation. **2** illuminate. □ **irradiation** *n.*

irrational *adj.* not guided by reason.

irrecoverable *adj.* unable to be recovered. □ **irrecoverably** *adv.*

irredeemable *adj.* unable to be set right or saved.

irrefutable *adj.* impossible to disprove. □ **irrefutably** *adv.*

irregular *adj.* **1** not even or smooth. **2** contrary to rules or custom. □ **irregularity** *n.*, **irregularly** *adv.*

irrelevant *adj.* not relevant. □ **irrelevance** *n.*, **irrelevantly** *adv.*

irreparable *adj.* unable to be repaired. □ **irreparably** *adv.*

irreplaceable *adj.* impossible to replace.

irrepressible *adj.* impossible to control or subdue. □ **irrepressibly** *adv.*

irreproachable *adj.* blameless, faultless. □ **irreproachably** *adv.*

irresistible *adj.* too strong or attractive to be resisted. □ **irresistibility** *n.*, **irresistibly** *adv.*

irresolute *adj.* unable to make up one's mind. □ **irresolutely** *adv.*

irrespective *adj.* □ **irrespective of** not taking (a thing) into account.

irresponsible *adj.* not showing a proper sense of responsibility. □ **irresponsibility** *n.*, **irresponsibly** *adv.*

irretrievable *adj.* impossible to retrieve or put right.

irreverent *adj.* lacking respect. □ **irreverence** *n.*, **irreverently** *adv.*

irreversible *adj.* impossible to alter or undo. □ **irreversibly** *adv.*

irrevocable *adj.* unalterable, irreversible. □ **irrevocably** *adv.*

irrigate *v.* supply (land) with water by streams, pipes, etc. □ **irrigation** *n.*

irritable *adj.* easily annoyed, bad-tempered. □ **irritability** *n.*, **irritably** *adv.*

irritant *adj.* & *n.* (something) causing irritation.

irritate *v.* **1** annoy. **2** cause to itch. □ **irritation** *n.*

irrupt *v.* make a violent entry.

ISBN *abbr.* international standard book number, a number indicating a book's publisher, country of origin, etc.

-ish *comb. form* approximately, roughly: *eightish*; rather, somewhat: *greyish*.

isinglass (Iz-ing-glahs) *n.* gelatin obtained from fish.

Islam *n.* the Muslim religion. □ **Islamic** *adj.*

island *n.* a piece of land surrounded by water.

islander *n.* an inhabitant of an island.

isle *n.* an island.

islet *n.* a small island.

ism *n. informal* a set of ideas, a movement. ● *comb. form* (**-ism**) a prejudice based on a specified factor.

isobar *n.* a line on a map, connecting places with the same atmospheric pressure. □ **isobaric** *adj.*

isolate *v.* place apart or alone; separate from others or from a compound. □ **isolation** *n.*

isolationism *n.* the policy of holding aloof from other countries or groups. □ **isolationist** *n.*

isomer (I-sŏ-mĕ) *n.* one of two or more substances whose molecules have the same atoms arranged differently.

isosceles (I-sos-i-leez) *adj.* (of a triangle) having two sides equal.

isotherm *n.* a line on a map, connecting places with the same temperature.

isotope *n.* one of two or more forms of a chemical element differing in their atomic weight. □ **isotopic** *adj.*

issue *n.* **1** a topic or problem for discussion. **2** supplying an item for sale, use, etc.; a quantity issued; one edition of a magazine etc. **3** *formal* children. **4** flowing out. **5** *dated* an outcome, a result. ● *v.* **1** supply for use; supply (someone) with something. **2** publish. **3** come or flow out; result. □ **at issue** being discussed or disputed.

isthmus (isth-mŭs, iss-mŭs) *n.* (*pl.* **isthmuses**) a narrow strip of land connecting two larger masses of land.

IT *abbr.* information technology.

it *pron.* **1** the thing mentioned or being discussed. **2** used as the subject of an impersonal verb; *it is raining*. **3** used to identify someone: *it's me*.

Italian *adj.* & *n.* (a native, the language) of Italy.

italic *adj.* (of type) sloping like *this*. ● *n.pl.* (**italics**) italic type.

italicize *v.* (also **-ise**) print in italics.

itch *n.* a tickling sensation in the skin, causing a desire to scratch; a restless desire. ● *v.* feel an itch; be the site or cause of an itch: *my skin itched*. □ **itchy** *adj.*

item *n.* **1** a single thing in a list or collection; a single piece of news. **2** *informal* a couple in a romantic relationship.

itemize *v.* (also **-ise**) list; state the individual items of. □ **itemization** *n.*

iterate *v.* repeat. □ **iterative** *adj.*

itinerant *adj.* travelling.

itinerary *n.* (*pl.* **-ies**) a route, a list of places to be visited on a journey.

its *poss. pron.* of the thing mentioned; belonging to it.

■ **Usage** The possessive pronoun *its* is written without an apostrophe. *It's* with an apostrophe is a contraction of *it is* or *it has*.

itself *pron.* the emphatic and reflexive form of **it**.

ITV *abbr.* Independent Television.

IUD *abbr.* intrauterine device; a contraceptive coil placed inside the womb.

IVF *abbr.* in vitro fertilization.

ivory *n.* (*pl.* **-ies**) a hard creamy-white substance forming the tusks of an elephant etc.; its colour; (**ivories**) *informal* piano keys. ● *adj.* creamy white.

ivory tower *n.* a place providing seclusion from the harsh realities of life.

ivy *n.* (*pl.* **-ies**) an evergreen climbing plant.

Jj

J *abbr.* joule(s).

jab *v.* (**jabbed, jabbing**) poke roughly with something pointed. ● *n.* a rough poke; *informal* an injection.

jabber *v.* talk rapidly, often unintelligibly.

jack *n.* **1** a portable device for raising heavy weights off the ground. **2** a playing card next below queen. **3** a ship's small flag showing nationality. **4** an electrical connection with a single plug. **5** a small ball aimed at in bowls. ● *v.* □ **jack up** raise with a jack.

jackal *n.* a dog-like wild animal.

jackass *n.* **1** a male ass. **2** a stupid person.

jackboot *n.* a military boot reaching above the knee.

jackdaw *n.* a bird of the crow family.

jacket *n.* **1** a short coat. **2** an outer covering; the skin of a potato.

jackknife *n.* (*pl.* **-knives**) a large folding knife. ● *v.* (of an articulated vehicle) fold against itself in an accident.

jackpot *n.* a large prize of money that has accumulated until won. □ **hit the jackpot** *informal* have a great and sudden success.

Jacobean (jak-ŏ-**bee**-ăn) *adj.* of the reign of James I of England (1603–25).

Jacobite *n.* a supporter of James II of England or of the exiled Stuarts.

jacuzzi (jă-**koo**-zee) *n. trademark* a large bath with underwater jets of water.

jade *n.* a hard green, blue, or white stone; a green colour.

jaded *adj.* tired and bored.

jagged (**jagg**-id) *adj.* having rough sharp projections.

jaguar *n.* a large animal of the cat family.

jail *n.* (also **gaol**) prison. ● *v.* put into jail.

jailbird *n.* (also **gaolbird**) *informal* a person who has been in prison; a habitual criminal.

jailer *n.* (also **gaoler**) a person in charge of a jail or its prisoners.

Jainism *n.* a religion of India. ▫ **Jain** *n.*

jalopy (jă-**lop**-i) *n.* (*pl.* **-ies**) *informal* an old battered car.

jam *n.* **1** a thick sweet substance made by boiling fruit with sugar. **2** a crowded mass making movement difficult; becoming jammed; *informal* a difficult situation. ● *v.* (**jammed, jamming**) **1** pack tightly into a space; block, crowd. **2** become stuck. **3** make (a broadcast) unintelligible by causing interference.

jamb *n.* the side post of a door or window.

jamboree *n.* a large party; a rally.

Jan. *abbr.* January.

jangle *n.* a harsh metallic sound. ● *v.* make or cause to make this sound; upset or be upset by discord.

janitor *n.* the caretaker of a building.

January *n.* the first month.

japanned *adj.* coated with a hard black varnish.

Japanese *adj.* & *n.* (a native, the language) of Japan.

jar[1] *n.* a cylindrical glass or earthenware container; *informal* a glass of beer.

jar[2] *v.* (**jarred, jarring**) strike with a painful shock; have a painful or disagreeable effect.

jardinière (*zh*ar-din-**yair**) *n.* a large ornamental pot for growing plants.

jargon *n.* words or expressions developed for use within a particular group of people and hard for others to understand.

jasmine *n.* a shrub with white or yellow flowers.

jasper *n.* a kind of quartz.

jaundice *n.* a condition in which the skin becomes abnormally yellow.

jaundiced *adj.* **1** affected by jaundice. **2** filled with resentment.

jaunt *n.* a short pleasure trip.

jaunty *adj.* (**jauntier, jauntiest**) cheerful, self-confident. ▫ **jauntily** *adv.*, **jauntiness** *n.*

javelin *n.* a light spear thrown in sport (formerly as a weapon).

jaw *n.* **1** the bones forming the framework of the mouth; (**jaws**) the gripping parts of a tool; (**jaws**) the opening of a valley etc. **2** *informal* lengthy talk. ● *v. informal* talk lengthily.

jay *n.* a bird of the crow family.

jaywalking *n.* crossing a road carelessly. ▫ **jaywalker** *n.*

jazz *n.* a type of music involving improvisation, strong rhythm, and syncopation.

JCB *n. trademark* a mechanical excavator.

jealous *adj.* envying and resenting another's success; suspiciously protecting possessions or a relationship. ▫ **jealously** *adv.*, **jealousy** *n.*

jeans *n.pl.* denim trousers.

jeep *n. trademark* a small sturdy motor vehicle with four-wheel drive.

jeer *v.* laugh or shout rudely or scornfully (at). ● *n.* a jeering shout.

jehad var. of **jihad**.

Jehovah *n.* the name of God in the Old Testament.

jejune *adj.* superficial; not satisfying; dull.

jell *v.* set as a jelly; *informal* (of plans etc.) become clear and fixed.

jelly *n.* (*pl.* **-ies**) a soft solid food made of liquid set with gelatin; a substance of similar consistency; jam made of strained fruit juice.

jellyfish *n.* a sea animal with a jelly-like body.

jemmy *n.* (*pl.* **-ies**) a short crowbar used by a burglar.

jenny *n.* (*pl.* **-ies**) a female donkey.

jeopardize (jep-er-dyz) *v.* (also **-ise**) endanger.

jeopardy (jep-er-di) *n.* danger.

jerbil var. of **gerbil**.

jerk *n.* a sudden sharp movement or pull. ● *v.* move, pull, or stop with a jerk. ◻ **jerkily** *adv.*, **jerkiness** *n.*, **jerky** *adj.*

jerkin *n.* a sleeveless jacket.

jerry-built *adj.* hastily and poorly built.

jerrycan *n.* a large can for petrol or water.

jersey *n.* (*pl.* **jerseys**) a knitted woollen pullover with sleeves; machine-knitted fabric.

jest *n.* a joke. ● *v.* make jokes.

jester *n.* a clown at a medieval court.

Jesuit *n.* a member of the Society of Jesus, a Roman Catholic religious order.

jet[1] *n.* a hard black mineral; glossy black.

jet[2] *n.* **1** a stream of water, gas, or flame from a small opening; a burner on a gas cooker. **2** an engine or aircraft using jet propulsion. ● *v.* (**jetted, jetting**) travel by jet aircraft.

jet lag *n.* delayed tiredness etc. after a long flight.

jet-propelled *adj.* propelled by jet engines.

jet propulsion *n.* forward movement provided by engines sending out jets of gas at the back.

jetsam *n.* goods jettisoned by a ship and washed ashore.

jet-skiing *n.* the sport of riding in a small jet-propelled vehicle that skims across water.

jettison *v.* throw overboard; eject; discard.

jetty *n.* (*pl.* **-ies**) a landing stage; a staircase for boarding an aircraft; a breakwater.

Jew *n.* a person of Hebrew descent or whose religion is Judaism. ◻ **Jewish** *adj.*

jewel *n.* a precious stone cut or set as an ornament; a highly valued person or thing. ◻ **jewelled** *adj.*

jeweller *n.* (*Amer.* **jeweler**) a person who makes or deals in jewels or jewellery.

jewellery *n.* (also **jewelry**) jewels or similar ornaments to be worn.

Jewry *n.* the Jewish people.

jib *n.* a triangular sail stretching forward from a mast; a projecting arm of a crane. ● *v.* (**jibbed, jibbing**) refuse to proceed. ◻ **jib at** object to.

jibe 1 var. of **gibe**. **2** Amer. sp. of **gybe**.

jiffy *n. informal* a moment.

Jiffy bag *n. trademark* a padded envelope.

jig *n.* **1** a lively dance. **2** a device that holds something and guides tools working on it. ● *v.* (**jigged, jigging**) move quickly up and down.

jiggery-pokery *n. informal* trickery.

jiggle *v.* rock or shake lightly.

jigsaw *n.* **1** (also **jigsaw puzzle**) a picture cut into pieces to be shuffled and reassembled for amusement. **2** a machine fretsaw.

jihad (ji-hahd) *n.* (also **jehad**) (in Islam) a holy war.

jilt *v.* abandon (a lover).

jingle *v.* (cause to) make a ringing or clinking sound. ● *n.* **1** this sound. **2** a simple rhyme, esp. one used in advertising.

jingoism *n.* excessive patriotism and contempt for other countries. □ **jingoistic** *adj.*

jinx *n. informal* an influence causing bad luck.

jitters *n.pl. informal* nervousness. □ **jittery** *adj.*

jiu-jitsu var. of **ju-jitsu**.

jive *n.* a lively dance to jazz music. ● *n.* dance in this style.

Jnr. *abbr.* Junior.

job *n.* a piece of work; a paid position of employment; a duty or responsibility; *informal* a difficult task, difficulty: *I had a job getting here.*

jobber *n. hist.* a principal or wholesaler dealing on the Stock Exchange, not with the public.

jobbing *adj.* doing single pieces of work for payment.

jobcentre *n.* (in the UK) a government office displaying information about available jobs.

jobless *adj.* out of work.

job lot *n.* miscellaneous articles sold together.

jockey *n.* (*pl.* **jockeys**) a person who rides in horse races. ● *v.* manoeuvre to gain advantage.

jockstrap *n.* a protective support for the male genitals, worn while taking part in sports.

jocose *adj. formal* joking.

jocular *adj.* joking. □ **jocularity** *n.*, **jocularly** *adv.*

jocund *adj. formal* merry, cheerful.

jodhpurs (jod-pŭz) *n.pl.* riding-breeches fitting closely from knee to ankle.

jog *v.* (**jogged, jogging**) **1** run at a steady gentle pace; carry on steadily and uneventfully. **2** nudge, knock; stimulate (someone's memory). ● *n.* **1** a steady run. **2** a nudge. □ **jogger** *n.*

joggle *v.* shake slightly. ● *n.* a slight shake.

jogtrot *n.* a slow regular trot.

joie de vivre (*zh*wah dĕ **veevr**) *n.* great enjoyment of life.

join *v.* **1** unite, connect, be connected. **2** become a member of; come into the company of. ● *n.* a place where things join. □ **join up** enlist in the forces.

joiner *n.* a maker of wooden doors, windows, etc. □ **joinery** *n.*

joint *n.* **1** a join; a structure where bones fit together; a large piece of meat. **2** *informal* a marijuana cigarette. **3** *informal* an establishment for meeting, eating, etc. ● *adj.* shared by two or more people. ● *v.* connect with a joint; cut into joints. □ **out of joint** dislocated; in disorder. □ **jointly** *adv.*

jointure *n.* an estate settled on a widow for her lifetime.

joist *n.* one of the beams supporting a floor or ceiling.

jojoba (hŏ-**hoh**-bă) *n.* a plant with seeds containing oil used in cosmetics.

joke *n.* something said or done to cause laughter; a ridiculous person or thing. ● *v.* make jokes.

joker *n.* **1** a person who jokes. **2** an extra playing card with no fixed value.

jollification *n.* merrymaking.

jollity *n.* (*pl.* **-ies**) lively celebration, being jolly.

jolly *adj.* (**jollier, jolliest**) happy and cheerful; *informal* enjoyable. ● *adv. informal* very. □ **jolly along** keep (a person) in good humour.

jolt *v.* shake or dislodge with a jerk; move jerkily; surprise or shock into action. ● *n.* a jolting movement; a shock.

josh *v. informal* hoax, tease.

joss stick *n.* a thin stick that burns with a smell of incense.

jostle *v.* push roughly.

jot *n.* a very small amount. ● *v.* (**jotted, jotting**) write down briefly.

jotter *n.* a notepad.

joule (jool) *n.* a unit of energy (symbol J).

journal *n.* a daily record of events; a newspaper or periodical.

journalese *n. informal* a clichéd style of writing associated with newspapers.

journalist *n.* a person employed to write for a newspaper or magazine. ▫ **journalism** *n.*

journey *n.* (*pl.* **journeys**) an act of travelling from one place to another. ● *v.* make a journey.

journeyman *n.* (*pl.* **-men**) a qualified craftsman who works for another.

joust *v. hist.* fight on horseback with lances.

jovial *adj.* cheerful and good-humoured. ▫ **joviality** *n.*, **jovially** *adv.*

jowl *n.* the lower part of the cheek; an animal's dewlap.

joy *n.* great pleasure; something causing delight. ▫ **joyful** *adj.*, **joyfully** *adv.*, **joyfulness** *n.*

joyous *adj.* very happy. ▫ **joyously** *adv.*, **joyousness** *n.*

joyride *n. informal* a fast and dangerous drive in a stolen car. ▫ **joyriding** *n.*

joystick *n.* an aircraft's control lever; a device for moving a cursor on a VDU screen.

JP *abbr.* Justice of the Peace.

Jr. *abbr.* Junior.

jubilant *adj.* joyful, rejoicing. ▫ **jubilantly** *adv.*, **jubilation** *n.*

jubilee *n.* a special anniversary.

Judaic (joo-**day**-ik) *adj.* of Jews or Judaism.

Judaism *n.* the religion of the Jewish people.

judder *v.* shake noisily or violently. ● *n.* this movement.

judge *n.* a public officer appointed to hear and try cases in law courts; a person who decides who has won a contest; a person able to give an authoritative opinion. ● *v.* try (a case) in a law court; act as judge of.

judgement *n.* (also **judgment**) the ability to make wise decisions; judging; a judge's decision on a case.

judgemental *adj.* (also **judgmental**) of judgement; severe, critical.

judicial *adj.* of the administration of justice; of a judge or judgement. ▫ **judicially** *adv.*

judiciary *n.* (*pl.* **-ies**) the whole body of judges in a country.

judicious *adj.* judging wisely, showing good sense. ▫ **judiciously** *adv.*

judo *n.* a Japanese system of unarmed combat.

jug *n.* **1** a container with a handle and a shaped lip, for holding and pouring liquids. **2** *informal* prison. ▫ **jugful** *n.*

juggernaut *n.* a very large transport vehicle; an overwhelmingly powerful object or institution.

juggle *v.* toss and catch several objects skilfully for entertainment; manipulate skilfully. ▫ **juggler** *n.*

jugular vein *n.* either of the two large veins in the neck.

juice *n.* the liquid in fruits and vegetables; fluid secreted by an organ of the body; *informal* electrical energy; petrol.

juicy *adj.* (**juicier, juiciest**) full of juice; *informal* exciting, scandalous.

ju-jitsu *n.* (also **jiu-jitsu, ju-jutsu**) a Japanese system of unarmed combat.

jukebox *n.* a coin-operated record player.

Jul. *abbr.* July.

julep *n.* a drink of spirits and water flavoured esp. with mint.

julienne *n.* a dish of vegetables cut into thin strips.

July *n.* the seventh month.

jumble *v.* mix in a confused way. ● *n.* jumbled articles; items for a jumble sale.

jumble sale *n.* a sale of second-hand articles to raise money for charity.

jumbo *n.* (*pl.* **jumbos**) *informal* something that is very large of its kind; (also **jumbo jet**) a very large jet aircraft.

jump *v.* move up off the ground etc. by movement of the legs; make a sudden upward movement; cross (an obstacle) with a jump; omit, pass over. ● *n.* **1** a jumping movement; a sudden increase or change. **2** an obstacle to be jumped. ▫ **jump at** seize or accept eagerly. **jump the queue** obtain something without waiting one's turn.

jumper *n.* **1** a knitted garment for the upper part of the body; *Amer.* a pinafore dress. **2** one who jumps; a short wire used to shorten or temporarily close an electrical circuit.

jump lead *n.* a cable for carrying electric current from one battery to another.

jumpsuit *n.* a one-piece garment for the whole body.

jumpy *adj.* (**jumpier, jumpiest**) *informal* nervous.

Jun. *abbr.* June.

junction *n.* a join; a place where roads or railway lines meet.

junction box *n.* a box containing a junction of electric cables.

juncture *n.* **1** a particular point in time or the development of events. **2** a join.

June *n.* the sixth month.

jungle *n.* **1** a tropical forest; a mass of tangled vegetation. **2** a scene of ruthless struggle.

junior *adj.* younger in age; lower in rank or authority; of or for younger people. ● *n.* a junior person.

juniper *n.* an evergreen shrub.

junk *n.* **1** *informal* useless or discarded articles, rubbish. **2** a flat-bottomed ship with sails, used in the China seas.

junket *n.* a sweet custard-like food made of milk and rennet.

junk food *n.* food with low nutritional value.

junkie *n.* *informal* a drug addict.

junk mail *n.* *informal* unrequested advertising matter sent by post.

junk shop *n.* *informal* a shop selling cheap second-hand goods.

junta (huun-tă, jun-tă) *n.* a military or political group ruling a country after seizing power.

jurisdiction *n.* the authority to administer justice or exercise power.

jurisprudence *n.* the theory or philosophy of law.

jurist *n.* an expert in law.

juror *n.* a member of a jury.

jury *n.* (*pl.* **-ies**) a group of people sworn to give a verdict on a case in a court of law.

jury-rigged *adj.* with makeshift rigging.

just *adj.* fair to all concerned; morally right; deserved, appropriate. ● *adv.* **1** exactly. **2** very recently. **3** by a small amount, barely. **4** only, merely. **5** very, absolutely: *just fine.* ▫ **just now** very recently. **just so** very tidy, immaculate. ▫ **justly** *adv.*

justice *n.* **1** just behaviour or treatment; legal proceedings. **2** a judge.

Justice of the Peace *n.* a non-professional magistrate.

justifiable *adj.* able to be defended as reasonable or acceptable. ▫ **justifiably** *adv.*

justify *v.* (**justified, justifying**) **1** show to be right or reasonable; be sufficient reason for. **2** adjust (a line of type) to fill a space neatly. ▫ **justification** *n.*

jut *v.* (**jutted, jutting**) ▫ **jut out** protrude; thrust forward.

jute *n.* fibre from the bark of certain tropical plants, used to make ropes etc.

juvenile *adj.* of or for young people; childish, immature; (of an animal) not adult. ● *n.* a young person or animal.

juvenile delinquent *n.* a young offender, too young to be held legally responsible for his or her actions.

juxtapose *v.* put (things) side by side. ▫ **juxtaposition** *n.*

Kk

K *abbr.* kelvin(s); one thousand; *Computing* kilobyte(s); *Chess* king. ● *symb.* potassium.

kaftan *n.* (also **caftan**) a long tunic worn by men in the Near East; a long loose dress.

kaiser (**kI**-zĕ) *n. hist.* an emperor of Germany or Austria.

Kalashnikov *n.* a Russian rifle or sub-machine gun.

kale *n.* a green vegetable.

kaleidoscope (kă-**lI**-dŏ-skohp) *n.* a tube containing coloured fragments reflected to produce changing patterns as the tube is rotated. □ **kaleidoscopic** *adj.*

kamikaze (kami-**kah**-zi) *n.* (in the Second World War) a Japanese explosive-laden aircraft deliberately crashed on its target. ● *adj.* reckless, suicidal.

kangaroo *n.* an Australian mammal with a pouch to carry its young and strong hind legs for jumping.

kangaroo court *n.* a court formed unofficially by a group to settle disputes among themselves.

kaolin (**kay**-ŏ-lin) *n.* fine white clay used in porcelain and medicine.

kapok (**kay**-pok) *n.* a fluffy fibre used as padding.

kaput (kă-**puut**) *adj. informal* broken; ruined.

karaoke (kari-**oh**-ki) *n.* entertainment in which people sing popular songs to pre-recorded backing tracks.

karate (kă-**rah**-ti) *n.* a Japanese system of unarmed combat using hands and feet to deliver blows.

karma *n.* (in Buddhism and Hinduism) a person's actions as affecting his or her next reincarnation.

kayak (**ky**-ak) *n.* a light covered canoe.

kc/s *abbr.* kilocycle(s) per second.

kebab *n.* small pieces of meat etc. cooked on a skewer.

kedge *n.* a small anchor.

kedgeree *n.* a cooked dish of fish, rice, hard-boiled eggs, etc.

keel *n.* a timber or steel structure along the base of a ship. □ **keel over** capsize; collapse, fall over.

keen *adj.* **1** eager, enthusiastic. **2** sharp; quick, intelligent; (of eyesight etc.) powerful; (of wind etc.) very cold. □ **keen on** *informal* fond of, interested in. □ **keenly** *adv.*, **keenness** *n.*

keep *v.* (**kept, keeping**) **1** retain possession of; reserve for future use; detain. **2** remain or cause to remain in a specified state or position; continue doing something: *keep talking*. **3** provide with food and other necessities; own and look after (animals); manage (a shop etc.). **4** fulfil (a promise). **5** prevent; restrain oneself: *I couldn't keep from laughing*. ● *n.* **1** a person's food and other necessities. **2** a strongly fortified structure in a castle. □ **keep off** avoid; abstain from. **keep on** continue. **keep up** progress at the same pace as others.

keeper *n.* a person who keeps or looks after something.

keeping *n.* custody, charge. □ **in keeping with** appropriate to.

keepsake *n.* something kept in memory of the giver.

keg *n.* a small barrel.

kelp *n.* a type of seaweed.

kelvin *n.* a degree of the **Kelvin scale** of temperature with zero at absolute zero (–273.15°C).

kennel *n.* a shelter for a dog; (**kennels**) a boarding place for dogs.

kept past & p.p. of **keep**.

keratin *n.* a protein forming the basis of horn, nails, and hair.

kerb *n.* a stone edging to a pavement.

kerchief *n.* a piece of fabric worn over the head.

kerfuffle *n. informal* a fuss, a commotion.

kernel *n.* a seed within a husk, nut, or fruit stone; the central or important part.

kerosene *n.* (also **kerosine**) paraffin oil.

kestrel *n.* a small falcon.

ketch *n.* a two-masted sailing boat.

ketchup *n.* (*Amer.* **catsup**) a thick tomato sauce.

kettle *n.* a container with a spout and handle, for boiling water.

kettledrum *n.* a drum with a membrane stretched over a large metal bowl.

key *n.* **1** a piece of shaped metal for moving the bolt of a lock, winding a clock, etc.; something giving access or insight; a list of answers; an explanatory list of symbols on a map etc. **2** a button on a panel for operating a typewriter etc.; a lever pressed by the finger on a piano etc. **3** a system of related notes in music. □ **keyed up** stimulated, nervously tense.

keyboard *n.* a set of keys on a piano, typewriter, or computer. ● *v.* enter (data) using a keyboard. □ **keyboarder** *n.*

keyhole *n.* a hole for a key in a lock.

keyhole surgery *n.* surgery carried out through a very small incision.

keynote *n.* **1** the note on which a key in music is based. **2** the prevailing idea of a speech, conference etc.

keypad *n.* a small device with buttons for operating electronic equipment, a telephone, etc.

keyring *n.* a ring on which keys are threaded for safe keeping.

keystone *n.* the central stone of an arch, locking others into position.

keystroke *n.* a single depression of a key on a keyboard.

keyword *n.* the key to a cipher etc.; a very significant word or concept.

kg *abbr.* kilogram(s).

KGB *abbr.* the secret police of the former USSR.

khaki (kah-ki) *adj.* & *n.* dull brownish yellow, the colour of some military uniforms.

khan (kahn) *n.* the title of rulers and officials in central Asia.

kHz *abbr.* kilohertz.

kibbutz *n.* (*pl.* **kibbutzim**) a communal settlement in Israel.

kick *v.* **1** strike or propel with the foot. **2** (of a gun) recoil when fired. **3** *informal* give up (an addictive habit). ● *n.* **1** an act of kicking; a blow with the foot. **2** *informal* a thrill. □ **kick out** *informal* expel, dismiss. **kick up a fuss** *informal* protest noisily and violently.

kick-off *n.* the start of a football game.

kick-start *n.* a lever pressed with the foot to start a motorcycle. ● *v.* start (an engine) using this; provide initial impetus for.

kid *n.* a young goat; *informal* a child. ● *v.* (**kidded, kidding**) *informal* tease, deceive. ● *adj.* made of leather from a kid's skin.

kidnap *v.* (**kidnapped, kidnapping**; *Amer.* **kidnaped**) carry off (a person) illegally to obtain a ransom. □ **kidnapper** *n.*

kidney *n.* (*pl.* **kidneys**) either of a pair of organs that remove waste products from the blood and secrete urine.

kill *v.* **1** cause the death of; put an end to. **2** spend (time) unprofitably when waiting. ● *n.* killing; an animal killed by a hunter. □ **killer** *n.*

killjoy *n.* *informal* a person who spoils others' enjoyment.

kiln *n.* an oven for hardening or drying pottery or hops, or burning lime.

kilo *n.* (*pl.* **kilos**) a kilogram.

kilo- *comb. form* one thousand.

kilobyte *n.* *Computing* 1,024 bytes.

kilocalorie *n.* the amount of heat needed to raise the temperature of 1Kg of water by 1°C.

kilogram *n.* a unit of weight or mass in the metric system (2.205 lb).

kilohertz *n.* a unit of frequency of electromagnetic waves, = 1,000 cycles per second.

kilojoule *n.* 1,000 joules.

kilometre *n.* 1,000 metres (0.62 mile).

kilovolt *n.* 1,000 volts.

kilowatt *n.* 1,000 watts.

kilt *n.* a knee-length pleated skirt of tartan, as traditionally worn by Highland men.

kimono *n.* (*pl.* **kimonos**) a loose Japanese robe worn with a sash.

kin *n.* a person's relatives.

kind *n.* a class of similar people or things. ● *adj.* gentle and considerate towards others. □ **in kind 1** (of payment) in goods etc., not money. **2** (of a response) similar, in the same way. □ **kind-hearted** *adj.*, **kindness** *n.*

kindergarten *n.* a school for very young children.

kindle *v.* light (a fire); arouse, stimulate (a feeling).

kindling *n.* small pieces of wood for lighting fires.

kindly *adj.* (**kindlier, kindliest**) kind. ● *adv.* in a kind way; please (used in polite requests). □ **kindliness** *n.*

kindred *n.* a person's relatives. ● *adj.* related; of a similar kind.

kinetic *adj.* of movement.

king *n.* **1** a male ruler of a country; a man or thing regarded as supreme. **2** the most important chess piece; a playing card next above queen.

kingdom *n.* **1** a country ruled by a king or queen. **2** one of the divisions into which natural objects are classified.

kingfisher *n.* a bird with bright blue feathers that dives to catch fish.

kingpin *n.* an indispensable person or thing.

king-size *adj.* (also **king-sized**) extra large.

kink *n.* a sharp twist in something straight; a flaw; a mental peculiarity. ● *v.* form or cause to form a kink or kinks.

kinky *adj.* **1** having kinks. **2** *informal* given to or involving unusual sexual behaviour.

kinsfolk *n.pl.* a person's relatives. □ **kinsman** *n.*, **kinswoman** *n.*

kiosk *n.* a booth where newspapers or refreshments are sold, or one containing a public telephone.

kip *n. informal* a sleep.

kipper *n.* a smoked herring.

kirk *n. Scot.* a church.

kirsch (keersh) *n.* a liqueur made from cherries.

kismet *n.* destiny, fate.

kiss *n.* & *v.* (a) touch or caress with the lips. □ **the kiss of life** mouth-to-mouth resuscitation.

kissogram *n.* a novelty greetings message delivered with a kiss.

kit *n.* a set of tools; a set of parts to be assembled; the clothing for a particular activity. ● *v.* (**kitted, kitting**) equip with kit.

kitbag *n.* a bag for holding kit.

kitchen *n.* a room where meals are prepared.

kitchenette *n.* a small kitchen.

kitchen garden *n.* a garden for vegetables, fruit, and herbs.

kite *n.* **1** a light framework with fabric stretched over it, attached to a string for flying in the wind. **2** a large hawk.

Kitemark *n.* an official mark on goods approved by British Standards.

kith and kin *n.* relatives.

kitsch (kich) *n.* objects etc. seen as in poor taste because garish, sentimental, or vulgar.

kitten *n.* a young cat; the young of a rabbit or ferret.

kitty *n.* (*pl.* **-ies**) a communal fund.

kiwi *n.* a flightless New Zealand bird.

kJ *abbr.* kilojoule(s).

klaxon *n. trademark* an electric horn.

Kleenex *n. trademark* a paper handkerchief.

kleptomania *n.* a compulsive desire to steal. ▫ **kleptomaniac** *n.*

km *abbr.* kilometre(s).

knack *n.* the ability to do something skilfully.

knacker *n.* a person who buys and slaughters old horses, cattle, etc. ● *v. informal* **1** tire out. **2** damage.

knapsack *n.* a bag worn strapped on the back.

knave *n.* **1** *archaic* a dishonest man. **2** a jack in playing cards.

knead *v.* press and stretch (dough) with the hands; massage.

knee *n.* the joint between the thigh and the lower leg; part of a garment covering this; a person's lap. ● *v.* (**kneed, kneeing**) hit with the knee.

kneecap *n.* the small bone over the front of the knee. ● *v.* (**kneecapped, kneecapping**) shoot in the knee as a punishment.

knee-jerk *adj.* (of a reaction) automatic and predictable.

kneel *v.* (**knelt** or **kneeled, kneeling**) support oneself on one's knees.

knees-up *n. informal* a lively party.

knell *n.* the sound of a bell tolled after a death.

knelt past & p.p. of **kneel**.

knew past of **know**.

knickerbockers *n.pl.* loose breeches gathered at the knee.

knickers *n.pl.* **1** *Brit.* underpants. **2** *Amer.* knickerbockers.

knick-knack *n.* a small worthless ornament.

knife *n.* (*pl.* **knives**) a cutting or spreading instrument with a blade and handle. ● *v.* stab with a knife.

knight *n.* **1** a man given a rank below baronet, with the title 'Sir'. **2** a chess piece shaped like a horse's head. **3** *hist.* a mounted soldier in armour. ● *v.* confer a knighthood on.

knighthood *n.* the rank of knight.

knit *v.* (**knitted** or **knit, knitting**) **1** make a garment from yarn formed into interlocking loops on long needles. **2** become united; (of a broken bone) grow together, heal; tighten (one's eyebrows) in a frown. ▫ **knitter** *n.*, **knitting** *n.*

knob *n.* a rounded lump; a round door handle. ▫ **knobbly** *adj.*

knock *v.* **1** hit with an audible sharp blow; strike a door to attract attention. **2** collide with; injure by hitting; drive in a particular direction with a blow. **3** *informal* criticize. ● *n.* a sharp blow; the sound of this; an injury caused by this; a setback. ▫ **knock about 1** treat roughly. **2** *informal* travel casually. **knock down** force to the ground with a blow or collision. **knock off** *informal* **1** finish work. **2** produce (a piece of work) quickly. **3** steal. **knock out 1** strike unconscious. **2** eliminate from a competition. **knock up 1** *Brit.* rouse by knocking at a door. **2** *informal* make hurriedly.

knock-down *adj.* (of a price) very low.

knocker *n.* a hinged device for knocking on a door.

knock-kneed *adj.* having knees that bend inwards.

knock-on effect *n.* a secondary, indirect effect.

knockout *n.* **1** striking someone unconscious. **2** a tournament in which the loser in each round is eliminated. **3** *informal* an outstanding person or thing.

knock-up *n.* a practice game at tennis etc.

knoll *n.* a small hill.

knot *n.* **1** a fastening made by tying a piece of thread, rope, etc.; a tangle; a cluster. **2** a hard round spot in timber formed where a branch joins the trunk. **3** a unit of speed used by ships and aircraft, = one nautical mile per hour. ● *v.* (**knotted, knotting**) tie or fasten with a knot; entangle.

knotty *adj.* (**knottier, knottiest**) **1** full of knots. **2** puzzling, difficult.

know *v.* (**knew, known, knowing**) **1** have in one's mind or memory; feel certain; have learned. **2** be acquainted, familiar, or friendly with (a person, place, etc.) □ **in the know** *informal* having inside information. **known as** called, referred to as (a particular name).

know-how *n.* practical knowledge or skill.

knowing *adj.* aware, cunning; showing that one has secret knowledge: *a knowing look.* □ **knowingly** *adv.*

knowledge *n.* the facts etc. that someone knows; knowing a fact or about a subject; familiarity with someone or something.

knowledgeable *adj.* intelligent; well-informed.

knuckle *n.* a finger joint; an animal's leg joint as meat. □ **knuckle under** yield, submit.

knuckleduster *n.* a metal device worn over the knuckles to increase the effect of a blow.

koala *n.* a bearlike Australian tree-climbing animal.

kohl *n.* black powder used as eye make-up.

kola var. of **cola**.

kookaburra *n.* an Australian giant kingfisher with a harsh cry.

kopeck, kopek (also **copeck**) *n.* a Russian coin, one-hundredth of a rouble.

Koran *n.* the sacred book of Islam.

kosher (koh-shĕ) *adj.* **1** conforming to Jewish dietary laws. **2** *informal* genuine, legitimate.

kowtow *v. informal* behave with exaggerated respect.

k.p.h. *abbr.* kilometres per hour.

Kr *symb.* krypton.

kremlin *n.* a citadel in a Russian town; (**the Kremlin**) the Russian government.

krill *n.* tiny plankton crustaceans that are eaten by whales etc.

krona *n.* the unit of money in Sweden (*pl.* **kronor**) and Iceland (*pl.* **kronur**).

krone *n.* (*pl.* **kroner**) the unit of money in Denmark and Norway.

krugerrand *n.* a South African gold coin.

krypton *n.* a chemical element (symbol Kr), a colourless, odourless gas.

kudos *n. informal* honour and glory.

kumquat *n.* (also **cumquat**) a tiny variety of orange.

kung fu *n.* a Chinese form of unarmed combat.

Kurd *n.* a member of a people of SW Asia. □ **Kurdish** *adj.*

kV *abbr.* kilovolt(s).

kW *abbr.* kilowatt(s).

Ll

L *abbr.* large; learner driver; lake. ● *n.* (Roman numeral) 50.

l *abbr.* litre(s).

La *symb.* lanthanum.

lab *n. informal* a laboratory.

label *n.* a piece of card, cloth, etc., attached to something and carrying information about it. ● *v.* (**labelled, labelling**; *Amer.* **labeled**) attach a label to; regard or describe as belonging to a specified category.

labia *n.pl.* the lips of the female genitals.

labial *adj.* of the lips.

labor etc. Amer. sp. of **labour** etc.

laboratory *n.* (*pl.* **-ies**) a room or building equipped for scientific work.

laborious *adj.* needing or showing much effort. □ **laboriously** *adv.*

labour *n.* (*Amer.* **labor**) **1** work, exertion; workers. **2** contractions of the womb at childbirth. ● *v.* work hard; move with effort; explain (a point) at unnecessary length.

laboured *adj.* (*Amer.* **labored**) done with great effort; not spontaneous.

labourer *n.* (*Amer.* **laborer**) a person employed to do manual work.

Labour Party *n.* a British political party formed to represent the interests of ordinary working people.

Labrador *n.* a large dog.

laburnum *n.* a tree with hanging clusters of yellow flowers.

labyrinth (lab-i-rinth) *n.* a maze. □ **labyrinthine** *adj.*

lace *n.* **1** decorative fabric made by looping thread in patterns. **2** a cord threaded through holes or hooks to pull opposite edges of a garment etc. together. ● *v.* **1** fasten with laces. **2** intertwine. **3** add alcohol to (a dish or drink).

lacerate *v.* tear (flesh); wound (feelings). □ **laceration** *n.*

lachrymose (lak-rim-ohs) *adj.* tearful.

lack *n.* an absence or insufficiency of something; not having something. ● *v.* be without (something needed or wanted).

lackadaisical *adj.* lacking vigour or determination, unenthusiastic.

lackey *n.* (*pl.* **lackeys**) a footman, a servant; a servile follower.

lacking *adj.* absent, missing, not available; without something; deficient.

lacklustre *adj.* (*Amer.* **lackluster**) lacking brightness, enthusiasm, or conviction.

laconic *adj.* using few words □ **laconically** *adv.*

lacquer *n.* a hard glossy varnish. ● *v.* coat with lacquer.

lacrosse *n.* a game similar to hockey played using sticks with small nets on the ends.

lactation *n.* secretion of milk for suckling.

lactic acid *n.* acid found in sour milk and produced in the muscles during exercise.

lactose *n.* a sugar present in milk.

lacuna *n.* (*pl.* **lacunas** or **lacunae**) a gap, a place where something is missing.

lacy *adj.* (**lacier**) of or like lace.

lad *n.* a boy; *informal* a young man with sexist attitudes and unrestrained behaviour.

ladder *n.* a set of crossbars between uprights, used for climbing up; a series of ascending stages in a career etc.; a vertical ladder-like flaw where stitches become undone in a stocking. ● *v.* cause or develop a ladder (in).

laden *adj.* loaded.

ladle *n.* a deep long-handled spoon for transferring liquids. ● *v.* transfer with a ladle.

lady *n.* (*pl.* **-ies**) a woman; a well-mannered woman; a woman of noble birth; (**Lady**) the title of wives, widows, or daughters of certain noblemen.

ladybird *n.* a small flying beetle, usu. red with black spots.

lady-in-waiting *n.* a lady attending a queen or princess.

ladylike *adj.* appropriate to a well-born or well-mannered woman; polite, decorous.

ladyship *n.* the title used in addressing or referring to a woman with the rank of *Lady*.

lag[1] *v.* (**lagged, lagging**) fall behind, fail to keep up. ● *n.* a delay.

lag[2] *v.* (**lagged, lagging**) cover (a boiler etc.) with insulating material.

lager *n.* a light-coloured beer.

lager lout *n. informal* a drunken rowdy youth.

laggard *n.* a person who makes slow progress.

lagging *n.* material used to lag a boiler etc.

lagoon *n.* a salt-water lake beside the sea.

lah *n. Music* the sixth note of a major scale, or the note A.

laid past & p.p. of **lay**[2].

laid-back *adj. informal* easygoing, relaxed.

lain p.p. of **lie**[2].

lair *n.* a place where a wild animal rests; a hiding-place.

laird *n. Scot.* a landowner.

laissez-faire (less-ay-**fair**) *n.* a policy of non-interference, esp. in politics or economics.

laity (lay-i-ti) *n.* lay people, not clergy.

lake *n.* a large body of water surrounded by land; a large pool of liquid.

lam *v.* (**lammed, lamming**) *informal* hit hard.

lama (lah-mă) *n.* a Buddhist priest in Tibet and Mongolia.

lamb *n.* **1** a young sheep; its flesh as food. **2** a gentle or endearing person. ● *v.* give birth to a lamb.

lambaste (lam-**bayst**) *v.* (also **lambast**) reprimand severely.

lame *adj.* **1** unable to walk normally. **2** unconvincing, feeble. ● *v.* make lame, disable. ◻ **lamely** *adv.*, **lameness** *n.*

lamé (lah-may) *n.* a fabric interwoven with gold or silver thread.

lament *n.* an expression of grief; a song or poem expressing grief. ● *v.* feel or express grief or regret (for) ◻ **lamentation** *n.*

lamentable (lam-ent-ă-bĕl) *adj.* regrettable, deplorable. ◻ **lamentably** *adv.*

laminate (**lam**-in-ăt) *n.* laminated material.

laminated *adj.* made of layers joined one upon another.

lamp *n.* a device for giving light.

lampoon *n.* a piece of writing that attacks a person with ridicule. ● *v.* ridicule in a lampoon.

lamp-post *n.* a tall post with a light on top as street illumination.

lamprey *n.* (*pl.* **lampreys**) a small eel-like water animal.

lampshade *n.* a shade on a lamp screening its light.

lance *n.* a long spear. ● *v.* prick or cut open with a lancet.

lance corporal *n.* an army rank below corporal.

lancet *n.* **1** a surgeon's pointed two-edged knife. **2** a tall narrow pointed arch or window.

land *n.* **1** the part of the earth's surface not covered by water; ground, soil; an area of ground as property or for a particular use. **2** a country or state. ● *v.* **1** come or bring ashore; come or bring down from the air. **2** *informal* succeed in obtaining or achieving. **3** *informal* come or cause to come into a specified state: *landed him in trouble*. **4** *informal* inflict (a blow).

landed *adj.* **1** owning land. **2** consisting of or including land: *landed estates*.

landfall *n.* the approach to land after a journey by sea or air.

landfill *n.* disposal of waste material by burying it, esp. to refill excavated pits; this material.

landing *n.* **1** coming or bringing ashore or to ground; a place for this. **2** a level area at the top of a flight of stairs.

landing stage *n.* a platform for coming ashore from a boat.

landlady *n.* (*pl.* **-ies**) **1** a woman who lets land or a house or room to a tenant. **2** a woman who runs a public house.

landlocked *adj.* surrounded by land.

landlord *n.* a person who lets land or a house or room to a tenant; one who runs a public house.

landlubber *n. informal* a person not accustomed to sailing.

landmark *n.* a conspicuous feature of a landscape; an event marking an important stage or turning point.

landscape *n.* the scenery of a land area; a picture of this. ● *v.* lay out (an area) attractively with natural-looking features.

landslide *n.* **1** a fall of earth and rock from a mountain or cliff. **2** an overwhelming majority of votes.

landslip *n.* a landslide.

landward *adj.* & *adv.* towards the land. ◻ **landwards** *adv.*

lane *n.* a narrow road, track, or passage; a division of a road for a single line of traffic; a track to which ships or aircraft etc. must keep; one of the parallel strips for runners etc. in a race.

language *n.* words and their use; a system of this used by a nation or group; gestures or symbols used for communication.

languid (lang-gwid) *adj.* lacking vigour or vitality.

languish (lang-gwish) *v.* lose or lack vitality; live under miserable conditions.

languor (lang-gě) *n.* tiredness, laziness, lack of energy. □ **languorous** *adj.*

lank *adj.* (of hair) long, limp, and straight.

lanky *adj.* tall and thin. □ **lankiness** *n.*

lanolin *n.* a fat extracted from sheep's wool, used in ointments.

lantern *n.* **1** a lamp protected by a transparent case, carried by a handle. **2** a structure at the top of a tower, with windows on all sides.

lanthanum *n.* a metallic element (symbol La).

lanyard (lan-yăd) *n.* a short rope for securing sails etc. on a ship; a cord for hanging a whistle etc. round the neck or shoulder.

lap *n.* **1** a flat area over the thighs of a seated person. **2** a single circuit of a racecourse; a section of a journey. ● *v.* (**lapped, lapping**) **1** take up (liquid) by movements of the tongue. **2** (of water) wash against something with a gentle sound. **3** be one or more laps ahead of (a competitor). **4** *poetic* wrap in something soft. □ **lap up** take or accept eagerly.

laparoscope (lap-ă-rŏ-skohp) *n.* a fibre-optic instrument inserted through the abdomen to view the internal organs. □ **laparoscopy** *n.*

lapdog *n.* a small pampered dog.

lapel (lă-pell) *n.* a flap folded back at the front of a coat etc.

lapidary (lap-id-ă-ri) *adj.* **1** (of language) concise and elegant. **2** of stones and gems.

lapis lazuli *n.* a blue semiprecious stone.

Lapp *n.* a native or the language of Lapland.

■ **Usage** The people prefer to be called *Sami*.

lapse *n.* **1** a temporary failure of concentration, memory, etc.; a decline in standard. **2** the passage of time. ● *v.* **1** (of a right or privilege) become invalid. **2** pass into an inferior state; fail to maintain one's standard.

laptop *n.* a portable computer.

larch *n.* a deciduous tree of the pine family.

lard *n.* a white greasy substance prepared from pig-fat. ● *v.* **1** put strips of fat bacon in or on (meat) before cooking. **2** use too many quotations, figures of speech, etc., in (speech or writing).

larder *n.* a storeroom for food.

large *adj.* of great size or extent. □ **at large 1** free to roam about. **2** as a whole, in general. □ **largeness** *n.*

largely *adv.* to a great extent.

largesse (lah-jess) *n.* (also **largess**) money or gifts generously given.

lariat (la-ri-ăt) *n.* a lasso.

lark *n.* **1** a small brown bird, a skylark. **2** *informal* something done for fun. □ **lark about** *informal* behave playfully.

larva *n.* (*pl.* **larvae**) an insect in the first stage of its life after coming out of the egg. □ **larval** *adj.*

laryngitis *n.* inflammation of the larynx.

larynx (la-rinks) *n.* the part of the throat containing the vocal cords.

lasagne (lă-zan-yă) *n.* a dish of pasta layered with sauces of cheese, meat, tomato, etc.

lascivious (lă-siv-i-ŭs) *adj.* lustful. □ **lasciviously** *adv.*, **lasciviousness** *n.*

laser *n.* a device emitting an intense narrow beam of light.

lash *v.* **1** strike with a whip; beat against; (of an animal) move (its tail) quickly to and fro. **2** tie down. ● *n.* **1** the flexible part of a whip; a blow with this. **2** an eyelash.

□ **lash out 1** strike at someone; attack someone verbally. **2** *informal* spend lavishly.

lashings *n.pl. informal* a lot.

lass *n.* (also **lassie**) *Scot. & N. Engl.* a girl, a young woman.

lassitude *n.* tiredness, lack of energy.

lasso (lă-soo) *n.* (*pl.* **lassos** or **lassoes**) a rope with a noose for catching cattle. ● *v.* (**lassoed, lassoing**) catch with a lasso.

last[1] *adj.* **1** coming after all others, final; lowest in importance. **2** most recent. ● *adv.* **1** most recently. **2** finally. ● *n.* the last person or thing; all that remains of something. ● *v.* continue; survive, endure; (of resources) be enough for a period of time. □ **at last, at long last** after much delay. **in the last resort** if all else fails. **the last straw** the final thing making a situation unbearable. □ **lasting** *adj.*

last[2] *n.* a foot-shaped block used in making and repairing shoes.

lastly *adv.* finally.

last post *n.* a military bugle call sounded at sunset or military funerals.

last word *n.* **1** the final statement in a dispute. **2** the latest, most fashionable example of something.

latch *n.* a bar lifted from its catch by a lever, used to fasten a gate etc; a spring-lock that catches when a door is closed. ● *v.* fasten with a latch. □ **on the latch** closed but not locked.

latchkey *n.* a key of an outer door.

latchkey child *n.* a child left at home without adult supervision.

late *adj.* **1** happening or coming after the proper or expected time. **2** far on in a day or night or period. **3** dead; no longer holding a position. **4** recent. ● *adv.* **1** after the proper or expected time. **2** at or until a late time. □ **of late** lately. □ **lateness** *n.*

lately *adv.* recently.

latent *adj.* existing but not active or developed or visible. □ **latency** *n.*

lateral *adj.* of, at, to, or from the side(s). □ **laterally** *adv.*

latex (lay-teks) *n.* a milky fluid from certain plants, esp. the rubber tree; a similar synthetic substance.

lath *n.* (*pl.* **laths**) a narrow thin strip of wood, in a trellis or partition wall.

lathe *n.* a machine for holding and turning pieces of wood or metal while they are worked.

lather *n.* froth from soap and water; frothy sweat. ● *v.* cover with or form lather.

Latin *n.* the language of the ancient Romans. ● *adj.* of or in Latin; of a people whose language is based on Latin, e.g. French or Spanish.

Latin America *n.* the parts of Central and South America where Spanish or Portuguese is the main language.

latitude *n.* **1** the distance of a place from the equator, measured in degrees; a region. **2** freedom from restrictions. □ **latitudinal** *adj.*

latrine *n.* a lavatory in a camp or barracks.

latter *adj.* towards the end, in the final stages; recent. □ **the latter** the second of two things to be mentioned.

latter-day *adj.* modern, recent.

latterly *adv.* **1** recently. **2** towards the end of a period.

lattice *n.* a framework of crossed strips.

laudable *adj.* praiseworthy.

laudanum (lord-ă-nŭm) *n.* opium prepared for use as a sedative.

laudatory (lord-ă-tŏ-ri) *adj.* praising.

laugh *v.* make sounds and facial movements expressing amusement or scorn. ● *n.* the act or manner of laughing; *informal* an amusing incident or person.

laughable *adj.* ridiculous.

laughing stock *n.* a person or thing that is ridiculed.

laughter *n.* the act or sound of laughing.

launch *v.* send (a ship) into the water; send (a rocket) into the air; start (an enterprise); introduce (a new product). ● *n.* **1** the process of launching something. **2** a large motor boat.

launder *v.* **1** wash and iron (clothes etc.). **2** transfer (money acquired illegally) to conceal its origin.

launderette *n.* an establishment fitted with washing machines to be used for a fee.

laundry *n.* (*pl.* **-ies**) a place where clothes etc. are laundered; clothes etc. for washing.

laurel *n.* an evergreen shrub; (**laurels**) victories or honours gained.

lava *n.* flowing or hardened molten rock from a volcano.

lavatory *n.* (*pl.* **-ies**) a fixture into which urine and faeces are discharged; a room equipped with this.

lavender *n.* a shrub with fragrant purple flowers; light purple.

lavish *adj.* generous; plentiful; luxurious and extravagant. ● *v.* give generously. □ **lavishly** *adv.*, **lavishness** *n.*

law *n.* a rule established by authority; a set of such rules; their influence or operation; a statement of what always happens in certain circumstances.

law-abiding *adj.* obeying the law.

law court *n.* a room or building in which legal trials are held.

lawful *adj.* permitted or recognized by law. □ **lawfully** *adv.*, **lawfulness** *n.*

lawless *adj.* disregarding the law. □ **lawlessness** *n.*

lawn *n.* **1** an area of closely cut grass in a garden or park. **2** fine woven cotton fabric.

lawnmower *n.* a machine for cutting grass.

lawn tennis *n.* tennis played with a soft ball on outdoor grass or a hard court.

lawrencium *n.* a radioactive metallic element (symbol Lw).

lawsuit *n.* the process of bringing a dispute before a court of law for settlement.

lawyer *n.* a person qualified in legal matters.

lax *adj.* slack, not strict or severe. □ **laxity** *n.*

laxative *adj.* & *n.* (a medicine) stimulating the bowels to empty.

lay[1] *adj.* not ordained into the clergy; non-professional.

lay[2] *v.* (**laid, laying**) **1** set down carefully; arrange for use; put cutlery etc. on (a table) for a meal. **2** cause to be in a certain condition: *laid him open to suspicion.* **3** (of a bird) produce (eggs). ● *n.* the appearance of a landscape; the way a carpet etc. lies. □ **lay bare** expose, reveal. **lay into** *informal* thrash; scold harshly. **lay off 1** discharge (workers) temporarily. **2** stop doing something. **lay on** provide. **lay out 1** spread out, arrange; prepare (a body) for burial. **2** *informal* knock unconscious. **3** *informal* spend (a sum of money). **lay up 1** store. **2** put (someone) out of action through illness. **lay waste** devastate.

■ **Usage** It is incorrect in standard English to use *lay* to mean 'lie', as in *She was laying on the floor*.

lay[3] past of **lie**[2].

layabout *n.* a lazy person.

lay-by *n.* (*pl.* **lay-bys**) an area beside the road where vehicles may stop.

layer *n.* **1** one of several sheets or thicknesses of a substance covering a surface. **2** a shoot fastened down to take root while attached to the parent plant. **3** a hen that lays eggs. ● *v.* **1** arrange in layers. **2** propagate (a plant) using layers.

layette *n.* an outfit for a newborn baby.

lay figure *n.* an artist's jointed model of the human body.

layman *n.* (*pl.* **-men**) someone not ordained as a clergyman; someone without professional knowledge of a subject.

layout *n.* an arrangement of parts etc. according to a plan.

laze *v.* spend time idly.

lazy *adj.* (**lazier, laziest**) unwilling to work or use energy; done without effort or care. □ **lazily** *adv.*, **laziness** *n.*

lb *abbr.* pound(s) weight.

LCD *abbr. Computing & Electronics* liquid crystal display; lowest common denominator.

LEA *abbr.* Local Education Authority.

lea *n. poetic* a piece of meadow or arable land.

leach *v.* remove (soluble minerals etc.) from soil through the action of liquid percolating through it; be drained away in this way.

lead[1] (leed) *v.* (**led, leading**) **1** go in front of and cause to follow one; guide. **2** be a reason or motive for (someone), influence. **3** be a route or means of access; result or culminate in something. **4** be in command of; be ahead of or superior to. **5** pass (one's life). ● *n.* **1** a leading position; being ahead. **2** a clue. **3** the chief part in a play or film; a person playing this. **4** a strap or cord for leading a dog. **5** a wire conveying electric current. □ **lead on** mislead, deceive. **lead up to** be an introduction to; result in; immediately precede.

lead[2] (led) *n.* **1** a chemical element (symbol Pb), a heavy grey metal; a lump of lead used for sounding depths. **2** graphite in a pencil.

leaden (led-ĕn) *adj.* **1** heavy, slow-moving. **2** dull grey like lead; *archaic* made of lead.

leader *n.* **1** a person who leads. **2** a newspaper article giving editorial opinions. □ **leadership** *n.*

leading question *n.* a question worded to prompt the desired answer.

leaf *n.* (*pl.* **leaves**) **1** a flat (usu. green) organ growing from the stem or root of a plant. **2** a single thickness of paper, a page; a very thin sheet of metal. **3** a hinged flap or extra section of a table. □ **leaf through** turn over the leaves of (a book).

leaflet *n.* **1** a printed sheet of paper giving information. **2** a small leaf of a plant.

leaf mould *n.* soil or compost consisting of decayed leaves.

leafy *adj.* (**leafier, leafiest**) having many leaves.

league *n.* **1** a group of people or countries united for a purpose; an association of sports clubs that compete against one another. **2** a class, a standard: *in a league of his own.* □ **in league with** conspiring with.

leak *v.* (of liquid, gas, etc.) pass through a crack; (of a container) lose contents through a crack or hole; disclose (secrets) or be disclosed. ● *n.* an escape of liquid or gas through a crack; a crack or hole through which this happens; an escape of an electric charge; a disclosure of secret information. □ **leakage** *n.*, **leaky** *adj.*

lean[1] *v.* (**leaned** or **lent, leaning**) put or be in a sloping position; (cause to) rest against something for support. □ **lean on 1** depend on. **2** *informal* intimidate, put under pressure.

lean[2] *adj.* thin, having no superfluous fat; (of meat) with little fat; (of a period) characterized by hardship. ● *n.* the lean part of meat. □ **leanness** *n.*

leaning *n.* a tendency, an inclination.

lean-to *n.* a shed etc. against the side of a building.

leap *v.* (**leaped** or **leapt, leaping**) jump vigorously. ● *n.* a vigorous jump. □ **leap at** seize (an opportunity) eagerly.

leapfrog *n.* a game in which each player vaults over another who is bending down. ● *v.* (**leapfrogged,**

leapfrogging) perform this vault (over); overtake another; pass over (an obstacle).

leap year *n.* a year with an extra day (29 Feb.), occurring once every four years.

learn *v.* (**learned** or **learnt, learning**) gain knowledge of or skill in; become aware of; memorize. □ **learner** *n.*

learned (ler-nid) *adj.* having or showing great learning.

learning *n.* knowledge obtained by study.

lease *n.* a contract allowing the use of land or a building for a specified time. ● *v.* obtain or grant (property) by lease. □ **leasehold** *n.*, **leaseholder** *n.*

leash *n.* a dog's lead.

least *adj.* smallest in amount or degree; lowest in importance. ● *n.* the least amount etc. ● *adv.* in the least degree. □ **at least 1** not less than. **2** if nothing else; anyway.

leather *n.* material made by treating animal skins; a piece of soft leather for polishing with. ● *v.* thrash.

leatherette *n.* imitation leather.

leathery *adj.* tough like leather.

leave *v.* (**left, leaving**) **1** go away (from); go away finally or permanently. **2** allow to remain; not take with one; abandon, desert; deposit, entrust to someone; bequeath **3** cause to remain in a specified state: *leave the door open*. ● *n.* permission; permission to be absent from duty; the period for which this lasts. □ **leave out** not insert or include.

leaven (lev-ĕn) *n.* a substance such as yeast, causing dough to rise; a transforming and improving influence. ● *v.* add leaven to; transform.

lecher *n.* a lecherous man.

lechery *n.* excessive sexual desire, lustfulness. □ **lecherous** *adj.*

lecithin *n.* a compound found in plants and animals used as a food emulsifier and stabilizer.

lectern *n.* a stand with a sloping top from which a bible etc. is read.

lecture *n.* a speech giving information about a subject; a lengthy reproof or warning. ● *v.* give a lecture or lectures; reprove at length. □ **lecturer** *n.*

LED *abbr.* light-emitting diode.

led past & p.p. of **lead**[1].

ledge *n.* a narrow horizontal projection or shelf.

ledger *n.* a book used for keeping accounts.

lee *n.* shelter from the wind given by a hill, building, etc.; the sheltered side of such an object.

leech *n.* a small blood-sucking worm.

leek *n.* a vegetable with an onion-like flavour.

leer *v.* look slyly, maliciously, or lustfully. ● *n.* a leering look.

lees *n.pl.* sediment in wine.

leeward *adj.* & *n.* (on) the side away from the wind.

leeway *n.* a degree of freedom of action.

left[1] past & p.p. of **leave**.

left[2] *adj.* & *adv.* of, on, or towards the side of the body which is on the west when one is facing north. ● *n.* **1** the left side or region; the left hand or foot. **2** people supporting socialism or a more extreme form of socialism than others in their group.

left-handed *adj.* using the left hand more easily than the right.

leftovers *n.pl.* things remaining when the rest is finished.

leg *n.* **1** each of the limbs on which a person, animal, etc. stands or moves; part of a garment covering a person's leg; a support of a table, chair, etc. **2** one section of a journey or contest. □ **leg it** *informal* run away.

legacy *n.* (*pl.* **-ies**) something left to someone in a will, or handed down by a predecessor.

legal *adj.* of or based on law; authorized or required by law. □ **legalistic** *adj.*, **legality** *n.*, **legally** *adv.*

legal aid *n.* help from public funds towards the cost of legal action.

legalize *v.* (also **-ise**) make permissible by law. □ **legalization** *n.*

legate *n.* an envoy.

legatee *n.* the recipient of a legacy.

legation *n.* a diplomatic minister and staff; their headquarters.

legato *adv. Music* smoothly and evenly.

legend *n.* **1** a story handed down from the past; such stories collectively. **2** a very famous person. **3** an inscription on a coin or medal; an explanation of the symbols on a map.

legendary *adj.* of or described in legend; famous.

legerdemain (lej-er-dĕ-mayn) *n.* skilful use of the hands in conjuring; trickery.

leggings *n.pl.* a close-fitting stretchy garment covering the legs.

legible *adj.* clear enough to be deciphered, readable. □ **legibility** *n.*, **legibly** *adv.*

legion *n.* a division of the ancient Roman army; a huge crowd. ● *adj.* very numerous.

legionnaire *n.* a member of a legion.

legionnaires' disease *n.* a form of bacterial pneumonia.

legislate *v.* make laws. □ **legislator** *n.*

legislation *n.* laws collectively.

legislative *adj.* making laws.

legislature *n.* a country's legislative assembly.

legitimate *adj.* **1** in accordance with a law or rule; justifiable. **2** born of parents married to each other. □ **legitimacy** *n.*, **legitimately** *adv.*, **legitimization** *n.*, **legitimize** *v.* (also **-ise**).

legless *adj.* **1** without legs. **2** *informal* drunk.

legume *n.* a plant of the family bearing seeds in pods. □ **leguminous** *adj.*

leisure *n.* time free from work. □ **at leisure** not busy. **at one's leisure** when one has time.

leisured *adj.* having plenty of leisure.

leisurely *adj.* & *adv.* without hurry.

leitmotif (lyt-moh-teef) *n.* (also **leitmotiv**) a recurrent theme in a musical or literary work, associated with a particular person or idea.

lemming *n.* a mouse-like Arctic rodent (said to rush headlong into the sea and drown in its migration).

lemon *n.* **1** a yellow oval fruit with acid juice; the tree bearing it; a pale yellow colour. **2** *informal* a stupid or unsatisfactory person or thing.

lemonade *n.* a lemon-flavoured fizzy drink.

lemur *n.* a nocturnal monkey-like animal of Madagascar.

lend *v.* (**lent, lending**) give (something) to (someone) for temporary use; provide (money) temporarily in return for payment of interest; add (an effect) to (something). □ **lend a hand** *informal* help. **lend itself to** be suitable for. □ **lender** *n.*

length *n.* **1** the measurement or extent from end to end; being long; the full extent; the length of something as a unit of measurement: *six lengths of the pool*; a piece of cloth etc. **2** an extreme effort: *go to great lengths.* □ **at length 1** in great detail. **2** at last, after a long time.

lengthen *v.* make or become longer.

lengthways *adv.* & *adj.* (also **lengthwise**) in the direction of a thing's length.

lengthy *adj.* (**lengthier, lengthiest**) very long □ **lengthily** *adv.*

lenient *adj.* merciful, not severe. □ **lenience** *n.*, **leniently** *adv.*

lens *n.* a piece of glass or similar substance shaped for use in an optical instrument; the transparent part of the eye, behind the pupil.

Lent *n.* the Christian period of fasting and repentance before Easter.

lent past & p.p. of **lend**.

lentil *n.* a kind of bean.

leonine *adj.* of or like a lion.

leopard (lep-erd) *n.* a large spotted animal of the cat family.

leotard (lee-ŏ-tahd) *n.* a close-fitting stretchy garment worn by dancers, gymnasts, etc.

leper *n.* a person with leprosy.

leprechaun *n.* (in Irish folklore) a small, mischievous sprite.

leprosy *n.* an infectious disease affecting the skin and nerves and causing deformities. □ **leprous** *adj.*

lesbian *n.* a homosexual woman. ● *adj.* of lesbians. □ **lesbianism** *n.*

lese-majesty (leez) *n.* an insult to a ruler; treason.

lesion (lee-*zh*ŏn) *n.* a region in an organ or tissue that is damaged by injury or disease.

less *adj.* & *pron.* not so much; a smaller amount of. ● *adv.* to a smaller extent. ● *prep.* minus.

lessee *n.* a person holding property by lease.

lessen *v.* make or become less.

lesser *adj.* not so great or important as the other.

lesson *n.* **1** an amount of teaching given at one time; something to be learnt by a pupil; an experience by which one can learn. **2** a passage from the Bible read aloud.

lessor *n.* a person who lets property on lease.

lest *conj.* for fear that.

let *v.* (**let, letting**) **1** allow, not forbid; allow to pass: *let me through.* **2** allow someone to use (accommodation) in return for payment. ● *v.aux.* used in requests, commands, suggestions, or assumptions: *let's try.* ● *n.* (in tennis etc.) an obstruction of the ball nullifying a service. **2** a period during which property is let: *a short let.* □ **let alone 1** refrain from interfering with. **2** used to introduce something more extreme and unlikely. **let down 1** disappoint. **2** deflate (a tyre etc.). **let go** stop holding on (to). **let off 1** fire or explode (a weapon, firework, etc.) **2** punish lightly; excuse. **let on** *informal* reveal a secret. **let out 1** utter; reveal. **2** make (a garment) looser. **let up** *informal* relax; become less intense or severe.

-let *comb. form* small; young.

lethal *adj.* causing death.

lethargy *n.* extreme lack of energy or vitality. □ **lethargic** *adj.*, **lethargically** *adv.*

letter *n.* **1** a symbol representing a speech sound. **2** a written message sent by post; (**letters**) literature. **3** the precise terms or interpretation of something: *the letter of the law.* ● *v.* inscribe letters (on).

letter box *n.* a slit in a door, with a movable flap, through which letters are delivered; a postbox.

letterhead *n.* a printed heading on stationery.

lettuce *n.* a plant with broad crisp leaves used as salad.

leucocyte (loo-ko-sIt) *n.* a white blood cell.

leukaemia (loo-kee-miă) *n.* a disease in which leucocytes multiply uncontrollably.

levee (le-vi) *n.* an embankment against floods; *Amer.* a quay.

level *adj.* **1** flat and even; without bumps or hollows. **2** horizontal. **3** at the same height or in the same relative position as something: *he drew up level with me.* **4** steady; unchanging. ● *n.* **1** a position on a scale; a degree: *unemployment levels.* **2** a height reached: *flood levels.* **3** an instrument to test a horizontal line. ● *v.* (**levelled, levelling**; *Amer.* **leveled**) **1** make or become level; knock down (a building). **2** aim (a gun). □ **on the level** honest.

level crossing *n.* a place where a road and railway cross at the same level.

level-headed *adj.* sensible.

level pegging *n.* equality in score.

lever *n.* a bar pivoted on a fixed point to lift something; a pivoted handle used to operate machinery; a means of power or influence. ● *v.* use a lever; lift by this.

leverage *n.* the action or power of a lever; power, influence.

leveret (lev-ĕr-et) *n.* a young hare.

leviathan (lĕ-vI-ă-thăn) *n.* something of enormous size and power.

levitate *v.* rise or cause to rise and float in the air. □ **levitation** *n.*

levity *n.* flippancy, humorous treatment of something serious.

levy *v.* (**levied, levying**) impose (a tax, fee, or fine). ● *n.* (*pl.* **-ies**) a tax; an act of levying a tax etc.

lewd *adj.* treating sexual matters vulgarly; lascivious. □ **lewdly** *adv.*, **lewdness** *n.*

lexical *adj.* of words.

lexicography *n.* the compiling of dictionaries. □ **lexicographer** *n.*

lexicon *n.* a dictionary; a vocabulary.

Li *symb.* lithium.

liability *n.* (*pl.* **-ies**) **1** being legally responsible. **2** a debt. **3** a person or thing putting one at a disadvantage.

liable *adj.* **1** held responsible by law; legally obliged to pay a tax etc. **2** likely to do something.

liaise (lee-ayz) *v.* establish a cooperative link or relationship.

liaison (lee-ayz-on) *n.* **1** communication and cooperation. **2** an illicit sexual relationship.

liana (lee-**ah**-nă) *n.* a climbing plant of tropical forests.

liar *n.* a person who tells lies.

libation *n.* a drink-offering to a god.

libel *n.* a published false statement that damages a person's reputation; the act of publishing it. ● *v.* (**libelled, libelling**; *Amer.* **libeled**) publish a libel against. □ **libellous** *adj.*

liberal *adj.* **1** tolerant; respecting individual freedom; (in politics) favouring moderate social reform. **2** generous. **3** (of an interpretation) not strict or exact. □ **liberally** *adv.*

liberalize *v.* (also **-ise**) make less strict. □ **liberalization** *n.*

liberate *v.* set free. □ **liberated** *adj.*, **liberation** *n.*, **liberator** *n.*

libertarian *n.* a person favouring absolute liberty of thought and action.

libertine *n.* a person who lives an irresponsible immoral life.

liberty *n.* (*pl.* **-ies**) freedom; a right or privilege. □ **at liberty** free; permitted to do something. **take liberties** behave with undue freedom or familiarity.

librarian *n.* a person in charge of or assisting in a library.

library *n.* (*pl.* **-ies**) a collection of books (or records, films, etc.) for consulting or borrowing; a room or building containing these.

libretto *n.* (*pl.* **librettos** or **libretti**) the words of an opera.

lice pl. of **louse**.

licence *n.* (*Amer.* **license**) **1** an official permit to own or do something; permission. **2** freedom to do as one likes.

license *v.* grant a licence to or for. ● *n.* Amer. sp. of **licence**.

licensee *n.* a holder of a licence.

licentiate (lI-sen-shĕt) *n.* a holder of a certificate of competence in a profession.

licentious *adj.* sexually immoral. □ **licentiousness** *n.*

lichee var. of **lychee**.

lichen (ly-kĕn) *n.* a low-growing dry plant that grows on rocks etc.

lich-gate *n.* (also **lych-gate**) a roofed gateway to a churchyard.

lick *v.* **1** pass the tongue over; (of waves or flame) touch lightly. **2** *informal* defeat; thrash. ● *n.* **1** an act of licking; *informal* a slight application (of paint etc.). **2** *informal* a fast pace.

licorice var. of **liquorice**.

lid *n.* a hinged or removable cover for a box, pot, etc.; an eyelid.

lie[1] *n.* a statement the speaker knows to be untrue. ● *v.* (**lied, lying**) tell a lie.

lie[2] *v.* (**lay, lain, lying**) **1** have or put one's body in a flat or resting position; be at rest on something. **2** be in a specified state; be situated. ● *n.* the pattern or direction in which something lies. □ **lie in** lie in bed late in the morning. **lie low** stay hidden.

■ **Usage** It is incorrect in standard English to use *lie* to mean 'lay', as in *Lie her on the bed.*

liege (leej) *n. hist.* **1** a feudal superior. **2** a vassal.

lien (leen, lee-ĕn) *n. Law* the right to hold another person's property until a debt on it is paid.

lieu (lew) *n.* □ **in lieu** instead.

lieutenant (lef-ten-ănt; *Amer.* looten-ănt) *n.* an army officer next below captain; a naval officer next below lieutenant commander; a rank just below a specified officer; a chief assistant.

life *n.* (*pl.* **lives**) **1** the ability of animals and plants to function and grow; being alive; living things. **2** the time for which an individual is alive; the time for which an object lasts. **3** a way of living. **4** vitality, enthusiasm; excitement. **5** a biography. **6** a sentence of imprisonment for life.

lifebelt *n.* a belt of buoyant material to keep a person afloat.

lifeboat *n.* a boat for rescuing people at sea; a ship's boat for emergency use.

lifebuoy (-boi) *n.* a buoyant device to keep a person afloat.

life cycle *n.* a series of changes undergone by an organism during its life.

lifeguard *n.* an expert swimmer employed to rescue bathers in danger.

life jacket *n.* a buoyant or inflatable jacket for keeping a person afloat in water.

lifeless *adj.* dead; unconscious; not animated; without living things.

lifelike *adj.* exactly like a real person or thing.

lifeline *n.* a rope thrown to a swimmer in danger; something essential to safety.

lifelong *adj.* lasting all one's life.

life sciences *n.pl.* biology and related subjects.

life-size *adj.* (also **life-sized**) (of a model etc.) of the same size as the person or thing represented.

lifestyle *n.* a way of spending one's life. ● *adj.* (of a product etc.) designed to appeal to customers with a particular lifestyle.

life support *n.* the artificial maintenance of the body's functions after physical failure or in a hostile environment.

lifetime *n.* the duration of a person's life.

lift *v.* **1** raise; turn to face upwards; move upwards; make larger, louder, or higher. **2** pick up and move; remove (legal restrictions etc.); steal, plagiarize. **3** raise (someone's spirits) or be raised. ● *n.* **1** an apparatus for moving people and goods from one floor of a building to another. **2** an act or manner of lifting. **3** a free ride in a motor vehicle. **4** a feeling of encouragement.

lift-off *n.* vertical take-off of a spacecraft etc.

ligament *n.* a tough flexible tissue holding bones together.

ligature *n.* a thing used for tying; thread used in surgery.

light[1] *n.* **1** a kind of radiation that stimulates sight; brightness; a source of illumination. **2** understanding, enlightenment. **3** a lighter or paler part or area of something. **4** a way of regarding something: *viewed the activities in a favourable light.* ● *v.* (**lit** or **lighted, lighting**) **1** illuminate, provide with light; switch on (an electric light). **2** ignite, set burning. ● *adj.* **1** well lit; not dark. **2** (of a colour) pale. □ **bring (or come) to light** reveal (or be revealed). **in the light of** when (something) is taken into account. **light on** discover by chance. **light up** brighten; put lights on at dusk; light a cigarette.

light[2] *adj.* **1** having little weight, not heavy; easy to lift; of less than usual or average weight. **2** not serious or profound; not solemn, sad, or worried. **3** (of sleep) not deep, easily broken. **4** (of food) easy to digest. □ **make light of** treat as unimportant. **travel light** take little luggage. □ **lightly** *adv.*, **lightness** *n.*

lighten[1] *v.* shed light on; make or become brighter.

lighten[2] *v.* make or become less heavy.

lighter *n.* **1** a device for lighting cigarettes and cigars. **2** a flat-bottomed boat for carrying ships' cargoes ashore.

light-fingered *adj.* apt to steal.

light-headed *adj.* dizzy and slightly faint.

light-hearted *adj.* cheerful, not serious.

lighthouse *n.* a tower with a beacon light to warn or guide ships.

light industry *n.* the manufacture of small or light articles.

lighting *n.* a means of providing light; the light itself.

lightning *n.* a flash of bright light produced from cloud by natural electricity. ● *adj.* very quick.

light pen *n.* a light-emitting device for reading bar codes; a pen-shaped device held to a computer screen to pass information to the computer.

lights *n.pl.* the lungs of certain animals, used as animal food.

lightship *n.* a moored ship with a light, serving as a lighthouse.

lightweight *adj.* not heavy; not important or influential; trivial, not serious or intellectual. ● *n.* a lightweight person; a boxing weight between featherweight and welterweight.

light year *n.* the distance light travels in one year, about 6 million million miles.

lignite *n.* a brown coal of a woody texture.

like[1] *prep.* resembling, similar to; in the same way as; typical of. ● *adj.* similar, the same. ● *conj. informal* **1** in the same way that. **2** as though. ● *adv. informal* in a way, rather. ● *n.* a person or thing resembling another.

like[2] *v.* **1** find pleasant, enjoy. **2** want, wish for: *I'd like a drink.* ● *n.pl.* (**likes**) things one likes or prefers.

likeable *adj.* (also **likable**) pleasant, easy to like.

likelihood *n.* a probability.

likely *adj.* (**likelier, likeliest**) **1** such as may reasonably be expected to occur or be true. **2** seeming to be suitable or have a chance of success. ● *adv.* probably. □ **likeliness** *n.*

liken *v.* point out the likeness of (one thing to another).

likeness *n.* being like; a copy, a portrait.

likewise *adv.* **1** also. **2** in a similar way.

liking *n.* a fondness. □ **to one's liking** suiting one's taste.

lilac *n.* a shrub with fragrant purple or white flowers; pale purple. ● *adj.* pale purple.

lilt *n.* **1** a rise and fall of the voice when speaking. **2** a pleasant swinging rhythm in a tune. □ **lilting** *adj.*

lily *n.* (*pl.* **-ies**) a plant growing from a bulb, with large flowers.

limb *n.* an arm, leg, or wing; a large branch of a tree.

limber *adj.* supple. □ **limber up** exercise in preparation for athletic activity.

limbo[1] *n.* a state of waiting unable to act or take a decision.

limbo[2] *n.* (*pl.* **limbos**) a West Indian dance in which the dancer bends back to pass under a bar.

lime *n.* **1** a white substance used in making cement etc. **2** a round yellowish-green fruit like a lemon; its colour. **3** a tree with heart-shaped leaves.

limelight *n.* the focus of public attention.

limerick *n.* a humorous poem with five lines.

limestone *n.* rock from which lime is obtained.

limit *n.* a point beyond which something does not continue; a restriction; the greatest amount allowed. ● *v.* set or serve as a limit to. ◻ **off limits** out of bounds; not allowed. ◻ **limitation** *n.*

limousine *n.* a large luxurious car.

limp *v.* walk or proceed lamely ● *n.* a limping walk. ● *adj.* not stiff or firm; wilting. ◻ **limply** *adv.*, **limpness** *n.*

limpet *n.* a small shellfish that sticks tightly to rocks.

limpid *adj.* (of liquids) clear.

linchpin *n.* **1** a pin passed through the end of an axle to secure a wheel. **2** a person or thing vital to an enterprise.

linctus *n.* a soothing cough mixture.

line *n.* **1** a long narrow mark; an outline as a feature of a design; a wrinkle. **2** a length of cord, rope, wire, etc., for a particular purpose; a telephone connection. **3** a row of people or things; a row of words; a brief letter; (**lines**) an actor's part. **4** a series of generations. **5** a railway track or route; a company providing ships, aircraft, or buses on a route. **6** an area or branch of activity: *my line of work.* **7** a series of military field works. ● *v.* **1** stand on either side of (a road etc.). **2** mark with lines. **3** cover the inside surface of. ◻ **line one's pockets** make money, esp. dishonestly. **line up** arrange or be arranged in a row.

lineage (lin-ee-ij) *n.* descent from an ancestor; one's ancestry.

lineal *adj.* of or in a line.

linear *adj.* extending along a line; formed with straight lines; proceeding straight forwardly from one stage to another.

linen *n.* cloth made of flax; household articles (e.g. sheets, tablecloths) formerly made of this.

liner *n.* **1** a passenger ship or aircraft. **2** a removable lining.

linesman *n.* (*pl.* **-men**) **1** an umpire's assistant at the boundary line. **2** a workman who maintains railway, electrical, or telephone lines.

ling *n.* heather.

linger *v.* stay longer than necessary; take a long time doing something.

lingerie (lahn-*zher*-ee) *n.* women's underwear.

lingua franca *n.* (*pl.* **lingua francas**) a common language used among people whose native languages are different.

lingual *adj.* of the tongue; of speech or languages.

linguist *n.* a person who is skilled in languages or linguistics.

linguistic *adj.* of language. ● *n.* (**linguistics**) the study of language. ◻ **linguistically** *adv.*

liniment *n.* an embrocation.

lining *n.* a layer of material or another substance covering an inner surface.

link *n.* **1** a connection; a means of contact; a person acting as messenger or intermediary. **2** each ring of a chain. ● *v.* connect; intertwine; represent as connected. ◻ **linkage** *n.*

lino *n. informal* linoleum.

linocut *n.* a design cut in relief on a block of linoleum; a print made from this.

linoleum *n.* a smooth covering for floors.

linseed *n.* the seed of flax, a source of oil.

lint *n.* a soft fabric for dressing wounds; fluff.

lintel *n.* a horizontal timber or stone over a doorway.

lion *n.* a large flesh-eating animal of the cat family.

lionize *v.* (also **-ise**) treat as a celebrity. ▫ **lionization** *n.*

lip *n.* **1** either of the fleshy edges of the mouth-opening. **2** the edge of a container or opening; a stight projection for pouring from. **3** *informal* impudence. ▫ **pay lip service** express approval but fail to act on it.

liposuction *n.* removal of fat from under the skin by suction, used in cosmetic surgery.

lip-read *v.* understand what is said from movements of a speaker's lips.

lipsalve *n.* ointment for the lips.

lipstick *n.* a cosmetic for colouring the lips.

liquefy *v.* (**liquefied, liquefying**) make or become liquid. ▫ **liquefaction** *n.*

liqueur (lik-**yoor**) *n.* a strong sweet alcoholic spirit.

liquid *n.* a flowing substance like water or oil. ● *adj.* **1** in the form of liquid. **2** (of assets) easy to convert into cash.

liquidate *v.* **1** close down (a business) and divide its assets among creditors. **2** convert (assets) into cash. **3** pay off (a debt). **4** kill. ▫ **liquidation** *n.*, **liquidator** *n.*

liquidity *n.* a company's possession of liquid assets.

liquidize *v.* (also **-ise**) reduce to a liquid.

liquidizer *n.* (also **-iser**) a machine for puréeing vegetables etc.

liquor *n.* **1** alcoholic drink. **2** juice from cooked food.

liquorice *n.* (also esp. *Amer.* **licorice**) a black substance used in medicine and as a sweet.

lira *n.* (*pl.* **lire**) a unit of money in Turkey (and formerly Italy).

lisp *n.* a speech defect in which *s* and *z* are pronounced like *th.* ● *v.* speak or utter with a lisp.

lissom *adj.* slim and supple.

list[1] *n.* a number of connected items or names following one another. ● *v.* make a list of; include in a list.

list[2] *v.* (of a ship) lean over to one side. ● *n.* a listing position.

listen *v.* make an effort to hear; pay attention; take notice of and act on what is said. ▫ **listen in** overhear a conversation; listen to a broadcast. ▫ **listener** *n.*

listeria *n.* a type of bacteria causing food poisoning.

listless *adj.* without energy or enthusiasm. ▫ **listlessly** *adv.*, **listlessness** *n.*

lit past & p.p. of **light**[1].

litany *n.* (*pl.* **-ies**) a set form of prayer; a long monotonous recital.

liter Amer. sp. of **litre**.

literal *adj.* taking the basic meaning of a word, not a metaphorical or exaggerated one. ▫ **literally** *adv.*, **literalness** *n.*

literary *adj.* of or associated with literature.

literate *adj.* able to read and write. ▫ **literacy** *n.*

literati *n.pl.* people interested in and knowledgeable about literature.

literature *n.* great novels, poetry, and plays; books on a particular subject; printed matter giving information etc.

lithe *adj.* supple, agile.

lithium *n.* a light metallic element (symbol Li).

litho *n. informal* lithography; a lithograph.

lithography *n.* printing from a plate treated so that ink sticks only to the design. ▫ **lithograph** *n.* **lithographic** *adj.*

litigant *adj.* & *n.* (a person) involved in or initiating a lawsuit.

litigate *v.* carry on a lawsuit; contest in law. ▫ **litigation** *n.*

litigious (lit-**ij**-ŭs) *adj.* fond of litigation.

litmus *n.* a substance turned red by acids and blue by alkalis.

litotes (**lI**-toh-teez) *n.* an ironic understatement.

litre *n.* (*Amer.* **liter**) a metric unit of capacity (1.76 pints) for measuring liquids.

litter *n.* **1** rubbish left lying about. **2** young animals born at one birth. **3** material used as bedding for animals or to absorb their excrement. **4** *hist.* a vehicle consisting of a curtained seat carried on men's shoulders. ● *v.* **1** scatter as litter; make untidy by litter. **2** give birth to (a litter).

little *adj.* small in size, amount, or degree; young, younger. ● *n.* & *pron.* a small amount; a short time or distance. ● *adv.* to a small extent; hardly.

littoral *adj.* of or by the shore.

liturgy *n.* (*pl.* **-ies**) a set form of public worship. □ **liturgical** *adj.*

live[1] (lyv) *adj.* **1** alive. **2** burning; unexploded; charged with electricity. **3** (of broadcasts) transmitted while actually happening.

live[2] (liv) *v.* **1** be or remain alive. **2** have one's home in a particular place. **3** spend one's life in a particular way; have a full and exciting life. □ **live down** live until (scandal etc.) is forgotten. **live on 1** eat (a type of food) as one's regular diet. **2** have (an amount of money) to buy necessities.

livelihood *n.* a means of earning or providing enough food etc. to sustain life.

lively *adj.* (**livelier, liveliest**) full of energy or action. □ **liveliness** *n.*

liven *v.* make or become lively.

liver *n.* a large organ in the abdomen, secreting bile.

liveried *adj.* wearing livery.

livery *n.* (*pl.* **-ies**) a distinctive uniform; a colour scheme in which a company's vehicles are painted.

livestock *n.* farm animals.

livid *adj.* **1** *informal* furiously angry. **2** bluish grey.

living *adj.* **1** alive; current, in use. **2** used as a home rather than for work. ● *n.* **1** an income; the means of earning it. **2** a particular life style.

living room *n.* a room for general daytime use.

lizard *n.* a reptile with four legs and a long tail.

llama (lah-mă) *n.* a South American animal related to the camel.

load *n.* **1** a thing or quantity carried; a burden of responsibility or worry; the amount of work someone has to do. **2** the amount of electric current supplied by a source. **3** (**loads**) *informal* a great deal. ● *v.* **1** put a load in or on; burden. **2** put ammunition into (a gun) or film into (a camera); put (data) into (a computer). **3** bias towards a particular outcome. □ **loaded** *adj.*

loaf *n.* (*pl.* **loaves**) **1** a quantity of bread baked as one piece; a similarly shaped mass of other food. **2** *informal* one's brains. ● *v.* spend time idly, saunter about. □ **loafer** *n.*

loam *n.* rich soil.

loan *n.* something lent, esp. a sum of money; lending. ● *v.* lend. □ **on loan** being borrowed.

loan shark *n. informal* a person lending money at very high rates of interest.

loath *adj.* unwilling.

loathe *v.* feel hatred and disgust for. □ **loathing** *n.*, **loathsome** *adj.*

lob *v.* (**lobbed, lobbing**) throw or hit (a ball) slowly in a high arc. ● *n.* a lobbed ball.

lobar *adj.* of a lobe, esp. of the lung.

lobby *n.* (*pl.* **-ies**) **1** a porch, entrance hall, or ante-room. **2** a body of people seeking to influence legislation. ● *v.* (**lobbied, lobbying**) seek to persuade (an MP etc.) to support one's cause.

lobbyist *n.* a person who lobbies an MP etc.

lobe *n.* a flat rounded part or projection; the lower soft part of the ear.

lobotomy *n.* (*pl.* **-ies**) an incision into the frontal lobe of the brain.

lobster *n.* a shellfish with large claws; its flesh as food.

local *adj.* of or affecting a particular place or small area; (of a telephone call) relatively cheap because made to somewhere nearby. ● *n.* **1** an inhabitant of a particular district. **2** *informal* one's nearest public house. □ **locally** *adv.*

locale (loh-**kahl**) *n.* the scene of an event.

local government *n.* the administration of a district by representatives elected locally.

locality *n.* (*pl.* **-ies**) the position of something; an area or neighbourhood.

localize *v.* (also **-ise**) confine within an area; decentralize. □ **localization** *n.*

locate *v.* discover the position of; situate in a particular place; set in a particular context.

location *n.* a place where something is situated; locating something. □ **on location** (of filming) in a setting away from the film studio.

loch *n. Scot.* a lake; an arm of the sea.

loci pl. of **locus**.

lock *n.* **1** a device (opened by a key) for fastening a door or lid etc. **2** a section of a canal enclosed by gates, where the water level can be changed. **3** a wrestling hold. **4** the extent to which a vehicle's front wheels can be turned using the steering wheel. **5** a piece of hair that hangs together; (**locks**) *poetic* a person's hair. ● *v.* fasten with a lock; shut into a locked place; make or become rigidly fixed. □ **lockable** *adj.*

locker *n.* a lockable cupboard where things can be stowed securely.

locket *n.* a small ornamental case worn on a chain round the neck.

lockjaw *n.* tetanus.

lockout *n.* the exclusion of employees from their workplace during a dispute.

locksmith *n.* a maker and mender of locks.

lock-up *n.* lockable premises; a place where prisoners can be kept temporarily; an act of locking a building's doors.

locomotion *n.* the ability to move from place to place.

locomotive *n.* a self-propelled engine for moving trains. ● *adj.* of or effecting locomotion.

locum *n.* a temporary stand-in for a doctor, clergyman, etc.

locus *n.* (*pl.* **loci**) **1** a particular position; something's location. **2** *Mathematics* a line or curve etc. formed by certain points or by the movement of a point or line.

locust *n.* a grasshopper that devours vegetation.

lode *n.* a vein of metal ore.

lodestar *n.* a star (esp. the pole star) used as a guide in navigation.

lodestone *n.* an oxide of iron used as a magnet.

lodge *n.* **1** a cabin for use by hunters, skiers, etc.; a gatekeeper's house; a porter's room at the entrance to a building. **2** the members or meeting place of a branch of certain societies. **3** a beaver's or otter's lair. ● *v.* **1** provide with sleeping quarters or temporary accommodation; live as a lodger. **2** present (a complaint, appeal, etc.) to an authority. **3** make or become fixed or embedded.

lodger *n.* a person paying for accommodation in another's house.

lodging *n.* a place where one lodges; (**lodgings**) a room or rooms rented for living in.

loft *n.* a space under a roof; a gallery in a church. ● *v.* hit, throw, or kick (a ball) in a high arc.

lofty *adj.* (**loftier, loftiest**) very tall; noble, exalted; proud, aloof. □ **loftily** *adv.*

log *n.* **1** a piece cut from a trunk or branch of a tree. **2** a systematic record; a logbook. **3** a device for gauging a ship's speed. **4** a logarithm. ● *v.* (**logged, logging**) enter (facts) in a logbook. □ **log on** or **off, log in** or **out** open or close one's on-line access to a computer system.

loganberry *n.* (*pl.* **-ies**) a large dark red fruit resembling a raspberry.

logarithm *n.* one of a series of numbers set out in tables, used to simplify calculations.

logbook *n.* a book for recording details of a journey.

loggerheads *n.pl.* □ **at loggerheads** disagreeing or quarrelling.

logic *n.* a science or method of reasoning; correct reasoning.

logical *adj.* of or according to logic; following naturally and sensibly; reasonable; reasoning correctly. □ **logicality** *n.*, **logically** *adv.*

logician *n.* a person skilled in logic.

logistics *n.pl.* the organization of supplies and services; the coordination of a large operation. □ **logistical** *adj.*

logo (loh-goh) *n.* (*pl.* **logos**) a design used as an emblem.

-logy *comb. form* the science or study of a particular subject.

loin *n.* the side and back of the body between the ribs and hip bone.

loincloth *n.* a cloth worn round the body at the hips.

loiter *v.* linger, stand about idly. □ **loiterer** *n.*

loll *v.* sit, lie, or stand in a relaxed way; hang loosely.

lollipop *n.* a large usu. flat boiled sweet on a small stick.

lollipop lady, lollipop man *n. informal* an official using a circular sign on a stick to stop traffic for children to cross a road.

lollop *v.* (**lolloped, lolloping**) move in clumsy bounds.

lolly *n. informal* **1** a lollipop. **2** money.

lone *adj.* solitary.

lonely *adj.* (**lonelier, loneliest**) **1** solitary; sad because one lacks friends. **2** (of a place) remote, unfrequented. □ **loneliness** *n.*

loner *n.* a person who prefers not to associate with others.

lonesome *adj.* lonely.

long[1] *adj.* of great length; of a specified length. ● *adv.* for a long time; throughout a specified period. □ **as** or **so long as** provided that.

long[2] *v.* feel an intense desire.

long-distance *adj.* travelling or operated between distant places.

longevity (lon-jev-iti) *n.* long life.

long face *n.* a dismal expression.

longhand *n.* ordinary writing, not shorthand or typing etc.

longing *n.* an intense wish.

longitude *n.* the distance east or west (measured in degrees on a map) from the Greenwich meridian.

longitudinal *adj.* **1** running lengthwise rather than across. **2** of longitude. □ **longitudinally** *adv.*

long johns *n.pl. informal* close-fitting underpants with long legs.

long-life *adj.* (of milk etc.) treated to prolong its shelf-life.

long-lived *adj.* living or lasting for a long time.

long-range *adj.* effective over long distances; relating to a long period of future time.

longshoreman *n.* (*pl.* **-men**) *Amer.* a docker.

long shot *n.* a venture or guess very unlikely to succeed.

long-sighted *adj.* able to see clearly only what is at a distance.

long-standing *adj.* having existed for a long time.

long-suffering *adj.* bearing provocation patiently.

long-term *adj.* of or for a long period.

long ton *see* **ton**.

long wave *n.* a radio wave of a wavelength above a kilometre and frequency less than 300 kHz.

longways *adv.* (also **longwise**) lengthways.

long-winded *adj.* talking or writing at tedious length.

loo *n. informal* a lavatory.

loofah *n.* the dried pod of a gourd, used as a rough sponge.

look *v.* **1** use or direct one's eyes in order to see, search, or examine. **2** seem. ● *n.* **1** an act of looking. **2** the appearance of something; a facial expression; (**looks**) a person's attractiveness. □ **look after** take care of; attend to. **look down on** despise. **look forward to** await eagerly. **look into** investigate. **look on** watch without being involved. **look out** be vigilant. **look round** go round and inspect (a building etc.) **look up 1** search for information about. **2** *informal* make contact with (someone). **3** (of a prospect) improve. **look up to** admire and respect.

looker-on *n.* (*pl.* **lookers-on**) a mere spectator.

lookout *n.* **1** an observation post; a person keeping watch. **2** *informal* a likely outcome. **3** *informal* a person's own concern.

loom *v.* appear, esp. close at hand or threateningly. ● *n.* an apparatus for weaving cloth.

loop *n.* a curve that is U-shaped or that crosses itself; something forming this shape. ● *v.* form into a loop; be loop-shaped. □ **loop the loop** fly an aircraft in a vertical circle.

loophole *n.* a means of evading a rule or contract.

loose *adj.* **1** not securely fixed in place; not tethered or shut up. **2** (of a garment) not fitting closely; (of a translation etc.) not exact; (of a walk) easy, relaxed. ● *v.* set free; unfasten; relax. □ **at a loose end** with nothing to do. **on the loose** having escaped from confinement. □ **loosely** *adv.*, **looseness** *n.*

loose box *n.* a stall for a horse.

loose-leaf *adj.* with each page removable.

loosen *v.* make or become loose or looser.

loot *n.* goods taken from an enemy or by theft. ● *v.* take loot (from); take as loot.

lop *v.* (**lopped, lopping**) cut off (branches) from a tree.

lope *v.* run with a long bounding stride. ● *n.* this stride.

lop-eared *adj.* with drooping ears.

lopsided *adj.* with one side lower, smaller, or heavier than the other.

loquacious (lŏ-kway-shŭs) *adj.* talkative. □ **loquacity** *n.*

lord *n.* a nobleman; the title of certain peers or high officials; a master or ruler; (**Lord**) God or Christ. □ **lord it over** behave in an arrogantly superior way towards.

lordship *n.* the title used of a man with the rank of lord.

lore *n.* a body of traditions and knowledge.

lorgnette (lorn-yet) *n.* eyeglasses held on a long handle.

lorry *n.* (*pl.* **-ies**) a large motor vehicle for transporting heavy loads.

lose *v.* (**lost, losing**) **1** cease to have; be deprived of. **2** become unable to find. **3** fail to win (a game etc.); waste, fail to use or take advantage of; earn less (money) than previously. **4** *informal* cause (someone) to be unable to follow one's argument. □ **lose heart** become discouraged. **lose oneself** become absorbed in something. **lose one's way** be unable to find the right direction to go in. **lose out** be disadvantaged, be deprived of an opportunity. **lose weight** become thinner and lighter. □ **loser** *n.*

■ **Usage** *Lose* has only one *o*. *Loose* as a verb means 'set free'.

---

loss *n.* losing, being lost; someone or something lost; someone or something badly missed when lost. □ **at a loss 1** not knowing what to do. **2** making less money than has been spent.

loss-leader *n.* an article sold at a loss to attract customers.

lost past & p.p. of **lose**. *adj.* **1** unable to find one's way; not knowing where one is. **2** having strayed; gone and not recoverable. □ **be**

lost on be unnoticed or unappreciated by.

lot *pron.* (**a lot, lots**) *informal* a large number or amount. ● *adv.* (**a lot, lots**) *informal* very much, greatly. ● *n.* **1** *informal* a group or set of people or things. **2** an item for sale at an auction. **3** each of a set of objects drawn at random to make a decision; a person's luck or condition in life. **4** a plot of land. □ **the lot** *informal* the total number or quantity.

lotion *n.* a medicinal or cosmetic liquid applied to the skin.

lottery *n.* (*pl.* **-ies**) a system of raising money by selling numbered tickets and giving prizes to holders of numbers drawn at random; something where the outcome is governed by luck.

lotus *n.* (*pl.* **lotuses**) a tropical water lily; a mythical fruit.

loud *adj.* **1** making a great deal of noise, easily heard. **2** gaudy, garish. ● *adv.* loudly. □ **loudly** *adv.*, **loudness** *n.*

loudhailer *n.* an electronically operated megaphone.

loudspeaker *n.* an apparatus that converts electrical impulses into audible sound.

lough (lok) *n. Irish* = **loch**.

lounge *v.* loll; sit or stand about idly. ● *n.* a sitting room; a waiting room at an airport etc.

lounge suit *n.* a man's ordinary suit for day wear.

lour (low-ĕ) *v.* (also **lower**) frown, scowl; (of clouds) look dark and threatening.

louse *n.* (*pl.* **lice**) a small parasitic insect; (*pl.* **louses**) a contemptible person.

lousy *adj.* (**lousier, lousiest**) **1** *informal* very bad. **2** infested with lice.

lout *n.* a clumsy ill-mannered person. □ **loutish** *adj.*

louvre (loo-vĕ) *n.* (also **louver**) each of a set of overlapping slats arranged to let in air but exclude light or rain. □ **louvred** *adj.*

lovable *adj.* endearing, inspiring love.

love *n.* **1** deep, intense affection; sexual passion; a beloved person or thing. **2** (in games) no score, nil. ● *v.* feel love for; like or enjoy greatly. □ **in love** feeling (esp. sexual) love for another person. **make love** have sexual intercourse.

love affair *n.* a romantic or sexual relationship between people who are in love.

lovelorn *adj.* pining with unrequited love.

lovely *adj.* (**lovelier, loveliest**) beautiful, attractive; delightful. □ **loveliness** *n.*

lover *n.* **1** a person in love with another or having a love affair. **2** a person who likes something specified.

loving *adj.* feeling or showing love. □ **lovingly** *adv.*

low[1] *adj.* **1** of little height from top to bottom; not far above the ground or sea level; of less than average amount or intensity. **2** ranking below others, inferior. **3** dishonourable. **4** depressed. ● *n.* a low point; an area of low atmospheric pressure. ● *adv.* in, at, or to a low level.

low[2] *v.* (of cattle) make a deep mooing sound.

lowbrow *adj.* not intellectual or cultured.

low-down *informal adj.* dishonourable. ● *n.* relevant information.

lower[1] *v.* let downwards; reduce the height, pitch, or degree of.

lower[2] var. of **lour**.

lower case *n.* letters that are not capitals.

low-key *adj.* not elaborate or ostentatious; restrained.

lowlands *n.pl.* low-lying land. □ **lowland** *adj.*, **lowlander** *n.*

lowly *adj.* (**lowlier, lowliest**) of humble rank or condition.

low-rise *adj.* (of a building) having few storeys.

low season *n.* the season that is least busy in a resort, hotel, etc.

low-tech *adj.* using relatively simple technology.

loyal *adj.* firm in one's allegiance. ▫ **loyally** *adv.*, **loyalty** *n.*

loyalist *n.* a person who is loyal, esp. while others revolt.

lozenge *n.* **1** a small medicinal tablet to be dissolved in the mouth. **2** a diamond-shaped figure.

LP *abbr.* a long-playing record.

Lr *symb.* lawrencium.

LSD *n.* a powerful hallucinogenic drug.

Ltd. *abbr.* Limited.

Lu *symb.* lutetium.

lubricant *n.* a lubricating substance.

lubricate *v.* oil or grease (machinery etc.) to allow smooth movement. ▫ **lubrication** *n.*

lubricious (loo-**bri**-shŭs) *adj.* **1** lewd. **2** slippery.

lucerne *n.* a clover-like fodder plant.

lucid *adj.* clearly expressed; sane. ▫ **lucidity** *n.*, **lucidly** *adv.*

luck *n.* good or bad fortune; chance thought of as a force bringing this.

luckless *adj.* unlucky.

lucky *adj.* (**luckier, luckiest**) having, bringing, or resulting from good luck. ▫ **luckily** *adv.*

lucky dip *n. Brit.* a game in which people draw small prizes at random from a container; a process determined by chance.

lucrative *adj.* profitable, producing much money.

lucre (loo-ker) *n. derog.* money.

Luddite *n.* a person opposing the introduction of new technology or working methods.

ludicrous *adj.* ridiculous. ▫ **ludicrously** *adv.*

lug *v.* (**lugged, lugging**) drag or carry with great effort. ● *n.* an ear-like projection; *informal* an ear.

luge *n.* a light toboggan, ridden sitting upright.

luggage *n.* suitcases and bags holding a traveller's possessions.

lugubrious (luu-**goo**-bree-ŭs) *adj.* dismal, mournful. ▫ **lugubriously** *adv.*

lukewarm *adj.* only slightly warm; not enthusiastic.

lull *v.* send to sleep; cause to feel deceptively confident; (of a storm etc.) become quiet. ● *n.* a period of quiet or inactivity.

lullaby *n.* (*pl.* **-ies**) a soothing song for sending a child to sleep.

lumbago (lum-**bay**-goh) *n.* rheumatic pain in muscles of the lower back.

lumbar *adj.* of the lower back.

lumber *n.* useless or unwanted articles, esp. furniture; *Amer.* timber sawn into planks. ● *v.* **1** move heavily and awkwardly. **2** burden with something unwanted.

lumberjack *n. Amer.* a person who cuts or transports lumber.

luminary *n.* (*pl.* **-ies**) **1** a natural light-giving body, esp. the sun or moon. **2** an eminent person.

luminescent *adj.* emitting light without heat. ▫ **luminescence** *n.*

luminous *adj.* emitting light, glowing in the dark. ▫ **luminosity** *n.*, **luminously** *adv.*

lump *n.* a hard or compact mass; a swelling. ● *v.* treat as alike, group together indiscriminately.

lumpectomy *n.* (*pl.* **-ies**) the surgical removal of a lump from the breast.

lumpy *adj.* (**lumpier, lumpiest**) full of or covered in lumps. ▫ **lumpiness** *n.*

lunacy *n.* (*pl.* **-ies**) insanity; great folly.

lunar *adj.* of the moon.

lunar month *n.* the period between new moons (29½ days), four weeks.

lunate *adj.* crescent-shaped.

lunatic *n.* an insane person; a very foolish or reckless person.

lunation *n.* a lunar month.

lunch *n.* a midday meal. ● *v.* eat lunch.

luncheon *n.* lunch.

luncheon meat *n.* tinned cured meat ready for serving.

luncheon voucher *n.* a voucher given to an employee as part of their pay, exchangeable for food.

lung *n.* either of the pair of breathing-organs in the chest.

lunge *n.* **1** a sudden forward movement of the body; a thrust. **2** a long rope attached to a horse while it is being trained. ● *v.* make a lunge forward.

lupine (loo-pIn) *adj.* like a wolf.

lupus *n.* a skin disease producing ulcers.

lurch *v.* & *n.* (make) an unsteady swaying movement, stagger. □ **leave in the lurch** leave (a person) in difficulties.

lure *v.* entice. ● *n.* an enticement; a bait to attract wild animals.

lurid *adj.* in glaring colours; vividly shocking or sensational. □ **luridly** *adv.*

lurk *v.* lie in ambush; (of something bad) be latent but threatening.

luscious (lu-shŭs) *adj.* delicious; voluptuously attractive. □ **lusciously** *adv.*, **lusciousness** *n.*

lush *adj.* (of grass etc.) growing thickly and strongly; very rich, luxurious. □ **lushly** *adv.*, **lushness** *n.*

lust *n.* intense sexual desire; any intense desire. ● *v.* feel lust. □ **lustful** *adj.*, **lustfully** *adv.*

lustre *n.* (*Amer.* **luster**) soft brightness of a surface; brilliance, glory; a metallic glaze on pottery. □ **lustrous** *adj.*

lusty *adj.* (**lustier, lustiest**) strong and vigorous. □ **lustily** *adv.*

lute *n.* a guitar-like instrument with a rounded body. □ **lutenist** *n.*

lutetium *n.* a metallic element (symbol Lu).

lux *n.* a unit of illumination.

luxuriant *adj.* growing profusely. □ **luxuriance** *n.*, **luxuriantly** *adv.*

luxuriate *v.* enjoy or indulge in as a luxury.

luxurious *adj.* very comfortable and elegant; giving self-indulgent pleasure. □ **luxuriously** *adv.*, **luxuriousness** *n.*

luxury *n.* (*pl.* **-ies**) great comfort and extravagance; something unnecessary but very pleasant.

LV *abbr.* luncheon voucher.

Lw *symb.* lawrencium.

lx *abbr.* lux.

lych-gate var. of **lich-gate**.

lychee *n.* (also **lichee**), a sweet white fruit with a brown spiny skin.

Lycra *n. trademark* an elastic fabric.

lye *n.* an alkaline solution used for cleaning.

lying present participle of **lie**[1], **lie**[2].

lymph (limf) *n.* a colourless fluid containing white blood cells. □ **lymphatic** *adj.*

lymphatic system *n.* the network of vessels carrying lymph, protecting against infection.

lymphoma (lim-foh-mă) *n.* (*pl.* **lymphomas** or **lymphomata**) a tumour of the lymph glands.

lynch *v.* (of a mob) kill (someone) for an alleged offence, without trial.

lynx *n.* (*pl.* **lynx** or **lynxes**) a wild animal of the cat family.

lyre *n.* an ancient musical instrument with strings in a U-shaped frame.

lyric *adj.* (of poetry) expressing the poet's feelings. ● *n.* a lyric poem; (**lyrics**) the words of a song.

lyrical *adj.* resembling or using language suitable for lyric poetry; *informal* expressing oneself enthusiastically. □ **lyrically** *adv.*

lyricist (li-ri-sist) *n.* a person who writes lyrics.

Mm

M *abbr.* motorway; mega-; Monsieur; male. ● *n.* (as a Roman numeral) 1,000.

m *abbr.* metre(s); mile(s); million(s); married; masculine.

MA *abbr.* Master of Arts.

ma'am *n.* madam.

mac *n.* (also **mack**) *informal* a mackintosh.

macabre (mă-**kah**-brĕ) *adj.* disturbingly interested in or involving death and injury.

macadam *n.* layers of broken stone used in road-making.

macadamize *v.* (also **-ise**) surface with macadam.

macaroni *n.* tube-shaped pasta.

macaroon *n.* a small almond biscuit.

macaw *n.* an American parrot.

mace *n.* **1** a ceremonial staff. **2** a spice.

macerate (**mas**-ĕ-rayt) *v.* soften by soaking.

Mach (mahk) *n.* (in full **Mach number**) the ratio of the speed of a moving body to the speed of sound.

machete (mă-**she**-ti) *n.* a broad heavy knife.

machiavellian *adj.* elaborately cunning or deceitful.

machinations *n.pl.* clever scheming.

machine *n.* an apparatus with several parts, using mechanical power to perform a particular task; an efficient group of powerful people. ● *v.* produce or work on with a machine.

machine code *n.* a computer language that controls the computer directly, interpreting instructions passing between the software and the machine.

machine-gun *n.* an automatic gun firing bullets in rapid succession.

machine-readable *adj.* in a form that a computer can process.

machinery *n.* machines; the parts of a machine; a system or structure.

machine tool *n.* a power-driven engineering machine such as a lathe.

machinist *n.* a person who works machinery.

machismo (mă-**kiz**-moh) *n.* aggressive masculine pride.

macho (**ma**-choh) *adj.* aggressively masculine.

mack var. of **mac**.

mackerel *n.* (*pl.* **mackerel** or **mackerels**) an edible sea fish.

mackintosh *n.* (also **macintosh**) a raincoat; a water-proof material of rubber and cloth.

macramé (mă-**krah**-mi) *n.* the art of knotting cord in patterns.

macro *n.* *Computing* a single instruction that expands automatically into a set of instructions for a particular task.

macro- *comb. form* large-scale; large; long.

macrobiotic *adj.* of a dietary system comprising wholefoods grown in close harmony with nature.

macrocosm *n.* the universe; a large complex whole.

mad *adj.* (**madder, maddest**) **1** not sane; extremely foolish; frantic, frenzied. **2** *informal* very enthusiastic. **3** *informal* angry. ▫ **madly** *adv.*, **madness** *n.*

madam *n.* a polite form of address to a woman.

Madame (mă-**dahm**) *n.* (*pl.* **Mesdames**) a title or form of address for a French-speaking woman, corresponding to Mrs or madam.

madcap *adj.* wildly impulsive.

mad cow disease *n.* *informal* = **BSE**.

madden *v.* make mad or angry.

madder *n.* a red dye.

made past & p.p. of **make**.

Madeira *n.* **1** a fortified wine from Madeira. **2** rich plain cake.

Mademoiselle (ma-dĕ-mwă-zel) *n.* (*pl.* **Mesdemoiselles**) a title or form of address for an unmarried French-speaking woman, corresponding to Miss or madam.

madonna *n.* a picture or statue of the Virgin Mary.

madrigal *n.* a part-song for unaccompanied voices.

maelstrom (mayl-strŏm) *n.* a powerful whirlpool; a scene of confusion.

maestro (my-stroh) *n.* (*pl.* **maestri** or **maestros**) a great musical conductor or composer; a master of any art.

Mafia *n.* an organized international body of criminals originating in Sicily; (**mafia**) a sinister secret group.

magazine 1 an illustrated periodical; a regular television or radio programme including a variety of items. **2** a chamber holding cartridges in a gun, slides in a projector, etc. **3** a store for arms or explosives.

magenta *adj.* & *n.* purplish red.

maggot *n.* a larva, esp. of the bluebottle.

magic *n.* the supposed art of controlling things by supernatural power; an exciting or delightful quality. ● *adj.* using or used in magic. □ **like magic** very effectively. □ **magical** *adj.*, **magically** *adv.*

magician *n.* a person with magical powers; a conjuror.

magisterial (maj-is-teer-i-ăl) *adj.* **1** authoritative; domineering. **2** of a magistrate.

magistrate *n.* an official or citizen with authority to hold preliminary hearings and judge minor cases. □ **magistracy** *n.*

magma *n.* molten rock under the earth's crust.

magnanimous *adj.* noble and generous, not petty. □ **magnanimity** *n.*, **magnanimously** *adv.*

magnate *n.* a wealthy influential business person.

magnesia *n.* a compound of magnesium used in medicine.

magnesium *n.* a white metallic element (symbol Mg) that burns with an intensely bright flame.

magnet *n.* a piece of iron or steel that can attract iron and point north when suspended; a powerful attraction.

magnetic *adj.* **1** having the properties of a magnet; involving magnetism. **2** fascinating, attractive. □ **magnetically** *adv.*

magnetic tape *n.* a strip of plastic coated with magnetic particles, used in recording, computers, etc.

magnetism *n.* the properties and effects of magnetic substances; great charm and attraction.

magnetize *v.* (also **-ise**) **1** make magnetic. **2** attract.

magneto (mag-nee-toh) *n.* (*pl.* **magnetos**) a small electric generator using magnets.

magnificent *adj.* **1** impressively beautiful, elaborate, or extravagant. **2** very good. □ **magnificence** *n.*, **magnificently** *adv.*

magnify *v.* (**magnified, magnifying**) **1** make (an object) seem larger than it is, esp. by using a lens; increase the volume or intensity of; exaggerate. **2** *archaic* praise. □ **magnification** *n.*

magnitude *n.* largeness, size; importance.

magnolia *n.* a tree with large white or pink flowers.

magnum *n.* a wine bottle of twice the standard size.

magpie *n.* a black and white bird of the crow family.

Magyar *adj.* & *n.* (a member, the language) of a people now predominant in Hungary.

maharaja *n.* (also **maharajah**) *hist.* an Indian prince.

maharanee *n.* (also **maharani**) a maharaja's wife or widow.

maharishi *n.* a Hindu man of great wisdom.

mahatma *n.* (in India etc.) a title of a man revered for his holiness and wisdom.

mah-jong *n.* (also **mah-jongg**) a Chinese game played with 136 or 144 pieces (tiles).

mahogany *n.* a very hard reddish-brown wood.

mahout (mă-**howt**) *n.* an elephant-driver.

maid *n.* a female servant.

maiden *n. archaic* a young unmarried woman, a virgin. ● *adj.* **1** unmarried. **2** first: *a maiden voyage.* □ **maidenhood** *n.*, **maidenly** *adj.*

maiden name *n.* a woman's family name before she married.

maiden over *n.* an over in cricket with no runs scored.

maidservant *n.* a female servant.

mail *n.* **1** post, letters; messages transmitted by computer from one user to another. **2** body-armour made of metal rings or chains. ● *v.* send by post or electronic mail.

mailbox *n. Amer.* a letter box.

mail order *n.* purchase of goods selected from a catalogue and ordered by post.

mailshot *n.* advertising material sent to potential customers.

maim *v.* injure so that a part of the body is useless.

main *adj.* chief in size or importance. ● *n.* a main pipe or channel conveying water, gas, or (usu. **mains**) electricity. □ **in the main** on the whole, generally. □ **mainly** *adv.*

main clause *n. Grammar* a clause that can stand as a complete sentence.

mainframe *n.* a large computer.

mainland *n.* a country or continent without its adjacent islands.

mainline *v. informal* take drugs intravenously.

mainmast *n.* a ship's principal mast.

mainsail *n.* the lowest sail or the sail set on the after part of the mainmast.

mainspring *n.* the chief spring of a watch or clock; the chief motivating force of a movement etc.

mainstay *n.* the cable securing a mainmast; something on which something else depends.

mainstream *n.* the dominant trend of opinion or style etc.

maintain *v.* **1** cause to continue, keep in existence; keep repaired and in good condition; bear the expenses of. **2** assert.

maintenance *n.* maintaining something; providing money for living expenses; money paid to a former spouse after a divorce.

maiolica (mI-**ol**-ik-ă) *n.* (also **majolica**) white pottery decorated with metallic colours.

maisonette *n.* part of a house (usu. not all on one floor) used as a separate dwelling.

maître d'hôtel *n.* a hotel manager; a head waiter.

maize *n.* a tall cereal plant bearing grain on large cobs; its grain.

majestic *adj.* stately and dignified, imposing. □ **majestically** *adv.*

majesty *n.* (*pl.* **-ies**) impressive stateliness; sovereign power; (**Majesty**) the title of a king or queen.

majolica var. of **maiolica**.

major *adj.* **1** important, serious. **2** greater. ● *n.* an army officer next below lieutenant colonel. ● *v.* (**major in**) *Amer.* specialize in (a subject) at college.

majorette *n.* = **drum majorette**.

major general *n.* an army officer next below lieutenant general.

majority *n.* (*pl.* **-ies**) **1** the greater number of a group; the number by which votes for one party exceed those for the next. **2** the age at which someone is legally considered adult.

make *v.* (**made, making**) **1** form, bring into being, create; prepare, produce. **2** cause to become of a specified nature; compose, be constituents of: *they make a good couple.* **3** earn (a sum of money).

4 perform (a specified action); arrange (an agreement). **5** compel to do something. **6** consider or calculate as being a specified number, age, etc. **7** put bedding on (a bed). **8** arrive at (a place). ● *n.* a brand of goods. □ **make do** manage with something inadequate or unsatisfactory. **make for 1** try to reach. **2** tend to result in. **make good 1** be successful. **2** repair or pay compensation for. **make it** *informal* **1** be successful. **2** arrive in time. **make off** leave hastily. **make off with** steal. **make out 1** decipher; interpret, understand. **2** write out (a document). **3** pretend, claim. **make over 1** transfer ownership of. **2** remodel, transform. **make up 1** constitute. **2** invent. **3** compensate for; complete (an amount). **4** become reconciled after a quarrel. **5** apply cosmetics to the face (of). **make up to** *informal* try to win favour with. **on the make** *informal* trying to make profits unscrupulously. □ **maker** *n.*

make-believe *n.* pretence.

make-up *n.* **1** cosmetics applied to the face. **2** the composition of something; a person's character.

makeshift *adj.* & *n.* (something) used as an improvised substitute.

makeweight *n.* something added to make up for a deficiency.

mal- *comb. form* bad, badly; faulty.

malachite (mal-ă-kyt) *n.* a green mineral.

maladjusted *adj.* unable to adapt to a social environment.

maladminister *v.* manage (business or public affairs) badly or improperly.

maladroit *adj.* bungling, clumsy.

malady *n.* (*pl.* **-ies**) an illness.

malaise *n.* a feeling of illness, discomfort, or uneasiness.

malapropism (mall-ă-prop-iz-ĕm) *n.* a comical confusion of words.

malaria *n.* a disease causing recurring fever. □ **malarial** *adj.*

Malay *adj.* & *n.* (a member, the language) of a people of Malaysia and Indonesia.

malcontent *n.* a dissatisfied and rebellious person.

male *adj.* of the sex that can fertilize egg cells produced by a female; of or characteristic of men; (of a plant) producing pollen, not seeds; (of a machine part) for insertion into a corresponding hollow part. ● *n.* a male person, animal, or plant.

malediction *n.* a curse. □ **maledictory** *adj.*

malefactor (mal-i-fak-ter) *n.* a wrongdoer.

malevolent *adj.* wishing harm to others. □ **malevolence** *n.*, **malevolently** *adv.*

malfeasance (mal-feez-ăns) *n. formal* misconduct.

malformation *n.* a deformity; being abnormal in shape. □ **malformed** *adj.*

malfunction *n.* faulty functioning. ● *v.* function faultily.

malice *n.* a desire to harm others. □ **malicious** *adj.*, **maliciously** *adv.*

malign (mă-lyn) *adj.* harmful; showing malice. ● *v.* say unpleasant and untrue things about. □ **malignity** *n.*, **malignly** *adv.*

malignant *adj.* **1** (of a tumour) growing harmfully and uncontrollably. **2** malevolent. □ **malignancy** *n.*, **malignantly** *adv.*

malinger *v.* pretend illness to avoid work. □ **malingerer** *n.*

mall (mal, morl) *n.* a large enclosed shopping precinct; a sheltered walk or promenade.

mallard *n.* a wild duck, the male of which has a glossy green head.

malleable *adj.* able to be hammered or pressed into shape; easy to influence. □ **malleability** *n.*

mallet *n.* a hammer, usu. of wood; an instrument for striking the ball in croquet or polo.

malmsey *n.* a strong sweet wine.

malnutrition *n.* weakness resulting from lack of nutrition.

malodorous *adj.* stinking. □ **malodour** *n.*

malpractice *n.* wrongdoing; improper professional behaviour.

malt (morlt) *n.* barley or other grain prepared for brewing or distilling; whisky made with this.

maltreat *v.* treat cruelly. □ **maltreatment** *n.*

mamba *n.* a poisonous snake.

mammal *n.* a member of the class of animals that suckle their young. □ **mammalian** *adj.*

mammary *adj.* of the breasts.

mammography *n.* the use of X-rays to detect tumours in the breasts.

mammoth *n.* a large extinct elephant ● *adj.* huge.

man *n.* (*pl.* **men**) **1** an adult male person; a male servant or employee; an ordinary soldier, not an officer. **2** a human being; the human race. **3** a small figure used in a board game. ● *v.* (**manned, manning**) provide (a place etc.) with people to work in or defend it. □ **man to man** directly, frankly.

manacle *n.* a shackle for the wrists or ankles. □ **manacled** *adj.*

manage *v.* **1** be in charge of, control; supervise (staff). **2** cope successfully with a task; succeed in doing or producing; succeed in dealing with. □ **manageable** *adj.*

management *n.* managing; the people who manage a business.

manager *n.* a person in charge of a business etc. □ **managerial** *adj.*

manageress *n.* a woman in charge of a business etc.

mañana (man-**yahn**-ă) *adv.* at some indefinite time in the future.

manatee *n.* a large tropical aquatic mammal.

mandarin *n.* **1** a senior influential official. **2** a variety of small orange. **3** (**Mandarin**) the literary and official form of the Chinese language.

mandate *n.* & *v.* (give) authority to perform certain tasks.

mandatory *adj.* compulsory.

mandible *n.* a jaw or jaw-like part.

mandolin *n.* a musical instrument like a lute.

mandrake *n.* a poisonous plant with a root said to resemble the human form.

mandrel *n.* a shaft holding work in a lathe.

mane *n.* long hair on the neck of a horse or lion.

maneuver Amer. sp. of **manoeuvre**.

manful *adj.* brave, resolute. □ **manfully** *adv.*

manganese *n.* a hard brittle grey metallic element (symbol Mn) or its black oxide.

mange *n.* a skin disease affecting hairy animals.

manger *n.* an open trough for horses or cattle to feed from.

mangetout (mornzh-**too**) *n.* a variety of pea, eaten with the pod.

mangle *n.* a clothes wringer. ● *v.* damage by cutting or crushing roughly, mutilate.

mango *n.* (*pl.* **mangoes** or **mangos**) a tropical fruit.

mangrove *n.* a tropical tree growing in swamps.

mangy *adj.* (**mangier, mangiest**) having mange; shabby.

manhandle *v.* **1** move by human effort alone. **2** *informal* treat roughly.

manhole *n.* an opening through which someone can enter a drain etc. to inspect it.

manhood *n.* the state of being a man; men collectively; qualities associated with men.

man-hour *n.* one hour's work by one person.

manhunt *n.* an organized search for a person, esp. a criminal.

mania *n.* violent madness; an extreme enthusiasm for something.

maniac *n.* a person behaving wildly; a fanatical enthusiast.

maniacal *adj.* of or like a mania or maniac.

manic *adj.* showing wild excitement; frantically busy; of or affected by mania.

manicure *n.* cosmetic care of the hands and fingernails. ● *v.* apply such treatment to. □ **manicurist** *n.*

manifest *adj.* clear and unmistakable. ● *v.* show clearly, give signs of. ● *n.* a list of cargo or passengers carried by a ship or aircraft. □ **manifestation** *n.*, **manifestly** *adv.*

manifesto *n.* (*pl.* **manifestos**) a public declaration of policy.

manifold *adj.* many and varied; having many elements. ● *n.* (in a machine) a pipe or chamber with several openings.

manikin *n.* **1** a very small person. **2** a jointed model of the human body.

manila *n.* brown paper used for envelopes and wrapping paper.

manipulate *v.* **1** handle or control skilfully; treat (a part of the body) by moving it by hand. **2** control or influence (someone) unscrupulously. □ **manipulation** *n.*, **manipulative** *adj.*, **manipulator** *n.*

mankind *n.* human beings in general.

manly *adj.* (**manlier, manliest**) brave, strong; considered suitable for a man. □ **manliness** *n.*

man-made *adj.* artificial, not produced or occurring naturally.

mannequin *n.* a dummy used to display clothes in a shop window; someone acting as a model.

manner *n.* **1** the way in which something is done or happens; a sort or kind: *what manner of man?* **2** a person's way of behaving towards others; (**manners**) polite social behaviour. □ **in a manner of speaking** in a sense.

mannered *adj.* **1** having manners of a specified kind. **2** stilted, unnatural.

mannerism *n.* a distinctive personal habit or way of doing something.

manoeuvre (măn-oo-vě) *n.* (*Amer.* **maneuver**) **1** a skilful movement; a crafty plan. **2** (**manoeuvres**) large-scale exercises of troops etc. ● *v.* **1** guide or manipulate. **2** perform manoeuvres. □ **manoeuvrability** *n.*, **manoeuvrable** *adj.*

manor *n.* a large country house, usu. with lands. □ **manorial** *adj.*

manpower *n.* the number of people available for work or service.

manqué (mahn-kay) *adj.* having failed to become something that one might have: *an artist manqué.*

manse *n.* a church minister's house, esp. in Scotland.

manservant *n.* (*pl.* **menservants**) a male servant.

mansion *n.* a large stately house.

manslaughter *n.* the act of killing a person unlawfully but not intentionally.

mantelpiece *n.* the shelf above a fireplace.

mantilla *n.* a lace veil worn over the hair and shoulders.

mantis *n.* (*pl.* **mantis** or **mantises**) a grasshopper-like insect.

mantle *n.* a loose cloak; a covering.

mantra *n.* a phrase repeated to aid concentration during meditation; a statement or slogan frequently repeated.

manual *adj.* of the hands; done or operated by the hand(s); working with one's hands. ● *n.* a handbook. □ **manually** *adv.*

manufacture *v.* make or produce (goods) on a large scale by machinery; invent (a story). ● *n.* the process of manufacturing. □ **manufacturer** *n.*

manure *n.* animal dung used as fertilizer. ● *v.* apply manure to.

manuscript *n.* a book or document written by hand or typed, not printed.

Manx *adj.* & *n.* (the language) of the Isle of Man.

many *adj.* numerous. ● *pron.* a large number of something ● *n.* the majority; most people.

Maori (mow-ri) *n.* & *adj.* (*pl.* **Maori** or **Maoris**) (a member, the language) of the aboriginal people of New Zealand.

map *n.* a representation of the earth's surface or a part of it; a diagram showing the arrangement of something. ● *v.* (**mapped, mapping**) make a map of. ◻ **map out** plan in detail.

maple *n.* a tree with broad leaves, and winged fruits.

mar *v.* (**marred, marring**) disfigure; spoil.

Mar. *abbr.* March.

maracas *n.pl.* club-like gourds containing beads etc., shaken as a musical instrument.

marathon *n.* a long-distance running race; a long-lasting or gruelling task of a specified kind.

marauding *adj.* going about in search of plunder. ◻ **marauder** *n.*

marble *n.* **1** crystalline limestone that can be polished; a piece of sculpture made of this. **2** a small ball of glass or clay used in children's games. ● *v.* give a veined or mottled appearance to.

March *n.* the third month.

march *v.* walk in a regular rhythm or an organized column; walk purposefully; force to walk somewhere quickly; progress steadily. ● *n.* the act of marching; the distance covered by marching; a piece of music suitable for marching to; progress. ◻ **marcher** *n.*

marches *n.pl.* border regions.

marchioness (mah-shĕn-ess) *n.* the wife or widow of a marquess; a woman with the rank of marquess.

mare *n.* the female of the horse or a related animal.

margarine *n.* a substance made from animal or vegetable fat and used like butter.

marge *n. informal* margarine.

margin *n.* **1** an edge or border; a blank space around the edges of a page. **2** an amount by which something is won or falls short.

marginal *adj.* **1** of or in a margin. **2** slight, unimportant.

marginally *adv.* very slightly.

marginalize *v.* (also **-ise**) make or treat as insignificant.

marguerite *n.* a large daisy.

marigold *n.* a plant with golden daisy-like flowers.

marijuana (ma-ri-**wah**-nă) *n.* (also **marihuana**) dried hemp, smoked as a hallucinogenic drug.

marina *n.* a harbour for yachts and pleasure boats.

marinade *n.* a flavoured liquid in which savoury food is soaked before cooking. ● *v.* soak in a marinade.

marinate *v.* marinade.

marine *adj.* of the sea; of shipping. ● *n.* a soldier trained to serve on land or sea.

mariner *n.* a sailor, a seaman.

marionette *n.* a puppet worked by strings.

marital *adj.* of marriage.

maritime *adj.* living or found near the sea; of seafaring.

marjoram *n.* a fragrant herb.

mark *n.* **1** a small area on a surface different in colour from the rest; a distinguishing feature. **2** a symbol; an indication of something's presence. **3** a point awarded for a correct answer; the total of such points achieved by someone in a test etc. **4** a target. **5** a particular model of a vehicle or other product: *a Mark 10 Jaguar*. **6** a Deutschmark. ● *v.* **1** make a mark on; stain or be stained. **2** write a word or symbol on (something) to indicate ownership, destination, etc.; show the position of; identify, indicate as being of a particular nature. **3** assess the merit of (school or college work). **4** notice, pay attention to. **5** (in football etc.) keep close to (an opponent) to prevent them from gaining the ball. ◻ **mark time** move the feet as though marching but without advancing. **quick off the mark** reacting quickly.

marked *adj.* clearly noticeable. □ **markedly** *adv.*

marker *n.* a person or object that marks something; a broad felt-tipped pen.

market *n.* **1** a place or gathering for the sale of provisions, livestock, etc. **2** demand for a commodity. ● *v.* (**marketed, marketing**) advertise; offer for sale. □ **on the market** offered for sale. □ **marketable** *adj.*

marketeer *n.* a specialist in promoting and advertising products.

market garden *n.* a small farm producing vegetables.

marking *n.* the colouring of an animal's skin, feathers, or fur; identifying marks.

marksman *n.* (*pl.* **-men**) a person who is a skilled shot. □ **marksmanship** *n.*

marl *n.* soil composed of clay and lime, used as a fertilizer.

marmalade *n.* a jam made from citrus fruit, esp. oranges.

marmoset *n.* a small bushytailed monkey

maroon *n.* **1** a brownish-red colour. **2** an explosive device used as a warning signal. ● *adj.* brownish red. ● *v.* put and leave (a person) ashore in a desolate place; leave stranded.

marquee (mah-**kee**) *n.* a large tent used for a party or exhibition etc.

marquess *n.* a nobleman ranking between duke and earl.

marquetry (**mah**-kit-ri) *n.* inlaid work in wood, ivory, etc.

marquis *n.* a rank in some European nobilities; a marquess.

marram *n.* a type of grass growing in sand.

marriage *n.* the legal union of a man and woman; the act or ceremony of marrying; a combination or blend.

marriageable *adj.* suitable or old enough for marriage.

marrow *n.* **1** a soft fatty substance in the cavities of bones. **2** a gourd used as a vegetable.

marry *v.* (**married, marrying**) join in marriage; take as one's spouse; enter into marriage; combine (different things or qualities).

marsh *n.* low-lying watery ground. □ **marshy** *adj.*

marshal *n.* a high-ranking officer; an official controlling an event or ceremony. ● *v.* (**marshalled, marshalling**; *Amer.* **marshaled**) arrange in proper order; assemble; guide, lead.

marshmallow *n.* a soft sweet made from sugar, egg white, and gelatin.

marsupial *n.* a mammal that carries its young in a pouch.

mart *n.* a market.

martial *adj.* of war, warlike.

martial law *n.* military government suspending ordinary law.

martinet *n.* a person who exerts strict discipline.

martyr *n.* a person who undergoes death or suffering for his or her beliefs; someone who ostentatiously displays their distress to gain sympathy. ● *v.* kill or torment as a martyr. □ **martyrdom** *n.*

marvel *n.* a wonderful thing. ● *v.* (**marvelled, marvelling**; *Amer.* **marveled**) feel wonder.

marvellous *adj.* (*Amer.* **marvelous**) amazing, extraordinary; very good or pleasing. □ **marvellously** *adv.*

Marxism *n.* the socialist theories of Karl Marx. □ **Marxist** *adj.* & *n.*

marzipan *n.* an edible paste made from ground almonds.

mascara *n.* a cosmetic for darkening the eyelashes.

mascot *n.* an object believed to bring good luck to its owner.

masculine *adj.* of, like, or traditionally considered suitable for men; *Grammar* of the gender of nouns and adjectives conventionally regarded as male. □ **masculinity** *n.*

mash *n.* a soft pulp of crushed matter; mashed potatoes. ● *v.* beat into a soft mass.

mask *n.* a covering worn over the face as a disguise or protection. ● *v.* cover with a mask; disguise, screen, conceal.

masochism *n.* pleasure in suffering pain. □ **masochist** *n.*, **masochistic** *adj.*

mason *n.* a person who builds or works with stone.

masonry *n.* stonework.

masque (mahsk) *n.* a musical drama with mime.

masquerade *n.* a false show or pretence. ● *v.* pretend to be what one is not.

mass *n.* **1** a coherent body of matter with no definite shape; the quantity of matter a body contains. **2** a large group of people or things; (**masses**) *informal* a large amount. **3** (**the masses**) ordinary people. **4** (usu. **Mass**) a celebration of the Eucharist, esp. in the RC Church; a form of liturgy used in this. ● *v.* gather or assemble into a mass.

massacre *n.* a great slaughter. ● *v.* slaughter in large numbers.

massage *n.* rubbing and kneading of the body to reduce pain or stiffness. ● *v.* **1** treat (the body) in this way. **2** manipulate (figures) to give a more acceptable result.

masseur *n.* a man who practises massage professionally.

masseuse *n.* a woman who practises massage professionally.

massif *n.* a compact group of mountain heights.

massive *adj.* large and heavy or solid; huge. □ **massively** *adv.*

mass-produce *v.* manufacture in large quantities by a standardized process.

mast *n.* **1** a tall pole, esp. supporting a ship's sails. **2** the fruit of the beech, oak, chestnut, etc., used as food for pigs.

mastectomy *n.* (*pl.* **-ies**) surgical removal of a breast.

master *n.* **1** a man who has control of people or things; a male teacher. **2** a person with great skill, a great artist. **3** a recording etc. from which a series of copies is made. **4** (**Master**) the title of a boy not old enough to be called *Mr.* ● *adj.* **1** highly skilled. **2** main, principal. ● *v.* **1** acquire complete knowledge of or expertise in. **2** gain control of; overcome.

masterclass *n.* a class given by a famous musician, artist, etc.

masterful *adj.* **1** powerful, commanding. **2** very skilful. □ **masterfully** *adv.*

master key *n.* a key that opens several different locks.

masterly *adj.* very skilful.

mastermind *n.* a person of outstanding mental ability; the person planning and directing an enterprise. ● *v.* plan and direct.

Master of Arts, Master of Science *n.* a university degree, above a first degree but below a Ph.D.

masterpiece *n.* an outstanding piece of work.

master stroke *n.* a very skilful act of policy.

mastery *n.* **1** thorough knowledge, great skill. **2** control, supremacy.

mastic *n.* **1** gum or resin from certain trees. **2** a type of cement.

masticate *v.* chew.

mastitis *n.* inflammation of the breast or udder.

mastoid *n.* a projecting piece of a bone behind the ear.

masturbate *v.* stimulate the genitals with the hand. □ **masturbation** *n.*

mat *n.* **1** a piece of material placed on a floor or other surface as an ornament or to protect it. **2** var. of **matt.** ● *v.* (**matted, matting**) make or become tangled into a thick mass. □ **matted** *adj.*

matador *n.* a bullfighter.

match *n.* **1** a short stick tipped with material that catches fire when rubbed on a rough surface. **2** a contest in a game or sport. **3** a person or thing exactly like or corresponding or equal to another; a marriage; a potential marriage partner. ● *v.* **1** correspond, be alike; find something or someone corresponding to. **2** equal in ability, extent, etc. **3** set against each other in a contest.

matchmaking *n.* scheming to arrange marriages. □ **matchmaker** *n.*

matchstick *n.* the stick of a match.

matchwood *n.* wood broken into splinters.

mate *n.* **1** a companion or fellow worker; each of a pair of mated animals. **2** a merchant ship's officer. **3** checkmate. ● *v.* (of animals) come together for breeding, copulate; bring (animals) together for breeding.

material *n.* a substance from which something can be made; facts to be used in a book etc.; cloth, fabric. ● *adj.* **1** of matter; of the physical (not spiritual) world. **2** significant, important. □ **materially** *adv.*

materialism *n.* **1** concentration on material possessions rather than spiritual values. **2** the belief that only the material world exists. □ **materialist** *n.*, **materialistic** *adj.*

materialize *v.* (also **-ise**) appear, become visible; become a fact, happen. □ **materialization** *n.*

maternal *adj.* of a mother; motherly; related through one's mother. □ **maternally** *adv.*

maternity *n.* motherhood. ● *adj.* of or for women in pregnancy and childbirth.

math *n. Amer. informal* mathematics.

mathematician *n.* a person skilled in mathematics.

mathematics *n.* (as *sing.*) the science of numbers, quantities, and measurements; (as *pl.*) the mathematical aspect of a subject or phenomenon. □ **mathematical** *adj.*, **mathematically** *adv.*

maths *n. informal* mathematics.

matinée *n.* an afternoon performance in a theatre or cinema.

matinée coat *n.* a baby's jacket.

matins *n.* (also **mattins**) morning prayer.

matriarch (may-tree-ahk) *n.* the female head of a family or tribe. □ **matriarchal** *adj.*

matriarchy *n.* (*pl.* **-ies**) a social organization in which a female is head of the family.

matrices pl. of **matrix**.

matricide *n.* killing one's mother; someone guilty of this. □ **matricidal** *adj.*

matriculate *v.* enrol at a college or university. □ **matriculation** *n.*

matrimony *n.* marriage. □ **matrimonial** *adj.*

matrix (may-triks) *n.* (*pl.* **matrices** or **matrixes**) **1** an environment in which something develops; a mould in which something is shaped. **2** *Mathematics* a rectangular array of quantities treated as a unit.

matron *n.* **1** a woman in charge of domestic and medical arrangements at a school etc.; *dated* the woman in charge of nursing in a hospital. **2** a married woman.

matronly *adj.* like or characteristic of a staid or dignified married woman.

matt *adj.* (also **mat**) dull, not shiny.

matter *n.* **1** physical substance occupying space; a specified type of substance. **2** a situation or affair; a problem, something causing distress. **3** pus. ● *v.* be important; be distressing or of concern to someone. □ **matter-of-fact** practical, unemotional.

mattins var. of **matins**.

mattress *n.* a fabric case filled with padding or springy material, used on or as a bed.

maturation *n.* maturing.

mature *adj.* fully grown or developed; mentally and emotionally developed, not childish; (of a life assurance policy etc.) due for payment. ● *v.* make or become mature. □ **maturely** *adv.*, **maturity** *n.*

matzo *n.* (*pl.* **matzos**) a wafer of unleavened bread.

maudlin (**mord**-lin) *adj.* sentimental in a silly or tearful way.

maul *v.* treat roughly, injure by rough handling.

maunder *v.* talk in a rambling way.

mausoleum (mor-so-**lee**-ŭm) *n.* a magnificent tomb.

mauve (mohv) *adj.* & *n.* pale purple.

maverick *n.* & *adj.* (someone) unorthodox and independent-minded.

mawkish *adj.* sentimental in a sickly way. □ **mawkishly** *adv.*, **mawkishness** *n.*

maxim *n.* a sentence giving a general truth or rule of conduct.

maximize *v.* (also **-ise**) make as great as possible. □ **maximization** *n.*

maximum *adj.* & *n.* (*pl.* **maxima**) the greatest (amount) possible. □ **maximal** *adj.*, **maximally** *adv.*

May *n.* the fifth month.

may[1] *v.aux.* used to express a wish, possibility, or permission: *it may be true*; *may I come in*?

■ **Usage** Both *can* and *may* are used for asking permission, as in *Can I move?* and *May I move?*, but *may* is better in formal English because *Can I move?* also means 'Am I physically able to move?'

may[2] *n.* hawthorn blossom.

maya *n.* (in Hinduism) illusion, magic.

maybe *adv.* perhaps.

mayday *n.* an international radio distress signal used by ships and aircraft.

May Day *n.* 1 May, esp. as a festival.

mayhem *n.* violent confusion and disorder.

mayonnaise *n.* a cold creamy sauce made with eggs and oil.

mayor *n.* the head of the municipal corporation of a city or borough. □ **mayoral** *adj.*, **mayoralty** *n.*

mayoress *n.* a female mayor; a mayor's wife.

maypole *n.* a tall pole for dancing round on May Day.

maze *n.* a network of paths etc. through which it is hard to find one's way.

MB *abbr.* Bachelor of Medicine; (*Computing*, also **Mb**) megabyte.

MBA *abbr.* Master of Business Administration.

MBE *abbr.* Member of the Order of the British Empire.

MC *abbr.* Master of Ceremonies; Member of Congress.

MD *abbr.* Doctor of Medicine; Managing Director.

Md *symb.* mendelevium.

ME *abbr.* myalgic encephalomyelitis, a condition characterized by prolonged fatigue.

me[1] *pron.* the objective case of *I*.

me[2] *n.* *Music* the third note of a major scale, or the note E.

mea culpa *int.* an acknowledgement of error or guilt.

mead *n.* an alcoholic drink made from honey and water.

meadow *n.* a field of grass.

meagre *adj.* (*Amer.* **meager**) scanty in amount.

meal *n.* **1** an occasion when food is eaten; the food itself. **2** coarsely ground grain.

mealy *adj.* of or like meal.

mealy-mouthed *adj.* afraid to speak frankly or straight forwardly.

mean[1] *adj.* **1** ungenerous, miserly; *informal* unkind; *Amer.* vicious. **2** of poor quality; of low rank. □ **meanly** *adv.*, **meanness** *n.*

mean[2] *adj.* & *n.* (something) midway between two extremes; an average.

mean[3] *v.* (**meant, meaning**) **1** convey, express; signify. **2** intend. **3** result in. □ **mean much to** be considered important by. **mean well** have good or kind intentions.

meander (mee-an-de) *v.* follow a winding course; wander in a leisurely way. ● *n.* a winding course; a wide bend in a river.

meaning *n.* what is meant. ● *adj.* expressive. ▫ **meaningful** *adj.*, **meaningless** *adj.*

means *n.* (as *sing.* or *pl.*) that by which a result is brought about; (as *pl.*) financial resources. ▫ **by all means** certainly. **by no means** certainly not.

means test *n.* an official investigation to establish need before giving financial help from public funds.

meant past & p.p. of **mean³**.

meantime *adv.* meanwhile.

meanwhile *adv.* in the intervening period; at the same time.

measles *n.* an infectious disease producing red spots on the body.

measly *adj.* (**measlier, measliest**) *informal* meagre.

measure *v.* find the size, amount, etc. of (something) by comparison with a known standard; be of a specified size; take or give (a measured amount); assess. ● *n.* **1** a course of action to achieve a purpose; a law. **2** a standard unit used in measuring; a size or quantity found by measuring; a certain quantity or degree: *a measure of freedom.* ▫ **measure up to** reach (a standard). ▫ **measurable** *adj.*, **measurably** *adv.*

measured *adj.* **1** with a slow steady rhythm. **2** carefully considered.

measurement *n.* measuring; a size etc. found by measuring.

meat *n.* animal flesh as food.

meaty *adj.* (**meatier, meatiest**) **1** like meat; full of meat. **2** *informal* full of interesting subject-matter. ▫ **meatiness** *n.*

mechanic *n.* a skilled workman who uses or repairs machines.

mechanical *adj.* of or worked by machinery; done or acting without conscious thought. ▫ **mechanically** *adv.*

mechanics *n.* the study of motion and force; the science of machinery; (as *pl.*) the way a thing works.

mechanism *n.* a system of parts in a machine; the way something works or happens.

mechanize *v.* (also **-ise**) equip with machinery; use machines for. ▫ **mechanization** *n.*

medal *n.* a coin-like piece of metal commemorating an event or awarded for an achievement.

medallion *n.* a pendant shaped like a medal; a circular ornamental design.

medallist *n.* (*Amer.* **medalist**) the winner of a medal.

meddle *v.* interfere in people's affairs or with an object. ▫ **meddler** *n.*, **meddlesome** *adj.*

media pl. of **medium**. ● *n.pl.* (**the media**) newspapers and broadcasting as conveying information to the public.

mediaeval *adj.* var. of **medieval**.

medial *adj.* situated in the middle. ▫ **medially** *adv.*

median *adj.* in or passing through the middle. ● *n.* a median point in a range of values; a median point or line.

mediate *v.* act as peacemaker between opposing sides; bring about (a settlement) in this way. ▫ **mediation** *n.*, **mediator** *n.*

medic *n.* *informal* a doctor.

medical *adj.* of the science of medicine. ● *n.* an examination to assess someone's health or fitness. ▫ **medically** *adv.*

medicament *n.* any medicine, ointment, etc.

medicate *v.* treat with a medicinal substance.

medication *n.* drugs etc. for medical treatment; treatment with these.

medicinal *adj.* having healing properties. ▫ **medicinally** *adv.*

medicine *n.* the science of the prevention and cure of disease; a substance used to treat disease.

medicine man *n.* a witch-doctor.

medieval *adj.* (also **mediaeval**) of the Middle Ages.

mediocre *adj.* second-rate. □ **mediocrity** *n.*

meditate *v.* think deeply; focus one's mind in silence for relaxation or religious purposes. □ **meditation** *n.*, **meditative** *adj.*, **meditatively** *adv.*

medium *n.* (*pl.* **media**) **1** a means of doing something; a substance through which something acts or is conveyed; a means of communication; (*pl.* **mediums**) a person claiming to be in contact with the spirits of the dead. **2** a middle quality, state, or size. ● *adj.* roughly halfway between extremes; average.

medium wave *n.* a radio wave between 300 kHz and 3 MHz.

medlar *n.* a fruit like a small brown apple.

medley *n.* (*pl.* **medleys**) an assortment; excerpts of music from various sources.

medulla *n.* the inner part of an organ or tissue. the hindmost segment of the brain. □ **medullary** *adj.*

meek *adj.* quiet and obedient, not protesting. □ **meekly** *adv.*, **meekness** *n.*

meerschaum (meer-shăm) *n.* a tobacco pipe with a white clay bowl.

meet *v.* (**met, meeting**) **1** come into contact (with); make the acquaintance of; assemble, gather; wait for and greet on arrival. **2** satisfy (a requirement etc.). **3** experience. ● *n.* an assembly for a hunt. ● *adj. archaic* suitable, proper. □ **meet with** receive (a particular response or reaction).

meeting *n.* coming together; an assembly for discussion.

mega *informal adj.* **1** huge. **2** excellent. ● *adv.* extremely.

mega- *comb. form* large; one million (as in *megavolts, megawatts*); *informal* extremely; very big.

megabyte *n. Computing* 1,048,576 (i.e. 2^{20}) bytes.

megahertz *n.* one million cycles per second, as a unit of frequency of electromagnetic waves.

megalith *n.* a large stone, esp. as a prehistoric monument. □ **megalithic** *adj.*

megalomania *n.* obsession with power, delusion about one's own power. □ **megalomaniac** *adj.* & *n.*

megaphone *n.* a funnel-shaped device for amplifying the voice.

megaton *n.* a unit of explosive power equal to one million tons of TNT.

melamine (mel-ă-meen) *n.* a resilient plastic used esp. for laminated coatings.

melancholy *n.* mental depression, sadness; gloom. ● *adj.* sad, gloomy; depressing.

melanin *n.* a dark pigment in the skin, hair, etc.

melanoma *n.* a malignant skin tumor.

meld *v.* merge, blend.

mêlée (mel-ay) *n.* a confused fight; a confused mass or crowd.

mellifluous *adj.* sweet-sounding.

mellow *adj.* (of fruit) ripe and sweet; (of sound or colour) soft and rich; (of people) having become kindly with age; relaxed, cheerful. ● *v.* make or become mellow.

melodeon *n.* (also **melodion**) a small organ or harmonium.

melodious *adj.* tuneful. □ **melodiously** *adv.*

melodrama *n.* a sensational drama. □ **melodramatic** *adj.*, **melodramatically** *adv.*

melody *n.* (*pl.* **-ies**) sweet music; the main part in a piece of harmonized music. □ **melodic** *adj.*, **melodically** *adv.*

melon *n.* a large sweet fruit.

melt *v.* make (something solid) liquid, esp. by heat; become liquid;

make or become less stern; leave unobtrusively, vanish.

meltdown *n.* the melting of an overheated reactor core.

member *n.* a person belonging to a particular group or society; part of a structure; *archaic* a limb.

membership *n.* being a member; the members of a group, their number.

membrane *n.* a thin flexible skin-like tissue. □ **membranous** *adj.*

memento *n.* (*pl.* **mementoes** or **mementos**) a souvenir.

memo *n.* (*pl.* **memos**) *informal* a memorandum.

memoir (mem-wah) *n.* a written account of events etc. that one remembers.

memorable *adj.* worth remembering, easy to remember. □ **memorability** *n.*, **memorably** *adv.*

memorandum *n.* (*pl.* **memoranda** or **memorandums**) a note written as a reminder; a written message from one colleague to another.

memorial *n.* an object or custom etc. established to commemorate an event or person(s). ● *adj.* serving as a memorial.

memorize *v.* (also **-ise**) learn (a thing) so as to know it from memory.

memory *n.* (*pl.* **-ies**) the ability to remember things; a thing remembered; the storage capacity of a computer, RAM. □ **in memory of** as a reminder of or memorial to.

men pl. of **man**.

menace *n.* something dangerous; a threatening quality; *informal* an annoying person. ● *v.* threaten. □ **menacingly** *adv.*

ménage (may-nah*zh*) *n.* a household.

menagerie (men-**aj**-ĕ-ree) *n.* a collection of wild animals for exhibition.

mend *v.* repair; heal; set right (a dispute etc.) ● *n.* a repaired place. □ **on the mend** getting better.

mendacious *adj.* untruthful. □ **mendaciously** *adv.*, **mendacity** *n.*

mendelevium *n.* a radioactive metallic element (symbol Md).

mendicant *adj.* & *n.* (a person) living by begging.

menfolk *n.* the men of a community or family.

menhir (men-heer) *n.* a tall upright stone set up in prehistoric times.

menial *adj.* lowly, degrading. ● *n.* a person who does menial tasks. □ **menially** *adv.*

meningitis *n.* inflammation of the membranes covering the brain and spinal cord.

meniscus *n.* the curved surface of a liquid in a tube; a lens convex on one side and concave on the other.

menopause *n.* the time of life when a woman finally ceases to menstruate. □ **menopausal** *adj.*

menorah (mi-**nor**-ă) *n.* a seven-armed candelabrum used in Jewish worship.

menstrual *adj.* of menstruation.

menstruate *v.* experience a monthly discharge of blood from the womb. □ **menstruation** *n.*

mensuration *n.* measuring; mathematical rules for this.

mental *adj.* **1** of, in, or performed by the mind. **2** *informal* mad. □ **mental age** a person's mental ability expressed as the age at which an average person reaches that ability. □ **mentally** *adv.*

mentality *n.* (*pl.* **-ies**) a characteristic attitude of mind.

menthol *n.* a peppermint-flavoured substance, used medicinally.

mentholated *adj.* impregnated with menthol.

mention *v.* speak or write about briefly; refer to by name. ● *n.* a reference to someone or something.

mentor *n.* a trusted adviser.

menu *n.* (*pl.* **menus**) a list of dishes to be served; a list of options displayed on a computer screen.

meow (also **miaow**) = **mew**.

MEP *abbr.* Member of the European Parliament.

mercantile (mer-kăn-tIl) *adj.* trading, of trade or merchants.

mercenary *adj.* working merely for money or reward; grasping. ● *n.* (*pl.* **-ies**) a professional soldier hired by a foreign country.

mercerized *adj.* (also **-ised**) (of cotton) treated with a slightly glossy substance that adds strength.

merchandise *n.* goods bought and sold or for sale. ● *v.* promote sales of (goods).

merchant *n.* a wholesale trader; *Amer.* & *Scot.* a retail trader.

merchantable *adj.* saleable.

merchant bank *n.* a bank dealing in commercial loans and the financing of businesses.

merchantman *n.* (*pl.* **-men**) a merchant ship.

merchant navy *n.* shipping employed in commerce.

merchant ship *n.* a ship carrying merchandise.

merciful *adj.* showing mercy; giving relief from pain and suffering.

mercifully *adv.* in a merciful way; *informal* to one's great relief, thank goodness.

mercurial *adj.* **1** liable to sudden changes of mood; lively. **2** of the element mercury.

mercury *n.* a heavy silvery usu. liquid metallic element (symbol Hg). □ **mercuric** *adj.*

mercy *n.* (*pl.* **-ies**) kindness shown to someone in one's power; something to be grateful for, a fortunate event or circumstance. □ **at the mercy of** wholly in the power of or subject to. □ **merciless** *adj.*, **mercilessly** *adv.*

mere[1] *adj.* no more or no better than what is specified. □ **merely** *adv.*

mere[2] *n. poetic* a lake.

merest *adj.* very small or insignificant.

meretricious (me-rĕ-**trish**-ŭs) *adj.* showily attractive but cheap or insincere.

merge *v.* combine into a whole; blend gradually.

merger *n.* the combining of commercial companies etc. into one.

meridian *n.* any of the great semicircles on the globe, passing through the North and South Poles.

meringue (mĕ-**rang**) *n.* a small cake made from a mixture of sugar and egg white.

merino (mĕ-ree-noh) *n.* (*pl.* **merinos**) a breed of sheep with fine soft wool.

merit *n.* a feature or quality that deserves praise; worthiness. ● *v.* (**merited, meriting**) deserve.

meritocracy *n.* (*pl.* **-ies**) government or control by people selected for ability.

meritorious *adj.* deserving praise.

merlin *n.* a small falcon.

mermaid *n.* an imaginary sea creature, a woman with a fish's tail instead of legs.

merry *adj.* (**merrier, merriest**) **1** cheerful and lively. **2** *informal* slightly drunk. □ **merrily** *adv.*, **merriment** *n.*

merry-go-round *n.* a roundabout at a funfair; a cycle of activities.

merrymaking *n.* happy celebrations.

mescaline *n.* (also **mescalin**) a hallucinogenic drug.

Mesdames pl. of **Madame**.

Mesdemoiselles pl. of **Mademoiselle**.

mesh *n.* material made of a network of wire or thread; the spacing of the strands in this: *wide mesh.* ● *v.* (of a toothed gearwheel) engage with another; make or become entangled; be in harmony.

mesmerize *v.* (also **-ise**) hypnotize, dominate the attention or will of. □ **mesmerizing** *adj.*

mesolithic *adj.* of the period between palaeolithic and neolithic.

meson *n.* an unstable elementary particle.

mess *n.* **1** a dirty or untidy condition; an untidy collection of things; a portion of pulpy food; a difficult or confused situation, trouble. **2** a room where members of the armed forces have meals. ● *v.* **1** (usu. **mess up**) make untidy or dirty; muddle, bungle. **2** (in the armed forces) eat with a group. ◻ **mess about 1** behave irresponsibly; potter. **2** interfere.

message *n.* a spoken or written communication; moral or social teaching.

messenger *n.* the bearer of a message.

Messiah *n.* the deliverer expected by Jews; Christ as this. ◻ **Messianic** *adj.*

Messrs pl. of **Mr.**

messy *adj.* (**messier, messiest**) untidy or dirty, slovenly; complicated and difficult. ◻ **messily** *adv.*, **messiness** *n.*

met past & p.p. of **meet**.

metabolism *n.* the process by which food is digested and energy supplied. ◻ **metabolic** *adj.*, **metabolically** *adv.*

metabolize *v.* (also **-ise**) process (food) in metabolism.

metacarpus *n.* (*pl.* **metacarpi**) the set of bones between the wrist and fingers.

metal *n.* **1** any of a class of mineral substances such as gold, silver, iron, etc., or an alloy of these. **2** road metal. ● *v.* (**metalled, metalling**; *Amer.* **metaled**) make or mend (a road) with road metal.

metallic *adj.* of or like metal. ◻ **metallically** *adv.*

metallography *n.* the study of the internal structure of metals.

metallurgy *n.* the study of the properties of metals; the science of extracting and working metals.

metamorphic *adj.* (of rock) changed in form or structure by heat, pressure, etc; of metamorphosis.

metamorphosis *n.* (*pl.* **metamorphoses**) a change of form or character. ◻ **metamorphose** *v.*

metaphor *n.* the application of a word or phrase to something that it does not apply to literally (e.g. the *evening* of one's life, *food* for thought). ◻ **metaphorical** *adj.*, **metaphorically** *adv.*

metaphysics *n.* the branch of philosophy dealing with the nature of existence and knowledge. ◻ **metaphysical** *adj.*

metatarsus *n.* (*pl.* **metatarsi**) the set of bones between the ankle and the toes.

mete *v.* ◻ **mete out** dispense (justice, punishments, etc.)

meteor *n.* a small body of matter entering the earth's atmosphere from outer space and appearing as a streak of light.

meteoric *adj.* of meteors; swift and brilliant. ◻ **meteorically** *adv.*

meteorite *n.* a meteor fallen to earth.

meteorology *n.* the study of atmospheric conditions in order to forecast weather. ◻ **meteorological** *adj.*, **meteorologist** *n.*

meter *n.* **1** a device measuring and indicating the quantity supplied, distance travelled, time elapsed, etc. **2** Amer. sp. of **metre**. ● *v.* measure by a meter.

methadone *n.* a narcotic painkilling drug.

methanal *n.* = **formaldehyde**.

methane *n.* a colourless inflammable gas.

methanol *n.* a colourless inflammable liquid hydrocarbon, used as a solvent.

method *n.* a procedure or way of doing something; orderliness.

methodical *adj.* orderly, systematic ◻ **methodically** *adv.*

Methodist *n.* & *adj.* (a member) of a Protestant religious denomination based on the teachings of John and Charles Wesley. ◻ **Methodism** *n.*

methodology *n.* (*pl.* **-ies**) a system of methods used in an activity or study.

meths *n. informal* methylated spirit.

methyl *n.* a chemical unit present in methane and many organic compounds.

methylated spirit a form of alcohol used as a solvent and for heating.

meticulous *adj.* careful and precise in attention to details. □ **meticulously** *adv.*, **meticulousness** *n.*

métier (met-ee-ay) *n.* one's profession; what one does best.

metre *n.* (*Amer.* **meter**) **1** a metric unit of length (about 39.4 inches). **2** rhythm in poetry.

metric *adj.* of or using the metric system.

metrical *adj.* **1** of or composed in rhythmic metre, not prose. **2** of or involving measurement.

metricate *v.* convert to a metric system. □ **metrication** *n.*

metric system *n.* a decimal system of weights and measures, using the metre, litre, and gram as units.

metric ton *see* **ton**.

metro *n.* (*pl.* **metros**) an underground railway.

metronome *n.* a device used to indicate tempo while practising music.

metropolis (mĕ-tro-pŏ-lis) *n.* the chief city of country or region. □ **metropolitan** *adj.*

mettle *n.* courage, strength of character.

mettlesome *adj.* spirited, brave.

mew *n.* a cat's characteristic cry. ● *v.* make this sound.

mews *n.* a set of stables converted into houses.

mezzanine *n.* an extra storey set between two others.

mezzo (mets-oh) *adv.* (in music) half; moderately: *mezzo forte.* ● *n.* a mezzo-soprano, a voice between soprano and contralto.

mezzotint (mets-oh-tint) *n.* a method of engraving.

Mg *symb.* magnesium.

mg *abbr.* milligram(s).

MHz *abbr.* megahertz.

mi. *abbr. Amer.* mile(s).

miaow (also **meow**) = **mew**.

miasma (mee-**az**-mă) *n.* an oppressive atmosphere; unwholesome air.

mica (my-kă) *n.* a mineral substance used as an electrical insulator.

mice pl. of **mouse**.

micro- *comb. form* extremely small; one-millionth part of (as in *microgram*).

microbe *n.* a micro-organism, esp. a bacterium. □ **microbial** *adj.*

microbiology *n.* the study of micro-organisms. □ **microbiologist** *n.*

microchip *n.* a small piece of a semiconductor holding a complex electronic circuit.

microclimate *n.* the climatic conditions of a small area, e.g. of part of a garden.

microcomputer *n.* a computer in which the central processor is contained on microchips.

microcosm *n.* something regarded as resembling something else but on a very small scale.

microfiche (my-kroh-feesh) *n.* (*pl.* **-fiche** or **-fiches**) a small sheet of microfilm.

microfilm *n.* a length of film bearing miniature photographs of documents. ● *v.* make a microfilm of.

microlight *n.* a very small, light one- or two-seater aircraft.

micromesh *n.* fine-meshed material, esp. nylon.

micrometer *n.* an instrument measuring small lengths or angles.

micron *n.* one-millionth of a metre.

micro-organism *n.* an organism invisible to the naked eye.

microphone *n.* an instrument for picking up sound waves for transmitting or amplifying.

microprocessor *n.* an integrated circuit containing the functions of a computer's central processing unit.

microscope *n.* an instrument with lenses that magnify very small things, making them visible.

microscopic *adj.* **1** tiny; too small to be seen without a microscope. **2** of or using a microscope. ▫ **microscopically** *adv.*

microsurgery *n.* intricate surgery using miniature instruments and a microscope.

microwave *n.* an electromagnetic wave of length between about 50 cm and 1 mm; an oven using such waves to heat food quickly.

mid *adj.* in the middle.

midday *n.* noon.

midden *n.* a heap of dung or rubbish.

middle *adj.* occurring at an equal distance from extremes or outer limits; intermediate in rank, quality, etc. ● *n.* the middle point, position, area, etc.; *informal* the waist and belly.

middle age *n.* the part of life between youth and old age. ▫ **middle-aged** *adj.*

Middle Ages *n.pl.* 5th c.-1453, or *c.* 1000–1453, as a period of European history.

middle class *n.* the class of society between upper and working classes. ▫ **middle-class** *adj.*

Middle East *n.* the area from Egypt to Iran inclusive.

middleman *n.* (*pl.* **-men**) a trader buying goods from producers and selling them to consumers.

middleweight *n.* a weight above welterweight, in amateur boxing between 71 and 75 kg.

middling *adj.* moderately good, large, etc.

midfield *n.* the part of a football pitch away from the goals.

midge *n.* a small biting insect.

midget *n.* a very small person or thing.

MIDI *n.* (also **midi**) an interface allowing electronic musical instruments and computers to be connected.

Midlands *n.pl.* the inland counties of central England. ▫ **midland** *adj.*

midnight *n.* 12 o'clock at night.

midriff *n.* the front part of the body just above the waist.

midshipman *n.* (*pl.* **-men**) a naval rank just below sub-lieutenant.

midst *n.* the middle.

midway *adv.* halfway.

midwife *n.* (*pl.* **midwives**) a person trained to assist at childbirth.

mien (meen) *n.* a person's manner or bearing.

might[1] *n.* great strength or power.

might[2] *v.aux.* **1** used to express possibility, esp. what would have been possible under different circumstances: *we might have gone out if it hadn't rained.* **2** used to request permission.

mighty *adj.* (**mightier, mightiest**) very strong or powerful; very great. ● *adv. informal* very, extremely. ▫ **mightily** *adv.*

migraine *n.* a severe form of headache.

migrant *adj.* migrating. ● *n.* a migrant animal; a person travelling in search of work.

migrate *v.* (of animals) regularly move from one area to another each season; move from one area and settle in another. ▫ **migration** *n.*, **migratory** *adj.*

mike *n. informal* a microphone.

mil *n.* one-thousandth of an inch.

milage var. of **mileage**.

milch *adj.* (of a cow) giving milk.

mild *adj.* gentle, not severe; not intense; (of an illness) not serious; (of weather) moderately warm; not strongly flavoured. ▫ **mildly** *adv.*, **mildness** *n.*

mildew *n.* tiny fungi forming a coating on things exposed to damp. ▫ **mildewed** *adj.*

mile *n.* a measure of length, 1760 yds (about 1.609 km).

mileage *n.* (also **milage**) a distance in miles.

milestone *n.* a stone showing the distance to a certain place; a significant event or stage reached.

milieu (meel-yer, meel-**yer**) *n.* (*pl.* **milieus** or **milieux**) environment, surroundings.

militant *adj.* & *n.* (a person) prepared to take aggressive action. □ **militancy** *n.*

militarism *n.* support for maintaining and using a military force. □ **militaristic** *adj.*

military *adj.* of soldiers or the army or all armed forces. ● *n.* (**the military**) the armed forces.

militate *v.* be a factor preventing (something).

■ **Usage** *Militate* is often confused with *mitigate*, which means 'to make less intense or severe'.

militia (mil-**ish**-ă) *n.* a military force, esp. of trained civilians available in an emergency.

milk *n.* a white fluid secreted by female mammals as food for their young; cow's milk; a milk-like liquid. ● *v.* draw milk from; gain all possible advantage from; exploit unfairly.

milkman *n.* (*pl.* **-men**) a person who delivers milk to customers.

milksop *n.* a weak or timid man.

milk teeth *n.* the first (temporary) teeth in young mammals.

milky *adj.* (**milkier, milkiest**) of or like milk; containing much milk.

mill *n.* machinery for grinding specified material; a building containing this; a building fitted with machinery for manufacturing. ● *v.* **1** grind in a mill. **2** produce markings on the edge of (a coin). **3** move about as a confused crowd. □ **go through the mill** undergo an unpleasant experience.

miller *n.* someone who owns and works a mill for grinding corn.

millennium *n.* (*pl.* **millenniums** or **millennia**) **1** a period of 1,000 years. **2** a time of great happiness for everyone.

■ **Usage** *Millennium* is spelt with two *l*s and two *n*s.

millepede var. of **millipede**.

millet *n.* a cereal plant; its seeds.

milli- *comb. form* one-thousandth part of (as in *milligram, millilitre, millimetre*).

millibar *n.* one-thousandth of a bar, a unit of meteorological pressure.

milliner *n.* a person who makes or sells women's hats. □ **millinery** *n.*

million *n.* one thousand thousand (1,000,000); (**millions**) *informal* very many. □ **millionth** *adj.* & *n.*

millionaire *n.* a person who has over a million pounds, dollars, etc.

millipede *n.* (also **millepede**) a small crawling creature with many legs.

millstone *n.* a heavy circular stone for grinding corn; a heavy burden of responsibility.

milometer *n.* an instrument measuring the distance in miles travelled by a vehicle.

milt *n.* sperm discharged by a male fish over eggs laid by the female.

mime *n.* acting with gestures without words. ● *v.* act in mime.

mimic *v.* (**mimicked, mimicking**) imitate, esp. playfully or for entertainment. ● *n.* a person who is clever at mimicking others. □ **mimicry** *n.*

minaret *n.* a tall slender tower on or beside a mosque.

mince *v.* **1** cut (meat) into very small pieces. **2** walk or speak with affected refinement. ● *n.* minced meat. □ **not mince one's words** be candid in criticism etc.

mincemeat *n.* a mixture of dried fruit, sugar, etc.

mince pie *n.* a small pie containing mincemeat.

mincer *n.* a machine with revolving blades for cutting food into very small pieces.

mind *n.* **1** the ability to be aware of things and to think and reason; the intellect; sanity: *losing my mind.* **2** attention, concentration; memory. ● *v.* **1** be distressed or worried by, object to. **2** remember to do something; take care. **3** look after temporarily. □ **be minded to** be inclined to. **be of one mind** share an opinion. **have it in mind to** intend to. **mind out** take care.

minded *adj.* having inclinations or interests of a certain kind: *scientifically minded.*

minder *n.* a person whose job is to have charge of someone or something; *informal* a bodyguard.

mindful *adj.* conscious or aware of something.

mindless *adj.* taking or showing no thought; not requiring thought or intelligence. □ **mindlessly** *adv.*, **mindlessness** *n.*

mine[1] *adj.* & *poss. pron.* belonging to me.

mine[2] *n.* **1** an excavation for extracting metal or coal etc; an abundant source. **2** an explosive device laid in or on the ground or in water. ● *v.* **1** extract (minerals) by excavating (an area). **2** lay explosive mines under or in.

minefield *n.* an area where explosive mines have been laid; a situation full of hazards.

miner *n.* a person who works in a mine.

mineral *n.* **1** an inorganic natural substance. **2** a fizzy soft drink. ● *adj.* of or containing minerals. □ **mineralogist** *n.*, **mineralogy** *n.*

mineral water *n.* water naturally containing dissolved mineral salts or gases.

minestrone *n.* (mini-**stroh**-ni) soup containing vegetables and pasta.

minesweeper *n.* a ship for clearing away mines laid in the sea.

mingle *v.* blend together; mix socially.

mini- *comb. form* miniature, small.

miniature *adj.* very small, on a small scale. ● *n.* a small-scale portrait, copy, or model.

miniaturize *v.* (also **-ise**) make a small version of.

minibus *n.* a small bus for about twelve people.

minicab *n.* a cab like a taxi that can be booked but not hailed in the street.

minicomputer *n.* a computer that is bigger than a microcomputer, but smaller than a mainframe.

minim *n.* a note in music, lasting half as long as a semibreve.

minima pl. of **minimum**.

minimal *adj.* very small, the least possible; negligible. □ **minimally** *adv.*

minimalism *n.* the use of simple basic design forms. □ **minimalist** *adj.* & *n.*

minimize *v.* (also **-ise**) reduce to a minimum; represent as small or unimportant.

minimum *adj.* & *n.* (*pl.* **minima**) the smallest (amount) possible.

minion *n.* a servant or follower.

miniskirt *n.* a very short skirt.

minister *n.* **1** the head of a government department; a senior diplomatic representative. **2** a member of the clergy. □ **minister to** attend to the needs of. □ **ministerial** *adj.*

ministration *n.* help, service.

ministry *n.* (*pl.* **-ies**) **1** a government department headed by a minister. **2** the work of a minister of religion. **3** a period of government under one Prime Minister.

mink *n.* a small stoat-like animal; its valuable fur; a coat made of this.

minnow *n.* a small fish.

minor *adj.* lesser; not very important. ● *n.* a person not yet legally of adult age.

minority *n.* (*pl.* **-ies**) **1** the smaller part of a group or class; a small group differing from or disagreeing with others. **2** being below the legal age of adulthood.

minster *n.* a large church.

minstrel *n.* a medieval singer and musician.

mint[1] *n.* a place authorized to make a country's coins. ● *v.* make (coins). □ **in mint condition** as new.

mint[2] *n.* a fragrant herb; peppermint, a sweet flavoured with this. □ **minty** *adj.*

minuet (min-yoo-**et**) *n.* a slow stately dance.

minus *prep.* with the subtraction of; (a specified number of degrees) below zero; *informal* without. ● *adj.* (of a number) negative, less than zero; (of a grade) lower than a specified grade: *B minus.* ● *n.* the sign (–).

minuscule *adj.* very small.

■ **Usage** The correct spelling is *minuscule*, not *miniscule*.

---

minute[1] (**min**-it) *n.* **1** one-sixtieth of an hour or degree; a moment of time. **2** (**minutes**) an official summary of the proceedings of a meeting. ● *v.* record in the minutes.

minute[2] (my-**newt**) *adj.* extremely small; very precise and detailed. □ **minutely** *adv.*, **minuteness** *n.*

minutiae (min-**yoo**-shi-ee) *n.pl.* very small details.

minx *n.* a mischievous girl.

miracle *n.* an event attributed to supernatural causes because not explicable in terms of natural laws, esp. one that is welcomed; a remarkable event or thing. □ **miraculous** *adj.*, **miraculously** *adv.*

mirage (**mi**-rah*zh*) *n.* an optical illusion caused by atmospheric conditions.

MIRAS *abbr.* mortgage interest relief at source.

mire *n.* swampy ground; mud.

mirror *n.* glass coated so that reflections can be seen in it. ● *v.* reflect in a mirror; correspond to, be the image of.

mirth *n.* merriment, laughter. □ **mirthful** *adj.*, **mirthless** *adj.*

mis- *pref.* badly, wrongly.

misadventure *n.* an accident, an unlucky occurrence.

misanthrope *n.* (also **misanthropist**) a person who dislikes people in general. □ **misanthropic** *adj.*, **misanthropy** *n.*

misapprehension *n.* a mistaken belief.

misappropriate *v.* take dishonestly. □ **misappropriation** *n.*

misbehave *v.* behave badly.

miscalculate *v.* calculate incorrectly. □ **miscalculation** *n.*

miscarriage *n.* an abortion occurring naturally.

miscarry *v.* (**miscarried, miscarrying**) **1** have a miscarriage. **2** (of a plan) go wrong, fail.

miscegenation (mis-i-jin-**ay**-shŏn) *n.* interbreeding of races.

miscellaneous *adj.* assorted.

miscellany *n.* (*pl.* **-ies**) a collection of assorted items.

mischance *n.* misfortune.

mischief *n.* playful misbehaviour; harm, trouble: *making mischief.*

mischievous *adj.* full of mischief. □ **mischievously** *adv.*, **mischievousness** *n.*

misconception *n.* a wrong interpretation.

misconduct *n.* bad behaviour; mismanagement.

misconstrue *v.* interpret wrongly. □ **misconstruction** *n.*

miscreant (**mis**-kree-ănt) *n.* a wrongdoer.

misdeed *n.* a wrongful act.

misdemeanour *n.* (*Amer.* **misdemeanor**) a misdeed, a wrongdoing.

miser *n.* a person who hoards money and spends as little as possible. □ **miserliness** *n.*, **miserly** *adj.*

miserable *adj.* very unhappy; wretchedly poor in quality or surroundings. □ **miserably** *adv.*

misery *n.* (*pl.* **-ies**) great unhappiness or discomfort; a cause of this; *informal* someone who is always complaining.

misfire *v.* (of a gun or engine) fail to fire correctly; (of a plan etc.) go wrong.

misfit *n.* a person not well suited to his or her environment.

misfortune *n.* bad luck, an unfortunate event.

misgiving *n.* a slight feeling of doubt, fear, or mistrust.

misguided *adj.* having or showing bad judgement.

mishap *n.* an unlucky accident.

misinform *v.* give wrong information to. ▫ **misinformation** *n.*

misinterpret *v.* interpret incorrectly. ▫ **misinterpretation** *n.*

misjudge *v.* form a wrong or unfair opinion of; estimate wrongly.

mislay *v.* (**mislaid, mislaying**) lose temporarily.

mislead *v.* (**misled, misleading**) cause to form a wrong impression. ▫ **misleading** *adj.*

mismanage *v.* manage badly or wrongly. ▫ **mismanagement** *n.*

misnomer *n.* a wrongly applied name or description.

misogynist (mis-**oj**-in-ist) *n.* a man who hates women. ▫ **misogyny** *n.*

misplace *v.* put in a wrong place; put (confidence) in someone who does not deserve it; mislay.

misprint *n.* an error in printing.

misquote *v.* quote incorrectly. ▫ **misquotation** *n.*

misread *v.* (**misread, misreading**) read or interpret incorrectly.

misrepresent *v.* represent in a false way. ▫ **misrepresentation** *n.*

misrule *n.* bad government; disorder, anarchy.

Miss *n.* (*pl.* **Misses**) the title of a girl or unmarried woman.

miss *v.* **1** fail to hit or reach; fail to catch; fail to see or hear; be too late to catch (public transport) or meet (someone who has left); fail to take (an opportunity). **2** notice or regret the absence of. ● *n.* a failure to hit or catch something. ▫ **miss out** omit, esp. accidentally. **miss out on** *informal* be deprived of.

misshapen *adj.* badly shaped.

missile *n.* an object thrown or fired at a target.

missing *adj.* not present; not in its place, lost.

mission *n.* **1** a task that a person or group is sent to perform; this group; a person's aim or vocation. **2** a missionaries' headquarters.

missionary *n.* (*pl.* **-ies**) a person sent to spread religious faith.

misspell *v.* (**misspelt** or **misspelled, misspelling**) spell incorrectly.

mist *n.* water vapour near the ground or clouding a window etc; a film over the eyes. ● *v.* cover or become covered with mist.

mistake *n.* an incorrect idea or opinion; a misguided or imprudent action. ● *v.* (**mistook, mistaken, mistaking**) misunderstand; identify wrongly.

mistletoe *n.* a plant with white berries, growing on trees.

mistral *n.* a cold north or northwest wind in southern France.

mistress *n.* a woman who has control of people or things; a female teacher; a man's female lover.

mistrial *n.* a trial invalidated by an error in procedure etc.

mistrust *v.* feel no trust in. ● *n.* lack of trust. ▫ **mistrustful** *adj.*

misty *adj.* (**mistier, mistiest**) full of mist; indistinct. ▫ **mistily** *adv.*, **mistiness** *n.*

misunderstand *v.* (**misunderstood, misunderstanding**) fail to understand correctly; misinterpret. ▫ **misunderstanding** *n.*

misuse *v.* (mis-**yooz**) **1** use wrongly. **2** treat badly. ● *n.* (mis-**yooss**) wrong use.

mite *n.* a very small spider-like animal; a small creature, esp. a child; a very small amount.

mitigate *v.* make less intense or severe; make (an offence) less serious. ▫ **mitigation** *n.*

▪ **Usage** *Mitigate* is often confused with *militate*, which means 'to have force or effect'.

mitre *n.* (*Amer.* **miter**) **1** the pointed headdress of bishops and abbots. **2** a join between pieces of wood that form a right angle. ● *v.* (**mitred, mitring**) join in this way.

mitt *n.* a mitten.

mitten *n.* a glove with no partitions between the fingers.

mix *v.* **1** combine (different things) or be combined; prepare by combining ingredients. **2** associate socially. **3** be compatible. ● *n.* a mixture. ▫ **mix up** mix thoroughly; confuse. ▫ **mixer** *n.*

mixed *adj.* composed of various elements; of or for both sexes.

mixed-up *adj. informal* muddled; not well adjusted emotionally.

mixture *n.* something made by mixing; the process of mixing things.

mizzenmast *n.* the mast that is next aft of the mainmast.

ml *abbr.* millilitre(s).

M.Litt. *abbr.* Master of Letters.

mm *abbr.* millimetre(s).

Mn *symb.* manganese.

mnemonic (nim-**on**-ik) *adj.* & *n.* (a verse etc.) aiding the memory.

Mo *symb.* molybdenum.

moan *n.* a low mournful sound; *informal* a grumble. ● *v.* utter a moan; *informal* complain. ▫ **moaner** *n.*

moat *n.* a deep wide water-filled ditch round a castle etc.

mob *n.* a large disorderly crowd; *informal* a group. ● *v.* (**mobbed, mobbing**) crowd round in a disorderly or violent way; (of birds) flock round and attack (a predator).

mobile *adj.* able to move or be moved easily. ● *n.* **1** an ornamental hanging structure whose parts move in currents of air. **2** a mobile phone. ▫ **mobility** *n.*

mobile phone *n.* a telephone that can be carried and used over a wide area without a physical connection to a network.

mobilize *v.* (also **-ise**) assemble (troops etc.) for active service. ▫ **mobilization** *n.*

moccasin *n.* a soft flat-soled leather shoe.

mocha (**mo**-kă) *n.* a kind of coffee.

mock *v.* tease, laugh at; imitate scornfully. ● *adj.* imitation, not authentic.

mockery *n.* (*pl.* **-ies**) mocking, ridicule; an absurd or unsatisfactory imitation.

mock-up *n.* a model for testing or study.

MOD *abbr.* Ministry of Defence.

mod cons *n.pl. informal* modern conveniences; appliances in a house making life easier and more comfortable.

mode *n.* **1** a way of doing something. **2** the current fashion.

model *n.* **1** a three-dimensional reproduction, usu. on a smaller scale. **2** someone or something seen as an example of excellence; a pattern to follow. **3** a person employed to pose for an artist or display clothes by wearing them. ● *adj.* exemplary. ● *v.* (**modelled, modelling**; *Amer.* **modeled**) **1** make a model of; shape. **2** work as an artist's or fashion model, display (clothes) in this way. ▫ **model oneself on** try to imitate.

modem *n.* a device for transmitting computer data via a telephone line.

moderate *adj.* (**mod**-er-ăt) medium; not extreme or excessive. ● *n.* (**mod**-er-ăt) a holder of moderate views. ● *v.* (**mod**-er-ayt) make or become moderate. ▫ **moderately** *adv.*

moderation *n.* avoidance of extremes. ▫ **in moderation** to a reasonable extent, not in excess.

moderator *n.* **1** an arbitrator. **2** a Presbyterian minister presiding over a church assembly.

modern *adj.* of present or recent times; in current style. ◻ **modernity** *n.*

modernist *n.* a person who favours modern ideas or methods. ◻ **modernism** *n.*

modernize *v.* (also **-ise**) adapt to modern ways or needs. ◻ **modernization** *n.*, **modernizer** *n.*

modest *adj.* **1** not vain or boastful; not elaborate or ostentatious. **2** small, moderate in size, amount, etc. **3** avoiding indecency. ◻ **modestly** *adv.*, **modesty** *n.*

modicum *n.* a small amount.

modify *v.* (**modified, modifying**) **1** make minor changes to, adapt. **2** make or become less extreme. ◻ **modification** *n.*

modish (moh-dish) *adj.* fashionable.

modulate *v.* regulate, moderate; vary in tone or pitch. ◻ **modulation** *n.*

module *n.* a standardized part or independent unit forming part of a complex structure; a unit of training or education. ◻ **modular** *adj.*

modus operandi *n.* a method of working.

mogul (moh-gŭl) *n. informal* an important or influential person.

mohair *n.* yarn made from the fine silky hair of the angora goat.

Mohammedan var. of **Muhammadan.**

moiety (moy-i-ti) *n.* each of two parts of something.

moist *adj.* slightly wet.

moisten *v.* make or become moist.

moisture *n.* water or other liquid diffused through a substance or as vapour or condensed on a surface.

moisturize *v.* (also **-ise**) make (skin) less dry. ◻ **moisturizer** *n.*

molar *n.* a back tooth with a broad top.

molasses *n.* syrup from raw sugar; *Amer.* treacle.

mold etc. Amer. sp. of **mould** etc.

mole *n.* **1** a small burrowing animal with dark fur. **2** *informal* a spy established within an organization. **3** a small dark spot on human skin. **4** a pier or breakwater.

molecule *n.* a group of atoms, the smallest unit that can take part in a chemical reaction; *informal* a tiny part or amount. ◻ **molecular** *adj.*

molehill *n.* a mound of earth thrown up by a mole.

molest *v.* pester, annoy; abuse sexually. ◻ **molestation** *n.*

mollify *v.* (**mollified, mollifying**) soothe the anger of.

mollusc *n.* an animal with a soft body and often a hard shell.

mollycoddle *v.* pamper.

Molotov cocktail *n.* an improvised incendiary bomb, a bottle filled with inflammable liquid.

molt Amer. sp. of **moult**.

molten *adj.* liquefied by heat.

molto *adv. Music* very.

molybdenum (mo-lib-di-nŭm) *n.* a hard metallic element (symbol Mo) used in steel.

moment *n.* **1** a point or brief portion of time. **2** importance.

momentary *adj.* lasting only a moment. ◻ **momentarily** *adv.*

momentous *adj.* of great importance.

momentum *n.* impetus gained by movement.

Mon. *abbr.* Monday.

monarch *n.* a ruler with the title of king, queen, emperor, or empress. ◻ **monarchic** *adj.*, **monarchical** *adj.*

monarchist *n.* a supporter of monarchy. ◻ **monarchism** *n.*

monarchy *n.* (*pl.* **-ies**) a form of government with a monarch as the supreme ruler; a country governed in this way.

monastery *n.* (*pl.* **-ies**) the residence of a community of monks.

monastic *adj.* of monks or monasteries. ◻ **monasticism** *n.*

Monday *n.* the day of the week following Sunday.

monetarist *n.* & *adj.* (a person) advocating control of the money supply to curb inflation. ▫ **monetarism** *n.*

monetary *adj.* of money or currency.

money *n.* current coins and banknotes; wealth; resources; payment for work; (*pl.* **moneys**) any form of currency.

moneyed *adj.* wealthy.

money-spinner *n.* a profitable thing.

Mongol *n.* & *adj.* **1** (a native) of Mongolia. **2** *offensive* (a person) suffering from Down's syndrome.

mongoose *n.* (*pl.* **mongooses**) a stoat-like tropical animal that can attack and kill snakes.

mongrel *n.* an animal (esp. a dog) of mixed breed. ● *adj.* of mixed origin or character.

monitor *n.* **1** a device checking or testing the operation of something; a person observing a process to ensure proper procedure. **2** a school pupil with special duties. ● *v.* keep watch over; record and test or control.

monk *n.* a member of a male religious community.

monkey *n.* (*pl.* **monkeys**) a small primate, usu. long-tailed and tree-dwelling; *informal* a mischievous person. ● *v.* (**monkeyed, monkeying**) *informal* behave mischievously; tamper with something.

monkey-nut *n.* a peanut.

monkey-puzzle *n.* an evergreen tree with needle-like leaves.

monkey wrench *n.* a wrench with an adjustable jaw.

mono *adj.* monophonic.

mono- *comb. form* one, alone, single.

monochrome *adj.* done in only one colour or in black and white.

monocle *n.* an eyeglass for one eye only.

monocular *adj.* with or for one eye.

monoculture *n.* the cultivation of only one crop in an area.

monogamy *n.* the system of being married to only one person at a time. ▫ **monogamous** *adj.*

monogram *n.* letters (esp. a person's initials) combined in a design. ▫ **monogrammed** *adj.*

monograph *n.* a scholarly treatise on a single subject.

monolith *n.* a large single upright block of stone; a large impersonal organization etc. ▫ **monolithic** *adj.*

monologue *n.* a long speech.

monomania *n.* an obsession with one idea or interest. ▫ **monomaniac** *n.*

monophonic *adj.* using only one transmission channel for reproduction of sound.

monoplane *n.* an aeroplane with only one set of wings.

monopolize *v.* (also **-ise**) have exclusive control or the largest share of; keep to oneself. ▫ **monopolization** *n.*

monopoly *n.* (*pl.* **-ies**) exclusive control of trade in a commodity; exclusive possession of something.

monorail *n.* a railway in which the track is a single rail.

monosodium glutamate *n.* a substance added to food to enhance its flavour.

monosyllable *n.* a word of one syllable. ▫ **monosyllabic** *adj.*

monotheism *n.* the doctrine that there is only one God. ▫ **monotheist** *n.*, **monotheistic** *adj.*

monotone *n.* a level unchanging tone of voice.

monotonous *adj.* dull because lacking in variety or variation. ▫ **monotonously** *adv.*, **monotony** *n.*

monoxide *n.* an oxide with one atom of oxygen.

Monsieur (mŏ-**syer**) *n.* (*pl.* **Messieurs**) a title or form of address for a French-speaking man, corresponding to Mr or sir.

monsoon *n.* a seasonal wind in South Asia; the rainy season accompanying this.

monster *n.* a large, frightening imaginary creature; something very large; a cruel person; something abnormal in shape. ● *adj. informal* very large.

monstrosity *n.* (*pl.* **-ies**) something very large and ugly; something very wrong.

monstrous *adj.* outrageous, shocking; huge; ugly and frightening. □ **monstrously** *adv.*

montage *n.* (mon-ta*zh*, mon-tah*zh*) the making of a composite picture from pieces of others; selecting and joining sections of film to form a whole.

month *n.* each of the twelve portions into which the year is divided; a period of 28 days.

monthly *adj.* & *adv.* (produced or occurring) once a month. ● *n.* a monthly periodical.

monument *n.* an object commemorating a person or event etc.; a structure of historical importance.

monumental *adj.* of great size or importance; of or serving as a monument.

moo *n.* a cow's low deep cry. ● *v.* make this sound.

mooch *v. informal* pass one's time aimlessly.

mood *n.* a temporary state of mind or spirits; a fit of bad temper or depression. □ **in the mood for** feeling inclined to.

moody *adj.* (**moodier, moodiest**) given to unpredictable changes of mood; sulky, gloomy. □ **moodily** *adv.*, **moodiness** *n.*

moon *n.* the earth's satellite, made visible by light it reflects from the sun; a natural satellite of any planet. ● *v.* behave dreamily. □ **over the moon** very happy and excited.

moonlight *n.* light from the moon. ● *v.* (**-lighted, -lighting**) *informal* have two paid jobs, one by day and the other in the evening.

moonlit *adj.* lit by the moon.

moonscape *n.* a landscape resembling the surface of the moon.

moonshine *n. informal* **1** foolish ideas. **2** illicitly distilled alcoholic liquor.

moonstone *n.* a pearly semi-precious stone.

Moor *n.* a member of a Muslim people of north-west Africa. □ **Moorish** *adj.*

moor[1] *n.* a stretch of open uncultivated land with low shrubs.

moor[2] *v.* secure (a boat etc.) to a fixed object by means of cable(s).

moorhen *n.* a small waterbird.

moorings *n.pl.* the cables or a place for mooring a boat.

moose *n.* (*pl.* **moose**) an elk of North America.

moot point *n.* a debatable or undecided issue.

■ **Usage** The correct spelling is *moot*, not *mute*.

---

mop *n.* a pad or bundle of yarn on a stick, used for cleaning things; a thick mass of hair. ● *v.* (**mopped, mopping**) clean with a mop; wipe (one's eyes, forehead, etc.); soak up (liquid) by wiping.

mope *v.* be unhappy and listless.

moped *n.* a low-powered motorcycle.

moraine *n.* a mass of stones etc. deposited by a glacier.

moral *adj.* concerned with right and wrong conduct; virtuous. ● *n.* **1** a moral lesson or principle derived from a story etc. **2** (**morals**) a person's standards of behaviour, esp. sexual conduct. □ **morally** *adv.*

morale (mŏ-**rahl**) *n.* the state of a person's or group's spirits and confidence.

moralist *n.* a person who expresses or teaches moral principles.

morality *n.* (*pl.* **-ies**) moral principles; the extent to which something is right or wrong; a system of values.

moralize *v.* (also **-ise**) comment on moral issues, esp. self-righteously.

moral support *n.* encouragement.

moral victory *n.* (*pl.* **-ies**) a defeat in which the defeated party gain credit, stand by their principles, etc.

morass *n.* a boggy area; a complicated situation from which it is hard to escape.

moratorium *n.* (*pl.* **moratoriums** or **moratoria**) a temporary ban on an activity.

morbid *adj.* **1** preoccupied with gloomy or unpleasant things. **2** of disease, unhealthy. ▫ **morbidity** *n.*, **morbidly** *adv.*, **morbidness** *n.*

mordant *adj.* (of wit) sharp, biting. ● *n.* a substance combining with a dye to fix it in material. ▫ **mordantly** *adv.*

more *n.* & *pron.* a greater quantity or degree; an additional quantity. ● *adv.* **1** to a greater extent. **2** again. ▫ **more or less** approximately. **no more** never again, no longer; dead.

moreish *adj.* (also **morish**) *informal* so pleasant to eat that one wants more.

moreover *adv.* besides.

mores (mor-ayz) *n.pl.* customs or conventions.

morgue (morg) *n.* a mortuary.

moribund *adj.* on the point of death.

morish var. of **moreish**.

Mormon *n.* a member of a Christian sect founded in the USA.

morning *n.* the part of the day before noon or the midday meal.

morning sickness *n.* nausea felt in early pregnancy.

morocco *n.* goatskin leather.

moron *n.* *informal* a stupid person. ▫ **moronic** *adj.*

morose *adj.* gloomy and unsociable, sullen. ▫ **morosely** *adv.*, **moroseness** *n.*

morphia *n.* *dated* morphine.

morphine *n.* a pain-killing drug made from opium.

morphology *n.* the study of forms of animals and plants or of words. ▫ **morphological** *adj.*

morris dance *n.* a traditional English dance performed in a costume decorated with ribbons and bells.

Morse code *n.* a code of signals using short and long sounds or flashes of light.

morsel *n.* a small piece of food; a small amount.

mortal *adj.* **1** subject to death. **2** causing death; fought to the death; hostile until death. ● *n.* a mortal being. ▫ **mortally** *adv.*

mortality *n.* (*pl.* **-ies**) being subject to death; loss of life on a large scale; the death rate.

mortar *n.* **1** a mixture of lime or cement with sand and water for joining bricks or stones. **2** a bowl in which substances are pounded with a pestle. **3** a short cannon.

mortarboard *n.* a stiff square cap worn as part of academic dress.

mortgage (mor-gij) *n.* a loan for the purchase of property, in which the property itself is pledged as security; an agreement effecting this. ● *v.* pledge (property) as security in this way.

mortgagee (mor-gij-ee) *n.* the borrower in a mortgage.

mortgager (mor-gij-ĕr) *n.* (also **mortgagor**) the lender in a mortgage.

mortician *n.* *Amer.* an undertaker.

mortify *v.* (**mortified, mortifying**) **1** humiliate, embarrass. **2** subdue (bodily desires) by self-discipline. **3** (of flesh) become gangrenous. ▫ **mortification** *n.*

mortise *n.* (also **mortice**) a hole in one part of a framework shaped to receive the end of another part.

mortise lock *n.* a lock set in a door, not attached to its surface.

mortuary *n.* (*pl.* **-ies**) a place where dead bodies are kept temporarily.

mosaic *n.* a pattern or picture made with small pieces of coloured glass or stone.

Moslem *adj.* & *n.* = **Muslim**.

mosque *n.* a Muslim place of worship.

mosquito *n.* (*pl.* **mosquitoes**) a bloodsucking insect.

moss *n.* a small flowerless plant forming a dense growth in moist places. □ **mossy** *adj.*

most *n.* & *pron.* the greatest amount or number; the majority. ● *adv.* **1** to the greatest extent. **2** very. □ **at most** not more than. **for the most part** in most cases **make the most of** use or enjoy to the best advantage.

mostly *adv.* for the most part.

MOT *abbr.* an annual test of motor vehicles over a certain age, checking safety etc.

motel *n.* a roadside hotel for motorists.

motet *n.* a short religious choral work.

moth *n.* an insect like a butterfly but usu. flying at night; a similar insect whose larvae feed on cloth or fur.

mothball *n.* a small ball of a pungent substance for keeping moths away from clothes.

mother *n.* a female parent; the title of the female head of a religious community; the origin of or inspiration for something. ● *v.* look after in a motherly way. □ **motherhood** *n.*

motherboard *n.* a printed circuit board containing the principal components of a micro-computer.

mother-in-law *n.* (*pl.* **mothers-in-law**) the mother of one's wife or husband.

motherland *n.* one's native country.

motherless *adj.* without a living mother.

motherly *adj.* showing a mother's kindness. □ **motherliness** *n.*

mother-of-pearl *n.* a pearly substance lining shells of oysters and mussels etc.

mother tongue *n.* one's native language.

motif (moh-teef) *n.* a pattern; a recurring feature or theme.

motion *n.* **1** moving; movement. **2** a formal proposal put to a meeting for discussion. **3** emptying of the bowels, faeces. ● *v.* direct (someone) with a gesture.

motionless *adj.* not moving.

motion picture *n.* a cinema film.

motivate *v.* give a motive to; stimulate the interest of, inspire. □ **motivation** *n.*

motive *n.* a person's reason for doing something. ● *adj.* producing movement; causing or being the reason for something.

mot juste (moh *zh*oost) *n.* (*pl.* ***mots justes***) the most appropriate word.

motley *adj.* varied, incongruously assorted. ● *n. hist.* a jester's particoloured costume.

motocross *n.* a motorcycle race over rough ground.

motor *n.* a machine supplying motive power; a car. ● *adj.* **1** driven by a motor. **2** producing motion. ● *v. informal* travel by car.

motorbike *n. informal* a motorcycle.

motorcade *n.* a procession or parade of motor vehicles.

motorcycle *n.* a two-wheeled motor-driven road vehicle. □ **motorcyclist** *n.*

motorist *n.* a car driver.

motorize *v.* (also **-ise**) equip with motor(s) or motor vehicles.

motor vehicle *n.* a vehicle with a motor engine, for use on ordinary roads.

motorway *n.* a road designed for fast long-distance traffic.

mottled *n.* patterned with irregular patches of colour.

motto *n.* (*pl.* **mottoes**) a short sentence or phrase expressing an ideal or rule of conduct; a maxim or joke inside a paper cracker.

mould (*Amer.* **mold**) *n.* **1** a hollow container into which a liquid is poured to set in a desired shape; something made in this. **2** a furry growth of tiny fungi on a damp surface. **3** a soft fine earth rich in organic matter. ● *v.* form into a particular shape; influence the development of.

moulder *v.* (*Amer.* **molder**) decay, rot away.

moulding *n.* (*Amer.* **molding**) an ornamental strip of plaster or wood.

mouldy *adj.* (*Amer.* **moldy**) (**mouldier, mouldiest**) **1** covered with mould; stale. **2** *informal* dull; depressing, unpleasant.

moult *v.* (*Amer.* **molt**) shed feathers, hair, or skin before new growth. ● *n.* this process.

mound *n.* a pile of earth or stones; a small hill; a large pile.

mount *v.* **1** go up (stairs, a hill, etc.); get up on to (a horse etc.); provide with a horse to ride. **2** organize and set in process; establish. **3** grow larger, more numerous, or more intense. **4** fix on or in a support or setting. ● *n.* **1** a support or setting. **2** a horse for riding. **3** a mountain (used in names).

mountain *n.* a mass of land rising to a great height; a large heap or pile. □ **move mountains** achieve amazing results; make a great effort.

mountain bike *n.* a sturdy bicycle suitable for riding on rough hilly ground.

mountaineer *n.* a person who climbs mountains. □ **mountaineering** *n.*

mountainous *adj.* **1** full of mountains. **2** huge.

mourn *v.* feel or express sorrow about (a dead person or lost thing). □ **mourner** *n.*

mournful *adj.* sorrowful. □ **mournfully** *adv.*

mourning *n.* dark clothes worn as a symbol of bereavement.

mouse *n.* **1** (*pl.* **mice**) a small rodent with a long tail; a quiet timid person. **2** (*pl.* also **mouses**) a small rolling device for moving the cursor on a VDU screen.

moussaka (moo-sah-kă) *n.* (also **mousaka**) a Greek dish of minced meat and aubergine.

mousse *n.* a frothy creamy dish; a soft gel or frothy preparation.

moustache (mŭs-tahsh) *n.* (*Amer.* **mustache**) hair on the upper lip.

mousy *adj.* (**mousier, mousiest**) **1** dull greyish brown. **2** quiet and timid.

mouth *n.* (mowth) the opening in the face through which food is taken in and sounds uttered; the opening of a bag, cave, cannon, etc; a place where a river enters the sea. ● *v.* (mow*th*) form (words) soundlessly with the lips; say (something unoriginal) □ **mouthful** *n.*

mouth-organ *n.* a small instrument played by blowing and sucking.

mouthpiece *n.* **1** the part of an instrument placed between or near the lips. **2** a spokesperson.

mouthwash *n.* a liquid for cleansing the mouth.

movable *adj.* able to be moved.

move *v.* **1** go in a specified direction, change position, change the position of; change one's residence. **2** prompt to action; provoke emotion in. **3** make progress; take action. **4** put to a meeting for discussion. ● *n.* an act of moving; the moving of a piece in chess etc.; a calculated action, an initiative. □ **get a move on** *informal* hurry up. **move in** take possession of a new home.

movement *n.* **1** an act of moving; being able to move; activity, bustle; (**movements**) someone's activities and whereabouts. **2** a group with a common cause. **3** a section of a long piece of music.

movie *n. Amer. informal* a cinema film.

moving *adj.* arousing pity or sympathy. □ **movingly** *adv.*

mow *v.* (**mowed, mown, mowing**) cut down (grass) on (an area of ground). □ **mow down** kill or destroy by a moving force. □ **mower** *n.*

mozzarella (mots-ă-**rell**-ă) *n.* a soft Italian cheese.

MP *abbr.* Member of Parliament.

m.p.g. *abbr.* miles per gallon.

m.p.h. *abbr.* miles per hour.

Mr *n.* (*pl.* **Messrs**) the title prefixed to a man's name.

Mrs *n.* (*pl.* **Mrs**) the title prefixed to a married woman's name.

MS *abbr.* multiple sclerosis; (*pl.* **MSS**) manuscript.

Ms *n.* the title prefixed to a married or unmarried woman's name.

M.Sc. *abbr.* Master of Science.

MS-DOS *trademark* Microsoft disk operating system.

Mt. *abbr.* Mount.

much *pron.* a large amount, a great quantity. ● *adj.* existing in great quantity. ● *adv.* to a great extent. □ **a bit much** *informal* excessive, unreasonable. **too much** an intolerable situation or event.

mucilage (**myoo**-si-lij) *n.* a sticky substance obtained from plants; an adhesive gum.

muck *n.* dirt, mess; farmyard manure; *informal* something worthless or unpleasant. □ **muck about** *informal* behave foolishly. **muck out** clean (a stable). **muck up** *informal* bungle; spoil. □ **mucky** *adj.*

muckraking *n.* seeking and exposing scandal.

mucous *adj.* like or covered with mucus.

mucus *n.* a slimy substance coating the inner surface of hollow organs of the body.

mud *n.* wet soft earth. □ **muddy** *adj.*

muddle *v.* confuse, mix up; progress in a haphazard way. ● *n.* a muddled state or collection.

mudguard *n.* a curved cover above a wheel on a vehicle, protecting the vehicle against spray.

muesli (**mooz**-li, **myooz**-li) *n.* food of mixed crushed cereals, dried fruit, nuts, etc.

muezzin (moo-**ez**-in) *n.* a man who proclaims the hours of prayer for Muslims.

muff *n.* a tube-shaped furry covering for the hands. ● *v.* *informal* bungle.

muffin *n.* a light round yeast cake eaten toasted and buttered; a cup-shaped cake.

muffle *v.* wrap for warmth or protection, or to deaden sound; make (a sound) less loud or less distinct.

muffler *n.* a scarf.

mufti (**muf**-tee) *n.* plain clothes worn by one who usually wears a uniform.

mug *n.* **1** a large drinking vessel with a handle, for use without a saucer. **2** *informal* the face. **3** *informal* a person who is easily outwitted. ● *v.* (**mugged, mugging**) rob (a person) with violence, esp. in a public place. □ **mug up** *informal* revise (a subject) intensively. □ **mugger** *n.*

muggy *adj.* (**muggier, muggiest**) (of weather) oppressively damp and warm. □ **mugginess** *n.*

Muhammadan *n.* & *adj.* (also **Mohammedan**) Muslim.

▪ **Usage** Muslims often find the term *Muhammedan* offensive.

mulberry *n.* (*pl.* **-ies**) a purple or white fruit resembling a blackberry.

mulch *n.* a mixture of wet straw, leaves, etc., spread on ground to protect plants or retain moisture. ● *v.* cover with mulch.

mule *n.* **1** an animal that is the offspring of a horse and a donkey; a stubborn person; *informal* a courier for illegal drugs. **2** a backless slipper. □ **mulish** *adj.*

mull *v.* heat (wine etc.) with sugar and spices, as a drink. □ **mull over** think over.

mullah *n.* a Muslim learned in Islamic law.

mullet *n.* a small edible sea fish.

mullion *n.* an upright bar between the sections of a window.

multi- *comb. form* many.

multicultural *adj.* of or involving several cultural or ethnic groups.

multifarious *adj.* very varied. ▫ **multifariously** *adv.*

multilateral *adj.* involving three or more parties.

multinational *adj.* & *n.* (a business company) operating in several countries.

multiple *adj.* having or involving many parts; numerous. ● *n.* a quantity divisible by another a number of times without remainder.

multiplex *adj.* having many elements; (of a cinema) having several separate screens within one building.

multiplicand *n.* a quantity to be multiplied by another.

multiplicity *n.* (*pl.* **-ies**) a large number; a great variety.

multiplier *n.* the number by which a quantity is multiplied.

multiply *v.* (**multiplied, multiplying**) add (a number) to itself a specified number of times; (cause to) become more numerous. ▫ **multiplication** *n.*

multiracial *adj.* of or involving people of several races.

multi-speed *adj.* progressing at different speeds towards the same goal.

multitasking *n. Computing* the performance of different tasks simultaneously.

multitude *n.* a great number of things or people.

multitudinous *adj.* very numerous.

mum *informal n.* mother. ● *adj.* silent = *keep mum.*

mumble *v.* speak indistinctly. ● *n.* indistinct speech.

mumbo-jumbo *n. informal* meaningless ritual; deliberately obscure language.

mummify *v.* (**mummified, mummifying**) preserve (a corpse) by embalming as in ancient Egypt. ▫ **mummification** *n.*

mummy *n.* (*pl.* **-ies**) **1** *informal* mother. **2** a corpse embalmed and wrapped for burial, esp. in ancient Egypt.

mumps *n.* a viral disease with painful swellings in the neck.

munch *v.* chew vigorously.

mundane *adj.* **1** dull, routine. **2** worldly.

municipal *adj.* of a town or city or its governing body.

municipality *n.* (*pl.* **-ies**) a self-governing town or district.

munificent *adj.* splendidly generous. ▫ **munificence** *n.*, **munificently** *adv.*

munitions *n.pl.* weapons, ammunition, etc.

muon *n.* an unstable elementary particle.

mural *adj.* of or on a wall. ● *n.* a painting on a wall.

murder *n.* intentional unlawful killing; *informal* a very difficult or unpleasant task or experience. ● *v.* kill intentionally and unlawfully. ▫ **murderer** *n.*

murderous *adj.* involving or capable of murder.

murk *n.* darkness, gloom.

murky *adj.* dark, gloomy; not clear, cloudy; involving dishonesty and deception.

murmur *n.* a low continuous sound; softly spoken words. ● *v.* make a murmur; speak or utter softly.

murrain (**mu**-rin) *n.* an infectious disease of cattle.

muscle *n.* a strip of fibrous tissue able to move a part of the body by contracting; physical strength; power or influence. ▫ **muscle in** *informal* force oneself on others.

Muscovite *n.* a person from Moscow.

muscular *adj.* of muscles; having well-developed muscles. ▫ **muscularity** *n.*

muscular dystrophy *n.* a condition causing progressive wasting of the muscles.

muse *v.* be deep in thought. ● *n.* a poet's source of inspiration.

museum *n.* a place where objects of historical or scientific interest are collected and displayed.

mush *n.* a soft pulp. ● *v.* crush to make this.

mushroom *n.* an edible fungus with a stem and a domed cap. ● *v.* spring up in large numbers; rise and spread in a mushroom shape.

mushy *adj.* (**mushier, mushiest**) **1** soft and pulpy. **2** *informal* sentimental. □ **mushiness** *n.*

music *n.* vocal or instrumental sounds combined to produce beauty and express emotion; the art of this; the written signs representing this; something very pleasant or welcome to hear.

musical *adj.* of or involving music; sweet-sounding; skilled or interested in music. ● *n.* a play with songs and dancing. □ **musically** *adv.*

musician *n.* a person skilled in music.

musicology *n.* the study of the history and forms of music. □ **musicologist** *n.*

musk *n.* a substance secreted by certain animals or produced synthetically, used in perfumes.

musket *n.* a long-barrelled gun formerly used by infantry.

Muslim (also **Moslem**) *adj.* of or believing in Muhammad's teaching. ● *n.* a believer in this faith.

muslin *n.* a thin cotton cloth.

mussel *n.* a bivalve mollusc.

must *v.aux.* **1** used to express necessity, obligation, or insistence. **2** used to express certainty or logical necessity. ● *n. informal* something that should not be missed or overlooked.

■ **Usage** The negative *I must not go* means 'I am not allowed to go'. To express a lack of obligation, use *I am not obliged to go, I need not go,* or *I haven't got to go.*

mustache Amer. sp. of **moustache**.

mustang *n.* a wild horse of Mexico and California.

mustard *n.* a sharp-tasting yellow condiment made from the seeds of a plant; this plant.

muster *v.* gather together, assemble; summon (energy, strength). ● *n.* a formal gathering of troops. □ **pass muster** be adequate or acceptable.

musty *adj.* (**mustier, mustiest**) smelling mouldy; stale. □ **mustiness** *n.*

mutable *adj.* liable to change; fickle. □ **mutability** *n.*

mutagen *n.* something causing genetic mutation.

mutant *adj.* & *n.* (a living thing) differing from its parents as a result of genetic change.

mutate *v.* change in form; undergo genetic change.

mutation *n.* a change in form; a mutant.

mute *adj.* silent; dumb. ● *n.* a device muffling the sound of a musical instrument; *dated* a dumb person. ● *v.* deaden or muffle the sound of. □ **mutely** *adv.*, **muteness** *n.*

mutilate *v.* injure or disfigure by cutting off a part. □ **mutilation** *n.*

mutineer *n.* a person who mutinies.

mutinous *adj.* rebellious, ready to mutiny. □ **mutinously** *adv.*

mutiny *n.* (*pl.* **-ies**) a rebellion against authority, esp. by members of the armed forces. ● *v.* (**mutinied, mutinying**) engage in mutiny.

mutter *v.* speak or utter in a low unclear tone; utter subdued grumbles. ● *n.* a low indistinct utterance.

mutton *n.* the flesh of sheep as food.

mutual *adj.* **1** felt or done by each of two or more people to the other(s): *mutual respect.* **2** common to two or more people: *a mutual friend* □ **mutuality** *n.*, **mutually** *adv.*

Muzak *n. trademark* recorded music played through loud speakers in public places.

muzzle *n.* the projecting nose and jaws of certain animals; a guard fitted over this to stop an animal biting; the open end of a firearm's barrel. ● *v.* put a muzzle on; prevent from expressing opinions freely.

muzzy *adj.* (**muzzier, muzziest**) confused, vague, dazed; (of vision or an image) blurred. □ **muzzily** *adv.*, **muzziness** *n.*

MW *abbr.* medium wave; megawatt(s).

my *adj.* belonging to me.

myalgia (mI-**al**-jă) *n.* muscle pain.

mycelium (mI-**see**-li-ŭm) *n.* microscopic threadlike parts of a fungus.

mycology (mI-**ko**-lŏ-ji) *n.* the study of fungi.

myelin (**mI**-ĕ-lin) *n.* a substance forming a protective sheath around nerve-fibres.

mynah *n.* (also **myna**) a bird of the starling family that can mimic sounds.

myopia (my-**oh**-piă) *n.* shortsightedness. □ **myopic** (my-**op**-ik) *adj.*

myriad (**mi**-ree-ăd) *n.* a vast number.

myrrh (mer) *n.* a gum resin used in perfumes, medicines, and incense.

myself *pron.* the emphatic and reflexive form of *I* and *me*.

mysterious *adj.* puzzling, hard to explain, enigmatic; (of an atmosphere) strange, secret, eerie. □ **mysteriously** *adv.*

mystery *n.* (*pl.* **-ies**) a matter that remains unexplained; the quality of being unexplained or obscure; a story dealing with a puzzling crime.

mystic *adj.* having a hidden or symbolic meaning, esp. in religion; inspiring a sense of mystery and awe. ● *n.* a person who seeks to obtain union with God by spiritual contemplation. □ **mystical** *adj.*, **mystically** *adv.*, **mysticism** *n.*

mystify *v.* (**mystified, mystifying**) puzzle, baffle. □ **mystification** *n.*

mystique (mis-**teek**) *n.* an aura of mystery or mystical power.

myth *n.* a traditional tale containing beliefs about ancient times or natural events and usually involving supernatural beings; an imaginary person or thing. □ **mythical** *adj.*

mythology *n.* myths; the study of myths. □ **mythological** *adj.*

myxomatosis (miks-ŏ-mă-**toh**-sis) *n.* a fatal viral disease of rabbits.

Nn

N *abbr.* **1** north, northern. **2** newton(s). **3** *Chess* Knight. ● *symb.* nitrogen.

Na *symb.* sodium.

NAAFI *abbr.* Navy, Army, and Air Force Institutes; (an organization running) canteen(s) for servicemen.

naan var. of **nan** (*sense* 2).

nab *v.* (**nabbed, nabbing**) *informal* catch (a wrongdoer) in the act, arrest; take; steal.

nadir (**na**-deer) *n.* the lowest point.

naevus (nee-vŭs) *n.* (*Amer.* **nevus**) (*pl.* **naevi**) a red birth-mark.

naff *adj. informal* lacking taste or style.

nag *v.* (**nagged, nagging**) scold continually; (of pain) be felt persistently. ● *n.* **1** a person who nags. **2** *informal* a horse.

nail *n.* **1** a layer of horny substance over the outer tip of a finger or toe. **2** a small metal spike driven into wood as a fastening. ● *v.* **1** fasten with nail(s). **2** *informal* catch, arrest.

naive (nah-**eev**) *adj.* showing lack of experience or judgement. □ **naively** *adv.*, **naivety** *n.*

naked *adj.* without clothes on; without coverings; (of feelings etc.) undisguised. ▫ **nakedness** *n.*

naked eye *n.* the eye unassisted by a telescope or microscope etc.

namby-pamby *adj.* feeble, cowardly, or effeminate.

name *n.* **1** the word(s) by which a person, place, or thing is known or indicated. **2** a reputation; a famous person. ● *v.* give a name to; identify; describe; nominate, specify. ▫ **name after** call by the same name as.

namely *adv.* that is to say.

namesake *n.* a person or thing with the same name as another.

nan *n.* **1** *informal* a grandmother. **2** (also **naan**) a flat leavened Indian bread.

nanny *n.* (*pl.* **-ies**) a child's nurse.

nano- *comb. form* one thousand millionth.

nap *n.* **1** a short sleep, esp. during the day. **2** short raised fibres on the surface of cloth or leather. ● *v.* (**napped, napping**) have a short sleep.

napalm (nay-pahm) *n.* a jelly-like petrol substance used in incendiary bombs.

nape *n.* the back part of the neck.

naphtha (naf-thă) *n.* an inflammable oil.

naphthalene *n.* a strong-smelling white substance used as a moth-repellent.

napkin *n.* **1** a piece of cloth or paper used at meals to protect clothes or for wiping one's lips. **2** a nappy.

nappy *n.* (*pl.* **-ies**) a piece of absorbent material worn by a baby to absorb or retain urine and faeces.

narcissism *n.* abnormal self-admiration. ▫ **narcissistic** *adj.*

narcissus *n.* (*pl.* **narcissi**) a flower of the group including the daffodil.

narcosis *n.* a state of drowsiness produced by drugs.

narcotic *adj.* & *n.* (a drug) causing drowsiness; (a drug) affecting moods and behaviour.

narrate *v.* tell (a story), give an account of. ▫ **narration** *n.*, **narrator** *n.*

narrative *n.* a spoken or written account of something. ● *adj.* of or forming a narrative.

narrow *adj.* **1** small in width, small from side to side. **2** limited in extent or scope; (of views or beliefs) limited and intolerant or inflexible. ● *v.* make or become narrow. ▫ **narrowly** *adv.*, **narrowness** *n.*

narrow-minded *adj.* intolerant.

narwhal *n.* an Arctic whale with a spirally grooved tusk.

nasal *adj.* of the nose; sounding as if breath came out through the nose. ▫ **nasally** *adv.*

nascent (nay-sĕnt) *adj.* just coming into existence. ▫ **nascence** *n.*

nasty *adj.* (**nastier, nastiest**) unpleasant; unkind; annoying, unwelcome. ▫ **nastily** *adv.*, **nastiness** *n.*

natal (nay-tăl) *adj.* of or from one's birth.

nation *n.* people of mainly common descent and history usu. inhabiting a particular country under one government.

national *adj.* **1** of a nation; common to a whole nation. **2** owned or supported by the state. ● *n.* a citizen of a particular country. ▫ **nationally** *adv.*

national curriculum *n.* a common programme of study for school pupils in England and Wales.

nationalism *n.* patriotic feeling; a policy of national independence. ▫ **nationalist** *n.*, **nationalistic** *adj.*

nationality *n.* (*pl.* **-ies**) **1** the status of belonging to a particular nation. **2** an ethnic group forming part of one or more political nations.

nationalize *v.* (also **-ise**) convert from private to state ownership. ▫ **nationalization** *n.*

native *adj.* belonging to a place by birth; associated by birth; (of a quality etc.) natural, inborn. ● *n.* a person born in a specified place; a local inhabitant.

nativity *n.* (*pl.* **-ies**) birth; (**the Nativity**) that of Christ; a representation of this in art.

NATO *abbr.* North Atlantic Treaty Organization; a defence association of European and North American States.

natter *v.* & *n. informal* chat.

natural *adj.* **1** of or produced by nature; not man-made; having a specified skill or quality from birth. **2** relaxed, spontaneous. ● *n.* **1** a person or thing that seems naturally suited for something. **2** *Music* (a sign indicating) a note that is not a sharp or flat. ◻ **naturalness** *n.*

natural history *n.* the study of animal and plant life.

naturalism *n.* realism in art and literature. ◻ **naturalistic** *adj.*

naturalist *n.* an expert in natural history.

naturalize *v.* (also **-ise**) admit (a person of foreign birth) to full citizenship of a country; introduce and acclimatize (an animal or plant) into a region to which it is not native. ◻ **naturalization** *n.*

naturally *adv.* **1** according to nature. **2** without affectation. **3** of course; as might be expected.

natural science *n.* a science studying the natural or physical world.

nature *n.* **1** the world with all its features and living things; the physical power producing these. **2** something's basic features and character, making it what it is; a person's character; a sort, a kind: *things of this nature.*

naturist *n.* a nudist. ◻ **naturism** *n.*

naught *n. literary* = **nought**.

naughty *adj.* (**naughtier, naughtiest**) **1** behaving badly, disobedient. **2** *informal* slightly indecent. ◻ **naughtily** *adv.*, **naughtiness** *n.*

nausea *n.* a feeling of sickness; revulsion.

nauseate *v.* affect with nausea.

nauseous *adj.* causing nausea; suffering from nausea.

nautical *adj.* of sailors or seamanship.

nautical mile *n.* a unit of 1,852 metres (approx. 2,025 yds).

nautilus *n.* (*pl.* **nautiluses** or **nautili**) a mollusc with a spiral shell.

naval *adj.* of a navy.

nave *n.* the main part of a church.

navel *n.* the small hollow in the abdomen where the umbilical cord was attached; the central point of a place.

navigable *adj.* (of a river) suitable for boats to sail in.

navigate *v.* **1** plan and direct the course of a ship, aircraft, etc.; travel along a planned course. **2** sail or travel over (water or land) or along (a route). ◻ **navigation** *n.*, **navigator** *n.*

navvy (na-vee) *n.* (*pl.* **-ies**) a labourer making roads etc. where digging is necessary.

navy (nay-vee) *n.* (*pl.* **-ies**) **1** a country's warships; the people serving in a naval force. **2** (in full **navy blue**) very dark blue.

NB *abbr.* (Latin *nota bene*) note well.

Nb *symb.* niobium.

Nd *symb.* neodymium.

NE *abbr.* north-east; north-eastern.

Ne *symb.* neon.

Neapolitan *adj.* & *n.* (a native or inhabitant) of Naples.

neap tide *n.* the tide when there is least rise and fall of water.

near *adv.* **1** at, to, or within a short distance or interval. **2** almost. ● *prep.* **1** a short distance or time from. **2** on the verge of. ● *adj.* **1** separated by only a short distance or time; closely related. **2** similar; close to being something specified: *a near disaster.* **3** on the side of a vehicle normally nearer the kerb. ● *v.* draw near. ◻ **nearness** *n.*

nearby *adj.* & *adv.* not far away.

nearly *adv.* **1** almost. **2** closely: *nearly related.*

neat *adj.* **1** clean and orderly in appearance or workmanship; skilful. **2** undiluted. □ **neatly** *adv.*, **neatness** *n.*

neaten *v.* make tidy.

nebula *n.* (*pl.* **nebulae**) a cloud of gas or dust in space. □ **nebular** *adj.*

nebulous *adj.* indistinct, having no definite form; vague.

necessarily *adv.* as a necessary result, inevitably.

necessary *adj.* **1** required to be done or possessed, essential. **2** inevitable; existing or happening by natural or logical laws or by fate. ● *n.* (**necessaries**) essential items; (**the necessary**) *informal* what is required.

necessitate *v.* make necessary; involve as a condition or result.

necessitous *adj.* poor, needy.

necessity *n.* (*pl.* **-ies**) **1** being required or essential; something essential. **2** being unavoidable; the principle by which something must be so according to logic or natural law. **3** a state of need or hardship.

neck *n.* the narrow part connecting the head to the body; the part of a garment round this; the narrow part of a bottle, cavity, etc. □ **neck and neck** running level in a race.

necklace *n.* a piece of jewellery worn round the neck.

neckline *n.* the outline formed by the edge of a garment at the neck.

necromancy *n.* the supposed art of predicting the future by communicating with the dead. □ **necromancer** *n.*

necrosis (ne-**kroh**-sis) *n.* death of bone or tissue. □ **necrotic** *adj.*

nectar *n.* a sweet fluid from plants, collected by bees; any delicious drink.

nectarine *n.* a kind of peach with a smooth shiny skin.

née (nay) *adj.* born (used in stating a married woman's maiden name).

need *v.* **1** require (something) as essential, not as a luxury. **2** have to, be obliged or required to. ● *n.* **1** something required; requiring something; necessity or reason for something: *no need to ask.* **2** lack of basic necessities, poverty.

needful *adj.* necessary.

needle *n.* a small thin pointed piece of steel used in sewing; something shaped like this; a pointer of a compass or gauge; the end of a hypodermic syringe. ● *v. informal* annoy, provoke.

needless *adj.* unnecessary. □ **needlessly** *adv.*

needlework *n.* sewing or embroidery.

needy *adj.* (**needier, neediest**) very poor.

nefarious *adj.* wicked or criminal. □ **nefariously** *adv.*

negate *v.* **1** nullify, make ineffective. **2** make (a statement) negative. **3** deny the existence of. □ **negation** *n.*

negative *adj.* **1** expressing denial, refusal, or prohibition; (of the results of a test) indicating that a substance is not present. **2** (of a quantity) less than zero. **3** (of a battery terminal) through which electric current leaves. **4** not optimistic; harmful, not helpful. ● *n.* **1** a negative statement or word; a negative quality or quantity. **2** a photograph with lights and shades or colours reversed, from which positive pictures can be obtained. □ **negatively** *adv.*, **negativity** *n.*

negative equity *n.* a situation in which the value of property falls below the debt outstanding on it.

negative pole *n.* the south-seeking pole of a magnet.

neglect *v.* pay insufficient attention to; fail to take proper care of; fail to do something. ● *n.* neglecting, being neglected. □ **neglectful** *adj.*

negligee (neg-li-*zh*ay) *n.* a woman's light flimsy dressing gown.

negligence *n.* lack of proper care or attention. □ **negligent** *adj.*, **negligently** *adv.*

negligible *adj.* too small to be worth taking into account.

negotiate *v.* **1** hold a discussion so as to reach agreement; arrange by such discussion. **2** get past (an obstacle) successfully. □ **negotiation** *n.*, **negotiator** *n.*

Negress *n.* a female Negro.

Negro *n.* (*pl.* **Negroes**) a member of the black-skinned race that originated in Africa. □ **Negroid** *adj.*

■ **Usage** The terms *Negro* and *Negress* are often considered offensive; *black* is usually preferred.

neigh *n.* a horse's long high-pitched cry. ● *v.* make this cry.

neighbour *n.* (*Amer.* **neighbor**) a person living next or near to another; a thing situated near another.

neighbourhood *n.* (*Amer.* **neighborhood**) a district.

neighbourhood watch *n.* systematic vigilance by residents to deter crime in their area.

neighbouring *adj.* (*Amer.* **neighboring**) situated nearby.

neighbourly *adj.* (*Amer.* **neighborly**) kind and friendly towards neighbours. □ **neighbourliness** *n.*

neither *adj.* & *pron.* not one nor the other of two. ● *adv.* & *conj.* **1** not either. **2** also not.

nem. con. *abbr.* unanimously, with nobody disagreeing.

nemesis (nem-i-sis) *n.* downfall; punishment for arrogance.

neo- *pref.* new.

neoclassical *adj.* of a style of art, music, etc. influenced by classical style.

neodymium *n.* a metallic element (symbol Nd).

neolithic *adj.* of the later part of the Stone Age.

neologism *n.* a new word.

neon *n.* a chemical element (symbol Ne), a gas used in illuminated signs.

neonatal *adj.* of the newly born.

neophyte (nee-o-fIt) *n.* a new convert; a novice.

nephew *n.* one's brother's or sister's son.

nephritis (nef-rI-tis) *n.* inflammation of the kidneys.

nepotism *n.* favouritism shown to relatives or friends in appointing them to jobs.

neptunium *n.* a radioactive metallic element (symbol Np).

nerd *n.* (also **nurd**) *informal* a foolish or uninteresting person.

nerve *n.* **1** a fibre carrying impulses of sensation or movement between the brain and a part of the body. **2** (**nerves**) agitation, anxiety, nervousness. **3** courage and steadiness; *informal* impudence. □ **get on someone's nerves** *informal* irritate someone. **nerve oneself** gather one's strength and courage.

nervous *adj.* **1** easily alarmed; slightly afraid or anxious. **2** of the nerves. □ **nervously** *adv.*, **nervousness** *n.*

nervy *adj.* (**nervier, nerviest**) easily alarmed; anxious. □ **nerviness** *n.*

nest *n.* **1** a structure or place in which a bird lays eggs and shelters its young; a breeding place, a lair; a snug place. **2** a set of articles (esp. tables) designed to fit inside each other. ● *v.* **1** build or use a nest. **2** fit (an object) inside a larger one.

nest egg *n.* a sum of money saved for future use.

nestle *v.* settle oneself comfortably; (of a place) lie in a sheltered and concealed position.

nestling *n.* a bird too young to leave the nest.

net[1] *n.* **1** open-meshed material of cord, wire, etc.; a piece of this for a particular purpose, eg. catching fish. **2** (**Net**) the Internet. ● *v.* (**netted, netting**) catch in a net.

net[2] *adj.* (also **nett**) remaining after all deductions; (of weight) not including wrappings etc. ● *v.* (**netted, netting**) obtain or yield as net profit.

netball *n.* a team game in which a ball has to be thrown into a high net.

nether *adj.* lower.

netting *n.* open-meshed fabric.

nettle *n.* a wild plant with leaves that sting when touched. ● *v.* irritate, provoke.

network *n.* an arrangement of intersecting lines; a complex system; a group of interconnected people or broadcasting stations, computers, etc.

networking *n.* interaction and exchange of ideas and information, as a business strategy or to further one's career.

neural *adj.* of nerves.

neuralgia *n.* a sharp pain along a nerve. ▫ **neuralgic** *adj.*

neural network *n.* a computer system modelled on the human brain and nervous system.

neuritis *n.* inflammation of a nerve.

neurology *n.* the study of nerve systems. ▫ **neurological** *adj.*, **neurologist** *n.*

neurosis *n.* (*pl.* **neuroses**) a mental disorder producing depression or abnormal behaviour.

neurotic *adj.* of or caused by a neurosis; subject to abnormal anxieties or obsessive behaviour. ● *n.* a neurotic person. ▫ **neurotically** *adv.*

neuter *adj.* **1** of a grammatical gender that is neither masculine nor feminine. **2** without developed sexual parts. ● *n.* **1** the neuter gender, a neuter word. **2** a castrated animal. ● *v.* castrate (an animal).

neutral *adj.* **1** not supporting either side in a conflict. **2** without distinctive or positive characteristics. ● *n.* **1** a neutral person, country, or colour. **2** (also **neutral gear**) a position of a gear mechanism in which the engine is disconnected from driven parts. ▫ **neutrality** *n.*, **neutrally** *adv.*

neutralize *v.* (also **-ise**) make ineffective. ▫ **neutralization** *n.*

neutrino (nyoo-tree-noh) *n.* (*pl.* **neutrinos**) an elementary particle with zero electric charge and probably zero mass.

neutron *n.* an elementary particle with no electric charge.

neutron bomb *n.* a nuclear bomb that kills people but does little damage to buildings etc.

never *adv.* **1** at no time, on no occasion. **2** not at all; *informal* surely not (expressing surprise or incredulity). ▫ **never mind** do not worry.

nevermore *adv.* at no future time.

nevertheless *adv.* in spite of this.

nevus Amer. sp. of **naevus**.

new *adj.* **1** not existing before, made recently. **2** acquired, discovered, or experienced for the first time; unfamiliar; replacing a former one of the same kind. ● *adv.* newly, recently. ▫ **newness** *n.*

New Age *n.* a set of beliefs replacing Western culture with alternative approaches to religion, medicine, the environment, etc.

newcomer *n.* a person who has arrived recently.

newel *n.* the top or bottom post of the handrail of a stair; the central pillar of a winding stair.

newfangled *adj.* objectionably new in method or style.

newly *adv.* recently, freshly.

newly-wed *n.* a recently married person.

new man *n.* a man who rejects traditional male attitudes and supports women's liberation, shares household chores, etc.

new moon *n.* the moon seen as a crescent.

news *n.* new or interesting information about recent events; a broadcast report of this. ▫ **be good news** *informal* be an asset, be welcome.

newsagent *n.* a shopkeeper who sells newspapers.

newscaster *n.* a newsreader.

newsflash *n.* an item of important news, broadcast as an interruption to another programme.

newsgroup *n.* a group of internet users exchanging messages about a shared interest.

newsletter *n.* a bulletin issued periodically to members of a society etc.

newspaper *n.* a printed daily or weekly publication containing news reports; the paper forming this.

newsprint *n.* cheap, low-quality paper on which newspapers are printed.

newsreader *n.* a person who reads broadcast news reports.

newsworthy *adj.* important or interesting enough to report as news. ▫ **newsworthiness** *n.*

newt *n.* a small lizard-like amphibious creature.

New Testament *see* **testament**.

newton *n. Physics* a unit of force.

new year *n.* the first days of January.

New Year's Day 1 Jan.

next *adj.* nearest in position or time; soonest come to. ● *adv.* immediately afterwards; on the next occasion; following in a scale: *next tallest.* ● *n.* the next person or thing. ▫ **next to 1** beside. **2** in comparison with. **3** apart from: *the quickest way next to flying.* **4** almost: *next to nothing.*

next door *adv.* in or to the next house or room. ● *adj.* living next door.

next of kin *n.* one's closest relative(s).

nexus *n.* (*pl.* **nexus** or **nexuses**) a link, a connection; a connected group; the central or most important point.

NHS *abbr.* National Health Service.

NI *abbr.* Northern Ireland; National Insurance.

Ni *symb.* nickel.

niacin *n.* = **nicotinic acid**.

nib *n.* the metal point of a pen.

nibble *v.* take small quick or gentle bites (at). ● *n.* a small quick bite; (**nibbles**) *informal* small snacks. ▫ **nibbler** *n.*

Nicam *n. trademark* a digital system used in Britain to produce high quality stereo television sound.

nice *adj.* **1** pleasant, satisfactory. **2** subtle, precise: *a nice distinction*; fastidious. ▫ **nicely** *adv.*, **niceness** *n.*

nicety *n.* (*pl.* **-ies**) a fine detail; precision. ▫ **to a nicety** exactly.

niche (neesh) *n.* **1** a shallow recess esp. in a wall. **2** a suitable or advantageous position in life or employment.

nick *n.* **1** a small cut or notch. **2** *informal* prison. ● *v.* **1** make a nick in. **2** *informal* steal; arrest. ▫ **in good nick** *informal* in good condition. **in the nick of time** only just in time.

nickel *n.* **1** a silver-white metallic element (symbol Ni) used in alloys. **2** *Amer. informal* a 5-cent piece.

nickelodeon *n. Amer. informal* a jukebox.

nickname *n.* a familiar or humorous name given to a person or thing instead of the real name. ● *v.* give a nickname to.

nicotine *n.* a poisonous substance found in tobacco.

nicotinic acid *n.* a vitamin of the B complex.

niece *n.* one's brother's or sister's daughter.

niggardly *adj.* stingy; meagre. ▫ **niggard** *n.*

nigger *n. offensive* a black person.

niggle *v.* cause slight but persistent discomfort; find fault with details.

nigh *adv.* & *prep. archaic* near.

night *n.* the period of darkness between sunset and sunrise; the onset of this, nightfall; the late evening.

nightcap *n.* an alcoholic or hot drink taken at bedtime.

nightclub *n.* a club open at night, providing refreshment and entertainment.

nightdress *n.* a woman's or child's loose garment worn in bed.

nightfall *n.* the onset of night.

nightgown *n.* a nightdress.

nightie *n. informal* a nightdress.

nightingale *n.* a small thrush, the male of which sings melodiously.

nightjar *n.* a night-flying bird with a harsh cry.

nightlife *n.* entertainment available in public places at night.

nightly *adj.* & *adv.* happening at night or every night.

nightmare *n.* a frightening dream; a very unpleasant experience. □ **nightmarish** *adj.*

night school *n.* instruction or education provided in the evening.

nightshade *n.* a plant with poisonous berries.

nightshirt *n.* a long shirt worn in bed.

nightspot *n. informal* a nightclub.

nihilism (*nI*-il-iz-ĕm) *n.* rejection of all religious and moral principles. □ **nihilist** *n.*, **nihilistic** *adj.*

nil *n.* nothing; zero.

nimble *adj.* able to move quickly. □ **nimbly** *adv.*

nimbus *n.* (*pl.* **nimbi** or **nimbuses**) **1** a halo. **2** a raincloud.

Nimby *n.* & *adj. informal* (a person) objecting to the siting of something unpleasant or dangerous in their own area. (from the phrase *not in my back yard*).

nincompoop *n.* a foolish person.

nine *adj.* & *n.* one more than eight (9, IX). □ **ninth** *adj.* & *n.*

ninepins *n.* a game of skittles played with nine objects.

nineteen *adj.* & *n.* one more than eighteen (19, XIX). □ **nineteenth** *adj.* & *n.*

ninety *adj.* & *n.* nine times ten (90, XC). □ **ninetieth** *adj.* & *n.*

ninny *n.* (*pl.* **-ies**) *informal* a foolish person.

niobium *n.* a metallic element (symbol Nb).

nip *v.* (**nipped, nipping**) **1** pinch or squeeze sharply; bite quickly with the front teeth. **2** *informal* go quickly. ● *n.* **1** a sharp pinch, squeeze, or bite. **2** a sharp coldness. **3** a small drink of spirits.

nipple *n.* the small projection at the centre of a breast; the teat of a feeding bottle.

nippy *adj.* (**nippier, nippiest**) *informal* **1** nimble, quick. **2** (of the weather) bitingly cold.

nirvana (neer-**vah**-nă) *n.* (in Buddhism and Hinduism) a state of perfect bliss achieved by the soul.

Nissen hut *n.* a tunnel-shaped hut of corrugated iron.

nit *n.* an egg of a louse or similar parasite.

nit-picking *n.* & *adj. informal* (given to) petty fault-finding.

nitrate *n.* a substance formed from nitric acid, esp. used as a fertilizer.

nitric acid *n.* a corrosive acid containing nitrogen.

nitrogen *n.* a chemical element (symbol N), a gas forming about four-fifths of the atmosphere.

nitroglycerine *n.* (also **nitroglycerin**) a powerful explosive.

nitrous oxide *n.* a gas used as an anaesthetic.

nitty-gritty *n. informal* the basic facts or realities of a matter.

nitwit *n. informal* a stupid or foolish person.

No *symb.* nobelium.

No., no. *abbr.* number.

no *adj.* **1** not any; hardly any: *no time at all.* **2** not of a specified kind: *no easy task.* ● *adv.* (used as a denial or refusal of something); not at all. ● *n.* (*pl.* **noes**) a negative reply, a vote against a proposal.

nobble *v. informal* **1** try to influence unfairly. **2** obtain dishonestly.

nobelium *n.* a radioactive metallic element (symbol No).

nobility *n.* (*pl.* **-ies**) **1** high character. **2** high rank; titled people.

noble *adj.* **1** belonging to the aristocracy. **2** having excellent moral qualities, generous, not petty. **3** grand, imposing. ● *n.* a member of the aristocracy. □ **nobleness** *n.*, **nobly** *adv.*

nobleman *n.* (*pl.* **-men**) a male member of the nobility.

noblesse oblige (noh-bless o-bleezh) privilege entails responsibility.

noblewoman *n.* (*pl.* **-women**) a female member of the nobility.

nobody *pron.* no person. ● *n.* (*pl.* **-ies**) a person of no importance.

nocturnal *adj.* of, happening in, or active in the night. □ **nocturnally** *adv.*

nocturne (nok-tern) *n.* a short romantic piece of music.

nod *v.* (**nodded, nodding**) **1** move the head down and up quickly; indicate (agreement or casual greeting) in this way; (of flowers) bend and sway. **2** let the head droop from drowsiness; make a mistake through lack of concentration. ● *n.* a nodding movement, esp. as a sign of agreement. □ **nod off** *informal* fall asleep.

node *n.* **1** a point in a network where lines intersect. **2** a point on a stem where a leaf or bud grows out. **3** *Anatomy* a small mass of tissue. □ **nodal** *adj.*

nodule *n.* a small rounded lump, a small node. □ **nodular** *adj.*

no-fly zone *n.* an area in which specified aircraft are forbidden to fly.

noggin *n.* a small measure of alcohol, usually ¼ pint.

no-go area *n.* an area to which entry is forbidden or restricted.

noise *n.* **1** a sound, esp. a loud, unpleasant, or disturbing one. **2** fluctuations accompanying and obscuring an electrical signal. □ **noiseless** *adj.*

noisome *adj.* evil-smelling; disgusting.

noisy *adj.* (**noisier, noisiest**) making much noise; full of noise. □ **noisily** *adv.*, **noisiness** *n.*

nomad *n.* a member of a tribe that roams seeking pasture for its animals; a wanderer. □ **nomadic** *adj.*

no man's land *n.* disputed ground between opposing armies; unowned land.

nom de plume *n.* (*pl.* **noms de plume**) a writer's pseudonym.

nomenclature *n.* the devising of a system of names, e.g. in a science.

nominal *adj.* **1** existing in name only. **2** (of a fee) very small. **3** of names. □ **nominally** *adv.*

nominal value *n.* the face value of a coin etc.

nominate *v.* name as candidate for or the future holder of an office; appoint as a place or date. □ **nomination** *n.*, **nominator** *n.*

nominative *n.* the grammatical case expressing the subject of a verb.

nominee *n.* a person nominated.

non- *pref.* not; an absence of.

nonagenarian (noh-nă-gĕn-air-ee-ăn) *n.* a person in his or her nineties.

non-aligned *adj.* not in alliance with another power.

nonchalant (non-shă-lănt) *adj.* calm and casual. □ **nonchalance** *n.*, **nonchalantly** *adv.*

non-committal *adj.* not expressing a definite opinion or commitment to a course of action. □ **non-committally** *adv.*

nonconformist *n.* a person not conforming to established practices; (**Nonconformist**) a member of a Protestant sect not conforming to Anglican practices.

non-contributory *adj.* (of a pension) funded by payments by the employer, not the employee; (of a benefit) paid to eligible people regardless of how much tax they have paid.

nondescript *adj.* lacking distinctive characteristics.

none *pron.* not any; no person. ● *adv.* to no extent, not at all: *none the worse.* □ **none too** not at all.

nonentity *n.* (*pl.* **-ies**) an unimportant or uninteresting person.

non-event *n.* an event that was expected to be important or exciting but proves disappointing.

non-existent *adj.* not existing. □ **non-existence** *n.*

nonplussed *adj.* surprised and confused.

nonsense *n.* words put together in a way that does not make sense; foolish talk, ideas, or behaviour. □ **nonsensical** *adj.*

non sequitur *n.* a statement or conclusion that does not follow from the previous statement or argument.

non-starter *n.* a horse entered for a race but not running in it; *informal* a person or idea with no chance of success.

non-stop *adj.* & *adv.* not ceasing; (of a train etc.) not stopping at places on the way to its destination.

noodles *n.pl.* pasta in narrow strips.

nook *n.* a secluded place; a recess.

noon *n.* twelve o'clock in the day.

no one *n.* no person, nobody.

noose *n.* a loop of rope etc. with a knot that tightens when pulled.

nor *conj.* and not; not either: *neither cheap nor convenient.*

norm *n.* a standard type; usual behaviour.

normal *adj.* conforming to what is standard or usual; free from mental or emotional disorders. □ **normality** *n.*, **normally** *adv.*

north *n.* the point or direction to the left of a person facing east; a northern part or region. ● *adj.* in the north; (of wind) from the north. ● *adv.* towards the north.

north-east *n.*, *adj.*, & *adv.* (in or towards) the point or direction midway between north and east. □ **north-easterly** *adj.* & *n.*, **north-eastern** *adj.*

northerly *adj.* towards or blowing from the north.

northern *adj.* of or in the north.

northerner *n.* a native of the north.

northernmost *adj.* furthest north.

northward *adj.* towards the north. □ **northwards** *adv.*

north-west *n.*, *adj.*, & *adv.* (in or towards) the point or direction midway between north and west. □ **north-westerly** *n.* & *adj.*, **north-western** *adj.*

Norwegian *adj.* & *n.* (a native, the language) of Norway.

Nos. *abbr.* numbers.

nose *n.* **1** the organ at the front of the head, used in breathing and smelling; the sense of smell; a talent for detecting something. **2** the front end of an aircraft, car, etc. ● *v.* **1** push the nose against something; sniff (something). **2** investigate, pry. **3** move forward slowly or cautiously.

nosebag *n.* a bag of fodder hung from a horse's head to allow it to eat at will.

nosedive *n.* a steep downward plunge, esp. of an aeroplane. ● *v.* make this plunge.

nosh *informal n.* food. ● *v.* eat.

nostalgia *n.* sentimental memory of or longing for things of the past. □ **nostalgic** *adj.*, **nostalgically** *adv.*

nostril *n.* either of the two external openings in the nose.

nostrum *n.* a remedy prepared by someone unqualified; a pet scheme.

nosy *adj.* (**nosier, nosiest**) *informal* inquisitive, prying. □ **nosily** *adv.*, **nosiness** *n.*

not *adv.* expressing a negative, denial, or refusal. □ **not at all 1** definitely not. **2** a polite response to thanks.

notable *adj.* worthy of notice; remarkable, eminent. ● *n.* an eminent person. □ **notably** *adv.*

notary *n.* (*pl.* **-ies**) (in full **notary public**) an official authorized to witness the signing of documents, perform formal transactions, etc.

notation *n.* a system of signs or symbols representing numbers, quantities, musical notes, etc.

notch *n.* **1** a V-shaped cut or indentation. **2** a degree on a scale: *a few notches higher*. ● *v.* make a notch in. ◻ **notch up** score, achieve.

note *n.* **1** a brief record written down to aid memory; a short or informal letter; a short written comment. **2** a banknote. **3** a musical tone of definite pitch; a symbol representing the pitch and duration of a musical sound; each of the keys on a piano etc. **4** a quality or tone expressing a mood: *a note of anger*. **5** importance, significance. ● *v.* **1** notice; remark upon. **2** write down.

notebook *n.* a book with blank pages on which to write notes.

notecase *n.* a wallet for banknotes.

noted *adj.* famous, well known.

notelet *n.* a small folded card for a short informal letter.

notepaper *n.* paper for writing letters on.

noteworthy *adj.* worthy of notice, remarkable.

nothing *n.* nothing, not anything; something unimportant; nought, no amount. ● *adv.* not at all: *cared nothing for it*. ◻ **for nothing 1** for no payment, at no cost. **2** achieving nothing. **nothing for it** no alternative.

notice *n.* **1** attention, observation. **2** warning, notification; the formal announcement of the termination of a job or an agreement. **3** a placard or sheet displayed to give information. **4** a review in a newspaper. ● *v.* become aware of. ◻ **take notice** show interest. **take no notice (of)** pay no attention (to).

noticeable *adj.* conspicuous, easily noticed. ◻ **noticeably** *adv.*

notifiable *adj.* (of a disease etc.) having to be reported to authorities.

notify *v.* (**notified, notifying**) inform (someone) of an intention etc.; report. ◻ **notification** *n.*

notion *n.* a belief, an idea; a concept; an impulse or desire.

notional *adj.* hypothetical. ◻ **notionally** *adv.*

notorious *adj.* famous, esp. for something bad. ◻ **notoriety** *n.*, **notoriously** *adv.*

notwithstanding *prep.* in spite of. ● *adv.* nevertheless.

nougat (noo-gah) *n.* a chewy sweet.

nought *n.* the figure 0; nothing.

noun *n.* a word used as the name of a person, place, or thing.

nourish *v.* feed so as to keep alive and healthy; cherish (a feeling).

nourishment *n.* food necessary for life and growth.

nous (nowss) *n. informal* common sense.

nouveau riche (noo-voh **reesh**) *n.* (*pl.* **nouveaux riches**) a person who has become rich recently and makes a display of it.

nouvelle cuisine (noo-vel kwi-**zeen**) *n.* a style of cooking avoiding heavy foods and emphasizing high quality.

Nov. *abbr.* November.

nova *n.* (*pl.* **novae** or **novas**) a star that suddenly becomes much brighter for a short time.

novel *n.* a book-length story. ● *adj.* new, unusual.

novelette *n.* a short (esp. romantic) novel.

novelist *n.* a writer of novels.

novelty *n.* (*pl.* **-ies**) **1** being new, unusual, or original. **2** a small toy or ornament.

November *n.* the eleventh month.

novice *n.* a person new to and inexperienced in an activity; a probationary member of a religious order.

now *adv.* **1** at the present time; immediately. **2** (with no reference to time) used to draw attention to a point or request: *now why didn't I think of that?* ● *conj.* once or because something has happened:

now you're here, let's start □ **for now** for the moment, until later. **now and again, now and then** occasionally.

nowadays *adv.* in present times.

nowhere *adv.* not anywhere.

noxious *adj.* unpleasant and harmful.

nozzle *n.* the vent or spout of a hosepipe etc.

Np *symb.* neptunium.

NSPCC *abbr.* National Society for the Prevention of Cruelty to Children.

nuance (nyoo-ahns) *n.* a subtle difference in meaning.

nub *n.* **1** the central or crucial point of a problem. **2** a small lump.

nubile *adj.* (of a young woman) sexually mature; sexually attractive. □ **nubility** *n.*

nuclear *adj.* of a nucleus; of the nuclei of atoms; using energy released in nuclear fission or fusion.

nuclear family *n.* (*pl.* **-ies**) a couple and their children as a basic social unit.

nucleic acid *n.* either of two complex organic molecules (DNA or RNA) present in all living cells.

nucleon *n.* a proton or neutron.

nucleus *n.* (*pl.* **nuclei**) the central part or thing round which others are collected; the central portion of an atom, seed, or cell.

nude *adj.* naked. ● *n.* a naked figure in a picture etc. □ **nudity** *n.*

nudge *v.* poke gently with the elbow to attract attention quietly; push slightly or gradually ● *n.* a slight push or poke.

nudist *n.* a person who believes that going unclothed is good for the health. □ **nudism** *n.*

nugget *n.* a rough lump of gold or platinum found in the earth.

nuisance *n.* an annoying person or thing.

nuke *v. informal* attack with nuclear weapons.

null *adj.* **1** having no legal force. **2** having the value zero. □ **nullity** *n.*

nullify *v.* (**nullified, nullifying**) make legally null; make ineffective, cancel out. □ **nullification** *n.*

numb *adj.* deprived of the power of feeling. ● *v.* make numb. □ **numbness** *n.*

number *n.* **1** a symbol or word indicating quantity, used in calculation and counting; a quantity. **2** a single issue of a magazine; an item in a performance; *informal* something such as an item of clothing. ● *v.* **1** amount to (a specified number). **2** mark with a number, assign a number to; count. □ **a number of** several.

numberless *adj.* too many to count.

number one *n.* the most important person or thing; *informal* oneself.

number plate *n.* a plate on a motor vehicle, bearing its registration number.

numeral *n.* a symbol representing a number.

numerate *adj.* having a good basic understanding of mathematics and science. □ **numeracy** *n.*

numerator *n.* the number above the line in a vulgar fraction.

numerical *adj.* of a number or series of numbers. □ **numerically** *adv.*

numerous *adj.* great in number.

numismatics (nyoo-miz-**ma**-tiks) *n.* the study of coins and medals.

nun *n.* a member of a female religious community.

nuncio (nun-see-oh) *n.* (*pl.* **nuncios**) a representative of the Pope.

nunnery *n.* (*pl.* **-ies**) a residence of a community of nuns.

nuptial *adj.* of marriage or a wedding. ● *n.pl.* (**nuptials**) a wedding ceremony.

nurd var. of **nerd**.

nurse *n.* **1** a person trained to look after sick or injured people. **2** *dated* a person employed to take charge of young children. ● *v.* **1** work as a nurse; act as nurse (to). **2** feed or be fed at the breast or udder. **3** hold carefully; give special care to; harbour (a belief or feeling).

nursery *n.* (*pl.* **-ies**) **1** a room for young children. **2** a place where plants are reared for sale.

nurseryman *n.* (*pl.* **-men**) a person growing plants at a nursery.

nursery rhyme *n.* a traditional verse for children.

nursery school *n.* a school for children below normal school age.

nursing home *n.* a privately run hospital or home for invalids, esp. elderly ones.

nurture *v.* care for and promote the growth or development of; cherish (a hope, belief, etc.). ● *n.* nurturing; upbringing and environment as an influence on character.

nut *n.* **1** a fruit with a hard shell round an edible kernel; this kernel. **2** a small metal ring with a threaded hole, for use with a bolt as a fastening. **3** *informal* the head. **4** *informal* a mad or fanatical person. ● *adj.* (**nuts**) *informal* crazy.

nutcase *n.* *informal* a crazy person.

nuthatch *n.* a small climbing bird.

nutmeg *n.* a spice.

nutrient *n.* a nourishing substance.

nutriment *n.* nourishing food.

nutrition *n.* providing or obtaining the food necessary for health; the study of nutrients and nourishment. □ **nutritional** *adj.*, **nutritionally** *adv.*

nutritious *adj.* nourishing.

nutshell *n.* the hard shell of a nut. □ **in a nutshell** expressed very briefly.

nutty *adj.* (**nuttier, nuttiest**) **1** full of nuts; tasting like nuts. **2** *informal* crazy.

nuzzle *v.* press or rub gently with the nose.

NVQ *abbr.* National Vocational Qualification.

NW *abbr.* north-west; north-western.

nylon *n.* a very light strong synthetic fibre.

nymph *n.* **1** a mythological semi-divine maiden. **2** a young insect.

nymphomania *n.* excessive sexual desire in a woman. □ **nymphomaniac** *n.*

NZ *abbr.* New Zealand.

O *symb.* oxygen.

oaf *n.* a stupid or clumsy person.

oak *n.* a deciduous forest tree bearing acorns; its hard wood. □ **oaken** *adj.*

oak apple *n.* (also **oak gall**) a growth on oak trees formed by the larvae of wasps.

OAP *abbr.* old-age pensioner.

oar *n.* a pole with a flat blade used to row a boat.

oasis *n.* (*pl.* **oases**) **1** a fertile spot in a desert, where there is water. **2** a peaceful area or period in the midst of uproar, violence, etc.

oast house *n.* a building containing a kiln for drying hops.

oat *n.* a hardy cereal plant; (**oats**) its grain.

oatcake *n.* a biscuit made of oatmeal.

oath *n.* **1** a solemn promise. **2** a swear word.

oatmeal *n.* **1** ground oats. **2** a greyish-fawn colour.

OAU *abbr.* Organization of African Unity.

obdurate *adj.* stubborn. □ **obduracy** *n.*, **obdurately** *adv.*

OBE *abbr.* Order of the British Empire.

obedient *adj.* doing what one is told to do. □ **obedience** *n.*, **obediently** *adv.*

obeisance (o-bay-săns) *n.* respect; a bow or curtsy.

obelisk *n.* a tall pillar set up as a monument.

obese *adj.* very fat. □ **obesity** *n.*

obey *v.* carry out the orders of; act in accordance with (a law etc.).

obfuscate *v.* make obscure or unclear. □ **obfuscation** *n.*

obituary *n.* (*pl.* **-ies**) an announcement of someone's death, often with a short biography.

object *n.* (**ob**-jekt) **1** something solid that can be seen or touched. **2** a person or thing to which an action or feeling is directed; *Grammar* a noun governed by a transitive verb or a preposition. **3** a goal or purpose. ● *v.* (ob-**jekt**) express disapproval or disagreement; protest. □ **no object** not influencing or restricting decisions. □ **objector** *n.*

objection *n.* disapproval, opposition; a statement of this; a reason for objecting.

objectionable *adj.* unpleasant. □ **objectionably** *adv.*

objective *adj.* **1** not influenced by personal feelings or opinions; actual, not dependent on the mind for existence. **2** *Grammar* of the form of a word used when it is the object of a verb or preposition. ● *n.* the thing one is trying to achieve, reach, or capture. □ **objectively** *adv.*, **objectiveness** *n.*, **objectivity** *n.*

object lesson *n.* a striking practical example of a principle.

objet d'art (ob-*zh*ay **dar**) *n.* (*pl.* **objets d'art**) a small decorative or artistic object.

oblation *n.* an offering made to God.

obligate *v.* oblige.

obligation *n.* a duty, something to which one is legally or morally bound; being obliged to do something; being indebted for a favour.

obligatory *adj.* compulsory, not optional.

oblige *v.* **1** require to do something, make legally or morally bound. **2** please or help (someone) by doing as they wish.

obliged *adj.* grateful; indebted.

obliging *adj.* polite and helpful. □ **obligingly** *adv.*

oblique (o-**bleek**) *adj.* **1** slanting, neither parallel nor at right angles. **2** not explicit or direct. □ **obliquely** *adv.*, **obliqueness** *n.*

obliterate *v.* blot out, destroy. □ **obliteration** *n.*

oblivion *n.* the state of being forgotten; the state of being unconscious or unaware.

oblivious *adj.* unaware. □ **obliviously** *adv.*, **obliviousness** *n.*

oblong *n.* & *adj.* (having) a rectangular shape with the length greater than the breadth.

obloquy (**ob**-lŏ-kwee) *n.* criticism, verbal abuse; disgrace.

obnoxious *adj.* very unpleasant. □ **obnoxiously** *adv.*

oboe *n.* a woodwind instrument of treble pitch, with a double reed. □ **oboist** *n.*

obscene *adj.* offensive in its treatment of sexual matters; offending against moral principles, repugnant. □ **obscenely** *adv.*, **obscenity** *n.*

obscure *adj.* not known about, uncertain; not easily understood; not well known; not easy to perceive distinctly. ● *v.* conceal; make unclear. □ **obscurely** *adv.*, **obscurity** *n.*

obsequies (**ob**-si-quiz) *n.pl.* funeral rites.

obsequious *adj.* excessively respectful, servile. □ **obsequiously** *adv.*, **obsequiousness** *n.*

observance *n.* the keeping of a law, custom, or festival.

observant *adj.* quick to notice things. □ **observantly** *adv.*

observation *n.* **1** watching carefully; noticing things. **2** a remark. □ **under observation** being watched. □ **observational** *adj.*

observatory *n.* (*pl.* **-ies**) a building equipped for the observation of stars or weather.

observe *v.* **1** perceive; watch carefully; pay attention to. **2** make a remark. **3** comply with (a rule etc.);

celebrate (a festival). ▫ **observable** *adj.*, **observer** *n.*

obsess *v.* occupy the thoughts of (someone) continually.

obsession *n.* the state of being obsessed; a persistent idea. ▫ **obsessional** *adj.*, **obsessive** *adj.*, **obsessively** *adv.*

obsolescent *adj.* becoming obsolete. ▫ **obsolescence** *n.*

obsolete *adj.* out of date, no longer used or of use.

obstacle *n.* something that obstructs progress.

obstetrics *n.* the branch of medicine and surgery dealing with childbirth. ▫ **obstetric** *adj.*, **obstetrician** *n.*

obstinate *adj.* not changing one's mind under pressure or persuasion; (of a problem) hard to overcome or get rid of. ▫ **obstinacy** *n.*, **obstinately** *adv.*

obstreperous *adj.* noisy, unruly. ▫ **obstreperously** *adv.*, **obstreperousness** *n.*

obstruct *v.* block; hinder the movement or progress of. ▫ **obstruction** *n.*, **obstructive** *adj.*

obtain *v.* **1** get, come into possession of. **2** *formal* be customary or prevalent. ▫ **obtainable** *adj.*

obtrude *v.* be annoyingly noticeable, intrude; force (something unwanted) on someone. ▫ **obtrusion** *n.*

obtrusive *adj.* obtruding oneself, unpleasantly noticeable. ▫ **obtrusively** *adv.*, **obtrusiveness** *n.*

obtuse *adj.* **1** blunt in shape; (of an angle) more than 90° but less than 180°. **2** slow at understanding. ▫ **obtusely** *adv.*, **obtuseness** *n.*

obverse *n.* the side of a coin bearing a head or the principal design; an opposite or counterpart.

obviate *v.* do away with (a need or problem).

obvious *adj.* easy to perceive or understand, self-evident; (of a remark or action) naturally chosen, predictable. ▫ **obviously** *adv.*, **obviousness** *n.*

ocarina *n.* an egg-shaped wind instrument.

occasion *n.* **1** the time at which an event takes place; a special event; a suitable time or opportunity. **2** *formal* reason, cause. ● *v. formal* cause.

occasional *adj.* **1** happening sometimes but not frequently. **2** for a particular occasion. ▫ **occasionally** *adv.*

Occident *n.* the West, the western world. ▫ **Occidental** *n.* & *adj.*

occlude *v.* stop up, obstruct. ▫ **occlusion** *n.*

occluded front *n.* an upward movement of a mass of warm air caused by a cold front overtaking it, producing prolonged rainfall.

occult *adj.* **1** of supernatural powers or magical practices. **2** secret, known to few.

occupant *n.* a person occupying a place or dwelling. ▫ **occupancy** *n.*

occupation *n.* **1** a job or profession; a way of spending time. **2** occupying, being occupied.

occupational *adj.* of or caused by one's employment.

occupational therapy *n.* activities designed to assist recovery from illness or injury.

occupy *v.* (**occupied, occupying**) **1** be in, live in; fill (a place or space). **2** take control of (a country) by force. **3** keep busy; fill (the mind or thoughts). ▫ **occupier** *n.*

occur *v.* (**occurred, occurring**) **1** happen. **2** exist in a particular place. ▫ **occur to** be thought of by.

occurrence *n.* an incident or event; occurring; the frequency with which something occurs.

ocean *n.* the sea surrounding the continents of the earth. ▫ **oceanic** *adj.*

oceanography *n.* the study of the ocean.

ochre (**oh**-kĕ) *n.* & *adj.* (*Amer.* **ocher**) pale brownish yellow.

o'clock *adv.* used in specifying an hour.

OCR *abbr.* optical character reader (or recognition).

Oct. *abbr.* October.

octagon *n.* a geometric figure with eight sides. ▫ **octagonal** *adj.*

octahedron *n.* a solid with eight sides. ▫ **octahedral** *adj.*

octane *n.* a hydrocarbon occurring in petrol.

octave *n.* the interval of eight notes between one musical note and the next note of the same name above or below it.

octavo *n.* (*pl.* **octavos**) the size of a book formed by folding a standard sheet three times to form eight leaves.

octet *n.* a group of eight voices or instruments; music for these.

October *n.* the tenth month.

octogenarian *n.* a person in his or her eighties.

octopus *n.* (*pl.* **octopuses**) a sea animal with eight tentacles.

ocular *adj.* of, for, or by the eyes.

oculist *n.* a specialist in the treatment of eye disorders and defects.

OD *n.* & *v. informal* (take) an overdose.

odd *adj.* **1** unusual, unexpected, strange. **2** (of a number) not exactly divisible by two. **3** occasional, happening rarely. **4** separated from or not part of a set or pair. ▫ **oddly** *adv.*, **oddness** *n.*

oddity *n.* (*pl.* **-ies**) an unusual person or thing; being strange.

oddment *n.* an isolated piece or item left over from a larger set.

odds *n.pl.* the ratio between the amounts staked by the parties to a bet; the likelihood of something's happening. ▫ **at odds with** in conflict with. **odds and ends** oddments.

odds-on *adj.* with success more likely than failure.

ode *n.* a poem addressed to a person or celebrating an event.

odious *adj.* hateful. ▫ **odiously** *adv.*, **odiousness** *n.*

odium *n.* widespread hatred or disgust.

odometer *n.* a milometer.

odoriferous (oh-dŏ-rif-ĕ-rŭs) *adj.* giving off a smell.

odour *n.* (*Amer.* **odor**) a smell. ▫ **in good (or bad) odour** in (or out of) favour. ▫ **odorous** *adj.*

odyssey *n.* (*pl.* **odysseys**) a long adventurous journey.

OECD *abbr.* Organization for Economic Cooperation and Development.

oedema (i-dee-mă) *n.* (*Amer.* **edema**) excess fluid in tissues, causing swelling.

oesophagus (i-sof-ă-gŭs) *n.* (*Amer.* **esophagus**) the tube from the mouth to the stomach.

oestrogen (ee-strŏ-jĕn) *n.* (*Amer.* **estrogen**) a sex hormone responsible for controlling female bodily characteristics.

of *prep.* **1** belonging to. **2** helping to form: *part of the body*; made up from: *a group of people*. **3** done, made, etc., by: *the decision of the committee*; done to: *the murder of the boys*. **4** consisting in, equivalent to. **5** expressing direction: *north of the river*. **6** concerning, involving.

off *adv.* **1** away; so as to be removed or separated: *took off his coat*. **2** not at work, absent; cancelled; unavailable. **3** so as to come or bring to an end: *finish off the work*. **4** not functioning, so as to cease functioning. ● *prep.* **1** moving away from; leading away from. **2** *informal* having a temporary dislike for: *off my food*. ● *adj.* **1** characterized by bad performance: *an off day*. **2** (of food) starting to decay. **3** *informal* unfair, annoying, impolite. **4** of the side of a vehicle furthest from the kerb. ▫ **on the off chance** just in case.

offal *n.* the edible organs from an animal carcass.

offbeat *adj. informal* unusual, unconventional.

off colour *adj.* **1** unwell. **2** slightly indecent.

offcut *n.* a piece of waste material left after cutting off a larger piece.

offence *n.* (*Amer.* **offense**) **1** an illegal act. **2** a feeling of annoyance or resentment.

offend *v.* **1** cause to feel indignant or hurt. **2** commit an illegal act. □ **offender** *n.*

offensive *adj.* **1** causing offence, insulting; disgusting. **2** used in attacking. ● *n.* an aggressive action; a campaign. □ **offensively** *adv.*, **offensiveness** *n.*

offer *v.* present for acceptance or refusal, or for consideration or use; state what one is willing to do, pay, or give; show an intention. ● *n.* an expression of willingness to do, give, or pay something; an amount offered; a reduction in the price of goods.

offering *n.* a gift; a contribution.

offertory *n.* (*pl.* **-ies**) **1** the offering of bread and wine at the Eucharist. **2** a collection of money at a religious service.

offhand *adj.* unceremonious, casual. ● *adv.* unceremoniously, casually.

office *n.* **1** a room or building used for clerical and similar work. **2** a position of authority or trust; tenure of an official position.

officer *n.* **1** a person holding authority in the armed forces; a policeman. **2** a holder of a public office.

official *adj.* of or authorized by a public body or authority; formally approved. ● *n.* a person holding public office. □ **officially** *adv.*

officialese *n. informal* formal, verbose, and obscure language seen as typical of official documents.

officiate *v.* act as an official in charge of an event; perform a religious ceremony.

officious *adj.* asserting one's authority, bossy. □ **officiously** *adv.*, **officiousness** *n.*

off-licence *n.* a shop with a licence to sell alcohol for consumption away from the premises.

off-line *adj.* & *adv.* (of a computer terminal or process) not directly controlled by or connected to a central processor.

offload *v.* unload.

off-putting *adj.* repellent; discouraging.

offset *v.* (**offset, offsetting**) **1** counterbalance, compensate for. **2** place out of line. ● *n.* **1** something counterbalancing something else. **2** the amount by which something is out of line. **3** a method of printing using an inked rubber surface.

offshoot *n.* a side shoot on a plant; something that has developed from something else.

offshore *adj.* at sea some distance from land; (of wind) blowing from the land to the sea.

offside *adj.* & *adv.* in a position where one may not legally play the ball (in football etc.).

offspring *n.* (*pl.* **offspring**) a person's child or children; an animal's young.

off-white *adj.* not quite pure white.

often *adv.* many times, frequently; in many cases.

ogee (oh-jee) *n.* a double continuous curve as in an S.

ogle *v.* look lustfully at.

ogre *n.* a man-eating giant in fairy tales; a terrifying person.

oh *int.* an exclamation of surprise, delight, or pain, or used for emphasis.

ohm *n.* a unit of electrical resistance.

OHP *abbr.* overhead projector.

oil *n.* **1** a thick slippery liquid that will not dissolve in water. **2** petroleum; a thick liquid derived from it. **3** an oil painting; (**oils**) oil paints. ● *v.* lubricate or treat with oil. □ **oily** *adj.*

oilfield *n.* an area where mineral oil is found in the ground.

oil paint *n.* paint made by mixing pigment in oil. □ **oil painting** *n.*

oil rig *n.* a structure for drilling and extracting mineral oil.

oilskin *n.* cloth waterproofed by treatment with oil; (**oilskins**) waterproof clothing made of this.

ointment *n.* a cream rubbed on the skin to heal injuries etc.

OK *adj.* & *adv.* (also **okay**) *informal* all right.

old *adj.* **1** having lived or existed for a long time or a specified time; worn and shabby with age. **2** of an earlier time, former.

old age *n.* the later part of life.

old-fashioned *adj.* no longer fashionable.

Old Testament *see* **testament**.

old wives' tale *n.* a traditional but unfounded belief.

oleaginous (oh-lee-**aj**-i-nŭs) *adj.* producing or covered in oil; unpleasantly complimentary, obsequious.

O level *n.* = **Ordinary level**.

olfactory *adj.* concerned with the sense of smell.

oligarchy *n.* government by a small group; a country governed in this way. ◻ **oligarch** *n.*, **oligarchic** *adj.*

olive *n.* **1** a small oval fruit from which an oil (**olive oil**) is obtained; a tree bearing this. **2** a greenish colour. ● *adj.* of this colour; (of the skin) yellowish brown.

olive branch *n.* something done or offered to show one's desire to make peace.

ombudsman (om-buudz-măn) *n.* (*pl.* **-men**) an official appointed to investigate people's complaints about maladministration by public authorities.

omega *n.* the last letter of the Greek alphabet (Ω, ω).

omelette *n.* a dish of beaten eggs cooked in a frying pan.

omen *n.* an event regarded as a prophetic sign.

ominous *adj.* threatening, suggesting that trouble is imminent. ◻ **ominously** *adv.*

omit *v.* (**omitted, omitting**) leave out, not include; neglect (to do something). ◻ **omission** *n.*

omnibus *n.* **1** a volume containing several works originally published separately. **2** *formal* a bus.

omnipotent *adj.* having unlimited or very great power. ◻ **omnipotence** *n.*

omnipresent *adj.* present everywhere. ◻ **omnipresence** *n.*

omniscient *adj.* knowing everything. ◻ **omniscience** *n.*

omnivorous *adj.* feeding on both plants and animals.

on *prep.* **1** attached to and supported by, on top of; moving to the surface of: *put it on the table*; coming into contact with: *hit his head on the ceiling*. **2** about, concerning; having as a basis: *depending on availability*. **3** aiming at, directed towards. **4** in the course of (a journey); travelling in (a public vehicle). **5** at (a point in time). **6** added to. **7** taking (medication). ● *adv.* **1** so as to be in contact with or covering something. **2** continuing: *carry on*; further forward, progressing: *move on*. **3** taking place, being presented: *What's on at the theatre?* **4** (of an electric appliance) functioning, so as to function. ◻ **not on** *informal* not acceptable. **on and off** from time to time, intermittently.

once *adv.* **1** on one occasion or for one time only. **2** formerly. ● *conj.* as soon as: *we'll start once he's arrived*. ◻ **at once 1** immediately. **2** simultaneously. **once upon a time** at some vague time in the past.

once-over *n.* *informal* a rapid inspection; a piece of work done quickly.

oncogene (ong-kŏ-jeen) *n.* a gene that transforms a cell into a cancer cell.

oncology *n.* the study of tumours.

oncoming *adj.* approaching.

one *n.* the smallest whole number (1, I). a single person or thing. ● *adj.* single, individual; only, unique, sole; a certain unidentified instance: *one day*; one of two or more; united, identical: *of one mind*. ● *pron*. **1** a person, anyone, the speaker as representative of people in general. **2** referring to a type of thing already mentioned: *do you want this book or the other one?* ◻ **at one** in agreement. **one another** each other. **one by one** separately and in succession.

onerous (oh-nĕ-rŭs) *adj*. burdensome.

oneself *pron*. the emphatic and reflexive form of *one*.

one-sided *adj*. biased; unfairly dealing with only one side of an issue.

one-upmanship *n*. *informal* maintaining an advantage over others.

one-way *adj*. allowing movement in one direction only.

ongoing *adj*. continuing, in progress.

onion *n*. a vegetable with a bulb that has a strong taste and smell.

online *adj*. & *adv*. *Computing* directly controlled by or connected to a central processor.

onlooker *n*. a spectator.

only *adj*. alone of its kind; single, sole. ● *adv*. **1** with no one or nothing besides; no more than: *only ten*. **2** no longer ago than: *only yesterday*. ● *conj*. *informal* except that, but: *I'd help, only I'm busy*. ◻ **only too** very much so.

onomatopoeia (onŏ-matŏ-pee-ă) *n*. the formation of words that imitate the sound of what they stand for. ◻ **onomatopoeic** *adj*.

onset *n*. **1** a beginning. **2** an attack.

onshore *adj*. (of wind) blowing from the sea to the land.

onslaught *n*. a fierce attack.

onto *prep*. to a position on, to a place on the surface of.

onus (oh-nŭs) *n*. a duty or responsibility.

onward *adv*. & *adj*. with an advancing motion; further on. ◻ **onwards** *adv*.

onyx (o-niks) *n*. a stone like marble.

oodles *n.pl*. *informal* a great amount.

oomph *n*. *informal* energy, vigour; enthusiasm.

ooze *v*. trickle or flow out slowly; exude. ● *n*. wet mud.

op. *abbr*. opus.

opal *n*. an iridescent precious stone.

opalescent *adj*. iridescent like an opal. ◻ **opalescence** *n*.

opaque *adj*. impossible to see through; difficult to understand. ◻ **opacity** *n*.

op. cit. *abbr*. in the work already quoted.

OPEC *abbr*. (oh-pek) Organization of Petroleum Exporting Countries.

open *adj*. **1** able to be entered or passed through; not closed or sealed. **2** not covered; not hidden or disguised. **3** (of a shop etc.) ready to admit customers. **4** (of a book) with the covers parted. **5** not finally settled or answered. ● *v*. **1** make or become open or more open; unfold, spread out; allow public access to (one's home etc.). **2** establish, begin. ◻ **in the open** **1** out of doors. **2** not hidden. **open to** **1** subject to; vulnerable to. **2** ready to accept. ◻ **openness** *n*.

opencast *adj*. (of mining) on the surface of the ground.

open-ended *adj*. with no fixed limit.

opener *n*. a device for opening tins, bottles, etc.

open-handed *adj*. giving generously.

open house *n*. hospitality to all comers.

opening *n*. **1** a gap. **2** a beginning, an initial part. **3** an opportunity.

open letter *n*. a letter addressed to a person by name but printed in a newspaper.

openly *adv*. without concealment or deception.

open-plan *adj*. (of a room) not divided, without partition walls.

open prison *n*. a prison with few physical restraints on prisoners.

open system *n. Computing* a system allowing software and hardware from different manufacturers to be used together.

open verdict *n.* a verdict not specifying whether a suspicious death is due to crime.

opera *n.* a play in which words are sung to music. ◻ **operatic** *adj.*

operable *adj.* **1** able to be operated. **2** suitable for treatment by surgery.

opera glasses *n.pl.* small binoculars used to give a better view of the stage in a theatre.

operate *v.* **1** control the functioning of (a machine or process); function. **2** perform a surgical operation.

operating system *n.* basic software allowing a computer program to run.

operation *n.* **1** functioning; being active. **2** an act of surgery performed on a patient. **3** a piece of planned activity to achieve a goal.

operational *adj.* **1** in or ready for use. **2** involved in functioning or activity.

operative *adj.* **1** working, functioning. **2** of surgical operations. ● *n.* a worker, esp. in a factory.

operator *n.* a person who operates a machine; one who connects lines at a telephone exchange; one who runs a business or enterprise.

operetta *n.* a short or light opera.

ophidian (o-fid-i-ăn) *adj.* & *n.* (a member) of the snake family.

ophthalmic *adj.* of or for the eyes.

ophthalmic optician *n.* an optician qualified to prescribe and dispense spectacles.

ophthalmology *n.* the study of the eye and its diseases. ◻ **ophthalmologist** *n.*

ophthalmoscope *n.* an instrument for examining the eye.

opiate *n.* a sedative containing opium.

opine (o-**pIn**) *v. formal* express or hold as an opinion.

opinion *n.* a belief or judgement held without actual proof; what one thinks on a particular point; one's estimate of someone's or something's merit or value.

opinionated *adj.* obstinate and arrogant in asserting one's opinions.

opium *n.* a narcotic drug made from the juice of certain poppies.

opossum *n.* a small tree-living marsupial.

opponent *n.* one who disagrees with or is hostile to another.

opportune *adj.* (of a time) favourable; well-timed. ◻ **opportunely** *adv.*, **opportuneness** *n.*

opportunist *n.* a person who exploits opportunities for immediate gain, esp. unscrupulously. ◻ **opportunism** *n.*, **opportunistic** *adj.*

opportunity *n.* (*pl.* **-ies**) a set of circumstances making it possible to do something.

oppose *v.* **1** argue or fight against; compete with. **2** place opposite; contrast with something; bring into opposition.

opposite *adj.* **1** on the further side; facing something. **2** totally different, contrasting. ● *n.* a person or thing totally different from another. ● *adv.* & *prep.* in an opposite position (to).

opposition *n.* **1** resistance, disagreement; a group of people who oppose something; (also **the Opposition**) the main parliamentary party opposing the one in power. **2** a difference or contrast.

oppress *v.* govern or treat harshly; distress, make anxious. ◻ **oppression** *n.*, **oppressor** *n.*

oppressive *adj.* exercising power harshly and unjustly; causing distress or anxiety; (of weather) sultry and tiring. ◻ **oppressively** *adv.*, **oppressiveness** *n.*

opprobrious (o-**proh**-bri-ŭs) *adj.* (of language) abusive.

opprobrium (o-**proh**-bri-ŭm) *n.* harsh criticism; disgrace due to shameful conduct.

opt *v.* make a choice. ◻ **opt out** choose not to participate; (of a school or hospital) withdraw from local authority control.

optic *adj.* of the eye or sight.

optical *adj.* of or aiding sight; visual. ◻ **optically** *adv.*

optical character reader *n.* *Computing* a scanner enabling text to be transferred to computer.

optical fibre *n.* a thin glass fibre used to transmit signals.

optician *n.* a maker or seller of spectacles.

optics *n.* the study of sight and of light as its medium.

optimal *adj.* the best or most favourable.

optimism *n.* a tendency to take a hopeful view of things. ◻ **optimist** *n.*, **optimistic** *adj.*, **optimistically** *adv.*

optimize *v.* (also **-ise**) make the best use of. ◻ **optimization** *n.*

optimum *adj.* & *n.* (*pl.* **optima** or **optimums**) the best or most favourable (conditions, amount, etc.).

option *n.* something that is or may be chosen; the freedom or right to choose; a right to buy or sell something at a specified price within a set time.

optional *adj.* not compulsory. ◻ **optionally** *adv.*

optometrist (op-tom-e-trist) *n.* an ophthalmic optician.

opulent *adj.* ostentatiously luxurious; very wealthy. ◻ **opulence** *n.*, **opulently** *adv.*

opus *n.* (*pl.* **opera**) a musical composition numbered as one of a composer's works.

or *conj.* used to link alternatives; also known as; otherwise, if not.

oracle *n.* a person or thing regarded as an infallible guide; an ancient shrine where a god was believed to answer questions.

oracular *adj.* of an oracle; authoritative; enigmatic, hard to interpret.

oral *adj.* **1** spoken not written. **2** of the mouth; taken by mouth. ● *n.* a spoken examination. ◻ **orally** *adv.*

orange *n.* a round juicy citrus fruit with reddish-yellow peel; its colour. ● *adj.* reddish yellow.

orang-utan *n.* (also **orang-outang**) a large ape

oration *n.* a long speech, esp. of a ceremonial kind.

orator *n.* a person who makes public speeches; a skilful speaker.

oratorio *n.* (*pl.* **oratorios**) a musical composition for voices and orchestra, usu. with a biblical theme.

oratory *n.* the art of public speaking. ◻ **oratorical** *adj.*

orb *n.* a sphere, a globe.

orbit *n.* **1** the curved path of a planet, satellite, or spacecraft round a star or planet. **2** a sphere of activity or influence. ● *v.* (**orbited, orbiting**) move in orbit round.

orbital *adj.* **1** of orbits. **2** (of a road) round the outside of a city.

orchard *n.* a piece of land planted with fruit trees.

orchestra *n.* a large body of people playing various musical instruments. ◻ **orchestral** *adj.*

orchestrate *v.* **1** compose or arrange (music) for an orchestra. **2** organize, manipulate (a situation or event). ◻ **orchestration** *n.*

orchid *n.* a showy flower.

ordain *v.* **1** appoint ceremonially to the Christian ministry. **2** order or decree authoritatively; determine.

ordeal *n.* a painful or difficult experience.

order *n.* **1** the arrangement of people or things in relation to each other; a sequence followed in determining this arrangement. **2** the following of the proper sequence or arrangement; a state of peace and obedience to law. **3** a command; a request to supply goods etc.; the things supplied; a written instruction. **4** a rank, kind, or quality; a group of plants or animals classified as similar. **5** a monastic organization. ● *v.* **1** give a command; request (something) to be supplied. **2** arrange methodically. □ **in order 1** properly arranged. **2** in accordance with the rules. **3** able to function. **in order to** or **that** with the purpose of or intention that. **on order** (of goods) requested but not yet supplied. **out of order** not functioning.

orderly *adj.* neatly arranged; disciplined, not unruly. ● *n.* (*pl.* **-ies**) an attendant in a hospital; a soldier assisting an officer. □ **orderliness** *n.*

order paper *n.* a programme of the day's business in Parliament.

ordinal *n.* (in full **ordinal number**) a number defining a thing's position in a series (e.g. *first, second,* etc.); contrast with **cardinal**.

ordinance *n.* a decree.

ordinand *n.* a candidate for ordination.

ordinary *adj.* usual, not exceptional. □ **ordinarily** *adv.*

Ordinary level *n.* (also **O level**) *hist.* the lower of the two main levels of GCE examination.

ordination *n.* ceremonial appointment to the Christian ministry.

ordnance *n.* mounted guns; missiles, bombs.

Ordnance Survey *n.* an official surveying organization preparing maps of the British Isles.

ordure *n.* dung.

ore *n.* solid rock or mineral from which metal is obtained.

oregano *n.* a herb.

organ *n.* **1** a keyboard instrument with pipes supplied with wind by bellows. **2** a body part with a specific function. **3** a medium of communication, esp. a newspaper.

organic *adj.* **1** of or derived from living matter. **2** of bodily organs. **3** (of farming methods) using no artificial fertilizers or pesticides. **4** forming or part of a system where all parts are essential and in harmony. □ **organically** *adv.*

organism *n.* a living being; an individual animal or plant.

organist *n.* a person who plays the organ.

organization *n.* organizing; arranging; an organized group of people with a shared purpose, e.g. a business. □ **organizational** *adj.*

organize *v.* (also **-ise**) **1** arrange into an ordered whole; form (people) into an association with a common purpose. **2** make arrangements for (an event). □ **organizer** *n.*

orgasm *n.* a climax of sexual excitement.

orgy *n.* (*pl.* **-ies**) a wild party; unrestrained indulgence in a specified activity. □ **orgiastic** *adj.*

Orient *n.* the East, the eastern world. □ **Oriental** *n.* & *adj.*

orient *v.* (also **orientate**) **1** position (something) relative to the points of the compass. **2** adapt to particular needs or circumstances; guide, direct. □ **orient oneself** find one's position in strange surroundings; become used to a new situation. □ **orientation** *n.*

orienteering *n.* the sport of finding one's way across country with a map and compass.

orifice *n.* an opening, esp. in the body.

origami (or-i-**gah**-mi) *n.* the Japanese decorative art of paper folding.

origin *n.* the point, source, or cause from which a thing begins its existence; a person's ancestry or parentage.

original *adj.* **1** existing from the beginning, not replaced or added; first. **2** created by a particular artist etc., not copied. **3** new and unusual; creative, not dependent on others' ideas. ● *n.* a model on which copies are based. □ **originality** *n.*, **originally** *adv.*

originate *v.* bring or come into being. □ **origination** *n.*, **originator** *n.*

ornament *n.* an object or detail designed to make something more attractive; decoration. ● *v.* decorate with ornaments. □ **ornamentation** *n.*

ornamental *adj.* serving as an ornament. □ **ornamentally** *adv.*

ornate *adj.* elaborately ornamented. □ **ornately** *adv.*, **ornateness** *n.*

ornithology *n.* the study of birds. □ **ornithological** *adj.*, **ornithologist** *n.*

orphan *n.* a child whose parents are dead. ● *v.* make (a child) an orphan.

orphanage *n.* an institution where orphans are cared for.

orthodontics *n.* correction of irregularities in teeth. □ **orthodontic** *adj.*, **orthodontist** *n.*

orthodox *adj.* of or holding conventional or currently accepted beliefs, esp. in religion. □ **orthodoxy** *n.*

Orthodox Church *n.* the Eastern or Greek Church.

orthography (or-**thog**-ră-fi) *n.* conventionally correct spelling. □ **orthographic** *adj.*

orthopaedics (orthŏ-**pee**-diks) *n.* (*Amer.* **orthopedics**) the surgical correction of deformities in bones or muscles. □ **orthopaedic** *adj.*, **orthopaedist** *n.*

Os *symb.* osmium.

oscillate *v.* move or swing to and fro. □ **oscillation** *n.*

osier (**oh**-zee-ĕ) *n.* willow with flexible twigs

osmium *n.* a hard metallic element (symbol Os.)

osmosis (oz-**moh**-sis) *n.* the diffusion of fluid through a porous partition into another more concentrated fluid. □ **osmotic** *adj.*

osprey *n.* (*pl.* **ospreys**) a large bird preying on fish

osseous (**os**-ee-ŭs) *adj.* like bone, bony.

ossify *v.* (**ossified, ossifying**) turn into bone; become rigid, cease to progress or develop. □ **ossification** *n.*

ostensible *adj.* apparent but not true; used as a pretext. □ **ostensibly** *adv.*

ostentation *n.* a showy display intended to impress people. □ **ostentatious** *adj.*, **ostentatiously** *adv.*

osteopathy *n.* the treatment of certain conditions by manipulating bones and muscles. □ **osteopath** *n.*, **osteopathic** *adj.*

ostracize *v.* (also **-ise**) exclude from a society or group. □ **ostracism** *n.*

ostrich *n.* a large flightless swift-running African bird.

OTE *abbr.* on-target earnings; a salesperson's expected salary together with bonuses and commission.

other *adj.* **1** distinct from one already present or mentioned; extra, further. **2** different. ● *n.* & *pron.* the one of two people or things not already mentioned or accounted for; (**others**) the members of a group not already accounted for. □ **other than** apart from; differently from. **the other day, week,** etc. a few days, weeks, etc., ago.

otherwise *adv.* **1** in different circumstances. **2** in other respects: *I'm tired, but otherwise I'm fine.* **3** in a different way.

otiose (**oh**-tee-ohs) *adj.* serving no practical purpose.

OTT *abbr. informal* over the top; extravagant, excessive.

otter *n.* a fish-eating water animal

ottoman *n.* a low seat without back or arms, also serving as a storage box.

OU *abbr.* Open University.

ought *v.aux.* **1** expressing duty, desirability, or advisability. **2** expressing strong probability.

Ouija board (**wee**-jă) *n. trademark* a board marked with letters and signs, over which a pointer is moved to indicate supposed messages from spirits.

ounce *n.* a unit of weight, one-sixteenth of a pound (about 28 grams); a very small amount.

our *adj.* of or belonging to us.

ours *poss.pron.* belonging to us.

ourselves *pron.* the emphatic and reflexive form of *we* and *us*.

oust *v.* drive out, eject.

out *adv.* **1** so as to leave a place; in or into the open. **2** away from one's home or base. **3** away from land: *out to sea*. **4** so as to be known: *find out*; so as to be heard: *call out*. **5** so as to be extinguished; so as to end or be completed. ● *adj.* **1** not at home; not at work, on strike. **2** known, public. **3** extinguished, not alight. **4** *informal* not possible. **5** unconscious. **6** in error. ● *n. informal* a way of escape. ● *v.* reveal the homosexuality of (a well-known person). □ **be out to** aim or intend to. **out and out** complete, thorough. **out of** having none left. **out of date** no longer current, valid, or fashionable. **out of the way 1** remote. **2** (of an obstacle) removed.

out- *pref.* more than, so as to exceed.

outback *n.* the remote inland areas of Australia.

outboard *adj.* (of a motor) attached to the outside of a boat.

outbreak *n.* a sudden onset of anger, war, disease, etc.

outbuilding *n.* an outhouse.

outburst *n.* a sudden release of feeling.

outcast *n.* a person driven out of a group or by society.

outclass *v.* surpass in quality.

outcome *n.* the way a process ends; a consequence.

outcrop *n.* part of an underlying layer of rock that projects on the surface of the ground.

outcry *n.* (*pl.* **-cries**) a loud cry; a strong protest.

outdistance *v.* get far ahead of.

outdo *v.* (**outdid, outdone, outdoing**) be or do better than.

outdoor *adj.* of or for use in the open air. □ **outdoors** *adv.*

outer *adj.* external; further from the centre or inside.

outermost *adv.* furthest outward.

outface *v.* disconcert (an opponent) by confronting them boldly.

outfit *n.* a set of clothes or equipment.

outfitter *n.* a supplier of equipment or men's clothing.

outflank *v.* get round the side of (an enemy).

outgoing *adj.* **1** sociable, talkative. **2** leaving an office or position.

outgoings *n.pl.* expenditure.

outgrow *v.* (**outgrew, outgrown, outgrowing**) grow too large for; grow faster than; leave behind or cease to be interested in as one grows or matures.

outhouse *n.* a shed, barn, etc.

outing *n.* a pleasure trip.

outlandish *adj.* looking or sounding strange or foreign.

outlast *v.* last longer than.

outlaw *n.* a fugitive criminal; *hist.* a criminal punished by being deprived of the law's protection. ● *v.* make illegal; *hist.* make (someone) an outlaw.

outlay *n.* money etc. spent.

outlet *n.* a way out; a means for giving vent to energies or feelings; a market for goods.

outline *n.* **1** a line showing a thing's shape or boundary. **2** a summary. ● *v.* draw or describe in outline; mark the outline of.

outlook *n.* a person's attitude to life; a view; the prospect for the future.

outlying *adj.* remote, far from the centre.

outmoded *adj.* no longer fashionable or accepted.

outnumber *v.* exceed in number.

outpace *v.* go faster than.

outpatient *n.* a person visiting a hospital for treatment but not staying overnight.

outplacement *n.* assistance in finding new employment, given to workers who have been made redundant.

outpost *n.* a small military camp at a distance from the main army; a remote settlement.

output *n.* the amount of electrical power, work, etc. produced. ● *v.* (**output** or **outputted, outputting**) (of a computer) supply (results etc.).

outrage *n.* extreme shock and anger; an action or event provoking this. ● *v.* provoke to shock and anger; blatantly break (a rule etc.).

outrageous *adj.* shockingly bad or excessive; exaggerated, improbable, unreasonable. □ **outrageously** *adv.*

outré (oo-tray) *adj.* eccentric, unseemly.

outrider *n.* a mounted attendant or motorcyclist escorting and guarding a vehicle.

outrigger *n.* a stabilizing strip of wood fixed outside and parallel to a canoe; a canoe with this.

outright *adv.* **1** totally, altogether. **2** frankly. **3** immediately; not gradually. ● *adj.* **1** total. **2** frank, direct.

outrun *v.* (**outran, outrun, outrunning**) run faster or further than.

outset *n.* □ **at** or **from the outset** at or from the beginning.

outside *n.* the outer side, surface, or part. ● *adj.* on or near the outside; coming from outside a group: *outside advice.* ● *adv.* to the outside; outside the boundaries. ● *prep.* not within; beyond the boundaries of; not a member of; beyond the scope of. □ **an outside chance** a remote possibility.

outsider *n.* **1** a non-member of a group. **2** a competitor thought to have no chance in a contest.

outsize *adj.* much larger than average.

outskirts *n.pl.* the outer districts.

outsource *v.* obtain (goods) from a supplier outside one's organization; contract (work) out.

outspoken *adj.* very frank.

outstanding *adj.* **1** conspicuous; exceptionally good. **2** not yet paid or dealt with. □ **outstandingly** *adv.*

outstrip *v.* (**outstripped, outstripping**) run faster or further than; surpass.

out-tray *n.* a tray for documents that have been dealt with.

outvote *v.* defeat by a majority of votes.

outward *adj.* **1** of or on the outside. **2** (of a journey) going away from a place. ● *adv.* towards the outside, away from the centre. □ **outwardly** *adv.*, **outwards** *adv.*

outweigh *v.* be of greater weight or importance than.

outwit *v.* (**outwitted, outwitting**) defeat by one's craftiness.

outwork *n.* work done away from the employer's premises.

ova pl. of **ovum**.

oval *n.* & *adj.* (having) a rounded elongated shape like that of an egg.

ovary *n.* (*pl.* **-ies**) an organ producing egg cells; that part of a pistil from which fruit is formed. □ **ovarian** *adj.*

ovate *adj.* egg-shaped.

ovation *n.* enthusiastic applause.

oven *n.* an enclosed chamber in which things are cooked or heated.

ovenware *n.* dishes for use in an oven.

over *prep.* **1** in or to a position higher than; directly upwards from. **2** moving across; to or on the other side of. **3** superior to; greater than, more than. **4** during, in the course of. **5** on the subject of. ● *adv.* **1** moving outwards or downwards: *lean over.* **2** from one side to another; across a space. **3** repeatedly. **4** at an end. ● *n.* *Cricket* a sequence of six balls bowled from one end of the pitch. □ **get something over with** complete an unpleasant task. **over**

and above in addition to. **over and over** again and again.

over- *pref.* **1** excessively; thoroughly. **2** extra; on top, upper.

overall *n.* a garment worn to protect other clothing; (**overalls**) a one-piece garment of this kind covering the body and legs. ● *adj.* total; taking all aspects into account. ● *adv.* taken as a whole.

overarm *adj.* & *adv.* (of a throw etc.) with the arm brought forward and down from above shoulder level.

overawe *v.* overcome with awe.

overbalance *v.* lose balance and fall; cause to do this.

overbearing *adj.* domineering.

overblown *adj.* **1** pretentious. **2** (of a flower) past its best.

overboard *adv.* from a ship into the water. □ **go overboard** *informal* be very enthusiastic; be excessive or immoderate.

overcast *adj.* covered with cloud.

overcharge *v.* ask too high a price from.

overcoat *n.* a warm full-length outdoor coat.

overcome *v.* succeed in dealing with (a problem); defeat (an opponent); (of an emotion) over whelm (someone).

overdo *v.* (**overdoes, overdid, overdone, overdoing**) take to excess; use too much of; cook for too long. □ **overdo it** tire oneself by overwork.

overdose *n.* a dangerously large dose of a drug. ● *v.* take an overdose.

overdraft *n.* a deficit in a bank account caused by overdrawing.

overdraw *v.* (**overdrew, overdrawn, overdrawing**) draw more money from (a bank account) than it holds.

overdrive *n.* a mechanism providing an extra gear above top gear.

overdue *adj.* not paid or arrived etc. by the required or expected time.

overestimate *v.* form too high an estimate of.

overflow *v.* flow over the edge or limits (of). ● *n.* an excess or surplus; a pipe to carry off excess water in a bath or sink.

overgrown *adj.* **1** covered with weeds. **2** grown beyond the proper size.

overhaul *v.* **1** take (a machine) apart to examine and repair it. **2** overtake. ● *n.* an examination and repair.

overhead *adj.* & *adv.* above the level of one's head; in the sky. ● *n.pl.* (**overheads**) the expenses involved in running a business etc.

overhead projector *n.* a projector producing an image from a transparency placed on it, using an overhead mirror.

overhear *v.* (**overheard, overhearing**) hear accidentally or without the speaker's knowledge.

overjoyed *adj.* very happy.

overkill *n.* excessive use or treatment; too much of something.

overland *adj.* & *adv.* (travelling) by land.

overlap *v.* (**overlapped, overlapping**) extend beyond the edge of (something) so as to cover part of it; partially coincide. ● *n.* overlapping; a part or amount that overlaps.

overleaf *adv.* on the other side of a leaf of a book etc.

overload *v.* put too great a load on or in. ● *n.* too great a load or amount.

overlook *v.* **1** fail to notice; ignore (a fault); fail to recognize the merits of. **2** have a view over.

overly *adv.* excessively, too.

overman *v.* (**overmanned, overmanning**) provide with too many staff or crew.

overnight *adv.* & *adj.* during or for a night.

overpass *n.* a road crossing another by means of a bridge.

overpower *v.* overcome by greater strength or numbers.

overpowering *adj.* (of heat or feelings) extremely intense.

overrate *v.* have too high an opinion of.

overreach *v.* □ **overreach oneself** fail through being too ambitious.

overreact *v.* respond more emotionally or extremely than is justified.

override *v.* (**overrode, overridden, overriding**) overrule; be more important than; interrupt the operation of (an automatic device).

overrule *v.* set aside (a decision etc.) by using one's authority.

overrun *v.* (**overran, overrun, overrunning**) **1** spread over and occupy in large numbers. **2** exceed (a limit).

overseas *adj.* & *adv.* across or beyond the sea, abroad.

oversee *v.* (**oversaw, overseen, overseeing**) supervise. □ **overseer** *n.*

overshadow *v.* cast a shadow over; be more important or prominent than, distract attention from.

overshoot *v.* (**overshot, overshooting**) pass beyond (a target or limit etc.).

oversight *n.* **1** an unintentional omission. **2** supervision.

overspill *n.* an excess; a district's surplus population looking for homes elsewhere.

oversteer *v.* (of a car) tend to turn more sharply than was intended. ● *n.* this tendency.

overstep *v.* (**overstepped, overstepping**) go beyond (a limit).

overt *adj.* done or shown openly. □ **overtly** *adv.*

overtake *v.* (**overtook, overtaken, overtaking**) **1** catch up with and pass (someone or something moving in the same direction as oneself). **2** (of misfortune) come suddenly upon.

overthrow *v.* (**overthrew, overthrown, overthrowing**) remove forcibly from power. ● *n.* a removal from power.

overtime *n.* time worked in addition to one's regular working hours; payment for this. ● *adv.* in addition to one's regular working hours.

overtone *n.* an additional quality or implication.

overture *n.* an orchestral composition forming a prelude to a performance; (**overtures**) an initial approach or proposal.

overturn *v.* **1** (cause to) turn upside down or onto its side. **2** cancel, reverse (a decision etc.).

overview *n.* a general survey.

overwhelm *v.* **1** bury beneath a huge mass. **2** overcome completely; make helpless with emotion. □ **overwhelming** *adj.*

overwrought *adj.* in a state of nervous agitation.

oviduct *n.* the tube through which ova pass from the ovary.

oviparous (oh-**vip**-ă-rŭs) *adj.* egg-laying.

ovoid *adj.* egg-shaped, oval.

ovulate *v.* produce or discharge an egg cell from an ovary. □ **ovulation** *n.*

ovule *n.* a germ cell of a plant.

ovum *n.* (*pl.* **ova**) an egg cell; a reproductive cell produced by a female.

owe *v.* be under an obligation to pay or repay (money etc.) in return for something received; have (something) through someone else's action: *I owe my life to him.*

owing *adj.* owed and not yet paid. □ **owing to** caused by; because of.

owl *n.* a bird of prey with large eyes, usu. flying at night. □ **owlish** *adj.*

own *adj.* belonging to a specified person: *her own home.* ● *v.* possess as one's own; acknowledge as one's own; admit. □ **of one's own** belonging to oneself. **on one's own** alone; independently. **own up** confess. ◻ **owner** *n.*, **ownership** *n.*

ox *n.* (*pl.* **oxen**) an animal of or related to the kind kept as domestic cattle; a fully grown bullock.

oxidation *n.* the process of combining with oxygen.

oxide *n.* a compound of oxygen and one other element.

oxidize *v.* (also **-ise**) combine with oxygen; coat with an oxide; make or become rusty. ◻ **oxidization** *n.*

oxyacetylene *adj.* using a very hot flame produced by mixing oxygen and acetylene, esp. in metal-cutting and welding.

oxygen *n.* a chemical element (symbol O), a colourless gas existing in air and necessary for life.

oxygenate *v.* supply or mix with oxygen.

oyster *n.* an edible shellfish.

oz. *abbr.* ounce(s).

ozone *n.* a colourless toxic gas with a strong odour.

ozone hole *n.* a thinning of the ozone layer in high latitudes, resulting in an increase in ultraviolet light reaching the earth.

ozone layer *n.* a layer of ozone in the stratosphere, absorbing ultraviolet radiation.

Pp

P *abbr.* (in road signs) parking. ● *symb.* phosphorus.

p *abbr.* **1** penny; pence (in decimal coinage). **2** *Music* piano.

PA *abbr.* **1** personal assistant. **2** public address system.

Pa *symb.* protactinium.

pa *n. informal* father.

p.a. *abbr.* per annum, yearly.

pace *n.* **1** a single step in walking or running. **2** a rate of progress. ● *v.* walk steadily or to and fro; measure (a distance) by pacing; lead (one's competitors) in a race, establishing the speed. ◻ **pace oneself** do something slowly and steadily so as not to tire oneself too quickly.

pacemaker *n.* **1** a runner etc. who sets the pace for another. **2** a device regulating heart contractions.

pachyderm (**pak**-i-derm) *n.* a large thick-skinned mammal such as the elephant.

pacific *adj.* peaceable.

pacifist *n.* a person totally opposed to war. ◻ **pacifism** *n.*

pacify *v.* (**pacified, pacifying**) calm the anger of; establish peace in (an area). ◻ **pacification** *n.*

pack *n.* **1** a collection of things wrapped or tied for carrying or selling. **2** a set of playing cards. **3** a group of hounds or wolves. ● *v.* **1** fill (a suitcase, bag, etc.); put (items) into a container. **2** press or crowd together; fill (a space) in this way. **3** cover or protect with something pressed tightly. ◻ **pack it in** *informal* stop what one is doing. **pack off** *informal* send away. **send packing** *informal* dismiss abruptly. ◻ **packer** *n.*

package *n.* **1** a parcel; a box etc. in which goods are packed. **2** a package deal. ● *v.* **1** put together in a package. **2** present so as to make more attractive. ◻ **packager** *n.*

package deal *n.* a set of proposals offered or accepted as a whole.

package holiday *n.* a holiday with set arrangements at an inclusive price.

packet *n.* **1** a small package. **2** *informal* a large sum of money. **3** *dated* a mailboat.

pact *n.* an agreement, a treaty.

pad *n.* **1** a piece of soft material used to protect against friction, absorb liquid, etc. **2** a set of sheets of paper fastened together at one edge. **3** a soft fleshy part under an animal's paw. **4** a flat surface for use by helicopters or for launching rockets. ● *v.* (**padded, padding**) **1** protect or make softer with a pad. **2** make larger or longer. **3** walk softly or steadily.

padding *n.* soft material used as a pad.

paddle *n.* a short oar with a broad blade. ● *v.* **1** propel by use of a paddle or paddles; row gently. **2** walk with bare feet in shallow water.

paddock *n.* a small field where horses are kept; an enclosure for horses at a racecourse.

padlock *n.* a detachable lock with a U-shaped bar secured through the object fastened. ● *v.* fasten with a padlock.

padre (**pah**-dray) *n. informal* a chaplain in the army etc.

paean (pee-ăn) *n.* (*Amer.* **pean**) a song of triumph or praise.

paediatrics (peed-i-**at**-riks) *n.* (*Amer.* **pediatrics**) the branch of medicine dealing with children's diseases. □ **paediatric** *adj.*, **paediatrician** *n.*

paella (py-**el**-ă) *n.* a Spanish dish of rice, seafood, chicken, etc.

pagan *adj.* & *n.* (a person) holding religious beliefs other than those of an established religion.

page *n.* **1** a sheet of paper in a book etc.; one side of this. **2** a young male attendant at a hotel; a boy attendant of a bride; *hist.* a boy training for knighthood. ● *v.* summon by name to pass on a message; contact using a pager. □ **page through** leaf through (a book).

pageant (**paj**-ĕnt) *n.* a public show or procession, esp. with people in costume. □ **pageantry** *n.*

pager *n.* a radio device with a bleeper for summoning the wearer.

pagoda *n.* a Hindu temple or Buddhist tower in India, China, etc.

paid past & p.p. of **pay**. □ **put paid to** end (hopes or prospects).

pail *n.* a bucket.

pain *n.* **1** physical discomfort caused by injury or disease; mental suffering. **2** (**pains**) careful effort: *he took pains over the job.* ● *v.* cause pain to.

painful *adj.* **1** causing or suffering pain. **2** laborious. □ **painfully** *adv.*

painkiller *n.* a drug for reducing pain.

painless *adj.* not causing pain. □ **painlessly** *adv.*

painstaking *adj.* very careful and thorough.

paint *n.* colouring matter for applying in liquid form to a surface; (**paints**) tubes or cakes of paint. ● *v.* **1** coat with paint; apply (liquid) to (a surface). **2** depict with paint; describe.

painter *n.* **1** a person who paints as an artist or decorator. **2** a rope attached to a boat's bow for tying it up.

painting *n.* a painted picture.

pair *n.* a set of two things or people; an article consisting of two parts: *a pair of scissors*; one member of a pair in relation to the other. ● *v.* arrange or be arranged in a pair or pairs.

paisley *adj.* patterned with feather-shaped figures.

pajamas Amer. sp. of **pyjamas**.

pal *n. informal* a friend.

palace *n.* an official residence of a sovereign, archbishop, or bishop; a splendid mansion.

palaeography (pali-**og**-răfi) *n.* (*Amer.* **paleography**) the study of ancient writing and inscriptions. □ **palaeographer** *n.*

palaeolithic (pali-ŏ-**lith**-ik) *adj.* (*Amer.* **paleolithic**) of the early part of the Stone Age.

palaeontology (pali-ŏn-**tol**-ŏji) *n.* (*Amer.* **paleontology**) the study of fossil animals and plants. □ **palaeontologist** *n.*

palatable (**pal**-ă-tă-bĕl) *adj.* pleasant to the taste; acceptable, welcome.

palate *n.* the roof of the mouth; the sense of taste.

■ **Usage** Do not confuse *palate* and *palette*.

palatial (pă-lay-shăl) *adj.* of or like a palace: splendid, grand.

palaver (păl-ah-vĕ) *n. informal* a fuss.

pale *adj.* light in colour; (of the face) having less colour than normal. ● *v.* turn pale; seem less important or prominent. □ **beyond the pale** outside the bounds of acceptable behaviour. □ **palely** *adv.*, **paleness** *n.*

paleo- Amer. sp. of words beginning with **palaeo-.**

Palestinian *adj.* & *n.* (a native) of Palestine.

palette *n.* a board on which an artist mixes colours; a range of colours used.

palette knife *n.* a knife with a flexible blade for spreading paint or for smoothing soft substances in cookery.

palindrome (pal-in-drohm) *n.* a word or phrase that reads the same backwards as forwards.

paling *n.* a fence made from pointed stakes; a stake.

pall (pawl) *n.* a cloth spread over a coffin; a heavy dark covering. ● *v.* come to seem less interesting.

palladium *n.* a rare metallic element (symbol Pd).

pall-bearer *n.* a person helping to carry or walking beside the coffin at a funeral.

pallet *n.* **1** a straw-stuffed mattress; a hard narrow or makeshift bed. **2** a tray or platform for goods being lifted or stored.

palliate (pal-i-ayt) *v.* make (a disease or its symptoms) less severe or painful; make (an offence) seem less serious. □ **palliative** *adj.*

pallid *adj.* pale, esp. from illness. □ **pallidness** *n.*, **pallor** *n.*

pally *adj.* (**pallier, palliest**) *informal* friendly.

palm *n.* **1** the inner surface of the hand. **2** a tree of warm and tropical climates, with large leaves and no branches. ● *v.* conceal in one's hand. □ **palm off** fraudulently persuade someone to accept.

palmist *n.* a person who tells people's fortunes from lines in their palms. □ **palmistry** *n.*

palomino (pal-ŏ-mee-noh) *n.* (*pl.* **palominos**) a golden or cream-coloured horse.

palpable *adj.* able to be touched or felt; obvious. □ **palpably** *adv.*

palpate *v.* examine medically by touch. □ **palpation** *n.*

palpitate *v.* throb rapidly; quiver with fear or excitement. □ **palpitation** *n.*

palsy *n.* (*pl.* **-ies**) *dated* paralysis, esp. with involuntary tremors. □ **palsied** *adj.*

paltry *adj.* (**paltrier, paltriest**) (of a sum) very small; worthless. □ **paltriness** *n.*

pampas *n.* vast grassy plains in South America.

pamper *v.* treat very indulgently.

pamphlet *n.* a leaflet or paper-covered booklet.

pamphleteer *n.* a writer of pamphlets.

pan *n.* a metal or earthenware container with a flat base, used in cooking; any similar container. ● *v.* (**panned, panning**) **1** *informal* criticize severely. **2** turn (the camera) horizontally in filming to give a panoramic effect. **3** wash gravel in a pan to separate (gold) from it. □ **panful** *n.*

pan- *comb. form* all, whole.

panacea (pan-ă-see-ă) *n.* a remedy for all kinds of diseases or troubles.

panache (păn-**ash**) *n.* a confident stylish manner.

panama *n.* a straw hat.

pancake *n.* a thin round cake of fried batter.

pancreas *n.* the gland near the stomach, discharging insulin into the blood. □ **pancreatic** *adj.*

panda *n.* a bear-like black and white animal.

pandemic *adj.* (of a disease) occurring over a whole country or the world.

pandemonium (pan-de-**moh**-ni-ŭm) *n.* uproar.

pander *v.* □ **pander to** gratify by satisfying a weakness or vulgar taste.

p. & p. *abbr.* postage and packing.

pane *n.* a sheet of glass in a window or door.

panegyric (pan-ĕ-**ji**-rik) *n.* a piece of written or spoken praise.

panel *n.* **1** a piece of wood or glass forming part of a door; a piece of metal forming part of a vehicle's body; any distinct part of a larger surface. **2** a group assembled to discuss or decide something; a list of jurors, a jury. ● *v.* (**panelled, panelling;** *Amer.* **paneled**) cover or decorate with panels.

panelling *n.* (*Amer.* **paneling**) a series of wooden panels in a wall.

panellist *n.* (*Amer.* **panelist**) a member of a panel.

pang *n.* a sudden sharp pain.

panic *n.* sudden strong fear; frenzied, unthinking action caused by this. ● *v.* (**panicked, panicking**) affect or be affected with panic. □ **panicstricken, panic-struck** *adj.*, **panicky** *adj.*

panjandrum (pan-**jan**-drŭm) *n.* a mock title for an important person.

pannier *n.* a large basket carried by a donkey etc.; a bag fitted on a motorcycle or bicycle.

panoply *n.* (*pl.* **-ies**) a splendid display.

panorama *n.* a view of a wide area or set of events. □ **panoramic** *adj.*

pan pipes *n.pl.* a musical instrument made of a series of graduated pipes.

pansy *n.* (*pl.* **-ies**) **1** a garden flower. **2** *offensive* an effeminate or homosexual man.

pant *v.* breathe with short quick breaths; utter breathlessly.

pantaloons *n.pl.* baggy trousers gathered at the ankles.

pantechnicon *n. dated* a large van for transporting furniture etc.

pantheism *n.* the doctrine that God is in everything. □ **pantheist** *n.*, **pantheistic** *adj.*

panther *n.* a leopard.

panties *n.pl. informal* underpants for women or children.

pantile *n.* a roof tile curved so as to overlap a neighbouring one.

pantograph *n.* a device for copying a plan etc. on any scale.

pantomime *n.* a Christmas play based on a fairy tale.

pantry *n.* (*pl.* **-ies**) a room for storing china, glass, etc.; a larder.

pants *n.pl.* underpants, knickers; *Amer.* trousers.

pap *n.* soft, bland food suitable for infants or invalids; undemanding reading matter.

papacy *n.* (*pl.* **-ies**) the position or authority of the pope.

papal *adj.* of the pope or papacy.

paparazzi *n.pl.* freelance photographers who pursue celebrities for pictures.

papaw, papaya *n.* = **pawpaw**.

paper *n.* **1** a substance manufactured in thin sheets from wood fibre, rags, etc., used for writing on, wrapping, etc. **2** a newspaper. **3** a document; a set of examination questions to be answered in one session; an essay. ● *v.* cover (walls) with wallpaper.

paperback *adj.* & *n.* (a book) bound in a flexible paper binding.

paperweight *n.* a small heavy object for holding loose papers down.

paperwork *n.* clerical or administrative work.

papier mâché (**pap**-ee-ay-**mash**-ay) *n.* moulded paper pulp used for making small objects.

papoose *n. offensive* a young North American Indian child.

paprika *n.* red pepper.

papyrus *n.* (*pl.* **papyri**) a reed-like water plant from which the ancient Egyptians made a kind of paper; this paper; a manuscript written on this.

par *n.* **1** *Golf* the number of strokes needed by a first-class player for a hole or course. **2** the face value of stocks and shares. □ **below par** not as good or well as usual. **on a par with** equal to in quality or importance. **par for the course** normal, to be expected under the circumstances.

parable *n.* a story told to illustrate a moral.

parabola *n.* a curve like the path of an object that is thrown into the air and falls back to earth. □ **parabolic** *adj.*

paracetamol *n.* a drug that relieves pain and reduces fever.

parachute *n.* a device used to slow the descent of a person or object dropping from a great height. ● *v.* descend or drop using a parachute. □ **parachutist** *n.*

parade *n.* a public procession; a formal assembly of troops; an ostentatious display of something; a public square or promenade. ● *v.* march in a parade; display ostentatiously.

paradigm (pa-ră-dym) *n.* an example; a model.

paradise *n.* heaven; a very beautiful or pleasant place or state.

paradox *n.* a statement that seems self-contradictory but contains a truth. □ **paradoxical** *adj.*, **paradoxically** *adv.*

paraffin *n.* oil from petroleum or shale, used as fuel.

paragliding *n.* a sport in which someone jumps from a height and glides through the air supported by a canopy resembling a parachute.

paragon *n.* an apparently perfect person or thing.

paragraph *n.* a distinct section of a piece of writing, begun on a new line. ● *v.* arrange in paragraphs.

parakeet *n.* a small parrot.

parallax (pa-ră-laks) *n.* an apparent difference in an object's position when viewed from different points. □ **parallactic** *adj.*

parallel *adj.* **1** (of lines or planes) going continuously at the same distance from each other. **2** existing at the same time and corresponding: *parallel worlds.* ● *n.* **1** someone or something similar to another; a comparison. **2** a line of latitude. ● *v.* (**paralleled, paralleling**) be parallel to; be comparable to. □ **parallelism** *n.*

parallelogram *n.* a four-sided geometric figure with its opposite sides parallel to each other.

paralyse *v.* (*Amer.* **paralyze**) affect with paralysis; bring (work, a system) to a standstill.

paralysis *n.* loss of power of movement.

paralytic *adj.* **1** affected with paralysis. **2** *informal* very drunk.

paramedic *n.* a person trained to do medical work but without a doctor's qualifications. □ **paramedical** *adj.*

parameter *n.* a numerical factor forming part of a set that defines a system; a limit defining the scope of an activity.

paramilitary *adj.* organized like a military force.

paramount *adj.* chief in importance.

paranoia *n.* a mental disorder in which a person has delusions of grandeur or persecution; an abnormal tendency to mistrust others. □ **paranoiac** *adj.*, **paranoid** *adj.*

paranormal *adj.* supernatural.

parapet *n.* a low wall along the edge of a balcony or bridge.

paraphernalia (pa-ră-fer-**nay**-li-ă) *n.* numerous belongings or pieces of equipment.

paraphrase *v.* express in other words. ● *n.* a rewording in this way.

paraplegia (pa-ră-**plee**-jă) *n.* paralysis of the legs and part or all of the trunk. □ **paraplegic** *adj.* & *n.*

parapsychology *n.* the study of mental perceptions that seem outside normal abilities.

paraquat *n.* an extremely poisonous weedkiller.

parasailing *n.* (also **parascending**) a sport in which a person wearing a parachute is towed behind a motor boat or vehicle.

parasite *n.* an animal or plant living on or in another; a person living off another or others and giving no useful return. □ **parasitic** *adj.*

parasol *n.* a light umbrella used to give shade from the sun.

paratroops *n.pl.* troops trained to parachute into an attack. □ **paratrooper** *n.*

parboil *v.* cook partially by boiling.

parcel *n.* **1** something wrapped in paper, to be posted or carried. **2** something considered as a unit. ● *v.* (**parcelled, parcelling**; *Amer.* **parceled**) **1** wrap as a parcel. **2** divide into portions.

parched *adj.* dried out with heat; *informal* very thirsty.

parchment *n.* writing material made from animal skins; paper resembling this.

pardon *n.* forgiveness. ● *v.* (**pardoned, pardoning**) forgive or excuse. □ **pardonable** *adj.*

pare *v.* trim the edges of; peel; reduce little by little.

parent *n.* **1** a father or mother. **2** an organization owning and controlling subsidiary ones. □ **parental** *adj.*, **parenthood** *n.*

parentage *n.* ancestry; origin.

parenthesis (pă-ren-thĕ-sis) *n.* (*pl.* **parentheses**) a word or phrase inserted into a passage; brackets (like these) placed round this. □ **parenthetic** *adj.*, **parenthetical** *adj.*, **parenthetically** *adv.*

parenting *n.* looking after and bringing up offspring.

par excellence *adv.* being a supreme example of its kind.

pariah (pă-ry-ă) *n.* an outcast.

parietal bone (pă-ry-i-tăl) *n.* each of a pair of bones forming part of the skull.

parings (pair-ingz) *n.pl.* thin strips pared off something.

parish *n.* **1** an area with its own church and clergyman. **2** a local government area within a county.

parishioner *n.* an inhabitant of a parish.

Parisian *adj.* & *n.* (a native) of Paris.

parity *n.* equality.

park *n.* **1** a public garden or recreation ground; the enclosed land of a country house. **2** an area for a specified purpose: *a science park*; an area for parking vehicles: *a car park*. ● *v.* stop and leave (a vehicle) temporarily; *informal* put down casually.

parka *n.* a hooded windproof jacket.

parking ticket *n.* a notice of a fine for illegal parking.

Parkinson's disease *n.* a disease causing trembling and weakness.

Parkinson's law *n.* the notion that work expands to fill the time available.

parlance (pah-lăns) *n.* a particular way of expressing oneself.

parley *n.* (*pl.* **parleys**) a discussion to settle a dispute. ● *v.* (**parleyed, parleying**) hold a parley.

parliament *n.* an assembly that makes a country's laws. □ **parliamentarian** *adj.* & *n.*, **parliamentary** *adj.*

parlour *n.* (*Amer.* **parlor**) **1** *dated* a sitting room. **2** a shop or business providing specified goods or services.

parlous *adj.* difficult; dangerous.

Parmesan *n.* a hard Italian cheese.

parochial *adj.* **1** of a church parish. **2** concerning or interested in only a limited area; narrow. □ **parochialism** *n.*, **parochially** *adv.*

parody *n.* (*pl.* **-ies**) an imitation using exaggeration for comic effect. ● *v.* (**parodied, parodying**) make a parody of.

parole *n.* the release of a prisoner before the end of his or her sentence on condition of good behaviour. ● *v.* release in this way.

paroxysm (pa-roks-iz-ĕm) *n.* an outburst of emotion; a sudden attack of an illness.

parquet (par-kay) *n.* flooring of wooden blocks arranged in a pattern.

parricide *n.* the killing of one's own parent. □ **parricidal** *adj.*

parrot *n.* a tropical bird with a short hooked bill, able to mimic human speech. ● *v.* (**parroted, parroting**) repeat mechanically.

parry *v.* (**parried, parrying**) ward off (a blow); evade (a question) skilfully.

parse (pahz) *v.* analyse (a sentence) in terms of grammar.

parsec (pah-sek) *n.* a unit of distance used in astronomy, about 3.25 light years.

parsimonious *adj.* mean, stingy. □ **parsimoniously** *adv.*, **parsimony** *n.*

parsley *n.* a herb with crinkled green leaves.

parsnip *n.* a vegetable with a large yellowish tapering root.

parson *n. informal* a clergyman.

parsonage *n.* a rectory or vicarage.

part *n.* **1** some but not all of something; a portion, a division; a constituent or element; a measure of relative amounts: *one part sugar to three parts flour*. **2** a character assigned to an actor; their words to be learned; the proper behaviour for someone: *not my part to criticize*. ● *v.* separate, be separated; divide. ● *adv.* partly. □ **in good part** without taking offence. **in part** partly. **part with** give up, give away. **take part** join in. **take someone's part** support someone.

partake *v.* (**partook, partaken, partaking**) **1** join in an activity. **2** take a portion, esp. of food. □ **partaker** *n.*

partial *adj.* **1** favouring one side or person, biased. **2** not complete or total. □ **be partial to** have a strong liking for. □ **partially** *adv.*

partiality *n.* bias, favouritism; a strong liking.

participate *v.* take part in something. □ **participant** *n.*, **participation** *n.*

participle *n. Grammar* a word formed from a verb, as a **past participle** (e.g. *burnt, frightened*), or a **present participle** (e.g. *burning, frightening*). □ **participial** *adj.*

particle *n.* a very small portion of matter; a minor part of speech.

particoloured *adj.* (*Amer.* **particolored**) coloured partly in one colour, partly in another.

particular *adj.* **1** individual, specific, singled out from others. **2** especially great: *particular care*. **3** insisting on high standards in every detail. ● *n.* a detail; a piece of information. □ **in particular** especially. □ **particularly** *adv.*

parting *n.* **1** leaving, being separated. **2** a line from which hair is combed in different directions.

partisan *n.* **1** a strong supporter. **2** a guerrilla. ● *adj.* prejudiced in favour of one side. □ **partisanship** *n.*

partition *n.* division into parts; a structure dividing a room or space, a thin wall. ● *v.* divide into parts or by a partition.

partitive *adj. Grammar* (of a word) denoting part of a group or quantity.

partly *adj.* to some extent; not completely.

partner *n.* a person sharing with another or others in an activity; each of a pair; a husband or wife or member of an unmarried couple. ● *v.* be the partner of; put together as partners. □ **partnership** *n.*

part of speech *n.* a word's grammatical class (noun, verb, adjective, etc.).

partridge *n.* a game bird.

part-time *adj.* for or during only part of the working week.

parturition (pah-tewr-**ish**-ŏn) *n.* the process of giving birth to young; childbirth.

party *n.* (*pl.* **-ies**) **1** a social gathering. **2** a formally constituted political group; a group travelling, working, etc. as a unit. **3** one side in an agreement or dispute.

party line *n.* the policy of a political party.

party wall *n.* a wall common to two buildings or rooms.

pascal (pas-kăl) *n.* a unit of pressure.

paschal (pas-kăl) *adj.* of the Passover; of Easter.

pass *v.* **1** move in a specified direction; change from one state into another. **2** go past, move in front of from one end to the other; overtake; go beyond, excel, outdo. **3** send or transfer to someone else. **4** (of time) elapse; while away (time). **5** be successful in an examination; be acceptable; judge to be acceptable or successful. **6** put (a law) into effect. **7** discharge from the body as excreta. **8** (in a game) refuse one's turn; decline to answer. ● *n.* **1** an act of moving past or through something. **2** a success in an examination. **3** a permit to enter a place. **4** a route over or through mountains. **5** (in football etc.) an act of passing the ball to another player on one's team. □ **a pretty pass** *informal* a bad state of affairs. **make a pass at** *informal* make sexual advances to. **pass away** die. **pass off as** represent falsely as being. **pass out** become unconscious. **pass over** disregard. **pass up** refrain from doing or taking.

passable *adj.* **1** just satisfactory. **2** able to be crossed or travelled on. □ **passably** *adv.*

passage *n.* **1** moving through or past something on one's way between places; the right to pass through. **2** a narrow access way, usu. with walls on either side; a duct etc. in the body. **3** an extract from a book etc. **4** a journey by sea. □ **passageway** *n.*

passbook *n.* a book recording a customer's deposits and withdrawals from a bank etc.

passé (pa-say) *adj.* old-fashioned.

passenger *n.* **1** a person (other than the driver, pilot, or crew) travelling in a vehicle, aircraft, etc. **2** a member of a team etc. who contributes less than the others.

passer-by *n.* (*pl.* **passers-by**) a person who happens to be going past.

passim *adv.* throughout a book, article, etc.

passing *adj.* not lasting long; casual.

passion *n.* **1** strong emotion; sexual love; great enthusiasm. **2** (**the Passion**) the sufferings of Christ on the Cross.

passionate *adj.* full of passion; intense. □ **passionately** *adv.*

passive *adj.* **1** acted upon and not active; not resisting; lacking initiative or forceful qualities. **2** *Grammar* (of a verb) of which the subject undergoes the action. □ **passively** *adv.*, **passiveness** *n.*, **passivity** *n.*

Passover *n.* a Jewish festival commemorating the escape of Jews from slavery in Egypt.

passport *n.* an official document for use by a person travelling abroad, certifying identity and citizenship; a means of achieving something: *a passport to success.*

password *n.* a secret word or phrase used to gain admission, prove identity, etc.

past *adj.* belonging to the time before the present; no longer existing or happening. ● *n.* the time before the present; a person's previous experiences. ● *prep.* **1** to or on the further side of. **2** in front of, going from one side to the other. **3** no longer capable of or able to benefit from. ● *adv.* going past or beyond. □ **past it** *informal* too old to be capable of anything.

pasta *n.* dried flour paste produced in various shapes, to be cooked in boiling water.

paste *n.* **1** a thick, moist substance. **2** an adhesive. **3** a glasslike substance used in imitation gems. ● *v.* **1** fasten or coat with paste. **2** *informal* thrash.

pasteboard *n.* cardboard.

pastel *n.* **1** a chalk-like crayon; a drawing made with this. **2** a light delicate shade of colour.

pasteurize *v.* (also **-ise**) sterilize by heating. □ **pasteurization** *n.*

pastiche (pas-teesh) *n.* a work in the style of another author; a medley of pieces imitating various styles.

pastille *n.* a small flavoured sweet; a lozenge.

pastime *n.* something done to pass time pleasantly.

past master *n.* an expert.

pastor *n.* a clergyman in charge of a church or congregation.

pastoral *adj.* **1** of country life. **2** (of a farm etc.) keeping sheep and cattle. **3** of spiritual and moral guidance.

pastrami (pas-**trah**-mee) *n.* seasoned smoked beef.

pastry *n.* (*pl.* **-ies**) a dough made of flour, fat, and water, used for making pies etc.; an individual item of food made with this.

pasturage *n.* pasture land.

pasture *n.* grassy land suitable for grazing cattle. ● *v.* put (animals) to graze.

pasty[1] (pas-ti) *n.* (*pl.* **-ies**) a pastry with a sweet or savoury filling, baked without a dish.

pasty[2] (pays-ti) *adj.* (**pastier, pastiest**) **1** of or like paste. **2** unhealthily pale.

pat *v.* (**patted, patting**) touch gently with the flat of the hand. ● *n.* **1** a patting movement or touch. **2** a small mass of a soft substance. ● *adj.* & *adv.* unconvincingly quick and simple. □ **off pat** known by heart.

patch *n.* a piece of cloth etc. put on something to mend or strengthen it; a part or area distinguished from the rest; a piece of drug-impregnated material worn on the skin so that the drug is gradually absorbed; a plot of land; *informal* a stretch of time with a particular character. ● *v.* mend with patches. □ **not a patch on** *informal* not nearly as good as. **patch up** repair; settle (a quarrel).

patchwork *n.* needlework in which small pieces of cloth are joined to make a pattern; something made of assorted pieces.

patchy *adj.* (**patchier, patchiest**) existing in patches; uneven in quality. □ **patchily** *adv.*, **patchiness** *n.*

pâté (pa-tay) *n.* a paste of meat etc.

patella *n.* (*pl.* **patellae**) the kneecap.

patent *adj.* **1** obvious. **2** patented. ● *v.* obtain or hold a patent for. ● *n.* an official right to be the sole maker or user of an invention or process; an invention etc. protected by this. □ **patently** *adv.*

patentee *n.* the holder of a patent.

patent leather *n.* leather with a glossy varnished surface.

paternal *adj.* of a father; fatherly; related through one's father. □ **paternally** *adv.*

paternalism *n.* a policy of making kindly provision for people's needs but giving them no independence or responsibility. □ **paternalistic** *adj.*

paternity *n.* fatherhood.

path *n.* **1** a way by which people pass on foot; a line along which a person or thing moves. **2** a course of action.

pathetic *adj.* arousing pity or sadness; *informal* miserably inadequate. □ **pathetically** *adv.*

pathogenic *adj.* causing disease.

pathology *n.* the study of disease. □ **pathological** *adj.*, **pathologist** *n.*

pathos *n.* a pathetic quality.

patience *n.* **1** calm endurance. **2** a card game for one player.

patient *adj.* showing patience. ● *n.* a person receiving medical treatment. ◻ **patiently** *adv.*

patina *n.* a sheen on a surface produced by age or use; a green film on bronze.

patio *n.* (*pl.* **patios**) a paved outdoor area by a house.

patisserie (pă-tee-sĕ-ree) *n.* fancy pastries; a shop selling these.

patois (pat-wah) *n.* a dialect.

patriarch *n.* the male head of a family or tribe; a bishop of high rank in certain Churches. ◻ **patriarchal** *adj.*, **patriarchate** *n.*

patriarchy *n.* (*pl.* **-ies**) a social organization in which a male is head of the family.

patricide *n.* the killing of one's own father; someone guilty of this. ◻ **patricidal** *adj.*

patrimony *n.* (*pl.* **-ies**) heritage.

patriot *n.* a patriotic person.

patriotic *adj.* loyally supporting one's country. ◻ **patriotically** *adv.*, **patriotism** *n.*

patrol *v.* (**patrolled, patrolling**) walk or travel regularly through (an area or building) to see that all is well. ● *n.* patrolling; a person or group patrolling.

patron (pay-trŏn) *n.* **1** a person giving influential or financial support to a cause. **2** a customer.

patronage *n.* **1** a patron's support; regular custom; the power to control appointments and privileges. **2** patronizing behaviour.

patronize *v.* (also **-ise**) **1** treat with apparent kindness that reveals one's sense of superiority. **2** be a customer of. ◻ **patronizing** *adj.*

patron saint *n.* a saint regarded as a protector.

patronymic (pat-rŏ-**nim**-ik) *n.* a name derived from that of a father or ancestor.

patter *v.* make a series of quick tapping sounds; run with short quick steps. ● *n.* **1** a pattering sound. **2** rapid glib speech.

pattern *n.* **1** a decorative design. **2** a model, design, or instructions showing how a thing is to be made; a sample of cloth etc.; an example to follow. **3** a regular sequence of events. ◻ **patterned** *adj.*

patty *n.* (*pl.* **-ies**) a small pie or pasty.

paucity *n.* lack, scarcity.

paunch *n.* a large protruding stomach.

pauper *n.* a very poor person.

pause *n.* a temporary stop. ● *v.* make a pause.

pave *v.* cover (a path, area, etc.) with flat stones or bricks.

pavement *n.* **1** *Brit.* a raised path at the side of a road. **2** *Amer.* the hard surface of a road.

pavilion *n.* **1** a building on a sports ground for use by players and spectators. **2** an ornamental building.

paw *n.* a foot of an animal that has claws. ● *v.* touch with a paw; scrape (the ground) with a hoof; *informal* handle awkwardly or indecently.

pawn *n.* a chess piece of the smallest size and value; a person whose actions are controlled by others. ● *v.* deposit with a pawnbroker as security for money borrowed.

pawnbroker *n.* a person licensed to lend money on the security of personal property deposited.

pawnshop *n.* a pawnbroker's premises.

pawpaw *n.* (also **papaw, papaya**) a tropical fruit.

pay *v.* (**paid, paying**) **1** give (money) to (someone) in return for goods or services; give what is owed; suffer (a penalty or misfortune) on account of one's actions. **2** be profitable or worthwhile. **3** give (attention etc.) to (someone or something). ● *n.* payment; wages. ◻ **pay off 1** pay (a debt) in full. **2** discharge (an employee). **3** be successful and profitable. ◻ **payer** *n.*

payable *adj.* which must or may be paid.

PAYE *abbr.* pay-as-you-earn; a system whereby tax is deducted from wages before payment.

payee *n.* a person to whom money is paid or is to be paid.

payload *n.* the part of a vehicle's load from which profit is derived.

payment *n.* paying; money etc. paid.

pay-off *n. informal* a payment on leaving a job; a bribe; a return on investment; a final outcome.

payola (pay-**oh**-lă) *n.* a bribe offered for dishonest use of influence to promote a commercial product.

payroll *n.* a list of a firm's employees receiving regular pay.

Pb *symb.* lead.

PC *abbr.* **1** police constable. **2** personal computer. **3** politically correct; political correctness.

Pd *symb.* palladium.

PDA *abbr.* personal digital assistant; a very small personal computer.

p.d.q. *abbr. informal* pretty damn quick.

PE *abbr.* physical education.

pea *n.* a round seed growing in pods, used as a vegetable.

peace *n.* a state of freedom from war or disturbance.

peaceable *adj.* avoiding conflict; peaceful. □ **peaceably** *adv.*

peace dividend *n.* public money made available when defence spending is reduced.

peaceful *adj.* free from war or disturbance; not involving violence. □ **peacefully** *adv.*, **peacefulness** *n.*

peacemaker *n.* a person who brings about peace.

peach *n.* a round juicy fruit with a rough stone; a pinkish-yellow colour; *informal* someone or something very good or attractive.

peacock *n.* a male bird with splendid plumage and a long fan-like tail.

peahen *n.* the female of the peacock.

peak *n.* a pointed top, esp. of a mountain; the projecting part of the edge of a cap; the point of highest value, intensity, etc. ● *v.* reach a highest point. ● *adj.* maximum. □ **peaked** *adj.*

peaky *adj.* (**peakier, peakiest**) looking pale and sickly.

peal *n.* the sound of ringing bells; a set of bells with different notes; a loud burst of thunder or laughter. ● *v.* sound in a peal.

pean Amer. sp. of **paean**.

peanut *n.* **1** the oval seed of a South American plant, commonly eaten as a snack. **2** (**peanuts**) *informal* a trivial sum of money.

pear *n.* a rounded fruit tapering towards the stalk.

pearl *n.* a round creamy-white gem formed inside the shell of certain oysters. □ **pearly** *adj.*

peasant *n.* a person working on the land, esp. in the Middle Ages.

peasantry *n.* peasants collectively.

peat *n.* decomposed vegetable matter from bogs etc., used in horticulture or as fuel. □ **peaty** *adj.*

pebble *n.* a small smooth round stone. □ **pebbly** *adj.*

pecan *n.* a smooth pinkish-brown nut.

peccary *n.* (*pl.* **-ies**) a small wild pig.

peck *v.* **1** strike, bite, or pick up with the beak. **2** kiss lightly and hastily. ● *n.* an act of pecking. □ **peck at** *informal* eat (food) in small amounts and without enthusiasm.

pecker *n. Amer. vulgar slang* the penis. □ **keep your pecker up** *informal* stay cheerful.

peckish *adj. informal* hungry.

pectin *n.* a substance found in fruits which makes jam set.

pectoral *adj.* of, in, or on the chest or breast. ● *n.* a pectoral fin or muscle.

peculiar *adj.* **1** strange, eccentric. **2** belonging exclusively to one person or place or thing; special. □ **peculiarity** *n.*, **peculiarly** *adv.*

pecuniary *adj. formal* of or in money.

pedagogue *n.* a person who teaches pedantically.

pedal *n.* a lever operated by the foot. ● *v.* (**pedalled, pedalling**; *Amer.* **pedaled**) operate by pedals; ride a bicycle.

pedalo *n.* (*pl.* **pedalos** or **pedaloes**) a small pedal-operated pleasure boat.

pedantic *adj.* insisting on strict observance of rules and details. □ **pedant** *n.*, **pedantically** *adv.*, **pedantry** *n.*

peddle *v.* sell (goods) as a pedlar.

peddler *n.* Amer. sp. of **pedlar**.

pedestal *n.* a base supporting a column or statue etc.

pedestrian *n.* a person walking, esp. in a street. ● *adj.* **1** of or for pedestrians. **2** unimaginative, dull.

pediatrics etc. Amer. sp. of **paediatrics** etc.

pedicure *n.* the care or treatment of the feet and toenails.

pedigree *n.* recorded ancestry; a line of descent. ● *adj.* (of an animal) descended from a known line of animals of the same breed.

pediment *n.* a triangular part crowning the front of a building.

pedlar *n.* (*Amer.* **peddler**) a person who sells small articles from door to door; a seller of illegal drugs.

pedometer *n.* a device for estimating the distance travelled on foot.

peduncle *n.* the stalk bearing a flower or fruit.

pee *informal v.* urinate. ● *n.* urine.

peek *v.* peep, glance. ● *n.* a peep.

peel *n.* the skin of certain fruits and vegetables. ● *v.* remove the peel or skin from; strip off (an outer covering); (of skin etc.) come off in flakes or layers; lose skin etc. in this way. □ **peeler** *n.*, **peelings** *n.pl.*

peep *v.* look through a narrow opening; look quickly or surreptitiously; show slightly. ● *n.* a brief or surreptitious look.

peephole *n.* a small hole to peep through.

peeping Tom *n.* a furtive voyeur.

peer[1] *v.* look searchingly or with difficulty or effort.

peer[2] *n.* **1** a duke, marquess, earl, viscount, or baron. **2** one who is the equal of another in rank, merit, age, etc.

peerage *n.* peers as a group; the rank of peer or peeress.

peeress *n.* a female peer; a peer's wife.

peerless *adj.* without equal, superb.

peeved *adj. informal* annoyed.

peevish *adj.* irritable. □ **peevishly** *adv.*

peg *n.* a wooden or metal pin or stake as a fastening or to hang things on; a clip for holding clothes on a line. ● *v.* (**pegged, pegging**) **1** fix or mark by means of pegs. **2** keep (wages or prices) at a fixed level. □ **off the peg** (of clothes) ready-made.

pejorative *adj.* expressing disapproval.

peke *n. informal* a Pekinese dog.

Pekinese *n.* (also **Pekingese**) a dog of a breed with short legs, a flat face, and silky hair.

pelican *n.* a waterbird with a pouch in its long bill for storing fish.

pelican crossing *n.* a pedestrian crossing with lights operated by pedestrians.

pellagra *n.* a disease involving cracking of the skin, caused by deficiencies in diet.

pellet *n.* a small round mass of a substance; a piece of small shot. □ **pelleted** *adj.*

pell-mell *adj.* & *adv.* in a hurrying disorderly manner, head-long.

pellucid *adj.* very clear.

pelmet *n.* a border of cloth or wood above a window.

pelt *v.* **1** throw missiles at. **2** *informal* run fast. ● *n.* an animal skin. □ **at full pelt** as fast as possible.

pelvis *n.* the framework of bones round the body below the waist. □ **pelvic** *adj.*

pen *n.* **1** a device with a metal point for writing with ink. **2** a small fenced enclosure, esp. for animals. **3** a female swan. ● *v.* (**penned, penning**) **1** write (a letter etc.). **2** shut in or as if in an animal pen.

penal (pee-năl) *adj.* of or involving punishment.

penalize *v.* (also **-ise**) inflict a penalty on; put at a disadvantage. □ **penalization** *n.*

penalty *n.* (*pl.* **-ies**) a punishment for breaking a law, rule, or contract.

penance *n.* an act performed as an expression of penitence.

pence pl. of **penny**.

penchant (**pahn**-shahn) *n.* a liking; a tendency.

pencil *n.* an instrument containing graphite, used for drawing or writing. ● *v.* (**pencilled, pencilling**; *Amer.* **penciled**) write, draw, or mark with a pencil.

pendant *n.* an ornament hung from a chain round the neck.

pendent *adj.* (also **pendant**) hanging.

pending *adj.* waiting to be decided or settled. ● *prep.* until, while waiting for.

pendulous *adj.* hanging loosely.

pendulum *n.* a weight hung from a cord and swinging freely; a rod with a weighted end that regulates a clock's movement.

penetrate *v.* make a way into or through, pierce; see into or through; understand. □ **penetrable** *adj.*, **penetration** *n.*

penetrating *adj.* **1** showing great insight. **2** (of sound) piercing.

penfriend *n.* a friend to whom a person writes regularly without meeting.

penguin *n.* a flightless seabird of Antarctic regions.

penicillin *n.* an antibiotic obtained from mould fungi.

peninsula *n.* a piece of land almost surrounded by water. □ **peninsular** *adj.*

penis *n.* the organ by which a male mammal copulates and urinates.

penitent *adj.* feeling or showing regret that one has done wrong. ● *n.* a penitent person. □ **penitence** *n.*, **penitently** *adv.*

penitential *adj.* of penitence or penance.

pen-name *n.* an author's pseudonym.

pennant *n.* a long tapering flag.

penniless *adj.* having no money.

pennon *n.* a pennant.

penny *n.* (*pl.* **pennies** for separate coins, **pence** for a sum of money) a British bronze coin worth one-hundredth of £1; a former coin worth one-twelfth of a shilling.

penny-pinching *adj.* niggardly, mean.

pen-pushing *n.* (*derog., informal*) clerical work.

pension *n.* an income paid by the government, an ex-employer, or a private fund to a person who is retired, disabled, etc. □ **pension off** dismiss with a pension.

pension (**pahn**-si-ahn) *n.* a guest house in Europe.

pensionable *adj.* entitled or (of a job) entitling one to a pension.

pensioner *n.* a person who receives a pension.

pensive *adj.* deep in thought. □ **pensively** *adv.*, **pensiveness** *n.*

pentagon *n.* a geometric figure with five sides. □ **pentagonal** *adj.*

pentagram *n.* a five-pointed star.

pentathlon *n.* an athletic contest involving five events.

Pentecost *n.* the Jewish harvest festival; Whit Sunday.

penthouse *n.* a flat on the top floor of a tall building.

penultimate *adj.* last but one.

penumbra *n.* (*pl.* **penumbrae** or **penumbras**) an area of partial shadow; the shadow cast by the earth or moon in a partial eclipse.

penury *n.* poverty. □ **penurious** *adj.*

people *n.pl.* **1** human beings; the subjects of a state. **2** persons of ordinary rank, the common people. **3** *dated* a person's relatives. ● *n.sing.* a race or nation. ● *v.* fill with people, populate.

PEP *abbr.* personal equity plan.

pep *n. informal* vigour. □ **pep up** (**pepped, pepping**) make livelier or more vigorous.

pepper *n.* **1** a hot-tasting seasoning powder made from the dried berries of certain plants. **2** a capsicum. ● *v.* sprinkle with pepper; scatter a large amount of something on or over; hit repeatedly with small missiles. □ **peppery** *adj.*

peppercorn *n.* a dried black berry from which pepper is made.

peppercorn rent *n.* a very low rent.

peppermint *n.* a mint producing a strong fragrant oil; a sweet flavoured with this.

pepsin *n.* an enzyme in gastric juice, helping in digestion.

pep talk *n. informal* a talk designed to encourage confidence and effort.

peptic *adj.* of digestion.

per *prep.* **1** for each. **2** in accordance with.

perambulate *v. formal* walk through or round (an area). □ **perambulation** *n.*

per annum *adv.* for each year.

per capita *adv.* & *adj.* for each person.

perceive *v.* become aware of; see, hear, etc.; regard in a particular way.

per cent *adv.* (*Amer.* **percent**) in or for every hundred.

percentage *n.* a rate or proportion per hundred; a proportion, a part.

perceptible *adj.* able to be perceived. □ **perceptibly** *adv.*

perception *n.* perceiving, the ability to perceive.

perceptive *adj.* showing insight and understanding. □ **perceptively** *adv.*, **perceptiveness** *n.*

perch[1] *n.* a branch or rod on which a bird lands and sits; a high seat. ● *v.* (of a bird) land on a perch; sit somewhere; balance (something) on a narrow support.

perch[2] *n.* (*pl.* **perch**) an edible freshwater fish.

percipient *adj.* perceptive. □ **percipience** *n.*

percolate *v.* filter, esp. through small holes; prepare in a percolator. □ **percolation** *n.*

■ **Usage** *percolate* and *percolator* are spelt with an *o*, not a *u*.

---

percolator *n.* a coffee-making pot in which boiling water is circulated through ground coffee in a perforated drum.

percussion *n.* the playing of a musical instrument by striking it with a stick etc.; instruments played in this way. □ **percussive** *adj.*

perdition *n.* eternal damnation.

peregrination *n. archaic* travelling.

peregrine *n.* a falcon.

peremptory *adj.* imperious; insisting on obedience. □ **peremptorily** *adv.*

perennial *adj.* lasting a long or infinite time; constantly recurring; (of plants) living for several years. ● *n.* a perennial plant. □ **perennially** *adv.*

perestroika (pe-ris-**troy**-kă) *n.* (in the former USSR) reform of the economic and political system.

perfect *adj.* (**per**-fekt) **1** without faults or defects; excellent. **2** exact, total, absolute: *a perfect stranger.* ● *v.* (per-**fekt**) make perfect. □ **perfection** *n.*, **perfectly** *adv.*

perfectionist *n.* a person who seeks perfection. □ **perfectionism** *n.*

perfidious *adj.* treacherous, disloyal. □ **perfidy** *n.*

perforate *v.* pierce, make holes in. □ **perforation** *n.*

perforce *adv. archaic* unavoidably, necessarily.

perform *v.* **1** carry out (a task etc.); function. **2** present (a form of entertainment) to an audience; act, sing, etc., to entertain others. □ **performance** *n.*, **performer** *n.*

perfume *n.* a sweet smell; a fragrant liquid for applying to the body. ● *v.* give a sweet smell to.

perfumery *n.* making perfumes; a shop selling perfumes.

perfunctory *adj.* done without thought, effort, or enthusiasm. □ **perfunctorily** *adv.*

pergola (per-gŏ-lă) *n.* an arbour or walkway with arches covered in climbing plants.

perhaps *adv.* it may be, possibly.

pericardium *n.* (*pl.* **pericardia**) the membranous sac enclosing the heart.

perigee (pe-ri-jee) *n.* the point nearest to the earth in the moon's orbit.

peril *n.* serious danger. □ **perilous** *adj.*, **perilously** *adv.*

perimeter *n.* the outline of a geometric figure; the outer edge of an area; the length of this.

perinatal *adj.* of the time immediately before and after birth.

period *n.* **1** a length or portion of time; a division of a school day, sports match, etc. **2** an occurrence of menstruation. **3** a complete sentence; a full stop in punctuation. ● *adj.* (of dress or furniture) belonging to a past age.

periodic *adj.* happening at intervals. □ **periodicity** *n.*

periodical *adj.* periodic. ● *n.* a magazine etc. published at regular intervals. □ **periodically** *adv.*

peripatetic (pe-ri-pă-te-tik) *adj.* going from place to place.

peripheral *adj.* of or on the periphery; of only minor importance.

periphery *n.* (*pl.* **-ies**) the outer limits of an area; the fringes of a subject.

periphrasis *n.* (*pl.* **periphrases**) a roundabout phrase or way of speaking.

periscope *n.* a tube attached to a set of mirrors, enabling one to see things above them and otherwise out of sight.

perish *v.* die, be destroyed; (of food, rubber, etc.) rot. □ **be perished** *informal* feel very cold.

perishable *adj.* liable to decay or go bad in a short time.

peritoneum (pe-ri-tŏ-nee-ŭm) *n.* (*pl.* **peritoneums** or **peritonea**) the membrane lining the abdominal cavity.

peritonitis *n.* inflammation of the peritoneum.

perjure *v.* □ **perjure oneself** lie under oath.

perjury *n.* the deliberate giving of false evidence while under oath; this evidence.

perk *n. informal* a benefit to which an employee is entitled. □ **perk up** make or become livelier, more cheerful, or more interesting.

perky *adj.* (**perkier, perkiest**) lively and cheerful. □ **perkily** *adv.*, **perkiness** *n.*

perm *n.* **1** a treatment giving hair a long-lasting artificial wave. **2** *informal* a permutation. ● *v.* **1** treat (hair) with a perm. **2** *informal* select (a specified number) from a quantity.

permafrost *n.* permanently frozen subsoil in arctic regions.

permanent *adj.* lasting indefinitely. □ **permanence** *n.*, **permanently** *adv.*

permeable *adj.* allowing liquid or gases to pass through it. □ **permeability** *n.*

permeate *v.* spread throughout, pervade.

permissible *adj.* allowable.

permission *n.* consent, authorization.

permissive *adj.* tolerant, esp. in social and sexual matters. □ **permissiveness** *n.*

permit *v.* (per-mit) (**permitted, permitting**) allow to do something or to be done or happen; make possible, provide an opportunity for. ● *n.* (per-mit) a written order giving permission, esp. for entry.

permutation *n.* one of several possible arrangements of things; *Brit.* a selection of a number of matches in a football pool.

pernicious *adj.* harmful.

pernickety *adj. informal* too fastidious, fussy.

peroration *n.* the concluding part of a speech.

peroxide *n.* a compound of hydrogen used to bleach hair.

perpendicular *adj.* at an angle of 90° to a line or surface; upright, vertical. ● *n.* a perpendicular line or direction. □ **perpendicularly** *adv.*

perpetrate *v.* commit (a crime), make (an error). □ **perpetration** *n.*, **perpetrator** *n.*

perpetual *adj.* never ending or changing; very frequent. □ **perpetually** *adv.*

perpetuate *v.* cause to continue or be preserved indefinitely. □ **perpetuation** *n.*

perpetuity *n.* □ **in perpetuity** for ever.

perplex *v.* puzzle, baffle.

perplexity *n.* not knowing how to deal with something.

per pro. *see* **p.p.**

perquisite *n. formal* a privilege or benefit given in addition to wages; a privilege derived from one's status.

■ **Usage** *Perquisite* is sometimes confused with *prerequisite*, which means 'a thing required as a precondition'.

perry *n.* a drink made from fermented pears.

per se *adv.* by or in itself; intrinsically.

persecute *v.* treat with hostility because of race or religion; harass. □ **persecution** *n.*, **persecutor** *n.*

persevere *v.* continue in spite of difficulties. □ **perseverance** *n.*

persimmon *n.* a tropical fruit.

persist *v.* continue in an opinion or course of action despite opposition; continue to exist. □ **persistence** *n.*, **persistent** *adj.*, **persistently** *adv.*

person *n.* (*pl.* **people** or **persons**) **1** an individual human being; an individual with a particular character or tastes. **2** an individual's body. **3** *Grammar* one of the three classes of personal pronouns and verb forms, referring to the person(s) speaking, spoken to, or referred to. □ **in person** oneself, physically present.

persona *n.* (*pl.* **personae**) the aspect of someone's character presented to others; a role adopted by someone.

personable *adj.* attractive in appearance or manner.

■ **Usage** Do not confuse *personable* with *personal.*

personage *n.* a person, esp. an important one.

personal *adj.* **1** belonging to or affecting an individual; one's own, private. **2** concerning one's emotions, relationships, etc. **3** of a person's body. **4** done by a particular person, not delegated. □ **personally** *adv.*

personal computer *n.* a computer designed for use by a single individual.

personal equity plan *n.* a scheme for tax-free personal investment.

personality *n.* (*pl.* **-ies**) **1** a person's distinctive character; a person with distinctive qualities. **2** a celebrity.

personalize *v.* (also **-ise**) **1** design to suit or identify as belonging to a particular individual. **2** cause (a discussion etc.) to be concerned with personalities rather than abstract topics. ▫ **personalization** *n.*

personal organizer *n.* a looseleaf folder or pocket-sized computer for keeping details of meetings, phone numbers, addresses, etc.

personal pronoun *see* **pronoun**.

personify *v.* (**personified, personifying**) represent in human form or as having human characteristics; embody in one's behaviour. ▫ **personification** *n.*

personnel *n.* employees, staff.

■ **Usage** Do not confuse *personnel* with *personal*.

---

perspective *n.* **1** the art of drawing so as to give an effect of solidity and relative position. **2** a particular attitude towards something; understanding of the relative importance of things. ▫ **in perspective** drawn according to the rules of perspective; not distorting a thing's relative importance.

perspex *n. trademark* a tough light transparent plastic.

perspicacious (per-spi-kay-shŭs) *adj.* showing great insight. ▫ **perspicaciously** *adv.*, **perspicacity** *n.*

perspicuous *adj.* expressing things clearly. ▫ **perspicuity** *n.*

perspire *v.* sweat. ▫ **perspiration** *n.*

persuade *v.* cause (someone) to believe or do something by reasoning. ▫ **persuader** *n.*

persuasion *n.* **1** persuading; persuasive argument. **2** a belief or set of beliefs.

persuasive *adj.* able or trying to persuade people. ▫ **persuasively** *adv.*, **persuasiveness** *n.*

pert *adj.* impudent, esp. in a lively and attractive way. ▫ **pertly** *adv.*, **pertness** *n.*

pertain *v.* be relevant; belong as a part.

pertinacious *adj.* persistent and determined. ▫ **pertinaciously** *adv.*, **pertinacity** *n.*

pertinent *adj.* relevant. ▫ **pertinence** *n.*, **pertinently** *adv.*

perturb *v.* make anxious or uneasy. ▫ **perturbation** *n.*

peruse *v.* read carefully. ▫ **perusal** *n.*

pervade *v.* spread throughout (a thing). ▫ **pervasive** *adj.*

perverse *adj.* obstinate in unreasonable or unacceptable behaviour; contrary to reason or expectation. ▫ **perversely** *adv.*, **perversity** *n.*

pervert *v.* (pĕ-**vert**) alter, distort, misuse or misapply; lead astray, corrupt. ● *n.* (**per**-vert) a person whose sexual behaviour is regarded as abnormal and unacceptable. ▫ **perversion** *n.*

pervious *adj.* permeable; penetrable.

peseta *n.* a former unit of money in Spain.

peso *n.* (*pl.* **pesos**) a unit of money in several South American countries.

pessary *n.* (*pl.* **-ies**) a vaginal suppository.

pessimism *n.* a tendency to take a gloomy view of things. ▫ **pessimist** *n.*, **pessimistic** *adj.*, **pessimistically** *adv.*

pest *n.* an insect or animal harmful to crops, stored food, etc.; *informal* an annoying person or thing.

pester *v.* annoy continually, esp. with requests or questions.

pesticide *n.* a substance used to destroy harmful insects etc.

pestilence *n.* a deadly epidemic disease. ▫ **pestilential** *adj.*

pestle (pess-ĕl) *n.* a club-shaped instrument for pounding things to powder.

pesto *n.* a sauce of basil, olive oil, Parmesan cheese, and pine nuts, often used on pasta.

pet *n.* **1** a tame animal kept for company and pleasure. **2** a favourite. ● *adj.* **1** kept as a pet. **2** favourite. ● *v.* (**petted, petting**) stroke affectionately; treat indulgently; kiss and caress.

petal *n.* one of the coloured outer parts of a flower head.

peter *v.* □ **peter out** gradually disappear, fade away.

pethidine *n.* a painkilling drug.

petite *adj.* small and dainty.

petition *n.* a formal written request signed by many people. ● *v.* present a petition to.

petrel *n.* a seabird.

petrify *v.* (**petrified, petrifying**) **1** change into a stony mass. **2** paralyse with astonishment or fear. □ **petrifaction** *n.*

petrochemical *n.* a chemical substance obtained from petroleum or gas. ● *adj.* of such a substance or the processing of it.

petrol *n.* an inflammable liquid made from petroleum for use as fuel in internal-combustion engines.

petroleum *n.* a mineral oil found underground, refined for use as fuel or in dry-cleaning etc.

petticoat *n.* a dress-length undergarment worn beneath a dress or skirt.

pettifogging *adj.* trivial; quibbling about unimportant details.

pettish *adj.* childishly bad-tempered.

petty *adj.* (**pettier, pettiest**) unimportant, trivial; of relatively low rank; spitefully or unfairly critical of details. □ **pettily** *adv.*, **pettiness** *n.*

petty cash *n.* money kept by an office etc. for small payments.

petulant *adj.* sulky, irritable. □ **petulance** *n.*, **petulantly** *adv.*

pew *n.* a long bench-like seat in a church; *informal* a seat.

pewter *n.* a grey alloy of tin with lead or other metal.

pfennig *n.* a German coin, one-hundredth of a mark.

PG *abbr.* (of a film) classified as suitable for children subject to parental guidance.

pH *n.* a measure of acidity or alkalinity.

phalanx (fal-anks) *n.* (*pl.* **phalanxes**) a compact mass of people or things; a body of troops or police officers.

phallus *n.* (*pl.* **phalluses** or **phalli**) (an image of) the penis. □ **phallic** *adj.*

phantom *n.* a ghost.

Pharaoh (**fair**-oh) *n.* the title of the kings of ancient Egypt.

pharmaceutical (fah-mă-**syoo**-tik-ăl) *adj.* of or engaged in pharmacy.

pharmacist *n.* a person skilled in pharmacy.

pharmacology *n.* the study of the action of drugs. □ **pharmacological** *adj.*, **pharmacologist** *n.*

pharmacopoeia (far-mă-kŏ-**pee**-ă) *n.* an official list of medicinal drugs with their effects.

pharmacy *n.* (*pl.* **-ies**) a shop or dispensary providing medicinal drugs; the preparation and dispensing of these drugs.

pharynx (**fa**-ringks) *n.* the cavity at the back of the nose and throat. □ **pharyngeal** *adj.*

phase *n.* a distinct period in a process of change or development. ● *v.* carry out (a programme etc.) in stages. □ **phase in** or **out** bring gradually into or out of use.

Ph.D. *abbr.* Doctor of Philosophy, a higher degree.

pheasant *n.* a game bird with bright feathers in the male.

phenomenal *adj.* extraordinary, remarkable. □ **phenomenally** *adv.*

phenomenon *n.* (*pl.* **phenomena**) **1** a fact, occurrence, or change perceived by the senses or the mind. **2** a remarkable person or thing.

pheromone *n.* a chemical secreted by an animal's body and influencing the behaviour of others of the same species when released into the air.

phial *n.* a small bottle.

philander *v.* (of a man) engage in many casual love affairs. □ **philanderer** *n.*

philanthropy *n.* benevolence, promotion of others' welfare. □ **philanthropic** *adj.*, **philanthropist** *n.*

philately *n.* stamp-collecting. □ **philatelic** *adj.*, **philatelist** *n.*

philistine *n.* an uncultured person.

philology *n.* the study of languages. □ **philological** *adj.*, **philologist** *n.*

philosopher *n.* a person who engages in philosophy.

philosophical *adj.* **1** of philosophy. **2** bearing misfortune calmly. □ **philosophically** *adv.*

philosophize *v.* (also **-ise**) theorize; moralize.

philosophy *n.* (*pl.* **-ies**) the study of the basic principles of existence, knowledge, morals, etc.; a particular system of beliefs about these; an outlook or set of principles.

philtre *n.* (*Amer.* **philter**) a magic potion.

phlegm (flem) *n.* a thick mucus in the bronchial passages, ejected by coughing.

phlegmatic *adj.* not excitable or emotional. □ **phlegmatically** *adv.*

phobia *n.* an extreme or irrational fear or dislike. □ **phobic** *adj.* & *n.*

phoenix (fee-niks) *n.* a mythical Arabian bird said to burn itself and rise young again from its ashes.

phone *n.* a telephone. ● *v.* telephone.

phonecard *n.* a card containing prepaid units for use in a cardphone.

phone-in *n.* a broadcast programme in which listeners telephone the studio with questions and comments.

phonetic *adj.* **1** of or representing speech sounds. **2** (of spelling) corresponding to pronunciation. ● *n.* (**phonetics**) the study or representation of speech sounds. □ **phonetically** *adv.*, **phonetician** *n.*

phoney (also **phony**) *informal adj.* false, sham. ● *n.* a phoney person or thing.

phonograph *n.* (*Amer.*) a record player.

phosphate *n.* a compound of phosphorous, esp. used in fertilizers.

phosphorescent *adj.* luminous. □ **phosphorescence** *n.*

phosphorus *n.* a chemical element (symbol P); a wax-like form of this appearing luminous in the dark and igniting in air.

photo *n.* (*pl.* **photos**) a photograph.

photocopier *n.* a machine for photocopying documents.

photocopy *n.* (*pl.* **-ies**) a photographic copy of a document. ● *v.* (**-copied, -copying**) make a photocopy of.

photoelectric cell *n.* an electronic device emitting an electric current when light falls on it.

photo finish *n.* a finish of a race so close that the winner has to be decided from a photograph.

photofit *n.* a likeness of a person made up of separate photographs of features.

photogenic *adj.* looking attractive in photographs.

photograph *n.* a picture made using a camera, formed by the chemical action of light on sensitive material on to which an image is focused. ● *v.* take a photograph of; come out (well or badly) when photographed. □ **photographer** *n.*, **photographic** *adj.*, **photographically** *adv.*, **photography** *n.*

photojournalism *n.* the reporting of news by photographs.

photon *n.* an indivisible unit of electromagnetic radiation.

photosensitive *adj.* reacting to light.

photostat *n. trademark* a photocopier; a photocopy. ● *v.* (**photostatted, photostatting**) make a photocopy of.

photosynthesis *n.* the process by which green plants use sunlight to convert carbon dioxide and water into complex substances. □ **photosynthesize** *v.*

phrase *n.* a group of words forming a unit; a short idiomatic expression; a unit in a melody. ● *v.* **1** express in words. **2** divide (music) into phrases. ▫ **phrasal** *adj.*

phraseology *n.* (*pl.* **-ies**) a mode of expression, a way of wording things.

phrenology *n.* the study of the shape of a person's skull, supposedly as an indication of their character.

phylum (fī-lŭm) *n.* (*pl.* **phyla**) a major division of the plant or animal kingdom.

physical *adj.* **1** of the body; of things perceived by the senses. **2** of physics; of natural forces and laws. ▫ **physically** *adv.*

physical education *n.* exercises and games as part of a school curriculum.

physical geography *n.* the study of the earth's natural features.

physical sciences *n.pl.* the sciences studying inanimate natural objects.

physician *n.* a doctor, esp. one specializing in medicine as distinct from surgery.

physicist *n.* an expert in physics.

physics *n.* the study of the properties and interactions of matter and energy.

physiognomy *n.* (*pl.* **-ies**) the features of a person's face.

physiology *n.* the study of the bodily functions of living organisms. ▫ **physiological** *adj.*, **physiologist** *n.*

physiotherapy *n.* treatment of an injury etc. by massage and exercises. ▫ **physiotherapist** *n.*

physique (fi-zeek) *n.* a person's physical build and muscular development.

pi *n.* a Greek letter (π) used as a symbol for the ratio of a circle's circumference to its diameter (about 3.14).

pianissimo *adv. Music* very softly.

pianist *n.* a person who plays the piano.

piano *n.* (*pl.* **pianos**) a musical instrument with strings struck by hammers operated by a keyboard. ● *adv. Music* softly.

pianoforte *n. formal* a piano.

piazza (pee-at-să) *n.* a public square or market place.

picador *n.* a mounted bullfighter with a lance.

piccalilli *n.* a pickle of chopped vegetables and hot spices.

piccaninny *n.* (*pl.* **-ies**) (*Amer.* **pickaninny**) *offensive* a black child; an Aboriginal child.

picaresque (pik-ă-resk) *adj.* (of fiction) recounting a series of adventures of a roguish hero.

piccolo *n.* (*pl.* **piccolos**) a small flute.

pick *v.* **1** take hold of and pull or lift from its place. **2** select. **3** pull at something repeatedly with the fingers; make (a hole) in this way. ● *n.* **1** an act of choosing; the right to choose; *informal* the best of a group. **2** a pickaxe. **3** *informal* a plectrum. ▫ **pick a lock** open a lock using something other than a key. **pick a pocket** steal from a pocket. **pick a quarrel** provoke a quarrel. **pick holes in** criticize. **pick off** single out and shoot. **pick on** unfairly single out for blame or criticism. **pick one's way** walk carefully over rough ground. **pick out 1** select. **2** mark, distinguish (a design etc.). **pick to pieces** criticize severely. **pick up 1** lift. **2** collect in a car, give a lift to. **3** become better or stronger. **4** casually become acquainted with. ▫ **picker** *n.*

pickaback var. of **piggyback**.

pickaninny Amer. sp. of **piccaninny**.

pickaxe *n.* (*Amer.* **pickax**) a tool with a pointed iron bar at right angles to its handle, for breaking ground etc.

picket *n.* **1** people stationed outside a workplace to dissuade others from entering during a strike; a party of sentries. **2** a pointed stake set in the ground. ● *v.* (**picketed, picketing**) **1** form a picket outside (a workplace). **2** enclose with stakes.

pickings *n.pl.* gains made easily or dishonestly.

pickle *n.* **1** vegetables preserved in vinegar or brine; this liquid. **2** *informal* a difficult or embarrassing situation. ● *v.* preserve in pickle.

pickpocket *n.* a thief who steals from people's pockets.

pickup *n.* **1** a small van with low sides. **2** *informal* a casual encounter with someone, esp. a sexual one. **3** a device producing an electrical signal in response to a change, e.g. the stylus holder on a record player.

picnic *n.* an informal outdoor meal. ● *v.* (**picnicked, picnicking**) take part in a picnic. □ **picnicker** *n.*

pictograph *n.* a pictorial symbol used as a form of writing.

pictorial *adj.* of, in, or like a picture or pictures; illustrated. ● *n.* a newspaper etc. with many pictures. □ **pictorially** *adv.*

picture *n.* a representation made by painting, drawing, or photography; an idea, a mental image; (**the pictures**) the cinema. ● *v.* represent, draw or paint; imagine. □ **be** (or **look**) **a picture** be very beautiful. **get the picture** *informal* understand a situation.

picturesque *adj.* forming a pleasant scene; (of words or a description) very expressive.

pidgin *n.* a simplified form of English or another language with elements of a local language.

pie *n.* a baked dish of meat, fish, or fruit covered with pastry or another crust.

piebald *adj.* (of a horse) with irregular patches of white and black.

piece *n.* **1** a portion; a part; an item in a set. **2** something regarded as a unit. **3** a musical, literary, or artistic composition. **4** a small object used in board games. □ **of a piece** of the same kind; consistent. **piece together** make by putting together pieces or parts.

pièce de résistance (pee-ess dă ray-zees-tahns) (*pl.* **pièces de résistance**) the most impressive feature, esp. of a creative work.

piecemeal *adj.* & *adv.* (done) part at a time, not as a systematic whole.

piecework *n.* work paid according to the quantity done.

pie chart *n.* a diagram representing quantities as sectors of a circle.

pied *adj.* particoloured.

pied-à-terre (pee-ayd a **tair**) *n.* (*pl.* **pieds-à-terre**) a small house for occasional use.

pie-eyed *adj. informal* drunk.

pier *n.* **1** a structure built out into the sea, used as a landing stage or a promenade. **2** a pillar supporting an arch or bridge.

pierce *v.* (of a sharp-pointed instrument) go into or through (something); make (a hole) in (something) in this way; force a way through.

piercing *adj.* **1** (of cold or wind) penetrating sharply. **2** (of sound) shrilly audible. □ **piercingly** *adv.*

piety *n.* being religious or reverent.

piffle *n. informal* nonsense.

pig *n.* **1** an omnivorous animal with cloven hooves and a blunt snout, domesticated for its meat. **2** *informal* a greedy or unpleasant person.

pigeon *n.* **1** a bird of the dove family. **2** *informal* a person's business or responsibility.

pigeon-hole *n.* a small compartment where mail can be left for someone; a similar compartment for documents in a desk. ● *v.* put (a document) in a pigeon-hole; assign to a category, esp. thoughtlessly.

piggery *n.* (*pl.* **-ies**) a pig-breeding establishment; a pigsty.

piggy *adj.* like a pig.

piggyback *n.* (also **pickaback**) a ride on a person's back.

piggy bank *n.* a money box shaped like a pig.

pig-headed *adj.* obstinate.

pig iron *n.* oblong blocks of crude iron from a smelting furnace.

piglet *n.* a young pig.

pigment *n.* colouring matter.

pigmy var. of **pygmy**.

pigsty *n.* (*pl.* **-ies**) a covered pen for pigs.

pigtail *n.* long hair worn in a plait at the back of the head.

pike *n.* **1** a spear with a long wooden shaft. **2** (*pl.* **pike**) a large voracious freshwater fish.

pilaf *n.* (also **pilaff, pilau**) a dish of rice with meat, spices, etc.

pilaster *n.* a rectangular usu. ornamental column.

pilchard *n.* a small sea fish.

pile *n.* **1** a number of things lying one on top of another; *informal* a large amount. **2** a large, imposing building. **3** a heavy beam driven vertically into the ground as a support for a building or bridge. **4** the surface of a carpet, velvet, etc., with many small projecting threads. **5** (**piles**) haemorrhoids. ● *v.* **1** lay (things) on top of one another. **2** get into or out of a vehicle in a disorganized group. ◻ **pile up** accumulate.

pile-up *n.* a collision of several vehicles.

pilfer *v.* steal (small items or in small quantities). ◻ **pilferer** *n.*

pilgrim *n.* a person who travels to a sacred place as an act of religious devotion. ◻ **pilgrimage** *n.*

pill *n.* a small piece of medicinal substance for swallowing whole; (**the pill**) a contraceptive pill.

pillage *n.* & *v.* plunder.

pillar *n.* a vertical structure used as a support or ornament.

pillar box *n.* a postbox.

pillbox *n.* **1** a small round hat. **2** a small concrete fort, partly underground.

pillion *n.* a passenger seat behind the driver of a motorcycle.

pillory *n.* (*pl.* **-ies**) *hist.* a wooden frame with holes for the head and hands, in which offenders were locked and exposed to public ridicule. ● *v.* (**pilloried, pillorying**) ridicule publicly.

pillow *n.* a cushion for supporting the head in bed. ● *v.* rest (one's head) as though on a pillow.

pilot *n.* **1** a person who operates an aircraft's flying controls; a person qualified to steer ships into or out of a harbour. **2** a television programme made to test audience reaction; an experimental project or scheme. ● *v.* (**piloted, piloting**) **1** act as pilot of (an aircraft or ship). **2** test (a project etc.).

pilot light *n.* **1** a small burning jet of gas which lights a larger burner. **2** an electric indicator light.

pimiento *n.* a sweet pepper.

pimp *n.* a man who finds clients for a prostitute or brothel.

pimple *n.* a small inflamed spot on the skin. ◻ **pimply** *adj.*

PIN *abbr.* personal identification number, a number for use with a cashcard machine.

pin *n.* **1** a short pointed piece of metal with a broadened head, used for fastening things together. **2** a peg or stake of wood or metal **3** (**pins**) *informal* legs. ● *v.* (**pinned, pinning**) fasten or attach with pins; hold (someone) so that they are unable to move. ◻ **pin down** force to be definite in a promise. **pin on** attach (blame) to someone. **pins and needles** a tingling sensation.

pinafore *n.* **1** an apron. **2** (in full **pinafore dress**) a sleeveless dress worn over a blouse or jumper.

pinball *n.* a game in which balls are propelled across a sloping board to strike targets.

pince-nez (panss-nay) *n.* spectacles that clip on to the nose.

pincers *n.pl.* a tool with pivoted jaws for gripping and pulling things; a claw-like part of a lobster etc.

pinch *v.* **1** squeeze between two surfaces, esp. between the finger and thumb. **2** *informal* steal. ● *n.* **1** an act of pinching. **2** a small amount. ◻ **at a pinch** if really necessary.

feel the pinch experience financial hardship.

pine[1] *n.* an evergreen tree with needle-shaped leaves.

pine[2] *v.* become ill and weak through grief; miss someone or something intensely.

pineapple *n.* a large juicy tropical fruit.

ping *n.* a short sharp ringing sound. ● *v.* make this sound.

pinger *n.* a device emitting short high-pitched sounds for detection, identification, or as a time signal.

ping-pong *n.* table tennis.

pinion *n.* **1** a bird's wing. **2** a small cogwheel. ● *v.* restrain by holding or binding the arms or legs.

pink *adj.* pale red. ● *n.* **1** a pink colour. **2** a garden plant with fragrant flowers. ● *v.* **1** cut a zigzag edge on (fabric); wound slightly with a sword etc. **2** (of an engine) make rattling sounds when running imperfectly. □ **in the pink** *informal* in very good health.

pinnacle *n.* a high pointed rock; a small ornamental turret; the highest point, the most successful moment.

pinpoint *v.* locate precisely.

pinstripe *n.* a very narrow stripe in cloth fabric. □ **pinstriped** *adj.*

pint *n.* a measure for liquids, one-eighth of a gallon (0.568 litre).

pin-up *n. informal* a poster of a famous or attractive person; such a person.

pioneer *n.* a person who is one of the first to explore a new region or subject. ● *v.* be the first to explore, use, or develop.

pious *adj.* devoutly religious; making a hypocritical display of virtue. □ **piously** *adv.*, **piousness** *n.*

pip *n.* **1** a small seed in fruit. **2** a star showing rank on an army officer's uniform. **3** a short high-pitched sound. ● *v.* (**pipped, pipping**) *informal* defeat by a small margin.

pipe *n.* **1** a tube through which something can flow. **2** a wind instrument; (**pipes**) bagpipes. **3** a narrow tube with a bowl at one end for smoking tobacco. ● *v.* **1** convey (water etc.) through pipe(s). **2** play (music) on a pipe. **3** utter in a shrill voice. □ **pipe down** *informal* be quiet. **piping hot** very hot.

pipe dream *n.* an unrealistic hope or scheme.

pipeline *n.* a long pipe for conveying petroleum etc. over a distance; a channel of supply or information. □ **in the pipeline** on the way, in preparation.

piper *n.* a player of pipes.

pipette *n.* a slender tube for transferring or measuring small amounts of liquid.

piquant (pee-kahnt) *adj.* pleasantly sharp in taste or smell; pleasantly ironic, mentally stimulating. □ **piquancy** *n.*

pique (peek) *n.* a feeling of hurt pride. ● *v.* **1** stimulate (curiosity etc.). **2** hurt the pride of.

piquet (pee-kay) *n.* a card game for two players.

piranha (pi-**rah**-nă, pir-**ahn**-yă) *n.* a fierce tropical American freshwater fish.

pirate *n.* **1** a person on a ship who robs another ship at sea or raids a coast. **2** one who infringes copyright or business rights, or broadcasts without authorization. ● *v.* reproduce (a book, video, etc.) without authorization. □ **piracy** *n.*, **piratical** *adj.*

pirouette (pi-roo-**et**) *v.* & *n.* (perform) a spin on one leg in ballet.

piss *vulgar slang v.* urinate. ● *n.* urine.

pissed *adj. Brit. vulgar slang* drunk.

pistachio (pis-**tash**-i-oh) *n.* (*pl.* **pistachios**) a type of nut.

piste (peest) *n.* a ski run.

pistil *n.* the seed-producing part of a flower.

pistol *n.* a small gun.

piston *n.* a sliding disc or cylinder inside a tube, esp. as part of an engine or pump.

pit *n.* **1** a hole in the ground; a coal mine; a sunken area. **2** a place where racing cars are refuelled etc. during a race. **3** the stone of a fruit. ● *v.* (**pitted, pitting**) **1** make pits or depressions in. **2** set against in competition. **3** remove stones from olives etc. ◻ **be the pits** *informal* be very bad or unpleasant.

pitch *n.* **1** an area of ground marked out for an outside game. **2** the degree of highness or lowness of a sound; the level of intensity of something. **3** the steepness of a slope. **4** a form of words used in trying to persuade someone to buy something. **5** a place where a street trader or performer is stationed. **6** an act of throwing. **7** a dark tarry substance. ● *v.* **1** throw; fall heavily. **2** set up (a tent). **3** set (one's voice, a piece of music) at a particular pitch; make suitable for a particular market, level of understanding, etc. **4** (of a ship) plunge forward and back alternately. **5** cause (a roof) to slope at a particular angle. **6** make a bid to obtain a contract. ◻ **pitch in** *informal* vigorously join in a task. **pitch into** *informal* attack; begin to deal with.

pitch-black, pitch-dark *adj.* completely black; with no light.

pitchblende *n.* a mineral ore (uranium oxide) yielding radium.

pitched battle *n.* a violent confrontation; a battle between large formations of troops.

pitcher *n.* **1** a baseball player who throws the ball to the batter. **2** a large usu. earthenware jug.

pitchfork *n.* a long-handled fork for lifting and tossing hay.

piteous *adj.* deserving or arousing pity. ◻ **piteously** *adv.*

pitfall *n.* an unsuspected danger or difficulty.

pith *n.* **1** spongy tissue in stems or fruits. **2** the essence of something. **3** concise expressive language.

pithy *adj.* (**pithier, pithiest**) **1** (of a plant) full of pith. **2** concise and expressive. ◻ **pithily** *adv.*, **pithiness** *n.*

pitiful *adj.* **1** deserving or arousing pity. **2** contemptibly small or inadequate. ◻ **pitifully** *adv.*

piton (**pee**-ton) *n.* a peg with a hole for a rope, used in rock-climbing.

pitta *n.* a flat bread, hollow inside.

pittance *n.* a very small allowance or wage.

pituitary gland *n.* a gland at the base of the brain, influencing bodily growth and functions.

pity *n.* (*pl.* **-ies**) a feeling of sorrow for another's suffering; a cause for regret: *what a pity you can't come.* ● *v.* (**pitied, pitying**) feel pity for. ◻ **take pity on** try to help, show compassion.

pivot *n.* a central point or shaft on which a thing turns or swings; someone or something with a crucial role. ● *v.* (**pivoted, pivoting**) turn on a pivot.

pivotal *adj.* **1** of a pivot. **2** vitally important.

pixel *n.* any of the minute illuminated areas making up the image on a VDU screen.

pixelate *v.* divide (an image) into pixels; display an image of (someone) as a number of pixels.

pixie *n.* (also **pixy**) a small supernatural being in fairy tales.

pizza *n.* a layer of dough baked with a savoury topping.

pizzeria *n.* a pizza restaurant.

pizzicato (pit-si-**kah**-toh) *adv.* plucking the strings of a violin etc. instead of using the bow.

pl. *abbr.* **1** plural. **2** (usu. **Pl.**) Place. **3** plate.

placard *n.* a poster or similar notice. ● *v.* put up placards on.

placate *v.* make less angry, soothe. ◻ **placatory** *adj.*

place *n.* **1** a particular portion of space or of an area; a particular town, district, building, etc. **2** a portion of space occupied by or available for someone; a person's rank; a position in a sequence; the behaviour appropriate to someone in a particular position: *not my place to argue.* ● *v.* **1** put in a particular position; find a home, job, etc. for; cause to be in a specified situation. **2** identify, classify. **3** make (an order for goods). ◻ **be placed** (in a race) be among the first three. **in place** established, in the correct position. **out of place** in the wrong position; inappropriate, incongruous. **take place** occur.

placebo (pla-see-boh) *n.* (*pl.* **placebos**) a substance with little or no physical effect, given to a patient for the psychological benefit of being given medicine.

placement *n.* putting someone or something in a place or home; posting someone temporarily in a workplace for experience.

placenta *n.* (*pl.* **placentae** or **placentas**) the organ in the womb that nourishes the foetus. ◻ **placental** *adj.*

place setting *n.* a set of dishes or cutlery for one person at a table.

placid *adj.* calm, not easily upset. ◻ **placidity** *n.*, **placidly** *adv.*

placket *n.* an opening in a garment for fastenings or access to a pocket.

plagiarize (pláy-jiă-ryz) *v.* (also **-ise**) take and use (another's writings etc.) as one's own. ◻ **plagiarism** *n.*, **plagiarist** *n.*

plague *n.* **1** a deadly contagious disease. **2** an infestation. ● *v.* cause continual trouble to; annoy, pester.

plaice *n.* (*pl.* **plaice**) an edible flatfish.

plaid (plad) *n.* cloth with a tartan pattern; a long piece of such cloth worn as part of Scottish Highland dress.

plain *adj.* **1** not elaborate or decorated, simple, ordinary; not patterned. **2** easy to perceive or understand; clear; frank, direct. **3** not beautiful or pretty. ● *adv.* clearly, directly; simply (used for emphasis): *plain wrong.* ● *n.* a large area of level country. ◻ **plainly** *adv.*, **plainness** *n.*

plain clothes *n.pl.* civilian clothes, not a uniform.

plain sailing *n.* an activity free from difficulties.

plainsong *n.* (also **plainchant**) medieval church music for voices, without regular rhythm.

plaintiff *n.* a person bringing an action in a court of law.

plaintive *adj.* sounding sad. ◻ **plaintively** *adv.*

plait (plat) *v.* weave (three or more strands) into one rope-like length. ● *n.* something plaited.

plan *n.* **1** an intention; a proposed means of achieving something. **2** a detailed diagram showing the relative positions of parts of a town etc. ● *v.* (**planned, planning**) **1** intend; work out the details of (an intended action). **2** draw a plan of. ◻ **planner** *n.*

plane *n.* **1** an aeroplane. **2** a level surface; a level of thought or development. **3** a tool for smoothing wood or metal by paring shavings from it. **4** a tall spreading tree with broad leaves. ● *v.* smooth or pare (wood or metal) with a plane. ● *adj.* level.

planet *n.* a celestial body orbiting round a star. ◻ **planetary** *adj.*

planetarium *n.* (*pl.* **planetaria** or **planetariums**) a room with a domed ceiling on which lights are projected to show the positions of the stars and planets.

plangent *adj.* **1** loud and resonant. **2** sad, mournful. ◻ **plangency** *n.*, **plangently** *adv.*

plank *n.* a long flat piece of timber.

plankton *n.* minute life forms floating in the sea, rivers, etc.

planning permission *n.* formal approval for construction of or changes to a building.

plant *n.* **1** a living organism such as a tree, grass, etc., with neither the power of movement nor special organs of digestion. **2** a factory; its machinery. **3** someone placed in a group as an informer; something placed in someone's belongings to incriminate them. ● *v.* place in soil for growing; place in position. □ **planter** *n.*

plantain *n.* **1** a tropical banana-like fruit. **2** a herb.

plantation *n.* an area planted with trees or cultivated plants; an estate on which cotton, tobacco, tea, etc. is cultivated.

planter *n.* **1** an owner or manager of a plantation. **2** a device for planting things. **3** a large container for plants.

plaque (plak, plahk) *n.* **1** a commemorative plate fixed on a wall. **2** a film forming on teeth, encouraging harmful bacteria.

plasma *n.* **1** the colourless fluid part of blood. **2** a kind of gas. □ **plasmic** *adj.*

plaster *n.* **1** a mixture of lime, sand, water, etc. used for coating walls. **2** a sticking plaster. ● *v.* cover with plaster; coat, daub. □ **plasterer** *n.*

plasterboard *n.* board with a core of plaster, for making partitions etc.

plastered *adj. informal* drunk.

plaster of Paris *n.* a white paste made from gypsum, for making moulds or casts.

plastic *n.* a synthetic substance that can be moulded to a permanent shape; *informal* credit cards or other plastic cards used to pay for things. ● *adj.* **1** made of plastic. **2** easily moulded. □ **plasticity** *n.*

plastic bullet *n.* a solid plastic cylinder fired as a riot-control device rather than to kill.

plasticine *n. trademark* a soft material for modelling.

plastic surgery *n.* the reconstruction or repair of parts of the body for medical or cosmetic reasons.

plate *n.* **1** an almost flat usu. circular utensil for holding food. **2** articles of gold, silver, or other metal. **3** a flat thin sheet of metal, glass, or other material. **4** an illustration on special paper in a book. **5** an orthodontic device. ● *v.* cover or coat with metal. □ **plateful** *n.*

plateau (plat-oh) *n.* (*pl.* **plateaux** or **plateaus**) **1** an area of level high ground. **2** a state of little change following rapid progress.

plate glass *n.* thick glass for windows etc.

platelet *n.* a small disc in the blood, involved in clotting.

platen (pla-těn) *n.* a plate in a printing press holding the paper against the type; the roller of a typewriter or printer.

platform *n.* a raised level surface or area, esp. for public speakers or performers; a raised structure beside a railway track at a station; the declared policy on which a political party bases its campaign.

platinum *n.* an element (symbol Pt), a silver-white metal that does not tarnish.

platinum blonde *n.* a woman with silvery-blonde hair.

platitude *n.* a commonplace remark. □ **platitudinous** *adj.*

platonic *adj.* involving affection but not sexual love.

platoon *n.* a subdivision of a military company.

platter *n.* a large plate for food.

platypus *n.* (*pl.* **platypuses**) an Australian animal with a duck-like beak which lays eggs but suckles its young.

plaudits *n.pl.* praise; applause.

plausible *adj.* seeming probable; persuasive but deceptive. □ **plausibility** *n.*, **plausibly** *adv.*

play *v.* **1** engage in activity for pleasure and relaxation rather than a practical purpose; take part in (a game or sport); compete against in a game; move (a piece) in a game. **2** act the part of. **3** perform on (a musical instrument); cause (a radio, recording, etc.) to produce sound. **4** move lightly and gently: *sunlight played on the ground.* ● *n.* **1** activity for relaxation and enjoyment; playing in a sports match. **2** action, operation: *luck comes into play.* **3** a dramatic work. **4** freedom of operation. □ **make a play for** *informal* attempt to attract or attain. **make play of** draw attention to ostentatiously. **play along** **1** perform a piece of music as it is being played on a record etc. **2** pretend to cooperate. **play at** do half-heartedly or frivolously. **play down** represent as unimportant. **play off** bring into conflict for one's own advantage. **play on** exploit (weakness etc.). **play safe** avoid risks. **play the game** behave honourably. **play up 1** *informal* cause pain or trouble; fail to work properly. **2** emphasize, represent as important. □ **player** *n.*

playboy *n.* a pleasure-loving usu. rich man.

playful *adj.* full of fun; for amusement, not serious. □ **playfully** *adv.*, **playfulness** *n.*

playgroup *n.* a group of pre-school children who play regularly together under supervision.

playhouse *n.* a theatre.

playing card *n.* one of a set of (usu. 52) pieces of card used in games.

playing field *n.* a field used for outdoor games.

playmate *n.* a child's companion in play.

playpen *n.* a portable enclosure for a young child to play in.

playwright *n.* a person who writes plays.

plaza *n.* a public square.

plc *abbr.* (also **PLC**) Public Limited Company.

plea *n.* **1** an earnest or emotional request. **2** an excuse. **3** a defendant's answer to a charge in a law court.

plead *v.* (**pleaded** (*Scot. & Amer.* **pled**), **pleading**) **1** give as one's plea; put forward (a case) in a law court. **2** make an appeal or entreaty. **3** put forward as an excuse.

pleasant *adj.* giving pleasure; having an agreeable manner. □ **pleasantly** *adv.*, **pleasantness** *n.*

pleasantry *n.* (*pl.* **-ies**) a friendly or humorous remark.

please *v.* **1** give pleasure to. **2** think fit, have the desire: *do as you please.* ● *adv.* a polite word of request. □ **please oneself** do as one chooses.

pleased *adj.* feeling or showing pleasure or satisfaction.

pleasurable *adj.* causing pleasure. □ **pleasurably** *adv.*

pleasure *n.* a feeling of satisfaction, enjoyment, or joy; a source of this. □ **at one's pleasure** whenever one wishes.

pleat *n.* a flat fold of cloth. ● *v.* make a pleat or pleats in.

pleb *n. informal* a rough uncultured person.

plebeian *adj.* of the lower social classes; uncultured, vulgar.

plebiscite (**pleb**-i-syt) *n.* a referendum.

plectrum *n.* (*pl.* **plectrums** or **plectra**) a small piece of plastic etc. for plucking the strings of a musical instrument.

pledge *n.* a solemn promise; something deposited as a guarantee that a debt will be paid etc.; a token of something. ● *v.* commit by a promise; give as a pledge.

plenary (**pleen**-ări) *adj.* entire; attended by all members.

plenipotentiary *adj.* & *n.* (*pl.* **-ies**) (an envoy) with full powers to take action.

plenitude *n.* abundance; completeness.

plentiful *adj.* existing in large amounts. □ **plentifully** *adv.*

plenty *pron.* enough or more than enough. ● *n.* a situation where necessities are available in large quantities. ● *adv.* fully, plentifully. □ **plenteous** *adj.*, **plenteousness** *n.*

plethora (**ple**-thŏ-ră) *n.* an oversupply or excess.

pleurisy *n.* inflammation of the membrane round the lungs.

pliable *adj.* flexible; easily influenced. □ **pliability** *n.*

pliant *adj.* pliable. □ **pliancy** *n.*

pliers *n.pl.* pincers with flat surfaces for gripping things.

plight *n.* a predicament.

plimsoll *n.* a canvas sports shoe.

Plimsoll line *n.* a mark on a ship's side showing the legal water level when loaded.

plinth *n.* a slab forming the base of a column or statue etc.

plod *v.* (**plodded, plodding**) walk doggedly, trudge; work slowly but steadily. □ **plodder** *n.*

plonk *informal n.* cheap or inferior wine. ● *v.* set down heavily or carelessly.

plop *n.* a sound like something small dropping into water with no splash.

plot *n.* **1** a conspiracy, a secret plan. **2** the story in a play, novel, or film. **3** a small piece of land. ● *v.* (**plotted, plotting**) **1** secretly plan (an illegal action). **2** make a map of, mark (a route) on a map. □ **plotter** *n.*

plough (plow) *n.* (*Amer.* **plow**) an implement for cutting furrows in soil and turning it up. ● *v.* **1** cut or turn up (soil etc.) with a plough. **2** make one's way laboriously. □ **ploughman** *n.*

ploy *n.* a cunning manoeuvre.

pluck *v.* pull at or out or off; pick (a flower etc.); strip (a bird) of its feathers. ● *n.* **1** a plucking movement. **2** courage.

plucky *adj.* (**pluckier, pluckiest**) brave, spirited. □ **pluckily** *adv.*

plug *n.* **1** something fitting into and stopping or filling a hole or cavity. **2** a device for making an electrical connection, consisting of an insulated casing with metal pins that fit into a socket. ● *v.* (**plugged, plugging**) **1** block or fill with a plug. **2** *informal* work steadily and laboriously. **3** *informal* promote (a product) by mentioning it publicly. □ **plug in** connect electrically by putting a plug into a socket.

plum *n.* **1** a fruit with sweet pulp round a pointed stone. **2** reddish purple. **3** *informal* something desirable, the best.

plumage *n.* a bird's feathers.

plumb (plum) *n.* a lead weight hung on a cord (**plumb line**), used for testing depths or verticality. ● *adv.* exactly; (*Amer.*) completely. ● *v.* **1** measure or test with a plumb line; reach (depths); get to the bottom of. **2** work or fit (things) as a plumber.

plumber (**plum**-er) *n.* a person who fits and repairs plumbing.

plumbing (**plum**-ing) *n.* a system of water and drainage pipes etc. in a building.

plume *n.* a feather, esp. as an ornament; something resembling this. □ **plumed** *adj.*

plummet *v.* (**plummeted, plummeting**) fall steeply or rapidly.

plump *adj.* having a full rounded shape. ● *v.* **1** make or become plump. **2** put down heavily. □ **plump for** choose, decide on. □ **plumpness** *n.*

plunder *v.* rob. ● *n.* plundering; goods etc. stolen.

plunge *v.* **1** jump or dive; fall suddenly; decrease rapidly. **2** push or go forcefully into something. ● *n.* plunging, a dive.

plunger *n.* a device that works with a plunging movement.

pluperfect *adj.* *Grammar* of the tense used to denote action completed before some past point of time, e.g. *we had arrived.*

plural *n.* the form of a noun or verb used in referring to more than one person or thing. ● *adj.* of this form; of more than one. □ **plurality** *n.*

plus *prep.* **1** with the addition of. **2** (of temperature) above zero. ● *adj.* **1** more than zero. **2** more than the amount indicated: *twenty plus.* ● *n.* **1** the sign (+). **2** an advantage.

■ **Usage** The use of *plus* as a conjunction, as in *they arrived late, plus they wanted a meal,* is considered incorrect except in very informal use.

---

plush *n.* cloth with a long soft nap. ● *adj.* **1** made of plush. **2** *informal* luxurious.

plushy *adj.* (**plushier, plushiest**) *informal* luxurious.

plutocracy *n.* government or control by the wealthy. ▫ **plutocrat** *n.*, **plutocratic** *adj.*

plutonium *n.* a chemical element (symbol Pu), a radioactive substance used in nuclear weapons and reactors.

pluvial (ploo-vi-ăl) *adj.* of or caused by rain.

ply[1] *n.* (*pl.* **plies**) **1** a thickness or layer of wood, cloth, etc. **2** plywood.

ply[2] *v.* (**plied, plying**) **1** use or wield (a tool etc.); work at (a trade). **2** travel regularly over a route for commercial purposes. **3** continually offer food etc. to.

plywood *n.* board made by gluing layers with the grain crosswise.

PM *abbr.* **1** Prime Minister. **2** postmortem.

Pm *symb.* promethium.

p.m. *abbr.* (Latin *post meridiem*) after noon.

PMS *abbr.* premenstrual syndrome.

PMT *abbr.* premenstrual tension.

pneumatic (new-**ma**-tik) *adj.* filled with or operated by compressed air. ▫ **pneumatically** *adv.*

pneumonia (new-**moh**-niă) *n.* inflammation of the lungs.

PO *abbr.* **1** Post Office. **2** postal order.

Po *symb.* polonium.

poach *v.* **1** cook (an egg without its shell) in or over boiling water; simmer in a small amount of liquid. **2** take (game or fish) illegally; trespass, encroach. ▫ **poacher** *n.*

pocket *n.* **1** a small bag-like part on a garment; a pouch-like compartment. **2** an isolated group or area. ● *adj.* small enough to carry in one's pocket. ● *v.* **1** put into one's pocket. **2** take dishonestly. ▫ **in** or **out of pocket** having made a profit or loss. ▫ **pocketful** *n.*

pocketbook *n.* **1** a notebook. **2** a small folding case for money or papers.

pocket money *n.* money for small personal expenses; money given regularly to children.

pock-marked *adj.* marked by scars or pits.

poco *adv. Music* a little, rather.

pod *n.* a long narrow seed case.

podgy *adj.* (**podgier, podgiest**) *informal* short and fat.

podium *n.* (*pl.* **podiums** or **podia**) a pedestal or platform.

poem *n.* a piece of creative writing expressing feelings etc. through diction, imagery, and sometimes rhyme and metre.

poet *n.* a person who writes poems.

poetic *adj.* (also **poetical**) of or like poetry. ▫ **poetically** *adv.*

poetry *n.* **1** poems; a poet's work. **2** a quality that pleases the mind in a poetic way.

po-faced *adj. informal* solemn.

pogrom *n.* an organized massacre.

poignant *adj.* evoking a keen sense of sadness. ▫ **poignancy** *n.*, **poignantly** *adv.*

poinsettia (pwahn-**set**-i-ă) *n.* a plant with large scarlet or cream bracts.

point *n.* **1** a tapered, sharp end; a tip. **2** a particular place or moment. **3** a single item in a discussion; an argument; a feature or characteristic: *her good points.* **4** advantage, purpose, reason to do something. **5** a unit of scoring. **6** a dot or other punctuation mark. **7** a promontory. **8** an electrical socket. **9** a movable rail for directing a train from one line to another. ● *v.* **1** direct, aim (a weapon, finger, etc.); direct or attract attention in this way; have a particular direction: *pointing north*; indicate a route etc.; emphasize: *point a moral.* **2** fill in (joints of brickwork) with mortar. ▫ **beside the point** irrelevant. **make a point of** take special care to do. **on the point of** about to do. **point out**

direct attention to. **point up** emphasize. **to the point** relevant.

point-blank *adj.* & *adv.* **1** at very close range. **2** without evasion or qualification; blunt and direct.

point duty *n.* traffic control by a policeman at a road junction.

pointed *adj.* **1** tapering to a point. **2** (of a remark or manner) expressing criticism clearly. □ **pointedly** *adv.*

pointer *n.* a thing that points to something; a dog that faces stiffly towards game which it scents.

pointing *n.* the mortar around the edges of bricks in a wall.

pointless *adj.* having no purpose or meaning. □ **pointlessly** *adv.*

point of view *n.* a way of considering an issue.

poise *n.* graceful bearing; self-assurance and dignity. ● *v.* be or cause to be balanced.

poison *n.* a substance that can destroy life or harm health. ● *v.* give poison to; put poison on or in; corrupt, fill with prejudice. □ **poisoner** *n.*, **poisonous** *adj.*

poison pen letter *n.* a malicious unsigned letter.

poke *v.* **1** prod with one's finger, a stick, etc.; push forward or into something. **2** search, pry. □ **poke fun at** ridicule.

poker *n.* **1** a stiff metal rod for stirring up a fire. **2** a gambling card game.

poker-face *n.* an expression concealing one's thoughts or feelings.

poky *adj.* (**pokier, pokiest**) small and cramped. □ **pokiness** *n.*

polar *adj.* **1** of or near the North or South Pole. **2** of magnetic or electrical poles. **3** (of opposites) extreme, absolute.

polar bear *n.* a white bear of Arctic regions.

polarize *v.* (also **-ise**) **1** confine similar vibrations of (light waves) to one direction or plane. **2** give magnetic poles to. **3** set at opposite extremes of opinion. □ **polarization** *n.*

Polaroid *n. trademark* **1** a material that polarizes light passing through it, used in sunglasses. **2** a camera that prints a photograph as soon as it is taken.

Pole *n.* a Polish person.

pole *n.* **1** a long rod or post. **2** the north (**North Pole**) or south (**South Pole**) end of the earth's axis. **3** one of the opposite ends of a magnet or terminals of an electric cell or battery. ● *v.* push along using a long rod. □ **poles apart** having nothing in common.

polecat *n.* a small animal of the weasel family; (*Amer.*) a skunk.

polemic *n.* a verbal attack on a belief or opinion. □ **polemical** *adj.*

polenta *n.* porridge made from maize meal.

pole position *n.* the most favourable starting position in a motor race.

pole star *n.* a star near the North Pole in the sky.

police *n.* a civil force responsible for keeping public order. ● *v.* keep order in (a place) by means of police.

policeman *n.* (*pl.* **-men**) a male member of the police force.

police state *n.* a country where political police supervise and control citizens' activities.

policewoman *n.* (*pl.* **-women**) a female member of the police force.

policy *n.* (*pl.* **-ies**) **1** a general plan of action. **2** an insurance contract.

polio *n.* poliomyelitis.

poliomyelitis *n.* an infectious disease causing temporary or permanent paralysis.

Polish *adj.* & *n.* (the language) of Poland.

polish *v.* make smooth and shiny by rubbing; refine, perfect. ● *n.* shininess; a substance for rubbing surfaces to make them shine; practised ease and elegance. □ **polish off** finish off. □ **polisher** *n.*

polished *adj.* (of manner or performance) elegant, perfected.

polite *adj.* having good manners, socially correct; refined. □ **politely** *adv.*, **politeness** *n.*

politic *adj.* showing good judgement.

political *adj.* of the government and public affairs of a country; of or promoting a particular party. □ **politically** *adv.*

political correctness *n.* avoidance of any expressions or behaviour that may be considered discriminatory.

politician *n.* an MP or other political representative.

politics *n.* the science and art of government; political affairs or life; (as *pl.*) political principles.

polity *n.* (*pl.* **-ies**) a form of civil government; a society.

polka *n.* a lively dance for couples.

poll *n.* **1** the votes cast in an election; a place for this. **2** an estimate of public opinion made by questioning people. ● *v.* record the opinions or votes of; receive a specified number of votes.

pollard *v.* cut off the top and branches of (a tree) to produce a close head of young branches. ● *n.* a pollarded tree.

pollen *n.* a fertilizing powder produced by flowers.

pollen count *n.* a measurement of the amount of pollen in the air.

pollinate *v.* fertilize with pollen. □ **pollination** *n.*

pollster *n.* a person conducting an opinion poll.

poll tax *n.* (*hist.*) a tax on each member of the population.

pollute *v.* make dirty or impure; corrupt. □ **pollutant** *n.*, **pollution** *n.*

polo *n.* a game like hockey played by teams on horseback.

polo neck *n.* a high turned-over collar on a jersey etc.

polonium *n.* a radioactive metallic element (symbol Po).

poltergeist *n.* a spirit believed to throw things about noisily.

polyandry *n.* a system of having more than one husband at a time.

polychrome *adj.* multicoloured. □ **polychromatic** *adj.*

polyester *n.* a synthetic resin or fibre.

polyethylene *n.* = **polythene**.

polygamy *n.* a system of having more than one wife or husband at a time. □ **polygamist** *n.*, **polygamous** *adj.*

polyglot *adj.* & *n.* (a person) knowing several languages.

polygon *n.* a geometric figure with many sides. □ **polygonal** *adj.*

polygraph *n.* a machine reading the pulse rate etc. used as a lie detector.

polyhedron *n.* (*pl.* **polyhedra** or **polyhedrons**) a solid with many sides. □ **polyhedral** *adj.*

polymath *n.* a person with knowledge of many subjects. □ **polymathy** *n.*

polymer *n.* a compound whose molecule is formed from a large number of simple molecules.

polymerize *v.* (also **-ise**) (cause to) combine into a polymer. □ **polymerization** *n.*

polynomial *adj.* consisting of three or more terms.

polyp *n.* **1** a simple organism with a tube-shaped body. **2** an abnormal growth projecting from a mucous membrane.

polyphony *n.* (*pl.* **-ies**) combination of melodies; a composition in this style. □ **polyphonal** *adj.*

polystyrene *n.* a synthetic resin, a polymer of styrene.

polytechnic *n.* a college offering courses up to degree level.

polytheism *n.* belief in or worship of more than one god. □ **polytheist** *n.*, **polytheistic** *adj.*

polythene *n.* (also **polyethylene**) a tough light plastic.

polyunsaturated *adj.* (of fat) not associated with the formation of cholesterol in the blood.

polyurethane *n.* a synthetic resin used in paint etc.

pomander *n.* a ball of mixed sweet-smelling substances.

pomegranate *n.* a tropical fruit with many seeds.

pommel (pum-ĕl) *n.* a knob on the hilt of a sword; an upward projection on a saddle.

pomp *n.* stately and splendid ceremonial.

pompom *n.* (also **pompon**) a small woollen ball as a decoration on a hat.

pompous *adj.* full of ostentatious dignity and self-importance. ▫ **pomposity** *n.*, **pompously** *adv.*

ponce *n.* **1** a pimp. **2** *offensive* a homosexual or effeminate man.

poncho *n.* (*pl.* **ponchos**) a cloak like a blanket with a hole for the head.

pond *n.* a small area of still water.

ponder *v.* be deep in thought; think over.

ponderous *adj.* heavy, unwieldy; laborious. ▫ **ponderously** *adv.*

pong *n.* & *v. informal* stink.

pontiff *n.* the Pope.

pontificate *v.* speak pompously and at length.

pontoon *n.* **1** a flat-bottomed boat supporting a temporary bridge; such a bridge. **2** a card game.

pontoon bridge *n.* a temporary bridge supported on pontoons.

pony *n.* (*pl.* **-ies**) a horse of any small breed.

ponytail *n.* long hair drawn back and tied to hang down.

poodle *n.* a dog with thick curly hair.

poof *n.* (also **poofter**) *informal, offensive* a homosexual or effeminate man.

pooh *int.* an exclamation of contempt.

pooh-pooh *v.* dismiss (a subject) scornfully.

pool *n.* **1** a small area of still water; a puddle; a swimming pool. **2** a shared fund or supply. **3** a game resembling snooker. **4** (**the pools**) football pools. ● *v.* put into a common fund or supply; share.

poop *n.* a ship's stern; a raised deck at the stern.

pooper scooper *n.* a device for clearing up dog faeces.

poor *adj.* **1** having little money or means. **2** not of high quality or standard. **3** deserving sympathy. ▫ **poorness** *n.*

poorly *adv.* in a poor way, badly. ● *adj.* unwell.

pop *n.* **1** a small explosive sound. **2** a fizzy drink. **3** pop music. ● *v.* (**popped, popping**) **1** make a sharp explosive sound; burst with this sound. **2** go or put something somewhere quickly. ● *adj.* of popular music or culture; made intelligible and accessible to the general public.

popadam var. of **poppadom**.

popcorn *n.* maize heated to burst and form puffy balls.

Pope *n.* the head of the Roman Catholic Church.

poplar *n.* a tall slender tree.

poplin *n.* a plain woven usu. cotton fabric.

pop music *n.* modern music appealing to young people.

poppadom *n.* (also **popadam, poppadam**) a large thin crisp savoury Indian bread.

popper *n. informal* a press stud.

poppy *n.* (*pl.* **-ies**) a plant with bright flowers on tall stems.

poppycock *n. informal* nonsense.

populace *n.* the general public.

popular *adj.* liked, enjoyed, or used by many people; of or for the general public. ▫ **popularity** *n.*, **popularly** *adv.*

popularize *v.* (also **-ise**) **1** make generally liked. **2** present in an accessible non-technical form.

populate *v.* fill with a population.

population *n.* the inhabitants of an area.

populous *adj.* thickly populated.

porcelain *n.* fine china.

porch *n.* a roofed shelter over the entrance of a building.

porcine *adj.* of or like a pig.

porcupine *n.* an animal covered with protective spines.

pore *n.* a tiny opening on skin or on a leaf, for giving off or taking in moisture. □ **pore over** study closely.

pork *n.* unsalted pig meat.

porn *n. informal* pornography.

pornography *n.* writings or pictures intended to stimulate erotic feelings by portraying sexual activity. □ **pornographer** *n.*, **pornographic** *adj.*

porous *adj.* letting through fluid or air. □ **porosity** *n.*

porpoise *n.* a small whale.

porridge *n.* a food made by boiling oatmeal or other cereal in water or milk.

port *n.* **1** a harbour; a town with a harbour. **2** an opening for loading a ship, firing a gun from a tank or ship, etc.; a socket in a computer network into which a device can be plugged. **3** the lefthand side of a ship or aircraft. **4** strong sweet wine.

portable *adj.* able to be carried. □ **portability** *n.*

Portakabin *n. trademark* a small portable building.

portal *n.* a door or entrance, esp. an imposing one.

portcullis *n.* a vertical grating lowered to block the gateway to a castle.

portend *v.* foreshadow.

portent *n.* an omen, a sign of a future event. □ **portentous** *adj.*

porter *n.* **1** a person employed to carry luggage or goods. **2** a doorkeeper of a large building. **3** a dark beer.

portfolio *n.* (*pl.* **portfolios**) **1** a case for loose sheets of paper. **2** a set of investments. **3** the area for which a Minister of State is responsible.

porthole *n.* a window in the side of a ship or aircraft.

portico *n.* (*pl.* **porticoes** or **porticos**) a roof supported by columns forming a porch or similar structure.

portion *n.* a part, a share; an amount of food for one person. ● *v.* divide; distribute portions of.

portly *adj.* (**portlier, portliest**) stout. □ **portliness** *n.*

portmanteau (port-man-toh) *n.* (*pl.* **portmanteaus** or **portmanteaux**) a travelling bag opening into two equal parts. ● *adj.* combining two or more separable elements, meanings, etc.

portrait *n.* a picture of a person or animal; a description.

portray *v.* make a picture of; describe; represent in a play etc. □ **portrayal** *n.*

Portuguese *adj.* & *n.* (a native, the language) of Portugal.

Portuguese man-of-war *n.* a jellyfish.

pose *v.* **1** constitute or present (a problem). **2** adopt or place in a particular position, esp. to be painted, photographed, etc.; pretend to be someone or something. ● *n.* an attitude in which someone is posed; a pretence.

poser *n.* **1** a puzzling problem. **2** a poseur.

poseur (poh-zer) *n.* a person who behaves affectedly.

posh *adj. informal* very smart, luxurious.

posit *v.* assume, esp. as the basis of an argument.

position *n.* **1** a place occupied by or intended for a person or thing. **2** a way in which someone or something stands, is arranged, etc. **3** a situation, a set of circumstances; a person's status; a job. **4** a point of view, an opinion about an issue. ● *v.* place, arrange. □ **positional** *adj.*

positive *adj.* **1** characterized by the presence of a quality rather than its absence; (of an utterance) affirmative, asserting; (of the results of a test) showing what was tested for to be present. **2** constructive, encouraging. **3** definite, not allowing doubt; convinced. **4** (of a battery terminal) through which electric current enters. **5** (of a photograph) showing lights and shades true to the original, not reversed. **6** (of a quantity) greater than zero. ● *n.* a positive quality, quantity, or photograph. □ **positively** *adv.*

positive discrimination *n.* the policy of favouring members of groups often discriminated against when appointing to jobs etc.

positive pole *n.* the north-seeking pole of a magnet.

positive vetting *n.* an intensive enquiry into the background of an applicant for a job relating to security.

positron *n.* a particle with a positive electric charge.

posse (poss-ee) *n. informal* a group or gang; *hist.* a body of law enforcers.

possess *v.* **1** own; hold as belonging to oneself. **2** dominate the mind of. □ **possessor** *n.*

possession *n.* owning; something owned; being controlled by an evil spirit. □ **take possession of** become the possessor of.

possessive *adj.* **1** jealously guarding one's possessions; demanding someone's total attention. **2** *Grammar* indicating possession. □ **possessively** *adv.*, **possessiveness** *n.*

possessive pronoun *see* **pronoun**.

possible *adj.* capable of existing, happening, being done, etc. □ **possibility** *n.*, **possibly** *adv.*

possum *n. informal* an opossum. □ **play possum** pretend to be asleep; feign ignorance.

post *n.* **1** the official conveyance of letters etc.; the letters etc. conveyed. **2** a piece of timber, metal, etc. set upright to support or mark something. **3** a place of duty; a job; an outpost of soldiers; a trading station. ● *v.* **1** send (letters etc.) by post. **2** put up (a notice); announce in this way. **3** send (someone) to take up employment in a particular place. □ **keep me posted** keep me informed.

post- *pref.* after.

postage *n.* a charge for sending something by post.

postal *adj.* of the post; by post.

postbox *n.* a box into which letters are put for sending by post.

postcard *n.* a card for sending messages by post without an envelope.

postcode *n.* a group of letters and figures in a postal address to assist sorting.

post-date *v.* **1** put a date on (a cheque etc.) that is later than the actual date. **2** occur later than.

poster *n.* a large picture or notice used for decoration or for announcing or advertising something.

poste restante (pohst rest-**ahnt**) *n.* a post office department where letters are kept until called for.

posterior *adj.* situated behind or at the back. ● *n.* the buttocks.

posterity *n.* future generations.

postern *n.* a small back or side entrance to a fortress etc.

postgraduate *n.* a student studying for a higher degree.

post-haste *adv.* with great speed.

posthumous *adj.* happening, awarded, published, etc. after a person's death. □ **posthumously** *adv.*

postman *n.* (*pl.* **-men**) a person who delivers or collects letters etc.

postmark *n.* an official mark stamped on something sent by post, giving place and date of marking. ● *v.* mark with this.

postmaster *n.* a male official in charge of a post office.

postmistress *n.* a female official in charge of a post office.

post-mortem *n.* an examination of a body to determine the cause of death; an analysis of something that has happened.

post-natal *adj.* after childbirth.

post office *n.* a building where postal business is carried on.

postpone *v.* cause (an event) to take place later than was originally planned. □ **postponement** *n.*

postprandial *adj. formal* after lunch or dinner.

postscript *n.* an additional paragraph at the end of a letter etc.

post-traumatic stress disorder (or **syndrome**) *n.* symptoms that typically occur after exposure to a stressful situation.

postulant *n.* a candidate for admission to a religious order.

postulate *v.* assume to be true as a basis for reasoning. □ **postulation** *n.*

posture *n.* the way a person stands, walks, etc. ● *v.* assume a posture, esp. for effect. □ **postural** *adj.*

posy *n.* (*pl.* **-ies**) a small bunch of flowers.

pot *n.* **1** a container for holding liquids or solids, or for cooking in. **2** *informal* cannabis. ● *v.* (**potted, potting**) **1** plant in a flowerpot. **2** preserve (food) in a pot. **3** send (a ball in billiards or snooker) into a pocket. □ **go to pot** *informal* deteriorate.

potable *adj. formal* drinkable.

potash *n.* potassium carbonate.

potassium *n.* a soft silvery-white metallic element (symbol K).

potation *n. archaic* drinking; a drink.

potato *n.* (*pl.* **potatoes**) a plant with starchy tubers used as food; one of these tubers.

pot belly *n.* (*pl.* **-ies**) a large protuberant belly.

potboiler *n. informal* a book, painting, etc. produced merely to make money.

poteen (poch-**een**) *n.* illegally distilled whisky.

potent *adj.* **1** having great natural power; having a strong effect. **2** (of a male) capable of sexual intercourse. □ **potency** *n.*, **potently** *adv.*

potentate *n.* a monarch or ruler.

potential *adj.* capable of being developed or used. ● *n.* an ability or capacity for development. □ **potentiality** *n.*, **potentially** *adv.*

pothole *n.* a hole formed underground by the action of water; a hole in a road surface.

potholing *n.* caving. □ **potholer** *n.*

pot luck *n.* □ **take pot luck** accept whatever is available.

potion *n.* a liquid medicine or drug.

pot-pourri (poh **poor**-ee) *n.* a scented mixture of dried petals and spices; a medley or mixture.

pot roast *n.* a piece of meat cooked slowly in a covered dish.

potsherd *n.* a broken piece of earthenware.

potshot *n.* a shot aimed casually.

potted past & p.p. of **pot**. ● *adj.* **1** preserved in a pot. **2** abridged.

potter[1] *n.* a maker of pottery.

potter[2] *v.* (*Amer.* **putter**) work on trivial tasks in a leisurely way.

pottery *n.* (*pl.* **-ies**) containers and other objects made of baked clay; a potter's work or workshop.

potty *informal adj.* (**pottier, pottiest**) **1** mad, stupid. **2** trivial, negligible. ● *n.* (*pl.* **-ies**) a chamber pot, esp. for a child.

pouch *n.* a small bag or bag-like formation.

pouffe (poof) *n.* a padded stool.

poult (pohlt) *n.* a young domestic fowl or game bird.

poulterer *n.* a dealer in poultry.

poultice (**pohlt**-is) *n.* a moist usu. hot dressing applied to inflammation.

poultry *n.* domestic fowls.

pounce *v.* swoop down and grasp or attack. ● *n.* a pouncing movement.

pound[1] *n.* **1** a measure of weight, 16 oz. avoirdupois (0.454 kg) or 12 oz. troy (0.373 kg). **2** a unit of money in Britain and certain other countries.

pound[2] *n.* an enclosure where stray animals, or vehicles officially removed, are kept until claimed.

pound[3] *v.* beat or crush with repeated heavy strokes; (of the heart) beat loudly; run heavily.

poundage *n.* a charge or commission per £ or per pound weight.

pour *v.* flow, cause to flow; rain heavily; come, go, or send in large quantities.

pout *v.* push out one's lips. ● *n.* a pouting expression.

poverty *n.* **1** lack of money and resources; scarcity. **2** inferiority.

POW *abbr.* prisoner of war.

powder *n.* a mass of fine dry particles; a medicine or cosmetic in this form; gunpowder. ● *v.* cover or sprinkle with powder. □ **powdery** *adj.*

powder room *n.* a ladies' lavatory.

power *n.* **1** the ability to do something. **2** vigour, strength. **3** control, influence, authority; an influential person or country etc. **4** a product of a number multiplied by itself a given number of times. **5** mechanical or electrical energy; the electricity supply. ● *v.* supply with mechanical or electrical power.

power dressing *n.* a style of dress for work intended to convey an impression of influence and efficiency.

powerful *adj.* having great power or influence. □ **powerfully** *adv.*

powerless *adj.* without power to take action, wholly unable.

power of attorney *n.* legal authority to act for another person.

power station *n.* a building where electricity is generated for distribution.

pp *abbr. Music* pianissimo.

pp. *abbr.* pages.

p.p. *abbr.* through the agency of, by proxy (indicating that a person is signing on behalf of another, e.g. 'T. Jones, p.p. P. Smith', meaning that P. Smith is signing on behalf of T. Jones).

PPS *abbr.* **1** Parliamentary Private Secretary. **2** post-postscript, an additional postscript.

PR *abbr.* **1** public relations. **2** proportional representation.

Pr *symb.* praseodymium.

practicable *adj.* able to be done. □ **practicability** *n.*

practical *adj.* **1** involving activity rather than study or theory. **2** suitable for use rather than decorative; sensible in approaching problems, doing things, etc. **3** almost, so nearly as to be accepted as being (something specified): *a practical certainty.* □ **practicality** *n.*

practical joke *n.* a humorous trick played on a person.

practically *adv.* **1** in a practical way. **2** virtually, almost.

practice *n.* **1** repeated exercise to improve skill. **2** action as opposed to theory. **3** a custom or habit. **4** a doctor's or lawyer's business. □ **in practice 1** in fact as opposed to wish or theory. **2** skilled through having practised. **out of practice** not having practised for a while.

practise *v.* (*Amer.* **practice**) **1** do something repeatedly or habitually. **2** (of a doctor or lawyer) perform professional work.

practised *adj.* (*Amer.* **practiced**) experienced; expert.

practitioner *n.* a professional worker, esp. in medicine.

praesidium var. of **presidium**.

pragmatic *adj.* treating things from a practical point of view. □ **pragmatically** *adv.*, **pragmatism** *n.*, **pragmatist** *n.*

prairie *n.* a large treeless area of grassland, esp. in North America.

prairie dog *n.* a North American rodent that lives in burrows.

praise *v.* express approval or admiration of; honour (God) in words. ● *n.* praising; approval expressed in words.

praiseworthy *adj.* deserving praise.

praline *n.* a sweet substance made by crushing sweetened nuts.

pram *n.* a four-wheeled conveyance for a baby.

prance *v.* move springily.

prang *v. informal* crash (a vehicle).

prank *n.* a piece of mischief.

prankster *n.* a person playing pranks.

praseodymium (pray-zi-o-**dI**-mi-ŭm) *n.* a metallic element (symbol Pr).

prat *n. informal* a fool.

prattle *v.* chatter in a childish way. ● *n.* childish chatter.

prawn *n.* an edible shellfish like a large shrimp.

pray *v.* say prayers; entreat.

prayer *n.* a solemn request or thanksgiving to God; an act of praying; an entreaty.

pre- *pref.* before; beforehand.

preach *v.* deliver a sermon; proclaim or teach (a religious belief); advocate (a course of action); talk in an annoyingly moralizing way. ▫ **preacher** *n.*

preamble *n.* a preliminary statement, an introductory section.

pre-arrange *v.* arrange beforehand. ▫ **pre-arrangement** *n.*

precarious *adj.* unsafe, not secure. ▫ **precariously** *adv.*, **precariousness** *n.*

precast *adj.* (of concrete) cast in shape before use.

precaution *n.* something done in advance to avoid a risk. ▫ **precautionary** *adj.*

precede *v.* come or go before in time, order, etc.

■ **Usage** Do not confuse *precede* and *proceed*.

precedence *n.* being more important than someone or something else.

precedent *n.* a previous case serving as an example to be followed.

precept *n.* a command or rule of conduct.

precinct *n.* **1** an area within a set of boundaries; a defined area round a cathedral etc. **2** an area closed to traffic in a town.

precious *adj.* **1** of great value; beloved. **2** affectedly refined.

precipice *n.* a very steep face of a cliff or rock.

precipitate *v.* (pri-**sip**-i-tayt) **1** cause to happen suddenly or prematurely; cause to move suddenly and uncontrollably. **2** cause (a substance) to be deposited. **3** condense (vapour) into drops falling as rain etc. ● *adj.* (pri-**sip**-i-tăt) rash, hasty. ● *n.* (pri-**sip**-i-tăt) a substance deposited from a solution. ▫ **precipitately** *adv.*

precipitation *n.* **1** rain or snow. **2** precipitating; being precipitated.

precipitous *adj.* very steep.

précis (pray-see) *n.* (*pl.* **précis**) a summary. ● *v.* make a précis of.

precise *adj.* exact, accurate over details. ▫ **precisely** *adv.*, **precision** *n.*

preclude *v.* exclude the possibility of, prevent.

precocious *adj.* having developed earlier than is usual. ▫ **precociously** *adv.*

precognition *n.* foreknowledge, esp. supernatural.

preconceived *adj.* (of an idea) formed beforehand. ▫ **preconception** *n.*

precondition *n.* a condition that must be fulfilled beforehand.

precursor *n.* a forerunner.

pre-date *v.* exist or occur at an earlier time than.

predator *n.* a predatory animal.

predatory (**pred**-ă-ter-i) *adj.* preying on others.

predecease *v.* die earlier than (another person).

predecessor *n.* a person who held an office, position, etc. before one.

predestination *n.* the doctrine that everything has been determined in advance.

predicament *n.* a difficult situation.

predicate (pre-di-kăt) *n. Grammar* the part of a sentence that says something about the subject (e.g. 'is short' in *life is short*). □ **predicative** *adj.*

predict *v.* foretell. □ **predictable** *adj.*, **predictably** *adv.*, **prediction** *n.*, **predictor** *n.*

predictive *adj.* foretelling or foreshowing something.

predilection *n.* a special liking.

predispose *v.* make liable or inclined to a particular attitude, action, etc. □ **predisposition** *n.*

predominate *v.* be most numerous or powerful; exert control. □ **predominance** *n.*, **predominant** *adj.*, **predominantly** *adv.*

pre-eminent *adj.* excelling others, outstanding. □ **pre-eminence** *n.*, **pre-eminently** *adv.*

pre-empt *v.* take action to prevent (an occurrence); forestall (someone); obtain (something) before anyone else can. □ **pre-emption** *n.*, **pre-emptive** *adj.*

preen *v.* (of a bird) smooth (feathers) with the beak. □ **preen oneself** groom oneself; show self-satisfaction.

prefabricate *v.* manufacture in sections for assembly on a site. □ **prefabrication** *n.*

preface *n.* an introductory statement. ● *v.* **1** introduce with a preface. **2** lead up to (an event).

prefect *n.* **1** a senior pupil authorized to maintain discipline in a school. **2** an administrative official in certain countries. □ **prefecture** *n.*

prefer *v.* (**preferred, preferring**) **1** choose as more desirable, like better. **2** *formal* put forward (an accusation).

preferable *adj.* more desirable. □ **preferably** *adv.*

preference *n.* **1** preferring; something preferred; favour to one person over others. **2** a prior right.

preferential *adj.* involving or showing favour or partiality. □ **preferentially** *adv.*

preferment *n.* promotion.

prefix *n.* a word or syllable placed at the beginning of a word to change its meaning. ● *v.* add as a prefix or introduction; add a prefix to.

pregnant *adj.* **1** having a child or young developing in the womb. **2** full of meaning. □ **pregnancy** *n.*

prehensile *adj.* (esp. of an animal's tail) able to grasp things.

prehistoric *adj.* of the ancient period before written records were made. □ **prehistorically** *adv.*

prejudge *v.* form a judgement on before knowing all the facts.

prejudice *n.* **1** a preconceived and irrational opinion; hostility and injustice based on this. **2** harm to someone's rights. ● *v.* **1** cause to have a prejudice. **2** cause harm to. □ **prejudiced** *adj.*

prejudicial *adj.* harmful to rights or interests. □ **prejudicially** *adv.*

prelate (pre-lăt) *n.* a clergyman of high rank. □ **prelacy** *n.*

preliminary *adj.* preceding and preparing for a main action or event. ● *n.* (*pl.* **-ies**) a preliminary action or event.

prelude *n.* an action or event leading up to another; an introductory part or piece of music.

premarital *adj.* before marriage.

premature *adj.* coming or done before the usual or proper time. □ **prematurely** *adv.*

pre-medication *n.* medication in preparation for an operation.

premeditated *adj.* planned beforehand. □ **premeditation** *n.*

premenstrual *adj.* occurring before a menstrual period.

premier *adj.* first in importance, order, or time. ● *n.* a prime minister, a head of government. □ **premiership** *n.*

premiere (prem-i-air) *n.* the first public performance of a play etc.

premise *n.* = **premiss**.

premises *n.pl.* a house or other building and its grounds.

premiss *n.* a statement on which reasoning is based.

premium *n.* **1** an amount to be paid for an insurance policy. **2** a sum added to a usual price or charge. □ **at a premium 1** above the nominal or usual price. **2** scarce and in demand.

premonition *n.* a feeling that something (bad) will happen. □ **premonitory** *adj.*

preoccupation *n.* being preoccupied; something that fills one's thoughts.

preoccupied *adj.* so absorbed in or anxious about something that one is inattentive to other matters.

prep. *abbr.* preposition.

preparation *n.* preparing; something done to make ready; a substance prepared for use.

preparatory *adj.* preparing for something. □ **preparatory to** as a preparation for.

preparatory school *n.* **1** *Brit.* a private school for pupils between seven and thirteen. **2** *Amer.* a private school preparing pupils for university.

prepare *v.* make ready for use, consumption, etc.; make ready to do or experience something; make oneself ready. □ **prepared to** willing to.

prepay *v.* (**prepaid, prepaying**) pay for in advance.

preponderate *v.* be greater in number, power, etc. □ **preponderance** *n.*, **preponderant** *adj.*

preposition *n. Grammar* a word governing a noun or pronoun and indicating its relation to other words in the sentence (e.g. She came *after* dinner, We went *by* train). □ **prepositional** *adj.*

prepossessing *adj.* attractive.

preposterous *adj.* utterly absurd, outrageous. □ **preposterously** *adv.*

prepuce (pree-pyoos) *n.* the foreskin.

prerequisite *n.* something that is required before something else can happen.

■ **Usage** *Prerequisite* is sometimes confused with *perquisite* which means 'an extra profit, right, or privilege'.

prerogative *n.* a right or privilege.

presage *v.* be an omen of. ● *n.* a sign, an omen, esp. of something bad.

Presbyterian *adj.* & *n.* (a member) of a Church governed by elders of equal rank, esp. that of Scotland. □ **Presbyterianism** *n.*

pre-school *adj.* of the time before a child is old enough to go to school.

prescribe *v.* **1** advise the use of (a medicine etc.). **2** lay down as a course or rule to be followed.

■ **Usage** *Prescribe* is sometimes confused with *proscribe*, which means 'to forbid'.

prescription *n.* prescribing; a doctor's written instructions for the preparation and use of a medicine.

prescriptive *adj.* imposing a rule to be followed.

presence *n.* being present; a person or thing that is present without being seen; an impressive manner or bearing. □ **presence of mind** ability to act sensibly in a crisis.

present[1] (pre-zĕnt) *adj.* **1** being in the place in question. **2** existing or being dealt with now. ● *n.* the present time, time now passing. □ **at present** now. **for the present** for now, temporarily.

present[2] *n.* (pre-zĕnt) a gift. ● *v.* (pri-**zent**) **1** give as a gift or award (to); cause (trouble, difficulty). **2** introduce (a broadcast); represent in a particular way. □ **present itself** become apparent. □ **presentation** *n.*, **presenter** *n.*

presentable *adj.* clean, smart, etc. enough to be seen in public. □ **presentably** *adv.*

presentiment *n.* a feeling of something about to happen, a foreboding.

presently *adv.* **1** soon. **2** *Scot.* & *Amer.* now, currently.

preservative *adj.* preserving. ● *n.* a substance that preserves perishable food.

preserve *v.* keep safe, unchanged, or in existence; treat (food) to prevent decay. ● *n.* **1** interests etc. regarded as one person's domain. **2** (also **preserves**) jam. □ **preservation** *n.*, **preserver** *n.*

preside *v.* be in authority or control.

president *n.* the head of an institution or club; the head of a republic. □ **presidency** *n.*, **presidential** *adj.*

presidium *n.* (also **praesidium**) the standing committee in a Communist organization.

press *v.* **1** (cause to) move into contact with something by applying force; push downwards or inwards; squeeze; flatten; iron (clothes). **2** urge; try hard to persuade or influence; insist on (a point). **3** move in a specified direction by pushing. **4** bring into use as a makeshift. ● *n.* **1** a device for flattening or squeezing. **2** a machine for printing; newspapers and periodicals; people involved in making these; publicity of a specified kind: *a bad press*. **3** an act of pressing. □ **be pressed for** have barely enough of. **press on** continue in one's activity.

press conference *n.* an interview given to a number of reporters.

press cutting *n.* an article cut from a newspaper.

press-gang *v.* force into service.

pressing *adj.* urgent.

press stud *n.* a small fastener with two parts that are pressed together.

press-up *n.* an exercise of pressing on the hands to raise the body while lying face down.

pressure *n.* **1** exertion of force against a thing; this force. **2** influence or persuasion of an oppressive kind; stress. ● *v.* pressurize (a person).

pressure cooker *n.* a pan for cooking things quickly by steam under pressure.

pressure group *n.* an organized group seeking to exert influence by concerted action.

pressurize *v.* (also **-ise**) **1** try to compel into an action. **2** maintain constant artificially raised pressure in (a gas or its container). □ **pressurization** *n.*

prestige *n.* respect resulting from good reputation or achievements.

prestigious *adj.* having or bringing prestige.

presto *adv. Music* very quickly.

prestressed *adj.* (of concrete) strengthened by wires within it.

presumably *adv.* it may be presumed.

presume *v.* **1** suppose to be true. **2** be presumptuous. □ **presume upon** treat as entitling one to greater privileges than is the case. □ **presumption** *n.*

presumptuous *adj.* impudently ignoring limits to one's rights, privileges, etc. □ **presumptuously** *adv.*

presuppose *v.* require as a precondition; assume at the beginning of an argument. □ **presupposition** *n.*

pre-tax *adj.* before tax has been deducted.

pretence *n.* (*Amer.* **pretense**) **1** pretending, make-believe. **2** a claim (e.g. to merit or knowledge).

pretend *v.* **1** speak or behave so as to make something seem to be the case when it is not. **2** lay claim to something. □ **pretender** *n.*

pretension *n.* **1** a claim or the assertion of it. **2** pretentiousness.

pretentious *adj.* trying to appear more important, intelligent, etc., than is the case. □ **pretentiously** *adv.*, **pretentiousness** *n.*

preterm *adj.* & *adv.* following an unusually short pregnancy.

preternatural *adj.* beyond what is natural. □ **preternaturally** *adv.*

pretext *n.* a reason put forward to conceal one's true reason.

prettify *v.* (**prettified, prettifying**) make (something) look superficially attractive.

pretty *adj.* (**prettier, prettiest**) attractive in a delicate way. ● *adv. informal* to a moderate extent: *pretty good.* □ **prettily** *adv.*, **prettiness** *n.*

pretzel *n.* a knot-shaped salted biscuit.

prevail *v.* **1** be victorious, gain mastery. **2** be widespread or current. □ **prevail on** persuade.

prevalent *adj.* existing generally, widespread. □ **prevalence** *n.*

prevaricate *v.* speak or act evasively or misleadingly. □ **prevarication** *n.*

■ **Usage** *Prevaricate* is often confused with *procrastinate*, which means 'to postpone action'.

---

prevent *v.* keep from happening; make unable to do something. □ **preventable** *adj.*, **prevention** *n.*

■ **Usage** In the sense 'make unable to do something', *prevent* should be used with *from*, as in *She prevented me from going*; use without *from* is informal. Another acceptable form is *She prevented my going*.

---

preventive (also **preventative**) *adj. & n.* (something) used to prevent something.

previous *adj.* coming before in time or order. □ **previously** *adv.*

prey *n.* an animal hunted or killed by another for food; a victim. □ **bird of prey** a bird that kills and eats birds and mammals. **prey on 1** kill and eat. **2** distress, worry.

price *n.* the amount of money for which something is bought or sold; an unpleasant experience etc. that is necessary to achieve something. ● *v.* decide the price of.

priceless *adj.* **1** invaluable. **2** *informal* very amusing or absurd.

prick *v.* **1** pierce slightly; feel a pain as from this; provoke to action. **2** erect (the ears). ● *n.* **1** an act of pricking; a sensation of being pricked. **2** *vulgar slang* the penis. □ **prick up one's ears** listen intently.

prickle *n.* a small thorn or spine; a pricking sensation. ● *v.* feel or cause a pricking sensation.

prickly *adj.* (**pricklier, prickliest**) **1** having prickles. **2** easily offended.

pride *n.* **1** a feeling of pleasure or satisfaction about one's actions, qualities, or possessions or those of someone close to one; a source of this; a sense of dignity. **2** a group of lions. □ **pride of place** the most prominent position. **pride oneself on** be proud of.

priest *n.* a member of the clergy; an official of a non-Christian religion. □ **priesthood** *n.*, **priestly** *adj.*

priestess *n.* a female priest of a non-Christian religion.

prig *n.* a self-righteous person. □ **priggish** *adj.*, **priggishly** *adv.*, **priggishness** *n.*

prim *adj.* (**primmer, primmest**) very formal and proper, easily shocked or disgusted. □ **primly** *adv.*, **primness** *n.*

prima ballerina *n.* a chief ballerina.

primacy *n.* pre-eminence.

prima donna *n.* **1** the chief female singer in an opera. **2** *informal* a temperamental and self-important person.

prima facie (pry-ma fay-shee) *adv.* at first sight. ● *adj.* based on first impressions.

primal *adj.* **1** primitive, primeval. **2** fundamental.

primary *adj.* **1** first in time, order, or importance. **2** (of a school or education) for children below the age of 11. ● *n.* (*pl.* **-ies**) (in the USA) a preliminary election to choose delegates or candidates. □ **primarily** *adv.*

primary colour *n.* a colour not made by mixing others, i.e. (for light) red, green, or blue, (for paint) red, blue, or yellow.

primate *n.* **1** an archbishop. **2** a member of the highly developed order of animals that includes humans, apes, and monkeys.

prime *adj.* **1** most important, main. **2** excellent. ● *n.* a state or time of greatest strength, success, excellence, etc.: *past his prime.* ● *v.* prepare for use or action; provide with information in preparation for something.

prime minister *n.* the head of a parliamentary government.

prime number *n.* a number that can be divided exactly only by itself and one.

primer *n.* **1** a substance used to prime a surface for painting. **2** an elementary textbook.

primeval *adj.* of the earliest times of the world.

primitive *adj.* of or at an early stage of evolution or civilization; simple, crude; fundamental.

primogeniture *n.* a system by which an eldest son inherits all his parents' property.

primordial *adj.* primeval.

primrose *n.* a pale yellow spring flower; its colour.

prince *n.* a male member of a royal family; a sovereign's son or grandson.

princely *adj.* of or appropriate to a prince; splendid; generous, lavish.

princess *n.* a female member of a royal family; a sovereign's daughter or granddaughter; a prince's wife.

principal *adj.* first in rank or importance. ● *n.* **1** a person with the highest authority in an organization; the head of a school or college; a leading performer in a play, concert, etc. **2** a capital sum as distinct from interest or income.

principality *n.* (*pl.* **-ies**) a country ruled by a prince.

principally *adv.* mainly.

principle *n.* a truth serving as the basis for a system of belief, reasoning, etc.; (**principles**) beliefs governing one's behaviour, moral standards; a scientific law applying across a wide field. □ **in principle 1** as a general idea. **2** theoretically though not necessarily in fact. **on principle** because of one's moral beliefs.

■ **Usage** *Principle* is sometimes confused with *principal*, which means 'most senior or important'.

print *v.* **1** press (a mark) on a surface, mark (a surface etc.) in this way; produce by applying inked type to paper. **2** write with unjoined letters. **3** produce a positive picture from (a photographic negative). ● *n.* a mark left by pressing; printed lettering or words; a printed design, picture, or fabric.

printed circuit *n.* an electric circuit with lines of conducting material printed on a flat sheet.

printer *n.* **1** a person who prints books, newspapers, etc. **2** a machine that prints.

printout *n.* printed material produced from a computer printer or teleprinter.

prior *adj.* coming before in time, order, or importance. ● *n.* a monk who is head of a religious community, or one ranking next below an abbot.

prioress *n.* a female prior.

prioritize *v.* (also **-ise**) treat as more important than other things; arrange in order of importance. □ **prioritization** *n.*

priority *n.* (*pl.* **-ies**) something regarded as more important than others; being treated as more important than others; the right to proceed before other traffic.

priory *n.* (*pl.* **-ies**) a monastery or nunnery governed by a prior or prioress.

prise *v.* (*Amer.* **prize**) force out or open by leverage.

prism *n.* a solid geometric shape with ends that are equal and parallel; a transparent object of this shape that separates white light into colours.

prismatic *adj.* of or like a prism; (of colours) rainbow-like.

prison *n.* a building used to confine people convicted of crimes; a place of confinement.

prisoner *n.* a person kept in prison; a person in confinement.

prissy *adj.* (**prissier, prissiest**) prim, prudish. □ **prissily** *adv.*, **prissiness** *n.*

pristine *adj.* in its original and unspoilt condition.

privacy *n.* being undisturbed or unobserved.

private *adj.* **1** belonging to a particular person or group, not public; confidential; free from intrusion. **2** not provided or owned by the state; not holding public office. ● *n.* a soldier of the lowest rank. □ **in private** privately. □ **privately** *adv.*

privation *n.* shortage of food etc.; hardship.

privatize *v.* (also **-ise**) transfer from state to private ownership. □ **privatization** *n.*

privet *n.* a bushy evergreen shrub much used for hedges.

privilege *n.* a special right granted to a person or group; a great honour. □ **privileged** *adj.*

privy[1] *n.* (*pl.* **-ies**) *dated* or *Amer.* a lavatory, esp. an outside one.

privy[2] *adj.* □ **privy to** sharing knowledge of (a secret).

prize *n.* an award for victory or superiority; something that can be won. ● *adj.* **1** winning a prize. **2** excellent. ● *v.* **1** value highly. **2** Amer. sp. of **prise**.

pro *n.* (*pl.* **pros**) *informal* a professional. □ **pros and cons** arguments for and against something.

pro- *pref.* in favour of.

proactive *adj.* gaining control by taking the initiative.

probable *adj.* likely to happen or be true. □ **probability** *n.*, **probably** *adv.*

probate *n.* the official process of proving that a will is valid; a certified copy of a will.

probation *n.* **1** observation to test someone's ability and suitability for a position. **2** the supervision of an offender by an official (**probation officer**) as an alternative to imprisonment. □ **probationary** *adj.*

probationer *n.* a person undergoing a probationary period in a new job.

probe *n.* a blunt surgical instrument for exploring a wound; an investigation; an unmanned exploratory spacecraft. ● *v.* examine with a probe; conduct an inquiry.

probity *n.* honesty.

problem *n.* something difficult to deal with or understand; something to be solved or dealt with. □ **problematic, problematical** *adj.*

proboscis (prŏ-**bos**-is) *n.* **1** a long flexible snout. **2** an insect's elongated mouthpart used for sucking things.

procedure *n.* a series of actions done to accomplish something, esp. an established or official one. □ **procedural** *adj.*

proceed *v.* **1** go forward or onward; continue. **2** start a lawsuit. **3** originate from a source.

■ **Usage** Do not confuse *proceed* and *precede*.

---

proceedings *n.pl.* a series of activities, a formal procedure; a lawsuit; a published report of a conference.

proceeds *n.pl.* the profit from a sale, performance, etc.

process *n.* a series of actions to achieve an end; a natural series of events or changes; a series of operations performed in manufacturing something. ● *v.* **1** change or preserve (something) by a series of mechanical or chemical operations. **2** deal with according to an official procedure.

procession *n.* a number of people or vehicles etc. going along in an orderly line.

processor *n.* a machine that processes things.

proclaim *v.* announce publicly. □ **proclamation** *n.*

proclivity *n.* (*pl.* **-ies**) a tendency, an inclination or preference.

procrastinate *v.* postpone action. □ **procrastination** *n.*

■ **Usage** *Procrastinate* is often confused with *prevaricate*, which means 'to speak or act evasively or misleadingly'.

procreate *v.* produce young, reproduce. □ **procreation** *n.*

procurator fiscal *n.* (in Scotland) a public prosecutor and coroner.

procure *v.* **1** obtain by care or effort, acquire. **2** act as procurer. □ **procurement** *n.*

procurer *n.* a person who obtains a prostitute for someone else.

prod *v.* (**prodded, prodding**) **1** poke. **2** stimulate to action. ● *n.* **1** a prodding action; an instrument for prodding things. **2** a stimulus.

prodigal *adj.* wasteful, extravagant. □ **prodigality** *n.*, **prodigally** *adv.*

prodigious *adj.* amazingly great, huge. □ **prodigiously** *adv.*

prodigy *n.* (*pl.* **-ies**) a person with exceptional abilities; an amazing or unnatural thing.

produce *v.* (prŏ-**dyoos**) **1** make, manufacture; bring into being; grow, yield (crops); result in. **2** present for inspection. **3** administer the staging, financing, etc. of (a performance). ● *n.* (**pro**-dyoos) things produced or grown. □ **production** *n.*

producer *n.* **1** a person who produces something. **2** a person responsible for the schedule, expenditure, and quality of a film, play, broadcast, etc.

product *n.* **1** a thing produced. **2** a number obtained by multiplying.

productive *adj.* producing things, esp. in large quantities.

productivity *n.* efficiency in industrial production.

profane *adj.* **1** not sacred. **2** not reverent, blasphemous. ● *v.* treat irreverently. □ **profanely** *adv.*, **profanity** *n.*

profess *v.* **1** falsely claim to have or feel (an emotion etc.). **2** affirm faith in (a religion).

professed *adj.* **1** self-acknowledged. **2** falsely claimed; falsely claiming to be something. □ **professedly** *adv.*

profession *n.* **1** an occupation requiring advanced learning; the people engaged in this. **2** a declaration.

professional *adj.* **1** belonging to a profession. **2** skilful and conscientious. **3** doing something for payment, not as a pastime. ● *n.* a professional worker or player. □ **professionalism** *n.*, **professionally** *adv.*

professor *n.* a university teacher of the highest rank; (in America) a university lecturer. □ **professorial** *adj.*

proffer *v.* offer.

proficient *adj.* competent, skilled. □ **proficiency** *n.*, **proficiently** *adv.*

profile *n.* **1** a side view, esp. of the face. **2** a short account of a person's character or career. **3** the extent to which someone or something attracts notice: *keep a low profile.*

profit *n.* money made in an enterprise or transaction; a gain, an advantage. ● *v.* (**profited, profiting**) make money; derive advantage.

profitable *adj.* bringing profit. □ **profitability** *n.*, **profitable** *adj.*

profiteer *n.* a person who makes excessive, unfair, or illegal profits. □ **profiteering** *n.*

profligate *adj.* wasteful, extravagant; dissolute. ● *n.* a profligate person. □ **profligacy** *n.*

profound *adj.* **1** (of an emotion, state, etc.) intense. **2** showing or needing great insight. □ **profoundly** *adv.*, **profundity** *n.*

profuse *adj.* lavish; plentiful. □ **profusely** *adv.*, **profusion** *n.*

progenitor *n.* an ancestor.

progeny *n.* offspring.

progesterone *n.* a sex hormone that stimulates the uterus to prepare for pregnancy.

prognosis *n.* (*pl.* **prognoses**) a forecast, esp. of the course of a disease. □ **prognostic** *adj.*

prognosticate *v.* forecast. □ **prognostication** *n.*

program *n.* **1** Amer. sp. of **programme**. **2** a series of coded instructions for a computer. ● *v.* (**programmed, programming**) instruct (a computer) by means of a program. □ **programmer** *n.*

programme *n.* (*Amer.* **program**) **1** a planned series of future events or actions. **2** a sheet giving details of a performance and performers. **3** a radio or television broadcast. ● *v.* arrange or include in a schedule.

progress *n.* (**proh**-gress) forward or onward movement; development. ● *v.* (prŏ-**gress**) move forward or onward; develop. □ **in progress** taking place. □ **progression** *n.*

progressive *adj.* **1** favouring progress or reform. **2** (of a disease) gradually increasing in its effect. □ **progressively** *adv.*

prohibit *v.* (**prohibited, prohibiting**) forbid. □ **prohibition** *n.*

prohibitive *adj.* **1** (of a price) too high, impossible to pay. **2** forbidding something.

project *n.* (**pro**-jekt) a plan, an undertaking; a piece of work involving research. ● *v.* (prŏ-**jekt**) **1** estimate; plan. **2** extend outwards beyond something else. **3** throw; cause (light etc.) to fall on a surface; make (one's voice) audible; present (an image of oneself); make (an impression).

projectile *n.* a missile.

projection *n.* **1** an estimate of future situations based on a study of present ones. **2** presenting an image on a screen; presenting a particular image of oneself etc. **3** something projecting from a surface.

projectionist *n.* a person who operates a projector.

projector *n.* an apparatus for projecting images on to a screen.

prolapse *n.* a condition in which an organ slips forward out of place.

proletariat *n.* working-class people. □ **proletarian** *adj.* & *n.*

pro-life *adj.* opposed to abortion and euthanasia.

proliferate *v.* reproduce rapidly, multiply. □ **proliferation** *n.*

prolific *adj.* producing things abundantly. □ **prolifically** *adv.*

prologue *n.* an introduction to a play, poem, etc.

prolong *v.* lengthen in extent or duration. □ **prolongation** *n.*

prolonged *adj.* continuing for a long time.

prom *n.* *informal* **1** a promenade concert. **2** a promenade.

promenade *n.* a paved public walk (esp. along a sea front).

promenade concert *n.* a concert where part of the audience is not seated and can move about.

promethium *n.* a radioactive metallic element (symbol Pm).

prominent *adj.* projecting from a surface; conspicuous; well known, famous. □ **prominence** *n.*, **prominently** *adv.*

promiscuous *adj.* **1** having sexual relations with many people. **2** indiscriminate. □ **promiscuity** *n.*, **promiscuously** *adv.*

promise *n.* a declaration that one will give or do something; signs of future excellence; an indication that something specified is likely to happen. ● *v.* **1** make a promise (to); say that one will do or give (a thing). **2** give reason to expect.

promising *adj.* likely to turn out well.

promissory *adj.* conveying a promise.

promontory *n.* (*pl.* **-ies**) high land jutting out into the sea.

promote *v.* **1** raise to a higher rank or office. **2** help the progress of; publicize in order to sell. □ **promoter** *n.*, **promotion** *n.*

promotional *adj.* of the publicizing of a product; of advertising.

prompt *adj.* done or acting without delay. ● *v.* **1** cause, give rise to (a feeling or action). **2** assist (an actor) by supplying forgotten words. ● *adv.* exactly (at a specified time). □ **promptly** *adv.*, **promptness** *n.*

prompter *n.* a person positioned off stage to prompt actors.

promulgate *v.* make widely known. □ **promulgation** *n.*, **promulgator** *n.*

prone *adj.* **1** lying face downwards. **2** likely to do or suffer something.

prong *n.* each of the pointed parts of a fork. □ **pronged** *adj.*

pronoun *n. Grammar* a word used as a substitute for a noun; *demonstrative pronouns*, e.g. this, that; *interrogative pronouns*, e.g. who?, which?; *personal pronouns*, e.g. I, you, her, it; *possessive pronouns*, e.g. my, your, her, its; *reflexive pronouns*, e.g. myself, oneself; *relative pronouns*, e.g. who, which, that. □ **pronominal** *adj.*

pronounce *v.* **1** utter (a sound or word) distinctly or in a certain way. **2** declare, announce. □ **pronunciation** *n.*

■ **Usage** Although *pronounce* has a second *o*, *pronunciation* is neither spelt nor pronounced with one.

---

pronounced *adj.* noticeable.

pronouncement *n.* a declaration.

proof *n.* **1** evidence that something is true or exists. **2** a copy of printed matter for correction. ● *adj.* able to resist penetration or damage: *proof against rain*. ● *v.* make (fabric) proof against something (e.g. water).

proof-read *v.* read and correct (printed proofs). □ **proof-reader** *n.*

prop *n.* **1** a support to prevent something from falling, sagging, or failing. **2** *informal* a stage property. **3** *informal* a propeller. ● *v.* (**propped, propping**) support with or as if with a prop.

propaganda *n.* publicity intended to persuade or convince people.

propagate *v.* **1** breed or reproduce (a plant) from parent stock. **2** spread (news etc.); transmit. □ **propagation** *n.*, **propagator** *n.*

propane *n.* a hydrocarbon fuel gas.

propel *v.* (**propelled, propelling**) push forwards or onwards. □ **propellant** *n.* & *adj.*

propeller *n.* a revolving device with blades, for propelling a ship or aircraft.

propensity *n.* (*pl.* **-ies**) a tendency; an inclination.

proper *adj.* **1** genuine, deserving a particular description: *a proper meal*. **2** of the required type, suitable. **3** according to or observing conventions of correct behaviour. □ **proper to** belonging naturally or exclusively to. □ **properly** *adv.*

proper name, proper noun *n. Grammar* the name of an individual person, place, or thing.

property *n.* (*pl.* **-ies**) **1** something owned; real estate, land. **2** a movable object used in a play or film. **3** a quality, a characteristic.

prophecy *n.* (*pl.* **-ies**) a prediction of future events.

prophesy *v.* (**prophesied, prophesying**) foretell (what will happen).

prophet *n.* **1** a person who foretells events. **2** a religious teacher inspired by God.

prophetic *adj.* prophesying.

prophylactic (pro-fil-**ak**-tik) *adj.* preventing disease or misfortune. ● *n.* **1** a preventive medicine or action. **2** *Amer.* a condom. □ **prophylaxis** *n.*

propinquity *n.* nearness.

propitiate (prŏ-**pish**-i-ayt) *v.* win or regain the favour of. □ **propitiation** *n.*, **propitiatory** *adj.*

propitious (prŏ-**pish**-ŭs) *adj.* auspicious, favourable. □ **propitiously** *adv.*, **propitiousness** *n.*

proponent *n.* a person putting forward a proposal.

proportion *n.* a fraction or share of a whole; a ratio; the correct relation in size or degree; (**proportions**) dimensions. □ **proportional** *adj.*, **proportionally** *adv.*

proportional representation *n.* an electoral system in which each party receives seats in proportion to the number of votes cast for its candidates.

proportionate *adj.* in proportion, corresponding. □ **proportionately** *adv.*

proposal *n.* **1** the proposing of something; something proposed. **2** an offer of marriage.

propose *v.* **1** put forward (an idea etc.) for consideration; nominate for a position. **2** ask someone to marry one. □ **proposer** *n.*

proposition *n.* **1** a statement or assertion. **2** a suggested plan. **3** a project considered in terms of the likelihood of success. **4** *informal* an offer of sexual intercourse. ● *v.* *informal* make a proposal to; suggest intercourse to.

propound *v.* put forward (an idea etc.) for consideration.

proprietary *adj.* made and sold by a particular firm, usu. under a patent; of an owner or ownership.

proprietor *n.* the owner of a business. □ **proprietorial** *adj.*

propriety *n.* correctness of behaviour.

propulsion *n.* the process of propelling or being propelled.

propylene *n.* a gaseous hydrocarbon.

pro rata *adj.* & *adv.* proportional(ly).

prorogue (proh-**rohg**) *v.* (**prorogued, proroguing**) discontinue the meetings of (a parliament) without dissolving it.

prosaic *adj.* plain and ordinary, unimaginative. □ **prosaically** *adv.*

proscenium (prŏ-**seen**-i-ŭm) *n.* (*pl.* **prosceniums** or **proscenia**) the part of a theatre stage in front of the curtain.

proscribe *v.* forbid.

■ **Usage** *Proscribe* is sometimes confused with *prescribe*, which means 'to impose'.

prose *n.* written or spoken language without metre or other poetic elements.

prosecute *v.* **1** take legal proceedings against (a person) for a crime. **2** continue with, carry on (a course of action). □ **prosecution** *n.*, **prosecutor** *n.*

proselyte *n.* a recent convert to a religion.

proselytize *v.* (also **-ise**) seek to convert.

prospect *n.* (**pross**-pekt) the likelihood of something's occurring; (**prospects**) chances of success. ● *v.* (prŏ-**spekt**) explore in search of something. □ **prospector** *n.*

prospective *adj.* expected to be or to occur; future, possible.

prospectus *n.* (*pl.* **prospectuses**) a document giving details of a school, business, etc.

prosper *v.* be successful, thrive.

prosperous *adj.* financially successful. □ **prosperity** *n.*

prostate gland *n.* the gland round the neck of the bladder in male mammals.

■ **Usage** *Prostate* should not be confused with *prostrate*.

prosthesis *n.* (*pl.* **prostheses**) an artificial body part. □ **prosthetic** *adj.*

prostitute *n.* a person who offers sexual intercourse for payment. ● *v.* make a prostitute of; put (talent etc.) to an unworthy use. □ **prostitution** *n.*

prostrate *adj.* (pross-**trayt**) **1** face downwards; lying horizontally. **2** overcome, exhausted. ● *v.* (pross-**trayt**) cause to be prostrate. □ **prostration** *n.*

protactinium *n.* a radioactive metallic element (symbol Pa).

protagonist *n.* **1** the chief person in a drama, story, etc. **2** a supporter of a cause etc.

protean (**proh**-ti-ăn) *adj.* variable; versatile.

protect *v.* keep from harm or injury. □ **protection** *n.*, **protector** *n.*

protectionism *n.* a policy of protecting home industries from competition by tariffs etc. □ **protectionist** *n.*

protective *adj.* protecting, giving protection. □ **protectively** *adv.*

protectorate *n.* a country that is under the official protection and partial control of a stronger one.

protégé (**prot**-i-*zh*ay) *n.* a person who is guided and supported by another.

protein *n.* an organic compound forming an essential part of humans' and animals' food.

pro tem *adj.* & *adv.* for the time being.

protest *n.* (**proh**-test) a statement or action indicating disapproval. ● *v.* (prŏ-**test**) **1** express disapproval. **2** declare firmly: *protested her innocence.*

Protestant *n.* a member of any of the western Christian Churches that are separate from the Roman Catholic Church. □ **Protestantism** *n.*

protestation *n.* a firm declaration.

protocol *n.* **1** official procedure governing affairs of state; accepted behaviour in a situation. **2** a draft of a treaty.

proton *n.* a particle of matter with a positive electric charge.

protoplasm *n.* the contents of a living cell.

prototype *n.* an original example from which others are developed.

protozoan (proh-tŏ-**zoh**-ăn) *n.* (also **protozoon**) (*pl.* **protozoa** or **protozoans**) a one-celled microscopic animal.

protract *v.* cause to last longer. □ **protraction** *n.*

protractor *n.* an instrument for measuring angles.

protrude *v.* project, stick out. □ **protrusion** *n.*, **protrusive** *adj.*

protuberance *n.* a bulging part.

protuberant *adj.* bulging.

proud *adj.* **1** feeling pride; giving cause for pride: *a proud history*; arrogant. **2** projecting slightly from a surface. □ **proudly** *adv.*

prove *v.* (**proved** or **proven, proving**) **1** demonstrate to be true. **2** turn out to be of a specified kind. **3** (of dough) rise because of the action of yeast.

provenance *n.* a place of origin.

provender *n.* fodder.

proverb *n.* a short well-known saying.

proverbial *adj.* **1** of or mentioned in a proverb. **2** well known.

provide *v.* **1** supply, make available (to). **2** stipulate in a legal document. □ **provide for 1** supply with necessities. **2** make preparations for. □ **provider** *n.*

provided *conj.* on condition (that).

providence *n.* **1** God's or nature's protection. **2** being provident.

provident *adj.* showing wise forethought for future needs, thrifty.

providential *adj.* happening very luckily. □ **providentially** *adv.*

providing *conj.* = **provided**.

province *n.* **1** an administrative division of a country. **2** (**the provinces**) all parts of a country outside its capital city. **3** a range of learning or responsibility.

provincial *adj.* **1** of a province or provinces. **2** having limited interests and narrow-minded views. ● *n.* an inhabitant of a province.

provision *n.* **1** the process of providing things. **2** a stipulation in a treaty or contract etc. **3** (**provisions**) food and drink.

provisional *adj.* arranged temporarily. □ **provisionally** *adv.*

proviso (prŏ-vyz-oh) *n.* (*pl.* **provisos**) a condition attached to an agreement.

provisory *adj.* provisional.

provoke *v.* **1** make angry. **2** rouse to action; produce as a reaction. □ **provocation** *n.*, **provocative** *adj.*, **provocatively** *adv.*

provost *n.* the head of a college; the head of a cathedral chapter.

prow *n.* a projecting front part of a ship or boat.

prowess *n.* great ability or daring.

prowl *v.* go about stealthily as though in search of prey. □ **on the prowl** prowling. □ **prowler** *n.*

proximate *adj.* nearest.

proximity *n.* nearness.

proxy *n.* (*pl.* **-ies**) a person authorized to represent or act for another; use of such a person.

prude *n.* a person who is too easily shocked, esp. by references to sex etc. □ **prudery** *n.*

prudent *adj.* showing thought for the future. □ **prudence** *n.*, **prudently** *adv.*

prudish *adj.* showing prudery. □ **prudishly** *adv.*, **prudishness** *n.*

prune *n.* a dried plum. ● *v.* trim (a tree etc.) by cutting away dead or unwanted parts; reduce.

prurient *adj.* having or stimulating lustful thoughts. □ **prurience** *n.*, **pruriently** *adv.*

pry *v.* (**pries, pried, prying**) inquire too inquisitively into someone's private affairs.

PS *abbr.* postscript.

psalm (sahm) *n.* a sacred song.

psalter (sawl-ter) *n.* a copy of the Book of Psalms.

psaltery *n.* (*pl.* **-ies**) an ancient musical instrument.

PSBR *abbr.* public sector borrowing requirement, the amount of money borrowed by government.

psephology (sef-ol-ŏji) *n.* the study of trends in voting. □ **psephologist** *n.*

pseudo- (syoo-doh) *comb. form* false.

pseudonym (syoo-dŏ-nim) *n.* a fictitious name used e.g. by an author. □ **pseudonymous** *adj.*

psoriasis (sŏ-ry-ăsis) *n.* a skin condition causing scaly red patches.

PSV *abbr.* public service vehicle.

psyche (sy-kee) *n.* the soul, the spirit; the mind.

psychedelic (sy-kĕ-**del**-ik) *adj.* **1** (of a drug) producing hallucinations. **2** with vivid colours or abstract patterns.

psychiatry (sy-**ky**-ătri) *n.* the study and treatment of mental illness. □ **psychiatric** (sy-kee-**at**-rik) *adj.*, **psychiatrist** *n.*

psychic (sy-kik) *adj.* of the soul or mind; of or having apparently supernatural powers. ● *n.* a person having or claiming psychic powers.

psycho (sy-koh) *n.* (*pl.* **psychos**) *informal* a psychopath.

psychoanalyse *v.* (*Amer.* **-yze**) treat by psychoanalysis. □ **psychoanalyst** *n.*

psychoanalysis *n.* a method of examining and treating mental conditions by investigating the interaction of conscious and unconscious elements.

psychology *n.* the study of the mind and how it works; a person's mental characteristics; the mental factors governing a situation or activity. □ **psychological** *adj.*, **psychologically** *adv.*, **psychologist** *n.*

psychopath *n.* a person suffering from a severe mental disorder resulting in antisocial or violent behaviour. □ **psychopathic** *adj.*

psychosis *n.* (*pl.* **psychoses**) a severe mental disorder in with the sufferer loses contact with reality. □ **psychotic** *adj.* & *n.*

psychosomatic *adj.* (of illness) caused or aggravated by mental stress.

psychotherapy *n.* treatment of mental disorders by psychological rather than medical methods. ▫ **psychotherapist** *n.*

PT *abbr.* physical training.

Pt *symb.* platinum.

pt. *abbr.* **1** pint. **2** part. **3** point.

PTA *abbr.* parent-teacher association.

ptarmigan (**tar**-mi-găn) *n.* a bird of the grouse family.

pterodactyl (terŏ-**dak**-til) *n.* an extinct reptile with wings.

PTO *abbr.* please turn over.

Pu *symb.* plutonium.

pub *n. informal* a public house.

puberty *n.* the stage in life when a person reaches sexual maturity and becomes capable of reproduction. ▫ **pubertal** *adj.*

pubic *adj.* of the abdomen at the lower front part of the pelvis.

public *adj.* of, for, or known to people in general. ● *n.* members of a community in general; people interested in the work of a particular author, performer, etc. ▫ **publicly** *adv.*

public address system *n.* a system of loudspeakers amplifying sound for an audience.

publican *n.* the keeper of a public house.

publication *n.* publishing; a published book, newspaper, etc.

public convenience *n.* a public lavatory.

public house *n.* a building (other than a hotel) licensed to serve alcoholic drinks.

publicity *n.* attention given to someone or something by the media; publicizing; material used in publicizing.

publicize *v.* (also **-ise**) bring to the attention of the public; promote, advertise. ▫ **publicist** *n.*

public relations *n.pl.* the promotion by a company or political party of a favourable public image.

public school *n.* **1** (in the UK) a private secondary school for fee-paying pupils. **2** (in the USA) a school supported by public funds.

public sector *n.* the part of the economy that is owned and controlled by the state.

public servant *n.* a state official, a civil servant, etc.

public-spirited *adj.* showing readiness to do things for the benefit of people in general.

publish *v.* **1** issue (a book etc.) for public sale. **2** make generally known. ▫ **publisher** *n.*

puce *adj.* & *n.* brownish purple.

puck *n.* a hard rubber disc used in ice hockey.

pucker *v.* contract into wrinkles. ● *n.* a wrinkle.

pudding *n.* **1** a sweet cooked dish; the sweet course of a meal. **2** a savoury dish containing flour, suet, etc. **3** a kind of sausage.

puddle *n.* a small pool of rainwater or other liquid.

pudenda *n.pl.* the genitals.

puerile *adj.* childish. ▫ **puerility** *n.*

puerperal *adj.* of or resulting from childbirth.

puff *n.* **1** a short burst of breath or wind; smoke, etc., blown out by this. **2** a light pastry case with a filling. **3** a soft pad for applying powder to the skin. **4** *informal* an over-complimentary review of a book etc. ● *v.* **1** emit or send out in puffs; breathe heavily, pant. **2** (cause to) swell. **3** review with excessive praise.

puffball *n.* a ball-shaped fungus.

puffin *n.* a seabird with a short striped bill.

puff pastry *n.* very light flaky pastry.

puffy *adj.* (**puffier, puffiest**) puffed out, swollen. ▫ **puffiness** *n.*

pug *n.* a dog of a small breed with a flat nose and wrinkled face.

pugilist (pew-ji-list) *n. formal* a professional boxer. ▫ **pugilism** *n.*

pugnacious *adj.* eager to fight, aggressive. ▫ **pugnaciously** *adv.*, **pugnacity** *n.*

puke *v.* & *n. informal* vomit.

pukka *adj. informal* real, genuine.

pull *v.* **1** exert force upon (someone or something that one is holding or attached to) so as to move it towards the source of the force; attract. **2** move steadily in a specified direction. **3** inhale deeply while smoking. **4** injure (a muscle etc.) by strain. ● *n.* **1** an act of pulling; a handle to hold while pulling. **2** an attraction; an influence or compulsion. **3** a deep drink. **4** a draw on a pipe etc. **5** an injury to a muscle etc. □ **pull down 1** demolish. **2** *informal* earn. **pull in** move to the side of a road; reach a station etc. **pull off** *informal* succeed in achieving. **pull out 1** leave a station; move out into the middle of a road. **2** withdraw from a contest etc. **pull through** come or bring through difficulty or danger. **pull to pieces** (or **apart**) criticize harshly. **pull up** stop.

pullet (**puu**-lit) *n.* a young hen.

pulley *n.* (*pl.* **pulleys**) a wheel over which a rope etc. passes, used in lifting things.

pullover *n.* a knitted garment covering the top half of the body.

pulmonary *adj.* of the lungs.

pulp *n.* **1** a soft, moist, shapeless substance; the soft moist part of fruit. **2** writing of poor quality. ● *v.* crush to pulp. □ **pulpy** *adj.*

pulpit *n.* a raised enclosed platform from which a preacher speaks.

pulsar *n.* a star emitting regular pulses of radio waves.

pulsate *v.* expand and contract rhythmically. □ **pulsation** *n.*

pulse *n.* **1** the rhythmical throbbing of arteries as blood is propelled along them, as felt in the wrists or temples. **2** a single beat, throb, or vibration. **3** the edible seed of beans, peas, lentils, etc. ● *v.* pulsate.

pulverize *v.* (also **-ise**) crush to powder; *informal* defeat utterly. □ **pulverization** *n.*

puma *n.* a large brown American animal of the cat family.

pumice *n.* (in full **pumice stone**) solidified lava used for scouring or polishing.

pummel *v.* (**pummelled, pummelling**; *Amer.* **pummeled**) strike repeatedly, esp. with the fists.

pump *n.* a machine for moving liquid, gas, or air. ● *v.* **1** force (air etc.) in a particular direction using a pump; inflate or empty using a pump. **2** move vigorously up and down. **3** pour forth. **4** *informal* question persistently.

pumpkin *n.* a large round orange-coloured fruit.

pun *n.* a humorous use of a word to suggest another that sounds the same. □ **punning** *adj.* & *n.*

punch *v.* **1** strike with the fist. **2** cut (a hole etc.) with a device. **3** press (a key on a machine); enter (information) in this way. ● *n.* **1** a blow with the fist. **2** a device for cutting holes or impressing a design. **3** a drink made of wine or spirits mixed with fruit juices etc.

punch-drunk *adj.* stupefied by repeated blows.

punchline *n.* words giving the climax of a joke.

punctilious *adj.* attending to details, esp. of correct behaviour. □ **punctiliously** *adv.*, **punctiliousness** *n.*

punctual *adj.* arriving or doing things at the appointed time. □ **punctuality** *n.*, **punctually** *adv.*

punctuate *v.* **1** insert the appropriate marks in (written material) to separate sentences etc. **2** interrupt at intervals. □ **punctuation** *n.*

puncture *n.* a small hole made by something sharp, esp. in a tyre or other object containing air. ● *v.* make a puncture in; suffer a puncture.

pundit *n.* an expert.

pungent *adj.* having a strong sharp taste or smell. □ **pungency** *n.*, **pungently** *adv.*

punish *v.* cause (an offender) to suffer for his or her offence; inflict a penalty for (an offence); treat roughly. □ **punishment** *n.*

punitive *adj.* inflicting or intended to inflict punishment; (of a tax or charge) damagingly high.

punk *n.* **1** (in full **punk rock**) a deliberately outrageous type of rock music, popular in the 1970s; a follower of this. **2** *informal* a hooligan, a lout.

punnet *n.* a small container for fruit etc.

punt[1] *n.* a shallow flat-bottomed boat with broad square ends. ● *v.* propel (a punt) by pushing with a pole against the bottom of a river; travel in a punt.

punt[2] *v.* kick (a dropped football) before it touches the ground. ● *n.* this kick.

punter *n. informal* **1** a person who gambles. **2** a customer.

puny *adj.* (**punier, puniest**) small and weak.

pup *n.* a young dog; a young wolf, rat, or seal. ● *v.* (**pupped, pupping**) give birth to pups.

pupa (pyoo-pă) *n.* (*pl.* **pupae**) a chrysalis.

pupate *v.* become a pupa.

pupil *n.* **1** a person who is taught by another. **2** the opening in the centre of the iris of the eye.

puppet *n.* a kind of doll made to move as an entertainment; a person, state, etc., controlled by another. □ **puppetry** *n.*

puppy *n.* (*pl.* **-ies**) a young dog.

purchase *v.* buy. ● *n.* **1** buying; something bought. **2** a firm hold or grip; a pulley etc. to move heavy objects. □ **purchaser** *n.*

purdah *n.* the Muslim or Hindu system of keeping women from the sight of men or strangers.

pure *adj.* **1** not mixed with any other substances; uncontaminated; not immoral, innocent, chaste. **2** sheer, utter, simple: *pure chance.* **3** (of mathematics or sciences) dealing with theory rather than practical considerations. □ **purity** *n.*

purée (pewr-ay) *n.* pulped fruit or vegetables etc. ● *v.* make into a purée.

purely *adv.* **1** in a pure way. **2** entirely; only.

purgative *adj.* strongly laxative. ● *n.* a purgative substance.

purgatory *n.* a place or condition of suffering, esp. (in RC belief) in which souls undergo purification before going to heaven. □ **purgatorial** *adj.*

purge *v.* **1** clear the bowels of by a purgative. **2** rid of undesirable people or things. ● *n.* the process of purging.

purify *v.* make pure. □ **purification** *n.*, **purifier** *n.*

purist *n.* a stickler for correctness. □ **purism** *n.*

puritan *n.* a person who is strict in morals and regards certain pleasures as sinful. □ **puritanical** *adj.*

purl *n.* a knitting stitch. ● *v.* **1** make this stitch. **2** (of a stream) flow with a rippling sound.

purlieu (perl-yoo) *n.* (*pl.* **purlieus** or **purlieux**) the area surrounding a place; a person's usual haunts.

purloin *v.* steal.

purple *adj.* & *n.* (of) a colour made by mixing red and blue.

purport *n.* (per-port) meaning. ● *v.* (per-**port**) pretend; be intended to seem. □ **purportedly** *adv.*

purpose *n.* the intended result of an action etc.; a feeling of determination. ● *v. formal* intend. □ **on purpose** intentionally. **to no purpose** pointlessly. **to the purpose** relevant.

purpose-built *adj.* designed and built for a particular purpose.

purposeful *adj.* showing determination; having a useful purpose; intentional. □ **purposefully** *adv.*

purposely *adv.* on purpose.

purr *n.* a low vibrant sound that a cat makes when pleased; any similar sound. ● *v.* make this sound.

purse *n.* **1** a small pouch for carrying money. **2** *Amer.* a handbag.

3 money available for use. ● *v.* pucker (one's lips).

purser *n.* a ship's officer in charge of accounts.

pursuance *n.* the performance (of duties etc.).

pursue *v.* (**pursued, pursuing**) **1** follow; try to catch or attain. **2** continue along (a route); engage in (an activity). ◻ **pursuer** *n.*

pursuit *n.* **1** pursuing. **2** an activity to which one gives time or effort.

purulent (pewr-yuu-lĕnt) *adj.* of or containing pus. ◻ **purulence** *n.*

purvey *v.* supply (food etc.) as a trader. ◻ **purveyor** *n.*

pus *n.* thick yellowish matter produced from an infected wound.

push *v.* **1** exert force on (someone or something) to move them away from the source of the force; move forward by exerting force. **2** make one's way forward forcibly. **3** press (a button or key). **4** make demands on; force to work hard. **5** *informal* promote the use or acceptance of; sell (drugs) illegally. ● *n.* **1** an act of pushing. **2** a vigorous effort; a military attack. ◻ **be pushed for** have little of. **be pushing** *informal* approach (a specified age). **push ahead** carry on, proceed. **push off** *informal* go away. ◻ **pusher** *n.*

pushchair *n.* a folding chair on wheels, in which a child can be pushed along.

pushy *adj.* (**pushier, pushiest**) *informal* self-assertive;. determined to get on. ◻ **pushiness** *n.*

pusillanimous (pyoo-si-**lan**-i-mŭs) *adj.* cowardly.

puss *n.* (also **pussy**) *informal* a cat.

pussyfoot *v. informal* move stealthily; act cautiously.

pussy willow *n.* a willow with furry catkins.

pustule *n.* a pimple or blister. ◻ **pustular** *adj.*

put *v.* (**put, putting**) **1** cause to be in a certain place, position, state, or relationship. **2** express, phrase. **3** throw (the shot or weight) as an athletic exercise. ● *n.* a throw of the shot or weight. ◻ **put by** (or **aside**) save for future use. **put down 1** snub; suppress. **2** kill (a sick animal). **3** record in writing. **4** pay (a deposit). **put down to** attribute to. **put off 1** postpone. **2** discourage; repel. **put on 1** put (a garment etc.) on one's body. **2** turn on (an electrical device etc.) **3** arrange (an event, entertainment, etc.). **put out 1** *informal* annoy; inconvenience. **2** extinguish. **3** dislocate. **put up 1** construct, erect. **2** raise (a price). **3** stay in or provide with temporary accommodation. **put upon** *informal* unfairly burdened. **put up with** tolerate.

putative *adj.* reputed, supposed. ◻ **putatively** *adv.*

putrefy *v.* (**putrified, putrifying**) rot. ◻ **putrefaction** *n.*

putrescent *adj.* rotting. ◻ **putrescence** *n.*

putrid *adj.* rotten; stinking; *informal* very unpleasant.

putt *v.* strike (a golf ball) gently to make it roll along the ground. ● *n.* this stroke.

putter *n.* a club used for putting. ● *v.* Amer. sp. of **potter**.

putty *n.* a soft paste that sets hard, used for fixing glass in frames, filling holes, etc.

put-up job *n. informal* a prearranged fraudulent scheme.

puzzle *n.* a difficult question or problem; a problem or toy designed to test knowledge or ingenuity. ● *v.* cause to feel confused or bewildered; (cause to) think hard about a problem. ◻ **puzzlement** *n.*

PVC *abbr.* polyvinyl chloride, a synthetic resin used in flooring, sheeting, etc.

PW *abbr.* policewoman.

PWR *abbr.* pressurized-water reactor.

pygmy *n.* (*pl.* **-ies**) (also **pigmy**) a member of a black African people of very short stature; an unusually small person or thing.

pyjamas *n.pl.* (*Amer.* **pajamas**) a loose jacket and trousers for sleeping in.

pylon *n.* a tall metal structure carrying electricity cables.

pyorrhoea (py-ŏ-ree-ă) *n.* (*Amer.* **pyorrhea**) a disease causing discharge of pus from the tooth-sockets.

pyramid *n.* a structure with triangular sloping sides that meet at the top. ▫ **pyramidal** *adj.*

pyre *n.* a pile of wood etc. for burning a dead body.

pyretic *adj.* of or producing fever.

Pyrex *n. trademark* a hard heat-resistant glass.

pyrites (py-**ry**-teez) *n.* a mineral sulphide of (copper and) iron.

pyromaniac *n.* a person with an uncontrollable impulse to set things on fire.

pyrotechnics *n.pl.* a firework display; a brilliant display or performance. ▫ **pyrotechnic** *adj.*

Pyrrhic victory (**pi**-rik) *n.* a victory gained at too great a cost to be worthwhile.

python *n.* a large snake that crushes its prey.

Qq

Q *abbr.* question.

QC *abbr.* Queen's Counsel.

QED *abbr.* quod erat demonstrandum, that which was to be proved.

qua (kway, kwah) *conj.* in the capacity of, as.

quack *n.* **1** a duck's harsh cry. **2** a person who falsely claims to have medical skill. ● *v.* (of a duck) make its harsh cry.

quad *n. informal* **1** quadrangle. **2** quadruplet.

quad bike *n.* a four-wheeled motorcycle used for racing.

quadrangle *n.* a four-sided courtyard bordered by large buildings.

quadrant *n.* **1** a quarter of a circle or of its circumference. **2** *hist.* a graduated instrument for taking angular measurements in astronomy.

quadraphonic *adj.* (also **quadrophonic**) (of sound reproduction) using four transmission channels.

quadratic equation *n.* an equation involving the square (and no higher power) of an unknown quantity or variable.

quadrilateral *n.* a geometric figure with four sides.

quadrille (kwo-**drill**) *n.* a square dance.

quadriplegia *n.* paralysis of both arms and legs.

quadrophonic var. of **quadraphonic**.

quadruped *n.* a four-footed animal.

quadruple *adj.* having four parts or members; four times as much as. ● *v.* increase by four times its amount.

quadruplet *n.* one of four children born at one birth.

quaff (kwoff) *v.* drink in large draughts.

quagmire *n.* a bog, a marsh; a situation full of hazards or difficulties.

quail *n.* a small game bird. ● *v.* flinch, show fear.

quaint *adj.* attractively strange or old-fashioned. ▫ **quaintly** *adv.*, **quaintness** *n.*

quake *v.* shake or tremble, esp. with fear.

Quaker *n.* a member of the Society of Friends, a Christian sect with no written creed or ordained ministers.

qualification *n.* **1** a pass in an examination etc. qualifying someone for something; qualifying, being eligible. **2** a restriction or condition on a statement, agreement, etc.

qualify *v.* (**qualified, qualifying**) **1** be entitled to a privilege or eligible for a competition; become or make an officially recognized practitioner of a profession etc. by meeting certain standards. **2** restrict, limit (a statement etc.). □ **qualifier** *n.*

qualitative *adj.* of or concerned with quality.

quality *n.* (*pl.* **-ies**) **1** a degree of excellence. **2** a characteristic, a distinctive attribute of a person or thing.

qualm (kwahm) *n.* an uneasy feeling of worry or fear.

quandary (kwon-dă-ri) *n.* (*pl.* **-ies**) a state of perplexity; a difficult situation.

quango *n.* (*pl.* **quangos**) an administrative body (outside the Civil Service) with senior members appointed by the government.

quantify *v.* (**quantified, quantifying**) express or measure the quantity of. □ **quantifiable** *adj.*

quantitative *adj.* of or concerned with quantity.

quantity *n.* (*pl.* **-ies**) an amount or number of a substance or things; (**quantities**) large amounts.

quantity surveyor *n.* a person who measures and prices building work.

quantum leap *n.* a sudden great increase or advance.

quantum theory *n.* a theory of physics based on the assumption that energy exists in indivisible units.

quarantine *n.* isolation imposed on those who have been exposed to an infectious disease. ● *v.* put into quarantine.

quark *n.* **1** a component of elementary particles. **2** low-fat curd cheese.

quarrel *n.* an angry argument; a reason for disagreement. ● *v.* (**quarrelled, quarrelling**; *Amer.* **quarreled**) engage in a quarrel.

quarrelsome *adj.* liable to quarrel.

quarry *n.* (*pl.* **-ies**) **1** an intended prey or victim; something sought or pursued. **2** an open excavation from which stone etc. is obtained. ● *v.* (**quarried, quarrying**) obtain (stone etc.) from a quarry.

quart *n.* a quarter of a gallon, two pints (1.137 litres).

quarter *n.* **1** one of four equal parts of something. **2** three months, a fourth part of a year; a point of time 15 minutes before or after every hour. **3** *Amer.* & *Canada* a coin worth 25 cents. **4** a district of a town etc. having a particular characteristic; the direction of a point of the compass. **5** (**quarters**) accommodation. **6** mercy to a defeated enemy: *give no quarter*. ● *v.* **1** divide into quarters. **2** put into lodgings.

quarterdeck *n.* the part of a ship's upper deck nearest the stern.

quarter-final *n.* a contest preceding a semi-final.

quarterly *adj.* & *adv.* (produced or occurring) once in every quarter of a year. ● *n.* (*pl.* **-ies**) a quarterly periodical.

quartermaster *n.* a regimental officer in charge of stores etc.; a naval petty officer in charge of steering and signals.

quartet *n.* a group of four instruments or voices; music for these.

quartz (korts) *n.* a hard mineral.

quartz clock *n.* a clock operated by electric vibrations of a quartz crystal.

quasar (kway-zah) *n.* a star-like object that is the source of intense electromagnetic radiation.

quash (kwosh) *v.* reject as invalid; suppress, put an end to.

quasi- *comb. form* seeming to be but not really so.

quatrain (kwo-trayn) *n.* a stanza or poem of four lines.

quaver *v.* tremble, vibrate; speak or utter in a trembling voice. ● *n.* **1** a trembling sound. **2** a note in music, half a crochet.

quay (kee) *n.* a landing place built for ships to load or unload alongside. □ **quayside** *n.*

queasy *adj.* (**queasier, queasiest**) feeling sick; causing nausea. □ **queasiness** *n.*

queen *n.* **1** a female ruler of a country by right of birth; a king's wife; a woman or thing regarded as supreme in some way. **2** a piece in chess; a playing card bearing a picture of a queen. **3** a fertile female bee, ant, etc. **4** *informal* a male homosexual. □ **queenly** *adj.*

queen mother *n.* the widow of a king and mother of a reigning sovereign.

queer *adj.* **1** strange, odd, eccentric. **2** *informal* slightly ill or faint. **3** *informal, offensive* homosexual. ● *n. informal, offensive* a homosexual. ● *v.* spoil □ **queer a person's pitch** spoil his or her chances.

quell *v.* suppress.

quench *v.* **1** satisfy (thirst). **2** extinguish (a fire); cool (red-hot metal) in water.

quern *n.* a hand mill for grinding corn.

querulous *adj.* complaining peevishly. □ **querulously** *adv.*, **querulousness** *n.*

query *n.* (*pl.* **-ies**) a question; a question mark. ● *v.* (**queried, querying**) ask a question or express doubt about.

quest *n.* a long search.

question *n.* a sentence requesting information; a matter for discussion or solution; a doubt. ● *v.* ask (someone) questions; raise questions about. □ **in question** being discussed or disputed. **no question of** no possibility of. **out of the question** completely impracticable.

questionable *adj.* open to doubt.

question mark *n.* a punctuation mark (?) placed after a question.

questionnaire *n.* a list of questions seeking information.

queue (kew) *n.* a line of people waiting for something. ● *v.* (**queued, queuing** or **queueing**) wait in a queue.

quibble *n.* a petty objection. ● *v.* make petty objections.

quiche (keesh) *n.* an open tart with a savoury filling.

quick *adj.* **1** moving or acting fast; taking only a short time. **2** able to learn or think quickly. **3** (of temper) easily roused. ● *n.* the sensitive flesh below the nails. □ **quickly** *adv.*, **quickness** *n.*

quicken *v.* make or become quicker or livelier.

quicklime *n.* = **lime** (*sense* 1).

quicksand *n.* an area of loose wet deep sand into which heavy objects will sink.

quicksilver *n.* mercury.

quickstep *n.* a ballroom dance.

quid *n.* (*pl.* **quid**) *informal* £1. □ **quids in** *informal* in a position of profit.

quid pro quo *n.* (*pl.* **quid pro quos**) a favour etc. given in return for another.

quiescent *adj.* inactive, quiet. □ **quiescence** *n.*

quiet *adj.* making little noise; free from disturbance; discreet, not elaborate or flamboyant. ● *n.* absence of noise or disturbance. ● *v.* make or become quiet. □ **on the quiet** *informal* secretly. □ **quietly** *adv.*, **quietness** *n.*

quieten *v.* make or become quiet.

quiff *n.* an upright tuft of hair.

quill *n.* **1** a large feather; a pen made from this. **2** each of a porcupine's spines.

quilt *n.* a padded bed-covering. ● *v.* line with padding and fix with lines of stitching.

quin *n. informal* a quintuplet.

quince *n.* a hard yellowish fruit.

quinine *n.* a bitter-tasting drug used to treat malaria.

quinsy *n.* (*pl.* **-ies**) an abscess on a tonsil.

quintessence *n.* a perfect example of a quality; an essential characteristic or element. □ **quintessential** *adj.*, **quintessentially** *adv.*

quintet *n.* a group of five instruments or voices; music for these.

quintuple *adj.* having five parts or members; five times as much as.

● *v.* increase by five times its amount.

quintuplet *n.* one of five children born at one birth.

quip *n.* a witty or sarcastic remark. ● *v.* (**quipped, quipping**) make a witty remark.

quire *n.* twenty-five (formerly twenty-four) sheets of writing paper.

quirk *n.* a peculiarity of behaviour; a trick of fate; a sudden twist or twitch.

quisling *n.* a traitor who collaborates with occupying forces.

quit *v.* (**quitted** or **quit, quitting**) **1** leave; *informal* resign from (a job). **2** *Amer.* cease, stop.

quite *adv.* **1** completely; exactly (expressing agreement). **2** to some extent, rather. □ **quite a few** a considerable number.

quits *adj.* on even terms after retaliation or repayment.

quiver *v.* shake or vibrate with a slight rapid motion. ● *n.* **1** a quivering movement or sound. **2** a case for holding arrows.

quixotic *adj.* idealistic; impractical. □ **quixotically** *adv.*

quiz *n.* (*pl.* **quizzes**) a series of questions testing knowledge, esp. as an entertainment. ● *v.* (**quizzed, quizzing**) interrogate.

quizzical *adj.* done in a questioning way, esp. humorously. □ **quizzically** *adv.*

quoit (koyt) *n.* a ring thrown to encircle a peg in the game of **quoits**.

quorate (**kwor**-ăt) *adj.* having a quorum present.

quorum (**kwor**-ŭm) *n.* a minimum number of people that must be present for a valid meeting.

quota *n.* a fixed share; a maximum or minimum number or amount that may be admitted, manufactured, etc.

quotable *adj.* worth quoting.

quotation *n.* quoting; a passage or price quoted.

quotation marks *n.pl.* punctuation marks (' ' or " ") enclosing words quoted.

quote *v.* **1** repeat or copy words from a book or speech; refer to as evidence or authority for a statement. **2** estimate (a price) for (a job).

quotidian (kwot-**id**-i-ăn) *adj.* daily.

quotient (**kwoh**-shĕnt) *n.* the result of a division sum.

q.v. *abbr.* which see (indicating that the reader should look at the reference given).

qwerty *adj.* denoting the standard layout of English-language keyboards.

Rr

R *abbr.* **1** Regina, Rex: *Elizabeth R.* **2** river. **3** registered as a trade mark. **4** *Chess* rook. □ **the three Rs** reading, writing, and arithmetic.

Ra *symb.* radium.

rabbi *n.* a religious leader of a Jewish congregation.

rabbinical *adj.* of rabbis or Jewish doctrines or law.

rabbit *n.* a burrowing animal with long ears and a short furry tail. ● *v.* (**rabbited, rabbiting**) *informal* talk at length in a rambling way.

rabble *n.* a disorderly crowd.

rabid *adj.* furious, fanatical; affected with rabies. □ **rabidity** *n.*

rabies *n.* a contagious fatal virus disease of dogs etc., that causes madness and can be transmitted to humans.

RAC *abbr.* Royal Automobile Club.

raccoon *n.* (also **racoon**) a small arboreal mammal of North America.

race *n.* **1** a contest of speed; (**the races**) a series of races for horses or dogs. **2** a large group of people with common ancestry and inherited physical characteristics; a genus, species, breed, or variety of animal or plant; belonging to a particular race, esp. as grounds for division or discrimination. ● *v.* compete in a race (with); move or operate at full or excessive speed. □ **racer** *n.*

racecourse *n.* a ground where horse races are held.

racetrack *n.* a racecourse; a track for motor racing.

raceme (ra-seem) *n.* a flower cluster with flowers attached by short stalks along a central stem.

racial *adj.* of or based on race. □ **racially** *adv.*

racialism *n.* racism. □ **racialist** *adj.* & *n.*

racism *n.* a belief in the superiority of a particular race; hostility or discrimination against members of a different race. □ **racist** *adj.* & *n.*

rack *n.* **1** a framework for hanging or placing things on. **2** a bar with teeth that engage with those of a wheel. **3** *hist.* an instrument of torture on which people were tied and stretched. ● *v.* (also **wrack**) subject to suffering or stress. □ **rack and ruin** destruction. **rack one's brains** try hard to think of something.

racket *n.* **1** (also **racquet**) a stringed bat used in tennis and similar games. **2** a din, a noisy fuss. **3** *informal* a fraudulent business or scheme.

racketeer *n.* a person who operates a fraudulent business etc. □ **racketeering** *n.*

raconteur (rak-on-ter) *n.* a person who is good at telling entertaining stories.

racoon var. of **raccoon**.

racquet var. of **racket** (*sense* 1).

racy *adj.* (**racier, raciest**) lively, entertaining, and mildly indecent. □ **racily** *adv.*

rad *n.* a unit of absorbed dose of ionizing radiation.

RADA *abbr.* Royal Academy of Dramatic Art.

radar *n.* a system for detecting objects by means of radio waves.

radial *adj.* **1** of rays or radii; having spokes or lines etc. that radiate from a central point. **2** (also **radial-ply**) (of a tyre) having the fabric layers parallel and the tread strengthened. ● *n.* a radial-ply tyre. □ **radially** *adv.*

radian *n.* an SI unit of plane angle; the angle at the centre of a circle formed by the radii of an arc equal in length to the radius.

radiant *adj.* **1** emitting rays of light or heat; emitted in rays. **2** looking very bright and happy. □ **radiance** *n.*, **radiantly** *adv.*

radiate *v.* **1** emit (energy) in rays; be emitted in rays. **2** spread outwards from a central point.

radiation *n.* **1** the process of radiating. **2** the sending out of rays and atomic particles characteristic of radioactive substances; these rays and particles.

radiator *n.* **1** an apparatus that radiates heat, esp. a metal case through which steam or hot water circulates. **2** an engine-cooling apparatus in a motor vehicle.

radical *adj.* fundamental, of or affecting the basic nature of something; extreme, thorough; advocating extreme political reform. ● *n.* someone holding radical views. □ **radically** *adv.*

radicchio (ră-dee-kioh) *n.* (*pl.* **radicchios**) a variety of chicory with reddish leaves.

radicle *n.* an embryo root.

radii pl. of **radius**.

radio *n.* (*pl.* **radios**) the process of sending and receiving messages etc. by electromagnetic waves; a transmitter or receiver for this; sound broadcasting. ● *adj.* of or involving radio. ● *v.* (**radioed, radioing**) transmit or communicate by radio.

radioactive *adj.* emitting radiation caused by the decay of atomic nuclei. □ **radioactivity** *n.*

radiocarbon *n.* a radioactive form of carbon used in carbon dating.

radiography *n.* the production of X-ray photographs. □ **radiographer** *n.*

radiology *n.* a study of X-rays and similar radiation, esp. of their use in medicine. □ **radiological** *adj.*, **radiologist** *n.*

radiophonic *adj.* relating to electronically produced sound.

radiotherapy *n.* the treatment of disease by X-rays or similar radiation. □ **radiotherapist** *n.*

radish *n.* a plant with a crisp root that is eaten raw.

radium *n.* a radioactive metallic element (symbol Ra) obtained from pitchblende.

radius *n.* (*pl.* **radii** or **radiuses**) **1** a straight line from the centre to the circumference of a circle; its length. **2** the thicker long bone of the forearm.

radon *n.* a chemical element (symbol Rn), a radioactive gas.

RAF *abbr.* Royal Air Force.

raffia *n.* fibre from the leaves of a palm tree, used for making hats, mats, etc.

raffish *adj.* slightly disreputable in appearance. □ **raffishness** *n.*

raffle *n.* a lottery with an object as the prize. ● *v.* offer as the prize in a raffle.

raft *n.* **1** a flat floating structure of timber etc., used as a boat. **2** a large collection.

rafter *n.* **1** one of the sloping beams forming the framework of a roof. **2** a person travelling on a raft.

rag *n.* **1** a torn or worn piece of cloth; (**rags**) old and torn clothes. **2** *informal* a newspaper, esp. one of poor quality. **3** a students' carnival in aid of charity. ● *v.* (**ragged, ragging**) *informal* tease.

ragamuffin *n.* a person in ragged dirty clothes.

rage *n.* **1** violent anger. **2** a fashion, something very popular: *his songs are all the rage.* ● *v.* **1** show violent anger. **2** (of a storm or battle) continue furiously.

ragged *adj.* (of clothes) old and torn; wearing ragged clothes; uneven, jagged.

raglan *n.* a sleeve that continues to the neck, without a shoulder seam.

ragout (ra-**goo**) *n.* a stew of meat and vegetables.

raid *n.* a brief attack to destroy or seize something; a surprise visit by police etc. to arrest suspected people or seize illicit goods. ● *v.* make a raid on. □ **raider** *n.*

rail *n.* **1** a horizontal bar. **2** any of the lines of metal bars on which trains or trams run; the railway system. ● *v.* **1** enclose or protect with a rail. **2** convey by rail. **3** utter angry reproaches.

railing *n.* a fence of rails supported on upright metal bars.

railroad *n. Amer.* a railway. ● *v. informal* force into hasty action.

railway *n.* a set of rails on which trains run; a system of transport using these.

raiment *n. archaic* clothing.

rain *n.* atmospheric moisture falling as drops; a fall of this; a shower of things. ● *v.* send down or fall as or like rain.

rainbow *n.* an arch of colours formed in rain or spray by the sun's rays.

raincoat *n.* a rain-resistant coat.

raindrop *n.* a single drop of rain.

rainfall *n.* the total amount of rain falling in a given time.

rainforest *n.* dense wet tropical forest.

rainy *adj.* (**rainier, rainiest**) in or on which much rain falls.

raise *v.* **1** move or lift to a higher level; increase the amount or level of; promote; multiply (a number). **2** move to an upright position. **3** bring to people's attention, cause to be felt, noticed, etc. **4** collect, earn, or procure (a sum of money). **5** bring up (children). ● *n. Amer.* an increase in salary.

raisin *n.* a dried grape.

raising agent *n.* a substance that makes bread etc. swell in cooking.

raison d'être (ray-zawn **detr**) (*pl.* **raisons d'être**) a reason for or purpose of a thing's existence.

Raj (rahj) *n.* the period of British rule in India.

raja *n.* (also **rajah**) *hist.* an Indian king or prince.

rake *n.* **1** a tool with prongs for gathering leaves, smoothing loose soil, etc. **2** a backward slope of an object. **3** a man who lives an irresponsible and immoral life. ● *v.* **1** gather or smooth with a rake; scratch and wound with a set of points; sweep with gunfire etc. **2** search; look over. **3** set (a stage etc.) at an angle. □ **rake up** revive the memory of (an unpleasant incident).

rake-off *n. informal* a share of profits.

rakish *adj.* dashing but slightly disreputable.

rallentando *adv. Music* with a gradual decrease of speed.

rally *v.* (**rallied, rallying**) **1** bring or come (back) together for a united effort. **2** revive; recover strength. ● *n.* (*pl.* **-ies**) **1** a mass meeting in support of a cause or pursuit of an interest. **2** a long-distance driving competition over public roads. **3** a recovery. **4** a series of strokes in tennis etc.

RAM *abbr. Computing* random-access memory, a temporary working memory.

ram *n.* **1** an uncastrated male sheep. **2** a striking or plunging device. ● *v.* (**rammed, ramming**) strike or push heavily, crash against.

Ramadan *n.* the ninth month of the Muslim year, when Muslims fast during daylight hours.

ramble *n.* a walk taken for pleasure. ● *v.* **1** take a ramble. **2** talk at length and in an incoherent way. □ **rambler** *n.*

ramekin (ram-ĕ-kin) *n.* a small individual baking dish.

ramification *n.* **1** a complex outcome of an action or event. **2** a subdivision of a complex structure.

ramify *v.* (**ramified, ramifying**) form branches or subdivisions.

ramp *n.* a slope joining two levels.

rampage *v.* (ram-**payj**) behave or race about violently. ● *n.* (ram-payj) violent behaviour. □ **on the rampage** rampaging.

rampant *adj.* **1** flourishing uncontrollably, unrestrained. **2** (of an animal in heraldry) standing on one hind leg with the opposite foreleg raised.

rampart *n.* a broad-topped defensive wall or bank of earth.

ram-raid *n.* a robbery in which a vehicle is crashed into a shop etc. ● *v.* rob in this way.

ramrod *n.* an iron rod formerly used for ramming a charge into guns.

ramshackle *adj.* tumbledown, rickety.

ran past of **run**.

ranch *n.* a cattle-breeding establishment, esp. in North America; a farm where certain other animals are bred. ● *v.* operate a ranch. □ **rancher** *n.*

rancid *adj.* smelling or tasting like stale fat. □ **rancidity** *n.*

rancour *n.* (*Amer.* **rancor**) a feeling of bitterness or ill will. □ **rancorous** *adj.*

rand *n.* a unit of money in South Africa.

R & B *abbr.* rhythm and blues.

R & D *abbr.* research and development.

random *adj.* done or occurring without method, planning, etc. □ **at random** without a particular aim or purpose. □ **randomness** *n.*

random-access *adj.* (of a computer memory or file) with all parts directly accessible, so that it need not be read sequentially. *See also* **RAM**.

randy *adj.* (**randier, randiest**) *informal* lustful, sexually aroused.

rang past of **ring**.

range *n.* **1** a set or series of similar or related things. **2** the limits between which something operates or varies. **3** the distance over which a thing can travel or be effective; the distance to an objective. **4** a large open area for grazing or hunting. **5** a place with targets for shooting practice. **6** a series of mountains or hills. ● *v.* **1** vary or extend between specified limits. **2** place in rows or in order. **3** travel or wander over a wide area.

rangefinder *n.* a device for calculating the distance to a target etc.

ranger *n.* an official in charge of a park or forest; a mounted warden policing a thinly populated area.

rangy *adj.* (**rangier, rangiest**) tall and thin.

rank *n.* **1** a position in a hierarchy, esp. in the armed forces; high social position. **2** a line of people or things. **3** (**the ranks**) ordinary soldiers, not officers. ● *v.* give a rank to; have a specified rank; arrange in ranks. ● *adj.* **1** growing too thickly and coarsely. **2** foul-smelling; unmistakably bad. □ **rank and file** the ordinary members of an organization. □ **rankness** *n.*

rankle *v.* cause lasting resentment.

ransack *v.* search thoroughly or roughly; rob or pillage (a place).

ransom *n.* a price demanded or paid for the release of a captive. ● *v.* demand or pay a ransom for.

rant *v.* make a violent speech.

rap *n.* **1** a quick sharp blow; the sound of this; *informal* criticism. **2** a monologue recited rhythmically to music. ● *v.* (**rapped, rapping**) strike with a quick sharp blow; *informal* reprimand. □ **take the rap** *informal* suffer the consequences.

rapacious *adj.* grasping, violently greedy. □ **rapacity** *adj.*

rape[1] *v.* have sexual intercourse with someone without consent. ● *n.* this act or crime; destruction or spoiling of a place.

rape[2] *n.* a plant with oil-rich seeds.

rapid *adj.* quick, swift. ● *n.pl.* (**rapids**) a swift current where a river bed slopes steeply. □ **rapidity** *n.*, **rapidly** *adv.*

rapier *n.* a thin light sword.

rapist *n.* a person who commits rape.

rapport (ra-**por**) *n.* a harmonious understanding or relationship.

rapprochement (ra-**prosh**-mahn) *n.* a resumption of friendly relations.

rapt *adj.* fascinated, absorbed. □ **raptly** *adv.*

rapture *n.* intense delight. □ **rapturous** *adj.*, **rapturously** *adv.*

rare *adj.* **1** very uncommon; exceptionally good. **2** (of meat) lightly cooked, still red inside. □ **rarely** *adv.*, **rareness** *n.*, **rarity** *n.*

rarebit *see* **Welsh rabbit**.

rarefied *adj.* **1** (of the atmosphere) of low density, thin. **2** (of an idea etc.) very subtle; esoteric. □ **rarefaction** *n.*

raring *adj. informal* very eager: *raring to go.*

rascal *n.* a dishonest or mischievous person. □ **rascally** *adv.*

rase var. of **raze**.

rash *n.* an eruption of spots or patches on the skin. ● *adj.* acting or done without due consideration of the risks. □ **rashly** *adv.*, **rashness** *n.*

rasher *n.* a slice of bacon or ham.

rasp *n.* **1** a coarse file. **2** a grating sound. ● *v.* scrape with a rasp; utter with or make a grating sound.

raspberry *n.* (*pl.* **-ies**) **1** an edible red berry. **2** *informal* a vulgar sound of disapproval.

rasterize *v.* (also **-ise**) convert (an image) into a set of points on a grid for display on a computer screen.

rat *n.* **1** a rodent like a large mouse. **2** *informal* an unpleasant or treacherous person. □ **rat on** (**ratted, ratting**) *informal* desert or betray.

ratable var. of **rateable**.

ratchet *n.* a bar or wheel with notches in which a device engages to prevent backward movement.

rate *n.* **1** a quantity, frequency, etc., measured against some other quantity. **2** a fixed price or charge; (**rates**) a tax levied according to the value of buildings and land. **3** a speed. ● *v.* **1** estimate the worth or value of; consider, regard as. **2** deserve; be of or regarded as of a specified nature. □ **at any rate** no matter what happens; at least.

rateable *adj.* (also **ratable**) liable to rates.

rateable value *n.* the value at which a business etc. is assessed for rates.

rather *adv.* **1** by preference: *I'd rather not.* **2** to a certain extent. **3** on the contrary; more precisely. **4** emphatically yes.

ratify *v.* (**ratified, ratifying**) confirm (an agreement etc.) formally. □ **ratification** *n.*

rating *n.* **1** the level at which a thing is rated. **2** a non-commissioned sailor.

ratio *n.* (*pl.* **ratios**) the relationship between two amounts, reckoned as the number of times one contains the other.

ratiocinate *v.* reason logically. □ **ratiocination** *n.*

ration *n.* a fixed allowance of food etc. ● *v.* limit to a ration.

rational *adj.* able to reason; sane; based on reasoning. □ **rationality** *n.*, **rationally** *adv.*

rationale (rash-ŏ-**nahl**) *n.* a fundamental reason; a logical basis.

rationalism *n.* treating reason as the basis of belief and knowledge. □ **rationalist** *n.*, **rationalistic** *adj.*

rationalize *v.* (also **-ise**) **1** invent a rational explanation for. **2** make more efficient by reorganizing. □ **rationalization** *n.*

rat race *n. informal* a fiercely competitive struggle for success.

rattan *n.* jointed stems of a palm, used in furniture making.

rattle *v.* **1** (cause to) make a rapid series of short hard sounds. **2** *informal* make nervous or irritable. ● *n.* a rattling sound; a device for making this, esp. as a baby's toy. □ **rattle off** utter rapidly.

rattlesnake *n.* a poisonous American snake with a rattling tail.

raucous (ror-kŭs) *adj.* loud and harsh. □ **raucously** *adv.*, **raucousness** *n.*

raunchy *adj.* (**raunchier, raunchiest**) *informal* coarsely outspoken; sexually provocative. □ **raunchily** *adv.*, **raunchiness** *n.*

ravage *v.* do great damage to. ● *n.pl.* (**ravages**) damage.

rave *v.* talk wildly or furiously; speak with rapturous enthusiasm. ● *n.* **1** an all-night party with loud music, attended by large numbers of young people. **2** *informal* a very enthusiastic review or reception.

ravel *v.* (**ravelled, ravelling**; *Amer.* **raveled**) complicate. □ **ravel out** untangle.

raven *n.* a black bird with a hoarse cry. ● *adj.* (of hair) glossy black.

ravenous *adj.* very hungry. □ **ravenously** *adv.*

ravine (ră-veen) *n.* a deep narrow gorge.

raving *adj.* **1** delirious. **2** *informal* utter, extreme: *a raving beauty.*

ravioli *n.* small square pasta cases containing a savoury filling.

ravish *v.* **1** rape. **2** delight.

ravishing *adj.* enchanting, delightful.

raw *adj.* **1** not cooked; not yet processed; inexperienced. **2** (of a part of the body) red and painful from friction. **3** (of weather) bleak, cold. **4** (of an emotion or quality) strong and undisguised. □ **rawness** *n.*

raw deal *n.* unfair treatment.

rawhide *n.* untanned leather.

ray *n.* **1** a line or narrow beam of light or other radiation. **2** one of a set of things arranged radially. **3** a large marine flat fish. **4** *Music* (also

re) the second note of a major scale, or the note D.

rayon *n.* a synthetic fibre or fabric, made from cellulose.

raze *v.* (also **rase**) tear down (a building).

razor *n.* a sharp-edged instrument used for shaving.

razzmatazz *n. informal* extravagant publicity and display.

Rb *abbr.* rubidium.

RC *abbr.* Roman Catholic.

RDA *abbr.* recommended daily allowance.

RE *abbr.* **1** religious education. **2** Royal Engineers.

Re *symb.* rhenium.

re[1] *prep.* concerning.

re[2] var. of **ray** (*sense* 4).

re- *pref.* again; back again.

reach *v.* **1** stretch out a hand to touch or take something. **2** arrive at; extend as far as; be able to touch; make contact with; achieve. ● *n.* **1** the distance over which someone or something can reach. **2** a section of a river. □ **out of reach** too far away to be touched; unattainable.

react *v.* cause or undergo a reaction. □ **reactive** *adj.*

reaction *n.* a response to a stimulus or act or situation etc.; a chemical change produced by substances acting upon each other; an occurrence of one condition after a period of the opposite; a bad physical response to a drug.

reactionary *adj.* & *n.* (*pl.* **-ies**) (a person) opposed to progress and reform.

reactor *n.* an apparatus for the production of nuclear energy.

read *v.* (**read, reading**) **1** look at and understand the meaning of (written or printed words or symbols); speak (such words etc.) aloud; study or discover by reading. **2** (of a passage of writing) have a certain wording. **3** (of an instrument) indicate as a measurement. **4** interpret mentally. ● *n.* a session of reading; *informal* a book considered in terms of its readability. □ **read into** see (a meaning) as implied by a situation or utterance when in fact it is not.

readable *adj.* **1** pleasant to read. **2** legible. □ **readably** *adv.*

reader *n.* **1** a person who reads. **2** a senior lecturer at a university. **3** a device producing a readable image from a microfilm etc. **4** a book containing passages of a particular author's work or designed to give practice in reading.

readership *n.* **1** the readers of a newspaper etc. **2** the position of a reader at a university.

readily *adv.* **1** willingly. **2** easily.

readjust *v.* adjust again; adapt oneself again. □ **readjustment** *n.*

ready *adj.* **1** in a suitable state for action or use, prepared; available; willing; inclined to or on the point of; quick or easy. ● *v.* (**readied, readying**) prepare. ● *n.* (**the ready**) *informal* cash. □ **readiness** *n.*

reagent (ree-ay-jěnt) *n.* a substance used to produce a chemical reaction.

real *adj.* existing as a thing or occurring as a fact; genuine, natural; actual, not ostensible or assumed.

real estate *n.* immovable assets, i.e. buildings or land.

realign *v.* align again; regroup in politics etc.

realism *n.* representing or viewing things as they are in reality. □ **realist** *n.*

realistic *adj.* showing realism; practical. □ **realistically** *adv.*

reality *n.* (*pl.* **-ies**) the quality of being real; something real and not imaginary; life and the world as they really are.

reality TV *n.* television programmes about real people and situations, made for entertainment rather than information.

realize *v.* (also **-ise**) **1** be or become aware of; accept as a fact. **2** fulfil (a hope or plan). **3** convert (an asset) into money; make (a profit). □ **realization** *n.*

really *adv.* **1** in fact. **2** thoroughly. **3** indeed; I assure you. **4** I protest.

realm *n.* **1** a kingdom. **2** a field of activity or interest.

realty (ree-ăl-ti) *n.* real estate.

ream *n.* a quantity of paper (usu. 500 sheets); (**reams**) a great quantity of written matter.

reap *v.* **1** cut (grain etc.) as harvest. **2** receive as the consequence of actions. □ **reaper** *n.*

reappear *v.* appear again.

rear *n.* the back part. ● *adj.* situated at the back. ● *v.* **1** bring up (children); breed and look after (animals); cultivate (crops). **2** (of a horse etc.) raise itself on its hind legs. **3** (of a building etc.) extend to a great height. □ **bring up the rear** be last. **rear one's head** raise one's head; emerge.

rear admiral *n.* a naval officer next below vice admiral.

rearguard *n.* troops protecting an army's rear.

rearm *v.* arm again. □ **rearmament** *n.*

rearrange *v.* arrange in a different way. □ **rearrangement** *n.*

rearward *adj., adv., & n.* (towards or at) the rear. □ **rearwards** *adv.*

reason *n.* **1** a motive, cause, or justification. **2** the ability to think and draw conclusions; sanity; good sense or judgement. ● *v.* use one's ability to think and draw conclusions. □ **reason with** try to persuade by argument.

reasonable *adj.* **1** ready to use or listen to reason; in accordance with reason, logical. **2** appropriate, moderate, not excessive. □ **reasonably** *adv.*

reassemble *v.* assemble again.

reassure *v.* restore confidence to. □ **reassurance** *n.*

rebate *n.* **1** a partial refund. **2** var. of **rabbet**.

rebel *n.* (re-bĕl) a person who rebels. ● *v.* (ri-**bel**) (**rebelled, rebelling**) fight against an established government; oppose authority or convention. □ **rebellion** *n.*, **rebellious** *adj.*

reboot *v.* start up (a computer) again.

rebound *v.* (ri-**bownd**) spring back after impact. ● *n.* (ree-bownd) the act of rebounding. □ **on the rebound** while still grieving over a failed relationship.

rebuff *v.* reject ungraciously. ● *n.* a snub.

rebuild *v.* (**rebuilt, rebuilding**) build again after destruction.

rebuke *v.* reprove. ● *n.* a reproof.

rebus (ree-bŭs) *n.* a representation of a word by pictures etc. suggesting its parts.

rebut *v.* (**rebutted, rebutting**) declare or show to be false. □ **rebuttal** *n.*

recalcitrant *adj.* obstinately disobedient. □ **recalcitrance** *n.*

recall *v.* **1** summon to return. **2** remember; remind someone of. ● *n.* recalling, being recalled.

recant *v.* withdraw and reject (one's former statement or belief). □ **recantation** *n.*

recap *informal v.* (**recapped, recapping**) recapitulate. ● *n.* a recapitulation.

recapitulate *v.* state again briefly. □ **recapitulation** *n.*

recapture *v.* capture again; experience again. ● *n.* recapturing.

recce (re-kee) *n. informal* a reconnaissance.

recede *v.* move back from a position; diminish; slope backwards.

receipt (ri-**seet**) *n.* the act of receiving; a written acknowledgement that something has been received or money paid.

receive *v.* **1** acquire, accept, or take in. **2** experience, be treated with. **3** greet on arrival.

receiver *n.* **1** a person or thing that receives something. **2** a person who deals in stolen goods. **3** the earpiece of a telephone; an apparatus that receives electrical signals and converts them into sound or images. **4** (in full **official re-**

ceiver) an official who handles the affairs of a bankrupt person or company.

receivership *n.* the office of official receiver; the state of being dealt with by a receiver.

recent *adj.* happening in a time shortly before the present. □ **recently** *adv.*

receptacle *n.* a container.

reception *n.* **1** an act or process of receiving; a reaction to something. **2** an assembly held to receive guests. **3** an area in a hotel, office, etc. where guests and visitors are greeted on arrival.

receptionist *n.* a person employed to receive and direct clients or guests.

receptive *adj.* quick to receive ideas. □ **receptiveness** *n.*

receptor *n.* a bodily organ able to respond to a stimulus and transmit a signal through a nerve.

recess *n.* **1** a part or space set back from the line of a wall or room etc. **2** a temporary cessation from business. ● *v.* set (a light etc.) in a recess.

recession *n.* a temporary decline in economic activity.

recessive *adj.* **1** (of a genetic characteristic) remaining latent when a dominant characteristic is present. **2** undergoing an economic recession.

recidivist (rĕ-**sid**-iv-ist) *n.* a person who persistently relapses into crime. □ **recidivism** *n.*

recipe (ress-ipi) *n.* directions for preparing a dish; something certain to lead to a particular outcome.

recipient *n.* a person who receives something.

reciprocal *adj.* both given and received; given in return; (of an agreement) binding both parties equally. □ **reciprocally** *adv.*, **reciprocity** *n.*

reciprocate *v.* **1** respond to (an action etc.) with a corresponding one. **2** (of part of a machine) move backwards and forwards. □ **reciprocation** *n.*

recital *n.* **1** a musical entertainment. **2** a listing of names etc.

recitative (ressi-tă-**teev**) *n.* a narrative part of an opera, sung in a rhythm imitating speech.

recite *v.* repeat aloud from memory; state (facts) in order. □ **recitation** *n.*

reckless *adj.* wildly impulsive. □ **recklessly** *adv.*, **recklessness** *n.*

reckon *v.* **1** count; calculate. **2** *informal* have as one's opinion. □ **reckon on** rely on. **reckon with** take into account.

reclaim *v.* **1** take action to recover possession of. **2** make (wasteland) usable. □ **reclamation** *n.*

recline *v.* lie back with one's back supported.

recluse *n.* a person who avoids contact with other people.

recognition *n.* recognizing.

recognizance (rĕ-**kog**-niz-ăns) *n.* a pledge made to a law court or magistrate; surety for this.

recognize *v.* (also **-ise**) **1** know again from one's previous experience; identify from knowledge. **2** acknowledge as genuine, valid, or worthy. □ **recognizable** *adj.*

recoil *v.* spring or shrink back in fear or disgust; rebound. ● *n.* the act of recoiling. □ **recoil upon** (of an action) have an adverse effect on (the originator).

recollect *v.* remember, call to mind. □ **recollection** *n.*

recommend *v.* praise or suggest as suitable; advise; (of a quality etc.) make (the possessor) desirable. □ **recommendation** *n.*

■ **Usage** *Recommend* is spelt with one *c* and two *m*s.

---

recompense *v.* repay, compensate. ● *n.* compensation.

reconcile *v.* make friendly after an estrangement; induce to tolerate something unwelcome; make compatible. □ **reconciliation** *n.*

recondite *adj.* obscure, dealing with an obscure subject.

recondition *v.* overhaul, repair.

reconnaissance (ri-**kon**-is-ăns) *n.* a preliminary survey, esp. exploration of an area for military purposes.

reconnoitre (rek-ŏn-oy-tĕ) *v.* (*Amer.* **reconnoiter**) (**reconnoitred, reconnoitring**) make a reconnaissance (of).

reconsider *v.* consider again; consider changing. ◻ **reconsideration** *n.*

reconstitute *v.* reconstruct; restore (dried food) to its original form. ◻ **reconstitution** *n.*

reconstruct *v.* **1** rebuild after damage. **2** enact (a past event). ◻ **reconstruction** *n.*

record *v.* (ri-**kord**) **1** set down in writing or other permanent form. **2** preserve (sound) on a disc or magnetic tape for later reproduction. **3** (of a measuring instrument) indicate, register. ● *n.* (**re**-kord) **1** information set down in writing etc.; a document bearing this. **2** a disc bearing recorded sound. **3** facts known about a person's past. **4** the best performance or most remarkable event etc. of its kind. ● *adj.* (**re**-kord) the best or most extreme hitherto recorded. ◻ **off the record** unofficially; not for publication.

recorder *n.* **1** a person or thing that records. **2** a barrister or solicitor serving as a part-time judge. **3** a simple woodwind instrument.

recount *v.* narrate, tell in detail.

re-count *v.* count again. ● *n.* a second or subsequent counting.

recoup *v.* regain (something lost or spent); reimburse.

recourse *n.* a source of help to which one may turn. ◻ **have recourse to** turn to for help.

recover *v.* **1** regain possession or control of. **2** return to health. ◻ **recovery** *n.*

recreation *n.* a pastime; relaxation. ◻ **recreational** *adj.*

recrimination *n.* an accusation in response to another. ◻ **recriminatory** *adj.*

recruit *n.* a new member, esp. of the armed forces. ● *v.* enlist (someone) as a recruit; form (an army etc.) from recruits. ◻ **recruitment** *n.*

rectal *adj.* of the rectum.

rectangle *n.* a geometric figure with four sides and four right angles, esp. with adjacent sides unequal in length. ◻ **rectangular** *adj.*

rectifier *n.* an electrical device converting an alternating current to a direct one.

rectify *v.* (**rectified, rectifying**) **1** put right. **2** convert (an alternating current) to a direct one. ◻ **rectification** *n.*

rectilinear *adj.* consisting of or bounded by straight lines.

rectitude *n.* correctness of behaviour or procedure.

rector *n.* **1** a clergyman in charge of a parish. **2** the head of certain schools, colleges, and universities.

rectory *n.* (*pl.* **-ies**) the house of a rector.

rectum *n.* (*pl.* **rectums** or **recta**) the last section of the intestine, between the colon and the anus.

recumbent *adj.* lying down.

recuperate *v.* recover from illness; regain. ◻ **recuperation** *n.*, **recuperative** *adj.*

recur *v.* (**recurred, recurring**) happen again or repeatedly. ◻ **recurrence** *n.*, **recurrent** *adj.*

recusant (rek-koo-zănt) *n.* a person who refuses to submit or comply.

recycle *v.* convert (waste material) for reuse.

red *adj.* (**redder, reddest**) **1** of or like the colour of blood; flushed, esp. with embarrassment; (of hair) reddish brown. **2** communist, favouring communism. ● *n.* **1** a red colour or thing. **2** a communist. ◻ **in the red** overdrawn. **see red** *informal* become very angry. ◻ **reddish** *adj.*, **redness** *n.*

red carpet *n.* privileged treatment for an important visitor.

redcurrant *n.* a small edible red berry.

redden *v.* make or become red.

redeem *v.* **1** compensate for the faults of; save from sin. **2** buy back; exchange (vouchers etc.) for goods. **3** fulfil (a promise). □ **redemption** *n.*, **redemptive** *adj.*

redeploy *v.* send to a new place or task. □ **redeployment** *n.*

red-handed *adj.* in the act of committing a crime.

redhead *n.* a person with red hair.

red herring *n.* a misleading clue or diversion.

red-hot *adj.* **1** glowing red from heat. **2** very exciting or popular.

redirect *v.* direct or send to another place. □ **redirection** *n.*

red-letter day *n.* a day that is memorable because of a success or happy event.

red light *n.* a signal to stop; a danger signal.

red-light district *n.* a district containing many brothels.

redolent *adj.* **1** strongly reminiscent or suggestive. **2** smelling strongly of something. □ **redolence** *n.*

redouble *v.* increase or intensify.

redoubtable *adj.* formidable.

redress *v.* set right. ● *n.* reparation, amends.

red tape *informal n.* excessive formalities in official transactions.

reduce *v.* **1** make or become smaller or less; lose weight. **2** bring to a weaker or worse state. **3** convert to a simpler or more basic form; state simply. **4** demote (an officer). □ **be reduced to** be forced by hardship to. □ **reducible** *adj.*, **reduction** *n.*

redundant *adj.* superfluous; no longer needed; no longer in employment. □ **redundancy** *n.*

redwood *n.* a very tall evergreen Californian tree.

reed *n.* **1** a water or marsh plant with tall hollow stems; its stem. **2** a vibrating part producing sound in certain wind instruments.

reedy *adj.* (**reedier, reediest**) (of the voice) having a thin high tone. □ **reediness** *n.*

reef *n.* **1** a ridge of rock or sand etc. reaching to or near the surface of water. **2** a part of a sail that can be drawn in when there is a high wind. ● *v.* shorten (a sail).

reefer *n.* **1** a thick double-breasted jacket. **2** *informal* a cannabis cigarette.

reef knot *n.* a symmetrical double knot.

reek *n.* a strong unpleasant smell. ● *v.* smell strongly.

reel *n.* **1** a cylinder on which something is wound. **2** a lively folk or Scottish dance. ● *v.* **1** wind on or off a reel. **2** stagger. □ **reel off** say rapidly without effort.

refectory *n.* (*pl.* **-ies**) the dining room of a monastery or college etc.

refer *v.* (**referred, referring**) □ **refer to 1** mention. **2** pass to an authority for decision; send to a specialist. **3** turn to for information.

referee *n.* **1** an umpire, esp. in football and boxing; a person to whom disputes are referred for decision. **2** a person willing to testify to the character or ability of one applying for a job. ● *v.* (**refereed, refereeing**) act as referee in (a match etc.).

reference *n.* **1** a mention or allusion. **2** use of a source of information; consultation. **3** a letter from a previous employer testifying to someone's suitability for a job; someone providing this. □ **in** or **with reference to** concerning.

reference book *n.* a book providing information.

reference library *n.* (*pl.* **-ies**) a library containing books that can be consulted but not taken away.

referendum *n.* (*pl.* **referendums** or **referenda**) the referring of a question to the people for decision by a general vote.

referral *n.* referring.

refill *v.* (ree-**fil**) fill again. ● *n.* (**ree**-fil) a second or later filling; material used for this.

refine *v.* remove impurities or defects from; make small improvements to.

refined *adj.* **1** with impurities removed. **2** elegant, cultured.

refinement *n.* **1** refining. **2** elegance of behaviour. **3** an improvement added. **4** a fine distinction.

refinery *n.* (*pl.* **-ies**) an establishment where crude substances are refined.

refit *v.* (**refitted, refitting**) renew or repair the fittings of.

reflate *v.* restore (a financial system) after deflation. □ **reflation** *n.*, **reflationary** *adj.*

reflect *v.* **1** throw back (light, heat, or sound); show an image of; bring (credit or discredit). **2** think deeply.

reflection *n.* **1** reflecting or being reflected. **2** a reflected image; reflected light etc. **3** thought; an idea. □ **a reflection on** a source of discredit to.

reflective *adj.* **1** reflecting (light etc.). **2** thoughtful.

reflector *n.* something that reflects light or heat.

reflex *n.* (also **reflex action**) an involuntary or instinctive movement in response to a stimulus.

reflex angle *n.* an angle of more than 180°.

reflexive *adj.* & *n. Grammar* (a word or form) showing that the action of the verb is performed on its subject (e.g. *he washed himself*).

reflexology *n.* the massaging of points on the feet as a treatment for stress and other conditions.

reform *v.* improve by removing faults; (cause to) give up bad behaviour. ● *n.* reforming. □ **reformation** *n.*, **reformer** *n.*, **reformist** *n.*

reformatory *adj.* reforming. ● *n.* (*pl.* **-ies**) *Amer., hist.* an institution to which young offenders were sent to be reformed.

refract *v.* (of water, air, or glass) make (a ray of light) change direction when it enters at an angle. □ **refraction** *n.*, **refractive** *adj.*, **refractor** *n.*

refractory *adj.* resisting control or discipline; resistant to treatment or heat.

refrain *v.* keep oneself from doing something. ● *n.* recurring lines of a song; music for these.

refresh *v.* **1** restore the vigour of by food, drink, or rest. **2** stimulate (a person's memory).

refreshing *adj.* **1** restoring vigour; cooling. **2** new and stimulating or welcome. □ **refreshingly** *adv.*

refreshment *n.* **1** relaxing; regaining vigour. **2** (**refreshments**) food and drink.

refrigerate *v.* make extremely cold, esp. in order to preserve. □ **refrigeration** *n.*

refrigerator *n.* a cabinet or room in which food is stored at a very low temperature.

refuge *n.* a shelter from pursuit or danger.

refugee *n.* a person who has left home and seeks refuge (e.g. from war or persecution).

refulgent *adj. literary* shining.

refund *v.* (ri-**fund**) pay back. ● *n.* (**ree**-fund) a repayment, money refunded.

refurbish *v.* make clean or bright again; redecorate. □ **refurbishment** *n.*

refuse[1] (ri-**fewz**) *v.* say or show that one is unwilling to do something; show unwillingness to accept or grant (something offered or requested). □ **refusal** *n.*

refuse[2] (**ref**-yooss) *n.* waste material.

refute *v.* prove (a statement or person) wrong. □ **refutation** *n.*

■ **Usage** *Refute* means 'disprove', not simply 'deny, contradict'.

---

regain *v.* obtain again after loss; reach again.

regal *adj.* like or fit for a king. □ **regality** *n.*, **regally** *adv.*

regale *v.* feed or entertain well.

regalia (ri-gay-li-ă) *n.pl.* emblems of royalty or rank.

regard *v.* **1** consider, think of as being of a specified kind. **2** look steadily at. ● *n.* **1** attention, concern. **2** liking, respect. **3** a steady gaze. **4** (**regards**) greetings conveyed in a message. □ **as regards** or **with regard to** concerning.

regarding *prep.* with reference to.

regardless *adv.* taking no notice of circumstances. □ **regardless of** despite; without regard for.

regatta *n.* boat races organized as a sporting event.

regency *n.* (*pl.* **-ies**) rule by a regent; a period of this.

regenerate *v.* regrow (new tissue); give new life or vigour to. □ **regeneration** *n.*, **regenerative** *adj.*

regent *n.* a person appointed to rule while the monarch is a minor or is unwell or absent.

reggae (reg-ay) *n.* a West Indian style of music with a strong beat.

regicide *n.* the killing or killer of a king.

regime (ray-*zh*eem) *n.* **1** a government. **2** a system of doing things; a regimen.

regimen *n.* a prescribed course of treatment etc.

regiment *n.* a permanent unit of an army. ● *v.* organize rigidly. □ **regimentation** *n.*

regimental *adj.* of an army regiment.

Regina *n.* **1** a reigning queen: *Elizabeth Regina.* **2** *Law* the Crown: *Regina v. Jones.*

region *n.* an area; an administrative division of a country; a part of a body or surface. □ **in the region of** approximately. □ **regional** *adj.*

register *n.* **1** an official list. **2** a range of a voice or musical instrument; a level of formality in language. ● *v.* **1** enter in a register; record in writing. **2** (of a measuring instrument) show (a reading); notice, be aware of; be noticed; convey (a feeling etc.). □ **registration** *n.*

register office *n.* a place where records of births, marriages, and deaths are kept and civil marriages are performed.

registrar *n.* **1** an official responsible for keeping written records. **2** a hospital doctor ranking just below specialist.

registry *n.* (*pl.* **-ies**) **1** registration. **2** a place where written records are kept.

registry office *n.* a register office.

regress *v.* (ri-**gress**) relapse to an earlier or more primitive state. ● *n.* (ree-gress) **1** regressing. **2** a series of statements in which the same logical procedure is constantly repeated and no conclusion can be reached. □ **regression** *n.*, **regressive** *adj.*

regret *n.* a feeling of sorrow, annoyance, or repentance. ● *v.* (**regretted, regretting**) feel regret about. □ **regretful** *adj.*, **regretfully** *adv.*

regrettable *adj.* unfortunate, undesirable. □ **regrettably** *adv.*

regular *adj.* **1** forming or following a definite pattern; occurring at uniform intervals; conforming to an accepted role or pattern. **2** frequent, repeated; doing something frequently. **3** even, symmetrical. **4** forming a country's permanent armed forces. ● *n.* **1** *informal* a regular customer. **2** a regular soldier etc. □ **regularity** *n.*, **regularly** *adv.*

regularize *v.* (also **-ise**) make regular; make lawful or correct. □ **regularization** *n.*

regulate *v.* control (something) so that it functions properly; control by rules; set (a clock etc.) by an external standard. □ **regulator** *n.*

regulation *n.* a rule; regulating.

regulo *n.* a point on the temperature scale of a gas oven; *cook at regulo 6.*

regurgitate *v.* bring (swallowed food) up again to the mouth; repeat (facts) without understanding. □ **regurgitation** *n.*

rehabilitate *v.* restore to a normal life or good condition. □ **rehabilitation** *n.*

rehash *v.* (ree-**hash**) put (old material) into a new form. ● *n.* (ree-hash) rehashing; something made of rehashed material.

rehearse *v.* practise (a play etc.) for later performance; state (a number of points). □ **rehearsal** *n.*

rehouse *v.* provide with new accommodation.

reign *n.* a sovereign's (period of) rule. ● *v.* rule as king or queen; be supreme.

reimburse *v.* repay (a person); refund. □ **reimbursement** *n.*

rein *n.* a long strap fastened to a bridle, used to guide or check a horse; a means of control. ● *v.* control with reins; restrain.

reincarnation *n.* the rebirth of a soul in another body after death. □ **reincarnate** *v.*

reindeer *n.* (*pl.* **reindeer** or **reindeers**) a deer of Arctic regions.

reinforce *v.* strengthen with additional people, material, or quantity. □ **reinforcement** *n.*

reinstate *v.* restore to a previous position. □ **reinstatement** *n.*

reiterate *v.* say or do again or repeatedly. □ **reiteration** *n.*

reject *v.* (ri-**jekt**) refuse to accept. ● *n.* (ree-jekt) a person or thing rejected. □ **rejection** *n.*

rejig *v.* (**rejigged, rejigging**) **1** rearrange. **2** *dated* re-equip with machinery.

rejoice *v.* feel or show great joy; *archaic* gladden.

rejoin *v.* **1** join again. **2** retort.

rejoinder *n.* a reply, a retort.

rejuvenate *v.* restore youthful appearance or vigour to. □ **rejuvenation** *n.*, **rejuvenator** *n.*

relapse *v.* fall back into a previous state; become worse after improvement. ● *n.* relapsing.

relate *v.* **1** narrate. **2** show to be connected. □ **relate to 1** concern, be to do with. **2** feel sympathy with.

related *adj.* having a common descent; causally connected; of a similar kind.

relation *n.* **1** a connection between people or things; people's behaviour towards one another. **2** a relative. **3** a narration. **4** (**relations**) sexual intercourse. □ **in relation to** as concerns, in connection with. □ **relationship** *n.*

relative *adj.* considered in relation to something else; true only in comparison with something else. ● *n.* a person related to another by descent or marriage. □ **relatively** *adv.*

relative pronoun *see* **pronoun**.

relativity *n.* **1** *Physics* Einstein's theory of the universe, showing that all motion is relative and treating time as a fourth dimension related to space. **2** absence of absolute standards.

relax *v.* make or become less tense; rest; make (a rule) less strict. □ **relaxation** *n.*

relay *n.* (ree-lay) **1** a group of workers etc., relieved after a fixed period by another group; a relay race. **2** a device activating an electrical circuit. **3** a device to receive and retransmit a broadcast; a broadcast transmitted by this. ● *v.* (ri-**lay**) receive and pass on or retransmit.

relay race *n.* a race between teams in which each person in turn covers part of the total distance.

release *v.* **1** set free; remove from a fixed position. **2** make (information, a film or recording) available to the public. ● *n.* **1** releasing; a handle or catch that releases part of a mechanism. **2** information or a film etc. released. □ **on release** (of a film) being generally shown.

relegate *v.* consign to a less important position or group. □ **relegation** *n.*

relent *v.* become less severe.

relentless *adj.* oppressively constant; harsh, inflexible. □ **relentlessly** *adv.*

relevant *adj.* related to the matter in hand. □ **relevance** *n.*

reliable *adj.* able to be relied on; consistently good. □ **reliability** *n.*, **reliably** *adv.*

reliance *n.* dependence on or trust in someone or something. □ **reliant** *adj.*

relic *n.* something that survives from earlier times; (**relics**) remains.

relief *n.* **1** relaxation following the removal of anxiety; alleviation of pain; a break in monotony or tension. **2** assistance to those in need. **3** a person replacing another on duty. **4** a carving etc. in which the design projects from a surface; a similar effect given by colour or shading.

relief road *n.* a road by which traffic can avoid a congested area.

relieve *v.* give or bring relief to; release from a task, burden, or duty; raise the siege of. □ **relieve oneself** urinate or defecate.

religion *n.* belief in and worship of a superhuman controlling power, esp. a god; a system of this; an interest of supreme importance to someone.

religious *adj.* **1** devout in religion; of religion. **2** (of a practice, belief, etc.) followed or held regularly or firmly. □ **religiously** *adv.*

relinquish *v.* give up, cease from. □ **relinquishment** *n.*

reliquary *n.* (*pl.* **-ies**) a receptacle for relics of a saint.

relish *n.* **1** great enjoyment of something. **2** a strong-tasting pickle, sauce, etc. ● *v.* enjoy greatly.

relocate *v.* move to a different place. □ **relocation** *n.*

reluctant *adj.* unwilling, grudging in one's consent. □ **reluctance** *n.*, **reluctantly** *adv.*

rely *v.* (**relied, relying**) □ **rely on** **1** have confidence in. **2** depend on for help etc.

REM *abbr.* rapid eye movement, jerky eye movements during dreaming.

remain *v.* stay; be left or left behind; continue in the same condition.

remainder *n.* the remaining people or things; a quantity left after subtraction or division. ● *v.* dispose of unsold copies of (a book) at a reduced price.

remains *n.pl.* what remains, surviving parts; a dead body.

remand *v.* send back (a prisoner) into custody while further evidence is sought. □ **on remand** remanded.

remark *n.* a spoken or written comment. ● *v.* **1** make a remark, say. **2** notice.

remarkable *adj.* worth noticing, unusual. □ **remarkably** *adv.*

remedial *adj.* **1** providing a remedy. **2** (of teaching) for slow or disadvantaged pupils.

remedy *n.* (*pl.* **-ies**) something that cures a condition or puts a matter right. ● *v.* (**remedied, remedying**) set right.

remember *v.* keep in one's mind and recall at will; act on a remembered instruction or need. □ **remembrance** *n.*

remind *v.* cause to remember.

reminder *n.* something that reminds someone; a letter sent for this purpose.

reminisce *v.* think or talk about past events.

reminiscence *n.* reminiscing; an account of what one remembers.

reminiscent *adj.* having characteristics that remind one (of something).

remiss *adj.* negligent.

remission *n.* **1** cancellation of a debt or penalty. **2** a reduction of force or intensity; a temporary recovery from an illness.

remit *v.* (ri-mit) (**remitted, remitting**) **1** cancel (a debt or punishment). **2** send (money). **3** refer (a matter for decision) to an authority. ● *n.* (**ree**-mit) **1** a task or field assigned to someone. **2** an item referred for decision.

remittance *n.* the sending of money; money sent.

remnant *n.* a small remaining quantity; a surviving piece or trace.

remold Amer. sp. of **remould**.

remonstrate *v.* make a protest. ◻ **remonstrance** *n.*

remorse *n.* deep regret for one's wrongdoing. ◻ **remorseful** *adj.*, **remorsefully** *adv.*

remorseless *adj.* pitiless; relentless. ◻ **remorselessly** *adv.*

remote *adj.* **1** far away in place or time; not close; aloof, unfriendly. **2** (of a possibility) very slight. ◻ **remotely** *adv.*, **remoteness** *n.*

remould (*Amer.* **remold**) *v.* (ree-**mohld**) mould again; reconstruct the tread of (a tyre). ● *n.* (**ree**-mohld) a remoulded tyre.

remove *v.* take off or away; dismiss from office; get rid of. ● *n.* a degree of remoteness or difference: *at one remove*. ◻ **removable** *adj.*, **removal** *n.*, **remover** *n.*

remunerate *v.* pay or reward for services. ◻ **remuneration** *n.*

■ **Usage** The correct spelling is *remunerate*, not *renumerate*.

---

remunerative *adj.* giving good remuneration, profitable.

Renaissance *n.* a revival of art and learning in Europe in the 14th–16th centuries; (**renaissance**) any similar revival.

renal (ree-năl) *adj.* of the kidneys.

rend *v.* (**rent, rending**) tear.

render *v.* **1** provide, give (help or service); submit (a bill etc.). **2** cause to become. **3** draw, represent; give a performance of. **4** translate. **5** melt down (fat).

rendezvous (ron-day-voo) *n.* (*pl.* **rendezvous**) a prearranged meeting or meeting place. ● *v.* (**rendezvoused, rendezvousing**) meet at a rendezvous.

rendition *n.* the way something is rendered or performed.

renegade *n.* a person who deserts from a group, cause, etc.

renege (ri-**nayg**) *v.* fail to keep a promise or agreement.

renew *v.* resume (an interrupted activity); repeat; replace with a new item of the same kind; extend the validity of (a licence etc.); give fresh life or vigour to. ◻ **renewal** *n.*

rennet *n.* a substance used to curdle milk in making cheese.

renounce *v.* give up formally; reject. ◻ **renouncement** *n.*

renovate *v.* repair, restore to good condition. ◻ **renovation** *n.*, **renovator** *n.*

renown *n.* fame.

renowned *adj.* famous.

rent[1] past & p.p. of **rend**. ● *n.* a torn place.

rent[2] *n.* periodical payment for use of land, rooms, machinery, etc. ● *v.* pay or receive rent for.

rental *n.* rent; renting.

renunciation *n.* renouncing.

reorganize *v.* (also **-ise**) organize in a new way. ◻ **reorganization** *n.*

reorient *v.* change the focus of. ◻ **reorient oneself** find one's position in relation to one's surroundings again.

rep *n. informal* **1** a business firm's travelling representative. **2** repertory.

repair *v.* **1** put right damage to; undo (damage). **2** *formal* go somewhere specified. ● *n.* **1** the process of repairing; a repaired place. **2** condition for use: *in good repair*. ◻ **repairer** *n.*

repartee *n.* an exchange of witty remarks.

repast *n. formal* a meal.

repatriate *v.* send or bring back (a person) to his or her own country. ◻ **repatriation** *n.*

repay *v.* (**repaid, repaying**) pay back. ◻ **repayable** *adj.*, **repayment** *n.*

repeal *v.* withdraw (a law) officially. ● *n.* the repealing of a law.

repeat *v.* say, do, or produce again; tell (a thing told to oneself) to another person. ● *n.* something that recurs or is repeated. □ **repeat itself** occur again in the same way. **repeat oneself** say the same thing again.

repeatedly *adv.* again and again.

repel *v.* (**repelled, repelling**) **1** drive away; disgust. **2** be impervious to (a substance).

repellent *adj.* causing disgust. ● *n.* a substance used to keep away pests or to make something impervious to water etc.

repent *v.* feel regret about (a wrong or unwise action). □ **repentance** *n.*, **repentant** *adj.*

repercussion *n.* an unintended consequence.

repertoire (rep-er-twah) *n.* a stock of songs, plays, etc., that a person or company is able to perform.

repertory *n.* (*pl.* **-ies**) **1** the performance of several plays etc. by a company at regular short intervals. **2** a repertoire.

repetition *n.* repeating; an instance of this.

repetitious *adj.* repetitive.

repetitive *adj.* characterized by repetition, esp. unneccessarily and tediously. □ **repetitively** *adv.*

repine *v.* (ri-**pIn**) *literary* be discontented.

replace *v.* **1** put back in place. **2** provide or be a substitute for. □ **replacement** *n.*

replay *v.* (ree-**play**) play again; repeat. ● *n.* (**ree**-play) replaying.

replenish *v.* refill; renew (a supply etc.). □ **replenishment** *n.*

replete *adj.* full; well-supplied.

replica *n.* an exact copy.

replicate *v.* make a replica of. □ **replication** *n.*

reply *v.* (**replied, replying**) answer. ● *n.* (*pl.* **-ies**) an answer.

report *v.* **1** give an account of; tell as news. **2** make a formal complaint about. **3** present oneself on arrival; be responsible to a superior. ● *n.* **1** a spoken or written account; a written statement about a pupil's work; a rumour. **2** an explosive sound.

reportage (re-por-**tah**zh) *n.* the reporting of news.

reported speech *n.* a speaker's words as reported by another person, not in the actual words.

reporter *n.* a person employed to report news for publication or broadcasting.

repose *n.* rest, sleep; tranquillity. ● *v.* rest, lie.

repository *n.* (*pl.* **-ies**) a storage place.

repossess *v.* take back (goods etc.) when payments are not made. □ **repossession** *n.*

reprehend *v.* reproach.

reprehensible *adj.* deserving reproach. □ **reprehensibly** *adv.*

represent *v.* **1** be entitled to speak or act on behalf of. **2** constitute, amount to; be an example of. **3** show in a picture etc.; act the part of; symbolize; describe as being of a particular nature.

representation *n.* **1** representing, being represented; a picture, diagram, etc. **2** (**representations**) statements made as an appeal, protest, or allegation.

representative *adj.* **1** typical of a group or class. **2** involving the representation of the public by elected spokesmen. ● *n.* a person's or firm's agent; a person chosen to represent others.

repress *v.* subdue, control; restrain the expression of (emotions). □ **repression** *n.*, **repressive** *adj.*

reprieve *n.* a postponement or cancellation of punishment (esp. a death sentence); a temporary relief from trouble. ● *v.* give a reprieve to.

reprimand *v.* reproach. ● *n.* a reproach.

reprint *v.* (ree-**print**) print again. ● *n.* (**ree**-print) a book reprinted.

reprisal *n.* an act of retaliation.

reproach *v.* express disapproval to (a person) for a fault or offence. ● *n.* an act of reproaching; (a cause of) discredit. ☐ **reproachful** *adj.*, **reproachfully** *adv.*

reprobate *n.* an immoral or unprincipled person.

reproduce *v.* produce again; produce a copy of; produce further members of the same species. ☐ **reproduction** *n.*, **reproductive** *adj.*

reproof *n.* an expression of condemnation for a fault.

reprove *v.* give a reproof to.

reptile *n.* a member of the class of cold-blooded animals with a backbone and rough or scaly skin. ☐ **reptilian** *adj.* & *n.*

republic *n.* a country in which the supreme power is held by the people's representatives, not by a monarch.

republican *adj.* of or advocating a republic. ● *n.* a person advocating republican government.

repudiate *v.* reject, disown; deny the truth of. ☐ **repudiation** *n.*

repugnant *adj.* distasteful, objectionable. ☐ **repugnance** *n.*

repulse *v.* drive back (an attacking force); reject, rebuff. ● *n.* a driving back; a rejection, a rebuff.

repulsion *n.* a strong feeling of distaste, revulsion.

repulsive *adj.* **1** arousing disgust. **2** able to repel. ☐ **repulsively** *adv.*

reputable *adj.* having a good reputation, respected.

reputation *n.* what is generally believed about a person or thing.

repute *n.* reputation.

reputed *adj.* said or thought to be.

reputedly *adv.* by repute.

request *n.* asking for something; something asked for. ● *v.* ask for; ask (someone) to do something.

requiem (**rek**-wi-em) *n.* a special Mass for the repose of the souls of the dead; music for this.

require *v.* **1** need; depend on for success or fulfilment. **2** order, oblige.

requirement *n.* a need.

requisite *adj.* required, necessary. ● *n.* something needed.

requisition *n.* a formal written demand, an order laying claim to the use of property or materials. ● *v.* demand or order by this.

requite *v.* make return for (a service or injury). ☐ **requital** *n.*

resale *n.* a sale to another person of something one has bought.

rescind (rĕ-**sind**) *v.* repeal or cancel (a law etc.).

rescue *v.* save from danger or capture etc. ● *n.* rescuing. ☐ **rescuer** *n.*

research *n.* study and investigation to discover facts. ● *v.* investigate; search for facts to use in (a book etc.). ☐ **researcher** *n.*

resemble *v.* be like. ☐ **resemblance** *n.*

resent *v.* feel bitter and indignant about. ☐ **resentful** *adj.*, **resentfully** *adv.*, **resentment** *n.*

reservation *n.* **1** reserving; reserved accommodation etc. **2** doubt. **3** an area of land set aside for a purpose.

reserve *v.* put aside for future or special use; order or set aside for a particular person; retain; delay the expression of (an opinion). ● *n.* **1** a supply of something kept for emergencies; a body of troops outside the regular armed forces; a substitute player in a sporting team. **2** land set aside for special use, esp. the protection of wildlife. **3** lack of friendliness or warmth. **4** the lowest acceptable price for an item at auction. ☐ **in reserve** kept unused for emergencies.

reserved *adj.* (of a person) showing reserve of manner.

reservist *n.* a member of a reserve force.

reservoir (**rez**-er-vwah) *n.* a lake used as a store for a water supply; a container for a supply of fluid.

reshuffle *v.* interchange; reorganize. ● *n.* a reorganization.

reside *v.* dwell permanently.

residence *n.* residing; the place where a person lives. ▫ **in residence** living in a specified place to perform one's work.

resident *adj.* residing, in residence. ● *n.* a permanent inhabitant; (at a hotel) a person staying overnight.

residential *adj.* designed for living in; lived in; providing accommodation.

residue *n.* what is left over. ▫ **residual** *adj.*

resign *v.* give up (one's job, claim, etc.). ▫ **resign oneself to** be ready to accept and endure. ▫ **resignation** *n.*

resigned *adj.* having resigned oneself. ▫ **resignedly** *adv.*

resilient *adj.* springing back when bent, pressed, etc.; readily recovering from shock or distress. ▫ **resilience** *n.*

resin *n.* a sticky substance from plants and certain trees; a similar substance made synthetically, used in plastics. ▫ **resinous** *adj.*

resist *v.* oppose strongly or forcibly; withstand; refrain from accepting or yielding to. ▫ **resistance** *n.*, **resistant** *adj.*, **resistible** *n.*

resistivity *n.* resistance to the passage of an electric current.

resistor *n.* a device having resistance to the passage of an electric current.

reskill *v.* retrain (workers) in the skills required by a modern business.

resolute *adj.* showing great determination. ▫ **resolutely** *adv.*

resolution *n.* **1** a firm decision; determination; a formal statement of a committee's opinion. **2** solving a problem etc.

resolve *v.* **1** find a solution to (a problem, dispute, etc.) **2** decide firmly on a course of action. **3** separate into constituent parts. ● *n.* determination.

resonant *adj.* deep, clear, and echoing; reinforcing sound, esp. by vibration. ▫ **resonance** *n.*

resonate *v.* be filled with deep reverberating sound; be able to evoke images and memories. ▫ **resonator** *n.*

resort *n.* **1** a popular holiday destination. **2** adopting a course of action to solve a problem. ▫ **resort to** turn to for help; adopt as a measure.

resound *v.* fill or be filled with sound; echo.

resource *n.* **1** a supply of an asset to be used when needed; (**resources**) available assets. **2** a strategy for dealing with difficulties; the ability to find such strategies.

resourceful *adj.* clever at finding ways of doing things. ▫ **resourcefully** *adv.*, **resourcefulness** *n.*

respect *n.* **1** admiration or esteem; politeness, regard for others' rights and wishes. **2** an aspect of a situation etc. ● *v.* feel or show respect for. ▫ **in respect of** or **with respect to** regarding, concerning.

respectable *adj.* **1** regarded as conventionally correct. **2** of some size, merit, or importance. ▫ **respectability** *n.*, **respectably** *adv.*

respective *adj.* belonging to each as an individual.

respectively *adv.* for each separately in the order mentioned.

respiration *n.* breathing.

respirator *n.* a device worn over the nose and mouth to prevent the inhalation of smoke etc.; a device for giving artificial respiration.

respiratory *adj.* of respiration.

respire *v. formal* breathe.

respite *n.* rest or relief from something unpleasant; a permitted delay before a punishment etc.

resplendent *adj.* brilliant with colour or decorations.

respond *v.* answer; react.

respondent *n.* a defendant in a lawsuit, esp. in a divorce case.

response *n.* **1** an answer. **2** an act, feeling, or movement produced by a stimulus or another's action.

responsibility *n.* being responsible; a duty resulting from one's job or position.

responsible *adj.* **1** being the cause of something; deserving blame or credit for it. **2** reliable, fulfilling duties conscientiously. **3** (of a job etc.) involving important duties. □ **responsible for** having control or care over. **responsible to** having to report to (a superior). □ **responsibly** *adv.*

responsive *adj.* responding readily to an influence. □ **responsiveness** *n.*

rest *v.* **1** (cause or allow to) cease from work or tiring activity; (of a subject) be left without further discussion. **2** place or be placed for support; be positioned. **3** place (hope etc.) or be placed in someone or something. **4** remain in a specified state: *rest assured.* ● *n.* **1** (a period of) inactivity or sleep. **2** a prop or support for an object. □ **the rest** the remaining part; the others.

restaurant *n.* a place where meals can be bought and eaten.

restaurateur (res-tě-rě-**ter**) *n.* a restaurant-keeper.

■ **Usage** There is no *n.* in *restaurateur.*

---

restful *adj.* giving rest; relaxing.

restitution *n.* **1** the restoring of a thing to its proper owner or original state. **2** compensation.

restive *adj.* restless; impatient.

restless *adj.* too anxious etc. to rest or keep still. □ **restlessly** *adv.*, **restlessness** *n.*

restorative *adj.* restoring health or strength. ● *n.* a restorative food, medicine, or treatment.

restore *v.* bring or give back (something lost or taken away); return to a former place or position; repair, return to a former state. □ **restoration** *n.*, **restorer** *n.*

restrain *v.* hold back from movement or action, keep under control. □ **restraint** *n.*

restrict *v.* put a limit on, subject to limitations. □ **restriction** *n.*, **restrictive** *adj.*

result *n.* **1** what comes about because of an action etc.; the product of calculation. **2** a final score or mark in a contest or examination. ● *v.* occur as a result. □ **result in** have as a result.

resultant *adj.* occurring as a result.

resume *v.* begin to do or be done again after a pause; take again, return to using. □ **resumption** *n.*, **resumptive** *adj.*

résumé (rez-yoo-may) *n.* **1** a summary. **2** *Amer.* = **curriculum vitae.**

resurface *v.* **1** put a new surface on. **2** return to the surface.

resurgent *adj.* rising or arising again. □ **resurgence** *n.*

resurrect *v.* bring back to life or into use.

resurrection *n.* **1** rising from the dead. **2** revival after disuse.

resuscitate *v.* restore to life or consciousness. □ **resuscitation** *n.*

retail *n.* selling of goods to the public for use rather than resale. ● *adj.* & *adv.* by retail. ● *v.* **1** sell or be sold by retail. **2** recount details of (a story). □ **retailer** *n.*

retain *v.* keep in one's possession; absorb and hold; hold in place; keep in one's service.

retainer *n.* a fee paid to a barrister etc. to secure service when required.

retaliate *v.* repay an injury, insult, etc. by inflicting one in return. □ **retaliation** *n.*, **retaliatory** *adj.*

retard *v.* cause delay to. □ **retardation** *n.*

retarded *adj.* backward in mental or physical development.

retch *v.* strain one's throat as if vomiting.

retention *n.* retaining.

retentive *adj.* able to retain things.

rethink *v.* (**rethought, rethinking**) reconsider; plan again and differently.

reticent *adj.* not revealing one's thoughts or feelings. □ **reticence** *n.*

retina *n.* (*pl.* **retinas** or **retinae**) a membrane at the back of the eyeball, sensitive to light.

retinue *n.* attendants accompanying an important person.

retire *v.* **1** give up one's regular work because of age; cause (an employee) to do this. **2** withdraw; retreat; go to bed. □ **retirement** *n.*

retiring *adj.* shy, avoiding society.

retort *v.* make (as) a witty or angry reply. ● *n.* **1** a reply of this kind. **2** a container or furnace for carrying out a chemical process on a large scale. **3** *hist.* a long-necked glass container used in distilling.

retouch *v.* touch up (a picture or photograph).

retrace *v.* go back over or repeat (a route).

retract *v.* pull back; withdraw (an allegation etc.). □ **retractable** *adj.*, **retraction** *n.*, **retractor** *n.*

retractile *adj.* able to be retracted.

retreat *v.* withdraw after defeat or from an uncomfortable situation; recede, move back. ● *n.* **1** retreating, withdrawal; a military signal for this. **2** a place of shelter or seclusion.

retrench *v.* reduce costs or spending. □ **retrenchment** *n.*

retrial *n.* a repeated trial.

retribution *n.* deserved punishment.

retrieve *v.* **1** regain possession of; bring back; extract (information) from a computer. **2** set right (an error etc.). □ **retrieval** *n.*

retriever *n.* a dog of a breed used to retrieve game.

retro *n.* a fashion imitating styles from the recent past. ● *adj.* imitating fashions of the recent past.

retroactive *adj.* operating retrospectively. □ **retroactively** *adv.*

retrograde *adj.* going backwards; reverting to an inferior state.

retrogress *v.* return to an earlier and worse state. □ **retrogression** *n.*, **retrogressive** *adj.*

retrospect *n.* □ **in retrospect** when one looks back on a past event.

retrospective *adj.* looking back on the past; (of a law etc.) made to apply to the past as well as the future. □ **retrospectively** *adv.*

retroussé (ri-troo-say) *adj.* (of the nose) turned up.

retroverted *adj.* turned backwards. □ **retroversion** *n.*

retsina *n.* a Greek resin-flavoured wine.

return *v.* **1** come or go back; bring, give, put, or send back. **2** make or yield (a profit). **3** elect to office. ● *n.* **1** an act of coming back etc.; a return ticket; a return match. **2** a profit. **3** an official report made by order.

return match *n.* a second match between the same opponents.

return ticket *n.* a ticket for a journey to a place and back again.

reunion *n.* a gathering of people who were formerly associated.

reunite *v.* bring or come together again.

reusable *adj.* able to be used again.

rev *informal n.* a revolution of an engine. ● *v.* (**revved, revving**) cause (an engine) to run faster; (of an engine) increase speed.

Rev. *abbr.* Reverend.

revalue *v.* reassess the value of. □ **revaluation** *n.*

revamp *v.* renovate, give a new appearance to.

Revd *abbr.* Reverend.

reveal *v.* make visible by uncovering; make known.

reveille (ri-va-li) *n.* a military waking signal.

revel *v.* (**revelled, revelling**; *Amer.* **reveled**) hold revels. ● *n.pl.* (**revels**) lively festivities, merrymaking. ▫ **revel in** take great pleasure in. ▫ **reveller** *n.*, **revelry** *n.*

revelation *n.* revealing; a surprising thing revealed.

revenge *n.* injury inflicted in return for what one has suffered. ● *v.* avenge.

revenue *n.* income; a country's income from taxes; the department collecting this.

reverberate *v.* be repeated as an echo; continue to have effects. ▫ **reverberation** *n.*

revere *v.* feel deep respect or religious veneration for.

reverence *n.* a feeling of awe and respect or veneration. ▫ **reverent** *adj.*, **reverently** *adv.*

reverend *adj.* **1** deserving to be treated with respect. **2** (**Reverend**) the title of a member of the clergy.

reverie *n.* a daydream.

reversal *n.* reversing.

reverse *v.* move backwards, cause to do this; undo, cancel; convert to its opposite; turn inside out or upside down etc. ● *adj.* opposite in direction, nature, order, etc. ● *n.* **1** a change of direction; the opposite side. **2** a setback. ▫ **reversely** *adv.*, **reversible** *adj.*

revert *v.* return to a former condition or habit; return to a subject in talk etc.; (of property etc.) return or pass to the original owner. ▫ **reversion** *n.*

review *n.* **1** a general survey of events or a subject; revision or reconsideration; a critical report on a book, play, etc. **2** a ceremonial inspection of troops etc. ● *v.* make or write a review of. ▫ **reviewer** *n.*

revile *v.* criticize angrily in abusive language.

revise *v.* **1** re-examine and alter or correct. **2** reread work already done in preparation for an examination. ▫ **reviser** *n.*, **revision** *n.*, **revisory** *adj.*

revivalist *n.* person who seeks to promote religious fervour. ▫ **revivalism** *n.*

revive *v.* come or bring back to life, consciousness, or strength; restore interest in or use of. ▫ **revival** *n.*

revivify *v.* (**revivified, revivifying**) give new life or strength to.

revoke *v.* withdraw (a decree, licence, etc.). ▫ **revocable** *adj.*, **revocation** *n.*

revolt *v.* **1** take part in a rebellion; be in a mood of protest or defiance. **2** cause strong disgust in. ● *n.* rebellion, refusal to submit or conform.

revolting *adj.* **1** causing disgust. **2** in revolt.

revolution *n.* **1** the forcible overthrow of a government and installation of a new one; a complete change in methods etc. **2** an instance of revolving; a single complete orbit or rotation.

revolutionary *adj.* of political revolution; involving dramatic change. ● *n.* (*pl.* **-ies**) a person who begins or supports a political revolution.

revolutionize *v.* (also **-ise**) alter completely.

revolve *v.* move in a circle on a central axis; move in an orbit.

revolver *n.* a type of pistol.

revue *n.* an entertainment consisting of a series of items.

revulsion *n.* strong disgust; a violent change of feeling.

reward *n.* something given or received in return for service or merit. ● *v.* give a reward to.

rewire *v.* renew the electrical wiring of.

rewrite *v.* (**rewrote, rewritten, rewriting**) write again in a different form or style.

Rex *n.* a reigning king.

Rf *symb.* rutherfordium.

RFC *abbr.* Rugby Football Club.

Rh *abbr.* rhesus. ● *symb.* rhodium.

rhapsodize *v.* (also **-ise**) talk or write about something very enthusiastically.

rhapsody *n.* (*pl.* **-ies**) **1** a very enthusiastic expression of feeling. **2** a romantic musical composition. □ **rhapsodic** *adj.*

rhenium *n.* a rare metallic element (symbol Re).

rheostat (ree-ŏ-stat) *n.* a device for varying the resistance to electric current.

rhesus *n.* a small monkey.

rhesus factor *n.* a substance usu. present in human blood. □ **rhesus-positive** having this substance. **rhesus-negative** not having this substance.

rhetoric *n.* the art of using words impressively; impressive language.

rhetorical *adj.* expressed so as to sound impressive. □ **rhetorically** *adv.*

rhetorical question *n.* a question used for dramatic effect, not seeking an answer.

rheumatism *n.* a disease causing pain in the joints, muscles, or fibrous tissue. □ **rheumatic** *adj.*, **rheumaticky** *adj.*

rheumatoid *adj.* having the character of rheumatism.

rhinestone *n.* an imitation diamond.

rhino *n.* (*pl.* **rhino** or **rhinos**) *informal* a rhinoceros.

rhinoceros *n.* (*pl.* **rhinoceroses** or **rhinoceros**) a large thick-skinned animal with one horn (or occasionally two) on its nose.

rhizome *n.* an underground stem producing roots and shoots.

rhodium *n.* a metallic element (symbol Rh).

rhododendron *n.* an evergreen shrub with large clusters of flowers.

rhombus *n.* a quadrilateral with opposite sides and angles equal (and not right angles). □ **rhomboid** *adj.* & *n.*

rhubarb *n.* a plant with red leaf-stalks used like fruit.

rhyme *n.* a similarity of sound between words or syllables; a word providing a rhyme to another; a poem with line-endings that rhyme. ● *v.* have a similar or the same sound.

rhythm *n.* a strong, regular, repeated pattern of movement or sound; the arrangement of musical notes according to duration and stress; a recurring sequence of events. □ **rhythmic, rhythmical** *adj.*, **rhythmically** *adv.*

rhythm method *n.* contraception by avoiding sexual intercourse near the time of ovulation.

rib *n.* **1** one of the curved bones round the chest; a structural part resembling this. **2** a pattern of raised lines in knitting. ● *v.* (**ribbed, ribbing**) **1** mark with raised lines. **2** *informal* tease.

ribald *adj.* humorously rude or vulgar in discussing sexual matters. □ **ribaldry** *n.*

riband *n.* a ribbon.

ribbon *n.* a decorative narrow strip of fabric; a narrow strip of something.

riboflavin *n.* (also **riboflavine**) a B vitamin found in liver, milk, and eggs.

ribonucleic acid *n.* a substance controlling protein synthesis in cells.

rice *n.* a cereal plant grown in marshes in hot countries; its seeds used as food.

rich *adj.* **1** having much money or many assets. **2** containing a large amount of something specified; abundant. **3** (of soil) fertile. **4** (of colour, sound, or smell) pleasantly deep and strong. ● *n.pl.* (**riches**) wealth. □ **a bit rich** *informal* (of a remark) unfair or unreasonable. □ **richness** *n.*

richly *adv.* generously, plentifully, splendidly; fully, completely.

rick *n.* **1** a large stack of hay etc. **2** a slight sprain or strain. ● *v.* sprain or strain slightly.

rickets *n.* a bone disease caused by vitamin D deficiency.

rickety *adj.* shaky, insecure.

rickshaw *n.* a two-wheeled vehicle used in the Far East, pulled along by a person.

ricochet (rik-ŏ-shay) *v.* (**ricocheted, ricocheting**) rebound from a surface after striking it with a glancing blow. ● *n.* a rebound of this kind.

ricotta *n.* a soft Italian cheese.

rid *v.* (**rid, ridding**) free from something unpleasant or unwanted. □ **get rid of** cause to go away; free oneself of; discard.

ridden p.p. of **ride.**

riddle *n.* **1** a question etc. designed to test ingenuity, esp. for amusement; something puzzling or mysterious. **2** a coarse sieve. ● *v.* **1** make many holes in; permeate. **2** pass through a coarse sieve.

ride *v.* (**rode, ridden, riding**) sit on and be carried by (a horse or bicycle etc.); travel in a vehicle; be carried or supported by. ● *n.* a spell of riding; a journey in a vehicle; a roller coaster or similar fairground amusement; a path through woods for riding.

rider *n.* **1** a person who rides a horse etc. **2** an additional statement or condition.

ridge *n.* a long narrow hilltop; a narrow raised strip; a line where two upward slopes meet; an elongated region of high barometric pressure. □ **ridged** *adj.*

ridicule *n.* mockery, derision. ● *v.* subject to ridicule, make fun of.

ridiculous *adj.* deserving to be laughed at, absurd. □ **ridiculously** *adv.*

rife *adj.* occurring frequently, widespread. □ **rife with** full of.

riff *n.* a short repeated phrase in jazz etc.

riffle *v.* flick through (pages etc.).

riff-raff *n.* rabble; disreputable people.

rifle *n.* a gun with a long barrel. ● *v.* **1** search hurriedly through something. **2** cut spiral grooves in (a gun barrel) to make the bullets spin.

rift *n.* a cleft in earth or rock; a crack, a split; a breach in friendly relations.

rift valley *n.* a steep-sided valley formed by the earth's subsidence.

rig *v.* (**rigged, rigging**) **1** fit (a ship) with rigging; set up (equipment), esp. in a makeshift way. **2** manage or run fraudulently. ● *n.* **1** the way a ship's masts and sails etc. are arranged; an outfit, a style of dress. **2** an apparatus for drilling an oil well etc.

rigging *n.* ropes etc. used to support a ship's masts and sails.

right *adj.* **1** morally good, in accordance with justice. **2** correct, true; suitable, appropriate to a need or purpose; satisfactory, in good condition. **3** of or on the side of the body which is on the east when one is facing north. **4** *informal* real, complete: *a right fool.* ● *adv.* **1** completely; directly, exactly. **2** correctly. **3** to or on the right-hand side. ● *n.* **1** that which is morally good. **2** an entitlement, something to which one is entitled. **3** the right-hand side or direction. **4** a party or group favouring conservative views and capitalist policies. ● *v.* restore to a normal or upright position; rectify, set right. □ **by rights** according to strict fairness. **in one's own right** by one's own merit etc., not by association with another. **in the right** having truth or justice on one's side. **right away** immediately. □ **rightly** *adv.*, **rightness** *n.*

right angle *n.* an angle of 90°.

righteous *adj.* morally justifiable; doing what is right. □ **righteously** *adv.*, **righteousness** *n.*

rightful *adj.* having a right to something; just, legitimate. □ **rightfully** *adv.*, **rightfulness** *n.*

right-handed *adj.* using the right hand.

right-hand man *n.* an indispensable assistant.

right of way *n.* **1** the right to pass over another's land; a path subject to this. **2** the right to proceed while another vehicle must wait.

rigid *adj.* unable to bend; strict, inflexible. □ **rigidity** *n.*, **rigidly** *adv.*

rigmarole *n.* a long rambling statement.

rigor mortis *n.* stiffening of the body after death.

rigour *n.* (*Amer.* **rigor**) being thorough and accurate; strictness, severity; harshness of weather etc. □ **rigorous** *adj.*, **rigorously** *adv.*, **rigorousness** *n.*

rile *v. informal* annoy.

rill *n.* a small stream.

rim *n.* an edge or border, esp. of something circular. ● *v.* (**rimmed, rimming**) form a border to; leave a circular stain on.

rime *n.* frost.

rind *n.* a tough outer layer on fruit, cheese, bacon, etc.

ring[1] *n.* **1** a small circular band worn on a finger; a circular outline; a circular device giving out heat on a gas or electric hob. **2** an enclosed area for a sport etc. **3** a group of people acting together dishonestly. ● *v.* put a ring on; surround.

ring[2] *v.* (**rang, rung, ringing**) give out a loud clear resonant sound; cause (a bell) to do this; ring a bell etc. as a signal; resound. ● *n.* **1** an act or sound of ringing. **2** a quality or impression conveyed by the tone of an utterance: *a ring of truth.* **3** *informal* a telephone call. □ **ring off** end a telephone call. **ring the changes** vary things. **ring up** make a telephone call (to).

ringleader *n.* a person who leads others in wrongdoing.

ringlet *n.* a long spiralling curl of hair.

ringside *n.* the area beside a boxing ring.

ringside seat *n.* a position from which one has a clear view of the scene of action.

ringworm *n.* a fungal infection producing round scaly patches on the skin.

rink *n.* an area of ice for skating; an enclosed area for roller skating.

rinse *v.* wash out soap etc. from; wash quickly. ● *n.* an act of rinsing; a mouthwash; a solution washed through hair to tint or condition it.

riot *n.* **1** a violent disturbance by a crowd of people. **2** a large and varied display. **3** *informal* a very amusing person or thing. ● *v.* take part in a riot. □ **run riot** behave in a violent and unrestrained way; grow in an uncontrolled way.

riotous *adj.* disorderly, unruly; boisterous. □ **riotously** *adv.*

RIP *abbr.* rest in peace.

rip *v.* (**ripped, ripping**) **1** tear apart; remove by pulling roughly; become torn. **2** rush along. ● *n.* an act of ripping; a torn place. □ **let rip** *informal* act or speak without restraint. **rip into** *informal* attack verbally. **rip off** *informal* defraud; steal.

ripcord *n.* a cord for pulling to release a parachute.

ripe *adj.* ready to be gathered and used; matured; ready for something; (of age) advanced. □ **ripeness** *n.*

ripen *v.* make or become ripe.

rip-off *n. informal* a swindle.

riposte (ri-posst) *n.* a quick counterstroke or retort. ● *v.* deliver a riposte.

ripple *n.* a small wave; a gentle sound that rises and falls. ● *v.* form ripples.

rise *v.* (**rose, risen, rising**) **1** move from a lower to a higher position; get up from lying or sitting. **2** become higher; increase in quantity, intensity, pitch, etc.; reach a higher rank or position. **3** rebel. **4** originate, have a source; (of the wind) start to blow. ● *n.* an act of rising; an increase, esp. in pay; an upward slope. □ **give rise to** cause.

risible *adj.* ridiculous. □ **risibility** *n.*, **risibly** *adv.*

risk *n.* a possibility of meeting danger or suffering harm; a person or thing representing a source of danger or harm. ● *v.* expose to the chance of injury or loss; accept the risk of.

risky *adj.* (**riskier, riskiest**) involving risk. ▫ **riskily** *adv.*, **riskiness** *n.*

risotto *n.* (*pl.* **risottos**) a dish of rice containing chopped meat, vegetables, etc.

risqué (riss-kay) *adj.* slightly indecent.

rissole *n.* a mixture of minced meat formed into a flat shape and fried.

rite *n.* a ritual.

ritual *n.* a series of actions used in a religious or other ceremony. ● *adj.* of or done as a ritual. ▫ **ritually** *adv.*

ritualism *n.* observance of ritual forms, esp. without regard to content. ▫ **ritualist** *n.*, **ritualistic** *adj.*

rival *n.* a person or thing that competes with or can equal another. ● *adj.* being a rival or rivals. ● *v.* (**rivalled, rivalling**; *Amer.* **rivaled**) be a rival of; seem as good as. ▫ **rivalry** *n.*

river *n.* a large natural stream of water; a great flow.

rivet *n.* a bolt for holding pieces of metal together, with its end beaten to form a head when in place. ● *v.* (**riveted, riveting**) **1** fasten with a rivet. **2** attract and hold the attention of, engross.

rivulet *n.* a small stream.

RN *abbr.* Royal Navy.

Rn *symb.* radon.

RNA *abbr.* ribonucleic acid.

RNLI *abbr.* Royal National Lifeboat Institution.

road *n.* a prepared track along which people and vehicles may travel; a series of events or actions leading to a particular outcome. ▫ **on the road** travelling.

road hog *n.* a reckless or inconsiderate driver.

roadie *n. informal* a person helping a touring band of musicians with their equipment.

road metal *n.* broken stone for making the foundation of a road or railway.

road rage *n.* aggressive behaviour by a driver, caused by the stress of driving in a heavy traffic etc.

roadster *n.* an open car with no rear seats.

roadway *n.* a road, esp. as distinct from a footpath beside it.

roadworks *n.pl.* construction or repair of roads.

roadworthy *adj.* (of a vehicle) fit to be used on a road. ▫ **roadworthiness** *n.*

roam *v.* wander.

roan *n.* & *adj.* (a horse) with a dark coat sprinkled with white hairs.

roar *n.* a long deep sound made or like that made by a lion; a loud sound of laughter. ● *v.* **1** give a roar. **2** (esp. of a motor vehicle) move very fast.

roaring *adj.* **1** noisy, giving a roar. **2** *informal* great and definite: *a roaring success.*

roast *v.* cook (meat etc.) in an oven; expose to great heat; undergo roasting; reprimand severely. ● *n.* a roast joint of meat.

rob *v.* (**robbed, robbing**) steal from using violence; deprive unfairly of something. ▫ **robber** *n.*, **robbery** *n.*

robe *n.* a long loose esp. ceremonial garment. ● *v.* dress in a robe.

robin *n.* a red-breasted bird.

robot *n.* a machine able to carry out a complex series of tasks automatically, esp. when programmed by a computer. ▫ **robotic** *adj.*

robotics *n.* the study of robots and their design and operation.

robust *adj.* sturdy; healthy. ▫ **robustly** *adv.*, **robustness** *n.*

rock *n.* **1** the hard part of the earth's crust below the soil; a mass of this, a large stone. **2** a hard sugar sweet made in sticks. **3** modern popular music with a heavy beat. **4** a rocking movement. ● *v.* **1** (cause to) move to and fro or from side to side. **2** shock, unsettle.

3 *informal* dance to rock music. □ **on the rocks 1** (of a drink) served with ice cubes. **2** *informal* in difficulties.

rock and roll *n.* rock music with elements of blues.

rock bottom *n.* the lowest or worst possible level. ● *adj.* (**rock-bottom**) very low.

rocker *n.* **1** a person performing or dancing to rock music. **2** something that rocks; a pivoting switch.

rockery *n.* (*pl.* **-ies**) a bank containing large stones planted with rock plants.

rocket *n.* **1** a structure that flies by expelling burning gases; a spacecraft propelled in this way. **2** a firework that rises into the air and explodes. **3** *informal* a severe reprimand. ● *v.* (**rocketed, rocketing**) move rapidly upwards or away.

rocketry *n.* the science or practice of rocket propulsion.

rock plant *n.* an alpine plant, a plant that grows among rocks.

rocky *adj.* (**rockier, rockiest**) **1** of or like rock; full of rock. **2** unstable; *informal* full of problems. □ **rockily** *adv.*, **rockiness** *n.*

rococo (rŏ-**koh**-koh) *adj.* & *n.* (of or in) an ornate style of decoration current in 18th-century Europe.

rod *n.* a slender straight round stick or metal bar; a fishing rod.

rode past of **ride**.

rodent *n.* an animal with strong front teeth for gnawing things.

rodeo *n.* (*pl.* **rodeos**) a competition or exhibition of cowboys' skill.

roe[1] *n.* a mass of eggs in a female fish's ovary.

roe[2] *n.* (*pl.* **roe** or **roes**) a small deer.

roentgen (runt-yĕn) *n.* a unit of ionizing radiation.

roger *int.* (in signalling) message received and understood.

rogue *n.* **1** a dishonest or mischievous person. **2** a wild animal living apart from the herd and unpredictably savage.

roguish *adj.* dishonest; mischievously playful. □ **roguishly** *adv.*, **roguishness** *n.*

roister *v.* make merry noisily.

role *n.* an actor's part; a person's or thing's function.

roll *v.* **1** (cause to) move by turning over and over on an axis; move on wheels. **2** turn (something flexible) over on itself to form a ball or cylinder. **3** move in waves; undulate; rock, oscillate; (of a deep sound) reverberate. **4** flatten with a roller. ● *n.* **1** a cylinder of flexible material turned over and over on itself. **2** an act of rolling; an undulating shape. **3** a reverberating sound of thunder etc. **4** a small individual loaf of bread. **5** an official list or register. □ **be rolling (in money)** *informal* be very wealthy. **roll-on roll-off** (of a ferry) that vehicles can be driven on to and off.

roll-call *n.* the calling of a list of names to check that all are present.

rolled gold *n.* a thin coating of gold on another metal.

roller *n.* **1** a cylinder rolled over things to flatten or spread them, or on which something is wound. **2** a long swelling wave.

roller coaster *n.* a switchback at a fair.

roller skate *n.* a boot or frame with wheels, strapped to the foot for gliding across a hard surface. ● *v.* move on roller skates.

rollicking *adj.* full of boisterous high spirits.

rolling pin *n.* a roller for flattening dough.

rolling stock *n.* railway engines and carriages, wagons, etc.

rolling stone *n.* a person who does not settle in one place.

rollmop *n.* a rolled uncooked pickled herring fillet.

roly-poly *n.* (*pl.* **-polies**) a pudding of suet pastry spread with jam, rolled up and boiled. ● *adj.* plump, podgy.

ROM *abbr. Computing* read-only memory, memory read at high speed but not capable of being changed by program instructions.

Roman *adj.* & *n.* (a native, an inhabitant) of Rome or of the ancient Roman republic or empire.

roman *n.* plain upright type.

Roman Catholic *adj.* & *n.* (a member) of the Church that acknowledges the Pope as its head.

romance *n.* a romantic atmosphere or quality; a love affair or love story; an imaginative story. ● *n.* **1** idealize, present unrealistically. **2** *informal* seek the favour of; engage in a love affair.

Romance language *n.* a language descended from Latin.

Romanesque *adj.* & *n.* (of or in) a style of architecture current in Europe about 900–1200.

Roman numerals *n.pl.* letters representing numbers (I=1, V=5, etc.).

romantic *adj.* appealing to the emotions by its imaginative, heroic, or picturesque quality; involving a love affair; enjoying romantic situations etc. ● *n.* a romantic person. □ **romantically** *adv.*

romanticism *n.* romantic style.

romanticize *v.* (also **-ise**) idealize, regard or represent as better or more beautiful than is the case.

Romany *n.* (*pl.* **-ies**) a gypsy; the gypsy language.

romp *v.* **1** play about in a lively way. **2** *informal* proceed to achieve something easily.

rondeau (ron-doh) *n.* (*pl.* **rondeaux**) a short poem with the opening words used as a refrain.

rondo *n.* (*pl.* **rondos**) a piece of music with a recurring theme.

rood-screen *n.* a screen separating the nave from the chancel in a church.

roof *n.* (*pl.* **roofs**) the upper covering of a building, car, cavity, etc. ● *v.* cover with a roof; be the roof of.

rook *n.* **1** a bird of the crow family. **2** a chess piece with a top shaped like battlements. ● *v. informal* defraud.

rookery *n.* (*pl.* **-ies**) a colony of rooks.

room *n.* **1** a division of a building, separated off by walls. **2** space for occupying or moving in; scope to act or happen.

roomy *adj.* (**roomier, roomiest**) having plenty of space.

roost *n.* a place where birds perch or rest. ● *v.* perch, esp. for sleep.

root *n.* **1** the part of a plant that grows into the earth and absorbs nourishment from the soil; the embedded part of a hair, tooth, etc. **2** the basis or origin of something. **3** a number in relation to another which it produces when multiplied by itself a specified number of times. **4** (**roots**) one's place of origin, esp. as the object of emotional attachment. ● *v.* **1** (cause to) take root; cause to stand fixed and unmoving. **2** (of an animal) turn up ground with the snout or beak in search of food; rummage, extract. □ **root for** *informal* support, cheer on. **root out** or **up 1** drag or dig up by the roots; get rid of. **2** find by rummaging. **take root** send down roots; become established. □ **rootless** *adj.*

rope *n.* a strong thick cord. ● *v.* fasten or secure with rope; fence off with rope. □ **know** or **show the ropes** *informal* know or show the procedure. **on the ropes** near to defeat or collapse. **rope in** persuade to take part.

rosary *n.* (*pl.* **-ies**) a set series of prayers; a string of beads for keeping count in this.

rose[1] *n.* **1** an ornamental usu. fragrant flower. **2** a reddish-pink colour.

rose[2] past of **rise**.

rosé (roh-zay) *n.* a light pink wine.

rosemary *n.* a shrub with fragrant leaves used as a herb.

rosette *n.* a round badge or ornament made of ribbons.

rosewood *n.* a dark fragrant wood used for making furniture.

rosin *n.* a resin.

roster *n.* a list showing people's turns of duty etc.

rostrum *n.* (*pl.* **rostra** or **rostrums**) a platform for standing on to make a speech, conduct an orchestra, etc.

rosy *adj.* (**rosier, rosiest**) **1** deep pink. **2** promising, hopeful.

rot *v.* (**rotted, rotting**) decompose through chemical action caused by bacteria; deteriorate through lack of use, attention, or activity. ● *n.* **1** rotting, rottenness. **2** *informal* nonsense.

rota *n.* a list of duties to be done or people to do them in rotation.

rotary *adj.* acting by rotating.

rotate *v.* (cause to) revolve; arrange, occur, or deal with in a recurrent series. □ **rotation** *n.*, **rotatory** *adj.*

rote *n.* □ **by rote** by memory without thought of the meaning; by a fixed procedure.

rotisserie (roh-tees-ĕ-ree) *n.* a revolving spit for roasting.

rotor *n.* a rotating part of a machine.

rotten *adj.* **1** decayed; breaking easily from age or use. **2** corrupt; *informal* very unpleasant. □ **rottenness** *n.*

rotund *adj.* plump; round or spherical. □ **rotundity** *n.*

rotunda *n.* a circular domed building or hall.

rouble *n.* (also **ruble**) a unit of money in Russia.

rouge *n.* a reddish cosmetic colouring for the cheeks. ● *v.* colour with rouge.

rough *adj.* **1** having an uneven or irregular surface; (of a voice) harsh. **2** not gentle or careful; violent; (of weather) stormy; (of water) with large waves; *informal* difficult, unpleasant. **3** not perfected or detailed; approximate; not refined or elegant. ● *n.* **1** a rough sketch. **2** long grass at the edge of a golf course. **3** a violent person. □ **in the rough** not polished, elaborated, or refined. **rough it** do without comforts or conveniences. **rough out** plan or sketch roughly. **rough up** attack, beat up. □ **roughly** *adv.*, **roughness** *n.*

roughage *n.* dietary fibre.

rough-and-ready *adj.* crude or simple but effective.

rough-and-tumble *n.* a haphazard struggle.

rough diamond *n.* a person of good nature but lacking polished manners.

roughen *v.* make or become rough.

roughshod □ **ride roughshod over** treat inconsiderately or arrogantly.

roulette *n.* a gambling game played with a small ball on a revolving disc with numbered compartments.

round *adj.* **1** curved, circular, spherical, or cylindrical. **2** (of a number) altered for convenience, e.g. to the nearest multiple of ten. ● *n.* **1** a circular piece of something. **2** a tour of visits or inspection; a recurring sequence of activities; one of a sequence of actions or events; one section of a competition. **3** a song for several voices starting the same tune at different times. **4** the amount of ammunition needed for one shot. ● *adv.* **1** in a circle or curve; so as to surround someone or something; so as to cover a whole area or group. **2** so as to face in a different direction; facing in a particular way: *the wrong way round.* **3** to a place by a particular route: *the long way round*; *informal* to someone's home: *come round tonight.* ● *prep.* **1** so as to surround or enclose. **2** going past (an obstacle) and curving to go back along the other side. **3** visiting in a series; seeing the whole of. ● *v.* **1** go round (a corner or obstacle). **2** alter (a number) for convenience. **3** make rounded. □ **in the round** with all sides visible. **round about** nearby; approximately. **round off**

complete. **round the clock** continuously through day and night. **round up** gather into one place. □ **roundness** *n.*

roundabout *n.* **1** a revolving platform at a funfair, with model horses etc. to ride on. **2** a road junction with a circular island round which traffic has to pass in one direction. ● *adj.* indirect; circuitous.

roundel *n.* a small disc.

rounders *n.* a team game played with bat and ball, in which players have to run round a circuit.

Roundhead *n. hist.* a supporter of Parliament against Charles I in the English Civil War.

roundly *adv.* **1** emphatically; thoroughly; bluntly or severely. **2** in a rounded shape.

round robin *n.* a petition signed with names in a circle to conceal the order of writing.

round trip *n.* a circular tour; an outward and return journey.

round-up *n.* a systematic rounding up; a summary (of news etc.).

roundworm *n.* a parasitic worm with a rounded body.

rouse *v.* wake; cause to become active or excited.

rousing *adj.* vigorous, stirring.

rout *n.* a complete defeat; a disorderly retreat. ● *v.* **1** defeat completely; put to flight. **2** fetch (out); rummage.

route *n.* a course or way from starting point to finishing point.

route march *n.* a training march for troops.

router (roo-tĕ) *n.* a device forwarding computer messages to the correct part of a network.

routine *n.* a standard procedure; a set sequence of movements. ● *adj.* in accordance with routine. □ **routinely** *adv.*

roux (roo) *n.* (*pl.* **roux**) a mixture of heated fat and flour as a basis for a sauce.

rove *v.* wander. □ **rover** *n.*

row¹ (roh) *n.* people or things in a line.

row² (roh) *v.* propel (a boat) using oars; carry in a boat that one rows. ● *n.* a spell or rowing. □ **rowboat, rowing boat** *n.*

row³ (*rhymes with* cow) *informal n.* a loud noise; an angry argument. ● *v.* quarrel, argue angrily.

rowan *n.* a tree bearing clusters of red berries.

rowdy *adj.* (**rowdier, rowdiest**) noisy and disorderly. ● *n.* (*pl.* **-ies**) a rowdy person. □ **rowdily** *adv.*, **rowdiness** *n.*

rowlock (rol-ŏk) *n.* a device on the side of a boat for holding an oar.

royal *adj.* **1** of or suited to a king or queen; of the family or in the service of royalty. **2** splendid. ● *n. informal* a member of a royal family. □ **royally** *adv.*

royal blue *n.* & *adj.* bright blue.

royalist *n.* a person supporting or advocating monarchy.

royalty *n.* (*pl.* **-ies**) **1** people of royal status; one such person; royal status. **2** payment to an author, patentee, etc. for each copy, performance, or use of his or her work.

RPI *abbr.* retail price index, a list showing monthly variation in the prices of basic goods.

rpm *abbr.* revolutions per minute.

RSI *abbr.* repetitive strain injury, injury to muscles or tendons from prolonged performance of repeated actions, esp. use of a keyboard.

RSJ *abbr.* rolled steel joint, a load-bearing beam.

RSPB *abbr.* Royal Society for the Protection of Birds.

RSPCA *abbr.* Royal Society for the Prevention of Cruelty to Animals.

RSVP *abbr.* (French *répondez s'il vous plaît*) please reply.

Ru *symb.* ruthenium.

rub *v.* (**rubbed, rubbing**) press (one's hand, a cloth, etc.) against (a surface) and move to and fro; polish, clean, dry, or make sore in this way. ● *n.* **1** an act of rubbing; an ointment to be rubbed on. **2** a difficulty. □ **rub along** *informal* manage without undue difficulty. **rub it in** constantly remind someone of something unpleasant. **rub out** erase (pencil marks).

rubber *n.* **1** a tough elastic substance made from the juice of certain plants or synthetically; a piece of this for rubbing out pencil or ink marks. **2** *Amer., informal* a condom. □ **rubber-stamp** *v.* approve automatically without consideration. □ **rubbery** *adj.*

rubberize *v.* (also **-ise**) treat or coat with rubber.

rubbish *n.* waste or worthless material; nonsense.

rubble *n.* waste or rough fragments of stone, brick, etc.

rubella *n.* German measles.

rubidium *n.* a soft silvery metallic element (symbol Rb).

ruble var. of **rouble**.

rubric *n.* words put as a heading or note of explanation.

ruby *n.* (*pl.* **-ies**) a red gem; a deep red colour. ● *adj.* deep red.

ruby wedding *n.* a 40th wedding anniversary.

RUC *abbr.* Royal Ulster Constabulary.

ruche (roosh) *n.* a decorative frill of fabric.

ruck *v.* crease, wrinkle. ● *n.* **1** a crease or wrinkle. **2** a tightly packed crowd; (in rugby) a loose scrum.

rucksack *n.* a bag carried on the back, used by walkers.

ructions *n.pl. informal* unpleasant arguments or protests.

rudder *n.* a vertical piece of metal or wood hinged to the stern of a boat or aircraft, used for steering.

ruddy *adj.* (**ruddier, ruddiest**) reddish.

rude *adj.* **1** impolite, showing no respect. **2** primitive, roughly made. **3** (of health) good, vigorous. □ **rudely** *adv.*, **rudeness** *n.*

rudiment *n.* a basic principle or element; an undeveloped part.

rudimentary *adj.* incompletely developed; basic, elementary.

rue *n.* a shrub with bitter leaves formerly used in medicine. ● *v.* regret deeply.

rueful *adj.* showing or feeling good-humoured regret. □ **ruefully** *adv.*

ruff *n.* a pleated frill worn round the neck; a projecting or coloured ring of feathers or fur round a bird's or animal's neck.

ruffian *n.* a violent lawless person.

ruffle *v.* disturb the calmness or smoothness of; annoy. ● *n.* a gathered frill.

rug *n.* a thick floor-mat; a piece of thick warm fabric used as a covering.

rugby *n.* (in full **rugby football**) a kind of football game played with an oval ball which may be kicked or carried.

rugged *adj.* **1** uneven, irregular, craggy. **2** rough but kindly. □ **ruggedly** *adv.*, **ruggedness** *n.*

rugger *n. informal* rugby football.

ruin *n.* destruction; complete loss of one's fortune or prospects; the damaged remains of a building etc.; a cause of ruin. ● *v.* cause ruin to; reduce to ruins. □ **ruination** *n.*

ruinous *adj.* bringing ruin; in ruins, ruined. □ **ruinously** *adv.*

rule *n.* **1** a statement or principle governing behaviour or describing a regular occurrence in nature etc.; a dominant custom; government, control. **2** a ruler used by carpenters etc. ● *v.* **1** govern; keep under control; give an authoritative decision. **2** draw (a line) using a ruler. □ **as a rule** usually. **rule of thumb** a rough practical method of procedure. **rule out** exclude.

ruler *n.* **1** a person who rules. **2** a straight strip used in measuring or for drawing straight lines.

ruling *n.* an authoritative decision.

rum *n.* an alcoholic spirit distilled from sugar cane or molasses. ● *adj.* (**rummer, rummest**) *informal* strange, odd.

rumba *n.* a ballroom dance.

rumble *v.* **1** make a low continuous sound. **2** *informal* detect, discover. ● *n.* a rumbling sound.

rumbustious *adj. informal* boisterous, uproarious.

ruminant *n.* an animal that chews the cud. ● *adj.* ruminating.

ruminate *v.* **1** think deeply. **2** chew the cud. □ **rumination** *n.*, **ruminative** *adj.*

rummage *v.* search clumsily. ● *n.* an untidy search through a number of things.

rummage sale *n. Amer.* a jumble sale.

rummy *n.* a card game.

rumour *n.* (*Amer.* **rumor**) a circulating story or report of doubtful truth. □ **be rumoured** be spread as a rumour.

rump *n.* the buttocks; a bird's back near the tail.

rumple *v.* make or become crumpled; make untidy.

rumpus *n. informal* an uproar, an angry dispute.

run *v.* (**ran, run, running**) **1** move with quick steps with always at least one foot off the ground; do this for exercise or in a race; move around hurriedly. **2** (cause to) move smoothly in a particular direction; flow; exude liquid; (of a road etc.) extend. **3** travel regularly along a route. **4** control, manage; function; continue, remain valid. **5** stand as a candidate in an election. **6** smuggle (goods). ● *n.* **1** a spell of running; a running pace; a journey. **2** a point scored in cricket or baseball. **3** a continuous spell or sequence: *a run of bad luck*. **4** unrestricted use of something: *the run of the house*. **5** an enclosed area where domestic animals can range. **6** a ladder in stockings etc. □ **in** or **out of the running** with a good or with no chance of winning. **in the long run** in the end; over a long period. **on the run** fleeing. **run across** happen to meet or find. **run a risk** take a risk. **run a temperature** be feverish. **run away** flee; leave secretly. **run down 1** reduce the numbers of. **2** speak of in a slighting way. **3** knock to the ground when driving. **run into** collide with; happen to meet. **run out** become used up; use up, have none left. **run over** knock down or crush with a vehicle. **run through** discuss or practise quickly. **run up** allow (a bill) to mount.

rundown *n.* a detailed analysis. ● *adj.* (**run-down**) weak or exhausted.

rune *n.* any of the letters in an early Germanic alphabet. □ **runic** *adj.*

rung¹ *n.* a crosspiece of a ladder etc.

rung² p.p. of **ring²**.

runner *n.* **1** a person or animal that runs; a messenger. **2** a creeping stem that roots. **3** a groove, strip, or roller etc. for a thing to move on. **4** a long narrow strip of carpet or ornamental cloth.

runner-up *n.* one who finishes second in a competition.

runny *adj.* (**runnier, runniest**) semi-liquid; tending to flow or exude fluid.

run-of-the-mill *adj.* ordinary.

runt *n.* an undersized person or animal.

run-up *n.* the period leading up to an event.

runway *n.* a prepared surface on which aircraft may take off and land.

rupee *n.* a unit of money in India, Pakistan, etc.

rupture *n.* a breaking, a breach; an abdominal hernia. ● *v.* burst, break; cause a hernia in.

rural *adj.* of, in, or like the countryside.

ruse *n.* a deception, a trick.

rush¹ *v.* (cause to) move with great speed; act or deal with hurriedly; force into hasty action; convey hurriedly; make a sudden assault on. ● *n.* a sudden quick movement; a very busy state or period; a sudden flow or surge.

rush[2] *n.* a marsh plant with a slender pithy stem.

rush hour *n.* one of the times of day when traffic is busiest.

rusk *n.* a biscuit, esp. for babies.

russet *adj.* soft reddish brown. ● *n.* a reddish-brown colour.

rust *n.* **1** a brownish corrosive coating formed on iron exposed to moisture. **2** a reddish-brown colour. ● *v.* make or become rusty. □ **rustproof** *adj.* & *v.*

rustic *adj.* of or like country life; simple, not sophisticated or elaborate; made of rough timber or untrimmed branches.

rustle *v.* **1** (cause to) make a sound like paper being crumpled. **2** steal (horses or cattle). ● *n.* a rustling sound. □ **rustle up** *informal* produce, find or make. □ **rustler** *n.*

rusty *adj.* (**rustier, rustiest**) affected by rust; deteriorating through lack of use; rust-coloured.

rut[1] *n.* **1** a deep track made by wheels. **2** a habitual dull pattern of behaviour.

rut[2] *n.* the periodic sexual excitement of a male deer, goat, etc. ● *v.* (**rutted, rutting**) be affected with this.

ruthenium *n.* a rare metallic element (symbol Ru).

rutherfordium *n.* an unstable element (symbol Rf).

ruthless *adj.* having no pity. □ **ruthlessly** *adv.*, **ruthlessness** *n.*

rye *n.* a cereal; whisky made from this.

Ss

S. *abbr.* **1** south; southern. **2** siemens. ● *symb.* sulphur.

s. *abbr.* **1** second(s). **2** *hist.* shilling(s).

SA *abbr.* **1** South Africa. **2** South Australia. **3** Salvation Army.

sabbath *n.* a day of worship and rest from work (Saturday for Jews, Sunday for Christians).

sabbatical *n.* leave granted to a university teacher for study and travel.

sable *n.* dark fur obtained from a small Arctic marten. ● *adj.* black.

sabotage (sab-ŏ-tahzh) *n.* wilful damage to machinery or materials, or disruption of work. ● *v.* commit sabotage on. □ **saboteur** *n.*

sabre *n.* (*Amer.* **saber**) a curved sword.

sac *n.* a hollow bag-like structure.

saccharin *n.* a sweet synthetic substance used instead of sugar.

saccharine *adj.* excessively sweet or sentimental.

sachet (sa-shay) *n.* a small bag or sealed pack.

sack *n.* **1** a large bag made of a strong coarse fabric. **2** (**the sack**) *informal* dismissal from one's employment. ● *v.* **1** *informal* dismiss. **2** plunder (a captured town). □ **sackful** *n.*

sackcloth *n.* (also **sacking**) coarse fabric for making sacks.

sacral (say-krăl) *adj.* **1** of the sacrum. **2** of or for sacred rites.

sacrament *n.* any of the symbolic Christian religious ceremonies. □ **sacramental** *adj.*

sacred *adj.* venerated as connected with God or religion, holy; not to be tampered with; dedicated to a person or purpose.

sacred cow *n.* *informal* an idea etc. which its supporters will not allow to be criticized.

sacrifice *n.* the slaughter of a victim or presenting of a gift to win a god's favour; this victim or gift; the giving up of a valued thing for the sake of something else; the thing given up, a loss entailed. ● *v.* offer, kill, or give up as a sacrifice. □ **sacrificial** *adj.*

sacrilege *n.* disrespect to a sacred thing. □ **sacrilegious** *adj.*

sacristan *n.* the person in charge of the sacred vessels etc. in a church.

sacristy *n.* (*pl.* **-ies**) the place where sacred vessels etc. are kept in a church.

sacrosanct *adj.* too important or precious to be harmed or interfered with.

sacrum (say-krum) *n.* (*pl.* **sacrums** or **sacra**) the triangular bone at the base of the spine.

SAD *abbr.* seasonal affective disorder, depression occurring in autumn and winter, supposedly due to lack of light.

sad *adj.* (**sadder, saddest**) feeling, causing, or expressing sorrow. ▫ **sadly** *adv.*, **sadness** *n.*

sadden *v.* make sad.

saddle *n.* **1** a seat for a rider. **2** a joint of meat consisting of the two loins. ● *v.* put a saddle on (an animal); burden with a task.

saddler *n.* a person who makes or deals in saddles and harness.

sadism *n.* a tendency to derive pleasure from inflicting or watching cruelty. ▫ **sadist** *n.*, **sadistic** *adj.*, **sadistically** *adv.*

s.a.e. *abbr.* stamped addressed envelope.

safari *n.* an expedition to observe or hunt wild animals.

safari park *n.* a park where exotic wild animals are kept in the open for visitors to see.

safe *adj.* not subject to risk or danger; not harmed; providing security. ● *n.* a strong lockable cupboard for valuables. ▫ **safely** *adv.*

safe conduct *n.* immunity or protection from arrest or harm.

safe deposit *n.* a strongroom or safe in a hotel, bank, etc., where valuables may be deposited.

safeguard *n.* a means of protection. ● *v.* protect.

safe sex *n.* the use of condoms during sexual activity as a precaution against Aids etc.

safety *n.* being safe, freedom from risk or danger.

safety belt *n.* a seat belt.

safety pin *n.* a pin with a point bent back towards the head and enclosed in a guard.

safety valve *n.* **1** a valve that opens automatically to relieve excessive pressure in a steam boiler. **2** a harmless outlet for emotion.

saffron *n.* orange food colouring and flavouring.

sag *v.* (**sagged, sagging**) gradually droop or sink. ● *n.* sagging.

saga *n.* a long story.

sagacious (să-gay-shŭs) *adj.* wise. ▫ **sagaciously** *adv.*, **sagacity** *n.*

sage *n.* **1** a herb. **2** an old and wise man. ● *adj.* wise. ▫ **sagely** *adv.*

sago *n.* the starchy pith of the sago palm, used in puddings.

said past & p.p. of **say**.

sail *n.* **1** a piece of fabric spread to catch the wind and drive a boat along. **2** a journey by boat. **3** the arm of a windmill. ● *v.* **1** travel by water; start on a sea voyage; control (a boat). **2** move smoothly. ▫ **sail through** do or succeed in easily. ▫ **sailboat, sailing ship** *n.*

sailboard *n.* a board with a mast and sail, used in windsurfing. ▫ **sailboarder** *n.*, **sailboarding** *n.*

sailcloth *n.* canvas for sails; a canvas-like material for clothes.

sailor *n.* a member of a ship's crew.

saint *n.* a holy person, esp. one venerated by the RC or Orthodox Church; a very good, patient, or unselfish person. ▫ **sainthood** *n.*, **saintly** *adj.*, **saintliness** *n.*

sake[1] *n.* ▫ **for the sake of** in order to please, help, or honour (a person) or to get or keep (a thing).

sake[2] (**sah**-ki) *n.* a Japanese fermented liquor made from rice.

salaam (să-**lahm**) *n.* an Oriental greeting meaning 'Peace'; a Muslim greeting consisting of a low bow.

salacious *adj.* lewd, erotic. ▫ **salaciously** *adv.*, **salaciousness** *n.*

salad *n.* a cold dish of (usu. raw) vegetables etc.

salamander *n.* a lizard-like animal.

salami *n.* a strongly flavoured sausage, eaten cold.

salaried *adj.* receiving a salary.

salary *n.* (*pl.* **-ies**) a fixed regular (usu. monthly) payment to an employee.

sale *n.* selling, the exchange of a commodity for money; an event at which goods are sold; the disposal of stock at reduced prices; (**sales**) the amount sold by a business or of a commodity. □ **for** or **on sale** offered for purchase.

saleable *adj.* fit to be sold, likely to find a purchaser.

salesman, salesperson, saleswoman *n.* (*pl.* **-men, -persons** or **-people, -women**) a person employed to sell goods.

salesmanship *n.* skill at selling.

salient (say-lee-ĕnt) *adj.* prominent; most noticeable. ● *n.* a piece of land or fortification jutting out to form an angle.

saline *adj.* salty, containing salt(s). □ **salinity** *n.*

saliva *n.* the colourless liquid that forms in the mouth. □ **salivary** *adj.*

salivate *v.* produce saliva. □ **salivation** *n.*

sallow *adj.* (of the complexion) yellowish. ● *n.* a low-growing willow tree.

sally *n.* (*pl.* **-ies**) a sudden charge from a besieged place; a witty remark or retort. □ **sally forth** (**sallied, sallying**) rush out in attack; set out on a journey.

salmon (sa-mŏn) *n.* (*pl.* **salmon**) **1** a large fish with pinkish flesh. **2** (also **salmon pink**) pale yellowish pink.

salmonella *n.* a bacterium causing food poisoning.

salon *n.* a place where a hairdresser, couturier, etc. receives clients; an elegant room for receiving guests.

saloon *n.* **1** a public room, esp. on board ship. **2** a saloon car.

saloon car *n.* a car with a separate boot, not a hatchback.

salsa *n.* **1** a style of music and dance of Cuban origin. **2** a spicy sauce.

SALT *abbr.* Strategic Arms Limitation Talks.

salt *n.* **1** sodium chloride used to season and preserve food. **2** (**salts**) a substance resembling salt in form, esp. a laxative. **3** a chemical compound of a metal and an acid. ● *adj.* tasting of salt; impregnated with salt. ● *v.* season with salt; preserve in salt. □ **take with a grain** (or **pinch**) **of salt** regard sceptically. **worth one's salt** competent. □ **saltiness** *n.*, **salty** *adj.*

salt cellar *n.* a small container for salt used at meals.

saltpetre *n.* (*Amer.* **saltpeter**) a salty white powder used in gunpowder, in medicine, and in preserving meat.

salubrious *adj.* health-giving.

salutary *adj.* producing a beneficial or wholesome effect.

salutation *n.* a greeting.

salute *n.* a gesture of greeting or acknowledgement; a prescribed movement made in the armed forces etc. to show respect. ● *v.* make a salute to.

salvage *n.* the recovery of a ship or its cargo from loss at sea, or of property from fire etc.; the items saved. ● *v.* save, rescue from loss or destruction. □ **salvageable** *adj.*

salvation *n.* saving from disaster, esp. from the consequences of sin.

salve *n.* a soothing ointment; something that soothes. ● *v.* soothe (conscience etc.).

salver *n.* a small tray.

salvo *n.* (*pl.* **salvoes** or **salvos**) a simultaneous discharge of guns; a series of actions performed simultaneously or in quick succession.

sal volatile (sal vŏ-lat-i-li) *n.* a solution of ammonium carbonate used as a remedy for faintness.

Samaritan *n.* a charitable or helpful person; a member of an organization counselling the distressed and suicidal.

samarium *n.* a metallic element (symbol Sm).

samba *n.* a ballroom dance.

same *adj.* identical; not changed or different. ● *pron.* the one already mentioned. ● *adv.* in the same way. □ **all the same** nevertheless. □ **sameness** *n.*

sami (sah-mi) *n.pl.* the Lapps of northern Scandinavia.

samosa *n.* a fried triangular pastry containing spiced vegetables or meat.

sampan *n.* a small flat-bottomed Chinese boat.

samphire *n.* a plant with edible fleshy leaves, growing by the sea.

sample *n.* a small part showing the quality of the whole; a specimen. ● *v.* test by taking a sample of.

sampler *n.* a piece of embroidery worked in various stitches to show one's skill.

samurai (sam-yuu-rI) *n.* (*pl.* **samurai**) a Japanese army officer.

sanatorium *n.* (*pl.* **sanatoriums** or **sanatoria**) an establishment for treating chronic diseases or convalescents; a room for sick pupils in a school.

sanctify *v.* (**sanctified, sanctifying**) make holy or sacred. □ **sanctification** *n.*

sanctimonious *adj.* ostentatiously righteous, hypocritical. □ **sanctimoniously** *adv.*, **sanctimoniousness** *n.*

sanction *n.* **1** permission, approval. **2** a penalty imposed on a country or organization. ● *v.* give sanction to, authorize.

sanctity *n.* sacredness, holiness.

sanctuary *n.* (*pl.* **-ies**) **1** a place of refuge; a place where wildlife is protected. **2** a sacred place.

sanctum *n.* a sacred place; a private place.

sand *n.* very fine loose fragments of crushed rock; (**sands**) an expanse of sand, a sandbank. ● *v.* **1** sprinkle with sand. **2** smooth with sandpaper or a sander.

sandal *n.* a light shoe with straps.

sandalwood *n.* a scented wood.

sandbag *n.* a bag filled with sand, used to protect a wall or building. ● *v.* (**sandbagged, sandbagging**) protect with sandbags.

sandbank *n.* a deposit of sand forming a shallow area in a sea or river.

sandblast *v.* treat or clean with a jet of sand driven by compressed air or steam.

sandcastle *n.* a model building of sand, made for fun.

sander *n.* a mechanical tool for smoothing surfaces.

sandpaper *n.* paper with a coating of sand or other abrasive substance, used for smoothing surfaces. ● *v.* smooth with this.

sandstone *n.* rock formed of compressed sand.

sandstorm *n.* a desert storm of wind with blown sand.

sandwich *n.* two or more slices of bread with a layer of filling between; something arranged like this. ● *v.* put between two other people or things.

sandy *adj.* (**sandier, sandiest**) **1** like sand; covered with sand. **2** (of hair) yellowish red.

sane *adj.* having a sound mind; rational. □ **sanely** *adv.*

sang past of **sing**.

sangria *n.* a Spanish drink of red wine, lemonade, and fruit.

sanguinary *adj.* full of bloodshed; bloodthirsty.

sanguine *adj.* optimistic.

sanitarium *n.* (*pl.* **sanitariums** or **sanitaria**) *Amer.* a sanatorium.

sanitary *adj.* of hygiene and health; clean, hygienic; of sanitation.

sanitary towel *n.* (*Amer.* **sanitary napkin**) a pad worn to absorb blood during menstruation.

sanitation *n.* arrangements to protect public health, esp. drainage and disposal of sewage.

sanitize *v.* (also **-ise**) clean, make hygienic; alter to make more palatable but less individual or authentic.

sanity *n.* the condition of being sane.

sank past of **sink**.

sap *n.* **1** the food-carrying liquid in plants. **2** *informal* a foolish person. ● *v.* (**sapped, sapping**) exhaust gradually. ◻ **sappy** *adj.*

sapling *n.* a young tree.

sapphire *n.* a blue precious stone; its colour.

saprophyte (sap-rŏ-fIt) *n.* a fungus or related plant living on decayed matter.

sarcasm *n.* ironically scornful language. ◻ **sarcastic** *adj.*, **sarcastically** *adv.*

sarcophagus (sah-**ko**-fă-gŭs) *n.* (*pl.* **sarcophagi**) a stone coffin.

sardine *n.* a young pilchard or similar small fish.

sardonic *adj.* humorous in a grim or sarcastic way. ◻ **sardonically** *adv.*

sari *n.* a length of cloth draped round the body, worn by Indian women.

sarong (să-**rong**) *n.* a strip of cloth worn round the body, esp. in Malaysia.

sartorial *adj.* of tailoring, clothing, or style of dress.

SAS *abbr.* Special Air Service; an armed regiment trained in commando techniques.

sash *n.* **1** a strip of cloth worn round the waist or over one shoulder. **2** a frame holding a pane of a window and sliding up and down in grooves.

sash window *n.* a window opened and shut by sliding up and down in grooves.

Sat. *abbr.* Saturday.

sat past & p.p. of **sit**.

Satan *n.* the devil.

satanic *adj.* **1** of Satan. **2** very evil or wicked.

Satanism *n.* the worship of Satan. ◻ **Satanist** *n.*

satchel *n.* a bag for school books, hung over the shoulder.

sateen *n.* a closely woven cotton fabric resembling satin.

satellite *n.* **1** a heavenly or artificial body revolving round a planet. **2** a country that is dependent on another.

satellite dish *n.* a dish-shaped aerial for receiving broadcasts transmitted by satellite.

satiate (say-shi-ayt) *v.* satisfy fully, glut. ◻ **satiation** *n.* **satiety** *n.*

satin *n.* a silky material that is glossy on one side. ● *adj.* smooth as satin.

satire *n.* criticism through ridicule, irony, or sarcasm; a novel or play etc. that ridicules something. ◻ **satirical** *adj.*, **satirically** *adv.*

satirize *v.* (also **-ise**) describe and criticize through satire. ◻ **satirist** *n.*

satisfactory *adj.* satisfying; adequate. ◻ **satisfactorily** *adv.*

satisfy *v.* (**satisfied, satisfying**) fulfil the needs or wishes of; make pleased or contented; fulfil (a need, requirement, etc.); convince. ◻ **satisfaction** *n.*

satsuma *n.* a small variety of orange.

saturate *v.* make thoroughly wet; fill or supply completely or to excess. ◻ **saturation** *n.*

Saturday *n.* the day following Friday.

saturnine *adj.* having a gloomy temperament or appearance.

satyr (sat-er) *n.* a woodland god in classical mythology, with a goat's ears, tail, and legs.

sauce *n.* **1** a liquid food added for flavour. **2** *informal* impudence.

saucepan *n.* a metal cooking pot with a long handle.

saucer *n.* a shallow curved dish on which a cup stands; something shaped like this.

saucy *adj.* (**saucier, sauciest**) impudent; mischievously or playfully provocative. □ **saucily** *adv.*

sauerkraut (sow-er-krowt) *n.* chopped pickled cabbage.

sauna (sor-nă) *n.* a specially designed hot room for cleaning and refreshing the body.

saunter *n.* & *v.* (take) a stroll.

sausage *n.* minced seasoned meat in a tubular case of thin skin.

sauté (soh-tay) *v.* (**sautéd** or **sautéed, sautéing**) fry quickly in shallow oil.

savage *adj.* wild and fierce; cruel, hostile; primitive, uncivilized. ● *n.* a primitive or uncivilized person; a very cruel person. ● *v.* maul, attack fiercely. □ **savagely** *adv.*, **savagery** *n.*

savannah *n.* a grassy plain in hot regions.

save *v.* **1** rescue or remove from harm or danger. **2** keep, store for future use; avoid wasting; keep money in this way. **3** prevent the scoring of (a goal). ● *n.* an act of saving in football etc. □ **saver** *n.*

savings *n.pl.* money put aside for future use.

saviour *n.* (*Amer.* **savior**) a person who rescues people from harm.

savoir faire (sav-wah fair) *n.* knowledge of how to behave; social tact.

savory *n.* a herb. ● *adj.* Amer. sp. of **savoury**.

savour (*Amer.* **savor**) *n.* flavour; smell. ● *v.* **1** enjoy fully, relish. **2** have a trace of a quality.

savoury (*Amer.* **savory**) *adj.* having an appetizing taste or smell; salty or piquant, not sweet. ● *n.* (*pl.* **-ies**) a savoury dish, esp. at the end of a meal.

saw[1] past of **see**.

saw[2] *n.* a cutting tool with a zigzag edge. ● *v.* (**sawed, sawn, sawing**) cut with a saw; make a to-and-fro movement.

saw[3] *n.* a saying.

sawdust *n.* powdery fragments of wood, made in sawing timber.

sawmill *n.* a mill where timber is cut.

sawn p.p. of **saw**[2].

sax *n. informal* a saxophone.

saxe blue *adj.* & *n.* greyish blue.

saxophone *n.* a brass wind instrument with finger-operated keys. □ **saxophonist** *n.*

say *v.* (**said, saying**) **1** utter (words); express, convey, state; have written or shown on the surface. **2** suppose as a possibility. ● *n.* the opportunity to express one's opinion or exert influence.

SAYE *abbr.* save-as-you-earn, a method of saving money that carries tax privileges.

saying *n.* a well-known phrase or proverb.

Sb *symb.* antimony.

Sc *symb.* scandium.

scab *n.* **1** a crust forming over a cut; a skin disease or plant disease causing similar roughness. **2** *informal, derog.* a blackleg. □ **scabby** *adj.*

scabbard *n.* the sheath of a sword etc.

scabies *n.* a contagious skin disease causing itching.

scabrous (skay-brŭs) *adj.* **1** rough-surfaced. **2** indecent.

scaffold *n.* **1** a platform for the execution of criminals. **2** a structure of scaffolding.

scaffolding *n.* poles and planks providing platforms for people working on buildings etc.

scald *v.* injure with hot liquid or steam; cleanse or peel using boiling water. ● *n.* an injury by scalding.

scale *n.* **1** an ordered series of units or qualities for measuring or classifying things; a series of marks at regular intervals, used in measuring. **2** relative size or extent. **3** (**scales**) an instrument for weighing. **4** a fixed series of notes in a system of music. **5** each of the overlapping plates of bony membrane protecting the skin of fish and reptiles; something resembling this. **6** a deposit caused in a kettle etc. by hard water; tartar on teeth. ● *v.* **1** climb. **2** represent in proportion to the size of the original. **3** remove scale(s) from. ◻ **scaly** *adj.*

scalene (skay-leen) *adj.* (of a triangle) having unequal sides.

scallion *n.* a shallot or spring onion.

scallop *n.* (also **scollop**) **1** a shellfish with a hinged fanshaped shell. **2** (**scallops**) semicircular curves as an ornamental edging. ◻ **scalloped** *adj.*

scallywag *n.* a rascal.

scalp *n.* the skin of the head excluding the face. ● *v.* cut the scalp from.

scalpel *n.* a surgeon's or painter's small straight knife.

scam *n. informal* a dishonest scheme.

scamp *n.* a rascal.

scamper *v.* run hastily or in play. ● *n.* a scampering run.

scampi *n.pl.* large prawns.

scan *v.* (**scanned, scanning**) **1** look at all parts of; read quickly. **2** pass a radar or electronic beam over; resolve (a picture) into elements of light and shade for transmission or reproduction. **3** (of verse) have a regular rhythm; analyse the rhythm of. ● *n.* scanning. ◻ **scanner** *n.*

scandal *n.* an action or event causing outrage; such outrage; malicious gossip about such actions. ◻ **scandalous** *adj.*, **scandalously** *adv.*

scandalize *v.* (also **-ise**) shock; outrage.

scandalmonger *n.* a person who spreads scandal.

Scandinavian *adj.* & *n.* (a native) of Scandinavia.

scandium *n.* a metallic element (symbol Sc).

scansion *n.* scanning of verse.

scant *adj.* barely enough.

scanty *adj.* (**scantier, scantiest**) small in amount or extent; barely enough. ◻ **scantily** *adv.*, **scantiness** *n.*

scapegoat *n.* a person made to bear blame that should fall on others.

scapula *n.* (*pl.* **scapulae** or **scapulas**) the shoulder blade. ◻ **scapular** *adj.*

scar *n.* the mark where a wound has healed. ● *v.* (**scarred, scarring**) mark with a scar; form scar(s).

scarab *n.* a sacred beetle of ancient Egypt.

scarce *adj.* not enough to supply a demand, rare.

scarcely *adv.* only just; only a short time before; surely or probably not.

scarcity *n.* a shortage.

scare *v.* frighten; be frightened. ● *n.* a fright; widespread alarm.

scarecrow *n.* a figure dressed in old clothes and set up to scare birds away from crops.

scaremonger *n.* a person who spreads alarming rumours. ◻ **scaremongering** *n.*

scarf *n.* (*pl.* **scarves** or **scarfs**) a piece or strip of material worn round the neck or tied over the head.

scarify *v.* (**scarified, scarifying**) **1** make cuts or scratches in; break up (grass or soil) with a rake. **2** criticize harshly.

scarlet *adj.* & *n.* brilliant red.

scarlet fever *n.* an infectious fever producing a scarlet rash.

scarp *n.* a steep slope on a hillside.

scart *n.* (also **Scart**) a 21-pin socket used to connect video equipment.

scary *adj.* (**scarier, scariest**) *informal* frightening.

scathing *adj.* (of criticism) very severe; scornful.

scatology *n.* an excessive interest in excrement ◻ **scatological** *adj.*

scatter *v.* throw in various random directions; (cause to) move off in different directions.

scatterbrain *n.* a careless or forgetful person. □ **scatterbrained** *adj.*

scatty *adj.* (**scattier, scattiest**) *informal* scatterbrained, disorganized.

scavenge *v.* search for (usable objects) among rubbish etc.; (of animals) search for decaying flesh as food. □ **scavenger** *n.*

scenario *n.* (*pl.* **scenarios**) **1** the script or summary of a film or play. **2** a possible or hypothetical sequence of events.

scene *n.* **1** the place where something occurs; a landscape, a place seen in a particular way; an event or episode characterized by a quality: *scenes of violence.* **2** a piece of continuous action in a play or film. **3** a display of temper or emotion. **4** *informal* one's area of interest or expertise: *not my scene.* □ **behind the scenes** hidden from public view.

scenery *n.* the general (esp. picturesque) appearance of a landscape; structures used on a theatre stage to represent the scene of action.

scenic *adj.* picturesque.

scent *n.* a pleasant smell; liquid perfume; an animal's trail perceptible to a hound's sense of smell. ● *v.* **1** apply scent to; make fragrant. **2** discover by smell; suspect or detect the presence of. □ **on the scent** making progress in an investigation.

sceptic (skep-tik) *n.* (*Amer.* **skeptic**) a sceptical person.

sceptical (skep-tik-ăl) *adj.* (*Amer.* **skeptical**) not easily convinced; having doubts. □ **sceptically** *adv.*, **scepticism** *n.*

sceptre *n.* (*Amer.* **scepter**) an ornamental rod carried as a symbol of sovereignty.

schadenfreude (shah-dĕn-froidĕ) *n.* enjoyment of others' misfortunes.

schedule *n.* a programme or timetable of events. ● *v.* **1** include in a schedule. **2** list (a building) for preservation.

scheduled flight *n.* a regular public flight, not a chartered flight.

schema *n.* (*pl.* **schemata** or **schemas**) a summary, outline, or diagram.

schematic *adj.* in the form of a diagram; simplified or simplistic. □ **schematically** *adv.*

schematize *v.* (also **-ise**) put into schematic form. □ **schematization** *n.*

scheme *n.* a plan of work or action; a system or arrangement. ● *v.* make plans, plot. □ **schemer** *n.*

scherzo (skair-tsoh) *n.* (*pl.* **scherzos**) a lively piece of music.

schism (skizm) *n.* division into opposing groups through a difference in belief or opinion. □ **schismatic** *adj.* & *n.*

schist (shist) *n.* a rock formed in layers.

schizoid (skits-oid) *adj.* abnormally introverted; *informal* having contradictory characteristics. ● *n.* a schizoid person.

schizophrenia *n.* a mental disorder involving failures of perception and withdrawal from reality; *informal* being subject to contradictory impulses etc. □ **schizophrenic** *adj.* & *n.*

schmaltz (shmawlts) *n.* sugary sentimentality.

schmuck *n. Amer. informal* a foolish person.

schnapps *n.* a strong alcoholic spirit.

schnitzel (shnit-sĕl) *n.* a fried cutlet.

scholar *n.* a learned person, esp. in a particular field; a pupil; the holder of a scholarship. □ **scholarly** *adj.*, **scholarliness** *n.*

scholarship *n.* **1** academic study, learning. **2** a grant of money supporting a student's education.

scholastic *adj.* of schools or education; academic.

school *n.* **1** an educational institution. **2** a group of people sharing the same ideas or following the same principles. **3** a shoal of whales. ● *v.* train, discipline. ▫ **schoolboy**, **schoolchild**, **schoolgirl** *n.*, **schoolteacher** *n.*

schooner *n.* **1** a sailing ship. **2** a measure for sherry.

sciatica (sI-at-ik-ă) *n.* a condition causing pain in the hip and thigh.

science *n.* a branch of knowledge requiring systematic study and method, esp. dealing with substances, life, and natural laws. ▫ **scientific** *adj.*, **scientifically** *adv.*

scientist *n.* an expert in a science.

scimitar (sim-i-tă) *n.* a short curved oriental sword.

scintilla (sin-til-ă) *n.* a trace.

scintillating *adj.* sparkling; witty, lively.

scion (sy-ŏn) *n.* **1** a plant shoot cut for grafting. **2** a descendant.

scissors *n.pl.* a cutting instrument with two pivoted blades.

sclerosis *n.* abnormal hardening of body tissue.

scoff *v.* **1** speak contemptuously, jeer. **2** *informal* eat greedily.

scold *v.* rebuke (esp. a child). ▫ **scolding** *n.*

scollop var. of **scallop**.

sconce *n.* an ornamental bracket on a wall, holding a light.

scone (skon, skohn) *n.* a soft flat cake eaten buttered.

scoop *n.* **1** an implement like a spoon, with a long handle and a deep bowl; a short-handled deep shovel. **2** *informal* an item of news published by one newspaper before its rivals. ● *v.* **1** lift or hollow with (or as if with) a scoop. **2** *informal* publish a news story before (a rival newspaper).

scoot *v. informal* move or leave quickly.

scooter *n.* **1** a lightweight motorcycle. **2** a child's toy consisting of a footboard on wheels, propelled by the foot and steered by a long handle.

scope *n.* the range of a subject, activity, etc.; opportunity.

scorch *v.* burn or become burnt on the surface.

scorching *adj.* very hot.

score *n.* **1** the number of points gained in a contest. **2** a set of twenty **3** a line or mark cut into something. **4** written or printed music; music for a film or play. ● *v.* **1** gain (points etc.) in a contest; keep a record of the score; *informal* achieve a success. **2** cut a line or mark into. **3** write or compose as a musical score. ▫ **score out** cross out. ▫ **scorer** *n.*

scorn *n.* the feeling that someone or something is worthless or despicable. ● *v.* feel or show scorn for; reject with scorn. ▫ **scornful** *adj.*, **scornfully** *adv.*

scorpion *n.* a creature related to spiders, with lobsterlike claws and a sting in its long tail.

Scot *n.* a native of Scotland.

Scotch *adj. dated* Scottish. ● *n.* Scotch whisky.

■ **Usage** *Scots* or *Scottish* is preferred to the adjective *Scotch* in Scotland.

---

scotch *v.* put an end to (a rumour).

scot-free *adv.* without injury or punishment.

Scots *adj.* Scottish. ● *n.* the Scottish form of the English language. ▫ **Scotsman, Scotswoman** *n.*

Scottish *adj.* of Scotland or its people.

scoundrel *n.* a dishonest person.

scour *v.* **1** cleanse by rubbing; clear out (a channel etc.) by flowing water. **2** search thoroughly. ● *n.* scouring, being scoured. ▫ **scourer** *n.*

scourge (skerj) *n.* **1** *hist.* a whip. **2** someone or something causing great suffering. ● *v.* **1** *hist.* flog. **2** cause suffering to.

scout *n.* a person sent to gather information, esp. about enemy movements. ● *v.* act as a scout, search.

scowl *n.* a sullen or angry frown. ● *v.* make a scowl.

scrabble *v.* scratch or search busily with the hands, paws, etc.

scraggy *adj.* (**scraggier**, **scraggiest**) thin and bony. □ **scragginess** *n.*

scram *v.* (**scrammed, scramming**) *informal* go away.

scramble *v.* **1** climb with difficulty; move hastily or awkwardly; struggle to perform or achieve; (of a fighter aircraft) take off quickly for action. **2** mix, muddle; make (a transmission) unintelligible except by means of a special receiver; cook (eggs) by mixing and stirring. ● *n.* **1** a scrambling walk or movement; an eager struggle. **2** a motorcycle race over rough ground. **3** a disordered mixture. □ **scrambler** *n.*

scrap *n.* **1** a fragment, esp. one left after use, eating, etc. **2** discarded metal suitable for reprocessing. **3** *informal* a fight or quarrel. ● *v.* (**scrapped, scrapping**) **1** discard as useless. **2** *informal* fight, quarrel.

scrapbook *n.* a book for newspaper cuttings or similar souvenirs.

scrape *v.* **1** clean, smooth, or damage by passing a hard edge across a surface; make a harsh sound doing this. **2** achieve (something) or manage to get by with difficulty; be very economical. ● *n.* **1** a scraping movement or sound; a scraped place. **2** *informal* a predicament caused by unwise behaviour. □ **scraper** *n.*

scrapie *n.* a disease of sheep causing loss of coordination.

scraping *n.* a fragment produced by scraping.

scrappy *adj.* (**scrappier, scrappiest**) made up of scraps or disconnected elements. □ **scrappily** *adv.*, **scrappiness** *n.*

scratch *v.* **1** mark or wound with a pointed object; rob or scrape with claws or fingernails; make a thin scraping sound by doing this. **2** obtain with difficulty. **3** cancel; withdraw from a competition. ● *n.* a mark, wound, or sound made by scratching; a spell of scratching. ● *adj.* collected from what is available; not of the highest quality. □ **from scratch** from the very beginning or with no preparation. **up to scratch** up to the required standard. □ **scratchy** *adj.*

scratch card *n.* a card with sections coated in a waxy substance which may be scraped away to reveal whether one has won a prize.

scratchings *n.pl.* crisp residue of pork fat left after rendering lard.

scrawl *v.* write in a hurried untidy way. ● *n.* bad handwriting; a scrawled note.

scrawny *adj.* (**scrawnier, scrawniest**) scraggy.

scream *v.* give a piercing cry, esp. of fear or pain; make a long piercing sound. ● *n.* **1** a screaming cry or sound. **2** *informal* a very amusing person or thing.

scree *n.* a mass of loose stones on a mountainside.

screech *n.* a harsh high-pitched scream or sound. ● *v.* make a screech.

screed *n.* **1** a tiresomely long piece of writing or speech. **2** a thin layer of cement.

screen *n.* **1** an upright structure used to give shelter, divide a room, hide something, etc. **2** a windscreen. **3** the surface of a television, VDU, etc., on which images and data are displayed; a blank surface on to which an image is projected. ● *v.* **1** shelter, protect, or separate with a screen. **2** show or broadcast (a film or television programme). **3** examine for the presence or absence of a disease, quality, etc.

screenplay *n.* the script of a film.

screen saver *n.* *computing* a program which, after a set time, replaces an unchanging screen display with a moving image to prevent damage.

screw *n.* **1** a metal pin with a spiral ridge round its length, fastened by turning; a thing twisted to tighten or press something; an act of twisting or tightening. **2** a propeller. **3** *informal* a prison officer. **4** *vulgar slang* an act of sexual intercourse. ● *v.* **1** fasten or tighten with screw(s); turn (a screw); twist, become twisted. **2** *informal* cheat; extort. **3** *vulgar slang* have sexual intercourse with. □ **screw up 1** summon up (courage) **2** *informal* bungle (something); cause (someone) to be emotionally disturbed..

screwdriver *n.* a tool for turning screws.

scribble *v.* write or draw hurriedly or carelessly. ● *n.* something scribbled.

scribe *n.* a person who (before the invention of printing) made copies of writings; (in New Testament times) a professional religious scholar.

scrimmage *n.* a confused struggle.

scrimp *v.* economize, save.

script *n.* **1** handwriting; a style of printed characters resembling this. **2** the text of a play, broadcast talk, etc.

scripture *n.* sacred writings; (**the Scriptures**) those of the Christians or the Jews. □ **scriptural** *adj.*

scroll *n.* a roll of paper or parchment; an ornamental design in this shape. ● *v.* move a display on a VDU screen up or down as the screen is filled. □ **scrollable** *adj.*

scrotum *n.* (*pl.* **scrota** or **scrotums**) the pouch of skin enclosing the testicles.

scrounge *v.* cadge; borrow; collect by foraging. □ **scrounger** *n.*

scrub *v.* (**scrubbed, scrubbing**) rub hard to clean, esp. with something coarse or bristly; *informal* cancel. ● *n.* **1** an act of scrubbing; a semi-abrasive skin cleanser. **2** vegetation consisting of stunted trees and shrubs; land covered with this.

scruff *n.* the back of the neck.

scruffy *adj.* (**scruffier, scruffiest**) *informal* shabby and untidy. □ **scruffily** *adv.*, **scruffiness** *n.*

scrum *n.* a scrummage; *informal* a disorderly crowd.

scrummage *n.* a grouping of forwards in rugby football to struggle for possession of the ball by pushing.

scrumptious *adj. informal* delicious.

scrunch *v.* crunch; crush, crumple. ● *n.* a crunching noise.

scruple *n.* a doubt as to whether something is morally right, hesitation caused by this. ● *v.* hesitate because of scruples.

scrupulous *adj.* very conscientious or careful. □ **scrupulously** *adv.*, **scrupulousness** *n.*

scrutinize *v.* (also **-ise**) examine carefully.

scrutiny *n.* (*pl.* **-ies**) a careful look or examination.

scuba *n.* an aqualung (acronym from *s*elf-*c*ontained *u*nderwater *b*reathing *a*pparatus). □ **scuba-diving** *n.*

scud *v.* (**scudded, scudding**) move along fast and smoothly.

scuff *v.* scrape the surface of (a shoe) against something; mark or scrape by doing this.

scuffle *n.* confused struggle or fight. ● *v.* take part in a scuffle.

scull *n.* one of a pair of small oars; an oar that rests on a boat's stern, worked with a screw-like movement. ● *v.* row with sculls.

scullery *n.* (*pl.* **-ies**) a room for washing dishes and similar work.

sculpt *v.* sculpture.

sculptor *n.* a maker of sculptures.

sculpture *n.* the art of carving or modelling; work made in this way. ● *v.* make or shape by carving or modelling. □ **sculptural** *adj.*

scum *n.* a layer of impurities or froth etc. on the surface of a liquid; *informal* a worthless person.

scupper *n.* an opening in a ship's side to drain water from the deck. ● *v.* sink (a ship) deliberately; *informal* thwart, spoil, stop.

scurf *n.* flakes of dry skin, esp. from the scalp; similar scaly matter.

scurrilous *adj.* making scandalous claims; humorously insulting. ◻ **scurrility** *n.*, **scurrilously** *adv.*

scurry *v.* (**scurried, scurrying**) run hurriedly, scamper. ● *n.* (*pl.* **-ies**) scurrying, a rush.

scurvy *n.* a disease caused by lack of vitamin C.

scuttle *n.* a box or bucket for fetching and holding coal. ● *v.* **1** scurry. **2** sink (a ship) by letting in water.

scythe (sy*th*) *n.* an implement with a curved blade on a long handle, for cutting long grass.

SE *abbr.* south-east; south-eastern.

Se *symb.* selenium.

sea *n.* the expanse of salt water surrounding the continents; a section of this; a large inland lake; the waves of the sea; a vast expanse. ◻ **at sea 1** in a ship on the sea. **2** perplexed.

seaboard *n.* the coast.

seaborgium *n.* a chemical element (symbol Sg).

seafaring *adj.* & *n.* working or travelling on the sea. ◻ **seafarer** *n.*

seafood *n.* fish or shellfish from the sea eaten as food.

seagoing *adj.* of or for sea voyages.

seagull *n.* a gull.

sea horse *n.* a small fish with a horse-like head.

seal[1] *n.* **1** an engraved piece of metal used to stamp a design; its impression. **2** a device used to join things or close something firmly. **3** an action etc. regarded as guaranteeing something. ● *v.* close or fasten securely; mark with a seal; settle (an agreement etc.).

seal[2] *n.* an amphibious sea animal with thick fur or bristles.

sealant *n.* a substance for coating a surface to make it airtight or watertight.

sea lion *n.* a large seal.

seam *n.* **1** a line where two pieces of fabric are sewn together; a join. **2** a layer of coal etc. in the ground. ● *v.* join by a seam.

seaman *n.* (*pl.* **seamen**) a sailor; a person skilled in seafaring. ◻ **seamanship** *n.*

seamless *adj.* with no obvious joins; smooth and continuous.

seamstress *n.* a woman who sews, esp. for a living.

seance (say-ahns) *n.* a meeting where people try to make contact with the spirits of the dead.

seaplane *n.* an aeroplane designed to take off from and land on water.

sear *v.* scorch, burn.

search *v.* try to find something; hunt through or over (a place or person). ● *n.* the process of searching.

searching *adj.* thorough.

searchlight *n.* an outdoor lamp with a powerful beam; its beam.

seascape *n.* a picture or view of the sea.

seasick *adj.* made sick by the motion of a ship. ◻ **seasickness** *n.*

seaside *n.* the coast as a place for holidays.

season *n.* one of the four divisions of the year associated with particular weather, length of daylight, etc.; the period when a specified event takes place or a specified food is plentiful. ● *v.* **1** add salt etc. to (food). **2** dry or treat (timber) to prepare it for use.

seasonable *adj.* suitable for the season.

■ **Usage** *Seasonable* is sometimes confused with *seasonal*.

---

seasonal *adj.* of a season or seasons; varying with the seasons. ◻ **seasonally** *adv.*

seasoned *adj.* experienced.

seasoning *n.* a substance used to enhance the flavour of food.

season ticket *n.* a ticket valid for any number of journeys or performances in a specified period.

seat *n.* **1** a thing made or used for sitting on; a place as a member of parliament, a committee, etc.; the site or base of something. **2** a country house. **3** the buttocks; the part of a garment covering these. ● *v.* cause to sit; have seats for.

seat belt *n.* a strap securing a person to a seat in a vehicle or aircraft.

sea urchin *n.* a sea animal with a round spiky shell.

seaward *adj.* & *adv.* towards the sea. □ **seawards** *adv.*

seaweed *n.* large algae growing in the sea.

seaworthy *adj.* (of ships) fit for a sea voyage. □ **seaworthiness** *n.*

sebaceous (si-**bay**-shŭs) *adj.* secreting an oily or greasy substance.

secateurs *n.pl.* clippers for pruning plants.

secede *v.* withdraw from membership. □ **secession** *n.*

seclude *v.* keep (a person) apart from others.

secluded *adj.* (of a place) not much visited, private.

seclusion *n.* privacy.

second[1] (**sek**-ŏnd) *adj.* **1** next after the first. **2** inferior or subordinate. ● *n.* **1** a second class in an examination. **2** an attendant at a duel or boxing match. **3** (**seconds**) goods of inferior quality. **4** (**seconds**) *informal* a second helping of food. ● *v.* formally support (a proposal etc.). □ **secondly** *adv.*

second[2] (**sek**-ŏnd) *n.* a sixtieth part of a minute of time or a degree of an angle.

second[3] (si-**kond**) *v.* transfer temporarily to another job or department. □ **secondment** *n.*

secondary *adj.* **1** coming after or derived from what is primary. **2** (of schools or education) for children who have had primary education, usu. between the ages of 11 and 18. ● *n.* a secondary thing. □ **secondarily** *adv.*

secondary colours *n.pl.* colours obtained by mixing two primary colours.

second-best *adj.* next to the best in quality; inferior.

second-class *adj.* & *adv.* next or inferior to first-class in quality etc.

second cousin *see* **cousin**.

second-hand *adj.* bought after use by a previous owner; passed on from someone else.

second nature *n.* a habit or characteristic that has become automatic.

second-rate *adj.* inferior in quality.

second sight *n.* the supposed power to foresee future events.

second thoughts *n.pl.* a change of mind after reconsideration.

second wind *n.* renewed capacity for effort.

secret *adj.* kept from the knowledge of most people. ● *n.* something secret; a mystery; a means of achieving something: *the secret of success.* □ **in secret** secretly. □ **secrecy** *n.*, **secretly** *adv.*

secretariat *n.* an administrative office or department.

secretary *n.* (*pl.* **-ies**) a person employed to deal with correspondence and routine office work; an official in charge of an organization's correspondence; an ambassador's or government minister's chief assistant. □ **secretarial** *adj.*

■ **Usage** *secretary* is spelt and pronounced with an *r* after the *c* (not *secetary*).

Secretary General *n.* (*pl.* **Secretary Generals**) a principal administrative officer.

secrete (si-**kreet**) *v.* **1** conceal, hide. **2** (of a cell, gland, etc.) produce and discharge (a substance). □ **secretion** *n.*, **secretor** *n.*

secretive *adj.* concealing information etc. □ **secretively** *adv.*, **secretiveness** *n.*

secretory *adj.* of physiological secretion.

sect *n.* a group with beliefs, esp. religious ones, that differ from those generally accepted.

sectarian *adj.* **1** of a sect or sects. **2** rigidly following the doctrines of a sect; promoting the interests of a sect.

section *n.* a distinct part; a cross-section; a subdivision. ● *v.* **1** divide into sections. **2** commit (a person) to a psychiatric hospital.

sectional *adj.* of a section or sections; made in sections.

sector *n.* a part of an area; a branch of an activity; a section of a circular area between two lines drawn from centre to circumference.

secular *adj.* of worldly (not religious or spiritual) matters.

secure *adj.* tightly fixed or fastened, certain not to slip, come undone, etc.; safe; confident ● *v.* **1** make secure, fasten securely; guarantee repayment of (a loan) by taking something as a pledge. **2** obtain. ◻ **securely** *adv.*

security *n.* (*pl.* **-ies**) **1** being secure. **2** precautions taken against espionage, theft, etc. **3** something given as a pledge of fulfilment of an obligation or repayment of a loan. **4** a certificate showing ownership of financial stocks etc.

sedate¹ *adj.* calm and dignified. ◻ **sedately** *adv.*, **sedateness** *n.*

sedate² *v.* treat with sedatives. ◻ **sedation** *n.*

sedative *adj.* having a calming effect. ● *n.* a sedative drug.

sedentary (sed-ĕnt-ă-ri) *adj.* seated; (of work) done while sitting.

sediment *n.* particles of solid matter in a liquid or deposited by water or wind. ◻ **sedimentary** *adj.*, **sedimentation** *n.*

sedition *n.* words or actions inciting rebellion. ◻ **seditious** *adj.*, **seditiously** *adv.*

seduce *v.* tempt into wrong or unwise action; persuade into sexual intercourse. ◻ **seducer** *n.*, **seduction** *n.*, **seductive** *adj.*, **seductress** *n.*

sedulous (sed-yuu-lŭs) *adj.* diligent and persevering. ◻ **sedulously** *adv.*

see¹ *v.* (**saw, seen, seeing**) **1** perceive with the eyes; learn from something seen; watch, look. **2** understand; deduce. **3** meet; escort: *see you home.* **4** experience; be the time when (something) happens. **5** regard in a particular way. **6** ensure: *see it gets done.* ◻ **see about** or **to** attend to. **seeing that** in view of the fact that. **see off** escort to the point of departure; drive away. **see through** not be deceived by.

see² *n.* a bishop's or archbishop's seat of authority.

seed *n.* **1** a plant's fertilized ovule, from which a new plant may grow; semen; the origin of something. **2** one of the stronger players in a sports tournament, scheduled to play in a particular order so they do not defeat one another early on. ● *v.* **1** plant with seeds; produce seeds. **2** remove seeds from (a fruit etc.) **3** give the status of seed to (a player). ◻ **go** or **run to seed** **1** cease flowering as seed develops. **2** deteriorate.

seedless *adj.* not containing seeds.

seedling *n.* a very young plant.

seedy *adj.* (**seedier, seediest**) **1** sordid, disreputable. **2** *informal* unwell. ◻ **seediness** *n.*

seek *v.* (**sought, seeking**) try to find or obtain; try (to do something).

seem *v.* appear to be or exist or be true. ◻ **seemingly** *adv.*

seen p.p. of **see¹**.

seep *v.* ooze slowly through porous material or small holes. ◻ **seepage** *n.*

seer *n.* a prophet.

see-saw *n.* a long board balanced on a central support so that children sitting on each end can ride up and down; a situation with repeated changes from one state to another. ● *v.* make this movement or change.

seethe *v.* bubble as if boiling; be very agitated or excited.

segment *n.* a part cut off, marked off, or separable from others; a part of a circle or sphere cut off by a straight line or plane. □ **segmented** *adj.*

segregate *v.* separate from others, isolate. □ **segregation** *n.*

seine (sayn) *n.* a fishing net that hangs from floats.

seismic (sIz-mik) *adj.* of earthquakes.

seismograph *n.* an instrument for recording earthquakes.

seismology *n.* the study of earthquakes. □ **seismological** *adj.*, **seismologist** *n.*

seize *v.* **1** take hold of forcibly or suddenly; take possession of by force or legal right. **2** (of a sensation, emotion, etc.) affect (someone) suddenly and strongly. □ **seize on** make use of eagerly. **seize up** (of a mechanism) become stuck, esp. through overheating.

seizure *n.* seizing; a sudden violent attack of an illness.

seldom *adv.* rarely, not often.

select *v.* pick out as the best or most suitable. ● *adj.* carefully chosen; exclusive. □ **selector** *n.*

selection *n.* selecting; things selected; things from which to choose.

selective *adj.* chosen or choosing carefully. □ **selectively** *adv.*, **selectivity** *n.*

selenium *n.* a chemical element (symbol Se).

self *n.* (*pl.* **selves**) a person's essential individual nature; a person as an individual; a person or thing as the object of reflexive action; one's own advantage or interests.

self- *comb. form* of or to or done by oneself or itself.

self-assured *adj.* confident.

self-centred *adj.* concerned primarily with one's own affairs and advantage.

self-confidence *n.* confidence in one's own worth and abilities. □ **self-confident** *adj.*

self-conscious *adj.* embarrassed from knowing that one is observed.

self-contained *adj.* **1** complete in itself; (of accommodation) having all the necessary rooms. **2** (of a person) quiet and independent.

self-control *n.* the ability to control one's feelings and act rationally. □ **self-controlled** *adj.*

self-denial *n.* deliberately going without things that one would like but thinks wrong or harmful.

self-determination *n.* a nation's choice of its own form of government, allegiances, etc.

self-evident *adj.* obvious, needing no argument or proof.

self-interest *n.* one's own advantage as a motive.

self-interested *adj.* pursuing one's own advantage.

selfish *adj.* acting or done according to one's own interests without regard to those of others; keeping good things for oneself. □ **selfishly** *adv.*, **selfishness** *n.*

selfless *adj.* unselfish. □ **selflessly** *adv.*

self-made *adj.* having risen from poverty by one's own efforts.

self-possessed *adj.* calm, controlled. □ **self-possession** *n.*

self-respect *n.* regard for one's own dignity and standards.

self-righteous *adj.* complacent about one's own virtue.

selfsame *adj.* the very same.

self-satisfied *adj.* excessively satisfied with one's qualities, achievements, etc.

self-seeking *adj.* aiming at one's own advantage before that of others.

self-service *adj.* (of a shop etc.) where customers help themselves and pay at a checkout.

self-styled *adj.* using a title or description that one has adopted without right: *self-styled experts.*

self-sufficient *adj.* able to provide what one needs without outside help. ▫ **self-sufficiency** *n.*

self-willed *adj.* obstinately doing what one wishes.

sell *v.* (**sold, selling**) **1** exchange (goods etc.) for money; keep (goods) for sale; (of goods) be sold, be for sale at a specified price. **2** persuade someone to accept. ● *n.* an act of selling or promoting. ▫ **sell off** dispose of by selling, esp. at a reduced price. **sell out** **1** sell all of one's stock. **2** betray. **sell up** sell one's house or business. ▫ **seller** *n.*

Sellotape *n. trademark* an adhesive usu. transparent tape.

selvedge *n.* (also **selvage**) an edge of cloth woven so that it does not unravel.

semantic *adj.* of meaning in language. ● *n.* (**semantics**) the study of meaning. ▫ **semantically** *adv.*

semaphore *n.* a system of signalling with the arms.

semblance *n.* an outward appearance or form.

semen *n.* the sperm-bearing fluid produced by male animals.

semester *n.* a half-year course or university term.

semi- *pref.* half; partly.

semibreve *n.* a note in music, equal to two minims or half a breve.

semicircle *n.* half of a circle. ▫ **semicircular** *adj.*

semicolon *n.* a punctuation mark (;).

semiconductor *n.* a substance that conducts electricity in certain conditions.

semi-detached *adj.* (of a house) joined to another on one side.

semi-final *n.* a match or round in a contest, preceding the final. ▫ **semi-finalist** *n.*

seminal *adj.* **1** of seed or semen. **2** giving rise to new developments. ▫ **seminally** *adv.*

seminar *n.* a small class for discussion and research.

seminary *n.* (*pl.* **-ies**) a training college for priests or rabbis.

semi-precious *adj.* (of gems) less valuable than those called precious.

semiquaver *n.* a note in music, equal to half a quaver.

Semite (see-mIt, sem-It) *n.* a member of the group of races that includes Jews and Arabs. ▫ **Semitic** *adj.*

semitone *n.* half a tone in music.

semolina *n.* hard particles left when wheat is ground and sifted, used to make puddings.

SEN *abbr.* State Enrolled Nurse.

senate *n.* the upper house of certain parliaments; the governing body of certain universities.

senator *n.* a member of a senate.

send *v.* (**sent, sending**) **1** order or cause to go to a particular destination; propel; send a message. **2** bring into a specified state: *sends me crazy.* ▫ **send for** order to come or be brought. **send up** *informal* make fun of by imitating.

senile *adj.* weak in body or mind because of old age. ▫ **senility** *n.*

senior *adj.* **1** older; for children above a certain age. **2** holding a higher rank or position. ● *n.* a senior person; a member of a senior school. ▫ **seniority** *n.*

senior citizen *n.* an elderly person; an old-age pensioner.

senna *n.* dried pods or leaves of a tropical tree, used as a laxative.

sensation *n.* **1** a feeling produced by stimulation of a sense organ or of the mind. **2** excited interest, a person or thing producing this.

sensational *adj.* causing great excitement or admiration. ▫ **sensationally** *adv.*

sensationalism *n.* use of or interest in exciting and shocking stories. ▫ **sensationalist** *n.*

sense *n.* **1** any of the special powers (sight, hearing, smell, taste, touch) by which a living thing becomes aware of the external world; the ability to perceive or be conscious of a thing. **2** a feeling that something is the case; awareness of or sensitivity to something; an impression received. **3** a sane and realistic outlook. **4** a meaning. **5** (**senses**) consciousness, sanity. ● *v.* perceive by a sense or intuitively. □ **make sense** have a meaning; be a sensible idea. **make sense of** find a meaning in.

senseless *adj.* **1** foolish. **2** unconscious.

sensibility *n.* (*pl.* **-ies**) sensitiveness.

sensible *adj.* **1** having or showing good sense. **2** aware. □ **sensibly** *adv.*

sensitive *adj.* **1** readily receiving impressions or responding to stimuli; easily damaged, injured, or distressed; tactful, appreciating others' feelings. **2** (of information) likely to endanger security. □ **sensitively** *adv.*, **sensitivity** *n.*

sensitize *v.* (also **-ise**) cause to respond readily to stimuli or a stimulus. □ **sensitization** *n.*, **sensitizer** *n.*

sensor *n.* a device for detecting a particular physical property.

sensory *adj.* of the senses; receiving and transmitting sensations.

sensual *adj.* gratifying to the body; indulging oneself with physical pleasures. □ **sensualism** *n.*, **sensuality** *n.*, **sensually** *adv.*

sensuous *adj.* of the senses rather than the intellect; affecting the senses pleasantly. □ **sensuously** *adv.*, **sensuousness** *n.*

■ **Usage** *sensuous* is a more neutral term than *sensual*, which suggests excessive physical indulgence, but the two are often used interchangeably.

sent past & p.p. of **send**.

sentence *n.* **1** a series of words making a single complete statement. **2** a punishment decided by a law court. ● *v.* pass sentence on (a person).

sententious *adj.* moralizing pompously. □ **sententiously** *adv.*, **sententiousness** *n.*

sentient *adj.* capable of perceiving and feeling things. □ **sentience** *n.*, **sentiently** *adv.*

sentiment *n.* **1** an opinion, view, or feeling. **2** sentimentality.

sentimental *adj.* full of romantic or nostalgic feeling, esp. excessively and self-indulgently so. □ **sentimental value** value derived from something's emotional associations rather than its objective worth. □ **sentimentalism** *n.*, **sentimentality** *n.*, **sentimentally** *adv.*

sentinel *n.* a sentry.

sentry *n.* (*pl.* **-ies**) a soldier posted to keep watch and guard something.

sepal *n.* each of the leaf-like parts forming a calyx.

separate *adj.* (sep-er-ăt) not joined or united with others. ● *v.* (**sep**-er-ayt) divide; set, move, or keep apart; cease to live together as a married couple. □ **separability** *n.*, **separable** *adj.*, **separately** *adv.*, **separation** *n.*, **separator** *n.*

■ **Usage** *Separate, separation*, etc. are not spelt with an *e* in the middle.

separatist *n.* a person who favours separation from a larger (esp. political) unit. □ **separatism** *n.*

sepia *n.* a reddish-brown colour or pigment.

sepsis *n.* septic condition.

Sept. *abbr.* September.

September *n.* the ninth month.

septet *n.* a group of seven instruments or voices; music for these.

septic *adj.* infected with harmful micro-organisms.

septicaemia (sep-ti-see-mia) *n.* (*Amer.* **septicemia**) blood poisoning.

septic tank *n.* a tank in which sewage is liquefied by bacterial activity.

septuagenarian (sept-ewr-jĕ-nair-i-ăn) *n.* a person in his or her seventies.

sepulchre (sep-ŭl-ker) *n.* (*Amer.* **sepulcher**) a tomb.

sequel *n.* what follows, esp. as a result; a novel or film etc. continuing the story of an earlier one.

sequence *n.* **1** an order in which related items follow one another; a set of things belonging next to each other in a particular order. **2** a section dealing with one event or topic in a film.

sequential *adj.* forming or following a logical sequence. □ **sequentially** *adv.*

sequester *v.* **1** isolate. **2** confiscate.

sequestrate *v.* confiscate; take temporary posession of until a debt is paid etc. □ **sequestration** *n.*

sequin *n.* a small shiny disc for decorating clothes. □ **sequinned** *adj.*

sequoia (si-**kwoi**-ă) *n.* a Californian tree growing to a great height.

seraglio (si-**rahl**-yoh) *n.* (*pl.* **seraglios**) a harem.

seraph *n.* (*pl.* **seraphim** or **seraphs**) a member of the highest order of angels. □ **seraphic** *adj.*

serenade *n.* music played for a lover, or suitable for this. ● *v.* sing or play a serenade to.

serendipity *n.* the fortunate occurrence of events by coincidence or chance. □ **serendipitous** *adj.*

serene *adj.* calm and cheerful. □ **serenely** *adv.*, **serenity** *n.*

serf *n.* a medieval farm labourer forced to work for his land-owner. □ **serfdom** *n.*

serge *n.* strong twilled fabric.

sergeant (sar-jĕnt) *n.* a noncommissioned army officer ranking just above corporal; a police officer ranking just below inspector.

serial *n.* a story presented in a series of instalments. ● *adj.* of or forming part of a series; repeated, doing something repeatedly. □ **serially** *adv.*

serialize *v.* (also **-ise**) produce as a serial. □ **serialization** *n.*

serial killer *n.* a person who murders repeatedly.

serial number *n.* a number identifying something by giving its position in a series.

series *n.* (*pl.* **series**) a number of similar things occurring, arranged, or produced in order; a set of related television or radio programmes.

serious *adj.* **1** solemn, thoughtful; sincere, in earnest. **2** requiring thought; important, not slight, significant; involving possible danger. □ **seriously** *adv.*, **seriousness** *n.*

sermon *n.* a talk on a religious or moral subject, esp. during a religious service.

sermonize *v.* (also **-ise**) give a long moralizing talk.

serpent *n.* a large snake.

serpentine *adj.* twisting like a snake.

SERPS *abbr.* state earnings-related pension scheme.

serrated *adj.* having a series of small projections; saw-like. □ **serration** *n.*

serried *adj.* placed or standing close together.

serum *n.* (*pl.* **sera** or **serums**) fluid left when blood has clotted; this used for inoculation; a watery fluid from animal tissue. □ **serous** *adj.*

servant *n.* a person employed to do domestic work in a household or as an attendant; an employee.

serve *v.* **1** perform duties or provide help for; be employed (in the army etc.). **2** be useful or suitable for something; help in achieving (a purpose). **3** present (food etc.) for others to consume; (of food) be enough for. **4** attend to (customers). **5** set the ball in play at tennis etc. **6** deliver (a legal writ etc.) to (a person). **7** spend (a period) in a post or in prison. ● *n.* a service in tennis etc.

server *n.* a computer or program managing access to a resource or service in a network.

service *n.* **1** an action helping someone; the action of working for someone, being employed; waiting on customers at a restaurant etc. **2** a system supplying a public need; a department run by the state. **3** (**the services**) the armed forces. **4** a religious ceremony. **5** a matching set of plates etc. **6** an act of serving in tennis etc. **7** maintenance and repair of machinery. ● *v.* **1** perform maintenance work on (machinery). **2** provide services for. **3** pay interest on (a debt). □ **at someone's service** ready to assist someone when required. **be of service** assist someone.

serviceable *adj.* useful, usable, functioning; hardwearing.

service area *n.* an area beside a motorway where petrol and refreshments etc. are available.

service flat *n.* a rented flat where domestic service is provided.

serviceman *n.* (*pl.* **-men**) **1** a member of the armed services. **2** a man providing a maintenance service.

service road *n.* a road giving access to houses etc. but not for use by through traffic.

service station *n.* a place beside a road selling petrol etc.

servicewoman *n.* (*pl.* **-women**) a woman in the armed services.

serviette *n.* a table napkin.

servile *adj.* excessively submissive. □ **servility** *n.*

servitude *n.* slavery; subjection to someone more powerful.

sesame (sess-ămi) *n.* a tropical plant with seeds that yield oil or are used as food.

session *n.* a meeting or meetings for discussing something; a period spent in an activity; an academic year or term.

set *v.* (**set, setting**) **1** put, place, or fix in position or readiness; bring into a specified state; cause to start doing something. **2** represent (a story etc.) as taking place in a particular location. **3** fix or appoint (a date); assign as a task or problem; establish (an example, record, etc.). **4** adjust (a clock) to show the right time. **5** make or become hard, firm, or solid; become fixed. **6** (of the sun etc.) be brought below the horizon by the earth's movement. **7** (of a tide) move in a specified direction. ● *n.* **1** a group or collection of things or people that are alike or form a unit. **2** the way something is positioned or arranged. **3** a radio or television receiver. **4** a group of games forming a unit in a tennis match. **5** scenery for a play or film. **6** the process of styling hair. **7** var. of **sett.** □ **be set on** be determined to do. **set about 1** begin doing. **2** *informal* attack. **set back 1** delay the progress of. **2** *informal* cost (someone) a specified amount. **set in** (of bad weather etc.) begin and become established. **set off 1** begin a journey. **2** cause to explode. **3** make more noticeable or attractive by contrast. **set out** or **forth 1** begin a journey. **2** declare, state systematically. **set sail** begin a sea voyage. **set up 1** establish; erect. **2** *informal* cause (an innocent person) to appear guilty.

setback *n.* a delay in progress; a problem.

set piece *n.* a formal or elaborate construction.

set square *n.* a right-angled triangular drawing instrument.

sett *n.* (also **set**) **1** a badger's burrow. **2** a paving block.

settee *n.* a sofa.

setter *n.* a dog of a long-haired breed.

setting *n.* **1** the place where something is positioned or takes place. **2** a speed etc. to which a machine can be adjusted. **3** a set of cutlery or crockery laid for one person.

settle[1] *v.* **1** arrange or resolve (a problem or dispute); pay (a bill); fix, decide on. **2** come to rest; adopt a more secure or steady life style; place in position; become familiar with and at ease in new surroundings; come to live somewhere permanently; occupy (a previously unoccupied area). **3** become quieter or calmer. **4** bestow (property) legally. □ **settle for** resign oneself to accepting. **settle up** pay what is owing. □ **settlement** *n.*

settle² *n.* a wooden seat with a high back and arms.

settler *n.* a person who settles in unoccupied territory.

set-up *n. informal* an organization or arrangement; a trick.

seven *adj.* & *n.* one more than six (7, VII). □ **seventh** *adj.* & *n.*

seventeen *adj.* & *n.* one more than sixteen (17, XVII). □ **seventeenth** *adj.* & *n.*

seventy *adj.* & *n.* seven times ten (70, LXX). □ **seventieth** *adj.* & *n.*

sever *v.* cut or break off. □ **severance** *n.*

several *adj.* **1** a few, more than two but not many. **2** separate, individual. ● *pron.* several people or things.

severally *adv.* separately.

severe *adj.* **1** strict, harsh; (of something bad or unpleasant) intense. **2** (of style) plain, without decoration. □ **severely** *adv.*, **severity** *n.*

sew (soh) *v.* (**sewed, sewn** or **sewed, sewing**) fasten by passing thread through material, using a needle etc.; make or fasten (a thing) by sewing. □ **sewer** *n.*, **sewing** *n.*

sewage (soo-ij) *n.* liquid waste drained from houses etc. for disposal.

sewer (soo-er) *n.* a drain for carrying sewage.

sewerage *n.* a system of sewers.

sewn p.p. of **sew**.

sex *n.* **1** either of the two main groups (*male* and *female*) into which living things are placed according to their reproductive functions; the fact of belonging to one of these. **2** sexual intercourse, sexual activity. ● *v.* judge the sex of.

sexagenarian *n.* a person in his or her sixties.

sexist *adj.* discriminating in favour of members of one sex; assuming a person's abilities and social functions are predetermined by his or her sex. ● *n.* a person who does this. □ **sexism** *n.*

sexless *adj.* **1** not involving sexual desire or activity. **2** neither male nor female.

sextant *n.* an instrument for finding one's position by measuring the height of the sun etc.

sextet *n.* a group of six instruments or voices; music for these.

sexton *n.* an official in charge of a church and churchyard.

sextuplet *n.* one of six children born at one birth.

sexual *adj.* **1** of sex; (of reproduction) occurring by fusion of male and female cells. **2** of the two sexes. □ **sexually** *adv.*

sexual intercourse *n.* sexual contact involving penetration, esp. the insertion of the penis into the vagina.

sexuality *n.* capacity for sexual feelings; a person's sexual orientation.

sexy *adj.* (**sexier, sexiest**) *informal* sexually attractive or stimulating. □ **sexily** *adv.*, **sexiness** *n.*

Sg *symb.* seaborgium.

Sgt. *abbr.* sergeant.

shabby *adj.* (**shabbier, shabbiest**) **1** worn; dilapidated; poorly dressed. **2** unfair, dishonourable. □ **shabbily** *adv.*, **shabbiness** *n.*

shack *n.* a roughly built hut.

shackle *n.* one of a pair of metal rings joined by a chain, for fastening a prisoner's wrists or ankles. ● *v.* put shackles on; impede, restrict.

shade *n.* **1** comparative darkness; a place sheltered from the sun; a screen or cover used to block or moderate light; (**shades**) sunglasses. **2** a colour, a degree of lightness or darkness in a colour; a slightly different variety of something; a trace, a slight amount. ● *v.* **1** block the rays of; give shade to; darken (parts of a drawing etc.). **2** pass gradually into another colour or variety.

shadow *n.* **1** a dark area produced by an object coming between light and a surface; partial darkness; a dark patch. **2** gloom; something spoiling happiness. **3** a slight trace. **4** an inseparable companion or follower. ● *v.* **1** cast shadow over. **2** follow and watch secretly. □ **shadower** *n.*, **shadowy** *adj.*

shadow-boxing *n.* boxing against an imaginary opponent as a form of training.

Shadow Cabinet *n.* members of the main opposition party in Parliament holding posts parallel to those of the government Cabinet.

shady *adj.* (**shadier, shadiest**) **1** giving shade; situated in shade. **2** disreputable, not completely honest. □ **shadily** *adv.*, **shadiness** *n.*

shaft *n.* **1** a long, slender, straight handle etc.; an arrow or spear; a ray or beam; a long rotating rod transmitting power in a machine; each of the two poles between which a horse is harnessed to a vehicle. **2** a vertical or sloping passage or opening.

shag *n.* **1** a shaggy mass. **2** a strong coarse tobacco. **3** a cormorant. ● *adj.* (of a carpet) with a long rough pile.

shaggy *adj.* (**shaggier, shaggiest**) having long rough hair or fibre; (of hair etc.) rough and thick. □ **shagginess** *n.*

shaggy-dog story *n. informal* a lengthy anecdote with a twist of humour at the end.

shah *n.* a title of the former ruler of Iran.

shake *v.* (**shook, shaken, shaking**) **1** (cause to) tremble or vibrate. **2** move quickly up and down or from side to side; dislodge by doing this. **3** shock or astonish; make (a belief or position) less firm. ● *n.* an act of shaking. □ **shake down** become settled. **shake hands** clasp right hands in greeting, parting, or agreement. **shake off** get rid of. **shake on** *informal* confirm (an agreement) by shaking hands. **shake up 1** mix by shaking. **2** rouse by startling or shocking. □ **shaker** *n.*

shake-up *n. informal* an upheaval, a reorganization.

shaky *adj.* (**shakier, shakiest**) shaking; unstable; unreliable. □ **shakily** *adv.*, **shakiness** *n.*

shale *n.* stone that splits easily. □ **shaly** *adj.*

shall *v.aux.* used with *I* and *we* to express future tense, and with *you, he, she, it*, or *they* to express obligation or determination.

shallot *n.* a small onion-like plant.

shallow *adj.* of little depth; not showing or requiring much thought, superficial. ● *v.* become less deep. ● *n.* (**shallows**) a shallow area in a river etc. □ **shallowness** *n.*

shalom (shă-**lom**) *n.* a Jewish expression of greeting or leave-taking.

sham *n.* a pretence; something that is not genuine. ● *adj.* pretended; not genuine. ● *v.* (**shammed, shamming**) pretend; fake.

shamble *v.* walk or run in a shuffling or lazy way.

shambles *n. informal* a scene or condition of great disorder.

shame *n.* a painful mental feeling aroused by having done something dishonourable or ridiculous; the ability to feel this; loss of respect; a cause of this; something regrettable: *it's a shame you can't stay.* ● *v.* cause to feel ashamed; provoke to action in this way. □ **shameful** *adj.*, **shamefully** *adv.*, **shameless** *adj.*, **shamelessly** *adv.*

shamefaced *adj.* looking ashamed.

shammy *n.* (*pl.* **-ies**) *informal* a chamois leather.

shampoo *n.* a liquid used to wash hair; a preparation for cleaning upholstery etc.; the process of shampooing. ● *v.* wash or clean with shampoo.

shamrock *n.* a clover-like plant.

shandy *n.* (*pl.* **-ies**) a mixed drink of beer and lemonade or ginger beer.

shank *n.* a leg, esp. from knee to ankle; the shaft or stem of a tool or implement.

shanty *n.* (*pl.* **-ies**) **1** a shack. **2** a sailors' traditional song.

shanty town *n.* an area of makeshift housing of rough shacks.

shape *n.* **1** an area or form with a definite outline; structure, orderly arrangement. **2** the condition of something: *in good shape.* ● *v.* give a shape to; influence the nature of. □ **shape up 1** develop in a particular way. **2** *informal* improve. □ **shapeless** *adj.*

shapely *adj.* (**shapelier, shapeliest**) having an attractive shape. □ **shapeliness** *n.*

shard *n.* a broken piece of pottery.

share *n.* **1** a part given to one person out of something divided among several; an amount that someone is entitled to or required to have. **2** one of the equal parts forming a business company's capital and entitling the holder to a proportion of the profits. ● *v.* give or have a share (of). □ **sharer** *n.*

shareholder *n.* an owner of shares in a company.

shareware *n.* computer programs freely available for trial, paid for by a fee to the author if used regularly.

shark *n.* **1** a large voracious sea fish. **2** *informal* an unscrupulous swindler or exploiter.

sharkskin *n.* a fabric with a slightly lustrous textured weave.

sharp *adj.* **1** having a fine edge or point capable of cutting; tapering to a point; (of a remark etc.) hurtful, intended to hurt. **2** distinct, well-defined. **3** abrupt, sudden. **4** alert; perceiving keenly. **5** (of tastes or smells) causing a smarting sensation. **6** unscrupulous. **7** above the correct or normal pitch in music. ● *adv.* **1** punctually, exactly. **2** abruptly; at a sharp angle. **3** above the correct pitch. ● *n. Music* (a sign indicating) a note raised by a semitone. □ **sharply** *adv.*, **sharpness** *n.*

sharpen *v.* make or become sharp or sharper. □ **sharpener** *n.*

sharp practice *n.* barely honest dealings.

sharpshooter *n.* a skilled marksman.

shatter *v.* break violently into small pieces; destroy utterly; distress greatly.

shave *v.* **1** cut (growing hair) from (the face or other part of the body). **2** cut (a thin slice) from a surface. **3** pass very close to. ● *n.* an act of shaving hair from the face. □ **a close shave** *informal* a narrow escape. □ **shaver** *n.*

shaven *adj.* shaved.

shaving *n.* a thin strip of wood etc. shaved from a surface.

shawl *n.* a large piece of soft fabric worn round the shoulders or wrapped round a baby.

she *pron.* the female previously mentioned. ● *n.* a female.

s/he *pron.* a written representation of 'he or she'.

sheaf *n.* (*pl.* **sheaves**) a bundle of corn stalks; a similar bundle.

shear *v.* (**sheared, shorn** or **sheared, shearing**) **1** cut or trim with shears or some other sharp device. **2** break because of strain. □ **shearer** *n.*

shears *n.pl.* a large cutting instrument shaped like scissors.

sheath (sheeth) *n.* a close-fitting cover, esp. for a blade or tool; a condom.

sheathe (shee*th*) *v.* put into a sheath; encase in a tight covering.

shed *n.* a building for storing things, or for use as a workshop. ● *v.* (**shed, shedding**) lose (leaves etc.) by a natural falling; discard; lose (a load) accidentally.

sheen *n.* gloss, lustre. □ **sheeny** *adj.*

sheep *n.* (*pl.* **sheep**) a grass-eating animal with a thick fleecy coat.

sheepdog *n.* a dog trained to guard and herd sheep.

sheepish *adj.* feeling shy or foolish. □ **sheepishly** *adv.*, **sheepishness** *n.*

sheepskin *n.* a sheep's skin with the fleece on.

sheer *adj.* **1** pure, not mixed or qualified. **2** very steep. **3** (of fabric) very thin, transparent. ● *adv.* straight up or down. ● *v.* swerve from a course. □ **sheerly** *adv.*, **sheerness** *n.*

sheet *n.* **1** a piece of cotton or other fabric used to cover a bed. **2** a large thin piece of glass, metal, paper, etc. **3** an expanse of water, flame, etc. **4** a rope securing the lower corner of a sail.

sheet anchor *n.* a very dependable person or thing.

sheikh (shayk) *n.* an Arab ruler. □ **sheikhdom** *n.*

shekel *n.* a unit of money in Israel; (**shekels**) *informal* money, riches.

shelf *n.* (*pl.* **shelves**) a flat piece of wood etc. fastened to a wall etc. for things to be placed on; a ledge of rock. □ **on the shelf** *informal* not wanted, esp. for marriage.

shelf-life *n.* the time for which a stored thing remains usable.

shell *n.* **1** the hard outer covering of eggs, nut kernels, and of animals such as snails and tortoises; the outer structure or form of something, esp. when hollow. **2** a metal case filled with explosive, fired from a large gun. ● *v.* **1** remove the shell(s) of. **2** fire explosive shells at. □ **shell out** *informal* pay (a sum of money).

shellac *n.* a resinous substance used in varnish. ● *v.* (**shellacked, shellacking**) coat with this.

shellfish *n.* (*pl.* **shellfish**) an edible water animal that has a shell.

shell shock *n.* psychological disturbance from exposure to battle conditions.

shelter *n.* a structure that shields against danger, wind, rain, etc.; protection. ● *v.* provide with shelter; find or take shelter.

shelve *v.* **1** put on a shelf. **2** postpone or cancel. **3** slope.

shelving *n.* shelves.

shepherd *n.* a person who tends sheep. ● *v.* guide (people).

shepherd's pie *n.* a pie of minced meat topped with mashed potato.

sherbet *n.* a sweet powder made into an effervescent drink.

sheriff *n.* the Crown's chief executive officer in a county; a judge in Scotland; *Amer.* the chief law-enforcing officer of a county.

Sherpa *n.* a member of a Himalayan people of Nepal and Tibet.

sherry *n.* (*pl.* **-ies**) a fortified wine.

shiatsu *n.* a Japanese therapy involving the application of pressure to points on the body.

shibboleth *n.* a principle etc. generally thought obsolete but considered essential by a particular group.

shield *n.* **1** a broad piece of metal etc. carried for protection; any source of protection. **2** a shield-shaped trophy. ● *v.* protect.

shift *v.* (cause to) move from one place or position to another; transfer (blame etc.); *informal* move quickly; *informal* sell. ● *n.* **1** a slight change in position etc. **2** a set of workers who start work when another set finishes; the time for which they work.

shiftless *adj.* lazy and inefficient.

shifty *adj.* (**shiftier, shiftiest**) *informal* evasive; untrustworthy. □ **shiftily** *adv.*, **shiftiness** *n.*

Shi'ite (shee-It) *n.* & *adj.* (a member) of a Muslim sect opposed to the Sunni.

shilly-shally *v.* (**-shallied, -shallying**) be indecisive.

shim *n.* a thin wedge used to make parts of machinery fit together.

shimmer *v.* & *n.* (shine with) a soft quivering light.

shin *n.* the front of the leg below the knee; the lower foreleg. □ **shin up (shinned, shinning)** climb quickly.

shindig *n. informal* a lively party; a noisy disturbance.

shine *v.* **1 (shone, shining)** give out or reflect light, be bright; direct (a torch etc.) a particular way; be excellent or outstanding. **2 (shined, shining)** polish. ● *n.* brightness. □ **take a shine to** *informal* develop a liking for.

shingle *n.* **1** a mass of small round pebbles on a beach etc. **2** a wooden roof tile. **3 (shingles)** a disease with a rash of small blisters. □ **shingly** *adj.*

Shinto *n.* a Japanese religion revering ancestors and nature spirits. □ **Shintoism** *n.*

shiny *adj.* **(shinier, shiniest)** shining, glossy. □ **shininess** *n.*

ship *n.* a large seagoing vessel. ● *v.* **(shipped, shipping)** transport on a ship. □ **ship off** take or send away. □ **shipper** *n.*

shipmate *n.* a person travelling or working on the same ship as another.

shipment *n.* the shipping of goods; a consignment shipped.

shipping *n.* ships collectively.

shipshape *adj.* in good order, tidy.

shipwreck *n.* the destruction of a ship by storm or striking rocks etc. □ **shipwrecked** *adj.*

shipyard *n.* an establishment where ships are built.

shire *n.* a county.

shire horse *n.* a horse of a heavy powerful breed.

shirk *v.* avoid (duty or work etc.) selfishly. □ **shirker** *n.*

shirt *n.* a lightweight garment for the upper part of the body.

shirty *adj.* **(shirtier, shirtiest)** *informal* annoyed, angry.

shit *vulgar slang n.* **1** faeces. **2** a contemptible person. ● *v.* **(shitted** or **shat** or **shit, shitting)** empty the bowels.

shiver *v.* **1** tremble slightly, esp. with cold or fear. **2** shatter. ● *n.* a shivering movement. □ **shivery** *adj.*

shoal *n.* **1** a large number of fish swimming together. **2** a shallow place; an underwater sandbank. ● *v.* form shoals.

shock *n.* **1** a sudden surprising and distressing experience, the feeling caused by this; acute weakness caused by injury, loss of blood, etc. **2** a violent impact or tremor. **3** a bushy mass of hair. ● *v.* surprise and distress; scandalize. □ **shocker** *n.*

shocking *adj.* causing outrage or indignation; very surprising and distressing; *informal* very bad or unpleasant.

shod past & p.p. of **shoe**.

shoddy *adj.* **(shoddier, shoddiest)** badly made or done. □ **shoddily** *adv.*, **shoddiness** *n.*

shoe *n.* **1** an outer covering for a person's foot. **2** a horseshoe. **3** the part of a brake that presses against a wheel. ● *v.* **(shod, shoeing)** fit with a shoe or shoes.

shoehorn *n.* a curved implement for easing one's heel into a shoe.

shoelace *n.* a cord for lacing up shoes.

shoeshine *n. Amer.* an act of polishing someone's shoes.

shoestring *n.* **1** *informal* a barely adequate amount of money. **2** *Amer.* a shoelace.

shoe tree *n.* a shaped block for keeping a shoe in shape.

shone past & p.p. of **shine**.

shoo *int.* a sound uttered to frighten animals away. ● *v.* **(shooed, shooing)** drive away.

shook past of **shake**.

shoot *v.* **(shot, shooting) 1** fire (a gun or missile); kill or wound with a missile from a gun etc.; hunt with a gun for sport. **2** (cause to) move swiftly and suddenly. **3** aim a ball at a goal. **4** film or photograph. **5** (of a plant) put out shoots. ● *n.* a young branch or new growth of a plant. □ **shoot up** rise suddenly; grow rapidly. □ **shooter** *n.*

shooting star *n.* a small meteor seen to move quickly.

shooting stick *n.* a walking stick with a small folding seat in the handle.

shop *n.* **1** a building where goods or services are sold to the public. **2** a workshop. ● *v.* (**shopped, shopping**) **1** buy things from shops. **2** *informal* inform against. □ **shop around** look for the best bargain. **talk shop** discuss one's work in a social setting. □ **shopper** *n.*

shop floor *n.* workers as distinct from management.

shoplifter *n.* a person who steals goods from a shop. □ **shoplifting** *n.*

shopping *n.* buying goods in shops; the goods bought.

shop-soiled *adj.* dirty or damaged from being on display in a shop.

shop steward *n.* a trade union official elected by workers as their spokesperson.

shore *n.* the land along the edge of the sea or a lake. ● *v.* prop or support with a length of timber.

shorn p.p. of **shear**.

short *adj.* **1** measuring little from end to end in space or time, or from head to foot. **2** not having enough of something; insufficient. **3** uncivilly curt. **4** (of pastry) crisp and easily crumbled. ● *adv.* not going far enough. ● *n.* **1** a small drink of spirits. **2** a short film. **3** a short circuit. **4** (**shorts**) trousers reaching only to the knee or thigh; *Amer.* underpants. ● *v.* short-circuit.

shortage *n.* a lack, an insufficiency.

shortbread *n.* (also **shortcake**) a rich sweet biscuit.

short-change *v.* cheat, esp. by giving insufficient change.

short circuit *n.* a fault in an electrical circuit when current flows by a shorter route than the normal one. ● *v.* (**short-circuit**) (cause to) malfunction because of a short circuit; shorten or speed up (a process) improperly.

shortcoming *n.* failure to reach a required standard; a fault.

short cut *n.* a quicker route or method.

shorten *v.* make or become shorter.

shortening *n.* fat used to make pastry etc.

shortfall *n.* a deficit.

shorthand *n.* a method of writing rapidly with quickly made symbols.

short-handed *adj.* having insufficient workers.

shortlist *n.* a list of selected candidates from which a final choice will be made. ● *v.* put on a shortlist.

shortly *adv.* **1** after a short time. **2** in a few words; curtly.

short-sighted *adj.* able to see clearly only what is close; lacking foresight.

short ton *see* **ton**.

short wave *n.* a radio wave of frequency greater than 3 MHz.

shot[1] past & p.p. of **shoot**. □ **shot through with** suffused or interspersed with.

shot[2] *n.* **1** a firing of a gun etc., the sound of this; a person of specified skill in shooting. **2** an attempt to hit a target, put a ball in goal, etc.; a stroke in tennis etc.; *informal* an attempt. **3** a heavy ball used as a missile or thrown as a sport; ammunition. **4** a photograph. **5** *informal* a measure of spirits; an injection. □ **like a shot** *informal* without hesitation.

shotgun *n.* a gun for firing small shot at close range.

should *v.aux.* used to express duty or obligation, a possible or expected future event, or (with *I* and *we*) a polite statement or a conditional or indefinite clause.

shoulder *n.* the part of the body where the arm or foreleg is attached; an animal's upper foreleg as a joint of meat. ● *v.* **1** assume (a burden or responsibility). **2** push with one's shoulder.

shoulder blade *n.* the large flat bone of the shoulder.

shout *n.* a loud cry or utterance. ● *v.* utter a shout; call loudly. □ **shout down** silence by shouting.

shove *n.* a rough push. ● *v.* push roughly; make one's way by pushing; put down carelessly. □ **shove off 1** push away from the shore in a boat. **2** *informal* go away.

shovel *n.* a spade-like tool for moving sand, snow, etc.; a mechanical scoop. ● *v.* (**shovelled, shovelling**; *Amer.* **shoveled**) shift or clear with or as if with a shovel; scoop or thrust roughly.

show *v.* (**showed, shown, showing**) **1** allow or cause to be seen, present to view; visibly or clearly possess (a characteristic); be visible; represent, depict. **2** demonstrate or prove (something) to (someone). **3** treat (someone) with (a specified characteristic): *show him mercy*. **4** guide, lead. ● *n.* a spectacle; a public exhibition or performance; outward appearance, esp. when misleading. □ **show off 1** display. **2** try to impress people. **show of hands** voting by raising hands. **show up 1** make conspicuous; emphasize the failings of. **2** *informal* arrive.

show business *n.* the entertainment profession.

showdown *n.* a confrontation that settles an argument.

shower *n.* **1** a brief fall of rain or of snow, stones, etc. **2** a device spraying water over someone's body; a cubicle containing this; a wash in this. **3** a sudden influx of letters or gifts etc. **4** *Amer.* a party for giving presents. ● *v.* **1** (cause to) fall in a shower; throw a number of things at or give a number of things to. **2** wash in a shower.

showerproof *adj.* (of fabric) able to keep out slight rain. ● *v.* make showerproof.

showery *adj.* with showers of rain.

showjumping *n.* the competitive sport of riding horses to jump over obstacles. □ **showjumper** *n.*

showman *n.* (*pl.* **-men**) an organizer of circuses or theatrical entertainments.

showmanship *n.* skill in presenting entertainment or goods etc. well.

shown p.p. of **show**.

showpiece *n.* an excellent specimen used for exhibition.

showroom *n.* a room where goods are displayed for inspection.

showy *adj.* (**showier, showiest**) striking; ostentatious or gaudy. □ **showily** *adv.*, **showiness** *n.*

shrank past of **shrink**.

shrapnel *n.* pieces of metal scattered from an exploding bomb.

shred *n.* a small strip torn or cut from something; a small amount. ● *v.* (**shredded, shredding**) tear or cut into shreds. □ **shredder** *n.*

shrew *n.* a small mouse-like animal.

shrewd *adj.* showing sound judgement, clever. □ **shrewdly** *adv.*, **shrewdness** *n.*

shriek *n.* a shrill cry or scream. ● *v.* utter (with) a shriek.

shrill *adj.* piercing and high-pitched in sound. □ **shrillness** *n.*, **shrilly** *adv.*

shrimp *n.* **1** a small edible shellfish. **2** *informal* a very small person.

shrine *n.* a sacred or revered place.

shrink *v.* (**shrank, shrunk, shrinking**) **1** make or become smaller. **2** draw back in fear or disgust. ● *n. informal* a psychiatrist.

shrinkage *n.* shrinking of textile fabric; loss by theft or wastage.

shrive *v.* (**shrove, shriven, shriving**) *archaic* hear the confession of and absolve.

shrivel *v.* (**shrivelled, shrivelling** *Amer.* **shriveled**) shrink and wrinkle from heat or cold or lack of moisture.

shroud *n.* **1** a cloth wrapping a dead body for burial; something that conceals. **2** one of the ropes supporting a ship's mast. ● *v.* wrap in a shroud; conceal.

shrub *n.* a woody plant smaller than a tree. □ **shrubby** *adj.*

shrubbery *n.* (*pl.* **-ies**) an area planted with shrubs.

shrug *v.* (**shrugged, shrugging**) raise (one's shoulders) as a gesture of indifference, doubt, or helplessness. ● *n.* this movement.

shrunk p.p. of **shrink**.

shrunken *adj.* having shrunk.

shudder *v.* shiver or shake violently. ● *n.* this movement.

shuffle *v.* **1** walk without lifting one's feet clear of the ground. **2** rearrange, jumble. ● *n.* **1** a shuffling movement or walk. **2** a rearrangement. □ **shuffle off** avoid (a responsibility).

shun *v.* (**shunned, shunning**) avoid.

shunt *v.* move (a train) to a side track; divert.

shush *int.* & *v. informal* hush.

shut *v.* (**shut, shutting**) move (a door or window etc.) into position to block an opening; be moved in this way; block an opening into (something); keep (someone or something) in a place by blocking an opening; bring together the sides of (a book etc.); make (a shop etc.) or become unavailable for business. □ **shut down** stop or cease working or business. **shut off** stop the supply of. **shut up** **1** close. **2** *informal* be quiet.

shutter *n.* a screen that can be closed over a window; a device that opens and closes the aperture of a camera. □ **shuttered** *adj.*

shuttle *n.* **1** a form of transport travelling frequently between places. **2** a spacecraft for repeated use. **3** a device carrying the weft thread in weaving. ● *v.* move, travel, or send to and fro.

shuttlecock *n.* a small cone-shaped feathered object struck to and fro in badminton.

shut-eye *n. informal* sleep.

shy *adj.* nervous in company, lacking self-confidence. ● *v.* (**shied, shying**) **1** jump in alarm; avoid something through nervousness. **2** *dated* throw. □ **shyly** *adv.*, **shyness** *n.*

SI *abbr.* Système International, the international system of units of measurement.

Si *symb.* silicon.

Siamese *adj.* of Siam, the former name of Thailand.

Siamese cat *n.* a cat with pale fur and darker face, paws, and tail.

Siamese twins *n.pl.* twins whose bodies are joined at birth.

sibling *n.* a brother or sister.

sibyl (sib-ŭl) *n.* a prophetess.

sic *adv.* thus (indicating that a quotation is exact though its wording or spelling appears wrong).

Sicilian *adj.* & *n.* (a native) of Sicily.

sick *adj.* **1** unwell; suffering from nausea. **2** tired of or bored with something. **3** finding amusement in misfortune or morbid subjects.

sicken *v.* **1** become ill. **2** distress; disgust. □ **be sickening for** be in the first stages of (a disease).

sickle *n.* a curved blade used for cutting corn etc.

sickly *adj.* (**sicklier, sickliest**) **1** often ill; weak. **2** causing nausea; distastefully sentimental. □ **sickliness** *n.*

sickness *n.* illness; vomiting.

side *n.* **1** a surface of an object, esp. one that is not the top, bottom, front, back, or end; a bounding line of a plane figure; a slope of a hill or ridge. **2** a part near the edge and away from the middle. **3** a position to the left or right of someone or something; either of the halves into which something is divided; an aspect of a problem etc. **4** one of two opposing groups or teams. ● *adj.* at or on the side. □ **on the**

side as a sideline; as a surreptitious activity. **side by side** close together. **side with** support in a dispute.

sideboard *n.* **1** a piece of dining-room furniture with drawers and cupboards for china etc. **2** (**sideboards**) *informal* sideburns.

sideburns *n.pl.* short whiskers on the cheeks.

side effect *n.* a secondary (usu. bad) effect.

sidelight *n.* one of two small lights on either side of a vehicle.

sideline *n.* **1** something done in addition to one's main activity. **2** (**sidelines**) lines bounding the sides of a football pitch etc.; a place for spectators; a position etc. apart from the main action. ● *v.* remove from the centre of activity or influence.

sidelong *adj.* & *adv.* sideways.

sidereal (sy-**deer**-iăl) *adj.* of or measured by the stars.

side-saddle *n.* a saddle on which a woman rider sits with both legs on the same side of the horse. ● *adv.* sitting in this way.

sideshow *n.* a small show forming part of a large one.

sidestep *v.* (**sidestepped, sidestepping**) avoid by stepping sideways; evade.

sidetrack *v.* divert; distract.

sidewalk *n. Amer.* a pavement.

sideways *adv.* & *adj.* to or from one side; with one side forward.

siding *n.* a short track by the side of a railway, used in shunting.

sidle *v.* advance in a timid, furtive, or cringing way.

SIDS *abbr.* sudden infant death syndrome; cot death.

siege *n.* the surrounding and blockading of a place by armed forces in order to capture it.

sienna *n.* a brownish clay used as colouring matter.

sierra (see-**air**-ă) *n.* a chain of mountains with jagged peaks, esp. in Spain or Spanish America.

siesta *n.* an afternoon nap or rest, esp. in hot countries.

sieve (siv) *n.* a utensil with a mesh through which liquids or fine particles can pass. ● *v.* separate out by putting through a sieve.

sift *v.* **1** sieve. **2** examine carefully and select or analyse.

sigh *n.* a long deep breath given out audibly in sadness, tiredness, relief, etc. ● *v.* give or express with a sigh.

sight *n.* **1** the ability to see; seeing; the distance within which one can see. **2** something seen or worth seeing; *informal* an unsightly thing. **3** a device looked through to aim or observe with a gun or telescope etc. ● *v.* **1** see, catch sight of. **2** aim at with a sight. □ **at** or **on sight** as soon as seen. **catch sight of** see, notice.

sightless *adj.* blind.

sight-read *v.* play or sing (music) without preliminary study of the score.

sightseeing *n.* visiting places of interest. □ **sightseer** *n.*

sign *n.* **1** something perceived that suggests the existence of a quality, a future occurrence, etc. **2** a notice displayed to give information or instructions. **3** an action or gesture conveying information etc. **4** any of the twelve divisions of the zodiac. ● *v.* **1** write (one's name) on (a document); indicate agreement to (something) by doing this. **2** make a sign. □ **sign in** sign a register on arrival. **sign on 1** take into one's employment. **2** register as unemployed. **sign up** commit oneself to a period of employment, education, etc.

signal *n.* **1** a sign or gesture giving information or a command; an apparatus indicating whether a railway line is clear. **2** a sequence of electrical impulses or radio waves transmitted or received. ● *v.* (**signalled, signalling**; *Amer.* **signaled**) make a signal or signals; communicate with or announce in this way. ● *adj.* noteworthy. □ **signaller** *n.*, **signally** *adv.*

signal box *n.* a small railway building with signalling apparatus.

signalman *n.* (*pl.* **-men**) a person responsible for operating railway signals.

signatory *n.* (*pl.* **-ies**) one of the parties who sign an agreement.

signature *n.* **1** a person's name or initials written by himself or herself in signing something. **2** an indication of key or tempo at the beginning of a musical score.

signature tune *n.* a tune used to announce a particular performer or programme.

signet ring *n.* a finger ring with an engraved design.

significance *n.* **1** being important. **2** meaning. □ **significant** *adj.*, **significantly** *adv.*

signification *n.* meaning.

signify *v.* (**signified, signifying**) indicate; have as a meaning; be important, matter.

signpost *n.* a post with arms showing the direction of and distance to certain places.

Sikh (seek) *n.* a member of an Indian religious sect. □ **Sikhism** *n.*

silage (sI-lij) *n.* green fodder stored and fermented in a silo.

silence *n.* the absence of sound or of speaking; the withholding of information. ● *v.* make silent.

silencer *n.* a device for reducing sound.

silent *adj.* without sound; not speaking; not giving information. □ **silently** *adv.*

silhouette (sil-oo-et) *n.* a dark shadow or outline seen against a light background. ● *v.* show as a silhouette.

silica *n.* a compound of silicon occurring as quartz and in sandstone etc. □ **siliceous** *adj.*

silicate *n.* a compound of silicon.

silicon *n.* a chemical element (symbol Si).

silicon chip *n.* a silicon microchip.

silicone *n.* an organic compound of silicon, used in paint, varnish, and lubricants.

silicosis *n.* a lung disease caused by inhaling dust that contains silica.

silk *n.* a fine strong soft fibre produced by silkworms; thread or cloth made from this. □ **silky** *adj.*

silken *adj.* made of silk; soft and lustrous like silk.

silkworm *n.* a caterpillar which spins its cocoon of silk.

sill *n.* a strip of stone, wood, or metal at the base of a doorway or window opening.

silly *adj.* (**sillier, silliest**) lacking good sense, foolish; frivolous. □ **silliness** *n.*

silo (sI-loh) *n.* (*pl.* **silos**) **1** a pit or airtight structure for holding silage. **2** a pit or tower for storing grain, cement, or radioactive waste. **3** an underground place where a missile is kept ready for firing.

silt *n.* sediment deposited by water in a channel or harbour etc. ● *v.* block or become blocked with silt.

silvan var. of **sylvan**.

silver *n.* a chemical element (symbol Ag), a white precious metal; articles made of this; coins made of an alloy resembling it; household cutlery; the colour of silver. ● *adj.* made of or coloured like silver.

silverfish *n.* (*pl.* **silverfish**) a small wingless insect.

silver jubilee *n.* the 25th anniversary of a significant event.

silverside *n.* a joint of beef cut from the haunch, below topside.

silver wedding *n.* the 25th anniversary of a wedding.

silvery *adj.* **1** like silver. **2** having a clear gentle ringing sound.

simian (sim-ee-ăn) *adj.* monkey-like, ape-like.

similar *adj.* alike but not identical. □ **similarity** *n.*, **similarly** *adv.*

simile (sim-i-lee) *n.* a figure of speech in which one thing is compared to another.

similitude *n.* similarity.

simmer *v.* **1** (cause to) boil very gently. **2** be in a state of barely suppressed anger or excitement. □ **simmer down** become calmer or quieter.

simper *v.* smile in an affected way. ● *n.* an affected smile.

simple *adj.* **1** easy to understand or do, not complicated. **2** not elaborate or showy; not proud or extravagant. **3** having only one element, not compound. **4** feeble-minded. □ **simplicity** *n.*, **simply** *adv.*

simpleton *n.* a foolish or feeble-minded person.

simplify *v.* (**simplified, simplifying**) make easier or less complex. □ **simplification** *n.*

simplistic *adj.* over-simplified. □ **simplistically** *adv.*

simulate *v.* imitate; pretend to feel; produce a computer model of. □ **simulation** *n.*, **simulator** *n.*

simultaneous *adj.* occurring at the same time. □ **simultaneity** *n.*, **simultaneously** *adv.*

sin *n.* the breaking of a religious or moral law; an act which does this. ● *v.* (**sinned, sinning**) commit a sin. ● *abbr.* sine. □ **sinner** *n.*

since *prep.* from (a specified time or event) until the present. ● *conj.* **1** from the time that. **2** because. ● *adv.* since that time or event.

sincere *adj.* without pretence or deceit. □ **sincerely** *adv.*, **sincerity** *n.*

sine *n. Maths* the ratio of the side opposite an angle (in a right-angled triangle) to the hypotenuse.

sinecure (sI-nĕ-kewr) *n.* a profitable or prestigious position requiring no work.

sine qua non (sinay kwah **nohn**) *n.* an indispensable condition.

sinew *n.* tough fibrous tissue joining muscle to bone; a tendon; (**sinews**) muscles, strength. □ **sinewy** *adj.*

sinful *adj.* wicked. □ **sinfully** *adv.*, **sinfulness** *n.*

sing *v.* (**sang, sung, singing**) make musical sounds with the voice; perform (a song); make a humming sound; recount, celebrate. □ **singer** *n.*

singe (sinj) *v.* (**singed, singeing**) burn slightly; burn the ends or edges of. ● *n.* a slight burn.

single *adj.* **1** only one; individual and distinct; designed for one person; unmarried. **2** having only one part, not complex or multiple; (of a ticket) valid for an outward journey only. ● *n.* an individual person or thing; a room for one person; a single ticket; a pop record with one piece of music on each side; (**singles**) unmarried people; (**singles**) a game with one player on each side. □ **single out** choose or distinguish from others. □ **singly** *adv.*

single figures *n.pl.* numbers from 1 to 9.

single-handed *adj.* & *adv.* without help.

single market *n.* an association of countries trading without restrictions.

single-minded *adj.* with one's mind set on a single purpose.

single parent *n.* a person bringing up a child or children without a partner.

singlet *n.* a sleeveless vest.

singleton *n.* a single thing or person of a particular kind.

singsong *adj.* with a monotonous rise and fall of the voice. ● *n.* informal singing by a group of people.

singular *n.* the form of a noun or verb used in referring to one person or thing. ● *adj.* **1** of this form. **2** uncommon, extraordinary. □ **singularity** *n.*, **singularly** *adv.*

sinister *adj.* suggesting that something evil or harmful is at hand.

sink *v.* (**sank, sunk, sinking**) **1** go down below the surface of a liquid, cause to do this; become lower, move downwards; gradually penetrate the surface of something; decrease in amount or value. **2** send (a ball) into a pocket or hole. **3** invest (money). ● *n.* a fixed basin with taps and a drainage pipe. □ **sink in** be realized or understood.

sinker *n.* a weight used to sink a fishing line etc.

sinking fund *n.* money set aside regularly for repayment of a debt etc.

sinuous *adj.* curving, undulating.

sinus (sy-nŭs) *n.* a cavity in bone or tissue, esp. that connecting with the nostrils.

sinusitis *n.* inflammation of the nasal sinus.

sip *v.* (**sipped, sipping**) drink in small mouthfuls. ● *n.* an amount sipped.

siphon *n.* a bent pipe or tube used for transferring liquid using atmospheric pressure; a bottle from which soda water etc. is forced out by pressure of gas. ● *v.* draw out (liquid) through a siphon; take from a source, esp. dishonestly.

sir *n.* a polite form of address to a man; (**Sir**) the title of a knight or baronet.

sire *n.* an animal's male parent. ● *v.* be the sire of.

siren *n.* **1** a device that makes a loud prolonged sound as a signal or warning. **2** a dangerously fascinating woman.

sirloin *n.* the upper (best) part of a loin of beef.

sirocco *n.* (*pl.* **siroccos**) a hot wind that reaches Italy from Africa.

sisal (sy-săl) *n.* rope-fibre made from a tropical plant.

sissy *n.* (*pl.* **-ies**) *informal* a weak or timid person.

sister *n.* **1** a daughter of the same parents as another person. **2** a woman who is a fellow member of a group. **3** a nun. **4** a senior female nurse. □ **sisterly** *adj.*

sisterhood *n.* **1** the relationship of sisters. **2** an order of nuns. **3** a group of women with common aims.

sister-in-law *n.* (*pl.* **sisters-in-law**) a sister of one's husband or wife; the wife of one's brother.

sit *v.* (**sat, sitting**) **1** take or be in a position with the body resting on the buttocks; cause to sit; (of animals) rest with legs bent and body on the ground; (of birds) perch; have room for (a specified number) to sit; pose for a portrait; (of birds) remain on the nest to hatch eggs. **2** be situated. **3** be a candidate; take (an examination); (of a committee etc.) hold a session. □ **sit tight** *informal* remain firmly in place.

sitar *n.* a guitar-like Indian musical instrument.

sitcom *n. informal* a situation comedy.

site *n.* the place where something is, was, or is to be located. ● *v.* locate, provide with a site.

sitter *n.* a babysitter; an artist's model.

sitting *n.* a period spent seated, esp. while engaged in a particular activity; a session of a committee etc.; a scheduled period for a group to be served in a restaurant.

sitting room *n.* a room in a house used for relaxed sitting in.

sitting tenant *n.* a tenant already in occupation.

situated *adj.* in a specified position or condition. □ **situate** *v.*

situation *n.* the place (with its surroundings) occupied by something; a set of circumstances; a position of employment. □ **situational** *adj.*

situation comedy *n.* (*pl.* **-ies**) a broadcast comedy involving the same characters in a series of episodes.

six *adj.* & *n.* one more than five (6, VI). □ **sixth** *adj.* & *n.*

sixteen *n.* one more than fifteen (16, XVI). □ **sixteenth** *adj.* & *n.*

sixty *adj.* & *n.* six times ten (60, LX). □ **sixtieth** *adj.* & *n.*

size[1] *n.* relative bigness, extent; largeness; one of a series of standard measurements in which things are made and sold. □ **size up** estimate the size of; *informal* assess.

size[2] *n.* a gluey solution used to glaze paper or stiffen textiles.

sizeable *adj.* (also **sizable**) large; fairly large.

sizzle *v.* make a hissing sound like that of frying.

skate *n.* **1** a boot with a blade or wheels attached, for gliding over ice or a hard surface. **2** an edible flatfish. ● *v.* move on skates. □ **skate over** make only a passing reference to. □ **skater** *n.*

skateboard *n.* a small board with wheels for riding on while standing. ● *v.* ride on a skateboard.

skedaddle *v. informal* leave hastily, run away.

skein (skayn) *n.* **1** a loosely coiled bundle of yarn. **2** a flock of wild geese etc. in flight.

skeletal *adj.* **1** of the skeleton. **2** very thin.

skeleton *n.* bones, cartilage, etc. forming the supporting structure of an animal body; the basic structure of something; the minimum number, structure, etc.

skeleton key *n.* a key made so as to fit many locks.

skeleton service, skeleton staff *n.* a service or staff reduced to the minimum.

skeptic Amer. sp. of **sceptic**.

sketch *n.* a rough drawing or painting; a brief account; a short usu. comic play. ● *v.* make a sketch or sketches (of).

sketchy *adj.* (**sketchier, sketchiest**) rough and not detailed or substantial. □ **sketchily** *adv.*, **sketchiness** *n.*

skew *adj.* slanting, at an angle. ● *v.* change direction; twist; distort, make biased.

skewbald *adj.* (of an animal) with irregular patches of white and another colour.

skewer *n.* a pin to hold pieces of food together while cooking. ● *v.* pierce with a skewer.

ski *n.* one of a pair of long narrow strips of wood etc. fixed under the feet for travelling over snow. ● *v.* (**skis, skied, skiing**) travel on skis. □ **skier** *n.*

skid *v.* (**skidded, skidding**) slide uncontrollably off course. ● *n.* a skidding movement. □ **put the skids on** *informal* hasten the decline of.

skid-pan *n.* a surface used for practising control of skidding vehicles.

skiff *n.* a small light rowing boat.

skilful *adj.* (*Amer.* **skillful**) having or showing great skill. □ **skilfully** *adv.*

skill *n.* ability to do something well. □ **skilled** *adj.*

skillet *n.* a long-handled cooking pot; *Amer.* a frying pan.

skim *v.* (**skimmed, skimming**) **1** take (matter) from the surface of (liquid). **2** glide. **3** read quickly.

skim milk *n.* (also **skimmed milk**) milk from which the cream has been skimmed.

skimp *v.* supply or use rather less than what is necessary.

skimpy *adj.* (**skimpier, skimpiest**) scanty. □ **skimpily** *adv.*, **skimpiness** *n.*

skin *n.* the tissue covering a human or other animal body; an animal skin used for clothing etc.; an outer covering; a film forming on hot milk etc. ● *v.* (**skinned, skinning**) strip the skin from.

skin diving *n.* the sport of swimming under water with flippers and breathing apparatus. □ **skin diver** *n.*

skinflint *n. informal* a miser.

skinny *adj.* (**skinnier, skinniest**) *informal* very thin.

skint *adj. informal* very short of money.

skip[1] *v.* (**skipped, skipping**) **1** move lightly with a hopping or bouncing step; jump with a skipping rope; jump over; *informal* omit, miss. **2** *informal* leave hastily or secretly. ● *n.* a skipping movement.

skip[2] *n.* a large open container for builders' rubbish etc.

skipper *n. informal* a captain.

skipping rope *n.* a rope turned over the head and under the feet while jumping.

skirmish *n.* a minor fight or conflict. ● *v.* take part in a skirmish.

skirt *n.* **1** a woman's garment hanging from the waist; this part of a garment; any similar part. **2** a cut of beef from the lower flank. ● *v.* form or go along the edge of; avoid (a subject).

skirting *n.* (in full **skirting board**) a narrow board round the bottom of the wall of a room.

skit *n.* a short parody or comedy sketch.

skittish *adj.* lively and unpredictable.

skittle *n.* one of the wooden pins set up to be bowled down with a ball in the game of skittles.

skive *v. informal* dodge a duty; play truant.

skulduggery *n.* trickery.

skulk *v.* loiter stealthily.

skull *n.* the bony framework of the head.

skullcap *n.* a small cap with no peak, for the crown of the head.

skunk *n.* **1** a black and white animal able to spray an evil-smelling liquid. **2** *informal* a contemptible person.

sky *n.* (*pl.* **skies**) the region of the clouds or upper air.

skydiving *n.* the sport of jumping from an aircraft and performing acrobatic movements in the sky before opening one's parachute.

skylark *n.* a lark that soars while singing. ● *v. informal* play mischievously.

skylight *n.* a window set in a roof or ceiling.

skyscraper *n.* a very tall building.

slab *n.* a broad flat piece of something solid.

slack *adj.* **1** not tight. **2** not busy; not fast; lazy or negligent. ● *n.* **1** a slack piece of rope. **2** coal dust. ● *v.* **1** slacken **2** *informal* work slowly or lazily. □ **slacker** *n.*, **slackly** *adv.*, **slackness** *n.*

slacken *v.* make or become slack.

slacks *n.pl.* trousers for casual wear.

slag *n.* **1** solid waste left when metal has been smelted. **2** *informal* a promiscuous woman. ● *v.* (also **slag off**) (**slagged, slagging**) *informal* criticize, insult.

slag heap *n.* a mound of waste matter.

slain p.p. of **slay**.

slake *v.* **1** satisfy (thirst). **2** combine (lime) with water.

slalom (**slah**-lŏm) *n.* a ski race down a zigzag course; an obstacle race in canoes etc.

slam *v.* (**slammed, slamming**) **1** shut forcefully and noisily; put or hit forcefully. **2** *informal* criticize severely. ● *n.* a slamming noise.

slander *n.* a false statement uttered maliciously that damages a person's reputation; the crime of uttering this. ● *v.* utter slander about. □ **slanderer** *n.*, **slanderous** *adj.*

slang *n.* very informal words and phrases, used for vividness and often restricted to a particular group, activity, etc.

slant *v.* **1** slope. **2** present (news etc.) from a particular point of view. ● *n.* **1** a slope. **2** a point of view, a bias. □ **slantwise** *adv.*

slap *v.* (**slapped, slapping**) strike with the open hand or with something flat; place forcefully or carelessly. ● *n.* a slapping blow. ● *adv.* suddenly and forcefully; directly.

slapdash *adj.* hasty and careless.

slap-happy *adj. informal* cheerfully casual.

slapstick *n.* boisterous comedy.

slap-up *adj. informal* lavish, first class.

slash *v.* cut with a sweeping stroke; *informal* reduce greatly. ● *n.* **1** a slashing stroke, a cut made by this.

2 an oblique line (/) used between alternatives.

slat *n.* a narrow strip of wood, metal, etc.

slate *n.* rock that splits easily into flat greyish plates; a piece of this used as roofing-material or (formerly) for writing on. ● *v.* **1** cover with slates. **2** *informal* criticize severely.

slaughter *v.* kill (animals) for food; kill ruthlessly or in great numbers ● *n.* killing in this way.

slaughterhouse *n.* a place where animals are killed for food.

Slav (slahv) *adj.* & *n.* (a member) of any of the peoples of Europe who speak a Slavonic language.

slave *n.* a person who is owned by and must work for another; a person dependent on or controlled by something; a mechanism directly controlled by another. ● *v.* work very hard.

slave-driver *n.* a person who makes others work very hard. □ **slave-driving** *n.*

slaver *v.* have saliva flowing from the mouth.

slavery *n.* being a slave; very hard work with inadequate reward.

slavish *adj.* excessively submissive or imitative. □ **slavishly** *adv.*

Slavonic *adj.* & *n.* (of) the group of languages including Russian and Polish.

slay *v.* (**slew, slain, slaying**) kill.

sleazy *adj.* (**sleazier, sleaziest**) corrupt, immoral; squalid. □ **sleaze** *n.*, **sleaziness** *n.*

sled *n. Amer.* a sledge.

sledge *n.* a cart with runners instead of wheels, used on snow. ● *v.* travel or convey in a sledge.

sledgehammer *n.* a large heavy hammer used with both hands.

sleek *adj.* smooth and glossy; looking well fed and thriving. □ **sleekness** *n.*

sleep *n.* the natural condition of rest with unconsciousness and relaxation of muscles; a spell of this. ● *v.* (**slept, sleeping**) **1** rest in this condition. **2** provide with sleeping accommodation. □ **sleep in** sleep until late. **sleep off** dispel (sickness etc.) by sleeping.

sleeper *n.* **1** one who sleeps. **2** a railway coach fitted for sleeping in. **3** a beam on which the rails of a railway rest. **4** a ring worn in a pierced ear to keep the hole from closing. **5** a film etc. that achieves sudden success after initially being unnoticed.

sleeping bag *n.* a padded bag for sleeping in.

sleepwalk *v.* walk about while asleep. □ **sleepwalker** *n.*

sleepy *adj.* (**sleepier, sleepiest**) feeling a desire to sleep; quiet, without stir or bustle. □ **sleepily** *adv.*, **sleepiness** *n.*

sleet *n.* hail or snow and rain falling together. ● *v.* fall as sleet.

sleeve *n.* the part of a garment covering the arm; a tube-like cover; the cover for a record. □ **up one's sleeve** concealed but available.

sleigh (slay) *n.* a sledge drawn by horses or reindeer.

sleight of hand (slyt) *n.* skill in using the hands to perform conjuring tricks etc.

slender *adj.* **1** slim and graceful. **2** small, barely enough. □ **slenderness** *n.*

slept past & p.p. of **sleep**.

sleuth (slooth) *n. informal* a detective.

slew[1] past of **slay**.

slew[2] *v.* (also **slue**) turn or swing round.

slice *n.* **1** a thin flat piece (or a wedge) cut from something; a portion; an implement for cutting and serving food. **2** a slicing stroke. ● *v.* **1** cut, esp. into slices. **2** strike (a ball) so that it spins away from the direction intended. □ **slicer** *n.*

slick *adj.* **1** efficient and effortless; glib, cunning. **2** smooth and glossy or slippery. ● *n.* a patch of oil on the sea; a smear of a glossy wet substance. ● *v.* make sleek.

slide *v.* (**slid, sliding**) (cause to) move along a smooth surface, always remaining in contact with it; move or pass smoothly. ● *n.* **1** a smooth surface for sliding on; a structure with a smooth slope for children to slide down. **2** a piece of glass for holding an object under a microscope. **3** a picture for projecting on to a screen. **4** a hinged clip to hold hair in place.

sliding scale *n.* a scale of fees or taxes etc. that varies according to the variation of some standard.

slight *adj.* not great or large; trivial, not profound; slender. ● *v.* insult by treating with lack of respect; snub. ● *n.* a snub. □ **slightly** *adv.*, **slightness** *n.*

slim *adj.* (**slimmer, slimmest**) attractively thin; of small girth or thickness; very slight. ● *v.* (**slimmed, slimming**) make oneself thinner by dieting and exercise; make smaller. □ **slimness** *n.*

slime *n.* an unpleasant thick liquid substance.

slimline *adj.* of slender design.

slimy *adj.* (**slimier, slimiest**) **1** like slime; covered with slime. **2** disgustingly dishonest or flattering. □ **slimily** *adv.*, **sliminess** *n.*

sling *n.* **1** a belt, chain, or bandage etc. looped round an object to support or lift it. **2** a looped strap used to throw a stone etc. ● *v.* (**slung, slinging**) **1** suspend (something) to hang loosely. **2** *informal* throw, put casually.

slink *v.* (**slunk, slinking**) move in a stealthy or shamefaced way.

slinky *adj.* (**slinkier, slinkiest**) smooth and sinuous.

slip *v.* (**slipped, slipping**) slide accidentally; lose one's footing; fall or slide out of place; move quietly and quickly, hand over (something) in this way; escape, elude; deteriorate gradually. ● *n.* **1** an act of slipping. **2** a slight mistake. **3** a small piece of paper. **4** a petticoat. **5** a liquid containing clay used in pottery. □ **give someone the slip** *informal* evade or escape from someone. **let slip** reveal by mistake. **slip up** *informal* make a mistake.

slipped disc *n.* a disc of cartilage between vertebrae that has become displaced and causes pain.

slipper *n.* a light loose shoe for indoor wear.

slippery *adj.* difficult to hold or stand on because smooth or wet; (of a person) not trustworthy. □ **slipperiness** *n.*

slip road *n.* a road for entering or leaving a motorway.

slipshod *adj.* done or doing things carelessly.

slipstream *n.* a current of air driven backward by a revolving propeller or jet engine.

slipway *n.* a sloping structure on which boats are landed or ships built or repaired.

slit *n.* a narrow straight cut or opening. ● *v.* (**slit, slitting**) cut a slit in; cut into strips.

slither *v.* slide unsteadily.

sliver *n.* a small thin strip.

slob *n. informal* a lazy, untidy person.

slobber *v.* slaver, dribble.

sloe *n.* a small bitter wild plum.

slog *v.* (**slogged, slogging**) **1** work hard; walk with effort. **2** hit hard. ● *n.* **1** a spell of hard steady work or walking. **2** a hard hit.

slogan *n.* a word or phrase adopted as a motto or in advertising.

sloop *n.* a small ship with one mast.

slop *v.* (**slopped, slopping**) overflow; spill; splash. ● *n.* an unappetizing liquid; (**slops**) liquid refuse.

slope *v.* lie or put at an angle from the horizontal or vertical. ● *n.* a sloping surface; the amount by which a thing slopes. □ **slope off** *informal* leave unobtrusively.

sloppy *adj.* (**sloppier, sloppiest**) **1** wet, slushy. **2** slipshod. **3** weakly sentimental. □ **sloppily** *adv.*, **sloppiness** *n.*

slosh *v.* **1** (of liquid) move with a splashing sound. **2** *informal* hit.

● *n.* **1** a splashing sound. **2** *informal* a heavy blow.

sloshed *adj. informal* drunk.

slot *n.* **1** a narrow opening into or through which something is to be put. **2** a place assigned to something in a schedule etc. ● *v.* (**slotted, slotting**) fit into a slot.

sloth (slohth) *n.* **1** laziness. **2** a slow-moving animal of tropical America. ◻ **slothful** *adj.*, **slothfully** *adv.*

slot machine *n.* a machine operated by inserting a coin into a slot.

slouch *v.* stand, sit, or move in a lazy way. ● *n.* a slouching movement or posture.

slough[1] (*rhymes with* cow) *n.* a swamp, a marsh.

slough[2] (sluf) *v.* shed (old or dead skin); be shed in this way.

slovenly (slu-vĕn-li) *adj.* careless and untidy. ◻ **slovenliness** *n.*

slow *adj.* not moving or working quickly; not learning quickly or easily; taking a long time; (of a clock) showing an earlier time than the correct one. ● *adv.* slowly. ● *v.* reduce the speed (of). ◻ **slowly** *adv.*, **slowness** *n.*

slowcoach *n. informal* a slow or lazy person.

slow-worm *n.* a legless lizard.

sludge *n.* thick mud.

slue var. of **slew**.

slug *n.* **1** a small slimy creature like a snail without a shell. **2** a small lump of metal; a bullet. ● *v.* (**slugged, slugging**) *informal* hit hard.

sluggard *n.* a slow or lazy person.

sluggish *adj.* slow-moving, not lively. ◻ **sluggishly** *adv.*, **sluggishness** *n.*

sluice (sloose) *n.* a sliding gate controlling a flow of water; a channel carrying off water; an act of rinsing with water.

slum *n.* a squalid house or district.

slumber *v.* & *n.* sleep.

slump *n.* a sudden great fall in prices or demand. ● *v.* **1** undergo a slump **2** sit down heavily and limply.

slung past & p.p. of **sling**.

slunk past & p.p. of **slink**.

slur *v.* (**slurred, slurring**) **1** utter (words) with one sound running into the next. **2** pass over, attempt to conceal. **3** make damaging allegations about. ● *n.* **1** a damaging allegation. **2** a slurred sound. **3** a curved line showing that notes of music are to be played legato or sung to one syllable.

slurp *v.* & *n.* (make) a noisy sucking sound.

slurry *n.* thin mud; thin liquid cement; fluid manure.

slush *n.* **1** partly melted snow on the ground. **2** *informal* silly sentimental talk or writing. ◻ **slushy** *adj.*

slush fund *n. informal* a fund of money for bribes etc.

slut *n.* a slovenly or immoral woman. ◻ **sluttish** *adj.*

sly *adj.* (**slyer, slyest**) cunning, deceitful; (of an expression) suggesting that one has secret knowledge. ◻ **on the sly** secretly. ◻ **slyly** *adv.*, **slyness** *n.*

Sm *symb.* samarium.

smack *n.* **1** a slap, the sound of this. **2** a loud kiss. **3** a flavour, a trace. **4** a single-masted boat. **5** *informal* heroin. ● *v.* **1** slap, hit hard. **2** close and part (lips) noisily. ◻ **smack of** taste of; suggest.

small *adj.* of less than normal size, not large; not fully grown; unimportant. ● *n.* **1** the narrowest part (of the back). **2** (**smalls**) *informal* underwear. ● *adv.* into small pieces; in a small size. ◻ **smallness** *n.*

smallholding *n.* a small farm. ◻ **smallholder** *n.*

small hours *n.pl.* the period soon after midnight.

small-minded *adj.* petty and narrow-minded.

smallpox *n.* a disease with pustules that often leave bad scars.

small talk *n.* social conversation on unimportant subjects.

small-time *adj. informal* minor, unimportant.

smarmy *adj.* (**smarmier, smarmiest**) *informal* distastefully flattering, fulsome. □ **smarmily** *adv.*, **smarminess** *n.*

smart *adj.* **1** neat and elegant; well dressed. **2** *informal* clever; (of a machine etc.) able to react independently of control. **3** brisk; sharp. ● *v.* feel or cause a stinging pain; feel distress. □ **smartly** *adv.*, **smartness** *n.*

smart card *n.* a plastic card on which information is stored in electronic form.

smarten *v.* make or become smarter.

smash *v.* break noisily into pieces; hit or collide with forcefully; destroy, ruin. ● *n.* an act or sound of smashing; a violent collision. □ **smash hit** *informal* something very popular and successful.

smashing *adj. informal* excellent.

smattering *n.* a slight knowledge; a small amount.

smear *v.* **1** spread with a greasy or dirty substance. **2** damage the reputation of. ● *n.* **1** a mark made by smearing. **2** a slander.

smell *n.* the ability to perceive things with the sense organs of the nose; a quality perceived in this way; an act of smelling. ● *v.* (**smelt** or **smelled, smelling**) perceive the smell of; give off a smell. □ **smelly** *adj.*

smelt *v.* heat and melt (ore) to extract metal; obtain (metal) in this way.

smidgen *n.* (also **smidgin**) *informal* a very small amount.

smile *n.* a facial expression indicating pleasure or amusement, with lips upturned. ● *v.* give a smile.

smirch *v.* & *n.* discredit, disgrace.

smirk *n.* & *v.* (give) a self-satisfied smile.

smite *v.* (**smote, smitten, smiting**) *literary* hit hard.

smith *n.* a person who makes things in metal; a blacksmith.

smithereens *n.pl. informal* small fragments.

smithy *n.* (*pl.* **-ies**) a blacksmith's workshop.

smitten p.p. of **smite**.

smock *n.* a loose shirt-like garment; a loose overall.

smog *n.* dense smoky fog.

smoke *n.* visible vapour given off by a burning substance; an act of smoking tobacco; *informal* a cigarette, a cigar. ● *v.* **1** give out smoke; inhale and exhale the smoke of tobacco or a drug, do this habitually. **2** preserve (meat or fish) by exposure to smoke. □ **smokeless** *adj.*, **smoker** *n.* **smoky** *adj.*

smokescreen *n.* something intended to disguise or conceal activities.

smolder Amer. sp. of **smoulder**.

smooch *v. informal* kiss and cuddle; dance slowly in a close hold.

smooth *adj.* **1** having an even surface with no projections; not harsh in sound or taste; moving evenly without bumping; free from difficulties or setbacks. **2** polite but perhaps insincere. ● *v.* make smooth. □ **smoothly** *adv.*, **smoothness** *n.*

smorgasbord (smor-găs-bord) *n.* a buffet meal with a variety of dishes.

smote past of **smite**.

smother *v.* suffocate, stifle; cover thickly; suppress.

smoulder *v.* (*Amer.* **smolder**) **1** burn slowly with smoke but no flame. **2** show silent or suppressed anger etc.

smudge *n.* a dirty or blurred mark. ● *v.* make a smudge on; become smudged; blur. □ **smudgy** *adj.*

smug *adj.* (**smugger, smuggest**) self-satisfied. □ **smugly** *adv.*, **smugness** *n.*

smuggle *v.* convey (goods) illegally into or out of a country, avoiding customs duties; convey secretly. □ **smuggler** *n.*

smut *n.* **1** a small flake of soot; a small black mark. **2** indecent pictures, stories, etc. □ **smutty** *adj.*

Sn *symb.* tin.

snack *n.* a small or casual meal.

snaffle *n.* a horse's bit without a curb. ● *v. informal* take without permission.

snag *n.* **1** a problem, a drawback **2** a jagged projection; a tear caused by this. ● *v.* (**snagged, snagging**) catch or tear on a snag.

snail *n.* a soft-bodied creature with a shell.

snake *n.* a reptile with a long narrow body and no legs. ● *v.* move in a winding course. □ **snakeskin** *n.*, **snaky** *adj.*

snap *v.* (**snapped, snapping**) **1** (cause to) break suddenly, esp. with a sharp sound; (cause to) make such a sound; (cause to) move or alter abruptly; speak suddenly and irritably. **2** take a photograph of. ● *n.* **1** a snapping sound or movement. **2** a snapshot. ● *adj.* done or happening at short notice. □ **snap up** take eagerly.

snapper *n.* an edible sea fish.

snappy *adj.* (**snappier, snappiest**) *informal* **1** irritable. **2** concise, pithy. **3** elegant. □ **make it snappy** hurry up. □ **snappily** *adv.*, **snappiness** *n.*

snapshot *n.* an informal photograph.

snare *n.* a trap, usu. with a noose. ● *v.* trap in a snare.

snarl *v.* **1** growl angrily with bared teeth; speak or utter in a bad-tempered way. **2** become entangled. ● *n.* **1** an act or sound of snarling. **2** a tangle.

snarl-up *n. informal* a traffic jam; a muddle.

snatch *v.* seize quickly or eagerly. ● *n.* an act of snatching; a fragment; a short spell of something.

snazzy *adj.* (**snazzier, snazziest**) *informal* stylish.

sneak *v.* **1** move or convey furtively; achieve or obtain furtively. **2** *informal* tell tales. ● *n. informal* a tell tale. □ **sneaky** *adj.*

sneaking *adj.* (of a feeling) persistent but not openly acknowledged.

sneer *n.* a scornful expression or remark. ● *v.* show contempt by a sneer.

sneeze *n.* & *v.* (give) a sudden audible involuntary expulsion of air through the nose.

snicker *v.* & *n.* = **snigger**.

snide *adj.* sneering slyly.

sniff *v.* draw air audibly through the nose; draw in as one breathes; try the smell of; make secret inquiries or investigations. ● *n.* the act or sound of sniffing. □ **sniffer** *n.*

sniffle *v.* sniff slightly or repeatedly. ● *n.* this act or sound.

snifter *n. informal* a small drink of alcohol.

snigger *v.* & *n.* (give) a sly giggle.

snip *v.* (**snipped, snipping**) cut with scissors or shears in small quick strokes. ● *n.* **1** the act or sound of snipping. **2** *informal* a bargain.

snipe *n.* (*pl.* **snipe** or **snipes**) a wading bird ● *v.* fire shots from a hiding place; make sly critical remarks. □ **sniper** *n.*

snippet *n.* a small piece.

snivel *v.* (**snivelled, snivelling** *Amer.* **sniveled**) cry; complain in a whining way.

snob *n.* a person with an exaggerated respect for social position or wealth, despising those he or she considers inferior. □ **snobbery** *n.*, **snobbish** *adj.*

snood *n.* a loose bag-like ornamental net, holding a woman's hair at the back.

snooker *n.* a game played on a table, with 21 balls to be pocketed in a set order.

snoop *v. informal* pry. □ **snooper** *n.*

snooty *adj.* (**snootier, snootiest**) *informal* snobbishly aloof. □ **snootily** *adv.*

snooze *informal n.* & *v.* (take) a nap.

snore *n.* a snorting or grunting sound made during sleep. ● *v.* make such sounds. □ **snorer** *n.*

snorkel *n.* a tube by which an underwater swimmer can breathe. ● *v.* (**snorkelled, snorkelling**, *Amer.* **snorkeled**) swim with a snorkel.

snort *n.* a sound made by forcing breath through the nose, esp. in indignation. ● *v.* make a snort; *informal* inhale (an illegal drug).

snout *n.* an animal's long projecting nose or nose and jaws.

snow *n.* frozen atmospheric vapour falling to earth in white flakes; a fall or layer of snow. ● *v.* fall as or like snow. □ **snowed under** overwhelmed with work etc. □ **snowstorm** *n.*, **snowy** *adj.*

snowball *n.* snow pressed into a compact mass for throwing. ● *v.* increase in size or intensity.

snowboarding *n.* the sport of sliding downhill over snow while standing on a single wide ski.

snowblower *n.* a machine that clears snow from a road by blowing it to the side.

snowdrift *n.* a mass of snow piled up by the wind.

snowdrop *n.* a plant with white flowers blooming in spring.

snowman *n.* (*pl.* **-men**) a figure made of snow.

snowplough *n.* (*Amer.* **snowplow**) a device for clearing roads by pushing snow aside.

snub *v.* (**snubbed, snubbing**) reject or ignore contemptuously. ● *n.* an act of snubbing. ● *adj.* (of the nose) short and turned up at the end. □ **snub-nosed** *adj.*

snuff *n.* powdered tobacco for sniffing up the nostrils. ● *v.* put out (a candle). □ **snuff it** *informal* die. □ **snuffer** *n.*

snuffle *v.* breathe with a noisy sniff. ● *n.* a snuffling sound.

snug *adj.* (**snugger, snuggest**) cosy; closefitting. ● *n.* a small comfortable room in a pub. □ **snugly** *adj.*

snuggle *v.* settle into a warm, comfortable position.

so *adv.* **1** to such a great extent; to the same extent, to the extent indicated. **2** also: *so do.* **3** in this way. ● *conj.* **1** for that reason. **2** in order that; with the result that. □ **so as to** in order to. **so that** with the aim or result that.

soak *v.* place or lie in liquid so as to become thoroughly wet; (of liquid) penetrate. ● *n.* **1** a soaking. **2** *informal* a heavy drinker. □ **soak up** absorb.

so-and-so *n.* **1** a person or thing that need not be named. **2** *informal* a person one dislikes.

soap *n.* **1** a substance used in washing things, made of fat or oil and an alkali. **2** *informal* a soap opera. ● *v.* wash with soap.

soap opera *n.* a television or radio serial dealing with the daily lives of a group of characters.

soapsuds *n.pl.* froth of soapy water.

soapy *adj.* (**soapier, soapiest**) **1** of or like soap; containing or smeared with soap. **2** fulsome, flattering. □ **soapiness** *n.*

soar *v.* rise high, esp. in flight.

sob *n.* an uneven drawing of breath when weeping or gasping. ● *v.* (**sobbed, sobbing**) weep, breathe, or utter with sobs.

sober *adj.* not drunk; serious and realistic; (of colour) not bright. ● *v.* make or become sober. □ **soberly** *adv.*, **sobriety** *n.*

sobriquet (soh-brik-ay) *n.* (also **soubriquet**) a nickname.

so-called *adj.* called by a specified name, but perhaps wrongly.

soccer *n.* football, Association football.

sociable *adj.* fond of company; characterized by friendly companionship. ◻ **sociability** *n.*, **sociably** *adv.*

social *adj.* **1** of society or its organization. **2** living in or suited to a community; of interaction between friends etc. ● *n.* a social gathering. ◻ **socially** *adv.*

socialism *n.* a political and economic theory that resources, industries, and transport should be owned and managed by the state. ◻ **socialist** *n.*, **socialistic** *adj.*

socialite *n.* a person prominent in fashionable society.

socialize *v.* (also **-ise**) mix with other people for pleasure.

socialization *n.* **1** accustoming someone to generally accepted behaviour. **2** organizing a society etc. on socialist principles.

social security *n.* financial assistance from the state for people with little or no income.

social services *n.* welfare services provided by the State.

social worker *n.* a person trained to help people with social problems.

society *n.* (*pl.* **-ies**) **1** an ordered community; a particular system of ordering the community. **2** an organization or club. **3** wealthy and fashionable people. **4** company.

sociology *n.* the study of human society or of social problems. ◻ **sociological** *adj.*, **sociologist** *n.*

sock *n.* **1** a covering of wool, cotton, etc., for the foot; a removable inner sole for a shoe. **2** *informal* a heavy blow. ● *v. informal* hit forcefully.

socket *n.* a hollow into which something fits.

sod *n.* **1** turf; a piece of this. **2** *vulgar slang* an unpleasant or awkward person or thing.

soda *n.* **1** a compound of sodium. **2** soda water.

soda water *n.* water made fizzy by being charged with carbon dioxide under pressure.

sodden *adj.* very wet.

sodium *n.* a soft silver-white metallic element (symbol Na).

sodomy *n.* anal intercourse. ◻ **sodomite** *n.*

sofa *n.* a long upholstered seat with a back.

sofa bed *n.* a sofa that can be converted into a bed.

soft *adj.* **1** yielding to the touch, not hard or firm; smooth, not harsh. **2** not loud; subtle, not strongly marked; gentle. **3** lenient, not strict. **4** (of drinks) non-alcoholic; (of drugs) not likely to cause addiction. **5** (of currency) likely to fall suddenly in value. ◻ **soft-hearted** *adj.*, **softly** *adv.*, **softness** *n.*

softball *n.* a form of baseball using a large soft ball.

soften *v.* make or become soft or softer. ◻ **softener** *n.*

soft fruit *n.* any small stoneless fruit (e.g. raspberry).

soft furnishings *n.pl.* cushions, curtains, rugs, etc.

softie *n.* (also **softy**) *informal* a soft-hearted or sentimental person.

soft option *n.* an easy alternative.

soft-pedal *v.* (**soft-pedalled, soft-pedalling**; *Amer.* **soft-pedaled**) refrain from emphasizing

soft spot *n. informal* a feeling of affection.

software *n.* computer programs.

softwood *n.* the soft wood of coniferous trees.

softy var. of **softie**.

soggy *adj.* (**soggier, soggiest**) very wet and soft. ◻ **sogginess** *n.*

soh *n. Music* the fifth note of a major scale, or the note G.

soigné (swahn-yay) *adj.* well-groomed and sophisticated.

soil *n.* the upper layer of the earth; a nation's territory. ● *v.* make dirty.

soirée (swah-ray) *n.* a social gathering in the evening for music etc.

sojourn (so-jĕn) *n.* a temporary stay. ● *v.* stay temporarily.

solace *v.* & *n.* (give) comfort in distress.

solar *adj.* of or from the sun; reckoned by the sun.

solar cell *n.* a device converting solar radiation into electricity.

solar plexus *n.* a network of nerves at the pit of the stomach.

solar system *n.* the sun with the planets etc. that revolve round it.

sold past & p.p. of **sell**.

solder *n.* a soft alloy used to cement metal parts together. ● *v.* join with solder.

soldering iron *n.* a tool for melting and applying solder.

soldier *n.* a member of an army. ● *v.* serve as a soldier. ◻ **soldier on** *informal* persevere doggedly.

sole[1] *n.* **1** the undersurface of a foot; the part of a shoe etc. covering this. **2** a flatfish used as food. ● *v.* put a sole on (a shoe).

sole[2] *adj.* one and only; belonging exclusively to one person or group. ◻ **solely** *adv.*

solemn *adj.* serious, not smiling; formal and dignified. ◻ **solemnity** *n.*, **solemnly** *adv.*

solemnize *v.* perform (a ceremony); mark with a ceremony. ◻ **solemnization** *n.*

solenoid (so-lĕ-noid) *n.* a coil of wire magnetized by electric current.

sol-fa *n.* the system of syllables (*doh, ray, me,* etc.) representing the notes of a musical scale.

solicit *v.* ask (someone) for (something); (of a prostitute) approach someone to offer sexual services. ◻ **solicitation** *n.*

solicitor *n.* a lawyer who advises clients and instructs barristers.

solicitous *adj.* anxious about a person's welfare or comfort. ◻ **solicitously** *adv.*, **solicitude** *n.*

solid *adj.* **1** keeping its shape, firm; not liquid or gas; strongly built; reliable. **2** not hollow; of a specified substance throughout: *solid gold*; (of time or an activity) uninterrupted. **3** three-dimensional; of three-dimensional objects. ● *n.* a solid substance, body, or food. ◻ **solidity** *n.*, **solidly** *adv.*

solidarity *n.* unity resulting from common aims or interests etc.

solidify *v.* (**solidified, solidifying**) make or become solid. ◻ **solidification** *n.*

solidus *n.* (*pl.* **solidi**) an oblique stroke (/).

soliloquize *v.* (also **-ise**) utter a soliloquy.

soliloquy *n.* (*pl.* **-ies**) a speech made aloud to oneself.

solitaire *n.* **1** a gem set by itself. **2** a game for one person played on a board with pegs.

solitary *adj.* alone; isolated; single, the only one. ● *n.* (*pl.* **-ies**) a recluse.

solitude *n.* being solitary.

solo *n.* (*pl.* **solos**) music for a single performer; an unaccompanied performance etc. ● *adj.* & *adv.* unaccompanied, alone.

soloist *n.* the performer of a solo.

solstice *n.* either of the times (about 21 June and 22 Dec.) when the sun reaches its highest or lowest point in the sky at noon.

soluble *adj.* **1** able to be dissolved. **2** able to be solved. ◻ **solubility** *n.*

solution *n.* **1** a liquid containing something dissolved; the process of dissolving. **2** the process of solving a problem etc.; the answer found.

solve *v.* find the answer to. ◻ **solvable** *adj.*

solvent *adj.* **1** having enough money to pay one's debts etc. **2** able to dissolve another substance. ● *n.* a liquid used for dissolving something. ◻ **solvency** *n.*

somatic (soh-**mat**-ik) *adj.* of the body as distinct from the mind or spirit.

sombre *adj.* (*Amer.* **somber**) dark, gloomy.

sombrero (somb-**rair**-oh) *n. pl.* **sombreros**) a hat with a very wide brim.

some *adj.* **1** an unspecified quantity or number of; a particular but unidentified: *some man called*; approximate: *some fifty people.* **2** considerable, great. **3** *informal* remarkable. ● *pron.* some people or things.

somebody *n.* & *pron.* **1** an unspecified person. **2** a person of importance.

somehow *adv.* in an unspecified or unexplained manner.

someone *n.* & *pron.* somebody.

somersault *n.* a leap or roll turning one's body upside down and over. ● *v.* move in this way.

something *n.* & *pron.* **1** an unspecified thing; an approximate point or number. **2** a notable thing: *quite something.*

sometime *adv.* at an unspecified time. ● *adj.* former.

sometimes *adv.* at some times but not all the time.

somewhat *adv.* to some extent.

somewhere *adv.* at, in, or to an unspecified place.

somnambulist *n.* a sleepwalker. □ **somnambulism** *n.*

somnolent *adj.* sleepy. □ **somnolence** *n.*

■ **Usage** *somnolent* is often confused with *soporific.*

son *n.* a male in relation to his parents.

sonar *n.* a device for detecting objects under water by reflection of sound waves.

sonata *n.* a musical composition for one instrument or two, usu. in several movements.

son et lumière (son ay loom-yair) *n.* a night-time entertainment dramatizing a historical event with lighting and sound effects.

song *n.* a set of words to be sung; singing. □ **going for a song** *informal* being sold very cheaply.

songbird *n.* a bird with a musical cry.

songster *n.* a singer

sonic *adj.* of sound waves.

sonic boom *n.* (also **sonic bang**) a loud noise caused by an aircraft travelling faster than the speed of sound.

son-in-law *n.* (*pl.* **sons-in-law**) a daughter's husband.

sonnet *n.* a poem of 14 lines.

sonorous *adj.* resonant, with a deep powerful sound. □ **sonority** *n.*, **sonorously** *adv.*

soon *adv.* **1** after a short time; early. **2** willingly, for preference. □ **sooner or later** at some time, eventually.

soot *n.* a black powdery substance produced by burning. □ **sooty** *adj.*

soothe *v.* calm; ease (pain or distress). □ **soothing** *adj.*

soothsayer *n.* a prophet.

sop *n.* a concession to pacify a troublesome person. ● *v.* (**sopped, sopping**) soak up (liquid) with something absorbent.

sophism *n.* sophistry.

sophisticated *adj.* **1** characteristic of or experienced in fashionable life and its ways. **2** complicated, elaborate. □ **sophistication** *n.*

sophistry *n.* clever and subtle but misleading reasoning. □ **sophist** *n.*

soporific *adj.* tending to cause sleep. ● *n.* a soporific drug etc.

■ **Usage** *Soporific* is often confused with *somnolent.*

sopping *adj.* very wet, drenched.

soppy *adj.* (**soppier, soppiest**) *informal* feebly or distastefully sentimental. □ **soppiness** *n.*

soprano *n.* (*pl.* **sopranos**) the highest female or boy's singing voice.

sorbet (sor-bay) *n.* a flavoured water ice.

sorcerer *n.* a magician. □ **sorcery** *n.*

sordid *adj.* dishonourable, contemptible; dirty. □ **sordidly** *adv.*, **sordidness** *n.*

sore *adj.* **1** causing or suffering pain from injury or disease.

2 *informal* distressed, vexed. ● *n.* a sore place; a source of distress or annoyance. □ **soreness** *n.*

sorely *adv.* very much, severely.

sorrel *n.* a sharp-tasting herb. ● *adj.* reddish brown.

sorrow *n.* mental suffering caused by loss, disappointment, etc.; an event or fact causing this. ● *v.* feel sorrow, grieve. □ **sorrowful** *adj.*, **sorrowfully** *adv.*

sorry *adj.* (**sorrier, sorriest**) **1** feeling pity or distress. **2** feeling regret or repentance. **3** wretched, pitiful.

sort *n.* a kind or category; *informal* a person of a specified nature. ● *v.* divide or arrange in classes, categories, etc. □ **sort out** solve (problems).

sortie *n.* an attack by troops from a besieged place; a flight of an aircraft on a military operation.

SOS *n.* an international distress signal; an urgent appeal for help.

sot *n.* a habitual drunkard.

sotto voce (sott-oh **voh**-chi) *adv.* in an undertone.

sou (soo) *n.* a former French coin of low value.

soubriquet var. of **sobriquet**.

soufflé *n.* a light dish made with beaten egg white.

sough ((suf) or *rhymes with* cow) *n.* & *v.* (make) a moaning or whispering sound as of wind in trees.

sought past & p.p. of **seek**.

souk (sook) *n.* a market-place in Muslim countries.

soul *n.* **1** the spiritual or immortal element in a person; a person's mental or emotional nature; a person. **2** someone embodying a quality: *the soul of discretion.* **3** (also **soul music**) black American music with elements of rhythm and blues, rock, and gospel.

soulful *adj.* showing deep feeling, emotional. □ **soulfully** *adv.*

soulless *adj.* lacking interest or individuality; lacking feeling.

sound[1] *n.* vibrations of air detectable by the ear; the sensation produced by these; what is or may be heard. ● *v.* **1** produce or cause to produce sound; utter, pronounce; give a specified impression when heard: *it sounded sweet.* **2** test the depth of (a river or sea etc.); examine with a probe. ● *adj.* **1** in good condition, not damaged or diseased; (of reasoning) valid. **2** (of sleep) deep. □ **sound off** express one's opinions loudly. □ **sounder** *n.*, **soundly** *adv.*, **soundness** *n.*

sound[2] *n.* a strait.

sound barrier *n.* the high resistance of air to objects moving at speeds near that of sound.

sound bite *n.* a short, pithy quotation extracted from a recorded interview.

sounding board *n.* **1** a board to reflect sound or increase resonance. **2** a person used to test opinion.

soundproof *adj.* not able to be penetrated by sound. ● *v.* make soundproof.

soup *n.* liquid food made from meat, vegetables, etc. □ **soup up** *informal* make more powerful or impressive.

soupçon (soop-son) *n.* a very small quantity.

soup kitchen *n.* a place where soup etc. is served free to the poor.

soupy *adj.* (**soupier, soupiest**) **1** like soup. **2** *informal* sentimental.

sour *adj.* **1** tasting sharp; not fresh, tasting or smelling stale. **2** bad-tempered. ● *v.* make or become sour. □ **sourly** *adv.*, **sourness** *n.*

source *n.* the place from which something comes or is obtained; a river's starting point; a person or book etc. supplying information.

sourpuss *n.* *informal* a bad-tempered person.

souse *v.* steep in pickle; drench.

south *n.* the point or direction to the right of a person facing east; a southern part. ● *adj.* in the south; (of wind) from the south. ● *adv.* towards the south.

south-east *n.* the point or direction midway between south and east. □ **south easterly** *adj.* & *n.*, **south-eastern** *adj.*

southerly *adj.* towards or blowing from the south. ● *n.* (*pl.* **-ies**) a wind blowing from the south.

southern *adj.* of or in the south.

southerner *n.* a native of the south.

southernmost *adj.* furthest south.

southpaw *n.* *informal* a left-handed person.

southward *adj.* towards the south. □ **southwards** *adv.*

south-west *n.* the point or direction midway between south and west. □ **south-westerly** *adj.* & *n.* **south-western** *adj.*

souvenir *n.* something serving as a reminder of an incident or place visited.

sou'wester *n.* a waterproof hat with a broad flap at the back.

sovereign *n.* **1** a king or queen who is the supreme ruler of a country. **2** a former British coin worth one pound. ● *adj.* supreme; (of a state) independent. □ **sovereignty** *n.*

Soviet *n.* & *adj.* (a citizen) of the former USSR.

sow[1] (soh) *v.* (**sowed, sown** or **sowed, sowing**) plant (seed, a particular type of seed) for growth; plant seeds in (land); suggest, give rise to. □ **sower** *n.*

sow[2] (*rhymes with* cow) *n.* an adult female pig.

soy *n.* = **soya**.

soya *n.* (in full **soya bean**) a plant from whose seed an edible oil and flour are obtained.

sozzled *adj.* *informal* drunk.

spa *n.* a place with a curative mineral spring.

space *n.* **1** the boundless expanse in which all objects exist and move; the universe beyond the earth's atmosphere. **2** an unoccupied area; room to be or move; a blank patch; an interval of time. ● *v.* arrange with gaps in between. □ **spaced out** *informal* disorientated, dazed.

spacecraft *n.* a vehicle for travelling in outer space.

spaceship *n.* a spacecraft.

spacious *adj.* providing much space, roomy. □ **spaciousness** *n.*

spade *n.* **1** a tool for digging, with a broad metal blade on a handle. **2** a playing card of the suit marked with black figures shaped like an inverted heart with a small stem.

spadework *n.* hard preparatory work.

spaghetti *n.* pasta made in long strings.

span *n.* something's extent from end to end; the distance or part between the uprights of an arch or bridge. ● *v.* (**spanned, spanning**) bridge; extend across.

spangle *n.* a small piece of glittering material decorating a dress etc. ● *v.* cover with spangles or sparkling objects.

Spaniard *n.* a native of Spain.

spaniel *n.* a dog with drooping ears and a silky coat.

Spanish *adj.* & *n.* (the language) of Spain.

spank *v.* slap on the buttocks.

spanking *adj.* **1** brisk, lively. **2** *informal* striking; excellent.

spanner *n.* a tool for gripping and turning the nut on a screw etc.

spar *n.* a strong pole used as a ship's mast, yard, or boom. ● *v.* (**sparred, sparring**) box, esp. for practice; quarrel, argue.

spare *adj.* **1** additional to what is needed; not being used, kept in reserve. **2** thin. ● *n.* an extra thing kept in reserve. ● *v.* **1** give from sufficient resources; be able to do without. **2** refrain from killing or hurting. □ **go spare** *informal* become distraught. **to spare** additional to what is needed.

sparing *adj.* economical, not generous or wasteful.

spark *n.* a fiery particle; a flash of light produced by an electrical discharge; a particle (of energy, genius, etc.). ● *v.* give off spark(s). ▫ **spark off** give rise to, provoke.

sparkle *v.* shine with flashes of light; be lively or witty. ● *n.* a sparkling light.

sparkler *n.* a hand-held sparking firework.

sparkling *adj.* (of wine or mineral water) effervescent, fizzy.

spark plug *n.* (also **sparking plug**) a device for making a spark in an internal-combustion engine.

sparrow *n.* a small brownish-grey bird.

sparse *adj.* thinly scattered. ▫ **sparsely** *adv.*, **sparseness** *n.*

spartan *adj.* (of conditions) simple and sometimes harsh.

spasm *n.* a strong involuntary contraction of a muscle; a sudden brief spell of activity or emotion etc.

spasmodic *adj.* occurring in brief irregular bursts; subject to spasms. ▫ **spasmodically** *adv.*

spastic *adj.* affected by cerebral palsy which causes jerky, involuntary movements. ● *n.* a person with this condition. ▫ **spasticity** *n.*

■ **Usage** The word *spastic* is frequently found offensive.

spat[1] past & p.p. of **spit**.

spat[2] *n. informal* a petty quarrel.

spate *n.* a sudden flood.

spatial *adj.* of or existing in space. ▫ **spatially** *adv.*

spatter *v.* scatter or fall in small drops (on). ● *n.* a splash; the sound of spattering.

spatula *n.* a knife-like tool with a broad blunt blade; a medical instrument for pressing down the tongue.

spawn *n.* the eggs of fish, frogs, or shellfish. ● *v.* **1** deposit spawn. **2** produce, generate.

spay *v.* sterilize (a female animal) by removing the ovaries.

speak *v.* (**spoke, spoken, speaking**) utter (words) in an ordinary voice; say something; have a conversation; be able to converse in (a language); express, be a sign of. ▫ **speak up for** speak in defence of.

-speak *comb. form* jargon; *computerspeak*.

speaker *n.* **1** a person who speaks, one who makes a speech. **2** a loudspeaker.

spear *n.* a weapon with a long shaft and pointed tip; a pointed shootor stem. ● *v.* pierce with or as if with a spear.

spearhead *n.* the foremost part of an advancing force. ● *v.* be the spearhead of.

spec *n.* ▫ **on spec** *informal* without instructions, on the off chance.

special *adj.* **1** better than or different from usual, outstanding. **2** for a particular purpose, recipient, etc. ▫ **specially** *adv.*

specialist *n.* an expert in a particular branch of a subject.

speciality *n.* (*pl.* **-ies**) a subject in which one specializes; something at which one excels.

specialize *v.* (also **-ise**) **1** be or become a specialist. **2** adapt for a particular purpose. ▫ **specialization** *n.*

species *n.* (*pl.* **species**) a group of similar animals or plants which can interbreed.

specific *adj.* particular; exact, not vague. ● *n.* a specific aspect. ▫ **specifically** *adv.*

specification *n.* specifying; details describing a thing to be made or done.

specify *v.* (**specified, specifying**) identify precisely; include in specifications.

specimen *n.* a part or individual taken as an example or for examination or testing.

specious (spee-shŭs) *adj.* seeming good or sound but lacking real merit. ▫ **speciously** *adv.*, **speciousness** *n.*

speck *n.* a small spot or particle.

speckle *n.* a small spot, esp. as a natural marking. ▫ **speckled** *adj.*

specs *n.pl. informal* a pair of spectacles.

spectacle *n.* **1** a visually striking performance, display, etc.; a ridiculous sight. **2** (**spectacles**) a pair of lenses in a frame, worn in front of the eyes to correct vision.

spectacular *adj.* visually striking. ● *n.* an event designed to be visually striking. □ **spectacularly** *adv.*

spectator *n.* a person who watches a game, incident, etc.

spectral *adj.* **1** of or like a ghost. **2** of the spectrum.

spectre *n.* (*Amer.* **specter**) a ghost; a haunting fear.

spectrum *n.* (*pl.* **spectra**) bands of colour or sound forming a series according to their wavelengths; an entire range of ideas etc.

speculate *v.* **1** form opinions by guessing. **2** buy in the hope of making a profit. □ **speculation** *n.*, **speculative** *adj.*, **speculator** *n.*

speculum *n.* (*pl.* **specula**) a medical instrument for looking into bodily cavities.

sped past & p.p. of **speed**.

speech *n.* speaking, the ability to speak; a spoken discourse; a manner of speaking.

speechless *adj.* unable to speak because of emotion or shock.

speed *n.* **1** the rate at which someone or something moves or operates; a fast rate, rapidity. **2** *informal* an amphetamine drug. ● *v.* **1** (**sped, speeding**) move, pass, or send quickly. **2** (**speeded, speeding**) drive at an illegal speed. □ **speed up** accelerate.

speedboat *n.* a fast motor boat.

speedometer *n.* a device in a vehicle, showing its speed.

speedway *n.* **1** an arena for motorcycle racing; racing in this. **2** *Amer.* a road for fast traffic.

speedy *adj.* (**speedier, speediest**) rapid. □ **speedily** *adv.*, **speediness** *n.*

speleology (spee-li-**o**-lŏ-ji) *n.* the exploration and study of caves. □ **speleologist** *n.*

spell *v.* (**spelt** or **spelled, spelling**) **1** give in correct order the letters that form (a word). **2** be a sign of; lead to inevitably. ● *n.* **1** words supposed to have magic power; their influence; a fascination, an attraction. **2** a period of time, weather, or activity. □ **spell out** state explicitly. □ **speller** *n.*

spellbound *adj.* entranced.

spend *v.* (**spent, spending**) **1** pay out (money) in buying something. **2** use up; pass (time etc.). □ **spender** *n.*

spendthrift *n.* a wasteful spender.

sperm *n.* (*pl.* **sperms** or **sperm**) a male reproductive cell; semen.

spermatozoon (sper-mă-tŏ-**zoh**-ŏn) *n.* (*pl.* **spermatozoa**) the fertilizing cell of a male organism.

spermicidal *adj.* killing sperm.

spew *v.* (also **spue**) vomit; cast out in a stream.

SPF *abbr.* sun protection factor.

sphere *n.* **1** a perfectly round solid geometric figure or object. **2** a field of action or influence etc.

spherical *adj.* shaped like a sphere.

sphincter *n.* a ring of muscle controlling an opening in the body.

sphinx *n.* **1** an ancient Egyptian statue with a lion's body and human or ram's head. **2** an enigmatic person.

spice *n.* a flavouring substance with a strong taste or smell; interest, excitement. ● *v.* flavour with spice. □ **spicy** *adj.*

spick and span *adj.* neat and clean.

spider *n.* a small creature with a segmented body and eight legs. □ **spidery** *adj.*

spiel (shpeel) *n. informal* a glib persuasive speech.

spigot *n.* a plug stopping the vent-hole of a cask or controlling the flow of a tap.

spike *n.* **1** a thin, pointed piece of metal, wood, etc. **2** a sharp increase. ● *v.* **1** impale on a spike; form into spikes. **2** *informal* add alcohol to (a drink). **3** put an end to, frustrate. □ **spiky** *adj.*

spill *v.* (**spilt** or **spilled, spilling**) cause or allow to run over the edge of a container; overflow; spread outside an allotted space. ● *n.* **1** spilling; an amount spilled. **2** a fall from a mount. **3** a thin strip of wood or paper for lighting a fire etc. □ **spillage** *n.*

spin *v.* (**spun, spinning**) **1** turn rapidly on an axis. **2** draw out and twist into threads; make (yarn etc.) in this way. ● *n.* **1** a spinning movement. **2** *informal* a short drive for pleasure. □ **spin out** prolong. □ **spinner** *n.*

spina bifida *n.* a condition in which part of the spinal cord is exposed, often causing paralysis.

spinach *n.* a vegetable with green leaves.

spinal *adj.* of the spine.

spindle *n.* a rod on which thread is wound in spinning; a revolving pin or axis.

spindly *adj.* long or tall and thin.

spin doctor *n. informal* a spokesperson employed to present a favourable interpretation of events to the media.

spindrift *n.* sea spray.

spine *n.* **1** the backbone; the part of a book where the pages are hinged. **2** a needle-like projection on a plant or animal.

spineless *adj.* **1** having no backbone. **2** lacking determination.

spinet *n.* a small harpsichord.

spinnaker *n.* a large extra sail on a racing yacht.

spinneret *n.* the thread-producing organ in a spider, silkworm, etc.

spinney *n.* (*pl.* **spinneys**) a thicket.

spin-off *n.* an incidental benefit.

spinster *n.* an unmarried woman.

spiny *adj.* (**spinier, spiniest**) covered in spines.

spiracle *n.* an opening through which an insect breathes; the blowhole of a whale etc.

spiral *adj.* forming a continuous curve round a central point or axis. ● *n.* **1** a spiral line or thing. **2** a progressive, usu. harmful, increase or decrease. ● *v.* (**spiralled, spiralling**; *Amer.* **spiraled**) **1** move in a spiral course. **2** increase or decrease progressively. □ **spirally** *adv.*

spire *n.* a tall pointed structure esp. on a church tower.

spirit *n.* **1** the mind as distinct from the body; the soul; a person's nature; something's characteristic quality; a person's mood; the prevailing mood at an event etc. **2** a ghost. **3** courage and determination. **4** the intended meaning of a law etc. **5** a strong distilled alcoholic drink. ● *v.* (**spirited, spiriting**) carry off rapidly and secretly.

spirited *adj.* courageous and determined. □ **spiritedly** *adv.*

spirit level *n.* a sealed glass tube containing a bubble in liquid, used to test that a surface is level.

spiritual *adj.* **1** of the human spirit or soul. **2** of the Church or religion. ● *n.* a religious folk song of American blacks. □ **spirituality** *n.*, **spiritually** *adv.*

spiritualism *n.* attempted communication with spirits of the dead. □ **spiritualist** *n.*, **spiritualistic** *adj.*

spirituous *adj. formal* strongly alcoholic.

spit *v.* (**spat** or **spit, spitting**) **1** eject saliva; eject (food etc.) from the mouth; utter aggressively. **2** (of rain) fall lightly. ● *n.* **1** saliva; the act of spitting. **2** a metal spike holding meat while it is roasted. **3** a narrow strip of land projecting into the sea.

spite *n.* malicious desire to hurt or annoy someone. ● *v.* hurt or annoy from spite. □ **in spite of** not being prevented by. □ **spiteful** *adj.*, **spitefully** *adv.*, **spitefulness** *n.*

spitfire *n.* a hot-tempered person.

spittle *n.* saliva.

splash *v.* **1** cause (liquid) to fall on something in drops; move, fall, or wet with such drops. **2** decorate with irregular patches of colour. **3** display (a story) prominently in a newspaper. ● *n.* **1** splashing, the sound of this. **2** a patch of colour; a striking display. □ **splash out** *informal* spend extravagantly.

splatter *v.* splash, spatter. ● *n.* a splash.

splay *v.* spread apart; become wider or more separate.

spleen *n.* **1** an abdominal organ involved in maintaining the proper condition of the blood. **2** bad temper; peevishness.

splendid *adj.* brilliant, very impressive; *informal* excellent. □ **splendidly** *adv.*

splendour *n.* (*Amer.* **splendor**) a splendid appearance.

splenetic *adj.* bad-tempered, peevish.

splice *v.* join by interweaving or overlapping the ends.

splint *n.* a rigid framework preventing a limb etc. from movement, e.g. while a broken bone heals. ● *v.* secure with a splint.

splinter *n.* a thin sharp piece of broken wood etc. ● *v.* break into splinters.

splinter group *n.* a small group that has broken away from a larger one.

split *v.* (**split, splitting**) break or come apart, esp. lengthwise; divide, share; separate. ● *n.* splitting; a split thing or place; (**splits**) an acrobatic position with legs stretched fully apart.

split infinitive *n.* an infinitive with a word placed between *to* and the verb, eg. *I want to really perfect my French.*

splodge *n.* & *v.* (make) a splash or blotch.

splotch *v.* & *n.* = **splodge**.

splurge *informal n.* an act of spending extravagantly. ● *v.* spend extravagantly.

splutter *v.* make a rapid series of spitting sounds; speak or utter incoherently. ● *n.* a spluttering sound.

spoil *v.* (**spoilt** or **spoiled, spoiling**) **1** make less good, pleasant, or useful; (of food) become unfit for eating. **2** harm the character of (esp. a child) by being indulgent. ● *n.* (also **spoils**) plunder. □ **be spoiling for** desire (a fight etc.) eagerly.

spoiler *n.* a device that slows down an aircraft by interrupting the air flow; a similar device on a vehicle, preventing it from being lifted off the road at speed.

spoilsport *n.* a person who spoils others' enjoyment.

spoke[1] *n.* any of the bars connecting the hub to the rim of a wheel.

spoke[2] past of **speak**.

spokesman *n.* (*pl.* **-men**) a person who speaks on behalf of a group.

spokesperson *n.* (*pl.* **-persons** or **-people**) a person who speaks on behalf of a group.

spokeswoman *n.* (*pl.* **-women**) a female spokesperson.

sponge *n.* **1** a water animal with a porous structure; its skeleton, or a similar substance, used for washing, cleaning, or padding. **2** (also **sponge cake**) a cake with a light, open texture. ● *v.* **1** wipe or wash with a sponge. **2** *informal* live off the generosity of others. □ **spongeable** *adj.*, **spongy** *adj.*

sponger *n. informal* a person who exploits others' generosity.

spongiform *adj.* with a porous sponge-like texture.

sponsor *n.* **1** a person who provides funds for an artistic or sporting event etc.; one who sponsors another for charity. **2** a person introducing a proposal for legislation. **3** a godparent. ● *v.* provide funds for; promise a sum of money to (someone) if they complete an activity raising funds for charity. □ **sponsorship** *n.*

spontaneous *adj.* not caused by outside influences; not rehearsed.

□ **spontaneity** *n.*, **spontaneously** *adv.*

spoof *n. informal* a hoax; a parody.

spook *n. informal* a ghost. □ **spooky** *adj.*

spool *n.* a reel on which something is wound. ● *v.* wind on a spool.

spoon *n.* an eating and cooking utensil with a rounded bowl and a handle. ● *v.* take or lift with a spoon. □ **spoonful** *n.*

spoonerism *n.* the interchange of the initial sounds of two words, e.g. *he's a boiled sprat.*

spoon-feed *v.* (**spoon-fed, spoon-feeding**) **1** feed from a spoon. **2** *informal* give excessive help to.

spoor *n.* a track or scent left by an animal.

sporadic *adj.* occurring at irregular intervals or in a few places. □ **sporadically** *adv.*

spore *n.* one of the tiny reproductive cells of fungi, ferns, etc.

sporran *n.* a pouch worn in front of a kilt.

sport *n.* **1** a physical activity engaged in for pleasure. **2** *informal* a sportsmanlike person. ● *v.* **1** wear, display prominently. **2** play.

sporting *adj.* **1** concerning or interested in sport. **2** fair and generous.

sporting chance *n.* a reasonable chance of success.

sportive *adj.* playful. □ **sportively** *adv.*

sports car *n.* an open low-built fast car.

sports jacket *n.* a man's jacket for informal wear.

sportsman *n.* (*pl.* **-men**) **1** a man who takes part in sports. **2** a fair and generous person. □ **sportsmanlike** *adj.*, **sportsmanship** *n.*

sportswoman *n.* (*pl.* **-women**) a woman who takes part in sports.

spot *n.* **1** a round mark or stain; a pimple. **2** a place. **3** *informal* a small amount. **4** a spotlight. ● *v.* (**spotted, spotting**) **1** notice, perceive. **2** mark with spots. □ **on the spot 1** at once. **2** at the scene of an action. **3** *informal* forced to answer or decide immediately. □ **spotter** *n.*

spot check *n.* a random check.

spotless *adj.* free from stain or blemish. □ **spotlessly** *adj.*

spotlight *n.* a lamp or its beam directed on a small area. ● *v.* (**spotlit** or **spotlighted, spotlighting**) direct a spotlight on; draw attention to.

spotty *adj.* (**spottier, spottiest**) marked with spots.

spouse *n.* a husband or wife.

spout *n.* a projecting tube or lip through which liquid is poured or conveyed; a jet of liquid. ● *v.* **1** come or send out forcefully as a jet of liquid. **2** utter or speak lengthily.

sprain *v.* injure by wrenching violently. ● *n.* this injury.

sprang past of **spring**.

sprat *n.* a small edible fish.

sprawl *v.* sit, lie, or fall with arms and legs spread loosely; spread out irregularly. ● *n.* a sprawling attitude or arrangement.

spray *n.* **1** liquid dispersed in very small drops; a liquid for spraying; a device for spraying liquid. **2** a branch with leaves and flowers; a bunch of cut flowers. ● *v.* come or send out in small drops; wet with liquid in this way. □ **sprayer** *n.*

spray-gun *n.* a device for spraying paint etc.

spread *v.* (**spread, spreading**) **1** open out, make wider; become longer or wider; cover an increasing area. **2** apply in an even layer; be able to be applied. **3** (cause to) affect or be known by increasing numbers. **4** distribute. ● *n.* **1** spreading; the extent to which something spreads; a range. **2** a paste for spreading on bread. **3** an article etc. covering several pages of a newspaper. **4** *informal* a lavish meal.

spreadeagled *adj.* with arms and legs extended.

spreadsheet *n.* a computer program that manipulates figures in tables for calculation.

spree *n.* a period of unrestrained indulgence in an activity.

sprig *n.* a twig, a shoot.

sprightly *adj.* (**sprightlier, sprightliest**) lively, full of energy. □ **sprightliness** *n.*

spring *v.* (**sprang, sprung, springing**) **1** jump; move rapidly; appear suddenly. **2** arise, originate. ● *n.* **1** the season after winter and before summer. **2** a device that reverts to its original shape or position after being pressed; elasticity, resilience. **3** a jump. **4** a place where water or oil flows naturally from the ground. □ **spring something on** confront or present unexpectedly with something.

springboard *n.* a flexible board giving impetus to a gymnast or diver.

spring-clean *v.* clean (one's home etc.) thoroughly.

spring roll *n.* a fried pancake filled with vegetables.

spring tide *n.* a tide when there is the largest rise and fall of water.

springy *adj.* (**springier, springiest**) resilient, elastic; (of a step) bouncy. □ **springiness** *n.*

sprinkle *v.* scatter small particles of (a substance) over (a surface); fall in this way.

sprinkler *n.* a device for spraying water on plants or to put out fires.

sprinkling *n.* a small thinly distributed amount.

sprint *v.* run at full speed. ● *n.* a fast run; a race over a short distance. □ **sprinter** *n.*

sprite *n.* an elf, fairy, or goblin.

spritzer *n.* a drink of white wine and soda water.

sprocket *n.* a projection on a wheel, engaging with links on a chain etc.

sprout *v.* begin to grow or appear; put forth (shoots etc.). ● *n.* **1** a plant's shoot. **2** a Brussels sprout.

spruce *adj.* neat, smart. ● *v.* smarten. ● *n.* a fir tree. □ **sprucely** *adv.*, **spruceness** *n.*

sprung p.p. of **spring**. *adj.* fitted with springs.

spry *adj.* (**spryer, spryest**) active, lively. □ **spryly** *adv.*, **spryness** *n.*

spud *n.* **1** *informal* a potato. **2** a narrow spade.

spue var. of **spew**.

spume *n.* froth.

spun past & p.p. of **spin**.

spur *n.* **1** a pricking device worn on a horse-rider's heel; a stimulus, an incentive. **2** a projection. ● *v.* (**spurred, spurring**) urge on (a horse) with one's spurs; urge on, incite; stimulate. □ **on the spur of the moment** on impulse. **win one's spurs** prove one's ability.

spurious *adj.* not genuine or authentic. □ **spuriously** *adv.*, **spuriousness** *n.*

spurn *v.* reject contemptuously.

spurt *v.* gush; send out (liquid) suddenly; increase speed suddenly. ● *n.* a sudden gush; a sudden burst of activity or speed.

sputter *v.* splutter. ● *n.* a sputtering sound.

sputum *n.* mixed saliva and mucus.

spy *n.* (*pl.* **spies**) a person who secretly watches or gathers information. ● *v.* (**spied, spying**) work as a spy for a government etc.; observe, catch sight of.

sq. *abbr.* square.

squabble *v.* quarrel pettily or noisily. ● *n.* a noisy and petty quarrel.

squad *n.* a small group working together.

squadron *n.* a division of a cavalry unit or an airforce; a detachment of warships.

squalid *adj.* dirty and unpleasant; morally degrading. □ **squalidly** *adv.*, **squalor** *n.*

squall *n.* a sudden storm or wind. □ **squally** *adj.*

squander *v.* spend wastefully.

square *n.* **1** a geometric figure with four equal sides and four right angles; an area or object shaped like this. **2** the product of a number multiplied by itself. **3** an instrument for testing right angles. ● *adj.* **1** of square shape. **2** right-angled; level, parallel. **3** of or using units expressing the measure of an area. **4** in good order; fair, honest. **5** *informal* old-fashioned. ● *adv.* directly, exactly. ● *v.* **1** make square. **2** mark with squares. **3** multiply (a number) by itself. **4** make or be compatible; balance (an account). **5** *informal* bribe. □ **square up to** face in a fighting attitude; face resolutely. □ **squarely** *adv.*, **squareness** *n.*

square dance *n.* a dance in which four couples face inwards from four sides.

square meal *n.* a substantial meal.

square root *n.* the number of which a given number is the square.

squash *v.* **1** crush; squeeze or become squeezed flat or into pulp. **2** suppress; silence with a crushing reply. ● *n.* **1** a crowd of people squashed together; a crowded place or state. **2** a fruit-flavoured soft drink. **3** (in full **squash rackets**) a game played with rackets and a small ball in a closed court. **4** a vegetable gourd. □ **squashy** *adj.*

squat *v.* (**squatted, squatting**) **1** crouch, sit on one's heels. **2** be a squatter. ● *n.* **1** a squatting posture. **2** a place occupied by squatters. ● *adj.* short and stout.

squatter *n.* a person who takes unauthorized possession of an unoccupied building.

squawk *n.* & *v.* (make) a loud harsh cry.

squeak *n.* a short high-pitched cry or sound. ● *v.* make or utter with a squeak. □ **narrow squeak** *informal* a narrow escape. □ **squeaky** *adj.*

squeal *n.* a long shrill cry or sound. ● *v.* **1** make or utter with a squeal. **2** *informal* become an informer.

squeamish *adj.* **1** easily sickened or disgusted. **2** scrupulous. □ **squeamishly** *adv.*, **squeamishness** *n.*

squeeze *v.* **1** press firmly; extract liquid from by doing this; obtain from someone with difficulty; *informal* extort money etc. from. **2** move or force into a tight space; crowd together. ● *n.* **1** an act of squeezing; an embrace; a crowded state. **2** liquid produced by squeezing. **3** restrictions on borrowing, spending, or investment. □ **squeezer** *n.*

squelch *v.* & *n.* (make) a sound like someone treading in thick mud.

squib *n.* a small exploding firework.

squid *n.* a sea creature with tentacles.

squiffy *adj.* (**squiffier, squiffiest**) *informal* slightly drunk.

squiggle *n.* a short curly line. □ **squiggly** *adj.*

squint *v.* have one eye turned abnormally from the line of gaze of the other; look sideways or through a small opening. ● *n.* a squinting condition of one eye; a sideways glance.

squire *n.* a country gentleman, esp. a landowner.

squirm *v.* wriggle; feel embarrassed.

squirrel *n.* a small tree-climbing animal with a bushy tail.

squirt *v.* send out (liquid) or be sent out in a jet; wet in this way. ● *n.* **1** a jet of liquid. **2** *informal* a contemptible person.

squish *v.* & *n.* (make) a soft squelching sound. □ **squishy** *adj.*

Sr *symb.* strontium.

SRN *abbr.* State Registered Nurse.

SS *abbr.* **1** steamship. **2** *hist.* the Nazi special police force.

St *abbr.* Saint.

St. *abbr.* Street.

st. *abbr.* stone (in weight).

stab *v.* (**stabbed, stabbing**) pierce, wound or kill with something pointed; poke. ● *n.* **1** a stabbing thrust; a sudden sharp sensation. **2** *informal* an attempt.

stabilize *v.* (also **-ise**) make or become stable. ▫ **stabilization** *n.*

stabilizer *n.* (also **-iser**) a device to keep something steady or stable.

stable *n.* a building in which horses are kept; an establishment for training racehorses; the horses, people, etc. from the same establishment. ● *v.* put or keep in a stable. ● *adj.* firmly fixed or established, not easily shaken or destroyed. ▫ **stability** *n.*, **stably** *adv.*

staccato *adv. Music* with each sound sharply distinct.

stack *n.* **1** an orderly pile or heap; *informal* a large quantity. **2** a tall chimney. **3** a storage section of a library; a storage system in a computer. ● *v.* **1** arrange in a stack; cover with stacks; cause (aircraft) to fly at different levels while waiting to land. **2** shuffle (cards) to allow one to cheat.

stadium *n.* a sports ground surrounded by tiers of seats for spectators.

staff *n.* **1** a stick used as a weapon, support, or symbol of authority. **2** the people employed by an organization. **3** a stave in music. ● *v.* provide with a staff of people.

stag *n.* a fully grown male deer.

stage *n.* **1** a point reached in a process, journey, etc. **2** a raised floor or platform for theatrical performances etc.; acting as a profession. ● *v.* present on the stage; organize and carry out. ▫ **go on the stage** become an actor or actress.

stagecoach *n. hist.* a large horse-drawn coach running on a regular route by stages.

stage fright *n.* nervousness on facing an audience.

stage whisper *n.* a whisper meant to be overheard.

stagflation *n.* a state of inflation without an increase in demand and employment.

stagger *v.* **1** move or go unsteadily. **2** surprise or shock deeply. **3** arrange so as not to coincide exactly. ● *n.* a staggering movement.

staggering *adj.* astonishing.

staging *n.* **1** a presentation of a play. **2** a set of temporary platforms; a platform for plants in a greenhouse.

stagnant *adj.* not flowing, still and stale; not active or developing. ▫ **stagnancy** *n.*

stagnate *v.* be or become stagnant. ▫ **stagnation** *n.*

stag-night *n.* an all-male party for a man about to marry.

staid *adj.* steady and serious.

stain *v.* discolour, mark with dirty patches; become discoloured; dye. ● *n.* **1** a mark caused by staining; a disgrace or blemish. **2** a dye. ▫ **stainless** *adj.*

stainless steel *n.* a steel alloy not liable to rust or tarnish.

stair *n.* one of a flight of fixed indoor steps; (**stairs**) a flight of these.

staircase *n.* a set of stairs with their supporting structure.

stairway *n.* a staircase.

stairwell *n.* the space for a staircase.

stake *n.* **1** a pointed stick or post for driving into the ground. **2** money etc. wagered; a share or interest in an enterprise etc. ● *v.* **1** support on a stake; mark (an area) with stakes. **2** wager. ▫ **at stake** being risked. **stake a claim** claim a right to something. **stake out** *informal* place under surveillance.

stalactite *n.* a deposit of calcium carbonate hanging like an icicle.

stalagmite *n.* a deposit of calcium carbonate standing like a pillar.

stale *adj.* not fresh; unpleasant or uninteresting from lack of freshness; spoilt by too much practice. ● *v.* make or become stale. ▫ **staleness** *n.*

stalemate *n.* a drawn position in chess; a situation where progress is impossible. ● *v.* bring to such a state.

stalk *n.* a stem or similar supporting part. ● *v.* **1** pursue stealthily; follow and harrass. **2** walk stiffly or proudly. ▫ **stalker** *n.*

stalking-horse *n.* a pretext concealing one's real intentions.

stall *n.* **1** a booth or stand for the display and sale of goods. **2** a stable or cowhouse; a compartment in this. **3** a fixed seat in a chancel. **4** (**stalls**) the ground floor seats in a theatre. **5** an engine's stalling. ● *v.* **1** (of an engine) stop running; (of an aircraft) begin to drop because the speed is too low; stop making progress; be obstructive or evasive. **2** put or keep (an animal) in a stall.

stallion *n.* an uncastrated male horse.

stalwart *adj.* loyal and hard-working. ● *n.* a stalwart person.

stamen *n.* the pollen-bearing part of a flower.

stamina *n.* the ability to withstand long physical or mental strain.

stammer *v.* speak with involuntary pauses or repetitions of a syllable. ● *n.* this act or tendency.

stamp *v.* **1** bring (one's foot) down heavily on the ground. **2** impress (a mark or pattern) on (a surface); mark out as having a particular characteristic. **3** fix a postage stamp to. ● *n.* **1** an instrument for stamping a mark; this mark; a characteristic quality. **2** a small adhesive label fixed to an envelope or document to show that postage or a fee has been paid. **3** an act of stamping the foot. ▫ **stamp out** suppress by force.

stampede *n.* a sudden rush of animals or people. ● *v.* (cause to) take part in a stampede.

stamping ground *n.* a place where someone regularly spends time.

stance *n.* a manner of standing.

stanch var. of **staunch**.

stanchion (stan-shĕn) *n.* an upright post or support.

stand *v.* (**stood, standing**) **1** have, keep, or take a stationary upright position; set upright; (of a building) be situated. **2** remain in a specified condition; remain undisturbed; remain valid or unaltered. **3** endure. **4** *Brit.* be a candidate in an election. **5** pay for (food, drinks) for (someone). ● *n.* **1** an attitude or policy; resistance to attack or pressure. **2** a support, a pedestal; a platform; a raised structure with seats at a sports ground; a stall for goods. **3** being stationary. ▫ **stand a chance** have a chance of success. **stand by 1** look on without interfering. **2** be ready for action. **3** support in difficulty; keep to (a promise). **stand down** withdraw. **stand for 1** represent; symbolize. **2** tolerate. **stand in** deputize. **stand one's ground** not yield. **stand out** be noticeable. **stand to reason** be logical. **stand up 1** get to one's feet; place upright. **2** be valid. **3** *informal* fail to keep an appointment with. **stand up for** speak in defence of. **stand up to** resist courageously; be strong enough to endure.

standard *n.* **1** a thing against which something may be compared for testing or measurement; a level of quality or achievement reached or required. **2** a principle of conduct. **3** a flag. ● *adj.* serving as or conforming to a standard; of average or usual quality, size, etc.

standardize *v.* (also **-ise**) cause to conform to a standard. ▫ **standardization** *n.*

standard lamp *n.* a household lamp set on a tall support.

stand by *n.* (*pl.* **stand bys**) readiness for action; a person or thing ready for immediate use or action in emergency; a system of allocating unreserved tickets.

stand-in *n.* a deputy, a substitute.

standing *n.* **1** status. **2** the length of time that something has lasted.

standing order *n.* an instruction to a bank to make regular payments.

stand-offish *adj. informal* cold or distant in manner.

standpipe *n.* a vertical pipe for fluid to rise in, esp. for attachment to a water main.

standpoint *n.* a point of view.

standstill *n.* inability to proceed.

stank past of **stink**.

stanza *n.* a verse of poetry.

staphylococcus (staf-il-ŏ-**kok**-ŭs) *n.* (*pl.* **staphylococci**) a pus-producing bacterium.

staple *n.* **1** a piece of wire driven into papers to fasten them together; a piece of bent metal used as a fastening. **2** a principal or standard food or product etc. ● *adj.* principal, most important. ● *v.* secure with staple(s). ▫ **stapler** *n.*

star *n.* **1** a heavenly body appearing as a point of light. **2** a mark with points or rays representing a star, an asterisk; this as a mark of quality. **3** a famous actor, performer, etc. ● *v.* (**starred, starring**) **1** be a star performer; have as a star. **2** mark with an asterisk.

starboard *n.* the right-hand side of a ship or aircraft.

starch *n.* **1** a carbohydrate occurring in cereals, potatoes, etc. **2** a preparation for stiffening fabrics; stiffness of manner. ● *v.* stiffen with starch. ▫ **starchy** *adj.*

stardom *n.* being a star actor etc.

stare *v.* gaze fixedly esp. in astonishment. ● *n.* a staring gaze.

starfish *n.* a star-shaped sea creature.

stark *n.* **1** desolate, bare. **2** sharply evident; downright. ● *adv.* completely. ▫ **starkly** *adv.*, **starkness** *n.*

starling *n.* a bird with glossy black speckled feathers.

starry *adj.* (**starrier, starriest**) set with stars; shining like stars.

starry-eyed *adj.* romantically enthusiastic or idealistic.

START *abbr.* Strategic Arms Reduction Talks.

start *v.* **1** come or bring into being; (cause to) begin to do something; (cause to) begin operating; set out on a journey. **2** make a sudden movement, esp. from pain or surprise. ● *n.* **1** beginning; the point at which something begins. **2** an advantage gained or given at the beginning of a race etc. **3** a sudden movement of surprise. ▫ **starter** *n.*

startle *v.* shock, surprise.

starve *v.* die or suffer acutely from lack of food; cause to do this; force by starvation; *informal* feel very hungry. ▫ **starvation** *n.*

stash *v. informal* store secretly.

state *n.* **1** the condition that someone or something is in; *informal* an agitated condition of mind. **2** a political community under one government or forming part of a federation; civil government. **3** grandeur, ceremony. ● *adj.* **1** of or provided by the state. **2** ceremonial. ● *v.* express in words; specify.

stateless *adj.* not a citizen or subject of any country.

stately *adj.* (**statelier, stateliest**) dignified, grand. ▫ **stateliness** *n.*

statement *n.* a clear expression of something; an official account of an event; a written report of a financial account.

stateroom *n.* a room used on ceremonial occasions; a captain's or passenger's private compartment on a ship.

statesman *n.* (*pl.* **-men**) an experienced and respected political leader. ▫ **statesmanship** *n.*

stateswoman *n.* (*pl.* **-women**) a woman who is an experienced and respected political leader.

static *adj.* **1** not moving or changing. **2** *Physics* of bodies at rest or forces in equilibrium. ● *n.* electrical disturbances in the air, causing interference in telecommunications; (in full **static electricity**) electricity present in a body, not flowing as current.

statics *n.pl.* the branch of mechanics concerned with bodies at rest or forces in equilibrium.

station *n.* **1** a place where trains stop for passengers to get on and off. **2** a place where a particular activity is carried on. **3** a broadcasting channel. **4** a place where someone stands, esp. on duty; a person's status. ● *v.* put at or in a certain place for a purpose.

stationary *adj.* not moving; not movable.

stationer *n.* a dealer in stationery.

stationery *n.* writing paper, envelopes, labels, etc.

■ **Usage** The noun *stationery* is spelt with an *e*, the adjective *stationary* with an *a*.

---

station wagon *n. Amer.* an estate car.

statistic *n.* an item of information obtained by studying numerical data; (*statistics*) the science of collecting and interpreting numerical information. □ **statistical** *adj.*, **statistically** *adv.*

statistician *n.* an expert in statistics.

statue *n.* a sculptured, cast, or moulded figure.

statuesque *adj.* like a statue in size, dignity, or stillness.

statuette *n.* a small statue.

stature *n.* bodily height; importance or reputation gained by ability or achievement.

status *n.* a person's position or rank in relation to others; high rank or prestige.

status quo *n.* the existing state of affairs.

statute *n.* a law passed by Parliament or a similar body.

statutory *adj.* fixed, done, or required by statute.

staunch *adj.* unshakeably loyal. ● *v.* (also **stanch**) stop the flow of (blood) from a wound. □ **staunchly** *adv.*

stave *n.* **1** a vertical wooden post; one of the strips of wood forming the side of a cask or tub. **2** a set of five horizontal lines on which music is written. ● *v.* (**stove** or **staved, staving**) dent, break a hole in. □ **stave off (staved)** ward off.

stay *v.* **1** remain in the same place; live temporarily; continue in the same state. **2** stop, postpone. ● *n.* **1** a period of staying somewhere. **2** a postponement. □ **stay the course** be able to reach the end of it.

STD *abbr.* subscriber trunk dialling; the connection of telephone calls without an operator's assistance.

stead (sted) *n.* □ **in someone's** or **something's stead** instead of him, her, or it. **stand in good stead** be of great service to.

steadfast *adj.* not changing or yielding. □ **steadfastly** *adv.*

steady *adj.* (**steadier, steadiest**) **1** firmly fixed; not shaking. **2** regular, not changing. **3** dependable, not excitable. ● *v.* (**steadied, steadying**) make or become steady. □ **steadily** *adv.*, **steadiness** *n.*

steak *n.* a thick slice of meat (esp. beef) or fish.

steal *v.* (**stole, stolen, stealing**) **1** take dishonestly. **2** move stealthily. ● *n. informal* **1** stealing. **2** a bargain. □ **steal the show** outshine other performers.

stealth (stelth) *n.* secrecy.

stealthy *adj.* (**stealthier, stealthiest**) quiet and cautious, avoiding notice. □ **stealthily** *adv.*, **stealthiness** *n.*

steam *n.* vapour into which water is changed by boiling; this as motive power. ● *v.* **1** give off steam; (cause to) become misted over with steam. **2** cook or treat with steam; move or function by the power of steam; move rapidly. □ **pick up steam** move or work faster. □ **steamy** *adj.*

steamer *n.* **1** a steam-driven ship. **2** a container in which things are cooked or heated by steam.

steamroller *n.* a heavy engine with a large roller, used in road-making.

steed *n. poetic* a horse.

steel *n.* a very strong alloy of iron and carbon; a steel rod for sharpening knives. □ **steel oneself** brace oneself to face difficulty or hardship etc. □ **steeliness** *n.*, **steely** *adj.*

steel wool *n.* a mass of fine shavings of steel used as an abrasive.

steep *adj.* **1** sloping sharply not gradually. **2** *informal* (of prices) unreasonably high. ● *v.* soak in liquid; permeate thoroughly. □ **steeply** *adv.*, **steepness** *n.*

steeple *n.* a tall tower with a spire, rising above a church roof.

steeplechase *n.* a race for horses or athletes, with fences to jump. □ **steeplechaser** *n.*, **steeplechasing** *n.*

steeplejack *n.* a person who climbs tall chimneys etc. to do repairs.

steer[1] *v.* direct the course of; be directed; guide.

steer[2] *n.* a bullock.

stellar *adj.* of a star or stars.

stem *n.* **1** the supporting part of a plant; a long thin supporting section. **2** *Grammar* the main part of a noun or verb, to which endings are added. ● *v.* (**stemmed, stemming**) stop the flow of. □ **stem from** have as its source.

stench *n.* a foul smell.

stencil *n.* a sheet of card etc. with a cut-out design, painted over to produce the design on the surface below; the design produced. ● *v.* (**stencilled, stencilling**; *Amer.* **stenciled**) produce (a design) on (a surface) in this way.

stenography *n.* shorthand. □ **stenographer** *n.*

stentorian *adj.* (of a voice) extremely loud.

step *v.* (**stepped, stepping**) lift and set down a foot or alternate feet; move a short distance in this way. ● *n.* **1** a movement of a foot and leg in stepping; the distance covered in this way; a short distance; a pattern of steps in dancing. **2** a level surface to place one's foot on in climbing; (**steps**) a stepladder. **3** one of a series of actions to achieve a goal; a stage in a process. □ **in step** stepping in time with others; conforming. **mind** or **watch one's step** take care. **step down** resign from a position of power. **step in** intervene; enter. **step up** increase.

step- *comb. form* related by remarriage of a parent, as *stepfather, stepmother, stepson*, etc.

stepladder *n.* a short ladder with a supporting framework.

steppe *n.* a grassy plain, esp. in south-east Europe and Siberia.

stepping stone *n.* a raised stone for stepping on in crossing a stream etc.; a stage in progress towards a goal.

stereo *n.* (*pl.* **stereos**) **1** stereophonic sound; a stereophonic hi-fi system. **2** a stereoscope.

stereophonic *adj.* (of sound recording and transmission) using two transmission channels so as to give the effect of sound from more than one source. □ **stereophony** *n.*

stereoscope *adj.* a device by which two photographs of the same object are viewed together to give an effect of depth. □ **stereoscopic** *adj.*

stereotype *n.* a standardized conventional idea or character etc. ● *v.* regard or represent as a stereotype. □ **stereotyped** *adj.*

sterile *adj.* **1** unable to produce fruit or young. **2** free from micro-organisms. □ **sterility** *n.* **sterilization** *n.*, **sterilize** *v.* (also **-ise**), **sterilizer** *n.*

sterling *n.* British money. ● *adj.* of standard purity; excellent.

stern *adj.* strict, severe. ● *n.* the rear of a ship or aircraft. □ **sternly** *adv.*, **sternness** *n.*

sternum *n.* (*pl.* **sternums** or **sterna**) the breastbone.

steroid *n.* any of a group of organic compounds that includes certain hormones.

stertorous (ster-tŏ-rŭs) *adj.* making a snoring or rasping sound.

stet *v.* (placed by a word that has been crossed out etc.) ignore the alteration.

stethoscope *n.* a medical instrument for listening to a patient's heart or breathing.

stevedore *n.* a docker.

stew *v.* **1** cook by simmering in a closed pot; (of tea) become strong. **2** *informal* worry. ● *n.* **1** a dish made by stewing meat etc. **2** *informal* a state of great anxiety.

steward *n.* **1** a person employed to manage an estate etc. **2** a passengers' attendant on a ship, aircraft, or train. **3** an official at a race meeting or show etc.

stewardess *n.* a female attendant on an aircraft, ship, etc.

stick *v.* (**stuck, sticking**) **1** thrust (something sharp) into or through something; *informal* put. **2** cling or adhere; cause to do this; remain without moving; become unable to move or work, jam; be unable to make progress. **3** *informal* endure. ● *n.* **1** a thin piece of wood; a similar piece of other material; an implement used to propel the ball in hockey, polo, etc. **2** a threat of punishment; *informal* criticism. □ **stick out** be prominent or conspicuous. **stick to** confine oneself to; remain faithful to. **stick together** *informal* remain loyal to one another. **stick to one's guns** refuse to yield. **stick up for** *informal* support.

sticker *n.* an adhesive label or sign.

sticking plaster *n.* an adhesive fabric for covering small cuts.

stick-in-the-mud *n. informal* a person who will not adopt new ideas etc.

stickleback *n.* a small fish with sharp spines on its back.

stickler *n.* □ **a stickler for** a person who insists on (something).

sticky *adj.* (**stickier, stickiest**) **1** sticking to what is touched. **2** humid. **3** *informal* difficult. □ **stickily** *adv.*, **stickiness** *n.*

stiff *adj.* **1** not bending or moving easily; formal in manner. **2** severe; (of a wind) blowing strongly; difficult, requiring effort; (of a drink) strong. ● *n. informal* a corpse. □ **stiff with** *informal* full of. □ **stiffly** *adv.*, **stiffness** *n.*

stiffen *v.* make or become stiff. □ **stiffener** *n.*

stiff-necked *adj.* obstinate.

stifle *v.* feel or cause to feel unable to breathe; suppress.

stigma *n.* **1** a mark of shame. **2** part of a flower pistil.

stigmata *n.pl.* marks corresponding to the Crucifixion marks on Christ's body.

stigmatize *v.* (also **-ise**) brand as disgraceful. □ **stigmatization** *n.*

stile *n.* steps or bars for people to climb over a fence.

stiletto *n.* (*pl.* **stilettos**) a dagger with a narrow blade.

stiletto heel *n.* a long tapering heel of a shoe.

still *adj.* **1** with little or no motion or sound. **2** (of drinks) not fizzy. ● *n.* **1** silence and calm. **2** a photograph taken from a cinema film. **3** a distilling apparatus. ● *adv.* **1** continuing the same up to the present or the time mentioned: *I'm still waiting.* **2** nevertheless. **3** even (used in comparisons): *still more.* □ **stillness** *n.*

stillborn *adj.* born dead.

still life *n.* a picture of inanimate objects.

stilted *adj.* stiffly formal.

stilts *n.pl.* a pair of poles with footrests, enabling the user to walk above the ground; piles or posts supporting a building.

stimulant *adj.* & *n.* (a substance) increasing the body's nervous activity.

stimulate *v.* rouse to action, make more active; motivate, encourage.

□ **stimulation** *n.*, **stimulative** *adj.*, **stimulator** *n.*

stimulus *n.* (*pl.* **stimuli**) something that rouses a person or thing to activity or energy.

sting *n.* a sharp wounding part of an insect etc.; a wound made by this; sharp bodily or mental pain. ● *v.* (**stung, stinging**) **1** wound or affect with a sting; feel or cause sharp pain; provoke by annoying or taunting. **2** *informal* overcharge, swindle.

stingy *adj.* (**stingier, stingiest**) spending or given grudgingly or in small amounts. □ **stingily** *adv.*, **stinginess** *n.*

stink *n.* **1** an offensive smell. **2** *informal* a row or fuss. ● *v.* (**stank** or **stunk, stinking**) **1** give off a stink. **2** *informal* seem very unpleasant or dishonest.

stinker *n. informal* an objectionable person; a difficult task.

stinking *adj.* foul-smelling; *informal* unpleasant. ● *adv. informal* extremely: *stinking rich.*

stint *v.* restrict to a small allowance; be thrifty or mean. ● *n.* an allotted period of work.

stipend (sty-pend) *n.* a salary.

stipendiary *adj.* receiving a stipend.

stipple *v.* (in painting, engraving, etc.) mark with numerous small dots.

stipulate *v.* demand or insist (on) as part of an agreement. □ **stipulation** *n.*

stir *v.* (**stirred, stirring**) **1** mix (a substance) by moving a spoon round in it. **2** move, begin to move; rouse, stimulate. ● *n.* **1** a slight movement. **2** a commotion. **3** an act of stirring.

stirrup *n.* a support for a rider's foot, hanging from the saddle.

stitch *n.* **1** a single movement of a thread in and out of fabric in sewing, or of a needle in knitting or crochet; the loop made in this way; a method of making a stitch. **2** a sudden pain in the side. ● *v.* sew; join or close with stitches. □ **in stitches** *informal* laughing uncontrollably.

stoat *n.* a weasel-like animal.

stock *n.* **1** goods kept in a shop etc. for sale; a supply of something. **2** livestock. **3** a business company's capital; a portion of this held by an investor. **4** reputation, status. **5** liquid made by stewing bones etc. **6** ancestry. **7** a plant into which a graft is inserted. **8** the handle of a rifle. **9** a cravat. **10** (**stocks**) a wooden frame with holes in which people had their feet locked as a punishment; a framework on which a ship rests during construction. ● *adj.* stocked and regularly available; predictable, said or made regularly and without thought. ● *v.* keep in stock; provide with a supply.

stockade *n.* a protective fence.

stockbroker *n.* a person who buys and sells shares for clients.

stock car *n.* a car used in races where deliberate bumping is allowed.

stock exchange *n.* the stock market.

stocking *n.* a close-fitting covering for the foot and leg.

stock-in-trade *n.* the commodity etc. used or traded in by a business; a characteristic quality.

stockist *n.* a firm that stocks certain goods.

stock market *n.* an institution for buying and selling stocks and shares; the transactions of this.

stockpile *n.* & *v.* (accumulate) a stock of goods etc. to hold in reserve.

stock-still *adj.* motionless.

stocktaking *n.* making an inventory of stock.

stocky *adj.* (**stockier, stockiest**) short and solidly built. □ **stockily** *adv.*, **stockiness** *n.*

stodge *n. informal* stodgy food.

stodgy *adj.* (**stodgier, stodgiest**) **1** (of food) heavy and filling. **2** dull.

stoic (stoh-ik) *n.* a stoical person.

stoical *adj.* calm and uncomplaining. □ **stoically** *adv.*, **stoicism** *n.*

stoke *v.* tend and put fuel on (a fire etc.). □ **stoker** *n.*

stole[1] *n.* a woman's wide scarf-like garment.

stole[2], **stolen** past, p.p. of **steal**.

stolid *adj.* not excitable. □ **stolidity** *n.*, **stolidly** *adv.*

stomach *n.* the internal organ in which the first part of digestion occurs; the abdomen; appetite. ● *v.* endure, tolerate.

stomp *v.* tread heavily.

stone *n.* **1** a piece of rock; stones or rock as a substance or material. **2** a gem. **3** a hard substance formed in the bladder or kidney etc. **4** the hard case round the kernel of certain fruits. **5** (*pl.* **stone**) a unit of weight, 14 lb. ● *adj.* made of stone. ● *v.* **1** pelt with stones. **2** remove stones from (fruit).

Stone Age *n.* a prehistoric period when weapons and tools were made of stone.

stoneground *adj.* (of flour) ground with millstones.

stonemason *n.* a person who carves or builds in stone.

stonewall *v.* obstruct (a process) by giving evasive replies.

stonewashed *adj.* washed with abrasives to give a worn faded look.

stony *adj.* (**stonier, stoniest**) **1** full of stones. **2** hard, unfeeling; unresponsive. □ **stonily** *adv.*

stood past & p.p. of **stand**.

stooge *n.* a comedian's assistant; *derog.* a person working for and controlled by others.

stool *n.* **1** a movable seat without arms or raised back. **2** (**stools**) faeces.

stool pigeon *n.* a person acting as a decoy, esp. to trap a criminal; an informer.

stoop *v.* bend forwards and down; condescend; lower oneself morally. ● *n.* a stooping posture.

stop *v.* (**stopped, stopping**) **1** come or bring to an end; cease doing something; (cause to) cease moving. **2** prevent; prevent from doing something. **3** block, close. ● *n.* **1** a cessation from movement or activity; a place where a train or bus etc. stops regularly; something that stops or regulates motion. **2** a row of organ pipes providing tones of one quality; the knob etc. controlling these.

stopcock *n.* a valve regulating the flow in a pipe etc.

stopgap *n.* a temporary substitute.

stopover *n.* an overnight break in a journey.

stoppage *n.* stopping; an obstruction.

stopper *n.* a plug for closing a bottle etc.

stop press *n. Brit.* late news inserted in a newspaper after printing has begun.

stopwatch *n.* a watch that can be started and stopped, used for timing races etc.

storage *n.* storing; a space for this.

storage heater *n.* an electric radiator accumulating heat in off-peak periods.

store *n.* **1** a supply of something available for use; a storehouse. **2** a large shop. ● *v.* collect and keep for future use. □ **in store 1** kept in a safe place while not in use. **2** coming in the future. **set store by** value greatly.

storehouse *n.* a place where things are stored.

storey *n.* (*pl.* **storeys** or **stories**) each horizontal section of a building. □ **storeyed** *adj.*

stork *n.* a large bird with a long bill.

storm *n.* a disturbance of the atmosphere with strong winds and usu. rain or snow; a heavy discharge of missiles; a violent outburst of feeling. ● *v.* **1** move angrily and violently; be angry. **2** suddenly attack and capture. □ **stormy** *adj.*

story *n.* (*pl.* **-ies**) an account of an incident (true or invented).

stout *adj.* **1** fat; thick and strong. **2** brave and determined. ● *n.* a strong dark beer. □ **stoutly** *adv.*, **stoutness** *n.*

stove[1] past & p.p. of **stave**.

stove[2] *n.* an apparatus for cooking or heating, burning fuel or using electricity.

stow *v.* place (something) somewhere for storage. □ **stow away** conceal oneself as a stowaway.

stowaway *n.* a person who hides on a ship or aircraft so as to travel free of charge.

straddle *v.* sit or stand with one leg on each side of (something); extend across; place (one's legs) wide apart.

strafe *v.* attack with gunfire from the air.

straggle *v.* grow or spread untidily; wander separately; lag behind others. □ **straggler** *n.*, **straggly** *adj.*

straight *adj.* **1** extending or moving in one direction, not curved or bent; level, even; tidy, ordered. **2** honest, frank, not evasive. **3** in continuous succession: *his fourth straight win*. **4** not modified, without additions. **5** *informal* heterosexual. ● *adv.* **1** in a straight line, directly; without delay. **2** clearly, without confusion. **3** frankly. ● *n.* the straight part of something, esp. of a racecourse. □ **go straight** live honestly after being a criminal. **straight away** without delay. **straight off** *informal* without hesitation. □ **straightness** *n.*

straighten *v.* make or become straight.

straight face *n.* a serious expression.

straight fight *n.* a contest between only two opponents.

straightforward *adj.* **1** simple, uncomplicated. **2** frank. □ **straightforwardly** *adv.*

straightjacket var. of **straitjacket**.

strain *v.* **1** make taut; injure by excessive stretching or over-exertion; make an intense effort (with). **2** sieve to separate solids from liquid. ● *n.* **1** a force stretching something; pressure, an excessive demand on strength etc.; an injury from straining. **2** a variety or breed of animal etc. **3** a tendency in someone's character. **4** the sound of music. □ **strainer** *n.*

strained *adj.* (of manner etc.) tense, not natural or relaxed.

strait *n.* **1** (also **straits**) a narrow stretch of water connecting two seas. **2** (**straits**) a difficult state of affairs.

straitened *adj.* (of conditions) poverty-stricken.

straitjacket *n.* (also **straightjacket**) a strong garment put round a violent person to restrain his or her arms. ● *v.* (**-jacketed, -jacketing**) restrict severely.

strait-laced *adj.* very prim and proper.

strand *n.* **1** a single thread, esp. one woven or plaited with others; one element in a complex whole. **2** a shore. ● *v.* run aground; leave in difficulties.

strange *adj.* **1** unusual, odd. **2** not known or met before. □ **strangely** *adv.*, **strangeness** *n.*

stranger *n.* a person one does not know; one who does not live in or know a place.

strangle *v.* kill by squeezing the throat; suppress, restrict the growth of. □ **strangler** *n.*

stranglehold *n.* a strangling grip; complete control.

strangulation *n.* **1** strangling. **2** the cutting off of blood supply to part of the body.

strap *n.* a strip of leather or other flexible material for holding things together or in place, or supporting something. ● *v.* (**strapped, strapping**) secure or support with strap(s). □ **strapped for** *informal* short of.

straphanger *n.* *informal* a standing passenger in a bus or train.

strapping *adj.* tall and robust.

strata pl. of **stratum**.

stratagem *n.* a cunning plan or scheme; a trick.

strategic *adj.* **1** of strategy. **2** (of weapons) directed against an enemy's territory rather than used in battle. □ **strategically** *adv.*

strategist *n.* an expert in strategy.

strategy *n.* (*pl.* **-ies**) the planning and directing of the whole operation of a campaign or war; a plan for achieving a major goal.

stratify *v.* (**stratified, stratifying**) arrange in strata; classify. □ **stratification** *n.*

stratosphere *n.* a layer of the atmosphere about 10–60 km above the earth's surface.

stratum *n.* (*pl.* **strata**) one of a series of layers or levels.

straw *n.* **1** dry cut stalks of corn etc.; a single piece of this. **2** a narrow tube for sucking up liquid to drink.

strawberry *n.* (*pl.* **-ies**) a soft edible red fruit with seeds on the surface.

strawberry mark *n.* a red birthmark.

straw poll *n.* an unofficial poll as a test of general feeling.

stray *v.* move from one's proper place; move idly or aimlessly; deviate from a subject. ● *adj.* having strayed; occurring or appearing by chance. ● *n.* a stray domestic animal.

streak *n.* **1** a thin line or band of a colour or substance different from its surroundings; an element in someone's character. **2** a continuous period of luck etc. ● *v.* **1** mark with streaks. **2** move very rapidly; *informal* run naked in a public place. □ **streaker** *n.*, **streaky** *adj.*

stream *n.* **1** a small river; a flow of liquid, things, or people; the direction of this. **2** a group into which schoolchildren of the same level of ability are placed. ● *v.* **1** flow; move in a particular direction; float in the wind. **2** run with liquid. **3** arrange (schoolchildren) in streams. □ **on stream** in active operation or production.

streamer *n.* a long narrow strip of material used for decoration.

streamline *v.* make (something) with a smooth shape offering little resistance to movement through water or air; make more efficient by simplifying.

street *n.* a public road lined with buildings.

streetcar *n. Amer.* a tram.

street cred *n. informal* (in full **street credibility**) a personal image of being fashionable and successful in city life.

streetwise *adj. informal* knowing how to survive in modern city life.

strength *n.* **1** being strong; the degree to which someone or something is strong or intense. **2** a good or advantageous quality. **3** the total number of people making up a group. □ **on the strength of** relying on as a basis or support.

strengthen *v.* make or become stronger.

strenuous *adj.* making or requiring great effort. □ **strenuously** *adv.*

streptococcus (strep-tŏ-**kok**-ŭs) *n.* (*pl.* **streptococci**) a bacterium causing serious infections.

stress *n.* **1** pressure; mental or emotional strain. **2** emphasis; extra force given to a syllable or note. ● *v.* **1** emphasize. **2** subject to pressure. □ **stressed** *adj.*, **stressful** *adj.*

stretch *v.* **1** pull out tightly or to a greater extent; become longer or wider without breaking; extend one's body or a limb. **2** extend over an area or period. **3** make demands on (a resource, ability, etc.). **4** exaggerate. ● *n.* **1** an act of stretching. **2** the ability to be stretched. **3** a continuous area or period. ● *adj.* able to be stretched. □ **at a stretch 1** continuously. **2** only just, in extreme cases. **stretch a point** agree to something not normally allowed. □ **stretchy** *adj.*

stretcher *n.* a framework for carrying a sick or injured person in a lying position.

strew *v.* (**strewed, strewn** or **strewed, strewing**) scatter over a surface; cover with scattered things.

striation *n.* each of a series of lines or grooves.

stricken *adj.* afflicted by an illness, shock, or grief.

strict *adj.* **1** requiring obedience to rules; severe in enforcing rules. **2** exact; total, without exception. □ **strictly** *adv.*, **strictness** *n.*

stricture *n.* **1** severe criticism. **2** a restriction; constriction of a duct in the body.

stride *v.* (**strode, stridden, striding**) walk with long steps. ● *n.* a single long step; a manner of striding; (**strides**) progress.

strident *adj.* loud and harsh. □ **stridency** *n.*, **stridently** *adv.*

strife *n.* quarrelling, conflict.

strike *v.* (**struck, striking**) **1** hit; knock; come into contact with. **2** attack suddenly, occur suddenly; afflict; come suddenly into the mind of. **3** stop work in protest. **4** ignite (a match) by friction. **5** indicate (the hour) by chiming. **6** agree on (a bargain). **7** find (oil, gold, etc.). **8** assume (a pose). **9** take down (a tent or flag). ● *n.* **1** a refusal by employees to work. **2** a sudden attack. □ **strike home** deal an effective blow. **strike off** or **out** cross out. **strike up** begin playing or singing; start (a friendship etc.) casually.

strikebound *adj.* immobilized by a workers' strike.

striker *n.* **1** a worker on strike. **2** a football player whose main function is to try to score goals.

striking *adj.* sure to be noticed; impressive. □ **strikingly** *adv.*

strimmer *n. trademark* a long-handled machine for cutting rough grass etc.

string *n.* **1** a narrow cord; a stretched piece of catgut or wire etc. in a musical instrument, vibrated to produce tones; (**strings**) stringed instruments. **2** a set of objects strung to gether; a series. **3** (**strings**) *informal* conditions or requirements. ● *v.* (**strung, stringing**) **1** hang up; thread on a string. **2** fit strings on (an instrument etc.) □ **pull strings** *informal* use one's influence. **string along** *informal* **1** accompany someone. **2** mislead. **string out** spread out on a line. **string up** hang up on strings; kill by hanging.

stringent *adj.* strict, with firm restrictions. □ **stringency** *n.*, **stringently** *adv.*

stringy *adj.* (**stringier, stringiest**) like string; tall and thin; (of food) containing tough fibres.

strip *v.* (**stripped, stripping**) remove clothes or covers from; pull off; deprive of property, rank, etc. ● *n.* **1** an act of undressing. **2** a long narrow piece or area.

strip cartoon *n.* = **comic strip**.

stripe *n.* a long narrow band on a surface, differing in colour or texture from its surroundings; a chevron on a sleeve, indicating rank. □ **striped** *adj.*, **stripy** *adj.*

strip light *n.* a tubular fluorescent lamp.

stripling *n.* a youth.

stripper *n.* **1** a device for stripping something. **2** a striptease performer.

striptease *n.* an entertainment in which a performer gradually undresses.

strive *v.* (**strove, striven, striving**) **1** make great efforts. **2** struggle; compete.

stroboscope *n.* (also *informal* **strobe**) an apparatus for producing a rapidly flashing light. □ **stroboscopic** *adj.*

strode past of **stride**.

stroganoff *n.* strips of meat etc. cooked in a sour cream sauce.

stroke *v.* pass the hand gently along the surface of. ● *n.* **1** an act of striking something; the sound of a striking clock. **2** an act of stroking. **3** a mark made by a movement of a pen, paintbrush, etc. **4** a movement, a beat; a style of swimming. **5** a loss of consciousness due to an interruption in the supply of blood to the brain. □ **at a stroke** by a single action.

stroll *v.* walk in a leisurely way. ● *n.* a leisurely walk.

stroller *n. Amer.* a pushchair.

strong *adj.* **1** able to move heavy weights or resist great pressure; having skills, qualities, or numbers assisting survival or victory; (of an argument or position) valid; able to bear distress. **2** intense; concentrated; containing much alcohol. **3** having a specified number of members: *fifty strong.* □ **going strong** *informal* continuing to be healthy or successful. **strong language** swearing. **strong on** good at. □ **strongly** *adv.*

stronghold *n.* a fortified place; the centre of support for a cause.

strong-minded *adj.* determined.

strongroom *n.* a room designed for safe storage of valuables.

strontium *n.* a silver-white metallic element (symbol Sr).

strontium 90 *n.* a radioactive isotope of strontium.

strop *n.* a leather strip on which a razor is sharpened.

stroppy *adj.* (**stroppier, stroppiest**) *informal* bad-tempered, awkward.

strove past of **strive**.

struck past & p.p. of **strike**. □ **struck on** *informal* fond of, attracted to.

structure *n.* the way a thing is constructed or organized; a thing's supporting framework or essential parts; a constructed thing, a complex whole. □ **structural** *adj.*, **structurally** *adv.*

strudel *n.* flaky pastry filled with apple etc.

struggle *v.* move violently to get free; make one's way or achieve something with difficulty; engage in conflict. ● *n.* a spell of struggling; a vigorous effort; a hard contest.

strum *v.* (**strummed, strumming**) play on (a stringed or keyboard instrument), esp. unskilfully or monotonously. ● *n.* a sound made by strumming.

strumpet *n. archaic* a prostitute or promiscuous woman.

strung past & p.p. of **string**.

strut *n.* **1** a bar of wood or metal supporting something. **2** a strutting walk. ● *v.* (**strutted, strutting**) walk stiffly and arrogantly.

strychnine (**strik**-neen) *n.* a bitter highly poisonous substance.

stub *n.* **1** a short stump. **2** a counterfoil of a cheque or receipt etc. ● *v.* (**stubbed, stubbing**) **1** strike (one's toe) against a hard object. **2** extinguish (a cigarette) by pressure.

stubble *n.* the lower ends of cornstalks left in the ground after harvest; short stiff hair or bristles growing after shaving. □ **stubbly** *adj.*

stubborn *adj.* obstinate, unyielding. □ **stubbornly** *adv.*, **stubbornness** *n.*

stubby *adj.* (**stubbier, stubbiest**) short and thick. □ **stubbiness** *n.*

stucco *n.* plaster used for coating walls or moulding into decorations. □ **stuccoed** *adj.*

stuck past & p.p. of **stick**. ● unable to move or make progress.

stuck-up *adj. informal* conceited, arrogantly aloof.

stud *n.* **1** a projecting nail-head or similar knob on a surface; a device for fastening e.g. a detachable shirt-collar. **2** an establishment where horses etc. are kept for breeding; these animals. ● *v.* (**studded, studding**) cover with studs or other small objects.

student *n.* a person who is studying at a college or university.

studied *adj.* achieved by deliberate effort, not natural.

studio *n.* (*pl.* **studios**) the workroom of a painter, photographer, etc.; premises where cinema films are made; a room from which broadcasts are transmitted or where recordings are made.

studio flat *n.* a one-room flat with a kitchen and bathroom.

studious *adj.* spending much time in study; deliberate and careful. □ **studiously** *adv.*, **studiousness** *n.*

study *n.* (*pl.* **-ies**) **1** effort and time spent in learning; a subject studied; a book or article on a topic. **2** a room for reading and writing. **3** a musical composition designed to develop a player's skill; a preliminary drawing. **4** an embodiment of a quality. ● *v.* (**studied, studying**) give one's attention to acquiring knowledge of (a subject); examine attentively.

stuff *n.* **1** *informal* matter, things; belongings. **2** the constituents or material for something. ● *v.* fill tightly; force into a confined space; fill the skin of (a dead animal) to make it lifelike. □ **stuff oneself** *informal* eat greedily.

stuffing *n.* padding used to fill something; a savoury mixture put inside poultry, vegetables, etc. before cooking.

stuffy *adj.* (**stuffier, stuffiest**) **1** lacking fresh air or ventilation. **2** narrow-minded, old-fashioned. □ **stuffily** *adv.*, **stuffiness** *n.*

stultify *v.* (**stultified, stultifying**) cause to lose enthusiasm and alertness. □ **stultification** *n.*

stumble *v.* trip and lose one's balance; walk with frequent stumbles; make mistakes in speaking etc. ● *n.* an act of stumbling. □ **stumble across** encounter accidentally.

stumbling block *n.* an obstacle, a difficulty.

stump *n.* **1** the base of a tree left in the ground when the rest has gone; a similar remnant of something cut, broken, or worn down. **2** one of the uprights of a wicket in cricket. ● *v.* **1** baffle, be too difficult for. **2** walk stiffly or noisily. □ **stump up** *informal* pay over (money required).

stumpy *adj.* (**stumpier, stumpiest**) short and thick. □ **stumpiness** *n.*

stun *v.* (**stunned, stunning**) knock unconscious; astonish.

stung past & p.p. of **sting**.

stunk past & p.p. of **stink**.

stunning *adj. informal* very attractive. □ **stunningly** *adv.*

stunt *n.* an action displaying skill and daring; something done to attract attention. ● *v.* hinder the growth or development of.

stupefy *v.* (**stupefied, stupefying**) make unable to think or feel; astound. □ **stupefaction** *n.*

stupendous *adj.* amazingly large or good. □ **stupendously** *adv.*

stupid *adj.* not clever; slow at learning or understanding; unable to think clearly. □ **stupidity** *n.*, **stupidly** *adv.*

stupor *n.* a dazed condition.

sturdy *adj.* (**sturdier, sturdiest**) strongly built, hardy, vigorous. □ **sturdily** *adv.*, **sturdiness** *n.*

sturgeon *n.* a large sharklike fish.

stutter *v.* stammer, esp. repeating consonants. ● *n.* a stammer.

sty *n.* (*pl.* **sties**) **1** a pigsty. **2** (also **stye**) an inflamed swelling on the edge of the eyelid.

style *n.* **1** a manner of writing, speaking, or doing something; a design, an appearance. **2** elegance. ● *v.* design, shape, or arrange, esp. fashionably. □ **in style** elegantly, luxuriously.

stylish *adj.* fashionable, elegant. □ **stylishly** *adv.*, **stylishness** *n.*

stylist *n.* **1** a fashion designer; a hairdresser. **2** a person who writes or performs with good style.

stylistic *adj.* of literary or artistic style. □ **stylistically** *adv.*

stylized *adj.* (also **-ised**) represented non-realistically.

stylus *n.* (*pl.* **styluses** or **styli**) a needle-like device for cutting or following a groove in a record.

stymie *v.* (**stymied, stymieing** or **stymying**) *informal* obstruct, thwart.

styptic (**stip**-tik) *adj.* checking bleeding by causing blood vessels to contract.

styrene (**stI**-reen) *n.* a liquid hydrocarbon used in plastics.

suave (swahv) *adj.* charming, confident, and elegant. □ **suavely** *adv.*, **suavity** *n.*

sub *n. informal* **1** a submarine. **2** a subscription. **3** a substitute. **4** a sub-editor.

sub- *pref.* under; subordinate.

subaltern (**sub**-ăl-tĕn) *n.* an army officer below the rank of captain.

sub-aqua *adj.* of underwater swimming.

subatomic *adj.* smaller than an atom; occurring in an atom.

subcommittee *n.* a committee formed from some members of a main committee.

subconscious *adj.* & *n.* (of) our own mental activities of which we are not aware. □ **subconsciously** *adv.*

subcontinent *n.* a large land mass forming part of a continent.

subcontract *v.* assign (work forming part of a contract) to someone outside one's company; undertake work in this way. □ **subcontractor** *n.*

subculture *n.* a culture within a larger one.

subcutaneous (sub-kyoo-**tay**-ni-ŭs) *adj.* under the skin.

subdivide *v.* divide (a part) into smaller parts. □ **subdivision** *n.*

subdue *v.* bring under control; make quieter or less intense.

subeditor *n.* a person who prepares newspaper etc. text for printing.

subhuman *adj.* less than human; not fully human.

subject *n.* (**sub**-jekt) **1** a person or thing being discussed or treated; a branch of knowledge taught in schools, universities, etc. **2** a citizen, a person ruled by a government etc. **3** *Grammar* the words in a sentence naming the person or thing performing the action of the verb. ● *adj.* (**sub**-jekt) not independent, ruled by another. ● *v.* (sub-**jekt**) cause to undergo an experience. □ **subject to** (**sub**-jekt) **1** liable to experience. **2** depending on. **3** under the authority of. □ **subjection** *n.*

subjective *adj.* **1** dependent on personal taste or views etc. **2** *Grammar* of the form of a word used when it is the subject of a sentence. □ **subjectively** *adv.*

subject-matter *n.* the topic treated in a book or speech etc.

sub judice (sub **joo**-di-si) *adj.* under judicial consideration, not yet decided.

subjugate *v.* bring under control or rule, esp. by conquest. □ **subjugation** *n.*

subjunctive *n. Grammar* of the form of a verb expressing what is imagined, wished, or possible; e.g. *were* in *if I were you.*

sublet *v.* (**sublet, subletting**) let (rooms etc. that one holds by lease) to a tenant.

sublimate *v.* divert the energy of (an emotion or impulse) into a culturally higher activity. □ **sublimation** *n.*

sublime *adj.* of the highest excellence or beauty. □ **sublimely** *adv.*

subliminal *adj.* below the level of conscious awareness.

sub-machine gun *n.* a handheld light-weight machine-gun.

submarine *adj.* under the surface of the sea. ● *n.* a vessel that can operate under water.

submerge *v.* go or cause to be under water; cover, obscure. □ **submersion** *n.*

submersible *adj.* designed to operate while submerged. ● *n.* a submersible craft.

submission *n.* **1** yielding, obeying. **2** presenting for consideration; a proposal etc. presented.

submissive *adj.* meek, obedient. □ **submissively** *adv.*, **submissiveness** *n.*

submit *v.* (**submitted, submitting**) **1** yield to authority or power; subject to a particular treatment. **2** present for consideration.

subordinate *adj.* (sub-**or**-di-năt) of lesser importance or rank; working under another's authority. ● *n.* (sub-**or**-di-năt) a subordinate person. ● *v.* (sub-**or**-di-nayt) treat as less important than something else. □ **subordination** *n.*

suborn *v.* induce by bribery to commit perjury or another unlawful act. □ **subornation** *n.*

subpoena (sŭ-pee-nă) *n.* a writ commanding a person to appear in a law court. ● *v.* (**subpoenaed, subpoenaing**) summon with a subpoena.

subscribe *v.* **1** pay in advance to receive a publication etc. regularly; contribute to a fund. **2** sign. □ **subscribe to** agree with, believe (a theory etc.). □ **subscriber** *n.*

subscription *n.* a sum of money contributed; a fee for membership etc.; a process of subscribing.

subsequent *adj.* occurring after something. □ **subsequently** *adv.*

subservient *adj.* **1** less important. **2** completely obedient. □ **subservience** *n.*, **subserviently** *adv.*

subset *n.* a set of which all the elements are contained in another set.

subside *v.* sink to a lower or normal level; become less intense. □ **subsidence** *n.*

subsidiarity *n.* the principle that a central authority should perform only those functions not performed more efficiently at local level.

subsidiary *adj.* of secondary importance; (of a business company) controlled by another. ● *n.* (*pl.* **-ies**) a subsidiary company.

subsidize *v.* (also **-ise**) pay a subsidy to or for.

subsidy *n.* (*pl.* **-ies**) money granted to support an industry and thus keep prices down; money granted to other enterprises.

subsist *v.* keep oneself alive, exist. □ **subsistence** *n.*

subsoil *n.* the soil lying immediately below the surface layer.

subsonic *adj.* of or flying at speeds less than that of sound.

substance *n.* **1** the matter of which something consists; a particular kind of matter. **2** an intoxicating or stimulating drug. **3** reality; importance. **4** something's essence or basic meaning.

substantial *adj.* **1** solid, real; large, strong; important. **2** concerning the essence of somethihg. **3** wealthy. □ **substantially** *adv.*

substantiate *v.* support with evidence. □ **substantiation** *n.*

substantive *adj.* genuine; existing in its own right.

substitute *n.* a person or thing that acts or serves in place of another. ● *v.* use or serve as a substitute. □ **substitution** *n.*

subsume *v.* bring or include under a particular classification.

subtenant *n.* a person to whom a room etc. is sublet.

subterfuge (sub-tĕ-fyooj) *n.* deceit used to achieve an aim.

subterranean *adj.* underground.

subtext *n.* an underlying theme.

subtitle *n.* **1** a caption displayed on a cinema or television screen to translate dialogue. **2** a subordinate title. ● *v.* provide with subtitle(s).

subtle (sutt-ĕl) *adj.* (**subtler, subtlest**) so slight or delicate as to be hard to analyse or identify; making fine distinctions; ingenious. □ **subtlety** *n.*, **subtly** *adv.*

subtotal *n.* the total of part of a group of figures.

subtract *v.* remove (a part or quantity or number) from a greater one. □ **subtraction** *n.*

subtropical *adj.* of regions bordering on the tropics.

suburb *n.* a residential area outside the central part of a town. □ **suburban** *adj.*, **suburbanite** *n.*

suburbia *n.* suburbs and their inhabitants.

subvention *n.* a subsidy.

subvert *v.* undermine the authority of, esp. by weakening people's trust. □ **subversion** *n.*, **subversive** *adj.*

subway *n.* a tunnel under a road, used by pedestrians; *Amer.* an underground railway.

succeed *v.* **1** achieve one's aim or wish. **2** take the place previously filled by; come next in order.

success *n.* the attainment of one's aims, or of wealth, fame, or position; a successful person or thing.

successful *adj.* accomplishing an aim; achieving wealth or popularity. □ **successfully** *adv.*

succession *n.* a series of people or things sharing a characteristic or position and following one another; succeeding to a throne or other position. □ **in succession** one after another.

successive *adj.* following in succession. □ **successively** *adv.*

successor *n.* a person who succeeds another.

succinct (suk-**sinkt**) *adj.* concise and clear. □ **succinctly** *adv.*

succour *v.* & *n.* (*Amer.* **succor**) help.

succulent *adj.* juicy; (of plants) having thick fleshy leaves. ● *n.* a succulent plant. □ **succulence** *n.*

succumb *v.* give way to something overpowering.

such *adj.* **1** of the type previously mentioned or about to be mentioned; similar. **2** to so high a degree. □ **as such** in the precise sense. **such as** for example. **such that** with the result that.

such-and-such *adj.* particular but not needing to be specified.

suchlike *adj.* of the same kind.

suck *v.* draw (liquid or air) into the mouth by contracting the lips to create a vacuum; draw liquid from in this way; hold in the mouth and roll with the tongue; draw in a particular direction. ● *n.* an act of sucking. □ **suck up to** *informal* behave in a servile way to (someone) to gain advantage.

sucker *n.* **1** an organ or device that can adhere to a surface by suction. **2** *informal* a person who is easily deceived. □ **a sucker for** *informal* very fond of or susceptible to.

suckle *v.* feed at the breast.

suckling *n.* an unweaned child or animal.

sucrose *n.* sugar.

suction *n.* sucking; the production of a partial vacuum so that external atmospheric pressure forces fluid etc. into the vacant space or causes adhesion.

sudden *adj.* happening or done quickly or without warning. □ **all of a sudden** suddenly. □ **suddenly** *adv.*, **suddenness** *n.*

sudorific (soo-dŏ-**rif**-ik) *adj.* causing sweating.

suds *n.pl.* soapsuds.

sue *v.* (**sued, suing**) take legal proceedings against.

suede (swayd) *n.* leather with a velvety nap on one side.

suet *n.* hard white fat from round an animal's kidneys, used in cooking.

suffer *v.* undergo (something unpleasant or harmful); experience pain or distress; tolerate. □ **suffering** *n.*

sufferance *n.* □ **on sufferance** tolerated but only grudgingly.

suffice *v.* be enough (for).

sufficient *adj.* enough. □ **sufficiency** *n.*, **sufficiently** *adv.*

suffix *n.* letters added at the end of a word to make another word.

suffocate *v.* kill by stopping the breathing; (cause to) have difficulty breathing. □ **suffocation** *n.*

suffrage *n.* the right to vote in political elections.

suffragette *n. hist.* a woman who campaigned for the right to vote.

suffuse *v.* spread throughout or over. □ **suffusion** *n.*

sugar *n.* a sweet crystalline substance obtained from the juices of various plants. ● *v.* sweeten; make more acceptable. ▫ **sugary** *adj.*

sugar beet *n.* white beet from which sugar is obtained.

sugar cane *n.* a tall tropical plant from which sugar is obtained.

sugar soap *n.* an abrasive cleaning compound.

suggest *v.* propose for consideration; imply; cause someone to think of.

suggestible *adj.* easily influenced. ▫ **suggestibility** *n.*

suggestion *n.* **1** suggesting; something suggested. **2** a slight trace.

suggestive *adj.* conveying a suggestion; suggesting something indecent. ▫ **suggestively** *adv.*

suicidal *adj.* likely or wanting to commit suicide; very risky, likely to cause death or ruin. ▫ **suicidally** *adv.*

suicide *n.* the intentional killing of oneself; a person who does this; an act destructive to one's own interests.

sui generis *adj.* unique.

suit *n.* **1** a set of clothes to be worn together, esp. jacket and trousers or skirt. **2** any of the four sets into which a pack of cards is divided. **3** a lawsuit. ● *v.* **1** be convenient for or acceptable to. **2** (of clothes etc.) enhance the appearance of.

suitable *adj.* right for the purpose or occasion. ▫ **suitability** *n.*, **suitably** *adv.*

suitcase *n.* a rectangular case for carrying clothes.

suite (sweet) *n.* **1** a set of rooms or furniture. **2** a group of attendants. **3** a set of musical pieces.

suitor *n.* a man who is courting a woman.

sulfur etc. Amer. sp. of **sulphur** etc.

sulk *v.* be sullen because of resentment or bad temper. ● *n.pl.* (**the sulks**) a fit of sulking. ▫ **sulkily** *adv.*, **sulkiness** *n.*, **sulky** *adj.*

sullen *adj.* bad-tempered; gloomy. ▫ **sullenly** *adv.*, **sullenness** *n.*

sully *v.* (**sullied, sullying**) stain, blemish.

sulphate *n.* (*Amer.* **sulfate**) a salt of sulphuric acid.

sulphide *n.* (*Amer.* **sulfide**) a compound of sulphur and an element or radical.

sulphite *n.* (*Amer.* **sulfite**) a salt of sulphurous acid.

sulphur *n.* (*Amer.* **sulfur**) a pale yellow chemical element (symbol S). ▫ **sulphurous** *adj.*

sulphuric acid *n.* (*Amer.* **sulfuric acid**) a strong corrosive acid.

sultan *n.* a ruler of certain Muslim countries.

sultana *n.* **1** a seedless raisin. **2** a sultan's wife, mother, or daughter.

sultanate *n.* a sultan's territory.

sultry *adj.* (**sultrier, sultriest**) hot and humid; (of someone's appearance) suggesting passion and sensuality. ▫ **sultriness** *n.*

sum *n.* **1** an amount of money; a total. **2** an arithmetical problem. ▫ **sum up** summarize; express an opinion of.

summarize *v.* (also **-ise**) make or be a summary of. ▫ **summarization** *n.*

summary *n.* (*pl.* **-ies**) a brief statement of the main points of something. ● *adj.* **1** brief, without unnecessary detail. **2** without legal formalities. ▫ **summarily** *adv.*

summation *n.* **1** adding up. **2** summarizing.

summer *n.* the warmest season of the year. ▫ **summery** *adj.*

summer time *n.* the time shown by clocks put forward in summer to give longer light evenings.

summit *n.* **1** the top of a mountain; the highest point. **2** a conference between heads of states.

summon *v.* send for; order to appear in a law court; arrange (a meeting); produce (a reaction or quality) with effort.

summons *n.* a command summoning a person; a written order to appear in a law court. ● *v.* serve with a summons.

sumo (soo-moh) *n.* Japanese wrestling.

sump *n.* a reservoir of oil in a petrol engine; a hole or low area into which liquid drains.

sumptuous *adj.* splendid, lavish, costly. ▫ **sumptuously** *adv.*, **sumptuousness** *n.*

Sun. *abbr.* Sunday.

sun *n.* the star around which the earth travels; the light or warmth from this; any fixed star. ● *v.* (**sunned, sunning**) expose to the sun.

sunbathe *v.* lie in the sun, esp. to tan one's skin. ▫ **sunbather** *n.*

sunbeam *n.* a ray of sun.

sunbed *n.* a device with ultraviolet lamps, for acquiring a tan artificially.

sunblock *n.* a cream protecting the skin against sunburn.

sunburn *n.* inflammation of the skin caused by exposure to sun. ● *v.* suffer sunburn. ▫ **sunburnt** *adj.*

sundae (sun-day) *n.* a dish of ice cream and fruit, nuts, syrup, etc.

Sunday *n.* the day after Saturday.

Sunday school *n.* a school for the religious instruction of Christian children, held on Sundays.

sunder *v. poetic* break or tear apart.

sundial *n.* a device that shows the time by means of a shadow cast by the sun on a plate marked with the hours.

sundown *n.* sunset.

sundry *adj.* various. ● *n.pl.* (**sundries**) various small items. ▫ **all and sundry** everyone.

sunflower *n.* a tall plant with large yellow flowers.

sung p.p. of **sing**.

sunk past & p.p. of **sink**.

sunken *adj.* lying below the level of the surrounding surface.

Sunni (suu-ni) *n.* & *adj.* (*pl.* **Sunni** or **Sunnis**) (a member) of a Muslim sect opposed to the Shiites.

sunny *adj.* (**sunnier, sunniest**) **1** full of sunshine. **2** cheerful. ▫ **sunnily** *adv.*

sunrise *n.* the rising of the sun.

sunset *n.* the setting of the sun; the sky full of colour at sunset.

sunshade *n.* a parasol; an awning.

sunshine *n.* direct sunlight.

sunspot *n.* a dark patch observed on the sun's surface.

sunstroke *n.* illness caused by too much exposure to sun.

super *adj. informal* excellent, superb.

superannuation *n.* an employee's pension; retiring someone on a pension.

superb *adj.* of the most impressive or splendid kind. ▫ **superbly** *adv.*

supercharge *v.* increase the power of (an engine) by a device that forces extra air or fuel into it. ▫ **supercharger** *n.*

supercilious *adj.* haughty and superior. ▫ **superciliously** *adv.*, **superciliousness** *n.*

supercomputer *n.* a very powerful computer.

superficial *adj.* of or on the surface; shallow, not profound. ▫ **superficiality** *n.*, **superficially** *adv.*

superfluous *adj.* more than is required. ▫ **superfluity** *n.*, **superfluously** *adv.*

superhighway *n.* an electronic network for the rapid transfer of information.

superhuman *adj.* having or requiring more than ordinary human capacity.

superimpose *v.* place on top of something else.

superintend *v.* oversee. ▫ **superintendence** *n.*

superintendent *n.* **1** a supervisor. **2** a police officer next above inspector.

superior *adj.* **1** of higher rank or quality; greater; thinking oneself better than others, haughty. **2** higher. ● *n.* a person or thing of higher rank or ability or quality. □ **superiority** *n.*

superlative *adj.* **1** of the highest quality. **2** of the grammatical form expressing 'most'. ● *n.* a superlative form of a word. □ **superlatively** *adv.*

supermarket *n.* a large self-service store selling food and household goods.

supernatural *adj.* of or attributed to a power outside the forces of nature. □ **supernaturally** *adv.*

supernova *n.* (*pl.* **supernovas** or **supernovae**) a star that suddenly increases in brightness because of an explosion.

supernumerary *adj.* extra.

superphosphate *n.* a fertilizer containing soluble phosphates.

superpower *n.* an extremely powerful nation.

superscalar *adj.* (of a computer microprocessor) able to execute more than one instruction at one time.

superscript *adj.* written just above and to the right of a word etc.

supersede *v.* take the place of; put or use in place of.

▪ **Usage** The correct spelling is *-sede*, not *-cede*.

supersonic *adj.* of or flying at speeds greater than that of sound. □ **supersonically** *adv.*

superstition *n.* a belief in magical and similar influences; an idea or practice based on this. □ **superstitious** *adj.*

superstore *n.* a large supermarket.

superstructure *n.* a structure that rests on something else; the upper parts of a ship or building.

supervene *v.* occur as an interruption or a change. □ **supervention** *n.*

supervise *v.* direct and inspect (workers etc.). □ **supervision** *n.*, **supervisor** *n.*, **supervisory** *adj.*

supine (soo-pIn) *adj.* **1** lying face upwards. **2** weakly or idly failing to act.

supper *n.* an evening meal, esp. a light or informal one.

supplant *v.* oust and take the place of.

supple *adj.* bending easily. □ **suppleness** *n.*, **supply** *adv.*

supplement *n.* something added as an extra part or to make up for a deficiency. ● *v.* provide or be a supplement to.

supplementary *adj.* serving as a supplement.

suppliant (sup-li-ănt) *n.* & *adj.* (a person) asking humbly for something.

supplicate *v.* ask humbly for something. □ **supplication** *n.*

supply *v.* (**supplied, supplying**) provide; make available to; satisfy (a need). ● *n.* (*pl.* **-ies**) a stock to be used; supplying; (**supplies**) necessary goods provided.

support *v.* **1** bear the weight of. **2** assist financially; encourage, approve of; comfort; suggest the truth of. **3** endure. ● *n.* the act of supporting; a person or thing that supports. □ **supporter** *n.*, **supportive** *adj.*

suppose *v.* assume, think; take as a hypothesis; presuppose. □ **be supposed to** be required to as a duty.

supposed *adj.* thought to exist, often wrongly.

supposedly *adv.* according to what is generally thought or believed.

supposition *n.* the process of supposing; what is supposed.

suppository *n.* (*pl.* **-ies**) a solid medicinal substance placed in the rectum or vagina and left to melt.

suppress *v.* **1** put an end to the activity or existence of. **2** keep from being known. □ **suppression** *n.*, **suppressor** *n.*

suppurate (sup-yuu-rayt) *v.* form pus, fester. □ **suppuration** *n.*

supra- *pref.* above; beyond.

supreme *adj.* highest in authority; greatest, most intense. ◻ **supremacy** *n.*, **supremely** *adv.*

supremo *n.* (*pl.* **supremos**) *informal* a person in overall charge of something; a person very skilled at something.

surcharge *n.* an additional charge. ● *v.* exact a surcharge from (someone).

sure *adj.* **1** confident, feeling no doubts. **2** reliable; certainly true or correct. ● *adv. informal* certainly. ◻ **make sure** act so as to be certain. **sure to** certainly going to do something. ◻ **sureness** *n.*

sure-footed *adj.* never slipping or stumbling.

surely *adv.* **1** used to emphasize a belief that something is true. **2** (as an answer) of course. **3** confidently; securely.

surety *n.* (*pl.* **-ies**) a guarantee; a guarantor of a person's promise.

surf *n.* white foam of breaking waves. ● *v.* ride on a surfboard; move between sites on (the Internet). ◻ **surfer** *n.*

surface *n.* the outside or uppermost layer of something; the top, the upper limit; an outward appearance. ● *adj.* on the surface; (of mail etc.) carried by sea, not air. ● *v.* **1** come to the surface of water etc.; become apparent. **2** put a specified surface on.

surfboard *n.* a narrow board for riding over surf.

surfeit (ser-fit) *n.* an excessive amount, esp. of food or drink. ● *v.* satiate, give more than enough to.

surfing *n.* the sport of riding on a surfboard.

surge *v.* move forward in or like waves; increase in volume or intensity. ● *n.* a surging movement or increase.

surgeon *n.* a doctor qualified to perform surgical operations.

surgery *n.* (*pl.* **-ies**) **1** treatment by cutting or manipulation of affected parts of the body. **2** a place where (or times when) a doctor or dentist or an MP etc. is available for consultation. ◻ **surgical** *adj.*, **surgically** *adv.*

surly *adj.* (**surlier, surliest**) bad-tempered and unfriendly. ◻ **surliness** *n.*

surmise *v.* guess, suppose. ● *n.* a guess, a supposition.

surmount *v.* overcome (a difficulty or obstacle); be on the top of. ◻ **surmountable** *adj.*

surname *n.* a family name.

surpass *v.* outdo; excel.

surplice *n.* a loose white garment worn by clergy and choir members.

surplus *n.* an amount left over after what is needed has been used.

surprise *n.* an emotion aroused by something sudden or unexpected; something causing this. ● *v.* cause to feel surprise; come upon or attack unexpectedly.

surreal *adj.* bizarre; dreamlike.

surrealism *n.* a style of art and literature seeking to express what is in the subconscious mind, characterized by unusual images. ◻ **surrealist** *n.*, **surrealistic** *adj.*

surrender *v.* cease to resist, submit to superior force etc.; hand over, give up. ● *n.* surrendering.

surreptitious *adj.* acting or done stealthily. ◻ **surreptitiously** *adv.*

surrogate (su-rŏ-găt) *n.* a deputy. ◻ **surrogacy** *n.*

surrogate mother *n.* a woman who bears a child on behalf of another.

surround *v.* come, place, or be all round, encircle. ● *n.* a border.

surroundings *n.pl.* things or conditions around a person or place.

surtax *n.* an additional tax.

surveillance (ser-vay-lăns) *n.* close observation.

survey *v.* (ser-vay) look at and take a general view of; examine the condition of (a building); measure and map out. ● *n.* (ser-vay) a general look at or examination of something; a report or map produced by surveying.

surveyor *n.* a person whose job is to survey land or buildings.

survival *n.* surviving; something that has survived from an earlier time.

survive *v.* continue to exist despite difficulty or danger; not be killed by; remain alive after the death of. □ **survivability** *n.*, **survivable** *adj.*, **survivor** *n.*

sus var. of **suss**.

susceptible *adj.* easily affected or influenced. □ **susceptibility** *n.*

sushi (soo-shi) *n.* a Japanese dish of flavoured balls of cold rice usu. garnished with fish.

suspect *v.* (sŭ-**spekt**) **1** feel that something may exist or be true. **2** believe (someone) to be guilty without proof. ● *n.* (**sus**-pekt) a person suspected of a crime etc. ● *adj.* (**sus**-pekt) suspected, open to suspicion.

suspend *v.* **1** hang up; keep from falling or sinking in air or liquid. **2** stop temporarily; deprive temporarily of a position or right; keep (a sentence) from being enforced if no further offence is committed within a specified period.

suspender *n.* an attachment to hold up a sock or stocking by its top; (**suspenders**) *Amer.* braces.

suspense *n.* anxious uncertainty while awaiting an event etc.

suspension *n.* **1** suspending. **2** the means by which a vehicle is supported on its axles.

suspension bridge *n.* a bridge suspended from cables that pass over supports at each end.

suspicion *n.* **1** an unconfirmed belief; a feeling that someone is guilty; distrust. **2** a slight trace.

suspicious *adj.* feeling or causing suspicion. □ **suspiciously** *adv.*

suss *v.* (also **sus**) *informal* realize; discover the true nature of.

sussed *adj.* *informal* well-informed; clever.

sustain *v.* **1** support; give strength to; keep alive or in existence. **2** undergo (injuries etc.). **3** uphold the validity of.

sustainable *adj.* (of development etc.) able to be continued without damage to the environment.

sustenance *n.* food, nourishment.

suture (soo-cher) *n.* surgical stitching of a wound; a stitch or thread used in this. ● *v.* stitch (a wound).

suzerain (soo-zĕ-rayn) *n.* a country or ruler with some authority over a self-governing country; an overlord.

svelte *adj.* slender and graceful.

SW *abbr.* south-west; south-western.

swab *n.* an absorbent pad for cleansing wounds or taking specimens; a specimen of a secretion taken on this; a mop. ● *v.* (**swabbed, swabbing**) cleanse with a swab.

swaddle *v.* swathe in wraps or warm garments.

swag *n.* **1** *informal* loot. **2** a decorative festoon of flowers, drapery, etc.

swagger *v.* walk or behave with aggressive pride. ● *n.* this gait or manner.

Swahili *n.* a Bantu language widely used in East Africa.

swallow *v.* cause or allow to go down one's throat; work the throat muscles in doing this; absorb, engulf; accept, believe; resist expressing. ● *n.* **1** an act of swallowing; an amount swallowed. **2** a small migratory bird with a forked tail.

swam past of **swim**.

swami (swah-mi) *n.* a Hindu male religious teacher.

swamp *n.* a marsh. ● *v.* flood or overwhelm with water; overwhelm with a mass or number of things. □ **swampy** *adj.*

swan *n.* a large usu. white waterbird.

swank *informal* *v.* show off, try to impress others. ● *n.* such behaviour.

swansong *n.* a person's last performance or achievement etc.

swap (also **swop**) ● *v.* (**swapped, swapping**) exchange. ● *n.* an exchange; a thing exchanged.

swarm *n.* a large cluster of people, insects, etc. ● *v.* move in a swarm; be crowded. □ **swarm up** climb by gripping with arms and legs.

swarthy *adj.* (**swarthier, swarthiest**) having a dark complexion. □ **swarthiness** *n.*

swashbuckling *adj.* & *n.* showing flamboyant daring. □ **swashbuckler** *n.*

swastika *n.* a symbol formed by a cross with ends bent at right angles.

swat *v.* (**swatted, swatting**) hit hard with something flat. □ **swatter** *n.*

swatch *n.* a sample of cloth etc.

swath (swawth) *n.* (also **swathe**) a strip cut in one sweep or passage by a scythe or mower.

swathe *v.* wrap with layers of coverings. ● *n.* var. of **swath**.

sway *v.* **1** (cause to) move gently to and fro. **2** control, influence. ● *n.* **1** a swaying movement. **2** influence.

swear *v.* (**swore, sworn, swearing**) **1** state or promise on oath; state emphatically. **2** use a swear word. □ **swear by** *informal* have great confidence in.

swear word *n.* a profane or indecent word used in anger etc.

sweat *n.* moisture given off by the body through the pores; a state of sweating; hard work, laboriousness; a state of anxiety. ● *v.* give off sweat or as sweat; work hard; be very anxious. □ **sweaty** *adj.*

sweatband *n.* a band of material worn to absorb sweat.

sweated labour *n.* work with low pay and bad conditions; workers engaged in this.

sweater *n.* a jumper, a pullover.

sweatshirt *n.* a long-sleeved cotton sweater with a fleecy lining.

sweatshop *n.* a place employing sweated labour.

Swede *n.* a native of Sweden.

swede *n.* a large variety of turnip.

Swedish *adj.* & *n.* (the language) of Sweden.

sweep *v.* (**swept, sweeping**) **1** clean by brushing away dirt; clear away with a broom; drive or push forcefully. **2** move smoothly and swiftly or majestically. **3** extend in a continuous line. ● *n.* **1** an act of sweeping; a sweeping movement or line; a long expanse of land etc. **2** a chimney sweep. **3** a sweepstake. □ **sweep the board** win all the prizes. □ **sweeper** *n.*

sweeping *adj.* comprehensive; making no exceptions.

sweepstake *n.* a form of gambling in which the money staked is divided among the winners.

sweet *adj.* **1** tasting as if containing sugar. **2** pleasant to hear or smell; delightful; kind; charming. ● *n.* a small shaped piece of sweet substance; a sweet dish forming one course of a meal. □ **sweetly** *adv.*, **sweetness** *n.*

sweetbread *n.* an animal's thymus gland or pancreas used as food.

sweetcorn *n.* sweet kernels of maize, eaten as a vegetable.

sweeten *v.* make or become sweet or sweeter.

sweetener *n.* **1** a sweetening substance. **2** *informal* a bribe.

sweetheart *n.* a girlfriend or boyfriend; a term of affection.

sweetmeal *n.* & *adj.* (made of) sweetened wholemeal.

sweet tooth *n.* a liking for sweet food.

swell *v.* (**swelled, swollen** or **swelled, swelling**) make or become larger from pressure within; curve outwards; make or become greater in amount or intensity. ● *n.* **1** a curving shape; a gradual increase. **2** the heaving movement of the sea. **3** *informal, dated* a person of wealth or high social position.

swelling *n.* a swollen place on the body.

swelter *v.* be uncomfortably hot.

swept past & p.p. of **sweep**.

swerve *v.* turn aside from a straight course. ● *n.* a swerving movement or direction.

swift *adj.* quick, rapid. ● *n.* a swiftly flying bird with narrow wings. □ **swiftly** *adv.*, **swiftness** *n.*

swill *v.* **1** wash, rinse; cause (liquid) to swirl in a container. **2** drink greedily. ● *n.* kitchen refuse mixed with water and fed to pigs.

swim *v.* (**swam, swum, swimming**) **1** travel through water by movements of the body. **2** be covered with liquid. **3** seem to be whirling or waving; be dizzy. ● *n.* an act or period of swimming. □ **swimmer** *n.*

swimming bath *n.* a building containing a public swimming pool.

swimmingly *adv.* easily and satisfactorily.

swimming pool *n.* an artificial pool for swimming in.

swindle *v.* cheat, deprive of money etc. fraudulently. ● *n.* a piece of swindling. □ **swindler** *n.*

swine *n.* **1** (as *pl.*) pigs. **2** (*pl.* **swine** or **swines**) *informal* a very unpleasant person or thing.

swing *v.* (**swung, swinging**) **1** (cause to) move to and fro while suspended or on an axis. **2** move by grasping a support and jumping; (cause to) move in a smooth curve. **3** (cause to) change from one mood or opinion to another; influence decisively. ● *n.* **1** a swinging movement; a hanging seat for swinging on. **2** a style of jazz music; its rhythm. **3** a change in opinion etc. □ **in full swing** with activity at its height. □ **swinger** *n.*

swing bridge *n.* a bridge that can be swung aside for boats to pass.

swingeing *adj.* severe; extreme.

swing-wing *n.* an aircraft wing that can be moved to slant backwards.

swipe *informal v.* **1** hit with a swinging blow. **2** snatch, steal. ● *n.* a swinging blow.

swipe card *n.* a plastic card carrying magnetically encoded information which is read when the card is slid through an electronic device.

swirl *v.* whirl, flow with a whirling movement.

swish *v.* (cause to) move with a hissing sound. ● *n.* this sound. ● *adj. informal* smart, fashionable.

Swiss *adj.* & *n.* (a native) of Switzerland.

Swiss roll *n.* a thin flat sponge cake spread with jam etc. and rolled up.

switch *n.* **1** a device operated to turn electric current on or off. **2** a shift in opinion or method etc. **3** a flexible stick or rod, a whip. **4** a tress of false hair. ● *v.* **1** change the direction or position of; change, exchange. **2** turn (an electrical device) on or off.

switchback *n.* a railway used for amusement at a fair etc., with alternate steep ascents and descents; a road with similar slopes.

switchboard *n.* a panel of switches for making telephone connections or operating electric circuits.

swivel *n.* a link or pivot enabling one part to revolve without turning another. ● *v.* (**swivelled, swivelling**; *Amer.* **swiveled**) turn on or as if on a swivel.

swizz *n.* (also **swiz**) *informal* a swindle, a disappointment.

swollen p.p. of **swell**.

swoop *v.* make a sudden downward rush; make a sudden attack. ● *n.* a swooping movement or attack.

swop var. of **swap**.

sword (sord) *n.* a weapon with a long blade and a hilt.

swordfish *n.* (*pl.* **swordfish**) an edible sea fish with a long swordlike upper jaw.

swore past of **swear**.

sworn p.p. of **swear**. *adj.* determined to remain as specified: *sworn enemies.*

swot *informal v.* (**swotted, swotting**) study hard. ● *n.* a person who studies hard.

swum p.p. of **swim**.

swung past & p.p. of **swing**.

sybarite (sib-ă-rIt) *n.* a person who is self-indulgently fond of luxury. ◻ **sybaritic** *adj.*

sycamore *n.* a large tree of the maple family.

sycophant (sik-ŏ-fant) *n.* a person who tries to win favour by flattery. ◻ **sycophantic** *adj.*, **sycophantically** *adv.*

syllable *n.* a unit of sound in a word. ◻ **syllabic** *adj.*

syllabub *n.* a dish of flavoured whipped cream.

syllabus *n.* (*pl.* **syllabuses** or **syllabi**) the subjects to be covered by a course of study.

syllogism (sil-ŏ-jiz-ĕm) *n.* an argument drawing a conclusion from two statements. ◻ **syllogistic** *adj.*

sylph (silf) *n.* a slender girl or woman; a spirit of the air.

sylvan *adj.* (also **silvan**) of woods; wooded; rural.

symbiosis (sim-bI-**oh**-sis) *n.* (*pl.* **symbioses**) a relationship between two organisms living in close, usu. mutually beneficial, association. ◻ **symbiotic** *adj.*

symbol *n.* something representing something else; a written character etc. with a special meaning.

symbolic *adj.* (also **symbolical**) of, using, or used as a symbol. ◻ **symbolically** *adv.*

symbolism *n.* the use of symbols to express things. ◻ **symbolist** *n.*

symbolize *v.* (also **-ise**) be a symbol of; represent by means of a symbol.

symmetry (sim-ĕt-ri) *n.* the state of having parts that correspond in size, shape, and position on either side of a dividing line or round a centre. ◻ **symmetrical** *adj.*, **symmetrically** *adv.*

sympathetic *adj.* feeling or showing sympathy; inspiring sympathy and affection; (of an effect) corresponding to or provoked by a similar action elsewhere. ◻ **sympathetically** *adv.*

sympathize *v.* (also **-ise**) feel or express sympathy. ◻ **sympathizer** *n.*

sympathy *n.* (*pl.* **-ies**) sorrow at someone else's misfortune; understanding between people; support, approval; responding to an event, action, etc., with a similar one.

symphony *n.* (*pl.* **-ies**) a long elaborate musical composition for a full orchestra. ◻ **symphonic** *adj.*

symposium (sim-**poh**-zi-ŭm) *n.* (*pl.* **symposia**) a meeting for discussing a particular subject.

symptom *n.* a sign of the existence of a condition, esp. a disease.

symptomatic *adj.* serving as a symptom.

synagogue *n.* a building for public Jewish worship.

synapse (**sI**-naps) *n.* a junction of two nerve cells.

synchronic *adj.* concerned with something as it exists at a particular time, not with its history.

synchronize *v.* (also **-ise**) (cause to) occur or operate at the same time; cause (clocks etc.) to show the same time. ◻ **synchronization** *n.*

synchronous *adj.* occurring or existing at the same time.

syncopate *v.* change the accents in (music) so that weak beats become strong and vice versa. ◻ **syncopation** *n.*

syndicate *n.* (sin-di-kăt) a group of people or firms combining to achieve a common interest. ● *v.* (**sin**-di-kayt) control or manage by a syndicate; arrange publication in many newspapers etc. simultaneously. ◻ **syndication** *n.*

syndrome *n.* a combination of signs, symptoms, etc. characteristic of a specified condition.

synod (sin-ŏd) *n.* a council of clergy and officials to discuss church policy, teaching, etc.

synonym *n.* a word or phrase meaning the same as another in the same language. ◻ **synonymous** *adj.*

synopsis (sin-**op**-sis) *n.* (*pl.* **synopses**) a summary, a brief general survey.

synovial (sin-**oh**-vi-ăl) *adj.* (of a joint) surrounded by a membrane secreting a thick lubricating fluid.

syntax *n.* the way words are arranged to form phrases and sentences. ◻ **syntactic** *adj.*, **syntactically** *adv.*

synthesis *n.* (*pl.* **syntheses**) **1** combining. **2** the production of chemical compounds by reaction from simpler substances.

synthesize *v.* (also **-ise**) **1** make by chemical synthesis. **2** combine into a coherent whole.

synthesizer *n.* (also **-iser**) an electronic musical instrument able to produce a great variety of sounds.

synthetic *adj.* made by synthesis; not natural or genuine. ● *n.* a synthetic substance or fabric. ◻ **synthetically** *adv.*

syphilis (si-fi-lis) *n.* a venereal disease. ◻ **syphilitic** *adj.*

syringe *n.* a tube with a nozzle and piston, for sucking in and ejecting liquid. ● *v.* wash out or spray with a syringe.

syrup *n.* a thick sweet liquid. ◻ **syrupy** *adj.*

system *n.* **1** a set of connected things that form a whole or work together; the animal body as a whole; a set of rules or practices used together; orderliness. **2** a method of classification, notation, or measurement.

systematic *adj.* methodical. ◻ **systematically** *adv.*

systematize *v.* (also **-ise**) arrange according to a system.

systemic *adj.* of or affecting an entire system.

Tt

T *symb.* tritium. ◻ **to a T** *informal* exactly; in every respect.

Ta *symb.* tantalum.

ta *int. informal* thank you.

tab *n.* a small projecting flap or strip. ◻ **keep tabs on** *informal* keep under observation.

tabard *n.* a short sleeveless tunic-like garment.

tabby *n.* (*pl.* **-ies**) a cat with grey or brown fur and dark stripes.

tabernacle (tab-ĕ-nak-ĕl) *n.* (in the Bible) a light hut, a portable shrine; (in the RC Church) a receptacle for the Eucharist; a meeting place for worship, used by Nonconformists or Mormons.

table *n.* **1** a piece of furniture with a flat top supported on one or more legs. **2** food provided. **3** a list of facts or figures arranged in columns. ● *v.* submit (a motion or report) for discussion.

tableau (tab-loh) *n.* (*pl.* **tableaux**) a silent motionless group arranged to represent a scene.

table d'hôte (tahbl **doht**) *n.* a restaurant meal at a fixed price and with a set menu.

tableland *n.* a plateau of land.

tablespoon *n.* a large spoon for serving food. ◻ **tablespoonful** *n.*

tablet *n.* **1** a slab bearing an inscription etc. **2** a measured amount of a drug compressed into a solid form.

table tennis *n.* a game played with bats and a light hollow ball on a table.

tabloid *n.* a small-sized newspaper, often sensational in style.

taboo *n.* (also **tabu**) a ban or prohibition made by religion or social custom. ● *adj.* prohibited by a taboo.

tabular *adj.* arranged in a table or list.

tabulate *v.* arrange in tabular form. □ **tabulation** *n.*

tachograph (tak-ŏ-grahf) *n.* a device in a vehicle to record speed and travel time.

tachometer (tak-o-mi-tĕ) *n.* an instrument measuring the speed of an engine.

tachycardia (taki-**kah**-diă) *n.* an abnormally rapid heart rate.

tacit *adj.* implied or understood without being put into words. □ **tacitly** *adj.*

taciturn *adj.* saying very little. □ **taciturnity** *n.*

tack *n.* **1** a small broad-headed nail. **2** a long stitch as a temporary fastening. **3** a change of course in sailing; an approach to a problem. **4** riding saddles, bridles, etc. ● *v.* **1** nail with tacks. **2** stitch with tacks. **3** change course by turning a boat into the wind; do this repeatedly. □ **tack on** add as an extra item.

tackle *n.* **1** a set of ropes and pulleys for lifting etc. **2** equipment for a task or sport. **3** an act of tackling in football etc. ● *v.* **1** try to deal with or overcome (an opponent or problem). **2** intercept (an opponent who has the ball in football etc.).

tacky *adj.* (**tackier, tackiest**) **1** (of paint etc.) sticky, not quite dry. **2** *informal* tasteless, vulgar. □ **tackiness** *n.*

taco (ta-koh, **tah**-koh) *n.* (*pl.* **tacos**) a folded tortilla with a savoury filling.

tact *n.* skill in avoiding offence or in winning goodwill. □ **tactful** *adj.*, **tactfully** *adv.*, **tactless** *adj.*, **tactlessly** *adv.*

tactic *n.* an action to achieve a particular end; (**tactics**) the organization of forces in battle and of operations; steps towards an overall goal.

tactical *adj.* of tactics; (of weapons) for use in a battle or at close quarters. □ **tactically** *adv.*

tactical voting *n.* voting for the candidate most likely to defeat the leading candidate.

tactician *n.* an expert in tactics.

tactile *adj.* of or using the sense of touch. □ **tactility** *n.*

tadpole *n.* the larva of a frog or toad etc. at the stage when it has gills and a tail.

taffeta *n.* a shiny silklike fabric.

tag *n.* **1** a label; an electronic device attached to someone or something so that they can be monitored. **2** a metal point on a shoelace etc. **3** a much-used phrase or quotation. ● *v.* (**tagged, tagging**) attach a label or electronic tag to. □ **tag along** follow without being invited. **tag on** add at the end.

tagliatelle *n.* pasta in ribbon-shaped strips.

t'ai chi (ty **chee**) *n.* a Chinese martial art and system of exercises.

tail *n.* **1** an animal's hindmost part, esp. when extending beyond its body; the rear or end of something. **2** *informal* a person tailing another. **3** (**tails**) the reverse of a coin as a choice when tossing. **4** (**tails**) *informal* a tail-coat. ● *v.* *informal* follow and observe. □ **tail off** become fewer, smaller, or slighter; end inconclusively.

tailback *n.* a queue of traffic.

tailboard *n.* a hinged or removable back of a lorry etc.

tailcoat *n.* a man's formal coat with a long divided flap at the back.

tailgate *n.* a rear door in a motor vehicle; a tailboard.

tail light *n.* a light at the back of a motor vehicle or train etc.

tailor *n.* a maker of men's clothes, esp. to order. ● *v.* **1** make (clothes) as a tailor. **2** make or adapt for a special purpose. □ **tailor-made** *adj.*

tailplane *n.* the horizontal part of an aeroplane's tail.

tailspin *n.* an aircraft's spinning dive.

taint *n.* a trace of decay, infection, or other bad quality. ● *v.* contaminate, pollute, spoil.

take *v.* (**took, taken, taking**) **1** get hold of; receive and keep; steal; capture. **2** cause to go with one, convey, remove; escort, guide. **3** accept; endure; react to, interpret. **4** measure (temperature etc.). **5** perform, make (a decision, an action); act on (an opportunity). **6** study or teach (a subject). **7** require (time etc.). **8** make (a photograph). ● *n.* **1** a sequence of film or sound recorded at one time. **2** the amount of something gained from a source. □ **be taken ill** become ill. **be taken with** or **by** find attractive. **take after** resemble (a parent). **take back** withdraw (a statement). **take down** write from dictation. **take in 1** make (a garment) smaller. **2** realize fully. **3** include. **4** deceive. **take off 1** become airborne. **2** *informal* mimic humorously. **take on 1** undertake; engage as an opponent. **2** employ. **take one's time** not hurry. **take out on** relieve (anger etc.) by mistreating (someone not to blame). **take over** take control of. **take part** join in an activity. **take place** occur. **take sides** support one party against another. **take to 1** develop a liking or ability for. **2** develop as a habit. **3** go to (a place) for refuge. **take up 1** adopt as a hobby. **2** use (time). **3** accept (an offer or the person making it). **take up with** begin to associate with. □ **taker** *n.*

takeaway *n.* a cooked meal bought at a restaurant etc. for eating elsewhere; (a place) selling this.

take-off *n.* **1** a piece of humorous mimicry. **2** the process of becoming airborne.

takeover *n.* the gaining of control of a business etc.

takings *n.pl.* money taken in business.

talc *n.* talcum powder; magnesium silicate used as a lubricator.

talcum powder (also **talcum**) *n.* talc powdered and usu. perfumed, for use on the skin.

tale *n.* a narrative, a story.

talent *n.* a special ability.

talented *adj.* having talent.

talisman *n.* (*pl.* **talismans**) an object supposed to bring good luck.

talk *v.* convey or exchange ideas by spoken words; use (a specified language) in talking. ● *n.* a conversation; talking; an informal lecture; rumour. □ **the talk of** widely discussed among. □ **talker** *n.*

talkative *adj.* talking very much.

talking book *n.* a recorded reading of a book.

talking shop *n. informal* a place for unproductive talk.

talking-to *n. informal* a reproof or reprimand.

tall *adj.* of great or specified height. □ **tallness** *n.*

tall order *n.* a difficult task.

tallow *n.* animal fat used to make candles, lubricants, etc.

tall story *n.* (*pl.* **-ies**) *informal* a fanciful and incredible account.

tally *n.* (*pl.* **-ies**) a total score etc.; a record of this. ● *v.* (**tallied, tallying**) agree, correspond.

Talmud *n.* the ancient writings on Jewish law and tradition. □ **Talmudic** *adj.*

talon *n.* a bird's large claw.

tambourine *n.* a percussion instrument with jingling metal discs.

tame *adj.* (of an animal) domesticated, not fierce towards or frightened of humans; unexciting. ● *v.* make tame or manageable. □ **tamely** *adv.*, **tameness** *n.*

Tamil *n.* & *adj.* (a member, the language) of a people of south India and Sri Lanka.

tamp *v.* pack down tightly.

tamper *v.* □ **tamper with** meddle or interfere with.

tampon *n.* a plug of absorbent material inserted into the body, esp. to absorb menstrual blood.

tan *v.* (**tanned, tanning**) **1** make or become brown by exposure to sun. **2** convert (hide) into leather. **3** *informal* thrash. ● *n.* yellowish brown; the brown colour of suntanned skin. ● *adj.* yellowish brown. ● *abbr.* tangent.

tandem *n.* a bicycle for two people one behind another. ● *adv.* together. □ **in tandem** arranged one behind another; together; alongside each other.

tandoori *n.* a style of Indian cooking.

tang *n.* a strong taste or smell. □ **tangy** *adj.*

tangent *n. Maths* **1** a straight line that touches the outside of a curve without intersecting it. **2** (in a right-angled triangle) the ratio of the sides (other than the hypotenuse) opposite and adjacent to an angle. □ **go off at a tangent** diverge suddenly from a line of thought etc. □ **tangential** *adj.*

tangerine *n.* a small orange.

tangible *adj.* able to be perceived by touch; clear and definite, real. □ **tangibility** *n.*, **tangibly** *adv.*

tangle *v.* twist into a confused mass. ● *n.* a tangled mass or condition. □ **tangle with** *informal* come into conflict with.

tango *n.* (*pl.* **tangos**) a ballroom dance.

tank *n.* **1** a large container for liquid or gas. **2** an armoured fighting vehicle moving on a continuous metal track.

tankard *n.* a one-handled usu. metal drinking container.

tanker *n.* a ship, aircraft, or vehicle for carrying liquid in bulk.

tanner *n.* **1** a person who tans hides. **2** *informal* a sixpence.

tannery *n.* (*pl.* **-ies**) a place where hides are tanned into leather.

tannic acid *n.* tannin.

tannin *n.* a substance (found in tree-barks and also in tea) used in tanning and dyeing.

tannoy *n. trademark* a public address system.

tantalize *v.* (also **-ise**) torment by the sight of something desired but kept out of reach or withheld.

tantalum *n.* a hard white metallic element (symbol Ta). □ **tantalic** *adj.*

tantamount *adj.* equivalent.

tantra *n.* a Hindu or Buddhist mystical or magical text. □ **tantric** *adj.*

tantrum *n.* an outburst of bad temper.

tap *n.* **1** a device for drawing liquid in a controlled flow. **2** a light blow; the sound of this. **3** a connection for tapping a telephone. ● *v.* (**tapped, tapping**) **1** knock gently. **2** draw liquid from through a tap; exploit (a resource). **3** fit a device in (a telephone), enabling one to listen secretly to conversations. **4** cut a thread in (something) to accept a screw. □ **on tap** *informal* readily available.

tapas *n.pl.* small Spanish-style savoury dishes.

tap dance *n.* a dance in which the feet tap an elaborate rhythm.

tape *n.* **1** a narrow strip of material for tying, fastening, or labelling things. **2** magnetic tape; a tape recording. **3** a tape measure. ● *v.* **1** record on magnetic tape. **2** fasten with tape. □ **have something taped** *informal* understand and be able to deal with something.

tape deck *n.* a machine for playing and recording audiotapes.

tape measure *n.* a strip of tape or flexible metal marked for measuring length.

taper *n.* a thin candle. ● *v.* make or become gradually narrower. □ **taper off** become gradually less.

tape recorder *n.* an apparatus for recording sounds on magnetic tape. □ **tape recording** *n.*

tapestry *n.* (*pl.* **-ies**) a textile fabric woven or embroidered ornamentally.

tapeworm *n.* a ribbon-like worm living as a parasite in intestines.

tapioca *n.* starchy grains obtained from cassava, used in making puddings.

tapir (tay-peer) *n.* a pig-like animal with a flexible snout.

taproom *n.* a room in a pub with alcoholic drinks (esp. beer) on tap.

tap root *n.* a plant's chief root.

tar *n.* a thick dark liquid distilled from coal etc.; a similar substance formed by burning tobacco. ● *v.* (**tarred, tarring**) coat with tar.

taramasalata *n.* a pâté made from the roe of mullet or smoked cod.

tarantella *n.* a whirling Italian dance.

tarantula *n.* a large black hairy spider.

tardy *adj.* (**tardier, tardiest**) late; slow. □ **tardily** *adv.*, **tardiness** *n.*

tare *n.* **1** a cornfield weed. **2** an allowance for the weight of the container or vehicle weighed with the goods it holds.

target *n.* an object or mark to be hit in shooting etc.; the object of criticism; an objective. ● *v.* (**targeted, targeting**) aim at; direct.

tariff *n.* a list of fixed charges; a duty to be paid.

tarmac *n. trademark* broken stone or slag mixed with tar; an area surfaced with this. □ **tarmacked** *adj.*

tarn *n.* a small mountain lake.

tarnish *v.* lose or cause (metal) to lose lustre; blemish (a reputation). ● *n.* loss of lustre; spoiling, damage.

tarot (ta-roh) *n.* a pack of 78 cards mainly used for fortunetelling.

tarpaulin *n.* a waterproof canvas.

tarragon *n.* an aromatic herb.

tarsus *n.* (*pl.* **tarsi**) the set of small bones forming the ankle and upper foot. □ **tarsal** *adj.*

tart *n.* **1** a pie or flan with a sweet filling. **2** *informal* a prostitute. ● *adj.* sour; sharp and sarcastic. □ **tart up** *informal* dress gaudily; smarten up. □ **tartly** *adv.*, **tartness** *n.*

tartan *n.* a checked pattern (originally of a Scottish clan); cloth marked with this.

tartar *n.* **1** a hard deposit forming on teeth; a deposit formed in a wine cask by fermentation. **2** (**Tartar**) *hist.* a member of a group of central Asian peoples. **3** a bad-tempered or difficult person.

tartare sauce *n.* a cold savoury sauce.

tartaric acid *n.* an acid used in baking powder.

tartrazine *n.* a yellow dye from tartaric acid, used as food colouring.

task *n.* a piece of work to be done. □ **take to task** rebuke.

task force *n.* a group organized for a special task.

taskmaster *n.* a person who makes others work hard.

tassel *n.* an ornamental bunch of hanging threads. □ **tasselled** *adj.*

taste *n.* **1** the sensation caused in the tongue by things placed on it; the ability to perceive this; a small quantity of food or drink tried as a sample; a slight experience. **2** a liking; a tendency to like certain things. **3** the ability to perceive beauty or quality. ● *v.* **1** discover or test the flavour of; have a certain flavour. **2** experience.

tasteful *adj.* showing good judgement of quality. □ **tastefully** *adv.*

tasteless *adj.* **1** having no flavour. **2** showing poor judgement of quality. □ **tastelessly** *adv.*, **tastelessness** *n.*

taster *n.* **1** a person who judges teas, wines, etc. by tasting them. **2** a small sample.

tasty *adj.* (**tastier, tastiest**) having a pleasant flavour.

tat *n. informal* tasteless ornaments etc.

tattered *adj.* ragged.

tatters *n.pl.* torn pieces.

tatting *n.* lace made by hand with a small shuttle.

tattle *v.* chatter idly, reveal private information in this way. ● *n.* idle chatter.

tattoo *v.* mark (skin) by puncturing it and inserting pigments; make (a pattern) in this way. ● *n.* **1** a tattooed pattern. **2** a military display or pageant. **3** a rhythmic tapping sound.

tatty *adj.* (**tattier, tattiest**) *informal* ragged, shabby and untidy. □ **tattily** *adv.*, **tattiness** *n.*

taught past & p.p. of **teach**.

taunt *v.* jeer at provocatively. ● *n.* a taunting remark.

taupe (tohp) *n.* pale greyish brown.

taut *adj.* stretched tightly, not slack.

tauten *v.* make or become taut.

tautology *n.* saying the same thing in different ways unnecessarily (e.g. *free, gratis, and for nothing*). □ **tautological** *adj.*, **tautologous** *adj.*

tavern *n. archaic* an inn, a pub.

taverna *n.* a Greek restaurant.

tawdry *adj.* (**tawdrier, tawdriest**) showy but tasteless and worthless. □ **tawdrily** *adv.*, **tawdriness** *n.*

tawny *adj.* orange-brown.

tax *n.* money compulsorily paid to the state; a strain or demand on strength etc. ● *v.* impose a tax on; strain, make heavy demands on. □ **taxable** *adj.*, **taxation** *n.*

tax evasion *n.* illegal nonpayment of tax.

taxi *n.* (also **taxicab**) a car with a driver which may be hired. ● *v.* (**taxied, taxiing**) (of an aircraft) move along the ground under its own power.

taxidermy *n.* the process of preparing, stuffing, and mounting the skins of animals in lifelike form. □ **taxidermist** *n.*

taxonomy *n.* the scientific classification of organisms. □ **taxonomical** *adj.*, **taxonomist** *n.*

tax return *n.* a form declaring income and expenditure for a particular year, used for tax assessment.

TB *abbr.* tuberculosis.

Tb *symb.* terbium.

t.b.a. *abbr.* to be announced.

T-bone *n.* a piece of loin steak containing a T-shaped bone.

tbsp *abbr.* tablespoonful.

Tc *symb.* technetium.

Te *symb.* tellurium.

te *n. Music* the seventh note of a major scale, or the note B.

tea *n.* **1** a drink made by infusing the dried leaves of a tropical plant in boiling water; these leaves. **2** an afternoon or evening meal at which tea is drunk.

tea bag *n.* a small porous sachet holding tea for infusion.

teacake *n.* a flat sweet yeasted bun served toasted and buttered.

teach *v.* (**taught, teaching**) impart information or skill to (a person) or about (a subject). □ **teacher** *n.*

tea chest *n.* a light metal-lined wooden box in which tea is exported.

tea cloth *n.* a tea towel.

teacup *n.* a cup from which tea etc. is drunk.

teak *n.* strong heavy wood of an Asian evergreen tree.

team *n.* a group of players forming one side in a competitive sport; a set of people or animals working together. ● *v.* combine into a team or set.

teamster *n.* **1** a driver of a team of animals. **2** *Amer.* a lorry driver.

teamwork *n.* organized co-operation.

teapot *n.* a container with a spout, for brewing and pouring tea.

tear[1] (tair) *v.* (**tore, torn, tearing**) **1** pull forcibly apart or to pieces; make (a hole) in (something) in this way; become torn. **2** *informal* move hurriedly. ● *n.* a hole etc. torn.

tear[2] (teer) *n.* a drop of liquid forming in and falling from the eye. □ **in tears** crying.

tearaway *n.* an unruly young person.

tearful *adj.* crying or about to cry. □ **tearfully** *adv.*

tear gas *n.* a gas causing severe irritation of the eyes.

tea room *n.* a tea shop.

tease *v.* **1** try to provoke in a playful or unkind way. **2** pick into separate strands. ● *n.* a person fond of teasing others.

teasel *n.* a plant with bristly heads.

tea set *n.* a set of cups and plates etc. for serving tea.

tea shop *n.* a small restaurant serving tea and light refreshments.

teaspoon *n.* a small spoon for stirring tea etc. □ **teaspoonful** *n.*

teat *n.* a nipple on a milk-secreting organ; a device of rubber etc. on a feeding bottle, through which the contents are sucked.

tea towel *n.* a cloth for drying washed crockery etc.

technetium (tek-**nee**-shŭm) *n.* an artificial radioactive element (symbol Tc).

technical *adj.* **1** of a particular subject, craft, etc.; requiring specialized knowledge to be understood. **2** of applied science and mechanical arts. **3** according to a strict legal interpretation.

technicality *n.* (*pl.* **-ies**) a small detail of a set of rules or of interpretation.

technically *adv.* **1** according to the facts, strictly. **2** with regard to technique or technology.

technician *n.* **1** an expert in the techniques of a subject or craft. **2** a person employed to look after technical equipment.

Technicolor *n. trademark* a process of producing films in colour; *informal* vivid colour.

technique *n.* a method of doing something; skill in an activity.

technocrat *n.* a technical expert perceived as having great social or political influence. □ **technocracy** *n.*

technology *n.* (*pl.* **-ies**) the application of scientific knowledge in industry etc.; equipment developed in this way. □ **technological** *adj.*, **technologically** *adv.*, **technologist** *n.*

teddy *n.* (*pl.* **-ies**) (in full **teddy bear**) a soft toy bear.

tedious *adj.* tiresome because of length, slowness, or dullness. □ **tediously** *adv.*, **tediousness** *n.*, **tedium** *n.*

tee *n.* a cleared space from which a golf ball is driven at the start of play; a small peg for supporting this ball. ● *v.* (**teed, teeing**) place a ball on a tee. □ **tee off** make the first stroke in golf.

teem *v.* be full of; be present in large numbers; (of water or rain) pour.

teenager *n.* a person in his or her teens. □ **teenage** *adj.*, **teenaged** *adj.*

teens *n.pl.* the years of age from 13 to 19.

teeny *adj.* (**teenier, teeniest**) *informal* tiny.

teepee var. of **tepee**.

tee shirt *n.* var. of **T-shirt**.

teeter *v.* balance or move unsteadily.

teeth pl. of **tooth.**

teethe *v.* (of a baby) have its first teeth appear through the gums.

teething troubles *n.pl. informal* problems in the early stages of an enterprise.

teetotal *adj.* abstaining completely from alcohol. □ **teetotaller** *n.*

TEFL *abbr.* teaching of English as a foreign language.

Teflon *n. trademark* a nonstick coating for saucepans etc.

tele- *comb. form* **1** at a distance. **2** by telephone. **3** television.

telecommunications *n.pl.* communication by telephone, radio, cable, etc.

telegram *n.* a message sent by telegraph.

telegraph *n.* a system or apparatus for sending messages, esp. by electrical impulses along wires. ● *v.* send (a message) to (someone) in this way.

telegraphic *adj.* **1** of telegraphs. **2** concise, omitting inessential words. □ **telegraphically** *adj.*

telegraphy *n.* communication by telegraph. □ **telegraphist** *n.*

telekinesis *n.* the supposed ability to move things without touching them.

telemarketing *n.* selling by unsolicited telephone calls.

telemessage *n.* a message sent by telephone or telex, delivered in printed form.

telemeter *n.* an apparatus for recording the readings of an instrument and transmitting them by radio. □ **telemetry** *n.*

telepathy *n.* supposed communication by means other than the senses. □ **telepathic** *adj.*

telephone *n.* a device for transmitting speech by wire or radio. ● *v.* speak to (a person) by telephone; send (a message) by telephone. □ **telephonic** *adj.*, **telephonically** *adv.*, **telephony** *n.*

telephonist *n.* an operator of a telephone switchboard.

telephoto lens *n.* a photographic lens producing a large image of a distant object.

teleprinter *n.* a device for transmitting, receiving, and printing telegraph messages.

teleprompter *n. Amer.* an autocue.

telesales *n.pl.* selling by telephone.

telescope *n.* an optical instrument for making distant objects appear larger. ● *v.* make or become shorter by sliding each section inside the next; compress or become compressed forcibly. □ **telescopic** *adj.*, **telescopically** *adv.*

teletext *n.* a service transmitting news and information to television screens.

telethon *n.* a long television programme broadcast to raise money for charity.

televise *v.* transmit by television.

television *n.* a system for reproducing on a screen a view of scenes etc. by radio transmission; televised programmes; (in full **television set**) an apparatus for receiving these. □ **televisual** *adj.*

telework *n.* work from home, communicating with an office by fax, modem, etc.

telex *n.* (also **Telex**) a system of telegraphy using teleprinters and public transmission lines. ● *v.* send a message to (a person) by telex.

tell *v.* (**told, telling**) **1** communicate information, ideas, etc. to (someone) in words; order, instruct; narrate; reveal a secret. **2** perceive, recognize; distinguish: *tell them apart.* **3** have an effect. □ **tell off** *informal* reprimand. **tell on** *informal* report the misdoings of. **tell tales** reveal secrets.

teller *n.* **1** a narrator. **2** a person appointed to count votes. **3** a bank cashier.

telling *adj.* having a noticeable effect.

tell tale *adj.* revealing something. ● *n.* a person who reveals secrets.

tellurium *n.* an element (symbol Te) used in semiconductors.

telly *n.* (*pl.* **-ies**) *informal* a television.

temerity *n.* audacity, rashness.

temp *n. informal* a temporary employee.

temper *n.* **1** a state of mind as regards calmness or anger. **2** a fit of anger. ● *v.* **1** reheat and cool (metal) to increase its strength and elasticity. **2** moderate, neutralize. □ **keep** or **lose one's temper** remain or fail to remain calm under provocation.

tempera *n.* a method of painting using colours mixed with egg.

temperament *n.* a person's nature as it controls his or her behaviour.

temperamental *adj.* of or relating to temperament; liable to unreasonable changes of mood. □ **temperamentally** *adv.*

temperance *n.* self-restraint, moderation; total abstinence from alcohol.

temperate *adj.* **1** (of a climate) without extremes. **2** self-restrained. □ **temperately** *adv.*

temperature *n.* the degree of heat or cold; a body temperature above normal.

tempest *n.* a violent storm.

tempestuous *adj.* stormy.

template *n.* a pattern or gauge, esp. for cutting shapes.

temple *n.* **1** a building dedicated to the worship of a god or gods. **2** the flat part between the forehead and the ear.

tempo *n.* (*pl.* **tempos** or **tempi**) the speed of a piece of music; the rate of motion or activity.

temporal *adj.* **1** secular. **2** of or denoting time. **3** of the temple(s) of the head.

temporary *adj.* lasting for a limited time. □ **temporarily** *adv.*

temporize *v.* (also **-ise**) avoid committing oneself in order to gain time. □ **temporization** *n.*

tempt *v.* persuade or try to persuade, esp. to do something wrong, by the prospect of pleasure or advantage; arouse a desire in. □ **temptation** *n.*, **tempter** *n.*, **temptress** *n.*

ten *adj.* & *n.* one more than nine (10, X).

tenable *adj.* able to be defended or held. □ **tenability** *n.*

tenacious *adj.* determined in holding a position etc. □ **tenaciously** *adv.*, **tenacity** *n.*

tenancy *n.* (*pl.* **-ies**) the use of land or a building as a tenant.

tenant *n.* a person who rents land or a building from a landlord.

tend *v.* **1** take care of. **2** have a specified tendency.

tendency *n.* (*pl.* **-ies**) the way a person or thing is likely to be or behave; an inclination.

tendentious *adj.* promoting a controversial point of view. □ **tendentiously** *adv.*

tender *adj.* **1** not tough or hard; delicate; painful when touched. **2** gentle and loving. ● *n.* **1** a formal offer to supply goods or carry out work at a stated price. **2** a container or vehicle conveying goods or passengers to and from a larger one. **3** a truck attached to a steam locomotive and carrying fuel and water etc. ● *v.* offer formally; make a tender for a piece of work. □ **legal tender** currency that must, by law, be accepted in payment. □ **tenderly** *adv.*, **tenderness** *n.*

tendon *n.* a strip of strong tissue connecting a muscle to a bone etc.

tendril *n.* a threadlike part by which a climbing plant clings; a slender curl of hair etc.

tenement *n.* a large house let in portions to tenants.

tenet *n.* a firm belief or principle.

tenfold *adj.* & *adv.* ten times as much or as many.

tenner *n.* *informal* a ten-pound note.

tennis *n.* a game in which players strike a ball over a net with rackets, with a soft ball on an open court (**lawn tennis**), or with a hard ball in a walled court (**real tennis**).

tenon *n.* a projection shaped to fit into a mortise.

tenor *n.* **1** general meaning; a settled course or character. **2** the highest ordinary male singing voice. ● *adj.* of tenor pitch.

tense *adj.* stretched tightly; nervous, anxious. ● *v.* make or become tense. ● *n.* *Grammar* any of the forms of a verb that indicate the time of the action. □ **tensely** *adv.*, **tenseness** *n.*

tensile *adj.* of tension; capable of being stretched.

tension *n.* **1** being stretched tight; strain caused by forces working in opposition; electromagnetic force. **2** anxiety, mental strain.

tent *n.* a portable shelter or dwelling made of canvas etc.

tentacle *n.* a slender flexible part of certain animals, used for feeling or grasping.

tentative *adj.* hesitant; not certain. □ **tentatively** *adj.*

tenterhooks *n.pl.* □ **on tenterhooks** in suspense because of uncertainty.

tenth *adj.* & *n.* next after ninth. □ **tenthly** *adv.*

tenuous *adj.* very slight; very thin. □ **tenuousness** *n.*

tenure *n.* the holding of an office or of land or accommodation etc.

tepee (tee-pee) *n.* (also **teepee**) a conical tent used by North American Indians.

tepid *adj.* slightly warm, lukewarm.

tequila (te-kee-lă) *n.* a Mexican liquor.

terbium *n.* a metallic element (symbol Tb).

tercentenary *n.* a 300th anniversary.

tergiversate (ter-ji-vĕ-sayt) *v.* **1** change one's party or principles. **2** make conflicting or evasive statements.

term *n.* **1** a fixed or limited period; a period of weeks during which a school etc. is open or in which a law court holds sessions. **2** a word or phrase; each quantity or expression in a mathematical series or ratio etc. **3** (**terms**) conditions offered or accepted; relations between people: *on good terms.* □ **come to terms with** reconcile oneself to (a difficulty etc.).

termagant *n.* a bullying woman.

terminal *adj.* **1** of or forming an end. **2** (of a disease) leading to death; of such a disease. ● *n.* **1** a terminus. **2** a building where air passengers arrive and depart. **3** a point of connection in an electric circuit. **4** an apparatus with a VDU and keyboard connected to a large computer etc. □ **terminally** *adv.*

terminate *v.* come or bring to an end. □ **terminator** *n.*

termination *n.* **1** coming or bringing to an end. **2** an induced abortion.

terminology *n.* (*pl.* **-ies**) the technical terms of a subject. □ **terminological** *adj.*

terminus *n.* (*pl.* **termini** or **terminuses**) the end; the last stopping place on a rail or bus route.

termite *n.* a small insect that is destructive to timber.

tern *n.* a seabird

ternary *adj.* composed of three parts.

terrace *n.* **1** a raised level place; a paved area beside a house. **2** a row of houses joined by party walls.

terracotta *n.* brownish-red unglazed pottery; its colour.

terra firma *n.* dry land, the ground.

terrain *n.* land with regard to its natural features.

terrapin *n.* a freshwater turtle.

terrarium (tĕ-rair-i-ŭm) *n.* (*pl.* **terrariums** or **terraria**) **1** a place for keeping small land animals. **2** a sealed glass container with growing plants inside.

terrestrial *adj.* of the earth; of or living on land; (of television) broadcast by land-based equipment, not satellite.

terrible *adj.* shockingly bad or serious; *informal* very unpleasant. □ **terribly** *adv.*

terrier *n.* a small dog.

terrific *adj.* **1** very great or intense. **2** *informal* excellent, wonderful. □ **terrifically** *adv.*

terrify *v.* (**terrified, terrifying**) fill with terror.

terrine *n.* a kind of pâté.

territorial *adj.* of territory or its ownership.

Territorial Army *n.* a volunteer reserve force.

territory *n.* (*pl.* **-ies**) **1** land under the control of a person, state, city, etc.; an area with a particular characteristic. **2** a sphere of action or thought.

terror *n.* extreme fear; someone or something causing this; control by intimidation; *informal* a very annoying person.

terrorism *n.* the use of violence and intimidation for political purposes. □ **terrorist** *n.*

terrorize *v.* (also **-ise**) fill with terror; coerce by terrorism.

terry *adj.* a towelling fabric.

terse *adj.* concise, curt. □ **tersely** *adv.*, **terseness** *n.*

tertiary (ter-sher-i) *adj.* third in order or level.

tessellated *adj.* decorated with or resembling mosaic.

test *n.* **1** something done to discover a person's or thing's qualities or abilities etc.; an examination (esp. in a school) on a limited subject; a procedure to determine the presence or absence of a disease, quality, etc. **2** a test match. ● *v.* subject to a test. □ **tester** *n.*

testament *n.* **1** a will. **2** evidence, proof. □ **Old Testament** the books of the Bible telling the history and beliefs of the Jews. **New Testament** the books of the Bible telling the life and teachings of Christ.

testate *adj.* having left a valid will at death. □ **testacy** *n.*

testator *n.* a person who has made a will.

testatrix *n.* (*pl.* **testatrices** or **testatrixes**) a woman who has made a will.

testes pl. of **testis**.

testicle *n.* a male organ that secretes sperm-bearing fluid.

testify *v.* (**testified, testifying**) give evidence in court; bear witness to something.

testimonial *n.* a formal statement testifying to character, abilities, etc.; a public tribute.

testimony *n.* (*pl.* **-ies**) a declaration (esp. under oath); supporting evidence.

testis *n.* (*pl.* **testes**) a testicle.

test match *n.* one of a series of international cricket or rugby matches.

testosterone *n.* a male sex hormone.

test tube *n.* a tube of thin glass with one end closed, used to hold material in laboratory tests.

test-tube baby *n. informal* a baby conceived by *in vitro* fertilization.

testy *adj.* (**testier, testiest**) irritable. □ **testily** *adv.*

tetanus *n.* a disease causing muscular spasms and rigidity.

tête-à-tête (tet-a-tet) *n.* a private conversation between two people. ● *adj.* & *adv.* together in private.

tether *n.* a rope or chain for tying an animal to a spot. ● *v.* fasten with a tether. □ **at the end of one's tether** having reached the limit of one's endurance.

tetrahedron *n.* (*pl.* **tetrahedra** or **tetrahedrons**) a solid with four sides.

Teutonic (Tyoo-ton-ik) *adj.* of Germanic peoples or their languages.

text *n.* **1** a written work; the main body of a book as distinct from illustrations etc. **2** a passage from Scripture used as the subject of a sermon. *v.* send a text message to. □ **textual** *adj.*

text message *n.* an electronic message sent and received via mobile phone.

textbook *n.* a book of information for use in studying a subject.

textile *n.* a woven or machine-knitted fabric. ● *adj.* of textiles.

texture *n.* the feel of a substance; the combination of threads or elements. □ **textural** *adj.*

textured *adj.* having a noticeable texture; (of a yarn or fabric) crimped, curled, or looped.

Th *symb.* thorium.

thalidomide *n.* a sedative drug found to have caused malformation of babies whose mothers took it during pregnancy.

thallium *n.* a toxic metallic element (symbol Tl).

than *conj.* & *prep.* used to introduce the second element in a comparison.

thank *v.* express gratitude to. ● *n.pl.* (**thanks**) expressions of gratitude; *informal* thank you.

□ **thank you** a polite expression of thanks.

thankful *adj.* feeling or expressing gratitude.

thankfully *adv.* **1** in a thankful way. **2** let us be thankful that.

■ **Usage** The use of *thankfully* to mean 'let us be thankful that' is considered incorrect by some people.

thankless *adj.* unpleasant and unlikely to inspire gratitude. □ **thanklessness** *n.*

thanksgiving *n.* an expression of gratitude, esp. to God.

that *adj.* & *pron.* (*pl.* **those**) a specific (person or thing); the (person or thing) referred to; the further or less obvious (one) of two. ● *adv.* to such an extent: *it's not that bad.* ● *rel.pron.* used to introduce a defining relative clause. ● *conj.* introducing a dependent clause expressing a statement, reason, hypothesis, etc.

thatch *n.* a roof made of straw or reeds etc. ● *v.* cover (a roof) with thatch. □ **thatcher** *n.*

thaw *v.* make or become unfrozen; become friendlier or less formal. ● *n.* a period of warm weather melting ice etc.

the *adj.* (called the definite article) **1** used with a noun denoting someone or something specific and known; identifying something unique. **2** identifying a class or group rather than an individual: *I play the piano.* **3** emphasizing importance or fame.

theatre *n.* (*Amer.* **theater**) **1** a place for the performance of plays etc.; plays and acting. **2** a lecture hall with seats in tiers. **3** a room where surgical operations are performed.

theatrical *adj.* of or for the theatre; exaggerated for effect. ● *n.pl.* (**theatricals**) theatrical (esp. amateur) performances. □ **theatricality** *n.*, **theatrically** *adv.*

thee *pron. archaic* the objective case of *thou.*

theft *n.* stealing.

their *adj.* of or belonging to them.

theirs *poss. pron.* belonging to them.

theism (th-ee-izm) *n.* belief in a god or gods, esp. as creator of the world. □ **theist** *n.*, **theistic** *adj.*

them *pron.* the objective case of *they.*

theme *n.* **1** a subject being discussed. **2** a melody which is repeated in a work. □ **thematic** *adj.*

theme park *n.* a park with amusements organized round one theme.

themselves *pron.* the emphatic and reflexive form of *they* and *them.*

then *adv.* **1** at that time. **2** next, afterwards. **3** in that case. ● *adj.* & *n.* (of) that time.

thence *adv. formal* from that place or source.

thenceforth *adv. archaic* from then on.

theocracy *n.* (*pl.* **-ies**) government by priests in the name of a divine being. □ **theocratic** *adj.*

theodolite *n.* a surveying instrument for measuring angles.

theology *n.* (*pl.* **-ies**) the study of God; a system of religious beliefs. □ **theologian** *n.*, **theological** *adj.*

theorem *n.* a mathematical statement to be proved by reasoning.

theoretical *adj.* concerning or based on theory rather than practice. □ **theoretically** *adv.*

theorist *n.* a person who theorizes.

theorize *v.* (also **-ise**) form theories.

theory *n.* (*pl.* **-ies**) a set of ideas formulated to explain something; the principles on which an activity is based.

theosophy *n.* a system of philosophy that aims at direct intuitive knowledge of God. □ **theosophical** *adj.*

therapeutic (the-ră-pew-tik) *adj.* contributing to the relief or curing of a disease etc. □ **therapeutically** *adv.*

therapist *n.* a specialist in therapy.

therapy *n.* (*pl.* **-ies**) a treatment for physical or mental disorders.

there *adv.* in, at, or to that place; at that point; in that respect. ● *int.* an exclamation of satisfaction, annoyance, or consolation.

thereabouts *adv.* near there; approximately then.

thereafter *adv.* after that.

thereby *adv.* by that means.

therefore *adv.* for that reason.

therein *adv. formal* in that place or point.

thereof *adv. formal* of that.

thereto *adv. formal* to that.

thereupon *adv. formal* immediately after that.

thermal *adj.* of or using heat; (of a garment) made of a special insulating fabric. ● *n.* a rising current of hot air.

thermodynamics *n.* the science of the relationship between heat and other forms of energy.

thermoelectric *adj.* producing electricity by a difference of temperatures.

thermometer *n.* an instrument for measuring temperature.

thermonuclear *adj.* of or using nuclear reactions that occur only at very high temperatures.

thermoplastic *adj.* & *n.* (a substance) becoming soft when heated and hardening when cooled.

thermos *n.* (in full **thermos flask**) *trademark* a vacuum flask.

thermosetting *adj.* (of plastics) setting permanently when heated.

thermostat *n.* a device that regulates temperature automatically. ◻ **thermostatic** *adj.*, **thermostatically** *adv.*

thesaurus (thi-sor-ŭs) *n.* (*pl.* **thesauri** or **thesauruses**) a dictionary of synonyms.

these pl. of **this**.

thesis *n.* (*pl.* **theses**) **1** a theory put forward and supported by reasoning. **2** a lengthy written essay submitted for a university degree.

thespian *adj.* of the theatre. ● *n.* an actor or actress.

theta *n.* the eighth letter of the Greek alphabet (Θ, θ).

they *pron.* the people already referred to; people in general; unspecified people.

thiamine *n.* (also **thiamin**) a vitamin of the B complex found in unrefined cereals.

thick *adj.* **1** of a great or specified distance between opposite surfaces. **2** composed of many closely-packed elements; fairly stiff in consistency. **3** *informal* stupid. **4** *informal* friendly. ● *adv.* thickly. ● *n.* (**the thick**) the busiest or most intense part. ◻ **thickly** *adv.*, **thickness** *n.*

thicken *v.* make or become thicker.

thicket *n.* a close group of shrubs or small trees.

thickset *adj.* stocky, burly.

thick-skinned *adj.* not sensitive to criticism or snubs.

thief *n.* (*pl.* **thieves**) a person who steals. ◻ **thievish** *adj.*

thieve *v.* be a thief; steal. ◻ **thievery** *n.*

thigh *n.* the upper part of the leg, between the hip and the knee.

thimble *n.* a hard cap worn to protect the end of the finger in sewing.

thin *adj.* (**thinner, thinnest**) **1** not thick; lean, not plump. **2** inadequate, lacking substance; (of a sound) faint and high-pitched. ● *adv.* thinly. ● *v.* (**thinned, thinning**) make or become thinner. ◻ **thinly** *adv.*, **thinness** *n.*

thine *adj.* & *poss. pron. archaic* belonging to thee.

thing *n.* **1** an object of unspecified type; an action, utterance, etc.; an inanimate object. **2** (**things**) belongings. **3** (**the thing**) an important fact about a situation; (**things**) circumstances, life in general.

think *v.* (**thought, thinking**) **1** have a belief or opinion. **2** use one's mind to form ideas, solve problems, etc. ● *n. informal* an act of thinking. ◻ **think better of it**

change a decision after thought. **think of 1** call to mind, remember. **2** have an opinion of. **think up** *informal* devise ingeniously. □ **thinker** *n.*

think-tank *n.* a group providing ideas and advice on national or commercial problems.

thinner *n.* a substance for thinning paint.

third *adj.* next after second. ● *n.* **1** a third thing, class, etc. **2** one of three equal parts. □ **the third degree** long and severe questioning. □ **thirdly** *adv.*

third-degree burn *n.* a burn of the most severe kind.

third party *n.* (*pl.* **-ies**) a person involved in a situation besides the two principals.

third-party insurance *n.* insurance covering injury by the person insured to someone else.

third-rate *adj.* of very poor quality.

Third World *n.* the developing countries of Asia, Africa, and Latin America.

thirst *n.* the feeling caused by a desire to drink; any strong desire. ● *v.* feel a strong desire. □ **thirstily** *adv.*, **thirsty** *adj.*

thirteen *adj.* & *n.* one more than twelve (13, XIII). □ **thirteenth** *adj.* & *n.*

thirty *adj.* three times ten (30, XXX). □ **thirtieth** *adj.* & *n.*

this *adj.* & *pron.* (*pl.* **these**) the person or thing near or present or mentioned.

thistle *n.* a prickly plant. □ **thistly** *adj.*

thistledown *n.* the very light fluff on thistle seeds.

thither *adv. archaic* to or towards that place.

thong *n.* a strip of leather used as a fastening or lash etc.

thorax *n.* (*pl.* **thoraces** or **thoraxes**) the part of the body between the neck and the abdomen. □ **thoracic** *adj.*

thorium *n.* a radioactive metallic element (symbol Th).

thorn *n.* a small sharp projection on a plant; a thorn-bearing tree or shrub. □ **thorny** *adj.*

thorough *adj.* complete in every way; detailed, careful. □ **thoroughly** *adv.*, **thoroughness** *n.*

thoroughbred *n.* & *adj.* (a horse etc.) bred of pure or pedigree stock.

thoroughfare *n.* a road forming the main route between two places.

those pl. of **that**.

thou *pron. archaic* you.

though *conj.* in spite of the fact that, even supposing. ● *adv.* however.

thought past & p.p. of **think**. *n.* an idea; the process of thinking; attention, consideration.

thoughtful *adj.* **1** thinking deeply; thought out carefully. **2** considerate. □ **thoughtfully** *adv.*, **thoughtfulness** *n.*

thoughtless *adj.* careless; inconsiderate. □ **thoughtlessly** *adv.*, **thoughtlessness** *n.*

thousand *adj.* & *n.* ten hundred (1000, M). □ **thousandth** *adj.* & *n.*

thrall *n.* □ **in thrall** in someone's power, captive.

thrash *v.* beat violently and repeatedly; *informal* defeat thoroughly; move wildly or convulsively □ **thrash out** discuss thoroughly.

thread *n.* **1** a thin length of spun cotton or wool etc.; a long or continuous strand of this. **2** the spiral ridge of a screw. ● *v.* **1** pass a thread through (a needle etc.); string together on a thread. **2** move between crowded obstacles. **3** cut a thread in (a screw). □ **lose the thread** forget the sequence of a story, argument, etc.

threadbare *adj.* (of cloth) thin and tattered with age; shabbily dressed.

threat *n.* an expression of intention to punish, hurt, or harm; a person or thing thought likely to bring harm or danger.

threaten *v.* make or be a threat (to).

three *adj.* & *n.* one more than two (3, III).

three-dimensional *adj.* having or appearing to have length, breadth, and depth.

threefold *adj.* & *adv.* three times as much or as many.

threesome *n.* a group of three people.

thresh *v.* beat out (grain) from husks of corn; make flailing movements.

threshold *n.* **1** a piece of wood or stone forming the bottom of a doorway; a point of entry. **2** the lowest limit at which a stimulus is perceptible.

threw past of **throw**.

thrice *adv. poetic* three times.

thrift *n.* economical management of resources. □ **thriftily** *adv.*, **thrifty** *adj.*

thrill *n.* a sudden feeling of excitement; something causing this; a wave of emotion. ● *v.* excite; be excited.

thriller *n.* an exciting story or play etc., esp. involving crime.

thrive *v.* (**throve** or **thrived, thriven** or **thrived, thriving**) grow or develop well; prosper.

throat *n.* the passage from the back of the mouth to the oesophagus or lungs; the front of the neck.

throaty *adj.* (**throatier, throatiest**) uttered deep in the throat; hoarse. □ **throatily** *adv.*

throb *v.* (**throbbed, throbbing**) beat or pulsate with a strong rhythm; feel regular bursts of pain. ● *n.* a regular pulsation.

throes *n.pl.* severe pangs of pain. □ **in the throes of** struggling with the task of.

thrombosis *n.* (*pl.* **thromboses**) the formation of a clot of blood in a blood vessel or organ of the body.

throne *n.* a ceremonial seat for a monarch, bishop, etc.; sovereign power.

throng *n.* a crowded mass of people. ● *v.* crowd (a place); move in a crowd.

throttle *n.* a device controlling the flow of fuel or steam etc. to an engine. ● *v.* strangle.

through *prep.* **1** from end to end or side to side of; from start to finish of. **2** by the agency, means, or fault of. ● *adv.* **1** from end to end or side to side; from beginning to end; entering at one point and coming out at another. **2** so as to have finished; so as to have passed (an examination). **3** so as to be connected by telephone. ● *adj.* going through a place without stopping; (of a means of transport etc.) going to one's final destination. □ **through and through** completely.

throughout *prep.* & *adv.* right through; from beginning to end (of).

throughput *n.* the amount of material processed.

throve past of **thrive**.

throw *v.* (**threw, thrown, throwing**) **1** propel through the air from one's hand; push forcefully in a specified direction; put (clothes) on or off hastily. **2** cause to be in a specified state; *informal* disconcert; have (a fit or tantrum). **3** operate (a switch or lever). **4** give (a party). **5** shape (pottery) on a wheel. ● *n.* an act of throwing; the distance something is thrown. □ **throw away** discard as useless or unwanted; fail to make use of. **throw in the towel** admit defeat or failure. **throw out 1** expel; discard. **2** cause (calculations) to become inadequate. **throw over** reject (a lover). **throw up 1** vomit. **2** bring to notice. **3** give up. □ **thrower** *n.*

throwback *n.* an animal etc. showing characteristics of an earlier ancestor.

thru Amer. = **through**.

thrum *v.* (**thrummed, thrumming**) make a rhythmic humming sound; strum.

thrush *n.* **1** a songbird with a speckled breast. **2** a fungal infection of the mouth, throat, or vagina.

thrust *v.* (**thrust, thrusting**) push forcibly; make a forward stroke with a sword etc. ● *n.* a thrusting movement or force.

thud *n.* a dull low sound like that of a blow. ● *v.* (**thudded, thudding**) make or fall with a thud.

thug *n.* a violent criminal. □ **thuggery** *n.*

thulium *n.* a metallic element (symbol Tm).

thumb *n.* the short thick finger set apart from the other four. ● *v.* **1** touch or turn (pages etc.) with the thumbs. **2** request (a lift) by signalling with one's thumb. □ **under the thumb of** completely under the influence of.

thumbnail *n.* the nail of the thumb. ● *adj.* brief, concise.

thump *v.* strike heavily; set down heavily and noisily; thud. ● *n.* a heavy blow; a sound of thumping.

thunder *n.* the loud rumbling or crashing noise that accompanies lightning; any similar sound. ● *v.* sound with or like thunder; utter loudly or angrily. □ **steal a person's thunder** forestall him or her. □ **thundery** *adj.*

thunderbolt *n.* **1** a lightning flash. **2** a sudden unexpected event or piece of news.

thunderclap *n.* a crash of thunder.

thundering *adj. informal* great, extreme.

thunderous *adj.* of or like thunder; threatening.

thunderstorm *n.* a storm accompanied by thunder.

thunderstruck *adj.* amazed.

Thur. *abbr.* (also **Thurs.**) Thursday.

Thursday *n.* the day after Wednesday.

thus *adv. formal* in this way; as a result of this; to this extent.

thwack *v.* strike with a heavy blow. ● *n.* this blow or sound.

thwart (thwort) *v.* prevent from doing what is intended; frustrate. ● *n.* a rower's bench across a boat.

thy *adj. archaic* belonging to thee.

thyme (tym) *n.* a fragrant herb.

thymus *n.* (*pl.* **thymi**) the ductless gland near the base of the neck.

thyroid *adj.* & *n.* (in full **thyroid gland**) a large ductless gland in the neck, secreting a growth hormone.

thyself *pron.* the emphatic and reflexive form of *thou* and *thee.*

Ti *symb.* titanium.

tiara *n.* a woman's jewelled semicircular headdress.

tibia *n.* (*pl.* **tibiae**) the inner shin bone.

tic *n.* an involuntary muscular twitch.

tick *n.* **1** a regular clicking sound, esp. made by a clock or watch. **2** *informal* a moment. **3** a mark (✓) used to show that an answer is correct or an item on a list has been dealt with. **4** a blood-sucking mite or parasitic insect. ● *v.* **1** (of a clock etc.) make a series of ticks. **2** mark with a tick. □ **on tick** *informal* on credit, with payment deferred. **tick off** *informal* reprimand. **tick over** (of an engine) run in neutral.

ticket *n.* **1** a marked piece of card or paper entitling the holder to a certain right (e.g. to travel by train etc.). **2** a label. **3** notification of a traffic offence. **4** a certificate of qualification as a ship's master or pilot etc. **5** a list of candidates for office. ● *v.* (**ticketed, ticketing**) give a ticket to; mark with a ticket. □ **just the ticket** *informal* exactly what is wanted or needed.

ticking *n.* strong fabric used for covering mattresses, pillows, etc.

tickle *v.* touch or stroke lightly so as to cause a slight tingling sensation; feel this sensation; amuse, please. ● *n.* the act or sensation of tickling.

ticklish *adj.* **1** sensitive to tickling. **2** (of a problem) requiring careful handling.

tic-tac *n.* a system of semaphore signals used by racecourse bookmakers.

tidal *adj.* of or affected by tides.

tidbit *n. Amer.* a titbit.

tiddler *n. informal* a small fish.

tiddly *adj.* (**tiddlier, tiddliest**) *informal* **1** very small. **2** slightly drunk.

tiddlywinks *n.* a game involving flicking small counters into a cup.

tide *n.* **1** the sea's regular rise and fall. **2** a trend of feeling or events etc. ▫ **tide over** help temporarily.

tidemark *n.* a mark made by the tide at high water; a line left round a bath by dirty water.

tidings *n.pl. literary* news.

tidy *adj.* (**tidier, tidiest**) neat and orderly. ● *v.* (**tidied, tidying**) make tidy. ▫ **tidily** *adv.*, **tidiness** *n.*

tie *v.* (**tied, tying**) **1** attach or fasten with cord etc.; form into a knot or bow; link, connect. **2** restrict, limit. **3** make the same score as another competitor. ● *n.* **1** a cord etc. used for tying; something that unites; a restriction. **2** a strip of cloth worn round the collar and knotted at the front of the neck. **3** an equal score between competitors. **4** a sports match in which the winners proceed to the next round of a competition. ▫ **tie in** link or (of information etc.) be connected with something else. **tie up** fasten with cord etc.; make (money etc.) not readily available for use; occupy fully.

tie-break *n.* a means of deciding the winner when competitors have tied.

tied *adj.* **1** (of a public house) bound to supply a particular brewer's beer. **2** (of a house) for occupation only by a person working for its owner.

tiepin *n.* an ornamental pin for holding a necktie in place.

tier (teer) *n.* any of a series of rows, ranks, or levels of a structure placed one above the other.

tie-up *n.* a connection, a link.

tiff *n.* a petty quarrel.

tiger *n.* a large striped animal of the cat family.

tight *adj.* **1** held or fastened firmly; stretched taut, not slack; fitting closely or too closely; leaving little room. **2** strict, thorough. **3** limited; *informal* stingy. **4** *informal* drunk. ● *adv.* tightly. ▫ **a tight corner** a difficult situation. ▫ **tightly** *adv.*, **tightness** *n.*

tighten *v.* make or become tighter.

tight-fisted *adj. informal* stingy.

tightrope *n.* a rope strung tightly high above the ground, on which acrobats balance.

tights *n.pl.* a garment closely covering the legs and lower part of the body.

tigress *n.* a female tiger.

tike var. of **tyke**.

tilde (til-dĕ) *n.* a mark (˜) put over a letter to mark a change in its pronunciation.

tile *n.* a thin slab of baked clay etc. used for covering roofs, walls, or floors. ● *v.* cover with tiles.

till[1] *prep. & conj.* up to (a specified time, event, etc.); until.

▪ **Usage** *Till* is less formal than *until.*

---

till[2] *n.* a cash register or drawer for money in a shop etc.

till[3] *v.* cultivate (land) for crops.

tiller *n.* a bar by which the rudder of a boat is turned.

tilt *v.* (cause to) move into a sloping position. ● *n.* a sloping position. ▫ **at full tilt** at full speed or force.

timber *n.* wood prepared for use in building or carpentry; trees suitable for this; a wooden beam used in constructing a house or ship.

timbered *adj.* **1** constructed of timber or with a timber framework **2** (of land) wooded.

timbre (tambr) *n.* the characteristic quality of the sound of a voice or instrument.

time *n.* **1** the dimension in which events etc. continue or succeed one another; past, present, and future; a period of this; a point of this measured in hours and minutes; an occasion. **2** a person's lifetime or prime. **3** rhythm in music. **4** (**times**) expressing multiplication. ● *v.* **1** arrange when (something) should happen. **2** measure the time taken by. □ **behind the times** out of date. **for the time being** until another arrangement is made. **from time to time** at intervals. **in time 1** not late. **2** eventually. **on time** punctually.

time-and-motion study *n.* (*pl.* **-ies**) a procedure measuring efficiency.

time bomb *n.* a bomb that can be set to explode at a particular time.

time-honoured *adj.* respected because of antiquity; traditional.

time lag *n.* an interval between two connected events.

timeless *adj.* not affected by the passage of time. □ **timelessness** *n.*

timely *adj.* (**timelier, timeliest**) occurring at a favourable time. □ **timeliness** *n.*

timepiece *n.* a clock or watch.

timeshare *n.* a share in a property that allows use by several joint owners at agreed different times.

time switch *n.* a switch operating automatically at a set time.

timetable *n.* a list showing the times at which trains, buses, or aeroplanes arrive and depart or at which events are scheduled to take place.

time zone *n.* a region (between parallels of longitude) where a common standard time is used.

timid *adj.* lacking courage or confidence. □ **timidity** *n.*, **timidly** *adv.*

timing *n.* **1** the deciding of when to do something for greatest benefit. **2** (in an engine) the times when the valves open and close.

timorous *adj.* timid. □ **timorously** *adv.*, **timorousness** *n.*

timpani *n.pl.* (also **tympani**) kettledrums. □ **timpanist** *n.*

tin *n.* **1** a metallic element (symbol Sn), a silvery-white metal. **2** a metal box or other container; one in which food is sealed for preservation. ● *v.* (**tinned, tinning**) **1** seal (food) in a tin. **2** coat with tin.

tincture *n.* **1** a solution of a medicinal substance in alcohol. **2** a slight tinge.

tinder *n.* any dry substance that catches fire easily.

tine *n.* a prong or point of a fork, harrow, or antler.

tinge *v.* (**tinged, tingeing**) colour slightly; give a slight trace of an element or quality to. ● *n.* a slight colouring or trace.

tingle *v.* have a slight pricking or stinging sensation. ● *n.* this sensation.

tinker *n.* **1** a travelling mender of pots and pans. **2** *informal* a mischievous child. ● *v.* work at something casually, trying to repair or improve it.

tinkle *n.* a series of short light ringing sounds. ● *v.* (cause to) make this sound.

tinnitus (tin-i-tŭs, tin-*I*-tŭs) *n.* ringing or buzzing in the ears.

tinny *adj.* (**tinnier, tinniest**) (of metal objects) flimsy; (of sound) thin and metallic.

tinpot *adj. informal* lacking value or power.

tinsel *n.* glittering decorative metallic strips or threads.

tint *n.* a variety or slight trace of a colour. ● *v.* colour slightly.

tiny *adj.* (**tinier, tiniest**) very small.

tip *v.* (**tipped, tipping**) **1** (cause to) overbalance and fall over; spill (contents) by doing this. **2** give a small present of money to (someone) in return for services. **3** name as a likely winner. **4** put a substance on the end of (something small or tapering). ● *n.* **1** a small money present. **2** a useful piece of advice. **3** the end of something slender or tapering. **4** a place where rubbish etc. is tipped. □ **tip off** *informal* give a warning or hint to. □ **tipper** *n.*

tip-off *n. informal* a warning or hint.

tippet *n.* a small cape or collar of fur with hanging ends.

tipple *v.* drink alcohol habitually. ● *n. informal* an alcoholic drink.

tipster *n.* a person who gives tips, esp. about likely winners in racing.

tipsy *adj.* (**tipsier, tipsiest**) slightly drunk.

tiptoe *v.* (**tiptoed, tiptoeing**) walk very quietly or carefully with one's weight on the balls of one's feet.

tiptop *adj. informal* first-rate.

tirade *n.* a long angry speech.

tire *v.* make or become tired; become bored. ● *n.* Amer. sp. of **tyre**.

tired *adj.* feeling a desire to sleep or rest. □ **tired of** bored or impatient with.

tireless *adj.* not tiring easily. □ **tirelessly** *adv.*, **tirelessness** *n.*

tiresome *adj.* annoying; tedious.

tiro var. of **tyro**.

tissue *n.* **1** a substance forming an animal or plant body. **2** tissue paper; a piece of soft absorbent paper used as a handkerchief etc.

tissue paper *n.* thin soft paper used for packing things.

tit *n.* **1** a small songbird. **2** *vulgar slang* a breast. □ **tit for tat** blow for blow.

titanic *adj.* enormous.

titanium *n.* a grey metallic element (symbol Ti).

titbit *n.* (*Amer.* **tidbit**) a small choice bit of food or item of information.

tithe *n.* one-tenth of income or produce, formerly paid to the Church.

titillate *v.* excite or stimulate pleasantly. □ **titillation** *n.*

titivate *v. informal* smarten up, put finishing touches to. □ **titivation** *n.*

title *n.* **1** the name of a book, poem, picture, etc. **2** a word denoting rank or office, or used in speaking of or to someone with a particular rank or office. **3** the position of champion in a sporting contest. **4** the legal right to ownership of property.

titled *adj.* having a title indicating high rank.

title deed *n.* a legal document proving a person's right to a property.

title role *n.* the part in a play etc. from which the title is taken.

titter *n.* & *v.* (give) a high-pitched giggle.

tittle-tattle *v.* & *n.* gossip.

titular *adj.* having a title but no real power.

tizzy *n.* (*pl.* **-ies**) *informal* a state of nervous agitation or confusion.

T-junction *n.* a junction where one road meets another at right angles but does not cross it.

Tl *symb.* thallium.

Tm *symb.* thulium.

TNT *abbr.* trinitrotoluene, a powerful explosive.

to *prep.* **1** towards; as far as; becoming: *the lights changed to green.* **2** affecting; for (someone) to hold or possess: *give it to me*; so as to be connected: *tied to a tree.* **3** resulting in (an emotion etc.). **4** in comparison with; as regarded by. **5** (with a verb) forming an infinitive; expressing purpose; used alone when the infinitive is understood: *come if you want to.* ● *adv.* into a closed position. □ **to and fro** backwards and forwards.

toad *n.* a froglike animal living chiefly on land.

toad-in-the-hole *n.* sausages baked in batter.

toadstool *n.* a mushroom-like fungus, often poisonous.

toady *n.* (*pl.* **-ies**) a person who flatters in order to gain advantage. ● *v.* (**toadied, toadying**) behave in this way.

toast *v.* **1** brown (bread) by heating on a grill etc. **2** drink in honour of (someone or something), express good wishes before drinking. ● *n.* **1** toasted bread. **2** an act of toasting someone; a person or thing toasted.

toaster *n.* an electrical device for toasting bread.

tobacco *n.* a plant with leaves that are used for smoking or snuff; its prepared leaves.

tobacconist *n.* a shopkeeper who sells cigarettes etc.

toboggan *n.* a small sledge used for sliding downhill. □ **tobogganing** *n.*

tocsin *n.* an alarm bell or signal.

today *adv.* & *n.* (on) this present day; (at) the present time.

toddle *v.* (of a young child) walk with short unsteady steps.

toddler *n.* a child who has only recently learnt to walk.

toddy *n.* a sweetened drink of spirits and hot water.

to-do *n. informal* a fuss or commotion.

toe *n.* any of the divisions (five in humans) of the front part of the foot; part of a shoe or stocking covering the toes. ● *v.* touch with the toe(s). □ **be on one's toes** be alert or eager. **toe the line** conform; obey orders.

toehold *n.* **1** a slight foothold. **2** a position from which one can progress.

toff *n. informal* a rich or upper-class person.

toffee *n.* a sweet made with heated butter and sugar.

toffee apple *n.* a toffee-coated apple on a stick.

tofu *n.* curd from crushed soya beans.

tog *n.* **1** a unit for measuring the warmth of duvets or clothing. **2** (**togs**) *informal* clothes. □ **tog out** or **up** (**togged, togging**) *informal* dress.

toga *n.* a loose outer garment worn by men in ancient Rome.

together *adv.* in company or conjunction; at the same time; so as to meet.

toggle *n.* **1** a short piece of wood etc. passed through a loop to fasten a garment. **2** a switch on a computer that turns a function on and off alternately.

toil *v.* work or move laboriously. ● *n.* laborious work. □ **toilsome** *adj.*

toilet *n.* **1** a lavatory. **2** (also **toilette**) the process of dressing and grooming oneself.

toiletries *n.pl.* articles used in washing and grooming oneself.

toilet water *n.* a light perfume.

token *n.* **1** something representing or expressing something else. **2** a voucher that can be exchanged for goods; a disc used as money in a slot machine etc. ● *adj.* for the sake of appearances, not effective or important in itself.

tokenism *n.* the making of concessions to a minority etc. that improve appearances rather than the situation.

told past & p.p. of **tell**. □ **all told** counting everything or everyone.

tolerable *adj.* **1** endurable. **2** fairly good. □ **tolerably** *adv.*

tolerance *n.* **1** willingness to tolerate. **2** an allowable variation in the size of machine parts etc. □ **tolerant** *adj.*, **tolerantly** *adv.*

tolerate *v.* permit without protest or interference; endure. □ **toleration** *n.*

toll *n.* **1** a tax paid for the use of a public road etc. **2** loss or damage caused by a disaster **3** a stroke of a tolling bell. ● *v.* (of a bell) ring with slow strokes, esp. to mark a death.

toll gate *n.* a barrier preventing passage on a road etc. until a toll is paid.

tom *n.* (in full **tomcat**) a male cat.

tomahawk *n.* a light axe used by North American Indians.

tomato *n.* (*pl.* **tomatoes**) a red fruit used as a vegetable.

tomb *n.* a grave or other place of burial.

tombola *n.* a lottery with tickets drawn for immediate prizes.

tomboy *n.* a girl who enjoys rough and noisy activities.

tombstone *n.* a memorial stone set up over a grave.

tome *n.* a large book.

tomfoolery *n.* foolish behaviour.

tommyrot *n. informal, dated* nonsense.

tomography *n.* a technique for displaying a cross-section through the body using X-rays or ultrasound.

tomorrow *adv.* & *n.* (on) the day after today; (in) the near future.

tom-tom *n.* a medium-sized cylindrical drum.

ton *n.* a measure of weight, either 2,240 lb (**long ton**) or 2,000 lb (**short ton**) or 1,000 kg (**metric ton**); a unit of volume in shipping; *informal* a great weight or large number.

tone *n.* **1** the quality of a musical or vocal sound; a musical note; an expression of an emotion or quality; the general character of an event or place. **2** an interval of a major second in music (e.g. between C and D). **3** a shade of colour. **4** proper firmness of muscles. ● *v.* **1** give firmness to (muscles). **2** harmonize. ◻ **tone down** make less intense. ◻ **tonal** *adj.*, **tonality** *n.*, **tonally** *adv.* **toneless** *adj.*

tone-deaf *adj.* unable to perceive differences of musical pitch.

tone poem *n.* an orchestral composition illustrating a poetic idea.

toner *n.* an ink-like substance used in a photocopier, printer, etc.

tongs *n.pl.* an instrument with two arms used for grasping things.

tongue *n.* **1** the muscular organ in the mouth, used in tasting and speaking; the tongue of an ox etc. as food. **2** a language. **3** a projecting strip; a tapering jet of flame.

tongue-in-cheek *adj.* ironic, insincere.

tongue-tied *adj.* silent from shyness etc.

tongue-twister *n.* a sequence of words difficult to pronounce quickly and correctly.

tonic *n.* **1** a medicine increasing energy and well-being. **2** tonic water. **3** a keynote in music. ● *adj.* invigorating.

tonic sol-fa *n.* the system of representing the notes of a musical scale by the syllables *doh, ray, me,* etc.

tonic water *n.* a carbonated soft drink flavoured with quinine.

tonight *adv.* & *n.* (on) the present evening or night, or that of today.

tonnage *n.* weight of cargo etc. in tons; a ship's carrying capacity expressed in tons.

tonne *n.* a metric ton, 1000 kg.

tonsil *n.* either of two small organs near the root of the tongue.

tonsillitis *n.* inflammation of the tonsils.

tonsorial *adj. formal* of hairdressing.

tonsure *n.* shaving the top or all of the head as a religious symbol; this shaven area. ◻ **tonsured** *adj.*

too *adv.* **1** to a greater extent than is desirable; *informal* very. **2** also.

took past of **take**.

tool *n.* an implement used for a particular task; a person controlled and exploited by another. ● *v.* **1** impress a design on (leather). **2** equip with tools.

toolbar *n. Computing* a strip of icons used to call up various functions when clicked on with a mouse.

toot *n.* a short sound produced by a horn or whistle. ● *v.* make or cause to make a toot.

tooth *n.* (*pl.* **teeth**) each of the white bony structures in the jaws, used in biting and chewing; a toothlike part or projection; (**teeth**) power, effectiveness. ◻ **toothed** *adj.*

toothpaste *n.* paste for cleaning the teeth.

toothpick *n.* a small pointed instrument for removing food from between the teeth.

toothy *adj.* (**toothier, toothiest**) having or showing many prominent teeth.

top *n.* **1** the highest point, part, or position; the upper surface; something forming the upper part or covering. **2** a garment for the upper part of the body. **3** the highest level of volume etc. **4** a toy that spins on its point when set in motion. ● *adj.* highest in position or rank etc. ● *v.* (**topped, topping**) **1** be more than; be at the highest place in (a ranking etc.); reach the top of. **2** put a top or cover on. ▫ **on top of** in addition to. **top up** fill up (something half empty).

topaz *n.* a semiprecious stone of various colours, esp. yellow.

topcoat *n.* **1** an overcoat. **2** a final coat of paint etc.

top dog *n. informal* the master or victor.

top-dress *v.* apply fertilizer on the top of (soil).

top hat *n.* a man's tall hat worn with formal dress.

top-heavy *adj.* liable to fall over because excessively heavy at the top.

topiary *n.* the art of clipping shrubs into ornamental shapes. ▫ **topiarist** *n.*

topic *n.* the subject of a discussion or written work.

topical *adj.* having reference to current events. ▫ **topicality** *n.*, **topically** *adv.*

topknot *n.* a tuft, crest, or bow on top of the head.

topless *adj.* wearing nothing on top, having the breasts bare.

topmost *adj.* highest.

top-notch *adj. informal* of the highest quality.

topography *n.* local geography, the position of the rivers, roads, buildings, etc., of a place or district. ▫ **topographical** *adj.*

topology *n.* the study of geometrical properties unaffected by changes of shape or size.

topper *n. informal* a top hat.

topple *v.* (cause to) overbalance and fall.

top secret *adj.* of the highest category of secrecy.

topside *n.* beef from the upper part of the haunch.

topsoil *n.* the top layer of the soil.

topspin *n.* a spinning motion given to a ball by hitting it forward and upward.

topsy-turvy *adv.* & *adj.* upside down; in or into great disorder.

tor *n.* a hill or rocky peak.

torch *n.* a small hand-held electric lamp; a burning piece of wood etc. carried as a light. ▫ **torchlight** *n.*

tore past of **tear**[1].

toreador *n.* a bullfighter (esp. on horseback).

torment *n.* (tor-ment) severe suffering; a cause of this. ● *v.* (tor-ment) subject to torment; tease, annoy. ▫ **tormentor** *n.*

torn p.p. of **tear**[1].

tornado *n.* (*pl.* **tornadoes** or **tornados**) a violent destructive whirlwind.

torpedo *n.* (*pl.* **torpedoes**) an explosive underwater missile. ● *v.* (**torpedoed, torpedoing**) attack or destroy with a torpedo.

torpid *adj.* sluggish and inactive. ▫ **torpidity** *n.*, **torpidly** *adv.*

torpor *n.* a sluggish condition.

torque (tork) *n.* a force that produces rotation.

torr *n.* (*pl.* **torr**) a unit of pressure.

torrent *n.* a fast and powerful stream of liquid; an outpouring. ▫ **torrential** *adj.*

torrid *adj.* intensely hot and dry; passionate.

torsion *n.* twisting, being twisted.

torso *n.* (*pl.* **torsos**) the trunk of the human body.

tort *n. Law* any private or civil wrong (other than breach of contract) for which damages may be claimed.

tortilla (tor-tee-yă) *n.* a Mexican flat maize cake eaten hot.

tortoise *n.* a slow-moving reptile with a hard shell.

tortoiseshell *n.* the mottled yellowish-brown shell of certain turtles, used for making combs etc.

tortuous *adj.* full of twists and turns; complex. ▫ **tortuously** *adv.*

> ■ **Usage** *Tortuous* is sometimes confused with *torturous*, meaning 'causing extreme pain'.

torture *n.* the infliction of pain on someone as a punishment or means of coercion; extreme pain. ● *v.* inflict severe pain upon. ▫ **torturer** *n.*

Tory *n.* (*pl.* **-ies**) a member or supporter of the Conservative Party.

toss *v.* throw lightly; throw up (a coin) to settle a question by the way it falls; (cause to) roll about from side to side; coat (food) by gently shaking it in dressing etc. ● *n.* an act of tossing. ▫ **toss off 1** drink rapidly. **2** produce rapidly and easily. **toss up** toss a coin to decide a choice etc.

toss-up *n. informal* an act of tossing a coin to settle an issue; a situation where two outcomes are equally likely.

tot *n.* **1** a small child. **2** a small quantity of spirits. ▫ **tot up** (**totted, totting**) add up.

total *adj.* including everything or everyone; complete. ● *n.* a total amount. ● *v.* (**totalled, totalling**; *Amer.* **totaled**). **1** amount to. **2** calculate the total of. ▫ **totality** *n.*, **totally** *adv.*

totalitarian *adj.* of a regime in which no rival parties or loyalties are permitted. ▫ **totalitarianism** *n.*

totalizator *n.* (also **totalisator, totalizer**) a device that automatically registers bets, so that the total amount can be divided among the winners.

tote *informal n.* a system of betting using a totalizator. ● *v. Amer.* carry.

totem *n.* a natural object adopted as a tribal emblem.

totem pole *n.* a pole decorated with totems.

totter *v.* walk or rock unsteadily. ● *n.* a tottering walk or movement. ▫ **tottery** *adj.*

toucan *n.* a tropical American bird with an immense beak.

touch *v.* **1** be, come, or bring into contact; feel or stroke; press or strike lightly. **2** handle, esp. so as to damage or harm. **3** affect; rouse sympathy or gratitude in. **4** *informal* request a gift or loan from. ● *n.* **1** an act, fact, or manner of touching; the ability to perceive things through touching them. **2** a slight trace; a detail. **3** a manner of dealing with something. ▫ **a touch** slightly. **in touch** in contact or communication. **lose touch** lose contact. **touch down 1** touch the ball on the ground behind the goal line in rugby. **2** (of an aircraft) land. **touch off** cause to explode; start (a process). **touch on** mention briefly. **touch up 1** make small improvements to. **2** *informal* touch sexually.

touch-and-go *adj.* uncertain as regards the result.

touché (too-**shay**) *int.* an acknowledgement of a hit in fencing, or of a valid criticism.

touching *adj.* rousing pity, affection, or gratitude. ● *prep.* concerning.

touchline *n.* the side limit of a football field.

touchstone *n.* a standard or criterion.

touchy *adj.* (**touchier, touchiest**) easily offended. ▫ **touchiness** *n.*

tough *n.* **1** strong, withstanding rough treatment or conditions; hard to chew or break; strong-minded, resolute, uncompromising; prone to violence. **2** difficult; unpleasant, unfair. ● *n.* a rough violent person. ▫ **toughness** *n.*

toughen *v.* make or become tough or tougher.

toupee (**too**-pay) *n.* a small wig.

tour *n.* a journey, visiting things of interest or giving performances. ● *v.* make a tour (of). ▫ **on tour** touring.

tour de force *n.* (*pl.* **tours de force**) a feat of strength or skill.

tourism *n.* the commercial organization of holidays and services for tourists.

tourist *n.* a person visiting a place for recreation.

tourmaline *n.* a mineral with unusual electric properties.

tournament *n.* a sporting contest consisting of a series of matches.

tourniquet (toor-ni-kay) *n.* a strip of material pulled tightly round a limb to stop the flow of blood from an artery.

tousle *v.* make (hair etc.) untidy by ruffling.

tout *v.* **1** sell (tickets etc.) by pestering people. **2** spy on (racehorses in training). ● *n.* a person who buys up tickets for popular events and resells them at high prices; a person who touts.

tow *v.* pull along behind. ● *n.* **1** the act of towing. **2** coarse fibres of flax or hemp.

towards *prep.* (also **toward**) **1** in the direction of. **2** in relation to. **3** as a contribution to.

towel *n.* a piece of absorbent material for drying things. ● *v.* (**towelled, towelling** *Amer.* **toweled**) rub with a towel.

towelling *n.* (*Amer.* **toweling**) fabric for towels.

tower *n.* a tall narrow building; a tall pile or structure. ● *v.* be very tall.

tower block *n.* a tall building with many storeys.

tower of strength *n.* a person who gives strong reliable support.

town *n.* a collection of houses, shops, etc. (larger than a village); its inhabitants; a central business and shopping area. □ **go to town** *informal* do something enthusiastically or extravagantly. □ **townsman** *n.*, **townswoman** *n.*

town hall *n.* a building containing local government offices etc.

township *n.* a small town; *S. Afr. hist.* an urban area set aside for black people under apartheid.

towpath *n.* a path beside a canal or river, originally for horses towing barges.

toxaemia (tok-see-miă) *n.* (*Amer.* **toxemia**) **1** blood poisoning. **2** abnormally high blood pressure in pregnancy.

toxic *adj.* poisonous; of or caused by poison. □ **toxicity** *n.*

toxicology *n.* the study of poisons. □ **toxicologist** *n.*

toxin *n.* a poison produced by a living organism.

toy *n.* a thing to play with. ● *adj.* (of a dog) of a small variety. □ **toy with** handle idly; deal with (a thing) without seriousness.

toyboy *n.* *informal* a woman's much younger male lover.

trace *n.* **1** a track or mark left behind; a sign of what has existed or occurred. **2** a very small quantity; a slight sign or appearance. **3** each of the two sidestraps by which a horse draws a vehicle. ● *v.* **1** follow or discover by observing marks or other evidence. **2** copy (a design etc.) by drawing over it on transparent paper; give an outline of. □ **kick over the traces** become insubordinate or reckless. □ **traceable** *adj.*, **tracer** *n.*

trace element *n.* a chemical element occurring or required only in minute amounts.

tracery *n.* (*pl.* **-ies**) a decorative pattern of interlacing lines, esp. in stone.

trachea (tră-kee-ă) *n.* (*pl.* **tracheae** or **tracheas**) the windpipe.

tracheotomy (tra-ki-ot-ŏmi) *n.* (*pl.* **-ies**) a surgical opening made in the trachea.

tracing *n.* a copy of a map or drawing etc. made by tracing it.

tracing paper *n.* transparent paper used for making tracings.

track *n.* **1** a rough path or road; a railway line; a racecourse. **2** marks left by a moving person or thing; a course followed. **3** a section on a CD, tape, etc. **4** a continuous band round the wheels of a tank, tractor etc. ● *v.* follow or find by observing marks left in moving. ◻ **keep** or **lose track of** keep or fail to keep oneself informed about. ◻ **tracker** *n.*

tracksuit *n.* a loose warm suit worn for exercise etc.

tract *n.* **1** a stretch of land. **2** a system of connected parts of the body, along which something passes. **3** a pamphlet with a short essay, esp. on a religious subject.

tractable *adj.* easy to deal with or control. ◻ **tractability** *n.*

traction *n.* **1** pulling something over a surface. **2** the grip of wheels on the ground. **3** the use of weights etc. to exert a steady pull maintaining an injured limb in position.

tractor *n.* a powerful vehicle for pulling farm equipment etc.

trad *adj. informal* traditional.

trade *n.* **1** the exchange of goods for money or other goods; exchanging. **2** a job requiring a particular skill; people engaged in this. ● *v.* engage in trade, buy and sell; exchange (goods) in trading. ◻ **trade in** give (a used article) as partial payment for a new one. **trade off** exchange as a compromise **trade on** take advantage of. ◻ **trader** *n.*

trademark *n.* (also **trade mark**) a company's registered emblem or name etc. used to identify its goods.

tradesman *n.* (*pl.* **-men**) a person engaged in trading or a trade.

trade union *n.* an organized association of employees formed to protect and promote their common interests. ◻ **trade unionist** *n.*

trade wind *n.* a constant wind blowing towards the equator.

tradition *n.* a belief or custom handed down from one generation to another; a long-established procedure. ◻ **traditional** *adj.*, **traditionally** *adv.*

traditionalist *n.* a person who upholds traditional beliefs etc. ◻ **traditionalism** *n.*

traduce *v.* misrepresent in an unfavourable way. ◻ **traducement** *n.*

traffic *n.* **1** vehicles, ships, or aircraft moving along a route. **2** trading. ● *v.* (**trafficked, trafficking**) trade in something illegal. ◻ **trafficker** *n.*

traffic warden *n.* an official who enforces parking restrictions for road vehicles.

tragedian *n.* a writer of tragedies; an actor in tragedy.

tragedienne *n.* an woman who acts in tragedy.

tragedy *n.* (*pl.* **-ies**) a serious drama with unhappy events or a sad ending; an event causing great suffering and sadness.

tragic *adj.* causing or suffering extreme grief; of dramatic tragedy. ◻ **tragically** *adv.*

tragicomedy *n.* (*pl.* **-ies**) a drama of mixed tragic and comic events.

trail *v.* **1** draw or be drawn along the ground behind someone or something; hang loosely; move slowly, lag behind. **2** track. ● *n.* **1** a track, a mark left by movement; a line of people or things; a beaten path. **2** something hanging or drawn behind someone or something.

trailer *n.* **1** an unpowered vehicle designed to be hauled by a vehicle. **2** a short extract from a film etc., shown in advance to advertise it. **3** a trailing part.

train *n.* **1** a railway engine drawing a set of trucks or carriages. **2** a line of pack animals or vehicles; a retinue; a sequence of events. **3** part of a long robe, trailing behind the wearer. ● *v.* **1** teach a particular skill to (someone); practise and exercise to reach a peak of fitness. **2** cause (a plant) to grow in a particular direction. **3** aim (a gun). ◻ **in train** in progress; organized.

trainee *n.* a person being trained.

trainer *n.* **1** a person who trains horses or athletes etc. **2** (**trainers**) soft sports or running shoes.

traipse *v.* move laboriously or by an unnecessarily long route.

trait (tray, trayt) *n.* a characteristic.

traitor *n.* a person who behaves disloyally, esp. to his or her country. □ **traitorous** *adj.*

trajectory *n.* (*pl.* **-ies**) the path of a projectile.

tram *n.* a public passenger vehicle powered by electricity and running on rails laid in the road.

tramcar *n.* a tram.

tramlines *n.pl.* **1** rails on which a tram runs. **2** *informal* a pair of parallel sidelines in tennis etc.

trammel *v.* (**trammelled, trammelling**); *Amer.* **trammeled**) hamper, restrain.

tramp *v.* walk with heavy footsteps; go on foot across (an area); trample. ● *n.* **1** a vagrant. **2** the sound of heavy footsteps. **3** a long walk. **4** a cargo boat that does not travel a regular route. **5** *informal* a promiscuous woman.

trample *v.* tread repeatedly, crush or harm by treading.

trampoline *n.* a sheet of canvas attached by springs to a frame, used for jumping on in acrobatic leaps. ● *v.* use a trampoline.

trance *n.* a sleeplike or dreamy state.

tranquil *adj.* peaceful, untroubled. □ **tranquillity** *n.*, **tranquilly** *adv.*

tranquillize *v.* (also **-ise**; *Amer.* **tranquilize**) make calm.

tranquillizer *n.* (also **-iser**; *Amer.* **tranquilizer**) a drug used to relieve anxiety and tension.

transact *v.* perform or carry out (business etc.). □ **transaction** *n.*

transatlantic *adj.* on or from the other side of the Atlantic; crossing the Atlantic.

transceiver *n.* a radio transmitter and receiver.

transcend *v.* go beyond the range of (experience, belief, etc.); surpass. □ **transcendence** *n.*, **transcendent** *adj.*

transcendental *adj.* of a spiritual or non-physical realm; mystical.

transcontinental *adj.* crossing or extending across a continent.

transcribe *v.* put into written form; write out (notes etc.) in full; arrange (music) for a different instrument etc. □ **transcription** *n.*

transcript *n.* a written version of a broadcast etc.

transducer *n.* a device that converts variations in a physical medium into an electrical signal or vice versa.

transept *n.* a part lying at right angles to the nave in a church.

transexual var. of **transsexual**.

transfer *v.* (trans-fer) (**transferred, transferring**) move from one position etc. to another. ● *n.* (trans-fer) transferring; a conveyance of property from one person to another; a design for transferring from one surface to another. □ **transferable** *adj.*, **transference** *n.*

transfigure *v.* transform into something nobler or more beautiful. □ **transfiguration** *n.*

transfix *v.* **1** pierce through, impale. **2** make motionless with fear or astonishment.

transform *v.* **1** change completely or strikingly in appearance or nature. **2** change the voltage of (electric current). □ **transformation** *n.*

transformer *n.* an apparatus for changing the voltage of an alternating current.

transfuse *v.* **1** give a transfusion of or to. **2** permeate; imbue.

transfusion *n.* an injection of blood or other fluid into a blood vessel.

transgenic *adj.* of an organism into which DNA from an unrelated organism has been artificially introduced.

transgress *v.* break (a rule or law). □ **transgression** *n.*, **transgressor** *n.*

transient *adj.* passing away quickly. ◻ **transience** *n.*

transistor *n.* a very small semiconductor device which controls the flow of an electric current; a portable radio set using transistors.

transit *n.* the process of travelling or conveying someone or something across an area.

transition *n.* the process of changing from one state to another. ◻ **transitional** *adj.*

transitive *adj. Grammar* (of a verb) used with a direct object.

transitory *adj.* lasting only briefly.

translate *v.* **1** express in another language or other words; be able to be translated. **2** transfer. ◻ **translation** *n.*, **translator** *n.*

transliterate *v.* convert to the letters of another alphabet. ◻ **transliteration** *n.*

translucent *adj.* allowing light to pass through but not transparent. ◻ **translucence** *n.*

transmigrate *v.* (of the soul) pass into another body after a person's death. ◻ **transmigration** *n.*

transmission *n.* **1** transmitting; a broadcast. **2** the gear transmitting power from engine to axle in a motor vehicle.

transmit *v.* (**transmitted, transmitting**) **1** pass on from one person, place, or thing to another. **2** send out (a signal or programme etc.) by cable or radio waves. ◻ **transmissible, transmittable** *adj.*, **transmitter** *n.*

transmogrify *v.* (**transmogrified, transmogrifying**) transform in a surprising or magical way.

transmute *v.* change in form or substance. ◻ **transmutation** *n.*

transom *n.* **1** a horizontal bar across the top of a door or window. **2** the flat surface forming the stern of a boat.

transparency *n.* (*pl.* **-ies**) **1** being transparent. **2** a photographic slide.

transparent *adj.* **1** able to be seen through. **2** easily understood or detected. ◻ **transparently** *adv.*

transpire *v.* **1** become known. **2** (of plants) give off vapour from leaves etc. ◻ **transpiration** *n.*

transplant *v.* (trans-**plahnt**) remove and replant or establish elsewhere; transfer (living tissue) to another body or part of the body. ● *n.* (**trans**-plahnt) transplanting of tissue; something transplanted. ◻ **transplantation** *n.*

transport *v.* (trans-**port**) convey from one place to another. ● *n.* (**trans**-port) **1** a means of conveying people or goods; the process of transporting. **2** (**transports**) strong emotion; *transports of joy.* ◻ **transportation** *n.*, **transporter** *n.*

transpose *v.* **1** cause (two or more things) to change places; move to a new position. **2** put (music) into a different key. ◻ **transposition** *n.*

transsexual *n.* (also **transexual**) a person who feels himself or herself to be a member of the opposite sex; a person who has had a sex change.

transubstantiation *n.* the doctrine that the bread and wine in the Eucharist are converted by consecration into the body and blood of Christ.

transuranic *adj.* having a higher atomic number than uranium.

transverse *adj.* crosswise.

transvestite *n.* a person who dresses in the clothes of the opposite sex for sexual pleasure. ◻ **transvestism** *n.*

trap *n.* **1** a device for capturing an animal; a scheme for tricking or catching a person. **2** a curved section of a pipe holding liquid to prevent gases from coming upwards. **3** a compartment from which a dog is released in racing; a trapdoor. **4** *informal* the mouth. **5** a two-wheeled horse-drawn carriage. ● *v.* (**trapped, trapping**) catch or hold in a trap.

trapdoor *n.* a door in a floor, ceiling, or roof.

trapeze *n.* a suspended swinging bar on which acrobatics are performed.

trapezium *n.* (*pl.* **trapezia** or **trapeziums**) **1** a quadrilateral with only two opposite sides parallel. **2** *Amer.* a trapezoid.

trapezoid *n.* **1** a quadrilateral with no sides parallel. **2** *Amer.* a trapezium.

trapper *n.* a person who traps animals, esp. for furs.

trappings *n.pl.* accessories; symbols of status.

trash *n.* worthless stuff. ● *v. informal* discard; damage, ruin. □ **trashy** *adj.*

trash can *n. Amer.* a dustbin.

trattoria (trat-ŏ-ree-ă) *n.* an Italian restaurant.

trauma *n.* a wound, an injury; an emotional shock having a lasting effect. □ **traumatic** *adj.*, **traumatize** *v.*

travail *n.* & *v. archaic* labour.

travel *v.* (**travelled, travelling**; *Amer.* **traveled**) go from one place to another; journey along or through. ● *n.* travelling, esp. abroad; (**travels**) journeys.

traveller *n.* (*Amer.* **traveler**) a person who travels; a person living the life of a gypsy.

traveller's cheque *n.* a cheque for a fixed amount, able to be cashed in other countries.

travelogue *n.* a book, film, etc., about someone's travels.

traverse *v.* travel or extend across. ● *n.* **1** an act of traversing. **2** a part of a structure that lies across another.

travesty *n.* (*pl.* **-ies**) a distorted or absurd imitation. ● *v.* (**travestied, travestying**) imitate in such a way.

trawl *n.* a large wide-mouthed fishing net. ● *v.* fish with a trawl; search thoroughly.

trawler *n.* a boat used in trawling.

tray *n.* a board with a rim for carrying small articles; an open receptacle for office correspondence.

treacherous *adj.* showing treachery; not to be relied on, deceptive. □ **treacherously** *adv.*

treachery *n.* (*pl.* **-ies**) betrayal, disloyalty; an act of betrayal.

treacle *n.* a thick sticky liquid produced when sugar is refined. □ **treacly** *adj.*

tread *v.* (**trod, trodden, treading**) set one's foot down, walk; walk on (a road etc.); press or crush with the feet. ● *n.* **1** the manner or sound of walking. **2** a horizontal surface of a stair. **3** the part of a tyre that touches the ground. □ **tread water** keep upright in water by making treading movements.

treadle *n.* a lever worked by the foot to drive a wheel.

treadmill *n.* **1** a mill-wheel formerly turned by people treading on steps round its edge. **2** monotonous routine work.

treason *n.* treachery towards one's country.

treasonable *adj.* involving treason.

treasure *n.* a collection of precious metals or gems; a highly valued object or person. ● *v.* value highly; store as precious.

treasurer *n.* a person in charge of the funds of an institution.

treasure trove *n.* treasure of unknown ownership, found hidden.

treasury *n.* (*pl.* **-ies**) **1** the revenue of a state, institution, etc.; the department managing this. **2** a place where treasure is stored.

treat *v.* **1** act or behave towards or deal with in a specified way; give medical treatment to; subject to a chemical or other process. **2** buy something for (a person) in order to give pleasure. ● *n.* something special that gives pleasure.

treatise *n.* a written work dealing with one subject.

treatment *n.* **1** a manner of dealing with a person or thing. **2** something done to relieve illness etc.

treaty *n.* (*pl.* **-ies**) a formal agreement, esp. between countries.

treble *adj.* **1** three times as much or as many. **2** (of a voice) high-pitched, soprano. ● *n.* **1** a treble quantity or thing. **2** a treble voice, a person with this. □ **trebly** *adv.*

tree *n.* a perennial plant with a single thick woody stem, usu. tall and having branches.

trefoil *n.* a plant with leaves divided into three parts; a design resembling this.

trek *n.* a long arduous journey. ● *v.* (**trekked, trekking**) make a trek.

trellis *n.* a light framework of crossing strips of wood etc.

tremble *v.* shake, shiver; be very frightened. ● *n.* a trembling movement. □ **trembly** *adj.*

tremendous *adj.* immense; *informal* excellent. □ **tremendously** *adv.*

tremolo *n.* (*pl.* **tremolos**) a trembling effect in music.

tremor *n.* a slight trembling movement; a thrill of fear etc.

tremulous *adj.* trembling, quivering. □ **tremulously** *adv.*

trench *n.* a deep ditch.

trenchant *adj.* (of comments, policies, etc.) strong and effective.

trend *n.* a general tendency; a fashion.

trendsetter *n.* a person who leads the way in fashion etc.

trendy *adj.* (**trendier, trendiest**) *informal* fashionable. □ **trendily** *adv.*, **trendiness** *n.*

trepidation *n.* nervousness.

trespass *v.* enter land or property unlawfully; intrude. ● *n.* the act of trespassing. □ **trespasser** *n.*

tress *n.* a lock of hair.

trestle table *n.* a board held on a set of supports with sloping legs, forming a table.

trews *n.pl.* close-fitting usu. tartan trousers.

tri- *comb. form* three times, triple.

triad *n.* **1** a group of three. **2** a Chinese secret society.

trial *n.* **1** an examination of evidence by a judge in a law court. **2** a test of quality or performance. **3** a person or thing that tries one's patience. □ **on trial** being tested and assessed.

triangle *n.* a geometric figure with three sides and three angles; a triangular steel rod used as a percussion instrument.

triangular *adj.* **1** shaped like a triangle. **2** involving three people.

triangulation *n.* the measurement or mapping of an area by means of a network of triangles.

tribe *n.* a community in a traditional society, consisting of a group of linked or related families. □ **tribal** *adj.*, **tribesman** *n.*

tribulation *n.* trouble, suffering.

tribunal *n.* a board of officials appointed to pass judgement on a particular problem.

tributary *adj.* & *n.* (*pl.* **-ies**) (a stream) flowing into a larger stream or a lake.

tribute *n.* **1** something said or done as a mark of respect. **2** a payment that one country or ruler was formerly obliged to pay to another more powerful one.

trice *n.* □ **in a trice** in an instant.

trichology (tri-**kol**-ŏ-ji) *n.* the study of hair and its diseases. □ **trichologist** *n.*

trick *n.* **1** something done to deceive someone; a mischievous act. **2** a clever act performed for entertainment; a knack of doing something. **3** a mannerism. ● *v.* deceive, outwit. □ **do the trick** *informal* achieve what is required.

trickery *n.* skilful deception.

trickle *v.* (cause to) flow in a thin stream; come or go gradually. ● *n.* a trickling flow.

tricky *adj.* (**trickier, trickiest**) **1** difficult. **2** deceitful. □ **trickiness** *n.*

tricolour *n.* (*Amer.* **tricolor**) a flag with three colours in stripes.

tricycle *n.* a three-wheeled pedal-driven vehicle.

trident *n.* a three-pronged spear.

triennial *adj.* happening every third year; lasting three years.

trier *n.* a person who tries hard.

trifle *n.* **1** something of only slight value or importance; a very small amount. **2** a sweet dish of sponge cake and jelly etc. topped with custard and cream. □ **trifle with** treat without seriousness or respect. □ **trifler** *n.*

trifling *adj.* trivial.

trigger *n.* a lever for releasing a spring, esp. to fire a gun. ● *v.* (also **trigger off**) set in action, cause.

trigger-happy *adj.* apt to shoot on slight provocation.

trigonometry *n.* a branch of mathematics dealing with the relationship of sides and angles of triangles.

trilateral *adj.* having three sides or three participants.

trilby *n.* (*pl.* **-ies**) a man's soft felt hat.

trill *n.* a vibrating sound, esp. in music or singing. ● *v.* sound or sing with a trill.

trillion *n.* a million million; (formerly, esp. *Brit.*) a million million million.

trilobite *n.* a fossil marine creature.

trilogy *n.* (*pl.* **-ies**) a group of three related books, plays, etc.

trim *v.* (**trimmed, trimming**) **1** cut untidy edges from; shorten and neaten. **2** decorate. **3** adjust (a sail); balance (a boat) by rearranging the cargo. ● *n.* **1** decoration. **2** an act of cutting. **3** good condition: *everything is in trim.* ● *adj.* (**trimmer, trimmest**) neat, smart, orderly. □ **trimly** *adv.*, **trimness** *n.*

trimaran *n.* a boat like a catamaran, with three hulls.

trimming *n.* **1** decoration; (**trimmings**) *informal* traditional accompaniments, extra items. **2** (**trimmings**) pieces cut off when trimming something.

trinity *n.* (*pl.* **-ies**) a group of three; (**the Trinity**) the three members of the Christian deity (Father, Son, Holy Spirit) as constituting one God.

trinket *n.* a small ornament or piece of jewellery.

trio *n.* (*pl.* **trios**) a group or set of three; music for three instruments or voices.

trip *v.* (**tripped, tripping**) **1** catch one's foot on something and fall; cause to do this. **2** move with quick light steps. **3** activate (a mechanism) by releasing a switch etc. ● *n.* **1** a journey or excursion, esp. for pleasure. **2** an act of stumbling. **3** *informal* a hallucinatory experience caused by a drug. **4** a device for tripping a mechanism. □ **trip up** (cause to) blunder.

tripartite *adj.* consisting of three parts.

tripe *n.* **1** the stomach of an ox etc. as food. **2** *informal* nonsense.

triple *adj.* having three parts or members; three times as much or as many. ● *v.* increase by three times its amount.

triplet *n.* one of three children born at one birth; a set of three.

triplex *adj.* having three parts.

triplicate *adj.* existing in three examples. ● *v.* make three copies of. □ **in triplicate** as three identical copies.

tripod *n.* a three-legged stand.

tripos *n.* the final examination for the BA degree at Cambridge University.

tripper *n.* a person who goes on a pleasure trip.

triptych (**trip**-tik) *n.* a picture or carving on three panels fixed or hinged side by side.

trite *adj.* unoriginal, overused.

tritium *n.* a radioactive isotope of hydrogen (symbol T).

triumph *n.* a great victory or achievement, joy at this. ● *v.* be successful or victorious; rejoice at this.

triumphal *adj.* celebrating or commemorating a triumph.

■ **Usage** *Triumphal*, as in *triumphal arch*, should not be confused with *triumphant*.

triumphant *adj.* victorious, successful; exultant. ◻ **triumphantly** *adv.*

triumvirate *n.* a group of three powerful people.

trivet *n.* a metal stand for a kettle or hot dish etc.

trivia *n.pl.* trivial things, trifles.

trivial *adj.* of only small value or importance. ◻ **triviality** *n.*, **trivially** *adv.*

trod, trodden past & p.p. of **tread**.

troglodyte (trog-lŏ-dIt) *n.* a cave dweller.

troika *n.* **1** a Russian vehicle pulled by a team of three horses. **2** an administrative group of three people.

troll *n.* a giant or dwarf in Scandinavian folklore.

trolley *n.* (*pl.* **trolleys**) a basket or frame on wheels for transporting goods; a small table on wheels.

trollop *n.* a promiscuous or disreputable woman.

trombone *n.* a large brass wind instrument with a sliding tube.

trompe l'oeil (tromp loi) *n.* a painting on a wall designed to give an illusion of reality.

troop *n.* a body of soldiers; a group of people or animals. ● *v.* move in a group, esp. a large one.

trooper *n.* a soldier in a cavalry or armoured unit; *Amer.* & *Austral.* a mounted or state police officer.

trophy *n.* (*pl.* **-ies**) something taken in war or hunting etc. as a souvenir of success; an object awarded as a prize.

tropic *n.* a line of latitude 23° 27' north or south of the equator; (**the tropics**) the region between these, with a hot climate. ◻ **tropical** *adj.*

troposphere *n.* the layer of the atmosphere between the earth's surface and the stratosphere.

trot *n.* a horse's pace faster than a walk; a moderate running pace. ● *v.* (**trotted, trotting**) (cause to) move at a trot. ◻ **on the trot** *informal* **1** in continuous succession. **2** constantly busy. **trot out** *informal* produce (a frequently repeated excuse etc.).

troth *n. archaic* faithfulness to a promise.

trotter *n.* a pig's foot, esp. as food.

troubadour (troo-bă-door) *n.* a medieval romantic poet.

trouble *n.* **1** difficulty, inconvenience; a cause of this; an unfortunate situation. **2** unrest, violence. ● *v.* **1** disturb, cause inconvenience to. **2** worry, distress. **3** make the effort to do something.

troubleshooter *n.* a person employed to deal with faults or problems.

troublesome *adj.* causing trouble.

trough (troff) *n.* **1** a long open receptacle, esp. for animals' food or water. **2** a depression between two waves or ridges; a region of low atmospheric pressure.

trounce *v.* defeat heavily.

troupe *n.* a company of actors or other performers.

trouper *n.* **1** a member of a troupe. **2** a reliable person.

trousers *n.pl.* a two-legged outer garment reaching from the waist usu. to the ankles.

trousseau (troo-soh) *n.* (*pl.* **trousseaux** or **trousseaus**) a bride's collection of clothing etc. for her marriage.

trout *n.* (*pl.* **trout** or **trouts**) a freshwater fish valued as food.

trowel *n.* a small garden tool for digging; a similar tool for spreading mortar etc.

troy weight *n.* a system of weights used for precious metals and gems.

truant *n.* a pupil who stays away from school without leave. ◻ **play**

truant stay away as a truant. □ **truancy** *n.*

truce *n.* an agreement to cease hostilities temporarily.

truck *n.* an open container on wheels for transporting loads; an open railway wagon; a lorry.

trucker *n.* a lorry driver.

truculent *adj.* defiant and aggressive. □ **truculence** *n.*, **truculently** *adv.*

trudge *v.* walk laboriously. ● *n.* a laborious walk.

true *adj.* **1** in accordance with fact; accurate; genuine. **2** loyal. ● *adv.* truly, accurately. □ **come true** be fulfilled, actually happen.

truffle *n.* **1** a rich-flavoured underground fungus valued as a delicacy. **2** a soft chocolate sweet.

trug *n.* a shallow wooden basket.

truism *n.* a statement that is obviously true, esp. a hackneyed one.

truly *adv.* **1** genuinely, really. **2** truthfully. **3** *archaic* loyally.

trump *n.* **1** (in card games) a card of a suit chosen to rank above the others. **2** *informal, dated* a helpful or admirable person. □ **trump up** invent fraudulently. **turn up trumps** *informal* be successful or helpful.

trumpet *n.* a metal wind instrument with a flared tube; something shaped like this. ● *v.* (**trumpeted, trumpeting**) proclaim loudly; (of an elephant) make a loud sound through its trunk. □ **trumpeter** *n.*

truncate *v.* shorten by cutting off the end. □ **truncation** *n.*

truncheon *n.* a short thick stick carried as a weapon.

trundle *v.* roll along, move along heavily on wheels.

trunk *n.* **1** a tree's main stem. **2** the body apart from the head and limbs. **3** a large box with a hinged lid, for transporting or storing clothes etc. **4** an elephant's long flexible nose. **5** *Amer.* the boot of a car. **6** (**trunks**) men's shorts for swimming etc.

trunk road *n.* an important main road.

truss *n.* **1** a framework supporting a roof etc.; a surgical support for a hernia. **2** a cluster of flowers or fruit. ● *v.* tie up securely.

trust *n.* **1** firm belief in the reliability, strength, or truth of someone or something; confident expectation. **2** responsibility; something for which one is responsible. **3** a legal arrangement whereby someone is made the nominal owner of property to use it for another's benefit; an organization administering funds to promote or protect something specified. ● *v.* **1** feel trust in; expect confidently. **2** entrust. □ **in trust** held by a legal trust. **on trust** without question or investigation. □ **trustful** *adj.* **trustfully** *adv.*, **trustworthiness** *n.*, **trustworthy** *adj.*

trustee *n.* a person who administers property held as a trust; one of a group managing the business affairs of an institution.

trusty *adj.* (**trustier, trustiest**) loyal, faithful.

truth *n.* the quality of being true; something that is true.

truthful *adj.* habitually telling the truth; accurate, realistic. □ **truthfully** *adv.*, **truthfulness** *n.*

try *v.* (**tries, tried, trying**) **1** attempt. **2** test the quality, taste, etc., of. **3** be a strain on. **4** subject to legal trial. ● *n.* **1** an attempt. **2** a touchdown in rugby, entitling the player's side to a kick at goal. □ **try on** put on (a garment) to see if it fits. **try out** test by use.

trying *adj.* annoying.

tsar *n.* (also **czar**) the title of the former emperors of Russia.

tsetse *n.* an African fly that transmits disease by its bite.

T-shirt *n.* (also **tee shirt**) a short-sleeved casual cotton top.

tsp *abbr.* teaspoonful.

T-square *n.* a large T-shaped ruler used in technical drawing.

tsunami *n.* a long high sea wave caused by an earthquake.

tub *n.* a wide, open, usu. round container for liquids etc.; a small container for food.

tuba *n.* a large low-pitched brass wind instrument.

tubby *adj.* (**tubbier, tubbiest**) *informal* short and fat. □ **tubbiness** *n.*

tube *n.* **1** a long hollow glass or metal cylinder; a similarly shaped container or vessel. **2** a cathode ray tube. **3** (**the Tube**) *trademark* the underground railway in London.

tuber *n.* a short thick rounded root or underground stem from which shoots will grow.

tubercle *n.* a small rounded swelling.

tubercular *adj.* of or affected with tuberculosis.

tuberculosis *n.* an infectious wasting disease, esp. affecting lungs.

tuberous *adj.* of or like a tuber; bearing tubers.

tubing *n.* tubular pieces of metal etc.

tubular *adj.* tube-shaped.

TUC *abbr.* Trades Union Congress.

tuck *n.* a flat fold stitched in a garment etc. ● *v.* fold or put (an edge of material) into or under something so that it is concealed or held in place; hide or put away neatly. □ **tuck in** *informal* eat heartily.

tuck shop *n. informal* a shop selling cakes and sweets etc. to schoolchildren.

Tues. *abbr.* (also **Tue.**) Tuesday.

Tuesday *n.* the day after Monday.

tufa *n.* porous rock formed round springs of mineral water.

tuft *n.* a bunch of threads, grass, hair, etc., held or growing together at the base. □ **tufted** *adj.*

tug *v.* (**tugged, tugging**) pull vigorously; tow. ● *n.* **1** a vigorous pull. **2** a small powerful boat for towing others.

tug of war *n.* a contest of strength with two teams pulling opposite ways on a rope.

tuition *n.* teaching or instruction, esp. of an individual or small group.

tulip *n.* a garden plant with a cup-shaped flower.

tumble *v.* **1** fall headlong; move in an uncontrolled way; rumple, disarrange. **2** perform somersaults etc. ● *n.* **1** a fall. **2** an untidy mass or state. □ **tumble to** *informal* understand, grasp.

tumbledown *adj.* dilapidated.

tumble-dryer *n.* (also **tumble-drier**) a machine for drying washing in a heated rotating drum.

tumbler *n.* **1** a drinking glass with no handle or stem. **2** an acrobat. **3** a pivoted piece in a lock, holding the bolt.

tumbril *n.* (also **tumbrel**) *hist.* an open cart, esp. used to take condemned people to the guillotine.

tumescent *adj.* swollen. □ **tumescence** *n.*

tummy *n.* (*pl.* **-ies**) *informal* the stomach.

tumour *n.* (*Amer.* **tumor**) a swelling of part of the body, caused by abnormal growth of tissue.

tumult (tyoo-mŭlt) *n.* a loud confused noise; confusion, disorder.

tumultuous *adj.* making an uproar.

tun *n.* a large cask; a fermenting vat.

tuna *n.* (*pl.* **tuna** or **tunas**) a large edible sea fish.

tundra *n.* a vast level Arctic region where the subsoil is frozen.

tune *n.* a melody. ● *v.* **1** put (a musical instrument) in tune. **2** set (a radio) to the desired wavelength. **3** adjust (an engine) to run smoothly. □ **in tune 1** playing or singing at the correct musical pitch. **2** in harmony or agreement. **out of tune** not in tune.

tuneful *adj.* melodious.

tuner *n.* **1** a person who tunes pianos etc. **2** a radio receiver as part of a hi-fi system.

tungsten *n.* a heavy grey metallic element (symbol W).

tunic *n.* a close-fitting jacket worn as part of a uniform; a loose garment reaching to the knees.

tunnel *n.* an underground passage. ● *v.* (**tunnelled, tunnelling**; *Amer.* **tunneled**) make a passage underground or through something; move forward in this way.

tunny *n.* (*pl.* **-ies**) = **tuna**.

tup *n.* a ram.

turban *n.* a Muslim or Sikh man's headdress of cloth wound round the head; a woman's hat resembling this.

turbid *adj.* (of a liquid) muddy, cloudy; confused, unclear. □ **turbidity** *n.*

■ **Usage** *Turbid* is sometimes confused with *turgid*, meaning 'swollen, pompous'.

turbine *n.* a machine or motor driven by a wheel that is turned by a flow of water or gas.

turbo- *comb. form* using a turbine; driven by such engines.

turbot *n.* a large edible flatfish.

turbulent *adj.* characterized by commotion, unrest, or violence; moving unevenly. □ **turbulence** *n.*, **turbulently** *adv.*

turd *n. vulgar slang* a lump of excrement.

tureen *n.* a deep covered dish from which soup is served.

turf *n.* (*pl.* **turfs** or **turves**) **1** short grass and the soil just below it; a piece of this. **2** (**the turf**) horse racing and race courses. ● *v.* cover (ground) with turf. □ **turf out** *informal* force to leave.

turf accountant *n.* a bookmaker.

turgid *adj.* swollen; (of language) pompous. □ **turgidity** *n.*

■ **Usage** *Turgid* is sometimes confused with *turbid*.

Turk *n.* a native of Turkey.

turkey *n.* (*pl.* **turkeys**) a large bird bred for eating.

Turkish *adj.* & *n.* (the language) of Turkey.

Turkish bath *n.* a hot-air or steam bath followed by massage etc.

Turkish delight *n.* a sweet of flavoured gelatin coated in powdered sugar.

turmeric *n.* a bright yellow spice.

turmoil *n.* a state of great disturbance or confusion.

turn *v.* **1** (cause to) move in a circular direction round a point or axis; (cause to) change direction or position; aim, direct; pass round (a corner etc.). **2** (cause to) change in nature, appearance, etc., reach a specified state; shape (wood) on a lathe; express elegantly; become or make (milk) sour. **3** pass (a specified age or time). ● *n.* **1** an act of turning; a change of direction; a new development in events; a bend in a road etc. **2** an opportunity or obligation coming to each of a group in succession: *it's my turn to pay*. **3** a short performance in an entertainment. **4** *informal* a shock; a brief feeling of illness. **5** a short walk. □ **a good** or **bad turn** a service or disservice. **in turn** in succession. **on the turn** about to turn or change. **out of turn** before or after one's proper turn; inappropriately. **take turns** (of two or more people) do something alternately or in succession. **to a turn** so as to be perfectly cooked. **turn against** make or become hostile to. **turn down 1** reject. **2** reduce the volume of. **turn in 1** hand over to an authority. **2** *informal* go to bed. **turn off 1** stop (a machine etc.) working. **2** *informal* cause to lose interest. **turn on 1** start (a machine etc.). **2** *informal* excite, esp. sexually. **turn out 1** prove to be the case. **2** go somewhere to attend or do something. **3** switch off (a light). **4** expel; empty, search, clean. **5** produce. **6** equip, dress. **turn the tables** reverse a situation so that one is in a superior position to those previously superior. **turn to 1** resort to for help. **2** move on to do or consider. **turn up 1** appear, be found; discover. **2** increase the volume of.

turncoat *n.* a person who changes sides in a dispute etc.

turner *n.* a person who works with a lathe.

turning *n.* a point where a road branches off another.

turning point *n.* a point at which a decisive change takes place.

turnip *n.* a plant with a round white root used as a vegetable.

turnout *n.* **1** the number of people attending or taking part in an event. **2** the way in which someone is dressed or equipped. **3** an act of clearing and tidying a room etc.

turnover *n.* **1** the amount of money taken in a business. **2** the rate at which employees leave or goods are sold and are replaced. **3** a small pie of pastry folded over a filling.

turnpike *n. hist.* a toll gate; a road on which tolls were levied.

turnstile *n.* a revolving barrier for admitting people one at a time.

turntable *n.* a circular revolving platform.

turn-up *n.* **1** the lower end of a trouser leg folded upwards. **2** *informal* an unexpected event.

turpentine *n.* oil used for thinning paint and as a solvent.

turpitude *n. formal* wickedness.

turps *n. informal* turpentine.

turquoise *n.* a blue-green precious stone; its colour.

turret *n.* a small tower; a revolving tower for a gun on a warship or tank. ▫ **turreted** *adj.*

turtle *n.* a sea creature like a tortoise. ▫ **turn turtle** capsize.

turtle dove *n.* a wild dove noted for its soft cooing.

turtleneck *n.* a high round close-fitting neckline.

tusk *n.* a long pointed tooth projecting from the mouth of an elephant, walrus, etc.

tussle *n.* a struggle, a conflict.

tussock *n.* a tuft or clump of grass.

tutelage (tyoo-tĕ-lij) *n.* guardianship; tuition.

tutor *n.* a private teacher; a teacher at a university. ● *v.* act as tutor to.

tutorial *adj.* of a tutor. ● *n.* a student's session with a tutor.

tutti *adv. Music* with all voices or instruments together.

tut-tut *int.* an exclamation of annoyance, impatience, or rebuke.

tutu *n.* a dancer's short skirt made of layers of frills.

tuxedo (tuk-see-doh) *n.* (*pl.* **tuxedos** or **tuxedoes**) *Amer.* a dinner jacket.

TV *abbr.* television.

twaddle *n.* nonsense.

twang *n.* **1** a sharp ringing sound like that made by a tense wire when plucked. **2** a nasal intonation. ● *v.* (cause to) make a twang.

tweak *v.* **1** pull or twist sharply. **2** *informal* make fine adjustments to. ● *n.* a sharp pull.

twee *adj.* (**tweer, tweest**) affectedly pretty or sentimental.

tweed *n.* a thick woollen fabric; (also **tweeds**) clothes made of tweed. ▫ **tweedy** *adj.*

tweet *v.* & *n.* (give) a chirp.

tweeter *n.* a small loudspeaker for reproducing high-frequency signals.

tweezers *n.pl.* small pincers for handling very small things.

twelve *adj.* & *n.* one more than eleven (12, XII). ▫ **twelfth** *adj.* & *n.*

twenty *adj.* & *n.* twice ten. ▫ **twentieth** *adj.* & *n.*

twerp *n.* (also **twirp**) *informal* a stupid person.

twice *adv.* two times; in double amount or degree.

twiddle *v.* twist idly about. ● *n.* an act of twiddling. ▫ **twiddle one's thumbs** have nothing to do.

twig *n.* a small shoot growing from a branch or stem. ● *v.* (**twigged, twigging**) *informal* realize or understand something.

twilight *n.* light from the sky after sunset; the period of this.

twill *n.* fabric woven so that parallel diagonal lines are produced. ▫ **twilled** *adj.*

twin *n.* one of two children or animals born at one birth; one of a pair that are exactly alike. ● *adj.* being a twin or twins. ● *v.* (**twinned, twinning**) combine as a pair; link with (another town) for cultural and social exchange.

twine *n.* strong thread or string. ● *v.* twist; wind or coil.

twinge *n.* a slight or brief pang.

twinkle *v.* shine with a flickering light. ● *n.* a twinkling light.

twin towns *n.pl.* two towns that establish special social and cultural links.

twirl *v.* spin round lightly or rapidly. ● *n.* a twirling movement; a spiralling shape. ▫ **twirly** *adj.*

twirp var. of **twerp**.

twist *v.* **1** bend; distort; shape by turning both ends; pervert the meaning of. **2** cause to move round each other or something stationary; wind (strands) round each other to form a single cord; wind, bend. ● *n.* an act of twisting; a twisted shape, a spiral; a distortion; an unexpected development in a story etc.

twister *n.* **1** *Brit. informal* a swindler. **2** *Amer.* a tornado.

twit *n. informal* a stupid person. ● *v.* (**twitted, twitting**) *dated* tease.

twitch *v.* give a short jerking or convulsive movement; pull sharply in a particular direction. ● *n.* a twitching movement.

twitcher *n. informal* a birdwatcher who tries to see as many species as possible.

twitter *v.* make light chirping sounds; talk rapidly in a high-pitched voice or in a trivial way. ● *n.* a twittering sound.

two *adj.* & *n.* one more than one (2, II).

twoc *v.* (**twocced, twoccing**) *informal* steal (a car).

two-dimensional *adj.* having or appearing to have length and breadth but no depth.

two-faced *adj.* insincere, deceitful.

twofold *adj.* & *adv.* twice as much or as many.

twosome *n.* two together, a pair.

two-time *v. informal* be unfaithful to (a lover)

tycoon *n.* a wealthy influential industrialist.

tying present participle of **tie**.

tyke *n.* (also **tike**) **1** *informal* a small mischievous child. **2** *dated* a coarse or unpleasant man.

tympani var. of **timpani**.

tympanum *n.* (*pl.* **tympana** or **tympanums**) **1** the eardrum. **2** a recessed triangular area above a door.

type *n.* **1** a kind, a category; *informal* a person of a specified nature. **2** a perfect example of something. **3** printed characters or letters; a piece of metal with a raised character, used in printing. ● *v.* **1** write using a typewriter. **2** classify according to type.

typecast *v.* (**typecast, typecasting**) cast (an actor or actress) repeatedly in the same type of role.

typeface *n.* a set of printing types in one design.

typescript *n.* a typewritten document.

typesetter *n.* a person or machine that sets type for printing.

typewriter *n.* a machine for producing printlike characters on paper by pressing keys. ▫ **typewritten** *adj.*

typhoid *n.* (in full **typhoid fever**) a serious infectious feverish disease.

typhoon *n.* a tropical storm.

typhus *n.* an infectious feverish disease transmitted by parasites.

typical *adj.* having the distinctive qualities of a particular type of person or thing. ▫ **typically** *adv.*

typify *v.* (**typified, typifying**) be a typical example of.

typist *n.* a person who types.

typography *n.* the art or style of printing. ▫ **typographical** *adj.*

tyrannize *v.* (also **-ise**) exercise power cruelly.

tyrannosaurus *n.* (also **tyrannosaur**) a large flesh-eating dinosaur

tyranny *n.* (*pl.* **-ies**) cruel exercise of power; absolute and arbitrary rule. ▫ **tyrannical** *adj.*, **tyrannically** *adv.*, **tyrannous** *adj.*

tyrant *n.* a ruler or other person who uses power in a harsh or oppressive way.

tyre *n.* (*Amer.* **tire**) a rubber covering round the rim of a wheel to absorb shocks.

tyro (tI-roh) *n.* (also **tiro**) (*pl.* **tyros**) a beginner.

tzatziki *n.* a Greek dish of yoghurt and cucumber.

Uu

U *symb.* uranium. • *abbr.* universal; a film classification indicating suitability for all ages.

UAE *abbr.* United Arab Emirates.

UB40 *abbr.* a card issued to people claiming unemployment benefit.

ubiquitous *adj.* found everywhere. ▫ **ubiquity** *n.*

UCAS *abbr.* Universities and Colleges Admissions Service.

udder *n.* a bag-like milk-secreting organ of a cow, goat, etc.

UDI *abbr.* unilateral declaration of independence.

UEFA *abbr.* Union of European Football Associations.

UFO *abbr.* unidentified flying object.

ugly *adj.* (**uglier, ugliest**) unpleasant to look at or hear; threatening, hostile. ▫ **ugliness** *n.*

UHF *abbr.* ultra-high frequency.

UHT *abbr.* ultra heat treated (esp. of milk).

UK *abbr.* United Kingdom.

ukulele (yoo-kŭ-**lay**-li) *n.* a small four-stringed guitar.

ulcer *n.* an open sore. ▫ **ulcerous** *adj.*

ulcerated *adj.* affected with an ulcer. ▫ **ulceration** *n.*

ulna *n.* (*pl.* **ulnae** or **ulnas**) the thinner long bone of the forearm. ▫ **ulnar** *adj.*

ult. *abbr.* ultimo.

ulterior *adj.* beyond what is obvious or admitted.

ultimate *adj.* final; extreme; fundamental. ▫ **ultimately** *adv.*

ultimatum *n.* (*pl.* **ultimatums** or **ultimata**) a final demand, with a threat of hostile action if this is rejected.

ultimo *adj. dated* of last month.

ultra- *pref.* beyond; extremely.

ultra-high *adj.* (of a frequency) between 300 and 3000 megahertz.

ultramarine *adj.* & *n.* brilliant deep blue.

ultrasonic *adj.* above the range of normal human hearing.

ultrasound *n.* ultrasonic waves.

ultraviolet *adj.* of or using radiation with a wavelength shorter than that of visible light rays.

ululate (ul-yuu-layt, **yoo**-yuu-layt) *v.* howl, wail. ▫ **ululation** *n.*

umbel *n.* a broad flat flower cluster.

umber *n.* a brownish natural pigment.

umbilical *adj.* of the navel.

umbilical cord *n.* a flexible tube connecting the placenta to the navel of a foetus.

umbra *n.* (*pl.* **umbrae** or **umbras**) an area of total shadow cast by the moon or earth in an eclipse.

umbrage *n.* annoyance. ▫ **take umbrage** be offended.

umbrella *n.* a circle of fabric on a folding framework of spokes on a central stick, used as a protection against rain.

umlaut (**uum**-lowt) *n.* a mark (¨) over a vowel indicating a change in pronunciation, used esp. in Germanic languages.

umpire *n.* a person appointed to supervise a sporting contest and see that rules are observed. ● *v.* act as umpire in.

umpteen *adj. informal* very many. ◻ **umpteenth** *adj.*

UN *abbr.* United Nations.

un- *pref.* not; reversing the action indicated by a verb, e.g. *unlock.* (*The number of words with this prefix is almost unlimited and many of those whose meaning is obvious are not listed below.*)

unaccountable *adj.* **1** not explicable or predictable. **2** not having to justify one's actions. ◻ **unaccountably** *adv.*

unadulterated *adj.* not mixed or diluted; absolute.

unalloyed *adj.* not spoiled or qualified; pure.

unanimous *adj.* with everyone's agreement. ◻ **unanimity** *n.*, **unanimously** *adv.*

unarmed *adj.* without weapons.

unassuming *adj.* not arrogant, unpretentious.

unattended *adj.* not supervised or guarded; not noticed.

unavoidable *adj.* unable to be avoided. ◻ **unavoidably** *adv.*

unawares *adv.* not realizing something, not aware.

unbalanced *adj.* **1** not balanced; not impartial. **2** mentally unstable.

unbeknown *adj.* (also **unbeknownst**) ◻ **unbeknown to** without the knowledge of.

unbend *v.* (**unbent, unbending**) **1** change from a bent position. **2** become relaxed or affable.

unbending *adj.* inflexible, refusing to alter one's demands.

unbidden *adj.* not commanded or invited.

unblock *v.* remove an obstruction from.

unbolt *v.* open (a door) by drawing back the bolt.

unborn *adj.* not yet born.

unbounded *adj.* without limits.

unbridled *adj.* unrestrained.

unburden *v.* ◻ **unburden oneself** reveal one's thoughts and feelings.

uncalled for *adj.* given or done impertinently or unjustifiably.

uncanny *adj.* (**uncannier, uncanniest**) mysterious and frightening; eerie. ◻ **uncannily** *adv.*

uncared-for *adj.* neglected.

unceasing *adj.* continuous.

unceremonious *adj.* without proper formality or dignity.

uncertain *adj.* not definitely known, not dependable; not knowing certainly.

uncle *n.* a brother or brother-in-law of one's father or mother.

unclean *adj.* not clean; ritually impure.

uncoil *v.* unwind.

uncommon *adj.* not common, unusual.

uncompromising *adj.* not allowing or not seeking compromise, inflexible.

unconcern *n.* lack of concern.

unconditional *adj.* not subject to conditions. ◻ **unconditionally** *adv.*

unconscionable *adj.* not right or reasonable; excessive.

unconscious *adj.* not conscious; not aware; done without conscious intention. ◻ **unconsciously** *adv.*, **unconsciousness** *n.*

unconsidered *adj.* **1** disregarded. **2** said or done without thought.

uncork *v.* pull the cork from.

uncouple *v.* disconnect (train carriages etc.).

uncouth *adj.* awkward in manner, boorish.

uncover *v.* remove a covering from; reveal, expose.

unction *n.* **1** anointing with oil, esp. as a religious rite. **2** effusive politeness.

unctuous *adj.* flattering, ingratiating. ◻ **unctuously** *adv.*, **unctuousness** *n.*

undeceive *v.* free (a person) from a misconception.

undecided *adj.* not having made a decision; not settled or answered.

undeniable *adj.* undoubtedly true. ▫ **undeniably** *adv.*

under *prep.* **1** extending below. **2** at or to a position or rank lower than; behind (a surface); less than. **3** governed or controlled by; affected by, undergoing. **4** subject to the rules of; in accordance with. ● *adv.* **1** in or to a position directly below something; under water. **2** in or into a state of unconsciousness. **3** below a required or specified number or amount. ▫ **under age** not old enough, esp. for some legal right; not yet of adult status. **under way** making progress.

under- *pref.* **1** below; lower, subordinate. **2** insufficiently.

underarm *adj.* & *adv.* (of a stroke in sport) with the hand brought forwards and upwards. ● *n.* the armpit.

underbelly *n.* (*pl.* **-ies**) the soft underside of an animal; an area vulnerable to attack.

undercarriage *n.* an aircraft's landing wheels and their supports; the supporting framework of a vehicle.

underclass *n.* the lowest and poorest social class in a country.

undercliff *n.* a terrace or lower cliff formed by a landslip.

underclothes *n.pl.* (also **underclothing**) underwear.

undercoat *n.* a layer of paint used under a finishing coat.

undercover *adj.* done or doing things secretly.

undercurrent *n.* a current flowing below a surface; an underlying feeling, influence, or trend.

undercut *v.* (**undercut, undercutting**) **1** offer goods or services for a lower price than (a competitor). **2** cut away the part below (a cliff edge etc.); weaken, undermine.

underdog *n.* a person etc. in an inferior or subordinate position.

underdone *adj.* not thoroughly cooked.

underestimate *v.* make too low an estimate (of).

underfelt *n.* felt for laying under a carpet.

underfoot *adv.* **1** on the ground. **2** getting in the way.

underfunded *adj.* provided with insufficient funds.

undergo *v.* (**undergoes, underwent, undergone, undergoing**) experience; be subjected to.

undergraduate *n.* a university student who has not yet taken a degree.

underground *adj.* & *adv.* under the surface of the ground; secretly. ● *n.* an underground railway.

undergrowth *n.* thick growth of shrubs and bushes under trees.

underhand *adj.* **1** done or doing things slyly or secretly. **2** underarm.

underlay *n.* material laid under another as a support. ● *v.* past of **underlie**.

underlie *v.* (**underlay, underlain, underlying**) be the cause or basis of. ▫ **underlying** *adj.*

underline *v.* **1** draw a line under. **2** emphasize.

underling *n.* a subordinate.

undermanned *adj.* having too few staff or crew etc.

undermine *v.* weaken gradually; weaken the foundations of.

underneath *prep.* & *adv.* below; hidden by (a surface).

underpants *n.pl.* an undergarment covering the lower part of the body and part of the legs.

underpass *n.* a road passing under another.

underpay *v.* (**underpaid, underpaying**) pay (a person) too little.

underpin *v.* (**underpinned, underpinning**) support, strengthen from beneath.

underprivileged *adj.* not having the normal standard of living or rights.

underrate *v.* underestimate.

underscore *v.* underline.

underseal *v.* coat the lower surface of (a vehicle) with a protective layer. ● *n.* this coating.

undersell *v.* (**undersold, underselling**) sell at a lower price than (a competitor).

undershoot *v.* (**undershot, undershooting**) fall short of (a target); land short of (a runway).

undersigned *adj.* who has or have signed this document.

underskirt *n.* a petticoat.

understand *v.* (**understood, understanding**) **1** grasp the meaning, nature, or cause of; see the significance of. **2** infer; assume without being told; interpret in a particular way.

understandable *adj.* able to be understood; able to be accepted or excused. □ **understandably** *adv.*

understanding *adj.* showing insight or sympathy. ● *n.* **1** ability to understand; sympathetic insight. **2** an agreement; a thing agreed.

understate *v.* represent as smaller, less good, etc., than is the case. □ **understatement** *n.*

understated *adj.* subtle, not exaggerated or flamboyant.

understudy *n.* (*pl.* **-ies**) an actor who studies another's part in order to be able to take his or her place if necessary. ● *v.* (**understudied, understudying**) be an understudy for.

undertake *v.* (**undertook, undertaken, undertaking**) commit oneself to (an action); promise to do something.

undertaker *n.* a person whose business is to organize funerals.

undertaking *n.* **1** work etc. undertaken. **2** a promise, a guarantee.

undertone *n.* **1** a low or subdued tone. **2** an underlying quality or feeling.

undertow *n.* an undercurrent moving in the opposite direction to the surface current.

underwear *n.* garments worn under indoor clothing, next to the skin.

underwent past of **undergo**.

underworld *n.* **1** a part of society habitually involved in crime. **2** (in mythology) the abode of the spirits of the dead, under the earth.

underwrite *v.* (**underwrote, underwritten, underwriting**) accept liability under (an insurance policy); undertake to finance. □ **underwriter** *n.*

undesirable *adj.* harmful or unpleasant. □ **undesirably** *adv.*

undies *n.pl.* *informal* women's underwear.

undo *v.* (**undoes, undid, undone, undoing**) **1** unfasten, unwrap. **2** cancel the effect of. **3** cause disaster to.

undone *adj.* **1** not fastened or tied. **2** not done.

undoubted *adj.* not disputed. □ **undoubtedly** *adv.*

undreamed *adj.* (also **undreamt**) not imagined, not thought to be possible.

undress *v.* take clothes off.

undue *adj.* excessive.

undulate *v.* move with a wave-like motion; have a wave-like shape. □ **undulation** *n.*

unduly *adv.* excessively.

undying *adj.* everlasting.

unearned income *n.* income from interest on investments, rent from tenants, etc.

unearth *v.* uncover or bring out from the ground; find by searching.

unearthly *adj.* **1** supernatural; mysterious. **2** *informal* absurdly early or inconvenient.

uneasy *adj.* (**uneasier, uneasiest**) anxious; uncomfortable; awkward. □ **unease** *n.*, **uneasily** *adv.*, **uneasiness** *n.*

uneatable *adj.* not fit to be eaten.

uneconomic *adj.* not profitable.

unemployable *adj.* not fit for paid employment.

unemployed *adj.* **1** without a paid job. **2** not in use. □ **unemployment** *n.*

unending *adj.* endless.

unequalled *adj.* (*Amer.* **unequaled**) without an equal; supreme.

unequivocal *adj.* clear and not ambiguous. □ **unequivocally** *adv.*

unerring *adj.* making no mistake.

UNESCO *abbr.* (also **Unesco**) United Nations Educational, Scientific, and Cultural Organization.

uneven *adj.* not level or smooth; not regular. □ **unevenly** *adv.*, **unevenness** *n.*

unexampled *adj.* without precedent.

unexceptionable *adj.* entirely satisfactory.

■ **Usage** *Unexceptionable* is sometimes confused with *unexceptional.*

unexceptional *adj.* not unusual or outstanding.

unexpected *adj.* not expected; surprising. □ **unexpectedly** *adv.*

unfailing *adj.* constant; never stopping or going wrong. □ **unfailingly** *adv.*

unfair *adj.* not impartial, not in accordance with justice. □ **unfairly** *adv.*, **unfairness** *n.*

unfaithful *adj.* not loyal; having committed adultery. □ **unfaithfully** *adv.*, **unfaithfulness** *n.*

unfeeling *adj.* unsympathetic, callous. □ **unfeelingly** *adv.*

unfit *adj.* **1** unsuitable. **2** not in perfect physical condition.

unflappable *adj. informal* remaining calm in a crisis.

unfold *v.* **1** open, spread out. **2** reveal; be revealed.

unforeseen *adj.* not predicted.

unforgettable *adj.* impossible to forget. □ **unforgettably** *adv.*

unfortunate *adj.* having bad luck; regrettable. □ **unfortunately** *adv.*

unfounded *adj.* with no basis.

unfrock *v.* dismiss (a priest) from the priesthood.

unfurl *v.* unroll; spread out.

ungainly *adj.* awkward-looking, not graceful. □ **ungainliness** *n.*

ungodly *adj.* **1** irreligious; wicked. **2** *informal* unreasonably inconvenient or early. □ **ungodliness** *n.*

ungovernable *adj.* uncontrollable.

ungracious *adj.* not courteous or kindly. □ **ungraciously** *adv.*

unguarded *adj.* **1** not guarded. **2** incautious.

unguent (ung-wĕnt) *n.* an ointment, a lubricant.

ungulate *n.* a hoofed animal.

unhand *v. literary* let go of.

unhappy *adj.* (**unhappier, unhappiest**) **1** not happy, sad. **2** unfortunate. **3** not satisfied. □ **unhappily** *adv.*, **unhappiness** *n.*

unhealthy *adj.* (**unhealthier, unhealthiest**) not healthy; harmful to health. □ **unhealthily** *adv.*

unheard-of *adj.* not previously known of or done.

unhinged *adj.* mentally unbalanced.

unholy *adj.* (**unholier, unholiest**) **1** wicked, irreverent. **2** *informal* dreadful, outrageous.

unicorn *n.* a mythical horselike animal with one straight horn on its forehead.

uniform *n.* distinctive clothing identifying the wearer as a member of an organization or group. ● *adj.* always the same; not differing from one another. □ **uniformity** *n.*, **uniformly** *adv.*

unify *v.* (**unified, unifying**) unite. □ **unification** *n.*

unilateral *adj.* done by or affecting only one person or group out of several. □ **unilaterally** *adv.*

unimpeachable *adj.* completely trustworthy.

uninterested *adj.* not interested; showing no concern.

uninviting *adj.* unattractive, repellent.

union *n.* uniting, being united; a whole formed by uniting parts; an association; a trade union.

Union Jack *n.* the national flag of the UK.

unionist *n.* **1** a member of a trade union; a supporter of trade unions. **2** one who favours union, esp. someone in Northern Ireland favouring union with Great Britain.

unionize *v.* (also **-ise**) organize into or cause to join a union. □ **unionization** *n.*

unique *adj.* **1** the only one of its kind; belonging only to one place, person, etc. **2** extraordinary. □ **uniquely** *adv.*

■ **Usage** Some people consider the use of *unique* to mean 'extraordinary', and expressions such as 'quite unique', to be incorrect.

unisex *adj.* suitable for people of either sex.

unison *n.* □ **in unison** speaking or acting together; singing or playing the same tune.

unit *n.* **1** an individual thing, person, or group, esp. as part of a complex whole. **2** a fixed quantity used as a standard of measurement. **3** a piece of furniture or equipment; part of an institution, having a specialized function.

Unitarian *n.* a person who believes that God is not a Trinity but one person.

unitary *adj.* single; of a single whole.

unite *v.* join together, make or become one; act together, cooperate.

United Kingdom *n.* Great Britain and Northern Ireland.

unit trust *n.* a trust managing a number of securities, in which small investors can buy units.

unity *n.* (*pl.* **-ies**) the state of being united or coherent; agreement; a complex whole.

universal *adj.* of, for, or done by all. □ **universally** *adv.*

universe *n.* all existing things, including the earth and its creatures and all the heavenly bodies.

university *n.* (*pl.* **-ies**) an educational institution for advanced learning and research.

unkempt *adj.* looking untidy or neglected.

unkind *adj.* cruel, harsh, hurtful. □ **unkindly** *adv.*, **unkindness** *n.*

unknown *adj.* not known. ● *n.* an unknown person, thing, or place.

unleaded *adj.* (of petrol etc.) without added lead.

unleash *v.* release, let loose.

unleavened *adj.* (of bread) made without yeast or other raising agent.

unless *conj.* except when; except on condition that.

unlettered *adj.* illiterate.

unlike *adj.* different. ● *prep.* different or differently from.

unlikely *adj.* (**unlikelier, unlikeliest**) improbable, not likely to happen, be true, etc.

unlimited *adj.* not limited; very great in number.

unlisted *adj.* not included in a (published) list.

unload *v.* **1** remove (a cargo) from (a vehicle etc.); *informal* get rid of. **2** remove ammunition from (a gun).

unlock *v.* release the lock of (a door etc.); make accessible or available.

unlooked-for *adj.* unexpected.

unmanned *adj.* operated without a crew.

unmask *v.* expose the true nature of; remove a mask from.

unmentionable *adj.* too shocking to be spoken of.

unmistakable *adj.* clear, not able to be doubted or mistaken for another. □ **unmistakably** *adv.*

unmitigated *adj.* not modified, absolute.

unmoved *adj.* not affected by emotion; not changed in intention.

unnatural *adj.* not natural; not normal. □ **unnaturally** *adv.*

unnecessary *adj.* not needed; excessive. □ **unnecessarily** *adv.*

unnerve *v.* cause to lose courage or determination.

unnumbered *adj.* **1** not marked with a number. **2** countless.

unobtrusive *adj.* not making oneself or itself noticed. □ **unobtrusively** *adv.*

unpack *v.* open and remove the contents of (a suitcase etc.); take out from its packaging.

unparalleled *adj.* never yet equalled.

unpick *v.* undo the stitching of.

unplaced *adj.* not placed as one of the first three in a race etc.

unpleasant *adj.* causing distaste or distress. □ **unpleasantly** *adv.*, **unpleasantness** *n.*

unplumbed *adj.* not fully investigated or understood.

unpopular *adj.* not popular; disliked. □ **unpopularity** *n.*

unprecedented *adj.* not done or known before; unparalleled.

unprepared *adj.* not ready or equipped for something; not prepared.

unprepossessing *adj.* unattractive, not making a good impression.

unpretentious *adj.* not trying to impress by artifice.

unprincipled *adj.* without good moral principles, unscrupulous.

unprintable *adj.* too indecent or libellous etc. to be printed.

unprofessional *adj.* contrary to the standards of behaviour for members of a profession. □ **unprofessionally** *adv.*

unprofitable *adj.* not profitable; useless. □ **unprofitably** *adv.*

unprompted *adj.* spontaneous.

unqualified *adj.* **1** lacking official qualifications. **2** absolute, unmodified.

unquestionable *adj.* too clear to be doubted. □ **unquestionably** *adv.*

unravel *v.* (**unravelled, unravelling** *Amer.* **unraveled**) disentangle; undo (knitted fabric); become disentangled.

unready *adj.* **1** not ready or prepared for something. **2** *archaic* not well advised.

unreal *adj.* imaginary, not real; *informal* incredible, amazing.

unreasonable *adj.* not guided by reason; unfair, excessive. □ **unreasonably** *adv.*

unrelenting *adj.* not becoming less intense, severe, or strict.

unremitting *adj.* not ceasing.

unrequited *adj.* (esp. of love) not returned or rewarded.

unreservedly *adv.* without reservation, completely.

unrest *n.* disturbance, violent disorder; dissatisfaction.

unrivalled *adj.* (*Amer.* **unrivaled**) having no equal incomparable.

unroll *v.* open out (something rolled).

unruly *adj.* (**unrulier, unruliest**) not easy to control, disorderly. □ **unruliness** *n.*

unsaid *adj.* not spoken or expressed.

unsaturated *adj.* (of fat or oil) capable of further reaction by combining with hydrogen.

unsavoury *adj.* (*Amer.* **unsavory**) disagreeable to the taste or smell; morally disgusting.

unscathed *adj.* without suffering any injury.

unscramble *v.* sort out; make (a scrambled transmission) intelligible.

unscrew *v.* unfasten (a lid etc.); unfasten by removing screws.

unscripted *adj.* without a prepared script.

unscrupulous *adj.* lacking moral scruples or principles.

unseasonable *adj.* not seasonable; untimely.

unseat *v.* dislodge (a rider); remove from a position of authority.

unseen *adj.* not seen, invisible; (of translation) done without preparation.

unselfish *adj.* not selfish; considering others' needs before one's own. ▫ **unselfishly** *adv.*, **unselfishness** *n.*

unsettle *v.* make uneasy, disturb.

unsettled *adj.* lacking stability; changeable; uneasy, anxious.

unshakeable *adj.* (also **unshakable**) firm.

unsightly *adj.* not pleasant to look at, ugly. ▫ **unsightliness** *n.*

unskilled *adj.* not having or needing skill or special training.

unsociable *adj.* disliking company.

▪ **Usage** *Unsociable* is sometimes confused with *unsocial.*

unsocial *adj.* **1** (of working hours) inconvenient because not conforming to the normal working day. **2** antisocial, disturbing to others.

unsolicited *adj.* not requested.

unsophisticated *adj.* simple and natural or naive.

unsound *adj.* not safe or strong; faulty, unreliable, invalid. ▫ **of unsound mind** insane.

unsparing *adj.* giving lavishly.

unspeakable *adj.* too bad to be described in words.

unstable *adj.* not stable; mentally or emotionally unbalanced.

unstick *v.* (**unstuck, unsticking**) detach (what is stuck). ▫ **come unstuck** *informal* suffer disaster, fail.

unstinting *adj.* given freely and generously.

unstudied *adj.* natural in manner, spontaneous.

unsung *adj.* not acknowledged or honoured.

unsuspecting *adj.* not expecting or aware of something.

unswerving *adj.* not turning aside; unchanging.

untenable *adj.* (of a theory or position) not valid because of strong arguments against it.

unthinkable *adj.* too bad or too unlikely to be thought about.

unthinking *adj.* thoughtless.

untidy *adj.* (**untidier, untidiest**) in disorder; not keeping things neat. ▫ **untidily** *adv.*, **untidiness** *n.*

untie *v.* (**untied, untying**) unfasten; release from being tied up.

until *prep. & conj.* up to (a specified time, event, etc.), till.

untimely *adj.* happening at an unsuitable time; premature. ▫ **untimeliness** *n.*

unto *prep. archaic* to.

untold *adj.* **1** not told. **2** too much or too many to be counted.

untouchable *adj.* not able or not allowed to be touched. ● *n.* a member of the lowest Hindu social group.

untoward *adj.* unexpected and inconvenient.

untried *adj.* not yet tried or tested.

untruth *n.* a lie; being false. ▫ **untruthful** *adj.*, **untruthfully** *adv.*

unusual *adj.* not usual; remarkable, rare. ▫ **unusually** *adv.*

unutterable *adj.* too great to be expressed in words. ▫ **unutterably** *adv.*

unvarnished *adj.* not varnished; plain and straightforward.

unveil *v.* remove a veil or drapery from; reveal, make known.

unwaged *adj.* not doing paid work.

unwarranted *adj.* unjustified, unauthorized.

unwary *adj.* not cautious.

unwell *adj.* not in good health.

unwieldy *adj.* (**unwieldier, unwieldiest**) awkward to move or control because of its size, shape, or weight.

unwilling *adj.* reluctant.

unwind *v.* (**unwound, unwinding**) draw out or become drawn out from being wound; *informal* relax from work or tension.

unwise *adj.* not sensible, foolish. □ **unwisely** *adv.*

unwitting *adj.* unaware; unintentional. □ **unwittingly** *adv.*

unwonted (un-wohn-tid) *adj.* not customary, not usual.

unworldly *adj.* spiritually-minded, not materialistic. □ **unworldliness** *n.*

unworthy *adj.* (**unworthier, unworthiest**) not deserving something; beneath someone's character, discreditable; worthless.

unwrap *v.* (**unwrapped, unwrapping**) remove the wrapping from; open, unfold.

unwritten *adj.* not written down; based on custom not statute.

unzip *v.* (**unzipped, unzipping**) open by the undoing of a zip fastener.

up *adv.* **1** to, in, or at a higher place or state; to a larger size or higher level of intensity, volume, etc. **2** to a vertical position; out of bed. **3** towards or as far as a stated place, position, etc. **4** so as to be closed or finished: *do up the buttons.* **5** *informal* happening, amiss: *what's up?* ● *prep.* upwards along, through, or into; to or at a higher part of. ● *adj.* **1** moving or directed upwards. **2** (of a train) travelling towards the capital or a major station. **3** (of a computer system) functioning. ● *v.* (**upped, upping**) *informal* **1** do something suddenly: *she upped and went.* **2** raise; increase. □ **it's all up with someone** *informal* someone is ruined or killed. **up against** *informal* confronted by (a difficulty). **up on** well informed about. **ups and downs** alternate good and bad fortune. **up to 1** as far as; as much as. **2** capable of, fit for. **3** the responsibility or choice of. **4** *informal* doing, occupied with.

upbeat *n. Music* an unaccented beat preceding an accented one. ● *adj. informal* cheerful, optimistic.

upbraid *v.* reproach.

upbringing *n.* training and education during childhood.

update *v.* bring up to date.

upend *v.* set on end or upside down.

upgrade *v.* raise to a higher grade; improve (equipment etc.).

upheaval *n.* a sudden violent change or movement.

uphill *adj.* & *adv.* going or sloping upwards.

uphold *v.* (**upheld, upholding**) support.

upholster *v.* put a fabric covering, padding, etc. on (furniture).

upholstery *n.* upholstering; material used in this.

upkeep *n.* keeping (a thing) in good condition and repair; the cost of this.

upland *n.* & *adj.* (of) the higher or inland parts of a country.

uplift *v.* raise; elevate mentally or morally. ● *n.* being raised; a mentally elevating influence.

upmarket *adj.* & *adv.* of or towards the more expensive end of the market; of or towards higher quality.

upon *prep.* on.

upper *adj.* higher in place, position, or rank. ● *n.* the part of a shoe above the sole. □ **the upper hand** mastery, dominance.

upper case *n.* capital letters in printing or typing.

upper class *n.* the highest social class. □ **upper-class** *adj.*

upper crust *n. informal* the aristocracy.

uppermost *adj.* & *adv.* in, on, or to the top or most prominent position.

uppish *adj.* (also **uppity**) *informal* self-assertive; arrogant.

upright *adj.* **1** in a vertical position. **2** strictly honest or honourable. ● *n.* a vertical part or support.

uprising *n.* a rebellion.

uproar *n.* an outburst of noise and excitement or anger.

uproarious *adj.* noisy; with loud laughter. □ **uproariously** *adv.*

uproot *v.* pull out of the ground together with its roots; force to leave an established home.

upset *v.* (up-set) (**upset, upsetting**) **1** distress, worry. **2** knock over; disrupt; disturb the digestion of. ● *n.* (**up**-set) a state of distress or disruption.

upshot *n.* an outcome.

upside down *adv.* & *adj.* with the upper part underneath; in or into great disorder.

upstage *adv.* & *adj.* at or towards the back of a theatre stage. ● *v.* divert attention from; outshine.

upstairs *adv.* & *adj.* to or on a higher floor.

upstanding *adj.* **1** honest, respectable. **2** strong, healthy.

upstart *n.* a person newly risen to a high position, esp. one who behaves arrogantly.

upstream *adj.* & *adv.* towards the source of a stream or river, against the current.

upsurge *n.* an upward surge, a rise.

upswing *n.* an increase; an upward trend.

uptake *n.* □ **quick on the uptake** *informal* quick to understand.

uptight *adj. informal* nervously tense; annoyed.

up to date *adj.* modern, fashionable.

upturn (**up**-tern) *n.* an improvement or upward trend. ● *v.* turn upwards or upside down.

upward *adj.* moving or leading up. ● *adv.* (also **upwards**) towards a higher place etc.

upwind *adj.* & *adv.* in the direction from which the wind is blowing.

uranium *n.* a metallic element (symbol U), a heavy grey metal used as a source of nuclear energy.

urban *adj.* of a city or town.

urbane (er-**bayn**) *adj.* courteous; having elegant manners. □ **urbanely** *adv.*, **urbanity** *n.*

urbanize *v.* (also **-ise**) change (a place) into an urban area. □ **urbanization** *n.*

urchin *n.* a mischievous child.

Urdu (**oor**-doo) *n.* a language related to Hindi.

ureter (yoo-**ree**-ter) *n.* the duct from the kidney to the bladder.

urethra (yoo-**ree**-thră) *n.* the duct which carries urine from the body.

urge *v.* encourage, advise strongly; recommend strongly; guide hurriedly. ● *n.* a strong desire or impulse.

urgent *adj.* needing or calling for immediate attention or action. □ **urgency** *n.*, **urgently** *adv.*

urinal *n.* a receptacle or structure for receiving urine.

urinate *v.* discharge urine from the body. □ **urination** *n.*

urine *n.* waste liquid which collects in the bladder and is discharged from the body. □ **urinary** *adj.*

urn *n.* **1** a vase, esp. for holding a cremated person's ashes. **2** a large metal container with a tap, for keeping water etc. hot.

ursine (**er**-sIn) *adj.* of or like a bear.

us *pron.* the objective case of *we*.

US, USA *abbr.* United States (of America).

usable *adj.* able or fit to be used.

usage *n.* **1** using, being used; the way in which something is used. **2** customary practice.

use *v.* (yooz) **1** cause to serve one's purpose or achieve one's end; exploit selfishly. **2** treat in a specified way. ● *n.* (yooss) using, being used; being helpful or useful; the power to control and use something; a purpose for which something is used. □ **use up** use all or the remains of, finish.

used (yoozd) *adj.* second-hand.

used to (yoost) *v.* was accustomed to (do). ● *adj.* familiar with by practice or habit.

useful *adj.* fit for a practical purpose; able to produce good results. □ **usefully** *adv.*, **usefulness** *n.*

useless *adj.* unable to serve a practical purpose; *informal* hopelessly incompetent. □ **uselessly** *adv.*, **uselessness** *n.*

user *n.* a person who uses something.

user-friendly *adj.* easy for a user to understand and operate.

usher *n.* a person who shows people to their seats in a public hall etc. ● *v.* lead, escort.

usherette *n.* a woman who ushers people to seats in a cinema etc.

USSR *abbr. hist.* Union of Soviet Socialist Republics.

usual *adj.* such as happens or is done or used etc. in many or most instances. □ **usually** *adv.*

usurp (yoo-serp) *v.* take (power, a position, or right) wrongfully or by force. □ **usurpation** *n.*, **usurper** *n.*

usury *n.* the lending of money at excessively high rates of interest. □ **usurer** *n.*

utensil *n.* an instrument or container, esp. for domestic use.

uterus *n.* the womb. □ **uterine** *adj.*

utilitarian *adj.* useful rather than decorative or luxurious.

utilitarianism *n.* the theory that actions are justified if they benefit the majority.

utility *n.* (*pl.* **-ies**) **1** being useful. **2** (also **public utility**) a company supplying water, gas, electricity, etc. to the community. ● *adj.* severely practical.

utility room *n.* a room for large domestic appliances.

utilize *v.* (also **-ise**) make use of. □ **utilization** *n.*

utmost *adj.* furthest, greatest, extreme. ● *n.* the furthest point or degree etc.

Utopia *n.* an imaginary place or state where all is perfect. □ **Utopian** *adj.*

utter[1] *adj.* complete, absolute. □ **utterly** *adv.*

utter[2] *v.* make (a sound or words) with the mouth or voice; speak. □ **utterance** *n.*

uttermost *adj.* & *n.* = **utmost**.

U-turn *n.* the driving of a vehicle in a U-shaped course to reverse its direction; a reversal of policy or opinion.

UV *abbr.* ultraviolet.

uvula (yoov-yoo-lă) *n.* (*pl.* **uvulae**) the small fleshy projection hanging at the back of the throat. □ **uvular** *adj.*

uxorious (uk-sor-i-ŭs) *adj.* excessively fond of one's wife.

V *n.* (as a Roman numeral) 5. ● *abbr.* volt(s). ● *symb.* vanadium.

v. *abbr.* **1** versus. **2** very.

vac *n. informal* **1** a vacation. **2** a vacuum cleaner.

vacancy *n.* (*pl.* **-ies**) an unoccupied position or job; empty space; emptiness.

vacant *adj.* **1** unoccupied. **2** showing no interest or understanding. □ **vacantly** *adv.*

vacate *v.* cease to occupy.

vacation *n.* **1** an interval between terms in universities and law courts; *Amer.* a holiday. **2** ceasing to occupy a place or position.

vaccinate *n.* inoculate with a vaccine. □ **vaccination** *n.*

vaccine (vak-seen) *n.* a substance used to stimulate the production of antibodies giving immunity against a disease by causing a mild form of it.

vacillate *v.* keep changing one's mind. □ **vacillation** *n.*

vacuous *adj.* unintelligent, inane; expressionless. □ **vacuity** *n.*, **vacuously** *adv.*

vacuum *n.* (*pl.* **vacuums** or **vacua**) a space from which air has been removed; a gap, a blank. ● *v. informal* clean with a vacuum cleaner.

vacuum cleaner *n.* an electrical apparatus that takes up dust by suction.

vacuum flask *n.* a container for keeping liquids hot or cold.

vacuum-packed *adj.* sealed after removal of air.

vagabond *n.* a wanderer; a vagrant.

vagary *n.* (*pl.* **-ies**) an unpredictable change or action.

vagina *n.* the passage leading from the vulva to the womb. □ **vaginal** *adj.*

vagrant *n.* a person without a settled home. □ **vagrancy** *n.*

vague *adj.* not clearly explained or perceived; not expressing oneself clearly. □ **vaguely** *adv.*, **vagueness** *n.*

vain *adj.* **1** excessively proud of one's appearance, abilities, etc. **2** useless, futile. □ **in vain** uselessly, without success. □ **vainly** *adv.*

vainglory *n.* great pride in oneself. □ **vainglorious** *adj.*

valance (val-ăns) *n.* a short curtain or hanging frill.

vale *n.* a valley.

valediction *n.* a farewell. □ **valedictory** *adj.*

valence (vay-lĕns) *n.* (also **valency**) the combining power of an atom as compared with that of the hydrogen atom.

valentine *n.* a romantic greetings card sent, often anonymously, on St Valentine's Day (14 Feb.); a person to whom one sends this.

valet (val-ay) *n.* a man's personal attendant. ● *v.* (**valeted, valeting**) **1** act as valet to. **2** clean (a car) thoroughly.

valetudinarian *n.* a person of poor health or unduly anxious about health.

valiant *adj.* brave. □ **valiantly** *adv.*

valid *adj.* **1** having legal force, legally acceptable. **2** actually supporting the intended conclusion, logically sound. □ **validity** *n.*

validate *v.* check the validity of; demonstrate the truth of; make valid. □ **validation** *n.*

valise *n.* a small suitcase.

valley *n.* (*pl.* **valleys**) a low area between hills.

valour *n.* (*Amer.* **valor**) bravery.

valuable *adj.* of great value or worth. ● *n.pl.* (**valuables**) valuable things.

valuation *n.* estimation or an estimate of a thing's worth.

value *n.* **1** the amount of money etc. considered equivalent to something; the extent to which something is considered useful, important, etc. **2** (**values**) moral principles, standards that one considers important. ● *v.* **1** consider precious. **2** estimate the value of.

value added tax *n.* a tax on the amount by which a thing's value has been increased at each stage of its production.

value judgement *n.* a subjective estimate of quality etc.

valuer *n.* a person who estimates values professionally.

valve *n.* **1** a device controlling flow through a pipe; a structure allowing blood to flow in one direction only. **2** each half of the hinged shell of an oyster etc. □ **valvular** *adj.*

vamoose *v. Amer. informal* depart hurriedly.

vamp *n.* the upper front part of a boot or shoe. ● *v.* play a short simple passage of music repeatedly.

vampire *n.* a ghost or reanimated body believed to suck blood from living humans.

van *n.* **1** a covered vehicle for transporting goods etc.; a railway carriage for luggage or goods. **2** the leading part, the front.

vanadium *n.* a hard grey metallic element (symbol V).

vandal *n.* a person who damages things wilfully. □ **vandalism** *n.*

vandalize *v.* (also **-ise**) damage wilfully.

vane *n.* **1** a weathervane. **2** the blade of a propeller, sail of a windmill, etc.

vanguard *n.* the foremost part of an advancing army etc.

vanilla *n.* a sweetish flavouring. ● *adj. informal* ordinary, not elaborate or special.

vanish *v.* disappear completely.

vanity *n.* (*pl.* **-ies**) **1** conceit. **2** futility.

vanity case *n.* a small case for carrying cosmetics etc.

vanquish *v.* conquer.

vantage point *n.* a position giving a good view.

vapid *adj.* insipid, uninteresting. □ **vapidity** *n.*, **vapidly** *adv.*

vaporize *v.* (also **-ise**) convert or be converted into vapour. □ **vaporization** *n.*

vapour *n.* (*Amer.* **vapor**) moisture suspended in air, into which certain liquids or solids are converted by heating. □ **vaporous** *adj.*

variable *adj.* changeable, not constant. ● *n.* a part or element liable to change. □ **variability** *n.*

variance *n.* □ **at variance** in disagreement.

variant *n.* a form of something differing from others or from a standard. ● *adj.* differing in this way.

variation *n.* a change, a slight difference; a variant; a repetition of a musical theme with changes and ornamentation.

varicose *adj.* (of veins) permanently swollen. □ **varicosity** *n.*

varied *adj.* of different sorts.

variegated *adj.* having irregular patches of colours. □ **variegation** *n.*

variety *n.* (*pl.* **-ies**) **1** not being uniform or monotonous; a selection of different things of the same type. **2** a sort or kind. **3** light entertainment made up of a series of short unrelated performances.

various *adj.* **1** differing from one another, not uniform. **2** several. □ **variously** *adv.*

■ **Usage** *Various* (unlike *several*) is not a pronoun and therefore cannot be used with *of*, as (wrongly) in *various of the guests arrived late.*

varlet *n. archaic* **1** a menial servant. **2** a rascal.

varnish *n.* a liquid that dries to form a shiny transparent coating. ● *v.* coat with varnish.

vary *v.* (**varied, varying**) make or be or become different.

vascular *adj.* of vessels or ducts for conveying blood or sap.

vase *n.* a decorative jar for holding cut flowers.

vasectomy *n.* (*pl.* **-ies**) a surgical removal of part of the ducts that carry semen from the testicles, esp. as a method of birth control.

Vaseline *n. trademark* a thick oily cream made from petroleum, used as an ointment or lubricant.

vassal *n.* a person or country subordinate to another.

vast *adj.* very great in area or size. □ **vastly** *adv.*, **vastness** *n.*

VAT *abbr.* value added tax.

vat *n.* a large tank for liquids.

vault *n.* **1** an arched roof. **2** an underground storage room; a burial chamber. **3** an act of vaulting. ● *v.* jump, esp. with the help of the hands or a pole. □ **vaulted** *adj.*

vaunt *v.* boast about. ● *n.* a boast.

V-chip *n.* a computer chip to be installed in a television receiver and block violent or sexually explicit material.

VCR *abbr.* video cassette recorder.

VD *abbr.* venereal disease.

VDU *abbr.* visual display unit.

veal *n.* calf's flesh as food.

vector *n.* **1** a quantity (e.g. velocity) that has both magnitude and direction. **2** the carrier of an infectious agent.

veer *v.* change direction.

veg *informal n.* vegetables. ● *v.* relax totally, be inactive and unthinking.

vegan (vee-găn) *n.* a person who eats no meat or animal products.

vegetable *n.* a plant grown for food. ● *adj.* of or from plants.

vegetarian *n.* a person who eats no meat or fish. ● *adj.* of or for such people. □ **vegetarianism** *n.*

vegetate *v.* live an uneventful life.

vegetation *n.* plants collectively.

veggie *n.* & *adj. informal* (a) vegetarian.

vehement *adj.* showing strong feeling. □ **vehemence** *n.*, **vehemently** *adv.*

vehicle *n.* a conveyance for transporting passengers or goods on land or in space; a means by which something is expressed or displayed. □ **vehicular** *adj.*

veil *n.* a piece of fabric concealing or protecting the face; something that conceals. ● *v.* cover with or as if with a veil.

vein *n.* **1** any of the blood vessels conveying blood towards the heart. **2** a narrow streak or stripe; a narrow layer of ore etc. **3** a mood or style: *something in a lighter vein.* □ **veined** *adj.*

Velcro *n. trademark* a fastener consisting of two strips of fabric which cling together when pressed.

veld *n.* (also **veldt**) open grassland in South Africa.

vellum *n.* fine parchment; smooth writing paper.

velocity *n.* (*pl.* **-ies**) speed.

velour (vĕ-**loor**) *n.* (also **velours**) a plush fabric resembling velvet.

velvet *n.* a woven fabric with a thick short pile on one side; a cotton fabric resembling velvet. ● *adj.* (of political changes) achieved without violence. □ **velvety** *adj.*

Ven. *abbr.* Venerable.

venal *adj.* susceptible to or influenced by bribery. □ **venality** *n.*

vend *v.* sell, offer for sale.

vendetta *n.* a feud.

vending machine *n.* a slot machine where small articles can be bought.

vendor *n.* a seller.

veneer *n.* a thin covering layer of fine wood; a superficial show of a quality. ● *v.* cover with a veneer.

venerable *adj.* worthy of great respect; (**Venerable**) the title of an archdeacon.

venerate *v.* respect deeply. □ **veneration** *n.*

venereal *adj.* (of infections) contracted by sexual intercourse with an infected person.

Venetian *adj.* & *n.* (a native) of Venice.

venetian blind *n.* a windowblind of adjustable horizontal slats.

vengeance *n.* retaliation, revenge. □ **with a vengeance** in an extreme degree.

vengeful *adj.* seeking vengeance.

venial *adj.* (of a sin) pardonable, not serious. □ **veniality** *n.*

venison *n.* deer's flesh as food.

Venn diagram *n.* a diagram using overlapping circles etc. to show relationships between sets.

venom *n.* **1** a poisonous fluid secreted by snakes etc. **2** bitter feeling or language. □ **venomous** *adj.*

venous (vee-nŭs) *adj.* of veins.

vent *n.* **1** an opening allowing gas or liquid to pass through. **2** a slit at the lower edge of a coat. ● *v.* give vent to. □ **give vent to** give an outlet to (feelings).

ventilate *v.* **1** cause air to enter or circulate freely in. **2** discuss or examine publicly. □ **ventilation** *n.*

ventilator *n.* **1** a device for ventilating a room etc. **2** a respirator.

ventral *adj.* of or on the abdomen.

ventricle *n.* a cavity, esp. in the heart or brain. □ **ventricular** *adj.*

ventriloquist *n.* an entertainer who can produce voice sounds so that they seem to come from a puppet etc. □ **ventriloquism** *n.*

venture *n.* an undertaking that involves risk. ● *v.* dare to do something or go somewhere; dare to say; expose to risk. □ **venturesome** *adj.*

venue *n.* an appointed place for a meeting, concert, etc.

veracious *adj.* truthful; true. □ **veraciously** *adv.*, **veracity** *n.*

veranda *n.* a roofed terrace.

verb *n.* a word indicating an action, state, or occurrence.

verbal *adj.* **1** of or in words; spoken. **2** of a verb. □ **verbally** *adv.*

verbalize *v.* (also **-ise**) express in words; be verbose. □ **verbalization** *n.*

verbatim (ver-**bay**-tim) *adv.* & *adj.* in exactly the same words.

verbiage (**ver**-bee-ij) *n.* an excessive number of words.

verbose *adj.* using more words than are needed. □ **verbosely** *adv.*, **verbosity** *n.*

verdant *adj.* (of grass etc.) green.

verdict *n.* a decision reached by a jury; a decision or opinion reached after testing something.

verdigris (**ver**-di-gree) *n.* a green deposit forming on copper or brass.

verdure *n.* green vegetation.

verge *n.* the extreme edge, the brink; a grass edging of a road etc. □ **verge on** come close to being.

verger *n.* a church caretaker.

verify *v.* (**verified, verifying**) check the truth or correctness of. □ **verification** *n.*

verisimilitude *n.* the appearance of being true.

veritable *adj.* deserving a specified description: *the book is a veritable goldmine.*

vermicelli *n.* pasta made in slender threads.

vermilion *adj.* & *n.* bright red.

vermin *n.* (*pl.* **vermin**) an animal or insect regarded as a pest. □ **verminous** *adj.*

vernacular *n.* the ordinary language of a country or district.

vernal *adj.* of or occurring in spring.

verruca (vĕ-**roo**-kă) *n.* (*pl.* **verrucas** or **verrucae**) an infectious wart on the foot.

versatile *adj.* able to do or be used for many different things. □ **versatility** *n.*

verse *n.* poetry, a poem; a group of lines forming a unit in a poem or hymn; a numbered division of a Bible chapter.

versed *adj.* □ **versed in** skilled or experienced in.

versify *v.* (**versified, versifying**) express in verse; compose verse. □ **versification** *n.*

version *n.* a particular form of something, differing from others; an account of events from a particular viewpoint; a translation or edition.

verso *n.* (*pl.* **versos**) the left-hand page of a book; the back of a leaf of manuscript.

versus *prep.* against.

vertebra *n.* (*pl.* **vertebrae**) any of the small bones forming the backbone. □ **vertebral** *adj.*

vertebrate *n.* & *adj.* (an animal) having a backbone.

vertex *n.* (*pl.* **vertices** or **vertexes**) the highest point of a hill etc.; an apex.

vertical *adj.* perpendicular to the horizontal, upright. ● *n.* a vertical line or position. □ **vertically** *adv.*

vertiginous (ver-**tij**-in-ŭs) *adj.* causing vertigo.

vertigo *n.* dizziness, esp. caused by heights.

verve *n.* enthusiasm, vigour.

very *adv.* to a high degree, extremely; absolutely: **the very best**. ● *adj.* **1** actual, precise: *this very moment*. **2** mere: *the very thought*. □ **very well** an expression of consent.

vesicle (**ves**-ik-ĕl, **vees**-ik-ĕl) *n.* a sac, esp. containing liquid; a blister.

vessel *n.* **1** a receptacle, esp. for liquid. **2** a ship, a boat. **3** a tubelike structure conveying blood or other fluid in the body of an animal or plant.

vest *n.* an undergarment covering the trunk; *Amer.* a waistcoat. ● *v.*

confer (power) as a firm or legal right.

vested interest *n.* a personal interest in a state of affairs, usu. with an expectation of gain.

vestibule *n.* an entrance hall; a porch.

vestige *n.* a small amount or trace. □ **vestigial** *adj.*

vestment *n.* a ceremonial garment, esp. of clergy or a church choir.

vet *n.* **1** a veterinary surgeon. **2** *Amer.* a military veteran. ● *v.* (**vetted, vetting**) examine critically for faults etc.

veteran *n.* a person with long experience, esp. in the armed forces.

veterinarian *n. Amer.* a veterinary surgeon.

veterinary *adj.* of or for the treatment of diseases and disorders of animals.

veterinary surgeon *n.* a person qualified to treat animal diseases and disorders.

veto *n.* (*pl.* **vetoes**) an authoritative rejection of something proposed; the right to make this. ● *v.* (**vetoed, vetoing**) reject by a veto.

vex *v.* annoy. □ **vexation** *n.*, **vexatious** *adj.*

vexed question *n.* a problem that is much discussed.

VHF *abbr.* very high frequency, (in radio) 30-300 MHz.

via *prep.* by way of, through.

viable *adj.* capable of working successfully, or of living or surviving. □ **viability** *n.*

viaduct *n.* a long bridge carrying a road etc. over a valley.

vial *n.* a small bottle.

viands (vI-ăndz) *n.pl. archaic* articles of food.

vibes *n.pl. informal* **1** an emotional state communicated to others; an atmosphere. **2** a vibraphone.

vibrant *adj.* full of energy and enthusiasm; quivering; resonant.

vibraphone *n.* a percussion instrument like a xylophone but with a vibrating effect.

vibrate *v.* move rapidly and continuously to and fro; sound with rapid slight variation of pitch. □ **vibrator** *n.*, **vibratory** *adj.*

vibration *n.* **1** vibrating. **2** (**vibrations**) *informal* mental influences; an atmosphere or feeling communicated.

vibrato *n.* (in music) a rapid slight fluctuation in the pitch of a note.

vicar *n.* a member of the clergy in charge of a parish.

vicarage *n.* the house of a vicar.

vicarious (vik-air-i-ŭs) *adj.* felt through sharing imaginatively in the feelings or activities etc. of another person; acting or done etc. for another. □ **vicariously** *adv.*

vice *n.* **1** great wickedness; criminal and immoral practices. **2** (*Amer.* **vise**) a tool with two jaws for holding things firmly.

vice- *comb. form* a substitute or deputy for; next in rank to.

viceroy *n.* a person governing a colony etc. as the sovereign's representative. □ **viceregal** *adj.*

vice versa *adv.* reversing the main terms in a statement, e.g. *from London to Oxford or vice versa.*

vicinity *n.* (*pl.* **-ies**) the surrounding district. □ **in the vicinity (of)** near.

vicious *adj.* deliberately cruel or spiteful; savage, dangerous. □ **viciously** *adv.*

vicious circle *n.* a bad situation producing effects that intensify its original cause.

vicissitude (vi-sis-i-tyood) *n.* a change of circumstances or luck.

victim *n.* a person injured or killed or made to suffer.

victimize *v.* (also **-ise**) single out to suffer ill treatment. □ **victimization** *n.*

victor *n.* a winner.

Victorian *n.* & *adj.* (a person) of the reign of Queen Victoria (1837–1901).

victorious *adj.* having gained victory.

victory *n.* (*pl.* **-ies**) success achieved by winning a battle or contest.

victualler (vit-ler) *n.* (*Amer.* **victualer**) a person licensed to sell alcohol.

victuals *n.pl.* food, provisions.

video *n.* (*pl.* **videos**) a recording or broadcasting of pictures; an apparatus for this; a videotape. ● *v.* (**videoed, videoing**) make a video of.

videotape *n.* magnetic tape for recording visual images and sound; a video cassette; a film recorded on this. ● *v.* record on videotape.

videotex *n.* (also **videotext**) teletext or viewdata.

vie *v.* (**vied, vying**) carry on a rivalry, compete.

view *n.* **1** the ability to see something or to be seen from a particular place; what can be seen from a particular place, esp. considered aesthetically. **2** an attitude or opinion. ● *v.* **1** look at, inspect; watch (a television programme). **2** regard in a particular way. □ **in view** visible. **in view of** because of, considering. **on view** displayed for inspection. **with a view to** with the hope or intention of. □ **viewer** *n.*

viewdata *n.* a news and information service from a computer source to which a television screen is connected by a telephone link.

viewfinder *n.* a device on a camera showing the extent of the area being photographed.

viewpoint *n.* **1** a point of view. **2** a place from which there is a good view.

vigil *n.* a period of staying awake to keep watch or pray.

vigilant *adj.* watchful. □ **vigilance** *n.*, **vigilantly** *adv.*

vigilante (vi-ji-**lan**-ti) *n.* a member of a self-appointed group trying to prevent crime etc.

vignette (veen-**yet**) *n.* a short written description.

vigour *n.* (*Amer.* **vigor**) active physical or mental strength; forcefulness. □ **vigorous** *adj.*, **vigorously** *adv.*, **vigorousness** *n.*

Viking *n.* an ancient Scandinavian trader and pirate.

vile *adj.* extremely disgusting or wicked. □ **vilely** *adv.*, **vileness** *n.*

vilify *v.* (**vilified, vilifying**) disparage, blacken the reputation of. □ **vilification** *n.*, **vilifier** *n.*

villa *n.* a large country residence; a house in a residential district; a rented holiday home.

village *n.* a collection of houses and other buildings in a country district. □ **villager** *n.*

villain *n.* a wicked person. □ **villainous** *adj.*, **villainy** *n.*

villein *n. hist.* a feudal tenant subject to a lord.

vim *n. informal* vigour.

vinaigrette *n.* a salad dressing of oil and vinegar.

vindicate *v.* clear of blame; justify. □ **vindication** *n.*

vindictive *adj.* showing a strong or excessive desire for vengeance. □ **vindictively** *adv.*, **vindictiveness** *n.*

vine *n.* a climbing plant on which grapes grow.

vinegar *n.* a sour liquid made from wine, malt, etc., by fermentation. □ **vinegary** *adj.*

vineyard *n.* a plantation of vines for wine-making.

vintage *n.* **1** the year in which a wine was produced; wine of high quality from a particular year; the date of something's origin. ● *adj.* of high quality, esp. from a past period.

vintner *n.* a wine-merchant.

vinyl (vy-nil) *n.* a kind of plastic.

viola[1] (vi-**oh**-lă) *n.* an instrument like a violin but of lower pitch.

viola[2] (vy-ŏ-lă) *n.* a plant of the genus to which violets and pansies belong.

violate *v.* break (a rule, promise, etc.); fail to respect (a right); treat irreverently; rape. □ **violation** *n.*, **violator** *n.*

violent *adj.* involving great force or intensity; using excessive physical force. □ **violence** *n.*, **violently** *adv.*

violet *n.* a small plant, often with purple flowers; a bluish-purple colour. ● *adj.* bluish purple.

violin *n.* a musical instrument with four strings of treble pitch, played with a bow. □ **violinist** *n.*

violoncello *n.* (*pl.* **violoncellos**) a cello.

VIP *abbr.* very important person.

viper *n.* a type of poisonous snake.

virago (vi-rah-goh) *n.* (*pl.* **viragos**) an aggressive woman.

viral (vy-răl) *adj.* of a virus.

virgin *n.* **1** a person (esp. a woman) who has never had sexual intercourse; (**the Virgin**) Mary, mother of Christ. **2** a person lacking experience in a specified area. ● *adj.* **1** never having had sexual intercourse. **2** untouched, not yet used. □ **virginal** *adj.*, **virginity** *n.*

virile *adj.* having masculine strength or procreative power. □ **virility** *n.*

virology *n.* the study of viruses. □ **virologist** *n.*

virtual *adj.* almost existing or being as described, but not strictly or officially so. □ **virtually** *adv.*

virtual reality *n.* a computer-generated simulation of reality.

virtue *n.* moral excellence of character or behaviour; an excellent characteristic; a good or useful quality; *dated* chastity. □ **by** or **in virtue of** because of, on the strength of.

virtuoso *n.* (*pl.* **virtuosos** or **virtuosi**) an expert performer. □ **virtuosity** *n.*

virtuous *adj.* morally good. □ **virtuously** *adv.*, **virtuousness** *n.*

virulent *adj.* (of poison or disease) extremely strong or violent; bitterly hostile. □ **virulence** *n.*, **virulently** *adv.*

virus *n.* **1** a minute organism capable of causing disease. **2** a destructive code hidden in a computer program.

visa (vee-ză) *n.* an official mark on a passport, permitting the holder to enter a specified country.

visage (viz-ij) *n. literary* a person's face.

vis-à-vis (veez-ah-vee) *prep.* in relation to; in comparison to.

viscera (viss-er-ă) *n.pl.* the internal organs of the body. □ **visceral** *adj.*

viscid (vi-sid) *adj.* thick and sticky. □ **viscidity** *n.*

viscose *n.* viscous cellulose; a fabric made from this.

viscount (vy-kownt) *n.* a nobleman ranking between earl and baron.

viscountess *n.* a woman holding the rank of viscount; a viscount's wife or widow.

viscous (vis-kŭs) *adj.* thick and gluey. □ **viscosity** *n.*

vise Amer. sp. of **vice** (*sense* 2).

visibility *n.* the state of being visible; the distance one can see under certain weather conditions etc.

visible *adj.* able to be seen or noticed. □ **visibly** *adv.*

vision *n.* **1** the ability to see; inspired and idealistic ideas about the future. **2** a dream, an apparition; an extraordinarily beautiful person.

visionary *adj.* idealistic; imaginative. ● *n.* (*pl.* **-ies**) a person with visionary ideas.

visit *v.* **1** go or come to see; stay temporarily with or at. **2** inflict (harm) on someone. ● *n.* an act of visiting. □ **visitor** *n.*

visitation *n.* **1** an official visit or inspection. **2** trouble regarded as divine punishment.

visor (vy-zer) *n.* (also **vizor**) a movable front part of a helmet, covering the face; a shading device at the top of a vehicle's windscreen.

vista *n.* an extensive view, esp. seen through a long opening.

visual *adj.* of or used in seeing. □ **visually** *adv.*

visual display unit *n.* a device displaying a computer output or input on a screen.

visualize *v.* (also **-ise**) form a mental picture of. □ **visualization** *n.*

vital *adj.* **1** essential to life; essential to a thing's existence or success. **2** full of vitality. ● *n.pl.* (**vitals**) the vital organs of the body, e.g. the heart and brain. □ **vitally** *adv.*

vitality *n.* liveliness, persistent energy.

vital statistics *n.pl.* **1** statistics of births, deaths, and marriages. **2** *informal* the measurements of a woman's bust, waist, and hips.

vitamin *n.* an organic compound present in food and essential for growth and nutrition.

vitiate (vish-i-ayt) *v.* make imperfect or ineffective. □ **vitiation** *n.*

viticulture *n.* vine-growing.

vitreous *adj.* like glass in texture, finish, etc.

vitrify *v.* (**vitrified, vitrifying**) change into a glassy substance. □ **vitrifaction** *n.*

vitriol *n.* **1** *archaic* sulphuric acid. **2** savagely hostile remarks. □ **vitriolic** *adj.*

vituperate *v.* insult, abuse. □ **vituperation** *n.*, **vituperative** *adj.*

viva[1] (vI-vă) *n. informal* a viva voce examination.

viva[2] (vee-vă) *int.* long live (someone or something).

vivace (vi-vah-chi) *adv. Music* in a lively manner.

vivacious *adj.* lively, highspirited. □ **vivaciously** *adv.*, **vivacity** *n.*

vivarium *n.* (*pl.* **vivaria**) a place for keeping living animals etc. in natural conditions.

viva voce (vy-vă **voh**-chi) *n.* an oral university examination.

vivid *adj.* bright, intense; clear; (of imagination) lively. □ **vividly** *adv.*, **vividness** *n.*

vivify *v.* (**vivified, vivifying**) put life into.

viviparous (vi-vi-pă-rŭs) *adj.* bringing forth young alive, not egg-laying.

vivisection *n.* performance of experiments on living animals.

vixen *n.* a female fox.

viz. *adv.* in other words; that is; namely.

vizor var. of **visor**.

V-neck *n.* a V-shaped neckline on a pullover etc.

vocabulary *n.* (*pl.* **-ies**) the words known by a person or group, or used in a particular field; a list of words and their meanings.

vocal *adj.* **1** of or for the voice. **2** expressing opinions freely; talking a great deal. ● *n.* a piece of sung music. □ **vocally** *adv.*

vocalist *n.* a singer.

vocalize *v.* (also **-ise**) utter. □ **vocalization** *n.*

vocation *n.* a strong desire or feeling of fitness for a certain career; a trade or profession. □ **vocational** *adj.*

vociferate *v.* say loudly, shout. □ **vociferation** *n.*

vociferous *adj.* making a great outcry. □ **vociferously** *adv.*

vodka *n.* an alcoholic spirit distilled chiefly from rye.

vogue *n.* current fashion; popularity. □ **in vogue** in fashion.

voice *n.* sounds formed in the larynx and uttered by the mouth; an expressed opinion, the right to express an opinion. ● *v.* express; utter.

voicemail *n.* an electronic system for storing messages left by telephone or transmitted through a digital computer network.

voice-over *n.* a narration in a film etc. without a picture of the speaker.

void *adj.* **1** empty. **2** not valid. ● *n.* an empty space, emptiness. ● *v.* make void; excrete.

voile *n.* a very thin dress fabric.

volatile *adj.* **1** evaporating rapidly. **2** liable to change unpredictably; changing quickly in mood. □ **volatility** *n.*

vol-au-vent (vol-oh-von) *n.* a small puff pastry case filled with a savoury mixture.

volcano *n.* (*pl.* **volcanoes**) a mountain with a vent through which lava is expelled. □ **volcanic** *adj.*

vole *n.* a small rodent.

volition *n.* the exercise of one's will.

volley *n.* (*pl.* **volleys**) **1** a simultaneous discharge of missiles etc.; an outburst of questions or other words. **2** a return of the ball in tennis etc. before it touches the ground. ● *v.* send in a volley.

volleyball *n.* a game for two teams sending a large ball by hand over a net.

volt *n.* a unit of electromotive force.

voltage *n.* electromotive force expressed in volts.

volte-face (volt-fass) *n.* a complete change of attitude to something.

voltmeter *n.* an instrument measuring electrical potential in volts.

voluble *adj.* speaking or spoken constantly and fluently. □ **volubility** *n.*, **volubly** *adv.*

volume *n.* **1** a book. **2** the amount of space held or occupied by a container or object; an amount, the quantity of something. **3** the loudness of a sound.

voluminous *adj.* having great volume, bulky; copious.

voluntary *adj.* done, given, or acting by choice; working or done without payment; maintained by voluntary contributions. □ **voluntarily** *adv.*

volunteer *n.* a person who offers to do something; one who works for no pay; one who enrols voluntarily for military service. ● *v.* freely offer to do something; offer (something) voluntarily.

voluptuary *n.* (*pl.* **-ies**) a person fond of luxury and sensual pleasure.

voluptuous *adj.* **1** full of or fond of sensual pleasure. **2** (of a woman) having a full attractive figure. □ **voluptuously** *adv.*, **voluptuousness** *n.*

vomit *v.* (**vomited, vomiting**) eject (matter) from the stomach through the mouth; emit in vast quantities. ● *n.* vomited matter.

voodoo *n.* a form of religion based on witchcraft. □ **voodooism** *n.*

voracious *adj.* greedy; ravenous; insatiable. □ **voraciously** *adv.*, **voracity** *n.*

vortex *n.* (*pl.* **vortexes** or **vortices**) a whirlpool or whirlwind.

vote *n.* a formal expression of one's opinion or choice on a matter under discussion; a choice etc. expressed in this way; the right to vote. ● *v.* express one's choice by a vote; elect to a position by votes. □ **voter** *n.*

votive *adj.* given to fulfil a vow.

vouch *v.* □ **vouch for** guarantee the accuracy or reliability etc. of.

voucher *n.* a document exchangeable for certain goods or services; a receipt.

vouchsafe *v.* give or grant.

vow *n.* & *v.* (make) a solemn promise, esp. to a deity or saint.

vowel *n.* a speech sound made without audible stopping of the breath; the letter representing this, e.g. *a* or *e*.

vox pop *n. informal* popular opinion represented by informal comments from the public.

voyage *n.* a journey made by water or in space. ● *v.* make a voyage. □ **voyager** *n.*

voyeur (vwah-yer) *n.* a person who gets sexual pleasure from watching others having sex or undressing.

vs. *abbr.* versus.

V-sign *n.* a sign of abuse made with the first two fingers pointing up and the back of the hand facing out; a similar sign with the palm facing outwards as a symbol of victory.

VSO *abbr.* voluntary service overseas.

vulcanite *n.* hard black vulcanized rubber.

vulcanize *v.* (also **-ise**) strengthen (rubber) by treating with sulphur. □ **vulcanization** *n.*

vulgar *adj.* lacking refinement or good taste. □ **vulgarity** *n.*, **vulgarly** *adv.*

vulgar fraction *n.* a fraction represented by numbers above and below a line (rather than decimally).

vulgarian *n.* a coarse person, esp. one with newly acquired wealth.

vulgarism *n.* a coarse word or expression.

vulnerable *adj.* able to be hurt or injured; exposed to danger or criticism. □ **vulnerability** *n.*

vulture *n.* a large bird of prey that lives on the flesh of dead animals.

vulva *n.* the external parts of the female genital organs.

vying present participle of **vie**.

Ww

W. *abbr.* **1** west; western. **2** watt(s). ● *symb.* tungsten.

wacky *adj.* (**wackier, wackiest**) *informal* mad, eccentric.

wad *n.* **1** a pad of soft material. **2** a bunch of papers or banknotes. ● *v.* (**wadded, wadding**) line, pad.

wadding *n.* padding.

waddle *v.* walk with short steps and a swaying movement. ● *n.* a waddling gait.

wade *v.* walk through water or mud; proceed slowly and laboriously (through work etc.).

wader *n.* **1** a long-legged waterbird. **2** (**waders**) high waterproof boots worn in fishing etc.

wadi (wo-di, wah-di) *n.* a rocky watercourse, dry except in the rainy season.

wafer *n.* a thin light biscuit; a very thin slice.

waffle *n.* **1** *informal* lengthy but vague or trivial speech or writing. **2** a small cake of batter eaten hot, cooked in a **waffle-iron**. ● *v. informal* talk or write waffle.

waft *v.* carry or travel lightly through air or over water. ● *n.* a gentle movement of air; a scent carried on it.

wag *v.* (**wagged, wagging**) (cause to) move briskly to and fro. ● *n.* **1** a wagging movement. **2** *dated* a humorous person.

wage *n.* (also **wages**) regular payment to an employee for his or her work. ● *v.* engage in (war).

waged *adj.* having paid employment.

wager *n.* & *v.* (make) a bet.

waggle *v. informal* wag. ● *n.* a waggling motion. □ **waggly** *adj.*

wagon *n.* (also **waggon**) a four-wheeled vehicle for heavy loads; an open railway truck. □ **on the wagon** *informal* abstaining from alcohol.

waif *n.* a homeless child; a thin and vulnerable person.

wail *v.* & *n.* (utter) a long sad cry.

wainscot *n.* (also **wainscoting**) wooden panelling on the lower part of a room's walls.

waist *n.* the part of the human body between ribs and hips; a narrow middle part.

waistcoat *n.* a close-fitting waist-length sleeveless jacket.

waistline *n.* the outline or size of the waist.

wait *v.* **1** stay where one is or refrain from acting until a specified time or event; expect someone or something, esp. when they are late; be left until later. **2** serve at table. ● *n.* an act or period of waiting. □ **wait on** serve food and drink to (a person) at a meal; fetch and carry things for.

waiter *n.* a man employed to serve customers in a restaurant etc.

waitress *n.* a woman employed to serve customers in a restaurant etc.

waive *v.* refrain from using (a right etc.). □ **waiver** *n.*

▪ **Usage** Do not forget the *i* in *waive.*

wake[1] *v.* (**woke** or **waked, woken** or **waked, waking**) **1** cease to sleep; cause to cease sleeping. **2** evoke. ● *n.* a watch by a corpse before burial; lamentations and merrymaking accompanying this. □ **wake up** wake; make or become alert.

wake[2] *n.* a trail of disturbed water left by a ship. □ **in the wake of** behind; following.

wakeful *adj.* unable to sleep; sleepless. □ **wakefulness** *n.*

waken *v.* wake.

walk *v.* progress by setting down one foot and then lifting the other(s) in turn; travel along (a path etc.) in this way; accompany in walking. ● *n.* a journey on foot; a manner or style of walking; a place or route for walking. □ **walk of life** social rank; occupation. **walk out** depart suddenly and angrily; go on strike suddenly. **walk out on** desert. □ **walker** *n.*

walkabout *n.* an informal stroll among a crowd by royalty etc.

walkie-talkie *n.* a small portable radio transmitter and receiver.

walking stick *n.* a stick carried or used as a support when walking.

walkout *n.* a sudden angry departure, esp. as a strike.

walkover *n.* an easy victory.

wall *n.* a continuous upright structure forming one side of a building or room or enclosing an area of land; a barrier; something that divides or encloses. ● *v.* surround or enclose with a wall.

wallaby *n.* (*pl.* **-ies**) a marsupial like a small kangaroo.

wallet *n.* a small folding case for banknotes or documents.

wallflower *n.* **1** a garden plant **2** *informal* a woman sitting out dances for lack of partners.

wallop *informal v.* (**walloped, walloping**) thrash, hit hard. ● *n.* a heavy blow.

wallow *v.* roll in mud or water etc. ● *n.* an act of wallowing. □ **wallow in** take unrestrained pleasure in.

wallpaper *n.* decorative paper for covering the interior walls of rooms.

wally *n.* (*pl.* **-ies**) *informal* a stupid person.

walnut *n.* a nut containing a wrinkled edible kernel.

walrus *n.* a large seal-like Arctic animal with long tusks.

waltz *n.* a ballroom dance; the music for this. ● *v.* dance a waltz; *informal* move easily and casually.

wan *adj.* pale, pallid. □ **wanly** *adv.*, **wanness** *n.*

wand *n.* a slender rod, esp. associated with the working of magic.

wander *v.* go from place to place with no settled route or purpose; stray; digress. ● *n.* an act of wandering. □ **wanderer** *n.*

wanderlust *n.* a strong desire to travel.

wane *v.* decrease in vigour or importance; (of the moon) show a decreasing bright area after being full. □ **on the wane** waning.

wangle *v. informal* obtain or arrange by trickery or scheming.

wannabe (won-ă-bee) *n. informal* a person who aspires to be like someone famous.

want *v.* desire, wish for or to; need; lack, fall short of. ● *n.* a desire; something desired or needed.

wanted *adj.* (of a suspected criminal) sought by the police.

wanting *adj.* lacking, deficient.

wanton *adj.* irresponsible, lacking proper restraint.

war *n.* (a period of) fighting (esp. between countries); open hostility;

conflict. ● *v.* (**warred, warring**) make war.

warble *v.* sing, esp. with a gentle trilling note. ● *n.* a warbling sound.

ward *n.* **1** a room with beds for patients in a hospital. **2** a division of a city or town, electing a councillor to represent it. **3** a child under the care of a guardian or law court. □ **ward off** keep at a distance; repel.

warden *n.* an official with supervisory duties.

warder *n.* a prison officer.

wardrobe *n.* a large cupboard for storing hanging clothes; a stock of clothes or costumes.

ware *n.* manufactured goods of the kind specified; (**wares**) articles offered for sale.

warehouse *n.* a building for storing goods or furniture; a large wholesale or retail store.

warfare *n.* making war, fighting.

warhead *n.* the explosive head of a missile.

warlike *adj.* aggressive; threatening war.

warm *adj.* **1** moderately hot; providing warmth. **2** readily feeling and expressing affection; enthusiastic, heartfelt. ● *v.* make or become warm. □ **warm to** become friendlier towards (someone) or more enthusiastic about (something). **warm up 1** heat or reheat; become livelier. **2** prepare for exercise by stretching muscles etc. □ **warmly** *adv.*, **warmness** *n.*

warm-blooded *adj.* having blood that remains at a constant temperature.

warmonger *n.* a person who seeks to bring about war.

warmth *n.* warmness.

warn *v.* inform about a present or future danger or difficulty etc., advise about action in this. □ **warn off** tell (a person) to keep away or to avoid (a thing).

warning *n.* something that serves to warn a person.

warp *v.* make or become bent by uneven shrinkage or expansion; distort, pervert. ● *n.* **1** a distortion, a warped state. **2** the lengthwise threads in a loom.

warrant *n.* a document giving legal authorization for an action; a voucher; justification. ● *v.* justify; guarantee.

warranty *n.* (*pl.* **-ies**) a guarantee of repair or replacement of a purchased article.

warren *n.* a series of burrows where rabbits live.

warrior *n.* a person who fights in a battle.

wart *n.* a small hard abnormal growth on the skin.

warthog *n.* an African wild pig with wart-like lumps on its face.

wary *adj.* (**warier, wariest**) cautious, suspicious. □ **warily** *adv.*, **wariness** *n.*

wash *v.* **1** cleanse with water or other liquid; wash oneself or clothes etc.; be washable. **2** flow past, against, or over; carry by flowing. **3** coat thinly with paint. **4** *informal* be convincing or persuasive: *that idea won't wash with him.* ● *n.* **1** the process of washing or being washed; clothes etc. to be washed; a solution for washing. **2** disturbed water or air behind a moving ship or aircraft etc. **3** a thin coating of paint. □ **wash down** accompany (food) with a drink. **wash one's hands of** refuse to take responsibility for. **wash out** (of heavy rain) make (a sporting event) impossible. **wash up 1** wash dishes etc. after use. **2** cast upon the shore.

washable *adj.* able to be washed without suffering damage.

washbasin *n.* a bowl (usu. fixed to a wall) for washing one's hands and face.

washed out *adj.* faded; pallid.

washed up *adj. informal* defeated, having failed.

washer *n.* a ring of rubber or metal etc. placed under a nut or bolt or in a tap to give tightness.

washing *n.* clothes etc. to be washed.

washing-up *n.* dishes etc. for washing after use; the process of washing these.

wash-out *n. informal* a failure.

washroom *n. Amer.* a room with a lavatory.

washy *adj.* (**washier, washiest**) (of food) watery; lacking vigour.

Wasp *n.* (also **WASP**) a middle-class American white Protestant.

wasp *n.* a stinging insect with a black and yellow striped body.

waspish *adj.* making sharp or irritable comments. □ **waspishly** *adv.*

wassail *archaic n.* revelry with a lot of drinking. ● *v.* celebrate in this way; sing carols.

wastage *n.* loss or diminution by waste; loss of employees by retirement or resignation.

waste *v.* **1** use more of (something) than is needed; use or spend to no purpose; fail to make use of. **2** become thinner and weaker. ● *adj.* left or thrown away because not wanted; (of land) unfit for use. ● *n.* **1** an act or process of wasting; waste material; a waste pipe. **2** a large expanse of usu. barren land. □ **waster** *n.*

wasteful *adj.* extravagant. □ **wastefully** *adv.*, **wastefulness** *n.*

waste pipe *n.* a pipe carrying off used or superfluous water or steam.

watch *v.* **1** look at attentively, observe; spy on; be careful about. **2** *archaic* stay awake for prayer etc. ● *n.* **1** a small device indicating the time, usu. worn on the wrist. **2** an act of observing or guarding. **3** a spell of duty worked by a sailor, police officer, etc. □ **on the watch** alertly looking out for something. **watch out** be careful. □ **watcher** *n.*

watchdog *n.* a dog kept to guard property; a guardian of people's rights etc.

watchful *adj.* vigilant, observant, alert. □ **watchfully** *adv.*, **watchfulness** *n.*

watchman *n.* (*pl.* **-men**) a person employed to guard a building etc.

watchtower *n.* a tower from which observation can be kept.

watchword *n.* a word or phrase expressing a group's principles.

water *n.* **1** a colourless odourless tasteless liquid that is a compound of hydrogen and oxygen; this as supplied for domestic use. **2** a watery secretion; urine. **3** a lake or other stretch of water; (**waters**) an area of sea controlled by a particular country; the level of the tide: *high water* ● *v.* **1** sprinkle water over; give a drink of water to. **2** produce tears or saliva. □ **by water** in a boat etc. **water down** dilute; make less forceful.

waterbed *n.* a mattress of rubber etc. filled with water.

water biscuit *n.* a thin unsweetened biscuit.

water butt *n.* a barrel used to catch rainwater.

water cannon *n.* a device giving a powerful jet of water to dispel a crowd etc.

water chestnut *n.* the edible corm from a sedge.

water closet *n.* a lavatory flushed by water.

watercolour *n.* (*Amer.* **watercolor**) artists' paint mixed with water (not oil); a painting done with this.

watercourse *n.* a stream, brook, or artificial waterway; its channel.

watercress *n.* a kind of cress that grows in streams and ponds.

waterfall *n.* a stream that falls from a height.

waterfront *n.* part of a town that borders on a river, lake, or sea.

water ice *n.* frozen flavoured water.

watering can *n.* a container with a spout for watering plants.

watering place *n.* a pool where animals drink; a spa, a seaside resort.

water lily *n.* (*pl.* **-ies**) a plant with broad floating leaves and flowers.

waterline *n.* the level normally reached by water on a ship's side.

waterlogged *adj.* saturated with water.

water main *n.* a main pipe in a water supply system.

watermark *n.* a manufacturer's design in paper, visible when the paper is held against light.

water meadow *n.* a meadow that is flooded periodically by a stream.

watermelon *n.* a melon with watery red pulp.

watermill *n.* a mill worked by a waterwheel.

water power *n.* power obtained from flowing or falling water.

waterproof *adj.* unable to be penetrated by water. ● *n.* a waterproof garment. ● *v.* make waterproof.

water rat *n.* a small rodent living beside a lake or stream.

watershed *n.* a line of high land separating two river systems; a turning point in the course of events.

water-skiing *n.* the sport of skimming over water on skis while towed by a motor boat.

waterspout *n.* a rotating column of water formed by a whirlwind over the sea.

water table *n.* the level below which the ground is saturated with water.

watertight *adj.* **1** made or fastened so that water cannot get in or out. **2** impossible to disprove.

waterway *n.* a navigable channel, a canal.

waterwheel *n.* a wheel turned by a flow of water to work machinery.

water wings *n.pl.* floats worn on the shoulders by a person learning to swim.

waterworks *n.* an establishment with machinery etc. for supplying water to a district.

watery *adj.* of or like water; containing too much water; pale, weak.

watt *n.* a unit of electric power.

wattage *n.* an amount of electric power expressed in watts.

wattle *n.* **1** interwoven sticks used as material for fences, walls, etc. **2** a fold of skin hanging from the neck of a turkey etc.

wave *n.* **1** a moving ridge of water; a curved shape compared to this. **2** an act of waving. **3** a slight curl in hair. **4** a burst of feeling; a sequence of a type of event: *a wave of strikes.* **5** a wave-like motion by which heat, light, sound, or electricity is spread; a single curve in this. ● *v.* **1** move one's hand or arm to and fro as a greeting or signal; (cause to) move loosely to and fro or up and down. **2** grow or cause (hair) to grow with a slight curl.

waveband *n.* a range of wavelengths.

wavelength *n.* the distance between corresponding points in a sound wave or electromagnetic wave. □ **on the same wavelength** in sympathy, understanding each other.

waver *v.* be or become unsteady; be undecided. □ **waverer** *n.*

wavy *adj.* (**wavier, waviest**) having waves or curves.

wax *n.* a soft fatty solid used for polishing, making models, etc. ● *v.* **1** coat or polish with wax; use wax to remove unwanted hair from (part of the body). **2** (of the moon) show an increasingly large bright area until becoming full; become stronger; *archaic* enter a specified state. □ **waxy** *adj.*

waxwork *n.* a wax model, esp. of a person.

way *n.* **1** a method or manner of doing something; someone's characteristic manner; (**ways**) habits. **2** a route, a path, a line of communication; progress: *make one's way*; a direction: *go the other way.* **3** a distance: *a long way to go.* **4** a respect or aspect: *wrong in every* *way*. ● *adv. informal* by a great deal, extremely: *way too much*. □ **by the way** incidentally, as an unconnected remark. **by way of 1** via. **2** as a form of, serving as. **have one's way** achieve what one wants. **in a way** to some extent, in a sense. **in the way** forming an obstacle. **make** or **give way** allow someone to pass. **on one's way** travelling somewhere. **on the way** travelling; (of a baby) conceived but not yet born. **out of one's way** not on one's intended route; going to particular trouble.

waybill *n.* a list of the passengers or goods being carried by a vehicle.

wayfarer *n.* a traveller.

waylay *v.* (**waylaid, waylaying**) lie in wait for.

way mark *n.* (also **way marker**) an arrow showing the direction of a footpath.

wayside *n.* the side of a road or path.

wayward *adj.* self-willed and hard to control or predict. □ **waywardness** *n.*

WC *abbr.* water closet.

we *pron.* used by a person referring to himself or herself and another or others; used instead of 'I' in newspaper editorials and by a royal person in formal proclamations.

weak *adj.* lacking physical strength or social etc. power; breaking easily; unconvincing; irresolute, easily influenced; much diluted; not bright or intense. □ **weakly** *adv.*

weaken *v.* make or become weaker.

weakling *n.* a feeble person or animal.

weakness *n.* being weak; a vulnerable point; a self-indulgent liking.

weal *n.* a ridge raised on flesh esp. by the stroke of a rod or whip.

wealth *n.* money and valuable possessions; possession of these; a great quantity. □ **wealthy** *adj.*

wean *v.* accustom (a baby) to take food other than milk; cause to give up something gradually.

weapon *n.* a thing designed or used for inflicting harm or damage; a means of coercing someone.

wear *v.* (**wore, worn, wearing**) **1** have on the body as clothing or ornament. **2** damage or become damaged by friction or use. **3** endure continued use: *the carpet has worn well*. ● *n.* **1** wearing, being worn; clothes of a specified type: *formal wear*. **2** damage by friction etc. □ **wear down** overcome (opposition) by persistence. **wear off** pass off gradually. **wear on** (of time) pass slowly. **wear out 1** use or be used until no longer usable. **2** tire out. □ **wearable** *adj.*, **wearer** *n.*

wearisome *adj.* causing weariness.

weary *adj.* (**wearier, weariest**) very tired; tiring, tedious. ● *v.* (**wearied, wearying**) make or become weary. □ **wearily** *adv.*, **weariness** *n.*

weasel *n.* a small slender carnivorous wild mammal.

weather *n.* the state of the atmosphere with reference to sunshine, rain, wind, etc. ● *v.* **1** wear away or change by exposure to the weather. **2** come safely through (a storm). □ **make heavy weather of** have difficulty in doing. **under the weather** feeling unwell or depressed.

weather-beaten *adj.* bronzed or worn by exposure to the weather.

weatherboard *n.* a sloping board at the bottom of a door, for keeping out rain.

weathervane *n.* (also **weathercock**) a revolving pointer to show the direction of the wind.

weave *v.* (**wove, woven, weaving**) **1** make (fabric etc.) by passing crosswise threads or strips under and over lengthwise ones; form (thread etc.) into fabric in this way. **2** compose (a story etc.). **3** move in an intricate course. ● *n.*

a style or pattern of weaving. □ **weaver** *n.*

web *n.* **1** a network of fine strands made by a spider etc.; a complex system of interconnected elements. **2** skin filling the spaces between the toes of ducks, frogs, etc. □ **webbed** *adj.*

webbing *n.* a strong band of woven fabric used in upholstery.

web page *n.* a document forming part of the World Wide Web.

web site *n.* a collection of web pages with a common theme or source.

Wed. *abbr.* (also **Weds.**) Wednesday.

wed *v.* (**wedded, wedding**) marry; unite, combine.

wedding *n.* a marriage ceremony and festivities.

wedge *n.* a piece of solid substance thick at one end and tapering to a thin edge at the other. ● *v.* force apart or fix in position with a wedge; force into a narrow space.

wedlock *n.* the married state.

Wednesday *n.* the day after Tuesday.

wee *adj. Scot.* little. ● *n.* & *v. informal* = **wee-wee**.

weed *n.* **1** a wild plant growing where it is not wanted. **2** a thin or feeble person. ● *v.* uproot and remove weeds from. □ **weed out** remove as inferior or undesirable. □ **weedy** *adj.*

week *n.* a period of seven successive days, esp. from Monday to Sunday or Sunday to Saturday; the weekdays of this; the working period during a week.

weekday *n.* a day other than Sunday or other than the weekend.

weekend *n.* Saturday and Sunday, esp. as leisure time.

weekly *adj.* & *adv.* (produced or occurring) once a week. ● *n.* (*pl.* **-ies**) a weekly periodical.

weeny *adj.* (**weenier, weeniest**) *informal* tiny.

weep *v.* (**wept, weeping**) shed tears; (of a sore etc.) exude liquid. ● *n.* a spell of weeping. □ **weeper** *n.*

weeping *adj.* (of a tree) having drooping branches.

weepy *adj.* (**weepier, weepiest**) prone to crying; inducing tears, sentimental.

weevil *n.* a small beetle that feeds on grain etc.

wee-wee *informal v.* urinate. ● *n.* urine, the act of urinating.

weft *n.* the crosswise threads in weaving.

weigh *v.* **1** find how heavy (someone or something) is; have a specified weight. **2** consider the relative importance or desirability of; have influence. **3** be a burden. □ **weigh anchor** raise the anchor and start a voyage. **weigh down** be a burden to; oppress, depress. **weigh up** form an estimate of.

weighbridge *n.* a weighing machine with a plate set in a road etc. for weighing vehicles.

weight *n.* **1** an object's mass, the heaviness of a person or thing; a unit or system of units for expressing this; a piece of metal of known weight used in weighing; a heavy object or load. **2** influence. ● *v.* **1** attach a weight to; hold down with a weight; burden. **2** attach importance to; bias. □ **weightless** *adj.*, **weightlessness** *n.*

weighting *n.* extra pay or allowances given in special cases.

weighty *adj.* (**weightier, weightiest**) heavy; serious, important; influential.

weir *n.* a small dam built to regulate the flow of a river.

weird *adj.* uncanny, bizarre. □ **weirdly** *adv.*, **weirdness** *n.*

welch var. of **welsh**.

welcome *adj.* gladly received; much wanted or needed. ● *n.* a kindly greeting; a manner of receiving someone. ● *v.* greet kindly; be glad to receive. ● *int.* a pleased greeting. □ **welcome to** willingly given the use of.

weld *v.* unite or fuse (pieces of metal) by heating or pressure; unite into a whole. ● *n.* a welded joint. □ **welder** *n.*

welfare *n.* well-being; organized efforts to ensure people's well-being.

welfare state *n.* a system attempting to ensure the welfare of all citizens by means of state operated social services.

well[1] *n.* a shaft sunk into the ground to obtain water, oil, etc.; an enclosed shaft-like space. ● *v.* (of liquid) rise to the surface.

well[2] *adv.* (**better, best**) **1** in a good or satisfactory way; in an appropriate or right way; in an advantageous way. **2** kindly; favourably. **3** thoroughly; extremely. **4** possibly, probably: *it may well be so.* ● *adj.* in good health; satisfactory. ● *int.* expressing surprise, relief, or resignation etc., or said when one is hesitating. □ **as well 1** in addition. **2** prudent, advisable. **as well as** in addition to. **might as well** have no reason not to.

well appointed *adj.* well equipped or furnished.

well-being *n.* good health, happiness, and prosperity.

well disposed *adj.* having kindly or favourable feelings.

well heeled *adj. informal* wealthy.

wellington *n.* a boot of rubber or other waterproof material.

well meaning *adj.* (also **well meant**) acting or done with good intentions.

well-nigh *adv.* almost.

well off *adj.* in a satisfactory or good situation; fairly rich.

well-read *adj.* having read much literature.

well spoken *adj.* speaking in a cultured way.

well-to-do *adj.* fairly rich.

Welsh *adj.* & *n.* (the language) of Wales. □ **Welshman** *n.*, **Welshwoman** *n.*

welsh *v.* (also **welch**) fail to keep a promise or pay a debt. □ **welsher** *n.*

Welsh rabbit *n.* (also **Welsh rarebit**) melted cheese on toast.

welt *n.* **1** a leather rim attaching the top of a boot or shoe to the sole. **2** a ribbed or strengthened border of a knitted garment. **3** a weal. ● *v.* **1** provide with a welt. **2** raise weals on, thrash.

welter *n.* a turmoil; a disorderly mixture. ● *v.* wallow; lie soaked in blood etc.

welterweight *n.* a boxing weight between lightweight and middleweight.

wen *n.* a benign tumour on the skin.

wend *v.* □ **wend one's way** go.

went past of **go**.

wept past & p.p. of **weep**.

werewolf *n.* (*pl.* **werewolves**) (in myths) a person who at times turns into a wolf.

west *n.* the point on the horizon where the sun sets; the direction in which this lies; a western part. ● *adj.* in the west; (of a wind) from the west. ● *adv.* towards the west. □ **go west** *informal* be destroyed, lost, or killed.

westerly *adj.* towards the west; blowing from the west.

western *adj.* of or in the west. ● *n.* a film or novel about cowboys in western North America.

westerner *n.* a native or inhabitant of the west.

westernize *v.* (also **-ise**) cause (a country etc.) to adopt European or North American economic, cultural, or political systems. □ **westernization** *n.*

westernmost *adj.* furthest west.

westward *adj.* towards the west. □ **westwards** *adv.*

wet *adj.* (**wetter, wettest**) **1** soaked or covered with water or other liquid; rainy; (of paint etc.) not having dried. **2** *informal* feeble, ineffectual. ● *v.* (**wetted, wetting**) make wet. ● *n.* wet weather; wetness. ◻ **wetly** *adv.*, **wetness** *n.*

wet blanket *n. informal* someone who spoils others' pleasure by being gloomy.

wether *n.* a castrated ram.

wet-nurse *n.* a woman employed to suckle another's child. ● *v.* act as wet-nurse to; *informal* treat like a helpless child.

wetsuit *n.* a rubber garment worn for warmth by divers, windsurfers, etc.

whack *informal v.* strike with a sharp blow. ● *n.* **1** a sharp blow. **2** an attempt. **3** an amount; a contribution.

whacked *adj. informal* exhausted.

whale *n.* a very large sea mammal. ◻ **a whale of a** *informal* an example of an exceedingly great or good thing.

whalebone *n.* a horny substance from the upper jaw of whales, formerly used as stiffening in corsets etc.

whaler *n.* a whaling ship; a seaman hunting whales.

whaling *n.* hunting whales.

wham *informal int.* & *n.* the sound of a forcible impact.

wharf (whorf) *n.* (*pl.* **wharfs** or **wharves**) a landing stage where ships load and unload.

what *adj.* **1** asking for something to be specified or identified. **2** how great or remarkable: *what luck.* ● *pron.* **1** what thing or things: *what is it?* **2** the thing that: *just what I need.* ● *adv.* to what extent or degree. ● *int.* an exclamation of surprise. ◻ **what for?** why?

whatever *pron.* anything or everything; no matter what. ● *adj.* of any kind or number. ● *adv.* not of any kind: *no help whatever.*

whatnot *n. informal* unspecified objects felt to form part of a group or series.

whatsoever *adj.* & *pron.* whatever.

wheat *n.* grain from which flour is made; the plant producing this.

wheaten *adj.* made from wheat.

wheatmeal *n.* wholemeal wheat flour.

wheedle *v.* coax.

wheel *n.* a disc or circular frame that revolves on a shaft passing through its centre, used to move a vehicle, as part of a machine, etc.; a turn or rotation. ● *v.* **1** push or pull (a cart or bicycle etc.) along. **2** turn; move in circles or curves. ◻ **at the wheel** driving a vehicle, directing a ship; in control of affairs. **wheel and deal** engage in scheming to exert influence.

wheelbarrow *n.* an open container with a wheel at one end and handles at the other, for moving small loads.

wheelbase *n.* the distance between a vehicle's front and rear axles.

wheelchair *n.* a chair on wheels for a person who cannot walk.

wheel-clamp *v.* immobilize (an illegally parked car etc.).

wheelwright *n.* a maker and repairer of wooden wheels.

wheeze *v.* breathe with a hoarse whistling sound. ● *n.* **1** this sound. **2** *informal* a clever scheme. ◻ **wheezy** *adj.*

whelk *n.* a shellfish with a spiral shell.

whelp *n.* a young dog, a pup. ● *v.* give birth to (whelps).

when *adv.* **1** at what time, on what occasion. **2** on the occasion on which. ● *conj.* **1** at the time that; whenever; as soon as. **2** although. ● *pron.* what or which time.

whence *adv.* & *conj. formal* from where; from which.

whenever *conj.* & *adv.* at whatever time; every time that.

where *adv.* & *conj.* at or in which place or circumstances; in what respect; from what place or source; to what place. ● *pron.* what place.

whereabouts *adv.* in or near what place. ● *n.* a person's or thing's approximate location.

whereas *conj.* **1** in contrast with the fact that. **2** *formal* seeing that.

whereby *conj.* by which.

whereupon *conj.* immediately after which.

wherever *adv.* & *conj.* at or to whatever place.

wherewithal *n.* the things (esp. money) needed for a purpose.

wherry *n.* (*pl.* **-ies**) a light rowing boat; a large light barge.

whet *v.* (**whetted, whetting**) sharpen (a knife etc.) by rubbing against a stone; stimulate (appetite or interest).

whether *conj.* introducing a choice between alternatives; expressing a question or investigation: *I'll see whether he's in.*

whetstone *n.* a shaped hard stone used for sharpening tools.

whey *n.* the watery liquid left when milk forms curds.

which *adj.* & *pron.* specifying a particular member or members of a set. ● *rel.pron.* introducing further information about something just referred to.

whichever *adj.* & *pron.* any which, no matter which.

whiff *n.* a puff of air or odour.

Whig *n. hist.* a member of the political party in the 17th–19th centuries opposed to the Tories.

while *conj.* **1** during the time that; at the same time as. **2** although; whereas. ● *n.* a period of time. ◻ **the while** meanwhile. **while away** pass (time) in an interesting way.

whilst *conj.* while.

whim *n.* a sudden fancy.

whimper *v.* make feeble crying sounds. ● *n.* a whimpering sound.

whimsical *adj.* impulsive and playful; fanciful, quaint; wrily humorous; capricious. ◻ **whimsicality** *n.*, **whimsically** *adv.*

whine *v.* make a long high complaining cry or a similar shrill sound; complain peevishly. ● *n.* a whining sound or complaint. ◻ **whiner** *n.*

whinge *v. informal* whine, complain.

whinny *n.* (*pl.* **-ies**) a gentle or joyful neigh. ● *v.* (**whinnied, whinnying**) utter a whinny.

whip *n.* **1** a cord or strip of leather on a handle, used for striking a person or animal. **2** a dessert made with whipped cream etc. **3** an official maintaining discipline in a political party. ● *v.* (**whipped, whipping**) **1** strike with a whip. **2** beat into a froth. **3** move rapidly; *informal* steal. ◻ **have the whip hand** have control. **whip up** incite.

whipcord *n.* **1** a cord of tightly twisted strands. **2** ribbed twilled fabric.

whiplash *n.* **1** the stroke of a whip. **2** injury caused by a jerk to the head.

whippet *n.* a small dog resembling a greyhound.

whipping boy *n.* a scapegoat.

whippy *adj.* flexible, springy.

whip-round *n. informal* a collection of money from a group.

whirl *v.* (cause to) spin round and round; move with bewildering speed. ● *n.* a whirling movement; a confused state; a state of activity. ◻ **give something a whirl** *informal* try something.

whirlpool *n.* a current of water whirling in a circle.

whirlwind *n.* a mass of air whirling rapidly about a central point.

whirr *n.* & *v.* (make) a continuous buzzing or vibrating sound.

whisk *v.* **1** convey or go rapidly; brush away lightly. **2** beat into a froth. ● *n.* **1** a whisking movement. **2** an instrument for beating eggs etc.; a bunch of bristles etc. for brushing or flicking things.

whisker *n.* a long hairlike bristle on the face of a cat etc.; (**whiskers**) hairs growing on a man's cheek. ◻ **whiskered** *adj.*, **whiskery** *adj.*

whisky *n.* (*Irish & Amer.* **whiskey**) a spirit distilled from malted grain (esp. barley).

whisper *v.* speak or utter softly, not using the vocal cords; rustle. ● *n.* a very soft tone; a whispered remark.

whist *n.* a card game usu. for two pairs of players.

whistle *n.* a shrill sound made by blowing through a narrow opening between the lips; a similar sound; an instrument for producing this. ● *v.* make such a sound; produce (a tune) in this way. □ **whistler** *n.*

whistle-stop *n.* a brief stop made during a tour. ● *adj.* (of a tour) hurried, with only short stops.

Whit *adj.* of or close to **Whit Sunday**, the seventh Sunday after Easter.

white *adj.* **1** of the colour of snow or common salt; having a light-coloured skin; pale from illness, fear, etc. **2** (of coffee or tea) served with milk. ● *n.* **1** a white colour or thing; a member of a race with light-coloured skin. **2** the transparent substance round egg yolk; the pale part of the eyeball around the iris. □ **whiteness** *n.*

white ant *n.* a termite.

whitebait *n.* (*pl.* **whitebait**) very small fish used as food.

whiteboard *n.* a white board which can be written on with coloured pens and wiped clean.

white-collar worker *n.* a person not engaged in manual labour.

white elephant *n.* a useless possession.

white gold *n.* gold mixed with platinum.

whiten *v.* make or become white or whiter.

white hope *n.* a person expected to achieve much.

white horses *n.pl.* white-crested waves on the sea.

white-hot *adj.* (of metal) glowing white after heating.

white lie *n.* a lie told to avoid hurting someone's feelings.

white noise *n.* noise containing many frequencies with equal intensities, a harsh hissing sound.

White Paper *n.* a government report giving information.

white sale *n.* a sale of household linen.

white spirit *n.* light petroleum used as a solvent.

whitewash *n.* **1** a liquid containing quicklime or powdered chalk, used for painting walls or ceilings etc. **2** deliberate concealment of mistakes. ● *v.* **1** paint with whitewash. **2** conceal (mistakes); present as blameless.

whither *adv. archaic* to what place.

whiting *n.* (*pl.* **whiting**) a small sea fish used as food.

whitlow *n.* an inflammation near a fingernail or toenail.

Whitsun *n.* Whit Sunday and the days close to it. □ **Whitsuntide** *n.*

whittle *v.* trim (wood) by cutting thin slices from the surface; gradually reduce by removing parts or elements.

whizz *v.* (also **whiz**) (**whizzed, whizzing**) make a hissing or whistling sound like something moving fast through air; move very quickly. ● *n.* a whizzing sound.

whizz-kid *n.* (also **whiz-kid**) *informal* a brilliant or successful young person.

who *pron.* **1** what or which person(s)? **2** introducing more information about someone just referred to.

whodunnit *n.* (*Amer.* **whodunit**) *informal* a detective story or play.

whoever *pron.* any or every person who, no matter who.

whole *adj.* with no part removed or left out; not injured or broken. ● *n.* the full amount, all parts or members; a complete system made up of parts. □ **on the whole** considering everything; in general.

wholefood *n.* food which has not been unnecessarily processed.

wholehearted *adj.* without doubts or reservations.

whole number *n.* a number consisting of one or more units with no fractions.

wholemeal *adj.* made from the whole grain of wheat etc.

wholesale *n.* selling of goods in large quantities to be retailed by others. ● *adj.* & *adv.* **1** in the wholesale trade. **2** on a large scale. □ **wholesaler** *n.*

wholesome *adj.* good for health or well-being. □ **wholesomeness** *n.*

wholism var. of **holism**.

wholly *adv.* entirely, fully, totally.

whom *pron.* the objective case of *who.*

whoop *v.* utter a loud cry of excitement. ● *n.* such a cry.

whooping cough *n.* an infectious disease esp. of children, with a violent convulsive cough.

whopper *n. informal* something very large; a great lie.

whore *n.* a prostitute.

whorl (werl, worl) *n.* a coiled form, one turn of a spiral; a circle of ridges in a fingerprint; a ring of leaves or petals.

who's who is, who has.

■ **Usage** Because it has an apostrophe, *who's* is easily confused with *whose*. They are each correctly used in *Who's there?* (= *Who is there?*), *Who's taken my pen?* (= *Who has taken my pen?*), and *Whose book is this?* (= *Who does this book belong to?*).

whose *pron.* & *adj.* belonging to whom or to which.

whosoever *pron.* whoever.

why *adv.* for what reason or purpose; on account of which. ● *int.* an exclamation of surprised discovery or recognition.

wick *n.* a length of thread in a candle or lamp etc., by which the flame is kept supplied with melted grease or fuel.

wicked *adj.* **1** morally bad, evil; *informal* very harsh or unpleasant. **2** playfully mischievous. **3** *informal* excellent. □ **wickedly** *adv.*, **wickedness** *n.*

wicker *n.* osiers or thin canes interwoven to make furniture, baskets, etc. □ **wickerwork** *n.*

wicket *n.* a set of three stumps with two bails across the top, used in cricket; the part of a cricket ground between or near the two wickets.

wide *adj.* **1** having a great or a specified distance between its sides. **2** including a variety of people or things. **3** far from the target. ● *adv.* widely; to the full extent. □ **wide awake** fully awake; *informal* alert. □ **widely** *adv.*, **wideness** *n.*

widen *v.* make or become wider.

widespread *adj.* found or distributed over a wide area.

widow *n.* a woman whose husband has died and who has not remarried. □ **widowhood** *n.*

widowed *adj.* made a widow or widower.

widower *n.* a man whose wife has died and who has not remarried.

width *n.* the extent of something from side to side; a piece of something at its full extent from side to side.

wield *v.* hold and use (a tool etc.); have and use (power).

wife *n.* (*pl.* **wives**) a married woman in relation to her husband. □ **wifely** *adj.*

wig *n.* a covering of hair worn on the head.

wiggle *v.* move repeatedly from side to side, wriggle. ● *n.* an act of wiggling. □ **wiggly** *adj.*

wigwam *n.* a conical tent used by some North American Indians.

wild *adj.* **1** not domesticated, tame, or cultivated; not civilized; desolate, bleak. **2** uncontrolled; unrestrained, unreasonable; *informal* very enthusiastic; *informal* very angry. **3** random: *a wild guess.* ● *n.* (**the wild, the wilds**) desolate places. □ **wildly** *adv.*, **wildness** *n.*

wildcat *adj.* (of a strike) sudden and unofficial.

wildebeest *n.* (*pl.* **wildebeest** or **wildebeests**) a gnu.

wilderness *n.* an uncultivated and uninhabited area.

wildfire *n.* □ **spread like wildfire** spread very fast.

wildfowl *n.pl.* birds hunted as game.

wild goose chase *n.* a useless quest.

wildlife *n.* wild animals and plants.

wiles *n.pl.* trickery, cunning.

wilful *adj.* (*Amer.* **willful**) intentional, not accidental; stubbornly self-willed. □ **wilfully** *adv.*, **wilfulness** *n.*

will[1] *v.aux.* used with *I* and *we* to express promises or obligations, and with other words to express a future tense.

will[2] *n.* **1** the mental faculty by which a person decides upon and controls his or her actions; determination; a person's attitude in wishing good or bad to others. **2** a legal document with instructions for the disposal of someone's property after their death. ● *v.* **1** exercise one's will-power, influence by doing this. **2** bequeath by a will. □ **at will** whenever one pleases. **have one's will** get what one desires.

willie var. of **willy**.

willing *adj.* ready to do what is asked; given or done readily. □ **willingly** *adv.*, **willingness** *n.*

will-o'-the-wisp *n.* **1** a phosphorescent light seen on marshy ground. **2** a hope or aim that can never be fulfilled.

willow *n.* a tree or shrub with flexible branches.

willowy *adj.* slender and supple.

will-power *n.* determination used to achieve something or restrain one's impulses.

willy *n.* (*pl.* **-ies**) (also **willie**) *informal* the penis.

willy-nilly *adv.* whether one desires it or not.

wilt *v.* droop through lack of water; become limp from exhaustion.

wily *adj.* (**wilier, wiliest**) cunning. □ **wiliness** *n.*

wimp *n. informal* a feeble or ineffective person.

win *v.* (**won, winning**) defeat an opponent in (a contest), be victorious; obtain as the result of a contest etc., or by effort. ● *n.* a victory, esp. in a game. □ **win over** gain the favour of.

wince *v.* make a slight movement from pain or embarrassment etc. ● *n.* this movement.

winch *n.* a machine for hoisting or pulling things by a cable that winds round a revolving drum. ● *v.* hoist or pull with a winch.

wind[1] (wind) *n.* **1** a natural current of air; breath as needed for exertion. **2** gas in the stomach or intestines. **3** empty talk. **4** an orchestra's wind instruments. ● *v.* **1** cause to be out of breath. **2** detect by smell. □ **get wind of** *informal* hear a hint or rumour of. **in the wind** happening or about to happen. **put the wind up** *informal* frighten. **take the wind out of a person's sails** take away an advantage, frustrate by anticipating him or her.

wind[2] (wynd) *v.* (**wound, winding**) move in a twisting or spiral course; wrap (something) repeatedly around something else or round upon itself; operate by turning a key, handle, etc.; hoist with a windlass etc. □ **wind down** *informal* become calmer, relax after stress. **wind up 1** set (a clock etc.) going by tightening its spring. **2** bring or come to an end; settle the affairs of and close (a business company). **3** *informal* provoke by teasing. □ **winder** *n.*

windbag *n. informal* a person who talks at unnecessary length.

windbreak *n.* a screen shielding something from the wind.

wind chill *n.* the cooling effect of the wind.

windfall *n.* **1** fruit blown off a tree by the wind. **2** an unexpected gain, esp. a sum of money.

wind farm *n.* a group of energy-producing windmills or wind turbines.

wind instrument *n.* a musical instrument sounded by a current of air, esp. by the player's breath.

windlass *n.* a winch-like device using a rope or chain that winds round a horizontal roller.

windmill *n.* a building with projecting sails or vanes that produce energy for grinding etc. when turned by the wind.

window *n.* **1** an opening in a wall etc. to admit light and air, usu. filled with glass; this glass; a space behind the window of a shop for displaying goods. **2** a framed area on a computer screen for viewing information.

window box *n.* a trough fixed outside a window, for growing flowers etc.

window dressing *n.* arranging goods attractively in a shop window; representing events in a misleadingly favourable way.

window-shopping *n.* looking at goods displayed in shop windows without buying.

windpipe *n.* the air passage from the throat to the bronchial tubes.

windscreen *n.* (*Amer.* **windshield**) the glass in the window at the front of a vehicle.

windsock *n.* a canvas cylinder flown at an airfield to show the direction of the wind.

windsurfing *n.* the sport of surfing on a board to which a sail is fixed. □ **windsurfer** *n.*

windswept *adj.* exposed to strong winds.

wind tunnel *n.* an enclosed tunnel in which winds can be created for testing the resistance of buildings etc.

windward *adj.* & *adv.* situated in or towards the direction from which the wind blows. ● *n.* this side or region.

wine *n.* **1** fermented grape juice as an alcoholic drink; a fermented drink made from other fruits or plants. **2** dark red. □ **wine and dine** entertain with food and drink.

wine bar *n.* a bar or small restaurant serving wine as the main drink.

wing *n.* **1** each of a pair of projecting parts by which a bird, insect, etc., is able to fly; each of the projections on an aircraft supporting it in the air. **2** a projecting part; the bodywork above the wheel of a car; a side or projecting part of a large building; (**wings**) the sides of a theatre stage. **3** either end of a battle array; a player at either end of the forward line in football or hockey etc., the side part of the playing area in these games; an extreme section of a political party. ● *v.* **1** travel on wings; move very quickly. **2** wound in the wing or arm. □ **on the wing** flying. **take wing** fly away. **under one's wing** under one's protection.

winged *adj.* having wings.

winger *n.* a wing player in football etc.

wingspan *n.* the measurement across wings from one tip to the other.

wink *v.* rapidly close and open one eye as a signal; (of a light) shine or flash intermittently. ● *n.* an act of winking. □ **not a wink** no sleep at all.

winkle *n.* an edible sea snail. □ **winkle out** extract, prise out.

winner *n.* a person or thing that wins; *informal* something successful.

winning *adj.* charming, persuasive. ● *n.pl.* (**winnings**) money won in betting etc.

winnow *v.* fan or toss (grain) to free it of chaff.

wino *n.* (*pl.* **winos**) *informal* an alcoholic.

winsome *adj.* charming.

winter *n.* the coldest season of the year. ● *v.* spend the winter in a particular place. ▫ **wintry** *adj.*

wipe *v.* rub (a surface) to clean or dry it; remove (dirt etc.) in this way; spread (liquid) over a surface by rubbing. ● *n.* an act of wiping; a piece of material for wiping. ▫ **wipe out** destroy completely.

wiper *n.* a device that automatically wipes rain etc. from a windscreen.

wire *n.* a strand of metal; a length of this used for fencing, conducting electric current, etc. ● *v.* **1** install electric wires in. **2** fasten or strengthen with wire.

wired *adj. informal* **1** using computers and information technology to transmit and receive information. **2** tense, nervous.

wire tapping *n.* tapping of telephone lines.

wiring *n.* a system of electric wires in a building, vehicle, etc.

wiry *adj.* (**wirier, wiriest**) like wire; thin but strong. ▫ **wiriness** *n.*

wisdom *n.* being wise, soundness of judgement; wise sayings.

wisdom tooth *n.* a hindmost molar tooth, not usu. cut before the age of 20.

wise *adj.* having experience, knowledge, and sound judgement; sensible, prudent. ▫ **wise to** *informal* alert to, aware of. ▫ **wisely** *adv.*

wiseacre *n.* a person who pretends to have great wisdom.

wisecrack *colloquial n.* a witty remark. ● *v.* make a wisecrack.

wish *n.* a desire, a hope; an expression of a desire, a request or instruction; (**wishes**) expressions of friendly feeling. ● *v.* feel a desire; desire or express a desire for (something) to happen to (someone).

wishbone *n.* a forked bone between a bird's neck and breast.

wishful thinking *n.* supposing that something desired but impossible or improbable is the case.

wishy-washy *adj.* weak in colour, character, etc.

wisp *n.* a small separate bunch; a small streak of smoke etc. ▫ **wispiness** *n.*, **wispy** *adj.*

wistful *adj.* full of sad or vague longing. ▫ **wistfully** *adv.*, **wistfulness** *n.*

wit *n.* amusing ingenuity in expressing words or ideas; a person who has this; intelligence. ▫ **at one's wits' end** worried and not knowing what to do.

witch *n.* a person (esp. a woman) who practises witchcraft; a fascinatingly attractive woman.

witchcraft *n.* the practice of magic.

witch doctor *n.* a magician and healer in traditional tribal societies.

witch hazel *n.* an astringent lotion made from a shrub.

witch-hunt *n. informal* persecution of people thought to be holders of unpopular views.

with *prep.* **1** accompanied by or accompanying. **2** having; characterized by; showing (a mood, emotion, etc). **3** using; employed by. **4** towards, in relation to: *I'm angry with her*. **5** indicating opposition or separation: *I won't part with this*. **6** affected by; because of: *weak with hunger*. **7** sharing the opinion of. ▫ **with it** *informal* **1** up to date in one's knowledge or behaviour. **2** alert.

withdraw *v.* (**withdrew, withdrawn, withdrawing**) **1** take back; remove (deposited money) from a bank etc.; cancel (a statement). **2** go away from a place or from company. ▫ **withdrawal** *n.*

withdrawn *adj.* (of a person) not communicative or sociable.

wither *v.* **1** shrivel, lose freshness or vitality. **2** subdue by scorn.

withhold *v.* (**withheld, withholding**) refuse to give; suppress (a reaction etc.).

within *prep.* inside; not beyond the limit or scope of; in a time no longer than. ● *adv.* inside.

without *prep.* not having; in the absence of; not doing (a specified action). ● *adv.* outside.

withstand *v.* (**withstood, withstanding**) endure successfully.

witless *adj.* stupid.

witness *n.* a person who sees or hears something; one who gives evidence in a law court; one who watches the signing of a document and signs to confirm this; something that serves as evidence. ● *v.* be a witness of.

witter *v. informal* speak lengthily about something trivial.

witticism *n.* a witty remark.

witty *adj.* (**wittier, wittiest**) clever, inventive, and funny. □ **wittily** *adv.*, **wittiness** *n.*

wives pl. of **wife**.

wizard *n.* a male witch, a magician; a person with great skill in a particular field. □ **wizardry** *n.*

wizened (wiz-ĕnd) *adj.* full of wrinkles, shrivelled with age.

woad *n.* a blue dye obtained from a plant.

wobble *v.* stand or move unsteadily; quiver. ● *n.* a wobbling movement; a quiver.

wobbly *adj.* (**wobblier, wobbliest**) unsteady; quivering. □ **throw a wobbly** *informal* have a fit of annoyance or panic.

wodge *n. informal* a large slice or lump.

woe *n.* sorrow, distress; trouble causing this, misfortune. □ **woeful** *adj.*, **woefully** *adv.*, **woefulness** *n.*

woebegone *adj.* looking unhappy.

wog *n. informal, offensive* a person who is not white.

wok *n.* a large bowl-shaped frying pan used esp. in Chinese cookery.

woke, woken past & p.p. of **wake**.

wold *n.* (esp. **wolds**) an area of open upland country.

wolf *n.* (*pl.* **wolves**) a wild animal of the dog family. ● *v.* eat quickly and greedily. □ **cry wolf** raise false alarms. □ **wolfish** *adj.*

wolfram *n.* tungsten or its ore.

wolf whistle *n.* a rising and falling whistle, expressing sexual admiration.

woman *n.* (*pl.* **women**) an adult female person; women in general.

womanhood *n.* the state of being a woman; women collectively.

womanize *v.* (also **-ise**) (of a man) engage in many casual affairs with women. □ **womanizer** *n.*

womankind *n.* women in general.

womanly *adj.* having qualities considered appropriate to a woman. □ **womanliness** *n.*

womb (woom) *n.* the hollow organ in female mammals in which the young develop before birth.

wombat *n.* a burrowing Australian marsupial like a small bear.

women pl. of **woman**.

womenfolk *n.* women in general; the women of one's family.

won past & p.p. of **win**.

wonder *n.* a feeling of surprise and admiration; an extraordinary and beautiful or admirable thing, person, etc. ● *v.* **1** feel curiosity. **2** feel amazement and admiration.

wonderful *adj.* very good; excellent, delightful. □ **wonderfully** *adv.*

wonderland *n.* a place full of wonderful things.

wonderment *n.* a feeling of wonder.

wonky *adj.* (**wonkier, wonkiest**) *informal* crooked; unsteady; not working.

wont (wohnt) *archaic adj.* accustomed to do something. ● *n.* one's usual practice.

woo *v.* seek to marry; seek the favour of.

wood *n.* the tough fibrous substance of a tree; this cut for use; (also **woods**) trees growing fairly densely over an area of ground. □ **out of the wood** clear of danger or difficulty.

woodbine *n.* wild honeysuckle.

woodcut *n.* a print made from a design cut in a block of wood.

wooded *adj.* covered with trees.

wooden *adj.* **1** made of wood. **2** stiff; showing no emotion. ▫ **woodenly** *adv.*

woodland *n.* wooded country.

woodlouse *n.* (*pl.* **woodlice**) a small wingless creature living in decaying wood etc.

woodpecker *n.* a bird that taps tree trunks with its beak to discover insects.

woodwind *n.* wind instruments made (or formerly made) of wood, e.g. the clarinet.

woodwork *n.* the art or practice of making things from wood; wooden parts of a room.

woodworm *n.* the larva of a kind of beetle that bores in wood.

woody *adj.* (**woodier, woodiest**) **1** wooded. **2** like or consisting of wood.

woof *n.* a dog's gruff bark. ● *v.* make this sound.

woofer *n.* a loudspeaker for reproducing low-frequency signals.

wool *n.* the soft hair from sheep or goats etc.; yarn or fabric made from this. ▫ **pull the wool over someone's eyes** deceive someone.

woollen *adj.* (*Amer.* **woolen**) made of wool. ● *n.pl.* (**woollens**) woollen cloth or clothing.

woolly *adj.* (**woollier, woolliest**) **1** covered with wool; like wool, woollen. **2** vague, confused. ● *n.* (*pl.* **-ies**) *informal* woollen garment. ▫ **woolliness** *n.*

woozy *adj.* (**woozier, wooziest**) *informal* dizzy, dazed.

word *n.* a unit of sound expressing a meaning independently and forming a basic element of speech; this represented by letters or symbols; something said; a message, news; a promise; a command. ● *v.* express in a particular style. ▫ **have a word with** speak briefly to. **have words** quarrel. **word of mouth** spoken, not written, words.

wording *n.* the way a thing is worded.

word-perfect *adj.* knowing every word of a speech etc.

word processor *n.* a computer or program designed for producing and altering text and documents.

wordy *adj.* (**wordier, wordiest**) using too many words.

wore past of **wear**.

work *n.* **1** the use of bodily or mental power in order to do or make something; such activity as a means of earning money; a task to be done. **2** something produced by work; a literary or musical composition; embroidery or other decorative articles of a particular kind. **3** (**works**) a factory; the operative parts of a machine; a defensive structure. **4** (**the works**) *informal* everything required or available. ● *v.* **1** perform work; be employed. **2** operate (a machine etc.); function. **3** bring about, accomplish: *working miracles.* **4** shape (material); produce, create; bring or come into a specified state. ▫ **work off** get rid of by activity. **work one's way** or **passage** fund oneself or pay for a journey by working. **work out 1** find or solve by calculation; plan the details of. **2** have a specified outcome. **3** take exercise. **work to rule** cause delay by over-strict observance of rules, as a form of protest. **work up 1** bring gradually to a more developed state; progress to a climax. **2** excite or make anxious.

workable *adj.* feasible, able to be put into practice.

workaday *adj.* ordinary, everyday; practical.

workbook *n.* a book with exercises for practice in a subject.

worker *n.* a person who works; a member of the working class; a neuter bee or ant etc. that does the work of the hive or colony.

workhouse *n.* a former public institution where people unable to support themselves were housed in return for work.

working *adj.* **1** engaged in work, esp. manual labour; working-class.

2 (of a theory etc.) used as the basis for work or argument but subject to revision. ● *n.* **1** a mine or part of a mine. **2** (**workings**) the way in which a system operates.

working class *n.* the class of people who are employed for wages, esp. in manual or industrial work. □ **working-class** *adj.*

working knowledge *n.* knowledge adequate to work with.

workman *n.* (*pl.* **-men**) a person employed to do manual labour.

workmanlike *adj.* efficient, practical.

workmanship *n.* skill in working or in a thing produced.

workout *n.* a session of physical exercise or training.

workshop *n.* **1** a room or building in which manual work or manufacture etc. is carried on. **2** a meeting for discussion or practice of a particular subject or activity.

workstation *n.* **1** a computer terminal and keyboard; a desk with this. **2** the location of a stage in a manufacturing process.

worktop *n.* a flat surface for working on, esp. in a kitchen.

world *n.* **1** the earth; all the people, creatures, etc., on it; everything. **2** an aspect of life; the people involved in a particular activity etc. □ **think the world of** respect highly.

worldly *adj.* of or concerned with earthly life or material gains, not spiritual. □ **worldliness** *n.*

worldwide *adj.* extending through the whole world.

World Wide Web *n.* a system of linked and cross-referenced documents for accessing information on the Internet.

worm *n.* **1** a creature with a long soft body and no backbone or limbs; (**worms**) internal parasites. **2** *informal* a feeble or contemptible person. **3** a spiral part of a mechanical device. ● *v.* **1** make one's way with twisting movements; insinuate oneself; obtain by crafty persistence. **2** rid (an animal) of parasitic worms. □ **wormy** *adj.*

worm cast *n.* a pile of earth cast up by an earthworm.

worm-eaten *adj.* full of holes made by insect larvae.

wormwood *n.* a woody plant with a bitter flavour.

worn p.p. of **wear**. *adj.* damaged or altered by use or wear; looking exhausted.

worn out *adj.* exhausted; damaged and thin from use.

worried *adj.* feeling or showing worry.

worry *v.* (**worried, worrying**) **1** feel anxious; cause anxiety to; annoy, trouble. **2** seize with the teeth and shake or pull about. ● *n.* (*pl.* **-ies**) anxiety, unease; something about which one worries. □ **worrier** *n.*

worse *adj.* & *adv.* more bad or badly, more evil or ill. ● *n.* something worse. □ **(none) the worse for** (not) harmed or impaired by.

worsen *v.* make or become worse.

worship *n.* reverence and respect paid to a god; adoration of or devotion to a person or thing. ● *v.* (**worshipped, worshipping**; *Amer.* **worshiped**) honour as a god; take part in an act of worship; idolize, treat with adoration. □ **worshipper** *n.*

worst *adj.* & *adv.* most bad or badly. ● *n.* the worst part, feature, event, etc. ● *v.* defeat, outdo. □ **get the worst of** be defeated in.

worsted (wuu-stid) *n.* a smooth woollen yarn or fabric.

worth *adj.* having a specified value; good enough for a specified treatment; likely to repay a specified treatment; possessing a specified sum as wealth. ● *n.* value, merit, usefulness; the amount that a specified sum will buy. □ **for all one is worth** *informal* with all one's energy. **worth one's while** worth the time or effort needed.

worthless *adj.* having no value or merit. □ **worthlessness** *n.*

worthwhile *adj.* worth the time or effort spent.

worthy *adj.* (**worthier, worthiest**) having great merit; deserving. ● *n.* (*pl.* **-ies**) a worthy person. □ **worthily** *adv.*, **worthiness** *n.*

would *v.aux.* used in senses corresponding to *will*[1] in the past tense, conditional statements, questions, polite requests and statements, and to express probability or something that happens from time to time.

would-be *adj.* desiring or pretending to be.

wound[1] (woond) *n.* an injury done to tissue by violence; injury to feelings. ● *v.* inflict a wound upon.

wound[2] (wownd) past & p.p. of **wind**[2].

wove, woven past & p.p. of **weave**.

wow *int.* an exclamation of astonishment. ● *n. informal* a sensational success.

WP *abbr.* word processor.

WPC *abbr.* woman police constable.

w.p.m. *abbr.* words per minute (specifying typing speed).

WRAC *abbr.* Women's Royal Army Corps.

wrack *n.* seaweed. ● *v.* var. of **rack**.

WRAF *abbr.* Women's Royal Air Force.

wraith *n.* a ghost, a spectral apparition of a living person.

wrangle *v.* argue or quarrel noisily. ● *n.* a noisy argument.

wrap *v.* (**wrapped, wrapping**) arrange (a soft or flexible covering) round (a person or thing). ● *n.* a shawl. □ **be wrapped up in** have one's attention deeply occupied by. **wrap up 1** dress warmly. **2** *informal* complete, conclude.

wrapper *n.* a cover of paper etc. wrapped round something.

wrapping *n.* material for wrapping things.

wrath *n.* anger, indignation. □ **wrathful** *adj.*, **wrathfully** *adv.*

wreak *v.* cause (damage); exact (revenge).

wreath (reeth) *n.* a decorative ring of flowers, leaves, and stems.

wreathe (ree*th*) *v.* encircle; twist into a wreath; wind, curve.

wreck *n.* the destruction esp. of a ship by storms or accident; a ship that has suffered this; something ruined or dilapidated; a person whose health or spirits have been destroyed. ● *v.* destroy; ruin; involve in shipwreck. □ **wrecker** *n.*

wreckage *n.* the remains of something wrecked.

Wren *n. hist.* a member of the WRNS.

wren *n.* a very small bird.

wrench *v.* twist or pull violently round; damage or pull by twisting. ● *n.* **1** a violent twisting pull. **2** pain caused by parting. **3** an adjustable spanner-like tool.

wrest *v.* wrench away; obtain by force or effort.

wrestle *v.* fight (esp. as a sport) by grappling with and trying to throw an opponent to the ground; struggle with a task or problem.

wretch *n.* a despicable person; a miserable person.

wretched *adj.* **1** very unhappy. **2** contemptible; infuriating. □ **wretchedly** *adv.*, **wretchedness** *n.*

wriggle *v.* move with short twisting movements; escape (out of a difficulty etc.) cunningly. ● *n.* a wriggling movement.

wring *v.* (**wrung, wringing**) twist and squeeze, esp. to remove liquid; squeeze (someone's hand) firmly or forcibly; obtain with effort or difficulty.

wrinkle *n.* **1** a small furrow in the skin, cloth, etc.; *informal* a minor fault or problem. **2** *informal* a useful hint or knack. ● *v.* make or become wrinkled. □ **wrinkly** *adj.*

wrist *n.* the joint connecting the hand and forearm; part of a garment covering this.

writ *n.* a formal written authoritative command; someone's power or influence.

write *v.* (**wrote, written, writing**) make letters or other symbols on a surface, esp. with a pen or pencil; compose in written form, esp. for publication; be an author; write and send a letter; write the necessary details on (a cheque etc.); *Computing* enter (data) into a storage medium. □ **write off 1** dismiss as insignificant. **2** acknowledge the loss of. **write up** write an account of; write entries in (a diary etc.).

write-off *n.* something written off as lost; a vehicle too damaged to be worth repairing.

writer *n.* a person who writes; an author.

writer's cramp *n.* cramp in the muscles of the hand.

write-up *n. informal* a published account of something, a review.

writhe *v.* twist one's body continually, esp. in pain; suffer because of embarrassment.

writing *n.* handwriting; literary work. □ **in writing** in written form.

writing paper *n.* paper for writing (esp. letters) on.

written p.p. of **write**.

WRNS *abbr. hist.* Women's Royal Naval Service.

wrong *adj.* **1** not true or correct; mistaken. **2** morally bad; unjust, dishonest. **3** unsuitable, undesirable; not the one desired or needed. ● *adv.* **1** mistakenly, incorrectly. **2** unjustly, wickedly. ● *n.* an immoral or unjust action. ● *v.* treat unjustly. □ **in the wrong** not having truth or justice on one's side. □ **wrongly** *adv.*

wrongdoer *n.* a person who behaves illegally or immorally. □ **wrongdoing** *n.*

wrongful *adj.* contrary to what is right or legal. □ **wrongfully** *adv.*

wrote past of **write**.

wrought (rawt) *adj.* (of metals) shaped by hammering. □ **wrought up** tense, distressed.

wrought iron *n.* a pure form of iron used for decorative work.

wrung past & p.p. of **wring**.

WRVS *abbr.* Women's Royal Voluntary Service.

wry *adj.* (**wryer, wryest** or **wrier, wriest**) **1** (of the face) contorted in disgust or disappointment. **2** (of humour) dry, mocking. □ **wryly** *adv.*, **wryness** *n.*

WYSIWYG *adj. Computing* indicating that the text is displayed on the screen as it will appear in print (from *what you see is what you get*).

X *n.* (as a Roman numeral) ten. ● *symb.* (of films) suitable for adults only.

X chromosome *n.* a sex chromosome, of which female cells have twice as many as males.

Xe *symb.* xenon.

xenon (zen-on) *n.* a chemical element (symbol Xe), a colourless, odourless gas.

xenophobia (zen-ŏ-**foh**-biă) *n.* a strong dislike or distrust of foreigners.

xenotransplantation *n.* the grafting or transplanting of tissues or organs between different species.

Xerox (zeer-oks) *n. trademark* a machine for producing photocopies; a photocopy. ● *v.* photocopy.

Xmas *n. informal* Christmas.

X-ray *n.* a photograph or examination made by electromagnetic radiation (**X-rays**) that can penetrate solids. ● *v.* photograph, examine, or treat by X-rays.

xylophone (**zI**-lŏ-fohn) *n.* a musical instrument with flat wooden bars struck with small hammers.

Y *symb.* yttrium.

yacht (yot) *n.* a light sailing boat; a boat used for private pleasure excursions. □ **yachting** *n.*, **yachtsman** *n.*, **yachtswoman** *n.*

yak *n.* a long-haired Asian ox.

yam *n.* the edible tuber of a tropical plant; a sweet potato.

yang *n.* (in Chinese philosophy) the active male principle.

yank *informal v.* pull sharply. ● *n.* **1** a sharp pull. **2** (**Yank**) an American.

yap *n.* a shrill bark. ● *v.* (**yapped, yapping**) bark shrilly.

yard *n.* **1** a measure of length, 3 feet (0.9144 metre). **2** a piece of enclosed ground, esp. attached to a building. **3** a pole slung from a mast to support a sail.

yardage *n.* length measured in yards.

Yardie *n.* a member of a Jamaican gang of criminals.

yardstick *n.* a standard of comparison.

yarmulke (yar-muul-kă) *n.* (also **yarmulka**) a skullcap worn by Jewish men.

yarn *n.* **1** any spun thread. **2** *informal* a story.

yashmak *n.* a veil worn by Muslim women in certain countries.

yaw *v.* (of a ship or aircraft) fail to hold a straight course.

yawn *v.* open the mouth wide and draw in breath, as when sleepy or bored; have a wide opening. ● *n.* the act of yawning.

Yb *symb.* ytterbium.

Y chromosome *n.* a sex chromosome occurring only in males.

yd *abbr.* yard.

year *n.* the time taken by the earth to orbit the sun (about 365¼ days); (also **calendar year**) the period from 1 Jan. to 31 Dec. inclusive; any consecutive period of twelve months.

yearbook *n.* an annual publication listing events or aspects of the previous year.

yearling *n.* an animal between 1 and 2 years old.

yearly *adj.* happening, published, or payable once a year. ● *adv.* annually.

yearn *v.* feel great longing.

yeast *n.* a fungus used to cause fermentation in making beer and wine and as a raising agent.

yell *n.* & *v.* (utter) a shout or scream.

yellow *adj.* **1** coloured like buttercups or ripe lemons. **2** *informal* cowardly. **3** (of reporting etc.) sensational. ● *n.* a yellow colour or thing. ● *v.* turn yellow. □ **yellowish** *adj.*

yelp *n.* & *v.* (utter) a shrill cry.

yen *n.* **1** (*pl.* **yen**) the basic monetary unit in Japan. **2** *informal* a longing, a yearning.

yeoman (yoh-măn) *n.* (*pl.* **-men**) *hist.* a man who owned and farmed a small estate.

yes *int.* & *n.* an affirmative reply; an expression of agreement or consent, or of reply to a summons etc.

yes-man *n.* (*pl.* **-men**) *informal* a person who is always ready to agree with a superior.

yesterday *adv.* & *n.* (on) the day before today; (in) the recent past.

yet *adv.* **1** up to the present or a specified time; this soon; for some time into the future. **2** even (used with comparatives): *yet more vain.* ● *conj.* nevertheless, in spite of that.

yeti *n.* a large manlike animal said to exist in the Himalayas.

yew *n.* an evergreen tree with dark needle-like leaves.

Y-fronts *n.pl.* *trademark* men's briefs with a Y-shaped seam at the front.

YHA *abbr.* Youth Hostels Association.

Yiddish *n.* the language used by Jews from eastern Europe.

yield *v.* **1** produce as a fruit, outcome of effort, etc. **2** surrender; hand over to another; move or give way when pushed or pressed. ● *n.* an amount yielded or produced.

yin *n.* (in Chinese philosophy) the passive female principle.

yippee *int.* an exclamation of delight or excitement.

YMCA *abbr.* Young Men's Christian Association.

yob *n. informal* an aggressive and coarse person.

yodel *v.* (**yodelled, yodelling**; *Amer.* **yodeled**) sing with a quickly alternating change of pitch. ● *n.* a yodelling cry. □ **yodeller** *n.*

yoga *n.* a Hindu system of meditation and self-control; exercises used in this.

yogurt *n.* (also **yoghurt**) food made of milk that has been thickened by the action of bacteria.

yoke *n.* **1** a wooden crosspiece fastened over the necks of two oxen pulling a plough etc.; a frame fitting over someone's shoulders and holding a load at each end; part of a garment fitting over the shoulders. **2** oppressive rule. ● *v.* harness with a yoke; join, link.

yokel *n.* a country person regarded as stupid or uneducated.

yolk *n.* the round yellow internal part of an egg.

yonder *adj.* & *adv. archaic* over there.

yonks *n.pl. informal* a long time.

yore *n.* □ **of yore** *literary* long ago.

Yorkshire pudding *n.* a baked batter pudding eaten with gravy or meat.

you *pron.* **1** the person(s) addressed. **2** one, people in general.

young *adj.* having lived or existed for only a short time; energetic and enthusiastic; immature. ● *n.* an animal's offspring.

youngster *n.* a young person, a child.

your *adj.* of or belonging to you.

yours *poss.pron.* belonging to you.

yourself *pron.* (*pl.* **yourselves**) the emphatic and reflexive form of *you.*

youth *n.* **1** the state or period of being young. **2** a young man; young people.

youth club *n.* a club providing leisure activities for young people.

youthful *adj.* young; characteristic of young people. □ **youthfulness** *n.*

youth hostel *n.* a hostel providing cheap accommodation for walkers or holidaymakers.

yowl *v.* & *n.* (make) a loud wailing cry.

yo-yo *n.* (*pl.* **yo-yos**) *trademark* a disc-shaped toy that can be made to rise and fall on a string that winds round it in a groove. ● *v.* (**yo-yoed, yo-yoing**) fluctuate, move up and down rapidly.

YTS *abbr.* Youth Training Scheme.

ytterbium (it-**er**-biŭm) *n.* a metallic element (symbol Yb).

yttrium (**it**-riŭm) *n.* a metallic element (symbol Y).

yuan *n.* (*pl.* **yuan**) the chief monetary unit in China.

yuck *int.* (also **yuk**) *informal* an expression of disgust.

Yuletide *n. archaic* the Christmas festival.

yummy *adj.* (**yummier, yummiest**) *informal* delicious.

yuppie *n.* (also **yuppy**) *informal* a young middle-class professional person working in a city.

YWCA *abbr.* Young Women's Christian Association.

Zz

zany *adj.* (**zanier, zaniest**) crazily funny. ● *n.* (*pl.* **-ies**) a zany person.

zap *informal v.* (**zapped, zapping**) **1** destroy. **2** (cause to) move suddenly. ● *n.* a burst of energy.

zeal *n.* enthusiasm, hearty and persistent effort. □ **zealous** *adj.*, **zealously** *adv.*

zealot (zel-ŏt) *n.* a person who is fanatical in support of a cause.

zebra *n.* an African horse-like animal with black and white stripes.

zebra crossing *n.* a pedestrian crossing where the road is marked with broad white stripes.

Zen *n.* a form of Buddhism.

zenith *n.* the part of the sky that is directly overhead; the highest point.

zephyr *n. literary* a soft gentle wind.

zero *n.* (*pl.* **zeros**) nought, the figure 0; nil; a point marked 0 on a graduated scale, a temperature corresponding to this. □ **zero in on** (**zeroed, zeroing**) take aim at; focus attention on.

zero-emission *adj.* (of a vehicle) not emitting pollutant gases in its exhaust.

zero hour *n.* the hour at which something is timed to begin.

zest *n.* **1** keen enjoyment or interest. **2** orange or lemon peel as flavouring. □ **zestful** *adj.*, **zestfully** *adv.*

zigzag *n.* a line or course turning right and left alternately at sharp angles. ● *adj.* & *adv.* as or in a zigzag. ● *v.* (**zigzagged, zigzagging**) move in a zigzag.

zilch *n. informal* nothing.

zinc *n.* a white metallic element (symbol Zn).

zing *informal n.* vigour. ● *v.* move swiftly.

Zionism *n.* a movement that campaigned for a Jewish homeland in Palestine. □ **Zionist** *n.*

zip *n.* **1** (in full **zip fastener**) a fastening device with teeth that interlock when brought together by a sliding tab. **2** *informal* energy. ● *v.* (**zipped, zipping**) **1** fasten with a zip fastener. **2** *informal* move with vigour or at high speed.

Zip code *n. Amer.* a postal code.

zipper *n.* a zip fastener.

zircon *n.* a bluish-white gem cut from a translucent mineral.

zirconium *n.* grey metallic element (symbol Zr).

zit *n. informal* a pimple.

zither *n.* a stringed instrument played with the fingers.

zloty *n.* (*pl.* **zloty** or **zlotys**) the unit of money in Poland.

Zn *symb.* zinc.

zodiac *n.* (in astrology) a band of the sky divided into twelve equal parts (**signs of the zodiac**) each named from a constellation. □ **zodiacal** *adj.*

zombie *n.* **1** (in voodoo) a corpse said to have been revived by witchcraft. **2** *informal* a person apparently without awareness, will, or energy.

zone *n.* an area with particular characteristics, purpose, or use. ● *v.* divide into zones. □ **zonal** *adj.*

zoo *n.* a place where wild animals are kept for exhibition, conservation, and study.

zoology *n.* the study of animals. □ **zoological** *adj.*, **zoologist** *n.*

zoom *v.* **1** move very quickly; increase sharply. **2** (in photography) make a distant object appear gradually closer by means of a zoom lens.

zoophyte (zoo-ŏ-fIt) *n.* a plantlike animal, esp. a coral, sea anemone, or sponge.

Zr *symb.* zirconium.

zucchini (zoo-kee-ni) *n.* (*pl.* **zucchini** or **zucchinis**) *esp. Amer.* a courgette.

Zulu *n.* a member of a Bantu people of South Africa; their language.

zygote (zI-goht) *n.* a cell formed by the union of two gametes.

Language tips

Spelling rules and tips 607

Frequently misspelled words 609

Commonly confused pairs of words 613

Punctuation 619

❶ Spelling rules and tips

English is full of inconsistencies and many spellings simply need to be learned by heart; but there are some rules and tips to help us.

- '*i* before *e* except after *c*': this rule is generally true when the pronunciation is *–ee-*, as in *believe*, *siege*, and *ceiling*, *deceive* [there are exceptions where the *e* is followed by *–in* or *–ine*, as in *caffeine* and *protein*]. The rule is not true when the syllable is pronounced in other ways, as in *beige* and *eiderdown*, or where the *i* and the *e* are pronounced separately, as in *holier*.

- Most verbs of one syllable ending in a single consonant double the consonant when *-ed*, *-ing*, *-able*, and *-er* are added, such as *beg*, *begged*, *begging* and *clap*, *clapped*, *clapping*. When the final consonant is *w*, *x*, or *y* this is not doubled, e.g. *tow*, *towed*, *towing* and *vex*, *vexed*, *vexing*. When the final consonant is preceded by more than one vowel the consonant is not normally doubled: *boil*, *boiled*, *boiling* and *clean*, *cleaned*, *cleaning*.

- Verbs of more than one syllable ending in a single consonant double the consonant when the stress is placed on the final syllable: *allot*, *allotted*, *allotting*; *begin*, *beginning*; *occur*, *occurred*, *occurring*. Where the final consontant is *w*, *x*, or *y* this is not doubled: *guffaw*, *guffawed*, *guffawing*; *relax*, *relaxed*, *relaxing*.

- Most verbs that do not have their stress on the final syllable do not double the consonant unless it is an *l*, as in *gallop*, *galloped*, *galloping*; *offer*, *offered*, *offering*; *target*, *targeted*, *targeting*. There are some exceptions to the rule in British English, for example *input*, *inputting*; *output*, *outputting*; *kidnap*, *kidnapped*, *kidnapping*; *worship*, *worshipped*, *worshipping*.

● Verbs ending in *l* normally double the *l* in British English, regardless of where the stress occurs: *enrol, enrolled, enrolling; travel, travelled, travelling, traveller*. Some exceptions include *appeal, appealed, appealing; conceal, concealed, concealing; reveal, revealed, revealing; parallel, paralleled, paralleling*.

● Words having a final silent *e* usually drop the *e* when an ending beginning with a vowel is added: *blue* + *-ish* = *bluish*; *brave* + *-est* = *bravest*; *refuse* + *-al* = *refusal*. However there are a number of exceptions. A final *e* is usually kept in *ageing* and in *changeable* (but not in *changing*), *twingeing*, and *whingeing*; and in *dyeing* (from *dye*), *singeing* (from *singe*), and *swingeing* (from *swinge*) to distinguish these from the words *dying* (from *die*), *singing* (from *sing*), and *swinging* (from *swing*).

● Nouns normally form plurals by adding *–s*, or *–es* if the singular form ends in *–s*, *-x*, *-z*, *-sh*, or soft *-ch* (as in *church* but not *loch*: *churches, lochs*).

● Words ending in *-y* form plurals with *-ies* (*policy, policies*) unless the ending is *-ey*, in which case the plural form is normally *-eys* (*valley, valleys*).

● Nouns ending in *-f* and *-fe* form plurals sometimes with *-fes*, sometimes *-ves*, and occasionally both *-fes* and *-ves*:

calf, calves
dwarf, dwarfs/dwarves
elf, elves
half, halves
handkerchief, handkerchiefs
hoof, hoofs/hooves
knife, knives
leaf, leaves
life, lives
proof, proofs
roof, roofs/rooves
scarf, scarfs/scarves
self, selves
sheaf, sheaves
shelf, shelves
thief, thieves
turf, turfs/turves
wharf, wharfs/wharves

loaf, loaves
oaf, oafs
wife, wives
wolf, wolves

❷ Frequently misspelled words

word	comment
abscess	*-scess*, not *-sess*
abseil	*-seil*, not *-sail*
accommodate, accommodation, etc	two *c*s, two *m*s
accumulate, accumulation, etc.	two *c*s, one *m*
achieve	*i* before *e*
acquaint, acquire, etc	*acq-*
address	two *d*s
ageing	preferred to *aging*
aggressive, aggression, etc.	two *g*s, two *s*'s
amateur	*-eur*, not *-uer*
anaesthetic	remember the *-ae-*
anoint	only one *n* in the middle
apartment	only one *p*
appal	two *p*s, one *l*; American *appall*
appalling	two *p*s, two *l*s
aqueduct	*aque-*, not *aqua-*
archaeology	remember the *-ae-*
artefact	*arte-* better than *arti-*
attach	not *-atch*
beautiful	not *beat-*
believe	*i* before *e*
besiege	*i* before *e*
biased	better than *biassed*
blatant	not *-ent*
broccoli	two *c*s, one *l*
cappuccino	two *p*s, two *c*s

Caribbean	one *r*, two *b*s
commemorate	two *m*s followed by one *m*
commitment	one *t* in the middle
committee	two *m*s, two *t*s
comparative	*-rative*, not *-ritive*
compatible	*-tible*, not *-table*
consensus	not *-census*
contemporary	*-porary*, not *-pory*
deceive	*e* before *i*
definite	*-ite*, not *-ate*
desperate	*-per-* not *-par-*
detach	not *-atch*
disappear	one *s*, two *p*s
disappoint	one *s*, two *p*s
ecstasy	ends *-asy*
eighth	two *h*s
embarrass, embarrassment, etc.	two *r*s, two *s*'s
enthral	one *l*; American *enthrall*
extraordinary	*extraor-*, nor *extror-*
extrovert	*extro-*, not *extra-*
fluorescent	*fluor-*, not *flour-*
fulfil	one final *l*; American *fulfill*
gauge	*-au-*, not *-ua-*
guarantee	*-ua-*, not *-au-*
guard, guardian, etc.	*-ua-*, not *-au-*
hamster	*ham-*, not *hamp-*
harass, harassment, etc.	one *r*, two *s*'s
humorous	*-or-*, not *-our-*
hygienic	*i* before *e*
independent	ends *-ent* (noun and adjective)
inoculate	one *n*, one *c*
instalment	one *l*; American *installment*
introvert	*-tro-*, not *-tra-*
itinerary	ends *-erary*
judgement	*-dge-* preferred to *-dg-*

label	*-el*, not *-le*
liaison	two *i*s: *-iai-*
licence	*-ence* in the noun
license	*-ense* in the verb
lightning	*-tn-*, not *-ten-*
manoeuvre	*-oeu-*; American *maneuver*
medieval	*-ev-* preferred to *-aev-*
Mediterranean	one *t*, two *r*s
memento	*mem-*, not *mom-*
millennium	two *l*s, two *n*s
millionaire	two *l*s, one *n*
miniature	*-ia-* in second syllable
minuscule	*-uscule*, not *-iscule*
mischievous	*-vous*, not *-vious*
misspell	two *s*'s
necessary	one *c*, two *s*'s
niece	*i* before *e*
occasion	two *c*s, one *s*
occurrence	two *c*s, two *r*s
omit	one *m*
parliament	*-ia-* in second syllable
peculiar	*-iar*, not *-ier*
permanent	*-nent*, not *-nant*
persistent	*-tent*, not *-tant*
pharaoh	*-aoh*, not *-oah*
pigeon	no *d*: *-igeon*
privilege	ends *-ilege*
pronunciation	*-nunc-*, not *-nounc-*
questionnaire	two *n*s
receive	*e* before *i*
recommend	one *c*, two *m*s
restaurateur	no *n* in the middle: *-ateur*
rhythm	begins *rhy-*, not *ry-*
risotto	one *s*, two *t*s
sacrilege	*-rilege*, not *-relige*
schedule	*sche-*, not *she-*

seize	*e* before *i*
separate	*-par-*
not	*-per-*
siege	*i* before *e*
sieve	*i* before *e*
skilful	single *l*s; American ***skillful***
successful	two *c*s, two s's, one *l*
supersede	not *-cede*
suppress	not *sur-*; two *p*s
surprise	begins *sur-*
threshold	one *h*
tomorrow	one *m*, two *r*s
until	just one *l*
unwieldy	*-dy*, not *-dly*
vegetable	*vege-*, not *vega-*
veterinary	note the *-er* in the middle
weird	*-ei-*, not *-ie-*
whinge	remember the *h*
wilful	single *l*s; American ***willful***
withhold	two *h*s

● DIFFERENT SPELLINGS FOR DIFFERENT PARTS OF SPEECH

word 1	part of speech	word 2	part of speech
annexe	noun	annex	verb
our rooms were in the annexe		*Germany annexed Austria in 1938*	
dependant	noun	dependent	adjective
a single man with no dependants		*he is dependent on drugs; households with dependent children*	

envelope	noun	envelop	verb
writing paper and envelopes		*darkness enveloped the town*	
licence	noun	license	verb
a gun licence		*he was licensed to fly a plane*	
practice	noun	practise	verb
she put her new ideas into practice		*you need to practise every day*	
thief	noun	thieve	verb
a car thief		*they began thieving again*	
wreath	noun	wreathe	verb
a holly wreath		*the mountains were wreathed in mist*	

❸ Commonly confused pairs of words

word 1	meaning	word 2	meaning
adverse	unfavourable	averse	opposed
affect	cause a change in	effect	bring about; a result
alternate	one after another	alternative	available instead
ambiguous	having more than one meaning	ambivalent	having mixed feelings
amend	change	emend	alter a text
amoral	having no moral sense	immoral	not conforming to moral standards
appraise	assess the quality of	apprise	inform

avoid	keep away from	evade	avoid by guile
biannual	twice a year	biennial	every two years
bought	past of *buy*	brought	past of *bring*
censor	act as censor of	censure	criticize harshly
climactic	forming a climax	climatic	relating to climate
complement	add to in a way that improves	compliment	politely praise
compose	make up a whole	comprise	consist of
continual	happening constantly or repeatedly	continuous	going on without a break
credible	believable	credulous	too ready to believe
decided	unquestionable	decisive	conclusive, unfaltering
definite	clear and distinct	definitive	conclusive, authoritative
defuse	remove the fuse from; reduce tension in	diffuse	spread out; not clear or concise
deprecate	disapprove of	depreciate	decrease in value
desert	a waterless area; abandon	dessert	a sweet course
discreet	careful to avoid attention	discrete	separate
disinterested	impartial	uninterested	not interested
draw	make a picture of; pull; have an equal score	drawer	sliding storage compartment
enormity	extreme seriousness; a grave crime	enormousness	great size or scale

ensure	make sure	insure	take out insurance on
especially	in particular, above all	specially	for a special purpose
exceptionable	causing disapproval	exceptional	unusually good
faint	hard to see or hear; temporarily lose consciousness	feint	paper with faint lines; a movement in boxing or fencing
flair	natural ability	flare	a burst of flame or light; become angry
flaunt	display ostentatiously	flout	disregard a rule or custom
flounder	(of a person) struggle or be in confusion	founder	(of an undertaking) fail or come to nothing
forego	(*old use*) go before	forgo	go without
forever	continually	for ever	eternally
fortuitous	happening by chance	fortunate	happening by good chance, lucky
gourmand	a glutton	gourmet	a food connoisseur
grisly	causing revulsion	grizzly	as in *grizzly bear*
hoard	a store of valuables	horde	(*disapproving*) a large group of people
illegal	against the law	illicit	not allowed
imply	suggest strongly	infer	deduce or conclude
impracticable	not able to be done	impractical	not sensible or realistic

incredible	(of a thing) not believable	incredulous	(of a person) unable to believe
ingenious	well thought out	ingenuous	innocent, honest
intense	extreme in force or degree	intensive	thorough or concentrated
interment	burial	internment	confinement
its	belonging to it	it's	it is, or it has
loath	reluctant, unwilling	loathe	dislike greatly
loose	not fixed; unfasten or relax	lose	be deprived of or no longer have
luxuriant	lush	luxurious	comfortable and rich
masterful	powerful, domineering	masterly	highly skilful
militate	be a powerful factor in preventing	mitigate	make less severe
naught	(*old use*) nothing (as in *come to naught*)	nought	the digit 0, nothing
naval	relating to a navy	navel	umbilicus
observance	the keeping of a law or custom	observation	a perception or remark
occupant	a person in a vehicle, seat, etc	occupier	the person living in a property
official	having authorized status	officious	aggressive in asserting authority
ordinance	an authoritative order	ordnance	mounted guns, military stores

palate	the roof of the mouth; the sense of taste	palette	an artist's mixing board
pedal	a lever that powers a bicycle	peddle	sell goods
perquisite	a special right or privilege	prerequisite	something needed in advance
perspicacious	having a ready understanding, perceptive	perspicuous	clearly expressed
pitiable	deserving pity	pitiful	causing pity; very small or poor
pore	(*pore over*) read closely	pour	flow, cause to flow
practicable	able to be done	practical	effective or realistic; (of a person) skilled at manual tasks
precipitate	hasty, headlong	precipitous	abruptly steep
prescribe	recommend with authority; issue a prescription	proscribe	forbid or condemn
prevaricate	avoid giving a direct answer	procrastinate	delay or post-pone action
principal	most important; main; the chief person	principle	a basis of belief or action
purposely	intentionally	purposefully	resolutely
refute	prove to be wrong	repudiate	refuse to accept or support
regrettable	causing regret, undesirable	regretful	feeling regret

sensual	relating to or giving physical pleasure	sensuous	relating to the senses rather than the intellect
shear	cut wool off, cut	sheer	utter, complete (as in sheer delight); swerve or avoid
site	a place where something happens	sight	the ability to see
sociable	friendly and willing to mix with people	social	relating to society
stationary	not moving	stationery	materials for writing
storey	part of a building on one level	story	an account of imaginary events
straight	extending without a curve	strait	narrow passage of water
titillate	excite pleasantly	titivate	adorn or smarten
tortuous	twisting, devious	torturous	causing torture, tormenting
triumphal	done or made to celebrate a victory	triumphant	victorious, jubilant after a victory
turbid	(of a liquid) cloudy; not clear	turgid	swollen or full; (of language) tediously pompous
unsociable	not willing to mix with people	unsocial	socially inconvenient
venal	open to bribery, corrupt	venial	(of a sin) minor
who's	who is	whose	belonging to which person

❹ Punctuation

● COMMA

The comma gives detail to the structure of sentences and makes their meaning clear by marking off words that either do or do not belong together. It usually represents the natural breaks and pauses that you make in speech, and operates at phrase level and word level.

at phrase level You should use a comma to mark off parts of a sentence that are separated by conjunctions (*and, but, yet,* etc.). This is especially important when there is a change or repetition of the subject:

> *Attempts to block him failed, and he went ahead on 23 June.*

It is not normally correct to join the clauses of a compound sentence without a conjunction:

> ☒ *His was the last house, the road ended with him.*

(In this sentence, the comma should either be replaced by a semicolon, or retained and followed by *and*.)

It is also incorrect to separate a subject from its verb with a single comma:

> ☒ *Those with the lowest incomes and no other means, should get the most support.*

(Remove the comma.)

A comma also separates parts of a sentence that balance or complement each other, and can introduce direct speech, especially in continuation of dialogue:

> *He was getting better, but not as fast as his doctor wished.*

Then Laura said, 'Do you mean that?'

An important function of the comma is to prevent ambiguity or momentary misunderstanding:

A hundred feet below, the woman in the red dress was gazing up at them.

Commas are used in pairs to separate elements in a sentence that are asides or not part of the main statement:

By then, however, it was very close to being dark.

It is important to remember *both* the commas in cases like this. Using only one can be worse than none at all:

☒ *By then, however it was very close to being dark.*

Commas are also used to separate a relative clause (one beginning with *which*, *who*, *whom*, or *whose*) when this is adding extra information and could be removed from the sentence without changing the meaning or producing nonsense:

The money, which totals more than half a million, comes from three anonymous donors.

But they are not used when the clause begins with *which* or *that* and is essential to the meaning by identifying a person or thing just mentioned:

What have you done with the money that I gave you?

A single comma sometimes follows adverbs (such as *already*, *moreover*, and *yesterday*), phrases, and subordinate clauses that come at the beginning of a sentence:

Moreover, they had lied about where they had been.

Next morning, the air glittered and the palm tree stood upright in the sun.

In these cases and many others this comma is optional, but one or more is always needed with *however* when it means 'by contrast' or 'on the other hand':

> *However, a good deal of discretion is left in the hands of area managers.*

at word level A comma is used to separate adjectives having the same range of reference coming before a noun:

> *a cold, damp, badly heated room*
>
> *a ruthless, manipulative person*

The comma can be replaced by *and* between a pair of adjectives to make a stronger effect:

> *a ruthless and manipulative person*

The comma is omitted when the adjectives have a different range of reference (for example, size and colour) or when the last adjective has a closer relation to the noun:

> *his baggy green jacket*
>
> *a distinguished foreign politician*
>
> *a dear little baby*

Commas are used to separate items in a list or sequence:

> *The visitors were given tea, scones, and cake.*

The comma before *and* is regarded by many people as unnecessary and left out; this dictionary always includes one. There are cases where the final comma is essential for clarity (for example, where one of the items in the list is a pair joined by *and*), and sometimes not having one produces ambiguity:

> ☑ *For breakfast they wanted tea, toast and marmalade, and eggs.*

☒ *I would like to thank my parents, Anne Smith and God.*

Leave out the comma between nouns that occur together in the same grammatical role in a sentence (called apposition):

My friend Judge Peters was not at home.

Her daughter Mary became a nurse.

But use one when the noun is a piece of extra information that could be removed from the sentence without any noticeable effect on the meaning:

His father, Humphrey V. Roe, was not so fortunate.

● SEMICOLON

The semicolon is the punctuation mark that causes most trouble in ordinary writing, and it is the one least noticeable if you skim the pages of a modern novel. But if you use it carefully, it can be extremely helpful.

Its main role is to mark a grammatical separation that is stronger in effect than a comma but less strong than a full stop. Normally the two parts of a sentence divided by a semicolon balance each other, as distinct from leading from one to the other (in which case a colon is usually more suitable, as explained below):

Honey looked up and glared; the man scurried away.

You can also use it as a stronger division in a sentence that already contains commas:

What has crippled me? Was it my grandmother, frowning on my childish affection and turning it to formality and cold courtesy; or my timid, fearful mother, in awe of everyone including, finally, me; or was it my wife's infidelities, or my own?

● COLON

The colon tends to be used much more in formal print than in everyday writing. Whereas a semicolon links two balanced statements, a colon leads from the first statement to the second. Typically it links a general or introductory statement to an example, a cause to an effect, or a premise to a conclusion. (In many cases a conjunction such as 'so' or 'for example' could be introduced between the two halves.)

> *He was being made to feel more part of the family: the children kissed him goodnight, like a third parent.*

> *I feel angry: do I look angry?*

You also use a colon to introduce a list:

> *The price includes the following: travel to London, flight to Venice, hotel accommodation, and excursions.*

● BRACKETS

The brackets you will use most often in writing are round brackets or parentheses ( ). You use round brackets:

- to show explanations and additional comment:

> *She let herself plan out what she would say, what her tone could be (easy but serious), how much need she could show (fatigue, strained loyalty).*

- to show optional words, implying doubt or caution about them:

> *There are many (apparent) difficulties.*

- to give references and statistical information:

> *a brass-rubbing of Sir Toby and Lady Falconer (c.1428)*

Square brackets [ ] are mostly used in formal printing. Their main use is to enclose extra information provided, often by someone other than the writer of the surrounding text, such as an editor, to clarify an obscure point or identity:

> *When Charles had spoken to Henry, he [Henry] withdrew graciously.*

● DASH

In formal printing there are two types of dash: the en-rule (–) and the longer em-rule (—). Most word-processing programs are able to distinguish the two lengths of rule, but in ordinary writing no distinction is usually made. In printing, the en-rule has certain special uses (e.g. to mark a range of numbers, as in pages 34–6), whereas the em-rule is the one corresponding to the dash in general use. The principal uses of the dash are:

- a single dash is used to introduce an explanation or expansion of what comes before it:

> *It is a kind of irony of history that I should write about the French Revolution in the very country where it has had the least impact—I mean England, of course.*

- a pair of dashes is used to indicate asides and parentheses, forming a more distinct break than commas would:

> *Helen has only seen her father once in her adult life and—until her flight from Grassdale—her brother is a virtual stranger to her.*

● QUESTION MARK

The main use of the question mark (?) is to indicate a direct question:

> *Are they leaving tomorrow?*

> *What time is it?*

You can sometimes use it even when the question is put in the form of a statement:

They told you that?

Surely it's the same one?

I wonder if you can help me?

You should not use a question mark in indirect questions in which the question is reported rather than expressed (*He asked what time it was*), but you should use it in tag questions of the kind *She's much taller now, isn't she?*.

A question mark is conventionally placed before a word about which there is some doubt, e.g. uncertain locations on maps and uncertain dates (*Thomas Tallis, ?1505–85*).

● EXCLAMATION MARK

An exclamation mark (!) shows in writing what you would normally say loudly or strongly in speech, to attract attention or to tell someone what to do. You will most often use it:

- to mark a command or warning:

Go to your room!

Be careful!

- to indicate the expression of a strong feeling of absurdity, surprise, approval, dislike, regret, etc., especially after *how* or *what*:

How awful!

Aren't they odd!

- to express a wish or a feeling of regret:

I'd love to come!

If only I had known!

The exclamation mark also occurs quite often in literature, especially in poetry, to express a strong feeling or idea:

Ah! parted lips and little pearly teeth,
Wide eyes, snub noses, shorts, divided skirts!
(Betjeman)

In ordinary writing, you do not often need to use the exclamation mark in this way. Avoid using it just to add a false sense of drama or sensation to writing that is otherwise routine or unexciting.

● QUOTATION MARKS

The main use of quotation marks (also called inverted commas) is to indicate direct speech and quotations. In writing it is common to use double quotation marks (" "), and in printing practice varies between the double and single style (' ').

In direct speech and quotations, the closing quotation mark normally comes after a final full stop, and after any other punctuation that forms part of the quotation, such as an exclamation mark:

Christie nodded her head as she said, 'A fine proposal this is, I must say.'

Then they shouted, 'Watch out!'

When the quoted speech is followed or interrupted by a reporting verb such as *say*, *shout*, etc., the punctuation that divides the sentence is put inside the quotation marks:

'No,' he said, slamming the suitcase shut.

'You must have read my mind,' she said, 'a good strong cup of tea is just what I need.'

If a quoted word or phrase comes at the end of a sentence or coincides with a comma, the punctuation that belongs to the sentence as a whole is placed outside the quotation marks:

What is a 'gigabyte'?

No one should 'follow a multitude to do evil', as the Scripture says.

When a quotation occurs within a quotation, the inner quotation is put in double quotation marks if the main quotation is in single marks (or vice versa):

'Have you any idea,' he asked, 'what a "gigabyte" is?'

● APOSTOPHE

The principal role of the apostrophe is to indicate a possessive, as in *Tessa's house* and *the town's mayor*. For its conventional role to indicate omitted letters, see below.

Singular nouns form the possessive by adding *'s* (*the dog's barks* = one dog), and plural nouns ending in *-s* add an apostrophe after the *-s* (*the dogs' barks* = more than one dog).

When a plural noun ends in a letter other than *-s*, the possessive is formed by adding *'s*: *the children's games*, *the oxen's hoofs*, etc.

Beware of the so-called 'grocers' apostrophe', an apostrophe wrongly applied to an ordinary plural, particularly in words ending in *-o* but also in quite harmless words such as *apples* and *pears* (e.g. ☒ *pear's 30p a pound*).

Beware also of confusing the possessive *whose* with *who's*, which is a contraction of *who is* (e.g. ☒ *Who's turn is it?*).

There is a problem with names ending in *-s*, because of the awkward sound that can result. Practice varies, but the best course is to add *'s* to names that end in *-s* when you would pronounce the resulting form with an extra *-s* in speech (e.g. *Charles's*, *Dickens's*, *Thomas's*, *The Times's*); and omit *'s* when the name is normally pronounced without the extra *s* (e.g. *Bridges'*, *Connors'*, *Mars'*, *Herodotus'*). With French names ending in (silent) *-s* or *-x*, add *'s* (e.g. *Dumas's, le Roux's*) and pronounce the modified word with a final *-z*.

An apostrophe should not be used in the pronouns *hers, its, ours, yours,* and *theirs*:

☑ *a friend of yours*

☒ *a friend of your's*

Be careful to distinguish *its* from *it's*. *Its* (no apostrophe) is a possessive meaning 'belonging to it', whereas *it's* (with an apostrophe) is a contraction meaning 'it is':

☑ *Give the cat its dinner.*

☒ *Give the cat it's dinner.*

☑ *It's hard to know where to start.*

☑ *It's been raining.*

An apostrophe is no longer normally used in the plural of abbreviated forms (e.g. *several MPs were standing around*), although it is used in the possessive (e.g. *the BBC's decision to go ahead with the broadcast*). It is used in plurals when clarity calls for it, e.g. *dot your i's and cross your t's*. The apostrophe is also rapidly disappearing in company names and other commercial uses, e.g. *Barclays Bank, Citizens Advice Bureau*.

Another important use of the apostrophe is to mark contractions such as *I'll, they've, couldn't,* and *she's*, and informally also in contractions involving nouns (e.g. *the joke's on them*).

The apostrophe is no longer needed in words that were originally shortened forms but are now treated as words in their own right, e.g. *cello, flu, phone,* and *plane*. Other words retain them in their spelling, usually in the middle of words rather than at the beginning, e.g. *fo'c'sle, ne'er-do-well, o'er, rock 'n' roll*.

HYPHEN

n print, a hyphen is half the length of a dash, but in writing here is often little noticeable difference. While the dash has he purpose of separating words and groups of words, the yphen is meant to link words and parts of words (apart from ts use as a printing convention to split a word at the end of a ine). Although the use of hyphens is very variable in English, he following guidelines reflect generally agreed principles.

s a so-called 'spelling hyphen', the hyphen is used to join two r more words so as to form a single word (often called a com-ound word), e.g. *free-for-all*, *multi-ethnic*, and *right-handed*, nd words having a grammatical relationship which form a ompound, e.g. *dive-bomb* (based on 'to bomb by making a ive'), *load-bearing* (based on 'bearing a load'), *punch-drunk* based on 'drunk from a punch'). Straightforward noun com-ounds are now much more often spelled either as two words *boiling point, credit card, focus group, garden party*) or as one, ven when this involves a collision of consonants, which used o be a reason for putting in the hyphen (*database*, *earring*, *reaststroke*, *radioisotope*). However, there are two cases in hich a compound spelt as two words is made into a hyphened orm or a one-word form:

- when a verb phrase such as *hold up* or *kick back* is made nto a noun (*hold-up*, *kick-back*).

- when a noun compound is made into a verb (e.g. *a date tamp* but *to date-stamp*).

hyphen is often used:

- to join a prefix ending in a vowel (such as *co-* and *neo-*) to nother word (e.g. *co-opt*, *neo-Impressionism*), although one-ord forms are becoming more usual (*cooperate*, *neoclassical*).

- to avoid ambiguity by separating a prefix from the main vord, e.g. to distinguish *re-cover* (= provide with a new cover) from *recover* and *re-sign* (= sign again) from *resign*.

- to join a prefix to a name or designation, e.g. *anti-Christian*, *ex-husband*. There is no satisfactory way of dealing with the type *ex-Prime Minister*, in which the second element is itself a compound, except to rely on the tendency of readers to use their knowledge of the world to choose the natural meaning. A second hyphen, e.g. *ex-Prime-Minister*, is not standard.

- to stand for a common second element in all but the last word of a list, e.g. *two-, three-, or fourfold*.

- to clarify meanings in groups of words which might otherwise be unclear or ambiguous:

> *Twenty-odd people came to the meeting.*
>
> *There will be special classes for French-speaking children.*

You should also use a hyphen to clarify the meaning of a compound that is normally spelled as separate words, when it is used before a noun: *an up-to-date record* but the *record is up to date*.

But there is no need to insert a hyphen between an adverb ending in *-ly* and an adjective qualified by it, even when they come before the noun: *a highly competitive market, recently published material*. When the adverb does not end in *-ly*, however, a hyphen is normally required to make the meaning clear: *a well-known woman, an ill-defined topic*.